CHILD AND ADOLESCENT PSYCHOLOGY

Child and Adolescent Psychology provides an accessible and thorough introduction to human development by integrating insights from typical and atypical development. This integration cements understanding since the same processes are involved. Knowledge about atypical development informs the understanding of typical development, and knowledge about typical development is a necessary basis for understanding atypical development and working with children with disorders.

Based on international research, and informed by biological, social and cultural perspectives, the book provides explanations of developmental phenomena, with a focus on how children and adolescents at different age levels actually think, feel and act. Following a structure by topic, with chronological developments within each chapter, von Tetzchner presents and contrasts the major theoretical ideas in developmental psychology and discusses their implications for different aspects of development. He also integrates information about sensory, physical and cognitive disabilities and the main emotional and behavioral disorders of childhood and adolescence, and the developmental consequences of these disabilities and disorders.

Child and Adolescent Psychology is accompanied by online resources for lecturers and students to enhance the book, including essay questions for each chapter, Powerpoint slides and multiple-choice questions. The book and companion website will prove invaluable to developmental psychology students.

Stephen von Tetzchner is Professor of Developmental Psychology at the Department of Psychology, University of Oslo, Norway.

CHILD AND ADOLESCENT PSYCHOLOGY

TYPICAL AND ATYPICAL DEVELOPMENT

STEPHEN VON TETZCHNER

Routledge
Taylor & Francis Group

LONDON AND NEW YORK

First published 2019
by Routledge
2 Park Square, Milton Park, Abingdon, Oxon OX14 4RN

and by Routledge
711 Third Avenue, New York, NY 10017

Routledge is an imprint of the Taylor & Francis Group, an informa business

© 2019 Stephen von Tetzchner

The right of Stephen von Tetzchner to be identified as author of this work has been asserted by him in accordance with sections 77 and 78 of the Copyright, Designs and Patents Act 1988.

British Library Cataloguing-in-Publication Data
A catalogue record for this book is available from the British Library

Library of Congress Cataloging-in-Publication Data
Names: Tetzchner, Stephen von, author.
Title: Child and adolescent psychology : typical and atypical development / Stephen von Tetzchner.
Description: 1 Edition. | New York : Routledge, 2019.
Identifiers: LCCN 2018018607 (print) | LCCN 2018020273 (ebook) | ISBN 9781317585190 (Adobe) | ISBN 9781317585176 (Mobipocket) | ISBN 9781317585183 (epub) | ISBN 9781138823389 (hardback) | ISBN 9781138823396 (pbk.) | ISBN 9781315742113 (ebook)
Subjects: LCSH: Child psychology. | Child development. | Adolescent psychology.
Classification: LCC BF721 (ebook) | LCC BF721 .T454 2019 (print) | DDC 155.4—dc23LC record available at https://lccn.loc.gov/2018018607

ISBN: 978-1-138-82338-9 (hbk)
ISBN: 978-1-138-82339-6 (pbk)
ISBN: 978-1-315-74211-3 (ebk)

Typeset in Sabon
by Florence Production Ltd, Stoodleigh, Devon, UK

Visit the companion website: www.routledge.com/cw/vonTetzchner

Printed in Canada

CONTENTS

The aim of the present book is to give insight into human development and guide the reader into a *developmental way of thinking*. This thinking is a tool for approaching developmental problems of a theoretical and an applied nature – be it in research or practical work with children and youths. Psychological science is characterized by numerous contrasts (and conflicts) in theoretical foundation and choice of method. This applies to developmental psychology as well: assumptions and explanations of the same developmental phenomena vary considerably and are frequently directly opposing. However, it is these differences and the insights from the various points of view that together contribute to an understanding of the complexity of human development.

It is the view of this author – and many others – that developmental explanations must apply to both typical and atypical developmental courses, and that an understanding of development must build on empirical studies and reflections on typical and atypical development. Discussion of atypical development is therefore a prominent feature of this book. There is one chapter about categorization of disorders of childhood and adolescence, and most conditions are discussed in several places where they contribute to the understanding of the developmental processes in general, as well as to understanding of the consequences of the particular disorder. Atypical functions do not simply reflect a neurological deficit, the whole developmental process and the child's interaction with the environment may change when a neurophysiological structure or process is incomplete or damaged. The present book gives an introduction to dis-abilities and disorders in childhood and adolescence but a full discussion of the complex issues relating to abnormal development and intervention is beyond the scope of this book. It gives a foundation for a developmental way of thinking but clinical work with a child with an impairment or disorder needs be based also on more specialized literature about the disability or disorder of the child.

The end of each chapter lists some core issues and suggestions for further reading. However, the text contains a large number of literature references to publications reporting on a particular research study and review publication comparing theories and empirical findings across studies. These allow the reader to obtain more details and go deeper into topics and studies of special interest. One useful way to follow up ideas and data presented in an article is to search for articles that cite that article (for example Google scholar has this function).

The terminology of developmental psychology is not always familiar to the general reader. Some words used in regular discourse might have a more technical application in developmental psychology. The book is therefore supplied with a glossary. The subject index makes it possible for the reader to read the book "cross-wise" and focus on topics and authors that are discussed in several places. An active use of these tools and the cross-references to other parts of the book will help the reader to construct the comprehensive perspective that a developmental way of thinking requires.

Working with a textbook is like engaging in a virtual dialogue with the large group of theoreticians and researchers who have contributed to the field of developmental psychology. Among the many developmentalists whose ideas have inspired this book, I would like to mention the diverse ideas of Renée Baillargeon, John Bowlby, Uri Bronfenbrenner, Joe Campos, Dante Cicchetti, Judy Dunn, Robert Fantz, Jerome Kagan, Annette Karmiloff-Smith, Richard M. Lerner, Andy Lock, Harald Martinsen, Katherine Nelson, Jean Piaget, Eleanor Rosch, Carolyn Rovee-Collier, Michael Rutter, Arnold Sameroff, Dan Slobin, Catherine Snow, L. Alan Sroufe, Stephen Suomi, Michael Tomasello, Jaan Valsiner and Lev Vygotsky.

I would like to thank Thilo Reinhard for help with the English language and Russell George, Lucy Kennedy, Sophie Crowe and Emma Brown at Routledge for a very friendly and constructive collaboration in the editorial process. Thanks also to the many researchers who generously have shared photographs and other material with me. Most of all I want to thank Karin for her patience and her support and engagement in my long-term writing projects.

Stephen von Tetzchner
Oslo, July 5th 2018

Contents

CHAPTER 1

DEVELOPMENTAL PSYCHOLOGY

Psychology is concerned with human beings' (and animals') understanding of the physical and social environment, and the bases for their actions, feelings and experiences, as well as their participation in greater and smaller social networks and in society. Developmental psychology is concerned with how all this comes about, how children gradually change socially, mentally and behaviorally, the underlying processes, and the factors that may influence these changes, for example how children's understanding of the world and thinking changes over time, what makes children develop different abilities, how children form relationships with parents and peers, why boys and girls tend to play in different ways and come to have different interests and behavior, why some children are socially active and extrovert while others are more shy and careful, and how emotional expressivity differs between cultures. Developmental psychology also includes the developmental courses of children with sensory and physical disabilities, as well as the vulnerability and risk factors that underlie the emergence of learning disorders and emotional and behavioral disorders in childhood and adolescence, and factors that may prevent the development of such disorders.

Development can be defined as an age-related process involving changes in the structure and functioning of human beings and animals as a result of interaction between biological structures, psychological states and ecological factors. While the organism adapts to its environment, the environment must also have properties that allow the organism to develop. At the core of the developmental process lies *transformation*: something new emerges, less becomes more, simplicity turns into complexity, limited skills evolve into advanced mastery (Overton, 2015). In all species, development toward adulthood implies a greater degree of autonomy and independence from the parent, and in human beings and many other species also increasing social affiliation (Keller, 2016). The main characteristic of development is change, but in most areas there is both change and continuity. The individual develops new ways of understanding and mastering the world, but always building on past experiences and remaining the same individual (Nelson, 2007a).

Development involves characteristics and abilities that are *common to all human beings*. Some are shared by humans and many other species, such as the ability to see, hear and walk, while others, such as talking and reflecting on the past and future, distinguish human beings. In addition, development entails processes that contribute to *individual differences* in particular traits and abilities. Some changes are *quantifiable*, such as children's physical growth or the number of words they say. Changes in areas such as reasoning ability, social adaptation and moral formation are not quite as easy to quantify. They represent *qualitative* differences. The particular objective of developmental theories is to explain the emergence of new abilities and qualitative changes, both common and individual differences, and change as well as continuity (Kagan, 2008a; Spencer and Perone, 2008; see Chapter 2).

With age, children engage in a growing number of activities and social relationships. They acquire the knowledge and values of their society, and adapt to the physical and social cultural landscape, a process known as *enculturation*. Some children grow up in a conglomerate of different cultures and their development reflects the multi-cultural background (Bronfenbrenner, 1979; Josephs and Valsiner, 2007).

THE HISTORICAL ROOTS OF DEVELOPMENTAL PSYCHOLOGY

Psychology is a relatively young scientific discipline. Its origins are often dated to 1879, the year in which Wilhelm Wundt opened the first psychological laboratory in Leipzig. This marked the transition from largely informal observations to a more systematic methodology in the study of human perception, thinking, feeling and action. Nonetheless, most key issues in psychology are deeply rooted in philosophy and medicine, and many of its main topics can be traced back to ancient reflections on human nature. Until the late nineteenth century, child development was primarily an educational field, and literature on children mostly dealt with upbringing and education (e.g., Herbart, 1841; Rousseau, 1763). A few researchers, like Tiedemann (1787) and Darwin (1877), described their children's development in detail, while Preyer published the first textbook with a general perspective on development in 1882. In 1900, Ellen Key proclaimed the twentieth century as *The Century of the Child*. It was equally to be the century of developmental psychology.

Developmental psychology encompasses widely different traditions that have moved toward and away from each other throughout history and influenced one another in varying degrees (see Chapter 2). The theories reflect the knowledge that was acquired, but also the spirit of the age and the overall development of the society. Many attempts have been made to unite different perspectives, but there is still disagreement about basic developmental issues, such as the organization and biological bases of cognition (see Chapter 9). Attempts at syntheses that integrate views from several directions and take into account the critique of others persist

Ellen Key.

into the twenty-first century. Present day "developmental science" crosses disciplinary boundaries and integrates perspectives from developmental psychology with anthropology, sociology, linguistics, medicine and technology (Witherington, 2014; Zelazo, 2013).

GLOBALIZATION

Globalization has become an integral part of modern societal development, and has also impacted the development of scientific thinking (Valsiner, 2012). Early in the history of developmental psychology, Western European psychology was dominant, and after World War II, American psychology assumed a leading role (Jensen, 2012). At the same time, theories were developed in other countries, which did not always receive international attention. Vygotsky's influential book *Thought and language*, for example, was first translated into English in 1962, 28 years after the author's death. Today the debate on development continues in Russia, but only a minor part of publications are translated into English (see Karpov, 2005; Vassilieva, 2010).

Development is global.

Cross-cultural studies are important for understanding the relationship between nature and nurture in development (see Bornstein, 2010; Nielsen and Haun, 2016). Similarly, cross-cultural discussions of scientific ideas are crucial to the advancement of developmental theories. For example, one-third of the world's children live in India and China, but since neither country engages in much systematic theoretical work, India and China have little influence on international research in developmental psychology. In China, this is partly due to the fact that psychology as a field, and individual-oriented psychology in particular, has essentially been an alien concept to the Chinese, since the group, rather than the individual, represent the natural unit in Chinese culture (Tardif and Miao, 2000). Moreover, during the Cultural Revolution (1966–1976), many psychology departments at universities were shut down (Blowers et al., 2009; Bond, 2010; Miao and Wang, 2003). In India, the British colonial powers had a considerable impact. Many of the studies involved children from upper middle class urban families and generalization to other social classes is uncertain (Saraswathi and Dutta, 2010). Today, both countries are establishing traditions with a stronger basis in their own values and cultures. Also in Africa, psychology has been an article of import, but the number of studies founded on African ecologies and perceptions of reality is steadily growing. Here, too, an important discussion concerns the relationship between a universal and a local cultural understanding of developmental processes (Marfo, 2011; Nsamenang and Lo-Oh, 2010).

While globalization and English as the *lingua franca* of academia contribute to more equality in the development of theories across national borders, they also highlight the differences between countries and contribute to the establishment of unique cultural scientific identities. In the age of globalization, developmental perspectives with an origin in African, Asian and other cultures will emerge and find their position in international developmental psychology, both locally and globally. The coming years will show how these perspectives position themselves.

TYPICAL AND ATYPICAL DEVELOPMENT

Some children acquire certain skills and abilities early on, while others have a late or unusual development in one or more areas. A smaller group of children have disabilities or disorders that inhibit all or some aspects of development, and have to perform many actions in unconventional ways. The most common course is typical development, with unimpaired functions and ordinary individual differences between children. Atypical development is a broad term used to describe all forms of irregular development, such as deaf children with a normal but unusual language development when they learn sign language instead of spoken language (Marschark et al., 2006), or children with intellectual disability who think and reason differently from their peers (Carr et al., 2016). Atypicality thus does not have to imply abnormality, only that something is done in less common ways. Knowledge of atypical development contributes to insight into developmental processes in general and there is a long tradition of comparing the developmental trajectories of children with different prerequisites. Many early researchers included children with visual impairment, hearing impairment and intellectual disability in their discussions of child development (e.g., Luria, 1961; Piaget, 1970).

Every age level sees the emergence of abilities and skills that are particularly prominent or important for that age and form the basis for further development. Early skills and characteristics involve among others the ability to grasp objects, followed a little later by independent mobility and attachment to a primary caregiver, and then to the development of language, understanding of minds, and morality. There are several ways of acquiring such skills and traits, both typical and atypical *developmental paths*. Children with severe mobility impairments may need a wheelchair to explore their surroundings, but their exploration has the same function and importance as for children without such impairments (Anderson et al., 2013; Campos et al., 2000). Blind children usually show normal language development, even though they have to learn

words with some other cues than sighted children (Pérez-Pereira and Conti-Ramsden, 1999).

It is the same basic principles that underlie all forms of development, regardless of whether it proceeds in an ordinary or unusual manner. Knowledge of typical development is necessary to understand atypical development, and knowledge of atypical development – of what can go wrong and how to compensate for impaired skills and abilities – is necessary to understand the developmental process in general (Cicchetti, 2013; Dekker and Karmiloff-Smith, 2011). The study of "theory of mind" in children with autism spectrum disorder and other disorders (see Chapter 13), for example, has been important in gaining insight into how children develop relationships and an understanding of how other people think and feel (Hughes and Leekam, 2004; Leekam, 2016). Most children with typical development will show positive development in quite different environments. Children with atypical development have a narrower range of possibilities and depend on an environment that fits their possibilities.

SOME RECURRENT ISSUES IN DEVELOPMENTAL PSYCHOLOGY

Many of the same issues appear in relation to descriptions and explanations of different developmental aspects.

Genes, environment and culture

The lay belief in genetic inheritance is strong and parents typically point to similarities between their children and various family members. The role of *heredity and environment* in the development of individual differences is also one of the most discussed themes in developmental psychology (see Chapter 5). Another issue is the *universality of abilities and traits*. Some characteristics and abilities seem to evolve in regular patterns across cultures, while others differ from one culture to the next. For example, children of all cultures learn to speak, but they speak different languages. Comparison of how children develop in different cultures is an important tool for understanding the biological and cultural bases of abilities and characteristics, including cultural differences in demographics, nutrition and lifestyle. Cultural differences underline the fact that genes alone have limited value in explaining developmental processes. A somewhat related issue is to what degree research findings can be generalized across species. Similarities and differences between species can provide important insights into the developmental process, including the fact that there are a number of factors that cannot be generalized across species. Culture and language separate humans from other species (Nielsen and Haun, 2016).

Learning and development

Although learning and development are often considered opposites, they are not always easily distinguished. Both have to do with continuity and change in knowledge and skills, with *becoming* as a continuation or transformation of what *is*. "Learning" is generally defined as a relatively permanent change in perception and behavior as the result of experience. The acquisition of factual or other explicit knowledge undoubtedly qualifies as learning, but learning at school also leads to the formation of new synapses and brain circuits (Demetriou et al., 2011). Changes due to maturation, illness, injury or fatigue are not learning. Some theorists would argue that development specifically involves new learning based on previous learning, independent of biological factors. Others consider biological factors to be essential to the development process (Zelazo, 2013).

Continuity and discontinuity

Continuity means that there is a direct relationship between earlier adaptation and functioning, and later ways of functioning. In *homotypic continuity*, form and function remain the same over time. Children and adults are both capable of running, but adults run faster. *Heterotypic continuity* means that the forms differ. One-year-olds stretch up their hands to be lifted onto mom's lap, while older children say *Can I sit on your lap?* to achieve the same thing. Since early childhood involves major changes in children's behavioral repertoire, heterotypic continuity is most pronounced at this age. *Differential continuity* or *stability* means that children maintain their relative position with respect to their peers in terms

of a particular ability or trait. A two-year-old with frequent temper tantrums may have fewer tantrums at the age of ten, but relative to his peers he may be characterized by a short temper and behavioral disorders (Rutter et al., 2006).

Stages

Some theorists describe children's development as a sequence of stages, such as Piaget for cognitive development (Chapter 9) and Kohlberg for moral development (Chapter 22). A stage is a period characterized by specific skills or characteristics, and has to fulfil certain formal criteria. In the transition from one stage to another, children achieve a higher and qualitatively different level of competence than before. The transition must occur relatively quickly and involve concurrent changes in several areas. All children must pass through the stages in the same order. For most stage theories, there is disagreement regarding whether the stages actually meet these criteria (Lourenço, 2016).

Critical and sensitive periods

During development there are periods where the child has a unique or particularly good opportunity for learning or development, or a particular vulnerability to harmful influences (see Chapter 7). An understanding of such "sensitive" or "critical" periods from prenatal life to biological maturity is important in order to prevent deviant development and initiate early intervention for children with developmental disorders. Related to this is a common view that experiences during early development are especially important and can install a form of vigilance or "preparedness," steer development in a certain direction and have long-term consequences (see Chapter 18). Theorists disagree on the significance of early experiences, but both the positive effects of a sound childhood environment and the harmful consequences of growing up in poor or unsupportive surroundings are used as arguments in favor of early intervention (Bush and Boyce, 2014). For example, the first years of childhood are generally considered to be a sensitive period for communication and language development, and communication and language intervention is often implemented at an early age (Kaiser and Roberts, 2011).

Equifinality and multifinality

Flexibility is a characteristic of human development and children and can follow different pathways, both typical and atypical. Equifinality means that different developmental paths can have the same developmental outcome, such as the various ways of self-propelled movement prior to walking (Largo et al., 1993). Children who become competent language users can follow somewhat different development courses (Bates et al., 1988). Multifinality occurs when developmental paths with a common point of departure lead to different developmental outcomes. Some children with adverse experiences in the early years continue to have problems into adult age, others with the same poor start do well in adulthood. Identity formation during adolescence can take different paths for individuals who initially shared the same group affiliation (see Chapter 21).

Process and outcome

Some descriptions of development place emphasis on the outcome, on the various traits and abilities children usually have developed at different age levels and their intercorrelations, while others focus on the processes that lead to new traits and abilities, and the transitions from one state to another (Valsiner, 1987). However, the *explanation* of developmental outcomes must address the process itself, and an understanding of the process will provide the best basis for designing interventions for children who may be vulnerable to deviant development.

Multiple levels of analysis

Human functioning can be analyzed on a number of different levels (e.g., Gottlieb, 1992). Humans have genes and neurons; they perceive the environment through their senses, perform motor actions and mental tasks, and live in physical, social and cultural surroundings. Modern developmental science includes all of these various levels and the complex relationships between them (Zelazo, 2013).

MODELING DEVELOPMENT

Developmental science seeks to model how biological and environmental factors affect children's development. A "developmental effect" will be the result of one or more influences. Developmental models distinguish between *main effects* and *interaction effects*, while *transaction effects* are the result of mutual influences between the child and the environment over time.

Main effects

A main effect is the direct result of an influence that is independent of other influences. A main effect can be caused by specific genes or environmental factors such as nutrition, exposure to certain events, and so on. Eye color, for example, is exclusively determined by genes and the result of a main effect. Genetic disorders like Rett syndrome and Huntington's disease are main effects (see Chapter 5), the presence of the disorders does not depend on other factors. An environmental main effect occurs when a sudden reduction in blood flow leads to brain damage resulting in motor impairment. The consequences of the impairment may vary depending on physio-therapy and other interventions, but the impairment itself cannot be "repaired." It may be argued that this is not development as such, but an external event with developmental consequences. Yet, there is no fundamental difference between this and other environmental influences: it is simply more dramatic than a condition such as malnutrition. In fact, it is precisely such dramatic events that may result in main effects, events that have such a pervasive effect on the course of development that other factors do not alter their effect.

Although a given trait can be the result of a main effect, a single factor alone does not necessarily determine the development of the trait, such as in the case of eye color. When several main effects act simultaneously, they are said to be *additive*. When trying to measure the extent to which height, intelligence, personality and other characteristics are the result of nature versus nurture, one usually proceeds from the assumption that genes and the environment operate independently, namely that two main effects (genes and environment) are added together (see Chapter 5).

Interaction models

An interaction effect occurs when the influence of a given factor is moderated by one or several other factors (Cicchetti, 2013). This implies that the effect of one factor cannot be determined without specifying one or more other factors. Figuratively speaking, interaction can be illustrated with the heat that melts the ice, causes the egg to harden.

Discussions about main and interaction effects are often concerned with the relationship between genes and environment. One example is when the gene variant determines the effect of characteristics of the environment (see Box 1.1).

This particular relationship is discussed in greater detail in Chapter 5. However, interaction effects can also occur between biological factors – including genes – and between several environmental conditions (Pennington et al., 2009). One example is when the relationship between a difficult temperament and the child's externalizing behavior is influenced by the mother's self-efficacy and her ability to manage the child's temperament (Coleman and Karraker, 1998).

An example of interaction between two environmental factors is demonstrated by a study that found a higher correlation between family income and children's academic performance in families

---

BOX 1.1 AN INTERACTION EFFECT BETWEEN GENES AND MATERNAL SENSITIVITY

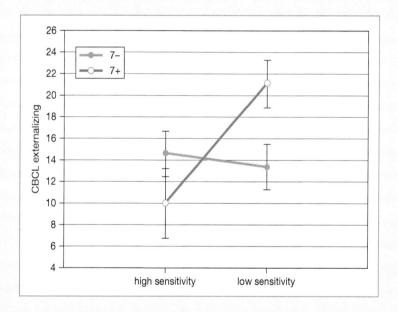

There are several different variants (alleles) of the dopamine receptor gene D4 (DRD4), each with a different number of DNA repeats. Forty-seven 10-month-old infants were observed with the mother in the home, and the mothers' sensitivity – how they reacted to their child – was assessed. When the children were 2–3 years old, the mothers completed a behavior questionnaire (CBCL) about their child. The children with the 7-repeat DRD4 and mothers who had been rated as insensitive were given higher scores for externalizing behavior than children with the 7-repeat allele and mothers who were rated as sensitive at 10 months, as well as of children without the 7-repeat allele, irrespective of their mothers' sensitivity. For the whole group, there was no significant difference between children whose mothers had been rated as sensitive and insensitive, the effect is only observable if one differentiates children with and without the 7-repeat allele of DRD4. There was thus an interaction between the DRD4 allele and the effect of maternal sensitivity: only the externalizing behavior of the children with the 7-repeat was influenced by the mother's sensitivity at this age (Bakermans-Kranenburg and van IJzendoorn, 2006).

with single parents than in those with two parents – good academic performance in children with single parents depended more on a solid household income (Zill, 1996). This may be due to the fact that a family with financial problems has more resources to follow up the child's education when two are sharing the task, than when a single parent struggles to make ends meet as well as provide the necessary help with schoolwork. Therefore, in order to predict how family income will most likely affect a child's academic performance, one needs to establish whether the child lives with one or with both parents. This shows that influences are not passively received, but integrated into the individual's own functioning, whether it be the influence of the parents on the child, or vice versa (Rutter, 2005).

No aspect of child development is simple, and an explanation based on main effects is rarely sufficient. When taking a more detailed look at the factors that may underlie the development of a given trait or ability, one will nearly always find interaction effects (Elman et al., 1996).

Transaction models

Transaction models deals with the *mutual* influence between an individual and the environment over time. Descriptions of main and interaction effects generally focus on the influences on the child, but children also influence their surroundings (Bell, 1968). Extroverted children, for example, meet with different reactions from their environment than shy children. Children with Noonan syndrome, who are small in stature, are met differently than children who are tall for their age (von Tetzchner, 1998). Boys and girls are treated differently (see Chapter 24). Children with different temperaments elicit different parenting behaviors. Just as a father can react to a child with a difficult temperament in a way that helps the child achieve better self-regulation and development, a child with an easy temperament can influence her temperamental father to reduce the likelihood of his verbal or physical outbursts and become a better parent (see Chapter 18). The experiences provided by the environment are thus not independent of the child, and a full understanding of the processes and conditions that shape the course of development must be based on how the individual and the environment influence one another over time. This

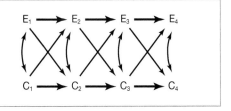

FIGURE 1.1 **Transaction (based on Sameroff, 2009).**

The transactional chain begins with the child and the environment at Time 1 (C_1 and E_1). The child's development at Time 2 is the result of the child's characteristics at Time 1 and the influences of the environment. The characteristics of the environment at Time 2 are the result of the environment's characteristics at Time 1 and the influences of the child. The child's development at Time 3 is the result of the child's characteristics at Time 2 and the influences of the environment, while the characteristics of the environment at Time 3 are the result of the environment's characteristics at Time 2 and the influence of the child. And so on.

requires a transactional model (Sameroff, 2010, 2014).

Figure 1.1 shows a simple transactional chain. Both the child and the environment change by mutual influence, so that the child's abilities and characteristics at various points on a timeline are the result of earlier development and new environmental influences, and the environment is the result of existing characteristics and new influences from the child. The chain continues, incorporating both stability and change.

Transaction entails that the characteristics of the child and those of the environment constantly gain new significance during the development process. The developed child is affected by environmental factors. The environment changes as a result of the child's influence, and the child changes with each new environmental influence. A common example of transaction is the mutual influence between parents and children over time. At some point in the transaction chain, a child causes her parents to react in a certain way. The child is affected by the parents' reactions, the child's reactions and actions in turn affect the parents, and so on, in increasingly longer chains (Sameroff, 2010). The study in Box 1.2 found a transactional relationship between disobedience in infants, depression in mothers, and behavioral disorders in adolescence (Gross et al., 2009). Another study found transactional effects between child externalizing behavior and maternal physical discipline

Arnold Sameroff.

(Gershoff et al., 2012). Studies show that maternal sensitivity to children with fragile X syndrome has an impact on language development, but also that the mother's sensitivity is dependent on the child's behavior (Carlier and Roubertoux,

2014; Warren et al., 2010). Hence, the child influences people in the environment who adapt in different ways to the child's characteristics as they perceive them. This in turn impacts their own influence on the child.

Ordinary age-related changes affect both children and adults. A 15-year-old is reprimanded differently by her parents than a 2-year-old or a child aged 8. Something that is forbidden by the parents and accepted by an 8-year-old straight-away may be perceived as unreasonably controlling by a 15-year-old. Similarly, parents often indulge toddlers who are stubborn or defiant, but react with anger and reprimands when older children behave the same way. Thus, a chain of influences can both be interactional and transactional.

The transactional model is a key element in the current understanding of development. The mutual influences between children and parents do not consist of isolated incidents, but interact with all the other influences children and parents are exposed to. Children engage in interactions and relationships with their peers and adults, take part in events and activities in and outside of school and kindergarten, and live under different physical and nutritional conditions (Wachs, 2003). Parents have different professions, engage in social relations in and outside of work, and involve themselves in community activities to varying degrees. Society's values, laws and practices will impact children's learning and development, education and peer relationships, and the way in which children and parents influence one another (Bronfenbrenner, 1979).

BOX 1.2 AN EXAMPLE OF TRANSACTION EFFECTS: TRAJECTORIES OF CHILD NON-COMPLIANCE, MATERNAL DEPRESSION AND ADOLESCENT ANTISOCIAL BEHAVIOR (from Gross et al., 2009)

A sample of 289 children from predominantly low-income families were followed longitudinally from 18 months to 13 years. At 18 months the mother–child interactions were observed and instances of non-compliance and infant aggression were registered in situations that varied in stress, such as free play, clean-up, no toy and a short separation from the mother (see p. 403). The mothers completed a scale for depressive symptoms at several time points, and teachers completed behavior scales when the children were 11, 12 and 13 years old. The researchers found that higher levels of child noncompliance were associated with more persistent and higher levels of maternal depressive symptoms. Persistent but moderate maternal depressive symptoms in turn, were associated with increased risk of adolescent antisocial behavior. However, it was not possible to predict adolescent antisocial behavior from toddler non-compliance. These results underline the dynamic interplay of transactional processes.

Analyses based on transactional models are important when the results of empirical studies are "translated" to practical work with children. Sameroff (2009) describes the three Rs of intervention: remediation, redefinition and re-education. *Remediation* aims to change the child's progress, and may include all aspects of the child's functioning, such as nutrition, cleft palate surgery or special education for dyscalculia. *Redefinition* attempts to change the parents' subjective perception of their child. Parents of children with atypical development may have to learn to understand their child's temperament, thoughts and experiences, for example that blind children explore the surroundings with their hands (Fraiberg, 1977). This may involve assigning new "labels" to what the child is doing. The aim of *re-education* is to provide parents with information about the possibilities and limitations of a child with a particular disorder, and how to best meet the child's needs. Parents of children with mobility impairments, for example, need to understand how the ability to move independently impacts the child's psychological space, exploration and attachment (see p. 406).

DYNAMIC SYSTEMS

Human development is complex and it is difficult to describe even a small number of the conglomerate of interrelated processes involved. Dynamic systems models may be used to go beyond individual interactional and transactional processes and capture more of the complex reciprocal changes among different levels of organization (Cox et al., 2010; Sameroff, 2010). A *system* can be defined as any collection of "objects" or components that interact by way of certain causal relationships between them. A *static* system describes the relationship between components irrespective of time, while a *dynamic* system also incorporates changes in the components and their function over time (Burton, 1994). Development involves different elements and processes, and dynamic systems models are therefore particularly well-suited to describe typical and atypical developmental pathways (Smith and Thelen, 2003; van Geert and Steenbeek, 2005). From a dynamic systems perspective, the ability to learn, for example, will gradually change as a result of the learning process itself and the situation in which it takes place, such as a physics

lesson that includes instructions, tool use and explorative interaction together with the teacher. Changes in children's learning thus are not merely quantitative, but also qualitative. Children acquire more knowledge and learn to think more and faster, but they also learn to understand the world around them in constantly new ways (van der Steen et al., 2012).

An important characteristic of dynamic systems is *self-regulation*. This means that a child's inherent characteristics can change based on previously existing characteristics or "knowledge" without external influence. For example, children can form new concepts by re-organizing already acquired concepts and knowledge that so far have remained uncoordinated. When the system becomes unbalanced, it self-regulates based on feedback from the environment and the system itself, and influences on the environment and the effects of these influences. It is thus *imbalance* that brings change (Schöner and Dineva, 2007). Neither external stimulation nor a predetermined structure alone can ensure internal stability or the imbalance needed to bring about change in the system (see Figure 1.2). Imbalances can result in positive or negative effects, and the course of development can be typical or atypical.

Developmental models can be *linear* or *non-linear*. A linear system involves a proportional relationship between a phenomenon and the conditions it results from – between what goes into the system and what comes out. When such a relationship is not proportional, it is said to be non-linear. Supposing there was a linear relationship between children's vocabulary and their age, a 4-year-old would know twice as many words as a 2-year-old (Figure 1.3). This is not the case, however – the relationship between vocabulary and age is non-linear (Dale and Goodman, 2005). Most children begin to use words around their first birthday. Acquiring the first words takes a long time, followed by rapid growth during childhood and adolescence, and finally adulthood with increasingly slower growth, although the acquisition of new words never stops entirely.

An important characteristic of dynamic systems is their ability to integrate processes at different levels and allow for interaction between many factors and mechanisms. The development of walking, for example, can be described as the result of children's intention to move, their neurological and perceptual development,

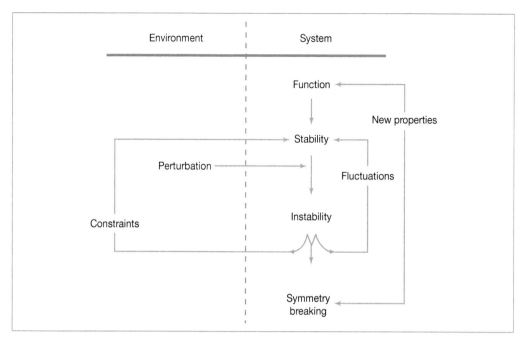

FIGURE 1.2 Dynamic model.

When the symmetry – or balance – between elements and processes in a dynamic system is disturbed, the resulting imbalance leads to the formation of qualitatively new characteristics. How the system behaves at any given time depends on the system's states at a previous point in time. Although the model does not include a timeline, the process of change always takes place over time (based on Hopkins and Butterworth 1997, p. 80).

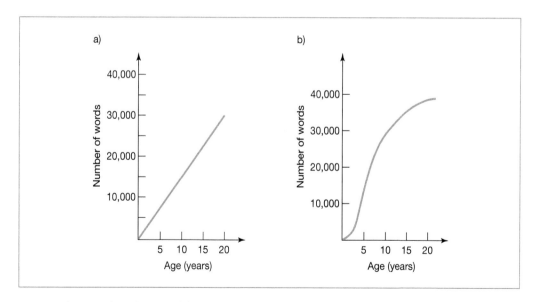

FIGURE 1.3 Linear and non-linear models.

The figure illustrates linear and non-linear models using a hypothetical growth in vocabulary. Model a is linear because the vocabulary increases by an equal amount each month until the age of 20. Model b shows a slow increase in vocabulary at the start, followed by a period of rapid growth; subsequently, the growth in vocabulary slows down, but without stopping completely.

their motor and other physical prerequisites, and the environmental conditions that make walking possible, such as a stable surface and something to hold on to for children who are not yet steady on their feet. In Piaget's theory, cognitive development is viewed as a continuation of the child's early perceptions, actions and general adaptation to the environment. Cognitive structures arise from the developmental process itself (see Chapter 9). Dynamic models are neither based on the notion of development as fixed and predetermined, nor on the assumption that all actions are shaped by the environment or based on imitation of an external model. They are not "deterministic" in the sense that there is a fixed relationship between input and output. Children's characteristics and actions are adaptive; they emerge from a complex and self-organizing system of physical, biological and psychological factors that can be either excitatory or inhibitory (Bates et al., 1998). The use of models capable of incorporating a wide range of different circumstances and details is problematic, however, in that they can become so extensive that little substance remains: the forest vanishes behind all the trees. A theoretical explanation is therefore called for when different factors are incorporated into one and the same model, and dynamic systems can be useful in generating new hypotheses about developmental mechanisms and relationships.

Cascades

The term "cascade" is closely associated with dynamic systems. It is used figuratively to describe how early traits or events lead to a sequence of stages, processes, operations or units. The outcome of one affects the next, leading to increasingly greater consequences across levels and for different domains at the same level (Cox et al., 2010). Inattention and restlessness in childhood, for example, can give rise to frustration, low self-efficacy and oppositional behavior. This in turn can lead to poor social skills, relational problems and learning problems at school, difficulties with boyfriends or girlfriends in adolescence, and in the workplace in adulthood. One study found cascade effects from social adaptation in preschool and externalizing behavior in middle childhood on adolescent cognitive, social and behavioral functioning (Racz et al., 2017).

Developmental cascades thus describe the cumulative impact of multiple interaction and transaction effects in a developing system. Although each in itself could possibly have been prevented, together they may reach a scale that becomes difficult to handle. This proliferation of problematic effects over time is sometimes referred to as a "chain reaction" or "snowball effect." The effects can be direct or indirect, unidirectional or bidirectional and follow different paths. An important characteristic is that their impact is not temporary: a developmental cascade alters the course of development, and the result can be positive or negative (Masten and Cicchetti, 2010).

VULNERABILITY, RISK, RESILIENCE AND PROTECTION

One of the main goals of developmental research and clinical work is to understand how various factors contribute positively and negatively to children's development. Some children have traits that make them *vulnerable* to particular developmental anomalies. A given environment can represent a developmental *risk* by not supporting a child's positive development or by directly counteracting it, and disability or injury resulting in unduly negative consequences. A typical environment will not always provide support for a positive atypical development. A severe hearing impairment, for example, always impacts the type of information children have access to as well as their ability to orient themselves in an acoustic environment, making interaction with others more difficult (Marschark et al., 2011). The consequences of a hearing impairment for a child's language development, however, will depend on the qualities of the environment, such as the availability and benefit of a cochlear implant (or other hearing aid), and a competent sign language environment. It is therefore essential to distinguish between an injury or a deficit of the organism and the resulting developmental consequences. An optimal environment cannot always be taken for granted. Children with attention deficit disorder are vulnerable to developing inadequate interaction strategies and social disorders. Structured activities together with guidance from parents and kindergarten personnel can have a protective effect and help them develop good social skills (Hinshaw and Scheffler, 2014). The timing of positive and negative experiences can be important, since the consequences of risk and protective factors depend on when they occur in the course of development. Children can be vulnerable or resilient at different times, for example during sensitive or critical periods when they are particularly vulnerable to negative environmental influences or dependent on specific influences to be able to develop normally.

Figure 1.4 illustrates an interaction model of risk and vulnerability. The development process is determined by the interaction between the child's characteristics and those of the environment. Even if children grow up under environmental conditions that represent a significant risk of aberrant or delayed development, they will develop normally as long as they are not vulnerable to these particular environmental conditions. If children are vulnerable to specific environmental factors, they need an environment free of such factors for normal development. Most children grow up under environmental conditions that do not represent a significant risk based on their prerequisites, and therefore develop normally. A sensitive and responsive caregiver can counteract the negative effects of early and severe deprivation (McGoron et al., 2012), but even under normal environmental conditions, some children with impairments or disabilities are vulnerable to a greater or lesser degree and will show atypical development under all or most environmental conditions, such as girls with Rett syndrome (Feldman et al., 2016).

In order to be able to prevent disorders in children, it is important to identify the factors and processes that may underlie vulnerability and risk. From a developmental perspective, it is natural to investigate the basis of children's positive development, also in the presence of vulnerability and risk factors. Even among children who are at serious risk of aberrant development, such as growing up in an unstable home environment and having little contact with trusted adults, there are always some who manage to cope relatively well. They seem to be "invulnerable" or resilient to negative influences (Garmezy, 1991; Luthar et al., 2014). Resilience is the complement to vulnerability and risk, and results from the same developmental processes (Supkoff et al., 2012).

Resilience is neither a general characteristic of children, nor does it provide clear guidelines for how to guard against problems. However, resilient children often take an active part in solving the problems they face and it is important that professionals look for such characteristics and support children's active participation (Rutter, 2013; Seligman and Darling, 2007). Furthermore, the environment itself can protect against vulnerability and other environmental risks. Studies of children adopted from war-torn countries, areas of drought and famine, and from mothers with drug problems provide insight into risk factors, children's resilience and the protection offered by the environment (Palacios and Brodzinsky, 2010).

The model in Figure 1.4 illustrates important aspects of development. It is based on a diathesis-stress model, which attempts to explain psychological disorders as the result of child

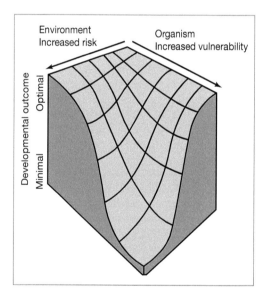

FIGURE 1.4 A developmental model of risk and vulnerability (based on Horowitz, 1987).

The figure shows the possible developmental consequences of the organism's vulnerability and risk factors in the environment. An optimal developmental outcome can be the result of invulnerability, absence of risk factors, or both. An organism with low vulnerability is protected against risk factors in the environment. Without risk, vulnerability is immaterial. Therefore, a non-optimal developmental outcome will always be the consequence of a certain vulnerability of the organism and a certain degree of risk in the environment.

vulnerability and stressful experiences. *Diathesis* is a congenital predisposition, and *stress* in this context is defined as negative experiences. The model deals exclusively with negative development or absence of negative development, however, and lacks promotive factors – positive development is merely the result of invulnerability and absence of risk (Roisman et al., 2012). Horowitz's model includes no positive forces, and makes no allowances for resilience and protection. Furthermore, Sameroff (2009) points to the presence of factors that promote a positive development, independent of any vulnerability and risk. In the same way that children differ in vulnerability to negative experiences, they react differently to positive experiences, for example praise (Brummelman et al., 2014; Pluess and Belsky, 2013). These are complex relationships.

THE DEVELOPMENTAL WAY OF THINKING

Developmental psychology comprises a wide range of issues, and as has been shown earlier, complexity in phenomena and processes is an inherent characteristic of all human development. The developmental way of thinking is a central tool in both research and practical work with children and adolescents. Within a developmental way of thinking the abilities and characteristics of the individual are not perceived as predetermined; they do not come ready made but are results of complex interactions and transactions between biological and environmental factors over time. It is not a question of genes *or* environment, but of how these interact in the different phases of development. At any point in time, the individual's abilities, characteristics and functioning must be understood as both results of the developmental process that the individual has passed through and a basis for the development that lies ahead, that is, what the individual *is* and *will become*. There is a continuous process of organization and reorganization of abilities and characteristics, where the individual both changes and remains the same. A developmental way of thinking implies seeing children both as they are and what they are in the process of becoming from biological, social and cultural perspectives. Children grow and develop physically and mentally, and are constantly becoming

involved in new activities and relating to new people. Also the extent and quality of these activities and relationships are changing. Within *applied developmental science* the developmental way of thinking is a tool for adapting society to support children's optimal cognitive, emotional and social development (Lerner and Castellino, 2002).

> A unifying conceptual framework of development – including what develops, how it develops, and what can hurt or help development – can give policymakers an understandable yet expansive framework that is anchored in science. When this framework replaces vague perspectives or models (e.g., child as blank slate), policy makers can use child development research to inform their decisions about policies and programs that serve children best.
>
> (Hogan and Quay, 2014, p. 247)

DEVELOPMENTAL PSYCHOPATHOLOGY

Developmental psychopathology is a multidisciplinary field that seeks to reveal and influence the processes that can give rise to mental problems in children and adolescents, and uncover factors that can promote or inhibit the development of psychological disorders (Lewis and Rudolph, 2014). Rather than a theory, it is a perspective with significance for research and practice (Rutter, 2014). Building on a developmental way of thinking, mental health problems and the absence of such problems are viewed as consequences of children's vulnerability and resilience, and of risk and protection in the childhood environment. It seeks to explain the developmental process itself, and thus differs from other approaches that place more emphasis on the presence of specific genes or traumatic experiences (Sroufe, 1997, 2007). One of the basic principles of this approach is that mental health problems do not arise spontaneously out of a void, but are the result of a developmental process. The roots of a disorder can go far back in time from the onset of symptoms and the establishment of a diagnosis. Toddler age, for example, can be a vulnerable period. At this age, children gradually become more mobile, but have yet to develop the cognitive skills to understand the consequences of their actions, as well as the ability to regulate their own emotions. Parents can find it difficult to deal with their child's behavior, and the first signs of internalizing and externalizing behaviors may begin to emerge. This may be the beginning of a developmental path with vulnerability of poor adaptation throughout life (Wiggins et al., 2015). To cite another example: usually there is a positive relationship between empathy and mental health, but a high degree of empathy can also increase children's worry and guilt and thus make them vulnerable to developing internalizing problems (Tone and Tully, 2014).

Since psychopathology represents a deviation from normal functioning, its identification, diagnosis, treatment and prevention must be based on knowledge of the normal course of development. Developmental psychopathology integrates knowledge of typical and atypical development, maintaining that any adaptation or lack of adaptation throughout an individual's life must be understood from a developmental perspective, where biological, psychological and social factors can contribute to healthy development under normal or difficult conditions, as well as to the development of psychopathology. It furthermore places emphasis on uncovering how different developmental paths can lead to the same end state (equifinality), and how a particular vulnerability or risk can lead to various mental problems (multifinality). The goal of developmental psychopathology is to "translate" research-based knowledge into clinical work, understand each child's unique developmental path and facilitate preventive and treatment measures that allow children and parents to take advantage of positive developmental opportunities (Cicchetti and Toth, 2009; Rutter and Sroufe, 2000).

SUMMARY

1   *Development* can be defined as age-related changes or transformations in the structure and functioning of human beings and animals as a result of biological and environmental factors. Development comprises both characteristics that are shared by humans and other animals, characteristics that are common to all humans and individual differences, and change as well as stability.

2   Most key issues in psychology are deeply rooted in philosophy and medicine, and many of its main topics can be traced back to ancient reflections on human nature. Developmental psychology encompasses widely different traditions, and there is disagreement about many of the basic issues.

3   *Cross-cultural discussions* are important for the development of new knowledge. *Globalization* contributes to the development of theories across national borders and to a more diverse cultural perspective on the development process.

4   Most children have a *typical development* with unimpaired functions and ordinary individual differences. *Atypical development* comprises all forms of unusual development.

5   *Main effects* are the result of an influence that acts independently of other influences. When several main effects act at the same time but independently of each other, they are said to be *additive. Interaction effects* occur when the impact of a given factor is moderated by one or more other factors.

6   *Transaction effects* are the result of mutual influences over time. Children are affected by the environment and affect the environment in turn. The environment changes as a result of the child's influence, and so on.

7   *Dynamic systems* models provide detailed descriptions of the developmental process. They *self-regulate* based on feedback from the environment and the system itself, and influences on

Continued

the environment and the effect of their impact. Regulation is brought about by *imbalance*. The term *cascade* is used to describe the way in which early traits or events lead to a sequence of stages, processes, operations or units. The outcome of one affects the next, leading to increasingly greater consequences.

8   All developmental theories make assumptions about characteristics that represent *vulnerability* in children or *risk factors* in the environment that can lead to aberrant development and developmental anomalies. Children may be *resilient* to stress and environments may have qualities that offer *protection*. The *diathesis-stress model* describes mental disorders as the result of predisposed vulnerability and stressful life events. However, positive development can also be the result of promotive factors, independent of any vulnerability and risk.

9   *A developmental way of thinking* implies seeing children both as they are and what they are in the process of becoming from biological, social and cultural perspectives. *Developmental psychopathology* is a multidisciplinary approach that views mental problems and the absence of such problems as developmental consequences of children's vulnerability and resilience, and risk and protection in the environment.

CORE ISSUES

• The role of main effects, interaction and transaction in modeling typical and atypical development.

• Usefulness and limitations of the diathesis-stress model.

SUGGESTIONS FOR FURTHER READING

Overton, W. F., & Lerner, R. M. (2014). Fundamental concepts and methods in developmental science: A relational perspective. *Research in Human Development, 11*, 63–73.

Rutter, M., & Sroufe, L. A. (2000). Developmental psychopathology: Concepts and challenges. *Development and Psychopathology, 12*, 265–296.

Sameroff, A. (2010). A unified theory of development: A dialectic integration of nature and nurture. *Child Development, 81*, 6–22.

Sternberg, R. J. (2014). The development of adaptive competence: Why cultural psychology is necessary and not just nice. *Developmental Review, 34*, 208–224.

Contents

This chapter provides a brief introduction to the foundations of theory formation and the most important theoretical perspectives in developmental psychology: *psychodynamic psychology*, *behaviorism*, *logical constructivism*, *social constructivism*, *evolutionary psychology*, *ethological psychology*, *ecological psychology*, *information processing* and *critical psychology*. They differ in their emphasis and explanations of developmental phenomena and together they illustrate the breadth of developmental thinking in the twenty-first century. Each of them comprises many assumptions and hypotheses, and constitutes a basis for many smaller theories.

The theories are presented in more detail in parts of the book where they are relevant, including critical comments. Chapter 10, for example, discusses the cognitive aspects of the theories, while Chapter 18 discusses the development of personality.

THE FUNCTION OF DEVELOPMENTAL THEORIES

Developmental theories are intellectual tools for categorizing and making sense of observations of children's actions and reactions and their environment, and explaining typical and atypical developmental trajectories. As all tools, they must be functional and solid. A good theory requires a coherent set of interconnected concepts and a terminology that can be used to describe the development of the psychological phenomena and explain the relevant processes, for example concepts that can characterize children's changing thinking or emotion understanding, and the processes that underlie these developmental changes (see Chapters 10 and 17). "The usefulness of theories may be evaluated in regard to its attributes of precision, scope and deployability" (Lerner, 2002, p. 11).

According to Popper (1959), a theory has to be testable in order to be scientific. The first test of whether a theory is sound and tenable is to establish if it can account for and integrate existing research findings (Lerner, 2002). Popper also points out that theories cannot be *proven* right, only wrong. A positive finding may be important

Richard M. Lerner.

but consistent with several explanations and unable to distinguish between even opposing theories. When findings contradict a hypothesis that is logically inferred from a theory, the theory must be revised or discarded. Negative evidence is therefore more decisive than positive in scientific inquiry, and when evaluating a theory it is necessary to ask what observations could possibly falsify the theory. A good theory must be able to generate hypotheses – statements about states of affairs that can be logically derived from the theory – that can be investigated in such a way that there is a potential result that would falsify the hypothesis and theory. If it is not possible to deduct hypotheses logically from a theory that will test its validity, the theory will remain speculative even if it is both interesting and sounds reasonable. In addition, most theories include some hypothetical constructs that are not directly observable – such as the existence of internal working models (p. 396) or defense mechanisms (p. 378). Their existence can only be inferred through interpretation of observations, and the interpretation may require corroborating evidence.

In the same way as a theory needs evidence, research results need a theory to be useful in a scientific inquiry. Without a theoretical framework results are empty facts without explanatory force (see Chapter 3). Practitioners also use theories when they try to explain the emergence of problems in a child who has been referred for example for severe social withdrawal or bullying. However, the dependence on a theoretical framework may also imply biases in the selection of observations and their inferences (Miller, 2011). To reduce the influence of such biases, both researchers and practitioners need to make their theoretical basis explicit and recognize their own possible biases when selecting and interpreting observations.

It is a major aim of research to distinguish between competing theories. However, because findings often are consistent with several explanations and theories, researchers may have to do many different studies before they can favor one theory over others – or abandon it. A theory may emerge from some basic assumptions derived from observations of children, existing developmental theories and philosophical ideas, and gradually grow into a larger and more complex theoretical construction. Theory building goes through a kind of scientific evolution with survival of the fittest, with reciprocal influences between theory and research findings. In this evolution, those theories will survive that have fewer unobservable constructs and have been widely studied with few findings contradicting their hypotheses. However, even if a theory's predictions are contradicted on some accounts and the theory eventually is revised or abandoned, it may not imply that the theory has been useless. Many aspects of Piaget's cognitive theory have been contradicted by research findings, for example his assumptions about logic and stages in the development of thinking (see Chapter 10), but the theory constitutes an invaluable foundation for the understanding of cognitive development because it has generated a lot of research questions and hypotheses. It has a clearly defined set of concepts and the most important feature of any theory – it can be tested.

PSYCHODYNAMIC PSYCHOLOGY

Psychodynamic psychology has its roots in the psychoanalytic theory of Sigmund Freud (1916) but most of Freud's original assumptions have been reformulated or replaced by new theoretical constructs. Within the over-arching psychodynamic framework, the disputes and differences of opinion are considerable, and there is no dominating psychodynamic approach (Luborsky & Barrett, 2006; Westen, 1998).

One knowledge base for psychodynamic theories is the causes of and treatments of psychological problems. Because psychodynamic psychology tends to assume that mental disorders largely originate in childhood experiences, clinically oriented psychodynamic theories also include assumptions about developmental processes. The other major knowledge base is studies of typical child development, often based on the assumption that psychological disorders reveal general features of development.

A central element of psychodynamic theory is the development of an *internal psychological structure* that determines the individual's perceptions of the world, actions and values. Individual mental functions are integrated into a coherent structure, as part of the child's adjustment to the surroundings. Many psychodynamic theories maintain that the primary course of development is predetermined and universal, and that the

Sigmund Freud.
Everett Historical/Shutterstock

formation of an individual's mental structure follows a set biological course. When complete, the personality has been shaped by individual experiences but genetic predispositions determine what experiences are significant at different age levels.

All psychodynamic theories emphasize the child's relationships with other people and especially with the parents, but they have different assumptions about the motivational bases for these relationships. Freud (1905) argues that all human motives are derived from two innate drives: *libido*, the sexual or life drive, and *thanatos*, the hatred or destructive drive. The drives must be released and children turn to their parents to satisfy their needs, for example for food or sucking. Children's future relationships with other people will depend on the ways in which their drives and needs have been met. At first, children are dominated by the *pleasure principle* and gradually adapt to the physical, social and cultural conditions that are necessary for reducing the drive levels and follow the *reality principle* (Freud, 1911). This development is

made possible by the creation of a psychological structure consisting of *id*, *ego* and *superego* (Freud, 1927). In newborn infants, this structure is made up of the *id* alone; they are controlled by their drives. The *ego* enables children to pay attention to external barriers and limitations and adjust to the realities of the world. The third element, the *superego*, develops in later childhood and ensures that actions are not only realistic but also acceptable in view of the norms and values of the culture. The superego is shaped by the norms and values transmitted by the parents, typically the values and norms that the parents themselves received from their parents. The superego therefore represents a relatively conservative set of attitudes and values.

According to the classical theory, children's development is characterized by conflicts between impulses deriving from the id, ego and superego. All children will experience such conflicts to a greater or lesser extent, because parents make demands that cross the child's own unconscious and drive-based desires. Initially, conflicts arise between the child's wishes and external demands, for instance the parental insistence on cleanliness. Gradually, the demands are *internalized* and become part of the child's own restraints on its actions and, consequently, conflicts between internal demands and internal desires emerge. According to Freud, it is the resolution of conflicts between id and superego that forms the basis of the personality, although many psychodynamic theoreticians regard the ego as the most important structure, because the ego regulates impulses from id and superego, and adjusts to the surroundings.

Freud's theory of drives has been taken up by others, notably Melanie Klein (1948) whose basic assumption is that children are born with a conflict between life and death drives. She represents *object relations theory* and in the psychodynamic sense, an "object" is a mental representation of a person or thing that is construed as the goal of a drive, or as a means for the drive to reach its goal. "Object relations" are abstractions, mental constructs of the roles the child and others have in interactions. Ronald Fairbairn (1952) argues that libido is not directed toward pleasure, as Freud thought, but toward "objects" – establishing relationships.

Other psychodynamic theoreticians are critical of the assumption that innate drives are the basis for the formation of relationships. Donald

Winnicott (1960) rejects the idea that children's social relationships are dependent on a need to satisfy primitive drives, and maintains that the wish to enter into relationships constitutes a drive in its own right. According to his theory, the relationship between mother and child is the natural unit in children's early development, and children only slowly become able to separate their own self from the union with the mother. Correspondingly, Margaret Mahler describes processes of *separation* and *individuation*, where children gradually separate their self from the mother and become independent individuals (Mahler et al., 1975). In more recent psychodynamic theories, early interaction between mother and child is given greater significance, among others by Daniel Stern (1998) and Robert Emde (1998).

Another core assumption in psychodynamic theory is the presence of unconscious motives and behavioral impulses, which may surface in slips of the tongue and similar failures of control, as well as in symbolic acts. It is the interactions between unconscious motives that constitute the "psychodynamics." Children may experience anxiety when impulses to act or think come into conflict with their internalized demands. According to Freud (1894), children develop a set of *defense mechanisms* for regulating impulses and keeping anxiety at bay, and making it possible for them to function within the community (see also A. Freud, 1966).

Ego psychology is an important strand within psychodynamic psychology. Among others Anna Freud (1966) and Erik Homburger Erikson (1963) assign the ego an independent role in personality development. In the theories of Donald Winnicott (1965) and Heinz Kohut (1977), the *self* replaces the tripartite structure of the psyche (id, ego and superego), and conflicts between id and superego therefore do not have the same central position as in Freud's theory. However, development is still considered to be characterized by internal conflicts, and defense mechanisms remain a critical element in psychodynamic psychology (Westen, 1998). The developmental importance of mental conflicts is a feature that distinguishes psychodynamic theory from many other schools of thought and hinders integration with other theories.

According to Freud (1916), childhood experiences are critically important for the mature personality. He maintains that there is a relationship between the experiences during three *psychosexual phases* that children pass through before the age of 4 to 5, and certain personality traits or psychological problems later in life (see Chapter 17). Erikson (1963) extends this idea in a theory of *social crises* that determine the development of normal and deviant personality traits. From yet another psychodynamic perspective, Stern (1998) describes how different aspects of the self are starting to be formed in different phases of development, and remain independent but integrated parts of the mature person's self image. At present, most psychodynamic theoreticians attribute importance to events in early childhood, but state that personality development continues well past preschool age, and that the personality can be changed, to a greater or lesser extent, throughout life (Westen, 1998).

Psychodynamic theories do not cover the full range of cognitive development, but the theory of a *tripartite consciousness* includes ideas about mental representations and memory organization (Freud, 1915). The thought processes of the aware mind make up the *conscious*. The *preconscious* is made up in part of cognitive activity that may be, but usually is not, under conscious control, and in part of mental representations that can be accessed, but only when the conscious mind focuses on them. The *unconscious* contains thoughts and feelings that are conflict-laden for the individual and enter the conscious only with difficulty, but which still may influence the individual's actions.

Psychodynamic theory has two main methodological approaches. One is based on clinical practice and typically consists of detailed case histories that often are assumptions about development derived from treatment of adults. Furthermore, there are many different ways in which the internal workings of the mind can manifest themselves symbolically in behavior. Two identical actions may well have quite different underlying meanings. Freud argues that developmental psychologists may well miss important elements of development and misunderstand the significance of a child's actions unless they see them as outcomes of unconscious motives.

The other methodological approach is direct studies of children. Among others, Stern, Emde and Fonagy seek to fuse experimental methods of infant psychology with psychodynamic interpretation. Stephen Mitchell (1988) describes *relational psychoanalysis* as an integration of ideas drawn from object relations theory, self psychology and infant research.

Psychodynamic theories have been of crucial importance for clinical psychology (Luborsky and Barrett, 2006). Although Sigmund Freud rarely worked with children, his theory dominated early child psychology to a greater extent than adult psychology, which has had to contend with several competing types of treatment. In the 1920s, Anna Freud and Melanie Klein began to develop psychoanalytical treatments for children. Psychodynamic developmental theory has also been highly influential on discussions about children's close relationships, and their motivation, personality, identity and emotional development. During the last century, psychodynamic psychology has also had a major influence on ideas about how to bring up children, although always in conflict with behaviorism.

BEHAVIORISM

Compared to other theories, behaviorism (also called *behavior analysis* or *learning theory*) attributes a greater role to learning processes. This does not mean that biology is without importance, also behaviorism assumes that humans are a result of evolution and biologically distinct from other species (Skinner, 1981, 1984). Genes constrain developmental trajectories but learning is decisive and all human functions can be explained on the basis of the same principles of learning, whether it be using language, solving problems, understanding emotions or entering into social relationships. Behaviorists often "translate" concepts from other theories – such as cognitive schema, attachment, joint attention and social referencing – into behavioristic terminology and explanations based on the relationship between stimuli and responses (Schlinger, 1995).

Behavior analysis concerns the relationship between behavior and environmental events. The environment is described as alterations of energy (stimuli) that reach the sensory receptors and trigger behaviors. Anything that the child reacts to in its surroundings is classified as a *stimulus*. A *response* is something the child does. Learning mechanisms include *respondent* (classical) and *operant* (instrumental) *conditioning*, and *imitation* (see Chapter 15). Behavior is regarded as an unbroken flow of actions that is constantly shaped, the incidence of actions increasing or decreasing in response to reactions in the environment. Sydney Bijou and Donald Baer (1961)

Burrhus Frederic Skinner at the Harvard Psychology Department, circa 1950.

https://commons.wikimedia.org/wiki/File:B.F._Skinner_at_Harvard_circa_1950.jpg. This file is licensed under the Creative Commons Attribution 3.0 Unported license. self-made (by User:Silly rabbit). Updated in the Gimp by User:Michaelrayw2.

define development as progressive change in the relationship between children's behavior and events in the environment. It is not the child who controls his or her own behavior; it is the surroundings that shape the child's responses (actions), and the responses are determined by the earlier learning history, that is, the conditions which over time influenced the child's pattern of responding (Skinner, 1971). While the child's reactions to people around her might contribute to shaping particular behaviors, the final result will also depend on the *motivating operations* in the child, her physiological status as well as other situational factors (Laraway et al., 2003).

Behaviorism proceeds from the assumption that the same fundamental learning processes can explain all developmental changes, regardless of species or individual biological differences within the species (Skinner, 1938). The human species is characterized by an inborn *sensitivity to consequences* (Skinner, 1977). This ability is so general that it does not imply any specific constraints on behavioral development. In Skinner's view, a basic *survival drive* underlies all behavior and thus development. Learning enables the individual to survive in different environments, and children learn from experience without innate predispositions. Individual differences in behavior are mainly the result of differences in learning conditions.

Bijou (1968) describes three stages in child development that reflect changes in the biology as well as in the activities of the child. The *universal stage* covers the period from fetal life beginning up to the age of 2. Children's behavior in this stage is termed *ecological*, and there are hardly any cultural differences. The reason is not only that development is controlled by biological factors that all infants share, but also that children aged 0 to 2 tend to be treated in similar ways. The *basic stage* lasts from age 2 to 6. The biological development has reached a level that allows children to use more resources for investigation and acquisition of new skills and knowledge. Different surroundings, and thus experiences, contribute to individual differences between children and establish the behavioral basis for the third stage. The *societal stage* lasts from early school age and onwards, throughout adulthood. Many different factors affect the child, expanding and altering the foundational behavior patterns. In many cultures, school plays an important role as it teaches children to read and count, complex problem solving and the history of the culture. At first children's social participation at home, in school, with peers and others is defined by society, but control gradually passes over to the children themselves. Bijou emphasizes that the age ranges only provide an indication, there are considerable differences between children with respect to the time they spend in the first two stages.

Albert Bandura (1978, 1986, 2006) is usually placed within behaviorism although his *cognitive* or *social* learning theory differs considerably from traditional behaviorism. He emphasizes that people are conscious, goal-oriented managers of their own lives and includes explanations based on cognitive processes traditionally avoided by behaviorists. Still, Bandura also starts with the fundamental idea of development as a cumulative learning process and maintains that differences between children reflect different learning conditions. However, he puts more emphasis on *modelling* and *observational learning*, that is, children's ability to learn by observing or hearing about the consequences certain behaviors have for other people. This implies that observed

Albert Bandura.

consequences contribute to how children later cognitively regulate their own behavior.

Skinner's theory assumes that the relationship between features in the surroundings (stimuli) and behaviors (responses) is solely an empirical issue. Behaviorists have always been occupied with methodology. As the very name implies, analyses of observed behavior is the core methodological focus. Bandura (2001, 2006) extends the behavioristic perspective by including cognitive factors in explaining why children of different ages pay attention to certain aspects of their surroundings, how they interpret events and store and organize event information for future use, and why some events have lasting effects, depending on their perceived value and meaning. In Bandura's theory, learning is *goal-directed*. For example, children imitate people they admire or value, whether they are pop stars or friends, and such "reference people" change with age. Children's self image and self efficacy are also given much weight in explanations of why children act as they do. However, Bandura does not base his ideas on an assumption that children develop a cognitive structure of the type proposed by Piaget, but sees both social and cognitive development as outcomes of learning, as a continuous growth that gradually expands the child's behavioral repertoire and renders it more complex. Skinner and Bandura thus have quite different views on how new behaviors are acquired and maintained.

Behaviorism has influenced nearly all areas of developmental psychology, and its ideas have had a major impact on education. However, due to the narrow explanatory system and resistance to "mentalist" concepts, behaviorism has made little inroads into the debates about cognitive and language development. Behavior therapy (BT) and applied behavior analysis (ABA) first developed by Ole Ivar Lovaas (1993) have had a large influence on intervention for children with autism spectrum disorders and severe intellectual disabilities. Bandura's cognitive theory has had considerable impact on personality and clinical psychology. Cognitive behavior therapy (CBT), which applies self-instruction and other cognitive strategies, is common intervention for mood and behavioral disorders in children (Kendall et al., 2015; Mendez, 2017). ABA has influenced parenting, especially the focus on consequences of children's behaviors (Sanders, 1996; Webster-Stratton, 2006). "Supernanny" and similar television series about raising children lean heavily on ideas from ABA.

LOGICAL CONSTRUCTIVISM

Logical constructivism is founded on the theory of Jean Piaget (1952, 1954). Constructivism assumes that children's understanding of the world does not depend on innate mechanisms but is constructed by the organism. Piaget's constructivism is called *logical* because his theory assumes that human thought follows logical principles. (Psychodynamic psychology is constructivist, too, in that the psychic structure determines how experiences are perceived and processed.) It was important for Piaget's views that his observations indicated that children perceive the world and its physical regularities differently from adults (see Figure 2.1). Hence, children are not small adults, their perception of the world is *qualitatively* different from that of the adult. They begin to perceive the world like adults only after a lengthy period of deveopment, involving both innate characteristics and life experiences.

Jean Piaget.

According to Piaget, development is *process of adaptation*, in which the child's own activity is a core component. Children develop knowledge and insight when they attempt new goals and have to overcome obstacles in order to reach them, for example move around a chair to get at a toy. Mental structures and processes are modified as children overcome challenges and acquire new experiences. They actively explore the environment, gain experiences and test the properties of the physical world. Piaget's vision of the

FIGURE 2.1　Children's representations of reality.

Children's drawings reflect the ideas they have formed about physical phenomena. When young children are asked to draw the water in a glass placed on a slope, they draw the line parallel to the top of the glass, and not horizontally as is the actual case.

child as active and creative was the critically important breach with contemporary views of cognitive development as the outcome of maturation and passive internalization of knowledge from adults.

According to Piaget, the cognitive structure provides the mental basis for all human understanding of and knowledge about the world. He compares it to a self-regulating (dynamic) system (see p. 10). Children exist in a state in which old notions are constantly challenged by new experiences and they will themselves seek out such challenges. If there is a *conflict* between new and existing ideas, the child experiences *disequilibrium*. The child solves the problem caused by a particular state of disequilibrium by altering its mental structure and thereby reinstating equilibrium. The new insight leads to new cognitive conflicts and disequilibriums. It is thus the cognitive conflict and the search for equilibrium which drive development. One example of conflict is if a child knows that two equal weights will balance a two-armed scale. He puts one weight on each side at random and discovers that the scale tips to one side. He did not realize that the distance to the middle matters and hence failed to take this into account when positioning the weights. The problem is solved by the child finding out that it matters how far from the center the weights are placed. By deducing that the weights must be placed at the same distance from the fulcrum, equilibrium is restored.

Piaget describes four cognitive stages characterized by qualitatively different functional capacities. At each stage, the cognitive structure sustains the logical operations that Piaget believes to be necessary to execute the tasks that children and young people learn to do at that stage. The stages are thus an ordering of children's developmental advances over time. However, Piaget's explanation of the developmental process is more important than the descriptions of stages, and especially what drives transitions from one level to the next, that is, cognitive conflict and equilibration.

Piaget's theory is still the only coherent theory of cognitive development and a starting point for almost all debate about cognitive development. Many developmental phenomena first described by Piaget, such as *object permanence* (that things exist when they are not perceived by the senses) and different forms of *conservation* (for example

that the volume of water remains the same when it is poured from a wide to a narrow glass), are still central to descriptions of cognitive development. Some theoreticians use Piaget's theory as a basis, others actively oppose it, but both are influenced by him (see Martí and Rodríguez, 2012). *Neo-Piagetians* such as Juan Pascual-Leone (1970), Robbie Case (1985), Graeme Halford (1989) and Kurt Fischer (1980) share Piaget's constructivist views and build on the idea that children's functioning reflects underlying cognitive structures which become gradually more complex and better integrated as the child grows older, that structures which develop later build on previously developed structures, and that children are themselves actively engaged in acquiring knowledge and insight. They however distance themselves from Piaget in that they do not incorporate logic into the model (Morra et al., 2008). However, Pascual-Leone, Case and Halford integrate Piaget's theory and concepts from information processing theory, such as *mental capacity*, *processing speed* and *executive functions*. Most of the neo-Piagetians have abandoned the assumption about general stages but share Piaget's view that children's thinking undergoes qualitative changes in the form of cognitive reorganizations which may be described as a series of levels. Piaget constantly revised his theory and thus became himself a neo-Piagetian. In what has been termed *the new theory* (Beilin, 1992), both the stages and the base of formal logic have become less important (Piaget et al., 1992).

Lawrence Kohlberg (1981) has elaborated Piaget's theory on moral development. Kurt Fischer has used Piaget's theoretical framework to describe the development of emotions and personality (Fischer et al., 1990; Fischer and Connell, 2003), and the theory has been important in education (deVries, 2000; Marchand, 2012), even though Piaget himself was not so interested in individual differences or whether his theory has practical applications.

SOCIAL CONSTRUCTIVISM

This school of thought, which is also called *cultural-historical*, originates in the writings of Lev Vygotsky (1962, 1978). He is usually seen as an opponent to Piaget, but social constructivism

Lev Vygotsky.

distances itself just as much from other theories. Vygotsky actually shared many of Piaget's views, even though their main lines of argument have diverged. Both are constructive and have a main focus on cognitive development. According to Piaget, the construction is an individual project, while Vygotsky views the construction as socially mediated. Children's cognition is shaped through cooperation with others and internalization of cultural tools and thought patterns. *Internalizing* means that external processes, for example in formats such as dialogues and collaborative problem solving, are absorbed and become part of the child's mind. Children thus do not construct reality on their own. They are guided into the culture's activities and use of strategies and mental tools by more competent members of the society (children and adults), at first together with others and later on their own. Cultural tools such as oral and written language, numbers and mathematical symbols, art and maps can be developed only through cooperation with other people. They do not only help or facilitate thinking but change the cognitive organization and

lead to qualitative changes in the child's cognition. Development thus consists in increasing internalization and increasingly complex handling of cultural tools.

Social constructivist theory assumes that children are born with biological mechanisms which also determine early cognitive development but that the individual cognitive resources are insufficient for the independent acquisition of the higher cognitive functions which characterize adults (Vygotsky, 1978). It is the influence of the cultural context which induces the biological organism to create meaning. The basis for human consciousness and action is not to be found in the brain or the mind, but in external conditions of life – the social, historical and cultural expressions of human existence. Children depend on people who make the necessary mental tools and knowledge available, and guide the children in using them. Enculturation happens first on a social, then on a psychological level. Children's mastery includes both what they can manage on their own, and what they can do with help from more competent persons (children or adults). It is precisely the "tasks" that children cannot do independently but with assistance from others, which according to Vygotsky reside in children's *zone of proximal development*, and it is within this zone that learning can take place as a cooperation between children and adults. Mastery within the zone of proximal development implies that the child understands the task, but also that the adults adapt the assistance they give to make it useful to the child. Also the help given must be within the zone of proximal development (Chaiklin, 2003).

Another main idea is that the cooperation between children and adults does not lead to abstract knowledge, independent of the context of the learning. Jean Lave and Etienne Wenger (1991) describe learning as *situated* within the activity to which the tools and strategies are relevant. Parents and children together take part in daily routines during which the child acquires different kinds of knowledge, for instance about lullabies by the bedside, food in the kitchen and wood in the workshop. It follows that acquisitions of specific skills depend on children taking part in interactions that have the necessary features.

Vygotsky describes four stages in development characterized by qualitatively different functional capacities. In these stages, children internalize cultural tools, develop more complex modes of thinking and integrate language and intellect. Vygotsky and Elkonin describe six phases in children's participation in activities, ranging from the first year of life, when the child joins in activities that typically provide intuitive and emotional contact between child and adult, to adolescence and the acquisition of vocational skills (Thomas, 2005).

Vygotsky's premature death at 38 years has meant that many of his theoretical ideas remain incomplete and unclear. Russian *neo-Vygotskians* such as Aleksei Leontiev, Alexander Zaporozhets, Piotr Galperin and Daniil Elkonin criticize several aspects of Vygotsky's theory, but also carry his ideas forward in *activity theory* (see Karpov, 2005). According to these theoreticians, children go through developmental phases characterized by various *main activities*, with their specific *motives*, *goals* and *actions*. Early on, one motive is to join in emotional interactions; while in adolescence one motive is to reflect on the self. In each phase, children have motives and behavioral resources which are appropriate for participation in the main activity but cannot manage on their own. The developmental phases are therefore characterized by activities which children and adults do together, with the adults acting as mediators. It is the mediation of the adults that drives development. When the adult has completed the mediation tasks in one phase, the child masters new mental tools and, together with the adult, is ready to enter into a new phase with main activities involving motives, goals and actions – and once more, the child will need the adult's help to manage. In this way, activity theory represents at the same time extension, modification and revision of Vygotsky's ideas. Outside Russia, Michael Cole, Barbara Rogoff, Jaan Valsiner and James Wertsch are leading proponents of this school of thought. Much of the research has been concerned with cognitive and language development, but social constructivist theories have influenced most areas of developmental psychology, including development of moral (Tappan, 2006), self (Stetsenko and Arievitch, 2004) and identity (Hammack, 2008), as well as developmental neuropsychology (Akhutina, 2003) and education (Kozulin et al., 2003). They have also inspired critical psychology (see p. 33).

EVOLUTIONARY PSYCHOLOGY

Evolution is central to the understanding of how children develop. All developmental theories assume that abilities and skills may have a genetic basis. It is also a common point of view that children who are alive today carry genes which during evolution conferred the possibility of developing characteristics which "fitted in" with their surroundings and increased their survival chances, and that many human characteristics can be explained by the significance they had in the evolution (see p. 77). However, evolutionary psychology assumes to a larger extent than other theories that psychological traits and behavioral tendencies are based on specific neurological mechanisms, *modules*, shared by all humans (Barrett and Kurzban, 2006; Lickliter and Honeycutt, 2015). The evolutionary process has been used to explain the development of aggression and altruism (Kurzban et al., 2015; Wilson, 1975). Steven Pinker (1994) writes about a "language instinct" that makes language a human biological necessity (unless brain damage has occurred in areas which the relevant genes helped to shape). There is no clear distinction between *nativism* and evolutionary psychology, and they are therefore presented together.

According to nativism, children are born with *core knowledge* in many areas and that development proceeds according to a plan represented in the genes (Carey, 2011; Spelke and Kinzler, 2007). Stimulation is usually necessary for activating the innate structures, but experiential differences have little influence on the developmental outcome (Scarr, 1992). Nativists assume that children are born with mental models which correlate with many aspects of the world, that a newborn's brain already "knows" how to go on to perceive certain types of stimuli and events in its surroundings. The argument is that experiences are not in themselves sufficient to provide a child with reliable knowledge about the world, nor how to relate to people. The child's own mind must be able to contribute already *before* assimilating experiences, thereby transcending knowledge imparted directly by external stimuli. For instance, Noam Chomsky (2000) and Steven Pinker (1994) believe that language acquisition would be impossible without a language module capable of limiting the ideas children might form about the functions of speech sounds or of the hand movements in sign language (see Chapter

15). Others maintain that infants are born with modules for face perception, numbers, spatial relationships and naive psychology (understanding of human relationships and feelings) (Spelke and Kinzler, 2007). An inborn mechanism that enables social learning by imitation has been suggested (Rizzolatti, 2005), and temperament and personality are also assumed to have a genetic basis (Buss and Penke, 2015).

That the basis for some characteristics have emerged as part of evolution however does not mean that they are independent of the individual's environment, only that a certain set of genes must be present for the individual to exhibit these traits. Genes make experience possible and experience allows the genes to function (see Chapter 5).

There is considerable disagreement within evolutionary psychology with regard to the specificity of the neurological bases for human cognitive functions. Many argue like Pinker (1997), Carruthers (2006, 2008) and Cosmides and Tooby (1994) that humans have a large number of specialized neurological modules because evolutionary adaptations require specific solutions. On the other hand, Bjorklund and Pellegrini (2002) maintain that human evolution implies the development of both modular and more general neural structures that enable adaption to different ecological niches. To suppose that evolution has created general neural structures is uncontroversial and in line with developmental theories in general. It is the assumption that many human functions to a large extent are determined by genes, which distinguishes evolutionary psychology from other theories.

Nativism has influenced thinking about most areas of development, from motor skills and object perception to emotions and personality. Evolution has been thought to explain, for instance, sexual identity, criminality and violence (Buss and Duntley, 2011; Durrant and Ward, 2012). During the last 50 years, research that shows infants to be more competent than previously thought has had considerable influence on the field. In the twenty-first century many nativist views have considerable support.

ETHOLOGICAL PSYCHOLOGY

Ethology is the study of animals in their natural setting. The basic idea of Robert Hinde (1992)

and other ethological psychologists is that the understanding of development and adaptation of the human and other species has to be based on knowledge about their biological capacities, the ecological niche in which characteristics have evolved and the ecological niche in which individual humans find themselves at present.

The ethological tenets influence the research methods. Ethologists prefer a natural science approach and emphasize the importance of describing children and young animals in different situations. One example is the observation by Konrad Lorenz (1935) that many young birds tend to follow whatever they first see moving within a time window which opens just after they hatched (imprinting). This makes it likely that they follow the mother and get food and protection, and thereby increases the survival of the species (see p. 397). In the theory of John Bowlby (1969, 1973, 1980), children's attachment behaviors are regarded as having the same function as imprinting in birds. Children with genes that contribute to their development of attachment behavior and physical proximity to a caregiver have increased likelihood that they will survive to sexual maturity and thereby transfer their genes to other individuals.

Bowlby's theory is the major theory within ethological psychology and has contributed decisively to shaping the insights of contemporary developmental psychology into the early social relationships of children (see Chapter 19). It has had a strong influence on clinical psychology, social work with children and attitudes to raising children in general. It has also been an inspiration for ecological psychology.

ECOLOGICAL PSYCHOLOGY

Ecological developmental psychology sets out from the premise that children are part of various social and cultural contexts, which they are affected by and also affect. Urie Bronfenbrenner is the key theoretician and his *bio-ecological theory* is made up of four elements – process, person, context and time – which are integral components of a model for development (Bronfenbrenner, 1979; Bronfenbrenner and Morris, 2006).

In Bronfenbrenner's theory, *proximal processes* include the interactions between the individual and the environment. He views development as an outcome of interactions over time between the active child and human beings, objects and symbols in the immediate surroundings, which invite attention, exploration, manipulation, elaboration and imagination. Children become more capable with age, and therefore the proximal processes must grow too. The activities in which children take part become more time-consuming and more varied, and development thus involves both the individual and the group.

The person is an individual's biological, cognitive, emotional and behavioral characteristics. Every individual has three sets of properties: first, predispositions that can initiate the proximal processes within a specific domain and in a defined situation or context; second, resources such as talents, experiences, knowledge and skills that are essential for the effective function of proximal processes at a given point in development; and third, demands that either promote or hinder reactions from people in the environment that can affect the proximal processes negatively or positively. Inspired by Kurt Lewin's (1931) concept "life space," Bronfenbrenner points out that the environment has both objective and subjective elements. The way in which a child is influenced by the environment, and influences it in turn, depends on the subjective understanding, which reflects the child's experiences, including the emotional aspects of the experiences. The person's characteristics contribute in their various ways to individual differences in development. Moreover, they are included in the definition of the microsystem (see below), such as characteristics of the child itself, the parents, siblings, friends, class mates and other significant persons.

The context consists of a hierarchy of four ecological levels, or systems, which combine to create the environment in which the child grows up (Figure 2.2). The *microsystem* is an individual's situation at a given time in his or her life, and consists of the relationships between the child and his or her surroundings. There are many microsystems, which interact and form a *mesosystem*. The mesosystem is the individual's developmental niche at a certain point in time and consists of the set of situations that are most important to that individual. How children function within their family and other significant environments affects how they function at school and with friends; and their school experiences affect the family situation. The *exosystem* comprises situations in which the child does not have an immediate role, but which all the same influence the child's behavior and development. The parents' employment situation, opportunities for holidays, social support, personal social network and other such factors (the exosystem) influence the care setting of the child as well as the functioning of the family (the microsystem). The parents of a child's friends (the exosystem) may matter to the interaction between the child and her friends (the microsystem). The *macrosystem* is a superordinate level and incorporates culture, community institutions and politics. The laws of the country (the macrosystem) regulate the organization of nursery schools and schools, and working conditions in general (the exosystem). They include duties, opportunities and rights which affect parents' care of their children (the microsystem). The influences also operate in the other direction: events in one or several families, nursery schools or school (in the micro- and mesosystems) can lead to changes in the laws and social attitudes (the macrosystem). The four levels interact, and what happens at one level relates with what happens elsewhere.

The ecological systems represent stepwise extensions of children's environment. As children grow older, their social networks expand and become more complex. Children who live in the same country have the same macrosystem. Children who live in the same local area are likely to share much of the same mesosystem, and also the exosystem if their parents often interact. It is however the mutual influences between all four levels which constitute an individual child's unique developmental environment. Besides, changes will take place, with time, at each level and also in the interactions between the levels. A child's world might come to include several siblings, or its parents might divorce and find new partners. Society's laws could change, as could its attitudes and values, changes which might deeply affect all four ecological levels.

Time is important in the bio-ecological model because the interactions must occur frequently over a period of time and are linked to the micro-, meso- and macro-levels. *Microtime* defines beginnings and ends of episodes of proximal processes. *Mesotime* is structured from such episodes, stretching over time intervals of days and weeks. *Macrotime* encompasses changes in expectations and events with life-long or generational durations.

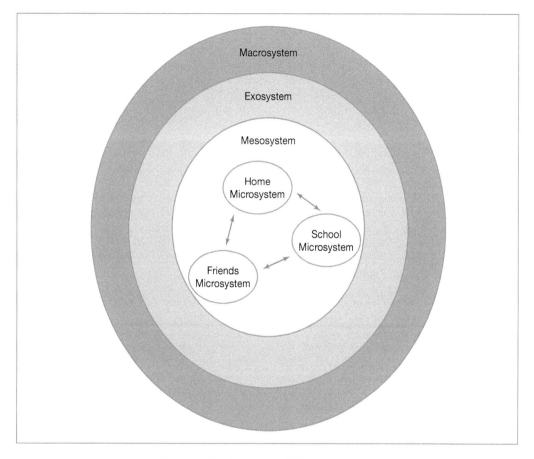

FIGURE 2.2 Four ecological levels (based on Bronfenbrenner, 1979).

Microsystem: consists of a child's intimate, daily relationships. In the Western world, these are usually with parents, siblings and other relatives who live with the family, as well as nursery school, school, after-school clubs and groups, friends in the neighborhood and similar.

Mesosystem: consists of links between two or several of the microsystems in which the child actively participates.

Exosystem: the wider social context in which the child is not active, but which matters for the functioning of the family and the child. It includes the parental places of work and their social networks, distant relatives, the parents of friends and similar.

Macrosystem: consists of social institutions, official services and similar, and includes the laws, customs and values of the society which affect the other systems.

The bio-ecological model of development thus concerns interactions between a child and its environment which take place at different levels and with different time-spans, and integrate the ecological systems and person characteristics within the framework of the transactional model (see p. 8).

Developmental psychology has mostly concentrated on close family relationships – and especially that between mother and child. Bronfenbrenner's theory has contributed to a shift in research to pay greater attention to chil-dren's development within a wider social and societal framework. The theory is important for social and health care practice, and community-oriented work in general (e.g., Ashiabi and O'Neal, 2015; Benson and Buehler, 2012). Moreover, it has helped to clarify the influence that higher-order political decisions can have on the development of individual children and hence why political decisions should be included as relevant environmental goals (Golden et al., 2015) and as starting points for studies of chil-dren's development.

INFORMATION PROCESSING

Theories based on information processing describe mental phenomena as information from the senses or memory being processed in various ways, and with various aims, including understanding of intentions and emotions, thinking and problem solving (Massaro and Cowan, 1993). Figure 2.3 describes a simple model of information processing. The computer serves as a conceptual metaphor: mental phenomena are calculations and cognitive development is changes in how calculations are made (Simon, 1962), and from this perspective, computer simulation of mental processes is an important research strategy (Schlesinger and McMurray, 2012). All mental functions are seen as involving the same set of processes and both the number of processes and their capacity are limited.

Information processing is used to explore what processes are active when children manage different tasks, how the children encode and process information, discriminate between new and old information, and create concepts about people, animals, objects, emotions and so on, and how the processes change over time. The theoreticians agree that differences in the information and the ways it is processed can explain social and cognitive differences between children and adults. There is however considerable disagreement about *what* it is that changes. According

to Pascual-Leone (1970), developmental changes are due to maturation-dependent increases in processing speeds and capacities, while Kail and Bisanz (1992) argue that the processes are constant and hence not susceptible to change. Michelene Chi (1978) represents a third view, that it is the organization of knowledge that changes. An "expert" in a particular area organizes knowledge differently to a novice. In addition, children learn new *strategies*. For example, children as young as 18 months can point to or name concealed objects in a hiding-game, but lack strategies for hiding things. Five-year-olds place objects in the corners of the room and in other obvious places which allow them to be easily found. Another example is that children as a rule begin to count on their fingers and gradually learn new strategies for adding and subtracting which can be used also with numbers greater than the number of fingers on both hands (Kail and Bisanz, 1992).

Models based on information processing are becoming increasingly influential in developmental psychology, especially in typical and atypical cognitive development (see Chapter 10), but other developmental areas also apply information processing models. The model of Crick and Dodge (1994) for processing *social information* has contributed to the understanding of the development of social functioning, personality and psychological problems by analyzing for instance

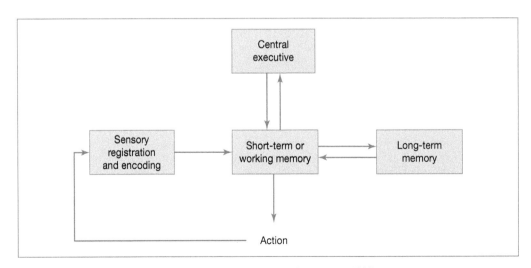

FIGURE 2.3 A simple model of information processing (based on Richardson, 1998).

The components act in conjunction when executing complex tasks and the model can be used for different types of information.

how aggressive or shy children or children with ADHD process social information, and is often applied in clinical work with children with behavioral disorders (e.g., Adrian et al., 2010; Fontaine, 2010; King et al., 2009). The process analytical approach of information processing is used in both mainstream and special education (van Nieuwenhuijzen and Vriens, 2012; Ziv, 2013).

CRITICAL DEVELOPMENTAL PSYCHOLOGY

Most of the developmental theories discussed are founded on a developmental way of thinking. Despite their many differences, they share assumptions about regular and age-related changes *within* children, which result from interactions between biological processes and environmental conditions. However, in the wake of radical social constructivism and gender studies, *critical developmental psychology* (also called *psychology of childhood*) has emerged, influenced by post-modern sociology and psychoanalytical ideas about interpretation and comprehension (Morss, 1996). Erica Burman (2008, 2017) aims to "deconstruct" developmental psychology and insists that there are no independent individual developmental processes – they are only a construction in the minds of developmental psychologists (see also Callaghan et al., 2015). "Critical" theoreticians argue against biology-based development and are particularly critical of evolutionary psychology. They argue that assumptions about regularities in the development of children's inner processes should be replaced by an understanding of children's thinking and actions as products of the social and cultural contexts in which the children take part and not on any assumptions about their internal functions being different to those of adults (Burman, 2001, 2013a). Similarly, Dion Sommer (2012) focuses on *childhood* rather than on the abilities which emerge from within the child. In his view, it is the *cultural histories* that define childhood, who children are, why they are the way they are, and their positions in society. Critical developmental psychology considers it as a main task to expose, in political and social terms, the implications and consequences of the other developmental theories. Burman (2017, 2013b) maintains that the traditional

schools of thought in developmental psychology have emerged less as a result of scientific research than of historical, economical and political conditions, especially the position of women and their function as a source of labor, and that these theories, as a consequence, help to underpin the current social system in the west. Critical psychology stresses the importance of gender as a cultural variable, but largely disregards age.

Critical psychology crucially insists that knowledge about development is not cumulative but constructed within a particular historical and cultural context and hence only is valid at that particular point in time. When changes take place in the social and cultural attitudes to children, previously acquired knowledge about them becomes invalid and must be revised. This contradicts the established scientific view that knowledge accumulates as part of an "evolutionary" process where some assumptions are not supported and hence abandoned, and others are supported and become accepted knowledge. For instance, it has been known for a long time that children start speaking during their first year of life. In medieval times, it was assumed that children would begin to speak even if they didn't hear speech, an assumption that is no longer accepted (O'Neill, 1980). In traditional developmental science, it is not the children who change throughout history but theories and empirical knowledge. In critical psychology there is no accumulated knowledge: children change when the theories change, because both are social constructs (Burman, 2017; Morss, 1996).

The critical perspective represents a radical break with the very foundation of developmental psychology, not least because it rejects the established understanding of the concept "development." There are relatively few critical psychologists and the critical approach has had only a limited influence on developmental psychology and the study of children. It has had more influence on the understanding of *childhood* as a sociological phenomenon, and especially in relation to variation in family structure and gender roles. However, questions raised by this perspective have been useful as counterweights to established views in developmental psychology and contributed to a more holistic appreciation of children in a social setting.

DISTINGUISHING BETWEEN THEORIES

This brief introduction demonstrates the considerable variation in theoretical approaches to developmental psychology, but also the many facets of children's capacities and the complexity of the developmental process. The theories differ but also encompass many similarities in their ways of describing development as a process of adaptation. Piaget (1952) and Freud (1916) both emphasize *conflict* as a driving force in development, but very different forms of conflict. In Piaget's theory, the conflicts are between elements of the child's perception of its surroundings, and the conflicts lead to integration of knowledge and cognitive development. In Freud's theory, the conflicts arise from children's motives and their demands on themselves, and the outcomes of the conflicts contribute to shaping personality. Freud (1930) and Vygotsky (1978) are both concerned with *culture*, but in Freud's theory culture represents distress to the child, something to which he must conform contrary to his own desires. Vygotsky (1978) sees culture as a positive component in development which enables thinking beyond the individual's own experience. Both also see *internalization* as an important mechanism, but in Freud's theory it is a case of internalizing external demands, while in Vygotsky's theory it is the acquisition of cultural skills and insights. Both Winnicott (1960) and Wertsch (1991) regard mother and child as a natural developmental *unit*, but for Winnicott this is a matter of mental representation and, for Wertsch, of collaboration to solve intellectual problems.

Theories differ in what factors they regard as more significant for children's development, but also, to some extent, in what aspect of development they emphasize. None of the theories can be said to cover the process as a whole. For instance, Piaget is particularly concerned with the development of cognition and morality, both of which he regards as a part of typical development. Freud was more interested in the development of personality and identity, and had a clinical orientation, but also presents his ideas as elements within a generalized theoretical model of development. Different theoretical views may thus neither agree nor disagree, but rather focus on different aspects of development. For instance, Piaget's views were clearly influenced by Freud

in areas which are relatively peripheral to his theory and he was for some time a member of the *International Psychoanalytic Association*. In his first book, Piaget writes: "Correspondingly, my indebtedness to psychoanalysis should be quite obvious. I believe these ideas to have revolutionized the primitive thinking in psychology" (Piaget, 1959, pp. xx–xxi). Psychodynamic accounts usually include a Piagetian approach to cognitive development.

New hypotheses often have their origin in some kind of behavior observation, and there may be consensus about what children do and what happens in a situation. It is the interpretation of the observation, the assumed motives and precursors, and the conclusions reached that differentiate the theories. A shared observational basis sometimes makes it difficult to decide which of several competing theories come closest to the truth. For instance, there is general agreement that some children are very shy and withdrawn, but disagreement about the reasons why children behave in this way. Behavioristic explanations would search for adult reactions to the child which may have contributed to maintaining the shy behavior. Cognitive learning theorists would in addition seek to gain insight into the child's self image and self efficacy. An ethologically oriented researcher may look for causes in the child's temperament and attachment relations. Finally, a traditional psychodynamic researcher may try to reveal unconscious psychological conflicts that have complicated the child's relationships to the mother and father.

When it becomes hard to discriminate between two contradictory but reasonable interpretations, both may be considered valid until there are grounds for excluding one of them. The theoretical selection process is however made more difficult still by the potential disagreement about the scientific basis and research methodology. Consequently, some of the knowledge remains uncertain and fragmented. Discussions about developmental psychology are characterized by phrases such as "on one hand . . . but on the other." A developmental way of thinking is a tool for reflecting on uncertain theoretical and methodological circumstances, as well as professional dilemmas during clinical work with children.

While studying developmental psychology, it may be useful to start by focusing on the phenomena – on what observations, experiments and other investigative approaches may tell about children. Once the phenomena are described, the next steps in the exploration of children's development are to compare the explanations and interpretations, identify the issues about which theories agree and disagree, and clarify their compatibility, that is, whether both could be true or if one excludes the other. The truth is not likely to be found somewhere halfway between two perspectives. Many theoretical views simply cannot be united: acceptance of one view will imply that other views must be rejected. A theory must be wrong if evidence supports a contradictory theory. And, often, there is no definite answer: one simply does not know which theory is the right one.

SUMMARY

1 Developmental theories attempt to explain the changes that take place between conception and adulthood. Modern developmental research has followed several different lines of thought and there is considerable variation between ideas and views within each perspective.

2 A good theory requires a coherent set of interconnected concepts and must be able to generate hypotheses that can test its validity.

3 *Psychodynamic psychology* is rooted in Sigmund Freud's psychoanalytic theory. Main elements are the importance of the *early years*, an *inner psychic structure* consisting of *id, ego* and *superego*, *unconscious motives* and *defense mechanisms*. However, Anna Freud and Erikson emphasize ego development, and Winnicott and Kohut, the development of the *self*. Psychodynamic theories are concerned with the child's relationships with other people, often seen in the form of *object relations*. Emde, Stern and Fonagy have integrated general infant psychology with psychoanalytical theory.

4 *Behaviorism* emphasizes the role of learning in development, but also that humans are different from other species. An important element of *cognitive learning theory* is that people are conscious and goal-oriented agents in their own life. It integrates cognitive processes, individual beliefs and assumptions about the self and the world but builds on the idea that development is a cumulative learning process and that learning is the basis for most of the individual differences between children.

5 In *logical constructivism,* the child's perception of the world is constructed by the organism, and cognitive development is thought to follow logical principles. Children perceive the world qualitatively differently from adults, actively seek knowledge and go through a long-lasting developmental process before they have acquired adult understanding and thinking. *Neo-Piagetians* such as Pascual-Leone, Case, Halford and Fischer share Piaget's constructivist basis, build on his ideas and integrate them with elements from other theories, notably information processing. Kohlberg extends Piaget's theory on moral development. Piaget's *new theory* takes earlier criticisms into account and is less based on logic.

6 According to *social constructivist theory* children's cognition is shaped through interaction with others and through *internalization* of the mental tools of the culture. Children are guided into the activities and using the strategies and mental tools of their culture, first together with others, then on their own. *Neo-Vygotskians* have made innovative changes and revisions and elaborated Vygotsky's ideas in *activity theory*.

7 *Nativism* assumes that important aspects of human development are constrained by the genetic endowment, and that experience has limited influence on many aspects of development. The main argument is that children's experiences alone are insufficient for adapting to the world, their own mind has to contribute from the start. According to *evolutionary psychologists* development of aggression, altruism and morality must be understood in terms of their significance

Continued

for survival in evolution. Bowlby's *ethological* theory of *attachment* has strongly influenced the understanding of children's early relations and has been important for clinical psychology, social work with children and raising children in general.

8   Bronfenbrenner's *bio-ecological* theory comprises *the proximal processes* with interactions between children and the people around them, and also meaningful objects or symbols. *The person* encompasses the individual's biological, cognitive, emotional and behavioral characteristics. *The context* consists of four systems: the *micro-*, *meso-*, *exo-* and *macrosystems*. *Time* encompasses the developmental time of the individual, as well as family time, historical time and so on.

9   *Information processing* models explain mental phenomena as information processed in one or several systems. Developmental change can be due to increases in processing speed or capacity and knowledge, and the use of new strategies. Information processing models have particularly influenced cognitive developmental psychology, but also social development and the development of emotions, personality and behavior disorders.

10   *Critical developmental psychology* or *childhood psychology* maintains that assumptions about developmental regularities in children's internal processes should be replaced by analyses of the cultural practices. The course of development does not depend on any biological givens, but on the child's social and cultural setting. Cultural narratives define childhood, who the child is and the reasons why, and her position in society. When social and cultural changes alter widely-held views about children, earlier knowledge about them is invalidated and has to be re-written.

11   Theories about developmental psychology differ markedly in their ways of describing and explaining what children are capable of, can perceive, feel, think and do at different ages. This reflects children's very varied capacities and the complexity of the developmental process. It can be difficult to establish which of the contradictory theories may be correct but the truth is not likely to be found somewhere halfway between two perspectives. If a theoretical assumption is shown to be correct, a contradictory assumption must be wrong.

CORE ISSUES

- The concepts that are needed for explaining human development in general and individual differences.
- The status of different theoretical models for understanding child and adolescence development.

SUGGESTIONS FOR FURTHER READING

Beilin, H. (1992). Piaget's new theory. In H. Beilin & P. B. Pufall (Eds), *Piaget's theory: Prospects and possibilities* (pp. 1–17). Hillsdale, NJ: Lawrence Erlbaum.

Bowlby, J. (1982). Attachment and loss: Retrospect and prospect. *American Journal of Orthopsychiatry*, *52*, 664–678.

Burman, E. (2001). Beyond the baby and the bathwater: Postdualistic developmental psychologies for diverse childhoods. *European Early Childhood Education Research Journal*, *9*, 5–22.

Geary, D. C., & Bjorklund, D. F. (2000). Evolutionary developmental psychology. *Child Development*, *71*, 57–65.

Gilmore, K. (2008). Psychoanalytic developmental theory: A contemporary reconsideration. *Journal of the American Psychoanalytic Association*, *56*, 885–907.

Karpov, Y. V. (2005). *The neo-Vygotskian approach to child development*. Cambridge: Cambridge University Press.

Martí, E., & Rodríguez, C. (Eds) (2012). *After Piaget*. New Brunswick, NJ: Transaction Publishers.

Yermolayeva, Y., & Rakison, D. H. (2014). Connectionist modeling of developmental changes in infancy: Approaches, challenges, and contributions. *Psychological Bulletin*, *140*, 224–355.

Contents

CHAPTER 3

METHODS OF GAINING KNOWLEDGE ABOUT CHILDREN

Both researchers and practitioners use systematic methods to collect information about children. Researchers investigate children's typical and atypical development, the presence of variation and how particular characteristics of children and the environment contribute to different developmental trajectories, using a variety of methods. Some map the development of traits and how they relate to each other in the general child population, others compare children who have different variants of the same gene or grow up under different environmental conditions, while others again describe the developmental course of individual children. The choice of method is closely related to the study's theoretical or practical basis, and what it intends to examine (Lerner et al., 2009). Theory and purpose thus act as "filters" that allow certain types of data to pass through and block out others. For practitioners, it is the child's possible problems or disorders that guide the collection of information.

OBSERVATIONS

Research is often about how children and adolescents act in a particular situation, for example when they are exposed to adult anger and aggression (see p. 359). This requires some kind of observation and a registration of the activities and behavior of one or more individuals. The observer may for instance see, hear or record what children say and do when they are playing, talking, arguing, and so on.

The observer may participate in the activity being observed, give instructions or simply observe, sometimes by using one or several video cameras. All observations involve *selection* and *interpretation,* and the adoption of one perspective where several are possible. Something is always left out. A good observer is aware of his or her own interests, perspectives and other factors that can lead to bias in the collection of information or unequal treatment of observations.

In planning an observation, it is common to prepare categories that define and specify the things to be observed. Such categories may describe where children are located (in the sandbox, on the swing, at the dining table), how they move (crawling, walking, running), what they are looking at (father, another child, a toy), what they are playing with (a car, a toy block, a ball) or the feelings they express (joy, anger, sadness) (see Table 3.1). The categories in each area should be unambiguous and mutually exclusive.

Naturalistic observations take place in the everyday environment where children usually spend their time, without influence by the observer. They may include observations of how children play and communicate with other children and adults, how they orient themselves in traffic, or how they use their mobile phones. Box 3.1 describes a study that compares how children play at home with their mothers and fathers.

Many of the earliest studies were *diary studies* in which the researchers (who were also the children's parents) wrote down what their children said or did in diary form (Bühler, 1928; Darwin, 1877; Stern, 1912). Piaget presents many systematic observations of his own children in his

An observation. (Photo: Tommy Næss)

early books (e.g., Piaget, 1950, 1952). In the field of language development, it is still common for researchers to study their own children, since this type of study requires close monitoring (Carpendale and Carpendale, 2010; Dromi, 1993; Tomasello, 1992).

Experiments

Experiments are often used when something is difficult to observe in ordinary situations. Investigations of causal relations for example in young children's memory for events may require systematic observation under controlled conditions (see Chapter 11). Here, "control" means that as many conditions as possible are kept constant so the results are likely to reflect the factors that are targeted in the study. Factors that are not part of the experiment should ideally not affect the outcome. All subjects should be observed in

the same way and treated equally, except when differential treatment is part of the experiment, such as in the experiment where two groups of children received different information about toys (p. 350), or when one group of children receives training, and another group does not.

Laboratory experiments are observations in customized environments and situations. One example is the "Strange Situation" which is used to elicit attachment behavior (see p. 402). The child is first separated from and then reunited with a caregiver, following a carefully planned procedure and using clearly defined categories for the child's behavior. One potential pitfall of laboratory studies that explore an otherwise naturally occurring situation is low *ecological validity*, because children may behave differently in unfamiliar surroundings. Many developmental experiments, however, do not aim to recreate a natural environment, but to test theoretical assumptions about how children act and react under very specific conditions. Robert Fantz's (1958) classic experiments provided new and pioneering knowledge about the visual acuity of infants and their focus of attention, and thereby also about the bases of cognitive and social development. Infants were shown visual patterns of varying complexity and without any other distracting stimulation, a situation that differs considerably from infants' normal visual environment. Despite all the informal observations of thousands of generations of parents and other adults, infant vision had been greatly underestimated until this point. The abilities of infants would hardly have been uncovered so convincingly without an experimental laboratory method (see p. 125).

TABLE 3.1   Common dimensions in the description of observations (based on Robson, 2002)

1	Space	Design of the physical environment, rooms, outside spaces, and so on
2	Persons	Names and relevant details of the persons included in the observations
3	Activities	The various activities in which the observed individuals participate
4	Objects	Physical elements, objects, furniture, and so on
5	Actions	Specific actions performed by each person
6	Events	Special events, such as gatherings and meetings
7	Time	Sequence of events
8	Goal	What the individuals being observed try to achieve
9	Emotions	Emotions shown or described by the individuals in particular contexts

BOX 3.1 CHILDREN'S PLAY WITH MOTHERS AND FATHERS (John et al., 2013)

Interested families were recruited from two centers for preschool-aged children. The home visits started by informing families of their rights as a participant and obtaining their consent. All observations began with a child–mother observation, which lasted for approximately 18–20 minutes, followed by child–father observation, which lasted for approximately 12–15 minutes, and took place at either the dining table or a play table in the living room. Both the child–mother and the child–father dyads chose from a set of toys comprising play dough and molds, building blocks, coloring book and markers, and a storybook. During the observation, only the participating dyad and the observer remained in the room. All observations were videotaped for
subsequent analysis, and each family received $75 for their participation. The researchers categorized each of the activities of the child–parent dyads, and rated parental sensitivity, structuring, non-intrusiveness and non-hostility, and child responsiveness and involvement, on a scale from low (1) to high (7). The analyses of the observations showed that the mothers tended to structure the children's play, "teach" them, guide their behavior and engage them in empathic conversations. The interactions with fathers included more physical play and child-led interactions, and the fathers tended to motivate and challenge the children, and behave more like age mates. However, the average emotional availability was not significantly different. With this methodology the researchers showed that young children have different interaction patterns in play with their mothers and fathers.

Field experiments combine naturalistic observation and experimental control by studying the consequences of a systematic change in a natural environment on child and adult behavior. One example is a study that demonstrated the *Rosenthal effect*. Teachers were told that some of the students in their class were expected to do well in school on the basis of their scores on intelligence tests, but the students' scores were actually drawn at random. The experiment showed that the false information had a bearing on both the teachers' assessment and the students' performance at school: those who were expected to do better on the basis of fake test results did in fact perform better in school (see p. 275).

Some common problems in observing children

Many factors can influence observations of children. The presence of an adult observer will always affect them. Children may be shy or have trouble understanding verbal instructions in an unfamiliar setting. In a study of the language of 4-year-olds, several children reacted to being

alone with an unfamiliar adult by answering almost exclusively in monosyllables, while the parents reported that their children usually spoke in sentences (Fintoft et al., 1983). Moreover, adults represent power and knowledge, and it is particularly difficult to observe children's spontaneous interactions without influencing them too much. Even adults behave slightly differently toward children when they are observed by an experimenter or recorded on video.

There is no simple formula for overcoming the problems that may arise in connection with observing children. Instead, it is a matter of being aware of potential problems, trying to reduce their impact and taking into account the uncertainty they create in drawing observation-based conclusions.

QUESTIONNAIRES AND INTERVIEWS

Sometimes researchers need to investigate a large number of children and adolescents to be sure that the information can be generalized to all boys and girls of that age, for example how many who are exposed to bullying and how they react when they see other students being bullied in school (see p. 477). It would be difficult to observe enough children and adolescents involved in bullying and it would take a lot of time and resources. It is more efficient to collect the information by interviewing the children themselves or their parents, or asking them to complete questionnaires (e.g., Baldry, 2003; Fekkes et al., 2005).

Questionnaires usually consist of close-ended questions with multiple-choice answers to be marked by the child or an adult, for example by indicating on a scale from 1 (never) to 5 (always) whether they see "Kids who hit or push others" (Pfeiffer and Pinquart, 2014). The advantage of questionnaires is that it is relatively easy to collect a large number of answers, sometimes with the help of the Internet (Gosling and Mason, 2015). The disadvantage is that the number of questions and alternative answers is limited and allows little insight into the reasoning behind the answers, even if informants can add comments.

Interviews are conversations between an interviewer and an interviewee, based on an interview guide. They can be as structured as a questionnaire, but are usually *semi-structured*, with room for clarifying questions and clearing up of potential misunderstandings. Although they are more time-consuming, the interviewer can collect more detailed information, respond with follow-up questions, and get deeper insight into the interviewee's thoughts and feelings. This is particularly important in interviewing children, who often interpret questions from their own point of view (Eder and Fingerson, 2001). Interviews are not commonly used in the study of younger children because they can have difficulty communicating their thoughts and ideas verbally, but are widely used in studies of older children and adolescents, and to gather information from parents, teachers and other adults. Interviews with children are important because they may give a quite different picture than information from their parents or teachers (Davies and Wright, 2008; Madge and Fassam, 1982) but they require sensitivity, ability to listen and good commutation skills.

ARCHIVAL RESEARCH

Many public institutions collect and store information routinely, and this material can to some extent be obtained, analyzed and interpreted (Scott and Attia, 2017). Public records with information about the population are available in most modern societies. Some are widely accessible in the form of a large amount of statistical material that makes it impossible to identify individuals, and analyses may give insight into the influences of different caregiving environments. Box 3.2 is an example of a study based on archival data. Other records have strict limitations on who can access them and how they can be used due to privacy protection laws. However, analyses of medical records or reports from health centers, hospitals, kindergartens, schools and school psychologists may give important information about the effect of different intervention measures. Archives represent an efficient and time-effective way of accessing information, but their drawback is that researchers cannot influence the information or ask follow-up questions.

BOX 3.2 PARENTAL DEMOGRAPHICS AND CHILDREN'S SOCIOECONOMIC ACHIEVEMENTS (Erola et al., 2016)

The researchers analyzed public data provided by Statistics Finland on the occupational position of 29,282 children and on the parents' education, occupational class and income when the children were 0–4, 5–9, 10–14, 15–19, 20–24 and 25–29 years old. They found that socioeconomic status in young adulthood was significantly related to parental education but not to parental income and social class. A large prospective study for investigating these kinds of relationships would have taken much time and resources.

METHODOLOGIES

Studies of children differ from one another along several dimensions: there are qualitative and quantitative studies, group and case studies, retrospective and prospective studies, and cross-sectional and longitudinal studies.

Quantitative and qualitative methods

Quantitative and qualitative methodologies are the two main classes of research methodologies. Quantitative methods are used when the phenomena in question can be counted or measured in other ways, and are often based on questions such as *who*, *where*, *when*, *what* and *how many*. For example, one can register the age at which a sample of children speak their first word, count how many words the children use at the age of 2 and calculate the average age and typical age range for the first word, the average number of words and the minimum and maximum number of words at 2 years, and the children's mean length of utterance (Brown, 1973). Based on these data, statistical relationships (correlations) can be established between the age at which the children spoke their first word and the size of their vocabulary and mean length of utterance at the age of 2 years. Statistics can be used to calculate whether there is more than a random difference in vocabulary among children from different social backgrounds or among the younger and older siblings in a family.

Qualitative methods are often used to describe processes, with research questions such as *how* and *why* something happens. Events are described with words, and analyses typically involve text rather than numbers. By performing qualitative analyses of children's and adults' contributions in early conversations, for example, one can study how children learn sentences (Scollon, 1976; Tomasello, 1992).

Both quantitative and qualitative methods are rooted in a scientific argument that makes a case for a given phenomenon to be worthwhile and viable for study. If the research questions are best answered by measurable results, a quantitative approach is indicated. If they are best answered by descriptions of processes that are difficult to quantify and measure, a qualitative approach is preferable. *Mixed methods* can often provide more information and a broader perspective than one of the methodologies alone

(Nelson, 2015a; Tolan and Deutsch, 2015). Experimental data are usually, but not necessarily, quantitative. The same applies to studies based on questionnaires, which are often analyzed using statistics. Tests and other assessment instruments are designed to rank children and quantify the differences between them. Observations and interviews of children can be analyzed quantitatively as well as qualitatively, for example by tallying up children's emotional statements as well as performing qualitative analyses that can shed light on their emotional involvement in a given situation (Lund, 2005; Yoshikawa et al., 2008). Thus, the lines between the two approaches are not always clear, and sometimes both methods are applied to the same observational data, such as in a study that surveyed parents and preschool teachers on when children should start in kindergarten (Undheim and Drugli, 2012). *Microgenetic* studies, which include both observations and conversations over time, are used to gain insight into how children think and solve problems (Siegler, 2006). Observations of quantitative changes in the occurrence of different child actions may direct the microgenetic "microscope" at processes in the transitional phases for a qualitative analysis of where the changes seem to occur, for example the point in development where children begin to express understanding of mind and false belief (Flynn et al., 2007).

Group and case studies

Many researchers are interested in the emergence and developmental consequences of specific traits, such as sociability or shyness (see Rubin and Coplan, 2010), and such studies may require a relatively large number of children. In order to investigate the relationship between shyness and social development, it is necessary to compare shy children with a group of children who are not shy and at the same time do not differ in other ways. If the groups differed in other areas, for example in relative numbers of boys and girls, any differences in social development could just as well be due to these factors as to the difference in shyness.

In some studies one of the groups is treated or influenced in a specific way, and compared with a group that has not been exposed to the same treatment or influence. One study, for example, found that a cod liver oil supplement had a positive effect on the cognitive development of infants (Helland et al., 2003). The "experimental group" received the supplement, while a similar substance was given to the "control group," a placebo. The control group corresponds to the experimental group in every other way, but "controls" the effect of the supplement by not receiving it. The children in this group had the same average birth weight and social background, and none of the parents were told whether their child received the supplement or the placebo, until after the study was finished. Only then could Helland be sure that the supplement made a difference.

Today, there is a general demand that educational and clinical practice should be evidence-based, that choice of assessment and intervention measures should be based on knowledge about documented effects and solid research (Berninger, 2015; Stoiber et al., 2016). This demand has partly emerged from the early disagreements between different theoretical approaches, in child mental health between psychodynamic treatment and behavioral and cognitive treatment, and has contributed to a wider use of interventions with documented effect (Forte et al., 2014). Clinical studies with a high degree of control, where similar subjects are randomly allocated to a treatment or non-treatment group, are considered the highest level of evidence. However, comparing treatment and no treatment may not be a good basis for deciding the efficacy of an intervention, as most interventions are better than nothing. Decisions about intervention for children with severe disabilities, for example, should be based on thorough knowledge about relevant interventions. New interventions should be compared with interventions that are already in use, and studies should thus have an experimental treatment group and a treatment-as-usual group (e.g., von Tetzchner et al., 2013).

Individual children can show a variation in development not otherwise found in the group. Descriptions of individual developmental trajectories can therefore supplement knowledge of development based on group studies (von Eye et al., 2015). Studies of individual children who show unusual abilities such as musicality or arithmetic skills can furthermore contribute knowledge about how these abilities develop in relation to other developmental areas. In a similar way, it can be useful to study children who are blind, deaf or have neurodevelopmental disorders.

Clinical descriptions of individual children are called *case studies*. One advantage of such studies is that they can go into greater depth and provide insight into the processes underlying the atypical development, also in a scientific sense. Their downside is that the findings can be difficult to generalize and apply to children in other contexts. Case studies typically include both qualitative and quantitative information, but most of the data tends to be qualitative. Case studies are of great importance to clinical developmental psychology (see Parker and Hagan-Burke, 2007; Yin, 2009).

Cross-sectional and longitudinal studies

There are two ways of obtaining information about the general development trajectory of a given characteristic in children. *Cross-sectional studies* try to map the development process by comparing children at different age levels (Figure 3.1), for example by observing the children's aggressive actions in typical situations or letting parents complete questionnaires about their children's behavior and background. Studies show that young children show a higher frequency of hitting than older children and positive relations between the number of aggressive actions and various environmental factors, such as family relations, time with violent computer games, and so on (see Chapters 23 and 26). The advantage of cross-sectional studies is that they are time-efficient. Researchers avoid having to wait for children to grow up, and children are spared some of the strain, since they are studied at only a single age level.

Cross-sectional studies can show what is typical for children at different age levels but reveal little about the actual course of development. If one has observed aggressive actions in 2-, 6- and 10-year-olds, it is impossible to know whether the same or different children exhibit most aggressive behaviors at these ages, whether their aggression is stable over time, or whether there is a relationship between their early characteristics, experiences and environment, and their later aggressive behavior. This requires a longiztudinal study in which the same children are observed at the ages of 2, 6 and 10 years. This approach would provide more insight into the developmental process and the developmental courses of children with different characteristics and experiences, their vulnerability and resilience.

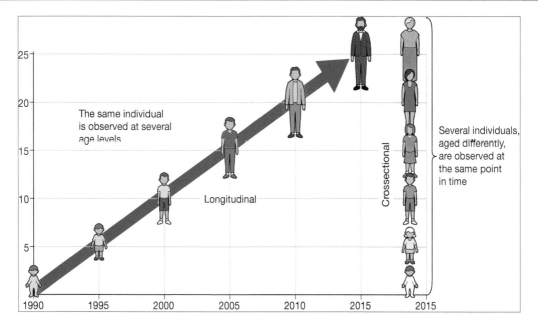

FIGURE 3.1 Longitudinal and cross-sectional studies.

Longitudinal studies examine the same individuals at different points in their lives. Here, the participants were observed at birth in 1990, and in 1995, 2000, 2005, 2010 and 2015. Cross-sectional studies examine a number of differently aged individuals at the same time. Here, the participants were newborns and 5, 10, 15, 20 and 25 years old in 2015.

Relatively short-term longitudinal studies are common (a search with "longitudinal" in Google Scholar creates over 4 millions hits) and several longitudinal studies have lasted for 30 years and longer (for example, Bergman et al., 2014; Block and Block, 2006; Caspi et al., 2016; Sroufe et al., 2010). In 1939, Sol Seim (1997) launched a unique longitudinal study that began when the participants were 13 years old, and continued until they were nearly 70 in 1994. Seim herself was over 80 years old at the time. Of the 100 original 13-year-olds, 49 were still part of the study when they turned 70.

Since longitudinal studies are very time-consuming, studies conducted over many years are relatively rare, but they are absolutely essential. Without such studies, there would be no basis for a developmental psychology based on scientific evidence (Campos et al., 2008; Kagan, 2008b).

Prospective and retrospective studies

When researchers follow one or several children over time, typically using observations, questionnaires and interviews, this is a *prospec-tive study. Retrospective studies* are based on information about passed events, such as children's earlier development and experiences. The source of information is usually parents and others who know the children well, but the informa-tion is often colored by the passage of time and therefore somewhat unreliable, especially when events and recollections go far back in time. In this case, archival information can provide a supplement to the information contributed by parents. For example, the diaries of family members and private videos have been used to document the development of children with autism spectrum disorder *before* they received the diagnosis (Zwaigenbaum et al., 2007).

Even though they are to a certain extent unreliable, retrospective studies are important. It can be difficult, for example, to map the development of children with a rare disorder before the disorder is detected. If one were to follow children with a rare disorder prospectively, from before the disorder makes its appearance, one would need to observe a group of children large enough to be likely to include children with the disorder in question. This would imply observing many children whose development is unrelated to the focus of study. The Norwegian Mother and Child Cohort Study (Magnus et al., 2016), that involves over 100,000 parents and children and includes regular information on the course of pregnancy and childhood, is an example of a prospective study large enough to incorporate information about the development of children with rare conditions.

Cross-cultural studies

Every child grows up in a society with certain values, norms, activities and ways of organizing and doing things, and styles and methods of parenting vary considerably between countries (Selin, 2014). Society is an important part of the childhood environment and impacts most developmental areas (see Bornstein, 2010). Comparing children growing up in different cultures is a way of studying the impact of both biological and cultural factors, and can yield information about the types of environmental factors necessary and adequate for normal development. The characteristics of child-directed speech, for example, are considered to be important for language development (see p. 327), but are not equally prominent in all cultures (Schaffer, 1989). Also how parents play with their children varies considerably between countries (Roopnarine and Davidson, 2015).

A consequence of such cultural differences is that the results of studies in one culture are not always transferable to other cultures. This is an important argument for studying children who grow up in different cultures. Asian and North American parents, for example, respond differently to the emotional expressions of their children (see Chapter 17). On the basis of either American or Chinese studies alone, an understanding of how children develop emotional regulation would be highly biased. In a similar vein, Robert Sternberg maintains that the study of culture is "necessary, not just nice," and that "developmental psychologists can do a better job of understanding and leveraging the strengths of people from diverse environmental contexts if those strengths are viewed in a cultural framework" (2014, p. 209).

SPECIAL METHODS FOR STUDYING INFANTS

Children's understanding of the world emerges gradually and how infants perceive their environment is of great interest to developmental research, but challenging from a methodological point of view. Since infants cannot directly communicate what they see or hear, or solve tasks involving complex verbal or non-verbal instructions, research methods are based on habituation and conditioning, visual exploration and physiological and neurophysiological measurements. Habituation and conditioning are also used in fetal research (see Chapter 6).

Habituation and dishabituation

Infants explore the world and are generally interested in what happens around them. They are typically attentive to new things and events but when they are repeatedly shown the same object or get to hear the same sound, they will gradually react less and less, and eventually stop responding altogether. They "lose" attention, or *habituate*. When children discover something new, they will respond more strongly once again, or *dishabituate*. Dishabituation thus requires the child to be able to distinguish between the original stimulation and the new one. This has been methodically exploited by researchers to discover the types of stimulation, situations and events infants are able to differentiate, such as their ability to distinguish between speech sounds (see p. 309).

Conditioning

Studies of infants make use of both classical and operant conditioning (see p. 285). An example of *classical conditioning* is a study in which a tone was played to infants right before a puff of air was blown onto their eyes and automatically caused them to blink. After several presentations, the children blinked when they heard the tone, "preparing" for the air they had learned would follow (Little et al., 1984). An example of *operant conditioning* is a study in which 3-month-olds learned to move a leg to activate a mobile hanging above the bed (Rovee-Collier and Cuevas, 2009a; see p. 198).

Visual exploration

Attention is selective and children's attention therefore gives information about what is and is not of interest to them. Head mounted cameras and equipment that records where infants look, pupil dilation and eye blink has become an important tool for studying how they explore and perceive their environment and react to events in the visual world (Eckstein et al., 2017; Gredebäck et al., 2010; Yoshida and Smith, 2008).

Visual preference

When infants are shown two pictures or objects, they often look longer at one of them than the other, and generally this is not a matter of chance. This tendency to look longer at one visual stimulus than another, also known as *preferential looking*, is used among other things to map the vision, memory and concepts of infants (Golinkoff et al., 2013). Fantz (1961) uses the preferential looking method to determine the types of stimulation most "interesting" to new-borns, that is, what they look at the longest (see p. 129).

Other studies build on the assumption that children will look longest at the picture or object that represents something new (novelty preference). When 3- to 4-month-olds are shown two pictures of a face with the same emotional expression, followed by the same picture together with a picture of a new facial expression, the infants will look longest at the new expression (provided they have had enough time to familiarize themselves with the first facial expression). Novelty preference shows that children remember the first facial expression and are able to see that it differs from the new facial expression (Fagan and Detterman, 1992).

Some studies are based on the assumption that unexpected phenomena have greater attention value than ordinary ones (e.g., Onishi and Baillargeon, 2005). Studies have found that infants look longer at a seemingly impossible event, such as a toy block hanging in the air without support, than they do in an otherwise identical situation in which the block is supported by a surface (Baillargeon et al., 1995; see p. 223). The results have been interpreted to mean that even at this age, infants have some understanding of physical forces and that toy blocks cannot float freely in the air (Baillargeon et al., 2009).

Physiological reactions

Children's physiological responses can also provide information on how they perceive what happens in their surroundings. For instance, infants react to novelty with a decrease in heart rate (orienting response). Loud noises and other forms of aversive stimulation leads to an increase in heart rate (Richards, 2001; Rovee-Collier and Barr, 2001). Cortisol levels are often used as a measure of stress but the production of cortisol is also affected by factors unrelated to stress (Reznick, 2013).

Neurophysiological measures

The methods for exploring brain functions are constantly improving (see p. 103) and open up new ways of studying infants. Just like dishabituation, the *mismatch response* (see p. 103) is used to determine when a child perceives something novel. One advantage of this method is that it requires no cooperation on the part of the child, who can be asleep during the procedure.

The methods are important but difficult to interpret

The methods are important for obtaining an empirical basis for theories about infant cognition. However, it is a narrow repertoire of reactions that is used to measure a broad range of hypothetical cognitive functions, including concept formation and reasoning about social and physical phenomena. Preferential looking in particular is frequently used (Baillargeon, 1987; Dahl et al., 2013; Fantz, 1956), but what children look at, and how long they look at different things and events, is affected by many factors and changes considerably throughout infancy (and later). Many interpretations of findings are controversial, and several researchers argue that far more knowledge and understanding is often ascribed to infants than warranted by the studies (Aslin, 2007; Bishop, 2007; Tafreshi et al., 2014). In an analysis of methods and conclusions, Kagan (2008a) points out that the results of infant studies commonly allow for widely differing interpretations, and that many of the studies lack observations that could corroborate the researchers' interpretations of the infants' preferential looking patterns.

CRITERIA FOR RESEARCH METHODOLOGY

Sound research methodology has to fill a number of special requirements to ensure that the results can be trusted, including transparency, representativeness, reliability and validity. These requirements are met in somewhat different ways, depending on whether they have to do with quantitative or qualitative methods.

Transparency means that all the details of the method are openly available. The main requirement of quantitative research is replicability, that the method is explained so clearly and unambiguously that another researcher can carry out an identical study and examine whether the outcome can be reproduced or was caused by accidental circumstances. Such replications are a necessary part of research, since the results of many frequently cited studies have shown themselves to be non-replicable, and therefore invalid (Asendorpf et al., 2013; Stroebe et al., 2012). However, when replications fail, this does not necessarily mean that all the results of the original study were wrong, but points to the need for further theoretical and empirical work (Reese, 1999; Stroebe, 2016). Replications are thus not only a control mechanism to decide whether a study's results were valid, but an important basis for driving science.

In qualitative research, transparency is quite different. The observer should make his or her subjective standpoint clear, including perceptions, opinions and attitudes, and a sufficiently "thick" description that allows other researchers to understand the findings and confirm that the conclusions are reasonable (Biggerstaff, 2012). A researcher may have personal experiences or qualifications that could be of significance to the study and therefore need reflection, but it is mainly the researcher's theoretical perspective that needs to be clarified, rather than his or her personal background. Piaget never discussed his own background, but always elucidated the theoretical assumptions behind the questions he asked children when applying his qualitative "clinical method" to find out how children reason in their problem solving (see p. 170).

Research is generally interested not only in the particular children being studied, but wishes to say something about the group or groups to which the children belong, for example the prevalence of language disorders in 4–5-year-olds (Harrison and McLeod, 2010). Therefore it is essential for the *sample* of children to be *representative* of the *population* they are part of. A population consists of all the children for whom the study results are intended to be valid. Depending on the population one wants to study, a representative sample may involve an equal number of girls and boys, an equal number of children from every age level, different social classes, and so on. If a study aims at investigating characteristics typical of girls, it is not enough to study girls. If the researcher's hypothesis for instance is that girls have better language skills than boys, the language of both boys and girls have to be studied (Leaper and Smith, 2004).

Qualitative research does not require the outcome to be quantitatively representative, meaning that the subjects of the study need not be representative of a larger group. However, observations must be considered adequate and typical enough by the researcher to be the target of research with validity beyond itself. Qualitative analyses of interviews with adolescents who have mobility impairments, for example, usually are not designed to say something about that particular group of adolescents, but to provide a more general insight into the living conditions of adolescents who grow up with mobility impairments (see Madge and Fassam, 1982; Wickenden, 2011). The observations must therefore be representative of the experiences of this group.

Reliability

A study may include many observations and several observers, and for the observations to be reliable, the observational categories and measurement methods used should yield the same result with all observers and with repeated observations. A common method of testing reliability is to let several observers rate the same situation or video recording independently of one another based on a specific set of observational categories (inter-observer reliability). If one observer claims to have seen a child smile five times and another observer has seen ten smiles in the same space of time, they clearly use different criteria for what they consider to be a smile. This leads to unreliable results, since the observers are not using the same categories. To meet the requirements of reliability, they must agree in advance on a common set of criteria, the only way of ensuring that measurements are consistent and comparable. This is not to say that observers are always entirely certain of the emotion shown by a child, but mutual uncertainty about a child's particular expression is also an indication of reliability.

Qualitative methods, too, require observations that are accurate enough to be trustworthy. Video and sound recordings must contain all relevant and necessary information. Observational notes must be sufficiently systematic and extensive, follow accepted standards, be written during or shortly after the observation, and be accessible to third parties (Wolcott, 1994).

Validity

Validity concerns whether the method measures what it is supposed to measure and the results can provide answers to the questions posed by the study (Boorsboom et al., 2004). Reliability is necessary but not sufficient for establishing validity. A method is of little use if it is reliable but does not measure what the study is about. Although children's height can be measured with great accuracy, height will never be a valid measure of intelligence. The question of validity is equally central to quantitative and qualitative research.

There are several types of validity. *Construct validity* is the degree to which something that is observed or measured is a true representation of what the study intends or claims to measure, for example that children's answers on a questionnaire about their routines at home match the observations of what they actually do at home. *Predictive validity* is the ability to foresee the future, whether measurements made at one point can predict later characteristics or performance. This type of validity is especially important for the use of tests and other assessment instruments. When Binet and Simon (1905) designed the first intelligence test, the aim was to find children who would need special help in school. For a test to be valid, children who have higher scores should do better in school than children who receive lower scores. Also today school psychologists try to find school starters who may need special help, and thus depend on tests that can give a valid assessment. If an assessment is not valid, it serves no purpose either. Construct validity is central to developmental psychology, since it concerns the way in which development in different areas is measured and described – the

particular observations that form the basis for conclusions about the mechanisms involved in development.

Internal validity describes the soundness of assumptions about causal relationships after finding some type of relation between two variables, for example between measures of working memory and reading (Cozby, 1993). There are many "threats" to internal validity that may lead to wrong conclusions. These can be coincidences, such as when the school bully drops out of school at the same time as the school takes action against bullying. It looks as if the school's initiative had an effect, while the decrease in bullying is actually due to the fact that the student who did the bullying is no longer in school. An evaluation of a program supposed to promote social development has to take into consideration that children continually develop and include observations of social development in a control group of children who do not attend the program. Without a control group, children's ordinary development during program attendance can mistakenly be ascribed to the program. And apparent changes in children's behavior can be due to the use of different routines or observational categories at different points in time (Cook and Campbell, 1979).

External validity concerns the extent to which information can be generalized, whether the same behavior or characteristics found in the study subjects will also be found in others. Non-representative samples, observations made under special circumstances and unique historical contexts can easily jeopardize external validity. A study of gross motor skills based on children's skiing abilities may have a high degree of validity in Nordic countries, but cannot be generalized to children living closer to the Equator.

The concept of validity is less clear in qualitative research (Creswell and Miller, 2000). Zambo (2004) includes establishing credibility (stability and plausibility of data), transferability (applicability to other situations), dependability (trustworthiness of the data) and confirmability (that the data are in accordance with other observations). In a study on the impact of dyslexia on school life, she tried to ensure validity by making observations over a long time period, interview with students and teachers, field notes and journal entries, reflecting on her own theoretical perspective and potential biases, using "triangulation" (comparing results from different methods) and by asking participants if they agreed with the descriptions and interpretations.

ASSESSMENT

The function of clinical assessment of children is usually to gather information on how they understand, think, feel and act, and on the characteristics of their physical and social environment, especially the quality of their relations within the family and with children and adults outside the family. The assessment is usually initiated on the basis of a concern and a referral, and these will guide the assessment. The goal is to examine whether the child has any disorders or difficulties in areas requiring treatment, special education or other measures, or whether changes need to be made in the child's environment. In a clinical context, assessment is nearly always individual, but the use of tests and other assessment instruments is common in research studies of both typical and atypical development.

Conversations and interviews

Most assessments of children begin with an anamnestic interview, a conversation with the parents about the child's developmental history and the observations that lead to the referral. This may include structured and standardized interviews about the child's functioning in specific areas. These conversations provide information about the child and the family, but also help professionals and parents get to know each other and establish an *alliance*, a shared understanding of the child's strengths and weaknesses and the types of measures that may be necessary. When possible, older children and adolescents should take part in the conversations and interviews, and be included in the alliance.

Observations

Observations at home, in kindergarten and at school can give the practitioner an impression for instance of the child's skills, play, working effort, attention and social functioning. It can be useful to observe the child in both structured and unstructured situations, together with other children and with adults. For some areas, there are checklists with predesigned categories that make it easier to record the child's actions, such as different types of play and activities (Barton, 2010; Kelly-Vance et al., 2002).

In some cases it can be helpful to use video recordings to document how the child functions in different situations. The child may behave differently in school and at home with the parents, and parents may use video to document the child's home behavior. Children with selective mutism are able to speak but do not speak with people outside the family (Steinhausen et al., 2006; see p. 66). An audio recording with the parents may be useful to get an impression of the child's expressive language.

Tests

Tests are designed to rank children. They contain tasks standardized to measure individual performance in a specific area and under standard conditions. A large number of tests are available, embracing a wide range of skills and abilities (see Miller, 2007; Sattler, 2002). Tests of intelligence and specific cognitive skills are often part of assessment (see Chapter 14), together with language testing (Chapter 16). Other tests include perceptual (Chapter 8) and motor skills (Chapter 9), attention and executive skills (Chapter 11), social cognitive skills (Chapter 13) and emotional understanding (Chapter 17).

It is important that tests be carried out according to the manual, and only by professionals with a license to use them. The instructions must be formulated so the child can understand them. This is often an issue in the assessment of immigrant children. If the child does not understand the instructions, the results will not reflect the child's ability to solve the tasks. In addition, the tasks must correspond to the child's level of competence. Tasks that are too easy or too difficult can be perceived as both boring and meaningless. The tester must maintain a pace adapted to the child and be sensitive to how the child experiences the test situation. The presentation of many difficult tasks should be followed by a break, even if highly motivated children might claim they do not need one.

Testing requires good communication. The tester must be thoroughly familiar with the test and so well prepared that there is no need to consult the manual or cause unnecessary delays during the test procedure. Before testing begins, it can be useful to inform the child about the test and the reasons for taking it, and ask whether the child has any questions. It is not unusual for children to have practical questions about how long the test will take, whether they will get a break, and so on. The tester should also engage in a bit of small talk before the test begins, and spend some time getting to know the child. However, there should be no small talk during the testing as this may take the child's attention away from the tasks.

Feedback has to focus on the child's *effort*. Ideally, the child should have a sense of doing well, even if the answers are wrong. Usually, it is enough to say something like "Good!" or "It's going very well." The tester must not tell the child whether the answer is right or wrong, except on trial tasks prescribed by the manual, since this would invalidate any future use of the test with the same child. Children can remember the answer even if they don't know why it is correct. Taking notes should also be done in such a way that the child cannot see whether the answer is right or wrong. The easiest way of doing this is to write down what the child says or does. It is important to get the child to focus on solving each task, not on whether the answer is correct.

Testing of special groups

All testing must be adapted to the individual child's abilities. Although tests are designed to be suitable for most children, it may still be necessary to adapt the test situation and the material being used. Children who are deaf and use sign language have to be given instructions in sign language. It is not always enough for a sign language interpreter to translate the instructions one by one. Translations of more complex instructions should be planned and prepared in advance (Reesman et al., 2014). Assessments of children with severe visual impairments often involve using the language part of the test alone. Tasks consisting of images with a missing item, categorization based on shape and colours, puzzles and checkerboard patterns are unsuitable for children with poor vision. However, there are tests with non-visual and non-verbal tasks for the assessment of children with visual impairments (Smith and Amato, 2012; Zebehazy et al., 2012).

Children with severe motor impairments cannot perform tasks requiring them to physically construct something or follow action instructions such as "put the doll on the chair," but some tests are adapted for computers with equipment for eye-tracking and the child or adolescent can answer by looking at the right response alternative (Kurmanaviciute and Stadskleiv, 2017; Stadskleiv et al., 2017). Children with less severe motor impairments may be able to perform such actions, but often use so many cognitive resources on the physical execution itself that they score below what their ability to reason would suggest. The same applies to children with developmental motor coordination disorder or dyspraxia (see p. 59). For these groups, it may be necessary to use tests that require a minimum of motor skills, allot more time and make allowances for motor problems in interpreting their cognitive skills.

Any special arrangements and adjustments must be taken into account in the interpretation of test results. When testing takes place under specially tailored conditions, the norms merely provide a guideline, since they are usually based on a representative group of children with typical development. Children with atypical development are rarely included in norm-referenced tests. Consequently, these norms do not apply to them and must be used with caution. However, the results can still be useful for optimizing the child's learning situation. Some children may benefit from a dynamic assessment as a supplement to regular testing (see below).

Checklists

Checklists have become a common element in assessment. They consist of questions about the child's skills, behavior and everyday functioning. They are usually completed by parents, teachers and other adults, but checklists can also be completed by older children and adolescents. In addition, checklists are used by professionals to structure their own observations. One example of this is an instrument for observing children's everyday language (Cordier et al., 2014). The *Vineland Adaptive Behavior Scale* (Sparrow et al., 2005) is used to map everyday skills, language, social-cognitive and social skills. The *Child Behavior Check List* (CBCL; Achenbach and Rescorla, 2000, 2001) assesses emotional and behavioral disorders. Other checklists measure temperament, life quality, characteristics of the environment and how parents and other people in the child's surroundings experience their situation.

Parents are an important source of information about the child, but should not be responsible for assessing their child's development. Their view of the child is colored by their own perspective as parents, and often there are considerable differences in how parents, professionals and the children themselves answer questions about the child's temperament, emotions and behavior (De Los Reyes and Kazdin, 2005; Rescorla et al., 2014; Seifer et al., 1994).

Many checklists are screening instruments designed to identify children who should be further assessed with regard to disorders in general (Macy, 2012). Others aim to identify a particular disorder, such as autism spectrum disorder. It is important to use checklists that have questions that address the child's problems at that age. M-CHAT, for example, does not work particularly well for 18-month-olds, but can be useful from the age of 2 years (Beuker et al., 2014; Stenberg et al., 2014).

Analysis and interpretation

Completing the testing procedure and filling out checklists is only the first stage in the assessment process. The main task is to analyze the results, describe functional profiles and collate test results, observations and information from interviews and conversations. It is especially important to compare the child's strengths and weaknesses as they emerge in a structured test situation with the child's functioning in structured and unstructured activities at home, in kindergarten and at school. Test scores are influenced by many factors and should not be considered a measure of the child's inborn abilities. In many countries it is therefore not usual to present scores but rather a broad characterization of the child's achievements, such as "average," "below average," "in the upper part of the normal variation," "gifted" or "mild intellectual disability." More important than the actual scores are their implications for the child's functioning in different domains and need for help or special education.

Dynamic assessment

Traditional use of tests is often referred to as "static" because the tests measure children's knowledge and skills at a particular point in time. From a social constructivist perspective on cognition, assessment should not only record which tasks the child does and does not master, but also the learning process. This implies identifying the child's zone of proximal development (see p. 183) – what the child is able to do with help, and how much help is needed to solve a given task (Jeltova et al., 2007; Lidz, 1997). Guthke (1993), for example, tested first-graders with a non-verbal cognitive test (Raven) in the traditional way; then the children received systematic and standardized help with tasks they were unable to solve on their own. Following this, they were tested once again with the Raven test, and the increase in their scores was interpreted as a measure of their *learning potential*. The study further showed that this increase correlated more closely with the children's math scores in later school grades than the ordinary test scores. Thus, dynamic testing does not merely measure the child's skills at a given time but what the child learns under standard conditions.

Instruments for dynamic assessment include the *Learning Potential Assessment Device* (LPAD) (Feuerstein et al., 1997) and *Dynamic Assessment of Children's Narratives* (Miller et al., 2001). Dynamic assessments can be especially useful when children score low on tests and the results are inconsistent with other observations, when children come from a different culture and have problems with language, when children's performance seems to be low due to learning disorders, emotional disorders and low motivation, and when the primary goal is not to categorize the child's ability level but to facilitate appropriate training. In this situation, it is important to know how the child understands and applies the principles associated with the tasks, and how much the child needs to learn in order to master different tasks (Tzuriel, 2005).

Response to intervention

The evaluation of any measures that may have been initiated is an essential part of the assessment process. "Response to intervention" monitors whether the child's education yields the desired results and if there is a need for modifications or supplementing the ordinary education with other measures. The "response" can consist of academic improvement, but also better social and emotional functioning (Fox et al., 2010).

Both response to intervention and dynamic assessment include training and testing, and thus share certain similarities. An important difference, however, is that dynamic assessment centers on the child's abilities using a *test–training–test* procedure, while response to intervention follows a *training–test–training* procedure. In a typical sequence of training and testing at different points in time, the two procedures are quite similar in practice, but the focus of dynamic assessment is on the child's abilities, while response to intervention focuses on the training (Lidz and Peña, 2009; Grigorenko, 2009).

Some researchers are critical to the widespread use of cognitive tests in schools. According to Floyd (2010), intelligence tests only serve as a general indication of whether a child has difficulties, a fact that is often known before the tests are taken. He believes that one gets more insight into children's problems by trying out different forms of intervention and observing the benefits of each, that is, the extent to which they reduce the child's difficulties. An assessment of this type can offer feedback to the child and help identify the learning strategies best suited to him or her (Clark, 2012). Positive feedback may also make the child more motivated to the extra efforts in the domain(s) where he is struggling.

ETHICAL CONSIDERATIONS

Any observation of children involves a certain degree of intrusion into their privacy, and sometimes into the family's life or the practice of professionals around the child. The most fundamental ethical issue is whether to conduct a study when weighing the potential benefits of gathering knowledge against the possible drawbacks and discomfort the study might entail. Because children are vulnerable and less able to assess the consequences of participating in a study than adults, a particular ethical responsibility rests with anyone conducting research on children. Parents must be given sufficient insight into the intent behind the research and the methods that will be used to be able to give their informed consent or refusal to the child's participation. Parents need to know that they can withdraw the child from the study at any time without the need for justification. Children must be given information they can understand and realize what they will be involved in, but children under 16 years of age should not give consent. Consent requires that they understand the consequences of saying yes or no to participation in the study, an understanding that children do not have (Koelch et al., 2009; Millum and Emanuel, 2007). Furthermore, it can be difficult for children to withdraw once they have given consent – they have promised an adult to participate, and are usually told that they should keep their promises. Children should know that their parents have given consent, so they can be sure that it is neither dangerous nor harmful for them to participate. Most countries have ethical research guidelines and ethical committees to assess whether a research project meets the necessary ethical criteria before the project can be launched.

SUMMARY

1   Choice of method is determined by the information one wishes to obtain, the purpose of the study and its theoretical framework.

2   Observations are about what children and adults do. An observer can participate in activities or merely observe. Observations imply choosing one of several possible perspectives. Observations are divided into *categories* that are specified and defined. Categories must be unambiguous and are often mutually exclusive.

3   *Naturalistic observation* takes place in children's own environment and without influence by the observer. *Experiments* are carried out under *controlled* conditions. Laboratory experiments consist of customized situations. *Field experiments* combine naturalistic observation and experimental control. *Questionnaires* with close-ended questions or *archival studies* are often

Continued

used to gather information about larger groups of children. *Interviews* can provide more detailed insight into children's and adults' thoughts and feelings.

4 *Quantitative methods* involve categorization, quantification, measurements and statistics, and are suitable for research questions such as *who*, *what*, *when* and *how many*. *Qualitative methods* are used to describe processes, and are suitable for research questions such as *why* and *how* something happens; processing typically involves text rather than numbers. *Microgenetic methods* combine quantitative and qualitative approaches. Mixed methods provide more information and a broader perspective.

5 *Group studies* compare children with different characteristics, or children who are, or are not, exposed to a certain influence. The *experimental group* should correspond to the *control group* in every way, except that the experimental group is exposed to the experimental treatment or influence.

6 *Case studies* describe individual children who have particular biological characteristics, grow up under particular conditions or receive a particular type of treatment. By going into greater depth, case studies represent a complement to group studies, but the findings can be difficult to generalize and apply to children in other contexts. Case studies are especially important to clinical developmental psychology.

7 *Cross-sectional studies* compare children at different age levels. *Longitudinal studies* observe the same group of children at two or more points in time. *Prospective studies* follow children over time. *Retrospective studies* are based on collecting past information, mostly from parents and others who know the children well. *Cross-cultural studies* compare children growing up in different cultures and offer a broad insight into the impact of the environment.

8 Studies of infants use *habituation* and *dishabituation, conditioning, visual exploration* (including *preferential looking*), as well as *physiological* and *neurophysiological measures*. The studies are important but the results are often difficult to interpret, and there is significant disagreement about their implications for infants' cognitive skills and perception of their surroundings.

9 Research must be *transparent*, and all the details of the method must be openly available. The *sample* of children must be *representative* of the *population* they are part of. Methods must be *reliable* and *valid*, measure what they are intended to measure and provide answers to the questions raised. It is the validity that relates observations of children to the understanding of their development.

10 An *assessment* is usually undertaken in response to a concern or referral. Methods include conversations and interviews, observations, tests and checklists. *Tests* are observations of children's ability to solve problems under predetermined conditions. Testing must be adapted to the individual child and requires test competency and good communication. *Dynamic assessment* focuses on the learning process and the child's learning potential. The results of an assessment are *interpreted*, *analyzed* and *collated*.

11 The most fundamental *ethical issue* behind all research is whether to conduct a study when weighing the potential benefits of gathering knowledge against any possible drawbacks and discomfort. Since children are vulnerable and unable to assess the consequences of participating in a study, a particular ethical responsibility rests with anyone conducting research on children. Parents must consent on behalf of their child, and children must be informed in a way they can understand. Ethical committees typically assess whether a research project meets the necessary ethical criteria before the project can be launched.

CORE ISSUES

- The role of quantitative and qualitative methodology in scientific research.
- The lack of replicating studies.
- Consent, assent and the involvement of children in research.

SUGGESTIONS FOR FURTHER READING

Danby, S., Ewing, L., & Thorpe, K. (2011). The novice researcher: Interviewing young children. *Qualitative Inquiry, 17,* 74–84.

Funamoto, A., & Rinaldi, C. M. (2015). Measuring parent–child mutuality: A review of current observational coding systems. *Infant Mental Health Journal, 36,* 3–11.

Nosek, B. A., & Bar-Anan, Y. (2012). Scientific utopia: I. Opening scientific communication. *Psychological Inquiry, 23,* 217–243.

Nosek, B. A., Spies, J. R., & Motyl, M. (2012). Scientific utopia: II. Restructuring incentives and practices to promote truth over publishability. *Perspectives on Psychological Science, 7,* 615–631.

Robson, C., & McCartan, K. (2016). *Real world research, Fourth edition.* Chichester, UK: Wiley.

Sroufe, L. A., Egeland, B., Carlson, E., & Collins, W. A. (2005). *The development of the person: The Minnesota study of risk and adaptation from birth to adulthood.* New York, NY: Guilford Press.

Contents

CHAPTER 4

CHILD AND ADOLESCENT DISORDERS

This chapter provides a brief description of the major diagnostic systems and the most common disorders in children and adolescents, and their prevalence. Issues related to the etiology and development of the disorders and their impact on development will be further discussed in the relevant chapters. The subject index at the end of the book is a useful tool for finding where a disorder is mentioned.

CATEGORIZATION OF DISORDERS

Knowledge about the basis for categorizing disorders is important for clinicians to be able to recognize, understand and communicate the problems children can experience (Rutter and Pine, 2015). Distinguishing characteristics are rarely absolute. Many disorders require the presence of only a certain number of the symptoms (Ortigo et al., 2010). Children who meet the criteria for a given disorder do not necessarily experience exactly the same problems or symptoms. In addition, there is a seamless transition between the normal variation in children's functioning and what constitutes a disorder.

Children with disorders are not characterized by their disorder(s) alone. In other areas they vary just as much as children without a disorder. Two children may meet the criteria for the same disorder and yet give very different impressions. Some children with autism spectrum disorders, for example, are passive and anxious, while others are active and seemingly without fear.

Some lack speech, while others talk incessantly. In describing a child, it is important to detail the way in which the disorder manifests, as well as other traits and characteristics exhibited by the child, both those related to diagnosis and those specific to the individual.

CLASSIFICATION SYSTEMS

There are two main international classification systems for mental and behavioral disorders. The eleventh edition of *The International Statistical Classification of Diseases and Related Health Problems* (ICD-11) was published by the World Health Organization in 2018. (The ICD-11 browser is accessible at http://www.who.int/classifications/icd/en/.) The fifth edition of the *Diagnostic and Statistical Manual of Mental Disorders* (DSM-5) was published by the American Psychiatric Association in 2013. With each new edition, the two systems have become more similar, and ICD-11 resembles DSM-5 more than ICD-10. Many disorder categories have become more or less identical. Critical voices, however, believe that ICD-11 should avoid the weaknesses of DSM-5 (Roessner et al., 2016), among other things the fact that the threshold for a number of diagnoses has either been lowered or raised, and that many of the categories in DSM-5 have not been sufficiently tested (Frances and Nardo, 2013). The differences between ICD and DSM and the changes in the diagnostic systems over time emphasize that diagnoses are not "natural" entities but conventional categories that can be changed with new theoretical and empirical insights.

DC 0-3: Diagnostic Classification of Mental Health and Developmental Disorders of Infancy and Early Childhood (Zero to Three; Wieder, 1994) is a supplement to ICD and DSM for the diagnosis of children below the age of 3 years.

The International Classification of Functioning, Disability and Health (ICF; World Health Organization, 2001) describes children's and adults' health by using a more comprehensive approach, independent of diagnosis. This includes both physical and mental functions, and distinguishes between *functioning and disability* on the one hand, and *environmental factors* on the other. Since *activity* and *participation* are directly associated with functioning and disability, an individual's activities and participation are key elements in the characterization of disabilities. *Disability* is defined as a deviation from what is possible or common, related to impaired body function, restricted activity or limited participation.

ICF is published in a separate version for children and young people: *International Classification of Functioning, Disability and Health, Children and Youth Version* (ICF-CY; World Health Organization, 2007). It includes a number of topics specifically related to childhood, such as *Temperament and personality functions*, *Acquiring language*, and *Learning through actions with objects*. The child's age is taken into account in the coding of functions and deviations (Björck-Åkesson et al., 2010).

It may be useful to combine ICF and ICF-CY with ICD and DSM (Selb et al., 2015).

SENSORY IMPAIRMENTS

Sensory impairment primarily involves vision and hearing, also in combination with each other. Milder impairments of vision and hearing can be difficult to detect, especially since children have no way of knowing how other children see and hear. Mostly, they have never experienced normal vision or hearing before. Early diagnosis is important for the creation of an environment that provides the children with access to experiences that allow them to establish social relations and create meaning based on their own perceptual abilities.

Visual impairment

Mild visual impairments are common, and most of them can easily be corrected with glasses. Approximately 1–2 percent of schoolchildren have reduced vision with functional consequences. In Western countries, congenital blindness and severe visual impairment have a prevalence rate of about one in 2,000. In countries with less favorable economic conditions, the prevalence rate is higher, about 15 in 10,000 (Dale and Edwards, 2015). Some children have *perceptual problems* caused by injury or disturbances in the eye's motor function or the development of the brain. Children with *cortical visual impairment* can see and follow objects, but have difficulty processing visual information and recognizing people and objects (Fazzi et al., 2012).

Many children with severe visual impairment have additional disorders, particularly mobility and hearing impairment, and intellectual disability (Geddie et al., 2013). Although rare, *juvenile neuronal ceroid lipofuscinosis* (JNCL, or Batten disease) continues to be the most common cause of blindness in many countries in children aged 5–15 years. Development is normal during the first few years, but a gradual loss of vision sets in at the age of 4–5 years, eventually followed by the loss of cognitive, language and motor functions. JNCL is associated with early death, usually in late adolescence or early adulthood (Mole et al., 2011).

Hearing impairment

Hearing impairment is commonly rated by the degree of hearing loss: deafness (above 95 dB), profound hearing loss (70–95 dB), severe hearing loss (60–70 dB), moderate hearing loss (40–60 dB) and mild hearing loss (10–40 dB). However, children's hearing shows major variations, and the decibel scale does not always provide a good indication of a child's hearing functions. *Hard of hearing* means that the child can comprehend and develop speech with a hearing aid, and *deafness* that the hearing loss is too great for speech to be perceived even with a hearing aid.

An important distinction is that between *prelingual* and *acquired hearing loss*. Hearing loss after children have developed spoken language has other developmental consequences than hearing loss that is congenital or occurs before speech has evolved. Another distinction is that between conductive and neurogenic hearing loss. *Conductive hearing loss* is usually caused by defects or injury to the middle ear, or by fluid obstructing the transfer of movement from the eardrum to the inner ear. It is easy to treat, but even minor but prolonged hearing loss can affect a child's vocabulary and knowledge acquisition. During preschool age, 12–14 percent of all children experience some form of reduced hearing for shorter or longer periods, mostly caused by ear infections and fluid in the inner ear. *Neurogenic hearing loss* refers to damage or defects in the inner ear, the auditory nerve or the brain. About two in every 1,000 children have a moderate hearing loss, and one in 1,000 is born deaf (Dietz et al., 2009).

Half of all incidents of profound early neurogenic hearing loss are probably related to genetic factors, but only 5–10 percent of deaf children have deaf parents. Infections and childhood diseases can lead to deafness (Dietz et al., 2009). About 40 percent of children with profound hearing impairment have other disorders such as ADHD, autism spectrum disorders, intellectual disabilities and learning disorders (Mitchell and Karchmer, 2006).

Deafblindness

A combination of early profound vision and hearing loss is quite rare, with a prevalence of one in 29,000 (Dammeyer, 2010). The cause is often unknown and may be related to genetic factors, prenatal infections, substance abuse by the mother or a number of different syndromes (Dammeyer, 2014; Wright, 2008). About 5 percent of all children with profound hearing loss have Usher syndrome, which leads to the eye disorder retinitis pigmentosa as well as problems with balance (Bitner-Glindzicz and Saihan, 2013).

MOTOR IMPAIRMENTS

Children may have reduced gross or fine motor control, or both (see Chapter 7). The most common causes of motor impairment in children and adolescents are cerebral palsy, spina bifida and injury from accidents. A number of illnesses and syndromes affect motor control, such as spinal muscular atrophy (Moultrie et al., 2016; Tisdale & Pellizzoni, 2015) and Duchenne muscular dystrophy (Emery et al., 2015; Flanigan,

2012). Additionally, neurological coordination disorders and dyspraxia can affect the performance of motor actions, but do not involve paralysis or motor impairment in the conventional sense (Gibbs et al., 2007a).

Cerebral palsy

Cerebral palsy (CP) is caused by a congenital or early acquired injury to the brain that results in various degrees of motor impairment (Rosenbaum et al., 2007). In the industrialized world, about two in every 1,000 children have cerebral palsy with widely varying degrees of severity (Blair, 2010). Some children's impairments are so mild as to be nearly invisible in daily life, while others must rely on a wheelchair. Spastic CP accounts for about 80 percent of all cases and is characterized by a general increase in muscular tension. It is graded according to the extent of motor impairment (Hoon and Tolley, 2012). Children with cerebral palsy have a higher prevalence of cognitive and language disorders than the general population but there is considerable variation within this group (Stadskleiv et al., 2017).

Spina bifida

Spina bifida, also called *cleft spine*, is a congenital sac-like bulge of nerve tissue due to an incomplete closing of the vertebrae during fetal development. Its prevalence is about one in 10,000 births. The impairment of primary motor functions is related to the location and size of the sac. The amount of cerebrospinal fluid around the brain and spinal cord is affected and many children need a surgical insertion of a *shunt*, a valve that regulates the pressure caused by the accumulation of fluid in the brain (Mitchell et al., 2004). Some children with spina bifida have problems with orientation, attention regulation, coordination of movements and speech (Dennis et al., 2006; Huber-Okrainec et al., 2005).

Developmental coordination disorder

Developmental coordination disorder in DSM-5, developmental motor coordination disorder in ICD-11, or *dyspraxia*, presents early in life, and children experience varying degrees of difficulty planning, organizing, executing and automating actions under voluntary control, especially when someone is watching them. Unintelligible speech is common. The prevalence rate is somewhat uncertain, estimated at 5–6 percent during infancy and 2 percent for more severe conditions. It is 2–7 times more common in boys than in girls (Gibbs et al., 2007a; Macintyre, 2000, 2001). Both ICD-11 and DSM-5 categorize this disorder under the broader heading of neurodevelopmental disorders and it occurs frequently together with other disorders in this group (Steinman et al., 2010).

NEURODEVELOPMENTAL DISORDERS

Neurodevelopmental disorders begin in early childhood and have a varied course of progression clearly related to the organism's maturation and development *as well as* to the influence of experience (Thapar and Rutter, 2015). They include intellectual disability, communication and language disorders, autism spectrum disorders, attention deficit disorders, reading and writing disorders, mathematics disorders, a number of motor disorders, tic disorders, schizophrenia and other psychoses, with some variation between ICD-11 and DSM-5.

An important reason for defining neurodevelopmental disorders as a higher-order category is the considerable coincidence in symptoms. Co-occurrence of two or more disorders is commonly referred to as *comorbidity*, based on the assumption that they are independent conditions. However, neurodevelopmental disorders occur far more frequently together than one would expect based on sheer coincidence, and there is reason to believe that they share some common basis or processes that affect each other during development. While different disorders can share underlying weaknesses or vulnerabilities, different developmental paths can also lead to the same disorder (Thapar and Rutter, 2015).

Language disorders

Approximately 6–12 percent of all children have delayed language development or language impairment, and 1–2 percent have severe language disorders. Some children have problems with speech, others with the language itself. The disorders are 2–3 times more common among boys than girls (Cummings, 2008; Weindrich et al., 2000).

Several systems for categorizing language disorders are in use. ICD-11 includes *developmental speech sound disorder*, *developmental speech fluency disorder*, and *language disorders* with impairment of a) receptive and expressive language, b) mainly expressive language, c) mainly pragmatic language, and d) other specified or unspecified language impairments. DSM-5 distinguishes between *language disorders*, *speech sound disorders*, *childhood-onset fluency disorders*, *social (pragmatic) communication disorders* and *unspecified communication disorders*. The categories listed in ICD-11 and DSM-5 are too general to be of use in practical work, however. Practitioners who work specifically with language disorders subdivide them in far greater detail (Cummings, 2008). Children with *phonological disorders* have difficulty perceiving and producing speech sounds, while children with *articulation disorders* have problems with the physical production of sound itself. *Grammatical impairments* involve problems with sentence formation and conjugation. *Semantic impairments* entail problems with the contents of language, and *pragmatic disorders* with the communication and use of language itself, such as understanding others' intentions, the choice of topic, repairing gaps in communication and maintaining a coherent conversation. Even children with good pronunciation or correct sentence structure may have an inadequate understanding of how language can be used (Cummings, 2014). Additionally, there are *voice difficulties* and *fluency disorders* such as *stuttering* and *cluttering* (Cummings, 2008; Simms, 2007). Language disorders are not necessarily linked to speech – some children with hearing impairments show similar difficulties when using sign language (Morgan et al., 2007).

Many factors can affect typical and atypical language development. When no clear evidence of a language disorder can be found and development proceeds normally in other areas, language impairments are considered to be "specific." Per definition, children with a specific language impairment do not have hearing loss, autism spectrum disorder, intellectual disability, brain damage, physical disabilities or other difficulties that could explain their language problems. Specific language impairment (SLI) is thus defined by exclusion (Bishop, 2006). Because language development is influenced by a large number of factors, language and communication problems can be found in children with various disorders such as ADHD, hearing impairment, motor impairment, intellectual disability and autism spectrum disorders (Conti-Ramsden et al., 2006; Turner and Stone, 2007).

Learning disorders

Learning disorders are related to the educational objectives of society. They include impairments in reading, written expression, mathematics, and other specified impairments of learning, or unspecified developmental learning disorders. Intellectual disability is not included in this category (see below). DSM-5 refers to them as "specific," meaning there is a gap between the expectations of the child's learning based on general cognitive functioning (usually based on IQ test scores) and the child's actual performance in a specific area of skill or knowledge. For example, a child can score well above average on an intelligence test, and at the same time have major difficulties learning to read, write or do arithmetic (Ruban and Reis, 2005). It can be problematic, however, to distinguish between specific and general disorders, such as between a mild intellectual disability and an emotional disorder, or between a learning disorder and underachievement (Algozzine et al., 2012; Kavale et al., 2005).

Reading and writing disorders

Many children struggle to learn how to read and write, but most of them manage to do so within the usual period of time (Åsberg et al., 2010). Inadequate training does not provide grounds for diagnosing a reading or writing disorder, such as in the case of children growing up in war without a functioning educational system. Prevalence is generally estimated at 7 percent, although this depends on the definition used (Peterson and Pennington, 2015). The prevalence rate diminishes with age, but a third of all children diagnosed with dyslexia at the age of 8 still meet the criteria years later. Some children have reading comprehension problems throughout school age (Woolley, 2010). There are many weak readers, but it is not known how many children fail to acquire basic reading skills altogether. Just like language disorders, reading and writing disorders are more common among boys than girls, and a number of boys develop persistent problems (Shaywitz et al., 2008; Wheldall and Limbrick, 2010).

Studies have found a clear connection between early language disorders and reading and writing disorders, although not all children with developmental language disorders experience persistent problems reading and writing (Ricketts, 2011). It appears that the types of problems associated with children's language acquisition also represent obstacles in learning how to read and write. Children with *phonological* problems may find it difficult to learn to read words and spell. Children with problems understanding the content of language also show similar problems in regard to reading (Bishop and Snowling, 2004). The importance of phonological problems can vary between languages, and it is by no means certain whether all results from the predominantly English-language research can be generalized to more phonetically written languages. Reading places relatively small demands on visual perception. The alphabet consists of a limited number of characters, and there is no evidence that visual processing represents an obstacle to learning how to read or that visual training will help children with reading disorders (Handler et al., 2011).

Some children can read aloud, but do not understand what they are reading. The precocious ability to read far above one's own comprehension level is known as *hyperlexia*. This group includes children with specific reading disorders, autism spectrum disorders, language disorders and intellectual disability (Grigorenko et al., 2003; Nation and Norbury, 2005).

Mathematics disorders

Mathematics disorders, or *dyscalculia*, involve major difficulties understanding numbers and mathematical concepts, and solving arithmetic problems. Children can experience difficulties with simple tasks such as counting small dots or using their fingers in basic addition or subtraction tasks at an age when other children remember the answer or quickly do a mental calculation. Three to 6 percent of all children are estimated to have a mathematics disorder, depending on the criteria used (Butterworth, 2008; Gifford and Rockliffe, 2012). A larger proportion of children and adolescents struggle with math and receive regular help without being considered to have a particular disorder. Special difficulties with mathematics can be found in many groups, among others in children with a low birth weight, ADHD, dyspraxia, dyslexia, cerebral palsy and epilepsy, and those who have problems with memory, perception and sequencing (Gifford and Rockliffe, 2012; Green and Gallagher, 2014). A relationship has been found between the degree of mathematical disorders on the one hand, and spatial perception, sense of direction, working memory and other executive functions on the other (Miller et al., 2013; Raghubar et al., 2010; Tosto et al., 2014).

Intellectual disability

The terminology used in connection with more extensive general disorders of development and learning is undergoing constant change. DSM-5 uses the term "intellectual disability" and ICD-11 "disorders of intellectual development."

ICD-11 includes four levels of intellectual disability, based on IQ and adaptive function. In mild intellectual disability, adaptive function and IQ is two to three standard deviations below the mean (IQ 69–55) (see p. 267), and in moderate 3–4 standard deviations below the mean (IQ 54–40). In both severe and profound disability, intellectual functioning is more than four standard deviations below the mean (IQ 39 and lower). Severe and profound disorders of intellectual development are differentiated exclusively on the basis of adaptive behaviour differences because existing standardized tests of intelligence cannot reliably or validly distinguish among individuals with intellectual functioning below four standard deviations. DSM-5 considers IQ to be an approximate expression for the ability to form concepts and to reason, and does not use IQ in the classification of intellectual disabilities. Instead, it describes conceptual, social and practical skills according to the same four levels of intellectual and adaptive functioning used by ICD-11: mild, moderate, severe and profound. Intelligence tests continue to be important tools for assessing problems, but in DSM-5, also children who achieve a full-scale IQ of over 70 can meet the criteria for intellectual disability. Caution is indicated, especially for younger children whose test scores tend to be less stable. In addition, one cannot use a full-scale IQ as a basis for the diagnosis when the profile is skewed, since this mean score may provide a false indication of both what the child masters and what the child is unable to do (Greenspan and Woods, 2014). For example, one 13-year-old girl scored average for her age on non-verbal subscales and did not master any items on the verbal subscales. An IQ in the middle would give a too low estimate of her non-verbal skills and a too high estimate of her verbal skills.

Based on a statistical definition, intelligence has a normal distribution curve. This means that about 2 percent of a population have an intellectual disability, meaning an IQ below 70 (see p. 267). Within this group, the distribution is about 85 percent mild, 10 percent moderate, 3–4 percent severe and 1–2 percent profound. However, prevalence studies of intellectual disability show a significantly lower percentage (less than 1 percent), and mild intellectual disability usually lies below 50 percent (Carr and O'Reilly, 2016a; Strømme and Valvatne, 1998). This is partly due to the fact that many children with a mild intellectual disability are able to manage on their own, possibly with the help of the family, and have therefore never been assessed or diagnosed.

Autism spectrum disorders

Autism spectrum disorder is a pervasive developmental disorder characterized by problems related to communication and social interaction, as well as restricted, repetitive and stereotyped interests and behaviors. The disorder emerges in childhood but the former requirement that symptoms should be present before the age of 3 has been abandoned in ICD-11 and DSM-5, since many of the problems of children with autism spectrum disorders and a high degree of language function may not become apparent and remain undiagnosed until early school age. Earlier subcatagories like *infantile autism*, *Asperger syndrome* and *atypical autism* are no longer part of the diagnostic group. In both ICD-11 and DSM-5, *autism spectrum disorder* has become a collective term with possibilities of specifying if the individual has intellectual disability and language impairment, or is lacking speech. Autism spectrum disorder is a heterogeneous condition with a genetic basis and significant variation in developmental trajectories (Lord et al., 2015).

Prevalence figures for autism spectrum disorder have increased significantly since childhood autism was first described by Kanner (1943), from 1 in 10,000 to 15 in 1,000 in 2015. The reason for this increase has been the subject of much discussion, and most experts agree that it partly reflects the expansion of diagnostic criteria, increasing attention on high-functioning children within this group, earlier diagnosis, and the awareness that autism spectrum disorder is a life-long condition (Matson and Kozlowski, 2011). At least twice as many boys as girls have autism spectrum disorder.

Children with autism spectrum disorder show considerable variation in intelligence and symptoms (Hughes, 2009; Volkmar et al., 2014). Approximately two-thirds score within or above the normal range (IQ 70) on intelligence tests. Language skills can vary from little communicative ability to the use of more or less well-formed sentences (Rapin et al., 2009). The diagnostic criteria entail that all children with the diagnosis have greater problems than other children understanding emotions and reasoning about how other people think and feel, and why they act as they do, including those with highly developed verbal abilities (Hoogenhout and Malcolm-Smith, 2014).

Attention deficit disorders

ICD-11 and DSM-5 categorize attention deficit hyperactivity disorder (ADHD) in the same manner. It consists of three elements that manifest in different ways throughout childhood and into adulthood: attention deficit, hyperactivity and impulsivity – they don't think before they act. Usually, children with this diagnosis are not characterized by a general lack of attention, but the inability to *sustain attention*. This, however, can vary significantly with activity and interests (Rothenberger and Banaschewski, 2007). Girls are less active and more inattentive than boys, and their attention deficits are frequently overlooked since they have a different expression than in restless boys (Cardoos and Hinshaw, 2011; Skogli et al., 2013).

One subtype presents predominantly with hyperactivity and impulsivity. Children with this subtype display a particularly high level of activity, impulsivity and little sustained attention. They are restless and may experience problems with emotional regulation, motor coordination, working memory, spatial perception, executive function and have a somewhat delayed language development. They typically score in the lower part of the normal range on intelligence tests (Shaw et al., 2014).

The second subtype presents predominantly with inattention. The children do not show the same degree of restlessness, but are poorly organized and have little perseverance, in addition to difficulties with working memory and motor coordination. Some hyperactive-impulsive symptoms may be present, but these are less significant compared to the symptoms of inattention (Sonuga-Barke and Taylor, 2015).

Children with the third subtype present with a combination, both innattention and hyperactivity and impulsivity are clinically significant.

There is a significant overlap between attention deficit disorder and other neurodevelopmental disorders (Biederman, 2005). Children with attention deficit disorders often show stronger emotional reactions than other children, and are susceptible to developing *oppositional defiant disorder* (Frick and Nigg, 2012; Lambek et al., 2017).

The prevalence of attention deficit disorder varies considerably, and in many countries has increased during the 2000s (Hinshaw, 2018). A prevalence rate of over 5 percent has been reported for preschool age children (Nomura et al., 2014). Common estimates are 2–5 percent between the ages of 6 and 16 years, and somewhat lower for adults. Approximately three times as many boys get an ADHD diagnosis compared with girls, resulting in a prevalence rate of about 9 percent for boys and under 3 percent for girls (Rothenberger and Banaschewski, 2004). There is no clear boundary between actions that are part of the common variation in activity level and actions that indicate a disorder in need of intervention. Some experts express concern that too many children receive this diagnosis (Cormier, 2008; Frick and Nigg, 2012).

BEHAVIORAL AND EMOTIONAL DISORDERS

Behavioral disorders and emotional disorders are broad diagnostic terms, and it is important to distinguish normal and slightly unregulated behavior from what may be defined as a disorder, such as common testing of limits or adolescent rebelliousness versus oppositional defiant disorders. *Externalizing disorders* include destructive, bullying, fraudulent and aggressive actions of such scope that they become disruptive to children and adults in the environment and require intervention. *Internalizing disorders* include mood and anxiety disorders.

Behavioral disorders

Behavioral disorders can assume many forms and varying degrees of severity. In ICD-11, *Disruptive behaviour and dissocial disorders* are characterized by persistent behaviour that range from defiant, disobedient, provocative or spiteful behaviours to actions that violate the basic rights of others or major age-appropriate societal norms, rules, or laws. The behaviour pattern is of sufficient severity to result in significant impairment in personal, family, social, educational, occupational or other important areas of functioning. Onset is usually but not always in childhood. In mild form, the child exhibits few negative actions beyond what is needed to establish a diagnosis, and actions are of little harm to others. In moderate form, the number of actions increases and their negative impact on others becomes clearer. The severe form includes numerous negative actions that can cause considerable harm to others. In a minority of cases, behavioral disorders are accompanied by an insufficiently developed sense of conscience and guilt, and at times also a lack of empathy or indifference in relation to the damage caused by the behavior (Williams and Hill, 2012).

There are two subtypes: Oppositional defiant disorder and conduct-dissocial disorder. *Oppositional defiant disorder* presents markedly defiant, disobedient, provocative or spiteful behaviour that occurs more frequently than is typically observed in individuals at the same developmental level and that is not restricted to interaction with siblings. It is a persistent pattern that has lasted 6 months or more. The disorder may be manifest in prevailing, persistent angry or irritable mood, often accompanied by severe temper outbursts or in headstrong, argumentative and defiant behaviour. *Conduct-dissocial disorder* is characterized by a repetitive and persistent pattern of behaviour in which the basic rights of others or major age-appropriate societal norms, rules, or laws are violated. This includes aggression towards people or animals; destruction of property; deceitfulness or theft; and serious violations of rules. To be diagnosed, the behaviour pattern must be enduring 12 months or more. Isolated dissocial or criminal acts are thus not in themselves grounds for the diagnosis.

In DSM-5, the main category *Disruptive, Impulse-Control, and Conduct Disorders* includes several disorders that need not be mutually exclusive. Children with *oppositional defiant disorder* have problems regulating their emotions, are irritable, easily throw tantrums and can be malicious and vindictive when they meet resistance. They are reluctant to do what authorities tell them to, and to follow normal rules. Conflicts with adults are common. Problems often begin to show up during preschool age, but can also appear as late as adolescence. Some children show behavioral problems in certain situations only, and the degree of severity depends on the number of situations in which the child shows negative behavior.

Intermittent explosive disorder is a type of *emotion regulation disorder* characterized by anger and poor impulse control, particularly in the form of language and physical actions that can harm others. The diagnosis requires the child to be above the age of 6 years and to function cognitively above this age level, since younger children usually are not able to self-regulate well enough. The disorder mostly occurs in later childhood, adolescence and adulthood. In certain situations, it may be natural for the child to react, but the reaction is completely out of proportion in relation to the event that triggered it.

The features of *conduct disorder* in DSM-5 are similar to those of *conduct-dissocial disorder* in ICD-11. They may include bullying, initiation of physical fights, use of a knife, a gun or other weapon that can cause serious physical harm, physical cruelty to people or animals, destruction, deceitfulness, theft, truant from school, and serious violations of rules.

There is considerable overlap between the characteristics of various behavioral disorders. It is possible that behavioral disorders represent a dimension that varies with the type and extent of negative actions, rather than distinct categories (Scott, 2015). Prevalence estimates vary, but mostly lie between 5 and 10 percent. The prevalence is 2–3 times higher among boys than girls (Odgers et al., 2008).

Mood disorders

Mood disorders, or *affective disorders*, are the most frequent psychological disorders among children and adolescents. They mainly include depression, mania and bipolar disorder. Mood disorders can occur at any age, and are also included in DC 0-3.

Depression

Most children and adolescents can feel sad or unhappy at times. To meet the criteria for depression, changes in mood must last for weeks or months. In toddlers, depression shows up in the form of despondency or irritability and reduced interest and pleasure in activities suited to the child's developmental level. The child may have decreased appetite and difficulty sleeping (Witten, 1997). Similarly, children and adolescents show less pleasure, interest and concentration than they normally would, and easily become tired. They sleep poorly and have little appetite, low self-esteem and little confidence. Depressed adolescents tend to ruminate and have problems coping with their emotions and taking pleasure in activities they usually enjoy. Depression can become deeper when it leads to social isolation and fewer friends. The inability of adolescents to solve the problems they meet may contribute to stress, a poor self-image and dysphoria (Hankin et al., 2018). Depression in children and adolescents must have lasted for a year to be considered *persistent*. Following the loss of a parent or other caregiver, toddlers can show a *prolonged grief reaction* lasting for more than 2 weeks (Lieberman et al., 2003; Tidmarsh, 1997). In *persistent depressive disorder* or *dysthymic disorder*, the depressive mood is persistent, lasting continuously 2 years or more, and for most of the day or for more days than not. In children and adolescents the depressed mood can manifest as pervasive irritability.

Depression can also express itself in agitated and disruptive behavior. According to DSM-5, *disruptive mood dysregulation disorder* is characterized by "severe recurrent temper outbursts manifested verbally and/or behaviorally," often as a reaction to frustration, but in a way that is inconsistent with the child's age. Because younger children generally have problems with self-regulation, children under the age of 6 years cannot receive this diagnosis, nor can young adults above the age of 18. The criteria require outbursts at least 3–4 times a week in connection with a minimum of three different situations, and having taken place for over a year. According to DSM-5, the prevalence rate is 2–5 percent and primarily includes boys.

Depression is relatively rare during childhood, but increases toward adolescence. In preschool age, the prevalence is estimated at 1 percent, and 3 percent in school age. With a prevalence rate of 10 percent during adolescence, depression is the most common reason for young people to seek help for their personal problems. Up to a quarter of all adolescents report having experienced at least one depressive episode (Garber and Rao, 2014). However, it is important to distinguish between depression that meets the diagnostic criteria, and the uncertainty and dysphoria that often characterize young people without justifying the term depression. In childhood, depression occurs just as frequently in boys as in girls, but during adolescence its prevalence is twice as high in girls (Hankin and Abramson, 2001).

Bipolar disorder

Bipolar disorder is characterized by depressive periods and periods of mania. Manic periods can include agitation, little need for sleep, impulsivity, risky behavior and uncritical thinking. Bipolar disorder usually first appears in early adulthood, but can also occur in children, in which case it is referred to as *paediatric bipolar disorder* (Fitzgerald and Pavuluri, 2015). However, there is considerable discussion about the existence of bipolar disorder in children, and DSM-5 emphasizes the difficulty of diagnosing the disorder during childhood. It is especially difficult to establish clear periods of euphoria and mania. Distinct episodes of depression and mania usually do not occur in childhood, but rather a mixture of depression, agitation and irritability (Carr, 2016). Symptoms related to ADHD in particular can be misinterpreted as bipolar disorder, since the two diagnoses share many traits, including distractibility, talkativeness and a high activity level (Leibenluft and Dickstein, 2015). Also in adolescents, bipolar disorder can be difficult to detect because it can develop gradually without any apparent periods of illness. Children and adolescents with this disorder frequently show problems across the entire social spectrum, and may additionally share common traits with autism spectrum disorder (Fitzgerald and Pavuluri, 2015). The prevalence rate is about 1 percent, and equally divided among boys and girls (Carr, 2016).

Anxiety or fear-related disorders

Anxiety disorders mainly consist of separation anxiety, phobias (including social phobia or anxiety) and generalized anxiety disorder. Anxiety disorders occur at all ages and are also listed in DC 0-3. The diagnosis is difficult to establish in younger children, however, because anxiety and fear are common at this age and may represent an adequate adaptation to an uncertain and potentially threatening situation, or one perceived as such by the child. It is the intensity of anxiety or fear and their persistence once the uncertain situation has passed that characterize abnormal fear (Pine and Klein, 2015). Toddlers may react by crying, screaming and throwing themselves on the floor, as well as by angry outbursts that lead them to throw their toys and bump their head in connection with transitions, separations and changes in routines. The prevalence of anxiety disorders in children and adolescents is estimated at somewhere between 6 and 10 percent, and slightly higher among boys than girls (Carr, 2016; Pine and Klein, 2015). Anxiety symptoms are common in children and adolescents with autism spectrum disorder (Kerns and Kendall, 2014).

Separation anxiety

Central to separation anxiety is the fear of being separated from attachment figures (see Chapter 19). In toddlers, the reactions to such a separation, or the worry that a separation will occur in the future, must be stronger and more persistent than normal. Children may cling to caregivers and react with angry outbursts, kicking, screaming and crying when someone tries to separate them. They may be reluctant or refuse to sleep away from the attachment figure, and have recurrent nightmares about separation. Children may also experience physical symptoms when leaving for kindergarten or school, or in other ways refuse to go to school. Adolescents can be anxious to be left at home alone. Symptoms usually appear in childhood and DSM-5 specifies 18 years as the upper age limit. Symptoms must last longer than 4 weeks in children and adolescents, and 6 months in adults. The prevalence rate is about 3 percent (Carr, 2016). Separation anxiety is the most common anxiety disorder in children below the age of 12 years, and symptoms can continue all the way into adult age, such as a reluctance to sleep away from home or go out alone, but separation anxiety is rare in adults (Pine and Klein, 2015).

Phobias

Childhood phobias are characterized by recurring fears that are more persistent and intense than normal fear in children. A diagnosis requires the fear to have consequences for the child's ability to function socially. The onset of phobias can occur at any age, but usually they first appear during childhood. Common phobias among children may involve things such as syringes, animals or blood, or specific locations such as elevators. Children can react with clinging behavior and crying, but also with anger and active avoidance, feeling that they do not get help regulating their response. The prevalence rate for simple phobias is 3 percent, and 1 percent for social phobia (Carr, 2016).

Social anxiety disorder

This disorder is characterized by a stronger fear of strangers than normal for a given age, and by apprehension or anxiety in unfamiliar social situations. The intensity of anxiety must be of such a degree as to create problems in social interaction with other children and adults. Occasional instances of anxiety are not enough. Children with social anxiety nearly always show great distress when they meet strangers, and may not be able to do anything when many people are present. In such situations, they tend to cry, cling to familiar adults, withdraw and turn silent. Older children and adolescents are afraid that others will perceive them negatively, such as being incompetent, stupid, weak and dull. Children with social anxiety generally try to avoid social situations. According to DSM-5, the prevalence rate lies well above 2 percent and decreases with age. The first symptoms of social anxiety usually appear between the ages of 8 and 15 years, and early development is often characterized by shyness (Kagan and Snidman, 2004).

Generalized anxiety disorder

Generalized anxiety disorder (GAD) is most common among adults, but can occur in children and adolescents. It is characterized by persistent anxiety and worry lasting for at least 6 months in connection with several situations that are difficult to cope with. Children may, for example, be unreasonably worried about disasters, not being liked, not managing their schoolwork or being teased. These concerns can be accompanied by fatigue, restlessness, irritability and sleep problems (Weems and Varela, 2011). The results may be little play and interaction with other children, and stress and worries that draw on cognitive resources and divert attention from other activities.

Selective mutism

Children with selective (or elective) mutism only speak at home and with their immediate family. Symptoms usually appear before the age of 5, with a prevalence rate below 1 percent (Carr, 2016; Bergman et al., 2002). Some children with selective mutism experience early difficulties with language, but the diagnosis requires the child to be able to talk. Lack of motivation is not an underlying factor. Children with selective mutism want to speak but are unable to do so. Many of them are generally shy and socially anxious, and therefore incapable of speaking with others, including friends, grandparents or more distant relatives. ICD-11 and DSM-5 require symptoms to persist for at least 1 month. Since many children do not speak for a long period after beginning at school, the diagnosis is usually given only once the child has failed to speak for far longer than a month (Cline and Baldwin, 2004; Steinhausen et al., 2006). The problem is specifically associated with speech, and it is possible in some cases to communicate via writing or graphic symbols.

Obsessive-compulsive disorder

The main characteristics of obsessive-compulsive disorder (OCD) consist of recurrent thoughts and impulses to perform specific actions, such as repeated hand washing or licking a dish. The disorder is usually accompanied by anxiety, and the individual's compulsive actions are intended to avert a situation that is perceived to be dangerous. Because they can be observed, compulsive actions are easier to identify than obsessive thoughts, which must be determined based on conversation. The average age for onset of initial symptoms is 19 years, but in a quarter of all cases symptoms appear before the age of 14 years. As a rule, the disorder is more serious when it shows up early (Anholt et al., 2014). Compulsive behavior is often permanent, but

can be more or less pronounced in periods. According to DSM-5, the prevalence rate is 1–2 percent. OCD is commonly associated with inhibition and internalizing disorders, and often comorbid with other conditions, including various anxiety disorders, attention deficit disorder, autism spectrum disorder and Tourette syndrome (Brem et al., 2014).

Eating disorders

Eating disorders have many similarities with OCD, but the obsessive thoughts revolve exclusively around food, body, appearance and weight. The most common among these disorders are *anorexia*, involving under-eating, and *bulimia*, involving binge-eating and "countermeasures" against food intake such as intentional regurgitation or use of a laxative. Eating disorders are often accompanied by fear of obesity (Clinton, 2010) and negative thoughts about oneself (Yiend et al., 2014). The prevalence rate is three in 1,000 for anorexia, nine in 1,000 for bulimia and 16 in 1,000 for binge-eating. The disorder typically appears around 14 to 18 years of age, but can occur as early as the age of 6. The prevalence rate during childhood, however, is merely three in 100,000. Problems tend to be more extensive and persistent when they appear early. Eating disorders occur in boys, but are six times more frequent in girls (Pinhas et al., 2011).

TRAUMA AND STRESSOR-RELATED DISORDERS

These types of disorders are the result of traumatic experiences or childhood environments with extremely poor caregiving.

Reactive attachment disorder

This disorder is characterized by grossly abnormal attachment behaviours in early childhood. The children are inhibited and emotionally withdrawn toward their caregivers. They rarely seek comfort when distressed, and show minimal response to comfort. They exhibit persistent social and emotional disturbance, with little social and emotional responsiveness, minimal positive affect, and episodes of unexplained fearfulness and irritability, even when interacting with adults in situations without apparent threat. Diagnosis requires that the child has experienced patterns of serious neglect and repeated changes of caregivers or limited opportunities to form selective attachment relationships. The disorder emerges between the ages of 9 months and 5 years (but should not be diagnosed before the age of 1), and may persist for several years. Its prevalence is unknown.

Disinhibited social engagement disorder

Children with this disorder actively seek interaction with unfamiliar adults. They show little reticence and can go off with a stranger without hesitation. They overstep the social boundaries of their culture, both physically by seeking excessive closeness, and verbally by asking personal and intrusive questions. Neither do they check back with their caregiver when venturing into unfamiliar surroundings. Diagnosis requires that the child has experienced patterns of serious neglect and repeated changes of caregivers or limited opportunities to form selective attachment relationships. Additionally, the child must have a mental age of at least 9 months and thus the cognitive prerequisites to form attachments. The disorder occurs only in connection with neg-lect before the age of 2 years; it emerges in the second year of life and lasts until adolescence (Guyon-Harris et al., 2018). Its prevalence is unknown.

Post-traumatic stress disorder

Post-traumatic stress disorder (PTSD) is a reaction to a stressful or traumatic event a child has experienced or learned about. The diagnosis requires the occurrence of a real event, such as divorce, death in the family or witnessing domestic violence. Children growing up in war are exposed to repeated traumatic events. Symptoms usually appear within 3 months of the event.

PTSD can occur at any age after the first year of life, and is included in DC 0-3R. DSM-5 has separate criteria for children below the age of 6, and symptoms must be assessed based on the child's age. Children can have intrusive memories and experience that the event repeats itself, including recurrent disturbing dreams with fear. They react with distress to anything reminiscent of the traumatic event, including people who talk about the event. The distress is persistent and intense, and the child finds it difficult to calm down. Affected children avoid places, things and

activities, including thoughts that remind them of the event, and may exhibit selective amnesia. They can feel a great deal of shame, guilt, fear and confusion, and express few positive emotions. They tend to be irritable and angry, are easily startled, and may have difficulty sleeping and concentrating. They also participate less in play and other positive activities. Symptoms must have lasted for over a month.

ICD-11 includes *complex post-traumatic stress disorder*, which may develop following exposure to an event or series of events of an extremely threatening or horrific nature, most commonly prolonged or repetitive events from which escape is difficult or impossible, such as prolonged domestic violence, or repeated childhood sexual or physical abuse. In addition to symptoms of PTSD, children with the complex disorder have severe and pervasive problems in affect regulation, persistent beliefs about themselves as diminished, defeated or worthless, accompanied by deep and pervasive feelings of shame, guilt or failure related to the traumatic event, and persistent difficulties in sustaining relationships and in feeling close to others.

The symptoms of PTSD involve unregulated emotions and can be reminiscent of behavioral problems. Because PTSD can be mistaken for depression, it is important to look for other causes in connection with changes in behavioral patterns.

ADDICTIONS

Adolescence is characterized by an increase in behavioral experimentation and participation in risky behavior, such as gambling and substance abuse. Although it usually does not indicate a disorder, this kind of behavior can become more extensive and persistent in some adolescents, and develop into a dependence on addictive substances such as alcohol and drugs, or gambling.

Alcohol and substance abuse

Problems with alcohol and other substances are most common during adulthood, but also occur in adolescence. According to DSM-5, the prevalence rate for alcohol problems lies above 4 percent among 12- to 17-year-olds, and higher among boys than girls. The prevalence of cannabis abuse is just over 3 percent. However, adolescents' experimentation with alcohol and drugs varies greatly between different countries. A majority of Norwegian 15- to 16-year-olds have tasted alcohol, but relatively few drink large amounts or consume alcohol regularly. In Denmark, consumption is significantly higher (Skretting et al., 2014).

Internet gaming addiction

Most children and adolescents occasionally participate in online games, and boys spend more time than girls on electronic games (Hastings et al., 2009). A significant minority spends 5 hours or more a day on computer games and Internet use. Some turn night into day and have major problems following up school work and taking part in the ordinary social life of their peer group. Accordingly, problems associated with this type of addiction are quite complex. Those spending a lot of time on online games have a higher incidence of depression and suicide attempts than adolescents with little or moderate time use (Johansson and Götestam, 2004; Messias et al., 2011). In ICD-11, gaming disorder has two subgroups: *predominantly online* (over the Internet) and *predominantly offline*. DSM-5 lists *Internet gaming disorder* among the conditions needing more research. The difficulty of defining and delimiting these types of problem is also the reason for the lack of an accepted formal diagnosis (King et al., 2013). The DSM-5 criteria for a possible *Internet gaming disorder* are an unusual preoccupation with gaming and withdrawal symptoms in the form of irritability, anxiety and sadness when there is no access to online play. Unregulated online gaming can thus be a separate disorder as well as a symptom of other disorders.

Internet gaming addiction does not include online gambling. *Gambling disorder* is a separate diagnosis in DSM-5, and in ICD-11, *gambling disorder* also has the two subgroups *predominantly online* and *predominantly offline*.

Internet addiction

Recent years have seen a dramatic increase in the use of social media (see Chapter 26). Some adolescents show clear signs of *Internet addiction*, also known as *dysfunctional*, *pathological* or *compulsive use of Internet*. Their thoughts are dominated by the Internet, which they use to escape negative thoughts, and they experience dis-comfort without online access, continuing their online activities even after having decided to stop for the day. Social media are a major contributing factor to dependency (Johansson and Götestam, 2004; van den Eijnden et al., 2011). Some users need to check social media all the time because they are afraid of being left out from something (Wallace, 2014). Neither ICD-11 nor DSM-5 include a formal diagnosis for general Internet addiction, since the nature of the addiction itself is difficult to define. Estimates vary widely, from less than 1 to over 26 percent (Kuss et al., 2013; Wallace, 2014).

ACQUIRED DISORDERS

The majority of childhood and adolescent disorders are developmental, but children can also have acquired disorders. For instance near-drowning, traffic accidents and radiation treatment of brain tumors can result in neurological damage leading to various disorders (de Ruiter et al., 2013). Landau-Kleffner syndrome is a form of epilepsy that leads to infantile acquired aphasia, the loss of early language skills (Campos and de Guevara, 2007).

Progressive disorders

Some diseases lead to dementia and loss of previously acquired skills during childhood and adolescence, including Sanfilippo syndrome and juvenile neuronal ceroid lipofuscinosis (Schoenberg and Scott, 2011).

DISORDERS CAN BE RELATED

Establishing that a child meets the criteria for a given disorder is only the beginning of the diagnostic process. It is always necessary to specify a child's strengths and weaknesses, as well as the pressures and opportunities afforded by the environment. Many children have more than one disorder or symptoms resulting from several disorders, but in addition they can have their particular strong areas. It is important to avoid *diagnostic shadowing* – the use of a single diagnosis to explain all of the child's problems. Initiating treatment based on a particular diagnosis without first examining how the child functions as a whole can lead to poor developmental results.

SUMMARY

1 A *disorder* is a relatively severe reduction or deviation in development, learning and function within a specific area. Children may have *difficulties* in meeting social or academic requirements without having a disorder. Some disorders are "specific," meaning they are characterized by a gap between expected performance and actual performance. There is a seamless transition between ordinary difficulties and disorders.

2 The two main international classification systems are ICD and DSM. DC 0-3 is for children below the age of 3 years. ICF and ICF-CY are used to describe children's and adults' overall functioning and participation.

3 *Sensory impairments* include *visual impairment, hearing impairment* and *combined visual and hearing impairment*. The most common causes of *motor impairment* are *cerebral palsy, spina bifida* and *brain damage* following accidents. In addition, various diseases and syndromes can affect motor control. *Developmental motor coordination disorder* and *dyspraxia* affect the performance of motor actions, but do not involve paralysis or mobility impairment.

4 *Neurodevelopmental disorders* begin early in childhood and have a varied course of progression clearly linked to the organism's maturation and development *as well as* to the influence of experience. They include *intellectual disabilities, communication* and *language disorders, autism spectrum disorders, attention deficit hyperactivity disorders, learning disorders,* some *motor disorders, tic disorders, schizophrenia* and other *psychoses*.

5 Delayed language development is common in preschool age, but *language disorders* can continue into school age. Children may have problems with different aspects of speech and language. The prevalence of *mental disorders* is higher among children with language disorders, and vice versa.

6 The most common *learning disorders* are *reading and writing disorders (dyslexia)* and *mathematics disorders (dyscalculia)*. *Intellectual disability* influences cognitive, language, motor and social abilities. There are considerable differences between children with regard to the causes, degree and symptoms of intellectual disabilities.

7 *Autism spectrum disorder* is characterized by problems related to communication and social interaction, as well as limited, repetitive and stereotyped interests and behaviors.

8 *Attention deficit hyperactivity disorder* includes two subgroups: *predominantly hyperactivity* and *impulsivity*, and *predominantly inattention*. It presents differently from childhood to adulthood, as well as in boys and in girls.

9 *Behavioral* or *externalizing disorders* include destructive, bullying, fraudulent and aggressive actions of such a scope that they become disruptive to children and adults in the environment.

10 *Internalizing disorders* include mood and anxiety disorders. *Mood disorders* include depression, mania and bipolar disorder, and are among the most frequent psychological disorders among children and adolescents. Depression is relatively rare during childhood, but its prevalence increases toward adolescence. *Anxiety disorders* occur at all ages and mainly include separation anxiety, phobias, social anxiety and *generalized anxiety disorder* (GAD). Children with *selective mutism* speak only at home and with their immediate family.

11 The most characteristic feature of *obsessive-compulsive disorder* (OCD) consists of recurrent thoughts and impulses to perform specific actions, such as repeated hand washing or licking a dish. The disorder is usually accompanied by anxiety, and the individual's compulsive actions are intended to avert a situation that is perceived to be dangerous. Because they can be observed, compulsive actions are easier to identify than obsessive thoughts, which must be determined based on conversation.

12 The most common eating disorders are *anorexia*, involving under-eating, and bulimia, involving binge-eating and "countermeasures" against food intake, such as intentional regurgitation or use of a laxative. Eating disorders are often accompanied by fear of obesity and negative thoughts about oneself.

13 *Reactive attachment disorder* and *disinhibited social engagement disorder* emerge in the first years of life and are related to severe neglect or abuse. Post-traumatic stress disorder can occur at all ages and is a reaction to a stressful or traumatic event a child has experienced or learned about.

14 Although problems with alcohol and substance abuse do occur in adolescence, they are not common. Some children and adolescents show signs of *gaming disorder* related to Internet, and some adolescents show signs of *Internet addiction*.

15 *Acquired disorders* are usually the result of injury or illness, and *progressive disorders* involve the loss of acquired skills.

CORE ISSUES

• The use of biological and behavioral features in defining disorders.

• The differentiation of overlapping disorders.

SUGGESTIONS FOR FURTHER READING

Carr, A. (2016). *The handbook of child and adolescent clinical psychology: A contextual approach.* Hove, UK: Routledge.

Carr, A., Linehan, C., O'Reilly, G., Walsh, P. N., & McEvoy, J. (Eds) (2016). *The handbook of intellectual disability and clinical psychology practice.* Hove, UK: Routledge.

Thapar, A., Pine, D. S., Leckman, J. F., Scott, S., Snowling, M., & Taylor, E. A. (Eds) (2015). *Rutter's child and adolescent psychiatry, Sixth Edition.* Chichester, UK: Wiley.

Contents

CHAPTER 5

GENES, EVOLUTION, HEREDITY AND ENVIRONMENT

The human genes have emerged through evolution (phylogeny) and are one of the essential biological foundations for individual development (ontogeny). Genes allow information to be transmitted from one generation to the next so that the fusion of a human sperm cell and an egg (ovum) results in an individual with the particular mix of properties that distinguish humans as a species with two legs, the ability to walk upright, color vision and language. Thus, genes form the basis for *shared* human characteristics.

At the same time, every individual is genetically unique, with the exception of identical twins, who share their genetic makeup. In addition to the traits shared by all – or nearly all – human beings, genes carry the potential for the development of a wide range of traits that vary from individual to individual. It is this genetic basis that constitutes the *individual heritage* and forms the basis for discussions about the contributions of heredity and environment, or nature versus nurture, for individual differences, for example in musicality or personality.

Today, genes are believed to be involved in the development of many traits, including intelligence and temperament, as well as the disposition for developing obesity, language disorders or schizophrenia (Gottesman and Hanson, 2005; Rutter, 2006). Some genes affect development starting with the first cell divisions or at specific times during fetal life, while others first take effect late in adult life. Spontaneous mutations or errors in the division of certain chromosomes can occasionally occur, such as in the case of *Down syndrome* (see Table 5.1, p. 76). More than 2,000 genetic syndromes are known to exist, and there is reason to believe that many severe impairments and conditions of unknown cause are due to genetic predisposition.

However, there is a complex interplay between genes and environment. Knowledge about *how* genes control species-specific development and contribute to individual characteristics remains limited. A gene can function in a number of ways, and some genes affect the activity of other genes (Rutter, 2014). Therefore, finding that particular genes are associated with a given developmental anomaly does not necessarily reveal the underlying developmental mechanisms, and consequently does not always make it possible to prevent or cure the anomaly.

CHROMOSOMES AND GENES

Chromosomes are thread-like structures that contain genes and are located inside the cellular nucleus. Human sperm and egg cells contain 23 chromosomes each. When they unite during conception, they form a single cell consisting of 23 pairs, or 46 chromosomes. With the exception of reproductive cells, or *gametes*, all of the body's cells thus normally contain 46 chromosomes. The arrangement in pairs applies to all but sex chromosomes: women have two X chromosomes, while men have an X and a Y chromosome (Figure 5.1). During cellular division, each of the genes on the 46 chromosomes is copied and the genetic information transferred to

FIGURE 5.1 Human chromosomes.
There are 22 autosomal chromosome pairs and two different pairs of sex chromosomes: one XY (male) and one XX (female).

both new cells (except during the production of gametes, which consist of only 23 chromosomes). The chromosome structure is retained as well.

Genes are made up of deoxyribonucleic acid, DNA, which consists of long, helical threads that contain over a million different proteins in human beings. As each chromosome consists of about 1,000 genes, every cell contains approximately 23,000 different genes, and the genes in one cell can have a length of almost 2 meters. A genome represents all the DNA sequences of a single species (Gerstein et al., 2007). The most important property of DNA is to provide a model for producing ribonucleic acid, RNA, which performs a variety of functions inside the cell, controls the formation of new proteins and catalyzes chemical reactions in the body.

Alleles are genes that share the same location on the two chromosomes in a chromosome pair and control the same genetic characteristics. Alleles are not identical, and different individuals can carry different alleles in a pair of genes. This gives rise to individual differences (Gottlieb et al., 2006). Although specific genes may have a particular task in the developmental process, it is rare that a characteristic is determined by a single gene. Even the eye color of the banana fly is the combined result of 13 genes. About 5,000 genes are

involved in cellular maintenance, and must therefore be expressed in all cells. Apart from minor variations, the same 5,000 genes are contained in all the cells of all species, but minute changes in the way these 5,000 genes interact allow for major structural differences. Moreover, there is no simple relationship between the number of genes two species have in common, and the degree of similarity between them. For example, humans and mice share 99 percent of their genes, while humans and chimpanzees share 98.4 percent (Gottlieb et al., 2006). It is the way in which genes interact, rather than the presence of specific genes, that results in the differences between species.

GENETIC INHERITANCE

Children get their genes from their parents. Inheritance in the genetic sense refers to the information transmitted to a human being or animal via the genes contained in the parent sperm and egg cell. The reproductive cells produced by an individual are not identical, however. They only contain one chromosome from each of the 23 chromosome pairs, and the particular chromosome that is passed on is random for each pair, coming either from the individual's biological father or mother. This means that every individual can produce some 8 million different combinations of chromosomes. Therefore, a large degree of genetic variation is possible even between siblings.

The unique combination of genes a child receives from her parents via their sperm and ovum is called the genotype. Not all of a child's genetic makeup is realized in full. The child's observable traits are known as the phenotype, and include both physical and psychological characteristics.

Children inherit genes, not behavioral patterns or psychological characteristics, but genetic factors can affect the likelihood of a child developing in a certain way. The term *behavioral phenotype* is used when a specific set of psychological characteristics seems to be linked to a known genetic syndrome or the presence of one or more genes. Only rarely, however, are children with a particular genetic syndrome or chromosomal anomaly characterized by a specific behavioral pattern (Hodapp, 1997).

Dominant and recessive traits

A wide range of traits and conditions are partially or completely determined by genes. This applies to eye color, skin color, and so forth. Mendel's laws of inheritance describe how genetically determined traits vary with the genes inherited from the parent generation. Some of the properties are dominant, others are recessive. A *dominant* trait will always assert itself when the gene is present on one of the chromosomes in a pair. A *recessive* trait must be transferred via both parents, meaning that the gene must be present on both chromosomes in a pair to be expressed. All people are carriers of recessive genes and thus able to pass on the genetic basis of traits they themselves do not have. Examples of dominant traits are brown eyes, curly hair and far-sightedness. Straight hair and normal vision are recessive. The same applies to blue eyes. Because the genetic basis for brown eyes is dominant, parents with completely blue eyes cannot have the gene for brown eyes and are therefore unable to conceive brown-eyed children.

The distribution of dominant and recessive genes can cause siblings to look quite different or differ considerably from each other in other ways. In some cases, a given genetic constellation can lead to serious illness or disability in one or more children in a family, while siblings with a different constellation develop normally. If the disease is caused by recessive genes, they can still be carriers, and genetic counselling is usually offered when a child in the family has a disability that may have a genetic basis.

Autosomal and sex-linked inheritance

All chromosomes other than sex chromosomes are *autosomal*. Conditions associated with the genes on these chromosomes occur as frequently in males as in females. When a gene located on a sex chromosome leads to an increased probability of a particular development, it is referred to as *sex-linked inheritance*. Genes located on the Y chromosome only affect the development of boys. Since most of the genes on this chromosome are recessive, the majority of recessive genes on the X chromosome of males will be expressed, while the recessive genes on the X chromosome of females will more likely be suppressed by a non-recessive allele on the other X chromosome. This means that conditions linked to the X chromosome are more frequent in males than in females. Twice as many boys as girls are color blind, for example. Sex chromosomes are involved in a number of known syndromes (see Table 5.1).

Mutation

A mutation is a sudden change of genetic code. Mutations are common to all living organisms and usually occur without any detectable reason, but may increase due to the influence of X-rays and certain chemical substances, for example. Some mutations lead to changes in gene expression, while others have little impact. Many chromosomal abnormalities and genetically determined conditions are caused by mutations. When mutations occur in gametes, their hereditary properties are changed, while the result of mutations in other cells cannot be inherited.

There is a positive correlation between mutations and parental age. For females, and to a lesser extent males, the risk of having a child with an extra chromosome in one pair of chromosomes (trisomy) increases with age, including a child with Down syndrome (trisomy 21). Males above the age of 35 have a slightly higher risk of new mutations, and thus of transferring certain autosomal dominant conditions (Hassold and Sherman, 2000; McIntosh et al., 1995).

TABLE 5.1 Some common chromosomal disorders and genetically determined conditions

Angelman syndrome is caused by a genetic defect on chromosome 15 inherited from the mother, the counterpart to Prader-Willi syndrome. Most affected children have severe or profound intellectual disability and lack speech. They are hyperactive, inquisitive and often have a happy demeanor. Their movements are stiff and puppet-like. Prevalence is estimated at 1 in 15,000.

Down syndrome is caused by a partial or complete extra chromosome 21. Common characteristics are a flat neck, slanted eyes, malformations of the outer ear, an increased incidence of heart disease and premature aging. This chromosomal defect is the most common cause of severe intellectual disability and makes up approximately 20 percent of this group of disorders. On average, 1 in 800 children have Down syndrome. The incidence increases with the mother's age at the time of birth.

Huntington disease is caused by a dominant gene located on chromosome 4. It is a neuro-degenerative brain disorder characterized by involuntary jerky movements, particularly involving the face, tongue, neck, shoulders, arms and legs. Speech is often slurred, and eating and swallowing are problematic. Initial symptoms may include changes in personality, impairment of memory, concentration and initiative, and emotional lability. In some cases, the disease appears before the age of 20, but generally symptoms first emerge around the age of 35–45. The prevalence varies from country to country, with an average of 5.7 per 100,000 in studies in Europe, North America and Australia, and significantly lower in Asian studies.

Klinefelter syndrome and *triple X syndrome* (also known as trisomy X) involve the presence of an additional X chromosome. Males with Klinefelter syndrome (XXY) have a feminine distribution of body fat, with long arms and legs and enlarged breast tissue. Females with triple X syndrome (XXX) look normal and often are slightly above medium height. They tend to score somewhat lower than average on intelligence tests. An extra X chromosome occurs in about 1 in 1,000 births.

Prader-Willi syndrome is caused by a genetic defect on chromosome 15 inherited from the father (see also Angelman syndrome). Common characteristics are low muscle tone (hypotonia), special facial features, small feet, delayed motor and language development, and mild or moderate intellectual disability. Children with this syndrome often have problems thriving during their first year of life. Later in life they tend to develop an insatiable appetite and major problems with being overweight. Prevalence is about 1 in 15,000.

Rett syndrome is believed to be caused by a defect in a gene on the X chromosome (mostly $MeCP_2$) that prevents some genes on this chromosome from being switched off when they should be (see genomic imprinting below). It is uncertain whether the syndrome can affect boys. Girls with Rett syndrome have profound intellectual disability as well as motor and language impairment. Most of them have a normal development during the first 6–18 months of life, and some develop speech. Following this, they experience a decline and lose their speech and other skills. Later development is extremely limited in most areas, but may show some improvement in social functioning. Prevalence is about 1 in 10,000 female births.

Juvenile neuronal ceroid lipofuscinosis (JNCL), also known as *Batten disease*, is an autosomal recessive neurodegenerative disorder. The first symptoms are usually loss of vision at 4–10 years of age. The disease is one of the most common causes of blindness between the ages of 5 and 15. Affected children gradually lose their cognitive, language and motor skills, and nearly all develop epilepsy. Many die in their twenties or earlier, but some can live beyond the age of 30 or even 40 years. Prevalence is about 1 in 30,000.

Turner syndrome is caused by a missing X chromosome (X0) in females. The chromosomal defect causes the degeneration of ovarian function, and a stop in the production of estrogen. Common characteristics are somewhat lower birth weight, heart defect, special facial features, short and broad fingers, a short stature and learning disorders. In some adults, hearing is partially impaired. Most of those affected only show some of the characteristics. Prevalence is about 1 in 2,500 female births.

Williams syndrome is caused by one or more genes on chromosome 7. Common characteristics are heart defects, special facial features, a short stature, delayed prenatal and later development, difficulties thriving in infancy and mild or moderate intellectual disability. Compared with other skills, their language skills tend to be good, and they are social and trusting. Prevalence is estimated at 1 in 7,500.

Some mutations reduce the cells' ability to survive and carry out their tasks, but mutations can also have a positive impact. They lead to changes in the gene pool and thus a species' ability to evolve. Every human being has an average of 300 mutations.

Genomic imprinting

According to Mendel's model, it is irrelevant whether a gene comes from the mother or the father. It has been found, however, that a gene can function differently depending on whether it is maternal or paternal. This is explained by the fact that one of the two alleles in a pair has been *imprinted*. Imprinting means that a gene is "silenced" or "switched off" if the child inherits the gene from one parent, but not if the same gene is passed on from the other parent. Both Angelman syndrome and Prader-Willi syndrome are caused by missing genetic material on chromosome 15 (see Table 5.1). Children develop Angelman syndrome when the relevant paternal genes are turned off and the maternal genes remain active, and Prader-Willi syndrome when the maternal genes are switched off and the paternal genes remain active (Davies et al., 2015; Kopsida et al., 2011). Genomic imprinting usually does not involve a permanent change or mutation in DNA, but a temporary or permanent change in the *function* of part of an individual's DNA (Choufani and Weksberg, 2016; Swaney, 2011).

The above example of Angelman and Prader-Willi syndromes illustrates genomic imprinting with abnormal development, but usually imprinting involves normal genetic mechanisms. It is a way of regulating the effect of different genes and hence related to epigenesis (see p. 78). So far, approximately 100 imprinted genes have been described (Choufani and Weksberg, 2016). The imprinting mechanism is believed to have played an important role in human evolution, as well as in individual development, especially in regulating prenatal and postnatal brain development (Perez et al., 2016). For example, genes that are switched off are activated during specific phases of development. By using the gene from a single parent only, the organism maintains a reserve gene that can be brought into play during periods of rapid growth, or in case of cellular mutations or dysfunctions (Kopsida et al., 2011; Wilkinson et al., 2007). Genomic imprinting shows that the mechanisms underlying the transfer of genetic information from one generation to the next, and the way in which the organism deals with this information, are both complex and flexible.

EVOLUTION

Evolution is the process by which different species have developed. According to Charles Darwin's theory of evolution (1859), a species undergoes constant changes over time. Certain genes contribute to properties that enable individuals in a given environment to grow up and reproduce more successfully in that environment than individuals lacking those genes. The prevalence of these genes increases because individuals carrying them generate offspring and spread their genes more than those who do not carry them. Other genes do not lead to the development of traits that result in increased reproduction in a given environment. Since these genes are propagated less, their incidence among the population declines. As a result of this process, species undergo constant transformation. Given the right conditions, individual differences can also evolve into differences between species. This is known

Charles Darwin.

as "natural selection," but it is important to emphasize that the process does not create new characteristics or skills, but simply ensures that individuals with certain existing characteristics and skills have a better chance of survival than others. Evolution does not explain *where* new traits and adaptations come from, but only *why* they propagate (Gottlieb, 2002).

Evolution thus entails a process of interaction between genes and the environment. Individual differences in genetic makeup are a prerequisite for evolution to take place, and any one environment will promote the spread of certain genes and inhibit that of others. The process is a slow one, however. Therefore, from a Darwinian perspective evolutionary adaptation can only take place when environmental characteristics are stable over many generations. Prior to Darwin, Lamarck (1809) maintained that acquired characteristics can be inherited – dependent on whether they are used or not used – and this view has been brought up in the recent discussion of epigenetic processes (see below) where genetic alternations in gene function are sometimes thought to be transmitted across generations. However, evidence of such transmission is limited and social inheritance seems a stronger process (Heard and Martienssen, 2014).

GENE REGULATION, EPIGENESIS AND DEVELOPMENT

The information contained in the genes of the very first cell (zygote), produced by the union of two germ cells (gametes), is a necessary prerequisite for the formation of an individual organism. The particular genes inherited by a child are determined by the parents' genetic makeup, but an optimal course of development requires environmental characteristics and genetic functioning to be adapted to one another. The individual's genetic structure or code sequence is stable but the function of the genes, their production of RNA, is adaptable and dynamic. Genes do not exist independently of the environment, but represent tendencies to react differently to specific environmental characteristics (Manuck and McCaffery, 2014). Epigenesis is a process which involves mechanisms that regulate the function of genes without changing their structure, includ-

ing imprinting (Zhang and Meaney, 2010). It is faster than structural genetic change and hence represents mechanisms for flexibility and adaption to the immediate environment (Heard and Martienssen, 2014). Studies show that the environment can influence gene activity by way of a "calibration" to the environment as it manifests itself through the child's experiences. The process can be compared with the activation of the immune system, which requires appropriate stimulation in order to prepare for the particular bacteria found in a child's environment. The ability to form antibodies is innate, but the specific antibodies developed by the child depend on the bacterial environment. Genes are innate, but it is the epigenetic process that determines how they are expressed. Early experiences prepare the individual for certain environmental conditions, a preparedness that continues throughout life, but the balance between gene function and expression may nevertheless change throughout the entire life cycle, and epigenetic effects may be reversible (McGowan and Szyf, 2010; Tammen et al., 2013). This emphasizes that gene function is a dynamic developmental process.

The role of the epigenetic process is to ensure typical development under different environmental conditions but the process sometimes goes wrong and leads to atypical development (Gapp et al., 2014). Brain development and function are particularly targeted by epigenetic influences, and disruption of epigenetic regulation is believed to be involved in profound disorders like Rett syndrome (Zahir and Brown, 2011) and neurodevelopmental disorders such as autism spectrum disorder (Geschwind, 2011; Millan, 2013). Rett syndrome is mainly related to mutation in the regulation gene $MeCP_2$, leading to dysregulation of gene expression and severely disturbed brain development with many cells and few synapses (Amir et al., 1999; Ehrhart et al., 2016; Lyst and Bird, 2015).

One of the fundamental questions regarding nature versus nurture is *how* genes function and impact the development of an individual, in other words how the genotype contributes to growth and change and to the formation of a phenotype. For example, it is estimated that several hundred genes have importance for the development of cognitive abilities (Kleefstra et al., 2014). This is not to say that these genes carry a predetermined IQ score. Genes produce nothing other than proteins, which in turn affect processes such as the production of nerve cells and cell connections in the brain, and thereby affect the ability to solve cognitive problems (Vaillend et al., 2008). One example of this is *phenylketonuria* (PKU), a hereditary defect in the production of one or more enzymes necessary to metabolize an essential amino acid (phenylalanine). Without treatment, affected children suffer neurological damage and severe intellectual disability, but a special diet low in phenylalanine allows them to develop normally (Crusio, 2015). All newborn children are screened for the disease. There is no doubt about the genetic cause of this metabolic disorder, but any damage to cognitive functioning would be the result of both genes and the environment. Although a basic vulnerability exists, the diet protects the child from any severe developmental consequences. The effect of genes is not absolute, but may involve an increased or reduced likelihood of a certain development (Rutter, 2006).

The formation of an individual by interaction between genes and environment means that a mechanism, or "meeting point," must exist for genes and experience to influence one other. Internal neurological activity and external stimulation can activate as well as inhibit the function of genes. This can occur when hormones susceptible to the influence of the organism's experiences penetrate the cellular nucleus and trigger gene activity. During very early development, for example, the activity of a number of genes depends on sensory stimulation. The ability of these genes to adjust their own function and that of other genes

allows the organism to achieve the same developmental result by making use of different genetic resources (Gottlieb, 2007). In a certain sense, every individual is created anew. In the course of development, the system creates its own genotype by activating and suppressing genes inherited from the parents and improving the proteins being produced (Elman, 2005; Hyde, 2015).

The fact that gene effects are not a one-way road is captured by the development model of Gottlieb (1992, 2007). It consists of four levels and genetic activity is represented by the lowest level (Figure 5.2). Nerve activity is located between genetic activity and behavior, and in turn influences both these levels. The connection between nerve activity and behavior forms the neurological basis for carrying out actions and creating mental representations of actions. Behavior affects the physical, social and cultural aspects of the environment, and is influenced by the latter. Experience based on action and perception affects neurological activity, which in turn affects genetic activity and gene regulation. At any one time, the organism is the result of previous genetic and environmental influences. This corroborates the fact that neither genes nor the environment are sufficient in themselves to ensure development. An organism depends on the functions and constraints dictated by its genes and the environmental influences it is able to exploit. The question of genes and the environment is – literally – the question of what came first: the chicken or the egg.

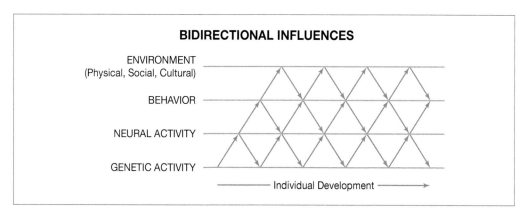

FIGURE 5.2 Mutual interaction between different levels.

Developmental model consisting of four levels that influence each other: genetic activity, nerve activity, behavior and environment. Behavior includes all forms of human mental activity (motor planning, perception, thinking, problem solving, etc.). The environment includes the physical, social and cultural characteristics of the individual's surroundings (based on Gottlieb, 1992, p. 186).

HEREDITY AND ENVIRONMENT IN INDIVIDUAL DIFFERENCES

The relationship between the impact of nature and nurture on individual differences in intelligence, personality, social ability and other areas may well be the most basic issue in developmental psychology, and is discussed in many places in this book. Heredity refers to the genes that are transferred to the child by the mother and father. The physical environment includes all of the chemical and physical influences an individual is exposed to from conception to death. The social and cultural environment consists of all the people in an individual's life, and includes the child's close social relations as well as broader societal contexts and cultural practices. There are two main ways of studying the influence of heredity and the environment on specific aspects of development: family studies and gene studies.

Family studies

These studies are based on the fact that people related to one another share all or part of the genes that contribute to individual differences, and that children growing up together are exposed to some of the same influences. The assumption is that individuals who share more genes will be more similar if a particular trait is influenced by genes. Family studies include comparisons of identical (monozygotic) and fraternal (dizygotic) twins, siblings who grow up together and separately, and children and their biological and/or foster parents. Identical twins come from the same fertilized egg and share identical genetic material (Figure 5.3). They therefore always have the same gender. Fraternal twins share 50 percent of their genes. The same is true of siblings. Since children receive their genes from their parents, they are genetically more similar than individuals who are not related.

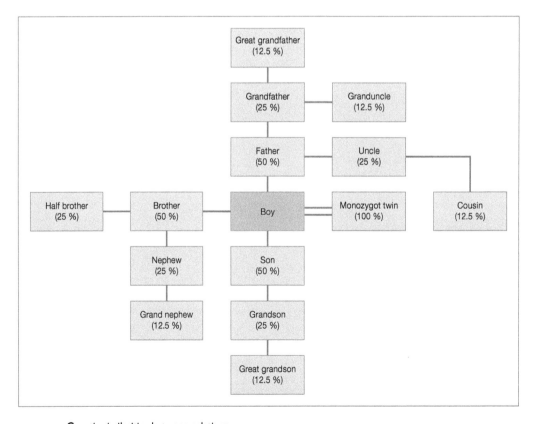

FIGURE 5.3 **Genetic similarities between relatives.**

The figure shows the percentage of genetic material shared between a boy and his male relatives. Due to the nature of sex chromosomes, percentages differ slightly across gender boundaries (based on Plomin et al., 1997, p. 29).

Twins can be difficult to distinguish.

Children of identical twins are half-siblings from a genetic point of view, since they genetically have a single parent in common.

Because identical twins share the same gene structure, twin studies have been particularly important in shedding light on the impact of genes and the environment. The similarity between identical twins who have grown up together reflects both their shared inheritance and environment. When identical twins who have grown up separately are less similar, it must be due to differences in their rearing environments. Assuming that the environments of identical twins growing up apart do not contribute to similarities between them, their similar traits must be caused by their shared genes.

A correlation is an expression of interdependence or agreement between variables (see p. 43), and may indicate how similar people are with regard to a specific characteristic, such as IQ of parents and children. Studies have shown that the correlations for height, intelligence, temperament, personality and many other human characteristics increase with the amount of shared genetic material (Table 5.2). There is thus little doubt that genetic inheritance influences the development of many characteristics, but the same is true of the environment. Children with different appearances and abilities are met in different ways and may therefore experience and react to the same environment in dissimilar ways. Identical twins, who physically resemble each other more than fraternal twins, most likely are being met more similarly by others, thereby reacting more equally to an environment than fraternal twins. Identical twins create more similar environments for themselves than fraternal twins, even if they grow up apart. On the other hand, epigenetic differences contribute to diversity in gene expression also among twins (Little, 2011). When fraternal twins are more similar to one another than to other siblings, it must be due to greater similarities in the environment, since they were born at the same time. After all, both fraternal twins and regular siblings share approximately 50 percent of their genes (Spinath et al., 2004).

TABLE 5.2 Examples of correlations between the characteristics of people with varying degrees of genetic and environmental similarity (correlations vary from study to study)

	Intelligence	Height	Weight	Extroversion	Neuroticism
Identical twins together	0.86	0.93	0.83	0.51	0.46
Identical twins apart	0.76	0.86	0.73	0.38	0.38
Fraternal twins together	0.60	0.66	0.46	0.18	0.20
Fraternal twins apart				0.05	0.23
Siblings	0.47		0.34	0.20	0.20
Adopted siblings	0.32		0.01	0.07	0.11
Biological parents and child(ren) together	0.42		0.26	0.16	0.16
Biological parents and adopted child(ren) apart	0.24		0.23		
Adoptive parents and adopted child(ren)	0.20		0.00	0.01	0.05

	Anxiety	Activity–impulsivity	Aggression	Religiosity	Masculinity–femininity	Heart rate	Blood pressure
Identical twins together	0.59	0.58	0.49	0.51	0.50	0.54	0.70
Identical twins apart				0.49		0.49	0.64
Fraternal twins together	0.18	0.22	0.28		0.33		

Family studies show that correlations within pairs of twins and between siblings change in the course of childhood and the life cycle (Lenroot and Giedd, 2008). In a longitudinal study of nearly 500 pairs of twins, Wilson (1983) found roughly the same correlations between intelligence scores for identical and fraternal twins during early childhood. By the age of 6, the identical pairs of twins had become significantly more similar to one another in intelligence than the fraternal pairs, a difference that remained stable until adolescence. One possible explanation may be that some genetically determined characteristics do not emerge until the child has reached a certain age. An alternative explanation is that the effects of gene environment interactions assert themselves more gradually over time, so that the combined effect of genes and the environment creates greater differences between fraternal than between identical twins.

Development does not occur equally in all areas, however: in some areas, the similarity between twins increases with age, in others it decreases, especially when twins do not grow up together. For example, the language of identical twins becomes somewhat more dissimilar with age, while that of fraternal twins becomes a little more similar. For certain personality traits, the differences between identical twins increase with age, for others they decrease (McCartney et al., 1990; Viken et al., 1994). A possible reason for this may be that monozygotic twins have a "twin identity" that leads them to seek out the same types of environments, while siblings who are similar to one another tend to deliberately try to be different.

Adoption studies have also been used to shed light on the influence of nature and nurture. The personality of adopted children correlates weakly with both their adoptive and their biological parents (Plomin et al., 1998). At the same time, studies show that children adopted into families with a high socioeconomic status achieve significantly higher average IQ scores than their biological parents (see p. 273). This indicates that the quality of the environment has an impact on intelligence.

In addition to such correlational studies of traits that vary among the general population, the influence of genes and the environment on psychiatric disorders has been studied by looking at their incidence among members of the same family. This is commonly expressed by indicating the degree of *concordance* – the presence of the same condition in different family members.

The concordance rate for severe depression, for example, is 40 percent for identical and 11 percent for fraternal twins. The concordance among close relatives is 10 percent for major depressive disorder. This means that a child has a 10-percent probability of experiencing major depression if the parents or siblings exhibit such symptoms. Among the population at large, the probability is 3 percent. Consequently, the risk of depression is more than three times greater for those who have family members with severe depression (Plomin et al., 2008). Similarly, language disorders (Bishop, 2003; Kang and Drayna, 2011), learning disorders (Landerl and Moll, 2010) and autism spectrum disorders (Persico and Napolioni, 2013) are often observed in families.

The emergence of specific family characteristics, particularly special talents such as musicality, has also been used as an argument in favor of a genetic basis for such characteristics – the many famous musicians in Johann Sebastian Bach's family have often been cited as an example. It is difficult, however, to separate genetic conditions from environmental factors in these types of studies. There can be no doubt about the existence of certain biological prerequisites, such as the ability to distinguish between musical pitches, but the influences of musical activities in a family may be just as important for developing an active relationship with music (Howe et al., 1998).

Heritability estimates

Behavioral genetics attempts to estimate the relative influence of genes and environment on the development of various traits and abilities (Plomin et al., 2013). Calculating a heritability estimate is typically based on the difference between the correlations for identical and fraternal twins. Pairs of twins growing up together are shaped by the same environment, but identical twins share twice as many genes as fraternal twins (100 vs. 50 percent). Table 5.2 shows the correlation of intelligence for identical twins (0.86) and fraternal twins (0.60), where 1.00 means full covariation, and 0.00 means no covariation. The difference in correlation is 0.26. Because only half of the genes differ between identical and fraternal twins, the heritability estimate for intelligence based on this table is two times the difference, or 0.52.

Heritability estimates are used in many contexts, but have also been criticized for creating an unrealistic picture of the influence of genes and environment (Gottlieb, 1995; Joseph, 2013; Lerner, 2015). This type of use of correlations is only valid if the influences of heredity and environment are made up of independent *main effects* that can be summed numerically (see p. 6). Most modern developmental theorists argue in favor of *interaction* between genes and the environment. Thus, the effect of the environment will depend on the individual's genes, and heritability will depend on the environment. Based on an interactive model, there is no fixed relationship between heredity and environment for a given trait, so that the genetic and environmental components are not independent (see p. 7). The rate of heritability will thus depend on variation in the environment. The more genetically alike two individuals are, the greater the influence of the environment on the differences between them. If their genes are exactly alike, such as in the case of identical twins, all of the differences must be caused by environmental factors. The same applies to differences in the environment. The more similar an environment twins grow up in, the greater the share of differences between them is caused by genes. A uniform environment will therefore yield high heritability estimates. Consequently, heritability estimates reveal as much about the contribution of the environment as that of genes. Calculating heritability estimates for different environments can still reveal useful information about the various environments' ability to realize positive and negative genetic potentials. If a characteristic is found to have major environmental variation in one place, and little such variation in another, it may be possible to identify the particular environmental aspects that contribute to the differences in that specific characteristic (Rose, 1997). An understanding of these mechanisms may enable society to promote positive and prevent negative development in children.

Gene studies of typical and atypical development

The family studies based on amount of shared genes indicate that some characteristics may have a genetic basis. But they say little about the underlying functions and the presence of a particular gene variant may be more important than the amount of shared genes. For example, girls with Rett syndrome (see Table 5.1, p. 76),

who mostly share a mutation in the MeCP$_2$ gene, are developmentally more similar to each other than to their parents and siblings even if they share around 50 percent of the genes with them. However, not all girls with the characteristics of the syndrome have the MeCP$_2$ mutation, and some with the mutation do not present with Rett syndrome, suggesting that there may be more than one genetic pathway to this severe disorder (Mari et al., 2005).

The mapping of the human genome in the first part of the twenty-first century lead to a search for genes or gene variants (alleles) that are associated with specific functions or disorders. The most common method has been the study of "candidate genes," where individuals with or without a particular trait or disorder are compared with regard to the presence of one or a few genes selected because existing knowledge about their function suggests that they may play a role in the development of the trait or disorder in question. The other method is the genome-wide search where the gene structure of subjects with a particular trait or disorder is compared to individuals without this trait or disorder. Many researchers aim to establish "functional genomics," that is, an overview of the functional consequences of DNA variation (Hudziak and Faraone, 2010). However, it has been difficult to document direct effects of individual genes and many initial findings have not stood the test of replication and are likely to be chance findings (Faraone et al., 2008; Latham and Wilson, 2010).

Studies have still contributed to new knowledge about how alleles of individual genes can influence development, for example the MAOA gene (Figure 5.4). Children with a low-activity allele of MAOA seem to be more sensitive to social rejection than children with other alleles of the gene (Kim-Cohen et al., 2006). They show a *greater* degree of behavioral problems, mental disorders and ADHD after having experienced neglect or physical abuse than children with other alleles of the gene. Under positive rearing conditions, however, they show *fewer* such problems (Caspi et al., 2002; Foley et al., 2004). Another example is the short allele of the 5-HTT gene, which also seems to entail a greater *susceptibility* to the influence of both good and bad environments than the long allele. Under unfavorable environmental conditions, children with a short variant develop more poorly than chil-

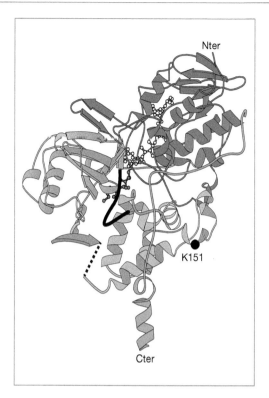

FIGURE 5.4 Monoamine oxidase A, MAOA, breaks down dopamine, norepinephrine and serotonin. (Photo from de Colibus et al., 2005)

of the gene. These studies demonstrate that development cannot solely be predicted based on knowledge of the child's genes or on the properties of the environment. Genes and environment always interact: the same gene can contribute negatively as well as positively, depending on the type of environment a child grows up in.

Many disorders have a genetic basis but there are no specific "intellectual disability genes," "language disorders genes," "autism genes" or "dyslexia genes." They are developmental disorders, not "natural" categories with corresponding genes, and many genes seem to be relevant for several disorders. More than 500 genes have been linked to intellectual disability (Kleefstra et al., 2014) and several genetic disruptions and mutations have been linked to language disorders and other disorders (Bishop, 2003; Kang and Drayna, 2011). Autism spectrum disorders have over time been linked to a large number of different genes. Some of these findings are likely to be unreplicable chance findings but they may also reflect that different genes may influence the development and severity of autism spectrum disorder (Bishop et al., 2014; Persico and Napolioni, 2013).

> To date, hundreds of genetic variants have been associated with ASD, and hundreds of "autism alleles" have been identified, with data on each available on a variety of autism genetic databases.
>
> Bishop et al. (2014, p. 1716)

dren with a long variant. Here, the short allele appears to represent vulnerability and the long allele *resilience* (see p. 13). Under potentially favorable rearing conditions, however, children with the short allele cope *better* than children with the long allele. In this case, the latter seem to be "vulnerable" in the sense that their development does not reflect their favorable environmental conditions. Therefore, none of the alleles can be said to represent vulnerability, as has often been suggested, but rather susceptibility – children with certain alleles are more susceptible to environmental influences in a particular domain than children with other alleles. Neither can long alleles be described as "resilience alleles," since they result in poorer development than the short alleles under favorable rearing conditions (Belsky et al., 2009; Pluess and Belsky, 2010). The findings thus suggest that children with a "susceptibility allele" of a gene are more dependent on favorable and relevant environmental conditions than children with other alleles

How genes may function in the neurological development of disorders is illustrated by the studies of an English family that was characterized by language disorders and a disruption of the FOX2 gene (see Box 5.1). The same gene was found only rarely in children with language disorders, thus demonstrating that different genes may be involved in such disorders. Moreover, the English family did not only have problems with language but with all actions that required a sequential organization. It is likely that the gene influenced their ability to construct spoken sentences because the ability to organize sequences of actions is *relevant* for the language function, in the same way as it is relevant for the organization of other action sequences in humans and

BOX 5.1 THE FOX2 GENE AND VERBAL APRAXIA

In an English family, 15 of 37 members had a severe form of verbal dyspraxia, problems performing the speech movement, and also many grammatical problems. A genome-wide search found that the family had a disruption of the FOX2 gene on chromosome 7 (Lai et al., 2001). The finding led to the assumption that the FOX2 gene was generally responsible for variation in language competence (Pinker and Jackendoff, 2005), but studies did not find the same mutation in other children with language disorders (Newbury et al., 2002). Further studies revealed that the FOX2 gene was not only related to language but to the organization of action sequences in general. The English family did not only have problems with speech but all actions that required a sequential organization (Karmiloff-Smith, 2011).

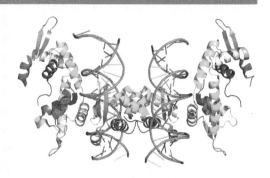

Structure of the FOXP2 protein. Based on PyMOL rendering of PDB 2ao9.

https://en.wikipedia.org/wiki/FOXP2#/media/File:Protein_FOXP2_PDB_2a07.png. CC BY-SA 3.0

other species (Karmiloff-Smith, 2011). Overall the studies seem to indicate that several genes may be relevant for the same pathological process, for example autism spectrum disorder or language disorder, and that the same gene may be relevant for different developmental disorders (Bishop et al., 2014).

Similarly, there is no specific personality gene: "Personality is heritable, but it has no genetic mechanism" (Turkheimer et al., 2014, p. 535), and with the exception of a few rare diseases, there is no direct relationship between individual genes and specific mental disorders (Abdolmaleky et al., 2005). It is more likely that a gene affects general brain properties, such as the ability to regulate emotional arousal, and that these properties can manifest themselves in different ways, depending on the child's other traits and the environment. Heritability estimates for antisocial behavior, for example, have been found to lie between 0.3 and 0.4. Relevant genes do not specify such behavior; they can influence traits such as temperament, activity level or attention, factors that in turn represent a vulnerability to developing antisocial behavior (Rutter, 2006).

Some variants of genes (alleles) are more prominent in certain geographic areas than in others, leading researchers to speculate about a possible relationship between genes and culture. It is common to distinguish between collectivist and individualist cultures. Studies have found that the short allele of MAOA, which seems to entail greater sensitivity to the social environment, is more frequent in collectivist than in individualist cultures. However, it is impossible to say whether collectivism has evolved as the result of the population's genes or whether individuals with this allele have reproduced more frequently in this type of society (Way and Lieberman, 2010).

It is important to emphasize that most research in this area is cutting-edge, and that knowledge of gene functions remains limited. Neither are the results unequivocal, and include both inconsistent and contradictory findings. Studies in different countries, for example, have found apparently contradictory relationships between genes and the characteristics and behavior of children with short and long 5-HTT alleles. Furthermore, the differences in behavior between groups with different alleles are relatively small, and the relationships between behavior and genes are often less pronounced than those between behavior and culture, class, ethnicity or gender (Kagan, 2009). Genes are important, but many factors contribute to an individual's development. Geschwind and Flint (2015) suggest that emotional and behavioral disorders are so complex that the search for genes may give limited results, and that more attention should be given to investigating environmental risk factors.

GENES AND DEVELOPMENT: CONSTRAINTS AND PLASTICITY

It is the species' genes that enable a human sperm cell and ovum to become a human being, and corresponding cells from dogs to become a dog. Genes must constrain the possibilities in such a way that certain developmental outcomes are likely or unavoidable (Keil, 1990). Therefore, the process initiated by the first cell in the fetal environment is guided by strict criteria and constraints. As described earlier, an individual's genes rarely determine a specific developmental result. Nor do cells divide and specialize according to a fixed pattern determined at the moment of conception through the unique set of genes passed on from the parents. The genetic architecture allows for sufficient flexibility to make survival possible when the environment changes. It allows room for more developmental possibilities, or plasticity. Instead of discussing the effects of heredity and environment, it has become more common to use the terms genetic and environmental constraint and plasticity. The question of nature and nurture, or maturation and learning, is thus reformulated into a question about constraints in children's potential traits and their plasticity and adaptability.

In discussing the functions of genes, it is important to distinguish between the importance of genes for developing a general trait, and the degree to which genes contribute to the differences between individuals. In some domains the constraints are quite strict, with little room for variation. This applies to processes that ensure that nearly all human beings have two eyes, two feet with five toes each, and so on. The design of details, on the other hand, has fewer constraints. There is considerable variation in head circumference, eye color, height, appearance, and so on. The greatest differences are in areas with a basis in neurological development, such as cognitive and social skills and personality. This means that the constraints on brain development are smaller and plasticity is greater than in other areas of growth. It is precisely such characteristics related to neurological function that cause the greatest disagreement from a biological point of view. Here, theories of general plasticity confront theories about genetically specified constraints. An intermediate position is that the brain's general structure and function are subject to strict constraints, while there is considerable plasticity within these constraints (Gottlieb et al., 2006; Johnson et al., 2002).

Behaviorism is located at one end of the scale in regard to nature versus nurture (see p. 23). Although the significance of genes for the development of the human organic structure is acknowledged, including the design of the brain, evolutionary selection is assumed to have provided neurological plasticity of such a magnitude that it does not imply any restrictions on behavioral development. Since, biologically speaking, plasticity is shared by all human beings, any variation in behavior must be caused by environmental differences, and thus learning.

At the other end of the scale lies the theoretical possibility that developmental changes are the result of genetically determined constraints and maturation, and that the primary function of the environment is to trigger innate knowledge. This means that the dissimilarities between children are solely due to differences in genetic makeup. Nativism is located at this end of the scale, but most theoreticians do not consider the constraints to be so strict as to assign no importance to the environment (see p. 28).

Nonetheless, some theorists ascribe nearly all importance to genes under normal development. According to Scarr (1992, 1996), genes not only contribute substantially and directly to development, but also to children's experiences: "genotypes drive experience" (1992, p. 9). By this she means that genes provide children with traits that lead them to seek out special experiences and thereby form their own environment. Assuming that a child grows up in an "average expected environment," including what Scarr calls a "normal home environment," parents will merely provide the environment that children themselves seek out based on their genetic dispositions. Consequently, the only function of the environment is to realize the child's genetic predisposition, and does not in and of itself contribute to the differences between children. It is principally the genetic basis that determines the developmental process, a process that, according to Scarr, is difficult to modify. Only when the environment differs dramatically from the norm and is "really deprived, abusive, and neglectful" does Scarr (1992, p. 3) believe it may be able to affect children negatively. She also believes that learning is most constrained early in life, and that plasticity increases with age because children are freer in their choice of environment.

Baumrind (1993) criticizes Scarr's one-sided emphasis on genes as the cause of individual differences. According to Scarr's model, children are passive agents for their genes, both in regard to intelligence and personality. It is the environment, not the individual, that is being adapted. Scarr's view furthermore implies that the differences between human races are mainly caused by variations in their genetic makeup, and only in extreme cases by different rearing conditions and cultural factors. This means that any attempt to improve the development of children growing up in a "normal" environment will have no effect, a view that is not supported by research (Baumrind et al., 2010; Flynn, 2016).

Most developmental psychologists position themselves between radical behaviorism and strong nativism, with major variations in the emphasis they place on genes versus the environment. In areas such as language, personality and intelligence, the theoretical differences are especially pronounced (see elsewhere in this book for discussions of these). Additionally, many theorists question the very notion of separating the effect of genes from those of the environment.

SUMMARY

1 *Genes* are an essential biological component in human functioning. How human genes have evolved through evolution (phylogeny) and how they contribute to the physical, perceptual, cognitive and social development of human beings (ontogeny) are key questions in developmental psychology.

2 With the exception of reproductive cells (gametes), every human cell normally contains 23 *pairs of chromosomes* with a total of approximately 23,000 different genes. Each gene can have several *alleles*.

3 *Genetic inheritance* refers to the information transmitted to a human being or animal via the genes contained in the parents' sperm and egg cell. A child's complete genetic material is called the *genotype*, its observable characteristics the *phenotype*. In order for *recessive genes* to affect development, children must inherit them from both parents. If a gene is *dominant*, it only needs to be transmitted by one of the parents in order to be expressed. A *mutation* is a sudden change in a gene structure.

4 *Genomic imprinting* means that a gene can be "switched off," and that the function of the gene depends on which parent it comes from. Genomic imprinting has an important function in regulating brain development.

5 Genes affect processes on other levels and are in turn affected by those processes. The genetic information inside the cells thus constantly interacts with what has previously been established via development and environmental influences. Plasticity is greatest in areas related to neurological function and development.

6 Genes affect and are in turn affected by other genes, as well as by external factors. *Epigenesis* refers to experience-driven changes in gene function without changes in gene structure. Gene expression seems to be "calibrated" early on, creating a preparedness that continues throughout life, but requires specific environmental conditions in order to be realized.

7 The influence of heredity and the environment on specific aspects of development are investigated with family studies and gene studies. Studies of twins, siblings and other biological and adopted family members show a complex interaction between genetic predisposition and environment in the development of *individual traits*. *Heritability estimates* are based on the difference in correlation between identical (monozygotic) and fraternal (dizygotic) twins. They

indicate the relative importance of genes for various traits, but there is disagreement about the usefulness of such estimates.

8   Studies of *candidate genes* compare individuals with or without a particular trait or disorder with regard to the presence of one or a few genes. In a *genome-wide search*, the gene structure of subjects with a particular trait or disorder is compared to individuals without this trait or disorder.

9   There is rarely a direct effect of a gene on human traits and disorders. Some studies have found that certain alleles of MAOA, 5-HTT and other genes cause an increased susceptibility to environmental influences, but many of the findings are inconsistent and contradictory. The behavioral differences between individuals with different alleles of a gene are often smaller than the differences caused by culture, class, ethnicity or gender.

10 Development is a balance between constraint and plasticity. Behaviorists maintain that development is plastic and the development of individual differences mainly a result of learning; while nativists believe that such differences are largely the result of genetic constraints and maturation. Other theorists believe development to be the result of interaction between genes and the environment, but vary in their emphasis on nature and nurture.

CORE ISSUES

• The relationship between nature and nurture in development.

• What methods to use to measure the influence of genes and environment.

SUGGESTIONS FOR FURTHER READING

Geschwind, D. H. (2011). Genetics of autism spectrum disorders. *Trends in Cognitive Sciences*, *15*, 409–416.

Gottlieb, G. (1995). Some conceptual deficiencies in "developmental" behavior genetics. *Human Development*, *38*, 131–141.

Lerner, R. M. (2015). Eliminating genetic reductionism from developmental science. *Research in Human Development*, *12*, 178–188.

Plomin, R., DeFries, J. C., Knopik, V. S., & Neiderhiser, J. M. (2016). Top 10 replicated findings from behavioral genetics. *Perspectives on Psychological Science*, *11*, 3–23.

Zhang, T. Y., & Meaney, M. J. (2010). Epigenetics and the environmental regulation of the genome and its function. *Annual Review of Psychology*, *61*, 439–466.

Contents

Development begins at conception when an egg and a sperm cell unite into a single cell. From here until birth, the fetus develops many characteristics and abilities, all made possible by the fetal environment – it protects the immature organism from injury and sensory stimuli the fetus cannot cope with, and facilitates stimulation and movement that prepare the organism for an independent life. A key question is how physiological and other factors during fetal development contribute to the differences among children. Although technical developments have opened up new possibilities, the opportunities for studying children in the womb are extremely limited, and both studies and possible interventions pose significant methodological challenges and ethical dilemmas.

FETAL DEVELOPMENT

Fetal development can be divided into three periods. *The germ* is the seed, the early embryo, and the *germinal period* includes the first 10 days of development. The egg and the sperm merge into a single cell and develop into 60 cells during the first 4 days. After a few days, the cells begin to cluster together into three layers. The outer layer (ectoderm) develops into the skin and nervous system. The middle layer (mesoderm) becomes the skeleton and muscles, while the inner layer (endoderm) evolves into the internal organs (Finne et al., 2001). During the first 8 weeks of development, the fetus is called an *embryo*. The 6-week period following the germinal period is the *embryonic period*, while the *fetal period* lasts until birth.

During the germinal period, all cells are identical and begin to specialize and form different organs during the embryonic period. The middle layer forms the heart, which begins to beat after 3 to 4 weeks. At 2 to 3 weeks, the outer layer forms a neural tube, but the nervous system does not begin to develop until the heart has started functioning. By 8 weeks, the fetus has grown to around 2 centimeters in length and weighs 1 gram. The beginning features of a human being become visible, including the limbs, nervous system and internal organs. At 12 weeks of age, the fetus is about 10 centimeters long and weighs 20 grams. Its human features can be clearly seen. At 20 weeks, its length is about 25 centimeters, weighing approximately 300 grams (see Figure 6.1). After that, the weight of the fetus increases significantly, on average from about 1,000 grams to 3,600 grams during the final 3 months. Because the brain is given priority during the fetal period, the size of the head is relatively large compared with the rest of the body. This also applies throughout childhood, and the head does not reach its final proportion in relation to the body until adulthood.

Birth usually occurs after about 40 weeks, and many functions are in place well before the child is born. Circulation is in place after 12 weeks. After 24 weeks, the fetus can breathe in air, but continues to rely on oxygen from the mother's blood because the lungs are still too immature to take up enough oxygen by breathing. Even children born more than 2 to 3 months prior to term and weighing very little at birth – under

There is an enormeous development in the fetal period.

1 kilo – can survive with medical help, but may have to be placed in an incubator.

The biochemical environment

It is the physiological environment that affects the development of the fetus in the womb. The fetus receives nourishment from the mother, whose nutrition and general health affect the fetus's uptake of nutrients and opportunities for growth. An appropriate and balanced diet increases the likelihood of pregnancy without complications, while malnutrition and deficiencies increase the risk of miscarriages, stillbirths and abnormalities. Malnutrition can affect the growth of brain cells, but may to some extent be counteracted if the child receives proper nutrition after birth (Fifer et al., 2004; Hales and Barker, 2001).

Maternal diseases can affect the development of the fetus. Maternal diabetes may reduce growth and delay development and it is therefore important to regulate the mother's glucose level during pregnancy (Mulder and Visser, 2016). Rubella can cause sensory impairment and other developmental disorders in the child during the first 3 months of pregnancy, in some cases also later. Because of the potentially serious consequences of the disease, girls in many countries are vaccinated against rubella (De Santis et al., 2006).

Substances that can harm the fetus are called teratogens. Children whose mothers smoke weigh less at birth, probably because nicotine causes the blood vessels in the uterus to contract and reduce the supply of nutrients. Maternal smoking during pregnancy also increases the risk of congenital heart conditions, premature birth and stillbirth, often in combination with other risk factors (Cnattingius, 2004; Mund et al., 2013).

Drinking relatively large quantities of alcohol during pregnancy leads to a greater risk of birth defects and developmental injuries in the child (Hepper, 2016; O'Leary and Bower, 2012). Particularly in the early stages of pregnancy, alcohol affects the development of the child's brain, often together with smoking and poor nutrition. The brain becomes smaller and the cortex develops fewer folds than normal (Guerrini et al., 2007). There is a relationship between the mother's alcohol consumption and later hyperactivity in the child. If the mother has consumed a lot of alcohol over time during pregnancy, the child may develop *fetal alcohol syndrome*, characterized by a small head, characteristic facial features and abnormalities of the heart and limbs. Additionally, the children are often irritable and hyperactive (Riley et al., 2011).

Some children are exposed to other substances such as cocaine and heroin during the fetal period. As newborns they may show withdrawal symptoms that include tremors, hypersensitivity, problems focusing the eyes and self-regulating, crying and sleeping problems. The symptoms eventually disappear, but can make the child's early interactions with adults difficult. Cocaine causes the mother's blood vessels to constrict and deprives the fetus of nutrition. Prolonged use increases the risk of delayed development, but the results of studies on the long-term effects on cognition, language and behavior vary. Children who have been exposed to heroin during the fetal period have problems with attention and perceptual and cognitive functioning in childhood, even if taken away from the mother and placed in a sound and nurturing environment. Boys are more vulnerable than girls (Behnke et al., 2013; Irner, 2012). Variations in the results most likely reflect differences in exposure and in the quality of follow-up care given to mothers and children.

The effects of various substances on fetal development depend on when and for how long the fetus has been exposed to them. Different organs and parts of the body are vulnerable at different times (Figure 6.2). Harmful exposure to teratogens, for example, tends to lead to heart

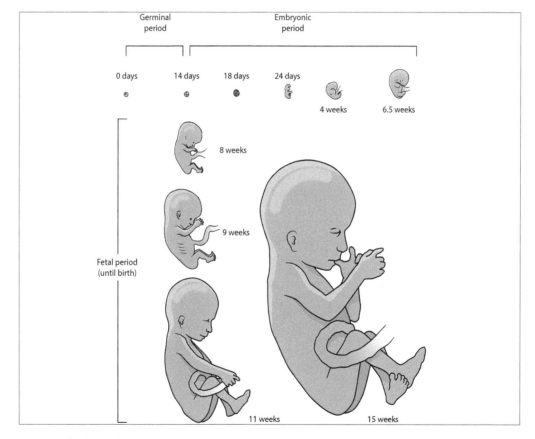

FIGURE 6.1 Fetal growth.
Changes in the relative size and shape of a fetus until 15 weeks of age (based on Butterworth and Harris, 1994, p. 38).

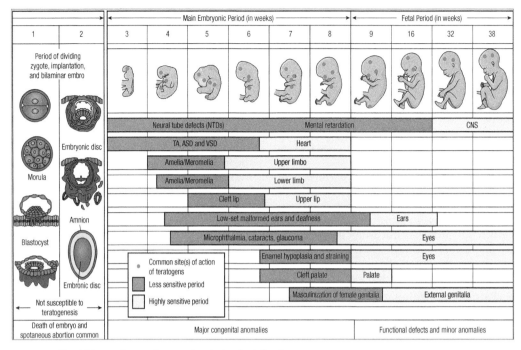

FIGURE 6.2 **Sensitivity to damage from toxins during fetal development.**
Different organs and parts of the body are vulnerable at various times during fetal development. The figure shows periods in which particular parts of the fetus are especially sensitive, somewhat sensitive and not sensitive to the influence of teratogenic agents such as nicotine, alcohol, drugs and various medications. Generally, the risk of major defects is greatest during the embryonic period. The figure also shows the effects of teratogens on other features at different stages of pregnancy (Moore and Persaud, 2008, p. 473).

failure early in the germinal period, while the brain is the organ most at risk during the final part of prenatal development. The effects of malnutrition and maternal smoking are greatest during the last 5 months, when the fetus increases most in weight.

Exposure to alcohol and drugs during fetal development also implies an increased vulnerability to environmental risk factors. This means that negative environmental factors can lead to more severe developmental consequences for children exposed to such substances than for other children (Yumoto et al., 2008).

PRENATAL STIMULATION

Perceptual and cognitive development begins with the fetal period. The cells divide and form a brain that is able to perceive, process and remember sensory information, and create simple patterns of movement. Sensory stimulation acti-

vates the nervous system and thereby fulfills an important function in neurological development. The development of the senses occurs in a fixed order: first the tactile sense and the sense of balance, followed by smell and taste, then hearing, and finally vision. All of these have begun to function before the fetus is 26 weeks old (Lecanuet and Schaal, 2002). This temporal sequence prevents competition between the different sensory systems, and facilitates their organization and integration (Turkewitz and Kenny, 1985).

The senses receive different types of stimulation during fetal development. The balance system is stimulated by the mother's movements, and her physical activity may cause pressure or vibration on the fetus (Ronca and Alberts, 1995). At 10–11 weeks, the fetus responds to *tactile stimulation* of the hands and arms, and after 14 weeks it responds to touch all over its body, except for the top of the head. The most common responses in studies of fetal development are changes in heart rate and amount of body movement (see Reissland and Kisilevsky, 2016). The neurological structures and chemical substances necessary to perceive *pain* are activated late in fetal life, although it is uncertain whether fetuses can feel pain (Piontelli et al., 2015). Moreover, the fetal environment includes little "acute" stimulation that could be painful (Hepper, 1992).

Over time, the fetus is able to perceive different chemical substances as precursors to *odor* and *taste*. A fetus swallows more amniotic fluid when a sweetener has been added than when the fluid is neutral, or when a bitter tasting substance has been added (Schaal et al., 1995).

The light that reaches the fetus is uniform and extremely weak, and provides little basis for visual learning. It is possible that the faint gleam of light that appears during late gestation helps to activate the optic nerves.

The fetus is exposed to a relatively high degree of acoustic stimulation from the mother's internal organs (60–85 dB), but the heartbeat and other sounds lie at a frequency range too low for the fetus to perceive. Other sounds in the child's environment are quite weak (8–32 dB) against the background noise. The child can react to outside sounds but these must penetrate several layers of tissue and fluids, and lose much of their energy in the transition from air to tissue. The liquid that fills the fetus's ears results in a distortion of sounds compared with how similar sounds are perceived after birth (Lecanuet and Schaal, 2002; Querleu et al., 1988). This means that the possibilities of a fetus gaining knowledge about the sounds it will meet in its surroundings after birth are generally poor during the time in the womb.

The mother's voice is a prominent sound in the fetal environment; it has the advantage of being transmitted through the body and can lie as much as 32 dB above other background sounds (Hepper, 1992). Right before term, the fetus will react to the mother's voice with changes in heart rate, a form of attention response (Voegtline et al., 2013). A number of experiments using conditioning and habituation have found that newborns are more attentive to their mother's voice than other female voices (see p. 137). This means that the fetus is able to perceive and remember some aspects of the mother's voice. In a study where the mother's speech was presented on tape, the fetus showed the same pattern of response when it was played forward and backward, indicating that the fetus is less attentive to temporal than non-temporal aspects of sounds, such as pitch, frequency and tone (Kisilevsky, 2016). Reduced fetal growth may be associated with delayed auditory development. Newborns who are small for gestational age more frequently fail to show preference for their mother's voice and score significantly lower on expressive language measures at 15 months (Kisilevsky et al., 2014).

The fetus reacts to sounds (or vibration) at 12–16 weeks of age, *before* the development of hearing. This suggests that the fetus experiences a form of *general* sensory stimulation that cannot be compared with hearing. Studies of visual perception performed during the first months after birth also show that newborn babies (and thus the fetus) perceive visual stimulation differently than infants only a few months of age (see p. 125).

The reactions to stimulation change in the course of fetal development. For example, early on, contact with the cheek will cause the fetus to withdraw from the source of stimulation. Later on, the fetus will turn toward the source of contact. This may be in preparation for the rooting reflex, which after birth helps children find their mother's nipple with their mouth in order to suck (see p. 150). Stimulation of the senses contributes to the development of fetal movements, and aids in the transition from the womb to the outside environment (Hepper, 1992; Ronca and Alberts, 1995). Hence, the function of fetal perception is not to remember certain experiences, but to prepare for the different types of stimulation the child will meet after birth. As the amount of amniotic fluid decreases toward the end of pregnancy, the fetus receives progressively more stimulation (Ronca and Alberts, 1995). Prematurely born babies are developmentally adapted to the protected fetal environment and have a limited ability to deal with stimulation from their surroundings and need help to shield themselves against overstimulation (McMahon et al., 2012; Yecco, 1993).

Movement and activity

With a length of 2–3 centimeters, the fetus begins to move by curling up and stretching out after about 7 weeks. After another 3 to 4 weeks, it begins to roll, turn its head and move individual limbs. After 16 weeks the movements are so distinct that mothers begin to notice them. The grasping reflex shows up after 28 weeks.

Fetuses generally move a lot, especially in the early fetal stage. At 16 weeks, a fetus makes up to 20,000 movements per day. Ultrasound studies have shown that *inactivity* increases with age, a phenomenon thought to be caused by the fact that higher parts of the brain assume motor control. Prior to week 24, the fetus never rests for more than five minutes at a time. At 32 weeks, most inactive periods last between 10 and 35 minutes, and only rarely more than 40 minutes (Pillai and James, 1990). The fetus also has a 96-minute wake-sleep cycle that is associated with the mother's own sleeping patterns and disappears after birth (de Vries et al., 1982, 1985, 1988).

The activity of the fetus strengthens its body, develops its senses, provides feedback about its physical growth and forms the basis for the development of behavior the child shows at birth. Fewer movements are associated with reduced mobility in the joints, growth disorders and malformations in the lungs and face (Ronca and Alberts, 1995). Children with *fetal alcohol syndrome* have abnormalities in the joints believed to be the result of sedation of the fetus by alcohol in the mother's blood, leading to reduced motor activity during a sensitive period in the development of the joints (Butterworth and Harris, 1994).

Initially, movement is *spontaneous*, that is, not caused by any external influence. Gradually, movement is progressively triggered by sensory stimulation. When the fetus is 20–27 weeks old, loud noises and vibrations begin to cause changes in the heart rate (Joseph, 2000). After 33 weeks, the fetus reacts with large movements when stimulated by sound (Gagnon, 1992), although the reaction time is quite slow: an increase in movement first occurs 10 minutes after stimulation and lasts for an hour. This delayed reaction most likely indicates that the fetus needs time to process stimulation.

Similar to studies conducted on sensory stimulation, research has found skills that are not easily detected in the fetal environment and will prove to be important in the external environment after birth. This emphasizes the fact that fetal development is about more than physical growth, and that it takes time for a child to develop the perceptual and motor skills shown by newborn children.

Prenatal learning

Prenatal learning – defined as a change in behavior (for example heart rate) as a direct result of experience – can entail habituation, conditioning and exposure. Most research has been conducted on animal fetuses (James, 2010). In humans, the onset of habituation – usually a decrease in reaction following repeated stimulation (see p. 46), for example an electric toothbrush placed on the maternal abdomen over the fetal head and activated in 5-second periods approximately every 20 seconds – appears to become established at roughly the same time as the senses begin to function, around week 25 to 28, and somewhat earlier in girls than in boys (Leader, 2016). Prenatal habituation requires a stimulus to be presented many times before the reaction becomes substantially reduced, but the number declines with age (McCorry and Hepper, 2007).

Towards the end of the prenatal period, the fetus also shows a capacity for long-term memory in connection with stimulation. In one study, the same auditory stimulus was repeated until the reactions of the fetus had decreased (habituation). When the experiment was repeated the following day, fewer iterations were needed to establish a corresponding degree of habituation. When the repetition took place after 3 days, no such learning effect was observable (Leader, 1995), indicating that the limit of fetal memory is more than 1 day and less than 3 days (see also p. 197).

The association between a stimulus and a response (see p. 286) is mainly based on animal studies using classical conditioning, and little research has been conducted on human fetuses. Although some studies have found evidence of this type of learning, others have not. Therefore, it remains uncertain whether the human fetus is sufficiently developed for this type of learning (James, 2010).

FETAL EXPERIENCES AND LATER DEVELOPMENT

Since the fetal period forms the basis for further development, it is assumed that the course of fetal development has a certain bearing on the child's future development. Also the fetus adapts to its environment, for example by reducing growth when nourishment is sparse (Gluckmann and Hanson, 2010; Wells, 2007). This is sometimes

BOX 6.1 FETAL HABITUATION AND LATER DEVELOPMENT (Leader, 2016)

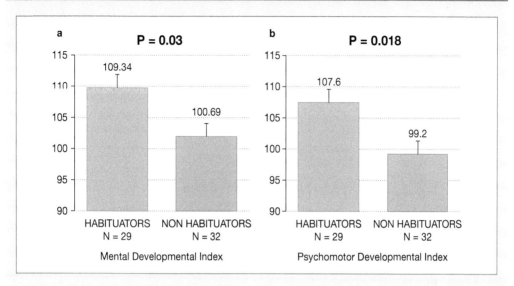

The study group consisted of 100 subjects who were tested for habituation with vibro-acoustic stimulation (a vibrator placed above the fetus on the mother's abdomen) 2 weeks before their delivery. Fifty-four of the mothers had uncomplicated pregnancies and 46 had pregnancies complicated by hypertension intrauterine growth retardation, or developed fetal distress in labor. The mean heart rate for 5 seconds before the stimulation was compared to the maximum heart rate achieved in the next 55 seconds. If the fetus did not increase its heart rate by more than ten beats per minute for five successive trials, it was regarded as habituation. The maximum number of trials to meet the habituation criterion was 50. Each fetus was classified as either a habituator or a non-habituator. At 3 years of age, 61 of the children were tested with the Bayley Scales of Infant Development (1993) by a developmental psychologist who was unaware of their earlier status as habituator or non-habituator. The average of both groups were within the normal range but the habituators had significantly higher scores than the non-habituators on a) Mental Developmental Index and b) Psychomotor Developmental Index. More of the non-habituators had scores one standard deviation below the mean or lower (below IQ 85). Similar differences were found at 7–8 years for a subgroup of 32 children but the results were less consistent and more pronounced for girls than for boys. The results show developmental continuation from fetal life into childhood.

referred to as "fetal programming," and includes *epigenetic* influences, the influence of environmental conditions on the expression of genes (Ellison, 2010; Monk et al., 2012; see also p. 78). For example, there is a correlation between fetal reactions to stimulation (measured by changes in the heart rate) and temperament during infancy (Werner et al., 2007). Continuity in development is also indicated by heart rate habituation before delivery and later cognitive development (Box 6.1). Similarly, children who are active in the womb tend to continue to be active after birth. It has also been suggested that some neurode-

velopmental disorders may have their origin in prenatal processes (van den Bergh, 2011). The prenatal environment may thus have a lasting effect on development.

> Throughout gestation, the mother and her offspring are exquisitely intertwined, forming an integrated, biological system within which the mother, gestating siblings, and fetus itself each contribute in significant and meaningful ways to the fetus's sensory milieu.
> (Ronca and Alberts, 2016, p. 21)

Another question is the extent to which a fetus can have specific experiences that are stored in memory and can be confirmed after birth. Studies have shown that fetal exposure to chemical substances can affect the child's taste preferences during the neonatal period. A fetus that is more attentive to its mother's voice than the voices of strangers right before birth (and after) indicates some kind of memory of the maternal voice (Kisilevsky et al., 2009). This type of recognition may increase the likelihood of newborns' attention to their mother. After all, it is the voice – along with the sense of smell – that forms the basis for the child's initial recognition (Hepper, 2015). It has been speculated that the mother's voice serves as a kind of preparation for the child's attachment, just as the sounds of brooding birds seem to prepare for imprinting (see p. 397). No research has been able to show whether this type of prenatal "preparation" affects the attachment process. However, studies show that the mother to some extent bonds with her child during pregnancy. Being able to see the fetus via ultrasound aids in this process (Alhusen, 2008; DiPietro, 2010).

Studies have also found that newborns showed a preference for the music of TV series their mothers had watched during pregnancy, but this disappeared after 3 weeks (Hepper, 1992). Thus, any early recognition of this type is short-lasting, and there is no reason to believe that it is possible to "imprint" children to like certain types of music by exposing them to it during the fetal stage. Neither is there evidence to suggest that additional auditory stimulation during the fetal period has any developmental benefits (James, 2010).

Children show a significant development in perceptual and cognitive functioning during the first months after birth. With the exception of the effect of teratogens, it is not known to what extent stimulation and experiences in the fetal period have significance beyond the general developmental stimulation brought about by activation. Correlations between fetal performance and later functioning indicate some degree of continuity but the factors influencing fetal performance are not always known. Therefore, one should be cautious in attributing a substantial impact of presumed specific experiences during fetal development on a child's subsequent cognitive and linguistic development. On the whole, the fetal environment is characterized by repetitive and relatively non-specific types of stimulation.

Maternal emotional states

There has been considerable discussion about the extent to which the mother's emotional state affects the fetal environment and influences the child's later development. When the mother experiences strong fear or anger, her autonomic nervous system is activated. Blood flows to the organs that are important for her defense, such as the brain, heart and muscles, while the blood supply to other parts of the body, including the uterus, decreases. If this state persists over time, it can deprive the fetus of needed nutrition. The fetus may respond with an increase in heart rate and a reduction in activity, a response that is interpreted as an attention reaction resulting from changes in the fetal environment, but there is no direct connection between the mother's physiological reactions and the reactions of the fetus (DiPietro, 2010).

Research indicates that the mother's state may have a more long-term effect. Several studies have found a relationship between stress and anxiety in mothers during pregnancy and the temperament of newborns and their later reactions to new experiences, as well as attentional and behavioral problems (Gutteling et al., 2005, 2006). A large longitudinal study found that mothers' prenatal anxiety and depression predicted elevated internalizing problems through childhood and adolescence (O'Donnell et al., 2014). Another study found that number of stressful life events during pregnancy predicted both internalizing and externalizing problems, suggesting that amount of maternal stress matters (Robinson et al., 2011). In addition, studies have found associations between maternal depression and fetal growth and activity, but the correlations are generally small (Field, 2011). Children seem to be particularly vulnerable to maternal stress during the first part of prenatal life; during later stages of pregnancy, maternal stress seems to have less impact on the child's development but this may be due to the fact that maternal responsiveness to stressful events gradually dampen over time due to pregnancy-related physiological changes in stress sensitive hormones (Lazinski et al., 2008; Robinson et al., 2011).

On the other hand, it has been suggested that non-optimal prenatal experiences do not have exclusively negative effects, but can prepare the child and contribute to more flexibility and adaptability in a somewhat "difficult" environment after birth (Pluess and Belsky, 2011). It is also possible that mothers who react more emotionally to different situations provide a more varied and stimulating physiological environment for the fetus (DiPietro, 2010).

Fetal development is complex and the interpretation of causal relationships in these types of studies is associated with considerable uncertainty. Statistical correlation says nothing about what is cause and what is effect. Development is transactional during fetal life as well (DiPietro, 2010). Depression and anxiety can lead mothers to smoke and drink more alcohol, substances which can affect the development of the fetus (see p. 93). Mothers with fetuses that are active or have developmental anomalies can experience pregnancy as more stressful. Studies showing increased stress in mothers of children with Down syndrome or cleft palate point in this direction (Drillien and Wilkinson, 1964; Stott, 1973). Such conditions cannot possibly have

been triggered by the mother's emotional state. Furthermore, mothers who are depressed or stressed during pregnancy tend to maintain these states after birth. It is therefore difficult to separate the effects of stress during pregnancy from the consequences of the mother's stress level and possible interaction problems during the child's first months of life (Field, 2011; Mulder et al., 2002).

It is sometimes argued that experiences during a normal birth can have a profound effect on children's development and lead to mental problems later in life (Winnicott, 1992). There is no scientific support for such claims and others argue that the powerful forces associated with labor and delivery fulfill an adaptive role that helps the newborn child begin to function independently, and thereby eases the transition from fetus to infant (Hepper, 1992; Ronca and Alberts, 1995).

SUMMARY

1   Development begins at conception. The characteristics and abilities of a child at birth emerge as the result of 9 months of development. The *germinal period* consists of the first 10 days. The 6 weeks following the germinal period are called the *embryonic period*, while the *fetal period* lasts until the child is born.

2   Several diseases can affect fetal development. In addition to the mother's use of alcohol, tobacco and drugs, chemical substances in the environment have also proved to be of importance. The particular effect of various substances depends on when and for how long the fetus has been exposed to them.

3   The sensory systems develop in a fixed order, and all senses are functional by week 26. Gradually, the fetus changes in its reactions to stimulation.

4   After about 7 weeks, the fetus begins to move and performs up to 20,000 movements per day by week 16. Following this, the inactive periods last progressively longer. Activity strengthens the body of the fetus, develops its senses, provides feedback about its physical growth and forms the basis for the behavior the child shows at birth.

5   Sensory stimulation of the fetus helps to activate the nervous system. On the whole, the fetal environment is characterized by repetitive and non-specific types of stimulation in preparation for the more intense and varied stimulation the child will meet after birth.

6   During the fetal period, learning can take place by means of habituation and exposure, but it is uncertain when the human fetus is sufficiently developed to form associations through conditioning. Newborns are more attentive to their mother's voice than the voices of strangers, and must therefore have formed some kind of memory of the maternal voice.

7   It is assumed that the course of fetal development has a certain bearing on the child's future development, "fetal programming" and epigenesis. There is a certain continuity in fetal activity, and a correlation between fetal reactions to stimulation and temperament during infancy. This can increase the probability of children attending to their own mother.

Continued

8   The mother's emotional state during pregnancy can affect the child's later development. For example, there is a relationship between the mother's emotions and fetal growth and activity, especially during the first part of fetal development, but the correlations are generally small and it is difficult to distinguish prenatal influences from later ones. On the other hand, fetuses whose mothers react more emotionally to different situations may have a more varied and stimulating physiological environment. Fetal development is complex and the interpretation of causal relationships in these types of studies is associated with considerable uncertainty.

9   There is no scientific support for the claim that particular experiences during birth can have a profound effect on a child's development and lead to psychiatric disorders later in life.

CORE ISSUES

• The influence of fetal experiences on later development.

• The influence of the mother's mental state on the fetus and the child's later development.

SUGGESTIONS FOR FURTHER READING

Behnke, M., Smith, V. C., & Committee on Substance Abuse (2013). Prenatal substance abuse: Short- and long-term effects on the exposed fetus. *Pediatrics, 131*, e1009–e1024.

James, D. K. (2010). Fetal learning: A critical review. *Infant and Child Development, 19*, 45–54.

O'Connor, T. G., Monk, C., & Fitelson, E. M. (2014). Practitioner review: Maternal mood in pregnancy and child development–implications for child psychology and psychiatry. *Journal of Child Psychology and Psychiatry, 55*, 99–111.

Contents

T he brain is the central organ responsible for human mental prowess, and its structure and large size relative to body size are defining features of *Homo sapiens* (Neubauer and Hublin, 2012). Ever since the birth of developmental psychology, an important goal has been to understand how the brain performs various functions and why it develops as it does (Preyer, 1882). There is a search for neurological processes that correspond with the various theoretical views on cognitive, social and emotional functions (e.g., Adolphs, 2009; Becker, 2006; Mahy et al., 2014; Meissner, 2008). Cultural differences are to some extent viewed in the context of brain development as well (Chiao et al., 2010). New technologies have led to an increasing use of brain function measurements in studies of both typical and atypical development (see Mareschal et al., 2007a,b; Nelson et al., 2006b). The understanding of brain structure and function and their development – and of the relationship between brain and mind – remains fairly limited, however (Miller, 2010). It is not likely that the human mind and the human brain are organized in the same way (Dekker and Karmiloff-Smith, 2011; Thomas et al., 2013). The basis for mapping the brain's functions is provided by psychological models that tell researchers what to look for.

METHODS OF STUDYING THE BRAIN

In order to find out how the brain is built up and performs various tasks, researchers investigate the brain of children who develop normally, search for the causes of attention deficit disorder, intellectual disability, autism spectrum disorder and other severe developmental disorders, and examine the functional consequences of cerebral hemorrhage and other physical damage in the brain of people who previously have functioned normally (Dennis and Thompson, 2013). Many studies have aimed to find out which parts of the brain and neural networks are involved in performing various mental functions. The most important methods are electroencephalography and magnetic resonance imaging, which make it possible to examine the brain while the subject performs various mental tasks (Brown and Jernigan, 2012; Hunt and Thomas, 2008).

Electroencephalography (EEG) is administered by attaching 20 or more sensors to the exterior of the head to record the electrical activity in the cerebral cortex. *Magnetoencephalography* (MEG) uses magnetic sensors inside a helmet to measure brain currents. The electrical activity of nerve cells, or neurons, creates weak magnetic fields, and when many thousands of neurons are activated simultaneously, it is possible to measure the magnetic field they create on the surface of the skull using MEG. EEG and MEG are often used to measure how the brain responds to sensory stimulation. The brain's response to visual stimulation is registered by measuring the activity in the visual cortex. Response to auditory stimulation is measured by placing sensors over the part of the cortex that processes auditory stimuli (Picton and Taylor, 2007). The *mismatch response* (MMR) is an example of such a use of

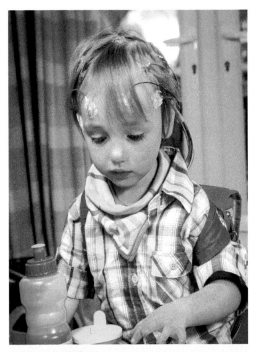

Child with EEG sensors.

blood is measured and compared with the oxygen level when the child is   rest or performs another task. MRI provides information about the brain's structural composition and fMRI whether one or more areas are active while the child is processing sensory stimulation or performing a specific task, such as talking or recognizing an object (Hunt and Thomas, 2008).

These methods are technically quite complex. They have different strengths and weaknesses, and supplement each other. fMRI provides precise information about active localizations, but results in inaccurate temporal data because the measurements are limited by the inertia of blood circulation and metabolism. Additionally, blood flow can be affected by factors that have nothing to do with the task at hand. EEG and MEG can measure the electrical activity in the brain down to a few milliseconds, but because measurement is done from the outside and only a small portion of the electrical impulses are registered, it can be difficult to determine where the signal stems from (Hari and Kujala, 2009; Mareschal et al., 2007a).

BRAIN STRUCTURE

EEG. MMR is a brain wave that appears 100–150 milliseconds after the subject has been exposed to an unknown or unexpected sound (Näätänen, 2003). The method can be used to assess whether a child recognizes or expects a particular sound, similar to dishabituation after habituation (see p. 46).

Magnetic resonance imaging (MRI) produces black-and-white images of the shape and size of the brain. Because MRI is sensitive to the cell differences in various types of tissues, such as white and gray brain matter, the images provide information about the structure of the brain and the composition of different tissue types. The brain depends on oxygen supplied by the blood, and blood flow is regulated so that active areas receive more oxygen. MRI can detect the oxygen level in the blood – whether it is oxygen-rich or oxygen-depleted – and provides a signal called BOLD (blood-oxygen-level-dependent). *Functional magnetic resonance imaging* (fMRI) measures oxygen content or changes in oxygen content in different areas of the brain while the child (or adult) performs a specific task, such as looking at something, listening to something or doing mental arithmetic. The oxygen level in the

The brain contains neurons, the specialized cells of the nervous system, each consisting of a *cell body* (nucleus), an axon and a substantial number of dendrites. *The axon* is a long, thin nerve fiber that sends impulses from the neuron to other cells. Although each neuron only has a single axon, it usually has many extensions, and can therefore reach up to several thousand other neurons. *Dendrites* are short, branch-like projections of the neuron whose function is to receive impulses from the axons of surrounding neurons, muscle cells or glands. The number of dendrites determines the number of cells from which a neuron can receive electrical impulses. The adult brain consists of some 86 billion cells and 150 trillion cell connections (Liao et al., 2017).

Nerve impulses are electrochemical signals that travel in the form of an electrical action potential at a speed of up to 300 kilometers per hour. The transition point between cells is called a synapse, and the small vesicles at the end of the axon are synaptic terminals. The electrical impulse triggers chemical compounds called *neurotransmitters* that are picked up by *recep-*

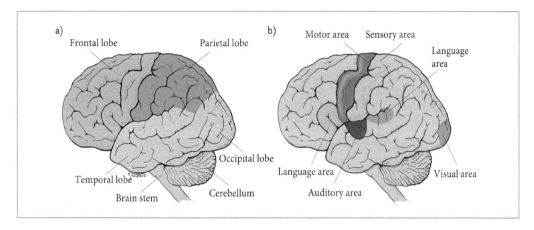

FIGURE 7.1 **The brain.**

(a) The cerebrum, the cerebellum and the brain stem. The cerebrum consists of two roughly equal parts connected by a broad band of nerve fibers in the *corpus callosum*, and is typically divided into four main areas: the top and front part is occupied by the *frontal lobes*, which are located in front of the *central sulcus*. The remaining parts of the brain lie behind this fold. The *parietal lobes* are located right behind the center of the head, while the *occipital lobes* occupy the lowest part and the back. The *temporal lobes* lie furthest down on the side of the head. (b) Parts of the left brain hemisphere that are particularly important for the development of perception, motor skills and language.

tors on the receiving neuron and briefly affect its activity. The effect of neurotransmitters can be *excitatory* (activating), meaning that the receiving nerve reacts more easily. They can also be *inhibitory*, making it more difficult for the nerve to pass on impulses. Inhibitory neurotransmitters are essential for the brain in order to suppress irrelevant information. Excitation and inhibition make up the brain's two basic processes, and the sum of all excitatory and inhibitory impulses that reach a neuron determines its activity (Brodal, 2004). The function of neurotransmitters is determined by genes as well as experience (see p. 110).

The central nervous system consists of the spinal cord, the cerebrum and the cerebellum (Figure 7.1). The cerebral cortex is about 2–5 millimeters thick and forms the outer layer of the brain. It consists of some 20 billion cells, each of which on average is connected to more than 1,000 other cells. The different parts of the brain fulfill various tasks and functions that are distributed in all directions: some functions involve the anterior part of the brain in particular, while others take place in the middle or the back, near the surface or further down, in the right or left hemisphere, and so on. Yet, none of these functions take place in one specific location. Just like the body, the brain constitutes a whole whose various parts work together (see the following).

The brain is not a model of the body. There is no direct and precise correspondence between the sensory and motor areas of the cerebral cortex and different parts of the body. Neurons responsible for adjacent body areas are often clustered around the same area. Cells that control the arm, elbow and shoulder, for example, can all work together, but not with cells that deal with the face and the body. Muscles that are used at the same time are thus controlled by the same area. This is a useful arrangement that facilitates a coordinated activation of neurons leading to the muscles that perform the complex movements of the arm. Although different movements generate different activation patterns, many of the same neural connections are involved (Barinaga, 1995).

THE BRAIN AND EXPERIENCE

The brain has a biological basis that evolved through evolution but depends on activity in order to develop (Cicchetti, 2002). Any minor or major new skill, experience or insight that is maintained involves the organization of cellular groups and processes. An individual's experiences affect the thickness, height, length and weight of the brain. Wild animals have larger brains than domesticated animals, probably because they have grown up in an environment with more varied activities. This cannot be caused by genetic differences, because the offspring of wild animals growing up in captivity also have smaller brains than those growing up freely in their natural environment (Schrott, 1997). Similarly, the cerebral cortex of children who have suffered neglect and early institutionalization is thinner than that of children who have grown up under normal conditions (Belsky and de Haan, 2011).

Experience affects the brain in various ways. Bourgeois (1997) describes the development of the cerebral cortex as progressing from experience-independent to experience-expectant processes, followed by experience-dependent processes. *Experience-independent* processes are controlled by genes and conditions in the organism, and are not dependent on stimulation. They mostly take place during the fetal period.

Experience-expectant processes depend on external stimulation that is present in most human environments and thus contribute to a similar design of the cerebral cortex in all humans who grow up under normal conditions. *Synapto-genesis* – the formation of new synapses – is predetermined, but the functional efficiency of many networks of neurons requires that they come into action in the right way at the right time. If the environment does not offer the expected experiences – as, for example, in cases of parental neglect – the result can be atypical brain development (Belsky and de Haan, 2011; Cicchetti, 2002).

Experience-dependent processes become prominent later in development. They involve the development of networks of cells and synapses as the result of experience and thus represent adaptation to the child's ecology. The more or less unique experiences of children affect the way in which the brain perceives and processes stimulation and initiates action, and thus contributes to individual differences in brain development and functioning (Cicchetti, 2002; Lewis, 2005).

BRAIN DEVELOPMENT

The development of the brain is a complex process that begins when the fetus is about 2 weeks old and continues all the way into adulthood, involving complementary processes of *producing* as well as *eliminating* neurons and neural connections. Brain development also includes *cell migration*, *myelination* and *specialization* (see below).

Prenatal development

The brain and the rest of the nervous system evolve from the outer layer of the embryo. After 2 to 3 weeks, this area begins to form an embryonic disc, which folds together into a closed neural tube. The cells in this tube produce new cells at an average rate of 250,000 *per minute* until birth (Ackerman, 1992). Gradually, the tube divides into layers, and cellular functions become more differentiated.

Cell migration

The overall structure of the brain is the same for all human beings. It is largely determined by genetic factors and has to do with which parts of the body the different areas of the brain are associated with. An important question is what causes cells to migrate and to specialize (see below). The instructions for cells to move to a particular area at the right time is probably part of the overall genetic blueprint, but this does not depend on the production of special cell types for each area by means of cell division. The cells are guided by other cells as well as chemical substances in the developing brain that cause certain neurons to cluster together and drive out foreign cells. This is how cells build up the brain from the inside out – at first there is nothing special about the cells that will perform a particular function, but as soon as they arrive where they are supposed to do their work, they begin to specialize. Experimental studies with animals in which cells were moved early during development show that cells from the brain's visual area begin to "hear" when they are moved to the area that is in charge of sound. Chemical compounds from the surrounding tissues stimulate further development within the cells. Therefore, the specialization of individual cells is the result of development, rather than a cause of it (Evrard et al., 1997). Cell migration is at its most active during fetal development, and most cells have found their place by the time a child is born.

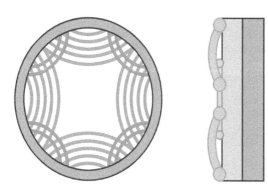

During the first 25 weeks of fetal developement, the cortex remains relatively smooth while the emerging neurons send pit fibers (coloured lines) to connect with neurons in other regions of the brain, where they become tethered.

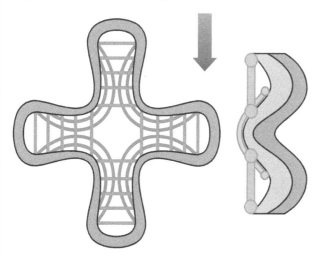

As the cortex continues to grow, mounting tension between regions connected via numerous fibers (orange) begins to draw them together, producing a bulge, or gyrus, between them. Weakly connected regions (green) drift apart, creating a valley of sulcus.
The folding is mostly comple by the time of birth.

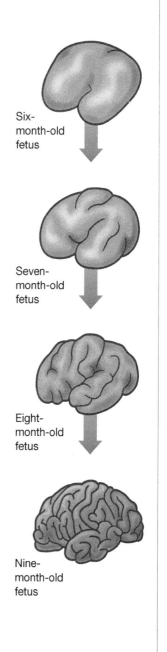

Six-month-old fetus

Seven-month-old fetus

Eight-month-old fetus

Nine-month-old fetus

FIGURE 7.2 The folds of the cerebral cortex.

The folds of the cerebral cortex are formed during the last 3 months of fetal development (based on Hilgetag and Barbas, 2009, p. 68).

The development of the cerebral cortex begins when the fetus is 8 weeks old, and continues until birth. At 6 months it is completely smooth, at 7 months it shows traces of folds, and at birth the folds are almost fully formed (Figure 7.2).

Brain development in childhood

The main structure of the brain is present at birth and the further development is characterized by the creation of smaller and larger functional networks. Figuratively speaking, the brain's "hardware" develops first, while new networks – the brain's "software" – are added and updated throughout childhood and adolescence (Liao et al., 2017; Menon, 2013; see Box 7.1).

Size

The brain of a newborn weighs about 20 percent of an adult brain, and has 25 percent of its volume. Its weight increases rapidly, however, from about 300 grams at birth to 900 grams at the age of 1 year – 60 percent of the weight of an adult brain. At the age of 6, its volume has reached 90 percent, and at age 10, the weight of the brain is about the same as that of an adult, on average 1,400 grams for men and 1,250 grams for women. But there is significant variation. A survey of 200 people aged 17–40 showed a range from 1,120 to 1,780 grams for men, and 1,070 to 1,550 grams for women (Stiles et al., 2015).

The thickness of the cerebral cortex increases by one-third in the first 2 years, reaching 97 percent of adult thickness. The cortical surface area more than doubles but still constitutes only about 70 percent of the adult surface at 2 years (Lyall et al., 2015).

Myelination

This is the formation of a layer of proteins and fat (myelin) around the nerve fibers. Myelin acts as an insulator, tripling the conduction velocity (up to 120 meters per second) and increasing the cells' efficiency and precision (Ackerman, 1992). Myelination begins during the fourth month of gestation, but has barely gotten started at birth and takes many years to complete. The process starts in the evolutionarily older neural pathways that manage the swallowing reflex and other basic functions. The sensory pathways are often myelinated before those responsible for motor functions. Myelination of the cerebral cortex happens last, beginning right after birth and continuing all the way into early adulthood. Furthermore, many axons remain unmyelinated (Couperus and Nelson, 2006). Since the number of neurons decreases during development (see below), the increase in weight must be caused by the myelination and the continuing growth of the remaining neurons and their dendrites.

Production and reduction of cells and connections

The function of the brain is to keep experiences for later use and every single experience forms

---

BOX 7.1 ESSENTIAL PHASES OF BRAIN DEVELOPMENT (based on Ackerman, 1992, p. 88; Menon, 2013, p. 628)

1. Proliferation of a vast number of undifferentiated brain cells.

2. Migration of the cells toward a predetermined location in the brain and the beginning of their differentiation into the specific type of cell appropriate to that location.

3. Aggregation of similar types of cells into distinct regions.

4. Formation of innumerable connections among neurons, segregation of functional circuits.

5. Dynamic pruning of functional circuits.

6. Refiguration; functional connectivity within and between spatially independent large scale functional networks undergoes significant changes with development.

7. Competition among cells and connections results in the stabilization of the 86 billion cells and 150 trillion connections or so that remain.

new synaptic patterns. During fetal development and early infancy, the brain overproduces cells, and in early infancy the brain has more neurons than at any other time in life. About half of the cells gradually disappear as the result of "cell death," a selective elimination of cells based on maturation and experience.

At birth, there are relatively few cell connections or synapses, but their number increases rapidly (Figure 7.3). Areas associated with the basic functions of perception and motor skills develop first, followed by associative skills, while areas central to learning and cognition develop last. The temporal differences in developmental progress help to divide tasks between the various parts of the brain (see p. 111). The visual cortex grows rapidly at 3–4 months of age, and in the period 4–12 months the synaptic density is 50 percent higher than in adults (Huttenlocher, 1990; Johnson, 1998). The extent of this process can be illustrated by the fact that the brain of a newborn macaque monkey forms about 40,000 new synapses in the visual cortex *every second* (Bourgeois, 1997). The brain of the human child forms several trillion excess connections. It would not be economical to keep all experiences that have formed a synaptic pattern. The connections between simultaneously activated neurons are strengthened while inactive synapses disappear, resulting in a significant amount of synaptic pruning (Casey et al., 2005). This process generally begins at around 6–7 months of age, but the exact time varies between the different areas of the cerebral cortex (Rakic et al., 1986). In some areas it happens right after birth, in others at 2 years of age. Around 4 years, the number of connections is at its highest.

The large number of cells and synapses means that learning conditions are ideal early in life, but the brain would be fairly inefficient if it were

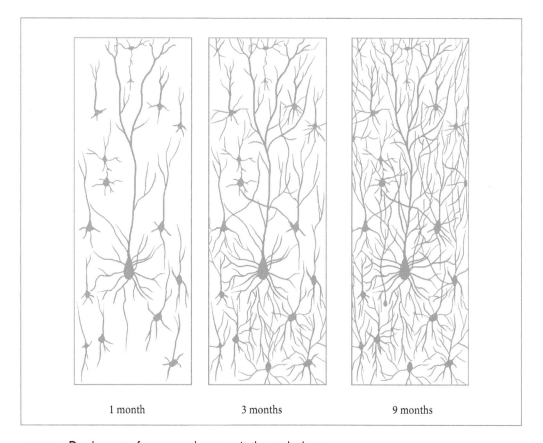

| 1 month | 3 months | 9 months |

FIGURE 7.3 **Development of neurons and synapses in the cerebral cortex.**
New neurons are created, and the number of connections between them increases during the first months of life.

to hold on to every single experience or action. The purpose of reducing the number of neurons and synapses is to strengthen those that persist, and avoid using energy on maintaining functions that are of little relevance. Nerve connections compete among each other so that the strong cells (frequently used) survive and the weak ones (rarely used) disappear. The cells that are much used are those that help the organism achieve its goals. The motivational and emotional state of the organism affects the cells' receptivity and is of importance to learning and the particular neural connections that are established. Since a number of basic brain functions are less dependent on experience, fewer synapses are pruned away in their locations.

The brain needs energy to produce and reduce cells and synapses, and metabolic processes provide the cells with the energy needed. In the child's first year of life, the brain's metabolism is about 50–70 percent lower than in adults. At age 2, it is the same as in adults, but continues to increase and reaches a peak around age 4, shortly after the number of synaptic connections is at its highest. At this age, children have twice as many neural connections as adults, after which the number gradually drops to an adult level. In most areas of the brain, the metabolism reaches adult levels by the age of 9, but in some areas it remains higher throughout adolescence (Johnson, 1998). This shows that the brain uses a great deal of energy to process stimulation and develop its various functions.

The enormous number of cells and synapses demonstrates the sheer workload involved in "producing" the brain of a human being, and the complexity of the neurodevelopmental process. It also demonstrates that experience is a necessary part of the process, not least because the 15,000 genes involved in the functioning of the brain are not enough to define such a complex structure in finite detail (de Haan and Johnson, 2003).

Brain development in adolescence

The period from adolescence to early adulthood is regarded as a transitional period constituting a second peak of human brain development (Zhong et al., 2017). There is considerable myelination, especially of the frontal parts, and reorganization of the brain. Many of the connections established in childhood are removed (Konrad et al., 2013). During puberty, pruning reduces synapses by 40 percent. As many as 10,000 synapses can be pruned every second in the prefrontal cortex once the decline in the number of synapses begins to exceed the formation of new synapses in early adolescence (Dawson, 1994; Lewis, 2005). The synaptic density of the prefrontal area reaches a comparable density to that of adults at 10–20 years of age (Huttenlocher, 1990; Johnson, 1998). The fine-tuning of overall connections continues into adulthood (Khundrakpam et al., 2013; Váša et al., 2017). There is a reduction of short-range connections and a strengthening of long-range connections, and functions are less defined to a local network and more to a network independent of location (Grayson and Fair, 2017).

The protracted development of the human prefrontal cortex during adolescence has been proposed to underlie the maturation of cognitive functions and the regulation of affective responses (Caballero et al., 2016), together with the influence from gonadal hormones during puberty, affecting the structuring of the adolescent brain (Guyer et al., 2016). Adolescent brain development is characterized by an imbalance caused by an earlier maturation of systems related to rewards and the not yet fully mature prefrontal control system. This imbalance may be the neural basis for the typical emotional reactive style of adolescence, and it may promote risky behavior (Konrad et al., 2013). These changes are assumed to be a basis for adolescents' increased susceptibility to social and emotional experiences and peer influence, and play a role in the higher frequency of anxiety and depressive disorders typical of adolescence (Guyer et al., 2016; Mills, 2015).

Specialization

It is a characteristic of the adult brain that there are areas that are particularly important for the performance of certain tasks or functions (see p. 105). The cerebellum, for example, is important for the performance of coordinated movements, as well as cognitive and affective regulation. The visual cortex is essential for interpreting and understanding visual impressions, and the auditory cortex for interpreting and understanding sounds. Some brain systems are involved in many cognitive tasks, such as attention, monitoring and maintaining goals. They also ensure that a number of tasks are executed while special systems are being developed to deal with them (Baillieux et al., 2008; Poldrack, 2010). Progressive specialization contributes to the increase in complexity that characterizes brain development in general (Stiles et al., 2015).

The question is, what causes the brain's organization? From a nativist point of view, the brain contains many innate modules whose predetermined functions emerge as a result of maturation (see p. 179). At the other extreme, the brain's organization is seen as the result of learning. Between these two extremes lies the view that the brain's organization is the result of an evolutionary process involving existing connections between different regions of the brain, and between the brain and the body. From this point of view, the brain has a body. It is not an isolated entity, but develops functionally through the body, which in turn both affects and becomes affected by the environment (Marshall, 2016).

There is a widespread and coordinated change in brain connectivity across much of the brain during the first two decades of life (Menon, 2013). Studies show that younger children often activate a larger area of the brain than older children when performing the same task, and many connections appear random (Johnson et al., 2009). In the early years, children develop many "small world networks" with high local clustering and short path length (Liao et al., 2017). Increasingly, the messages between these cell systems allow the brain's functions to be carried out by the areas best suited to the task, consolidating them and ensuring their survival. When adult brains show *less* activation in specialized areas than those of children, it may be due to the fact that they have developed specialized systems that are smaller and more efficient. Once specialization has taken place, including cell death and synaptic pruning, new cognitive functions are not merely the result of activating smaller areas in the cerebral cortex, but equally of a renewed collaboration between specialized cellular systems and areas. Under such circumstances, the adult brain sometimes activates more systems than that of children.

The brain of children thus shows little specialization to begin with. With a basis in both genetic influences and experience, they develop a number of specialized systems that are organized into integrated networks capable of solving increasingly complex tasks (Tomasi and Volkow, 2011). It is an efficient and self-organizing system: the brain is shaped by its own activity (Sirois et al., 2008).

Lateralization

Lateralization means that certain functions are allocated to one of the cerebral hemispheres and is a core element in the brain's specialization. Each hemisphere primarily controls perception and motor skills in the opposite side of the body, but also fulfills functions not directly related to perception or motor skills. Injury to the left hemisphere, for example, often causes language impairments in adults, while injury to the right hemisphere typically affects spatial perception. However, studies have found little relation between lateralization and language skills in children, and weak lateralization may be a consequence rather than a cause of impaired language learning (Bishop, 2013).

A certain degree of functional lateralization is already present during the embryonic period, and the differences become more pronounced with age. The perception of language and faces, for example, seems to activate areas in both hemispheres during early development, but later mostly on one side alone (Geschwind and Galaburda, 1985; Karmiloff-Smith, 2010).

When only one of the hemispheres assumes a specific function, it may be due to a difference in the pace of development. Since the brain does not have the capacity to develop all areas simultaneously, it constantly prioritizes some areas in favor of others. Areas that are ready to perform a given task in one hemisphere attend to this task. Lateralization thus does not originate in a functional genetic specification of different areas of the brain, but is the result of temporal regulation and prioritizing certain areas and processes (Johnson, 2011). This allows for flexibility during development and may explain why lateralization is reversed or uncertain in some people. Nearly all right-handers have important centers for processing language in their left hemisphere, while a third of all left-handers have similar centers on the right side (Bishop, 2013). For example, other parts of the brain can take over in case those normally used have been damaged (see below). This kind of functional transfer would not be possible if functions were hardwired to a specific area. The temporal organization of different processes, however, depends on genetic information. Thus, the development of the brain itself is largely predetermined, but the developmental process is subject to environmental factors and any possible injury. This makes it possible for children to grow up and cope under very different conditions.

Mirror neurons

The brain is a receiving as well as an executive organ. It processes and interprets sensory impressions, and plans and regulates actions. *Mirror neurons* are activated both when an action is carried out and when the same action is observed (seen, heard or felt) (Gallese et al., 1996; Hunter et al., 2013). However, the term "mirror" is not a particularly fitting analogy. It is not enough to observe a movement; mirror neurons are only activated once the *intention* of a physical action becomes apparent. The cells are not activated by a "vacant" stretching motion alone, for example, but only once the goal of the movement becomes evident, such as taking a glass of water. Nor is it only the sight of the movement that can activate the cells, as the term "mirror neurons" seems to suggest: in addition the sounds usually associated with an action lead to an activation of the cells. Therefore, mirror neurons do not function as a mirror reflection of an action, but rather as a concept-forming mechanism that includes various aspects of a given action (Jacob, 2009, 2013).

There has been much discussion about the significance of mirror neurons for human development. Some claim that this type of mirroring is necessary in order to understand or imitate the actions of others and experience empathy. They allow humans to understand the actions of others "from the inside" – as if they were their own (Rizzolatti and Sinigaglia, 2010). Others are skeptical of such an interpretation and point out that mirror neurons are not unique to human beings. Therefore, the presence of these cells does not explain the development of exclusively human functions (Hickok, 2013; Steinhorst and Funke, 2014).

There is also disagreement about the development of mirror neuron systems. Some believe they are genetically determined, and that observing and executing an action will automatically lead to the activation of the same cells (Fogassi and Ferrari, 2011). An alternative explanation is that mirror neuron systems originate through learning via the concerted execution and observation of an action (Cook et al., 2014). At present, the results of studies of mirror neurons do not distinguish between different explanations of cognitive development (Caramazza et al., 2014).

Mirror neurons represent an important discovery, showing that the brain has complex and efficient mechanisms to identify important environmental conditions and facilitate action. At the same time, it illustrates the difficulties of transferring knowledge about the brain in order to draw conclusions about the mind.

The brain functions as a whole

Although some brain areas are specialized to a certain degree, the brain nevertheless functions as a whole. The cerebral cortex changes with context, experience and expectation, and rarely is a task done in one location alone – several areas are usually necessary for a function to be performed (Singer, 2013). Even a simple event such as the unexpected sound of a flute leads to the activation of 24 different brain areas (Kagan, 2007).

Activation of the frontal lobes is affected by many other parts of the brain and illustrates that the division of labor is a complex process. Emotional regulation includes intention, planning, communication, motor skills and behavior, and one of the tasks of the frontal lobes is to coordinate these processes. The right frontal lobe is more associated with negative affects such as agitation, anxiety, crying and withdrawal, and the left with joy, interest, anger and approach behavior. However, they are not symmetrical: a high level of activation in one of the frontal lobes does not lead to a low level of activation in the other. They represent different emotional qualities, and it is the combined pattern of activation between the two areas that determines an individual's emotional reactions (Johnson et al., 2009; Nelson and Bosquet, 2000).

The brain's division of labor requires cooperation. Areas that need to collaborate on sensory input, actions involving both sides of the body or different functional tasks must be able to communicate efficiently. A substantial increase in connections between the two brain hemispheres takes place from 3 to 6 years of age. Reduced capacity of these connections can lead to delayed development, and also seems to be associated with a number of developmental disorders (Horwitz and Horovitz, 2012).

EARLY AND LATER PLASTICITY

Plasticity refers to the brain's ability to change as a result of experience. Many areas of the brain are more *plastic* or more *malleable* during early development than later in life (Kolb et al., 2013). The functions of many areas of the brain are not yet finally determined, and the course of development can follow somewhat different paths (Menon, 2013). This opens up for other alternatives in case a particular developmental path is closed due to defect or injury. Both children and adults can experience illness or accidents that result in injury to the brain, but children often have a better prognosis than adults. In some areas, injuries in children barely seem to have any developmental consequences. In fact, it is possible to remove one brain hemisphere at an early age without severe consequences for language and

cognitive functions, and in special cases it can lead to better functioning when the hemisphere is removed because the child has epilepsy that cannot be controlled with medication (Battro, 2000; Bulteau et al., 2017; Immordino-Yang, 2007; Vargha-Khadem et al., 1997; see Box 7.2).

It is assumed that damaged areas in the brains of children heal more easily (restitution), and that "vacant" areas are able to assume the tasks of areas that have been injured (substitution). However, there is considerable variation in the development of children following brain injury (Anderson et al., 2011). Children with brain damage often show difficulties and disorders in many areas. When the removal of a hemisphere leads to more typical development the reason may be that the child's functions have mainly developed in the good hemisphere and removal of the bad hemisphere takes away the pathological processes related to the epilepsy.

Later difficulties do not always involve functions normally located in the injured area. One study found that children who had experienced brain injury showed improvement over a long time, but that the development of some children

---

BOX 7.2 A CHILD WITH HALF A BRAIN (Borgstein and Grootendorst, 2002)

A girl had a hemispherectomy (removal of one hemisphere) at the age of 3 for Rasmussen syndrome because intractable epilepsy had led to right-sided hemiplegia and severe regression of language skills (see photograph). Though the dominant hemisphere was removed, with its centers for language and motor control of the left side of her body, at 7 years her hemiplegia has partially recovered and is only noticeable by a slight spasticity of her left arm and leg. She had normal hearing on both ears but a reduced field of vision which she was not aware of (Haak et al., 2014). She was fully bilingual in Turkish and Dutch, attended school and was leading a normal life. She scored low on intelligence tests (IQ 50) but gave an impression of higher potential once she was moved from a special school to mainstream school, and her general school performance improved remarkably.

Thanks to Johannes Borgstein for photograph and supplementary information.

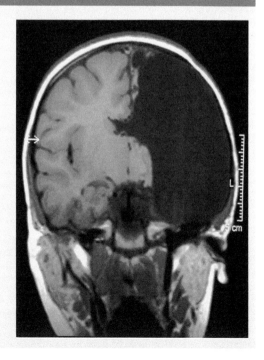

seemed to come to a halt when they reached the level at which the injury had occurred. They regained much of what they had learned before the injury, but had great difficulties coping with tasks above the level of the corresponding school grade (Basser, 1962). A possible explanation may be that an area assuming the functions of a damaged area usually fulfills a different function, and now is unable to follow a normal development because the area usually allocated to that function is completely or partially occupied (Taylor and Alden, 1997). This means that the consequences of an injury may first show up at the age when the new function was to be established. Since reorganization may take place at the expense of the later development of a different function, it may be necessary to monitor children's development over a long time in order to assess the possible consequences of an injury.

In the longer term, the consequences of an injury can therefore be more serious for younger children than for older children and adults, since it interferes with a long developmental process. It seems that young children are both more vulnerable *and* sufficiently plastic for many functions to be re-established. Plasticity thus changes in different ways. Some functions are more vulnerable to early injury, others have more serious consequences when they occur later on. The brain is unable to compensate for all functions that may be impaired. Especially basic functions such as motor skills are difficult to compensate for because the areas responsible for these functions are myelinated during early development. Damage to areas having to do with plasticity may lead to a global deterioration that is difficult to counteract. The developmental arrest of girls with Rett syndrome (see p. 76) is an example of such an injury. Moreover, compensation often has a cost, like when the function usually carried out by an area which has taken over the function of a damaged area is not as well developed (Kolb et al., 2013; Pennington, 2015).

Critical and sensitive periods

During development there are periods of plasticity when the child has a unique or particularly good opportunity for learning or development. The organism may require specific forms of stimulation within a certain *time window* to develop the ability to process this stimulation. For example, the development of stereoscopic depth perception depends on the simultaneous stimulation of both eyes during the first years of life (see p. 128). In order to speak a language without an accent, it must be acquired during a time window for phonological categorization (Hensch, 2004; see also p. 310). Following a critical period, stimulation is unable to restore functions that were not developed at the right time. However, the plasticity of a critical period may also imply vulnerability to harmful influences. Various periods during fetal development, for example, are characterized by vulnerabilities to different teratogens (see p. 94).

A sensitive period implies a heightened susceptibility to environmental influences; the brain is particularly vulnerable or capable of learning something more easily than during other developmental periods (Roth and Sweatt, 2011). There is a sensitive period for learning language, for example. New languages can be learned throughout life, but it seems to be particularly easy from the age of 1 until school age. While critical periods are rare, many assumptions have been made about sensitive periods, such as the development of perception, attachment and personality (Bailey et al., 2001).

One of the key questions is what leads a critical or sensitive period to start and end. From a functional point of view, the brain is unable to keep all opportunities for development open at all times, as this would require too many resources. Instead, the brain creates neural networks for a given area during a specific period. This is not determined by age and its onset is flexible, with some variation in age. It is the brain's development of other neurological structures and the balance between excitatory and inhibitory neurons that determine when an area is ready for a critical or sensitive period to take place (Takesian and Hensch, 2013).

The purpose of terminating the plasticity of a critical or sensitive period is to save resources and stabilize the functional neurological structures that have been established so they are not easily lost. If the brain has not received a particular stimulation by the time it is ready, development will proceed on the assumption that this stimulation is not significant. The lack of stimulation tells the brain that no systems or resources are necessary to process this type of stimulation. Its resources can be used for something else. Part of the auditory cortex, for example, could be used for visual processing in case a child is deaf (see

p. 105). In blind children, the visual cortex is sometimes used for language processing (Pennington, 2015). The same principle that applies to cell death and synaptic pruning also applies to sensitive and critical periods: the neurological structures that are used at the right time will be maintained.

A critical or sensitive period implies that once the functional organization of the brain has taken place, it may be impossible to reverse the process and assign other functions to established systems. For instance, the brain creates neurological connections for the language or languages a child has been exposed to during the sensitive period of language development, and does not maintain the possibility of learning additional languages with similar ease. The brain no longer creates separate neurological structures for new languages; the learning process must make use of previously established language structures. This makes it more difficult to learn other languages later in life, but as far as the brain is concerned, it is an economical use of resources. Once the critical and sensitive periods have passed, the individual is also more vulnerable to physical injury, since it is more difficult to establish a new function – or replace a lost function – than during periods with more brain plasticity (Takesian and Hensch, 2013).

The regulation of critical and sensitive periods is an extremely complex process that can be affected by many factors. However, these periods are important to children's ability to adapt based on their own prerequisites and the ecological niche they grow up in (Thomas and Johnson, 2008). By keeping or discarding various neurological connections, the brain prepares to cope in the world as it appears to the individual based on his or her experiences. Critical and sensitive periods are a natural consequence of the brain's ability to specialize and adapt, and thus of the development process itself. They also reflect the fact that development is about timing and providing children with the experiences they need to develop at the time they are ready to cope with them (Elman et al., 1996).

Side by side with the establishment of brain structures as the result of interaction between biology and experience, biological processes become more flexible in themselves and thus capable of processing the entire range of individual experiences. To a certain degree, there is an inverse relationship between neurological plasticity and the flexible processing of experiences. Although reduced plasticity makes the brain more vulnerable to physical injury, the developmental outcome takes advantage of a multitude of integrated mechanisms and complex processes that allow the brain to use the sum of all previous experience and knowledge in order to face new challenges in a flexible way.

GENDER DIFFERENCES

Gender is an important developmental factor, and studies have investigated whether there are developmental differences in the brain structure and organization of men and women. Female brains reach their maximum volume three years earlier than those of males (11;6 and 14;6 years), and are on average 9 percent smaller than the brains of men (Lenroot and Giedd, 2006). Studies have also found a somewhat different organization in male and female brains, but the results are uncertain and sometimes contradictory (Fine, 2014). In some areas, women show a lesser degree of lateralization and seem to have somewhat more connections between the brain hemispheres, while men have more connections within each hemisphere itself (Ingalhalikar et al., 2014). This may indicate that women do more processing involving both hemispheres than men do (Kimura, 1992, 1999).

Sex hormones affect the brain's prenatal development and a small group of girls have a congenital disorder that results in an excess of male hormones during the fetal period. Even with hormone treatment, these girls have a tendency to act more like boys in their selection of toys, such as preferring cars to dolls (see Chapter 24). They generally score higher than other girls on tasks involving spatial concepts, something boys are somewhat better at than girls as well. Studies have found that male sex hormones inhibit the growth of the left hemisphere and give priority to the right hemisphere, a fact that may explain differences in the degree of lateralization, and why girls on average are better at language and perform lower at spatial skills than boys (Servin et al., 2003; Swaab, 2007).

Although the brain is affected by sex hormones, there is no such thing as a male or a female brain, or one particular gender-specific dimension. Sex hormones affect different areas of the brain in different ways, and each area can be "male" or "female." Every individual brain is a mosaic of neurological structures – some are male, others female, and some are unisex (McCarthy et al., 2015). Besides, many other factors affect the development of males and females. Studies are rarely able to show behavioral differences that correlate with the gender-specific differences in brain connections. It has also been shown that men and women activate somewhat different brain areas when solving identical tasks that both are able to perform equally well.

It is likely that some of the differences between male and female brains are the consequence of developmental factors that appear too early to be the result of social and cultural conditions. At the same time it is important to emphasize that they represent average values with a wide range and significant overlap between cognitive and social attributes in boys and in girls. In addition, gender-related factors represent a small proportion of all the biological factors that, along with social and cultural influences, seem to make up the unique set of abilities and interests of each individual boy or girl.

BRAIN ORGANIZATION AND ATYPICAL DEVELOPMENT

The development of the human brain is complex and takes many years. The fact that development mostly works out well demonstrates the brain's extraordinary ability to safeguard and adjust. Sometimes, however, the dynamics of brain development can take a wrong turn and lead to "developmental miswiring," abnormal development of neural connections (Di Martino et al., 2014). The basic processes of brain development are the same in typical and atypical development and neuroimaging studies show that children with cognitive and behavioral disorders have atypical organization and activity in various brain regions (Dennis and Thompson, 2013; Menon, 2013).

It has been suggested that defects in cell proliferation, reduced or abnormal patterns of neural connections, and variation in timing during cell migration, synaptic pruning or the organization of neurological networks may be linked to the development of epilepsy, autism spectrum disorder, conduct disorder and other severe disorders, as well as to the differences in trajec-

tories of the these disorders (Jiang et al., 2015; Kolb et al., 2013; Pennington, 2015). Compared to children with typical development, children with Williams syndrome (see p. 76) have 20 percent smaller brain volume and cortical malformations, and show atypical chemistry and activity patterns (Karmiloff-Smith, 1998). Girls with Rett syndrome (see p. 76) have many cells and few synapses in the central part of their brain (Bauman et al., 1995), indicating that neither the elimination of cells nor the formation of synapses functions properly. The connections between amygdala (a structure located in the temporal lobes) and the prefrontal cortex are typically immature in children. The finding that maturation of these connections were accelerated in previously institutionalized and maternally deprived children and adolescents and associated with reduced anxiety reactions was interpreted as an adaptation to the early adversity (Gee et al., 2013). Also other studies have found that neurological networks involving the amygdala may lead to a vulnerability for mood disorders (Pessoa and Adolphs, 2010). Another example is the smaller than normal head circumference of many children who have spent their early childhood in poor institutions. This may be due to a lack of experience-expectant processes required by the brain, or an excess of stress hormones with a damaging influence on brain development (Pennington, 2015).

> The vast majority of mental illnesses are conceptualized as neurodevelopmental disorders, rooted in disturbances of typical brain development.
> (Di Martino et al., 2014, p. 1335)

Still, particular brain characteristics do not provide a sufficient basis for diagnosis. One cannot simply "translate" cognitive processes into neurological processes, or vice versa. Undoubtedly, many disorders have an atypical neurological basis, and many different factors can influence such a development. Children with neurodevelopmental disorders (see p. 60) often show signs of several such disorders, and presumably they include some of the same pathological brain processes. Most disorders have yet to be charted when it comes to identifying the point at which atypical connections and activation patterns originate, and how they contribute to the development of children's experiences and behavior (Horwitz and Horovitz, 2012; Miller, 2010). Moreover, many different forms of atypical brain connectivity have been associated with, for example, autism spectrum disorders (Kana et al., 2014; Thomas et al., 2016). A developmental disorder is not simply the result of an injury or a defect, but appears gradually as the result of irregular and abnormal processes in brain development (Johnson et al., 2002; Karmiloff-Smith, 2009). Many disorders are neurodevelopmental in the literal sense of the term.

The current presentation is in line with the *neuroconstructivist* approach, which integrates elements from cognitive constructivism (see p. 188), neuroscience and computer simulation of developmental processes (Karmiloff-Smith, 1998; Mareschal et al., 2007a, b). This approach is critical to nativist assumptions about genetically predetermined modules, and views the development of the brain (and mind) as a dynamic structure that gradually grows more complex. Although children do not start as a blank slate, basic congenital factors do not determine the brain's final functions, but instead initiate a process that allows the brain to develop based on genetic predisposition and the child's perception and actions. The interaction of genes and experience in brain development can result in typical as well as atypical functioning (Sirois et al., 2008).

STIMULATING DEVELOPMENT

The brain's ability to regulate development, and the fact that experience is of significance to its development, are important arguments for adopting suitable measures for children with developmental disabilities. Interventions are likely to be effective, and research also suggests that it is important to start at an early age when possible (Grossman et al., 2003).

More difficult, however, is determining what types of experiences are important to children when genetic and other factors increase the probability of atypical brain development. Moreover, intervention may differ with the presence of a sensitive or critical period. When brain plasticity is high, the aim is to promote problem solving that may stimulate the creation of new smaller and larger patterns of neural connections. After the critical period, the aim may be to guide the child to address challenges with means allowed by the established neural connection patterns (Immordino-Yang, 2007; Nahum et al., 2013). Some children need more or less of certain types of stimulation, others need a general increase or reduction in stimulation. Timing is also important, that stimulation occurs at the right moment during development. Early stimulation is mostly indirect by influencing how people in the environment perceive and react to a child. Thus, the design of early interventions for children at risk of abnormal and delayed neurological development should be based on a transactional model (see p. 8) (Cicchetti, 2002; Sameroff, 2010).

There are a number of commercially available computerized training programs claiming to train the brain and improve general cognitive function, but these claims are controversial and although the performance on training tasks may improve, a transfer to everyday functioning mostly lack empirical support (Owen et al., 2010; Rabipour and Raz, 2012).

SUMMARY

1   An important task is to identify how the brain works, and psychological models provide the basis for mapping the brain's functions. However, there is no simple relationship between the structure of the brain and the mind.

2   The brain is examined using advanced *electroencephalography* (EEG and MEG) and *magnetic resonance imaging* (MRI and fMRI). MRI and fMRI provide precise localization but inaccurate temporal data, while MEG and EEG result in inaccurate localization and precise time resolution.

Continued

3   A neuron consists of a *cell body* (nucleus), an *axon* and a substantial number of *dendrites*. The transition point between cells is called a *synapse*. *Excitation* and *inhibition* are fundamental brain processes, and the activity of a neuron is determined by the excitatory and inhibitory impulses it receives. *The central nervous system* consists of the *brain stem*, the *cerebrum* and the *cerebellum*. The *cerebral cortex* is 2–5 millimeters thick and forms the outer layer of the brain.

4   Experience affects the thickness, height, length and weight of the brain. An environment offering little stimulation results in a smaller brain size than under normal upbringing conditions. *Experience-independent* processes are not dependent on stimulation and mostly occur during the fetal period. *Experience-expectant* processes depend on external stimulation for the brain to develop in a typical way. *Experience-dependent* processes are the result of an individual's experiences, represent adaptation to the child's ecology and contribute to individual differences in brain development and functioning.

5   The nervous system evolves from the outer layer of the embryo, forming a neural tube after 2–3 weeks. Cells migrate to different areas at different times, while their functions become more differentiated. The cerebral cortex begins to develop at around 8 weeks, and the folds are almost fully formed at birth. The weight of the brain at birth is about 20 percent of that of an adult, with 25 percent of its volume. At 6 years of age, its volume has reached 90 percent of that of an adult brain. At 10 years, the brain's weight is the same as in adults. Myelination begins during the fourth month of gestation, but has barely gotten started at birth and takes many years to complete.

6   During fetal development and early infancy, the brain *overproduces* cells. About half of the cells disappear as a result of experience and maturity, with an uneven distribution throughout the brain. Newborns have relatively few *synapses*, but between the ages of 9 and 24 months, the cerebral cortex has about 50 percent more synaptic connections than that of an adult. Inactive synapses disappear, while the connection between simultaneously activated neurons is strengthened. The reduction in neurons and synapses strengthens those that are left, and prevents the brain from using energy on maintaining unused functions.

7   The period from adolescence to early adulthood is a transitional period with considerable myelination and reorganization. The fine-tuning of overall connections continues into adulthood, with a reduction of short-range connections and a strengthening of long-range connections. Adolescent brain development is characterized by an imbalance caused by an earlier maturation of systems related to rewards and the not yet fully mature prefrontal control system, which may play a role in the higher frequency of mood disorders typical of adolescence.

8   The brain functions as a whole, but also distributes its tasks. The two hemispheres control perception and motor skills in the opposite side of the body, and some functions are *lateralized*. A child's brain shows little specialization to begin with, but develops a number of specialized systems that are organized into networks capable of solving increasingly complex tasks.

9   "Mirror neurons" are activated both when performing an action and observing an action with the same intention. Some researchers argue that mirror neurons are necessary in order to understand or imitate the actions of others and experience empathy. Others have pointed out that mirror neurons are not unique to human beings, and therefore do not explain exclusively human development. There is also disagreement as to whether mirror neurons are genetically determined or originate through experience.

10 Many areas of the brain are more plastic during early development than later in life. Children have a better prognosis than adults when the brain is injured. This may be due to superior restitution of injured areas or functional substitution by "vacant" areas. However, compensation may lead to slower development or the impairment of other functions. In the longer term, the consequences of some injuries may be more severe for younger children than for older children and adults, since they interfere with a long development.

11 A *critical period* entails that the organism needs specific forms of stimulation within a certain *time window* to develop the ability to process it. A *sensitive period* means that the brain is particularly malleable for a certain period of time, and that some things are more easily learned than during other developmental periods. Critical periods are rare, sensitive periods are more common. Critical and sensitive periods save resources and stabilize established functions. They are a natural consequence of the brain's increasing tendency to specialize and adjust.

12 There are some differences in the brain development of men and women. Studies indicate that their brains are somewhat differently organized, but the results are uncertain and sometimes contradictory. The number of connections within and between the hemispheres differs to a certain extent. Some of the differences appear to be related to sex hormones, and appear too early to be the result of social and cultural conditions. However, there is no such thing as a male or a female brain; the brain is a mosaic of different "male" and "female" functions, and every individual has a unique mosaic of "masculine" and "feminine" features. There is a wide range of abilities and significant overlap between cognitive and social attributes in boys and in girls.

13 The brain is a complex organ, and many different factors can lead development in the wrong direction. The cause of developmental disorders is as complex as any other development, and developmental disorders emerge gradually as the result of irregular and abnormal processes in the development of the brain. According to neuroconstructivism, basic congenital factors do not determine the brain's final functions, but instead may initiate a process that allows the brain to develop typically or atypically, based on genetic predisposition and the child's perception and action.

14 The brain's ability to regulate development, and the fact that experience is of significance to its development, are important arguments for adopting suitable measures for children with developmental disabilities. Early stimulation is usually indirect by influencing how people in the environment perceive and react to the child.

CORE ISSUES

- The role of genes and experience in the formation of the brain.
- The development and function of mirror neurons in human imitation and action understanding.
- Gender differences in brain development.

SUGGESTIONS FOR FURTHER READING

Ingalhalikar, M., Smith, A., Parker, D., Satterthwaite, T. D., Elliott, M. A., Ruparel, K., Hakonarson, H., Gur, R. E., Gur, R. C., & Verma, R. (2014). Sex differences in the structural connectome of the human brain. *Proceedings of the National Academy of Sciences, 111,* 823–828.

Johnson, M. H., Grossmann, T., & Cohen Kadosh, K. (2009). Mapping functional brain development: Building a social brain through interactive specialization. *Developmental Psychology, 45,* 151–159.

Karmiloff-Smith, A. (1998). Development itself is the key to understanding developmental disorders. *Trends in Cognitive Sciences, 2,* 389–398.

Liao, X., Vasilakos, A. V., & He, Y. (2017). Small-world human brain networks: Perspectives and challenges. *Neuroscience and Biobehavioral Reviews, 87,* 286–300.

Menon, V. (2013). Developmental pathways to functional brain networks: Emerging principles. *Trends in Cognitive Sciences, 17,* 627–640.

Contents

CHAPTER 8

PERCEPTUAL DEVELOPMENT

Perception is the ability to distinguish and identify sensory information, to direct and sustain attention to various aspects of the environment, and to lend meaning to them. Children use their senses to explore the physical and social world, establish a basis for action, and to monitor and regulate their own actions. The sensory systems facilitate interaction with other people early in life.

Vision, the sense that provides the majority of information about the environment, is the most studied among the senses. Hearing, too, is of major importance for a child's ability to adapt, and auditory development is described fairly thoroughly. To some extent, these two senses can compensate for one another in children with severe visual or hearing impairment. A severe reduction in both senses has major consequences for a child's development. Developmental changes also take place in the ability to smell, taste and feel by touch, and in the coordination of impressions from multiple senses.

Research has largely focused on children's early perception. This is due to an interest in the biological and experiential foundations of human cognition, and the fact that sensory functions by and large become fully developed in the course of early childhood.

TWO THEORETICAL EXPLANATIONS

The two central theories within the study of perceptual development have mainly focused on vision. One of the key questions is how children learn to coordinate sensory information with their actions, and how action and perception relate to one another.

Piaget's constructivism

According to Piaget (1952), perception of the outside world is constructed by the individual itself. Children primarily gain knowledge of the perceptual properties of materials and objects by performing actions on them in the broadest sense. Here the term action does not merely include physical actions, but any type of internal (mental) or external behavior. For example, an object assumes the property "graspable" when a child grasps it with the hand. In this way, action turns into a perceptual property. Perception entails a progressively more precise understanding of physical reality. Children differ from adults in their perception of the world, and only begin to perceive the world like an adult once they have developed the corresponding cognitive skills.

Gibson's ecological theory

According to Gibson (1979), perception involves an active search for information in the environment. Perception does not need to be constructed, since the correspondence between perceptual-cognitive structures and the properties of the outer world makes the information provided by sensory stimulation directly meaningful to infants. Vision is designed for seeing, just as the fingers of the hand are designed for grasping.

A child's direct perception also incorporates a relationship between characteristics of the physical environment and any *possibilities for action*, referred to as "affordances" by Gibson. Unlike properties ascribed to the environment by the individual, an affordance is something "offered" by the environment, and therefore depends on the environment as well as the organism. A surface, for example, may be perceived as "standable" or "walkable" based on the physical apparatus human beings use when they stand or walk, in the same way a surface is perceived as having a color (cats and many other animals do not have color vision). Even children who have just begun to walk seem to be able to differentiate between surfaces that are suitable for walking and those that are not (Gibson et al., 1987). "Graspability" is a property directly associated with what is being perceived. Thus, perception leads to action, the opposite of what Piaget's theory proposes.

Gibson's theory is called "ecological" because it is based on the correspondence between perception and the properties of the physical world. Different species perceive the world in different ways, and a particular possibility for action will only be valid for some species. A fly sees the ceiling as being "walkable." For a monkey, a tree is "climbable," but not for a horse. According to Gibson, the properties perceived by humans have been adapted to the species' ecological niche through evolution. Since perception is a priori, it does not represent a developmental problem: children perceive the world directly in a human way because they are human beings. These views are in line with other evolution-based theories (see Chapter 2).

Comparison between the two theories

Gibson's theory is based on the assumption that children are born with significant perceptual skills that continue to evolve. Perception is "direct" because it does not involve drawing inferences or learning. Piaget's theory considers perception to be "indirect" because sensory stimulation is converted by cognitive structures, knowledge and expectation. Piaget acknowledges the innate quality of only a number of basic perceptual abilities, such as reflexes that ensure adaptation to sensory stimulation (like pupil contraction in bright light), the ability to perceive

movement and contrast, and to distinguish between figure and ground. According to Gibson, the ability to perceive three dimensions lies fully formed in the dynamic flow of information from sensory stimulation. While Piaget's theory assumes that perception is constructed by the child itself, Gibson's model is based on a process whereby children are able to perceive constantly new details using their visual sense. Yet Gibson's theory, too, incorporates clear connections between perception and action: an affordance is a relation between properties of the environment and the structure of children's actions. When children's motor skills improve, new affordances emerge. At first, the floor becomes "crawlable," followed by "walkable" once the child is able to walk. These affordances appear automatically through children's natural interaction with the environment.

Although these two theories seem to stand in stark contrast to one another, it is not easy to design experiments that clearly differentiate between them, and arguments can be found in favor of both. Some species are born with well-developed perceptual skills, such as goat kids that stay away from abysses right after birth. The perceptual skills that can be observed in early infancy (see the following sections) speak in favor of Gibson's theory. However, they do not furnish a sufficient basis to conclude that Gibson's affordance-based model is correct, but only that action and experience do not seem to be required for the development of perception to the extent argued by Piaget.

On the other hand, a classic experiment demonstrates the importance of autonomous action for the development of visually guided behavior. Held and Hein (1963) designed an experiment in which one kitten in a pair was able to move on its own and the other was a passive recipient of visual stimulation (Figure 8.1). The active kitten showed better perceptual development than the one sitting in the gondola. Thus, Held and Hein's study supports Piaget's assumption about the relationship between perception and action.

Assuming that perception and action mutually affect each other, the two theories may actually describe different aspects of the same process. According to Bremner (1997), the most important milestone in children's perceptual development is their ability to use perceptual knowledge

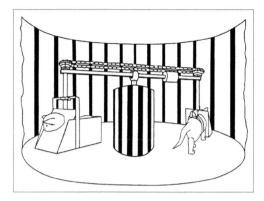

FIGURE 8.1 **The importance of action in perceptual development.**

Five pairs of kittens grew up with the same visual stimulation, but one kitten in each pair was able to move unrestricted, while the other sat in a gondola that was moved by the first kitten's movements. Subsequently, the kittens were placed on a bridge between a deep visual cliff on one side and a shallow part on the other. The kittens that had been able to move independently went down the shallow side, while the passive kittens just as often tried to climb down the deep side. Only the active kittens extended their paws when they were moved in such a way that they seemed to be about to collide with something. However, this need not be due to a lack of depth perception, but the fact that the kitten in the basket had learned that its movements had no influence on the actions surrounding it (learned helplessness) (Held and Hein, 1963, p. 873). (Copyright © 1963, American Psychological Association)

to guide their actions and integrate sensory and action-related knowledge. Perception is neither as direct as Gibson claims, nor as dependent on action as Piaget assumes.

VISION

Vision is important for recognizing people, things and places in one's surroundings, and for monitoring and regulating one's own actions such as walking or reaching for something. It is commonly assumed that these two types of tasks are handled separately – that the *perceptual system* (the "what" system) and the *action system* (the "how" system) are in different parts of the visual cortex of the brain, that they develop relatively independently (the perceptual system before the action system) and that injury or abnormalities in the two systems will have different consequences (Dilks et al., 2008).

Early development of vision

The retina and the central visual system are still incomplete at birth, and full functionality of vision can only be acquired through experience. Objects are projected onto the retina in different ways, depending on light conditions and their location relative to the viewer. In order to experience the world as stable, children have to develop constancy and be able to disregard irrelevant variations. They must be able to perceive objects as being identical, independent of distance, angle, lighting conditions, and so on. Piaget considers the acquisition of constancy to be one of the key factors in perceptual development (see p. 170).

Research has above all focused on visual acuity, perception of motion, object perception, depth perception, color vision and facial recognition. During the first year of life, children acquire basic skills, but the development of visual strategies continues all the way to adulthood.

Visual acuity

For a long time it was believed that infants perceive very little of the world around them. William James (1890) referred to the perceptual experience of infants as "blooming, buzzing confusion." The view on infant competence was revolutionized when Fantz and his colleagues in 1958 used a visual preference technique (see p. 47) in connection with paired line patterns and white surfaces to examine the visual acuity of children a few months of age, that is, the spatial resolution of their visual system. The children spent more time looking at the lines than the white surface, meaning that they had to have sufficient visual acuity to perceive the lines. Since then, studies have shown that the visual acuity of newborn children is inferior to that of adults, partly due to a smaller retina and a poorer ability to adjust the lens of the eye to distance and produce a sharp image (von Hofsten et al., 2014). Newborns do not see details, but they are able to perceive the outline of faces (see Figure 8.2) and larger movements. The optimal distance for infants to produce a sharp image is 20–40 centimeters. This is usually also the distance between the face of a newborn and an adult during interaction (von Hofsten, 1993). At 6 months of age, visual acuity has improved, and by the end of the preschool period it is comparable to that of

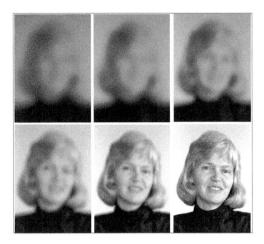

FIGURE 8.2 **Visual acuity in children of different ages.**
The photographs illustrate how newborns, children aged
1–2, 3 and 6 months, 2 years and adults perceive faces. The
photographs have been produced using filters that simulate
the visual process based on what is known about infant
vision. (Photo: Tony Young)

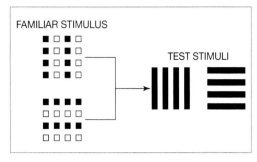

FIGURE 8.3 **Early Gestalt organization of visual
stimulation.**

Three-month-olds seem to perceive black and white squares
as a pattern. Those who had been shown horizontal rows of
black and white squares spent more time looking at the
vertical stripes, while those who had been shown vertical
columns spent more time looking at the horizontal stripes.
Five to 6-month-olds – but not those in the 3–4 month
group – showed a similar preference for horizontal and
vertical lines when the rows and columns consisted of circles
and squares that the children had been habituated to (based
on Quinn, 2006).

adults (Lewis and Maurer, 2005; Skoczenski and
Norcia, 2002).

Movement

Infants are generally more aware of something
that moves than something that is stationary. In
one study, when infants were shown two similar patterns – one of them static, the other one
moving – they looked twice as long at the moving
patterns. They also habituated more rapidly to
shapes they had previously seen in motion than
to new objects. This shows that the infants had
perceived the shape of the moving objects (Slater
et al., 1985). In their first few months of life,
infants become better at perceiving and following the movements of people and things with their
eyes, and begin to show that they expect an
object disappearing behind a screen to reappear
on the other side of the screen by anticipating the
movement and moving their eyes to that side
before the object has appeared (Rosander and von
Hofsten, 2004).

Children must also be able to distinguish
between visual changes caused by their own
movements and those that result from the physical movement of objects, two situations that
produce different types of visual information.
When an object moves, it changes position rela-

tive to its background in a different way than
when the observer moves (Britten, 2008).

Shape and pattern

Studies based on visual preference show that
newborns are able to distinguish between simple
squares, triangles, circles and crosses, between
patterns in which only the orientation of the
lines differs (vertical and horizontal), and between
sharp and blunt angles (Slater, 2001). Children
seem to organize visual impressions in line
with *Gestalt principles*, where "similarity,"
"proximity" (grouping) and "good continuity"
determine what is perceived to belong together.
Three-month-olds perceive identically colored
shapes as a pattern (Figure 8.3), and 6-month-
olds organize rows and columns with identical
shapes in a similar way (Quinn, 2006).

Children also develop a gradual preference for
more complexity. One-month-old children look
longer at eight large squares while 2-month-olds
spend more time looking at an equally sized
board containing 32 smaller squares (Fantz and
Fagan, 1975). One-month-olds, however, do not
seem to perceive square patterns and other visual
patterns as a whole. They focus on a small part
of the board, while 2-month-olds look at larger
board areas.

Object recognition

The world contains many objects and to identify objects, children must be able to perceive the *extent* of objects and the *boundaries* between them. A dog with a body, four legs, a head and a tail, for example, is *one* object, while a rider on horseback consists of two. In the first months of life, children have difficulty distinguishing the boundaries between objects. In one study, 3-month-olds did not seem to perceive two objects when one object was stationary within the boundaries of a larger object – such as a toy animal in a car – even when the toy animal's color and texture differed from that of the car (Kestenbaum et al., 1987). With increasing age, children make better use of various clues, but even 10 to 12-month-olds do not seem to perceive a toy animal in a toy car as two objects (Spelke and Newport, 1998; Xu and Carey, 1996).

Objects are rarely seen in isolation, but are usually part of a larger "visual scene" in which they partially occlude other objects and in turn are partially occluded themselves, so that the objects' visual boundaries do not coincide with their actual physical limits. Studies indicate that children early on perceive a partially occluded object as a single unit if its visible parts move at the same time. The results of the study in Figure 8.4 suggest that the 4-month-old children perceived the object moving behind a block as one object. That they looked longer at the broken rod than the complete one was interpreted as indicating that the two pieces of broken rod were not expected by the children (Kellman and Spelke, 1983).

According to Spelke (1990), children are born with *core knowledge* about objects (see p. 28), including an innate strategy that allows them to form an understanding of partially overlapping objects. This strategy does not include information about where one object begins and another ends, but *limits* the possible boundaries of objects and helps children form a more comprehensive and meaningful understanding of what they see. One problem with Spelke's theory, however, is that in similar experiments, newborns looked longest at the complete rod, and 2-month-olds did not show any preference, but looked equally long at the complete rod and the broken rod. Thus, there seems to be a gradual development in the perception of objects (Slater, 2001). Shared movement appears to be an important clue, and infants quickly gain experience with moving objects.

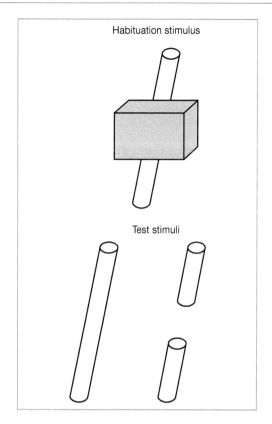

Habituation stimulus

Test stimuli

FIGURE 8.4 **Infant perception of partly occluded objects.**

Four-month-olds were shown a rod that was partially occluded by a block until they became habituated (looked at it less often). In some of the experiments, the rod moved behind the block, at other times the block and the rod moved together. Then the children were shown either an entire rod or two smaller rods with a space between them. When the rod and the block were stationary during habituation, the children looked equally long at the complete rod as they did at the two pieces. When the rod had moved behind the block, the children looked longer at the two separate parts of the rod than at the complete rod (based on Kellman and Spelke, 1983, p. 508).

Nevertheless, Condry and associates (2001) argue that newborns cannot demonstrate their innate knowledge of objects because they still do not have the necessary perceptual skills. Other theorists believe that the perception of objects is governed by certain genetically determined factors, but that experience and learning play a more important role than assumed by Spelke (Johnson, 2004, 2005; Kagan, 2008a). Thus, there continues to be considerable disagreement on the innate basis of object perception (see also Chapter 12).

Size

Knowledge of the size of objects is important, since size determines what can be done with them. The image projected onto the retina represents a relative size, however, and depends on the distance between the eye and the object. Studies suggest that *size constancy* does not depend on experience, but is present at birth. In one study, newborns first habituated to either a large or a small block. Then they were shown the same, a larger or a smaller block, but the distance between the child and the object was adjusted so that the object's projected size on the retina remained the same. The children spent more time looking at one of the differently sized blocks (dishabituation) than the one they had been shown during habituation. Thus, they were able to perceive a difference between the objects even if the image on the retina remained the same, probably because the eyes focus differently at various distances (Kellman, 1996; Slater et al., 1990). The results suggest that children have an innate ability to integrate visual information on distance adaptation (accommodation) with information about the size of the retinal image. But development continues until school age before children acquire size constancy for objects located further away (Granrud and Schmechel, 2006).

Depth perception

To orient themselves in a three-dimensional world children must become able to judge distance and to understand how objects are located and move relative to each other and themselves. Depth perception is based on *stereoscopic vision* and *pictorial depth cues*.

The distance between the eyes results in a small difference between the images projected onto each retina when the eyes are directed at the same point (hold a finger in front of your face and look at it with first the left eye closed, then the right one). When the brain combines these two images, space is perceived as three-dimensional. Children begin to develop stereoscopic vision at 3 months of age, and usually it is fully developed about 3 months later. When two appealing objects are placed at different distances from 5-month-olds, they will reach for both objects to an equal extent, regardless of whether they are viewing them with both eyes (binocular) or with one eye covered (monocular).

Children who are 2 months older reach for the nearest object when viewing with both eyes, but equally for both when one eye is covered. This shows that they have developed the ability to exploit the difference between the images in each eye, or stereoscopic vision. This development is dependent on appropriate stimulation: both eyes must be stimulated equally and simultaneously before the age of 2. If the stimulation remains uncoordinated or if one eye is prevented from being used over a longer period during early development, children will not develop stereoscopic vision (Lewis and Maurer, 2005).

Pictorial depth cues, such as light, surface and relative height, provide cues to how objects are positioned relative to each other. For example, when objects partially or completely cover other objects located behind them in space, the latter appear to be located "above" the objects that are closer to the viewer. Children's use of such cues is based on experience and begins at the age of 5 months. The way in which children make use of different cues varies with each type of cue and shows greater individual differences than in connection with stereoscopic vision (Kavšek et al., 2009; Yonas et al., 2002).

In a classic experiment on depth perception in infants, Gibson and Walk (1960) built a table with a glass top and placed a checkerboard pattern underneath part of the glass plate to give the impression of depth (see Box 17.1, p. 345). Children aged 6–14 months who had begun to crawl or otherwise move independently were placed on the "shallow" part of the table and encouraged by their mother to come to her. When the mother was positioned in such a way that the children did not have to move beyond the apparent edge of the cliff, they quickly moved toward her. Only a few of the children moved toward their mother when they had to move past the visual cliff. The results suggest that children at this age are able to perceive depth and will try to avoid places that are too deep.

Depth perception is also important for the perception of size constancy – the ability to perceive changes in the size of an object that moves in space seems to develop at an early age. One-month-olds respond by blinking when an object appears to be approaching ("appears to be" because blinking may otherwise be a response to the air pressure caused by actual moving objects). At the age of 2 weeks, children raise their arms as if to protect themselves when a block seems to be approaching (Nanez, 1988). This suggests that children are able to perceive objects moving toward them at an earlier stage than they are capable of perceiving depth in general.

Color vision

Color vision is somewhat incomplete at birth, but children aged 1–2 months are able to distinguish colors about as well as adults (Bornstein, 1992). Four-month-olds seem to categorize the color spectrum into the main categories blue, green, red and yellow, similar to the way adults do. The transitions between colors are less pronounced in infants, but the development continues, and at 3–4 years of age, the boundaries between color categories have become clearly more distinct (Raskin et al., 1983).

Facial perception

By the time a child is born, the visual system has developed in such a way that the infant is attentive to other people, especially their faces. Newborns prefer stimulation with curved lines, strong contrasts, varied edges, movement and complexity (Fantz and Miranda, 1975; Goren et al., 1975). The preference for faces temporarily disappears at 1 month of age and returns at around 3 months (Johnson et al., 1991; Turati et al., 2005). At this age, a change takes place in the processing of faces from the deeper parts of the brain to the cerebral cortex (Nelson et al., 2008). Figure 8.5 shows that infants look longest at images that resemble a face, but also that the characteristics of visual stimulation preferred by children change rapidly. This suggests that children do not have an innate preference for faces as such, but for the typical features of many faces. Infants must learn to recognize faces, but are initially aided by their preference for the type of complex stimulation faces convey.

Newborns are most attentive to the outer edges of the face. At 2 months of age, they begin to focus more on the central part of the face. At this age, parents usually report that their children begin to make eye contact. Eye movement tracking furthermore shows that 1-month-olds look at only a small part of the face, while 2-month-olds look at several parts. Children thus gradually develop a more comprehensive and detailed ability to perceive faces (Slater and Butterworth, 1997). Between the ages of 3 and 6 months, the

ability to distinguish between different faces and facial expressions increases as well (see p. 348).

Some theorists believe that infant's aptitude for recognizing faces suggests that humans have an innate module for facial recognition. According to Carey (1996), the way in which sensory stimulation is processed does not change – changes in facial recognition are solely the result of maturation and increased experience with faces. Other theorists believe that infants do not have a special ability to recognize faces, but that early facial recognition is the result of a general ability for perceptual learning. They point out that most people are "experts" on faces, and that some are experts on dogs, cars and other things as well. The ability to recognize faces is similar to other types of specialized forms of recognition, and faces are extremely prominent in an infant's environment and immediately gain importance through the interaction with caregivers. It is the human environment itself, with its prominence of voices and faces, that gives rise to specialized knowledge and furnishes the basis for what may appear to be a separate "mechanism" (Nelson et al., 2008; Slater and Butterworth, 1997). The "expert theory" is supported by the fact that

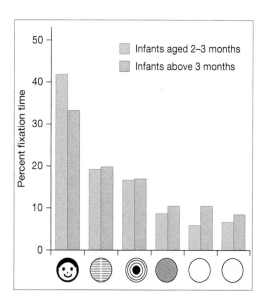

FIGURE 8.5 **Viewing time of infants exposed to different types of stimulation.**

In the first months of life, infants spend more time looking at patterned stimulation than at monochrome images and give most attention to faces and stimulation with facial characteristics (Fantz, 1961, p. 72).

children under the age of 4 months do not react differently to faces that are presented right-side up or upside down. After this age, facial recognition becomes orientation-specific (Fagan, 1979).

During the first weeks of life, infants usually see their mother's face more than any other. The sound of her voice helps the child direct the gaze and learn to recognize her quickly (Sai, 2005). In one study, 5-day-old infants spent more time looking at their mother than at an unfamiliar woman, but this changed when the stranger put on a wig that matched the mother's hair, suggesting that children initially use the outline of their mother's head as a clue for recognition (Bushnell et al., 1989). Thus, children's earliest clues contain little detail, a natural consequence of infants' limited visual acuity. Gradually, the individual features of the face gain more importance, but the combination of contour and facial features always provides the best basis for recognition, also in adults (Want et al., 2003).

Studies show that infants typically recognize the faces of women better than those of men. In one study, 3 to 4-month-olds spent more time looking at female faces than male faces when they were presented in pairs. In another study, infants habituated (see p. 46) to a female face and dishabituated when they were shown a different female face, but did not dishabituate when they were shown a different male face after having habituated to a male face. However, all of the infants had spent most of their time together with their mother. Similar studies involving infants who were mostly together with their father showed that they reacted the same way to male faces as the other children did to female faces (Quinn et al., 2002). This indicates that children's early experience with faces has significance for how they distinguish between faces.

Adults generally find it more difficult to distinguish between people from other races than those belonging to their own race. Early in life there is no such difference. Between the ages of 4 and 8 months, children begin to improve at recognizing people of their own rather than other races, no matter what race they belong to (Ferguson et al., 2009; Kelly et al., 2009). Six-month-olds are able to distinguish between races other than their own, while 9-month-olds seem to group all other races into a single category – "we" and "they" (Quinn et al., 2016). Children who grow up in homes with several races naturally do not show such differences (Bar-Haim et al., 2006). Kinzler and Spelke (2007) believe that humans have an innate core system (see p. 28) to distinguish between "us" and "them," but this type of intrinsic mechanism is not required to explain facial recognition in infants. The results are entirely consistent with the general development of the perceptive system, as many areas undergo a *reduction* in the ability to discriminate. Children's ability to distinguish between the characteristics of people, sounds and common objects in the environment is preserved, while the ability to distinguish between features that occur rarely, or not at all, disappears (Scott et al., 2007). This is part of the brain's tendency to "economize" and maintain systems for what is most common and familiar (see p. 108).

Critical visual stimulation

The visual system has developed through evolution in a physical and human environment, so

FIGURE 8.6 **Growing up with vertical or horizontal stripes.**

Kittens grew up in an environment with either vertical or horizontal stripes. The kittens that grew up with vertical stripes had difficulty perceiving horizontal stripes later on. Kittens that grew up with horizontal stripes had similar problems with vertical stripes (Blakemore and Cooper, 1970, p. 478. Reprinted with permission from *Nature*, Macmillan Magazines Ltd.).

that growing up in a normal environment ensures the type of stimulation needed for normal development. A number of experimental animal studies have shown that visual stimulation early in life is necessary for the development of visual function. One study found that chimpanzees that had grown up in darkness during the first 16 months of life were able to respond to light, but could not differentiate between various visual patterns (Riesen, 1947). Under such conditions, the cells of the retina and the brain's visual cortex deteriorate due to lack of use (atrophy). Studies show that atypical visual stimulation may result in a neurological organization that differs from the norm, such as when kittens grow up with either vertical or horizontal stripes only (Figure 8.6). The results show that the kittens' experiences affected the processing of visual information, since the brain can only process impressions based on some degree of prior experience and formation of the necessary nerve connections (see p. 111).

Studies of children with illness or injury of the visual system have contributed important information about the development of vision. A *cataract* is a clouding of the eye's natural lens. The usual treatment is to remove the lens and replace it with an artificial one that creates a sharp image on the retina. When children whose vision was severely impaired to the illness during the first weeks or months of their lives were examined 10 minutes after removal of the bandages, they showed the same visual acuity as newborns, regardless of whether they were 1 week or 9 months old. After only 1 hour, their visual acuity was equivalent to that of a 6-week-old child (Lewis and Maurer, 2005, 2009). This shows that visual acuity is not related to maturation alone, but also that its development requires little stimulation. At the age of 6 months, the children's vision mostly fell within the normal range for this age group, but their visual acuity continued to be slightly reduced compared with that of their peers all the way into adolescence. The visual acuity of children who developed cataracts somewhat later and were left without the ability to see for a period of time was also impacted. Moreover, each eye develops relatively independently of the other, so that the vision of one eye is equally affected by a lack of stimulation regardless of whether the other eye is normal or not. In order to prevent one eye from taking over completely, children with strabismus and binocular vision

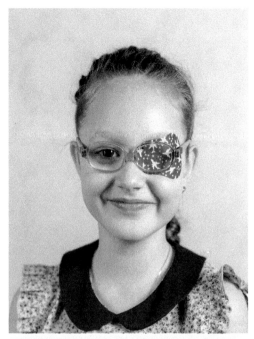

The use of an eye patch ensures functional vision in both eyes.

problems therefore alternately have to cover one of their eyes with a patch.

Later development of the visual sense

Basic visual functions are established early on, and with increasing age children generally become faster, less distractible and more efficient at processing visual stimulation. Especially the integration of various types of visual information undergoes a development. *Optical illusions* are a result of how the mature visual system organizes stimulation that consists of several different elements (Carbon, 2014). Four to 5-year-olds *surpass* adults at judging whether two circles are of equal or different size when one of the circles is surrounded by larger or smaller circles (Figure 8.7). Adults are "fooled" by illusions because their visual system perceives different elements in context. Since visual information is not yet fully integrated in children, they are less influenced by the elements that surround the circles they are comparing (Doherty et al., 2009; Káldy and Kovács, 2003). From the age of 7–8 years, their perception gradually approaches that of adults.

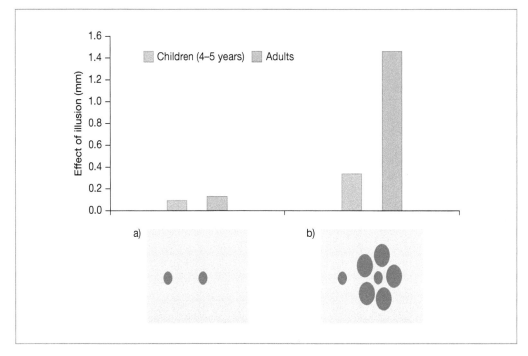

FIGURE 8.7 Perception of optical illusions in children and adults.

Children aged 4–5 years and adults were asked to judge whether two circles were equal or different in size. The two circles were shown by themselves (a) or with one circle surrounded by circles of a different size (b). Adults were more influenced by the presence of visual elements surrounding the circle than children (Kovács, 2000, p. 1306).

Studies have found that many people with autism spectrum disorder have particular problems with perception (Dakin and Frith, 2005; Simmons et al., 2009). Some, but not all, studies have found that they are less susceptible to optical illusions than others (Happé, 1996; Ropar and Mitchell, 2001). This suggests that the processing of visual stimulation is somewhat differently organized, and that the integration of perception in persons with autism spectrum disorder differs from that of other people.

The development of visual integration is also evident in children's perception of parts and wholes in drawings (see Figure 8.8). At age 6–11, children generally improve at differentiating and identifying visual information (Gibson, 1982). This development is related to issues involving vision, attention and other cognitive functions, but cultural differences also seem to play a role in the integration of visual elements. For example, adults in Japan are more susceptible to optical illusions than adults in the UK (Doherty et al., 2008).

Children improve at recognizing faces and facial expressions throughout childhood (Karayanidis et al., 2009). In one study, children aged 6–16 years were first shown 36 pictures of faces for 5 seconds each. Then they were shown the same pictures together with pictures of other faces and asked to point out the faces they had seen before. Six-year-olds were able to identify 70 percent of the faces, just above chance level, which would have resulted in 50 percent correct answers. Ten-year-olds identified 90 percent of the faces correctly. The same was true of 16-year-olds, while those aged 12–14 years were able to identify approximately 75 percent of the faces. One explanation is that the decline in recognition among the 12- to 14-year olds is related to maturation and the hormonal changes that occur during puberty (Carey, 1996). Another explanation is that adolescents begin to notice new features in other people's faces in connection with puberty, which is supported by the fact that they become better to recognize faces of peers than of adults (Picci og Scherf, 2016).

FIGURE 8.8 Integration of visual information.

Children aged 4–9 years were asked to tell what they saw when presented with drawings such as the ones shown here. The answers were divided into parts, wholes and both (both parts and wholes for the same drawing). If the child did not mention either a part or a whole, they were asked once again whether they saw anything else. About 71 percent of children aged 4–5 years named parts only. The remaining responses consisted of wholes or both wholes and parts. Six-year-olds named parts about half of the time. Only at the age of seven did parts account for less than half of the responses, and even among 9-year-olds, 21 percent of the responses referred to parts only, without responding to wholes when they were asked if they saw anything else (Elkind et al., 1964 p. 84). (Permission granted by Elsevier)

Pictorial competence

An understanding of images (photographs, drawings, films, etc.) is a necessary skill in modern society. It entails the ability to recognize and lend meaning to what is depicted in an image or a film (e.g. a cat), and to understand that what is depicted corresponds to what exists in reality – that photographs and film can provide information about the environment, for example where something is located (Troseth et al., 2004).

Early pictorial competence

Children show early on that they are able to perceive what is depicted in an image, a form of recognition that probably requires little experience with images. With no little effort, Hochberg and Brooks (1962) raised their own son with minimal exposure to images until the age of 19 months. At this age, their son had acquired many words for objects, and when he was shown images of items that corresponded to these words, he was readily able to name them. In another study, 5-month-olds with normal pictorial experience were habituated to one of two different dolls and showed a preference for the other (new) doll, regardless of whether they were shown the actual doll or a picture of it. When they were shown a doll, a black-and-white photograph and a color photograph of it, they nonetheless looked longest at the doll (DeLoache et al., 1979; Slater et al., 1984). This suggests that infants are both able to recognize an object depicted in an image, and to perceive that there is a difference between the object and the image.

Children's reactions to images change during early childhood. Nine-month-olds try to explore the objects in the pictures, while 15- and 19-month-olds vocalize and point. This is probably related to the fact that older children have developed new communicative skills, and that parents in many cultures like to point at pictures in books while talking to their children about them. Children also improve at using pictorial information. Eighteen-month-olds are able to use actions to show what happens in photographs and drawings, an ability that improves rapidly until the age of 30 months. Eighteen-month-olds are also more dependent on the realistic depiction of images. They show more actions based on photographs than drawings, while 24- and 30-month-olds show an equal number (Simcock and DeLoache, 2006).

An important aspect of pictorial competence is the relationship between the content of an image or a film, and reality. This type of understanding develops long after the ability to recognize things on pictures. In one study, children aged 18–44 months saw an adult performing an action, and were asked to point out which of three pictures corresponded to the action. One example was an adult splashing ketchup onto a toy pig. Each child was shown photographs of a clean pig, a pig with a white patch on its neck, and a pig with a splash of ketchup, and asked which of the pictures most resembled the pig. Despite the fact that the pig with ketchup stood right in front of the child, children below 2 years seemed to respond fairly randomly to the question (Harris et al., 1997).

In a series of studies, DeLoache and her colleagues surveyed children's use of pictorial information to locate an item, much like using a map. Children aged 24 and 30 months were shown photographs or drawings of a room in which a Snoopy dog or something else was hidden. The room included only a few furnishings that were easily visible in the pictures. In the first part of the study, the experimenter pointed to a location in the picture and said: *Snoopy would like to sit here. Can you go and put him there?* Seventy-five percent of the younger and all of the older children were able to perform this task. The next task was to find the Snoopy dog, which had been hidden by one of the experimenters. The experimenter pointed at the picture in which Snoopy was hidden, and almost all of the children approached the task with great enthusiasm, but only 13 percent of the 24-month-olds went straight to the correct location, while 72 percent of the children who were 6 months older were able to do so (DeLoache and Burns, 1994). This suggests that a major change takes place in children's ability to use graphical representations between the ages of 24 and 30 months, a result that may partly be explained by the fact that older children have been mobile for longer and are more familiar with exploring the environment. Studies using videos have led to similar results. Despite being given instructions and help, less than half of the 24-month-olds were able to use the information in a video to find a toy, while nearly 80 percent of the 30-month-olds achieved this task. When 2-year-olds could observe through a window that the experimenter was hiding a toy, all of them went straight to the toy, and over 60 percent managed to do so after looking through a "video window" (Deocampo and Hudson, 2005; Troseth and DeLoache, 1998). Studies have also shown that children under the age of 3 are unable to use a model of a room to find an item (Figure 8.9), about 6 months later than in the case of images (DeLoache, 1987; Troseth et al., 2007). Compared with images, toddlers seem to have relatively more difficulty understanding that a physical model represents something other than itself.

These studies show that children recognize objects in images and on video early on, and that they can name the items without any particular

FIGURE 8.9 **A 3-year-old observes the experimenter** hiding a small frog in a model of the room and finds a large frog in the "real" room (photographs courtesy of Judy DeLoache).

previous experience once they are able to talk. It takes some time for them to understand that there may be a direct relationship between an image and reality. In studies involving 2- to 3-year-olds, the children were startled to see themselves on video, and were often unable to recognize themselves. For instance, they did not react to the fact that photographs or videos taken a few moments earlier showed that they had a sticker on their head, put there by the experimenter without their knowledge (see also Box 21.1, p. 436). Four-year-olds reacted immediately by reaching for the sticker (Povinelli et al., 1999). One possible reason for this may be that most videos watched by children have nothing to do with themselves, but rather with a fantasy world far removed from everyday life. When the families of a number of 2-year-olds connected a camera to their TV so the children were able to see their parents, siblings, pets and themselves on television for 2 weeks, they became as proficient at using the information on video as other 2½-year olds (Troseth, 2003). The widespread use of digital cameras with instant viewing possibilities has probably allowed many of today's children to form an earlier understanding of the relationship between image and reality.

Later development of pictorial understanding

Children's ability to perceive drawings as well as their preferences change throughout childhood. Toddlers prefer clear and unambiguous images, but also complexity and strong contrasts. Preschool children prefer bright colors without regard to realism. Until the age of 7 to 8, distinctness is the most important requirement, while the demand for realism becomes stronger toward the age of 14 (Holm and Thau, 1984).

Also the perception of detail undergoes a development during school age. At first, children generally see only the main motif or figure in a picture, and only later develop the ability to perceive the background. Children's understanding of pictorial content also develops quite slowly. Constable and associates (1988) found that students all the way up to the first year of middle school had trouble understanding the illustrations and pictures in their biology textbooks, all of which were designed to make it *easier* to absorb the material. This may indicate that many of the illustrations used in textbooks are not well

enough adapted to children's pictorial understanding and thus do not provide the educational benefits they potentially could (Carney and Levin, 2002; Cook, 2008).

Visual impairment

Many children have a visual impairment that is easily corrected with glasses, but may be difficult to detect at an early age. After all, children have no way of knowing that others see better than they do. Therefore it is important for all children to undergo an eye examination.

Severe visual impairment affects all areas, but blind children with no additional problems generally show relatively normal cognitive and language development. Due to their difficulties with orientation and mobility, these areas are central to early intervention for visually impaired children (Kesiktas, 2009). Their motor development is typically somewhat delayed, probably because they cannot move with the same confidence as other children and because they lack the incentive for locomotion and exploration of the environment provided by visual impressions (Fazzi et al., 2002). During early development, blind children can often be passive, with little mobility and a tendency to listen and explore with their ears. It is difficult for them to perceive things at a distance, and it takes some time before they begin to reach for the source of a sound. Tactile exploration is initially limited to what they are able to reach (Fazzi et al., 2011), and they spend little time playing with objects. Constructive play is more limited, and they prefer toys that produce sounds, household items and common objects in their surroundings (Pérez-Pereira and Conti-Ramsden, 1999; Webster and Roe, 1998). Compared with sighted children, many everyday skills such as drinking from a regular cup, pouring liquid into a cup or building towers with Duplo bricks are acquired later (Brambring, 2007).

Blind children use human and other sounds to orient themselves. They may say the names of others, for example when playing in kindergarten, in order to discover who is there and where they are located. Their lack of overview leads to lower participation in many activities and also impacts social functioning. In addition, many blind children and adolescents need time to develop a mental map in order to navigate independently in familiar surroundings. This can inhibit participation in ordinary child and adolescent activities (Salminen and Karhula, 2014).

Blind and severely visually impaired children can access emotional information through sound, but social referencing can be difficult in many situations because they do not always fully comprehend the situation and the connotations of emotional words or expressions. They express joy and anger early on, but have a smaller repertoire of emotional expressions (Tröster and Brambring, 1992). Because their social smile is more uncertain and less frequent (see p. 345), parents can be affected in their reactions and interactions with the child. During the earliest developmental period, parents can feel rejected when their child does not turn its head toward them, rather than seeing it as an expression of the child's effort to concentrate and listen. They may react with disappointment and withdraw instead of establishing interaction. Parents need help to understand the inner world of their child, which is why guidance to parents and a "redefinition" of the child's actions are particularly important (Fraiberg, 1977; Sameroff, 2009).

Despite the lack of visual information, blind children engage in joint attention (see p. 300) and show a relatively normal language development, although many words have a somewhat different conceptual content and usage than for sighted children. When blind children say they want to "look at" something, they do not refer to vision, but to experience in a more general sense (Landau and Gleitman, 1985). They may confound "I" and "you" – words whose reference change depending on who is talking (Pérez-Pereira and Conti-Ramsden, 1999). Nonetheless, language is the main source of information about social factors and the physical world, and early language skills are one of the strengths of many blind children.

The demands on children vary through development. Toward the end of preschool age, for example, many activities involve a great deal of running and moving about. During this period, children with visual impairments can lag behind, drop out from play and become passive because they are unable to follow the changes in activity and cannot move fast enough. Once they start school, the number of stationary activities increases, and they can choose friends and join groups of children who are more verbally oriented and not as physically active. Parents of

blind children are often overprotective. During later school age, children with severe visual impairment are often passive and suffer from low self-esteem (Hodge and Eccles, 2013; Roe, 2008).

Many children with severe visual impairment have a number of other disorders, particularly motor impairments, auditory impairments and intellectual disabilities, and may need extensive support and adaptive measures (Geddie et al., 2013). The incidence of autism spectrum disorder among children with severe visual impairment is often rated to be high, and some believe that these children develop pragmatic disorders, problems with mind understanding, and autism-like conditions since they are unable to observe other people's interactions and emotional reactions (Hobson and Bishop, 2003). Others are critical of these claims and believe that blind children's use of language must be understood based on their particular experience of the world (Pérez-Pereira, 2014).

Many children with disabilities are able to perceive visual impressions, but have trouble processing sensory input. Although there is considerable variation ranging from slight impairment to near functional blindness, it is always important to assess and account for any possible disturbances in visual perception in connection with intervention and adaptive strategies for children with more extensive developmental disorders (Zihl and Dutton, 2015). Juvenile neuronal ceroid lipofuscinosis (Batten disease) is a neurodegenerative disorder involving the gradual loss of vision, and eventually cognitive and motor skills as well. They require an altogether different type of developmental support and environmental adaptation than for children with visual impairments who show a slow but positive development (von Tetzchner et al., 2013).

HEARING

Children explore the auditory environment with their ears just as they explore the visual environment with their eyes. Hearing is used to analyze "auditory scenes," listen to speech and to identify and locate people, things and events (Werner et al., 2012). The perception of speech sounds is especially important, and will be described in Chapter 16 in connection with language development.

Early perception of sound

At birth, the development of hearing has progressed further than vision and dominates children's attention during the first few months of life (Robinson and Sloutsky, 2004). However, the peripheral auditory system (outer and inner ear) is more developed than the central auditory system, and a significant development has yet to take place in the brain's processing of auditory information (Morrongiello, 1990). Children are able to recognize and distinguish between sounds early on, but need varied experiences to be able to process sounds and understand their meaning (Werner, 2007).

Studies based on habituation and conditioning show that newborns are able to distinguish between all aspects of acoustic stimulation, but require higher audio levels and greater differences. While they show little reaction to sounds below 55–60 decibels (dB), above this level their reaction increases with the *intensity* of the sound (Steinschneider et al., 1966). At 1 month of age, the threshold lies 35 dB above that of adults (at 4,000 Hertz, Hz) and at 6 months 15 dB above. In addition to a certain intensity, sounds must also have a minimum duration of 1 second in order to create a reaction in young infants (Johnson and Hannon, 2015).

Similarly, a gradual development occurs in the ability to distinguish between tones of different *pitch*. Three-month-olds react to differences greater than 120 Hz at around 4,000 Hz, a difference of 3 percent. Adults are able to notice a difference of 40 Hz, or 1 percent (Olsho et al., 1987). Six-month-olds react to differences in frequency from 1.5 to 3 percent, depending on the pitch (Trainor and He, 2013). Children's perception of sound is less detailed than that of adults, and they also have greater difficulty detecting a tone against a background of sound (auditory figure-ground), even if the background frequencies do not lie within the same bandwidth as the tone (Leibold, 2012).

Human voices

Attention to voices is important for social orienting and creating affective ties between children and caregivers. A female voice saying "baby" elicits more motor activity in 3- to 8-day-old infants than pure tones (Hutt et al., 1968). Studies also show that newborns are especially sensitive to their mother's voice right after birth. When sucking on a pacifier is followed by the sound of a voice, children suck more when they hear their mother's voice than any other voice (Fifer and Moon, 1995). In a survey of 2-day-old children of English and Spanish speaking mothers, the children sucked more on the pacifier when they heard their mother's language. It is possible that the children remembered and recognized certain voice properties from their time in the womb, but since they were exposed to their mother's language during the first 2 days, their preference may be due to early exposure and learning. Not all speech is equally interesting, however. Children aged 2–4 weeks preferred their mother's voice when she spoke with the exaggerated intonation typical of adults talking to children, but not when she read the words of a text backwards, resulting in a monotonous tone of voice (Mehler et al., 1978). This suggests that intonation is important for recognition.

Localization

Sound is an important cue to the localization of people and things and hearing enables children to find things that produce sound, such as identifying the source of a familiar voice. The brain localizes sounds by using the minute time and phase differences between each ear when a sound is heard. Newborn babies can roughly distinguish between left, right and straight ahead. Only a few hours after birth, children turn their heads to the right or to the left, depending on where the sound comes from (Wertheimer, 1961). The reaction disappears after about 6 weeks, but returns at 3 months of age. This pause in development suggests that the turning of the head toward the sound, like many other early skills, changes from a primarily reflexive reaction to a voluntary response. At around 3 months of age, the movement toward sound also begins to be accompanied by visual exploration. In early infancy, children smile at the sound of their mother's voice alone; 3-month-olds do not smile until they see the face of their mother (see p. 348). At 6 months, children show a noticeably greater interest in sounds accompanied by interesting visual stimulation, such as a brightly colored music box. They have learned more about the connection between sounds and their sources, such as humans, animals and other things, and sounds have become more meaningful to them.

Nevertheless, it is not until the end of the first year of life that auditory and visual localization seem to be fairly well integrated (Neil et al., 2006).

The development of hearing throughout childhood and adolescence

In many areas, children approach adults in their ability to distinguish between sounds as early as infancy, but generally distinguish higher frequencies better than lower ones. Their ability to differentiate between the intensity of lower frequency sounds continues to develop until the age of 10 (Johnson and Hannon, 2015).

At around 18 months, children can locate an isolated sound almost as precisely as adults under good acoustic conditions, but do not do equally well in noisier environments. Five-year-olds have significantly greater problems localizing a sound than adults in somewhat more complex sound environments such as a busy street, a room full of people, or when the radio and television are turned on (Trainor and He, 2013). They also have more difficulty analyzing auditory scenes, separating sounds, identifying and localizing sounds when there are several people or things that produce sound, and when sounds change and partially coincide in time. The perception of auditory figure-ground remains difficult all the way into adolescence (Leibold, 2012).

Until the age of 10, children continue to be more affected by noise and irrelevant sounds. Older children and adults are more selective in their perception of sounds in the environment. Younger children's auditory attention is less affected by expectations, and they filter out relevant information to a lesser degree than adults (Werner, 2007). Thus, hearing shares many of the same developmental characteristics as vision.

Hearing impairment

Congenital or early acquired hearing impairment has developmental consequences for the ability to orient oneself and explore the environment, as well as for social awareness, communication and language. However, the impact on various developmental areas is not merely the result of the hearing loss itself, but equally of how the environment is adapted to compensate for the lack of hearing, particularly in regard to language and social factors (Lederberg et al., 2013; Mitchell and Karchmer, 2004). Studies have documented that early detection along with appropriate measures for both child and family are important to ensure an optimal development (Yoshinaga-Itano, 2013). Lack of visual communication early in life before the child's hearing may be restored can result in fewer resources for other developmental tasks, and make later language acquisition more difficult.

A key question has been how to best support the development of communication and language in children with severe hearing impairments. Hearing loss can be detected early (Lang-Roth, 2014), and it is possible to improve the perception of speech sounds, support the development of visual forms of communication and combine these two measures (see p. 331). High-quality hearing aids are available for mild to moderate hearing impairments, and in many countries deaf and severely hearing-impaired children can get a cochlear implant that converts sound into electrical impulses that are sent directly to the inner ear. Many children with severe hearing impairments use these hearing aids (which are not suitable for children with milder hearing loss) to good advantage and are able to function on the level of moderate hearing impairment, while they are deaf without the hearing aid. For best results, children are operated on both ears before the age of 18 months (van Wieringen and Wouters, 2015) and followed up with visual support and various forms of training (Yoshinaga-Itano, 2013). Nevertheless, most of them are delayed in their speech development and have problems understanding and producing more complex utterances (Geers et al., 2009). Children (and adults) with cochlear implants also have greater difficulty perceiving emotions in the voice than children without hearing loss (Chatterjee et al., 2015).

Even a minor hearing loss can affect the ability to acquire spoken language (Spencer and Marschark, 2010). Both speech and common auditory scenes involving a number of people and background noise can result in a lack of clarity and be more difficult to analyze for children with hearing impairments (van Wieringen and Wouters, 2015). Some children have good hearing in only one ear, a fact that is often discovered late. It may influence orientation and attention, and studies show that children with hearing loss in one ear tend to have delayed language development and educational difficulties, and an increased prevalence of behavior disorders (Lieu et al., 2012).

For some children, cochlear implants do not function well. Because it is impossible to know in advance whom this may apply to, children with hearing impairments should always be followed up in different ways (van Wieringen and Wouters, 2015). Bilingual competence in spoken and sign language in the child's environment is an important element of optimal language support (Becker and Erlenkamp, 2007). A shared language is important for the child's cognitive and emotional development. Since only 5 percent of all deaf children have deaf parents, most parents with a deaf child need training and guidance (Lederberg et al., 2013). Children who use visual communication or need visual support must alternate between looking at the person they communicate with and the particular aspect of the situation they are communicating about. Deaf parents have experience with visual communication, while hearing parents must receive help to develop good visual strategies in communicating with their deaf child. Unlike deaf children with deaf parents, those with hearing parents are delayed in solving theory of mind tasks (see p. 258).

Children with relatively severe hearing impairments also need ergonomic support to allow their vision to compensate for the lack of hearing. In kindergarten and school, this involves creating good acoustic conditions and correct placement in relation to light and overview of the room. When children with unilateral hearing loss try to turn toward the sound in order to listen with their good ear, this can be perceived as restlessness and give rise to conflicts, for example during circle time when the child is positioned in the circle with the good ear facing out. This group of children benefit from attending small classes and seating in the classroom so the good ear faces away from noise (Kuppler et al., 2013).

Severe hearing impairment in itself does not lead to cognitive defects. Deaf children without other disorders receive normal scores on nonverbal cognitive tests (Spencer and Marschark, 2010). However, a large minority have additional disorders (see p. 59). Language disorders also occur in deaf children, and some show signs of delayed language development (Woll and Morgan, 2012). Many hearing-impaired children have difficulty learning written language,

both among those using sign language and those with hearing aids, but there is considerable variation depending on the general environment and the quality of the reading instruction (Lederberg et al., 2013). This is of great importance to their entire education.

Sound can direct a child's visual attention toward specific events. The loss of hearing can affect situational awareness and social participation, and communication with peers outside the home is often difficult. The incidence of mental disorders is higher in children with hearing impairments than in children with normal hearing (Stevenson et al., 2015). Hard-of-hearing children seem to be more vulnerable than deaf children, perhaps because they are expected to perform as well as others. People in the surroundings may pay little attention to the major and minor difficulties that hearing impairment always brings with it, making it difficult for hearing-impaired children to find an identity as either a deaf or a hearing person (Spencer and Marschark, 2010).

Deafblindness

The consequences of early deafblindness are exceptionally severe because tactile and haptic information cannot compensate for more than a small part of the information loss from the two most important senses during development. Although the consequences are major, they are far less severe once language (sign or spoken) has been acquired and merely needs to be translated to another modality such as tactile signing or Braille. The time at which deafblindness presents is therefore of great importance. Among others, Helen Keller and Laura Bridgeman lost their ability to see and hear at about 1½ years of age (see Fukushima, 2011), and their early communicative experiences may have been crucial for their positive development. Children with *precommunicative deafblindness* have difficulty establishing joint attention, and their lack of social experience limits their language development. The number of deafblind children is low, but an optimal development depends on a physical and social environment that is completely adapted to each child, in addition to individualized and intensive instruction and other measures (Nafstad and Rødbroe, 2016; Vervloed et al., 2006).

Development of musical skills

Musical ability is usually regarded a separate area of development. Gardner (1993) believes musicality to be a unique form of intelligence, but most authorities consider musicality to be a type of ability other than intelligence (see p. 264). Unusual musical abilities are also found in people with severe learning disabilities or developmental disorders (Miller, 1989). Studies of people with congenital or acquired impairment in the ability to differentiate pitches and recognize melodies show that there is no connection between musicality and language ability. Children who have difficulty recognizing melodies or hearing that melodies are played incorrectly have no problems perceiving differences in the intonation of speech (Peretz and Hyde, 2003).

Studies on the development of musicality have particularly focused on the ability to distinguish between and produce pitched tones and melodies. Musicality undergoes a development from the perception and production of simple to more complex pitch patterns (see Table 8.1).

Perception of music and singing

Starting at an early age, children seem to react selectively to music and recognize short melodies and tone patterns. They also seem to perceive melody constancy early on, as a pattern independent of the key (Chang and Trehub, 1977). Hearing forms the basis for melodic recognition, and musical perception is enculturated early on. Six-month-olds dishabituated equally to an incorrect note in melodies based on Western (major and minor) and Javanese musical scales, while 1-year-olds (as well as older children and adults) from Western cultures did better at Western scales (Lynch and Eilers, 1992). Six-month-olds were also better at perceiving music based on foreign scales than adults. This suggests that children begin with an unbiased ability to recognize melodies based on different scales, and lose the ability to recognize scales they are not exposed to. Thus, there seems to be a development from melodic perception based on general auditory characteristics to culture-specific musical perception without any special training. This is similar to the process of recognizing speech sounds (see p. 308). Toward the end of preschool

TABLE 8.1 Milestones in musical development (age ranges are approximate (Hargreaves, 1986))

Age (years)	
0–1	Respond to sound.
1–2	Make up music spontaneously.
2–3	Begin to reproduce parts of songs they have heard.
3–4	Perceive a general outline of the melody. May develop perfect pitch if they learn an instrument.
4–5	Are able to distinguish between pitches and tap out simple rhythms they have heard.
5–6	Understand high and low and are able to differentiate between simple pitch patterns and rhythms (similar/dissimilar).
6–7	Sing more in tune. Perceive tonal music better than atonal music.
7–8	Prefer consonance to dissonance.
8–9	Keep a steadier rhythm.
9–10	Perceive the rhythm and remember the melody better. Perceive two-part melodies; have developed a sense for cadences (conclusion of a phrase or melody).
10–11	Establish a sense of harmony and appreciate more subtle musical aspects.
12–17	Increasingly appreciate music and show a more sophisticated cognitive and emotional response.

BOX 8.1 ATTENTION TO CONSONANT AND DISSONANT MUSIC IN 6-MONTH-OLDS (Plantinga and Trehub, 2014)

The attention of 64 infants aged 6 months was directed to a loudspeaker with flashing lights, and music was presented as long as the infants looked at the loudspeaker. When they looked away, the music stopped, the infant's gaze at the loudspeaker thus maintained the music. The figure shows that the infants looked slightly longer at dissonant than at consonant music but the differences were not significant. In another experiment, the children were first exposed to 3 minutes of either consonant or dissonant music. When using the same procedure as in the first experiment, the infants looked longer at the loudspeaker that played the music they had heard just before, independent of consonance.

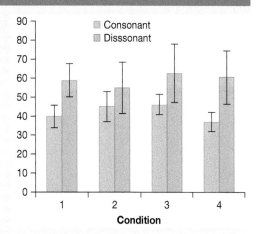

Mean cumulative looking time (seconds) to consonant and dissonant stimuli in each of four pairwise tunes. The bars represent standard errors, which indicate the variation in distribution of responses.

age and the start of school age, children begin to master many aspects of music. An understanding of harmony and more complex melodies, however, is first acquired during adolescence. Music education and other forms of musical experience are important for this development (Trainor and Unrau, 2012).

There is considerable disagreement about children's preference for *consonant* rather than *dissonant* melodies. Some experts argue that this is an innate ability and that infants have a "built in" sense for consonance (Masataka, 2006; Trainor and Unrau, 2012) but this is contradicted by Plantinga and Trehub (2014) who found preference for familiar music rather than consonance in 6-month-olds (Box 8.1). They point out that preference is chiefly an expression of recognition and that consonance is culturally determined. Children's preferences become clearer toward the end of preschool age, and there are major changes in musical perception up to the end of school age, and an increasing preference for consonance and aversion to dissonance. Five-year-olds, for example, can detect incorrect notes outside of a scale, but not within a scale, such as 7-year-olds and adults are able to (Trainor and Trehub, 1994). This development occurs earlier

and is more pronounced in children with relatively good musical abilities (Winner, 2006).

Around the age of 1 year, some children begin to stamp their feet and move their hands up and down when they hear music, and by 18 months such motor reactions are common (Moog, 1963). At the age of 2 years, children are able to tap rhythms with their hand with about 21 percent accuracy, and almost 50 percent at the age of 5. A significant improvement in rhythmic perception occurs between the ages of 5 and 11. Adults have a rhythmic accuracy rate of about 87 percent (Hannon and Johnson, 2005; Jersild and Bienstock, 1935).

Children of all cultures are generally exposed to music from an early age, especially by adults who sing for them (Trehub and Schellenberg, 1995). Songs for infants are usually simple and emotive with a leisurely tempo, a falling melodic line and repetitions of the same pattern. They are also sung in the same mode (major, minor, etc.) every time. Infants are more attentive to songs sung in this child-oriented way than to the same songs when sung in a conventional way, as well as to songs at a higher than at a lower pitch (Winner, 2006). It has been argued that certain types of music (especially Mozart) have a positive effect on intellectual development, especially the ability to solve tasks that require good spatial perception (Hetland, 2000; Rauscher and Hinton, 2006; Rauscher et al., 1993). Belief in the "Mozart effect" has led to large sales of "intelligence-enhancing" music for parents who wish to stimulate their children's intellectual development, even during pregnancy. However, studies of children who have listened to Mozart and other types of music have not found evidence of such an effect (McKelvie and Low, 2002; Waterhouse, 2006 a, b). Children's own music making has a better effect (Trainor and Unrau, 2012).

Production of songs and music

Children begin to react to music early on by producing song-like sounds or moving to rhythms (Simons, 1964). Some children begin to make "babbling songs" by vocalizing at different pitches around the age of 6 months. At 9 months, the majority of children produce such babbling songs. At 1½ to 2 years of age, children begin to produce songs with a certain similarity to the songs sung for them by adults, and from 2 to 5 years, spontaneous singing undergoes a development from simple to more complex "melodies" (Werner, 1961). Older preschoolers spontaneously sing children's songs and fragments of pop songs. When somewhat older children are asked to sing back simple songs, they make more mistakes in the most complex songs. Throughout childhood, the number of mistakes decreases, and children progressively improve at singing melodies correctly and in more detail. Practice has a significant effect, but in younger preschoolers, it merely leads to an improvement in the direct imitation of melodies. Children's spontaneous singing does not change, and practice first has an actual effect on their singing once they approach school age. The age at which children start singing melodies correctly varies considerably, and some never acquire this ability (Søbstad, 1974).

Individual differences

Musical ability varies greatly from one child to the next. Often – but not always – several members of the same family share a high level of musical skills, as in the case of J. S. Bach's family. Outstanding musicians and singers have musical parents more often than others. For example

Jussi, Rolf and Raymond Björling are three generations of opera singers. Although musicality undoubtedly involves biological factors, the prevalence of musicality within a family may just as well be the result of social influences. Twin studies suggest that there is a certain genetic basis, but that the contribution of genes is moderate (Shuter-Dyson and Gabriel, 1981). Howe and colleagues (1998) conclude that individuals who become prominent musicians do not seem to have a special innate talent compared to musicians in general, but that it is the amount of practice that distinguishes this group from others. Both special and more ordinary musical abilities depend on certain biological prerequisites, but the development of musicality also requires an environment that provides experiences and promotes the development of these skills.

OTHER SENSES

Observations of everyday life show that newborns respond differently to various forms of *tactile* stimulation. They cry when they receive a vaccine shot and calm down when gently stroked on the back. Knowledge about the development of tactile perception is limited, but early in life the mouth is sensitive to tactile stimulation, and infants tend to explore objects with their mouths. The use of the mouth gradually decreases during the second half of the first year and manual exploration increases (Ruff, 1984).

Smell

The sense of smell plays an important role in identifying people and food, and is well developed already at birth (Monnery-Patris et al., 2009). Children are able to recognize different odors early on, and prefer certain odors to others. Cernoch and Porter (1985) found that 12- to 18-day-old breastfeeding children preferred the odor of their mother's sweat – collected on gauze pads from her underarm the night before – to that of another woman. Bottle-feeding children who were not breastfeeding showed no similar preference for their mother's or father's odor. This suggests that children learn to recognize their mother's odor in connection with breastfeeding, while bottle-feeding children are not as close to their mother's underarm and therefore not equally familiar with her odor.

Newborns also show preferences for familiar non-maternal odors, and gender differences seem to be present early on. Balogh and Porter (1986) fastened a gauze pad with the odor of cherry or ginger to the inside of newborn infants' bassinets for one day. When they were tested shortly after, the girls, but not the boys, preferred the familiar odor. This may be because girls are physiologically somewhat more mature at birth than boys. The importance of odors is also demonstrated by the fact that children aged 7–15 months spent less time exploring unknown objects, especially with their mouths, when unfamiliar odors had been added to the objects. The unfamiliar odor caused the children to be cautious (Durand et al., 2008).

Although children show an ability to distinguish between important odors early on, older children are far better at recognizing odors than younger children, and adults are better than older children. Throughout childhood, girls exceed boys in their ability to distinguish odors, and are also more aware of them (Ferdenzi et al., 2008).

Taste

Taste and nutrition are related. During the first week of life, children develop a complex system to regulate their own food intake. Newborns show a consistent preference for foods with a sweet taste rather than for sour, salty, bitter or tasteless foods (Steiner et al., 2001). They generally respond to sweet-tasting liquids with a relaxed expression reminiscent of a smile, and often lick themselves around the lips. Sour liquids result in pursed lips and a wrinkled nose. Bitter liquids cause infants to gape open and stick out their tongue as if to squeeze out the bitter taste (Rosenstein and Oster, 1988). The common preference for sweet tastes is easy to change, however. Infants who are allergic to milk are often given a substitute that does not taste as sweet. They get used to it quickly and soon prefer the substitute to regular milk. Since the flavor of breast milk varies somewhat depending on the mother's diet, infants become used to different flavors and will accept food more easily if they are already familiar with its taste from their mother's breast milk (Nicklaus, 2009). The enculturation of taste thus already begins with breast milk.

Children are born with a set of innate preferences and aversions that dominate at an early age, while new impressions and experiences become more important after the first 3 months (Harris, 1997). During the first 2 years of life, a change takes place from internal to external cues, from congenital and hunger-driven to socially determined preferences. Around the age of 2, children's preferences begin to become established. They become more discerning, begin to reject food and eat less varied foods. While only 19 percent of 4- to 6-month-olds are considered to be picky by their mothers, the number rises to 50 percent at the age of 2 (Carruth et al., 2004; Nicklaus, 2009). However, 2-year-olds who eat different types of food have the most varied diet at the age of 5 (Cox et al., 1997). It is also at the age of 5 that children first begin to show the same dislike of the kinds of foods that are generally disliked by people in their culture (Rozin, 1989). The period in which children eat less varied lasts until the age of 8, after which they slowly become more willing to try out new foods. Studies nevertheless show that a varied diet is important early on, as the differences between 2- to 3-year-olds can actually be traced all the way into adulthood (Nicklaus et al., 2005).

INTERMODAL PERCEPTION

Intermodal perception is the ability to recognize the same "object" with more than one sense, such as recognizing something by touch one has previously only seen. This is necessary in order for children to form a comprehensive understanding of the world as well as to establish experiential *constancy* across the senses. They must be able to distinguish between "natural" relationships, such as the connection between the movement and sound of a bouncing ball, and incidental relationships, such as when a dog barks and the phone rings at the same time. The question is how the child comes to relate information from one sense with information from other senses.

Here, too, Gibson and Piaget take opposing views. Gibson's theory (1979) is based on *differentiation*, arguing that the senses initially constitute a primitive unity and gradually become differentiated. At first, all the senses are equal in that they provide information about the qualities of the same object, but directed at different types of energy. It is possible to demonstrate an emerging intermodal organization at birth, such as when children only a few hours after being born turn in the direction of a sound (see p. 137). According to Piaget's (1952) *integration theory*, the senses are initially separate and become integrated through a child's actions and the experience of simultaneous impressions from several senses. His view is supported by the finding that 6-month-olds showed visual recognition of objects they had seen before, but not of similar objects they had only explored by touch (Rose and Ruff, 1987).

Gottlieb and associates (2006) argue that both theories are too simple. They point to the fact that the senses do not develop simultaneously – neither during fetal development nor later – and therefore cannot derive from a single sense as suggested by Gibson. By the time a child is born, the auditory sense has already begun to develop, while their visual sense is first put to functional use after birth. Although partly agreeing with Piaget, they add that intermodal perception is not a uniform process but a result of interaction between the senses in different situations and for different purposes. The temporal differences in development may be of importance to the processing of sensory stimulation. Moreover, the senses are specialized for different types of sensory input from the outset. The auditory system, for example, is specialized to process sequentially organized stimulation, while the visual system is best at spatial perception. Visual and auditory perception are thus characterized by altogether different properties, and any one of the two senses will be more prominent depending on the context (Lewkowicz, 1994).

Studies of children's reactions to *amodal information* contribute to an understanding of the development of intermodal integration, information that does not derive from a single sensory modality, but across two or more senses such as time, space, rhythm and intensity. The movements and sounds of a speaking mouth or a bouncing ball are completely synchronous. Bahrick and Lickliter (2000, 2014) agree with Gibson that integration is inherent in the senses. The perceptual system is constructed in such a way that amodal information recruits attention, and young infants are more attentive to amodal information than to information from only a single sense. In one study, 4-month-olds were shown two superimposed videos of two pairs of clapping hands. When adults look at such double images of two hands clapping without sound, they perceive both pairs of hands as ambiguous and vague. When they hear the sound of one hand pair, they perceive the movement of that hand pair more clearly, while the movement of the second hand pair fades into the background. After the superimposed video without sound had been shown to the children, they looked equally long at both pairs of hands when these were shown simultaneously, but with each pair on its own screen. After the children had heard the sound of one pair of hands clapping on the superimposed video, they looked longer at the screen with the other pair of hands. Preference for novelty is typical for this age (see p. 47). The results therefore suggest that the pair of hands with sound visually stood out for the children as well, just as it does for adults. The clapping hands without synchronous sound receded into the background and received less attention, and were thus perceived as novel when shown by themselves on a screen (Bahrick et al., 1981).

According to Bahrick (2004), amodal experiences form a basis for the development of intermodal perception and an understanding of the relationships between different aspects of the complex sensory environment. When stimulation is not amodal, infants focus on a single sense, thereby promoting the development of detailed perception within that particular sense. Unimodal and amodal experiences thus complement each other during development. Toward the end of the first year, children become better at regulating their own perceptual exploration of the environment. Adults, too, are sensitive to the synchronicity of amodal perceptual stimulation and may experience discomfort when dubbing or poor synchronization results in mouth movements that are out of synch with the sounds of speech in a movie.

Hearing or vision impairments will influence intermodal perception it is not known how this may impact other sensory modalities and the development of perception in general.

SUMMARY

1   The senses are functional at birth, but not fully developed. It takes time for a child to use its senses in the same way as an adult. Children get better at perceiving what is common in their environment and worse at perceiving things that occur only rarely. The visual and auditory systems have characteristics that promote children's social orientation.

2   According to Piaget, perception occurs "indirectly" – children construct their perception by interacting with objects (in the broadest sense). Gibson's ecological theory maintains that infants' perceptual equipment "fits" the environment and thus allows them to perceive "directly" without learning. Children automatically perceive possibilities for action or *affordances*. Perception leads to action, the opposite of Piaget's view. There is research to support both views, and a number of theorists believe that the development of perception includes elements of both theories. According to Bremner the most important milestone in perceptual development is children's ability to use their perceptual knowledge to guide their own actions.

3   Most aspects of visual perception show a rapid development during the first year. There is disagreement about the importance of innate abilities and experience for this development. Normal development of vision is dependent on relevant visual experiences.

4   Right after birth, infants "prefer" the visual features typical of faces. According to Carey, children have an innate module for facial recognition, while Slater and Butterworth maintain that early facial recognition is an expression of children's overall aptitude for learning. With increasing age, children improve at distinguishing faces in their own environment, while their ability to recognize faces of people from races with which they have less experience declines.

5   Children get better at integrating multiple visual elements and gradually become more susceptible to optical illusions. Throughout infancy, children improve at using representations of reality in images and videos as a "map," and begin to understand when a photo or a video depicts themselves.

6   Visual impairment affects all areas of development, particularly orientation and mobility. Children with visual impairments often have a delayed motor development and can be passive. They use sound to orient themselves physically, emotionally and socially. Blind children engage in joint attention, and language is often one of their strengths. Because of their unique experience, they use words in a somewhat different way. Many children with severe visual impairment have multiple disorders.

7   Newborns are able to distinguish between all aspects of auditory stimulation, but have higher hearing thresholds than older children and adults and require varied acoustic stimulation to develop full auditory perception. Early auditory attention is directed at human voices.

8   Newborns can *localize* sound approximately, and are able to locate sounds with increasing accuracy in the course of the first 2 years of life. At the end of the first year, visual and auditory localization are fairly well integrated.

9   Hearing impairments affect children's orientation in the environment and their speech. Communication and speech can be supported by improving the perception of sound and facilitating visual communication. Many children with a severe hearing impairment benefit from a cochlear implant, but need additional visual support. Some function best by using sign language. Many children with hearing impairments also have other disorders such as ADHD and learning disorders. Children with hearing impairments are socially vulnerable and have a higher rate of behavioral and emotional problems than others.

10 Children show an early interest in music. They are able to recognize short melodies and tonal patterns, and make up "babbling songs." Musical ability has a certain genetic basis, but

Continued

musicality also requires an environment that fosters the development of such skills. Musical preferences emerge gradually and reflect the child's experiences and culture.

11 The development of *smell* and *taste* is largely controlled by innate preferences and aversions at an early age, while new impressions and experiences gradually become more important. Later eating habits can be traced back to a varied diet during early childhood.

12 According to Gibson's *differentiation theory*, the senses initially constitute a primitive unity and gradually become differentiated, while Piaget's *integration theory* maintains that the senses are separate at first and gradually become integrated. Gottlieb and colleagues propose that the development of *intermodal perception* is a *dynamic process* that incorporates both differentiation and integration. *Amodal information* can be experienced with several senses at the same time. It assumes attentional precedence during early perception and lays the foundation for a child's understanding of what belongs together and to establish context.

CORE ISSUES

- The role of action in the development of perception.
- Developmental differentiation or integration of the senses.

SUGGESTIONS FOR FURTHER READING

Bahrick, L. E., Walker, A. S., & Neisser, U. (1981). Selective looking by infants. *Cognitive Psychology*, 13, 377–390.

Fantz, R. L. (1961). The origin of form perception. *Scientific American*, 204, 66–72.

Fraiberg, S. (1977). *Insights from the blind*. New York, NY: Basic Books.

Leibold, L. J. (2012). Development of auditory scene analysis and auditory attention. In L. A. Werner, A. N. Popper, & R. R. Fay (Eds), *Human auditory development* (pp. 137–161). New York, NY: Springer.

Contents

CHAPTER 9

MOTOR DEVELOPMENT

P hysical actions are movements with an intention and a goal. Motor development is an adaptive process that allows children to gradually overcome the gravitational forces, to plan, coordinate, perform and evaluate actions, and to create new physical and social opportunities for action. Action forms the basis for developing cooperative skills as well as autonomy. During the first years of life, children go through a significant motor development that leads to important changes in how they explore and relate to their physical and social surroundings.

Compared with many newborn animals, the motor skills of human children are extremely limited at birth. The most important early skills are a rudimentary head control and the ability to suckle when nourishment is offered, but infants make increasing use of the actions required by different situations and the opportunities they provide. Action control, however, is not confined to the brain alone. Movements are performed by the body, and physical growth implies a continuous adaptation of these movements to a body that grows in size and changes in proportion.

Action means planning. Actions must be adapted to the properties of things and expected movements, or *prospective control*. When children catch a ball, they must assess its size in order to gauge the correct distance between their hands and anticipate the ball's movement. Unless the movement is "planned" and has been initiated before the ball arrives, the child's hands will react too late. Therefore, the development of motor skills is largely a matter of coordinating perception and movement (Adolph and Robinson, 2015; von Hofsten, 2007). Although severely impaired vision affects a child's motor development (see p. 135), it is not dependent on the child's ability to see, but on some way of perceiving the environment.

Motor development affects children's functioning in many ways. Their ability for independent locomotion increases their room for action and entails psychological reorganization (Anderson et al., 2014; Campos et al., 2000). It allows children access to new experiences and activities, to explore people, things and events more independently and to investigate the properties of objects. Children can take a more active role in play and interaction and approach caregivers, other children and adults they may be interested in on their own. They become more aware of people and things that are farther removed from them, develop a greater need for emotional information about what may be dangerous and what may be positive, about what to stay away from and what they might explore. They look more toward their mother when she moves away, and begin to seek out emotional information from her and from others (social referencing; see p. 350). Greater mobility means greater freedom, but also more constraints. Adults must be more attentive to children's whereabouts, and guide as well as limit their exploration.

Children's development of motor skills also affects the *transactional* processes. When children acquire new motor skills and a larger repertoire of actions, parents gain more insight into their child's perception, thoughts and feelings about the world and surrounding activities, and the

Joe Campos.

child's interests and intentions. This affects the parent's reactions, expectations and demands of their child, which in turn affects the child's actions, and so on (see p. 8). Parents experience that their child's increasingly independent mobility changes the family's interaction patterns, both due to the need for increased monitoring and limitation of the child's actions, and the child's development of independence, self-reliance and autonomy (Biringen et al., 2008; Campos et al., 2000).

FROM ACTION SYSTEMS TO COMPLEX ACTIONS

Some of children' earliest movements are *developmental reflexes* that only occur during infancy. They are the result of evolutionary processes and provide early action tendencies that have been and continue to be important for a child's survival (Table 9.1). A touch on the lips, for example, induces a newborn to suck. Once the *rooting reflex* has helped a child find its mother's nipple (see the following), the *sucking reflex* ini-

tiates the intake of food. A child's early repertoire of actions contributes to nourishment and survival, but also initiates the development of movement and provides children with experience of the environment (von Hofsten, 2007).

Some developmental reflexes are activated by internal and external factors. The rooting reflex, for example, causes the infant to turn his head toward the side being stimulated. It is usually elicited when the infant is stroked across the cheek, but not when he does so himself or when he is not hungry. Placing the infant's cheek near the mother's breast will help him find the nipple, while trying to push the infant's opposite cheek to get his mouth in the right place is counterproductive, since he will search for the nipple on the side being touched. This illustrates how developmental reflexes lead to self-initiated actions rather than actions imposed on the infant by others. Neither is the infant's suckling action automatic, but adapted to the amount of milk. Infants do not begin to suckle reflexively once they are satiated, even if their lips are stimulated.

Developmental reflexes are thus not entirely reflexive, but rather form a set of *action systems* that are activated under certain external conditions. They gradually lose their reflexive character to be replaced by more deliberately controlled actions. Children continue to suck after the sucking reflex has disappeared; the difference is that the sucking is not as easily activated by external factors alone. Similarly, newborns can only grip with their hand when something touches their palm. Only a few months later, infants will reach for objects and adapt their grip to the object's size, and not try to reach for objects that clearly are too far away (von Hofsten, 2007). These early action tendencies are important because they help children develop exploratory movements and learn. Their disappearance, or the loss of their reflexive character, is nonetheless a significant developmental milestone, and children's learning gains momentum around the age of 3 months, coinciding with their growing social awareness.

Children's earliest engagement in activities typically involves the whole body. An interesting event causes a child to watch actively, but also to move her mouth, tongue and arms (Smitsman, 2001). An important part of development is for children to learn to confine themselves to movements that are relevant to the situation to be explored, and the actions to be taken.

TABLE 9.1 Some developmental reflexes (based on Gallahue and Ozmun, 2006)

Babinski reflex	The child's big toe flexes upwards and the other toes fan out when a sharp object is stroked backwards along the lateral side of the foot. Usually begins to disappear at 3 months of age.
Palmar grasp reflex	The fingers close when the child's palm is lightly touched. Usually disappears at 2–4 months of age.
Moro reflex	The child stretches out her arms and moves them toward the body's midline when the head suddenly loses support. Usually disappears at 5–6 months of age.
Plantar reflex	Replaces the Babinski reflex around the age of 4 months. The toes flex down when the ball of the foot is stimulated. Usually disappears at 9–10 months of age.
Rooting reflex	The child turns her head toward the side being stimulated when lightly touched on the cheek. Most pronounced at 3 weeks of age; gradually subsides and disappears at around 11 months of age.
Sucking reflex	Stimulation of the lips and the mouth elicits a sucking action. Present at birth, disappears at around 3 months of age.
Asymmetric tonic neck reflex	When the child herself or someone else turns the child's head to one side, the arm and the leg on that side will extend. Usually disappears at around 6 months of age.

Children's early repertoire of developmental reflexes and action systems forms the basis for developing a broad and varied repertoire of actions. The transition from simple to more complex actions is often characterized by a reduced level of efficiency. Children are able to move much faster by crawling, for example, than by walking when taking their first steps. Although children do occasionally crawl during this phase when they want to get somewhere quickly, they will mostly try to move on two legs, even if it means that they fall. This illustrates the importance of independent action and the intrinsic motivation provided by physical mastery, and perhaps also by moving just like older children and adults. In addition, it is faster to walk across longer distances, and walking increases the child's range and makes it easier to carry things. There are thus many advantages to walking versus crawling (Adolph and Tamis-LeMonda, 2014).

GROSS MOTOR DEVELOPMENT

Gross motor skills include control of the body's posture, crawling, walking and other forms of locomotion.

Early development

During early gross motor development, children gradually overcome the forces of gravity. Some early milestones are shown in Figure 9.1. Newborns are able to turn their head from one side to the other when lying on their stomach, for example to orient themselves to a sound. At 3 months, children are usually able to hold their head up and look straight ahead. They support themselves by leaning on their forearms and are able to turn their face to both sides. The ability to maintain an upright head position is important for children to visually explore the surroundings. It also makes it easier for parents and others to discover the child's interests and further encourage these through interaction. Early motor development thus affects the interaction between children and parents (Prechtl, 1993).

Usually, children are able to turn from side to back when they are about 2 months old. A little later, they can sit with the support of their arms, and about half of all 6- to 7-month-olds can sit without supporting themselves. At 9 months, they are able to move from a lying to a sitting position, and at 11 months, most infants can stand on their own.

The first independent locomotion usually occurs by rolling at the age of 5–6 months of age. At 10 months, children can walk with help and support, and a little later by themselves. This changes the perception of the surroundings as children look down when they crawl and ahead when they walk (Kretch et al., 2014). At 2 years of age children begin to climb stairs. However, the acquisition of these and other skills shows significant variation in age (see Figure 9.1). The specified ages should therefore be understood to be typical ages, and somewhat earlier or later acquisition of skills generally does not indicate an abnormal development. Additionally, there is considerable variation in how children solve the challenge of independent locomotion. They scoot, roll, jump, kick and crawl forward using their arms, legs, chest, elbows, stomach and back. Children also use different strategies when they learn to walk; some use a "stepping" strategy, others twist their body back and forth, some move sideways while holding onto furniture or initiate movement by letting their body "fall" forward (Snapp-Childs and Corbetta, 2009). The reasons for this variation are unknown. Some of them probably reflect children's active exploration of possible actions in their physical surroundings, others seem to be the result of sheer coincidence, lack of mastery or "sensory-motor noise." Thus, variation represents an important developmental element here as well. Each child chooses the strategies that work best (Adolph and Robinson, 2015). Blind children move less to explore, and their motor skills develop later due to a lack of visual incentives for exploration and movement (Freedman and Cannady, 1971).

Further gross motor development

Motor development continues after the child has passed the first milestones and learned to walk. Most children learn to run, jump and hop, and to walk on various surfaces as well as uphill and downhill. At 18 months, children begin to run and improve until the age of 2–3 years, but running first becomes effective at the age of 4–5. Children are generally about 3 years old before they can hop three times on one foot. Around the age of 5, they can jump a distance of about 1 meter and 30 centimeters in height. Until the age of 12, boys jump only a little farther than girls, but from here on the differences become increas-

ingly pronounced. More culture-bound motor skills such as riding a bike, playing soccer or swimming continue to evolve throughout school age, and even longer for those who pursue it as a sport. Development is about more than simply mastering or not mastering a skill – the *qualitative* execution of many established motor skills improves throughout childhood and adolescence (Largo et al., 2001a, b).

DEVELOPMENT OF FINE MOTOR SKILLS

Fine motor skills include all the movements of the hands, such as pointing, gripping and drawing. Fine motor skills make it possible for children to manually handle and explore things.

Early development

Early development is above all characterized by the ability to grip and hold with increasing precision, and to adjust the grip of the hand to objects of various shapes and sizes (Figure 9.2). Even a fetus brings its hand to its mouth, and the coordination of this movement increases rapidly during the first 6 months of life. If an object is placed in the hand of a child at this age, they will usually move it to their mouth. It is not necessary for them to see the object first, since they perform just as well in darkness.

The ability to let go develops later; children are unable to let go of objects until they are about 4 months old. At this age, children also begin to look at the object they hold in their hand before moving it to their mouth. As the child's grip improves, the movement of the hand adjusts to the object about to be grasped, and at the end of the first year the shape of the hand anticipates the object's size, an ability that requires visual control. At 9 months, children begin to use the pincer grip, which enables them to pick up very small objects (Bertenthal and Clifton, 1998; Rochat, 1993).

A parallel development takes place in children's hand movements toward objects. To begin with, the movements are brief, imprecise and depend on suitable physical conditions. The hand rarely reaches its goal. Furthermore, newborns automatically open their hand when extending it and thus fail to close it around objects that are further away. At 2 months, infants will generally

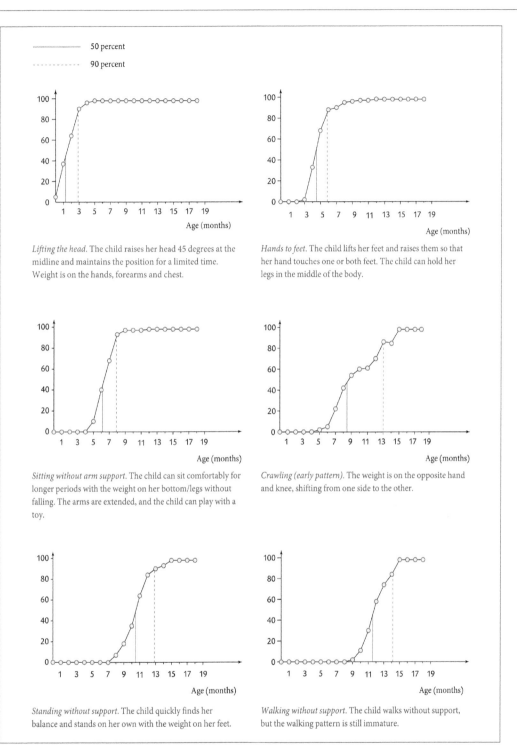

—————— 50 percent

- - - - - - - - 90 percent

Lifting the head. The child raises her head 45 degrees at the midline and maintains the position for a limited time. Weight is on the hands, forearms and chest.

Hands to feet. The child lifts her feet and raises them so that her hand touches one or both feet. The child can hold her legs in the middle of the body.

Sitting without arm support. The child can sit comfortably for longer periods with the weight on her bottom/legs without falling. The arms are extended, and the child can play with a toy.

Crawling (early pattern). The weight is on the opposite hand and knee, shifting from one side to the other.

Standing without support. The child quickly finds her balance and stands on her own with the weight on her feet.

Walking without support. The child walks without support, but the walking pattern is still immature.

FIGURE 9.1 **Selected gross motor skills and their development.**
The curves indicate the percentage of children who master a given skill at different ages. Age levels at which 50 and 90 percent of all children master a skill are highlighted (after Piper and Darrah, 1994, pp. 84, 130, 162 and 171).

clench their hand when reaching for something, while at the same time extending less frequently than before. When manual extension once again increases in frequency 1½ months later, their hand is open, and at 4–5 months of age they begin to succeed when reaching out to grasp an item. The ability to grasp moving objects requires forward control and coordination of information about the object's path and the infant's own movements. Nevertheless, infants begin to anticipate and reach for the location of moving objects at around the same time as they begin to grasp stationary items (von Hofsten, 2004, 2007).

The fact that infants begin to reach for things is also important for the interaction with other children and adults. Exactly what they reach for provides the most important clue to what infants are interested in.

Further development of fine motor skills

Around the age of 2–3 years, children develop the ability to throw and catch a ball, but around the age of 6 they are able to perform these skills in a more competent way (Gallahue and Ozmun, 2006).

At the end of their first year of life, children begin to use tools to extend their reach, such as a small rake to get hold of something they cannot reach with their hands. Other tools at this age are usually used for eating, drinking and drawing. Learning to eat with a spoon illustrates this gradual process. Toward the end of the first year, children begin to use a spoon in different ways: putting it on a plate, pounding it on the table, switching it from hand to hand and occasionally putting it in their mouth. A little later they try to eat with it, but even if they are able to hold the spoon, they find it difficult to fill it with food and move it to their mouth. The spoon does not become an independent eating utensil until they approach the age of 2 years. Chinese children master the necessary motor skills for chopstick use at 4½ years but need 2 more years before they can eat half of their meal independently (Wong et al., 2002).

Toward the end of the second year, children also begin to use pencils and crayons. Until the age of 3–4 years, most children use a fist grip to hold a pencil. This grip develops until children are taught to use an "adult" writing grip in kindergarten or school. Writing is a complex process, and children's handwriting progressively becomes faster, more coherent and more automatized in the course of the first years of school, in line with their general motor development. A 12-year-old writes about 50 percent faster than a 9-year-old. Girls' handwriting is generally somewhat "neater" than that of boys (Connolly and Dalgleish, 1993; Søvik, 1993).

FINE AND GROSS MOTOR SKILLS ARE RELATED

The development of fine and gross motor skills is part of the same process, and the distinction between them is more a matter of convenience than fact. Body control is necessary for children to be able to perform independent actions with their arms and hands, and the loss of balance when reaching for an interesting object will lead the child to find sturdy ways of sitting and moving. An important development thus takes place when children handle objects as a result of changes in gross motor skills, which in turn are motivated by the desire to perform fine motor actions. Being able to sit for longer periods without support is a prerequisite for children's ability to reach for objects without tumbling over. Children who are not yet able to sit upright without help reach for objects with both hands when they are supported, while children who can sit on their own reach for objects with one hand. The same applies to the development of independent locomotion: once children begin to slide forward on their belly and start to crawl, objects lying beyond reach provide an incentive for locomotion. Children who can walk on their own carry things in a different way than children who crawl or who have to support themselves (Adolph and Robinson, 2015; Goldfield and Wolff, 2004).

Children's early movements are frequently exploratory and often performed with a high degree of self-control, demanding considerable attention and cognitive resources. Gradually, their movements become *automatized*. This is a prerequisite for the fluid performance of motor skills, and also reduces the amount of cognitive resources involved in performing movements. A well-acquired skill thus requires fewer resources. Children with motor difficulties need to use more cognitive resources to perform movements, and are thus left with fewer resources for actual play and the solving of "tasks."

Age	Behavior
0.2–0.4	Waves arms when excited
0.2–0.4	Waves arms at objects
0.2–0.4	Holds both hands in front of the body
0.3–0.5	Gradually moves hands towards an object
0.4–1.0	Dominant hand becomes noticeable
0.4–1.0	Moves objects to mouth
0.5–0.8	Grasps objects with the dorsum of the hand
0.6–0.9	Grasps using the fingers
0.6+	Grasps objects and examines them
0.6+	Shifts an object from one hand to the other
0.6+	Lets go of objects and throws them
0.9+	Pincer grip (grasping an object between thumb and forefinger)
1–2	Scribbles
1.6	Throws a ball into a box
1.6	Builds a tower with three blocks
2	Runs after a ball, but does nothing to catch it
2	Builds a tower with six blocks
2	Places blocks in a row to make a train
2–3	Turns body towards the target, using only the forearm to throw with
3	Makes a basket shape with body and hands to catch a ball
3	Draws crosses with two lines
4	Draws the sun with circles and lines
4–5	When throwing, takes a step forward in sync with the movement
5	Catches a small ball with hands
5	Draws trees
6	Able to draw triangles
9	Able to draw three-dimensional shapes
11	Line perspective in drawings

FIGURE 9.2 Some milestones in the development of fine motor skills.

Children begin to use their hands for many different purposes early on. Age indicates when the action is observed in the majority of children.

INDIVIDUAL AND CULTURAL DIFFERENCES

Children show significant differences with regard to when they master various skills, as well as the quality of execution (Adolph and Robinson, 2015). Although some of these differences are due to biological factors, experience is important as well. This becomes evident when comparing cultures with different routines of childcare. In some African cultures, mothers believe it is necessary to teach their children to overcome gravity and train them in motor skills such as sitting and standing. They develop these skills earlier than North American children, whose mothers do not instruct their children in a similar way, but they do not show a correspondingly early development in other motor skills (Konner, 1976; Super, 1981). Similarly, environments that do not promote children's independent locomotion may delay the development of children's ability to walk. Children who are swaddled much of the day – wrapped tightly in cloth or a similar material – have a delayed motor development. Chinese children who spend much of their time in a bed with fluffy pillows that are difficult to walk on generally begin to walk about 3 months later than children in the US (Adolph and Robinson, 2015; Campos et al., 2000).

Many motor skills develop in a more or less fixed order, but there is always some variation. Most children crawl before they begin to walk, but some of them follow other developmental paths. Some children move by pushing themselves forward on their buttocks and start to walk without ever having crawled (Hopkins et al., 1993). It has been argued that children who do not crawl or otherwise deviate from the typical sequence of development may have difficulty reading and writing at school because of this (Holle, 1981), but this is not supported by research (White et al., 2006). Some children will indeed have difficulty learning to read and write, both among those who crawl and those who do not crawl. Therefore, absence of crawling is neither a defect nor a sign of abnormal development, but an expression of the fact that children follow different developmental paths toward the same goal (Largo et al., 1985). It is the biological foundation, together with the childcare routines (for example how the child is usually placed), that determines a child's path of development (Hopkins and Butterworth, 1997; Iverson, 2010).

THEORIES OF MOTOR DEVELOPMENT

Maturation has traditionally been emphasized in motor development, but recent theories give experience a greater role.

Maturation

For a long time, motor development was generally seen as the result of neurological maturation based on a genetically determined timetable, while experience was considered to be of limited importance (Schmuckler, 2013). New movements were believed to originate as a result of the brain's formation of nerve structures that control the performance of these movements (see McGraw, 1943). In a classic experiment, one of two identical female twins was trained to walk a staircase 10 minutes every day for 6 weeks between the ages of 46 and 52 weeks. At the end of this period, it took her 26 seconds to walk the stairs. The other twin, who had not received training, began to climb stairs by herself when she was 49 weeks old, and was able to walk the training stairs in 45 seconds 4 weeks later. At this point, she received the equivalent training her sister had been given, 10 minutes a day for two weeks. After that, she could walk the stairs in 10 seconds, faster than her sister, with far longer experience, was able to do (Gesell and Thompson, 1929). Experience thus played a role, but Gesell interpreted the result to indicate that although training does have an effect, it is of limited value before neurological maturation has progressed far enough.

Dynamic models

From the perspective of dynamic models, children's movements develop as part of a self-organizing system that consists of many internal and external processes and sub-processes (see p. 10). Although general neurological development is of importance, it is only one of several interacting processes. Every movement involves a number of conditions: adequate neurological maturation, related motor functions, muscle strength, experience and the physical environment. The underlying processes originate at different times and develop at a somewhat different pace. Only once the necessary processes are functional are children able to develop new movements, which in turn are adapted to constantly new objects and environments. All motor activity is dependent on a complex hierarchy of support structures in the form of body posture and affordances in the environment. Their organization varies depending on the action chosen by a child, and whether the child is in a lying, sitting or standing position (Adolph and Robinson, 2015).

Thelen and Smith (1994) use a dynamic systems approach to explain the emergence of walking. In their view, walking is the result of an infant's intention to move toward something, its neurological and perceptual development and physical prerequisites, such as sufficient leg muscle strength to support the body as well as move the legs. In addition, environmental conditions must allow for the possibility of walking, for example something the child can hang on to while still unable to walk steadily, or an adult who supports some of the weight while the child's muscle power still lacks the necessary strength. If any of these conditions are not sufficiently met, the child will not walk.

Newborns perform walking movements with their legs when they are held upright and a light pressure is applied to the bottom of their feet. Although these movements disappear after about 2 months and do not return until the child learns to walk a few months later, Thelen and Smith believe that their neurological basis is maintained, but that the movements are suppressed because children must first develop sufficient muscle strength and body control to overcome gravity. To support their view, they point out that a 3-month-old placed upright in water that provides buoyancy will perform the same walking movements with the feet as a newborn. Other scientists argue that these early walking movements have not been "preserved" as Thelen and Smith claim, but that they have an altogether different neurological basis precisely because the legs have the power to carry the body under normal gravitational conditions (Adolph and Robinson, 2015).

Primary movement patterns, variation and selection

The theory of *neuronal group selection* is based on the assumption that a structure of primary neuron groups (nerve cell connections) responsible for motor functions has formed in the course of evolution, and that this structure changes as the result of experience based on variation, explo-

ration and selection of movements (Edelman, 1989). A genetically determined starting repertoire of general movement patterns emerges at different age levels. These patterns are further selected through experience and adapted to the environment. The *phase of primary variability* begins early in fetal development and continues throughout the first few months after birth. The infant tries out different movements and chooses the most appropriate among them. Yet these early movements entail only a rough adaptation to the environment. They are followed by the *phases of selection*, involving different age levels for various skills such as grasping, crawling and walking. Each selection phase is followed by a *phase of secondary variability* in which variation in movement leads to a more specific adaptation to different environments (Hadders-Algra, 2002).

In contrast to dynamic models, Edelman's theory places more emphasis on maturation due to the assumption of an innate basic set of movement patterns. It differs from other theories of maturation in that maturation alone does not bring about the infant's final movements, but only general movement patterns that must be further developed through experience (Piek, 2002).

DEVELOPMENT OF DRAWING

In many cultures, children begin to use pencils and crayons early – during their second year of life – but drawing takes time to learn. The earliest drawings mostly consist of scribbles that gradually become more distinct and detailed. Barely half of the drawings of human figures made by 4-year-olds include the feet and arms; at 6 years of age, over 90 percent of the drawings include the feet. About 70 percent of all 6-year-olds and 90 percent of 10-year-olds draw the arms. Very few 4-year-olds draw the neck and hair. First at the age of 8, half of all children include the neck. A similar percentage include the hair a year later (Aronsson, 1997).

The development of drawing skills reflects general motor development, changes in the ability to perceive and abstract characteristics of people and things in the environment, and the development of interests and creativity. Children's drawings reflect both their perception of reality and the particular aspects of the environment that capture their attention. At 3 years of age, children are able to explain what their drawings represent

Painting is a popular child activity in many cultures.

when asked about them. Before this age, it is not always easy to recognize realistic elements in their drawings. However, scribbling does not merely produce scribbles: it represents mom, a house, a cat, and so on. Scribbling also has its own aesthetic and reflects the way in which a child tries to represent a three-dimensional world on a two-dimensional sheet of paper (Arnheim, 1974). When children create a graphical representation, they choose certain aspects of the object they want to draw (Aronsson, 1997). When asked to depict a potato field, a 7-year-old drew potatoes that were visible through the soil (Figure 9.3). The main characteristic of a potato field is after all potatoes, which is why they had to be visible.

Children's drawings are influenced by the environment they live in, including general cultural influences as well as the culture's particular drawing traditions. In industrialized countries,

young children spend a lot of time drawing, and with increasing age their drawings gradually become more culturally conventional (Winner, 2006). Training and drawing traditions are of major importance. A survey conducted in a remote region of Papua New Guinea, an area with no tradition of graphic art, found major differences between human figure drawings made by children who had gone to school and received drawing instruction, and children who had not attended school (Martlew and Connolly, 1996). The children who attended school drew conventional drawings, while many of those who were unschooled produced scribbles and shapes. A few children drew relatively advanced human figures. The study demonstrates the importance of training and experience for developing drawing skills. Drawing is not merely a matter of learning how to use a pencil, the general graphic culture is of significance as well. Studies

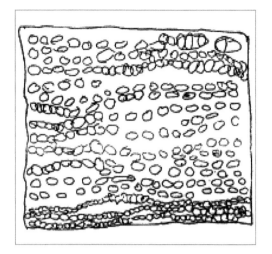

FIGURE 9.3 **Potato field.**
Children often draw elements that are important for the picture's theme, although not visible in reality. In this picture, a 7-year-old depicting a potato field drew potatoes that can be seen through the soil (from Luquet, 1927).

of children's drawings show the important influence of the kinds of drawings children are exposed to, such as comic strips (Wilson and Wilson, 1977).

There are considerable individual differences in drawing skills and artistic ability. Edvard Munch and many other famous painters showed signs of talent early on. Some children with Down syndrome, autism spectrum disorders and other forms of atypical development also show exceptional drawing skills (Mullin, 2014; Xia, 2014).

ATYPICAL MOTOR DEVELOPMENT

Motor disorders impact children's independent mobility and use of hands, as well as their participation in many common activities. Gross motor skills are of particular importance for exploring the surroundings, participating socially and feeling secure. Fine motor skills are used for exploring things in the environment, handling objects, building and constructing, using eating utensils, drawing and other things, and thus are important for a child's ability to independently participate in meals, play and other activities. For children with motor impairment many ordinary

skills are more difficult to acquire and have a delayed development. They take more cognitive resources and when fewer resources are available for other purposes, such as paying attention to what happens in one's surroundings while performing an action, it can impact children's understanding of social relationships and the development of language and social skills. Motor training may be necessary at the expense of other activities. For children with more severe disabilities this can involve considerable amounts of time.

Children with motor impairments have a higher incidence of many types of disorders, with major variations in cognitive and language functioning (Odding et al., 2006; Stadskleiv et al., 2017). Symptoms of attentional problems are common among children with cerebral palsy (Bjørgaas et al., 2012). Some of them have learning disorders, including problems with mathematics and learning how to read and write (Dahlgren Sandberg, 2006). Also boys with Duchenne muscular dystrophy have difficulty reading and writing (Banihani et al., 2015). Children with more severe motor impairments have a greater number of cognitive disorders – especially intellectual disability – than children with more moderate motor impairments, but there is no direct relationship between motor impairment and general cognitive functioning. While studies have found that 60 percent of all children with cerebral palsy and impairment in both arms and legs score below 70 on intelligence tests, the results indicate that 40 percent scored within or above the normal range (Andersen et al., 2008; Sigurdardottir et al., 2008). Thus, motor functioning does not provide a basis for drawing conclusions about the individual child's cognitive functions (Blair, 2010). The disorders may have a neurological basis, but like all other development, disorders are the result of interaction between biology and experience (see p. 12). Theories of cognitive development and self-regulation place emphasis on children's actions. Distinguishing between what is directly attributable to a brain injury and what is related to changes in motor experiences is not always possible. There may be cognitive cascade effects (see p. 12), from individual motor experiences with fewer possibilities for action, less automatization and increased use of cognitive resources to the execution of the earliest actions in infancy. It is commonly observed that children "grow into" their disability, and that the differences between them and their peers increase with age.

Minor motor impairments usually have less influence on children's development. They are generally able to perform the same actions as others, but have to use more resources in connection with locomotion, handling objects, drawing and the like. Many children with intellectual disability are clumsy and have coordination problems beyond what one would expect from their intellectual disability.

Children with moderate motor impairments can participate in most activities, but need to be more selective in their choice of activities and acquire less experience in many areas. The need to use additional cognitive resources in the performance of activities means that they have less time and get tired more quickly. Often they are less active and function more as observers than participants. They can be left out in some social settings and lose part of the common social life, especially in the phases when children tend to be physically active.

More severe motor disorders impact all areas of the developmental process and affect the child's cognition, language, social interaction and emotional life. Children with severe gross motor impairments participate less actively in play, exploration of the environment and other interactions, and find it more difficult to establish contact with other children and adults they may be interested in. The impairment can place major demands on planning and other executive functions (see p. 210) and prevent the child from participating in activities that promote these functions (Stadskleiv et al., 2014). Some of these problems can be prevented through early intervention and by adopting measures that afford similar experiences in other ways. A walker or a wheelchair provides better opportunities for exploring the environment and can help children extend their psychological space and autonomy, just as other children experience once they develop independent mobility (Gudgeon and Kirk, 2015). Children with cerebral palsy whose speech is impeded or unintelligible can use communication aids

The wheelchair gives children with motor impairment acces to mobility and sports.

(see p. 331). Despite being unable to speak, language can be their strongest asset, also in connection with play, and they can instruct others to perform play actions they themselves are unable to participate in – language for action.

The developmental consequences of motor impairment thus reach far beyond the motor execution of various actions alone. Even moderate gross and fine motor problems can affect the interaction with parents, siblings and other children and adults, and the child's emotional development, relationships and personality. A child's inability to explore and regulate the distance to her parents may affect the bonding process (see p. 401). The need for help has an impact on the development of self-image and autonomy. The constant presence of a parent or other adult affects the child's relations with its peers. Children who use a wheelchair state that they feel less disabled when helped by a peer than by an adult (Madge and Fassam, 1982). For children with severe motor impairments, the environment needs to be adapted and must include training for parents and siblings.

Parents of children with cerebral palsy report more emotional and behavioral problems among their children than parents of children without motor disorders (Brossard-Racine et al., 2012). This may reflect the children's frustration over not being able to cope, training fatigue, problems with self-regulation and a difficult social situation with few supportive resources.

SUMMARY

1   Newborns have a limited repertoire of *reflex actions* that are activated under certain external conditions. They are essential for survival and help initiate movements that allow children to experience the environment. The coordination of perception and movement is important in the development of an action repertoire, and motor precision requires *forward control*.

2   *Gross motor skills* overcome the forces of gravity and control body posture, crawling, walking and other forms of locomotion. The ability to move independently alters the psychological environment and affects areas such as attachment, language, self-perception and autonomy.

3   The development of *fine motor skills* includes all use of the hands such as grasping, exploring, handling objects and using *tools*, including pencils for drawing and writing. With increasing age, many movements become *automatized*.

4   The development of motor skills follows a relatively stable pattern with individual variation in relation to how and when skills develop. These differences are the result of both biological factors and different cultural practices.

5   Traditional explanations of motor development have been based on *maturation*. *Dynamic systems theories* view motor development as the result of interaction between the child's individual traits and the physical environment. According to the theory of *neuronal group selection*, motor development is the result of an evolutionary-based set of actions and variation, exploration and selection of movements in connection with the environment.

6   The development of drawing skills reflects general motor development, the ability to perceive and abstract characteristics of people and things, and the child's interests and creativity. Children's drawings reflect their culture, perception of reality and the particular aspects of the environment that capture their attention.

7   Motor disorders affect independent locomotion and the use of hands, as well as attachment, social participation and autonomy. While many children with severe motor impairments have other disorders, it is uncertain what is caused by neurological damage and what is due to the developmental consequences of their motor impairment.

CORE ISSUES

- Biology and experience in motor development.
- The association between motor ability, cognition and learning disorders.

SUGGESTIONS FOR FURTHER READING

Adolph, K. E., Tamis-LeMonda, C. S., Ishak, S., Karasik, L. B., & Loboet, S. A. (2008). Locomotor experience and use of social information are posture specific. *Developmental Psychology, 44,* 1705–1714.

Campos, J., Anderson, D. I., Barbu-Roth, M. A., Hubbard, E. M., Hertenstein, M. J., & Witherington, D. (2000). Travel broadens the mind. *Infancy, 1,* 149–219.

Largo, R. H., Molinari, L., Weber, M., Pinto, L. C., & Duc, G. (1985). Early development of locomotion: Significance of prematurity, cerebral palsy and sex. *Developmental Medicine and Child Neurology, 27,* 183–191.

Thelen, E. (1995). Motor development: A new synthesis. *American Psychologist, 50,* 79–95.

von Hofsten, C. (2004). An action perspective on motor development. *Trends in Cognitive Sciences, 8,* 266–272.

Contents

CHAPTER 10

THEORIES OF COGNITIVE DEVELOPMENT

ognition plays a role in everything human beings do – playing, eating, working out school assignments, designing space crafts, developing strategies for a football game, taking a walk and enjoying the view, sending messages on a cell phone or reading a book. Cognitive development is an essential part of developmental psychology. Children are not merely "incomplete" adults and theories of cognitive development aim to explain how children's cognitive processes initially arise and develop into adult comprehension, thinking and problem solving (Newcombe, 2013).

The theories are as complex as cognition itself. They describe dissimilar processes and emphasize different factors in explaining the development of a mature mind. The current chapter discusses four main approaches to cognitive development: *logical constructivism*, *information processing*, *nativism* and *social constructivism*. (Their main features are presented in Chapter 2 and will not be repeated here.) Comparisons between them provide an insight into the different ways of understanding changes in children's cognitive functioning, and a sound basis for discussing the various aspects of cognitive development presented in the following chapters. Piaget's theory is the most influential as well as the most criticized among the theories, and most other theories incorporate elements from Piaget's theory, challenge it, or both (Barrouillet, 2015). Therefore, it is presented first and treated in some detail, and the others are discussed in relation to it.

DOMAINS, MODULES AND ACTIVITIES

Cognitive development concerns the organization, structure, and biological and cultural basis of cognition. One of the key questions is whether all areas undergo a general change in level, or whether development varies between different knowledge areas, or *domains*. Domain-general development means that knowledge areas share the same foundation and evolves more or less in parallel. When development is domain-specific, it progresses differently in separate areas, such as language, spatial perception or mathematics. Therefore, the question is whether cognition is driven by a single large "machine," or by multiple "machines" of varying size for each individual domain.

Modules

Some theorists believe that domain-specific development has its basis in *modules*, neurological units with a specific function that include a set of categories and processes capable of interpreting external stimulation in one particular way only, just as the heart, the liver and other organs have their specific functions. One module perceives language only, another spatial relationships, a third social relationships, and so on. A module can cover a broader or narrower area of knowledge, and modules can incorporate independent sub-modules. These modules are considered important for development because they are specialized to deal with particular aspects of the world and thereby put restrictions on learning and lead it in the right direction. Without such restrictions, human experience would be too ambiguous and inadequately structured, the world would appear chaotic, and children would be unable to distinguish aspects of the environment that are and are not relevant for a particular task (Butterfill, 2007). There is, however, considerable disagreement about the number of modules. Spelke and Kinzler (2007) believe there are four or five, while Carruthers (2006, 2008) and Sperber (2001) argue in favor of "massive modularity," meaning that the mind (and the brain) contains a large number of modules.

Because modules are independent, they can be damaged without affecting the function of other modules. Both developmental disorders and acquired injuries are used as an argument for the possible existence of modules. For example, many theorists assume there is a module for language, since brain injury can result in impaired language function (aphasia) without affecting other areas in any significant way. The same applies to the ability to recognize faces.

Most modularists adopt a nativist view and believe that modules were formed in the course of evolution, since they led to skills that ensured a higher survival rate. They mainly develop through maturation, while experience merely functions as a "trigger mechanism." Chomsky (2000) and Pinker (1994), for example, believe that human beings have an innate language module and that children under normal circumstances only need to be exposed to linguistic stimulation in order to develop language (see p. 305). Other theorists argue that any potential modular properties of the brain are not present at birth, but emerge through a *process of modularization* where experience and genes interact. The modules are thus the result of development, rather than being mechanisms that determine the developmental course of knowledge, such as the nativists claim (Karmiloff-Smith, 2015). In line with this view, atypical development can occasionally lead to inadequate modularization. While persons with typical development activate different areas of their brain when they see faces and other objects, people with Williams syndrome seem to activate the same area when looking at cars and faces (D'Souza and Karmiloff-Smith, 2011).

Activities

An alternative to the notion that the mind consists of domains or modules is the view that different abilities have their origin in experiences related to various activities, and that the developmental process may be activity-specific in some areas. Activities are here not isolated acts, but constitute a stable and complex system of practices that have evolved in response to society's needs and opportunities. Play, education and different types of work are examples of activities (Cole, 2006; Karpov, 2005). A tailor may be good at calculating how much fabric is needed for a dress, or a butcher at calculating the weight of a piece of meat, without either of them being able to solve a problem of similar difficulty outside their professional activities, for example when presented in a classroom (see p. 186). The math skills of the tailor, the butcher and the pupil in the classroom belong to the same knowledge domain, but develop in different ways nonetheless. Domain-specific knowledge exists independently of a given activity and it would therefore be incorrect to say that their math skills are domain-specific. Instead, learning arithmetic appears to be activity-based and to some extent remain activity-specific knowledge.

Embodiment

Although cognitive psychology has largely focused on the brain, cognitive development is not a process that merely occurs in the brain, independent of the body. Many theorists emphasize how human (and other species') perception of the world, thinking and problem solving are determined by the very design of the body, its interaction with the physical forces of nature and participation in social interaction. According to this view, the human body itself imposes limitations on the development of the human mind. Organisms with different bodies would also have had a different type of cognition and other ways of categorizing, thinking and solving problems. The nervous system is the body's connection with the environment. Human beings do not have "a brain or a mind in a box," but are organisms with a nervous system that exists *within* rather than separate from the environment. Children do not learn to perform an action isolated from a situation, but as an adaptation to and within the situation. Hence, the body and the physical and social environment are part of the human cognitive apparatus and development (Clark, 2008; Glenberg, 2010).

LOGICAL CONSTRUCTIVISM

This chapter discusses Piaget's standard theory, including the cognitive structure, the developmental processes and the stages, its critical reception, and "the new theory."

Cognitive structure

According to Piaget (1950, 1952), cognitive development involves the formation of a *cognitive structure* based on logic and mathematics that enables increasingly complex and abstract thinking. The cornerstones of this structure consist of schemas that are formed when actions become generalized and transformed through mental processing. *Action schemas* can be compared with action strategies. When children face obstacles in achieving a goal, their past actions – previously incorporated into schemas – will determine how they try to overcome these obstacles, for example by using a stick to get hold of something that is out of reach. Schemas are abstractions that include aspects of actions not specifically related to a given situation, and that can be transferred to other situations. "Throwing" is an example of an action schema formed early in life. A child can throw a rattle, a ball, a cap or something else. Since the act of throwing is adapted to different objects, it can vary a good deal – high or low, long or short, and so forth. However, the schema includes only what is common to or *constant* in throwing. Activating a schema rather than merely repeating the execution of an earlier action allows the child's execution to be more flexible and adapted to the situation.

According to Piaget's theory, action and thinking have the same function: to achieve goals and overcome obstacles. Thoughts are internalized actions, and action knowledge provides the foundation for all thinking. It is by exploring and engaging with objects in space and time that children discover how they can predict, understand and master the world around them.

Symbolic schemas represent something other than themselves. Words are an example of symbolic schemas. When children pretend that a

wooden block is a toy car, the block becomes a non-linguistic symbol for "car." The development of symbolic schemas enables children to solve problems and think about objects and events without directly linking them to actions.

Action schemas and symbolic schemas involve abstraction, meaning that certain characteristics are extracted and reassembled into new categories. *Operational schemas* keep track of the changes that occur when experiences are transformed from concrete experience to mental categories. Operational schemas are necessary for children to understand the connection between events and to construct a coherent and consistent world.

The assumption that children develop the same cognitive structure independent of their specific experiences is one of the cornerstones of Piaget's standard theory. Just like the other schemas, operational schemas are not products of learning in the conventional sense, but mental constructs formed by abstracting and processing physical and mental actions. The knowledge children acquire is neither determined by an innate mental structure nor is it a replica of the world formed through sensory experiences. Instead, it arises from the interaction between the child and the external environment. According to Piaget, it is the human biological equipment that makes abstraction possible, but children must have experience in order for abstraction and the formation of structure to take place (Piaget, 1950, 1983).

The development process

Children's quest to understand the world is a basic life function, a *process of adaptation* whereby mental schemas and processes undergo a gradual change as children respond to challenges and gather new experiences. According to Piaget, development is determined by three factors: maturation, training and social transfer. Maturation is of particular importance during early development, and is also a prerequisite for the particular order between the stages (see below). Development based on maturation alone would, according to Piaget, be static and fail to provide a sufficient basis for the adaptive abilities that distinguish children's development. Thus, development is not simply the result of learning or social transfer, but requires the presence of a cognitive structure able to perceive and interpret

– humanize – experience. An attempt to determine what may be the result of maturation and what is learned is considered to be of little importance by Piaget. It is the *interaction* between maturational processes and children's active interaction with the environment, their adaptation to constantly new surroundings and conditions, that determine development in Piaget's theory: experience leads to challenges, mastering challenges leads to new experiences that provide new challenges, and so on.

Assimilation and accommodation

When children perceive events, objects and people, they select or interpret things and events in the external world based on the schemas they have acquired. Piaget calls this *assimilation*. Because younger children's cognitive schemas and structures differ from those of adults and older children, they perceive the physical and social world in a different way. In order for children to gain new knowledge and develop new actions, their schemas must be adapted to experiences with new people, objects and events. Piaget calls this process *accommodation*. It is accommodation that leads to changes in cognitive schemas, but assimilation entails adaptation as well. The assimilation of new objects and events forces children's thinking to adapt, to be accommodated. Assimilation and accommodation thus are complementary aspects of the same process, rather than distinctly separate processes. The internal structure (accommodation) and children's perception of the world (assimilation) change in tandem with each other.

Equilibration and conflict

According to Piaget, cognitive development is driven by an innate ability to perceive cognitive contradictions and seek to create *equilibrium* between established schemas and new experiences. When children experience a *conflict* between beliefs they have formed, they encounter a state of cognitive *disequilibrium* that leads them to resolve the problem. Disequilibrium represents a state of incomplete adaptation but which enables the child to perceive the contradiction. Based on their own schemas, children are unable to perceive the same contradictions as adults. An adult knows, for example, that an object cannot float one moment and sink the

next. Toddlers might claim that a toy they have just observed sinking will float the next time they throw it into the water. It is only once children understand that these two events are incompatible that a cognitive conflict takes place and becomes a problem they can relate to. Children must have acquired the necessary prerequisites to recognize a problem before they can solve it.

Piaget's theory thus views development as being driven by an intrinsic motivation to establish equilibrium or structural order. Children's perceptions are constantly challenged by new experiences, and they actively seek out such challenges. When a child has solved the problem created by a given state of disequilibrium, the new understanding brought about by equilibration forms the basis for new insights, which in turn lead to new conflicts and disequilibrium. A final state of equilibrium is essentially impossible to achieve, since new and unresolved problems will emerge on new levels.

Organization

The earliest schemas evolve individually and independently of one another. They represent knowledge about the world that is as yet fragmented and disjointed. It is the *organization* process that makes the cognitive structure function as a whole. It coordinates established schemas and creates superordinate schemas in accordance with logico-mathematical principles. This is the logic in logical constructivism. Reorganization leads to a greater degree of equilibrium by solving former contradictions or conflicts, and at the same time to disequilibrium as the child discovers new contradictions. One consequence of this model is that new experiences affect the structure and organization of past experiences, which in turn are adapted to the new knowledge. Following each new organization, the child is unique and different from the person he was before, and will be in the future. Some reorganizations imply a transition to a new cognitive stage.

Stages

Piaget describes four domain-general stages of cognitive development. Each stage represents an extensive reorganization and a qualitatively new way of thinking and reasoning, that enables children to understand and solve new tasks. Since the completion of a stage leads to the ability to recognize new cognitive conflicts, one stage always functions as preparation for the next.

The sensorimotor stage (0–2 years)

In this stage, children develop *sensorimotor schemas* based on perception and external actions. It includes approximately the first 2 years of life and is divided into six sub stages. In the first sub stage (0–1 months), the child has a small repertoire of reflexive actions that are elicited by primary needs. Adaptation to the environment begins as early as during the first few days of life. Newborns quickly improve at finding their mother's nipple and begin to suck.

In the second sub stage (1–4 months), children produce spontaneous actions they can perceive to lead to a goal. Piaget (1952) describes how his son Laurent learned to suck his thumb after accidentally putting it into his mouth for the first time. However, children do not yet distinguish between means and ends. The goal is achieved because a particular sequence of movements leads to it. It is only during the third sub stage (4–8 months) that children are able to use the same action to achieve other goals. At the same time, this sub stage forms the basis for being able to distinguish between means and ends, and choose from a variety of actions to reach a goal, something children do during the fourth sub stage (8–12 months). In the fifth sub stage (12–18 months), children are able to use tools to achieve a goal, such as grasping the edge of a tablecloth

and pulling it toward them to reach an object (Figure 10.1).

The acquisition of object permanence is an important cognitive milestone in the fourth sub stage. At 7–8 months, children will stop looking for a toy when it has been hidden under a blanket so they cannot see it. Children who are 2 months older will search for the object and look underneath the blanket. This reflects an understanding of the permanent existence of objects, and shows that children are beginning to "handle" objects mentally. Their understanding remains limited, however, and the search is unsystematic. During the fifth sub stage children begin to show understanding of how objects behave under different conditions. In the sixth sub stage (18–24 months), children will also look in other places if they cannot find the toy where they thought it would be (see p. 217).

The sixth sub stage represents the completion of basic sensorimotor skills and lays the groundwork for the development of operational thinking. Of particular importance is the development of mental representations and symbolic schemas. Children no longer need to perform concrete actions, but are able to solve problems mentally by imagining actions and objects. They can show sudden insight and make use of new solutions as the result of thinking without physical trial and error. This marks the beginning of dissociation from the immediately perceptible situation. Once children have developed object permanence, they are able to look for objects they have just observed being hidden, such as a toy under a

FIGURE 10.1 **Using a tool to achieve a goal.**
Once children have reached the fifth sensorimotor stage, they are able to pull on a tablecloth to reach an object placed on it (Willatts 1989, p. 162). (Thanks to Peter Willatts.)

pillow. Symbolic representation enables them to look for objects that were not part of a given situation some moments earlier.

According to Piaget's theory, the ability to *imitate* plays an important role in cognitive development. Although children show imitation-like behavior as early as the first sensorimotor stage, Piaget does not consider this to be *genuine* imitation. During the second and third sub stage, children repeat their own actions when these are imitated by adults. True imitation emerges in the fourth stage, first in the form of *immediate imitation*, followed by *deferred imitation*, meaning that an action is carried out some time after the original action, such as when a child sweeps the floor like dad did the day before. Children show deferred imitation of simple actions toward the end of the sensorimotor stage (see Chapter 15). Imitation is not a passive form of replication – deferred imitation requires the child to store an action mentally and recreate it completely or in part. It is an active and creative process that leads to independently constructed mental representations.

A tremendous development takes place during this first stage, "no less than a conquest by perception and movement of the entire practical universe that surrounds the small child," to quote Piaget. External actions have become internalized mental actions, and children have acquired and organized basic knowledge of the physical and social world around them.

The preoperational stage (2–7 years)

The preoperational stage forms the transition from sensorimotor to operational thinking. Piaget calls this stage "preoperational" because the cognitive structure includes schemas that are not aimed at coordinating external actions and thus are not sensorimotor, but not abstract enough either to be operational. During this stage, thinking begins to detach itself from action, but continues to be unstable and characterized by the immediate perception of a situation: children think what they see.

Object permanence is the understanding that objects continue to exist even when they cannot be seen at the moment. This stage sees the development of a new type of *constancy* that enables children to retain specific qualities of objects, such as color and shape. They are able to categorize objects by a single property, but unable to take into account several at the same time (Inhelder and Piaget, 1964). A 5-year-old (B) shows typical preoperational thinking in conversation with the experimenter (E):

E: *What do we have here?*
B: *Blue circles and blue and red squares.*
E: *Are all the circles blue?*
B: *No, because there are blue circles and squares.*
E: *Are all the squares red?*
B: *Yes, because there are only squares.*
E: *Are all the circles blue?*
B: *No, there are circles and squares.*

The development of *symbolic function* is one of the key elements of this stage. It allows children to influence the coordination of perception and action-based knowledge with their own thought processes and thereby overcome the limits of sensorimotor knowledge and free their thought from their actions. This is reflected in children's deferred imitation, use of words and symbolic play. Words are symbols, but the use of symbols is not necessarily related to language. A piece of clay is also a symbol when it represents the mother or the baby during play. According to Piaget, language does not structure thinking; it is the cognitive development that lays the foundation for a child's understanding of complex linguistic content. Nonetheless, Piaget considers language important for children's acquisition of knowledge.

In the course of this extended process, while the cognitive structure is still incomplete, children solve a number of tasks by using "intuitive" pre-logical thinking and mental trial and error. Children often know the answer, but are unable to explain it. The following answers are typical:

Piaget: *What is wind?*
Child: *Something that blows in the sky.*
Piaget: *How do you know that?*
Child: *I just know.*

An incomplete cognitive structure thus characterizes children's thinking during this stage. This is also apparent in their failure to fully separate between fantasy and reality – both their thoughts and their dreams can appear real to them.

The concrete operational stage (7–11 years)

It is the formation of *operational schemas* that distinguishes the cognitive structure formed during the operational stages from the structure of the first two stages. These schemas enable children to organize and link together other schemas, and provide them with a "mental space" to move around in and solve new problems in entirely new ways.

In contrast to earlier stages, descriptions of children's problem solving during the concrete operational stage place greater emphasis on what they are capable of rather than not. Many advanced cognitive skills emerge for the first time during this stage. For example, children become able to arrange objects according to a given dimension and eventually also to compare information. They can draw a map that shows the way to school, something younger children are unable to do even if they know the way and can walk to school on their own. Five-year-olds can usually differentiate between the right and the left side of their body, but first during the concrete operational stage are they able to do so for others as well. Yet children's thinking continues to be limited and relies on being supported by experience. The stage is concrete-operational because they are only able to carry out operations in relation to "concrete" objects.

During this operational stage, children begin to master various forms of *conservation*. This is a type of *mental constancy*, an understanding that the material or mass of an object does not change even if external aspects of the object do. This underscores that children's perception of the world is not a passive registration of external characteristics. Conservation of number is usually acquired first, followed by mass, weight and volume. Figure 10.2 shows two typical experiments studying conservation in children.

In experiments on conservation, younger children are unable to pay attention to more than one aspect at a time. They fail to understand that quantity, weight and volume remain constant even if the object's outward appearance changes. They focus on the characteristics that attract their attention the most and experience no cognitive conflict due to lack of constancy. First at the age of about 7 years are they able to overcome the object's immediate visual impact.

At about 7–8 years, children begin to understand that an object can belong to two classes simultaneously, such as being both black and round, and can therefore be assigned both piles if the task is to categorize objects by shape and by color. A related conceptual development is the understanding of *class inclusion*, the fact that one class of objects can be a subcategory of another class. Tulips and roses are two distinct categories, but also subcategories of the category "flowers" (see p. 231).

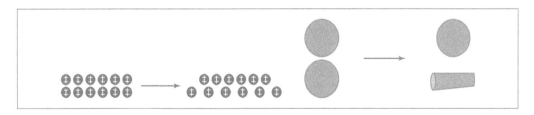

FIGURE 10.2 **Two conservation experiments.**

1 Number

Together, the experimenter and the child place two rows of buttons so they lie in pairs of two. The experimenter asks whether both rows contain an equal number of buttons and receives a positive response from the child. The experimenter then increases the distance between the buttons in one row so the row becomes a little longer. He asks which of the rows contains most buttons. Children below the age of 6–7 years usually respond that there are a greater number of buttons in the longer row.

2 Mass and weight

The child is given a lump of clay that is divided into two precisely equal parts by the experimenter and rolled into two clay balls. He asks the child whether there is an equal amount of clay in each ball and gets an affirmative answer. Next he rolls one of the balls into a sausage and asks which of them contains the most clay. Children below the age of 7 years point to the sausage. Older children respond that there is an equal amount. A corresponding procedure is used for weight, with the experimenter asking what weighs the most. Children are usually 7–8 years old before they are able to correctly answer the question on mass, and 9–10 years before they correctly answer the question on weight.

The formal operational stage (11+ years)

Around the age of 11, children begin to think more like adults, and at the age of 15 they have acquired a stable system of formal mental operations, according to Piaget. The formal operational stage is characterized by a new ability to combine several features or elements. "Formal" here means that operations can be applied to abstract and hypothetical problems. Concrete operations involve thinking about the world; formal operations involve thinking about thinking.

Adolescents who have reached this stage therefore do not need concrete support. Thought is liberated from specific content, and adolescents are able to deduce logical consequences of an issue or a situation without first deciding whether it is true or false. They are, for example, able to reason about what would happen *if* they were in a different country. While children in the concrete operational stage will dismiss such a counterfactual question by answering that they are not in the other country, thought is only limited by possibilities rather than by what actually is during the formal operational stage. Adolescents begin to understand proportion, probability and analogy, and are able to take into account several dimensions at the same time, such as the width and the height of a glass to estimate its contents. In addition to actual problems, the final cognitive structure is capable of processing hypothetical obstacles and objectives.

In this stage adolescents also become able to form theories and make use of hypothetical-deductive reasoning, formulating hypotheses and testing them out in a systematic manner. It is precisely this capacity for "scientific" thinking that characterizes the formal operational stage, the culmination of Piaget's description of cognitive development. Thinking becomes more advanced and complex even after the age of 15, but according to Piaget, later development is characterized only by an increase in knowledge, not by qualitative changes in cognitive structure. When adults draw incorrect conclusions it is due to a lack of knowledge rather than an inadequate logical structure (see also p. 236).

Domain-general development

According to Piaget, development is domain-general (see p. 165). Once the cognitive structure

has been established and conservation can be demonstrated in one area, children will also be able to master similar tasks in other areas. However, the ability to solve different tasks does not always occur at the same age, a fact Piaget explains by suggesting that children's thinking in the concrete operational stage is not yet fully detached from concrete situations, but more or less related to specific types of experiences. Because the occurrence of such experiences varies, some areas may be delayed compared with others. Only once children enter the formal operational stage does their thinking become entirely liberated from specific objects and experiences and reach the same general cognitive level.

Status of the standard theory

Piaget's theory was the major theory in the twentieth century, and in the twenty-first century, neo-Piagetians and others continue to develop theories and conduct research building directly on it (Barrouillet, 2015; Morra et al., 2008). However, Piaget's standard theory and his empirical findings have been challenged by all the other theoretical views on cognitive development. Criticism against him is as essential to the debate as his theory. Yet Piaget continues to occupy a central position, both because his theory remains to be the only comprehensive and detailed theory of cognitive development, and because it includes many positions that can be scientifically verified (see p. 20). The basic assumption that children develop a cognitive structure based on logic is generally disputed, but many of Piaget's concepts and his terminology are still frequently used to describe children's cognitive development. The experimental tasks used by Piaget have in themselves been important for an understanding of cognitive development. Piaget described them in great detail, and they represent an original and well-founded approach to children's thinking and reasoning.

Age

Much research has been aimed at establishing whether the various age specifications Piaget arrived at are correct. A common objection to Piaget is that he underestimates younger children. Studies show that by using other methods or changing the instructions, children are able to solve similar tasks at a lower age level than specified by Piaget. For example, using the visual preference method, Baillargeon (1987) found evidence of object permanence in children much younger than what Piaget found (see p. 217). McGarrigle and associates (1978) studied class inclusion in an experiment involving a teddy bear walking up a staircase made up of red and white steps to reach a table. Children were able to determine whether there were a greater number of red steps or total steps at a much earlier age than in Piaget's study, in which they were asked whether there were more red flowers or more flowers (see p. 231). McGarrigle believes the difference can be explained by the fact that the teddy bear task was based on a play activity the children were familiar with. A similar difference was found between Piaget's and Donaldson's studies of children's ability to adopt different visual perspectives (see Chapter 13).

However, not all tasks are mastered simply because the instructions change, and the age levels Piaget found for mastering certain tasks still generally hold true (Bjorklund, 1995). What the studies conducted by Hundeide (Box 10.1), Donaldson and others show is that changes in the conditions of tasks may change the age at which children are able to master them. Together, Piaget's and the other studies contribute to an understanding of what it takes for children at various age levels to solve different types of tasks. The fact that studies show children to be capable of solving many tasks at an earlier age when combined with familiar activities, emphasizes the importance of designing tasks that are meaningful to children based on their own experience. This also indicates that children's ability to solve

many cognitive tasks is more *activity based* than suggested by Piaget's standard theory.

While Piaget underestimates younger children, he seems to overestimate the capacity for systematic and logical thinking among adolescents and adults. Far from all teenagers are able to master formal operational tasks (Shayer and Wylam, 1978). Also adults frequently provide answers that reflect a concrete operational way of thinking, especially in connection with tasks related to areas they have little experience with (see p. 235). Most people never develop a fully consistent level of logical thinking, but their reasoning to some extent remains dependent on the given situation.

Piaget himself was relatively uninterested in specifying age. He considered age indications to be approximate, and mastering a skill earlier or later than usual is not critical to his theory as such. Only a change in the sequence of skills associated with the different stages would represent a decisive blow to his ideas. When differences in the age at which children acquire a particular skill show major discrepancies, the question nevertheless arises whether cognitive development truly is domain-general and can be explained based on the acquisition of a higher-level cognitive structure relatively independent of children's concrete experiences.

Stages and domains

Developmental stages must comply with certain formal criteria. Children have to acquire a certain competence that differs qualitatively from the competence they have previously shown. The

The experimenter showed a picture of five cups and two glasses to preschool-age children, and asked them whether there were more cups or more things to drink from. Seventeen of the 36 children who were shown the picture before they were asked the question answered correctly. Thirty-six other children were asked the question before they saw the picture, and 31 of them answered correctly. Hundeide's explanation of the results is that the children who were shown the picture first were naturally aware that it included two types of objects and many had therefore formed an *expectation* that the two objects were going to be compared, since this is something adults often ask children to do. They expected a question about the differences between cups and glasses, and "forgot" that both are used to drink from. The children who had not seen the photograph first had no such expectation to influence their reasoning.

transition from one stage to another should occur relatively quickly and be accompanied by changes in several aspects of children's thinking. Every child must move through the stages in the same order (Flavell, 1971). Research shows that these criteria are not always being met, and most developmental theorists reject the types of stages described by Piaget. However, stages are still considered useful for describing children's cognitive development (Carey et al., 2015; Lourenço, 2016). The models of neo-Piagetians Case (1985, 1998) and Feldman (2004) represent an adaptation of Piaget's theory by integrating the concept of stages with more recent research about children's thinking and conceptual formation. According to Feldman's model, the first half of each stage is used to build new skills and structures, the second to develop the ability to apply them. The distinction between construction and application provides more room for individual and cultural differences.

The stages in Piaget's theory are domain-general, but research suggests that many areas involve domain-specific and activity-specific development. Tasks that according to Piaget reflect the same cognitive structure are mastered at different age levels (Bidell and Fischer, 1992). There is also cultural variation as to when children master different tasks. Price-Williams and colleagues (1969) compared children from two Mexican villages. The population in one of the villages made a living by producing pottery, and children in this village acquired conservation of mass with clay earlier than conservation of number. The other village did not produce pottery and the children showed the usual pattern of developing conservation of number before mass. This contradicts Piaget's thesis that all experiences lead to the same cognitive end result. Examples of activity-specific reasoning can be found at all age levels, including adults, as illustrated by Wason's experiment (p. 231). The study of "street mathematics" and "school mathematics" shows the importance of the particular sphere of activity in which knowledge is acquired (see p. 186). In fact, Overton and colleagues (1987) point out that variation in performance is an expression of the fact that the capacity for formal reasoning does not arise in a vacuum: logical thinking must act on and in connection with the individual's knowledge of the world.

In Piaget's theory, a child's cognitive development represents a personal and individual project. Language and social interaction provide knowledge, but have little impact on the development of cognitive structure. Although Piaget acknowledges the fact that some children and adults develop more knowledge in certain areas than in others, depending on the challenges and problems they face, his objective was to describe common elements in children's development rather than individual variation.

The new theory

The theory presented here so far is known as the *standard theory*. It represents Piaget's views in their essential form during the 1950s and 60s. In what is referred to as the *new theory* (Beilin, 1992), he takes into account some of the criticism launched against the standard theory, especially the problems associated with his assumptions about domain-general development. The theory itself is not "new," Piaget continued to revise the theory throughout his life (Burman, 2013). The foundation of the standard theory has largely been preserved, but with less emphasis on action and logic, and incorporating *meaning* and *interpretation*, concepts that are central to social constructivist theories (see Piaget et al., 1992). The theory's main elements will be described here to show its development.

In Piaget's new theory, detecting *novelty*, comparing objects and events, and finding similarities are basic cognitive abilities. Children form schemas by detecting *correspondences* between various "forms" in the outside world, for example that cups have the same shape or that several actions can fulfill the same function. In order to correspond, there has to be a similarity between several elements. The sentence "John is Peter's uncle," for example, expresses a single relationship. A correspondence first arises when several such individual relations share a common feature. In this case it could be "Bill is John's uncle," "Anders is Tom's uncle," and so on.

The simplest correspondences are those between completely identical objects or events, followed by objects or events that resemble each other. Correspondences that go beyond a comparison of identical features are called morphisms. They are tools for establishing *constants*, attributes that do not vary across the phenomena in question. An example of such a constant is that the same number sequence can be used for all months: 1 January, 2 January, 1 February,

2 February, and so on. Morphisms that span across objects and relations are called *categories*. Thus, categories are abstract qualities.

Correspondences are the result of children's organization of experiences in the external world. *Transformations* are internal processes that make it possible to see more abstract similarities, for example similarity between a zebra and a striped crosswalk. They have their origin in the correspondences or relationships the child has discovered, and without correspondences, transformation would not be possible (Barrouillet and Poirier, 1997; Beilin, 1992).

While children's thinking initially is focused on external characteristics and consequences of actions, mental processing gradually becomes more important. Just as in the standard theory, the distance between perception and thinking constantly increases. Children's use of morphisms and transformations passes through three levels of development: from *intramorphic* via *intermorphic* to *transmorphic*, from immediate experience to mentally processed information (Barrouillet and Poirier, 1997). The course of development can be exemplified by the acquisition of class inclusion, meaning that a category can be part of a different category (see p. 231). In one experiment, children were shown seven raspberries and three strawberries and asked whether there were mostly raspberries or mostly berries. Children who reason at the *intramorphic* level are able to compare aspects that lie within one and the same morphism. They can count the number of raspberries and the number of strawberries, but fail to see them in context. Children at this level do not show class inclusion and will reply that there are mostly raspberries.

Children who reason at the *intermorphic* level are able to coordinate simple morphisms and establish correspondences across multiple morphisms. They can compare a subcategory with the category it is part of, such as "raspberries" and "berries," and correctly answer that there are mostly berries. Children process the simple correspondences they have discovered in the world around them. Consequently, the new theory is able to explain why children at this level manage this type of task better with known than with unknown materials. It is, for example, more difficult for children to include "ducks" in the category "animals" than to include "yellow flowers" in "flowers." They don't usually refer to ducks

as animals. Such results were critical to the standard theory, which was based on domain-general development, while the new theory opened up for domain-specific and activity-specific knowledge (Acredolo, 1997; Barrouillet and Poirier, 1997).

A *qualitative* change takes place in children's thinking from the intermorphic to the transmorphic level. Children at the intermorphic level are merely able to coordinate morphisms. At the *transmorphic* level, they are capable of generalizing this knowledge and change – transform – morphisms into more abstract correspondences. Transmorphisms are also *operations*, processing of mental content. Children can link together morphisms into a comprehensive system so that their knowledge exceeds the specific content of these morphisms, which is based on their individual experiences. This marks the transition to a general system similar to formal operational thinking, but via a process that is more varied and whose results are less predetermined than in the standard theory.

Roughly speaking, preoperational thinking is comparable to the intramorphic level, concrete operational thinking to the intermorphic level, and formal operational thinking to the transmorphic level. An important difference, however, lies in the fact that the three levels of Piaget's new theory do not represent general stages of development. Compared with the standard theory, cognitive functioning is to a greater extent determined by the child's individual experiences. A child's thinking can involve different levels in different areas, depending on the child's specific experiences. The performance of different tasks may furthermore depend on the material being used, and is therefore to some extent activity-specific (Acredolo, 1997).

INFORMATION PROCESSING

The common denominator of information processing theories is the notion that all cognitive phenomena can be described and explained based on a model whereby *information flows through one or more processing systems*, and increasing *complexity* is a major organizing principle of cognitive development (Halford and Andrews, 2011). According to Cohen and associates (2002), six principles explain how children come to understand the world:

1. Infants are endowed with an innate information-processing system.
2. Learning is hierarchical – infants form higher units from lower units.
3. Higher units serve as components for still-higher units.
4. Children will always take advantage of the highest-formed units.
5. If higher units are not available, lower-level units are utilized.
6. This learning system applies throughout development and across domains.

Thus, information processing can involve individual processes. An example of this is memory, which can be broken down into *encoding*, *decoding*, *storage*, *recall* and *feature identification* (see Chapter 10), while executive processes and other metacognitive processes monitor and regulate the processing. Metacognitive processes can be compared with Piaget's operations, although the underlying approach is quite different. In Piaget's theory, cognitive development centers on the formation of a unified structure. Information processing takes the opposite view and searches for a set of individual processes involved in all forms of cognitive functioning. Some mental tasks can be solved by individual processes, while others require coordination and multiple parallel processes (Welsh et al., 2006). Complexity may be defined as the number of relations that can be processed in parallel and schemes needed to coordinate (Halford and Andrews, 2011).

The developmental process

Information processing theorists have different views on *what* it is that changes during cognitive development. One view is that basic processes increase in speed or capacity with age, while at the same time children acquire more knowledge and better strategies and use of rules (Demetriou et al., 2002; Kail and Miller, 2006; Luna et al., 2004). Pascual-Leone (1970), for example, argues that changes in children's thinking are the result of maturational increases in memory capacity that allow children to store more information in their working memory and encode it into long-term memory. Information processing can also become more complex and efficient as the result of *parallel processing*, a gradual increase in the ability to perform multiple processes simultane-

ously. Others, like Case (1985), believe that after infancy the fundamental processes remain the same throughout life, and that development is a result of more efficient use of the capacities. Many tasks require more conscious attention and cognitive resources in children than in adults where the performance of the task has become automatized, a development that entails that much routine processing takes place outside of the individual's conscious attention. When fundamental processes are constant and cannot be affected by the environment, they are per definition innate (Halford and Andrews, 2011).

Also the view on domains varies within this tradition. When children solve mental tasks faster as they grow older, it may either be due to the increasing speed of individual cognitive processes, or to a general speed increase across different processes. In some models, basic processes operate across domains and therefore are domain-general (Cohen et al., 2002; Gathercole et al., 2004). Other models include differential processing of domains, and domain-specific development (Demetriou et al., 2002). Kail (2004) suggests that development includes both global (domain-general) and domain-specific processes.

Knowledge

From the perspective of information theory, knowledge is information, and changes in the extent and organization of information are important elements in cognitive development. Multiple processing allows the information to become more efficiently organized and take up fewer resources. An individual with extensive experience of a particular type of information becomes an "expert." Experts in a particular area have more knowledge of a certain type and are therefore able to solve problems in this area faster than non-experts – novices. According to Chi, problem solving, that in Piaget's model is assumed to reflect qualitative changes in cognitive structure, can be the result of a child's expanding knowledge and an increase in the speed of processing information when the subject area is known. Adults usually have more knowledge than children, but children are nevertheless able to surpass adults in certain areas. Many children know more than adults about dinosaurs. Children who are good at chess remember the position of more pieces on the board than adults who know the rules, but have little experience with the game (Chi and Koeske, 1983). Knowledge and strategies for organizing information thereby affect how it is perceived, memorized and processed.

Rules and strategies

The use of strategies for managing cognitive tasks is an important element of information processing (see Box 10.2). New rules and strategies of solving tasks lead to changes in cognitive performance. Throughout childhood, children acquire a large repertoire of action strategies and create rules that can be more or less useful for different types of problem solving tasks. Younger children have few strategies, and their application is often inefficient or inappropriate. As they get older, they adopt and reject new rules and strategies. Some of these are short-term, others long-term, and are used to varying degrees at different age levels (Figure 10.3). The particular strategies children choose depend on previous experience, the types of problems they intend to solve and how successful they eventually turn out to be (Siegler and Jenkins, 1989; Siegler, 1994).

Strategic choices and the establishment of rules gradually become more well-adapted with age. School-age children adopt various strategies spontaneously, and many strategies are explicitly communicated by teachers at school. The use of rules is not always permanent, however, and some strategies are rarely applied unless children are reminded of them. One explanation may be that complex strategies demand too great a part of children's limited cognitive resources. Therefore, the use of new strategies does not always lead to improved performance in younger children, and sometimes they perform even worse. In one study, children in third and seventh grade were taught a memory strategy based on collecting words into categories and trying to recall all the words in the category, such as animals, clothing or furniture. Having received instruction, all of the children used the strategy they had been taught, but only the seventh graders recalled more words. Bjorklund and Harnishfeger (1987) interpret this to mean that the third graders spent so many of their cognitive resources on applying the strategy that there were few resources left for the memorization task itself. This shows that there is little point in teaching children conscious strategies before they have developed the capacity to handle both task and strategy at the same time.

The development of early arithmetic skills can progress from applying a rule to a specific problem via a set of rules for similar problems to the formulation of general rules:

Rule 1: If the goal is to add (1 + 2), then count one finger, followed by two fingers, and say the result.

Rule 2: If the goal is to add (3 + 4), then count three fingers, followed by four fingers, and say the result.

Rule 3: If the goal is to add two numbers, m and n, then count m fingers, followed by n fingers, and say the result.

Rule 1 is only valid for solving the problem 1 + 2 = ? Rule 2 is a new unique rule with an equally narrow scope (3 + 4). Rule 3 is a general rule, but is restricted by confining itself to the number of available fingers. When children learn higher numbers, they need new rules because rule 3 is not broad enough.

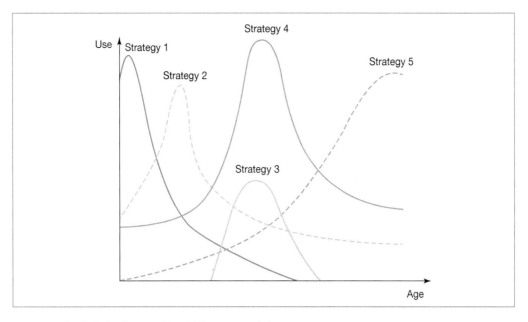

FIGURE 10.3 **Siegler's developmental model for strategy choice.**
According to Siegler, children develop a repertoire of strategies to choose from over time. In this example, strategy 2 fairly quickly takes over for strategy 1. Strategies 3 and 4 occur simultaneously, while strategy 4 is used the most. In the end, strategy 5 almost completely takes over, but strategies 2 and 4 continue to be used (based on Bjorklund, 1995, p. 117).

The path to using adult rules and strategies is a long one. Children must choose between different strategies and identify the one that fits best. The ability to inhibit strategies that do not fit the situation and abandon previously acquired strategies that no longer are suitable is also part of development. Particularly during adolescence, the monitoring of one's own deliberate choice and use of strategies – metacognitive strategies – becomes progressively more pronounced (Kuhn and Franklin, 2008).

Connectionism

Connectionism is an approach within the information-processing tradition. Connectionists attempt to describe the fundamental processes behind various functions and their development by modeling and simulating these processes using computer programs. They believe that computer simulations can help bridge the gap between cognitive models of the mind and neurological models of the brain and nervous system. Connectionist models of cognitive functions consist of networks of processing units that are assumed to correspond to similar units in the

brain. When simulating an external stimulation, the model's units are activated to varying degrees and transmit activating or inhibitory impulses to other units in the network, thereby generating a *representation* or "model" of the incoming stimulation. Similarly, the model incorporates networks of units that activate or inhibit simulated action. When combined, the networks replicate the perception and actions of a simulated "child" (Elman et al., 1996; Schultz, 2003).

There are similarities between unit patterns of connectionist models and Piaget's schemas. Both describe how sensory stimulation and action are represented in the mind. Many connectionists have a background in the Piagetian tradition and view the simulation of children's learning processes as one of assimilation and accommodation (see p. 168). Unlike Piaget, however, they make no assumptions about predetermined structures or stages. Connectionists have demonstrated that the simulation of skill acquisition can result in a developmental curve similar to that of stages, since many small developmental changes can lead to sudden higher-level changes. An example of this is the simulation of the "vocabulary spurt," an increase in the rate of word learning that usually occurs at the end of the second year of life (see p. 312). According to connectionist simulations, the rate of word acquisition will increase once the system has learned a certain number of words (Elman et al., 1996). However, connectionist models never deal with domain-general development, but rather a stage-like development within clearly defined domains.

Connectionists are generally critical to assumptions about innate domain-specific knowledge. They acknowledge the existence of certain genetic factors, but by using computer simulations they have been able to show that cognitive skills can be acquired through experience in areas where nativists insist on the presence of certain innate abilities because a given skill cannot be learned. For example, the use of simulations has made it possible to demonstrate that children can quickly learn to recognize faces, an ability that consequently need not be innate, as many nativists claim (see p. 129).

Status of the information-processing tradition

Information processing is the dominant school of thought in twenty-first century cognitive psychology. Although many scientists base their study of development on information and processing systems, the tradition remains somewhat incomplete in its perspective on development. Greater focus has been placed on identifying individual processes than on the developmental changes they bring about, and on creating models and simulating processes than on theoretical explanations of development (Munakata, 2006). No single unified model exists, it is rather a general approach to the understanding of cognitive functioning that slowly introduces developmental aspects, and there is considerable disagreement as to what development actually involves. This may be the very reason that information processing is often integrated with other approaches, including logical and social constructivism (Halford and Andrews, 2004; Morra et al., 2008; Russell, 1999).

While the strength of connectionist simulations lies in their ability to specify all processes and elements of development, it simultaneously limits the type of development that can be simulated. They primarily center on the acquisition of relatively simple perceptual, cognitive and language skills, but include atypical develop-

ment. Additionally, the simulations do not sufficiently account for the child's own active role in development (Elman, 2005). Many critics have raised the question of whether the computer metaphor is suited to describe the cognitive development of children. Computers neither grow nor change the way children do. The information-processing tradition makes little allowance for the learning situation itself and for social and cultural factors that have proven to be important for cognitive functioning. The focus is on isolated processes and information, and socially constructed meaning is not considered to be central to an understanding of cognitive functioning (Nelson, 2007a).

NATIVISM

According to nativist views on cognitive development, infants are born with a pre-programmed, or "hard-wired," mental "model" of various aspects of the world. Modern nativists ascribe some degree of importance to the environment, but nativism is based on the fundamental assumption that the development of many cognitive functions are *experience-independent* or *experience-expectant* (see p. 106). In their view, human genes impose *constraints* on what children can perceive and learn, and provide a framework for the development of *domain-specific* processing modules, but not for their detailed contents. The rationale behind this is that these constraints ensure a developmental pathway that is domain-relevant rather than domain-irrelevant (Newcombe, 2002). Strong and weak forms of nativism are distinguished by the specific degree to which development is determined by genes.

Strong nativism

Strong forms of nativism ascribe the basis of cognition to genetic factors. There are no structural cognitive changes as a result of experience as described by Piaget and others. The emergence of neurological processes and the way in which knowledge is represented are predetermined. Experience may be necessary for a given function to be utilized, but has little significance for the design of the function, for example how human beings perceive spatial relationships. Children's acquisition of knowledge depends solely on an input that allows processing by the module.

Assumptions about pre-programmed modules are central to strong nativist theories (see p. 165). According to Fodor (1983, 1985), the sensory system translates information to fit the relevant module. For example, stimulation of the eye is translated in a way that enables the geometry module to process it. Following such processing, knowledge is forwarded to higher cognitive processes that guide the actions of children (and adults). Gardner (2006) believes there are different forms of intelligence with a basis in a limited number of modules (see p. 264).

Some theorists distinguish between *core domains* with a genetic basis that leaves little room for variation, and *non-core domains* that are more dependent on experience. Core domains have developed because they represent areas in which the human species and its predecessors have needed to solve specific problems over a large number of generations (Gelman and Williams, 1998). Carey (1992), for example, suggests that the ability to distinguish and recognize members of one's own species has been of such great advantage that humans in the course of evolution have formed a separate neurological module to process facial information. This allows newborn infants to quickly learn to differentiate between the face of their own mother and that of another female. Specific problems with facial recognition due to brain injury during adulthood are also considered evidence of an innate modular ability (see p. 166). Spelke and Kinzler (2007) propose that children are born with four or five modules constituting a core knowledge that forms the basis for further cognitive development. These are modules for understanding objects, actions, numbers and spatial relationships (geometry), and perhaps also social relationships (social cognition).

Weak nativism

In weaker forms of modern nativism, development is more affected by experience. The most important innate cognitive function in Gopnik and Meltzoff's (1997) *theory-theory* is the ability to form "theories." A theory can be defined as a "coherent conceptual system used to understand and explain a set of related conditions and to predict future events." A theory arguing that infants form "theories" is based on the assumption that infants possess cognitive resources enabling them to form hypotheses, make infer-

ences about specific causal relationships in the outside world, and determine whether the theory's inferences are correct or not, based on their own experience.

The ability to develop and try out theories is domain-general and used to produce theories in different areas of knowledge, according to Gopnik and Meltzoff. Infants are born with certain innate assumptions or "theories" about the world that they use as the basis for analyzing "data" from different domains, including an implicit "theory of mind." These theories are not permanent but subject to later modifications and revisions. To begin with, they provide an insufficient basis, and infants draw conclusions that future experience or "evidence" will show to be incorrect. When the infant gains new evidence, she creates new theories, which in turn are tried out and revised. The theories an individual ends up with as an adult may therefore have very little in common with the infant's initial theories. The earliest theories are nevertheless required in order to initiate the developmental process and enable children to recognize the world and form new theories.

The theory-theory represents a weak form of nativism because it does not assume that children are born with modules or "theories" that represent final cognitive functions. Instead, they constitute an innate starting point. In this way, the theory-theory allows more room for developmental variation and qualitative changes in children's thinking not determined by maturation. It nevertheless stands in sharp contrast to Piaget's theory by claiming that children are born with a cognitive structure that enables them to form and try out hypotheses. Piaget's theory views this type of "scientific" ability as the final result of development, first acquired through the development of operational schemas late in childhood. Yet, the theory-theory's conjecture that children's theories – and consequently their conceptual system and reasoning – are changed through experience is not entirely unlike Piaget's theory of equilibration. The theory-theory hypothesizes that qualitative changes occur in children's thinking because the "data" (what children learn about the world) require a new theory and way in which to perceive the world, just as Piaget's theory states that children's experiences lead to the formation of new cognitive structures that cause them to perceive the world differently than before. According to the theory-theory, the types of theories children form depend to some extent on their specific experiences. The theory thus allows for different developmental pathways and individual differences in abilities and knowledge.

No clear boundaries exist between weak forms of nativism and what are considered to be non-nativist points of view. All theories assume that genetic factors play a determining role in the development of human cognition and thinking, but weak nativists place greater emphasis on these predetermined factors than non-nativists.

Status of nativism

Nativism plays a significant role in twenty-first century developmental psychology, but no one today views cognitive development as being exclusively determined by maturation. Nor does anyone entirely reject the importance of genes. A key objection to nativist assumptions is that they do not contribute to a better understanding of development by sidestepping the developmental process and ascribing all essential factors to the influence of genes. Strictly speaking, there is no development when all is predetermined (Kuo, 1967; Stotz, 2008). This is also Piaget's objection to a theory based exclusively on maturation. Others have pointed out that nativists underestimate the structural importance of children's actions and their environment, and the brain's ability to form patterns within these structures (Blumberg, 2008; Elman et al., 1996).

Many nativist theories are based on infant studies using habituation and visual preference (see Chapter 3). Infants have certain ways of organizing their experiences of the environment, but the nature of this organization and the associated competence are uncertain (Newcombe, 2002). Critics argue that nativists ascribe greater cognitive skills to infants and toddlers than empirically warranted. After all, cognitive development does not end at birth. Compared to older children and adults, infant knowledge is partial and as yet unfinished. Something must be developed, and maturation does not sufficiently explain the process (Campos et al., 2008; Kagan, 2008a; Karmiloff-Smith, 2007). Studies show, for example, that much of the mind understanding ascribed to toddlers on the basis of visual exploration is not yet explicit or consciously accessible at the age of 4 years (see Chapter 13). Just as important as it is to establish what perceptual and cognitive knowledge infants have, is being able to explain *how* this initial knowledge can develop into mature cognitive functioning and reflection (Halford, 1989). This is precisely what developmental models attempt to do. Innate knowledge in itself is relatively inflexible. The more genetically specific one assumes early recognition to be, the more important it is to explain the flexibility that characterizes later cognitive development. The development of specific modules furthermore requires interaction between an extremely large number of genes. Researchers with a background in biology believe it is unlikely that the human organism would use a large proportion of its 23,000 genes or less (Ezkurdia et al., 2014) to develop dedicated processes for number comprehension or facial recognition. Genes have to take care of many other tasks (Nelson et al., 2006b).

Karmiloff-Smith (2009) points out that many theorists seem quick to assume that something is innate when a developmental process is difficult to describe, rather than searching for alternative *developmental* explanations. The nativists' claim that certain forms of knowledge cannot be taught or acquired seems paradoxical in light of their view that the basis of this knowledge can be formed through evolution. The explanation as to why evolution has led to a higher occurrence of some genes than of others is that they contribute to properties that improve the individual's chance of survival. Since the wheels of biology grind slowly, such properties must be useful over a large number of generations. Because environmental conditions tend to constantly change, it is likely that the evolutionary process has taken place based on general environmental characteristics, rather than highly specialized knowledge that mostly improves the chance of survival within a limited ecological niche.

SOCIAL CONSTRUCTIVISM

From a social constructivist perspective, the culture children grow up in affects their thinking through informal interaction as well as formal training (Vygotsky, 1935a, b). One of the key points is that children construct knowledge on their own: "An individual's abilities do not arise from the exercise of individually possessed 'cognitive processes,' but are constructed out of the social interactions an individual is immersed in" (Service et al., 1989, p. 23). *Dialogue, cooperation with others* and the *internalization of cultural tools* provide the main basis for cognitive development, rooted in the activities that incorporate these tools and strategies (Karpov, 2005; Vygotsky, 1962, 1978). Development is therefore characterized by a greater degree of *activity-specific* processes. When social constructivists criticize Piaget for failing to account for social conditions, it is not primarily his lack of interest in the importance of social factors on the development of individual differences. The criticism is directed at the fact that he underestimates the role of social and cultural aspects in cognitive development in general.

Development

Although social constructivists, too, argue that children are born with a biological makeup that determines much of their early cognitive development, it is more a matter of processes that contribute to a child's social orientation rather than of domains of abstract knowledge (Gauvain and Perez, 2015). Individual cognitive resources are not sufficient for the development of higher forms of cognitive functioning. Children depend on adults to convey the knowledge their culture considers important, as well as mental tools and how to use them. It is worth noting that this is the same argument used by nativists to argue that knowledge must be innate – that children are unable to acquire enough knowledge through individual experience with the physical environment alone (see p. 28).

In social-constructivist explanations, cognitive development occurs on two levels: first on the social, second on the psychological level. Initially, it is an interpersonal (intermental) process, followed by an individual (intramental) process. Children are guided to acquire the culture's knowledge and interpretation of the environment, and their cognition changes qualitatively with the activities and social interactions they engage in (Vygotsky, 1962). This point of view differs radically from the Piagetian tradition, in which the child herself develops knowledge at increasingly higher and more conscious levels by processing and organizing experiences.

Cultural tools

While Piaget emphasizes the development of the child's own cognitive structure, the social constructivist theories emphasize the way in which

cultural cognitive tools facilitate thinking. Tools like symbols, calendars and mathematics reflect human knowledge developed over many generations. Children must acquire the use of these tools just as they must learn to use a hammer, a spade and other tools of labor the culture has developed for use by human hands (Karpov, 2005). The most important mental tool is language: children solve practical tasks as much by using language as with their eyes and hands. Language enables children to plan actions and carry out mental actions and causes human memory to work fundamentally differently from that of other species. It is a tool for autonomous thinking and reflection, but also a tool that makes it possible to gain and communicate knowledge, and that facilitates the acquisition of other tools. According to Vygotsky, language is a requirement for developing higher mental functions, while Piaget attributed less importance to language precisely because it is socially acquired, through observing the outside world.

Internalization

Internalization may be the most important process in Vygotsky's developmental model. It entails the transformation of external processes, for example in the form of dialogue or collaboration on problem solving, into internalized psychological processes. The internalization of tools depends on children's participation in social interaction and adult guidance and mediation, since the children are unable to "discover" these tools on their own. The internalization of language and other cognitive tools mediates increased awareness and higher cognitive functioning. By engaging in conversations and collaboration, children acquire new ways of solving problems and gradual mastery of the tools used by their culture. Initially, they use language in interaction with others, subsequently as a tool for abstract reflection. The process of internalization happens gradually, and during early development, children speak out loud when planning and regulating their own behavior or solving tasks because the tool is not yet fully internalized (see p. 243).

This process is illustrated by the development of memory. While the memory of toddlers is based purely on a biological ability to store what is being perceived, adults use language and various other strategies and aids to remember (for example by categorizing things or writing them down). Through interaction with adults, children gradually learn the memory strategies of their culture and integrate the basic functions of memory with conceptual skills, reasoning and narratives.

The types of tools that shape cognition vary from culture to culture. The way in which a culture organizes knowledge forms the basis for the developmental reorganization of categories and the structure of thought. Therefore, the internalization of cultural tools and knowledge from more competent peers and adults is an important basis for continuity across generations as well as cultural variation.

The zone of proximal development

According to Vygotsky, the gradual process of social internalization makes it necessary to distinguish between what children master independently and what they are able to do in collaboration with adults and more competent peers. Things children are unable to master on their own, but together with others, are within their zone of proximal development. In Vygotsky's own words: what children are capable of with help today, they do on their own tomorrow. Children will always be able to do more with help than on their own, but two children capable of doing equally much independently may not be equally susceptible to help – they have different zones of proximal development. Take, for example, two 8-year-olds, both capable of independently solving arithmetic problems typically mastered by children of their age. With help, one of the children can solve arithmetic problems that children are usually able to solve when they are 9 years old, that is, 1 year older. The other child can solve problems that children usually are unable to master before the age of 12. Within this domain, the first child has a zone of proximal development of 1 year and the second child one of 4 years. It is within the zone of proximal development that learning can take place (see p. 291). When one child is able to do more than another and both receive equal help, the first child has a greater *learning potential* in that particular area and at that particular moment than the second child. Vygotsky believes that what children are able to do with help is a better measure of cognitive development than what they can do on their own. This principle is used in dynamic assessment (see p. 52).

In other words, internalization is not the result of a passive intake of socially mediated knowledge, but of a collaborative effort that gradually changes character. Help and guidance from adults (and more competent peers) is part of children's cognitive development and mastery of new tasks. To begin with, it may be the adult who is in charge of nearly all the cognitive resources necessary to solve a task. By interacting, children receive confirmation of previously established skills, acquire new tools and knowledge, and gradually need less help to solve the task. In the end, the necessary tools and their use become internalized and provide children with sufficient cognitive resources to master tasks on their own.

The beginning of the zone of proximal development is defined based on what a child is able to do independently. The point at which children no longer master a task on their own marks the beginning of the zone. Its extent is defined by what the child can do with help. When a maximum amount of help from more competent peers and adults does not enable the child to attempt to solve a task, it means that the task lies outside the child's developmental zone. The child must be able to understand the task and have a strategy in order to try to solve it. The strategy may well be incorrect, but for a task to lie within the zone of proximal development, the child must show an understanding of what the task is about and somehow attempt to approach the task. It is not enough that an adult solves the problem while the child looks on with interest.

In social constructivist theory, development is not domain-general, neither independent performance nor the zone of proximal development. Instead, different zones are associated with separate domains and skills, and children can have strengths and weaknesses in different areas (see Figure 10.4). When children acquire new competence, their independent competence increases and their zone of proximal development changes. Children do not move through the zone, it is the zone itself that changes with the child's growing expertise. For a period of time, a child's development in a given area may consist of an increase in independent performance, while the developmental zone for that domain decreases correspondingly. At other times, only the developmental zone increases. The child is able to do more with help, but does not master more tasks within the domain more independently. At other times, there is an increase in children's independent performance and in what they can do with help (see Figure 10.4).

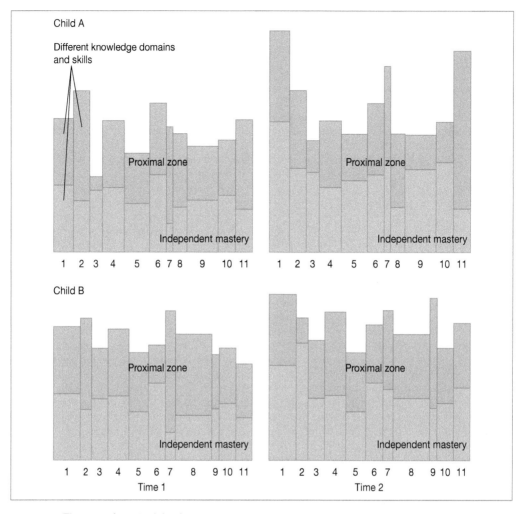

FIGURE 10.4 **The zone of proximal development.**

The figure shows independent performance and the zone of proximal development (what children are able to do with help) for two children at different ages within several knowledge domains and skills. At age level I, these areas show a difference in "width" and "length," and the development within the different domains is also somewhat dissimilar until age II. In domain I, both independent performance and the developmental zone (problem solving with help) have increased from age I to age II in both children. Independent performance has increased in domain 2 and the developmental zone has decreased correspondingly in both children. They have become more independent, but are unable to do more with help than at age level I. In domain 4, the developmental zone of child B has increased (can do more with help), but there is no increase in the child's independent performance. For child A neither independent performance nor the developmental zone have increased in this domain, but child A shows a similar development in domain 11 as child B in domain 4. Child B shows a corresponding development in domain 5 as child A in domain 4. Consequently, the children have different strong and weak domains and skills, and also show a dissimilar development between the two age levels.

Scaffolding

According to social constructivist developmental theories, it is mediation by adults that enables children to acquire the cognitive tools and knowledge of their culture, and the collaboration between adults and children represents an important part of the developmental process. Adults must be able to introduce "tasks" and adapt their mediation to the child's zone of proximal development. If children encounter a task with a degree of difficulty above this zone, they will not understand the task and thus not be able to contribute to its solution. If the task is too easy, solving it will not contribute to the children's development or changes in their zone of proximal development. For tasks located within a given zone, the strategies contributed by adults are known as *scaffolding*, they constitute a flexible external structure that can support the development of the child's ability to solve problems. Scaffolding is mediation: adults attempt to clarify what is required to solve a task, limit those aspects of the task that the child is unable to master – for example by holding an object stationary while the child tries to take something from it – and shield the child from distractions that can draw attention from the task at hand. The scaffold – help and support – is gradually disassembled or reduced, and once the child is able to master a task independently, scaffolding is no longer needed. This means that adults guide the child toward tasks at the child's own level *as well as* offer help that the child actually benefits from.

Too little help can prevent children from being able to solve the task. Too much help can reduce children's trust in their own ability, because the help provided by adults also reflects an evaluation of the child's competence (von Tetzchner, 2009). Both task and help must therefore lie within a child's zone of proximal development if adults are to contribute to the child's development.

Development of leading activities

From a social constructivist point of view, children's cultural participation and activities are part of their cognitive development. Vygotsky and Elkonin describe six phases of children's participation in activities, from intuitive and emotional contact between children and adults to the acquisition of vocational expertise (Box 10.3). Each phase is comprised of a *leading activity* with spe-

---

BOX 10.3 PHASES OF LEADING ACTIVITIES

Vygotsky and Elkonin describe six phases in children's development that are characterized by different leading activities:

1 *The activity of intuitive and emotional contact between the child and adults (0–1 years)*
   This includes a feeling for the need to interact with other people, the expression of emotions, learning to grasp things and a variety of perceptual actions.

2 *Object-manipulation activity (1–3 years)*
   Children adopt socially acceptable ways of handling things, and through interaction with adults they develop speech and visual-perception thinking.

3 *Game-playing activity (3–7 years)*
   Children engage in symbolic activities and creative play. They now have some comprehension of how to cooperate together in group endeavors.

4 *Learning activity (7–11 years)*
   Children develop theoretical approaches to the world of things, a function that involves their considering laws of reality and beginning to comprehend psychological preconditions for abstract theoretical thought (intentional mental operations, schemes for problem solving, reflective thinking).

5 *Social-communication activity (11–15 years)*
   Adolescents gain skills in initiating types of communication needed for solving life's problems, understanding other people's motives and submitting to group norms.

6 *Vocational-learning activity (15–17 years)*
   Older adolescents develop new cognitive and vocational interests, grasp elements of research work and attempt life projects.

The development of activities is characterized by fluctuations between periods of stability and periods of change. The transition from one developmental phase to another disrupts the stability of the child's thinking and interaction with the environment, thereby producing crises as the child struggles to comprehend the next activity that is to occupy the leading role (based on Thomas, 2005).

BOX 10.4 STREET MATHEMATICS AND SCHOOL MATHEMATICS (Nunes et al., 1993)

The study includes four boys and one girl from the poor quarter of the city of Recife in northeastern Brazil. They were between 9 and 15 years of age and had received 1–8 years of schooling, but classroom teaching had been limited. Their arithmetic skills were studied using both informal and formal tests. The informal test was conducted in their natural environment – on the street corner or in the market where they sold coconuts and other goods. The experimenter was the "customer" and purchased goods or inquired about the price of goods she considered buying. The formal test took place at the children's home. The math problems were dictated to the subject (for example 105 + 105) or presented in word form of the type: *Mary bought x bananas; each banana cost y; how much did she pay altogether?* The results showed that the children were able to solve a far greater number of problems in the natural street vending situation than in the more formal tests.

Subject	Informal test	Arithmetic operations	Word problems
M	10.0	2.5	10.0
P	8.9	3.7	6.9
Pi	10.0	5.0	10.0
MD	10.0	1.0	3.3
S	10.0	8.3	7.3

EXAMPLE 1 (M, 12 YEARS)

Informal test

Customer: *I'm going to take four coconuts. How much is that?*
M: *There will be one hundred five, plus thirty, that's one thirty-five . . . one coconut is thirty-five . . . that is . . . one forty!*

Formal test

M solves the item 35×4, explaining out loud: *Four times five is twenty, carry the two; two plus three is five, times four is twenty.* Answer written: 200.

EXAMPLE 2 (MD, 9 YEARS)

Informal test

Customer: *OK, I'll take three coconuts* (at a price of 40 cruzeiros each).
MD: (Calculates out loud) *Forty, eighty, one twenty.*

cific *motives*, *goals* and *actions* that are central to a particular age level and prepare the child for the next phase with a new leading activity. The particular activities are not predefined, and will depend on the culture a child grows up in. In industrialized societies, for example, role play prepares preschool-age children for school, while children in many other societies participate in adult activities from an early age (Morelli et al., 2003). These phases also reflect the way in which social constructivist theories describe children's cognitive functioning on two levels. One level includes the activities children engage in together with more competent adults or peers. This rep-

resents children's "external" thinking. The second level incorporates the changes that occur in children's "internal" thinking. Because the activities in a society are not stable over time, Rogoff (1998) suggests that an understanding of development requires a third level, the *community level*, which includes the technological and cultural development of a society. The cell phone, for example, has changed the patterns in children's social interactions (see Chapter 22). Leontiev and other neo-Vygotskians are further developing the phases in *activity theory* (Karpov, 2005).

When knowledge is acquired only within a specific area or activity, it is not automatically

Formal test

MD solves the item 40 × 3 and obtains 70. She then explains the procedure: *Lower the zero; four and three is seven.*

EXAMPLE 3 (MD, 9 YEARS)

Informal test

Customer: *I'll take twelve lemons* (one lemon is 5 cruzeiros).
MD: *Ten, twenty, thirty, forty, fifty, sixty* (while separating out two lemons at a time).

Formal test

MD has just solved the item 40 × 3. In solving 12 × 15, she explains what she does while trying to solve the problem, and proceeds by lowering first the 2, then the 5 and then the 1, obtaining 152.

EXAMPLE 4 (S, 11 YEARS)

Informal test

Customer: *What would I have to pay for six kilos* (of watermelon at 50 cruzeiros per kilo)?
S: *(Without any appreciable pause) Three hundred.*
Customer: *Let me see. How did you get that so fast?*
S: *Counting one by one. Two kilos, one hundred. Two hundred. Three hundred.*

Formal test

The task: A fisherman caught 50 fish. The second one caught five times the amount of fish the first fisherman had caught. How many fish did the lucky fisherman catch?

S writes down 50 × 6 and 360 as the result, then answers *36*. Examiner (E) repeats the problem and S does the computation again, writing down 860 as the result and answering: *86*.

E: *How did you calculate that?*
S: I did it like this. Six times six is thirty-six. Then I put it there.
E: *Where did you put it?* (S had not written down the number to be carried.)
S: (Points to the digit 5 in 50) That makes eighty-six (apparently adding 3 and 5 and placing this sum in the result).
E: *How many did the first fisherman catch?*
S: Fifty.

transferred to other activities. One study found that 9–15-year-old street vendors in Brazil were able to solve math problems when they sold fruit on the street, but were unable to do so outside the confines of their familiar street vending activities, even if the problems by and large required the same level of math skills (Box 10.4). Similarly, British children who have learned to work out pre-formulated math exercises may encounter difficulties when confronted with practical math problems in text form (Desforges, 1998).

Other studies have demonstrated that different cultural activities can lead to cognitive differences, for example in the development of conservation (see p. 174). Moreover, Vygotsky himself emphasizes the importance of formal education and considers it to be part of the cultural foundation that shapes cognitive development (Karpov, 2014).

Individual and social exploration

By focusing on social and cultural activities, social constructivists have made a unique contribution to the understanding of cognition and cognitive development. Piaget is frequently criticized for his view of children as self-reliant explorers of the physical world, and for failing to take sufficient account of the social context that provides a framework for cognitive development. Yet a similar criticism of bias can be directed at many theorists within the social constructivist tradition. They place little emphasis on the independent and direct exploration of objects that characterizes early development in particular. Children engage with other people, but it takes time before they realize that they can use others to solve the problems they encounter. Even when they are able to ask for such help, they do not always want it. "Do it myself" is virtually a standard phrase among 2–3 year olds. More often it is older children who seek help with problems they are unable to cope with. Part of the reason that children's independent exploration of the physical environment has received little attention within this tradition may be found in the fact that Vygotsky himself rarely studied children under the age of 4 years. Moreover, social constructivist studies have focused specifically on language and cultural activities that involve interaction, such as group play and meals. A theory of cognitive development must include both the exploration children engage in on their own *and* the knowledge that is communicated through cooperation with adults (Gauvain and Perez, 2015).

Status of social constructivism

Social constructivism plays a central role in modern developmental psychology, and is often applied as a counterweight to both logical constructivism and nativism. Although many researchers base their study on the concepts of this tradition, it has lead them down somewhat different paths in Russia, Europe and the US. Many theorists of the Russian school are critical to Western European and North American interpretations of Vygotsky's writings, which they found to be too static (Karpov, 2005). Compared with the other theories, social constructivist ideas seem to have somewhat less influence on research based on brain functioning, which today represents a significant part of developmental science.

The social constructivist tradition has major influence on educational theories and practices. At the same time, it has been criticized for its bias toward adult-communicated knowledge. Damon (1984) emphasizes that also the cooperation with peers provides a unique contribution to children's cognitive development through the exchange of ideas with equal partners. In addition, many studies based on social constructivist theory focus on the interaction between a single adult and child, a fact that most likely reflects the small family size of industrialized countries. Many activities involve numerous participants, particularly in developing countries, but also in highly industrialized societies, children's activities occur in the context of larger groups, such as educational settings (Sommer, 2012).

DISPARITY AND INTEGRATION

Today, the four main traditions of developmental cognitive psychology continue to evolve in different ways. The complexity of cognitive development is reflected in the fact that so far no single description and explanation exist that all can agree on. At the same time, the different theories are expanded and integrated with ideas that lie outside the individual tradition. Several current approaches combine Piaget's constructivist ideas with concepts based on information processing (Barrouillet, 2015; Morra et al., 2008). Concepts from neuroscience are commonly included as well. Both *neuroconstructivism* (Mareschal et al., 2007a, b) and *neoconstructivism* (Johnson and Hannon, 2015) integrate elements from Piaget's theory, connectionism and neuroscience. Nelson's developmental theory (1996, 2007a) uses *events* as a basic unit and is inspired by both Piaget and Vygotsky. Children begin by participating in and learning to master events that are part of their social and cultural world, and subsequently form an understanding of these events. The most important cognitive task is to create *meaning* of events, and it is this search for meaning that drives children's cognitive development.

A discussion of the basic ideas behind these traditions is important in order to reveal disparities between their various explanations (Sokol and Martin, 2006). Nelson (2007a) points out that each tradition in itself is insufficient to explain cognitive development. She is critical of nativism due to its lack of focus on development, as well as to the information-processing tradition, which she believes describes isolated mental processes without accounting for the sense of meaning and coherence that characterizes the human mind.

SUMMARY

1 The central question of theories of cognitive development is how children perceive and adapt to the world around them, retain experiences and develop new knowledge and new ways of categorizing, thinking and reasoning.

2 The theories place varying emphasis on modules, domains and activities. Cognitive processes can be *domain-general*, *domain-specific* or *activity-specific*. Some theorists argue for the existence of innate *neurological modules* that correspond to specific areas of knowledge. Others believe that development is based on a *process of modularization*.

3 *Piaget's theory* has a decisive impact on most approaches to cognitive development. His is the only major theory to describe the development from infant to adult as a coherent developmental pathway of qualitative changes in thinking and reasoning, and to explain how this development takes place. Piaget's key concepts are that thought has its roots in action and that children *construct* their understanding of the world through their experiences with the physical and social environment. Children develop a *cognitive structure* that consists of *schemas*, enabling children to abstract and store experiences. The basic processes are *assimilation*, *accommodation* and *organization* – mental schemas and processes undergo change as children solve problems and acquire new experiences. Development is driven by an innate ability to perceive contradictions and a search for *equilibrium* between established schemas and new experiences. Piaget divides cognitive development into four universal stages: *sensorimotor*, *preoperational*, *concrete operational* and *formal operational*. The cognitive structure manifests itself in the types of tasks children are able to understand and solve in the different stages.

4 Piaget's theory has also received more criticism than any other in the field of cognitive development. Many are skeptical about the role of domain-specific processes and the division into stages, but stage thinking is still present in many theories. Studies show that children are capable of solving similar tasks at a much earlier age than Piaget found by facilitating a different set of circumstances, and often there are significant differences in age levels at which tasks with the same presumed operational structure are mastered. Additionally, there are major differences in how various cultures solve cognitive tasks. Piaget's ideas are being further developed by neo-Piagetians, including his stage theory.

5 The main principle behind Piaget's *new theory* is that schemas are formed when children discover *correspondences* in the external world. Correspondences that go beyond a comparison of identical features are called *morphisms*. They are tools for establishing *constants*, conditions that do not vary across the phenomena in question. Thinking traverses three levels: *intramorphic*, *intermorphic* and *transmorphic*. They do not represent general stages of development; instead, a child's thinking can involve different levels in different domain-specific areas.

6 *Information-processing theories* build on the assumption that all cognitive phenomena can be described as information that flows through one or more processing systems, and search for a set of *basic processes* of human cognition. There are different views on what development consists of. As children develop, they may increase the capacities, perform several processes simultaneously, gain more knowledge and organize it in new ways, develop metacognition and acquire new strategies for solving problems. Critics claim that the computer is not suitable as a model for children's cognitive development and that information processing has a biased focus on children's performance of isolated tasks without placing them in the social and cultural context to which they belong.

7 *Connectionism* uses computer models and simulations to investigate the basic processes underlying different abilities, based on models where external stimulation lead to various

Continued

activating or inhibitory processes. These processes determine what an individual perceives and how he or she acts. Critics point out that connectionism to date has focused mainly on the acquisition of relatively simple perceptual, cognitive and linguistic skills, and not taken sufficient account of the child's own active role in development.

8   *Nativism* is based on the assumption that children are born with a mental "model" of various aspects of the world, and that the brain "knows" something about how to interpret certain forms of stimulation. Genes impose *constraints* on what children can perceive and learn. Studies of cognitive abilities in infants and toddlers constitute an important but also disputed empirical basis. In *strong forms of nativism*, it is largely genes that determine the design of cognition, often in the form of *neurological modules*. Spelke and Kinzler suggest that children begin with a core knowledge of 4–5 modules that form the basis for further development. *Weaker forms of nativism* attribute a somewhat lesser role to genes. According to Gopnik and Meltzoff's *theory-theory*, children are born with a domain-general cognitive structure that enables them to form hypotheses and try them out. Children begin with *innate theories* that are revised as the children gain more experience. Nativism has a strong position in twenty-first century cognitive developmental psychology. Critics point out that there is little room for development because the structure is predetermined. They also argue that nativists ascribe greater cognitive skills to infants than empirically warranted, and that there are major differences between the infant competence inferred from indirect methods and the explicit understanding and ability to apply knowledge in older children.

9   From a *social constructivist* perspective, cognitive development is the result of collaboration between children and adults. Social interaction and cultural knowledge and activities become a part of a child's cognitive structure, and there are cognitive differences between children who grow up under different social and cultural conditions. The acquisition of *cultural cognitive tools*, like language and other symbolic systems, facilitates thinking and makes it possible for children to plan actions, act mentally and reflect, and develop higher mental functions. The internalization of cultural tools requires social interaction, since children are unable to create these tools on their own. The social process of internalization makes it necessary to distinguish between what children master independently and what they are able to do in collaboration with others, their *zone of proximal development*. The strategies contributed by adults are figuratively known as *scaffolding*, a flexible external structure that can support and promote the child's functioning and development. Vygotsky and Elkonin describe six phases or levels of children's participation in activities, further developed by Leontiev and other neo-Vygotskians. Social constructivism has been criticized for placing too little emphasis on the independent exploration that characterizes an infant's early development in particular, and for its bias towards adult-communicated knowledge and the interaction between a single adult and child. Many child activities involve numerous participants, such as educational settings.

10 There is today no single description or explanation of cognitive development that everyone can agree on. All the four main traditions of cognitive development continue to be developed today. They represent significant theoretical and empirical differences, but are also further expanded and integrated with ideas that lie outside the individual tradition.

CORE ISSUES

- The presence of domain-general, domain-specific and activity-specific processes.
- The role of nature and nurture in cognitive development.
- The role of culture in cognitive development.

SUGGESTIONS FOR FURTHER READING

Acredolo, C. (1997). Understanding Piaget's new theory requires assimilation and accommodation. *Human Development, 40*, 235–237.

Cohen, L. B., Chaput, H. H., & Cashon, C. H. (2002). A constructivist model of infant cognition. *Cognitive Development, 17*, 1323–1343.

Karmiloff-Smith, A. (2015). An alternative to domain-general or domain-specific frameworks for theorizing about human evolution and ontogenesis. *AIMS Neuroscience, 2*, 91–104.

Karpov, Y. V. (2005). *The neo-Vygotskian approach to child development*. Cambridge: Cambridge University Press.

Morra, S., Gobbo, C., Marini, Z., & Sheese, R. (2008). *Cognitive development: Neo-Piagetian perspectives*. New York, NY: Lawrence Erlbaum.

Nunes, T., Schlieman, A. D., & Carraher, D. W. (1993). *Street mathematics and school mathematics*. Cambridge: Cambridge University Press.

Piaget, J. (1954). *The construction of reality in the child*. New York, NY: Routledge and Kegan Paul.

Spelke, E. S., & Kinzler, K. D. (2007). Core knowledge. *Developmental Science, 10*, 89–96.

Vygotsky, L. S. (1962). *Language and thought*. Cambridge, MA: MIT Press.

Contents

CHAPTER 11

ATTENTION, MEMORY AND EXECUTIVE FUNCTION

Attention, memory and executive functions are the basis for all daily activities and are necessary for the child to adapt to and cope with the environment. Attention has to do with being alert, obtaining an overview of one's surroundings and focusing on what is important and relevant to the situation. Experiences are processed and stored; they can be recognized or recalled, or otherwise influence children's thoughts and actions. Executive functions serve to regulate attention, plan and monitor the performance of voluntary actions, and inhibit inappropriate action impulses. Since executive functions include attention and working memory, there are no clearly defined boundaries between them.

ATTENTION

Attention is about directing awareness toward what is relevant – like a spotlight – and to confine or expand the attention depending on the activity and the objective. When playing football, a broad attention is functional, while focused attention is more appropriate when solving math problems. Attention is important in the regulation of thoughts and feelings, but the ability to disengage and shift attention to something else can be just as important as focusing attention (Reynolds et al., 2013; Ristic and Enns, 2015). While research on early attention often centers on how long children look at something (Colombo, 2001), hearing and other senses are also governed by attention (Karns et al., 2015).

Attention in the first year of life

The development of attention proceeds through three phases that reflect the different functions of attention (Colombo, 2001). The first phase includes the first 2 months of life and is characterized by increasing alertness and the ability to sustain attention over gradually longer periods of time. Infants gradually look at things for longer, but they have difficulty shifting attention away from something once they have become aware of it (Reynolds et al., 2013).

During the second phase from 3 to 6 months there is an increase in infants' ability to orient themselves and explore their surroundings. Due to faster and more efficient processing of sensory information, they are able to shift attention more frequently. The third stage begins around 7 months; the time infants need to familiarize themselves with new things becomes more stable and increases in duration for more complex stimulation. Throughout the first year of life, infants learn to use attention to regulate their own emotional arousal and distress, for example by looking away when they get too emotionally aroused by what they are looking at, or shifting visual attention away from stimulation that makes them distressed to neutral or positive stimulation (Swingler et al., 2015).

The child's attention focus is also important for the infant's interaction with adults. Parents observe their child's focus of attention, interpret the child's behavior and general state, and direct the child's attention to something neutral or positive when the child seems upset or agitated by something. Development thus progresses from

Solving a puzzle requires attention and working memory.

attention controlled by external stimulation to a greater degree of voluntary attention regulation. Children also improve at filtering stimulation and focusing on what is relevant (Ristic and Enns, 2015), and toward the end of the first year, they begin to become attentive to the attention of others as well (see p. 299).

There are considerable differences between children with typical development, and research has found a relationship between early individual differences in attention and the development of language, cognition and play during later childhood (Reynolds et al., 2013).

Attention development during childhood and adolescence

Younger children have difficulties adapting their attention. With increasing age, their ability to maintain and shift focus improves – they become better at both confining and expanding the boundaries of their attention to a given activity or situation, and to perceive what is relevant and maintain attention there. Children's ability to filter and prioritize stimulation gradually improves during early school age. They are increasingly able to refrain from reacting to stimulation that is not relevant to what they are engaged in, and thus less distractible. There are, however, individual differences in how well children are able to sustain attention on a task and how easily they become distracted by more peripheral stimulation (Ristic and Enns, 2015).

The ability to regulate attention is important in school, where children need to sit still and maintain focused attention on the subject in the classroom. Research shows that young schoolchildren perform many tasks involving attention as well as adults, such as finding specific letters or patterns on a page. However, their attention depends on motivation and content, and on the ability to understand context and meaning. For example, children notice a change in pictures better when the change makes sense or is central than when the change is more peripheral (Fletcher-Watson et al., 2009). Even for adolescents it is difficult to sustain attention when they do not understand the meaning of what is being taught. There may be quite different reasons why a teacher struggles to maintain the attention of a class, but it might be because the children do not understand what the teacher is trying to tell them.

Certain types of stimulation promote attention more than others. Children (and adults) generally react differently to social and non-social stimulation, for example faces and geometric shapes. They are more attentive to faces that express fear or anger than to faces with a neutral or positive emotional expression, and find it difficult to ignore faces that look angry or frightened, perhaps because they convey information that can create both fear and empathy (see Chapter 17). Children are more likely to discover spiders and snakes hidden among mushrooms and flowers in a picture than mushrooms and flowers hidden among spiders and snakes (Waters et al., 2008). However, although infants show high attention to snakes, there is no evidence that they are afraid of snakes or find them aversive (Thrasher and LoBue, 2016).

Children also develop general attention tendencies that determine how they filter stimulation and weigh different cues. This in turn affects how they perceive or misperceive their surroundings. Social cues are often ambiguous, and children develop different tendencies in regard to perceiving emotional cues. Physically aggressive children, for example, tend to be particularly aware of social hostility and to perceive others as threatening (see p. 483) (Arsenault and Foster, 2012; Gouze, 1987). Children who have developed such a tendency may find it difficult to filter out or not react to potential signs of hostility, even when other aspects of the situation indicate that they are irrelevant (Ristic and Enns, 2015). Similarly, shy children tend to be aware of potential cues for social rejection. They have fewer expectations that others might be glad when they look at them, and are more likely to perceive interactions as negative (Kokin et al., 2016).

Attention in atypical development

Children with ADHD have problems sustaining attention and are easily distracted by more peripheral stimulation, but do not necessarily perform poorly on tasks that require them to be alert and orient themselves. Problems are evident in daily life, especially in the educational domain, and many children and adolescents with ADHD perform below their skill level at school (Rogers et al., 2015). Even when symptoms of inattention and hyperactivity decline, children may have significant academic difficulties throughout school, possibly because early inattention impeded acquisition of the basic knowledge and skills that form the basis for later learning (Pingault et al., 2011, 2014; Sasser et al., 2016).

Helping children gain better control over their attention may be effective in early intervention (Posne and Rothbart, 2000). The trajectories of ADHD are related to family characteristics and inconsistent parenting may negatively influence development (Sasser et al., 2016). Early parent education can affect parents' response to their child's behavior and thereby contribute to preventing the development of behavioral problems (Campbell et al., 2014; Danforth et al., 2016). The effectiveness of cognitive behavior therapy for children with ADHD is well documented, but only in connection with the presence of behavioral problems (Antshel and Olszewski, 2014; Tamm et al., 2014). There have been many attempts at attention training but results are modest (Cortese et al., 2015; van der Donk et al., 2015).

Studies suggest that some children with ADHD are sensitive to certain food substances and can benefit from a change in diet (Pelsser et al., 2011). ADHD is often treated with medication but the use of medication is controversial. For some children, drugs can be of help, but they should only be administered once other treatment initiatives have been tried for several months without satisfactory results, and should also always be accompanied by other therapeutic approaches (Rothenberger and Banaschewski, 2004; Sibley et al., 2014). Additionally, drugs have a greater impact on behavior than on learning (Doggett, 2004). Therefore, both with and without medication, it is important to tailor education at school and adopt strategies that reduce the cognitive load to allow children with ADHD to master the daily academic and social challenges they face (Hinshaw and Scheffler, 2014; Tannock, 2007). Many children with ADHD struggle with learning to read and may benefit from intensive reading intervention, independent of their use of medication (Tannock et al., 2018).

Attention deficits are classified as a separate group of disorders (see Chapter 4) but problems with attention are also associated with other neurodevelopmental disorders (Karns et al., 2015). They are not always a matter of attention regulation being better or worse but also of what children and adolescents pay attention to (Burack et al., 2016). Children with autism spectrum disorders are characterized by atypical filtering and focus, and they are often attentive to other aspects of the situation than their peers (Fan, 2013; Keehn et al., 2013). An intervention study with heterogeneous groups of children with intellectual and developmental disabilities did not find positive effects of attention training (Kirk et al., 2017). Attention and distractibility is furthermore affected by problems related to vision (Tadić et al., 2009) and hearing (Dye and Hauser, 2014). Behaviorally inhibited children and adolescents with anxiety tend to pay attention to threat and not to reward, and attentional bias modification is used in anxiety intervention (MacLeod and Clarke, 2015; Shechner et al., 2012).

MEMORY

The mind always makes use of earlier experiences and learning. Memory makes it possible to anticipate the future and create continuity between past, present and future. Speech, writing and other cultural tools also allow for the organization and storage of knowledge beyond the limits of each individual's memory.

The human memory consists of several elements with different functions. The function of short-term memory is to store information for a short period of time, seconds or minutes, often in connection with the performance of another task, such as when children think of the shape of a puzzle piece cut-out while looking for the piece that fits. Working memory also stores information for a short time, but additionally involves some type of processing or organizing information, such as when children learn to pronounce and use a new word. Working memory is about the here-and-now, and has a limited capacity for storing and processing information. It registers information from both the environment and long-term memory, and helps tie together new and previously stored information. At any given time, working memory only contains what is needed at the moment, and forms an integral part of all learning and thinking (Cowan, 2014).

Long-term memory stores information over time, in some cases throughout life. It is considered to have unlimited capacity, and represents the individual's personal and cultural knowledge base. In order to make use of what is stored, children must be able to recall the information whenever it is needed. *Recognition* may be measured by asking children to indicate whether they have seen a particular photograph or action before. Infants, for example, will typically look longer at an unfamiliar image than at one they have seen before (see p. 47). *Recall* is a process of recreation or reconstruction, the individual tells or shows what was observed or experienced. The focus of attention, knowledge and past experiences determine what is being recalled. However, also forgetting and unlearning are important functions of the memory system. They are necessary so that children do not act the same way all the time, but are capable of adapting to constantly changing environments (Bauer, 2014; Cuevas et al., 2015).

From a developmental point of view, the question is how the various parts of the memory system change with age. The most important developmental changes seem to happen between birth and early school age, but changes in memory function continue all the way until adulthood.

Memory in infancy

Memory is functional very early but initially both working memory and long-term memory are severely limited in capacity, and the ability for recall is still lacking.

Working memory

A common method of measuring working memory is to set up a situation with a time gap between an incident and the child's reaction or response to it, such as looking for something that has been hidden after a short delay. The number of seconds a child can be delayed or distracted and still maintain the search for the hidden object is considered to be a direct measure of working memory capacity. Studies using this method indicate a memory span of about 2 seconds for 7-month-old children, 7–8 seconds for 1-year-olds, and 30 seconds for 2½-year-olds (Reznick,

2009). Six-month-olds are able to hold one thing in mind, while 1-year-olds can maintain about three different things in working memory at the same time (Rose et al., 2004; Oakes and Luck, 2014).

Long-term memory

As early as the womb, experiences slowly become embedded in fetal long-term memory. The fact that children only a few days old prefer their mother's voice to unfamiliar voices (see p. 95) shows that certain aspects of the mother's voice are represented in the child's mind.

A common experiment with infants aged 2–6 months is to attach a ribbon to one of their ankles so that they trigger a mobile when kicking with their legs, and see how long they remember the mobile and the movement (Box 11.1). The results show that the duration of children's memory increases significantly in the first 18 months of life but also show early memory is context dependent. Objects used for later recognition had to be identical to those used during training. It is possible to teach 3- and 6-month-old children to move two different mobiles in two different situations, but the learning from one context is not transferred to the other. Infants seem to remember them as independent events (Rovee-Collier and Cuevas, 2009a; Watanabe and Taga, 2006). However, at this age, context-dependence may also have certain advantages. It prevents children from resorting to actions they have learned in situations where they are inappropriate. Infants have poor control over action impulses, and actions should therefore not be too easily activated (Rovee-Collier and Cuevas, 2009b). At 6 months of age, infants begin to draw connections between these types of independent memories, and by the age of 9 months their learning begins to become less context-specific. At this point, infants also become more mobile and exploratory, and need to be able to apply the knowledge they have and learning to new situations (Campos et al., 2000).

Infant memory is dependent on repetition. Repeated actions or events are preserved, while anything that is not repeated disappears or becomes difficult to reactivate, consistent with the brain's synaptic processes (see p. 108). *Refreshment*, whereby children are exposed to all or part of the same incident, therefore has a major impact on how long infants remember. The best effect is achieved while the infant performs the original task, but even a reminder in the form of short exposure to the mobile or the train without triggering their movement leads to a significant increase in the duration of infants' memories. When the mobile was shown to 3-month-old infants for 2 to 3 minutes at a later point, they remembered it for about a week – longer than when they initially learned how to set it in motion. The effect is further increased by using several reminders (Rovee-Collier et al., 1999). In one study, 3-month-old infants were given several reminders and showed no sign of forgetting after 6 weeks (Hayne, 1990). In another study, 6-month-olds learned to start an electric train by pushing a lever. At this age, and without refreshment of memory, infants usually remember the action for 2 weeks. Children who received a 2-minute reminder at the ages of 7, 8, 9, 12 and 18 months showed no signs of forgetting by the age of 2 years (Hartshorn, 2003).

These experiments show that infants can integrate information from two different points in time. However, refreshment must be presented within a certain *window of time*. If no refreshment is given, the original situation will be forgotten, and the next repetition is as a new situation. The retention interval furthermore increases when refreshment occurs at the end, rather than at the beginning of this time window (Rovee-Collier et al., 1993).

The development of memory during childhood and adolescence

Throughout childhood, children continue to explore and expand their knowledge base as the memory system becomes more efficient.

Working memory

The capacity of working memory is commonly measured by the individual's ability to recall numbers. Memory span lies at around two at the age of 2 years, four at the age of 5, five at the age of 7 and six at the age of 12. Many adults have a memory span for numbers of around seven (Dempster, 1981). Another way of testing working memory is to ask children to imitate an action sequence. Children as young as 11 months of age are capable of performing a sequence of two tasks that are demonstrated to them and that they have never carried out before, such as

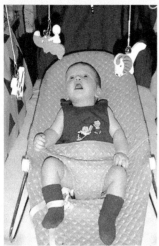  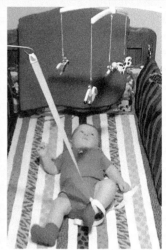

Left: the ribbon is attached to the infant's ankle, but not to the mobile, so the infant can get used to it. The infant looks at the mobile, but the leg is at rest.

Centre: the infant has learned how to move the mobile with the leg.

Right: the ribbon is attached to something else. The infant pulls the ribbon with the leg while looking at the mobile, but the mobile does not move.

(Thanks to the child's parents and Carolyn Rovee-Collier for the use of these photos.)

Infants aged 2–6 months had a ribbon attached to one of their ankles, so that the mobile moved when they kicked their legs. Once the infants had learned this motor activity, the ribbon with the mobile was once again attached to the ankle after a certain length of time. If the infants kicked more with their legs than they did in a similar situation without the ribbon and mobile, the action was considered to be remembered.

Two-month-olds remembered the mobile and leg movement for 1 day, but not for 3 days. Three-month-olds remembered perfectly for 3 to 4 days, but had forgotten the mobile and the movement after 6 to 8 days. However, objects in the mobile had to be identical to those used during training. When more than one of the objects on the mobile was replaced, infants no longer showed any retention after 1 day. Three-month-olds recognized the mobile after 1 day, even in a new environment, but after 3 days they only recognized it as long as an identical ribbon was attached to their ankle or wrist. When the color of the ribbon was changed, the infants' recognition was significantly reduced, and when it was placed in a different room, they showed no recognition.

After as little as 1 day, even older infants did not recognize the mobile used during training if it was presented in a new context. It is possible to teach 3- and 6-month-old children to move two different mobiles in two different situations, but the learning from one context is not transferred to the other. Infants seem to remember them as independent events.

putting a button inside a box and shaking it like a rattle. At 20 months of age, children are able to imitate tasks consisting of three parts, and 4 months later, five parts. Children aged 2½ years are nevertheless able to imitate the construction of a house in eight parts: pour sand on the house, put a nail into a precut hole, hammer in the nail, use a saw on the house, load up a truck with blocks, put a pipe on the roof and paint the house (Bauer and Fivush, 1992). This reflects the fact that these types of tasks depend less on language skills and carry more meaning for children.

The development of children's performance on tasks requiring the use of working memory is also linked to the formation of concepts. Children aged 7–9 years who know a lot about soccer, for example, remember more objects from an image related to soccer (such as the soccer ball, shoes and goal) than an image with objects unrelated to soccer (such as a bike, a banana and a hammer), while there is no corresponding difference among children who have little knowledge of soccer (Schneider and Bjorklund, 1992). When the things to be remembered are less familiar, more of the capacity of working memory is used for encoding and organization, and less for storage (Alexander and Schwanenflugel, 1994).

As they grow older, children improve at making use of *memory strategies*, such as saying aloud or silently the things to be remembered (Bjorklund et al., 2009). In an experiment with 5- to 10-year-old children, only two 5-year-olds out of 20 verbally articulated what they had seen for themselves, compared with half of the 7-year-olds and 17 of the 10-year-olds (Flavell et al., 1966). Organizing objects that belong together into groups is also a common memory strategy. Younger children who are encouraged to do so, however, or who try to group objects on their own in connection with memory tasks, go about it in such an unsystematic way that it is of little help in practice. Only from about the age of 10 do children begin to apply this type of categorization effectively (Bjorklund et al., 2009). This shows that children's use of strategies is less automatized than that of adults. Even when younger children have learned a number of strategies, they do not always apply the best strategy when performing a task. Working memory capacity and utility therefore continue to develop into adolescence (Isbell et al., 2015; Luciana et al., 2005).

Long-term memory

Children are aware of and remember much of what goes on around them, thus keeping what they are learning about the world. At the end of the first year of life it is not unusual for them to observe someone's action and perform it themselves at a later time. Thirteen-month-olds are to some degree able to remember a sequence of actions shown to them. After 1 week they remember less, although it is still possible to detect some recollection. Twenty-month-olds show few signs of forgetting short actions after 2–6 weeks – their recollection is as good as it was

right after the action (Bauer, 1997). Thus, toddlers are able to remember individual actions for a considerable length of time, while the temporal sequence of actions is more difficult to recall, especially if it is non-functional. When preschoolers recount baking cookies together with someone, they follow the course of events. When they talk about a shopping trip, the order is random (Fivush, 1997). This is not only because the sequence of baking cookies must occur in a certain order. Children who had not seen the event sequence were unable to find out how to perform the actions on their own.

It is not always necessary to show an action sequence several times for it to be remembered, but children who have seen it repeatedly will remember more of it for a longer time. Children aged 13–15 months who were shown an action once were able to remember it for a week, but had largely forgotten it after a month. Children who were shown the action three times in the course of 1 week remembered the action just as well after a month as after a week (Bauer et al., 1995). Similarly, children aged 2–2½ who had seen an action twice remembered as much after 3 months as they did after 2 weeks, and far more than children who had seen it only once (Fivush and Hamond, 1989). These findings show that repetition and refreshment continue to be important for memory retention during toddler age as well, especially if the actions are complex and consist of several parts. Repetition also implies that an action is important and worth remembering. Toddlers often ask for stories that engage them to be told over and over again (Nelson, 2014).

Toddlers are not as dependent on similarity with the original situation as infants, but similarity continues to be of importance. Eighteen-month-olds where shown a puppet action with a toy cow and were able to reproduce the action sequence with the cow the next day. But when the children were asked to perform the action sequence with a toy duck, they seemed to have forgotten everything. Children who were 3 months older had no difficulty performing the action sequence with a different puppet (Hayne et al., 1997). When children aged 3 and 5 years were asked to verbally recall or demonstrate a play action they had participated in, the older children told more about it than the younger ones, but both groups conveyed an equal amount of information by demonstrating the action. This was only the case, however, as long as the situations were identical. When new toys and small changes were introduced to the action during repetitions, the group of 5-year-olds recalled far more than the younger children. When asked to perform a similar but not identical task, 5-year-olds were able to do so without a problem, while the 3-year-olds seemed not to know what to do (Fivush et al., 1992).

In order to recall an action, infants must perform or observe it once again on their own, while older children can also be reminded verbally or by using videos and images. Photographs along with verbal narration were an effective reminder for 2-year-olds, but not for children 6 months younger. A verbal reminder about a previous activity had an effect on the memory of 3-year-olds, but not on that of 2-year-olds (Hudson, 1993; Hudson and Sheffield, 1995).

Just like adults, children remember best things that are important and meaningful to them (Nelson, 2007a, 2014). One study found that 4-year-olds remembered more grocery items when this involved foods they were supposed to make lunch with than when they were simply asked to remember items read to them from a list (Mistry et al., 2001). Events that are perceived to be important can be remembered for a long time, like a popcorn fire (Box 11.2). The earliest interviews suggested that the 4-year-olds had understood far more of the fire situation than the 3-year-olds. Since the incident was more meaningful to them, they had better recall, even at the age of 11. In addition, it is likely that the 4-year-olds talked more about the incident at home and thus established it more firmly in their memory (Neisser, 2004).

During school age, the development of memory is primarily associated with the formation of concepts and cognitive development in general. Throughout childhood, children become faster and more efficient at processing, storing and recalling information, and able to remember more complex events and details. In adolescence, memory reaches its peak and has become integrated, coherent and consistent (Howe, 2015; Schneider, 2015).

Memory and language

Language is important for the organization of memory – it is language that makes it possible

---

BOX 11.2 REMEMBERING A FIRE IN THE KINDERGARTEN (Pillemer et al., 1994)

In 1984, a kindergarten at Wellesley College Child Study Center was abruptly evacuated because the popcorn someone was making had caught fire. The children were told to sit by the sandboxes in the outside playgrounds while the firefighters entered the building and turned off the alarm. The teachers and children then returned to their classrooms.

Two weeks later, 12 children with an average age of 3;8 and 16 children aged 4;7 years were interviewed individually, and asked: "What happened when you heard the fire alarm?" This open-ended question was followed by six direct questions about the child's personal circumstances at the time, such as where he or she had been and what they were doing. The narratives of the 3-year-olds and the 4-year-olds differed considerably. Of the 4-year-olds, 15 of the 16 said they were inside the building when the alarm went off, while of the 3-year-olds, seven of the 12 said they were already assembled outside at that point. Twelve of the older children and four of the younger ones told that they had felt it was important to leave the building. Seven of the 4-year-olds mentioned the cause of the fire alarm, compared with only one of the 3-year-olds.

The children were interviewed 7 years later, when children from the younger group were 10;11 and the older group 11;11 years old. The children were asked open-ended questions about their memories of (1) anything special or unusual that happened in preschool, (2) a very loud noise at school and (3) hearing the fire alarm. The 25 children who reported having a memory were asked six direct questions about a) the child's location when the alarm sounded, b) the child's ongoing activity, c) the cause of the alarm, d) the child's feelings at the time, e) other people's feelings and f) what happened after hearing the alarm. Eight of the 14 children in the older group remembered the incident, and four were able to provide a coherent description of what had happened. Nine of the 11 younger children had forgotten the incident and only two children were able to give a fragmentary account of the event sequence.

for people to "travel" in time and reflect on the past and future. Language also makes it possible to take part in the experiences of others, share one's own experiences, and refresh one's memory without reliving the event (Nelson, 2007b, 2014).

Studies show that children can remember some of what they experienced before they learned to speak and in the earliest stages of language development, but also that there is a connection between children's ability to express themselves verbally when they experience something, and their ability to tell about it at a later point. Bauer and Werkera (1995, 1997) observed 13- to 20-month-old children at regular intervals for a year after the children had seen a specific action for the first time, such as someone hanging up a metal gong and striking it. Most of the children spoke spontaneously in all of the situations, and approximately half of what they talked about had to do with the action they had observed. There was a significant statistical rela-

tionship between children's verbal ability at the time they observed the action and how much they told about it later on. Their understanding of language, however, had little impact on how much they were able to describe later, and their expressive verbal skills were not decisive for how much of the action they performed, only for what they told about the action. The children who gave the most complete verbal descriptions were not always the ones who performed most of the original action.

Similarly, another study found that 27- to 39-month-old children were unable to "translate" a spectacular pre-linguistic experience into verbal narrative (Box 11.3). The decisive element was the children's ability to express themselves verbally at the time the event was stored, rather than when it was recalled from memory. Nevertheless, children's understanding of language may have an impact on how well they can take advantage of language support from their parents in remembering past events (Lukowski et al., 2015).

BOX 11.3 TODDLERS REMEMBERING THE MAGIC SHRINKING MACHINE (Simcock and Hayne, 2002)

Children aged 27 to 39 months were shown a "magic shrinking machine" that could turn big toys into small ones. Each child was visited at home and invited to play with the machine. First the child was shown how to turn on the machine by pulling down a lever that activated an array of lights on the front panel. Then the experimenters took a toy from a large case and placed it inside the Magic Shrinking Machine, where it disappeared from view. The experimenter then turned a handle on the side of the machine to produce a series of unique sounds. When the sounds stopped, the child was shown how to retrieve a smaller, yet identical toy from a door on the front of the machine.

This was a fascinating experience for the children, and all of them remembered it 6 and 12 months later, although fewer after 12 than after 6 months, and the amount remembered increased with the age of the child at the event. The children were asked first to describe (verbally) what they had observed, then asked if they remembered more when they were shown a photograph of the original event, and finally to re-enact it (non-verbally). They remembered the greatest proportion of information when they reenacted the event, and the smallest proportion when they had to use language to tell about it. Their performance with the photograph was intermediate between these two. The verbal accounts were related to the children's expressive language skills at the time they first observed the "shrinking process." Even though they had acquired the necessary words in the meantime, they were not able to "translate" pre-linguistic experiences into verbal narrative. This shows that the decisive element was children's verbal ability at the time the event was stored, rather than when it was recalled from memory.

Memories of personally experienced events need not be verbal, but can include visualizing an event in the form of mental imagery. Nevertheless, language is an important tool for organizing events, and a requirement for personal narratives. There is, in other words, a close relationship between the organization of event memories and language. The previous studies also demonstrate that the extent to which children are capable of expressing themselves verbally does not always reflect their ability to remember. Several studies have found that 5-year-old children were able to communicate twice as much information when asked to perform what they had seen rather than describe the event in words (Goodman et al., 1990). Younger children's limited language skills can therefore easily result in underestimating their ability to remember.

Scripts

Children's lives do not consist of individual and unique events alone, but include many routines that involve recurring actions with larger and smaller variations (Hudson and Mayhew, 2009). These routines seem to be organized in the form of script-based memory. A script is a mental representation of what usually happens within a given context – the sequence of events, what is being said, and so on (Nelson, 2007a; Schank and Abelson, 1977). Some scripts reflect special family routines, but many scripts relate to common cultural practices.

The question is: When and how do children begin to acquire this type of knowledge? The earliest scripts consist of simple interaction routines children engage in, such as mealtime, shopping, visiting grandma, various forms of play, dressing and undressing, relaxing, going on a car trip, and so on (Nelson and Gruendel, 1981). Over time, children create an extensive inventory of scripts for various events.

A common method of gaining insight into script knowledge is to ask children to describe their everyday events, such as dinner at home, their day at school or a birthday party. When children describe these types of situations, they usually use the second-person singular (you) and present tense, rather than the first-person (I) and past tense, as they do when describing a particular event they have experienced. Younger children have shorter and less elaborate scripts than older children (see Box 11.4).

The question is how script is formed. One possibility is that children initially acquire a large number of experiences and subsequently abstract a script based upon them. However, the fact that children seem to begin to acquire scripts at an early age suggests that the script is a basic way for human beings to organize experiences, with age-related changes in content. Children appear to begin with a schematic script that grows in detail as they gain more experience, rather than a script that arises as an abstraction of several similar experiences. Although older children have more elaborate scripts than younger children, presumably the result of greater experience as well as more advanced linguistic and cognitive development, their scripts have the same basic temporal characteristics. Their scripts are described in essentially the same manner, but older children's experience contributes to more complexity and detail.

Autobiographical memory

There are major differences between a personally experienced event and one communicated by someone else. Events children have merely been told about, or which they have seen on video, result in far less robust memories. Even stories that are told repeatedly are not remembered as well as those experienced by children themselves (Fivush, 2011).

Autobiographical memory consists of temporal sequences of significant personal events, something that happened to one's self – me – at a particular time and place (Prebble et al., 2013). While autobiographical memory forms the basis for the development of a temporally extended self (see Chapter 21), this self is also integrated with the organization of memories of personally experienced events (Howe, 2015). This form of memory seems to emerge around the age of 3 to 4 years (Nelson, 2007a; Peterson, 2002). Fivush and Hamond (1990) found that 2½-year-olds had relatively little interest in talking about their experiences, while the same children were more than willing to do so at the age of 4.

To begin with, children's stories consist of fragments, such as *food for breakfast*, *luggage for the trip* or *a special toy* (Nelson, 2014). Early representations of personal events are not always chronological, but organized around a theme, such as this monologue by 21-month-old Emmy (Nelson, 1996):

BOX 11.4 SCRIPT FOR BIRTHDAY PARTIES FROM CHILDREN AGED 3–8 YEARS (Nelson and Gruendel, 1981, p. 135)

3;1   *You cook a cake and eat it.*

4;9   *Well, you get a cake and some ice cream and then some birthday (?) and then you get some clowns and then you get some paper hats, the animal hats and then and then you sing "Happy Birthday to you", and then then then they give you some presents and then you play with them and then that's the end and they go home and they do what they wants.*

6;7   *First, uhm... you're getting ready for the kids to come, like puttin' balloons up and putting out party plates and making cake. And then all the people come you've asked. Give you presents and then you have lunch or whatever you have. Then... uhm... then you open your presents. Or you can open your presents anytime. Uhm...*

you could... after you open the presents, then it's probably time to go home, if you're like at Foote Park or something, then it's time to go home and you have to drive all the people home. Then you go home too.

8;10   *Well, first you open your mail box and get some mail. And then you see that there's an invitation for you. Read the invitation. Then you ask your parents if you can go. Then you ... uhm ... go to the birthday party and after you get there you usually wait for everyone else to come. Then usually they always want to open one of the presents. Sometimes then they have three games, then they have the birthday cake then sometimes they open the other presents or they could open them up all at once. After that they like to play some more games and then maybe your parents come to pick you up. And then you go home.*

The broke, car broke, the . . . Emmy can't go in the car. Go in green car. No. Emmy go in the car. Broken. Broken. Their car broken, so Mommy Daddy go in their their car, Emmy Daddy go in the car, Emmy Daddy Mommy go in the car, broke. Da . . . da, the car . . . their, their, car broken.

Emmy is using private speech to reflect and make sense of her experiences; the monologue is private in a double sense: it is directed at herself and recorded without anybody being present (Nelson, 2015b). Nine months later, at the age of 2½ years, Emmy was able to describe her experiences in a far more organized and coherent way:

We bought a baby, . . . cause, . . . the, well because, when she, well, we thought it was for Christmas, but when we went to the s-s-store we didn't have our jacket on, but I saw some dolly,

and I yelled at my mother and said I want one of those dolly. So after we were finished with the store, we went over to the dolly and she bought me one. So I have one.

Thus, children's descriptions gradually become more coherent, although they contain little detail during early childhood. One boy summed up his camping trip as follows: *First we eat dinner, then go to bed, and then wake up and eat breakfast.* With increasing age, knowledge of oneself and one's surroundings becomes more firmly integrated and permanent (Howe, 2015).

What children spontaneously talk about when asked to describe earlier experiences becomes curtailed over time, but if they are shown objects or pictures of the event, they are able to remember many details. What they describe can also change. One study found that preschool children related equally much about holiday trips and birthday parties after a few weeks and 1 year. Most of what the children described was correct, but relatively little of what they talked about during each of these two periods dealt with the same events (Peterson, 2002). Another study of children who had visited the emergency room between the ages of 12 and 33 months followed up with interviews after 6, 12 and 18 months. The youngest children (12–18 months) did not remember anything about the visit 18 months later, while the middle group (20–25 months) remembered certain details. The older children (26–33 months) remembered a good deal after 1 year, and even more after 2 years. They told many things that were incorrect, but the proportion of correct information remained the same. This means that they added both correct and incorrect elements (Peterson and Rideout, 1998). Older children are able to remember events for many years, but they, too, change the content of their stories. Children's accounts of events that lie far back in time often contain more general information (Peterson, 2002), illustrating that children (and adults) combine event-specific knowledge with script elements when describing something they experienced long ago.

Children must learn to talk about the past in general before they can construct a personal narrative. By talking with parents and other adults about events that have occurred, children construct the basis for their autobiographical memory by internalizing these conversations (Nelson, 2007a; Nelson and Fivush, 2004). In the case of preschoolers, personally experienced events and coherent stories in conversation with parents result in the best recall and description by children afterwards. Four-year-olds had better recall of those parts of an event their mothers had talked about than of the rest of the event. In addition, they remembered the information they had discussed with their mother better than that described by the mother or by themselves alone (Tessler and Nelson, 1994). This demonstrates how children create their own world through conversations with adults. Children can remember events they have experienced on their own, but the memories of these events are generally neither as complete nor as accurate.

In line with this, parents' conversational style affects children's autobiographical memory, and thus how they perceive themselves, other people

and events in the world. When parents use a *high elaborative style*, they help their child remember by expanding and verbally elaborating the child's narratives, emphasizing key elements, providing situational details, evaluating events and asking many questions. A *low elaborative style* means that parents are more passive and ask fewer, more general, and partly redundant questions. The parents' style seems to remain relatively stable, even if parents tend to become more elaborative as children get older, but can be changed. Children of mothers who had received elaborative-style training remembered more from a camping trip than children of mothers who had not received such training (Boland et al., 2003). Children of parents with a high elaborative style talk about their experiences in a more coherent and evaluative way (Fivush et al., 2006). In addition, conversations reflect the child's temperament, gender and other traits. Both mothers and fathers talk more about shared experiences and use a more elaborative style with their daughters than with their sons, at least in Western cultures. Neither do children share their experiences with their parents alone – also grandparents, siblings and friends help to shape children's autobiographical memories (Fivush et al., 2006; Fivush and Nelson, 2004).

In childhood and adolescence, the process that began in early infancy is brought to completion, and the autobiography gains more context and detail. Older children and adolescents get better at structuring their descriptions, talk more about the causes and contexts of actions rather than merely describing them, and position their experiences on a personal timeline. In addition to who was involved, what happened, how it was done and where and when it occurred, personal narratives also involve a subjective perspective and evaluation. Seven-year-olds typically include three such narrative elements, while 11-year-olds use twice as many, and girls generally a few more than boys. In adolescence, personally experienced events are increasingly associated with both earlier experiences and possible future events (Bauer, 2013). At this age, the development of identity also assumes a central role (see Chapter 21).

Autobiographical memories are about a self in a world of other people, a development that is also shaped by culture (Alea and Wang, 2015; Nelson, 2014). Cultural differences manifest themselves in personal narratives as early as preschool age. In China, mothers typically use conversation to emphasize the moral aspects of an event, while mothers in the United States ask more questions and focus more on the child's personal views. US mothers are, in other words, characterized by a higher elaborative style than Chinese mothers. When US and Chinese children were asked to describe an important event such as a birthday or an occasion when their mother scolded them, US schoolchildren told long and detailed stories that focused on themselves and their feelings, while the stories of the Chinese children were more frail and emotionally neutral, with greater focus on social interaction and routines, and their own social role in the event (Wang, 2001, 2004).

Memories of negative and traumatic events

Children's lives consist of minor and major joys and sorrows, of positive, negative and neutral events. Some children experience dramatic and traumatic events such as getting hurt in an accident, being hit by a tsunami or other natural disaster, or being subjected to physical and sexual abuse (Quas and Fivush, 2009). When comparing children's memories of emotionally neutral and positive events with their memories of stressful and traumatic events, it appears that moderately stressful events are remembered better than positive and more neutral events (Bauer, 2006). Therefore, it has been speculated that negative events are remembered better because knowledge of such events may be more important for the individual's protection and survival than knowledge of positive and neutral events (Howe, 2015; Cordón et al., 2004; Wallin et al., 2009). This may also be related to the fact that increased arousal or motivation lead to better recall – up to a certain point. Beyond this point, memory is weakened. Children who cried a great deal during a stressful medical examination, for example, remembered less than children who did not cry as much, but what they remembered was accurate (Peterson and Warren, 2009). Negative events may create an attentional bias and preparedness for negative events (McLaughlin and Lambert, 2017; see p. 386). However, even children growing up in dangerous environments like the Gaza Strip report more early memories of play and visits to nice places than of traumatic events (Peltonen et al., 2017).

Many dramatic events are remembered for a long time. Sometimes children are able to recall more after a long time than they did immediately following the incident. Children who had experienced Hurricane Andrew in New Orleans in 1992, for example, were able to give twice as much information about the event when they were interviewed at 10–11 years of age, compared with their interviews right after the hurricane at the age of 3–4 years. There was much talk about the event at the time, and it is likely that the children's stories were equally based on the descriptions of others as on their own experiences, in addition to the fact that they had gained more knowledge about the world in general (Fivush, 2009; Fivush et al., 2004). The importance of working through experiences together with adults is also demonstrated by the fact that children of mothers who frequently talk about everyday and non-stressful events remember more details than children whose mothers do not talk as much. However, it is not certain whether the children actually remember more, or whether they simply are willing to talk more, and therefore also provide more information (Peterson and Warren, 2009).

Childhood amnesia

The research presented here leaves no doubt that children under the age of 3 years are able to remember and recount specific experiences both verbally and by acting them out. Adults, on the other hand, rarely remember experiences from before the age of 3, although some can remember events from their second year of life (Rubin, 2000). They remember considerably more from the ages of 3 to 6 years, but memories from this period are difficult to recall for adults, and generally fragmented (Hayne and Jack, 2011; Pillemer and White, 1989). In a classic study, Sheingold and Tenney (1982) asked students about events surrounding the birth of a younger sibling that could be verified by the mother and other family members. Students who were under the age of 3 years at the time the sibling was born were unable to answer some of the questions, while those who were 7 years and above at the time of their sibling's birth were able to answer most of the questions.

Early memories seem to begin to fade by the age of 4–6 years; from 8–10 years of age, children and adolescents remember approximately as much of their first 3 years of life as adults do (Howe, 2015). In one study on early memories in children aged 4–13 years, many of the youngest children (4–7 years) remembered events from before the age of 2, but most of them did not remember the event 2 years later, even though they had talked about it at the time. New events had taken their place, and the average age for the earliest memory increased from 32.0 to 39.7 months. The oldest children were between 10 and 13 years old at the time of the original interview, and 2 years later mostly recalled the same events as in the first interview (Peterson, 2012; Peterson et al., 2011). Bauer and Larkina (2014) found that children aged 5–7 years remembered 70 percent of events from the age of 3, while 8- to 9-year-olds remembered somewhat less than 40 percent of the same events. There was also a marked transition between the age of 8 and 9 years.

Freud (1905) was the first to use the term "childhood amnesia" about the fact that individuals rarely remember anything from their 3 first years of life. He believed childhood amnesia was caused by the repression of sexual and aggressive feelings toward the parents. This is an unlikely explanation, since memories of many different types of events are affected, rather than only events involving feelings toward the parents. A more up-to-date explanation is that the neurological structures responsible for storing memories undergo significant development during the first 2 years of life, and that early memories are not adequately stored and integrated (Olson and Newcombe, 2014). Bauer and Larkina (2014) suggest that childhood amnesia is not caused by a failure to store events, but rather that events are forgotten because the memories are too unstable and contain too few cues to become firmly embedded in memory. The youngest children in their study remembered a great deal for a long time, but were unable to clearly position the events in time. The memory structure and cognitive abilities of older children and adults differ to such a degree from those of infants that they are unable to recall events based on the same cues they used for storage at an earlier age, causing them to be forgotten (Bauer, 2015). In addition, the lack of linguistic labels during storage can make it difficult to recall the events (Peterson, D. J. et al., 2016).

Another type of explanation is that infants do not have the mental capacity to deal with perceptions of the world that are in conflict with each other. Therefore, it is a functional advantage to forget past conceptions when new ones take their place (Freeman and Lacohée, 1995). This view is corroborated by experiments in which children were shown a Smarties box and asked what they think it contains. Naturally, the children answered *Smarties*. When the box was opened, the children saw that it contained pencils instead of chocolate. When asked what they thought was in the box, children under 3–4 years of age insisted that they themselves had said they thought it was pencils (see p. 247). In the very first years of life, children often encounter events that invalidate their assumptions in a similar, although less clear, way as in the Smarties experiment. Besides, much of what children learn in the first years of their lives is not as useful at a later age and replaced by new knowledge as part of children's adaptive process (Rovee-Collier and Gerhardstein, 1997). Therefore, children rarely remember anything from this time in their lives. It is not an expression of a deficit or failure on the part of the child, but of the functionality of the cognitive system.

False memories

Recall is a form of re-creation, and can occasionally be affected by later acquired knowledge, resulting in incorrect memories. It has been shown that false memories – intentionally or unintentionally – can be grafted onto memory long after an incident allegedly occurred, providing the event is a likely one (Belli, 2012; Howe, 2015). Piaget (1951) recounts that he himself for 10 years had distinct memories of having been the subject of a kidnapping attempt as an infant. In reality, it was his nanny who had invented the story. Loftus (1993) describes an experiment in which a (collaborating) adolescent got his 14-year-old brother, Chris, to "remember" that he got lost in a department store at the age of 5 years (Box 11.5). The study demonstrates that it is not easy to distinguish between real and false memories, especially when the false memories are reinforced by a well-known and trusted person.

BOX 11.5 **AN EXPERIMENT OF INDUCED MEMORY (Loftus, 1993, p. 532)**

In this experiment Jim implanted a false memory in his 14-year-old brother, Chris. Jim told his younger brother the following story as if it was true:

It was 1981 or 1982. I remember that Chris was 5. We had gone shopping at the University City shopping mall in Spokane. After some panic, we found Chris being led down the mall by a tall, oldish man (I think he was wearing a flannel shirt). Chris was crying and holding the man's hand. The man explained that he had found Chris walking around crying his eyes out just a few moments before and was trying to help him find his parents.

Just 2 days later, Chris recalled his feelings about being lost:

That day I was so scared that I would never see my family again. I knew that I was in trouble.

On the third day, he recalled a conversation with his mother:

I remember mom telling me never to do that again.

On the fourth day:

I also remember that old man's flannel shirt.

On the fifth day, he started remembering the mall itself:

I sort of remember the stores. I remember the man asking me if I was lost.

A couple of weeks later, Chris described his false memory and he greatly expanded on it.

I was with you guys for a second and I think I went over to look at the toy store, the Kay-bee toy and uh, we got lost and I was looking around and I thought, "Uh-oh. I'm in trouble now." You know. And then I ... I thought I was never going to see my family again. I was really scared you know. And then this old man, I think he was wearing a blue flannel, came up to me ... he was kind of old. He was kind of bald on top ... he had like a ring of gray hair ... and he had glasses.

When the experiment was completed, Chris was told that his memory of getting lost was false. He replied:

Really? I thought I remembered being lost ... and looking around for you guys. I do remember that. And then crying. And mom coming up and saying "Where were you. Don't you ... Don't you ever do that again."

Intentional inducing of false memories is rare, but the integration of earlier and more recent memories, or the filling in of missing event information, can lead to "memory illusions." The incidence of spontaneous false memories increases with age, probably because older children have more knowledge than younger children, who are not able to fill in missing information to the same extent. Studies have furthermore shown that negative false memories result in greater susceptibility to memory illusions than positive memories (Howe, 2015). Claims of recalling memories from a very early age should therefore be treated with skepticism, and should not be taken at face value in evaluating a given course of events. In recent years, newspapers and magazines have written about cases in which adults have brought accusations against their parents, claiming that they were sexually abused as infants and toddlers. These memories usually emerged in therapy or under hypnosis. Unfortunately, the abuse of young children occurs all too frequently, but based on such newly established recollections, it is difficult to distinguish memories of actual experiences from false memories, such as those elicited by leading questions from a psychologist, psychiatrist or other professional (Loftus and Davis, 2006; McNally, 2012).

Memory and atypical development

Memory is central to all cognitive and social activity. Therefore, problems related to the functioning of the memory system can be found in many different types of disorders (Peterson, C. et al., 2016). Learning and reading place high demands on the ability to remember. Children's memory thus has a major impact on their academic performance, and measurement of working memory is a better predictor of academic achievement than IQ (DeMarie and López, 2014). Children with ADHD and other attention disorders often have reduced working memory capacity (Martinussen et al., 2005). Limited capacity of working memory and difficulty finding and activating words are considered important underlying factors in language disorders and dyslexia (Montgomery et al., 2009; Vulchanova et al., 2014). A relation has also been found between math disorders and working memory (Raghubar et al., 2010).

Children with intellectual disabilities generally have problems storing, organizing, and recalling memories. Also children with severe epilepsy can experience difficulties with working memory and storage in long-term memory (Peterson, C. et al., 2016). Problems with memory is a core characteristic of childhood dementia in children and adolescents with juvenile neuronal ceroid lipofuscinosis (see p. 58). High functioning children with autism spectrum disorder have more problems with verbal recall than their peers. Their descriptions of past events typically lack both detail and emotional content (Andersen et al., 2013). Children who have been subjected to severe neglect and abuse can be vulnerable to memory impairment (Peterson, C. et al., 2016).

There exists a number of programs for training working memory in children with typical development and with ADHD, autism spectrum disorders and learning disorders, and promising results have been reported (Holmes and Gathercole, 2014; Hovik et al., 2013; Klingberg et al., 2002; Wass et al., 2012). However, the results are inconsistent and larger analyses of working memory training studies indicate that the training produces short-term, specific training effects that do not generalize to general problem solving and behavior, and thus may have little clinical relevance (Cortese et al., 2015; Melby-Lervåg et al., 2016; Morra and Borella, 2015; Roberts et al., 2016; van der Donk et al., 2015; von Bastian and Oberauer, 2014).

Children as witnesses

Sometimes it is necessary to gain precise knowledge about a child's experiences. This can involve aspects of the child's daily life, but the need for knowledge about children's ability to relate events they have been involved in arises particularly in connection with possible sexual or other abuse, sometimes murder of close relatives (Christianson et al., 2013; McWilliams et al., 2013). In abuse cases, children are usually the only witnesses, and their testimony may be decisive for the outcome (Roberts and Powell, 2001). Many countries have seen dramatic court cases in which the way children were interrogated, and how their testimony was interpreted, has been a central issue (see Bruck et al., 2006).

Children can be reliable witnesses, sometimes more so than adults. Exactly how much children remember, however, depends on whether they perceived a given event as important and meaningful. Children can also have difficulty keeping events apart (Nelson, 2007b; Roberts, 2002). Information about the time of events often play an important role in legal proceedings but can be difficult to ascertain, especially from young children (Friedman et al., 2010, 2011; Orbach and Lamb, 2007). In addition, testimony can concern aspects that are difficult for children to understand and relate to, and giving evidence can be a stress factor in itself.

With open questions such as "Tell me what happened," younger children provide less information than older children. They often omit information that adults would consider important, but what they say is generally correct. They tell what they understand and are able to put into words. It is possible to increase the amount of information provided by the child, for example by rephrasing what the child says and encouraging her to tell more about it (Pipe and Salmon, 2009; Qin et al., 1997). Adults provide the most information, but also some inaccuracies. They tend to fill in missing information based on their own experience and knowledge of scripts. Specific questions can take the place of open-ended questions, and also here the proportion of correct answers increases with age (Eisen et al., 2002; Pipe and Salmon, 2009).

Younger children are vulnerable to social pressure, such as when adults make claims about persons the child is supposed to talk about, or when they use leading or misleading questions (Peterson, C. et al., 2016). Children are used to reconstructing events with the help of their parents and other adults. They try to find the answer they think the adult is expecting, and that they believe to be the correct one. Younger children also tend to agree with leading questions such as "He asked you to come along, right?" This is how adults typically phrase questions when they want children to agree (Bruck et al., 2006). In one study, 3- to 6-year-olds and adults were presented with 17 neutral and four leading questions of the type: "He wore a sweater, right?" There were only minor differences between adults and children on the neutral questions, but the children were more susceptible to the influence of leading questions than the adults (Goodman and Reed, 1986).

Adults often repeat questions to be sure of the child's answer. However, repeating a question the child has already answered can have a leading effect. Typically, it is a signal that the answer was wrong, and often leads children to change their response, particularly on *yes/no* questions (Poole and White, 1991). Repeated interviews can refresh children's memory and produce more correct details in later interviews. Similarly, leading questions that are repeated in the course of several interviews can increase the likelihood that children respond in line with the question's bias (Quas et al., 2007). Thus, adults who mistakenly believe they know the sequence of events can – without intending to do so – get children to confirm something that never happened (Ceci et al., 2007; Cronch et al., 2006). The situation in which children find themselves has significance as well. Saywitz and Nathanson (1993) found that 9- to 10-year-olds remembered less and provided more incorrect answers to leading questions when they were interrogated in a "courtroom" in which the judges, lawyers and spectators were played by actors than when they were interviewed alone at school. Children are used to getting help from adults when reconstructing events. Therefore, any suggestion by an adult about the factual circumstances can affect children's perception and interpretation of an event that has occurred. Children's suggestibility increases when they do not fully understand

what they are being asked about, and the information is uncertain or vaguely coded in memory (Warren et al., 1991).

Another important element is the interviewer. Children are more susceptible to influence when questioned by an authority figure such as a parent, teacher or the police (Bruck et al., 2006; Perry and Wrightsman, 1991). In one study, some of the children were interviewed by a "cold" man who neither smiled, made eye contact or encouraged the children, while the other group met a "warm" interviewer who appeared to be open, smiled and encouraged the children in a friendly way. The children who were interviewed by the "cold" interviewer made more incorrect statements and changed explanation more often than those who had met the "warm" interviewer (Goodman et al., 1991). This suggests that a feeling of safety and emotional support increases the likelihood of children maintaining their version of what they experienced. They are no more susceptible to the influence of adults who appear warm and positive than to persons who provide little support. Studies in which children were exposed to stress – a characteristic feature of many real interrogations – have shown both better and poorer recall (Bruck et al., 2006). A possible explanation for these conflicting results may be that a small amount of stress sharpens the mind, while too much stress leads to insecurity and poor concentration.

A number of aids have been developed for questioning children in connection with abuse and other violations, such as the Cognitive Interview and the National Institute of Child Health and Human Development Investigative Interview, designed to help the child and prevent the interviewer from asking leading questions (Memon et al., 2010; Lamb et al., 2011). These tools are most effective when used with older children, since they require strategies that are difficult for lower age groups (Cronch et al., 2006; Memon et al., 1993). The child's age and language and cognitive development are important factors to take into account. Children with intellectual disability have less knowledge and can be more susceptible than children of the same age with typical development (Agnew and Powell, 2004; Henry and Gudjonsson, 2003). Children with autism spectrum disorder can be reliable witnesses but may provide less information to open questions and may need questions to help recall (McCrory et al., 2007).

In the past, "anatomically detailed dolls" were used in questioning children about sexual abuse, but such dolls seem to increase the likelihood of errors. Younger children can be influenced by the dolls and give false information about the course of events, especially in connection with leading questions (Melinder et al., 2010; Pipe and Salmon, 2009). When 2½- to 3-year-olds were interviewed about a medical examination, the children pointed at random points on the doll. They seemed not to understand that the dolls were supposed to represent themselves (Bruck et al., 1995b). Infants and preschool children have difficulty representing both their own and the doll's body at the same time, and it may be easier for them to use their own body to demonstrate where they have been touched than to use an anatomically detailed doll (DeLoache and Marzolf, 1995).

Some years ago, testimony from children under the age of 10 to 14 years was not heard because it was thought to be unreliable. Today, the age limit has been lowered considerably, and the way in which children are questioned has changed somewhat (Cronch et al., 2006; Thoresen et al., 2006, 2009). Even information from preschool children can be relied upon as long as they have adequate knowledge of the topic in question, and the "interrogation" is conducted in a way suitable to children. A child does not remember everything, even if no pressure or misdirection is used. Just as with any other witnesses, testimony must be considered based on children's prerequisites and knowledge. It is especially important to take into account what children at different ages can respond to with relative certainty, and what types of questions may be difficult for them and lead to inconsistent answers, such as questions about time and the sequence of events (Ceci et al., 2007; Peterson, 2002).

EXECUTIVE FUNCTIONS

In the first years of life, children act spontaneously based on what they have learned and what they perceive to be prominent in a situation. They can suddenly take hold of a toy and do things without considering whether it fits the situation. With age, children become more aware and selective in their actions and get better at planning and performing complex actions in different environments. They do not merely act,

but consider the context and adapt their actions to the situation. They choose a target for their action and a sequence of sub-actions, such as putting on their socks before their shoes, monitor their actions and evaluate their effectiveness based on the objective. The executive functions are a foundation for children's planning and mastery of everyday tasks in general, as well as for learning and school work (Blair, 2016; Carlson et al., 2013).

Executive functions consist of several elements, including attention and working memory. Attention to one's own voluntary actions is sometimes referred to as "executive attention." Since executive functions are not automated, they require more of the child's cognitive resources than actions that more easily can be carried out on "automatic pilot" (Diamond, 2013). It is common to distinguish between "hot" and "cold" functions. Cold executive functions include cognitive processes, while hot executive functions involve emotional and motivational factors. It is difficult for children (and adults) to plan and make good decisions when motivation and emotional involvement are high. Even toddlers perform better when choosing a reward for adults rather than for themselves. Executive functions largely develop during preschool age, but their development continues throughout childhood and adolescence (Best et al., 2009).

A particular focus has been on children's ability to inhibit action impulses, change solution strategy and plan in advance. *Inhibitory control* is the ability not to let oneself be distracted and to inhibit thought and action impulses. It is important for replacing previously learned actions with new ones, as well as maintaining concentration on a given task, resisting temptation and distractions, and postponing pleasurable actions. In experiments on inhibitory control, children can typically choose between a smaller immediate reward and a larger delayed reward. In a classical experiment, the child could eat the one marshmallow placed in front of him or her on the table, or wait and eat two marshmallows when the experimenter returned after 15 minutes. The 3-year-olds typically chose immediate gratification, while the 5-year-olds waited for the larger delayed reward (Mischel et al., 1989). However, another study showed that how long the child waited was not only dependent on the child's self-control but also on how reliable the child believed the promise to be. If the experimenter had "forgotten" something in an earlier situation, more older children ate the marshmallow instead of waiting for the larger reward (all the children got three marshmallows whether they had eaten the one or not) (Kidd et al., 2013).

Another type of task to measure inhibitory control is to ask children to point to something they do not want in order to get what they want, or to say "day" when shown a picture of the moon, and "night" when shown a picture of the sun. Children's performance on these types of tasks shows a marked change between the age of 3 and 4 years. By the time children start school, they have become less inattentive, impulsive and distractible. It is an important aspect of children's school-readiness and becoming able to master progressively more complex and cognitively challenging situations on their way to adolescence and adulthood (Best et al., 2009; Shaul and Schwartz, 2014). However, adolescence seems to be a period with increased impulsivity and impatience, possibly related to both brain development and physiological changes related to puberty (Steinberg and Chein, 2015; van den Bos et al., 2015).

The ability to inhibit thoughts and actions contributes to *cognitive flexibility*. This helps children pursue complex tasks and find novel solutions, adapted to changing demands (Ionescu, 2012). This ability is often measured by using tasks in which children have to switch from one sorting dimension to another, for example by sorting cards with images of different shapes and colors. Three-year-olds have no problem sorting the cards by image shape *or* color, but experience difficulties when they have to switch to sorting by shape after having sorted by color, or by color after they have sorted by shape. Four-year-olds have no trouble switching from one sorting dimension to another (Carlson et al., 2013). Nevertheless, younger children have greater difficulty switching when more categories are introduced, such as size in addition to shape and color. Children's efficiency and speed on this type of task increases throughout childhood and adolescence.

Planning is necessary in order to solve more intricate tasks and perform complex actions. Early planning ability may be observed in how children put on their clothes, build with blocks, make a drawing or play a game. Studies often make use of simple or more complex versions of the Tower of London or Hanoi. Children have to copy a pattern by moving a number of discs

Young children find it difficult to resist taking the marshmallow.

or orbs from one peg to another according to certain rules. The task must be solved in as few moves as possible, and planning becomes more difficult and time-consuming the more moves it requires. At the age of 3 years, children get better at correcting themselves when their attempts do not lead to results. Younger children continue to try the same solution, even if it leads nowhere. Four-year-olds handle tasks with two moves equally well as adults, but tasks with three or more moves take time to master. Between the ages of 7 and 13 years, a gradual development takes place with regard to how quickly and correctly children solve this type of task (Best et al., 2009; Carlson et al., 2013).

The development of executive functions is believed to be related to neurological development in general and the development of the brain's frontal lobe in particular (Barrasso-Catanzaro & Eslinger, 2016). There are however also cultural developmental differences. Children and adolescents in Hong Kong develop executive functions earlier than in the UK, while among adults there is no difference (Ellefson et al., 2017). Children's participation in different social contexts as well as their school work help develop these functions, while at the same time placing new demands on their executive abilities (Rueda and Cómbita, 2013). A relationship has been found between late or inadequate development of executive functions and both social functioning and academic performance at school (see also below).

Executive functions and atypical development

Children's executive functions affect all areas of their lives. A reduction in executive functioning is associated with disorders such as Tourette syndrome, epilepsy and fetal alcohol syndrome,

as well as malnutrition and severe deprivation (Carlson et al., 2013). Since executive functions include attention and working memory, many – but not all – children with difficulties in these areas will show a reduction in executive functioning. Many children with ADHD, autism spectrum disorders or learning disorders have difficulty planning, monitoring and performing actions in a flexible way (Crippa et al., 2015; Goldstein and Naglieri, 2014; Tillman et al., 2009). Math disorders are linked to cold executive functions and distractibility (Miller et al., 2013; Raghubar et al., 2010), while inattention, overactivity and behavioral problems are primarily linked to hot executive functions (Zelazo, 2015). Children who have social problems in interaction with their peers often score lower on executive functions than other children (Holmes et al., 2016). The important role of executive functions in learning and social adaptation is also reflected in the statistical correlation between early executive function disorders and difficulties coping with adult life, criminal behavior and mental problems (Carlson et al., 2013).

The importance of executive function for learning and adaptation has led to a search for interventions that can improve functioning in children and adolescents with executive problems. Since working memory is also part of executive functions, many of the same training program are applied for problems with working memory and executive functions (Rapport et al., 2013). Research indicates that executive functions are influenced by the environment and can be improved at all age levels, but it is not clear how much they can be improved and whether improvements will be maintained (Diamond and Lee, 2011; Diamond and Ling, 2016). A review of executive function training in children with ADHD show limited efficacy (Rapport et al., 2013).

SUMMARY

1 Attention is an active, alert state that affects children's perception and priorities in the here-and-now. During the first year of life, children become more alert and better at orienting themselves, filtering stimulation and shifting as well as sustaining attention. Throughout childhood, attention is increasingly directed at what is relevant in a situation, but children can also develop a tendency to take particular notice of either positive or negative emotional cues. Atypical attention processes are a key element in attention disorders and many other neurodevelopmental disorders. Results at attention training are modest. Medication may help some but not

all children and is controversial. Intervention directed at behavior disorder in children with attention problems are often useful.

2 Memory is the mental representation and recognition or recall of experiences. *Short-term memory* can store material for a few seconds or minutes. *Working memory* stores and processes and is used when an individual tries to remember something for a short period of time or works on a problem. *Long-term memory* is the relatively permanent storage of experiences. *Autobiographical memory* includes personally experienced events that are meaningful to the individual.

3 Memory is functional even before birth, but initially the capacity of working memory is severely limited. Through childhood and adolescence, it increases with the formation of concepts, the ability to process larger units and improved *memory strategies*.

4 Early long-term memory is limited and depends on perfect uniformity – infants quickly forget once the circumstances or the situation change. *Refreshment* in the form of full or partial repetition increases the length of time for which children remember, provided it takes place within a certain *time window*. The extent of what children remember, and for how long, increases with age. The recall of action sequences depends on their meaningfulness, the relationship between the actions and how many times the child has seen them. With age, memory can be refreshed by partial repetition, images or language.

5 In toddlers, expressive language at the time of the experience affects their ability to recount the event at a later age, but not their ability to imitate the action that took place. It is difficult for children to "translate" pre-linguistic memories into verbal form.

6 A *script* is a mental representation of something that usually happens in a given context. Children start to form scripts at an early age, and with time they accumulate a large supply of scripts that make up an important part of their social and cultural knowledge.

7 *Autobiographical memory* consists of temporal sequences of significant personal events, and forms the basis for the development of the self. It begins at the age of 3 to 4 and continues to develop throughout life. The elaboration style of the parents affects what children remember. Also cultural differences affect children's autobiographical memory. Some children experience dramatic and traumatic events; exactly how they remember and recall these events is related to the types of events they were exposed to, how often they occurred, how much stress they caused, the child's past experiences and how parents and others talk about the events.

8 *Childhood amnesia* is the phenomenon that older children and adults rarely recall events from before the age of three. The reason may be that the neurological structures involved in storing memories undergo significant development during the first 2 years of life, and that the organization of memory material differs so much between adults and children that adults are unable to activate memories of events that were coded when they were young children. In addition, much of the knowledge of infants and younger children is replaced by new knowledge.

9 *False memories* can occur as the result of intentional or unintentional influence by other people, and can be difficult for a person to distinguish from actual memories.

10 Learning and reading place high demands on the ability to remember, and memory problems may be found in many developmental disorders, including attention disorders, language disorders, learning disorders and autism spectrum disorder. Also children who have been subjected to severe neglect and abuse can be vulnerable to memory impairment.

11 Children can be reliable *witnesses*, but younger children often provide fewer details and are more *susceptible* to influence from adults. They are used to reconstructing events together with

Continued

adults and are vulnerable to leading questions, especially about things they do not fully understand, and when questioned by an authority figure.

12 *Executive functions* have to do with the planning, execution and monitoring of voluntary actions. "Cold" executive functions are associated with cognitive processes, and "hot" executive functions with emotional and motivational factors. *Inhibitory control* shows a marked increase in preschool age, but continues to develop all the way to adolescence and adulthood. The ability to inhibit thoughts and actions contributes to the development of *cognitive flexibility* that characterizes adolescence and adulthood. *Planning* is necessary to solve intricate tasks and perform complex actions. A reduction in executive functioning is associated with many disorders. The development of executive functions is influenced by experience but results of training is modest.

13 Relations have been found between delayed or inadequate development of executive functions and social functioning and academic performance at school. An early reduction in executive functioning is associated with many developmental disorders, later criminal behavior, difficulty coping with adult life and mental problems.

CORE ISSUES

- Medical and behavioral treatment of attention disorders.
- The relationship between memory and language.
- Effects of training of working memory and executive functions.

SUGGESTIONS FOR FURTHER READING

Barrasso-Catanzaro, C., & Eslinger, P. J. (2016). Neurobiological bases of executive function and social-emotional development: Typical and atypical brain changes. *Family Relations, 65*, 108–119.

Kidd, C., Palmeri, H., & Aslin, R. N. (2013). Rational snacking: Young children's decision-making on the marshmallow task is moderated by beliefs about environmental reliability. *Cognition, 126*, 109–114.

Ristic, J., & Enns, J. T. (2015). The changing face of attentional development. *Current Directions in Psychological Science, 24*, 24–31.

Rovee-Collier, C., & Cuevas, K. (2009a). Multiple memory systems are unnecessary to account for infant memory development: An ecological model. *Developmental Psychology, 45*, 160–174.

Waters, A. M., Lipp, O., & Spence, S. H. (2008). Visual search for animal fear-relevant stimuli in children. *Australian Journal of Psychology, 60*, 112–125.

Contents

CHAPTER 12

CONCEPTUAL DEVELOPMENT AND REASONING

hildren develop an understanding of the world as structured and meaningful. Impressions from the senses are organized, arranged and mentally processed in different ways depending on the child's cognitive abilities, personal and cultural experiences and knowledge. Children notice similarities and differences that form the basis for their categorizations and conceptual development. They create categories based on their own experiences and their concepts differ in various ways from those of adults. A 6-year-old who invites children to a birthday party, even though it is not her birthday but because she wants to get presents, has understood one of the central elements in the concept "birthday party" (getting presents), but lacks another element (celebrating the day of one's birth). However, the "mistakes" children make in forming concepts do not necessarily reflect an inadequate ability to categorize, but rather that they use this ability.

Reasoning is a form of thinking or mental problem solving that involves drawing conclusions about imagined situations, including both *actual* ones (what is) and *counterfactual* ones (what could be, but isn't). Children show an early ability to reason. They might say that apes have a heart because people have a heart, and apes are similar to people. "If humans were four meters tall, doorways would be five meters high," is an example of a counterfactual statement. Children's understanding of conditional promises such as, "if it's sunny, we'll go for a swim" also depends on reasoning. In addition, reasoning forms the basis for scientific thinking. The question is how children develop the abilities to draw inferences and to reason.

EARLY CONCEPTIONS OF SPACE, TIME AND CAUSALITY

Three factors are basic to an understanding of the physical world: it has a *spatial dimension*, a *temporal dimension* and it includes *causal relationships*.

Space

Spatial perception is necessary to orient oneself and remember where events took place (Moser and Moser, 2016). It allows children to know where they are and to locate people, things and events. The perceptual field is structured by spatial concepts, including relative positions such as "behind," "above," "below" and "between." An understanding of physical space as permanent is also an important element in spatial cognition.

Object permanence

Piaget was the first to discuss the development of object permanence the understanding that objects continue to exist and have a physical location even when they cannot be experienced directly. He observed that children aged 7–8 months stopped looking for a toy when a screen was placed between them and the toy, so the toy could no longer be seen. In some cases, children showed disappointment, but did nothing to try to find the toy. Piaget interpreted this as a lack of object permanence in children at this age – objects do not exist for them when they cannot experience them with their senses. Children who were 2 months older searched for the toy and tried to get behind the screen to get hold of it (Piaget, 1950).

Others maintain that young infants' failure to search is not related to the fact that they do not remember an object, but that they do not know how to get hold of it. Using a method that places low demands on motor skills, Baillargeon (1987) found that 3½-month-olds reacted differently to two events in a way that implied that they had object permanence and remembered the location of objects in space even if they did not see them, far earlier than what Piaget found (Box 12.1).

There are, however, important differences between Piaget's and Baillargeon's experiments. Baillargeon based her experiment on where the infants *looked*, while Piaget observed how children *acted* when interesting objects disappeared. Baillargeon's method may be suitable to demonstrate children's emerging understanding of space and the objects in it, while Piaget's method reflects a more advanced understanding that also includes knowledge of how to get hold of things that cannot be directly perceived with the senses (Cohen and Cashon, 2006; Gómez, 2005). This is supported by observations showing that children continue to have difficulty locating objects they cannot see, even after developing object permanence. An important observation was that when infants repeatedly have found a particular

EARLY OBJECT PERMANENCE (Baillargeon, 1987)

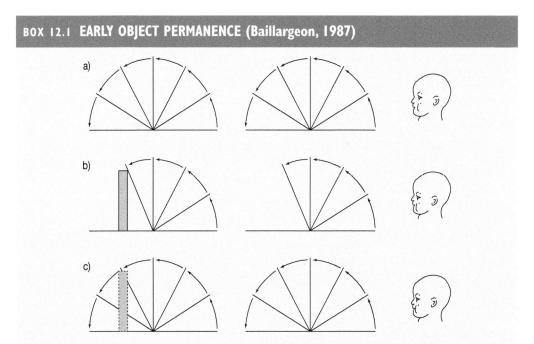

Infants aged 3½ months watched a plate moving in a half-circle from one side to the other (Figure a) until they lost interest and looked at it less (habituation). While the children watched, a box was placed in the path of the moving plate in such a way that the children could not see the box when the plate was moving. Following this, each child was shown one of two possible scenarios: either a *possible* action in which the plate stopped moving and returned to where the box most likely was located (Figure b), or an *impossible* action in which the plate seemed to continue along its former path as if there were no box to prevent its movement (Figure c). The infants looked longer at the impossible (c) than the possible (b) action. This was interpreted as a surprise that the plate did not stop, implying that the infants were aware of the presence of the box even though they could not see it, and thus had object permanence (Baillargeon, 1987, p. 191. Reprinted with permission from Excerpta Medica Inc.).

toy in one place, they will look in the same spot, even if they have just seen an adult hiding the toy somewhere else, like in this example from Piaget (1950, p. 52).

Lucienne is seated on a sofa and plays with a plush duck. I put it on her lap and place a small red cushion on top of the duck (this is position A); Lucienne immediately raises the cushion and takes hold of the duck. I then place the duck next to her on the sofa in [position] B, and cover it with another cushion, a yellow one. Lucienne has watched all my moves, but as soon as the duck is hidden she returns to the little cushion A on her lap, raises it and searches. An expression of disappointment; she turns it over in every direction and gives up.

A number of studies have since confirmed that infants make the same type of error as Lucienne. It is called "A-not-B error" because children search in position A (where they have previously found the object) rather than in position B (where they saw the object being hidden). The error is not caused by motor limitations since it is no more difficult to look in position B than A. Instead, it reflects how complex a task it is for infants of this age to look in a different place than they are used to, leading them to repeat actions that previously have been successful. It is first around the age of 1 year that insight prevails over habit – until then, children always start by looking where they last saw the object disappear. Somewhat older children will also continue to search if they cannot find the toy where they believe it to be. Thus, it takes time for children to integrate new knowledge about an object's location in space with earlier experiences of getting hold of the object. This is contrary to Spelke and Kinzler's (2007) assumption that object localization has its basis in an innate geometry module.

Further development of spatial perception

Children mainly use two types of cues to orient themselves in space. Geometric cues include surface, direction, distance, angle and the like, and depend on the viewer's perspective. Landmarks include characteristics such as wall color and placement of windows, doors and objects (Ferrara and Landau, 2015). Children use both types of cues. Clear geometric cues and landmarks are important to children's early development, and it takes some time before they are able to take advantage of less prominent physical details to orient themselves (Newcombe et al., 2013). Sometimes children have to take a physical perspective not based on their own body to locate an object (Vasilyeva and Lourenco, 2012).

In an experiment with 12-month-old children, a toy was hidden underneath one of 58 pillows scattered on the floor. The pillows were blue, but sometimes the pillow with a toy under it would have a different color and thus serve as a landmark. The children found the toy when it was lying under a pillow with a different color or under a pillow between two pillows with a different color, and succeeded less often when the toy was hidden under a blue pillow near a pillow with a different color (indirect landmark) (Bushnell et al., 1995). Another study found that children under the age of 22 months used geometric cues and made little use of landmarks when they attempted to find a toy they had observed being hidden in a sandbox and had to move around the sandbox. Somewhat older children (22–36 months) did better on these tasks when they also had access to landmarks (Newcombe et al., 1998). This indicates a change in children's use of spatial cues around the age of 21 months and an improvement in their use of directional cues (beacons) from the age of 2 to 4 years (Sutton, 2006).

Children gradually orient themselves better in both larger and smaller spaces, but are well into their second year before they are able to take alternative "routes" between two objects, such as moving around an obstacle to reach a target. When children try to find a hidden object, they can remember its location in relation to themselves (egocentric cue), a particular landmark (external cue) or based on where a target is in relation to a hidden object (internal cue), for example if the object is located in a table drawer and the table has been moved. Three-year-olds can take advantage of the first two cues, but children are 5–6 years old before they are able to use internal cues (Negen and Nardini, 2015). In one experiment, children aged 3–6 years hid a toy duck in a corner together with the experimenter. The task of the child was to find the duck after having been blindfolded and slowly turned around. The youngest children used landmarks in large spaces and geometric cues in small spaces,

Children gradually become able to use maps to find the way.

but geometric cues were of limited use in finding the duck because their relative position and perspective changed when they were turned around. Six-year-olds used landmarks in both types of spaces (Learmonth et al., 2008). Children's ability to remember where events take place improves considerably between the ages of 4 to 8 years (Bauer et al., 2012).

With age, children learn to use maps and other aids to orient themselves. Toddlers can use simple maps to find something in a small space (see p. 134). One study found that 5-year-old children had an emerging understanding of maps as a representation of a wider geographical area. When asked to make a map of their daily route from home to school, the map consisted of a single straight line. Slightly older children included landmarks in their maps, but many of these were of no help in finding the target, such as flowers and friends. The maps produced by 8-year-olds were more functional, and over half of them included intersecting roads and clearly identifiable buildings (Thommen et al., 2010).

Six- to 8-year-olds have difficulty finding their way based on a map without landmarks, while 10-year-olds can find their way without landmarks (Lingwood et al., 2015). Although children learn to measure distances in early school age (Nunes and Bryant, 2015), the map reading skills of 9- to 12-year-olds remain limited, with large individual variations (Hemmer et al., 2015).

Individual differences in spatial cognition

The development of spatial cognition shows major individual differences. Some children develop abilities that are suitable for a career as an engineer or a pilot. Boys generally do better than girls on spatial tasks, and differences widen around puberty (Reilly et al., 2017). Others show atypical development. Children with Turner syndrome (Vicario et al., 2013) and Williams syndrome (Landau and Ferrara, 2013), among others, have special problems with spatial perception and orienting themselves in space. Blind children need more time to explore and form mental representations of space based on their experiences with locomotion, non-visual strategies and landmarks, and this may have consequences for their development of exploration and independence (Gibson and Schmuckler, 1989; McAllister and Gray, 2007).

Time

There are two main approaches to time: either as a dimension of events themselves, or as a "framework" in which events can be located on a timeline from past to future (McCormack, 2015).

Time in events

Piaget (1969a, 1970) was primarily concerned with the development of children's concept of time as a dimension of the physical world, inspired by a question Albert Einstein asked him in 1928 about when children form a concept of time and speed. According to Piaget, this concept of time is based on three operations: the temporal ordering of events, the coherence of event durations and the intervals between them, and the partitioning of time in a way analogous to spatial units (seconds, minutes, etc.). A number of experiments conducted by Piaget and others included two toy trains that rode on parallel tracks. The children's task was to determine which train had moved the furthest, the fastest or for the longest time. The results showed that preschool children understood the individual concepts, but failed to integrate time, speed and distance and infer one of the variables (such as time) based on knowledge of the other two (speed and distance). Many of them answered that the train that had travelled furthest also had the greatest speed or had been moving for the longest time, since they only took into account one variable at a time. Slightly older children were able to include two variables at a time, and from the age of 9 years, many children consistently solved this type of task correctly (Matsuda, 2001; Piaget, 1970).

However, when they used a stopwatch to measure time, 7-year-old children, and some 5-year-olds, were able to solve tasks in which cars travelling at different speeds started and stopped in different places. Without the stopwatch, the children first managed these tasks at 8–9 years of age (Nelson, 1996). Six-year-olds were able to

integrate the duration of different events after having been taught to use counting as a strategy (Wilkening et al., 1987). This shows that children need to manage cultural "tools" (counting or stopwatch) to master these types of tasks before their concept of time is sufficiently internalized. However, 5- to 7-year-olds often count unevenly, and their time estimates can be inaccurate even if they use a counting strategy. This type of task is easier when it does not involve movement and thus has one less dimension. Five-year-olds, for example, are able to determine which of two dolls has slept the longest when one of the dolls went to sleep earlier than the other, and both woke up at the same time (Levin, 1977, 1989).

Events in time

Children's earliest understanding of events in time is based on their own experiences, especially their participation in events with a fixed order and schedule (Nelson, 2007a). Children's conversations with parents about past and future events are also important for the development of temporal understanding. Quite early on, parents introduce expressions such as *early*, *late*, *morning*, *evening* and *bedtime* in conversations with their children (Lucariello and Nelson, 1987). Some children use words such as *before*, *after*, *today* and *yesterday* at an early age, but most children do not show a conventional understanding of these words before the age of 4 (Harner, 1975). They have some understanding of time based on temporal distance, and are able to say whether Christmas or their birthday was "most recent" if one of them occurred during the last 60 days and the other before that. Until the age of around 9 years, children are usually unable to tell which of two events occurred last if both occurred in the past 60 days (Friedman et al., 1995).

Time is perceived both forward and backward from the present. It is easier for preschool children to judge the temporal relationship between two events that have already occurred than between events that will occur, even in cases of recurring events such as Christmas or their birthday (McCormack and Hanley, 2011). Children also continue to have problems placing events earlier or later on a timeline, for example whether Wednesday or Thursday comes first when they go backward or forward in time (Friedman, 2005).

Acquiring the temporal concepts of one's own culture is the result of formal and informal training in dividing up time and arranging events temporally. Learning to read a clock is an important part of this process. When 3- to 5-year-old children were asked "When do you get up?", the answers were linked to routines such as "When Mom wakes me up." Seven-year-olds answered either "In the morning" or specified a certain time, but many of them did not know the correct time for their routine activities (Nelson, 1996). This shows that development is characterized by the gradual transition from an event-based concept of time to a temporal understanding related to formal divisions of the day into larger (morning, evening, etc.) and smaller units (hours, minutes, etc.). The temporal arrangement of events into weeks and months gradually becomes more precise all the way to adolescence (Friedman, 2014). Children's script knowledge and autobiographical memory are important elements in the development of this ability (see Chapter 11).

Causality

An understanding of cause and effect, the relationship between events that necessitate one another, is fundamental to gaining overview and control of the environment, and thus an essential part of cognition (Corrigan and Denton, 1996). Causality cannot be observed directly, but is a concept related to the perception of relationships between events (Saxe and Carey, 2006).

Early understanding of physical causality

A number of innovative studies have attempted to map infants' understanding of how objects behave and interact. They typically consist in showing children physically *possible* and (apparently) *impossible* events. When the children spend more time observing one event than another, it is interpreted to mean that they perceive them to be different, for example that one is expected and the other unexpected. The fact that objects fall when they lack support, and that colliding objects affect each other's movement, are prototypical examples of causal relationships. These types of events have therefore been widely used in studies on infants' understanding of physical causality. Many studies are based on the assumption that infants will look longer at events that violate their expectations than at events that do not (Baillargeon, 2004).

In a classic study, 3-month-olds looked longer at a wooden block placed by a hand into thin air in front of a larger block (without falling down), than when it was placed on the larger block (Box 12.2).

Another core aspect of physical causation is what happens when a moving object collides with an object at rest. In one study, 2½-month-old children spent less time looking when a ball hit a small toy animal and pushed it forward a little (possible event) than when the toy animal moved forward even though an obstacle stopped the ball before it reached the toy animal (impossible event). Baillargeon and colleagues (1995) suggest that this indicates that the children had formed an expectation that stationary objects move when they are hit by an object in motion, and that they remain stationary when they are not hit. Another study found that 6½-month-old children looked longer when a small rather than a large ball pushed an object forward, while 9-month-olds also reacted differently depending on the width of the object being hit. This is interpreted as a gradual development: children first develop a concept about the difference between a collision and a non-collision, and later integrate the properties of the objects involved in the collision event (Wang et al., 2003).

Explanations of how children begin to understand cause and effect vary with regard to the specific innate characteristics they build on. The standard nativist argument of Newman and colleagues (2008) is that this type of understanding is too complex for infants to acquire on their own, and that they must have an innate module capable of perceiving causality. Similarly, Spelke and Kinzler (2007) suggest that infants are born with basic assumptions about how objects move in space and that this *core knowledge* forms the basis for children's further development of a naive theory of physical laws, which in turn relies on experience (see p. 28).

In contrast to these hypotheses, Baillargeon (2008) maintains that the development of physical causality is governed by a more general and innate *principle of persistence*: things have a continuous existence in time and space and retain their physical properties (this also includes object permanence). Over time, infants form concepts about the relationships between objects and spaces, objects and surface support, objects and barriers,

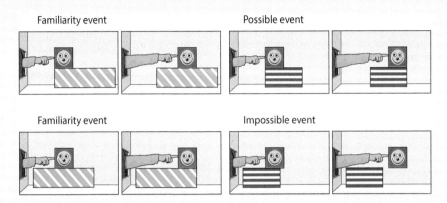

Three months old infants were first familiarized with the situation where a smaller block was moved along a larger block. Then they were shown a block that was pushed with a hand a) along a large block without losing support (possible event) or b) equally long along a shorter block and into thin air without falling (impossible event). The children looked longer at the block hanging in thin air than at the possible event. The interpretation of Baillargeon and associates is that infants look longer at what is unexpected, and that the longer look indicated that the infants had an emerging understanding of physical causality that made them expect objects to fall if not supported from below.

and so on. They discover different types of causal relations between objects, such as "occlusion phenomena," "passing-through phenomena," "support phenomena" and "unveiling phenomena," and show astonishment when things behave in ways that violate their expectations. It is an experience-based development that changes in line with children's motor development, among other things. For example, children gain new knowledge about what happens when objects collide once they begin to develop hand-eye coordination at 4 months of age and interact more consciously with objects (p. 152). Since adults rarely let objects collide in such a way that children can observe the process "systematically," their experience is not primarily based on watching others. Baillargeon's theory suggests that the acquisition of causal relationships is a rapid process rather than a realization of innate knowledge. An understanding of individual physical events is integrated much later together with a more general understanding of physical causality and the forces that affect the movement of objects (Baillargeon, 1994, 2008; Baillargeon et al., 2009).

Oakes (1994) explains this development from an information processing perspective, arguing that children notice events that occur together and gradually form a causal understanding based on what happens when objects collide and similar events.

Further development of causal cognition

Infants' early understanding of cause and effect is *implicit* and does not involve the *sense of causal necessity* that a conceptual understanding of physical causality implies (Baillargeon et al., 2009; Piaget and Inhelder, 1975). It is not enough for children to discover that certain events tend to occur together, a conscious understanding of causality requires that they *comprehend* the connection between the events, and this develops slowly. Around the age of 3, children become very interested in causality and begin to ask "why?" about many things, such as why water is shiny. Their questions are often impossible to answer, and demonstrate children's limited understanding of cause and effect in many areas.

An emerging understanding of causality does not mean that children immediately understand the mechanism of cause and effect in a given area; this depends on relevant knowledge and experience. Children may show an understanding of causes in some areas and lack the necessary knowledge in others. In a study, half of the 4½- to 6-year-olds answered "yes" to the question whether a toothache can be contagious and be passed from one child to another. A similar number thought they could get a toothache by playing with a forbidden pair of scissors (Siegal, 1991). Since the children responded yes and no equally often, it seemed as if they were simply guessing. In a somewhat older group of children (7½ to 8½ years), 90 percent ruled out both possibilities. On the other hand, 22 of 24 children between the ages of 4½ and 5½ years knew that a knee wound is not infectious. Thus, the study shows that children gradually develop a deeper and more conscious understanding of cause and effect, based on greater insight into specific areas of knowledge.

OBJECT CONCEPTS

Conceptual development also includes children's perception and categorization of people, animals and objects and their characteristics. The extension of a concept consists of all the exemplars that fall under the concept; poodles and bulldogs, for example, belong to the concept "dog." The intension of a concept is its meaning or content, the set of distinguishing characteristics that are encompassed by the concept, for example that most exemplars of "dog" have four legs, a fur and a shorter or longer tail that can wag.

> One of the most basic functions of living creatures is to categorize, that is to treat distinguishable objects and events as equivalent. Humans live in a categorized world; from household items to emotions to gender to democracy, objects and events, although unique, are acted toward as members of classes. Some theories would say that without this ability it would be impossible to learn from experience and thus that categorization is one of the basic functions of life.
>
> (Rosch, 1999, p. 61)

Children develop concepts gradually, and their conceptual extensions and intensions tend to vary somewhat from those of adults. Some concepts largely reflect the physical characteristics and sensory apparatus of human beings and are relatively similar across cultures. Others are defined by the culture and communicated through language. Children must learn how the culture they grow up in categorizes people, animals, objects and other things.

Theories of object categorization

There are two main approaches to object concept formation: feature-based theories and prototype theories. Both include different views on *how* children form concepts.

Feature-based theories

According to feature-based theories, categorization relies on specific traits or characteristics. These can be physical (such as the fact that a ball is usually round) or functional (a ball can be thrown or kicked). For every category, there is a set of common features that are necessary and sufficient for that category alone, and therefore can be used to determine whether an object should be included in the concept. Conceptual development comes about by collecting different traits into categories and getting to know the particular traits that characterize a given category.

One main hypothesis is that children's earliest categorizations are based on *perceptually prominent characteristics* of objects, in particular their shape (Clark, 1973). To begin with, children are attentive to certain features and create categories based on these; the concept "ball," for example, can be based on the property "round" and include balls, the moon, oranges, dinner plates, and so on (see Figure 12.1, left). As children gain more experience, they create more concepts by dividing up larger categories and adding more features. Their concepts become more differentiated and gradually more similar to those of adults. The features that are added are not exclusively perceptual, however. With the exception of geometric forms, external physical characteristics alone are not enough to lend meaning to a concept.

Functional features have to do with what objects do and what they can be used for, such as sitting on them or riding on them (Figure 12.1,

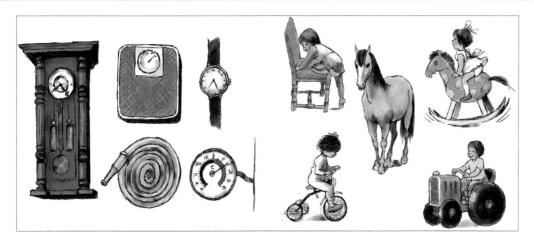

FIGURE 12.1 Concept formation based on perceptual and functional features.

The objects in the left hand image represent a category based on perceptually prominent features. The objects in the right hand image are categorized according to functional similarity.

right). During early conceptual development, children are aware of only a few features that form the *core* of a concept, such as what they can do with an object, how it moves, and so on. "Ball," for example, can be categorized as "something that can be thrown and bounced around." As children gain more experience with objects, functional features become more differentiated, their division more complex, and the number of concepts increases (Nelson, 1996, 2007a).

Although Nelson suggested that perceptual traits are too abstract in relation to the cognitive abilities of toddlers, the physical appearance of things is important nevertheless. External features are clues to internal characteristics or usage and help children identify things that belong to different concepts. For example, children assume that something that looks like an animal must have a heart, blood and other qualities they associate with animals (see p. 232).

Mandler (2004, 2010) integrates perceptual and functional features. According to her, children form concepts by experiencing the perceptible world and have an innate ability to create *perceptual categories* of how things look, sound, and the like. Perceptual categorization allows children to remember people and things in the earliest stage of life. Since perceptual categories often are extremely detailed, children will react to subtle differences. The perceptual categories are determined by the design of the human sensory apparatus and result from children's nearly passive registration of sensory impressions, an implicit or non-conscious registration of the perceptual similarity between things. As a next step, children use *perceptual meaning analysis* to categorize things according to different characteristics, such as the way in which they move, whether they can contain or enclose anything, or whether anything can rest on them. These features form the basis for pre-linguistic concepts. Since they represent global features, children's early concepts are global as well, such as "animal" and "vehicle" rather than "dog" and "car." Mandler suggests, for example, that infants use "self-initiated movement" to distinguish the category "animal" from "inanimate objects."

Mandler (2008, 2012) suggests that there are two parallel systems that handle information from the sensory systems. The first generates purely perceptual categories without conceptual content, the second creates categories based on the function and spatial behavior of objects. These two systems begin to be integrated as early as 3 months of age, but are far from complete at 18 months. Language helps children divide the world into smaller global categories and thus serves a crucial function in the formation of concepts. As an example, Mandler mentions children's pre-linguistic global concept "living being" (animals). From a purely perceptual point of view, however, children are able to distinguish between dogs and cats, and learn that some animals say *meow* and others say *woof*. When children hear other people call these animals by different names, it tells them that the differences are significant, and that dogs and cats belong to different categories.

Prototype theories

One fundamental objection to feature theories is the difficulty of describing enough necessary and sufficient features to define even simple categories like "table" or "chair." Possible features for "table" might include "has a flat surface," "things can be put on top," "has legs," and so on. But even after listing these three features one runs into problems, since some tables have a solid base and the feature "legs" no longer represents a common property. When it comes to "flat surface" and "things can be put on top," it is difficult to include all tables while at the same time excluding benches, planks and trays.

Prototype theories are therefore an alternative to the feature-based theories (Lakoff, 1987; Rosch, 1999). Rather than grouping by common features, children assign different categories to people, animals, objects, and so on. The category "bird," for example, may initially contain only sparrow and crow. They represent the prototype. As time goes by, hen and penguin are added to the category as well. Studies show that children, when asked to determine whether a picture shows

a bird, take a longer time to respond to more peripheral exemplars like hen and duck than when the picture shows a swallow or a thrush. According to feature-based theories, it should take the same amount of time, since all category members share the same traits (Rosch, 1973).

Mervis and Rosch (1981) describe three conceptual levels: a superordinate level (animal, furniture), a basic level (dog, chair) and a subordinate level (poodle, rocking chair). According to Mervis and Rosch, objects belonging to the basic level are easier to perceive as perceptual units and physically more similar than objects at the superordinate level. At the same time, they are not as similar as objects at the subordinate level, which can be difficult to keep apart. Although a chow-chow and a German shepherd are quite different, dogs are nevertheless more alike than a dog, a horse and an elephant. Therefore, children naturally begin by forming concepts of objects at the basic level, rather than broad superordinate concepts or narrow subordinate concepts. When forming a prototype category, the first exemplars the child meets will constitute the prototype.

Elaborating on this theory, Quinn (2002) describes early conceptual development as proceeding from collections of individual exemplars to the creation of prototypes, which in turn give rise to "magnets" that form the core of categories and attract new exemplars (Figure 12.2). For instance, children first form a prototype "chair"

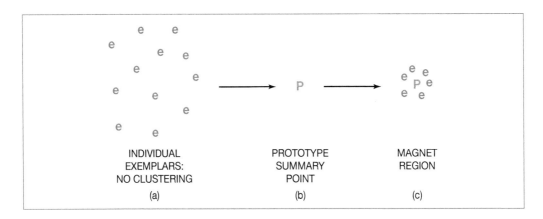

INDIVIDUAL
EXEMPLARS:
NO CLUSTERING

(a)

PROTOTYPE
SUMMARY
POINT

(b)

MAGNET
REGION

(c)

FIGURE 12.2 **Quinn's model of early categorization and concept formation.**

a) Children begin by grouping a number of exemplars that seem to belong together based on perceptual similarity. b) The sum of these exemplars forms the basis for a prototype. c) Categories are developed by the addition of new exemplars that are attracted to the prototype like a "magnet" (based on Quinn, 2002, p. 186).

based on their concrete experiences with chairs, maybe also the word *chair*. An unfamiliar object is perceived as a "chair" and included in the concept to the extent that the child perceives it to resemble the prototype. Whether the resemblance is perceptual or functional is not a decisive factor.

According to Quinn, the earliest categories are based on perceptual information, but instead of traits, they build on summary-level representations or prototypes. "Dog," for example, is initially defined by all the visual characteristics of animals the child perceives to belong to the category "dog," such as four legs, a snout and a tail. Quinn disagrees with Mandler's division between perceptual and conceptual characteristics, maintaining that there is *continuity* in conceptual development despite the fact that concepts change, new ones appear and categories are split up and combined in increasingly complex ways. The characteristics children initially use can make it difficult to assign exemplars to the correct concept. Many animals have four legs, a snout and a tail. When the visual prototype "dog" is augmented with the knowledge that dogs bark, eat bones, are called *dog*, and so on, the content of the concept will change but still maintain the perceptual characteristics that were included in its initial formation and that contribute to the recognition of exemplars belonging to the concept (Quinn, 2002, 2008).

The theories presented here illustrate the range of different views and at the same time reflect the continuing lack of agreement on the processes underlying the formation of concepts.

Early categorization of objects

Researchers have designed innovative experiments to find an answer to the question of what types of categories children begin with. Since infants are not yet able to talk, or are in their earliest language development, researchers have to use non-verbal methods. Studies based on preferential looking (see p. 47) suggest that 3-month-olds are able to distinguish between cats and horses, tigers and cats and lions and cats, but not between horses and zebras or horses and giraffes (Eimas and Quinn, 1994). Because 3- to 6-month-olds have no understanding of the types of "beings" cats, horses, tigers, lions and elephants are (living creatures, mammals, and so on), Eimas and Quinn suggest that children at this age distinguish between them based on visual features alone, and still have to develop broader conceptual categories (see Figure 12.2).

The study in Box 12.3 illustrates how the breadth of children's experiences influences what is included in their conceptual categories. The perceptual differences are usually greater between dogs than between cats, children therefore tend to develop broader dog concepts and more narrow cat concepts. This may explain why children more often call cats *woof-woof* than they call dogs *kitty*.

Another method is based on the fact that studies have found that 18-month-old children touch the objects in a certain pattern, and according to Mandler this pattern is motivated by their interest and therefore reflect their conceptual system. Objects from different categories are placed in front of children without leading them to do anything specific with them. If the objects for example include toy animals and vehicles, and the child consecutively touches the toy animals more often than chance would suggest, Mandler interprets this to mean that the child has formed a category "animals" as distinct from "vehicles." By using this method, Mandler found that 18-month-olds distinguished between exemplars of the categories "bird" and "airplane," even though birds and airplanes are perceptually quite similar, as well as between "bird" and "animal." First at the age of 2½ years, they consistently differentiated between exemplars from different basic-level concepts, such as "hare" and "dog" (Mandler et al., 1991).

Early concepts also include functions, what things do and what one usually does with them. Mandler and McDonough (1996) began by observing what 14-month-old children spontaneously did with different animals and vehicles that were put in front of them. Then the children were shown a normal play action with one of the items, such as feeding an animal with a small spoon or opening the door of a toy car with a key (Figure 12.3). When the children got to play with an animal and a vehicle shortly after, they imitated the action with the object that belonged to the same higher-level category, although it was quite unlike the one they had observed (such as a dog and a fish). Only rarely did they imitate actions that did not fit with the item. They did not feed the plane or open the bird with a key, not even when they were only given a single toy after watching the experimenter demonstrate the

BOX 12.3 ASYMMETRIES IN CATEGORIZATION OF DOGS AND CATS (Quinn, 2002; Quinn et al., 1993)

In an experiment based on preference looking, 3- to 4-month-olds were first shown either a set of photographs of different cats *or* of different dogs, two at a time. By observing the photographs, the children developed either a "dog" category or a "cat" category. Then all the children were shown a pair of photographs with a new dog and a new cat. The infants who had been shown different cats looked longer at the picture of the dog than that of the cat (novelty preference), while the other group, that had been shown different dogs, looked equally long at the dog and the cat.

One explanation for this difference may be that cats resemble each other more than dogs. The children who were shown pictures of different cats therefore formed a relatively narrow category "cat." They looked longest at the dog, perceiving it as new compared with the cat, which in turn they perceived to belong to the category they had habituated to. The dogs in the pictures were so different, however, that the children who were shown dogs formed a category broad enough to also include cats, and therefore did not assign the cat to a different category than the new dog.

This explanation is supported by an analysis of ten surface measurements on the photographs of the dogs and cats, which showed that half of the cats perceptually fit into the dog category, while only two of 18 dogs fit into the cat category. When the dog category was narrowed down by removing the most atypical dogs and the experiment was repeated, the children showed novelty preference for the image of the cat after having habituated to the narrower range of dogs.

action. Mandler explains the results by inferring that the children's categorizations were based more on knowledge about animals and vehicles than on visual similarity.

Mandler's results suggest a development from global to more specific categories, but other studies have not supported this conclusion. For example in one study, 3-year-olds were able to find two objects that belonged together when two of them belonged to the same basic-level concept and a third belonged to a different superordinate category (for example, two cats and a car). When the objects belonged to different basic-level categories (car, motorcycle, cat), the children seemed to make random selections (Rosch et al., 1976). The results suggest that children at this age do not have a clear understanding of things that belong to the same superordinate category, the opposite of Mandler's findings.

Rakison (2003) explains the conflicting results by proposing that young children do not have

global concepts like "animal" or "vehicle," and only appear to categorize objects based on global traits because they focus on one or two prominent features (Box 12.4). Rakison's results suggest that children initially are aware of one or a few prominent features, but that the object as a whole is important as well. Somewhat older children had difficulties forming categories when things appeared to violate the object's familiar integrity as a whole. Rakison suggests that children have an innate tendency to pay attention to parts of objects and a general ability to form associations. Over time, children associate the objects' parts with movement and other functions and form concepts of complex feature patterns that usually are connected. This leads to a continuous development from infants' earliest categorizations based on one or two features to the complex concepts of adults.

Exactly how children begin to categorize things and form concepts is one of the funda-

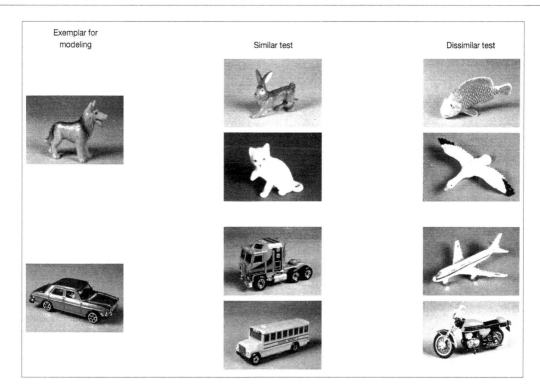

Exemplar for modeling   Similar test   Dissimilar test

FIGURE 12.3 Photographs of animals and vehicles used in Mandler and McDonough's study (1996).

mental questions of developmental psychology, but the results are ambiguous and partly seem to contradict one another. Mandler interprets her findings to mean that children form global concepts before they begin to categorize at the basic level. Quinn and Eimas' studies show that infants are able to distinguish between animals at the basic level based on perceptual analysis alone. The question is, why children do not seem to use this ability. Mandler's explanation is that they represent different levels of categorization, while Eimas and Quinn's studies merely show a simple form of perceptual categorization. Eimas and Quinn disagree with this view. They consider the formation of perceptual prototypes to be an early stage in conceptual development as such. Rakison argues that the results are consistent with the view that children form concepts from prominent perceptual and functional features by means of *associative learning*, grouping together characteristics that tend to occur together. This is similar to Quinn and Eimas' explanation, except that children start with a few perceptual characteristics instead of single exemplars, which in turn form

the basis for later prototypes and broader categories. Both explanations involve a continuous process by which concepts constantly become more specific and varied.

These different explanations illustrate how difficult it can be to interpret the results of infant studies (see Kagan, 2008a). Perhaps the results of these experiments say more about how infants perceive a collection of things shown to them than the types of categories they form in the course of early development. This is important knowledge, but it is possible that children use other characteristics to create functional categories in a world where many objects appear together with constantly new things and in different situations (Walker-Andrews, 2008). Children most likely form concepts in more than one way, and variations in culture determine which of them they use the most. Both similarities and differences between objects determine the distinguishing characteristics for their categorization. Among a group of different objects, any similarity will stand out. If, for example, some triangles and rectangles are blue, it will be their shape that

BOX 12.4 CATEGORIZATION OF BLENDS OF ANIMALS AND VEHICLES (Rakison, 2003)

The study included children aged 14, 18 and 22 months. Rakison (2003) observed how they behaved when there were:

a) different exemplars of "animals" (cow, dog, goose and walrus) and "vehicles" (terrain vehicles, trains, buses and motorcycles)

b) different animals without legs and vehicles without wheels

c) animals and vehicles with either legs only or wheels only

d) animals and vehicles with wheels or legs.

He found that the children touched the typical exemplars in line with common categories, as other studies have found as well. However, the children did not seem to form two separate categories for animals without legs and vehicles without wheels, or when both animals and vehicles had either legs or wheels. When the parts were mixed, that is, animals with wheels and legs and vehicles with wheels and legs, the 14- and 18-month-olds categorized the toys based on their functional parts independent of the body – "things with legs" and "things with wheels" – while the oldest children (22 months) showed no systematic categorization (Rakison and Butterworth, 1998).

In a similar study with objects at the basic level (cows and cars), 18- and 22-month-old children distinguished between cows and cars when they had no legs or wheels. Children aged 14 and 18 months did not seem to form any categories when all the objects had either wheels or legs. The oldest children distinguished between cows and cars on all the tasks (Rakison and Cohen, 1999). (Thanks to David Rakison for photographs).

distinguishes them and be the property that stands out the most. If two identical triangles have different colors, their color will be more salient than their shape and receive more attentional weight (Sloutsky, 2003). And although children's earliest concepts do not involve object categories alone, it is these categories that have been studied the most (Nelson, 2011).

Conceptual development in childhood and adolescence

Through development children's physical and social environment expands, and they take part in more varied activities. These activities play an important role in concept development. Over time, children develop a complex conceptual structure with greater internal consistency and structural relationship between concepts. In preschool age, many of their concepts are based on the role things have in activities and events. Lucariello and Nelson (1985) call these concepts slot-fillers because they involve things that can fulfill the same role in an event or activity, such as putting on X (pants, shirt, socks) in the morning, or eating X (cheese, jam, salami) for breakfast. Therefore, a slot-filler category for food at this age is not a global concept such as "all edible things," but rather "what is eaten during a particular activity," for example at lunch or breakfast. Evidence for such concepts is provided by a study of preschool children who were able to list more items when asked for examples of "breakfast foods" or "snacks" than of "food." School-age children listed more items when asked about "food" (Lucariello, 1998). The fact that things are exchangeable at a certain point in a daily activity or routine helps children see similarities and group them together.

The number of slot-fillers decreases with age, and many of them are later reorganized into hierarchical structures (Nelson, 1988). Between the ages of 5 and 7 years, a conceptual shift seems to take place whereby hierarchical or scientific concepts become more prominent (Nguyen and Murphy, 2003; Perraudin and Mounoud, 2009). These are related to each other in a hierarchy that includes more wide-ranging concepts with many subordinate concepts, as well as others that are more narrowly defined. Some are superordinate to others in the sense that all members of one category are members of the other, but not vice versa. For example, all cats are animals, but not all animals are cats. "Dog" and "cat" are different categories, but belong to the same superordinate category "animal" (Sloutsky, 2015).

The relationship between two classes or categories in which one class is part of another is called class inclusion. Since this involves the coordination of many concepts, an understanding of class inclusion is considered an important milestone in conceptual development, and there are differing views on when children pass this milestone. Inhelder and Piaget (1964) performed a series of experiments showing that class inclusion – such as the inclusion of "rose" in the category "flower" in Figure 12.4 – was difficult to understand for children before they had reached the concrete operational stage at around 7 years of age (see also p. 171). Other studies, however,

have found class inclusion in younger children. In a much cited study, children were shown a teddy bear that was supposed to walk up a staircase with four red and two white steps to reach a table. The children were asked whether there were more red steps or steps. Children as young as 4 years old answered correctly, far earlier than what Piaget and Inhelder had found (McGarrigle et al., 1978). The results are interpreted to suggest that class inclusion develops more gradually and at an earlier age when it concerns toys and other areas that are familiar to children (see p. 173). However, others have pointed out that this task may not measure class inclusion and that the children instead solve it by comparing two lengths (Halford and Andrews, 2006).

From an early age, language becomes increasingly important in the formation of concepts. Words are referents to meanings that contribute both to the formation of new concepts and the reorganization of preexisting ones (Lupyan, 2016). Words lead the attention to important events and situational characteristics, and the words children hear people use about different objects in the environment tell them what does and does not belong together according to their culture. It is not certain that toddlers would place cats and dogs in different categories if adults' use of language had not led them to do so. Words can also draw children's attention to various forms of categorization. When an adult uses a noun to refer to a toy such as *teddy bear* or *doll*, the word is likely to be the name of the toy. If the adult uses an adjective such as *soft*

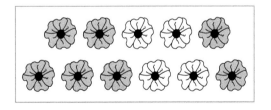

FIGURE 12.4 **Class inclusion.**

Each child was shown a collection of 11 flowers – seven roses and four white flowers, and asked: *Are there more roses or more flowers?* Children who had not yet reached the concrete operational stage answered *roses*, while older children answered *flowers*. The youngest children were able to tell that some of the flowers were roses and that the others were a different type of flower. They did not understand, however, that roses are flowers as well and must be included when counting "flowers" (Inhelder and Piaget, 1964).

or *raggedy*, it tells the child that the toy has characteristics that place it in a group with other soft and raggedy things (Waxman and Gelman, 2009). The importance of conceptual knowledge also shows up in the fact that 4-year-old children remember the name of a greater number of new objects when they are told how they work, and younger children themselves often ask how a thing works when they are told the name of a new object (Nelson et al., 2008). In addition, language is a prerequisite for forming abstract concepts such as "politics" or "democracy."

Since children's use of words also reflects their concepts, many studies of conceptual development have focused on how children use language. Children under the age of 2½ years rarely use words that refer to global concepts; when they do, their understanding and use of them usually differs from that of adults (Griffiths, 1986). Neither are the global categories of a culture necessarily identical with those formed by children early on. In a certain sense, "vehicle," "furniture" and "animal" are a cultural construct and do not exist in the real world. Children learn such categories when they turn up during conversation. Macnamara (1982) found that 2- to 3-year-olds seemed to follow a prototype strategy in acquiring global concepts, whereby new members are gradually assigned to a concept. Initially, the children used the word *animals* for only a group of different animals, and objected strongly when Macnamara held up a toy horse and asked whether it was an animal. Observations showed that children's understanding of *animals* was related to the way their parents used the word in conversation with their children. They only used the word *animal* when they talked about several different types of animals. A herd of horses, for example, was called *horses* by the parents, not *animals*. Gradually, children learn that dogs are "animals," cats are "animals," horses are "animals," and so on. The point at which animals are assigned to this category will depend on the animals children encounter during play and in reality. In more exotic parts of the world, elephants and giraffes may be among the earliest members of children's "animal" category.

The research of Carey (1985), gives insight to other aspects of concept development. She asked children aged 4–10 years about the characteristics of real animals and of dolls. The 4-year-olds differentiated between real animals and dolls, and attributed a number of relevant characteristics to animals, such as internal organs. None of the 4- to 7-year-olds commented that all animals and plants are living things, and that "dead" things are not alive. The children who said that dead things are dead also said the same thing about plants. The children's answers seemed to reflect a prototype rather than a feature-based strategy: the characteristics they attributed to animals were based on how similar they were to people. Four-year-olds attributed characteristics to new animals only if they were told that people also had these characteristics, and did not generalize in the same way from other animals. Neither did they transfer knowledge of people to things, even if the same rules could be applied, such as the weight of rocks and people. The 7-year-olds generalized both ways (Heyman et al., 2003). In addition, the younger children's categories were *asymmetrical*: animals are more like people than people are like animals.

Gradually, the children transferred more human characteristics to other living beings. The more familiar they were with the animals, the more human qualities they attributed to them. Carey concludes that children's early biological understanding is based on their perception of *similarities* between individual species rather than the taxonomic categorization used by older children and adults. Not until the age of 10 did the children consider plants to be living things and appeared to be using the term "living" in a way similar to adults. They understood that the body represents a whole and that the body's organs cooperate. The asymmetry typical of younger children's understanding was largely absent among the 10-year-olds. The children's answers thus reflected the general principle that children make use of their previous knowledge when learning something new. Because human characteristics are so prominent in children's experiences, assumptions about these characteristics often form the basis for younger children's exploration of animal characteristics.

The transition from non-hierarchical to hierarchical categorization is important for the formation of new structures and coherence in children's conceptual network. The studies conducted by Nelson and Carey suggest that children do not form larger hierarchical structures before entering school age. Education exerts a systematic and profound influence on children's conceptual structure by supplementing their "spontaneously" formed concepts through participation in various activities (Wells, 2008). A lot of schoolwork implies categorization – much time is spent, for example, on reviewing and clarifying the biological taxonomy (Wertsch, 1991). It is at school that children learn that whales are mammals rather than fish, the way children tend to classify them spontaneously. Nevertheless, not all concepts undergo this type of reorganization. Many adolescent and adult concepts are non-hierarchical or associated with certain situations as well (Perraudin and Mounoud, 2009). Conceptual metaphors often form a cluster or chain-like structure, such as the concept "mother," which includes biological mother, foster mother, surrogate mother, step-mother, and so on. Some cultures do not base their biological categories on a taxonomy of species, genus, family, order and class. The Australian Dyirbal tribe, for example, assigns women, dogs, some snakes, some fish, the sun, the moon, shields, some spears, some trees and many things associated with water and fire to the same category *balan* (Lakoff, 1987). A group of farmers in Central Asia did not seem to form concepts based on hierarchy, but rather on their association with different activities. *Axe, saw* and *log,* for example, were considered part of the same conceptual category since they belonged to the same activity: cutting down trees and chopping them up for firewood (Luria, 1976).

Adolescents have developed a better understanding of the boundaries between different knowledge domains, but also an increasing ability to see similarities or correspondences between them. Nonetheless, conceptual development is not an unfinished jigsaw puzzle to which missing pieces are added and the totality reorganized to create a conceptual hierarchy. Most domains undergo extensive minor and major reorganization before a large and varied conceptual structure is established – a structure that continues to be impacted by experience and changes in society.

REASONING

The most common forms of reasoning are analogy, induction and deduction. All three are important in everyday thinking and scientific work, and hence also how they develop (Kuhn, 2013). *Analogical reasoning* means that children apply a familiar solution to a new "task," such as when toddlers are aware of the fact that

humans have a heart and deduce that apes have a heart as well. *Inductive reasoning* involves making a general assumption on the basis of one or a few cases, such as an assumption that all swans are white because every swan one has ever seen has been white. Induction leads to more or less probable assumptions depending on the observations they are based on (Hayes et al., 2010). *Deductive reasoning* moves from a general rule to a specific conclusion that must be true if the rule is correct. If the rule says that all swans are white, the swans in the park must be white. Thus, deduction is a "top-down" process whose logical conclusion *must* be true. Observations that do not conform to the rule require the rule to be rejected. If a single black swan is observed, the rule that all swans are white must be incorrect (Johnson-Laird, 1999). Reasoning is a resource-efficient way of solving problems because it allows one to arrive at decisions about what to do without first having to try out several scenarios. More advanced forms of reasoning include *metacognitive* skills – thinking about thinking.

The reasoning of children and adolescents undergoes age-related changes. However, both children and adults occasionally draw wrong conclusions, and their errors reflect the knowledge they have (and don't have) as well as how they analyze tasks and choose solution strategies. In addition, reasoning can take place individually or in collaboration with others.

Analogical reasoning

Analogy is a kind of similarity (Holyoak, 2005). The earliest reasoning is based on observations of perceptual or functional similarities. Young children may notice a similarity in the relationship between things and properties, such as between "wide–narrow" and "high–low" (Bulloch and Opfer, 2009). When a 2-year-old uses a rake to get hold of a toy after having seen an adult use a candy cane for the same purpose, a form of analogical reasoning tells the child that using the rake can be another way of achieving the same goal. Children do not choose a shorter candy cane that more closely resembles the cane used by the adult, but that is too short to reach the target (Brown, 1989).

Goswami (1992) maintains that the ability to notice similarities is innate and that children can perceive similarities between relations as early as the first months of life. The basic mechanism is thus in place, but children's reasoning depends on sufficient relevant knowledge and analogical relations that are not too abstract. When children first begin to use analogies depends on the context and the child's experience in each domain. A 3-year-old who says "Gasoline is milk for the car" bases his knowledge on the milk he himself drinks to explain why cars need to be refueled. Five-year-old Ross was at the cemetery together with his mother, asking her whether the big tombstones were meant for kings. He applied his knowledge of the relationship between "kings" and "ordinary people" to "large tombstones" and "small tombstones" (DeLoache et al., 1998). In another study, children were asked: "Food is to body as rain is to . . .?" (ground). To respond correctly, the children had to know that food nurtures the body and rain nurtures the ground. The children who did not have this knowledge gave associative answers related to rain, such as "water", "storm" and "coat" (Goswami, 1992). A lack of knowledge makes younger children feel more insecure and easily leads them to change the correct answer. One girl chose "eyes" on the pairing task "Radio–ears, television–?", but quickly changed "eyes" to "plug" at the experimenter's suggestion.

The task complexity increases as the number of relational items grows. The pairing task "Horse–foal, dog–?" (puppy), for example, consists of two binary relationships. Two-year-olds are able to manage this task, but only if there are distinct similarities (Singer-Freeman and Bauer, 2008). The task "Peter is fairer than Tom, John is fairer than Peter; who is fairer – John or Tom?" includes three binary relations: Peter–Tom, John–Peter and John–Tom. Five-year-olds are usually able to solve this type of task. Younger children can easily be distracted by irrelevant information, especially when tasks are complex; it is not until the age of 9–11 years that they are able to cope with both complexity and distraction (Richland et al., 2006).

Older children have more knowledge, are more aware of the relationships between things, and hold on to their own answers to a greater degree. Adolescents give more correct answers, justify their answers based on relational similarity, and resist counter-suggestions. Even so, it is not difficult to create analogies that many adults are unable to work out because they

lack knowledge in the domains from which the analogy is taken.

According to Halford (1992), analogical thinking arises from the ability to form mental models. As children's cognitive capacity increases, they form new and more advanced mental models and become capable of mastering more complex and abstract analogical relationships. While early analogical thinking is implicit, children become more aware of their own thinking with age (meta-knowledge). Younger children often make use of the first model that comes to mind. If the model is wrong, the answer will be wrong as well. Older children can keep several models in mind and consider them at the same time (Halford and Andrews, 2004).

Explanations based on analogy are a key element in all teaching. Students' ability to reason by analogy is therefore of great importance for how they manage their schoolwork, and teachers need to ensure that the students understand the analogies they use in teaching (Vendetti et al., 2015).

Logical and pragmatic reasoning

In logical reasoning, all inferences are restricted to the rules of logic. It is the logic of reasoning itself, rather than its content, that is of importance. Whether a deductive inference is correct does not depend on whether a condition actually is or may be a certain way, but on the agreement between a set of premises and a conclusion. Given two premises: a) there are more eggs in basket X than in basket Y, and b) there are more eggs in basket Y than in basket Z, more eggs must be in basket X than in Z by *necessity*. Anything else would be impossible. If basket Z actually contained more eggs than basket X, it would be *incompatible* with the two premises. One of them would have to be wrong. If the premises are correct, the conclusion *must* also be correct (Johnson-Laird, 1999).

In logic, a *syllogism* is a statement about the relation between two objects or conditions, based on two independent statements about the relation between them (Johnson-Laird, 1999). According to Donaldson (1978), even toddlers are able to draw (implicit) syllogistic inferences based on their – often limited – knowledge, as in the following example (DeLoache et al., 1998):

Three-year-old Laura takes an opened can of soda from the refrigerator and says to her mother: "Whose is this? It's not yours, cause it doesn't have lipstick".

Laura's reasoning can formally be described as follows:

a Her mother's soda can always has lipstick marks after she has drunk from it.
b The opened soda can has no lipstick marks.
c The soda can is not her mother's.

Expressed more generally, the logic behind this example is: If *p*, then *q*. Not *q*, therefore *not p* (no lipstick, therefore not her mother's can). Logic is a mental tool that makes it possible to disregard issues involving content and experience, and to ensure internal consistency between a premise and a conclusion. But there is little reason to ascribe an understanding of logic to a 3-year-old. It is more likely that Laura's conclusion was based on her observations of soda cans her mother had drunk from. With clear instructions, 4-year-olds can learn how to pick one of four flowers that gets a monkey to sneeze when observing the monkey's reaction to different flower combinations (Schulz and Gopnik, 2004). But without clear guidance younger children's reasoning is intuitive and unsystematic. Their answers – like Laura's – are based on their experience and knowledge of circumstances without considering the necessity inherent in logic (Kuhn, 2013).

A qualitative change in reasoning across knowledge areas seems to take place around the age of 11 or 12 (Marini and Case, 1994; Richland et al., 2006). Children become more attentive to logical connections, and around 13 years of age, adolescents improve at solving problems based on internal logical consistency (Markovits et al., 1989).

This is not to say that logic takes over reasoning completely. The reasoning of adolescents and adults is not exclusively based on logic, but equally much on experience and knowledge of what usually is true. Wason (1977) and other researchers have shown that adolescents and adults often reason in a similar way as children when the material is new and unfamiliar. They manage tasks involving areas they have experi-ence with better than more abstract tasks. In tasks like the first in Box 12.5, people tend to search *positive evidence*: if a vowel is opposite a blue square, and a blue square is opposite a vowel, the hypothesis is confirmed. If a consonant is opposite a blue square, it has no bearing on the evaluation of the rule since the rule says nothing about it. The tasks must be solved by looking for *negative evidence* (such as 3-year-old Laura did to determine whether the soda can belonged to her mother). Only a white square opposite a vowel and a vowel opposite a white square would invalidate the rule that there must be a blue square opposite a vowel. The need for negative evidence seemed clearer to the participants in the second task. The percentage of correct answers increased dramatically for a task with a corresponding logical structure, but related to an activity that the participants were familiar with.

Cheng and Holyoak (1985) explain these results by proposing that both children and adults instead of logic make use of *pragmatic reason-ing schemas*. These schemas are abstracted from past experience and the answers depend on the individual's ability to associate a given problem with experience from earlier tasks and situations with a similar goal. Children are able solve this type of task if they have the relevant experience and can base their reasoning on related mental models (Halford and Andrews, 2004; Chen and Klahr, 2008). For example, in a study, children aged 3–4 years were told the rule "If Sally wants to play outside, she must put her coat on." When asked to point out where Sally is being naughty and not doing what her mom told her, most of the children pointed to the picture of a girl playing outside without wearing a coat (Harris and Núñez, 1996). The presentation of this task is not entirely comparable to the tasks in Box 12.5, but 6- to 7-year-olds are able to solve this type of task when the material is familiar and meaningful to them, such as breaking a rule about when trucks are allowed to drive into town (Girotto et al., 1988; Light et al., 1990). Younger children, however, have difficulty gen-eralizing and applying their knowledge to new situations, and begin to reason all over again in the next situation (Kuhn, 2013). The variation in children's reasoning demonstrates that they do not develop the ability for formal reasoning in a vacuum: logical knowledge must operate on

BOX 12.5 LOGICAL AND PRAGMATIC REASONING (based on Wason, 1977)

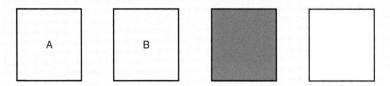

PROBLEM 1 (LOGICAL)

The participant was shown the cards above and given the following rule: "If there is a vowel on one side of the card, there is always a blue square on the other side." The task was to find out which of the four cards need to be turned to determine whether the rule is true.

The typical answer was A only, or A and the blue square. The correct answer is A and the white square. The rule can only be rejected if a white square is opposite a vowel, or a vowel opposite a white square. Only about 10 percent of the participants gave the correct answer to this task.

Drinks beer	Drinks mineral water	Is 16 years old	Is 22 years old

PROBLEM 2 (PRAGMATIC)

The participant was shown the cards above and asked to imagine a policeman who checks whether a restaurant adheres to the following rule for serving alcohol: "Only those above the age of 18 years are allowed to drink beer." The cards included information about four restaurant guests. One side listed their age, the other what they were drinking. The task was to find out which of the four cards needed to be turned to determine whether the rule for serving alcohol had been broken.

About 75 percent of the participants answered this task correctly: they checked the card of the person drinking beer and the card of the 16-year-old. The task has precisely the same logical structure as Problem 1, but relates to an area the subjects had concrete experience with. When they were familiar with the situation, the participants also understood the need for negative evidence.

and in the context of the child's knowledge of the world (Overton et al., 1987).

Some types of tasks cannot be solved through pragmatic reasoning and require logical knowledge. Children and adults most likely use both logical and pragmatic rules in their reasoning. Pragmatic schemas have their origin in children's individual experiences, which are largely shaped by cultural activities. Cultural differences suggest that the application of logical rules depends on the introduction to formal reasoning

as part of the regular school curriculum in industrialized countries (Richland et al., 2010). It is also likely that dialectical reasoning is important for the ability to reach beyond one's own experiential rationale (see below). Logic thus becomes a cultural tool in the Vygotskian sense rather than an individual trait as described by Piaget's theory. Furthermore, it is a tool that different cultures have developed in different ways and to varying degrees (Nisbett and Norenzayan, 2002).

Dialectical reasoning

Dialectical reasoning is a form of shared problem solving, involving two or more people who argue on behalf of their individual views. Taking a social constructivist perspective, Salmon and Zeitz (1995) describe dialectical reasoning as a fundamentally social process. The individual child's capacity for this type of reasoning and reflection is the result of internalized social processes that in turn affect the child's dialectical reasoning in social contexts. Therefore, conscious reasoning is not merely the product of joint reflection, but also forms the basis for renewed social and individual dialectical reasoning and cognitive development. However, younger children have difficulty maintaining attention on both their own opinion and that of others. Dialectical reasoning is therefore mostly relevant to older children and adolescents (Kuhn, 2013). Dialectical reasoning and argumentation in the classroom may support the development of scientific and critical reasoning (Osborne, 2010).

ATYPICAL DEVELOPMENT

The research presented in this chapter shows that children, adolescents and adults do not think and reason in any one particular way, but approach problems from different angles, depending on the situation and the knowledge and strategies they have acquired through personal experience and informal and formal training. Disorders that affect children's cognitive functioning can also affect their reasoning, including intellectual disability (Harris and Greenspan, 2016). One study showed that children with specific learning disorders who scored within the normal range on intelligence tests had greater problems with analogical reasoning than children without learning disorders; this was particularly true of children who struggled with math at school (Schiff et al., 2009). Other studies have found that children with autism spectrum disorders have difficulty drawing inferences (Grant et al., 2004; Leevers and Harris, 2000). At the same time, it is important to map the types of tasks children with different forms of atypical development do *not* have particular difficulties with. Some studies, for example, have found that children with autism spectrum disorder are able to master analogical reasoning as well as their peers, but that they do not always make use of this ability, even in areas they are quite familiar with. They need explicit instructions to understand the nature of the problem (Green et al., 2014).

SUMMARY

1 Children's developing understanding of the world includes a *spatial dimension*, a *temporal dimension* and *causal relationships*. From an early age, children perceive that objects exist and have a physical location even when they cannot be experienced directly (*object permanence*). "A, not B-error" means that children search where they recently found an object rather than where they last saw it being hidden. With age, children make increasingly precise use of *geometric cues* and *landmarks*. Independent locomotion and exploration of the physical environment are important elements in this development.

2 Children in preschool age understand time, speed and distance as separate entities. Closer to school age, children are able to manage two dimensions at a time, and three by the age of 9. By counting, using a stopwatch or other "timing aid," children are able to manage this type of task earlier.

3 Children's initial understanding of time comes from their own experiences with routines and schedules. Conversations with parents and other adults help children organize days and events on a timeline between past and future. Formal and informal training are important for a cultural understanding of time.

Continued

4 *Physical causality* has to do with the physical behavior of objects and how they interact. Studies have found an emerging understanding of physical causality in 3-month-olds, but children are much older before the concept of causality includes a sense of physical *necessity*. According to a nativist view, it is an understanding too complex to be acquired and must therefore be innate. In contrast to this, Baillargeon suggests that the development of physical causality is based on an innate *principle of persistence*. Children's early understanding of individual events is later transformed into a general understanding of physical causality. From an *information processing* perspective, children are assumed to notice events that occur simultaneously and gradually form an understanding of physical causality, for example what happens when objects collide.

5 According to *feature-based theories*, children's earliest object categorizations are based on the *perceptual* or *functional* properties of objects. Mandler describes a development that moves from *perceptual* to *conceptual categories* by way of *perceptual meaning*. Features and categories are initially global and gradually become more differentiated.

6 From the perspective of *prototype theory*, Rosch suggests that people, animals, things and so forth are assigned to three conceptual levels: superordinate, basic and subordinate, and that children develop basic level categories first. Quinn describes a development from collections of individual exemplars to the creation of prototypes that form conceptual "magnets." New objects are assigned to concepts that are perceived to have important similarities with the prototype. Prototypes are summary-level representations, traits are perceived in context.

7 Mandler interprets her results to mean that children acquire global categories before categories at the basic level. Quinn and Eimas' findings suggest that children's early differentiations mainly occur at the basic level. According to Rakison, children initially become aware of one or two perceptually prominent features. Gradually, they form overall categories with complex patterns of perceptual and functional traits. Early categorization is affected by the characteristics of the things children are aware of in the moment.

8 Nelson describes *slot-filler categories* in children's transition from "spontaneous" to "scientific" concepts. Slot-fillers are linked to a particular situation and do not form hierarchies based on their own function, but consist of things that can fill the same place in an event or activity. *Class inclusion* is a necessary property in any hierarchical system.

9 Beginning in early childhood, language becomes increasingly important for children's categorizations. Words are cues to meaning and contribute to both the formation of new concepts and to the reorganization of previously established concepts. Children under the age of 2½ years rarely use superordinate terms generally in the same way as adults, but in the way their parents use them in conversation with the child.

10 *Analogical reasoning* is based on relational similarity. Goswami suggests children have an innate ability to notice such similarities, and that relations continue to become more complex with age. Others believe development to be the result of an age-related increase in cognitive capacity. Compared with younger children, older children are able to keep several models in mind and consider them at the same time. Analogy is a key element in all teaching and the development of analogical reasoning is of importance for children's schoolwork.

11 Younger children are able to draw *deductive* inferences, but their reasoning is mostly based on experience rather than logic. Adolescents and adults make more use of logic, but studies based on *selection tasks* and similar problems show that also adults are able to master reasoning tasks better when they can relate them to events they have experience with. One explanation is that children and adults use *pragmatic reasoning schemas* abstracted from past

experience. Another explanation is that reasoning has a basis in mental models formed in connection with certain situations, and that it is easier to activate mental models that lie closer to the individual's own experiences. Children are able to solve reasoning tasks that are not too complex and for which they have the relevant mental models. Pragmatic schemas underline the importance of activities for children's knowledge about the world.

12 *Dialectical reasoning* sets the perspectives of two or more persons against each other. Children's ability to reason and reflect is the result of internalized dialectical social processes.

13 *Cognitive disorders* can affect children's concept formation and reasoning, including children with learning disorders, intellectual disability and autism spectrum disorders.

CORE ISSUES

- The development of physical causality.
- Features and prototypes in object concepts.
- Logic and pragmatics in reasoning.

SUGGESTIONS FOR FURTHER READING

Baillargeon, R. (2008). Innate ideas revisited: For a principle of persistence in infants' physical reasoning. *Perspectives on Psychological Science*, 3, 2–13.

Friedman, W. J. (2005). Developmental and cognitive perspectives on humans' sense of the times of past and future events. *Learning and Motivation*, 36, 145–158.

Learmonth, A. E., Newcombe, N. S., Sheridan, N., & Jones, M. (2008). Why size counts: Children's spatial reorientation in large and small enclosures. *Developmental Science*, 11, 414–426.

Rosch, E. (1999). Reclaiming concepts. *Journal of Consciousness Studies*, 6, 61–77.

Schulz, L. E., & Gopnik, A. (2004). Causal learning across domains. *Developmental Psychology*, 40, 162–176.

Contents

CHAPTER 13

MIND UNDERSTANDING

umans seem to have a *species-specific* ability to understand and reason about people, a *social cognitive* ability that other species lack. It forms the basis for human interaction and understanding of one another's actions, intentions, desires, thoughts and feelings, of sympathy and empathy, but also to deceive or mislead, as well as to expose trickery and deceit.

Thus, children develop a *mind understanding*, an understanding that they themselves and others perceive the world around them and form mental representations of people, things and events. The ability to perceive that others see something represents an emergent understanding of other people's minds, and gradually also of *what* they see. This includes an understanding of the fact that others may lack or have knowledge different from one's own, and that this knowledge will determine how the other person reasons and acts. Because the mind cannot be observed directly, an understanding of other people's minds requires the child to draw inferences about their perceptions, thoughts, desires and emotions beyond what she can observe directly. Therefore, this type of understanding is sometimes referred to as "theory of mind" (Premack and Woodruff, 1978). It is also referred to as *mentalizing*, defined as the interpretation of one's own and others' behavior as an expression of mental states, desires, feelings, beliefs, and so on. In a broader sense, mentalizing is described as a process that involves all thinking about relations, human interaction and psychological processes in human beings (Allen, 2003; Fonagy et al., 2004). Others talk about the development of "commonsense psychology," "mindreading" or "social understanding" (Carpendale and Lewis, 2015). I have chosen to use the term "mind understanding" because it is concise and theoretically neutral.

VISUAL PERSPECTIVE

In the second half of their first year, most children become increasingly attentive to others looking at them and to what others are looking at, and follow their gaze to look in the same direction as the other person (see p. 299). One-year-olds show a nascent ability to take the perspective of others when they leave their mother's lap and crawl to see what an adult is looking at behind a wall that prevents the child from seeing what is there (Moll and Tomasello, 2004). When they are a little older, they also understand that the adult may see something different than they do (Flavell, 2004).

Two levels of visual perspective-taking

Flavell (1992, 2004) describes two levels of visual perspective knowledge. At *Level 1*, children understand that other people see the world around them, while *Level 2* involves an understanding of *what* they see, the fact that the same thing can appear differently depending on the viewpoint, and that people may see things in different ways.

Children who perceive the visual perspective of others on Level 1 know that they themselves and others do not necessarily see the same thing. With sufficient cues, they can infer what others do and do not see. A development in the ability to assume someone else's visual perspective seems to take place between the ages of 2 and 3 years. In a study of 2- to 3-year-olds, even the youngest children were able to place a toy in such a way that the experimenter *could see it*, even when this meant that the children had to place the toy out of their own line of sight. The 2-year-olds, however, had difficulty hiding a toy so the experimenter on the other side of a screen *could not see it*. Some of the children hid the toy behind the screen so the experimenter could see the toy, while they themselves could not see it. The 3-year-olds had no problems with this task. After hiding the toy correctly, several of them went to the experimenter's side of the screen to make sure that it was not visible from that side (Gopnik and Meltzoff, 1997).

In another study, children aged 2–5 years were shown a card with a picture of a cat on one side and a dog on the other. The 3-year-olds had no difficulty saying that the experimenter saw the cat while they saw the dog when the card was held between them (Masangkay et al., 1974). The same study also included a picture of a turtle that could be positioned so the turtle seemed to be standing on its legs when viewed from one side of the table, while it seemed to be upside-down from the other. In this case, most of the 3-year-olds were unable to say what the experimenter was seeing, even when they could go around the table and view the picture from the other side. They lacked the cognitive skills of Level 2 perspective-taking, which this task requires. Almost all of the 4- to 5-year-olds managed this task.

According to Flavell, Levels 1 and 2 require the same skills and knowledge, but children at Level 2 additionally know that things can look different from different viewpoints. If given sufficient cues, they can infer approximately how things look from another visual angle. Four-year-olds rarely fail on any of the previously mentioned tasks.

The three mountain task

In a classic experiment, Piaget and Inhelder (1956) found that children below the age of 7 had difficulties taking a visual perspective different from their own (Box 13.1). Their explanation of these results is that children below this age are *egocentric* and unable to take the perspective of

BOX 13.1 THE THREE MOUNTAIN TASK (Piaget and Inhelder, 1956)

Children aged 4–11 years were first allowed to examine a model of three mountains from all sides. Then they were seated in front of the model at one of its sides. A doll was placed on a chair at one of the other sides. The children were then shown photographs taken from all sides, and asked to identify the photograph of the mountain as the doll was seeing it.

Children below the age of 7 years had difficulty saying which of the photographs showed the mountains from a doll's point of view, while older children accomplished these tasks.

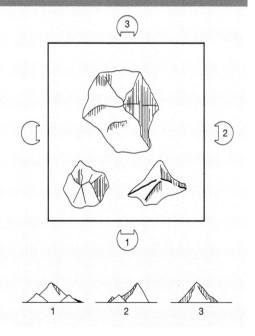

others in addition to their own. Donaldson (1978) disagrees with the assumption that children are egocentric, and suggested that much younger children have the necessary skills to solve this type of task, which requires perspective-taking skills at Level 2. She maintained that the mountain task was only difficult because the children lacked the relevant experience. Therefore, she conducted a similar experiment using a model of a house with several rooms and a boy doll and a policeman doll placed in different parts of the house (Box 13.2). Like in Piaget's experiment, the child was sitting in one place and nearly all of the youngest children accomplished this task. Donaldson explains these results by the fact that her task – unlike the mountain task – represented a meaningful context for the children. Children at this age have been playing hide and seek and know that the police can look for someone who is hiding, while they have little experience working out how mountains look from different sides.

Another possible explanation for children's problems with the mountain task is that they lacked clear cues for the mountains' placements. When Newcombe and Huttenlocher (1992) placed various stickers on the sides of the mountains in the model, children as young as 3 years succeeded in the task. The stickers functioned as "landmarks" for where the doll was looking

(see also p. 219). In effect, Donaldson's visual cues were simpler as well: all sides were equal, and the children only needed to look at the location of the police doll in relation to the walls to solve the task.

Whatever the reason for younger children's difficulties with the mountain task may be, these studies show that their difficulties are hardly caused by an egocentric worldview, as Piaget claims. Also more recent studies have found that children under the age of 7 have problems when the task is presented according to Piaget's model. In one study, children aged 4–8 years were shown two dolls photographing a scene with a pyramid, a cylinder and a cube from different sides. Most of the youngest children were unable to say which of the dolls had taken the pictures, while a majority of the 8-year-olds managed to do so well above the level of chance (Frick et al., 2014). Children are not egocentric, but find it difficult to take multiple perspectives in unfamiliar situations with indistinct cues.

PRIVATE SPEECH

When listening to conversations between toddlers, one can occasionally wonder whether they are talking about the same subject or with each other at all. Often children do not convey enough

---

BOX 13.2 THE DOLLHOUSE EXPERIMENT (from Donaldson, 1978)

Thirty children aged 3½–5 years participated in the study. The child was sitting in front of a doll house and was told that a police doll was trying to catch a boy doll, and that he or she was supposed to help the boy doll hide so the police doll could not find him. The child sat in one place, while the police doll was moved around. The child's task was to say where the boy had to hide from the police in order not to be seen. Nearly 90 percent of a group of the youngest children with an average age of 3;9 years were able to tell correctly where the boy doll should hide.

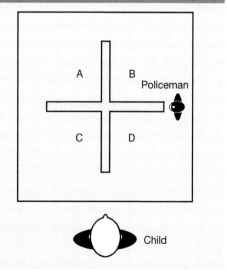

information for a listener to be able to understand what they are talking about. They may begin by describing an event without giving any background information such as where it happened, who was involved, and so on. Or they may refer to *him* without having mentioned a male person. Children also talk when they are engaged in something without anyone else being present.

There are many contradictory explanations for these forms of language use. Piaget (1959) associates this type of private speech with *egocentricity*, an inability to take the perspective of others. According to Piaget, 50 percent of preschool children's speech is egocentric in the sense that it does not lead to effective communication, and consists of what he calls *collective monologues*. Vygotsky (1962) offers a different explanation: private speech shows that children often do not speak to communicate something to others, but to solve problems and to plan and regulate their own actions. Such use of language may *seem* egocentric, but since it is not intended to be communicative, it is not egocentric. Instead, it is part of children's internalization of conversations with others, a step on the way to *internal speech*, a transition from solving problems in conversation with others to solving them independently without talking aloud (Alderson-Day and Fernyhough, 2015).

The difference between Piaget's individual constructivism and Vygotsky's social constructivism becomes clear in the context of this debate (see Chapters 2 and 10). Piaget's theory claims that cognitive knowledge comes from within. Toddlers talk side by side rather than with each other because they are not yet able to communicate in a way that takes into account other people's perspective. Their speech is egocentric and will be replaced by rational and social speech once they become aware that they need to adapt their speech to the listener and have acquired the cognitive tools for doing so. According to Vygotsky's theory, cognitive skills are formed through interaction with other people. Language is culturally imparted knowledge. It comes from outside and does not need to be socialized, but to be internalized. Private speech disappears once language has become fully internalized as a tool for thinking.

In line with Piaget's theory, there are many examples of children not taking sufficient account of the other person's knowledge in situations where they seem to try to communicate with someone, as in this telephone conversation between 3-year-old Alice (A) and her grandmother (G) (Warren and Tate, 1992, p. 258):

A: *I got a green one* (opening topic).
G: *You got a what?*
A: *A green one.*
G: *A green one . . .*
A: *There's a baby out there* (points out window).
G: *There is . . .*
A: *Is a baby out there.*
G: *My goodness.*

Piaget's explanation that children lack the cognitive skills to take the perspective of others is also supported by a study in which children from second through eighth grade were to teach a new game to a group of adults. Half of the adults were blindfolded while the other half could see. Children in the lowest grade did not take into account whether the adult could see, but gave the same description in both situations. Eighth-graders used many more words when describing the game to the blindfolded adults (Flavell et al., 1968).

Vygotsky's theory, on the other hand, is supported by the fact that younger children often talk while doing something else. Their speech does not seem to be directed at anyone, and often no one else is present (McGonigle-Chalmers et al., 2014). Sound recordings made of toddlers before falling asleep show that they may lie in bed and talk to themselves about the day's events and what will happen the next day, as in this monologue of 24-month-old Emily (Nelson, 2015b, p. 174):

That Daddy brings down basement washing,
I can hold Emmy, so,
Daddy brings down the,
the washing on the basement,
washing,
so my can.

Similarly, while most gestures used by toddlers have a clear communicative intent, toddlers also point without such an intent – *private pointing* – in connection with memory and problem solving in situations in which there is no one to communicate with (Delgado et al., 2009, 2011). Deaf children use *private sign language* similar to how hearing children use private speech (Winsler, 2009). The incidence of private speech or sign increases when children have to solve complex tasks, resist temptations, experience difficulties or become frustrated, and use language to regulate both their actions and their feelings (Bono and Bizri, 2014; Luria, 1961; Manfra et al., 2014).

Research thus lends a certain amount of support to both Vygotsky and Piaget, and a practical differentiation between their theories is not entirely unproblematic in this context. A possible explanation could be that children at this age are egocentric in the sense that they lack the necessary insight to take sufficient account of the person they are talking to, *as well as* using gestures and language "privately" in non-communicative contexts to manage *executive functions* that regulate attention, actions and emotions (see Chapter 11).

The proportion of children who talk while engaged in tasks and other activities steadily decreases from preschool age to adolescence: from nearly half of all 5-year-olds to 10 percent of 17-year-olds. Children with attention deficit disorder (ADHD) and behavioral problems use speech to control attention, actions and emotions in a similar way as other children, but continue to use overt private speech for somewhat longer. They seem to benefit from regulating themselves through speech, and it may be useful to encourage them to use speech as a self-regulatory strategy, even if they talk out loud because their speech has yet to be internalized (Winsler, 2009).

Private speech after childhood also occurs in typical development – adolescents speak quietly when working out problems, and many of them report that they use inner speech while solving difficult tasks (Winsler and Naglieri, 2003). Even adults sometimes talk to themselves when faced with a difficult task or making plans (Duncan and Tarulli, 2009).

EARLY UNDERSTANDING OF DESIRES AND BELIEFS

Mind understanding is about subjective experience, the fact that other people are thinking beings who reason and act according to their own desires and perception of a situation (Doherty, 2009).

Desires

Children become aware of other people's desires early on. Unlike 14-month-olds, 18-month-old children understand that people can desire different things and that others can have the same or different wishes as their own, for example that an adult wants broccoli while they prefer a cracker (Repacholi and Gopnik, 1997). They expect other people to act according to their own desires, for example that an adult will choose the same thing she usually chooses. At the end of their second year, children often speak with their parents about desiring or wanting something, but it is not until the age of 2½ that they understand that people can have conflicting desires about something, for example that Peter wants ice cream and Mary doesn't (Poulin-Dubois et al., 2009). Three-year-olds have difficulty separating a person's action goals – their *intention* – from the action as such. Four-year-olds have a better understanding of the mental and subjective aspects of desires, the fact that someone could wish to do something and try without succeeding, for example that a person can end up somewhere else than where he intended to travel (Feinfield et al., 1999).

Beliefs

Understanding the minds of others involves recognizing that the mental world can differ from the real world and that people can have false beliefs about something – such as Little Red Riding Hood who *thinks* it is her grandma lying in bed – and that they will act based on their *beliefs* about the world rather than how it actually is. The question is, at what point in their development children acquire this type of understanding. The standard test for assessing the development of mind understanding is based on tasks showing whether children understand that other people act according to their own perception, especially tasks involving false beliefs. These are often called theory-of-mind tasks and deal with two types of events: unexpected transfer and unexpected content.

Unexpected transfer

In this kind of task, something is moved unknown to a person. In Wimmer and Perner's (1983) original experiment, children were told a story about

BOX 13.3 **THE FIRST MAXI EXPERIMENT (Wimmer and Perner, 1983)**

Children between the ages of 4–9 years were told and shown a story in which a boy named Maxi put his chocolate in a gray cupboard before going out to play. While outside, his mother moves the chocolate to a blue cupboard. Then the children were asked: "Where will Maxi look for the chocolate when he comes back?" The 3- to 4-year-olds replied that he would look in the blue cupboard where the chocolate, unknown to Maxi, was moved. Fifty-seven percent of children aged 4–6 years and 86 percent of children 6 years and older correctly answered that Maxi would look in the gray cupboard, where he believed it to be.

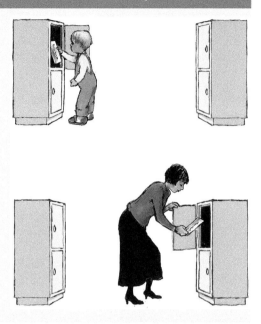

Maxi's chocolate, which was moved without his knowledge (Box 13.3).

When asked where Maxi will look for the chocolate, the youngest children answered that Maxi will look in the place where the chocolate was moved, while over half the children between 4 and 6 years and most of the older children answered that he will look where he put the chocolate before leaving, in other words where he *thinks* it is. Wimmer and Perner interpreted their findings to mean that children under the age of 4–5 years lack the cognitive skills to understand that other people will act based on their perception of the situation, even when it contradicts the facts. Therefore, they understand the question of where Maxi will look as a question about where the chocolate is, and base their response on that. Many subsequent studies with different variations on the Maxi task have shown that children usually begin to master this type of task around the age of 3–5 (Wellman et al., 2001).

Some researchers have pointed out that children's responses do not necessarily reflect a lack of mind understanding, but that limited language comprehension can lead children to misunderstand the question. Therefore, researchers have varied the verbal instructions and implementation in trying to identify the factors that are decisive for children's ability to solve the problem. For example, when Siegal and Beattie (1991) changed the question to "Where will Maxi first look for his chocolate when he comes back?" twice as many 3- to 4-year-olds were able to answer correctly. Including "first" in the question seemed to make them aware of the possibility that Maxi would look in several places, and that he looks in the wrong place before looking where the chocolate is actually located. This interpretation is supported by a relation between children's ability to retell stories and their answers to tasks of the Maxi type, independent of age (Lewis et al., 1994).

Unexpected content

The second type of experiment deals with children's understanding of having acted on a false belief *themselves*. These studies typically are based on asking children about the content of a box that is clearly labeled, for example with a brand of chocolate. Then they get to see that it contains something completely different and are asked what they thought was in the box

(Box 13.4). Children under the age of 4 years usually answer that it was the actual content of the box, rather than what they previously said it contained.

Children generally like to do well and give the right answers. One possible explanation for why the younger children in the experiment answered *pencils* when asked what they had thought was in the Smarties box may be that they were embarrassed to have given the wrong answer and did not want to say so. Therefore, Wimmer and Hartl (1991) conducted a similar experiment with "Kasperl," a puppet most Austrian children know from children's televi-

sion. Kasperl is notorious for making mistakes, so it would not be strange if he had a false belief about something. It turned out, however, that it made no difference whether the children were asked what Kasperl had thought was in the box or whether they were asked what they themselves had thought.

A significant change in mind understanding thus seems to occur around the age of 4. Wimmer and Hartl (1991) suggest that 3-year-olds have yet to form a notion of what it means to assume or believe something and therefore do not distinguish between assumption and reality. It seemed as if the children in the study understood

BOX 13.4 SMARTIES EXPERIMENT (Astington and Gopnik, 1988; Gopnik and Astington, 1988)

Children aged 3;0–6;3 years were shown a Smarties box and asked what they thought was in the box. Even the youngest children were familiar with the box and answered *Smarties*. The experimenters opened the box so the children could see that it contained pencils instead of Smarties. When the children were asked what the box contained, all of them answered *pencils*. Then the box was closed again and the children were asked what they themselves had thought was in the box before it was opened. The following dialogue between the experimenter (E) and a child (C) aged 3;8 years is a typical protocol for children under the age of 4 years:

E: Look. Here's a box.
C: Smarties!
E: Let's look inside.
C: Okay.
E: Let's open it and look inside.
C: Oh . . . holy moly . . . pencils!
E: Now I'm going to put them back and close it up again. *[does so]*
E: Now . . . When you first saw the box, before we opened it, what did you think was inside it?
C: Pencils.
E: Nicky *[friend of the subject]* hasn't seen inside this box. When Nicky comes in and sees it . . . When Nicky sees the box, what will he think is inside it?
B: Pencils.

About half of the youngest children (3;0–4;0 years) and most of the older children (4;1–6;3 years) gave the correct answer, saying they had thought the box contained Smarties.

the question "When you first saw the box, what did you think was in it?" to mean, "When you first saw the box, what was in it?" Winner and Hartl therefore conducted a new experiment in which the children could observe the contents of the box being replaced. The children were asked about the contents of the Smarties box and could see that it contained Smarties. These were taken out of the box and exchanged with pencils while the children watched. This time, when the children were asked what they had first thought, twice as many answered correctly: 87 instead of 43 percent when the box contained pencils when they opened it. Wimmer and Hartl interpret the higher number of correct answers to indicate that the children understood the question as, "When you first saw the box, what was in it?" Thus, they did not reply to a question about what they thought, but about the contents of the box. In the standard task, the children did not get to see the pencils in the box throughout the experiment and therefore answered incorrectly.

Freeman and Lacohée (1995) view these results in connection with *childhood amnesia*, the fact that older children and adults do not remember what happened early in life (see p. 205). They believe that toddlers have a limited mental capacity and that the results of the Smarties experiments reflect a cognitive mechanism that prevents children from incorporating all of their previous misconceptions. Since only the most recent belief is preserved, and everything contradicting it is forgotten, children form consistent beliefs. False beliefs are preserved as well, but only as long as no new beliefs are formed that run contrary to the old ones. This is why children are unable to reconcile their initial belief that the box contains Smarties with the fact that they know there are no Smarties in it. Freeman and Lacohée thus view younger children's failure to remember earlier beliefs as an expression of a *positive* developmental mechanism.

Over the past 30 years, thousands of studies have been conducted with preschool-age children and tasks of the Maxi and Smarties type. Although the results vary depending on language instructions and implementation, most studies have found that by around 4 years of age, children have developed a mind understanding that younger children do not have. They understand that people may lack knowledge or believe something that does not correspond to reality, and that this determines how people act in a given situation (Schaafsma et al., 2015; Wellman et al., 2001). A number of studies involving much younger children, however, have raised doubts about this conclusion (Baillargeon et al., 2010).

Very early understanding of others' beliefs

A number of studies have been founded on the assumption that the traditional theory-of-mind tasks require cognitive and linguistic skills that go beyond the ability to perceive what others know (Caron, 2009). Researchers have therefore tried to find new methods capable of revealing an *implicit* mind understanding, that is, an understanding that does not require children to formulate their responses explicitly (through language or by pointing). Instead of questioning the children, their spontaneous reactions to events are observed, similar to studies of early spatial concepts (see p. 218).

The first study involved an *unexpected transfer* of a toy watermelon slice from one box to another, and a woman who either sees it or does not see it (Box 13.5). Onishi and Baillargeon (2005) interpret the results as indicating that the children were able to understand that the woman believed the watermelon to be where it was when she left and not where it actually was, and that she therefore had a false belief about the location of the watermelon. Other studies involving unexpected transfer have used children's *gaze direction* – where they look – based on the assumption that children have an implicit tendency to anticipate the actions they expect others to perform. One example of this is a study in which a woman was supposed to find a ball in one of two boxes. She saw the ball being placed inside the box, but in some of the trials it was moved while she appeared to be distracted by a ringing telephone. Since she did not see what happened, she formed a false belief of where the ball was located. Seventeen out of 20 children aged 25 months first looked at the box in which the woman had to believe the ball to be, based on what she had seen. They did not look at the box in which the ball was actually hidden, but anticipated where the woman would look *based on her own knowledge* (Southgate et al., 2007a). Another study using measurements of brain activity found similar differences in response patterns as early as 6 months of age (Southgate and Vernetti, 2014).

BOX 13.5 MAXI EXPERIMENT WITH 15-MONTH-OLDS (based on Onishi and Baillargeon, 2005)

Fifty-six children aged around 15 months participated in the experiment. Each child was seated in front of a small puppet theater stage. (a) In order to familiarize the children with the material, they first watched a woman play with a toy watermelon slice for a few seconds and hide it inside a green or yellow box, always the same for each child. The woman wore a visor so the children could not use her eyes as a cue. (b) The following two trials ended with the woman putting her hand into the box with the watermelon, but without removing it and holding it in place until a curtain was lowered and the trial ended. Then the children were shown two different events that were to provide them with a basis for assumptions about where the woman would believe the watermelon to be. (c) Someone moves the watermelon without the woman seeing it, or the woman sees someone move the watermelon to the other box. (d) The woman reaches into the yellow or the green box. On some occasions, she reaches inside the box into which she had seen the watermelon being moved, or into the box that contained the watermelon before it was moved without her seeing it. Her actions are consistent with what she was able to know. At other times, she reaches inside the box to which the watermelon has been moved without her seeing it, or into the box from which she has seen the watermelon being moved. Both actions are in conflict with her knowledge of the watermelon's location. The children looked a little longer at the woman when she put her hand into the empty box after having seen the watermelon being moved, or into the box that contained the watermelon when she had not seen it being moved. This is interpreted as caused by the woman acting in a way not expected by the children.

Studies based on gaze direction assume that children at this age have acquired a certain degree of mind understanding, but are unable to apply it in practice. Buttelmann and associates (2009) use a method that builds on children's general tendency to help adults. Together with a helper, children aged 16 and 18 months saw a man put a toy caterpillar in either a yellow or a green box. The box lids had a special locking mechanism and the helper had shown the child how to open and close the boxes. Then the helper moved the caterpillar to the other box, either while the man was watching or while he was away for a short while (with the pretext of picking up his keys). Afterwards, the man tried to open the now empty box (where the caterpillar had been), but without succeeding. He sat down right between the boxes and behaved as if he was at a loss about what to do. The children either took initiative to help the man themselves or were encouraged to do so by the helper, more often when he had been away than when he had seen the caterpillar being moved. A greater percentage of children tried to tell him where the caterpillar was located when it had been moved without his knowledge, than when the man had been present when the caterpillar was moved. Therefore, it seems the children assumed that the man was looking for the caterpillar when he had not seen it being moved, and

for something else when he tried to open the box after having seen it being moved. The difference was most pronounced among the 18-month-olds (Buttelmann et al., 2009). In similar experiments with *unexpected content*, 18-month-old children also seemed to use their knowledge of what another person could know, based on what they had seen (Buttelmann et al., 2014).

Ever since Onishi and Baillargeon's first experiment, many studies have been conducted with similar results. They show that children to some extent are able to implicitly infer other people's knowledge earlier than previously thought. But there is no disagreement about the fact that children aged 3 years or younger consistently fail in tasks of the Maxi type when they *explicitly* need to describe or show what people or dolls will do based on the knowledge these can have and how a particular situation is shown and described. There is, however, wide disagreement on what children actually understand and how the results should be interpreted (Low and Perner, 2012; Rakoczy, 2017).

Theoretical explanations

Any theory of the development of mind understanding must be able to explain both the fact that toddlers seem to react to the knowledge others have about something *and* the problems much older children have in solving tasks that require mind understanding (Caron, 2009; Rakoczy, 2012, 2017). These theories mainly deal with very early and early mind understanding. Most of them assume a certain innate basis but vary considerably with regard to the particular innate mechanisms at play and the importance of experience (Baillargeon et al., 2016; Carpendale and Lewis, 2015).

From a nativist point of view, Leslie suggests that human beings have a neurological module with a *theory-of-mind mechanism* that is functional by the age of 18 months. When children fail on Maxi and Smarties tasks before the age of 4, it is not due to a lack of mind understanding but because it takes too many cognitive resources for children to inhibit the tendency to respond based on their own knowledge and formulate a correct answer (Leslie, 2005; Leslie et al., 2004). Expanding on this view, Baron-Cohen (1995) assumes that human beings have an *intentionality detector*, an *eye direction detector* and a *shared-attention mechanism*. These modules are independent and together make up what he calls a *mindreading system*. The two detectors are functional in early infancy while the shared-attention mechanism becomes operative at the end of the first year. The theory-of-mind mechanism is functional by the age of 18–24 months.

The *theory-theory* asserts that children are born with certain assumptions or "theories" about the world that they use to analyze statistical and other "data" from different domains (see p. 180). These innate "theories" only represent a starting point, however, and change in line with development in other areas and children's specific experiences (Gopnik and Bonawitz, 2015). According to Wellman, *theory of mind* is one such domain-specific theory. It represents a kind of "commonsense psychology," a system of assumptions used by children and adults to explain and predict the actions of others. Children start with a theory of other people's desires and motives, but it first develops into a full theory of mind once it also includes other people's beliefs. This happens around the age of 4–5 years and leads to qualitatively new insights into other people's thoughts that 3-year-olds lack. Wellman thus considers the age of 4 to mark the beginning of a new stage in social cognition (Rhodes and Wellman, 2013; Wellman, 1990).

The *simulation theory* represents a slightly different approach (Goldman and Mason, 2007; Gordon, 1986; P.L. Harris, 1992). The understanding of other people's minds is based on children's knowledge of their own mind. An innate mechanism enables infants to take part in activities with shared emotions and joint attention (see p. 350). Based on their experiences with these activities, they become aware of other people's *intentionality*, discover that perceptions and feelings are directed at specific goals, and begin to *simulate* such relationships between intention and goal – what others believe and feel about particular things – using memories of their own former mental states. A parallel development takes place in children's imagination that allows them to reach beyond their own experiences and conceive of the mental state of others. Children simulate their own beliefs and feelings while imagining what they assume to be other people's desires and beliefs. Their continued development is the result of more complex thoughts and correspondingly more powerful simulations. Experiences with language play a significant role. One objection to the simulation theory is its implicit assumption about children's understanding of their own mental state. However, children do not seem to have any more insight into their own misconceptions than into those of others. This is not only demonstrated by the Smarties experiments, but it is altogether difficult to understand how children should be able to simulate their own mental states (Hala and Carpendale, 1997). A criticism of the theory-theory and simulation theory is that it has proven difficult to design experiments that distinguish between them (Apperly, 2008).

Several theories address the paradox of very early mind understanding and difficulties with mind understanding in toddler age by suggesting that children have two social cognitive systems – often based on Flavell's two levels of visual perspective-taking (see p. 241). Baillargeon and her colleagues (2010, 2013) describe two innate and independent social cognitive conceptual systems. *System 1* is intuitive and allows children to immediately grasp what others see, and thus know, and to ascribe motives to them. This system deals with children's perception of reality. *System 2* enables children to understand that others may have a belief about something that differs from reality, and to predict and explain others' actions based on the knowledge they seem to have. It is this system that enables children to correctly answer Maxi tasks.

Apperly (2011) proposes that children initially develop a system that allows for *minimal* mind understanding. System 1 is a distinct modular system that includes processes capable of quickly registering people's actions and their perception of reality. The system needs few cognitive resources but is also correspondingly inflexible. System 2 is more flexible and requires more cognitive resources. System 1 is innate and develops in the course of the first year while System 2 emerges more gradually, depending on experience. According to Apperly's model, children need System 2 to solve tasks of the Maxi type. However, if two such systems exist, it is uncertain whether System 1 is replaced by System 2, whether System 2 is a continuation and expansion of System 1, or whether both systems continue to function in parallel (Rakoczy, 2017). These systems also share similarities with the two modes of thinking described by Kahneman (2011). In his model, System 1 is fast, instinctive and emotional while System 2 is slow and reflective.

Social constructivist theories of mind understanding argue against innate modules, theory-theories and simulations, which all build on internal characteristics as a primary basis. They maintain that the mind is not an innate container capable of holding thoughts, desires and feelings, and that mind understanding is not a theoretical but a social construct with a basis in social processes. Social constructivists thus do not base their ideas on individually predetermined knowledge. Although not rejecting the presence of parallel neurological maturation, they believe it only offers a limited explanation of the differences in children's performance on various tasks. Mind understanding is viewed in the context of developing cultural awareness, a mentally shared world that arises from joint attention, the experiences children form through conversations with adults about past and future in various events and activities, and their role as members of a "society of minds" (Carpendale and Lewis, 2004; Nelson, 2007a). Increasing language skills and gradually more complex conversations with adults about situations involving the human mind allow children to realize that people can believe different things and that these differences are related to the experiences of each individual (Carpendale et al., 2009; Turnbull et al., 2009). Like Harris,

they emphasize language and conversation, but their basic theoretical assumptions about the underlying processes differ considerably.

The psychoanalytic tradition views the ability to mentalize – including mind understanding – as the result of attachment and early relational experiences. Mentalizing (also called "reflective function") is the primary developmental goal of the attachment process. Secure attachment is a prerequisite for mature mind understanding, while insecure attachment will lead to inadequate mentalizing or understanding of one's own and others' minds (Fonagy et al., 2002). This view differs radically from both other theories of mind and theories of attachment (see Chapter 19). A number of studies have found a relation between children's early attachment and their later performance on traditional tasks of the Maxi and Smarties type, but this can be explained by coexisting factors such as language skills, parenting style and parental sensitivity and mind-mindedness. Most studies find no connection between the developmental paths of attachment and mind understanding, and research generally provides little support for Fonagy's theory. Critics argue that since attachment has to do with security and mind understanding with social insight, they do not share the same motivational basis (Cortina and Liotti, 2010; Symons, 2004).

This brief presentation illustrates the complexity of mind understanding and its theories. There is agreement about the fact that children show some degree of mind understanding early in life, but researchers disagree on how to interpret children's gaze patterns and actions, the types of processes and knowledge actually involved in early mind understanding, and the relationship between early and more advanced later mind understanding. However, a two-level theory of mind understanding seems best to explain the paradox of early mind understanding and later problems with theory of mind tasks.

Pretense and lies

Many theorists presume there is a connection between mind understanding and the ability to pretend, *to make believe*, since pretense involves performing a targeted action on another person in a make-believe way. The ability to understand that someone is pretending also involves insight into the *intention* behind the action. It is the intention that turns a banana into a phone when someone talks while holding a banana to their ear and mouth. Correspondingly, a child playing with a wooden block as if it were a car must have a mental representation of the car represented by the block (Lillard, 2001). Studies have found a relation between children's pretend play with peers and their mind understanding (Dunn and Cutting, 1999; LaBlonde and Chandler, 1995). Sometimes the goal of pretense is to create a wrong perception in someone else's mind, such as when one person tries to get another to believe he has not done something when he actually has. In verbal form, this type of pretense is generally called "lying" (Lee, 2013). Deliberate lying therefore requires mind understanding.

Pretense

The earliest form of what might be called *make-believe* is when children at the end of their first year hold out an object and withdraw their hand when an adult reaches for it (Reddy, 1991). Piaget (1951) describes how his 15-month-old daughter Jacqueline used a piece of cloth as a pillow, laughing and saying "no-no." (It was clear that she had not simply made a mistake, but actually pretended the cloth was a pillow.) Around 18 months, pretend play becomes common and children begin to understand when others are "kidding around," an understanding that rapidly develops. One study found that 21-month-olds had few problems when asked to use a yellow wooden block as a piece of soap while pretending to wash a teddy bear. But only half of a group of 28-month-olds were able to shift from make-believe soap to make-believe bread by pretending that the same block was a piece of bread when they were told to feed the teddy bear right after (Harris, 1994).

This early understanding of pretense means that younger children have some understanding of the difference between what is real and what is make-believe, but not of the full implications of pretense. This is illustrated by a study of 4- to 5-year-olds who were told a story about Moe, a troll who jumped like a hare although he had never heard of hares. Most of the 4-year-olds thought that Moe pretended to be a hare, even though they had been told that he had never heard of hares and therefore could not know how a hare jumps. Twice as many 5-year-olds answered that Moe did not pretend to be a hare, but one-third nevertheless responded that he did

pretend (Lillard, 1993, 2001). The results suggest that many 4- to 5-year-olds perceive pretense as an action, while older children perceive it more as a mental function. Lillard explains this development as the result of better language skills, and of children eventually coming to view *pretend* as a mental verb rather than as an action verb.

Lying

It is uncertain when children start to be able to tell lies. Studies have shown that children as young as 2 years of age lie about things they have done, but at this point they probably do not understand that lying affects someone else's knowledge and instead perceive it as a way of avoiding the consequences of a prohibited action, such as being scolded or losing a privilege. In one study, the experimenter told 3-year-old children that a play zoo was hidden behind a curtain and that they would get to see it in a little while. The experimenter then made an excuse to leave the room and the children were left by themselves. Only four of 33 children resisted the temptation to peek. Among the 29 children who peeked, 11 later answered "true" when asked whether they had looked. Seven of them lied, and 11 did not answer the question (Lewis et al., 1989). Relatively few of the children thus told a direct lie. Similar studies have found that a third of all 3-year-olds lied, while a majority of 4- to 7-year-olds and almost all 6- to 11-year-olds did so in the same situation (Talwar et al., 2007; Talwar and Lee, 2002). In one study, 4–8-year-olds were asked not to look at a toy while the experimenter was away for one minute. About two thirds of the children peeked at the toy. When the experimenter returned, some of the children were told that they might be punished for lying, others were told it was right to tell the truth, and some were not given any such appeal. More than 80 percent of the children in the no-appeal group and slightly fewer in the punishment group lied about peeking. Only the positive appeal reduced lying significantly (Talwar et al., 2015).

Another study investigated the use of lying among 3- to 4-year-olds to prevent a "villain" from getting a reward that otherwise would be given to themselves (Box 13.6). The children enthusiastically locked the box containing the reward and some spontaneously tried to prevent the villain from opening it when it was not locked. However, the younger children honestly

BOX 13.6 **STRATEGIC LYING (Sodian, 1994)**

Children aged 3–4;6 years were told they would receive a reward contained in one of two cardboard boxes. The other box was empty. They were also told that there was a villain who would try to take the reward for himself, and a friend with whom they should share the reward. They were told that they could prevent the villain from taking the reward by locking the box containing the reward (sabotage), or by pointing to the empty box (deceit). Similarly, they were told that they could lock the empty box and point to the one with the reward when their friend came. Nearly half the children aged 3;0–3;6 years and over 60 percent of the older children locked the box with the reward when the villain came and the empty box when their friend came. Approximately half the 4-year-olds also quickly pointed to the wrong box to trick the villain, while **85 percent of the 3;0- to 3;6-year-olds** honestly answered the villain's question about which box contained the reward.

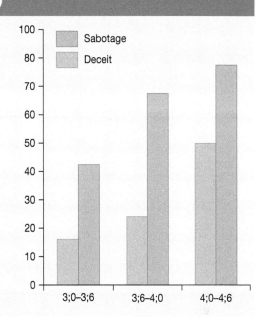

told the villain where the reward was hidden, while many of the 4-year-olds pointed at the wrong box to fool the villain. The 3-year-olds did not seem to understand that they could prevent the villain by giving him faulty information and use mind knowledge in addition to action knowledge (Sodian, 1994). In a similar study, children could choose a toy, but the study was set up in such a way that there was always another child who wanted exactly the same toy and he was the one to choose first. However, the children could secure the toy for themselves by saying that they wanted a different toy than the one they actually wanted, since this meant that the other child would choose that toy. More than 80 percent of the 5-year-olds used this strategy compared with less than 20 percent of the 3-year-olds (Peskin, 1992).

Lying is not only for concealing mischief or obtaining something, lying may also be a positive expression of politeness. Even 3-year-olds lied and said that they liked a gift they did not like, for example that they really needed the piece of soap they got. Older children were more likely to tell such white lies, and they were also better at explaining why they did so (Lee, 2013; Talwar et al., 2007).

These studies on pretense and lying suggest that a development takes place from using action understanding to using mind understanding between the ages of 3 and 5. This agrees well with other studies of mind understanding in children of this age. Studies have also found a relationship between the development of mind understanding and lying (Ding et al., 2015). Telling a lie to hide one's knowledge of something or portray one's thoughts in a more positive light requires second-order understanding (see below), since it involves a deliberate attempt to influence what another person thinks about one's own thoughts (Miller, 2009).

FURTHER DEVELOPMENT OF MIND UNDERSTANDING

In the studies cited previously, children make first-order belief attributions. They solve explicit tasks involving what another person thinks, such as the Maxi tasks. Second-order belief attribution requires an understanding of what a person thinks about someone else's thoughts. This is often studied by using the following type of story (slightly abbreviated):

Mary and John have gone to the park together, where an ice cream vendor is standing with his van. Mary wants to buy an ice cream, but has left her wallet at home. The ice cream vendor tells her that he will also be there in the afternoon, and she goes home. After a while, the ice cream vendor tells John that he will be selling ice cream near the church, because more people are buying ice cream there. He drives off. On his way to the church, the ice cream vendor passes Mary's house. She sees his van and goes out to ask him where he is going. He tells her that he will be selling ice cream near the church. John does not know that Mary talked to the ice cream vendor. A little later, John goes to visit Mary. Her mother opens the door and tells him that Mary has gone out to buy ice cream.

Children aged 5–10 years were told the story and then asked where John will go to look for Mary. Most of the 5-year-olds answered incorrectly (to the church), while many of the 6-year-olds and a majority of the older children responded correctly that John will go to the park, at least after being reminded that John did not know that Mary had talked to the ice cream vendor. Thus, they understood the consequence of John's belief – that he did not know Mary had met the ice cream vendor and believed that she believed the ice cream vendor was still in the park (Perner and Wimmer, 1985).

Second-order belief attribution involves a greater degree of awareness (Nelson, 2007a). Children who manage this type of task are usually able to explain why they responded the way they did, what knowledge or beliefs the people in the story have and why they acted the way they did (Miller, 2009). It is uncertain, however, whether 5-year-olds have an incomplete mind understanding or whether second-order belief attribution tasks simply are more complex. A larger percentage of children answer correctly when the stories are shorter, involve fewer people and events, and when the language is simpler and they are given more reminders (Coull et al., 2006; Sullivan et al., 1994). Similarly, children are older before they are able to solve more complex first-order tasks, such as including emotional or moral content (Lagattuta et al., 2015).

With age, children also become better at understanding the wider implications of holding a certain belief. An understanding of the relationship between belief and feeling (what someone with a particular belief will feel) develops somewhat later than that of the relationship between belief and action (how someone with a particular belief will act) (Lagattuta et al., 2015). In a study with tasks of the Smarties type, most 5- to 7-year-olds correctly answered questions about a belief they had, but only a few of them were also able to describe the feelings related to this belief. The results were interpreted to mean that it is easier for children to suppress what they see in the moment and activate memories of a past situation than to suppress what they feel in the moment and reconstruct a past emotion. There was little difference between the youngest and the oldest children, and it made little difference whether the situation dealt with their own or someone else's past emotion (de Rosnay et al., 2004).

The combination of pretense and false belief is difficult for children below school age. In one study, 5- to 6-years-olds managed common tasks of the Maxi and Smarties type, but had trouble with tasks in which someone had a false belief about an object because it looked like something other than it actually was, such as an eraser that looks like a die. Although the children were told that the puppet Heinz believed the object was only a die, many of them answered that Heinz will look in the box with the die-eraser when he needs an eraser (Apperly, 2011).

Around the age of 7–8, children develop a more flexible mind understanding. They begin to understand that human beings have interpretative minds, meaning that they can perceive the same information in different ways and react differently to the same situation (Lagattuta et al., 2015). The spectators at a football match, for example, might disagree with the judgment call of the referee, depending on which team they are rooting for. Compared with 5-year-olds, 9-year-olds are better able to accept that people can have different beliefs that are equally valid, but this also depends on the topic. Both 5- and 9-year-olds are more absolute – believing that only one point of view can be correct – when it comes to moral issues than issues concerning facts or taste (Carpendale and Chandler, 1996; Wainryb et al., 2004). Adolescents show more advanced mind understanding in positive than in negative relations (O'Connor and Hirsch, 1999). Activities that can be important to later development of mind understanding include jokes and other forms of humor, conversations about causality and internal states, parents' handling of conflicts, and moral reasoning. Thus, mind understanding is not a general ability that emerges fully formed during childhood, but continues to evolve all the way into adulthood (Hay, 2014).

INDIVIDUAL AND CULTURAL DIFFERENCES

The development of mind understanding is affected by both individual and environmental factors, including cultural issues. Twin studies suggest that genetic differences generally do not contribute to individual differences in this area (Hughes and Devine, 2015), but some disorders associated with mind understanding problems have a high degree of heritability (see below).

Individual differences

The social environment contributes to individual differences in mind understanding. Studies have found a relationship between parental behavior and children's mind understanding (Pavarini et al., 2013). In one study, 33-month-old children whose mothers talked about mental states when explaining the actions of others showed better insight into such states 6 months later (Brown and Dunn, 1991; Dunn et al., 1991). In another study, how much mothers talked about cognitive states to 2-year-old children was related to the children's mind understanding measures at 6 and 10 years of age (Ensor et al., 2014). In a third study, 4-year-olds who often referred to the mental states of others when talking with their friends mastered tasks requiring mind understanding better after 12 months than children who did not talk about mental states as often (Hughes and Dunn, 1998). The relationship between language and mind understanding seems to be reciprocal. There is a relationship between early language skills and later performance on tasks involving mind understanding, but also between early mind understanding and later language development (Milligan et al., 2007).

Studies have furthermore found a relationship between parents' early *mind-mindedness*, the proclivity to treat their child as an individual with a mind, and children's later mind understanding (Meins and Fernyhough, 1999). In one study, maternal mind-mindedness when the child was 6 months old correlated significantly with the child's mind understanding at 4 years of age.

Mind-mindedness is reflected in the way mothers speak with their children, but at the age of 6 months children could not possibly have understood what their mother was saying. The mother's language therefore did not communicate knowledge but rather reflected her attitude toward her child (Meins et al., 2003). Shy children typically show mind understanding earlier than other children, possibly reflecting a particular sensitivity to other people's intentions and actions (Mink et al., 2014).

Other studies have found that children with siblings develop mind understanding somewhat earlier than only-children (Perner et al., 1994). The daily interactions between siblings promote an understanding that children can have different beliefs, for example about where something is located, and that only one of these can be correct. After all, it is quite common for siblings to argue about where they have put things (McAlister and Peterson, 2007; Randell and Peterson, 2009). It is also likely that parents with more than one child talk about the different needs and abilities of their children more often than parents with only a single child, and thus add to the siblings' own experiences.

Cultural differences

Cultures differ in their language, activities and way of interacting, and this may influence children's development of mind understanding. Studies generally show consistent age agreement across cultures, but also a certain age variation in the ability to solve Maxi and Smarties tasks (Callaghan et al., 2005; Wellman et al., 2001). Avis and Harris (1991) designed a Maxi task adapted to Baka children, a group of pygmies living in the rainforests of southeast Cameroon. The children saw the experimenter move mango kernels from a pot to a hiding place while the adult who was cooking the mango was away. They found that most of the children above the age of 5 years said that the adult would look for the mango in the pot when he came back.

On the other hand, many studies have found cultural differences in age. British children scored slightly higher than Italian children on tasks that measure mind understanding (Lecce and Hughes, 2010). Children in Samoa manage unexpected transfer tasks considerably later than in the classic studies, but it is not clear why they pass these tasks later (Mayer and Träuble, 2013). In another study, children from Cameroon who had attended school showed better mind understanding than those who had not gone to school (Vinden, 2002). In line with this, British children did better on theory of mind tasks than children in Hong Kong, but only those who attended Chinese schools. Children who attended international schools did as well as the British children (Wang et al., 2016). Education thus seems more important than the general culture. However, is has also been suggested that fewer opportunities for play may contribute to the delay in mind understanding (Wang et al., 2017). Moreover, the British mothers were also more mind-oriented than the mothers in Hong Kong, and both in the UK and Hong Kong there was a significant association between the mother's mind-mindedness and the children's performance on theory of mind tasks (Hughes et al., 2017). The results of these studies emphasize that many aspects of cultural practice may influence the developmental course of mind understanding.

ATYPICAL DEVELOPMENT OF MIND UNDERSTANDING

Problems with social understanding and interaction are a characteristic of people with autism spectrum disorders, and a large number of studies have investigated mind understanding in this group. However, children with different disorders seem to have social cognitive problems that also include mind understanding.

Autism spectrum disorders

The diagnostic criteria for autism spectrum disorder require impaired social cognitive skills (see p. 62), and studies have shown that children with this diagnosis have greater problems with tasks involving mind understanding than other children. In one of the earliest studies, children with autism spectrum disorder, Down syndrome and typical development were told and shown a story about unexpected transfer (Box 13.7), and although the children with autism spectrum disorder scored higher on assessment of language and intelligence, they had far greater difficulties with this task than the children with Down syndrome and typical development (Baron-Cohen et al., 1985). In a related study, the same children should arrange three sets of picture cards in the right order to create meaningful stories (Box 13.7). One of the story sets required mechanical insight, another behavioral and the third mind understanding. The children with autism spectrum did well on the two first sets

Unexpected Transfer
A study with unexpected transfer tasks included 20 children with autism spectrum disorder aged 6;1–16;6 years, 14 children with Down syndrome aged 6;3–17 years, and 27 children with typical development aged 3;5–5;9 years. The children with autism spectrum disorder scored slightly higher on assessments of intelligence and language than the children with Down syndrome and typical development. The children were told and shown a story about two dolls, Sally and Anne. Sally puts a marble into a basket and leaves, and Anne moves the marble somewhere else while Sally is away. Then Sally returns and the children are asked: "Where will Sally look for her marble?".

Figure 1 shows that approximately 20 percent of the children with autism spectrum disorder and over 80 percent of the other children answered correctly (Baron-Cohen et al., 1985).

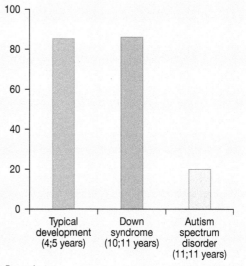

Figure 1

BOX 13.7B MIND UNDERSTANDING IN CHILDREN WITH AUTISM SPECTRUM DISORDER

Stories

In a follow-up study, the same children were given three sets of picture cards and asked to arrange each of them in the right order to create meaningful stories. In Figure 2, sequence a is mechanical, sequence b is behavioral and sequence c is a mind story. Arranging the pictures in the mechanical stories requires an understanding of physical conditions; the behavioral stories require an understanding of the actions being carried out, while the mind stories require the ability to attribute mental states to the people in the pictures.

Figure 2

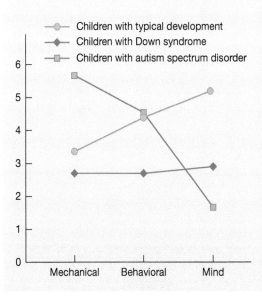

Figure 3 shows the number of correct answers for each of the three groups. The children with Down syndrome performed equally well on all three types of stories, while the children with typical development did best on stories that required behavioral knowledge and mind understanding. The children with autism spectrum disorder did best on the mechanical stories, where they almost achieved full scores, and poorly on the story that required mind understanding. The results show that the children with autism spectrum disorder had particular difficulties understanding the context of actions if this means they have to infer the thoughts of the people in the pictures (Baron-Cohen et al., 1986).

Figure 3

compared to the two other groups but much poorer on the story that required mind understanding (Baron-Cohen et al., 1986).

Following these early studies, a large number of studies have demonstrated that children with autism spectrum disorder do not develop mind understanding in the same way as other children, but there is no generally accepted explanation of these difficulties (Hoogenhout and Malcolm-Smith, 2014). This is a heterogeneous group with frequent problems in other areas, including perception and emotion understanding and regulation. They have restricted interests and depend on regular routines (Happé and Ronald, 2008). Most likely, their problems are caused by impairment in perceptual, communicative and cognitive processes and the interaction between them, rather than impairment in a particular module, as Leslie and Baron-Cohen suggest. Moreover, since about 20 percent among this group are able to solve theory-of-mind tasks (Hamilton, 2009; Happé, 1994), performance on these tasks alone cannot be used to include or exclude a diagnosis of autism spectrum disorder (Belmonte, 2009; Charman, 2000), although problems with such tasks may indicate the level of severity of the disorder (Hoogenhout and Malcolm-Smith, 2017). Moreover, most children in this group manage to solve tasks requiring first-order understanding, but they may be 9 years or older before they are capable of tasks that other children usually master around the age of 4 years. Some adults with autism spectrum disorder are able to solve tasks requiring second-order understanding, but children with typical development do so as early as 6–7 years of age (see p. 253). Practical training in mind understanding has shown mixed results and they are often not generalized to everyday situations (Fletcher-Watson et al., 2014; Kimhi, 2014).

Thirty years of studying mind understanding in individuals with autism spectrum disorders have been extremely important to an understanding of the types of problems they face, but also for the understanding of human mind understanding in general (Happé and Conway, 2016). Without such studies, the scope of this research as well as the insights it provides would have been much the poorer. The study of mind understanding in children and adolescents with autism spectrum disorder is therefore a good example of how atypical development can lead to insights that are important for the understanding of typical development.

Other disorders

Many types of disorders can affect social cognitive development. Most research is based on visual tasks and interpretations of why children see what they see, but the development of mind understanding is not dependent on vision alone. Lack of visual experiences may make the acquisition of mind understanding more difficult but most blind children develop mind understanding and manage to solve Maxi and Smarties tasks (tailored to their visual impairment), although somewhat later than sighted children (Brambring and Asbrock, 2010; Green et al., 2004). They also seem to catch up with sighted peers (Pijnacker et al., 2012). Studies of children with language disorders support the assumption of a relationship between language and mind understanding. Children with specific language disorders have a delayed mind understanding (Miller, 2001; Nilsson and de López, 2016), performing similar to children at the same language level (Andrés-Roqueta et al., 2013). The differences to peers may persist into school age (Spanoudis, 2016). Also children with severe motor impairments and speech disorders are delayed in mind understanding (Dahlgren et al., 2010). Deaf children with hearing parents have a delayed development in both language and mind understanding. Deaf children with deaf parents and a good sign language environment at home, and who are taught sign language at school, show a development similar to children with normal hearing. Deaf children with deaf parents who attend a school without a sign language environment do not develop as well. This may partly be due to fewer opportunities for play and conversations with peers in a predominantly speech-oriented environment (Peterson, 2009, 2016).

Consequences of problems with mind understanding

Experimental studies using the types of tasks discussed previously lend important insights into the development of mind understanding, and also point to possible causes of problems in everyday life. Although inadequate social skills lead to major problems in the daily life of children with autism spectrum disorders, studies have not found a relationship between mind understanding and empathy in this group (Peterson, 2014). Many high-functioning children with autism spectrum disorder are sensitive to criticism, and anxiety and depression, as well as behavioral disorders, are extremely common (Joshi et al., 2010). These disorders may be related to confusion originating in the children's lack of mind understanding and general cognitive problems. By facilitating positive social interaction with other children, this group can be supported in the development of social skills and learning in general (Conn, 2014).

Studies show that good mind understanding is associated with positive friendships (Fink et al., 2015). Deaf children with higher scores on mind understanding have better peer relations and are more popular in class than deaf children with lower scores (Peterson, C. et al., 2016). A great deal of schoolwork concerns psychological causes and motives (Wellman and Lagattuta, 2004), and mind understanding generally makes it easier to handle criticism from teachers (Lecce et al., 2017). Good insight into other people's thinking is not always an advantage, however. Some children with good mind understanding are sensitive to criticism from teachers and others (Cutting and Dunn, 2002). Spitefulness is associated with difficulties in mind understanding (Ewing et al., 2016). Some imprisoned juvenile offenders have inadequate social insight and have profited from measures to promote mind understanding and social problem solving (Noel and Westby, 2014).

SUMMARY

1 *Mind understanding* is people's understanding of each other's perceptions, thoughts, attitudes and feelings. Since the mind is not directly observable, children must be able to make inferences beyond what they can observe directly and become "mind readers."

2 *Visual perspective-taking* at *Level 1* involves the understanding that other people see the world around them. *Level 2* additionally involves the understanding that something can appear differently from various viewpoints. According to Piaget and Inhelder younger children are egocentric and unable to take a *visual perspective* other than their own. Donaldson and others have found that children are able to solve perspective-taking tasks earlier when they include more familiar situations and distinctive *landmarks*.

3 According to Piaget, toddlers use *private speech* because they are *egocentric*. Vygotsky points to the fact that younger children talk aloud to solve problems and to plan and regulate their own actions. Their speech is private but not egocentric. Both may be true to a certain extent – children may be a little egocentric *and* use speech for self-regulation in non-communicative contexts. Children with ADHD and behavioral disorders use overt private speech longer than other children.

4 Children become aware of others' *desires* early on. Eighteen-month-olds understand that people's desires affect their actions; at 2½ years, they understand that people can have conflicting opinions about the same thing. Three-year-olds have difficulty distinguishing between intention and action, while 4-year-olds understand that a person can try to do something without succeeding.

5 Children develop an understanding of the fact that people can have a *false belief* about a situation. Most children begin to solve *theory-of-mind tasks* involving *unexpected transfer* and *content* between the ages of 3 and 5 years. Studies based on non-verbal tasks suggest that children as early as their second year of life have an implicit understanding of what others know. Theories must be able to explain early mind understanding as well as problems with explicit mind understanding in early childhood.

Continued

6   One explanation is that mind understanding is rooted in an innate neurological module for *meta-representation* or a *theory-of-mind mechanism*. According to the *theory-theory*, children form a domain-specific *commonsense theory* about other people's minds that they use to explain and predict the actions of others. According to the simulation theory, children use their understanding of their own mind to *simulate* the relationship between other people's feelings and beliefs about particular things. Several researchers suggest that there are two social cognitive systems: *System 1* is intuitive and allows children to immediately grasp what others see, and thus know, and to ascribe motives to them. *System 2* enables children to understand that others may have a belief about something that differs from reality. From a *social-constructivist* point of view, mind understanding is a social construction of a mentally shared world that arises from the experiences children form in conversation with adults about situations involving the human mind. They discover that people can believe different things, and that these differences are related to the experiences of each individual. From a psychoanalytic perspective, *mentalizing* is seen as the primary developmental objective of the attachment process.

7   The earliest forms of *make-believe* suggest that young children have an understanding of the difference between what is real and what is pretense. Toddlers do not seem to understand that pretense does not have to involve an external action, while children aged 4–5 years perceive it more as a mental function.

8   Relatively few 3-year-olds tell outright *lies*, while 5-year-olds are able to use lying as a strategy to prevent someone else from getting hold of something desirable. Telling a lie to hide one's own knowledge of something or portray one's thoughts in a more positive light involves a deliberate attempt to influence what others think about one's own thoughts, and thus requires second-order mind understanding.

9   Children show *second-order belief attribution* once they understand what a person thinks about what another person is thinking. It develops 1–2 years after first-order understanding and somewhat earlier if simpler stories and language are used. At around 7–8 years of age, children begin to understand that the mind is *interpretative*. Development of mind understanding in later childhood and adolescence also involves the ability to infer how a particular belief affects another person emotionally, and the understanding that different people can perceive the same event in different ways.

10 The development of mind understanding is affected by many environmental factors. There is a relationship between children's mind understanding and their language skills, their parents' *mind-mindedness* and how the parents talk with their children about mental states. Children with siblings develop mind understanding earlier than only-children. Also the effects of practical training have shown that experience is of importance in the development of mind understanding.

11 Although the development of mind understanding appears relatively consistent across cultures, there are also a number of age differences in the development of children from different cultures.

12 Children with autism spectrum disorders have difficulty with mind understanding, but there is considerable variation in the group. Some never develop second-order understanding, and there are different theories about the underlying mechanisms. Their problems are most likely caused by an interaction between basic deficiencies in perceptual, linguistic and cognitive processes, rather than damage to a particular module for mind understanding. The studies of mind understanding have been extremely important to gain insight into the problems faced by children with autism spectrum disorder, as well as for a general understanding of human mind understanding.

13 Blind children develop mind understanding somewhat later than sighted children since their lack of visual experience makes its acquisition more difficult. Compared with their peers, children with specific language disorders have a delayed mind understanding; this also applies to children with severe motor impairment and speech disorders. Deaf children with hearing parents show a later development in both language and mind understanding, while deaf children with deaf parents and a good sign language environment show a development similar to children with normal hearing.

14 A slow or deficient development of mind understanding may create problems in the daily life of children with autism spectrum disorders. Sensitivity to criticism, anxiety, depression and behavioral disorders may be related to confusion originating in the children's problems with mind understanding and general cognitive problems. By facilitating positive social interaction with other children, this group can be supported in the development of social skills and learning in general. Results from training mind understanding are mixed.

15 Good mind understanding is associated with good peer relations, friendship and popularity in class. Good mind understanding can make it easier to deal with criticism from teachers but can also involve greater sensitivity to criticism from teachers and others. Spitefulness is associated with deficits in mind understanding. Some juvenile offenders have inadequate social skills and have profited from measures to promote mind understanding and social problem solving.

CORE ISSUES

• The functions of private speech.

• The biological bases of mind understanding.

• The connection between implicit early mind understanding and later explicit abilities.

SUGGESTIONS FOR FURTHER READING

Buttelmann, D., Carpenter, M., & Tomasello, M. (2009). Eighteen-month-old infants show false belief understanding in an active helping paradigm. *Cognition, 112,* 337–342.

Grant, C. M., Grayson, A., & Boucher, J. (2001). Using tests of false belief with children with autism: How valid and reliable are they? *Autism, 5,* 135–145.

Lillard, A. S. (1993). Pretend play skills and the child's theory of mind. *Child Development, 64,* 348–371.

Low, J., & Perner, J. (Eds) (2012). Special issue: Implicit and explicit theory of mind. *British Journal of Developmental Psychology, 30,* 1–223.

Talwar, V., Murphy, S. M., & Lee, K. (2007). White lie-telling in children for politeness purposes. *International Journal of Behavioral Development, 31* (1), 1–11.

Wellman, H. M., Cross, D., & Watson, J. (2001). Meta-analysis of theory of mind development: The truth about false belief. *Child Development, 72,* 655–684.

Contents

urrently, there is no widely accepted definition of intelligence (Goldstein, 2015; Nisbett et al. 2012). It is generally agreed that intelligence involves reasoning and problem solving, but aside from this, definitions vary considerably. Some view intelligence as a general ability to solve problems while others see it as the sum of many different abilities. Some believe there are multiple forms of intelligence. It is not easy to define, but this description seems to catch the essence: "The ability to understand complex ideas, to adapt effectively to the environment, to learn from experience, to engage in various forms of reasoning, to overcome obstacles by taking thought" (Neisser et al., 1996, p. 77).

Intelligence is about individual differences and closely related to testing. The development of tests has shaped the concept of intelligence as it is generally used today (van der Maas et al., 2014) and intelligence tests have been of major importance in assessing children's learning and development. When Binet and Simon designed the first intelligence test for children in 1905, some special classes had just been established, and their aim was to find a way to identify children who needed remedial education (Binet, 1975). Also today, the most common reason for testing children is to reveal skills and abilities that can affect academic achievement, as well as other areas.

THEORIES OF INTELLIGENCE

Theories of intelligence deal with the foundation and structure of intelligence. One of the key questions is whether there is one or several forms of intelligence. Spearman (1927) suggested that humans have a domain-general ability, the *g-factor*, as well as some more specific abilities, *s-factors*. The *g* is the common factor in all subtests on intelligence tests, and Spearman maintains that the *g-factor* is most important to assess. Some researchers associate g with IQ and intelligence as a general ability measured by intelligence tests; others distinguish intelligence from factor analysis of tests results, emphasizing that intelligence is more than a psychometric concept (Neisser et al., 1996; Nisbett et al., 2012). For example, a central processing capacity, an abstract reasoning ability, or processing speed (Neisser et al., 1996). A different view is that intelligence consists of many domain-specific components. Guilford (1988) describes 180 different factors.

An important distinction is between crystallized and fluid intelligence (Cattell, 1963). *Fluid intelligence* may be defined as the ability to solve problems in unfamiliar domains, using inductive and deductive reasoning (Kyllonen and Kell, 2017). It is predominantly biologically determined and includes basic skills such as memory and spatial perception. It shows especially in problem solving requiring adaptation to new situations, where crystallized skills are of no particular advantage. *Crystallized intelligence* consists of experience-based cultural and personal knowledge, such as vocabulary and factual knowledge, and reflects schooling and learning. The name comes from the notion that "skilled judgment habits have become crystallized" (Cattell, 1963, pp. 2–3). The different views on intelligence also determine how it is measured (Conway and Kovacs, 2015).

A triarchic model

More recent theories emphasize the role of intelligence in adapting, learning, using skills and coping in a particular environment. Sternberg's (1997, 2015) model of intelligence comprises three parts, or sub theories: process, experience and adaptation, which is why it is called triarchic. *Process* involves the mental processes that form the basis for all intelligent action and includes a number of components. *Metacomponents*, or *executive processes*, consist of a limited number of higher-order processes that detect and define problems, choose strategies, plan what to do, distribute cognitive resources, monitor things as they are being done and evaluate results. *Performance components* are lower-order processes that carry out the instructions dictated by the metaprocesses. There are a great number of these and many are specific to a particular type of task. The *knowledge-acquisition components* consist of processes used to learn which tasks the metacomponents and performance components are meant to carry out. They include, among other things, selective attention, shift of attention and choice of certain types of information above others.

The *experiential sub theory* (also *facet* or *aspect*) of Sternberg's model deals with applying these processes in the outer world. The various components always come into play in situations the individual has some prior experience with, and their function is closely linked to individual experience. How well the components serve as a measure of intelligence depends on the experiences of the person being tested. Intelligence is best measured by tasks that are relatively novel but not altogether unfamiliar to the child (Raaheim, 1969). Performing a task that lies too far below or above the child's level of experience will not yield any insight into the child's intelligence. A simple addition problem that allows plenty of time is as ineffectual in measuring a six-grader's intelligence as an equation with three variables. The first type of task is too easy, the second too difficult. The experiential sub theory also includes usage-based automation. Children who have not automated the basic reading process, for example, have fewer cognitive resources to interpret the content of what they are reading and will perform worse on tasks requiring reading comprehension.

The basis for the *contextual sub theory*, sometimes called the *practical sub theory*, is that intelligent behavior is not accidental, but has a purpose or a goal and must be seen in the context of the child's situation. According to Sternberg, the goal of intelligent thought is to adapt the individual's actions to the environment, change the environment or choose an environment to suit the individual's needs and possibilities. The content of these goals will depend on the culture and the child's situation. Knowledge that is important to a child growing up in Paris is not necessarily helpful to a child growing up in New York or in Tonga, but the same underlying components contribute to intelligent behavior in all cultures. Differences in intelligence are the result of differences in how effectively processes can be applied in the child's culture. What may be intelligent adaptive behavior in one culture is not necessarily so in another.

Despite its division into three sub theories of intelligence, each with its own components and processes, the triarchic model constitutes a whole, and any assessment of a child's intelligence must take into account all three aspects. According to Sternberg's theory, it would be insufficient and little meaningful to measure processes not related to a purpose and a cultural context. Intelligent behavior must always be assessed based on the child's culture and specific situation. This is necessary to take into consideration when making a cognitive assessment of a child who is seeking asylum and has limited experience with the country where the family is seeking asylum (Whitaker, 2017).

Multiple intelligences

Gardner (1993, 2006) refutes the notion of a *g-factor*. In his theory, human intelligence is not a unitary construct or ability, but consists of several functionally independent intelligences, which may work together. They include linguistic, spatial (spatial perception and recognition of visual patterns), logical-mathematical, interpersonal (cooperation and understanding of others' intentions, motives, needs and desires), intrapersonal (self-understanding), naturalistic (recognition and categorization of living organisms and objects), bodily-kinesthetic (use of body and movement) and musical intelligence. Each intelligence has a computational capacity to process a certain kind of information that originates in human biology and human psychology, and is assumed to reside in a module with its basis in evolution and with separate neurological processes and individual developmental histories (see p. 165). Each intelligence implies problem-solving skills that allow the individual to approach a situation in which a goal is to be obtained and to locate the appropriate route to that goal. According to Gardner, intelligences must be universal but he also emphasizes social and cultural contexts, and that an intelligence should enable the person to solve problems or create products that are valued in one or more cultural contexts or communities. Moreover, according to Gardner, an intelligence must also be susceptible to encoding in a symbol system – a culturally contrived system of meaning that captures and conveys important forms of information. All humans have all the eight forms of intelligence but may have individual strengths or weaknesses. Chen and Gardner (1997) maintain that traditional intelligence tests disfavor many children by focusing on school-oriented linguistic and mathematical intelligence and do not place sufficient emphasis on other abilities valued by culture.

The theory of multiple intelligences is controversial (Willingham, 2004). There is no disagreement about the existence of many competencies, for example that some people are more musical or socially adept than others, and that it is important to encourage these types of abilities. Disagreements concern whether the various areas of competence can be considered forms of intelligence. Inasmuch as cognition is the core concept of intelligence, body control, important as it may be to athletes and dancers, is not usually viewed as a cognitive ability. The same goes for musicality, which is generally regarded an ability independent of intelligence (Willingham, 2004). There is further disagreement on whether Gardner's eight types of intelligence reflect independent biological modules (Almeida et al., 2010; Waterhouse, 2006a). The evidence Gardner (1983, 2006) presents for separate intelligences is similar to other module theorists (see p. 165) that each can be impaired by brain damage without consequence for the other intelligences, the existence of individual variation, including individuals with exceptional abilities, as well as impaired functioning and savants with special abilities in spite of low general abilities. However, critics point out that the evidence Gardner cites does not support his claims or distinguish his theory from others (Waterhouse, 2006a, b; Willingham, 2004).

INTELLIGENCE TESTS

Internationally there exists a large number of standardized tests that measure intellectual functioning in children and adolescents, and rank their performance in relation to their peers. Most of the tests are originally in English and constructed in North America and Western Europe, but many countries also have local tests (Oakland, 2004). The major intelligence tests like the *Wechsler Intelligence Scale for Children* (WISC; Wechsler, 2014) and the *Stanford-Binet Intelligence Scales* (Roid, 2003) are translated and standardized in several languages.

The major tests include several subscales with different tasks. They provide an overall (full-scale) intelligence quotient (IQ) and a number of sub scores that together give a broad profile of the child's ability structure. Other tests measure only some aspects of intelligence, *Leiter International Performance Scales* (Roid et al., 2013) and *Raven Progressive Matrices* (Raven et al., 1998) measure non-verbal cognitive abilities, while *Peabody Picture Vocabulary Test* (Dunn and Dunn, 2007) and *Test of Reception of Grammar* (Bishop, 2005) measure language comprehension. *Bayley Scales of Infant Development* (Bayley, 2006), *Mullen Scales of Early Learning* (Mullen, 1995) and other tests of development in the early years measure a broader set of abilities than intelligence tests, such as motor skills. They are often called "developmental scales," but essentially fulfill the same function as intelligence tests.

Intelligence cannot be measured directly as an ability in its own right, although some tests aim to measure more basic cognitive processes (Naglieri, 2015). Intelligence tests measure children's performance on knowledge and skill tasks at a particular point in time. Testing is based on the assumptions that a) the test items are representative of children's abilities, and b) that their performance is an expression of the cognitive ability or abilities called intelligence. Intelligence tests use a variety of tasks (see Table 14.1), but the tasks are merely "samples." It is not important whether a child knows for example the exact meaning of "comical," or is able to repeat "3-8-6" after the tester has said the three digits. It is the correspondence between the knowledge and skills probed by the tests and the child's abilities that makes the tasks useful. If the tasks are not representative of the child's abilities, the test is of little value.

TABLE 14.1 Examples of types of tasks often found in intelligence tests for children and adolescents

None of the questions below are part of an actual test, but they are similar to those found in intelligence tests.	
Knowledge	Questions such as: *Where is your left hand? How many grams are there in a kilo?*
Encoding	Mark the correct graphic shapes or digits based on a code key (time limit).
Word understanding	Questions such as: *What is a jacket? What is a saw? What does horizontal mean? What does comical mean?*
Completing pictures	Point at the place in a picture where something is missing (time limit).
Categorizing pictures	Indicate which pictures belong together.
Comparing and finding similarities	Questions such as: *You put on a winter hat and you put on . . .? In what way are a cow and a horse similar?*
Searching	Mark pictures of things that belong to a particular category.
Completing patterns	Find a missing picture in an array of several pictures.
Labyrinth	Trace the way out of a maze with a pencil.
Arithmetic	Indicate which object is largest or smallest, greatest or smallest in number; addition and traditional arithmetic problems.
Drawing	Copy a shape.
Copy a pattern	Copy a pattern consisting of blocks or squares of different color (time limit).
Puzzle	Work out a jigsaw puzzle (time limit).
Reasoning	Questions such as: *Why do trains have doors? Why do streets have names?*
Sentence memory	Repeat a sentence read by the tester.
Number memory	Repeat rows of numbers forwards and backwards.

To avoid cultural or other biases, in constructing intelligence tests, one tries to use tasks requiring a minimum of specific experience or formal education. However, children's skills and knowledge – and thus their performance on a test – always reflect their education and cultural background. If children do not have the education and cultural experience required by a test, this will influence the correspondence between test tasks and child abilities, and hence may not measure the children's underlying abilities (intelligence). This will include children who grow up in an environment using a different language and belong to another culture than those for whom the test is norm-referenced. In designing test tasks, one therefore tries to make them as culturally "fair" as possible (Shuttleworth-Edwards et al., 2004). Non-verbal test items measuring fluid intelligence, like

Raven's Matrices, usually show smaller differences between ethnic groups than test items measuring crystallized intelligence, which reflect more cultural knowledge (Naglieri, 2015). However, it is important to distinguish between *tests of non-verbal intelligence* and *non-verbal testing*, that is, test administration without complex verbal instruction, such as with the Leiter test. Many of the performance items of standard intelligence tests require that the child understands a lengthy verbal instruction (Franklin, 2017).

Many children and adolescents with disabilities participate less in social activities with peers and other everyday activities. They may therefore have an experience background so different from those of children without disabilities that their performance on a regular test can give a false impression of their intelligence (Bedell et al., 2013; King et al., 2013; Martin, 2014).

Standardization

The standard measure of intelligence is the *intelligence quotient* (IQ). Some developmental scales use a "developmental quotient" (DQ) rather than IQ. The *raw scores* of a test are the points the child gets on each subtest. The age score or mental age is the average age when children obtain a particular raw score. Originally, the IQ was calculated with the formula: IQ = mental age/chronological age × 100. This implies that a mental age of 9 years and a chronological age of 10 would give an IQ of 90. With the same mental age, an 8-year-old would get an IQ of 112.5. The IQ difference of a year in mental age would thus change through development, and with adolescents and adults, the formulae would not make sense.

Today, intelligence tests are standardized or norm-referenced by testing a large representative sample of individuals in the age group for which the test is intended. This is based on the assumption that intelligence has a *normal statistical distribution* among the population, and that IQ scores are symmetrically distributed around the mean with a fixed percentage of the population within each standard deviation (see Figure 14.1). It is the distribution of raw scores in the standardization group that determines the size of the standard deviation and thus the IQ resulting from a particular raw score at different ages. The standard deviation indicates the child's relative placement in relation to the statistical average and the score distribution in the standardization sample, or norm group, which should be the same as his peer group. The mean is 100 and the standard deviation 15 IQ points on most intelligence tests. An IQ within ± 1 standard deviation from the statistical mean (IQ 100 and standard

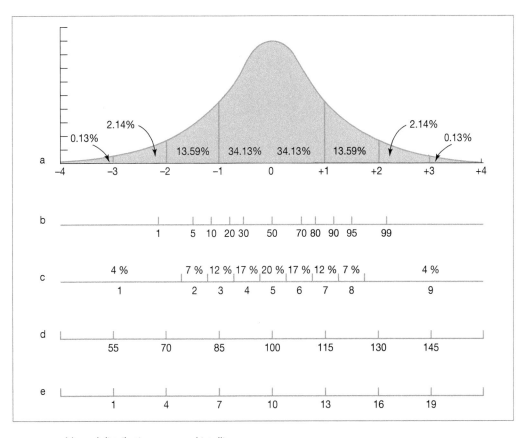

FIGURE 14.1 **Normal distribution curve and intelligence.**

The figure shows a) the normal distribution curve (or Bell curve) with percentages and standard deviation, b) percentiles, c) stanine scores consisting of nine different scores or test categories and their percentage distribution, d) IQ based on the Wechsler test and e) scores for each Wechsler subtest.

score 0) is considered within the typical range of variation. An IQ one standard deviation below the mean for the age group (IQ 85) is a low normal score often used in clinical work as a threshold to identify the need for further assessment. The curve in Figure 14.1 shows that about 68 percent of the population score between 85 and 115 and about 95 percent between 70 and 130. Only 2.3 percent score two standard deviations or more above the mean, or IQ 130 and above. An equal number score lower than minus two standard deviations, or 70 and below.

Many children show a relatively even performance across subscales, while others have more pronounced strengths and weaknesses in cognitive functioning. Some are quick at solving puzzles, others are strong in language or particularly fast at mental arithmetic. To understand a child's functioning, it is necessary to assess his *cognitive profile*. WISC and other major intelligence tests have a verbal and a performance part. It is also possible to calculate different indexes by adding the scores of different combinations of subtest. WISC includes indexes for "verbal comprehension," "visual spatial," "fluid reasoning," "working memory" and "processing speed." The Stanford-Binet includes "fluid reasoning," "knowledge," "quantitative reasoning," "visual-spatial processing," and "working memory," which have both verbal and non-verbal items. In addition, there are tests made up exclusively of verbal tasks or non-verbal tasks. Raven Matrices are considered a good test of fluid intelligence.

Two children can achieve the same full-scale IQ and still have very different test profiles. In assessing children, emphasis is therefore placed on their profile (Greenspan and Woods, 2014). A child may have a clear language delay, but it is not enough to assess his language skills compared to his peers, also his non-verbal cognitive functioning must be assessed. A language delay may be part of an intellectual disability but may also be a specific language impairment (see p. 268). In some extreme cases, children show near-normal performance on non-verbal tasks without managing any of the verbal tasks; this is the case for some children with Landau-Kleffner syndrome (Caraballo et al., 2014). A full-scale IQ based on the average scores from the verbal and performance parts would give an overly positive impression of verbal abilities and an overly negative impression of non-verbal intelligence.

Other observations of intelligent action

Cognitive assessments of children never rely on tests alone. Test results must always be collated with observations of how children cope with familiar and unfamiliar everyday situations. With younger children, observing their play may give useful information (Vig, 2007). Chen and Gardner (1997) are skeptical to the use of tests and believe one should identify domain-specific skills by observing preschool children in their normal environment and in familiar contexts. Examples of observations include children's body control during physical play, perception and use of colors and materials in arts and crafts, comprehension and use of words about objects and events in the environment, counting and arithmetic during regular activities, ability to notice physical changes in their surroundings and understanding of other people's social interests and reactions. Such observations can reveal children's practical understanding in a way standardized tests are poorly designed to capture, and may be a useful supplement to cognitive assessment. Nonetheless, in the absence of some type of standard, they cannot replace traditional intelligence tests altogether.

STABILITY AND VARIATION IN IQ SCORES

In most cases, the purpose of using an intelligence test is to find out whether a child needs special training or support in certain areas to ensure an optimal future development. Implicit in this objective is the assumption that the test is able to predict how children will function in the future if their environment is not changed in a significant way, and that the scores will help develop appropriate intervention measures.

Early prediction

Correlations are generally low between early test scores and later performance on intelligence tests. On average, developmental scores from the first 6 months of life correlate around 0.1 with IQ at 5–7 years of age and 0.06 with IQ between 8 and 18 years. For tests conducted between 12 and 18 months, the correlation is 0.3 with IQ at 5–7 years and 0.2 with IQ at 8–18 years. Scores at

3–4 years of age correlate around 0.3–0.4 with IQ at 10–12 years (Bishop et al., 2003; McCall and Carriger, 1993; Sternberg et al., 2001).

In addition to collating early and later test results, researchers have searched for relationships between more basic and presumably stable information-processing mechanisms and later cognitive functioning (McCall, 1994). Visual processing, attention and memory have been a particular focus of study using tasks based on habituation and novelty preference (see p. 47). Habituation means that the child is gradually reacting less to the same stimulation. In studies of novel preference, infants are shown two identical pictures for a certain length of time, after which they get to see one of the pictures together with a new picture. Novelty preference is when they spend longer looking at the new picture than the one they saw first (Fagan and Detterman, 1992).

The amount of time it takes children to habituate during their first year of life correlates on average 0.35–0.40 with their IQ between age 1 and 11. The corresponding value for early memory is 0.35 (Kavšek, 2004; McCall and Carriger, 1993). Some studies have found even higher correlations. Slater and colleagues (1989), for example, found that the habituation time at the age of 1½–6 months correlated –0.58 with a full-scale WISC IQ when the children were 8½ years old. The negative correlation means that children who needed less time to habituate in infancy tended to achieve higher WISC scores 8 years later. However, the correlation was much higher for the verbal part of the WISC (–0.75) than for the performance part (–0.28). This suggests that the time infants spend habituating does not reflect a possible general ability (*g-factor*), but rather that the child's capacity for visual processing and orientation toward novel objects may have an impact on establishing joint attention and thereby on the acquisition of communication and language skills (see p. 299). This is supported by another study that found a correlation of 0.26 between novelty preference at 7–12 months and a vocabulary test at 21 years of age (Fagan et al., 2007).

Early prediction and transaction

One of the main objectives of clinical developmental psychology is to identify factors of importance to children's development and be able to predict how development will proceed under different conditions. At the same time, it is not the goal of early tests and other observations to predict *too* well. This would imply a deterministic view of children's cognitive functioning and intelligence as something fixed and immutable. To the contrary, interventions are based on the assumption that children's developmental problems and disorders can be mitigated by changes to their environment (training is also a form of environmental influence). In line with a transactional model (Sameroff, 2010), innate characteristics and early development of skills lay the foundation for future skills and abilities, but do not determine them (see p. 8).

One reason for the low correlation between very early test scores and later intellectual functioning may be that children at this age still are so "incomplete" that many abilities have yet to develop for individual differences to become noticeable. In addition, some genes that are relevant remain inactive and are not expressed until later in life (Briley and Tucker-Drob, 2013). A low statistical relationship can also indicate *discontinuity*, a lack of a direct relationship between skills measured during infancy and children's later cognitive functions. Some early skills reflect infants' unique adaptation to the environment and are only relevant for that age. Other skills form the developmental basis for future skills and therefore show a higher correlation (McCall, 1989; Slater, 1995). A low statistical relationship between infants' habituation time and their concurrent performance on the infant scales suggests that the skills measured by these scales do not necessarily reflect processes that affect future performance on intelligence tests (Berg and Sternberg, 1985), but they may still give important information about the present state of the child. The ability to follow an object with one's eyes or pick up a wooden block at 4 months of age may not be related to the ability to turn the pages of a book or build a tower with three blocks at 12 months, abilities that in turn differ considerably from the broad set of tasks on modern intelligence tests (see Table 14.1).

Prediction of future intelligence based on tasks involving information processing, such as the Fagan test (Fagan and Detterman, 1992), appears to work best when children are between the ages of 2 and 8 months. After that, the correlation with future cognitive functioning declines (McCall and Carriger, 1993). At this early age, children almost can't help but look at the pictures they are shown in such studies. Once they have grown a little older, other activities begin to compete for their attention, even in the relatively unstimulating environment of a research lab. For example, since children usually sit on their parent's lap during the test, they have a familiar partner to communicate and interact with. This can be more attractive than the study material even if the researcher does her best to attract the attention of the child. More-over, a study of children with low birth weight found a higher correlation between early socio-economic background and IQ at age 8 than between novelty preference in the first year of life (Fagan Test of Infant Intelligence) and IQ at age 8 (Smith et al., 2002). Hence, the social back-ground of infants is a better predictor of intelli-gence than early visual processing.

Some types of early injury or developmental anomalies are so severe that they are decisive for children's further development. In such cases, it is possible to estimate future skills with some confidence. There is also developmental variation in IQ among children with intellectual disability, but developmental processes are slower and change curves have been found to be longer in young children with Down syndrome (Smith and von Tetzchner, 1986). It should be noted, how-ever, that most developmental tests are not designed to measure individual differences among children with IQ scores lower than 50, and are therefore not capable of predicting individual differences in the development of this group of children.

Stability and variation in later childhood

For children above preschool age, test results usually correlate relatively high with test scores at later age levels. Tests from 7 years correlate usually 0.6 or higher with IQ at age 10–12 years (Bishop et al., 2003; Schneider et al. 2014; Sternberg et al., 2001). The higher correlations from school age to late adolescence is partly due to the diminishing time interval up to the age of 18, but statistical correlations increase relatively little between the age of 6 to 7 and the beginning of adolescence. A unique long-term study showed a correlation of 0.54 in IQ at 11 years and 90 years (Deary et al., 2013).

At the same time, a relatively high correla-tion does not mean that children's IQ remains stable throughout childhood. In one longitudinal study, children's IQ varied on average by a good 28 IQ points between the ages of 2 and 17 years, even though the average for the entire group was well over 100, which is the standard mean (Box 14.1). In another study, 794 children were tested every other year over a 7-year period. Among them was a "labile" group of 107 children whose average IQ varied by 38 points over the entire period. Some of them alternated between an IQ in the typical range and intellectual disability, while others varied between the typical and very high range. Variation was significant even over relatively short time spans, with an average change of 16 IQ points for each 2-year period (Moffitt et al., 1993).

The studies mentioned above do not furnish a basis to establish the cause of variation in IQ with certainty. Genetic and epigenetic factors emerging over time, as well as transactional changes related to age and the environment, can contribute to variation in development. Most studies have not used the same tests at different age levels, and the children's motivation may have varied during testing. Since a number of studies show that many children do not perform con-sistently on intelligence tests over time, it is important that professionals do not rely on earlier test results alone when assessing cognitive devel-opment, and compare current results and former results.

NATURE, NURTURE AND INTELLIGENCE

Intelligence can have major consequences for an individual's prospects and place in society. The debate about nature and nurture has a central position in the study of intelligence. The basic issues are the same as in other discussions about nature and nurture in development (see also Chapter 5).

Genetic variation

The most common approach to the study of nature and nurture in intelligence has been to compare the correlation between IQ scores among identical and fraternal twins, siblings growing up together and apart, and children and their biological and adoptive parents (see p. 80). Figure 14.2 shows that the correlation increases

BOX 14.1 IQ CAN VARY CONSIDERABLY OVER TIME (McCall et al., 1973)

Eighty children, 38 boys and 42 girls, were assessed with the Stanford-Binet test at 2½, 3, 3½, 4, 4½, 5, 5½, 6, 7, 8, 9, 10, 11, 12, 14, 15 and 17 years of age. The group average was well above 100, and the average difference between highest and lowest score from 2 to 17 years of age was 28 IQ points. For 21 percent of the children, the difference between their highest and their lowest IQ scores from 2 to 17 years was less than 20 IQ points, 43 percent had a difference between 21 and 30 IQ points, and 36 percent had more than 30 points between their highest and lowest IQ. One child had a difference of 74 IQ points.

The figure shows the average variation in IQ over time for five groups, each consisting of children who showed a similar progression. Four of the groups obtained similar results around the age of 17 years, the differences between them during school age may have been related to conditions in the home. Some of the children may also have developed slightly earlier than others, with a leveling-out during adolescence. Children in Group 2 showed a very different development than the other groups. Their IQ initially declined between the ages of 2 and 6 years, after which their scores increased throughout school age and declined once again as they approached the age of 17. It is possible that these children had a difficult situation at home, and that the school contributed positively to their development until they dropped out of school.

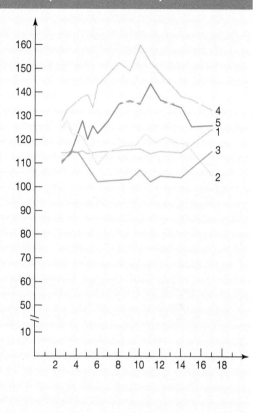

with amount of shared genetic material. It is highest for identical twins growing up together and lowest for adopted children and their adoptive parents. Age also matters, in one twin study, the heritability estimate (see p. 83) at 10 months was 2 percent, at 24 months, 23 percent (Tucker-Drob et al., 2011). Based on several twin studies, the hereditability estimate for intelligence seems to increase from 20 percent in infancy to 40 percent in adolescence and 60 percent in adulthood (Plomin and Deary, 2015; Tucker-Drob et al., 2013). The influence of genes thus increases with age.

On the other hand, Figure 14.2 also shows that the IQ of siblings growing up together is closer than that of siblings growing up apart. Furthermore, heredity estimates for intelligence are not consistent, but vary with the individuals' socioeconomic background. In one study, the dif-

ferences in IQ among 7-year-old twins with a low socioeconomic background showed little relationship with genes (low heritability), while genes were of great importance among twins with a high socioeconomic background (high heritability) (Turkheimer et al., 2003). These findings may suggest that the genetic influences contribute most when the environment is good enough and differences contribute little to development, or that genetic differences are suppressed by environmental factors, that children from lower socioeconomic backgrounds do not develop their full potential (Nisbett et al, 2012). One implication of this would be that children from a lower socioeconomic background will benefit most from intervention (Hanscombe et al., 2012).

It should be noted that some studies have not found the same influence of socioeconomic background (Hanscombe et al., 2012). One

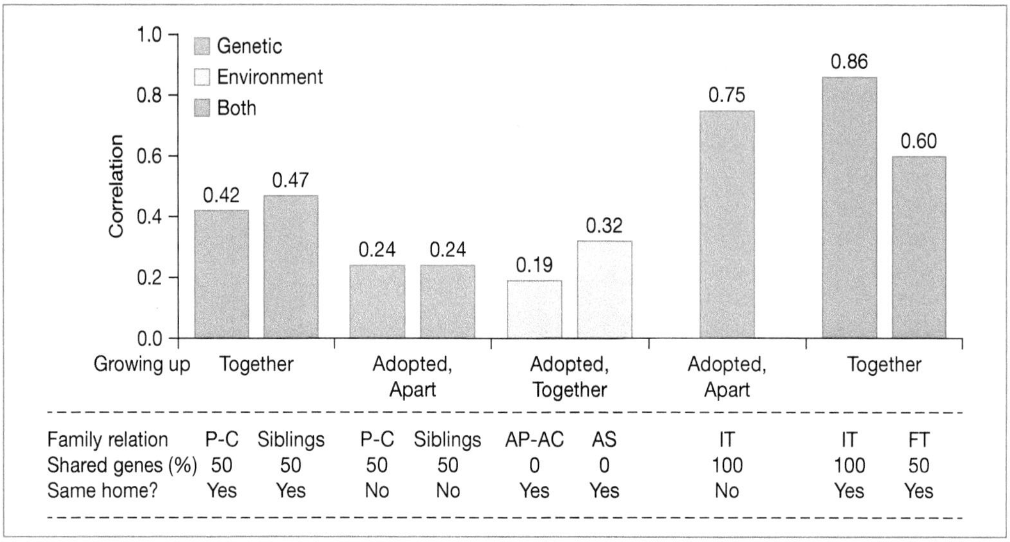

FIGURE 14.2 Family studies on intelligence.

The figure shows the mean correlations between IQ in persons with varying degrees of genetic and environmental similarity. Identical twins (IT) share twice as many genes (100 percent) as fraternal twins (FT) (50 percent). Biological parents (P) and children (C) also share 50 percent of their genes, while adopted children (AC) and adoptive parents (AP) as well as adoptive siblings (AS), do not share any genes (based on Plomin et al., 1997, p. 140).

reason may be societal differences in education and provision of social and health services.

> It is noteworthy that these failures to replicate have predominantly been in northern European nations, where social welfare systems are more comprehensive, whereas most of the positive results have been obtained in the United States, where social class differences in educational opportunity are vast. Socioeconomic disadvantage may not disrupt gene-environment transactions to the same extent in countries that ensure access to adequate medical care and high-quality education.
>
> (Tucker-Drob et al., 2013, p. 353)

Moreover, if the environment does not have the same importance in different socioeconomic groups, the socioeconomic backgrounds of the sample has consequences for the size of the heritability estimate. As pointed out in Chapter 5, heritability estimates – the influence attributed to genes – is dependent on the environmental variation. If there is little environmental variation, the differences between individuals must mainly be caused by their genes, and vice versa. It is therefore of relevance that individuals from lower socioeconomic backgrounds are typically underrepresented in behavioral-genetic studies. The consequence will be a more narrow range of environmental variation, which will increase the heritability estimate and attribute less importance to environmental factors (Nisbett et al., 2012).

Many hundreds of different genes are believed to be involved in cognitive development. Although thousands of children have been compared with regard to intelligence and genetic makeup, it has been difficult to single out the effects of individual genes, and many of the findings have not been replicable, indicating that they are chance findings (Chabris et al., 2012; Kleefstra et al., 2014). One finding in need of explanation is the fact that culture-dependent skills like vocabulary knowledge show a higher degree of heritability than skills that are not as culture-dependent, such as memory for digits and the ability to reconstruct a visual pattern (Kan et al., 2013). A possible explanation may be that some of the genes believed to be related to intelligence result in different degrees of environmental susceptibility. This is in line with research showing that children with a high IQ are more susceptible to experience than children with a low IQ (Brant et al., 2013).

Environmental factors

Studies show that many environmental factors influence the development of intelligence. Nutrition during prenatal development and childhood has an impact on children's intellectual development (Prado and Dewey, 2014). Long-term malnutrition can have permanent consequences, whereas the effect of shorter periods is reversible. However, it is not easy to distinguish the effect of nutrition from other factors: children who suffer from poor nutrition usually have parents who are undernourished themselves, live under difficult conditions and have little energy for interaction and play. The children may receive less stimulation and encouragement to pursue activities that promote intellectual development (Sigman and Whaley, 1998). In industrialized societies, lead and other contaminants are a possible source of cognitive problems (Dapul and Laraque, 2014; Needleman, 2004).

Classical studies of children in overcrowded orphanages with few personnel have clearly demonstrated that under stimulation and lack of social contact lead to low cognitive functioning and in extreme cases to death, even if the children were not malnourished (Provence and Lipton, 1962; Spitz, 1946). However, the studies also show that delay due to severe under stimulation can be reversed. In one study, severely under stimulated and developmentally delayed 18-month-olds were moved to an institution for women with intellectual disability. After 15 months, during which the children received stimulation and care from the women with intellectual disability and staff, the children showed normal functioning (Skeels and Dye, 1939). Similar results have been found in more recent studies of children who lived under extremely unstimulating conditions in Romanian orphanages. The children showed dramatic progress when they were adopted by British families, and those who were youngest at the time of adoption showed the most cognitive progress. Children who were adopted after the age of 6 months, however, scored 15 IQ points lower at the age of 11 years than children who had been adopted before this age (Beckett et al., 2007).

The impact of environmental factors is also apparent in the relationship between IQ and socioeconomic background, and the effect becomes more apparent with age (Huston and Bentley, 2010). One longitudinal study found an increase in correlation between children's IQ and their socioeconomic status from 0.17 at 6 months to 0.51 at 3 years of age (Wilson, 1983). A large study summarizing results from many countries found that children growing up in orphanages scored on average 20 IQ points lower than children reared in foster or biological families (van IJzendoorn et al., 2008). It was not clear what qualities of the orphanages made a difference for the children's development. The statistical effect of caregiver-child ratio was not significant, but when the ratio was three children per caregiver or less, the children did not show developmental delay compared to children living in families. In addition, some of the children in orphanages were more resilient (see p. 12) and showed positive development in spite of poor environmental conditions (van IJzendoorn et al., 2011).

Another study found significant differences in IQ (112 vs. 100) between children adopted by parents with high and low socioeconomic backgrounds (Capron and Duyme, 1989). The socioeconomic background of the biological parents was of importance as well. Children with biological parents from a higher socioeconomic background scored higher than children with parents from a low socioeconomic background (114 vs. 98).

Exactly how socioeconomic background affects children's intelligence is not entirely clear. Poverty may imply non-optimal nutrition and care even if low socioeconomic status does not always lead to poor cognitive development (and lower IQ). Families with a low socioeconomic status often come from a minority language background, have little education, are more often unemployed and have a greater number of psychological problems. The more such factors are present, the greater the risk that children will score low on intelligence tests (Figure 14.3). Furthermore, the incidence of environmental risk factors are often the same from preschool age to adolescence – children usually remain in the same environment (Huston and Bentley, 2010; Sameroff et al., 1993).

Many countries have designed programs to improve the developmental opportunities

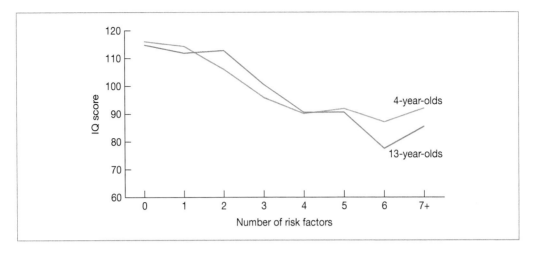

FIGURE 14.3 **IQ in relation to risk factors.**

A longitudinal study tested 152 children growing up in high-risk environments using WPPSI at 4 years and WISC-R at 13 years. The study included a total of ten risk factors: minority background, parental provider with low-status job, mother with low level of education (had not completed US high school), large family (four or more children), single parent (neither father nor stepfather), many stressful life events (e.g., parents lose their jobs, death in the family), parents with main-effect perspective on the importance of child rearing (suggesting that children's fate is determined by a single cause, either constitution or environment), anxious mother, mother with mental health problems, interaction between mother and child characterized by negative or undifferentiated emotions (based on Sameroff et al., 1993, p. 89).

of children growing up under difficult social conditions. In 1965, half a million US children enrolled in *Head Start*, a relatively short-term preschool initiative that was to give children some basic knowledge and skills to get a better start in school. The results of the effort are controversial, partly due to the inconsistent quality of follow-up studies. There seems to be agreement, however, that children who took part in Head Start showed fewer learning disorders, did better in school and completed middle school to a greater extent than their peers with a similar background who did not participate in the program (Lazar and Darlington, 1982; Zigler and Valentine, 1979). The reason for these differences is not only what children learned through Head Start, but equally the fact that they developed more positive attitudes toward learning from the start, which in turn affected their teachers' expectations of them (see also Rosenthal effect, below). A more recent study of children born between 1995 and 1998 suggests a primary relation between development and environmental risk factors, such as unemployment and low quality of parent–child interaction (Ayoub et al., 2009). Between 1972 and 1977, the *Abecedarian Project* implemented early educational intervention for

111 children from birth until the age of 5. The results showed that preschool initiatives were more effective both in terms of IQ and academic performance at school than initiatives introduced during school age. At the same time, the effect of preschool initiatives was strengthened when the education was especially adapted to the children's needs during the first years of school (Campbell and Ramey, 1994; Campbell et al., 2002).

The studies of orphanages and adopted children above show that environmental factors can have positive as well as negative – and sometimes dramatic – consequences for children's intellectual (and emotional) development. The fact that genes are of importance in the development of intelligence does not change this.

Zone of modifiability

Genes and environment impose both possibilities and constraints on intellectual development (Rinaldi and Karmiloff-Smith, 2017). Gottesman (1963) suggests that genes limit the degree of environmental impact in the form of a *reaction range* within a given developmental domain. Figure 14.4 shows the reaction range for

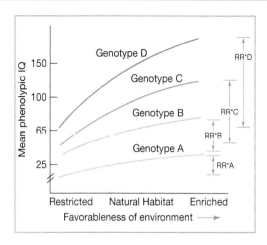

FIGURE 14.4 Reaction range.

The figure shows the reaction range curves for IQ with four hypothetical genotypes (A–D). The genotype that would result in the lowest intelligence in a normal environment (A) is least susceptible to the environment, both in a positive and a negative sense. The genotype that would result in the highest intelligence in a normal environment (D) has the greatest reaction range. A genotype with a wide reaction range can thus lead to large variations in IQ (Gottesman, 1963, p. 255).

cognitive development based on four different hypothetical genotypes, indicating a relationship between intelligence and reaction range. In line with this model, one study found a higher environmental susceptibility in children with high than with low IQs, and that development spans over a longer period of time in the high-IQ group (Brant et al., 2013). Another study found IQ scores to be stable earlier in a group of children with an average IQ of 93 than in another group with an average IQ of 121 (Schneider et al., 2014).

The notion of a reaction range implies that children's intellectual development is constrained rather than prescribed by genes, and that competence can change over time as a result of environmental influences. According to Ramey and Ramey (1998a) a reaction range represents the child's *zone of modifiability*, which is important to utilize to promote optimal development for the child. They further argue that modifiability may be higher earlier than later in development, and that appropriate preschool programs should be introduced to accelerate cognitive development in children at biological or social risk of developmental delay (Ramey and Ramey, 1998b).

The Rosenthal effect

Knowledge of how children perform on intelligence tests can be useful, but also brings with it certain dangers, since the results are often viewed as a "true" expression of children's abilities. It has been shown, for example, that this type of knowledge can affect teachers' expectations of children and in turn children's performance at school. Rosenthal and Jacobsen (1968) gave a non-verbal IQ test to all the students in an elementary school. The teachers were told that the test could predict which of the children would be "intellectual bloomers" at the end of the school year. They were also given a list of these bloomers, but the children were actually picked at random. When they were tested 8 months later, the scores of the group on the list had increased by comparison with the other children, with the greatest effect among the youngest children. Since this group presumably had received more interest and follow-up from the teachers, the "prediction" about a more positive development became a self-fulfilling prophecy. Similar effects have been found in other studies (Rosenthal, 1994; Rubie-Davies, 2006), demonstrating the potential damage negative attitudes among teachers can do to children's cognitive development. It is likely that teachers' positive and negative assumptions about children have a similar impact in non-experimental situations.

GENDER DIFFERENCES

The cognitive profiles of boys and girls show some differences. These differences do not involve general intelligence (*g-factor*) but mostly language, mathematics and spatial abilities. Girls are generally better at language and begin to read and write earlier, and fewer girls than boys have reading and writing disorders (Calvin et al., 2010; Kimura, 1999). Furthermore, average differences tend to be greater among the male group than the female group (Arden and Plomin, 2006; Johnson et al., 2008, 2009), and more boys than girls receive special education (Hibel et al., 2010).

When it comes to math abilities, boys on average do better than girls, but the differences change with age. Girls are slightly ahead of boys in early childhood. In elementary school, there is no difference in math skills between boys and girls, but in secondary school boys start to be ahead. Among those starting at university, males perform better in this area than females. This is consistent with the fact that the differences seem to be greater among those with high scores on intelligence tests. Children with more average IQ scores show no clear gender differences (Hyde et al., 1990), suggesting that there is no general difference between genders. It seems rather as males and females with higher education make different choices, probably based on cultural factors, which is also supported by the finding that gender differences in the high-scoring group have been reduced (Wai et al., 2010).

Boys are clearly better at spatial tasks than girls, such as reading maps and imaging three-dimensional objects in their mind, a difference that has also been related to male sex hormones (testosterone). This is not to imply that the difference depends on biology alone, but that hormonal differences between males and females affect brain development and in turn contribute to the differences between them (Halpern et al., 2007). Girls and boys may also differ in the strategies they apply on such tasks (Lawton, 2010).

When it comes to intelligence, the similarities between males and females are more prominent than the differences. Although consistent, the differences between the groups are too small to have any bearing on the assessment of individuals. Differences are far greater among boys and among girls than between the mean scores of boys and girls as groups (Arden and Plomin, 2006). However, it is still discussed whether these differences are due to evolutionary biological factors or to differences in upbringing (Bleie, 2003; Jones et al., 2003; Kimura, 2004). In this context, it is important to mention that some gender differences gradually seem to disappear in tandem with changes in society. Most likely, the differences are not related to upbringing alone, for example that males and females are encouraged to enroll in different school subjects, but equally to the experiences they gain through the activities in which they participate. Traditionally, boys are physically more active and play with technically more complex toys. As girls progressively take part in more traditional boy play, and boys in girl play, some of these differences diminish.

ETHNICITY AND INTELLIGENCE

Many studies have found variation in average IQ scores among different ethnic groups, and there is considerable controversy about what the intelligence scores measure and the bases for this variation (Dramé and Ferguson, 2017; Fagan and Holland, 2007; Neisser et al., 1996; Nisbett et al., 2012; Rushton and Jensen, 2010). In the USA, some maintain that genetic differences were the basis for an observed difference of around 15 IQ points between Black and White adults (Herrnstein and Murray, 1994; Jensen, 1985; Rushton and Jensen, 2005, 2010). However, a division into "races" is a socially and not a biologically constructed concept (Sternberg et al., 2005), and there is no reason why the genetic basis of skin color should influence cognitive development. The opposing view is that the difference in average IQ is a consequence of environmental and cultural factors, of differences in the life conditions of Black and White individuals (Nisbett, 2005). To explain such results, Lewontin (1970) uses an analogy about two corn fields planted with seeds that have the same genetic variation but only one is watered and cared for. It is not surprising that the field that is cared for gives a better harvest. However, it is not due to different genes but the growth environments of the seeds. Similarly, the economic and social conditions of the Black and White populations in the USA are so large that they have consequences for the populations' scores on intelligence tests. In line with Lewontin's analogy, and in accordance with an environmental explanation, relatively recent evidence suggests that the difference in IQ has narrowed by around five IQ points (Dickens and Flynn, 2006a, b). A change process is also supported by an even more recent finding that 4-year-old Black children are five points behind their White peers, compared to 17 IQ points among 24-year-olds (Nisbett et al., 2012).

CHANGING NORMS: THE FLYNN EFFECT

Average scores on intelligence tests have steadily increased over many years, making it necessary to re-standardize the tests at regular intervals to maintain a normal distribution of IQ scores with a mean of 100 (Flynn, 2007). In the USA, the average total score on the Stanford-Binet test and on Wechsler tests has increased by about three IQ points per decade (Baron, 2004). Similar and larger changes have been found in European as well as developing countries (Daley et al., 2003), although the gains vary somewhat between countries and domains (Pietschnig and Voracek, 2015).

This increase in scores must be the result of environmental changes, since the genetic pool of a population would not be able to change over such a short time period. Although the particular environmental factors responsible for this development have not been mapped, it is likely that economic conditions, changes in nutrition and child rearing, higher levels of education, increased literacy and the influence of radio and television have had an impact (Ceci and Kanaya, 2010). At the same time, the increase in IQ is greater for non-verbal than for verbal intelligence, that is, tests or subtests believed to be relatively unaffected by cultural factors. The average IQ on the non-verbal Raven test – which is also considered a good measure of fluid intelligence – increased by 21 points over 30 years, with equal differences among 10-year-olds and 20-year-olds (Flynn, 1998). One possible explanation is that children growing up in the 1980s and later have had more exposure to graphic patterns through film, television and computer games than earlier generations (Greenfield, 1998). More recently, the Flynn effect seems to have declined somewhat, and is even on the reverse in some countries (Flynn and Shayer, 2018; Sundet et al., 2004).

Due to this "inflation" in test scores, children's cognitive abilities are assessed slightly differently, depending on when the test used was last standardized (Fletcher et al., 2010). This also applies to children who score well below or above the mean. With each new standardization of the Wechsler tests, studies show a rapid increase in the proportion of children and adolescents classified as intellectual disabled (even though many specialists continue to use older versions of the tests). After that, the proportion gradually decreases over time until the appearance of a new standardization (Kanaya and Ceci, 2012). Similarly, the proportion of children classified as gifted increases with the length of time since the most recent standardization (Wai et al., 2012).

SCHOOL PERFORMANCE AND INTELLIGENCE

By and large, there is a clear statistical relationship between IQ and academic performance at school. Access to education contributes positively to IQ, and interrupted and reduced schooling – which is often the case for children living in war areas and when the family is seeking refuge in another country – can lead to lower intellectual performance (Ceci, 1991; Nisbett et al., 2012). However, the effect of schooling interacts with general maturity: In spite of the fact that they had been equally long in school, the youngest children in fourth grade and in the eighth grade scored a few percentiles lower than the oldest (Bedard and Dhuey, 2006). Mass education is considered one of the factors contributing to the Flynn effect (Baker et al., 2015). In Norway, a reform that increased obligatory schooling by 2 years increased the population mean among 19-year-olds by 3.7 IQ points (Brinch and Galloway, 2012).

Children with higher IQ scores typically do better in school than children with lower scores, but the relationship varies with the subject (Mayes et al., 2009; Roth et al., 2015). At the same time, a high IQ does not ensure academic success. Studies of children with an IQ above 130 show that also social factors, motivation and self-regulation are of importance. Some gifted children have specific learning disorders, and in many cases their positive skills as well as their learning disorders remain undetected (Lovett and Lewandowski, 2006; McCoach et al., 2001). Moreover, the best predictor of future grades is not IQ, but earlier school grades (Minton and Schneider, 1980).

ATYPICAL DEVELOPMENT

Intellectual disability

Intellectual disability is a complex condition involving low intelligence (see p. 62), and its developmental consequences are discussed in several sections of this book. These include low tolerance for novelty, complexity and uncertain situations, and difficulty understanding social and emotional cues (Whitman et al., 1997). The incidence of motor impairment, sensory impairment, epilepsy, autism spectrum disorder, attention deficit disorder and other disorders is often several times higher in children with intellectual disability than among children in general (Carr and O'Reilly, 2016a, b). Children with intellectual disability show a delayed development in most areas and the differences to typically developing children increase with age (Hall et al., 2005). However, they only share a general difficulty with learning, but otherwise they are as different as other children. Regarding them as a homogeneous group would mask important differences in their possibilities and limitations and their needs for an adapted environment (Leonard and Wen, 2002).

There are five main causes of intellectual disability: lack of oxygen (hypoxia) or exposure to toxins during pregnancy, disturbances in brain development, genetic conditions, metabolic diseases, and neglect and psychosocial influences (Jimenez-Gomez and Standridge, 2014). Genetic factors are thought to have a major impact on severe intellectual disability. Mutations in individual genes, such as *phenylketonuria* (PKU) and fragile X syndrome, are of particular importance in moderate to profound intellectual disability. A single gene, however, can have many mutations, and the same gene can be involved in a number of conditions (Kleefstra et al., 2014). Mild intellectual disability seems more associated with variation in several genes and to be part of the normal variation among the population. Siblings of children with severe intellectual disability have the same average IQ as the general population (around 100), indicating that they do not share the genetic disorder. Siblings of children with mild intellectual disability score about one standard deviation lower than the population mean, or roughly 85, which may reflect that they share relevant genes or environmental influences (Nichols, 1984).

The largest single group with a known cause for intellectual disability is represented by people with Down syndrome. With an incidence of one in 720 births, they make up about 6–8 percent of children with intellectual disability (Presson

Down syndrome is a common cause of intellectual disability.

et al., 2013; Vissers et al., 2016). Other common syndromes involving various degrees of intellectual disability are Rett syndrome, Lesch-Nyhan syndrome, Williams syndrome, Cornelia de Lange syndrome, Prader-Willi syndrome and Angelman syndrome (see p. 76). In about half the cases, the cause of the intellectual disability is unknown, but new syndromes are constantly being identified (Anazi et al., 2017; Udwin and Kuczynski, 2007; Vissers et al., 2016). There are, however, large individual differences among children with the same diagnosis, both with regard to their biological basis and their environment, and each child follows a unique developmental pathway.

For optimal development, children with intellectual disability depend more than other children on a specially adapted environment. Their developmental progress must be individually planned in far more detail than for other children. The child's individual education plan (IEP) can differ substantially from the school's usual curriculum, with greater emphasis on everyday skills and practical tasks. Children with intellectual disability often take an *outer directed* approach to problem solving. This means that they, more than other children, make use of the immediate situation and other external cues when solving problems, and to a lesser extent internal reflection or mental trial and error. They often lack the necessary concepts and mental strategies to reason beyond what they are able to perceive in the moment. They are unable to try out mental solutions and have to take a practical approach to problem solving (Bybee and Zigler, 1998). Children with intellectual disability may need a lot of help in developing the ability to play and interact with other children, as well as to explore their surroundings, learn to dress, eat, and cope with the minor and major challenges of daily life. Special education at school also includes social skills and opportunities for interacting with other children.

For children with intellectual disability, the first 5 years of life are often a period of early intervention that typically includes direct intervention with the child and parent guidance (Baker et al., 2016). Early intervention is an important tool in leading children onto the best possible path of development (Guralnick, 2011, 2017; Ramey and Ramey, 1998b). They are partly based on the assumption of sensitive periods, that the brain is more plastic and that children learn more easily during their first few years of life (see p. 113).

Notwithstanding the possible presence of such periods, it is better to support a positive development early on, both in terms of development and resources, than having to attempt to change the child's developmental course at a later point.

A child with an intellectual disability requires time and effort and can take many of the family's resources, partly because of the child's problems with comprehension and self-regulation, and partly because the intellectual disability itself involves training, adaptation and care beyond the age required by other children (Blacher et al., 2007; Carr and O'Reilly, 2016b). At the same time, the family represents the most important resource and social network for children and adolescents with intellectual disability. Help and support for the family are therefore important in any work involving children with intellectual disability.

Giftedness and talent

Although they represent a small group, especially gifted children may also need special support and adaptation for an optimal development:

Albert Einstein.

one in 1,000 is highly gifted and one in 10,000 is exceptionally gifted (Gagné, 2004). Their school may need to provide an individually tailored plan that incorporates opportunities for learning and social development that go beyond the school's ordinary curriculum and routines. The number of mildly gifted and moderately gifted children is considerably higher (1 in 10 and 1 in 100, respectively). They are often academically strong and may need some form of adaptation, but within the framework of the regular curriculum.

Traditional support for talented children has included starting earlier at school or skipping a grade (in some cases with a certain degree of curricular adaptation). Since strong intellectual ability typically goes hand in hand with the ability to work independently, support may be directed at the children's own active learning. Encouraging exploration and curiosity is often a good way of exploiting the intellectual potential of gifted children (Porath, 2014). Tailored education for this group should therefore not simply consist of more work and more challenging tasks, but has to be rooted in an active engagement in the student's particular learning style and interests (VanTassel-Baska and Stambaugh, 2008).

For gifted children with specific learning disorders or behavioral disorders there is a risk of failing to identify both their talent and their disorders, and hence for them to become underachievers in school. They need follow-up strategies that can promote their talent and reduce the impact of learning disorders, emotional problems and adjustment disorders (Buică-Belciu and Popovici, 2014; Gilman et al., 2013).

SUMMARY

1 There is no widely accepted definition of intelligence, but intelligence involves the understanding of complex ideas, adaption to the environment, learning from experience, reasoning, overcoming and problem solving. Some believe intelligence is a *domain-general* ability, others that it consists of many *domain-specific* abilities, while others yet believe that it includes both a *g-factor* and several *s-factors*.

2 Sternberg's *triarchic theory of intelligence* consists of three parts: process, experience and adaptation. *Process* involves the mental processes that form the basis for intelligent action; the *experiential sub theory* deals with the application of processes in the outer world. The *contextual sub theory* is based on the notion that intelligent actions have a purpose and that human beings use cognitive mechanisms to adapt to the world they live in.

3 Gardner's theory of *multiple intelligences* includes eight domain-specific modular *intelligences*. It is controversial and there is disagreement on whether the different areas of competence can be called intelligence.

4 Intelligence tests build on the assumption that intelligence has a *normal distribution*. Tests are norm-referenced by testing a large, representative sample of children in the relevant age groups. IQ is a measure of how children perform on a test compared with their peers. Most intelligence tests consist of various types of task and provide a *cognitive profile* in addition to a full-scale IQ. The *age score* indicates the age at which children on average achieve a specific raw score. Experience, culture and language background affect the test results.

5 The most common reason for testing intelligence is to assess whether a child needs special education or support, based on the assumption that tests are able to *predict future development*. Correlations between early test scores and later childhood IQ are low. Measures of information processing in the first year – but not later – have a higher average correlation with later IQ scores. After toddler age, IQ scores correlate relatively high with later IQs, although there is also significant variation. It is not the goal of tests to predict *too* well, since this would imply a predetermined view of intelligence. Interventions are based on the assumption that developmental problems and disorders can be remediated by training and adaptation.

6 Twin studies and other family studies show that genes are important to intellectual development, *and* that improvement to the environment results in higher IQ. The correlations between IQ scores increase with the amount of shared genetic material. Many genes have been associated with intelligence, but the effect of individual genes is very small. Children who are adopted into families with a higher socioeconomic background have higher IQs than children adopted into families with a lower socioeconomic background. Heredity estimates have been found to vary with socioeconomic background.

7 Many environmental factors impact children's intellectual development, including nutrition. *Orphanage studies* have shown that environmental factors can have a dramatic effect on children's intellectual development. Although lack of stimulation and social contact can lead to decreased cognitive functioning, the effects can be reversed. A low socioeconomic status is associated with risk factors that result in lower IQ. Most environments are stable, and the majority of children grow up in the same good or bad environment. Many countries have programs to support children who grow up in high-risk environments.

8 Based on the hypothesis of a *reaction range*, genes determine the amount of environmental impact on the development of a given area. The reaction range is also a *zone of modifiability* with possibilities and constraints. The *Rosenthal effect* illustrates how assumptions about a child's intelligence can become a self-fulfilling prophecy.

9 The ability profiles of boys and girls show certain differences, most likely due to differences in biology, culture and experience. The differences among boys and among girls are greater than the average difference between boys and girls as a group.

10 Many studies have found variation in average IQ scores among different ethnic groups. Some attribute differences to genes, others to environmental factors. The difference between average IQ in the Black and the White populations is best explained by environmental factors.

11 The mean raw score on intelligence tests has increased in most countries over time, making it necessary to standardize tests at regular intervals. The *Flynn effect* is probably caused by changes in economic factors, nutrition, parenting, education, reading ability and the influences of media. In many countries, the effect is currently declining or even on the reverse. The Flynn effect has an impact on the number of people categorized as intellectually disabled or especially gifted.

12 Performance on intelligence tests is positively influenced by education. Higher intelligence is associated with better academic achievement, but also the achievement of gifted children is dependent on social factors, motivation and self-regulation. Some gifted children have learning disorders.

13 *Intellectual disability* is a complex condition that affects all aspects of a child's functioning, and cognitive profiles vary as much as those of children with typical development. For optimal development, children with intellectual disability rely on a specially adapted environment. Child rearing requires more time and effort from parents, and parent guidance and support are important elements in any work involving children in this group.

14 Especially gifted children may require individually tailored programs beyond the school's ordinary curriculum. Other gifted children who do well in school may need some form of adaptation within the regular curriculum.

CORE ISSUES

- The role of genes and environment in intelligence.
- The bases of ethnic differences in average IQ.
- The effect of public early intervention programs.

SUGGESTIONS FOR FURTHER READING

Dickens, W. T., & Flynn, J. R. (2006a). Black Americans reduce the racial IQ gap: Evidence from standardization samples. *Psychological Science*, *17*, 913–920.

Drevon, D. D., Knight, R. M., & Bradley-Johnson, S. (2017). Nonverbal and language-reduced measures of cognitive ability: A review and evaluation. *Contemporary School Psychology*, *21*, 255–266.

Guralnick, M. J. (2011). Why early intervention works: A systems perspective. *Infants and Young Children*, *24*, 6–28.

Jensen, A. R. (1985). The nature of the Black-White difference on various psychometric tests: Spearman's hypothesis. *Behavioral and Brain Sciences*, *8*, 193–219.

Ramey, C. T., & Ramey, S. L. (1998). Early intervention and early experience. *American Psychologist*, *53*, 109–120.

Sternberg, R. J. (2015). Multiple intelligences in the new age of thinking. In S. Goldstein, D. Princiotta, & J. A. Naglieri (Eds), *Handbook of intelligence* (pp. 229–241). New York, NY: Springer.

Contents

CHAPTER 15

LEARNING AND INSTRUCTION

Learning may be defined as an experiential process which leads to relatively permanent changes in the knowledge, skills and behavior of an organism, and which are not caused by maturation, disease, fatigue or injury (Kolb, 1984). Learning is a central part of children's lives and adaptation (Siegler, 2000), and it is not always easy to distinguish learning and developmental processes (see p. 5). The individual learns throughout the lifespan but the acquisition of new knowledge and skills is especially important in childhood and adolescence. In new situations, adults can to a greater extent use the knowledge and skills they already have.

Children learn from their individual actions and exploration, but much of children's learning is social as other children and adults guide them toward what is important and relevant in their society (Tomasello, 2005). The transfer of knowledge across generations is basic to the evolution of human societies, and every society has ways of equipping children with knowledge, including children with atypical learning and development. Some have educational difficulties, and the most common learning disorders involve problems with reading, writing and math.

Among the developmental theories, logical and social constructivism have had a particular impact on education.

TYPES OF LEARNING

Learning is an adaptive process and can take different forms, both formal in educational settings and informal in play and other everyday activities. Learning is related to cognitive development but also to emotional development and motivation. Early forms of learning are habituation, conditioning and imitation. As children grow older, reasoning and insight become more important in acquiring knowledge and skills (see Chapter 12).

Habituation and conditioning

Habituation and conditioning are basic simple forms of learning and adaptation to the environment. Habituation can be demonstrated as early as the embryonic stage and is used in research on newborns (Leader, 2016). The particular types of stimulation to which infants habituate and dishabituate provide important insights into the characteristics of the physical and social surroundings they are aware of and capable of differentiating. In *classical conditioning*, children form associations between two stimuli that follow each other closely in time. *Operant conditioning* leads to learning when a child's action is followed by *reinforcement*, defined as an event that increases the likelihood of repeating the action. Good grades act as a reinforcement when they lead a child to spend more time on homework. An important characteristic of operant conditioning is that the reinforcing event need not take place every time the action is performed. Once an action has been learned, it often leads to more effective learning as long as it is reinforced at certain intervals (Skinner, 1969).

Imitation and observational learning

Imitation is the deliberate execution of an action performed by another person, and is rooted in social learning (Tomasello, 2005). Observing and then imitating others reduce the need for time-consuming trial and error, lays the foundation for learning from others and their experiences, and makes it easier to establish social and emotional relationships. Of special interest from a developmental point of view are imitation in newborns and the emergence of immediate and deferred imitation as a tool for learning new skills.

Imitation in newborns

One of the major points of contention among developmental psychologists is the question of when children are able to "translate" actions they see others perform into movements they perform themselves (Oostenbroek et al., 2013). Meltzoff and Moore (1983) observed that 1- to 3-day-old infants spent more time mouth opening when the adult opened and closed the mouth, and more time in tongue protrusion when the adult engaged in this activity. In another experiment, newborns were differentially influenced by adult tongue-protrusion and head turning (Figure 15.1). Other studies have reported similar findings (Meltzoff and Moore, 1997; Nagy et al., 2013), including the observation that the finger movements of 2-day-old children were affected by the number of fingers shown to them (Nagy et al., 2014). Meltzoff and Moore explain their observations by suggesting that children have an innate ability to imitate other people's actions that they are able to master themselves.

Other studies have been unable to find a consistent correspondence between actions performed by the adult and the infant (Abravanel and DeYong, 1997; Anisfeld et al., 2001; Heimann et al., 1989; Ullstadius, 1998), and a number of theorists have questioned whether the infants in Meltzoff and Moore's studies actually imitated the adult's actions (Anisfeld, 2005; Jones, 2009; Oostenbroek et al., 2016). In a similar experiment, Jones (1996) found that 4-week-olds stuck out their tongue more often

Young children like to do the same as adults do.

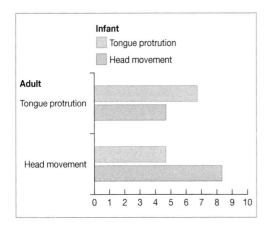

Infant
- Tongue protrution
- Head movement

Adult

Tongue protrution

Head movement

0 1 2 3 4 5 6 7 8 9 10

FIGURE 15.1 Tongue protrusion and head rotation in newborns.

Forty infants aged 1–3 days saw an adult either protruding the tongue or rotating the head. The figure shows that the infants more often stuck out their tongue when the adult performed a tongue-protrusion gesture, and turned their head more often when the adult rotated his or her head (based on Meltzoff and Moore, 1989).

in response to tongue protrusion than to a mouth-opening gesture, consistent with the observations of Meltzoff and Moore (1983). Jones, however, also found that infants looked longer at a tongue-protruding face than at a mouth-opening face. Her interpretation is that tongue protrusion is more interesting for a newborn than mouth opening, and that tongue movements involve *oral exploration* (Jones, 2006). There is no doubt that the infants' tongue movements were elicited by the adult's actions, but they were not imitative – it was not the specific outward appearance of the adult's action that determined the child's behavior, but rather the interest aroused by seeing the tongue-protruding gesture. Furthermore, imitative behavior gradually diminishes: imitation of hand movements disappears at 2 months of age and returns once again at 7 months, while imitation of mouth movements disappears around 3 months and returns around 12 months. This suggests that the elicited actions of newborns and the later imitation of actions have different functions, and that early "imitation" needs a separate explanation (Elsner, 2005).

For newborns to be able to copy the actions of others, they must be born with a neurological structure that allows them to recognize and perform actions carried out by others without any previous experience. A number of researchers suggest that the mirror-neuron system (see p. 112) is the neurological basis for imitation (Fabbri-Destro and Rizzolatti, 2008; Iacoboni, 2005; Stern, 2007). Such a system may possibly be of importance for the later development of imitation, but it can hardly explain imitation in newborns. One of the characteristics of mirror-neuron systems is that they are activated once the *goal* of a perceived action becomes clear, such as stretching out the hand to pick up an apple or pour water out of a glass (Jacob, 2009). The small action repertoire of newborns has no clear purpose, and infants only a few days of age have little knowledge about the intent of different actions. Moreover, mirror neurons have been found in a number of species that do not imitate (Oostenbroek et al., 2013; Suddendorf et al., 2013).

Another hypothesis is that the areas of the brain that control motor skills are generally activated when an individual observes the actions of others (Cattaneo and Rizzolatti, 2009). This implies the possibility of a rudimentary link between perception and action at birth that does not provide a basis for imitation in the narrow sense, but with an activating function that increases the likelihood of the infant being attentive and acting in concert with other people. Conceivably, this could help ensure social attachment through mutual attention, or represent a form of early "calibration" between external stimulation and individual action that later enables the child to acquire new skills by observing others.

Most researchers agree that newborns have a small repertoire of actions and that children's actions can be triggered by those of adults. The point in question is how to explain the correspondences that have been found between the actions of newborns and adults. On the one hand, Meltzoff and Moore (1994) maintain that these actions are a form of imitation, performed with such effort as to suggest they have a purpose. Anisfeld (2005) and Jones (2009), on the other hand, suggest that watching the actions of adults activates part of infants' behavioral repertoire, although not in the way imitation is commonly defined. No matter which explanation may be right, actions elicited at this age do not seem to lead infants to learn new actions or where a particular action may be appropriate.

Imitation after the age of 6 months

By around 6 months, the behavioral repertoire of infants has grown and they gradually begin to imitate new actions, although imitation in the first year of life generally remains sparse. Children and adults often interact by vocalizing, but it is usually the adult who imitates the child (Jones, 2009). One study investigated at what age more than 50 percent of children imitate some common actions (Jones, 2007). The mothers of 162 children aged 6 to 20 months performed different actions in front of their child. The age when half of the children performed the mother's action was 6 months for hitting the table when their mother did, 8 months for waving good-bye and vocalizing the sound *ah*, 10 months for clapping hands, 14 months for vocalizing the sound *eh-eh*, 16 months for performing sequential finger movements and putting one hand on their head, and 18 months for protruding their tongue when the mother protruded her tongue. However, the children rarely reiterated a specific action before the age of 1 year. Two-thirds of the 6-month-olds knocked on the table when their mother did, but did so just as often when their mother performed a different action. Only the mother's *ah*-sound had a specific matching response before the age of 12 months, while the other actions matched between 12 and 18 months. It is worth noting that the children generally protruded their tongue quite often. While 40 percent of the 6-month-olds protruded their tongue when their mother did, it was not until 18 months that they did so significantly more often when observing their mother's tongue protrusion than when she performed other actions. This supports the assumption that the imitation of actions after the age of 6 months has a different basis than the earliest tongue-protruding gestures (Elsner, 2005; Jones, 1996, 2007).

It is an important milestone in children's development when they begin to imitate actions they have not mastered earlier – imitation becomes a functional aspect of the learning process. This imitation is not random: children imitate actions more often when they have a clear goal, have an effect on something or trigger an action than when the action has no clear objective, such as just moving an object in a circle (Elsner, 2007). Children first imitate functional actions such as drinking from a cup or brushing their hair with a brush, and not until 2 years of age are they able to imitate non-functional actions such as using a toy car as a cup or a brush (Guillaume, 1926; Uzgiris, 1999). Children under 2½ years of age find it difficult to start using a new action to reach a goal without having seen the goal as well as the action that leads to it (Carpenter and Call, 2002). What children imitate also depends on their development and interests, and with age their imitation becomes progressively more selective (Harris and Want, 2005). Imitation is also reduced when the action is marked as undesired by an adult (Seehagen et al., 2017).

Deferred imitation means that children perform an action some time after having observed it, and thus that the action must be remembered. Deferred imitation and memory is limited in the first year of life. With age, children need fewer demonstrations, recall more complex actions and their order, and remember for longer (Elsner, 2007).

Learning consists not only of acquiring new skills, children also use cues to learn *when* particular skills can be used. In many situations, imitating another person's action may be neither functional nor practical. A counter-imitation mechanism has therefore been suggested inhibiting "automatic" imitation, which is assumed to be part of the mirror neuron system and self-regulation (see p. 340) in general (Campbell and Cunnington, 2017).

The fact that a child uses an action or a strategy that has worked well for someone else does not always involve imitation in a straightforward sense. The actions of adults also provide information about the properties of objects. When a child presses a button the way Daddy did, the action is not necessarily imitated directly, but the result of having discovered new action possibilities afforded by the object (Yang et al., 2010). Deferred imitation can entail either direct copying of an action or the use of new knowledge in exploring the environment. Both are the result of *observational learning*.

Children do not imitate adults only, they start early to follow each other's example. A major diary study found that only-children and children with siblings imitate with about the same frequency around the age of 1, but that only-children almost exclusively imitate adults. Children with siblings imitate more spontaneously and more in the context of play, with fewer actions and routines based on instruction than only-children. Thus, having a sibling affects what a child is imitating (Barr and Hayne, 2003). Two-year-olds often copy each other's actions, for example by taking the same toy another child has taken (Nadel-Brulfert and Baudonniere, 1982). This suggests that imitation may be a tool for children to establish joint play and other activities.

Around the age of 1 year, children learn one-two new skills per day by imitating others (Barr and Hayne, 2003). Much of children's play consists of copying the activities of adults, while adults adapt to children by imitating and expanding *their* actions. Imitation is especially important during the first years of life, but continues as a learning strategy throughout life. The emergence of culture would be impossible to imagine without cooperation, imitation and observational learning, and the fact that children imitate other people and are guided in modeling the actions of others (Rogoff, 2014; Tomasello, 2016).

Learning by trial and error, insight and heuristics

Children use a variety of strategies when they encounter "problems" they need to solve, depending on their development and experience (Schunk, 2012; Siegler, 2000). During early development, an important strategy is trial and error. The child is trying different solutions without a clear plan until one works, for example turning a triangle around or moving between holes when trying to put it into a box with differently shaped holes. This is typically a novice strategy. Since younger children are new to many situations, they lack appropriate strategies to solve everyday problems. At first, they may use strategies that are not particularly adequate, but over time, their exploratory trial and error leads to better understanding and a larger action repertoire, as well as to more systematic and deliberate "guess and check" (Fessakis et al., 2013).

Young children learn about the physical world by trying out different solutions.

Four-year-old Mary is looking at a jigsaw puzzle. Suddenly she puts a piece exactly where it belongs. She has had an insight into how it fits. Insight is characterized by a sudden shift in skills. Sometimes it is the result of mental trial and error, other times it is the result of reasoning, combining different elements, arranging the situation in different ways, and the like (Schunk, 2012). It is precisely this type of understanding Piaget and other researchers explore in their conversations with children about problem solving – their conscious reflection on the challenges they meet (see p. 170).

In heuristic problem solving, older children employ a set of general strategies, such as thinking of a similar problem, making a plan, drawing a conceptual map or working backward, that may help the child be systematic and reach a solution when encountering new problems. A child may start by identifying the problem, asking what she knows and needs to know to solve the problem, and searching for strategies and solutions that were useful in the past. Heuristics functions best with new material, in familiar situations the child may already have established useful strategies (Gigerenzer and Gaissmaier, 2011; Schunk, 2012).

TWO DEVELOPMENTAL PERSPECTIVES ON EDUCATION

Children learn in a large variety of formal and informal situations. Informal learning is most common, but formal training and education in kindergarten and at school ensure that knowledge considered important by society is conveyed to the coming generation (Cole, 2005; Olson, 2003). Both logical and social constructivism have had a significant impact on education (deVries, 2000; Green and Gredler, 2002; Stoltz et al., 2015), each with its own perspective: Piaget views cognition as the basis for learning and education, while Vygotsky views learning and education as the basis for cognition (see Chapter 10).

Logical constructivism

According to Piaget (1969b, 1972), children's thinking is qualitatively different from adult thinking and limits what children are able to learn. Therefore, education can only be effective as long as it takes into account these differences.

Educational objectives at school must be based on the child's level of development, for example by paying attention to the order in which basic concepts such as conservation of mass, weight, volume and causality are acquired (Elkind, 1976). Cognitive assessment of children who struggle or excel in school is an integral part of educational practice (see Chapters 3 and 14).

According to Piaget, schools should promote children's thinking – factual knowledge is of secondary importance. The goal of education is to foster autonomous intellectual explorers rather than vessels of information to be reproduced, and schools should strive to encourage the best possible quality of thinking in children. This is in line with modern educational approaches, except that Piaget places relatively little emphasis on children's interactions. In his view, learning mostly concerns individual exploration of the laws and rules of natural science. However, individual experience is not enough and children must also learn to reconstruct knowledge selected by the school system (Martí, 1996).

The emphasis on children's abilities is also closely connected with Piaget's view of children as active participants in their own learning. In educational approaches based on Piaget's theory, the teacher is not an agent who fills passive children with the knowledge they lack. The teacher should adapt the situation and ask questions that promote children's independent learning based on their own prerequisites, but it is the individual child itself who creates intellectual growth (Furth and Wachs, 1975). Piaget has contributed to leading school education from blackboard and lecture to a more activity-oriented approach. Teachers should give students time to "work" rather than merely talking in front of the class all day. This does not represent a downgrading of the teacher's importance, but, to the contrary, places greater demands on teachers' knowledge about children's cognitive functioning. Although the teacher's function described above is less collaboration-oriented, it is not unlike the role of the teacher in Vygotsky's theory (see below).

Social constructivism

In social constructivism, formal education is seen as an integral aspect of cognitive development, and educational work at all levels is a natural part of this (Karpov, 2014; Kozulin, 2002). "Instruction" is a central concept in Vygotsky's theory:

> Studying child thought apart from the influence of instruction, as Piaget did, excludes a very important source of change and bars the researcher from posing the question of the interaction of development and instruction peculiar to each age level. Our own approach focuses on this interaction.
>
> (Vygotsky, 1962)

Like Piaget, Vygotsky (1935a, b) places emphasis on the independent and active child. Adults should not simply tell or show children what to do, but facilitate the child's own discovery of the problem as well as the solution together with the adult. In Vygotsky's theory, "independent" means that children themselves seek out knowledge, not that they find it on their own. They need the help of adults, and it is the adult's responsibility to guide the child to seek knowledge that is considered important by society. The learning process is not merely a matter of transferring information from teacher to student, but of guiding the student's construction of scientific concepts and theoretical understanding. In contrast with Piaget's theory, it is not the child's individual exploration that yields the best result, but the collaboration between the child and others. Children learn better when the adult takes part as committed and active participants in the children's exploration (Kozulin, 2002).

Vygotsky argues that education must be based on the child's *zone of proximal development*, the area in which a child is able to master new tasks with help (see p. 184). The children in a school class are different both with respect to independent coping and the extent of their zone of proximal development in different fields of knowledge. The zone determines the types of tasks and activities that are meaningful for a child and the kind of instruction and guidance the child requires. Tasks children are able to manage independently lie below the zone and are therefore too simple. No matter how many such tasks a child solves, they will not lead to new knowledge. If a task lies above the zone of proximal development, the child will not be able to understand it, and watching somebody else solve the problem will not provide new knowledge. When a child or adolescent struggles or has atypical development, a thorough assessment will be necessary to ensure that the teaching is appropriate for their zone of proximal development in relevant areas. This

zone thus acts as a bridge between the known and the unknown. Being within the child's proximal zone ensures that the instruction does not turn into tedious repetitions of familiar knowledge or frustrating encounters with the unfamiliar, but makes new insights achievable.

COOPERATION AMONG CHILDREN

Much of children's and adolescents' learning takes place in vertical relationships with teachers and other adults. It is an asymmetric relationship where the adult possesses the knowledge and skills, and the child or adolescent is the recipient. This is not to say that children are usually passive learners. They actively seek knowledge and help from more competent persons, both inside and outside of kindergarten and school. In a horizontal relationship, both parts are equal. Peer collaboration is based on a reciprocal relationship and can involve competition as well as cooperation.

Damon and Phelps (1989) distinguish between three types of collaboration between children. *Peer tutoring* means that older or more competent children help children who are novices. They assume the role of the teacher and create a vertical relationship. This can occur within the scope of a class, but often peer tutoring involves students from higher grades who act as "mentors" in cross age tutoring. In *cooperative learning*, a group of children joins forces to solve an assignment given by the teacher. The assignment is often divided into smaller tasks that are distributed among individual children. Every child works toward the same final goal, however, and the group members are a source of support and inspiration for each other. In *peer collaboration*, everyone is equal. The learning process consists of jointly exploring a topic, and the task is based on the group's interests rather than the teacher's authority. This also represents a more integrated and joint process in which preliminary ideas and proposals are discussed by all the group members. An important part of the process is that children gain a better understanding of their own as well as others' reasoning and have to adapt to different perspectives on the same topic.

Studies have shown that two or more children solve tasks of which they had no prior knowledge better in collaboration than separately (Battistich and Watson, 2003; Gillies, 2014; Johnson and Johnson, 2009). For example, Light and Glachan (1985) found that pairs of children aged 7–8 or 12–13 years needed on average about one-third-fewer entries to solve Mastermind tasks than a group of children who solved the tasks individually. In fact, studies of adults have found that the "group intelligence" can be higher than the achievement of the highest scoring individual (Woolley et al., 2015). However, studies have also found that the effect of collaboration depends on the task and the interaction between the children. For example, in group mathematics, those who master mathematics best may dominate and hinder true collaboration. Children need help in learning to work together, as much of the group activity that goes on in classrooms may be distracting and have little educational value. In addition, peer collaboration in school also puts significant demands on the teacher (Gillies, 2014; Mercer, 2013).

The question is how and why collaboration makes learning more effective, why a collaborative solution can be better than the best individual solution. Howe (2010) suggests that a need to find a common solution elicits more in-depth discussions and hence better solutions. According to Doise (1978), collaborative learning is driven by "socio-cognitive conflicts" that arise because children have different perspectives and experiences. Since children initially only have their own perspective (or perspectives, but nevertheless only their own), the individual child cannot achieve a similar level of problem solving. Another important factor is that the children themselves are active in the production of knowledge and therefore have a greater sense of ownership. A teacher would not be able to present different perspectives to the same extent. It should also be noted that in this context, the word "conflict" should not be taken literally. It is not as if serious disagreement between children necessarily promotes learning. Children who accept each other's viewpoints without expressing disagreement learn more than children who quarrel. Howe (2009) emphasizes the importance of unresolved contradictions, analogous to the process of equilibration in Piaget's theory (see p. 169). Conflict entails a certain polarity between children's views that provides opportunity for agreement and disagreement in their dialogue, and that requires a mental reshuffling for conflicting views to be united (Kruger, 1993). Perspectives must neither be too different, nor so similar as to leave no room for contradiction. Effective collaborative learning furthermore requires that children understand their role and have the opportunity to explore each other's views constructively (Gillies, 2003). In line with this, Mercer (2013) suggests that collaborative learning builds on mind understanding and the ability to share ideas and compare different perspectives.

ATYPICAL DEVELOPMENT: LEARNING DISORDERS

The school is society's main tool for providing shared knowledge and competence to all children, as well as ensuring the competence society needs. A learning disorder implies that the child has difficulty achieving some of the school's educational objectives beyond general cognitive resources and in spite of appropriate education. Low performance due to poor education is not considered a learning disorder. When a child has a learning disorder, teaching needs to be adapted to the child's problems, and severe disorders can necessitate an entirely different educational approach than other children benefit from. Moreover, a learning disorder can represent a significant emotional burden and require psychological support.

In line with a developmental understanding, multiple factors interact in the development of learning disorders (Kaufmann et al., 2013). A child may have early signs indicating vulnerability for a learning disorder, such as delayed language development or a high frequency of family members with dyslexia, and these may be a strong reason for preventive measures. However, correlations between early signs of vulnerability and later development are often small and moderate and many vulnerable children show resilience and do not develop a learning disorder (Lee and Johnston-Wilder, 2015). A learning disorder does not present and cannot be diagnosed before the child has actually shown difficulties in school learning.

Reading and writing disorders

Disorders related to the comprehension and production of written language are common and a major problem in school (see p. 61). There is considerable discussion about the definition of dyslexia but core features are problems with word decoding, poor reading fluency and spelling problems, and can appear in children with high as well as low intelligence (Elliott and Grigorenko, 2014; Snowling, 2013). Written text is the basic tool in most school work and problems with understanding and composing written text may therefore have major influences on motivation and academic achievement.

Research shows a clear relationship between language and reading skills, and developmental language disorders entail a vulnerability for developing reading and writing disorders (Grigorenko, 2007; Simkin and Conti-Ramsden, 2006). Children with dyslexia who learn an alphabet-based language usually recognize the letters but have difficulty combining the sounds that correspond to the individual letters into words (Peterson and Pennington, 2015). Chinese children can have problems distinguishing written words with differences in stress (tonemes) (Li and Ho, 2011). Dyslexia may be seen as a language disorder because the reading problems seem to be a developmental extension of the problems children have in language processing. Children with phonological problems tend to have problems with word reading and spelling; children with semantic problems have difficulties understanding text meaning (Bishop and Snowling, 2004; Nation et al., 2010). However, children with dyslexia understand and use spoken language much better than written. Reading must therefore imply additional impaired processes, and reading is related to many non-verbal cognitive skills (Ricketts, 2011).

Reading problems are common in a variety of disorders. Among children with severe motor impairments and unintelligible speech (dysarthria), reading and writing disorders are the rule rather than the exception (Smith, 2005). Many children with ADHD have problems with reading and writing (McGrath et al., 2011). There are often several family members with dyslexia, indicating that it is hereditary, but also influences from the environment (Bishop, 2015; Shaywitz and Shaywitz, 2013). Children with dyslexia more often than other children have parents who left school early, do little reading, and lack the resources to follow up their child's disorders (Bonifacci et al., 2016).

Most often, reading disorders are noted when a child is unable to read out loud, especially when it comes to new words and text with more complex content. One exception is children with hyperlexia, who have good mechanical reading abilities and read the text correctly aloud, but do not comprehend what they are reading and cannot answer even simple questions about the content (Grigorenko et al., 2003). If they had heard someone else say the same sentences, they would have been able to answer these questions without difficulty. They seem to be attentive to only a part of the reading process, the production of speech on the basis of letters. This emphasizes that the understanding of meaning of a text involves more processes than just letter-sound decoding.

Some children are not hyperlexic but have *reading comprehension problems*. They appear to be able readers, and the people around them do not always notice their problems. After all, they are able to read out loud and understand what others say to them. As a result, they often do not receive the support they need for an adequate development of vocabulary and reading comprehension (Woolley, 2010). Reading comprehension problems can persist throughout adolescence and adulthood (Vaughn et al., 2014).

Prevention and learning support

Reading and writing are so fundamental to a child's future that early help is indicated for anyone with an increased risk of problems. For children with early language disorders or ADHD and other groups known to be at risk, early intervention is essential *before* the disorder appears, often already in kindergarten (Schulte-Körne, 2010). Shaywitz and colleagues (1998) found that 80 percent of children diagnosed with dyslexia in first grade did not meet the criteria for the disorder 4 years later. This underlines not only the importance of intervention and the fact that early difficulties do not necessarily predestine later problems, but also that care should be taken in giving this type of diagnosis during early school age. In later school age, learning disorders tend to stabilize. Most children diagnosed with dyslexia at 9 years of age remain poor readers 5 years later (Rutter et al., 1976).

Intervention and adaptation may be important throughout school life, but intervention seems to be more effective when implemented early rather than later in school age. A number of programs are available to help children with reading and writing disorders, and different methods seem to be effective in early and later interventions (Scammacca et al., 2015; Shaywitz et al., 2008; Schiff and Joshi, 2016). Some children derive only limited benefits from ordinary interventions (Shaywitz and Shaywitz, 2013). A large repertoire of strategies is essential, since a larger dose of what does not work serves little purpose. Audiobooks can be effective in countering the inevitable loss of knowledge brought about by poor reading skills; special assistive technology and text-to-speech computer programs can also be of help (Saine et al., 2011; von Tetzchner et al., 1997). It is important, however, to distinguish between children who simply read slowly, and children who struggle with the process of reading itself. Slow readers may need additional training to automate the reading process, preferably by using books that are exciting and easy to read and naturally speed up the child's reading pace. Children who struggle with the process of reading itself need support in learning the relationship between letters and speech sounds.

Research has found associations between reading disorders and emotional and behavioral problems. This demonstrates the impact such disorders can have on stress and self-esteem (Halonen et al., 2006; Mugnaini et al., 2009). Strategies for reducing or preventing severe reading and writing problems are thus crucial to a child's entire course of school as well as to prevent emotional and behavioral problems (Halonen et al., 2006).

Mathematics disorders

Mathematics learning disorder, or *developmental dyscalculia*, implies math performance significantly below grade level, often operationally defined as two school grades below peers (see p. 61). Therefore, the severity of problems often does not become noticeable until late in the second or third grade (Gifford and Rockliffe, 2012). Many children struggle with mathematics and it is discussed whether children with a math disorder represent the extreme end of a continuum (or several continua) of mathematical ability or whether the arithmetic difficulties associated with dyscalculia are qualitatively different from more common mathematics difficulties. Some children are able to solve mathematical exercises but are slow performers and use far more time than their peers.

Dyscalculia was first described by Kosc (1974) and the fact that many children have difficulties with math may be one reason why these types of problems were only more recently acknowledged as a learning disorder (Butterworth, 2008). In addition, there are different types of mathematical problems, and there is still disagreement on how to diagnose dyscalculia and whether a uniform complex of math disorders actually exists (Emerson, 2015; Gillum, 2012). Studies show a relation between math performance and different cognitive skills but there is no specific test profile capable of determining whether a child has a math disorder (Munro, 2003). Recent research has investigated the involvement of different brain areas and processes in mathematical thinking, which may give new insights into math learning and problems, and in the future contribute to the design of special educational interventions (Bugden and Ansari, 2015; Gillum, 2012).

Mathematics also includes a linguistic aspect. Relational terms such as prepositions and words for quantity and size are part of early math language (Donlan, 2015). In addition, math requires a high degree of precision in both comprehension and expression. When children struggle with language, their ability to establish numeracy is also reduced (Landerl, 2015). Children with a minority language background, for example, can develop language skills that function well in daily life but are too rudimentary to acquire mathematical knowledge (Levels et al., 2008).

There is no consensus on the causes of mathematical disorders, but they can reflect individual differences in both numerical and non-numerical functions (Kaufmann et al., 2013). Working memory appears to be important for mathematics learning and children with mathematics learning disorders have special difficulties with tasks involving working memory (Menon, 2016). However, this is also the case for children with autism spectrum disorder (Kercood et al., 2014) or ADHD (Martinussen et al., 2005). Butterworth (2008) suggests that a deficiency in an innate "number module" leads to a decrease in the ability to handle all types of mathematical operations. However, the assumption about a number module is inconsistent with brain studies (Bugden and Ansari, 2015) and the fact that many children with math disorders also have ADHD and problems in reading and writing. Math problems are found in many groups, with slight variations among children with different syndromes and disorders (Green and Gallagher, 2014; Reeve and Gray, 2015). Therefore, it is more likely that a number of different functions are involved in the development of mathematical skills and disorders (Fias et al., 2013; Henik et al., 2011). The heterogeneity in problems shows the complexity of mathematics and comparison of different syndromes and disorders may shed light on the many factors influencing learning of mathematics (Bugden and Ansari, 2015; Kaufmann et al., 2013; Reeve and Gray, 2015).

Prevention and learning support

It seems possible to identify 5–6-year-olds who later show mathematical learning disabilities in the first and second grade (Stock et al., 2010). There is a large number of intervention programs for moderate problems as well as severe mathematical disorders (Dowker, 2017; Reeve and Waldecker, 2017). The consequences of poor school-entry quantitative knowledge can be life-long without appropriate intervention (Geary, 2015). One study found that first graders who were more than one standard deviation below average in the understanding of numerals had a four times higher probability of being functionally innumerate as adolescents than children with average numerical understanding in the first grade. The vulnerable children improved their math skills to a similar degree as their peers but did not gain on them and the gap in mathematical competence remained (Geary et al., 2013). Although genes have been shown to influence the acquisition of mathematical skills, development is not determined by genes only but depends on education and other environmental factors. Studies on the prevention of mathematical disorders suggest that early detection of potential problems and remedial follow-up can reduce the incidence and consequences of disorders (Clarke et al., 2016; Gersten et al., 2015; Salminen et al., 2015). In primary school, there is no age effect, indicating that there is no "critical period," mathematics intervention can be effective at any age. However, the long-term effects may be small (Dowker, 2017). School instruction geared at demonstrating visual spatial relationships and strengthening executive reasoning skills can be of help (Cheng and Mix, 2014; Raghubar et al., 2010), as can language support (Gersten et al., 2009).

> It is worth acknowledging, while we are discussing the heterogeneous nature of children, that teachers, too, are a heterogeneous group.
>
> (Chinn, 2015, p. 7)

Some children receive special education in order to achieve the corresponding level of math skills as their peers, while others need lower educational targets (Holmes and Dowker, 2013). Number knowledge is important in many daily activities, and an appropriate goal for children with severe math disorders may be to provide them with the skills necessary to manage most practical situations, and possibly compensatory strategies and assistive technology. Teaching can focus on a practical understanding of length, weight, time and money, for example. Also the home environment can support the child's development, for example if parents focus children's attention on the numerical features of routine activities, such as counting children in a game or plates as they are put on the table (Hannula et al., 2010). Counseling can be of help in strengthening children's self-esteem and self-efficacy in tandem with more intensive and specially adapted math lessons (Green and Gallagher, 2014).

LEARNING DISORDERS AND MENTAL DISORDERS

Many children and adolescents with learning disorders find school emotionally stressful and are vulnerable to developing internalizing and externalizing disorders (Alesi et al., 2014; Jenson et al., 2011). Learning disorders influence education and employment in adult life (Gerber, 2012). As adults, they also have a higher incidence of internalizing disorders (Klassen et al., 2013). Although some children are anxious about math, anxiety does not seem to be the main cause of their math disorder. At the same time, problems with math can lead to considerable emotional distress (Butterworth, 2008).

Since many children with a learning disability are diagnosed late, they do not know what is wrong and may experience the first years of school as stressful. The situation can improve once they get better insight into their own difficulties in adolescence and realize that they are no less smart than their peers (Ingesson, 2007).

Meanwhile, children's self-image is increasingly affected by their academic achievements. While there is little connection between math disorders and self-image in second grade, it is relatively high in eighth grade (Linnanmäki, 2004). Many adolescents with dyslexia and mathematics learning disorders experience low self-esteem and a sense of despondency (Alexander-Passe, 2006; Graefen et al., 2015).

Some degree of emotional strain is probably unavoidable for children and adolescents with learning disorders, but the negative consequences of these disorders can be significantly reduced by early diagnosis and adequate educational and psychological support (Ingesson, 2007). When learning disorders are accompanied by social and emotional disorders, academic performance can be improved through parallel interventions aimed at these disorders (Alesi et al., 2014). Although learning disorders will not simply disappear with an improvement in the child's social and emotional life, better social and emotional functioning frees up resources that in turn allow the child to take better advantage of learning in school.

SUMMARY

1   *Learning* is commonly defined as a relatively permanent change in knowledge and skills that result from experience. *Instruction* includes both formal and informal strategies to provide children with knowledge and skills.

2   *Habituation* means that children react less after repeated presentations of a stimulus. *Dishabituation* occurs when the presentation of a new stimulus once again leads to an increase in reaction. Children regulate the stimulation from the environment.

3   *Classical conditioning* involves the association of two stimuli. In *operant conditioning*, learning occurs when a child's action is followed by *reinforcement*, an event that increases the likelihood of repeating the action.

4   *Imitation* is social learning, the deliberate replication of someone else's action. One point of discussion is *when* infants are able to "translate" other people's actions into movements they themselves perform. After the age of 6 months, infants learn many skills through *immediate* and *deferred imitation* and by observing and copying the actions of others. Imitation is particularly important during the first years, but remains a learning strategy throughout life. The development of cultural knowledge is based on cooperation, imitation and instruction.

5   Children are new to many situations and often have to use *trial and error* to find the strategy in their repertoire best suited to solving the problems they face. *Insight learning* is characterized by a sudden shift in skills as the result of mental trial and error, reasoning, or by combining different elements.

6   A pedagogy based on *logical constructivism* assumes that children's development sets limits to what they are capable of learning. Learning in the narrow sense comes *after* development. *Social constructivism* centers on children's active participation in the process while the adult lays the groundwork for the child to discover the problem and find a solution together with the adult. Training must remain within the child's *zone of proximal development* for different areas.

7   *Learning disorders* imply a difficulty meeting the school's educational objectives. Even milder forms of *reading and writing disorders* (dyslexia) can have major consequences for children's learning and development. Some children struggle most during childhood, but disorders can persist throughout adolescence and adulthood. Various strategies can mitigate and prevent reading and writing disorders, and different methods seem to be useful at earlier and later stages. Although many children struggle with math, some have such severe problems that they are diagnosed with *dyscalculia*. Early detection of potential disorders and remedial follow-up

with or without compensatory strategies and assistive technology can reduce the incidence and consequences of these disorders.

8   Children and adolescents with learning disorders often have low self-esteem and are vulnerable to developing internalizing and externalizing disorders. When learning disorders are accompanied by social and emotional disorders, academic performance can be improved by parallel interventions.

9   *Vertical learning relationships* involve children together with adults or more competent children, while *horizontal learning relationships* are reciprocal. *Peer tutoring* means that more competent children teach children who need help. In *cooperative learning*, a group of children jointly solves an assignment given by the teacher. In *peer collaboration*, the learning process consists of jointly exploring an area of knowledge based on the group's interests rather than the teacher's authority. The fact that two or more children solve a task better together than on their own may be related to "socio-cognitive conflicts," where children have to integrate different perspectives and experiences.

CORE ISSUES

- The basis and function of early imitation.
- The presence of domain-specific core functions in mathematical learning disorders.
- The relationship between cognition and learning.

SUGGESTIONS FOR FURTHER READING

Alexander-Passe, N. (2006). How dyslexic teenagers cope: An investigation of self-esteem, coping and depression. *Dyslexia, 12,* 256–275.

Jones, S. S. (2007). Imitation in infancy: The development of imitation. *Psychological Science, 18,* 593–599.

Kaufmann, L., Mazzocco, M. M., Dowker, A., von Aster, M., Goebel, S. M., Grabner, R. H., Henik, A., Jordan, N. C., Karmiloff-Smith, A., Kucia, K., et al. (2013). Dyscalculia from a developmental and differential perspective. *Frontiers in Psychology, 4,* 516.

Meltzoff, A. N., & Moore, M. K. (1983). Newborn infants imitate adult facial gestures. *Child Development, 54,* 702–709.

Mercer, N. (2013). The social brain, language, and goal-directed collective thinking: A social conception of cognition and its implications for understanding how we think, teach, and learn. *Educational Psychologist, 48,* 148–168.

Contents

CHAPTER 16

THE DEVELOPMENT OF COMMUNICATION AND LANGUAGE

anguage consists of a unique system of symbols and grammar that only humans use to communicate, and distinguishes human beings from other species. The length of this chapter reflects both the complexity of the language development process and the fact that language is a core element in human social life. The development of communication precedes that of language and represents the core function of language. For children to be able to learn to comprehend and use spoken language, they must be able to divide the flow of speech into meaningful units and understand the relevance of objects, people and events in the environment to the speech sounds they hear. Children who learn sign language must be able to divide the stream of hand movements they observe and attribute meaning to them. They must understand their use and the intentions behind them when other people – and eventually they themselves – use language.

EARLY DEVELOPMENT OF COMMUNICATION

In **communication** development the human ability to regulate attention is integrated with *social orientation*. Visual and auditory preferences lead children to direct their attention at stimulation from other people (see Chapter 8), while children's early emotional signals, such as smiling and crying, attract the attention of adults (see Chapter 17). Communication emerges as children become able to engage in *joint attention*, seek to direct the attention of others and let their own atten-

tion be directed by others, that is, when the child's action is based on a *communicative intention*, or when the child perceives that others have such an intention (Rommetveit, 1974). It is a transactional process where child and parent influence each other.

Joint attention

Infants are aware of other people's faces and eyes at an early age, and even newborns look longer at faces that are turned toward them than at faces that look away (Csibra, 2010). At the same time, the direction in which the child gazes provides parents with an important *clue* to the child's focus of attention. They often pick up toys their child is looking at (Collis and Schaffer, 1975), and 50–70 percent of the time they introduce the name of the child's object of interest (Woodward and Markman, 1998).

The first sign that children begin to become aware of others' attention is that they begin to follow their facial orientation and gaze direction. There seems to be a development from attention to the adult to attention to the environment and to what the attention of the adult informs about the environment. Observations of interactions between 6-week-olds and their mothers showed that they were oriented toward one another 70 percent of the time. At 6 months of age, this had decreased to 30 percent, and a greater proportion of interaction involved objects within reaching distance (Kaye and Fogel, 1980). These changes are also reflected in parental speech, which at this age begins to revolve less around the child's state and more on the child's actions, as well as on objects and events in the environment (Snow, 1977).

There is a gradual change in the alignment and function of attention. While interacting, parents and children often look at the same object, but during the first few months it is the parents who follow the child's focus of attention. At 6 months, children begin to move their gaze toward the same side of the room the adult is looking at, but stop at the first thing that catches their interest. At 9 months, children are able to locate the object an adult is looking at as long as it lies within their field of vision. At this age, children also begin to check whether the adult is looking at them or at what they themselves are looking at. At 12 months, a child's ability to follow an adult's gaze direction is relatively well established, but still depends on where the object is located in relation to the child. Around 18 months, children are mostly – but not always – able to follow another person's gaze, independent of the direction in which the other person is looking (MacPherson and Moore, 2007; Mundy et al., 2007). There are, however, significant individual differences in when children begin to follow the gaze direction of others.

Other people are children's main source of knowledge about the world; children need strategies to monitor and capture the attention of others in order to understand and react to the events around them (Nelson, 2007b). In joint attention the child and the adult are both attentive to the same thing, for example a toy, *and* aware of each other's attention (Carpenter and Liebal, 2011). Adults often use the child's visual attention and interest as clues to ensure that the child perceives the relevant communicative expressions, and they lead the child's awareness to those aspects of the situation that are relevant to what the adult is saying. Activities involving verbal communication provide children with cues to what the adult is saying and how their own expressions are understood.

Most descriptions of early communicative development focus on joint visual attention because visual situational cues are most prominent for children at this age (Begeer et al., 2014). Nonetheless, the use of vision is not an essential condition for joint attention. Blind children, too, establish joint attention to objects and events with other people, but for the children to understand what the parents are communicating about, they must be given non-visual cues (Bigelow, 2003;

Pérez-Pereira and Conti-Ramsden, 1999). The parents must use the child's listening behavior and manual exploration as clues to the child's focus of attention – blind children use the fingers to explore (Fraiberg, 1977). Thus, joint attention is equally important to blind and sighted children, but differs in the use of experiential modalities. This also demonstrates that communication is extremely robust. Even if children are unable to see, they will attribute communicative intent to the sounds of their parents' voices.

In early infancy, children are used to having the attention of the people around them when they are awake. As children begin to move independently, they find that this is less and less the case. Once they begin to take direct action to establish joint attention – they may even turn their mother's head in their own direction while she talks to someone else – it not only reflects their awareness of other people's attention, but also the discovery that others may have a different focus of attention than their own.

Joint attention and autism

Children with autism spectrum disorder are characterized by problems related to communication and social interaction (see p. 62). Inadequately developed non-verbal communication and joint attention skills are important early indications when screening for or diagnosing autism (Kim and Lord, 2013; Stenberg et al., 2014). However, the problems are not absolute. With increasing age, most children with autism engage in situations involving joint attention but are less likely than other children to lead the attention of other people to something just to show them what has captured their interest. Their early communication is usually more instrumental than declarative (Camaioni et al., 2003; Naber et al., 2008). Why children with autism develop these types of problems is still unknown, but there is reason to believe that their difficulties acquiring language are related to their problems with communication (Sarria et al., 1996). When children have difficulties following the cues to other people's attention, they will generally also struggle with the formation of meaning itself. Therefore, many early intervention programs for children with autism spectrum disorder aim to engage them in situations involving joint attention (Chang et al., 2016; Jones et al., 2006; Murza et al., 2016).

THEORIES OF COMMUNICATIVE DEVELOPMENT

Most theorists believe that communication has an innate basis, that there is something about human biology that makes communication possible, but precisely what is assumed to be innate varies considerably. According to Bloom (1998), human beings have an innate motive to create and maintain *intersubjectivity* – a drive to share knowledge about facts, ideas, emotions and so on, and thereby establish their self in a social world. Trevarthen (1979, 2015) explains joint attention by proposing that intersubjectivity is innate and that children are intrinsically motivated to share emotions and experiences. The ability to communicate evolves in a way comparable to the heart and other internal organs. According to Trevarthen, infants as young as 2–3 months of age are capable of *primary intersubjectivity*, in which attention is directed at the person they are engaged with and they can understand communicative expressions as well as the effect of their own expressions on others, for example that they can tease someone. However, Trevarthen's theory of primary intersubjectivity remains controversial since it implies that 2-month-olds are able to perceive their effect on others as well as the fact that others are aware of them. Most theorists believe that this type of communicative understanding and insight into the minds of other people develops much later. *Secondary intersubjectivity* appears around the age of 9 months, according to Trevarthen. It manifests itself when children and adults are attentive to something outside themselves, for example, an object or animal, and each is aware of the other's attention. There is general agreement about this form of intersubjectivity.

Tomasello (1999, 2003) argues that human beings have a species-specific ability to "read" the *intentions* of others, an ability present from the moment the child exhibits the first communicative expressions at the end of the first year. He points to the fact that the child's perception of a movement or a sound as a communicative act always requires the attribution of communicative intent. Otherwise, the sounds coming from another person's mouth, or their gestural movements, would remain meaningless. According to Tomasello (2008), this type of understanding does not have its origins in an innate social motive, such as Trevarthen and Bloom argue, but in the human propensity for cooperation and children's general cognitive and social skills.

EARLY DIALOGUES

A *dialogue* is a communicative interaction – verbal or non-verbal – between two people who share the same focus of attention and somehow convey something and adapt to each other. The earliest dialogues largely take place in the context of play and daily routines in which the child and adult take turns and the adult facilitates and helps the child solve communicative "problems" (see Scollon, 1976, 2001). Often it is the adult who initiates play and routines that involve turn-taking, but it is precisely the adult's ability to adapt that allows the child to take the lead and contribute to early dialogue (Bruner, 1975). The routines themselves are not the goal of communication but provide a framework that allows children to acquire skills they later can apply outside of these routines. Early interactions require a certain degree of repetition and stability, based as they are on the child's knowledge of the world, and routine activities provide this stability (Nelson, 2007a). Many early intervention programs are based on routine activities (Hughes-Scholes and Gavidia-Payne, 2016).

Infants exhibit many actions and expressions before they show actions with a communicative intent. They do not yet communicate in the strict sense of the word – communication requires expressions to be intentional, and there is no evidence that children actually attempt to convey information or otherwise influence the attention of the adult. However, the actions help adults attribute interests and emotional reactions to the child, and see infants as social individuals and engage them in dialogues (Goldstein and West, 1999).

GESTURES

Manual gestures are hand movements primarily used for communication, and interpreted consistently within a social system (Kendon, 2004; Morris et al., 1979). *Deictic* or *pointing gestures* direct attention in a certain direction or toward something in the environment without naming it, and can be translated as "there" or "that." *Symbolic gestures* function more like words and specify or name what the gesture refers to. Children may, for example, ask to be picked up by stretching their hands up to the adult. Later, the same wish may be expressed by saying *Up!* or *Sit lap!* The acquisition of gestures is an important milestone in the development of communication, since the goal of the child's actions goes beyond mere physical interaction with the environment. The function of gestures is to direct the attention – or the mind – of another human being (Tomasello et al., 2007).

Pointing

When the child starts to follow pointing gestures, this provides the first clue that a child understands someone else's communication. Pointing indicates a direction for the child's attention, and an understanding of pointing involves the ability to perceive the intent behind the pointing gesture. When adults points at something, infants initially look at the extended hand without moving their eyes in the direction of the point, suggesting that they do not understand the gestural properties of the pointing handshape. Some 9-month-olds are able to look in the right direction when this does not involve having to turn around, but most infants look at the hand. If a little older children have to shift their gaze further to the side or turn their head to see where the adult is pointing, they just as often look in another direction (Desrochers et al., 1995). When infants look in the right direction, but do not follow the pointing gesture all the way to its target, it may indicate that their perception of the other person's intentions continues to be vague (Lock et al., 1990; Tomasello et al., 2007). Not until the age of about 14 months do the majority of children consistently follow the direction of the point, and somewhat later they usually look in the right direction no matter where the adult is pointing (Desrochers et al., 1995).

Pointing is usually also the child's first communicative gesture and the clearest form of prelinguistic communication about objects in the environment. Pointing with an extended index

Pointing is a core element of early dialogues.

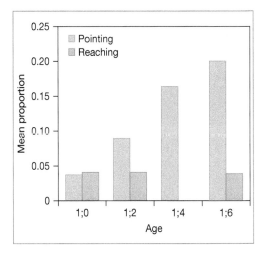

FIGURE 16.1 **The communicative function of pointing.**
Pointing and reaching undergo different functional
developments. Pointing has a communicative function: to lead
others to do or become attentive to something. The purpose
of reaching is to obtain something for oneself. Between 12
and 18 months, children increasingly look at the adult when
pointing, while the incidence of gazing at the adult when
reaching for something does not increase (based on Franco
and Butterworth, 1996, p. 320).

finger usually does not occur until the age of 9–10
months and becomes more common after the age
of 12 months, with major individual differences.
Some 8-month-olds exhibit this type of pointing
gesture, but it is not unusual for children to start
pointing as late as 16 months of age (Butterworth,
2003). Unlike reaching, the communicative function of pointing becomes evident in that children
increasingly look at the adult when pointing
(Figure 16.1). At around 12 months of age, children also vocalize more often in connection with
pointing and gaze when an adult looks in a direction other than that of the object they are interested in themselves, making their attempts to
communicate become more effective because the
sound draws the adult's attention to the pointing gesture (Legerstee and Barillas, 2003).

Pointing is *referential* and always involves a
meaningful context. The purpose of *declarative*
pointing is to inform or share an experience.
Many 12-month-olds will point at the item an
adult pretends to be looking for, and may also
point when something disappears (Liszkowski
et al., 2006; Tomasello, 2008). *Instrumental*
or *imperative* pointing aims to induce the other
person to carry out a specific action, such as

giving something to the child or removing something. In addition, pointing may be *exploratory*.
When pointing at an object the adult is already
looking at, the child seems to request information: get an object label, find out how something
works, if it safe or dangerous, and so on. Pointing
thus becomes a tool for cultural learning that provides the child with new or corroborating information from knowledgeable adults (Southgate
et al., 2007b).

There are several explanations for how children learn to point. According to Vygotsky
(1962), pointing gestures arise from what he
calls the "ritualization of action": the child tries
to reach for something but cannot get hold of it.
An adult observes the reaching action and
retrieves the object for the child. Consequently,
the child discovers that the movement can be used
to get others to fetch things that are out of reach.
This, however, only explains the development of
imperative pointing – pointing to get something.
Another explanation is that children learn to
point by imitating others, but observations of
children's interactions with adults who point do
not indicate that imitation plays a major role.
Besides, children often use pointing movements
before showing an understanding of others'
pointing gestures (Carpendale and Carpendale,
2010; Tomasello, 2008).

Shinn (1900) views pointing as an extension
of children's earliest experiences with touch and
exploration with their fingertips. This is in line
with studies that have found a significant increase
in the incidence of pointing gestures around 18
months, an age that sees a corresponding increase
in explorative behavior (Goldin-Meadow, 2015).
Carpendale and Carpendale (2010) integrate the
theories of Vygotsky and Shinn, based on the
assumption that the precursors to pointing can
both be found in children's attempts to reach for
things and their exploration of things with the
fingertips. By interacting with adults, children discover how adults react to pointing in different
contexts and thus become aware of the various
usages of pointing. Based on this theory, pointing is not primarily social, but part of a child's
early behavioral repertoire that gains social functions through activities involving pointing
actions. Consequently, the communicative insight
shown by infants when they point does not have
an innate basis, but emerges as the result of
social interaction. This theory is supported by the
fact that infants often point when they are alone

and do not always seem to care whether others follow their points. Toddlers who are alone seem to point at things they try to remember, using *private pointing* analogous to the function of *private speech* in problem solving (see p. 243) (Delgado et al., 2011). These examples demonstrate how pointing changes throughout the first year of life and gradually emerges as a social and referential tool. The notion of physical exploration as a basis for pointing can furthermore contribute to an understanding of joint attention and communicative development in blind children, whose early proximal pointing involves physical touch (von Tetzchner and Sedberg, 2005).

Symbolic gestures

Symbolic gestures are characterized by the fact that they can be translated by a word, such as when a child shakes her head to say "no," flaps her arms for "bird," or turns her hand in a locking movement for "key." Hence, their use is more specific and less dependent on the immediate situation than pointing, which merely indicates a direction. Children usually but not always begin to point before they say their first words (McGillion et al., 2017), while symbolic gestures appear around the same time as the first words, and occasionally a little earlier (Petitto, 1992). However, some children with severe language and communication disorders find it easier to learn symbolic gestures and signs than speech (Lederer and Battaglia, 2015) (see also p. 331).

The use of symbolic gestures increases after the age of 2 years, once children have begun to understand what words can be used for and their vocabulary begins to grow. Goldin-Meadow (2015) found that many early gestures are associated with objects and reflect their physical properties (iconicity). She believes children use symbolic gestures not as "labels" in the way words are used, but to describe a visual property of an object when they lack the word. Iconic gestures conveying actions come later, often long after the child has begun to use the word associated with the gesture, and serve as supplemental descriptions to spoken words. In an experiment with 18- and 26-month-olds who were taught new spoken words and gestures, both groups learned the words, but only the youngest children learned the gestures (Namy and Waxman, 1998). The older children thus did not

seem to accept that a gesture can have the equivalent status of a word.

Symbolic gestures vary from culture to culture (Morris et al., 1979). Therefore it is likely that children primarily learn symbolic gestures from observing their parents and other adults (Tomasello and Camaioni, 1997). Children sometimes make their own gestures when they lack words, and some child gestures are not commonly used by adults. In addition, some of the child's hand movements may have been over interpreted by the adult and assigned a meaning that in turn has been adopted by the child. These types of idiosyncratic gestures are comparable to *vocables* (see p. 309).

Animal gestures

Many species use communicative expressions to relay information about food, danger and the like (Håkansson and Westander, 2013). Dogs, dolphins, apes and many other species can also be trained to obey human gestures and spoken words (Herman, 2010). The chimpanzee Nim Chimpsky (named after Noam Chomsky), for example, learned 125 signs in the course of 4 years of training (Terrace, 1979). Other studies have shown that apes are capable of using non-vocal communication systems, but even with extensive training, communication remains extremely limited compared with human language (see Herrmann et al., 2007; Håkansson and Westander, 2013). This underlines the biological foundation of human communication.

THE DEVELOPMENT OF LANGUAGE

Three important characteristics distinguish human language from the communicative expressions of other species: It consists of linguistic *symbols* that represent social conventions to draw attention to specific people, things, events and ideas. It has *grammar*, which allows the symbols to be arranged in patterns according to certain conventions – *sentence structures* – that create meaning beyond the individual symbols themselves. And thirdly, more than 6,000 different human languages exist, while other species mostly have one small common set of communicative expressions (Tomasello, 2006). This implies that humans have a very different and more flexible basis for communication development than other species.

Spoken language includes a system of speech sounds (phonology), an inventory of words (vocabulary), a grammar that governs word order (syntax) and inflection (morphology), and different areas of application (pragmatics). *Sign language* incorporates the same features, but here the hands take over the function of the speech organs (see p. 331).

Main theories

No generally accepted "standard theory" of language development exists. Instead, many theories abound, and there is considerable disagreement about the biological basis and the underlying mechanisms of how children develop grammatical competence. Following is a brief presentation of the most important theories that also shows the range of different viewpoints, and a discussion of their status.

Nativism

Nativism represents one theoretical extreme in that it considers language to be based on innate linguistic knowledge, facilitated by a language module in the brain specialized to perceive language stimulation (see p. 165). According to Chomsky (1986), the language module contains a *language acquisition device* (LAD) that enables children to divide the flow of speech and identify word classes and grammatical categories in the language or languages they grow up with. The language module has been shaped by evolution and its function is predetermined, just like the function of the heart, liver, and other organs. Pinker (1994) calls it the "language instinct," much like the spider's instinct for spinning a web.

The fact that children learn the language that surrounds them is in itself evidence that experience determines the type of language a child acquires, but according to Chomsky (1968, 2000), these are merely "surface differences." The "deep structure" of language that all sentences are derived from places such tight constraints on how the human brain can perceive and process linguistic stimulation, that all languages closely resemble each other from a formal point of view. The language acquisition device includes a *universal grammar* with a limited set of options for each existing grammatical aspect or "parameter,"

for example whether language expresses a spatial relationship such as "in" or "on" as a preposition (preceding nouns and verbs), postposition (following nouns and verbs) or an inflection of a noun or a verb. It thus limits the possible functions of specific words and parts of words in a sentence.

The main nativistic argument for innateness of linguistic structure is "the poverty of the stimulus." The claim is that the language children are exposed to is too impoverished to provide the necessary basis for forming the grammatical rules that competent language users must know. Universal grammar enables children to learn a language with all its complexities from a minimal language input. Similar to how the eye perceives different colors, the child perceives some words as the subject of a statement, others as adjectival, and so on. As long as a child is exposed to language, the universal grammar will quickly establish a grammar in the child with the properties of the language in the surroundings. The universal grammar thus also determines the kind of language a child can learn: human beings are incapable of developing a language not specified by universal grammar (Jackendoff, 2002; Wexler, 1999; Wunderlich, 2004).

Behaviorism

Behaviorism represents another theoretical extreme. It completely rejects the notion of language acquisition as genetically determined, modular knowledge. In "Verbal behavior," Skinner (1957) explains the acquisition of language with the same basic learning mechanisms as any other type of behavior: conditioning, reinforcement and imitation (see p. 23). This position is maintained by more recent behaviorists (Greer and Keohane, 2005; Novak and Peláez, 2004). *Relational frame theory* is an extension of Skinner's descriptions and theoretical explanations which retains the basic mechanisms suggested of his theory and also includes processes like analogue reasoning (see p. 233) and perspective taking (see p. 241) (Barnes-Holmes et al., 2001).

Social constructivism

The central claim of *social constructivist theories* (see p. 26) is that language is a *cultural tool* that cannot be created by children on their own but must be learned through others (Lisina, 1985; Vygotsky, 1962). According to Bruner (1975, 1983), the use of words and structure of language is learned through social interaction with more competent children and adults. His response to Chomsky's ideas is that children need a *language acquisition support system* (LASS) in order for any supposed language acquisition device (LAD) to function. The support system is not a form of "training," but a scaffold that takes place in the context of social activities in which children and adults participate together, often involving every-day routines and other activities that recur with some variation. Language development is guided through these interactions (Lock, 1980; Thorne and Tasker, 2011).

Emergentism

Emergentism has its basis in cognitive develop-ment, including Piaget's theory and information processing, and connectionism in particular (MacWhinney and O'Grady, 2015). Language is not rooted in a specific linguistic mechanism, but gradually emerges as the result of interaction between *general* cognitive mechanisms and linguistic experience (Karmiloff-Smith, 2011; MacWhinney, 2015). Then there is no need for any language acquisition device or universal grammar. Contrary to Chomsky, emergentism considers the language environment to be "rich" enough to provide sufficient information to allow children to learn a language. By using computer simulations, connectionists have demonstrated that it is possible for a computer – a far simpler device than the human brain – to learn gram-matical rules based on the equivalent experi-ences a child would have (Elman et al., 1996; Vogt and Lieven, 2010).

Usage-based theory

The usage-based theory of Tomasello (2003, 2009) belongs to the tradition of functionalism. It is closely related to social constructivism in its stress on the importance of social mediation and co-construction, while at the same time empha-sizing general cognitive processes and children's ability to recognize the perceptual and social patterns of linguistic stimulation. Children learn language from the language they hear (or see) and by communicating and using language for dif-ferent reasons and in different contexts. The reg-ularities of grammar arise from these experi-ences. This is how the theory is "usage-based." According to usage-based theory children have an innate basis for communication that manifests itself in the human propensity for community and cooperation. The developmental trajectory is determined by the child's experiences in situations involving communication and language, allow-ing room for individual developmental variation (Lieven, 2014, 2016).

Theoretical status

There are many good descriptions of typical development and of some of the variation in typical and atypical acquisition of spoken lan-guage and sign language. Based on current know-ledge, it is nevertheless impossible to determine which theories provide the most accurate descrip-tion of language development.

Nativism has always had a strong standing among theories of language development and is the most established theory from a historic point of view. It was long believed that children would develop spoken language even if they were not exposed to language (O'Neill, 1980). One main criticism of nativism is that language does not develop but is "prefabricated." Children are learning language by activating an innate gram-mar – all a child needs is a modicum of exposure to language, analogous to making coffee by pouring hot water into a cup filled with instant coffee. But language is not an instinct: instinc-tive behavior is generally quite stereotyped and appears even if an animal grows up isolated from the normal experiences of the species. This does not apply to language (Evans, 2014; Tomasello, 1995).

The fact that the human species alone has lan-guage supports the likelihood of a unique human biological predisposition for developing language. However, this need not be a universal grammar or any other specifically linguistic feature (Tomasello, 2005). It may just as well be a neu-rological structure with significance for human perception, cognition and learning in general. The argument that language is too complex to be learned without detailed genetically determined knowledge does not seem to be valid (Braine, 1994; Tomasello, 2003, 2005). Not only has human language evolved too recently for evolu-tion to select genes that ensure the development of a detailed mechanism such as universal grammar, but the human brain and body must also be able to produce the communicative expressions that develop into language. It is therefore more likely that communicative expressions reflect the human brain and body, rather than being the result of an evolutionary neurological adaptation to a language environment that did not yet exist (Christiansen and Chater, 2008). However, in spite of considerable criticism, nativism has maintained a solid position in language development.

The behavioristic account of language development (Skinner, 1957) met with considerable opposition from the outset (Chomsky, 1959), and behaviorism has exerted little influence on contemporary research into children's language. Critics maintain that conditioning and imitation are inadequate mechanisms to explain the development of language, and that behavioral explanations ignore the meaning of language. Inhelder and Piaget (1964) point out that if language learning merely involved conditioning, children would start to learn language in their second month of life. Children are rarely corrected in their use of language and construct many sentences they have never heard before, such as *ball up* or *there boy*. Neither do children's errors suggest that they simply imitate. Instead, they acquire a language system that may be described as a set of grammatical constructions. This is evident in children's overgeneralizations of such constructions, such as when they say *goed* instead of *went* during a certain period (see p. 321). In view of this unanimous criticism, it is difficult to understand why language instruction for children with autism spectrum disorders, intellectual disability and other severe developmental disorders is often based on Skinner's ideas in applied behavior analysis (see Bondy and Frost, 2002; Durand and Merges, 2001; Mirenda, 1997).

Most developmental theorists of the twenty-first century position themselves somewhere between nature and nurture in regard to the development of language. They believe that human genes allow language to be acquired via cognitive and social functions, but without a genetic linguistic basis in the way proposed by Chomsky and Pinker. *Functionalism* has a long history of challenging the nativist view of language development, and Tomasello's usage-based theory is the most important non-nativist theory today. Based on a large number of studies, Tomasello (2003, 2009) and others have shown

that the acquisition of vocabulary and grammar can be explained by children's social and cognitive skills and interactions with more competent children and adults. According to Tomasello, it is children's understanding of intention that provides the innate decisive element in language development, from the earliest communicative efforts to the development of grammar.

By using computer simulations of the language learning process, *connectionists* have demonstrated that language learning does not need to depend on genetically specified categories (Chang et al., 2006). Connectionism argues that children are able to analyze sensory stimulation and that their overall learning capacity is sufficient to detect regularities in the language from what they hear or see in their environment (Elman et al., 1996; Westermann et al., 2009). A certain innate basis remains nonetheless. Some theorists maintain that children have an innate sensitivity to probability structure – an awareness of things that often occur together, that allows them to discover linguistic regularities (Erickson and Thiessen, 2015). At the same time, theories based on *information processing* are met with the objection that language development cannot be explained based exclusively on the processing of information, independent of other human factors. Such processes must incorporate meaning and direction, and can therefore only be understood within a social context (Campbell, 1986; Nelson, 2007a).

Karmiloff-Smith (2005) argues that Bruner (1983) and other social constructivists place too much emphasis on social interaction and too little on cognitive processes. She and Bruner represent the two basic twenty-first-century perspectives on what language development is about. Karmiloff-Smith focuses mainly on neurology and the underlying cognitive processes, as well as on the "technical" aspects of language: its conceptual foundation, the structure of vocabulary and the rules of grammar. Bruner emphasizes the social cognitive basis of language, its pragmatic aspects and its function in social interaction. The *emergentist coalition model* is one of several theories attempting to reconcile these two perspectives. According to this model, language development has its origins in purely perceptual and associative processes, followed by linguistic and social processes that furnish the basis for word use and sentence structure (Hollich et al., 2000; Parish-Morris et al., 2013).

The emergence of speech

During the first months of life, the infant's sounds consist of crying and cooing. Children usually begin to babble around the age of 6 months, but here, too, there is considerable variation. Since infants with profound deafness vocalize as well, their sound production cannot be used as an early clue to normal hearing. Babbling, however, is delayed in deaf children and is somewhat different in quantity as well as quality from the babbling sounds of children with normal hearing, and babbling may not appear without a cochlear implant (see p. 138) (Fagan, 2015).

Initially, the babbling sounds of hearing children consist of series of identical consonant-vowel syllables, for example *dadadada* or *nanana*. Gradually, these sounds become more varied and incorporate several different consonants into the same sound sequence. Additional sounds include pure vowel sequences, vowel-consonant sequences and consonant-vowel-consonant sequences. Accentuation patterns and intonation contours become more differentiated, and gradually render the production of sound more varied and similar to speech. Children with early onset of babbling also tend to say their first words early (McGillion et al., 2017).

Early babbling is identical across languages, but around the age of 10 months it begins to absorb the sound of the surrounding language, for example whether the child grows up in a French, Swedish, English or Japanese language environment (Vihman, 1993). During the babbling phase, children also "play" with speech sounds and practice pronouncing the sounds they have heard (Kuczaj, 1982).

Studies have found that deaf infants who are exposed to early sign language produce hand movements with hand shapes that do not constitute manual signs but have the same similarity to the hand movements and shapes found in sign language as babbling has to speech. This kind of manual activity, which they call *grabling*, is not found in hearing children (Petitto and Marentette, 1991).

Perception of speech sounds

Every language has its own unique set of speech sounds, or phonemes, the smallest sound units that distinguish words with different meanings. /M/ and /p/ belong to different phonemes because *mark* and *park* are different words. The number of phonemes in a language vary from 12 to just under 100. On a global scale, about 600 consonants and 200 vowels are in use (Ladefoged, 2004). Many animals communicate by using sounds, but none of them with a system that corresponds to human phonemes (Collier et al., 2014).

All children with normal hearing share the same basis for perceiving speech sounds, and must learn to differentiate, recognize and produce exactly those speech sounds that distinguish meaning in the language or languages they grow up with. In English, /r/ and /l/ belong to different phonemes. Japanese and Chinese speakers have great difficulty distinguishing between /r/ and /l/ because they belong to the same phoneme and thus do not yield different words in Japanese or Chinese. Therefore, many Chinese speakers say *low* instead of *row*, or *lice* instead of *rice*. A child of Japanese origin growing up in an English-speaking environment usually has no trouble detecting the difference between /l/ and /r/ or other sounds that differentiate the meaning of English words. Very early in development, infants are able to distinguish most speech sounds, regardless of language. Box 16.1 shows a typical experiment examining the ability of infants to distinguish between speech sounds (see also p. 138).

Young infants are capable of discriminating between speech sounds that do not change the meaning of a word in their own language, but later find it difficult to distinguish between these sounds. Two- to 3-month-old Japanese children, for example, are able to tell the difference between /l/ and /r/ just like infants of the same age in other language cultures (Kuhl, 1992).

The actual perception of phonemes only occurs once the sounds are incorporated into a meaningful context, that is, once children learn that different sound combinations have unique meanings and functions, for example that the sound *Teddy* refers to a dog and *Siam* to a cat. As children's vocabulary increases, the acoustic differences between the words they learn are perceived as being worthy of attention, while differences that do not give rise to different words are perceived as carrying no meaning and eventually are no longer differentiated. Since it would interfere with children's understanding of language if they were to notice differences between speech sounds that did not also involve a difference in meaning, children actively ignore them. At the same time, children become more sensi-

BOX 16.1 EARLY DISCRIMINATION OF SPEECH SOUNDS (based on Eimas, 1985, p. 47)

Four-month-old infants were exposed to a speech sound such as *ba* or *pa* from a loudspeaker whenever they sucked on a pacifier. The speech sound was interesting to the infants and made them suck more. After listening to the same sound repeatedly, the infants lost interest and their sucking slowed (habituation). Some of the infants continued to hear the same sound while others heard a new sound. After 5 minutes, the sucking rate had decreased significantly and kept declining among those infants who continued to hear the same sounds. Infants who were exposed to a different speech sound showed an increase in their sucking rate instead (dishabituation). By using this method, it has been possible to show that infants at this age are able to hear the difference between *ba* and *pa*, *ba* and *ma*, and other phonemic contrasts.

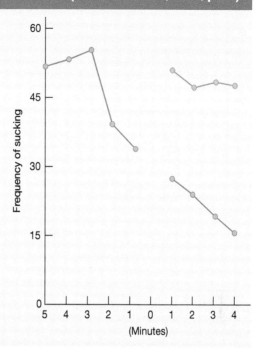

tive to the differences between sounds that result in different meanings (Maurer and Werker, 2014). In this way, recognition gradually becomes more enculturated and adapted to the language or languages in the child's surroundings (Kuhl, 1993; Werker, 1991). Studies have shown that infants exhibit differences in brain activation when they hear their own language compared with the sounds of languages they have never experienced before (Kuhl, 2010).

During the first years of life, children comprehend a fast growing number of words. Consequently, the ability to recognize sequences of speech sounds is well enough developed in most children not to impose significant constraints on the acquisition of words. With increasing age, children also improve at recognizing new words even if they are pronounced somewhat differently than when they first heard the word (McQueen et al., 2012).

Production of speech

Many of the first words uttered by children resemble babbling sounds, such as *mama* and *papa* (Lewis, 1936). Children continue to babble for some time after producing their first words, and it is not always easy to hear whether an infant is babbling or attempting to say a word, and what the intended word may be. Since many common words resemble babbling sounds, adults may interpret these sounds as acoustically similar words that make sense in a given situation (Bjerkan et al., 1983). At the same time, children begin to produce simple sound combinations – *vocables* – that are not found in the language spoken by adults (Ferguson, 1978). The first words children utter are therefore not always a direct copy of what they hear. Children are highly creative in how they acquire language and invent their own vocables early on while trying to find out what different words can be used for. The very existence of vocables emphasizes the gradual transition from babbling to adult-like speech, and from prelinguistic to linguistic communication.

The ability to articulate speech sounds develops gradually. Words require rapid and complex motor movements that take time to learn. /b/, /d/ and /m/ are mastered early, while /r/ is one of the last sounds acquired by English-speaking children and can pose challenges all the way until school age (McLeod and Bleile, 2003). During their first years, many children simplify the articulation of many words, for example by saying *tootie* for *cookie*, or *dod* for *dog*. As children learn more words, their repertoire of sounds increases, but during early development children are often selective and choose words they are able to pronounce (Clark, 2016). It takes time to develop an awareness of the sounds words are composed of and the differences between them, an insight children often gain in connection with learning how to read.

Perception and production of speech

Although perception and use of speech are related, they can develop in slightly different ways. Children can perceive acoustic differences they themselves are not yet capable of producing. As a rule, the more articulation errors children make, the greater their problems perceiving the differences between words, although many children are able to differentiate words despite not being able to articulate them differently when they speak (Strange and Broen, 1980). Hence, the relationship between perception and production can vary from one child to the next.

A developmental trend is the gradual reduction in children's ability to hear the difference between what they themselves say and what others are saying. They can hear the articulation errors of others without being aware that they themselves say the same words incorrectly, such as in the following example in which a father and his son are watching ships in the harbor (MacWhinney, 2015, p. 306):

Child: *Look at this big sip.*
Father: *Yes, it is quite a big sip.*
Child: *No, Daddy, say "sip" not "sip."*

Although the boy said "sip," he thought he had said "ship," which is what it sounded like to him. Had he heard what he actually said on a recording, he would probably have realized that his own articulation was wrong. Another study found that 3-year-olds perceived words spoken by adults better than the same words spoken by themselves on a recording. The more their own articulation deviated from that of the adult, the

more difficult it was for the children to understand the words (Dodd, 1975).

The difficulties involved in hearing one's own articulation cause problems in connection with learning to pronounce foreign languages. Because over time children increasingly lose the ability to correct their own articulation, infants born with a cleft lip or palate receive surgery in the first few months of life to allow them as much time as possible to take advantage of this ability (Kuehn and Moller, 2000).

Early word learning

The transition from prelinguistic to linguistic communication takes place once the child begins to understand and apply words to communicate about people, animals, objects, actions, events, and so on. Children must be able to infer a word's *reference*, based on their knowledge and their perception of the situation. They must be able to understand whether the word represents the name of something that is or is not present in the environment, whether it refers to something to do with the child itself or with something else, and so on. Besides, word learning is about far more than linking a word form to a conceptual category. Children must understand the relevant communicative action, the intent behind the words others say, such as why they name something or comment on an event or a characteristic. The phrase "it's hot" entails completely different meanings depending on whether it refers to the weather or to a bowl of soup (Brown, 1958; Tomasello, 2003).

The first words

Children comprehend words before they themselves begin to use words in a way others can understand. Saying a word demands more of a child than merely showing an understanding of it. In investigations of word comprehension, the child usually has to point at something or react in another meaningful way when a word is spoken. Studies of language use require children to activate and produce a word, as well as to show an underlying intention. Imitation is not enough – children imitate many words they do not understand. Additionally, it is difficult to assess children's partial comprehension of words while they are still progressing to a more mature understanding. It is easier to register how children use words. This may be one reason why comprehension has been far less studied than usage, and why knowledge remains quite limited (Bishop, 2006).

Children usually say their first words around the age of 1, but with major variation. Some children are 9 months, while others begin at 17 months or later. Girls generally begin to speak slightly earlier than boys. In one study, parents registered that their children had used an average of ten words by the age of 13 months, and 50 words 3 months later, but 10 percent of the children had used fewer than five words at 16 months (see Figure 16.2). By the age of 2 years, the average lies at around 150 words, and children can have learned anywhere from 10 to 450 words (MacWhinney, 2015). Nelson (1988) describes three periods in the early development of words (Box 16.2).

Word learning not only builds on the child's previously acquired concepts, but also encourages the child to form new concepts – a word can act as an invitation to form a category (Brown, 1958; Nelson, 2007a). As early as the beginnings

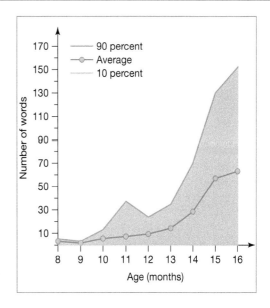

FIGURE 16.2 **Early vocabulary.**

The blue line shows the average vocabulary size and number of words of 8-16-month-old children, based on a checklist filled out by their parents. The red line shows the boundary for the 90th percentile (based on Bates et al., 1995, p. 103).

BOX 16.2 **THREE PERIODS IN EARLY LEXICAL DEVELOPMENT (from Nelson, 1988)**

The acquisition of words is characterized by periods posing different challenges.

PERIOD 1

The child faces the problem of finding a way into the language system: understanding what words are, what they refer to, and what they can be used for. This period begins once children first become sensitive to language forms and consistently respond to some of them, and continues until the production of 30 or more words. It usually lasts for 6–12 months, with considerable spread: for some children it begins as early as 9 months, for others it lasts until the age of 2.

PERIOD 2

The start of this period is when children have acquired about 30 words and have a basic knowledge of words and conceptual categories. It is marked by an increase in the rate of acquiring new words (and possibly a vocabulary spurt). By now, children have developed an understanding of what words are and want to know the name of everything they see. Their main challenge is to discover the meaning behind the words they hear and associate the conceptual categories they have formed of people, objects and events in their physical and social world with the corresponding words. During this period, children also seem to assume that a single word corresponds to a single category, and vice versa. It is a two-way process: children try to find the right words for existing categories, and categories for the words they hear. This period lasts several years.

PERIOD 3

The third period generally begins around the age of 3–4 years and is characterized by increasing insight into language. It is a period of revision, reorganization and consolidation of lexical items within domains of related words. There is an increase in the use of previously limited word classes, such as relational terms.

of language development, children perceive toy animals with identical names to belong to the same category, while toy animals with dissimilar names are perceived as being different (Waxman and Braun, 2005; Xu, 2002). Thus, words form a bridge that links together the perception of children and adults about the world and its concepts.

Fast mapping

The first time children hear a word, they must – without any awareness on their own part – form an assumption about its meaning and use. This first attribution of meaning to a word is called "fast mapping" (Dollaghan, 1985). By fast mapping, the child starts to turn an unknown word into a known one by creating a mental representation of the word's form and use, such as *cat* referring to a small four-legged animal. This is necessary in order to recognize the word later and make use of it in other situations. Without this first attribution of meaning, the word would appear to be new every time the child heard it. Sometimes, fast mapping leads to a correct understanding of the word's meaning, but for most early words, fast mapping merely provides the child with a partial clue to begin using the word. The complexity of the sound and the meaning of a new word will influence the fast mapping, and children with language disorders have more difficulties with fast mapping and learning new words than children without language disorders (Alt and Plante, 2006). The process from perceiving a word for the first time to the adult's understanding and nuanced use of it can take a long time (Dollaghan, 1985).

Overextension and underextension

Many words take time to learn and children's early use of a word can be both broader, narrower and different from that of an adult. The *extension* of a word consists of all the exemplars that pertain to and can be represented by the word. Overextension occurs when a word is used beyond its conventional meaning. When my nephew Fredrik was 3 years old, he pointed at my cat and enthusiastically said *woof-woof*. For a while he used the same word for cats and dogs (see also p. 228). When Dromi's (1993) daughter Keren was about 16 months old, she used the term *broom* for all items stored in a particular cupboard in the kitchen.

Underextension occurs when words are used in a narrower sense than usual. The word may be correct when it is used but it is not always used when it would be appropriate (Griffiths, 1986). When Keren was between 12 and 15 months, her white toy elephant was the only thing she called *elephant*. She never said *elephant* when playing outside on a small slide with the shape of an elephant, or when her mother showed her pictures of elephants or toy elephants made of plastic. For a certain period, when Keren had gotten a little older, she said *walk* only while walking around the house wearing one of her parents' pair of shoes. She never said *walk* in response to her mother's question about people passing by or when she herself was walking barefoot. Dromi (1993) observed approximately the same number of overextensions and underextensions in her daughter.

Over time, the language environment usually provides children with sufficient clues to correct their own use of words and understanding of the categories particular words refer to. The use of a word is therefore not static, but changes over time. When young children make "errors" these do not reflect an inability to categorize or learn words, but rather the fact that children make use of this ability. The nuanced use of words by older children and adults is the result of long experience with words in different communicative situations.

The vocabulary spurt

Acquiring the first words can take time. For children with typical language development it can take up to 5 months from when they utter their first recognizable word until they have used ten words (Harris, M., 1992). Often children use only a few words, as if trying to find out what those words can be used for. This is illustrated in a diary study of Jessie's development. From the age of 15 to 20 months, her utterances were dominated by *cat* and *mom*. She said each word over 5,000 times – more than 30 times a day. Between the age of 17 and 20 months, she only used a handful of other words: *hi, dad, blow, apple* and *there* (Labov and Labov, 1978).

Toward the end of the second year of life, the rate of learning new words usually increases. The beginning of what is known as the *vocabulary spurt* is often defined as the first month in which vocabulary increases by at least 15 words (Poulin-

Dubois and Graham, 1994). It can occur at different ages: some children show an increase in word learning as early as 13 months of age, while others are 25 months before the vocabulary spurt sets in (Bloom, 1993). However, some children show a more gradual increase in vocabulary rather than a sudden and rapid surge (Bloom, 2004; Reznick and Goldfield, 1992).

The content of children's first words

Children's early vocabulary reflects their cognitive development and knowledge about the world, their interests and preferences, what adults talk about with children, and physical and emotional aspects of the situations they participate in. The names of animals, for example, including exotic animals like alligators and zebras, stand for a relatively large proportion of toddler vocabulary (Gleason et al., 2009). This is related to the interest children often show in animals, but also the fact that Western adults tend to give toddlers picture books about animals.

Children learn the words they hear in their surroundings (or see, in the case of sign language), but word learning is not merely an imitative process. In a study of how a group of children used the first ten words they had learned (40 different words in all), as many as 37 of the words could be traced to how each child's mother had used the word right before. A little later, the children used 29 of the words in a new way, while 11 words were used exactly as before. Seventeen of the 29 new word uses were related to how each child's mother had used the word just moments before the child used it, while 12 of the words were used in ways the children had not heard from their mother, at least not recently (Barrett et al., 1991). This means that children make active use of familiar words for their own communicative purposes even during the earliest language development.

Words are used to talk about many different things. One of the key questions is how children are able to understand what a word used in a given situation refers to. A number of researchers believe this to be such a difficult task, that there must be limitations to the types of assumptions a child can form about the meaning of a word during early language development. Some suggest that children have an innate tendency to assume that words refer to whole objects unless the situation clearly indicates something else,

and that this is why object words dominate children's early vocabulary (Golinkoff et al., 1995; Markman, 1992). However, this could just as well reflect adults' tendency to name whole objects when talking to children. Observations show that mothers tend to name whole objects rather than parts of objects and characteristics when they introduce new things to toddlers (Masur, 1997). The results in Box 16.3 show that an assumption of innate constraints is unnecessary in explaining toddlers' tendency to learn the names of whole objects; neither is there agreement about the time frame in which any possible constraints may be in effect (Clark, 2016). Adults' use of language is sufficient to allow children to learn many new words for whole objects.

Toddlers spend much of their time exploring objects in the environment and often ask adults about the names of things. However, although they typically first label the whole object, parents and other adults do not simply name the objects children are engaged with, that would quickly become repetitive. They talk about what children do with the objects, such as throwing or kicking a ball, cuddling with a doll, pushing a toy car, and about how objects behave – the ball rolls, the music box plays a melody and the down quilt keeps you warm. They also talk about the characteristics of people, animals, objects and actions, for example that the kitty is cute, the baby is small, the ball is red and the boy runs fast (Nelson, 2007a; Tomasello, 2008). Although object words make up a significant portion of children's vocabulary during the second year of life, they make up less than 50 percent of all words (Bates et al., 1995; Bornstein et al., 2004).

Cultural differences in early vocabulary also support the assumption that the proportion of object words reflects children's language environment. The large number of object words among toddlers in Western countries may reflect that joint activities between children and adults typically include many toys and picture books. Children in Korea and China experience fewer such activities and have a smaller proportion of object words in their early vocabulary compared with children in the USA and Europe. This runs counter to the assumption that vocabulary is determined by an innate tendency to interpret words as the names of whole objects (Gopnik and Choi, 1995; Tardif, 1996, 2006).

The other major category in early vocabulary is made up of action words that refer to what

BOX 16.3 LANGUAGE INPUT: MATERNAL LABELING OF NOVEL ANIMALS (Masur, 1997)

Ten boys and ten girls aged 10–21 months were observed for 10–15 minutes in farm and zoo play with their mothers. The mothers produced 667 names of animals previously unknown to the children and whose name they had never heard before. Nearly all the first names provided by the mothers labelled the whole animal. Reference to parts before giving the animal name, such as *What's this? A long, long neck*, occurred only three times. Forty-one times, the first name was accompanied by a reference to parts of the animal (e.g., arm, tail) or its characteristics (e.g., color, size), for example *a little dog*. In a further 27 cases, the first naming was immediately followed by a reference, for example, *That's a bird, a bird with a large beak*. In addition, for 51 animals, reference to parts or other characteristics followed two or more statements after the animal had first been named. When all were included in the count, parts of animals or their characteristics were mentioned in 119 of 667 cases.

humans and animals do, such as *run, cry, play, wait* or *think*. In a study of 20-month-old children, these made up about 20 percent of all words (Bornstein et al., 2004). Since actions have different durations, they are not always readily perceived as clearly defined units. Children ask adults more often about the names of things rather than the names of actions, although the question *What is she doing?* is not uncommon among toddlers. Also the situations associated with objects words and action words differ to some degree. Mothers use more object words when looking at a picture book together with their child, and more verbs when playing with toys (Altınkamış et al., 2014). In addition, children use various situational cues to determine whether a word refers to an object or an action (Box 16.4). Toddlers tend to associate unknown words with what is new in the situation.

Children's early vocabulary also contains some words that refer to characteristics and qualities such as shape, color, temperature, size, height and kindness. At 20 months, these words make up about one-tenth of children's vocabulary (Bornstein et al., 2004). *Function words* include words that express relationships between objects, people, places and events, such as the prepositions *in* and *on*. Unlike many objects and to some extent action words, they cannot be pointed at or physically differentiated, and their acquisition is more related to sentence formation (Thorseng, 1997).

Individual styles

Although people share a common language, the development of language is individual. *Mama* and *papa* are not always among the first ten words (Tardif et al., 2008). Nelson (1973) found that some children had more than 25 object words among their first 50 words. For other children, first names and social words and phrases such as *please, hi, stop, yes, no* and *ouch* made up the largest share. Nelson suggested that the differences in word use have their origin in different cognitive styles and the way in which children organize their experiences, and that children at this age have different "theories" about how language is used. The first group she calls *referential*, since most of children's words referred to objects. The second group she calls *expressive*, meaning that children in this group used more words referring to social situations and their own experiences. Children in the expressive group seemed to perceive language more as a tool for social interaction, while the referential group mostly used language to communicate about things in the environment. Both groups showed

BOX 16.4 CONTEXT GUIDES CHILDREN'S UNDERSTANDING OF NEW WORDS (Tomasello and Akhtar, 1995)

Thirty-six children aged 20–26 months participated in the study. There were two conditions with two objects that were unknown to the children (a small wooden toy that wobbled when rolled or a complex string of blocks with bells inside) and two novel actions (throwing the object down a chute or shooting it out with a "catapult"). In both conditions, the experimenter was sitting together with the child. With 12 of the children, the experimenter first threw several familiar objects down the chute or shot them out with the catapult, and then said *modi* when doing the action with the new object. With 12 other children, the experimenter carried out a number of familiar play actions with the object before saying *modi* and performing the new play action. A control group of 12 children (six in each condition) went through the same procedures but the experimenter said only *Watch!* or *Look there!* and *modi* was not mentioned until they were asked the test question (below).

Somewhat later, the experimenter and the child sat down together with all the objects used in the two situations. The experimenter said to the child: *Look over there. Can you show me modi?* Seven of the 12 children who had taken part in the situation with the chute took the object and showed it to the experimenter, implying that they had perceived *modi* as the name of the object. Nine of the 12 children who had been involved in the situation with different play actions performed the new action they had observed, and thus seemed to have perceived *modi* as the name of the action. One of the children in the control group performed the new action when asked to modi. Two in each experimental group and 11 children in the control group made other responses.

The results indicate that the children perceived the new word as the label of what was new in the situation. In the first situation, the object was new, in the second situation the action.

typical development and the study illustrates that there is more than one way to language competence (Nelson, 1981).

The contrast principle

In a certain sense, an infant's first words consist of isolated units, while words acquired later also take on meaning because they are different from words already contained in the vocabulary (de Saussure, 1974). According to Clark (1992), word learning follows the *principle of contrast*, meaning that a difference in form always entails a difference in meaning. Children assume that every new word has a meaning different from the words they have previously learned. The discovery that two or more words can be *synonyms* with roughly the same meaning comes relatively late, according to Clark. Yet, studies have shown that toddlers both perceive and use new words about objects whose names they already know (Gathercole, 1987; Merriman, 1986). Nelson (1988), on the other hand, suggests that children first begin to use the principle of contrast later in childhood as the result of word learning, rather than as one of its requirements. Adults often use contrasting terms when explaining the meaning of a word to children, for example, that

one car is *big* and another *small*, or that something is *above* and something else *below* a bridge (Clark, 2016).

Further growth in vocabulary

Both toddlers and older children spend much of their time talking. Not only do children learn how to speak, they also speak in order to learn. By using wireless microphones attached to children's clothing, Wagner (1985) registered all the words spoken by seven children aged 1½–9 years in the course of one day. The youngest child used 1,860 different words for a total of 13,800 words. The most talkative child that day used 37,700 words (Table 16.1).

Following the vocabulary spurt, or alternately a more gradual growth in vocabulary, word learning increases at a formidable pace. Estimates vary anywhere from an average of 5.5 to 9 words per day until the age of 18 years. Around 6 years of age, children are usually able to comprehend between 10,000 and 15,000 words, and produce somewhat fewer (Anglin, 1993; Carey, 1978). Both the situation and the linguistic context provide guidelines for the possible interpretation of words, such as the meaning of *helicopter* when the child's mother says *The helicopter makes a lot*

TABLE 16.1 Children's word production in the course of one day (the number of different words and the total number of words used in the course of one day by seven German children aged 1;5–9;7 years (Wagner, 1985))

	Age (years;months)	Total number of word forms	Number of different word forms
Katrin	1;5	13,800	1,860
Andreas	2;5	20,200	2,210
Carsten	3;6	37,700	4,790
Gabi	5;4	30,600	2,490
Fredrik	8;7	24,700	4,960
Roman	9;2	24,400	3,860
Teresa	9;7	25,200	3,520

of noise when something is flying past. The word's placement in the sentence and the adult's inflection of it are important clues to the type of word that may be involved, for example whether it is a noun, a verb or an adjective (Nagy and Townsend, 2012; Snow, 2010).

As children grow older, their conversations increase in length and complexity. They learn the entire range of different word classes and their word use becomes more diverse and flexible. Adolescents improve at varying words, use more words to refer to the same thing, understand that the same word can be used in many different contexts, and that it has a number of different meanings, including its figurative use (see below). School is an important source for new words, and the child's vocabulary is an important tool in academic learning (Nagy and Townsend, 2012). Printed school English consists of approximately 88,500 distinct words, but few children understand all of them (Nagy and Anderson, 1984). It is estimated that English-speaking children learn between 3,000 and 5,400 words a year during primary and secondary school (Berman, 2007). In the course of 12 years of school, this adds up to anywhere between 36,000 and 64,800 words. This shows the tremendous capacity of children and adolescents to learn new words and the complexity of the knowledge they acquire, but also the enormous vocabulary requirements in school.

Figurative language

Figurative language refers to words that are used in a nonliteral or indirect way, including metaphors, similes, irony and humor. Metaphors often incorporate knowledge from one area in order to understand new areas (Rakova, 2003). Modern examples of linguistic innovation based on metaphor is the word "memory" in connection with computers, or "surfing" on the Internet. Metaphor is a key element in later language development. Although preschoolers occasionally use metaphors spontaneously, for example by saying that *gasoline is milk for the car*, the development of metaphors has barely begun by the time a child starts in school (Levorato and Cacciari, 2002; Nippold, 1998). Children use words in innovative nonliterate ways when they have difficulty retrieving a known word form, like *pourer* for cup or *sleeper* for bed (Clark, 1981). Keil (1986) describes four stages in children's perception of metaphors (Table 16.2). During early development, metaphors are interpreted *literally* rather than *figuratively*. When asked to explain the statement *My sister is a rock*, the 6-year-olds said things like, *She is hard, like if you felt her hand, you couldn't squish it or anything*, or *She just sits there without moving*. The 8-year-olds realized that the statements had to do with behavioral characteristics, and answered that the sister did not give up. The 10-year-olds tended to interpret it as a psychological trait, answering that the sister was mean. However, it is not until 11 or 12 years of age that children are able to formulate the relationship between a hard thing and a hard person in the sense that "both a hard thing and a hard person are difficult to handle" (Asch and Nerlove, 1960). In the transition to adolescence there is a change in the quantity and quality of figurative language, which may be related to the general increase in knowledge and development of more complex metalinguistic abilities. Adolescents are also better at constructing new figurative expressions (Levorato and Cacciari, 2002; Nippold, 1998).

The studies previously mentioned show that metaphor comprehension is not simply a matter of experience, but also of children's depth of understanding. Although children in early school age have ample experience with both people and things that are hot, cold, smooth and hard, they have difficulty understanding the relationship between personal characteristics and physical expressions. The complex nature of figurative language is also reflected in the challenges experienced by children and adolescents with language impairments (Abrahamsen and Smith, 2000; Kerbel and Grunwell, 1998a, b) and autism spectrum disorder (Happé, 1995). They seem to have difficulty integrating linguistic, social and contextual elements and infer the intended meaning, and the difference between adults is more pronounced than between older children with and without autism – also children without autism struggle with metaphorical language (Chahboun et al., 2016).

Teachers use metaphors to explain scientific concepts and other subjects to students; teaching without metaphors is nearly impossible to imagine (Aubusson et al., 2006; Pramling, 2015). Unfamiliar metaphors can make textbooks inaccessible to children, especially if they struggle with comprehension. At the same time, studies show that children develop a better understanding and usage from texts containing metaphors than from similar texts without metaphors (Winner, 1988). This shows the importance of metaphors in acquiring knowledge and underlines the fact that metaphors in a text (and in language in general) must be designed so children can actually understand them.

Cultural differences in word extension

Languages differ greatly with regard to word extension, that is, the extent of what a word can encompass. This often becomes apparent when translating from one language to another – even actions such as cutting or breaking are not necessarily assigned to the same categories in different languages (Majid et al., 2008).

The differences between languages offer important insights into the development of language, as they reveal the relationship between basic human concepts and words. For example, there is no universal correspondence between the characteristics of physical space and the words that describe these properties. Different cultures not only use dissimilar words, but also divide the world in different ways (Lakoff, 1987). Figure 16.3 shows five ways in which various languages indicate spatial relationships represented by *in* and *on* in English. This means that children who grow up with different languages both use different words when they describe identical spatial relationships and describe different spatial relationships (Bowerman and Choi, 2001; Gentner and Bowerman, 2009).

Expanding social activities

The gradual expansion of children's language environment affects their vocabulary. Kindergarten

TABLE 16.2 Children pass through four levels in their comprehension of metaphors involving personality traits (based on Keil, 1986)

Level 1	Children take metaphors literally. A "smooth person" is described as someone who has just shaved.
Level 2	Children realize that the statement relates to two areas, both physical and psychological, but fail to juxtapose them. "The idea bloomed" is explained by saying that "it went away."
Level 3	Children juxtapose the two domains along basic inferred dimensions. A "sour person" is someone who is "not very nice," while a "smooth person" is someone who is thoughtful.
Level 4	Children are able to identify the interaction between different domains and interpret the statements correctly. A "sour person" is someone who "doesn't want to do things," a "smooth person" is someone who "takes things without yelling or jumping at people," and an "idea that wasn't ripe yet" is an idea that needed "some more planning."

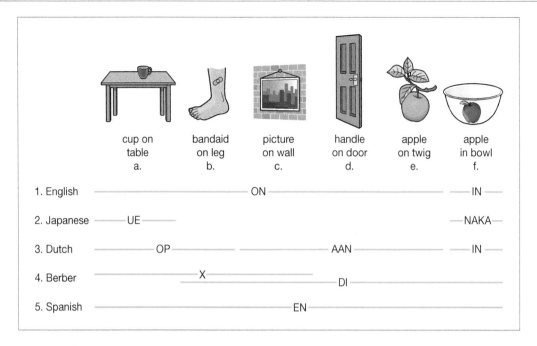

FIGURE 16.3 **Spatial relationships in various languages.**
English, Japanese, Dutch, Berber and Spanish speakers refer to the spatial relationships shown in illustrations a–f. 1) In English, Norwegian, Hungarian and several other languages, a, b, c, d and e are *on*, while f is *in*. 2) Japanese uses an unspecified generic term that simply indicates the presence of some spatial relationship that applies to all the illustrations; *ue* (a) is a noun that can be translated as "upper region" or "top," while *naka* (f) can be translated as "inner space." 3) Dutch uses three prepositions: *op* for a and b, *aan* for c, d and e, and *in* for f. 4) Berber uses the preposition *x* for a and *di* for d, e and f. Both can be used for b and c. 5) Spanish uses the same preposition *en* for all the illustrations (based on Bowerman and Choi, 2001).

usually represents a broader and more varied language environment than the home. The school introduces many new words, at the same time, as it creates the need for new words. The vocabulary learned at school is a basis for gaining access to education, employment and the general public debate in newspapers and other media. Another part of children's vocabulary comes from magazines and books. Adolescence is marked by a major change in interests and activities. Adolescents spend a lot of time talking together, and their language is typically characterized by many new words and expressions. The variation in children's activities leads to individual differences in word learning, and there is a clear relationship between social background and vocabulary (Hoff, 2013). Culture, too, has an impact on word learning. To some extent, children in Great Britain and the USA talk about other things than children in Uganda and Japan. In adulthood, the growth in vocabulary diminishes. This is partly the result of word learning itself – many words have already been learned – but also of the fact that individual activity patterns become more stable with age.

From single words to sentences

The ability to express an infinite number of different meanings by combining words is the very essence of human language. The transition from single to multi-word utterances is the most important qualitative milestone in language development. Once children begin to combine two or more words, they are able to communicate more specific and complex messages.

Early understanding of multi-word utterances

Children show understanding of multi-word utterances before they themselves begin to use them. Many children who mostly use single-word utterances will perform instructions such as *kiss teddy* and *teddy kiss* in different ways (Sachs and Truswell, 1978). Although children's earliest sentences are typically incomplete and in "telegram style," their comprehension is best when adults use short but complete sentences (Petretic and Tweney, 1977). Toddlers generally do not understand sentences with several embedded clauses (Clark, 2016).

To interpret what they hear, young children use both their language skills and their general knowledge about the world. The study in Box 16.5 shows that from 3 to 5 years, children increasingly relied on sentence structure when inferring meaning from sentences (Strohner and Nelson, 1974). However, children's interpretations can be influenced by inducing a particular perspective. In a similar study, most of a group of 3–4-year-olds let the cat bite the duck when they carried out *The cat was bitten by the duck*, which was the expected action based on their knowledge about cats and ducks. With another group of children, the researcher said *naughty duck* or *poor cat* before the sentence was presented, and these children let the duck bite the cat (MacWhinney, 1982). Whether they noticed the word order at all is uncertain – children are usually closer to school age by the time they understand passive sentences.

Early sentence construction

The age when children start to use sentences varies widely. Some children use many utterances with two or more words before the age of 16 months; others have few or no such utterances even past the age of 2 years (Bates et al., 1995). In addition, the transition from single to multi-word utterances can take quite a long time. Ramer (1976) found that the time between the child's first two-word utterances until 20 percent of the utterances consisted of two or more words ranged from 1½ to 9 months. Since all the children developed normal speech, the variation in time did not reflect any permanent difference in language skills.

In moving to multi-word utterances, children use thematically related *successive single-word utterances*. In the following example Allison is 18 months old and her father had used a knife to cut up a piece of peach lying in the bowl of a spoon (Bloom, 1973). Allison hands him a new peach and a spoon, and says:

Daddy.
Peach.
Cut.

This type of successive single-word utterance differs from children's later multi-word utterances

---

BOX 16.5 EVENT PROBABILITY AND SENTENCE STRUCTURE IN YOUNG CHILDREN'S INTERPRETATION OF SENTENCES (Strohner and Nelson, 1974)

Children aged 3 to 5 years (15 in each age group) were asked to act out sentences that were active or passive, and describing probable or improbable events. There were an actor and an object or a recipient in each sentence, and the children had two dolls for each sentence they should act out. The figure shows that all the children correctly acted out active and probable sentences like *The boy throws the ball* without problems. The 3-year-olds had problems with acting out all the sentences describing improbable events. They let the tiger bite the turtle when acting out *The turtle bites the tiger*, seemingly basing their interpretation on what they knew about turtles and tigers. The 4-year-olds

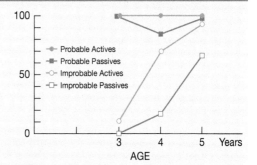

Permission from Keith E. Nelson.

correctly acted out most of the active sentences with improbable events but failed on most of the passive sentences. The 5-year-olds based their interpretation on the language sentence content but also had some problems with the passive sentences describing improbable events.

in that the words are not connected by an intonation contour. Little by little, the pace of children's word production increases, inter-word pauses get progressively shorter and several words fall within the same intonation contour (Peters, 1995; Scollon, 1976).

According to Tomasello (1992, 2003), verbs have a core function in children's grammatical constructions as structural elements that express *intent*. Because a verb implies that someone performs an action and someone or something else may receive it, verbs represent an early conceptual framework for constructing sentences. The verb *to kick* entails that someone does the kicking and something or someone else is being kicked, such as a boy kicking a ball. The verb *to give* implies that someone gives, that something is given and that someone else is the recipient of what is being given, for example a girl who gives an apple to her teacher. With verbs as a basis, children learn to use constructions such as "X kicks Y," "X gives Y," "X pushes Y," and so forth, linking verbs to words that indicate specific people, places, objects, points in time, and so on. Once children's utterances include a greater number of words, more elements become explicit as well, for example, *The boy kicks the ball through the window*, or *The girl gives a red apple to the math teacher*.

Children's language is creative but young children have a small language repertoire. One study involving four 2-year-olds found that 20–40 percent of their utterances were word sequences that they had used before, and 40–50 percent of their utterances were identical to a previous utterance except for one single point of variation (Lieven et al., 2009). This means that they use strategies that worked for them in the past when solving communicative challenges. They also use utterances they themselves have frequently used or heard others use for a particular purpose as *formulas* or models for constructing new sentences (Bannard and Lieven, 2012). The sentence *Can I have apple?*, for example, can provide the formula "Can I have X?", where X can be apple, juice, book, ball, and so on. Other typical early formulas are "Where is X?" and "Shall we X?" (Tomasello, 2006).

Formulas are useful during very early development, but if children were to base their language exclusively on formulas, their language would become fairly stereotyped – as in the case of many children with autism spectrum disorder

(Boucher, 2012). Children notice that other people use different types of sentence constructions and assume that there is a reason for doing so, analogous to the *principle of contrast* in word learning (p. 315). The child wants to find out why the other person chooses a particular sentence construction, that is, the intent behind using structure A rather than structure B (Tomasello, 2006). Formulas thus make it possible to exploit previously established sentence structures, while the principle of contrast encourages the use of new grammatical constructions.

Young children thus construct their own sentences from observing the language of others. They take notice of single words and larger parts of sentences, and use them actively, even if they fail to understand the entire sentence. Some of the sentences children use consist of adults' expansions of their own utterances (see p. 327), but they produce many sentences they have never heard before. Children constantly create more or less new meaningful structures based on the context of the conversation and their own goals and objectives in what they express.

More complex sentences

At the age of 2, most children have started to use simple sentences, and the length and complexity of their utterances gradually increases toward school age. Their initial sentence-building strategies continue to develop and expand, and their own productivity becomes increasingly important. Complex utterances begin to emerge as combinations of simpler sentences. Sentences that previously were uttered separately turn into a single sentence. *Daddy car* and *Daddy drive* becomes *Daddy drive car*, so that the common element *Daddy* is only used once. Tomasello's daughter Travis combined the formulas *Look at X* and *Pete eat X* into the sentence *Look at Pete eating a bone* (Tomasello, 1992). The children's language becomes more efficient because they can include more information in a single utterance.

Children produce increasingly more intricate sentences, such as *I saw the neighbor's horse jump over the fence, which is broken*. An increase in complexity is particularly pronounced between the ages of 5 and 7, but complexity continues to increase throughout school age (Berman, 2007; Nippold, 1998). The context also influences sentence structure: young adolescents used much longer and more complex sentences when they retold fables than when they engaged in conversations about topics like family, friends, hobbies, sports and travel (Nippold et al., 2014).

Word classes and inflections

Word inflections mark important information about the word – for example tense or plurality – and its role in the utterance. To master the language, children have to learn the inflections of their language. Children learning English and many other languages have to learn that verbs can either be conjugated regularly (e.g., *play – played – have played*) or *irregularly* (e.g., *go – went – have gone*). Children learning Chinese or other East Asian languages have to learn the functions of classifier inflections. To ask for one apple, they have to say *yi ge pinguo* ('one unit apple'). Without the classifier *ge* (which would be ungrammatical), it is not clear if the child means one apple, a piece of apple or a bag of apples (Allan, 1977; Li et al., 2010).

The words in children's earliest utterances are without inflections. It is only once children are well underway to using sentences that they begin to inflect words and include function words such as *over* and *under*. During early language development, children use both regular and irregular verbs, but only in their simple form. They appear to perceive conjugations of the same verb as different words, such as *do* and *did*. Around the age of 2–3, children begin to *overregulate* the conjugation of verbs (Marcus, 1995). They may say *goed* instead of *went*, even if they previously said *went*. It seems that children first begin to learn the general rules of verb conjugation at around this age, and that they still have not understood that there are exceptions. Other word classes are treated similarly, for example *two mouses*. This also has to do with the fact that children are used to making mistakes and adjust what they say during early language development. Their "errors" are the result of new insights, and they need time to identify the boundaries of these new regularities they have discovered.

Some of the systematic aspects of language take a long time to learn. Related words belonging to different word classes, for example, usually share the same stem, such as in *saw* and *sawing*, making it possible to *derive* a word class based on the stem of a word from a different word class. Derwing and Baker (1986) found that 25 of 40 English-speaking children between the age of 6 and 8 had learned to add *-er* to the end of a verb in order to indicate an individual performing an action, such as *to run* and *a runner*. Twenty-two of 40 11-year-olds were able to derive adjectives from nouns by adding *-y*, such as *greed* and *greedy*, while 32 of 40 adolescents aged 12–17 managed to derive adverbs by attaching the suffix *-ly*, as in *serious* and *seriously*. Younger children are only able to derive words from well-familiar verbs, while older children are also able to do so with recently learned verbs (Lieven et al., 2003).

Different views on children's sentence construction

The transition from single words to sentences and the acquisition of syntax and grammar is the most discussed topic in language development. The main division runs between nativism, which claims that children acquire abstract grammatical rules by way of an innate *universal grammar*, and usage-based theory and emergentism, which maintain that children *construct* language based on their cognitive resources and experience with language. Nativism and usage-based theory thus have very different views on how children come to master grammar. *Overregulation* (see above) has been given special attention because children produce word inflections they have not heard from adults. Nativists argue that the overregulation reflects the development of a linguistic rule system based on universal grammar. Children forget the exceptions and use the rules on them as well (Pinker, 1994). According to the usage-based theory, children initially learn to inflect one item at a time, rather than starting with a general rule, and use *analogy* when they inflect new words. Overregulation occurs because children have not yet learned the different conjugations of verbs and overregulate by choosing the most common ones. Thus, usage-based theory views overregulation as a result of the learning process itself. Both nativism and usage-based theory are able to explain children's overregulation and the presence of overregulation can therefore not be used to distinguish between the theories (Ambridge and Lieven, 2011).

On the other hand, according to the theory of a universal grammar, a child who has learned to use a particular grammatical structure should be able to use it in any linguistic context – the content is irrelevant (Radford, 1990). One study, however, found the mastery of passive sentence structure was not the same across verbs: 80 percent of a group of 5-year-olds understood passive sentences with *to hit*, while only 30 percent understood sentences with *to follow*. This supports a usage-based theory (Tomasello, 2003).

LANGUAGE IN USE

The functions of language are rooted in the intention to communicate something to someone else. The object may be to give or to obtain information, to get someone to do something, to maintain the conversation, and so on. Toddlers talk mostly to adults, and their conversations often revolve around the child's activities together with the adult. Their language use typically involves getting someone else to do something (*take*), expressing agreement or disagreement with someone else's suggestion (*yes*, *no*), expressing what something is (*that car*), and what they intend to do (*I throw*). They also respond to their parents' *yes/no* questions (Snow et al., 1996). About a third of all toddlers' utterances consist of descriptions and statements, compared with 80–90 percent among adults (Dore, 1977; Miller, 1981).

Children also use language as a tool to explore the environment and regulate their own behavior by commenting on objects and their own actions without any apparent communicative intent (see p. 244). Vygotsky (1962) considers this a step toward children's internalization of language and other people's regulation of their behavior. In one study, 21 percent of the utterances of 4-year-olds in dialogue with each other had elements of self-regulation, including the use of "monologues" to guide themselves through play activities such as building a house. However, it varied considerably: some of the 4-year-olds used a lot of self-regulating speech, others almost none (Schober-Peterson and Johnson, 1991).

Conversation skills

Conversation requires many skills. Conversation partners must have a common focus, agree on a topic, understand what the other person can understand and communicate, and provide a relevant response to the other person's input. Conversation skills include strategies to express communicative intent and regulate the conversation, such as taking initiative, answering, turn-taking, clearing up misunderstandings and ending the conversation. In early dialogues, the adult assumes practically all responsibility for keeping the conversation going, such as in the following dialogue between Sean and his mother (Dore, 1986):

M: *Okay, let's go play bally?* (Both go toward family room)
Wanna play bouncy ball?
S: *Ba(ll). /b_/*
M: *Okay. You get the ball there.* (Points to ball)
S: (Hands the ball to her)
M: *Sit down. Here. Like this.* (Positions Sean in front of her and spreads out legs in V-shape)
Here we go. (Rolls ball to Sean)
S: (Clutches the ball)
Ba(ll). /b_/ (Pushes ball toward his mother)
M: *Nice. Good boy, Sean. That a boy.* (Rolls ball back to him).

During early conversations, the adult is in control while at the same time supporting the child's participation. Once children's vocabulary increases, adults ask many questions they usually know the answer to. This helps children take turns and produce a relevant utterance, even if they do not remember the entire context. Even 18-month-olds seem to understand that the rising intonation of a question means that it is their turn. Generally, toddlers respond far more often to questions than to purely narrative statements by the adult. Twenty-month-olds respond to about one-third of their parents' questions, whereas 29–36 month-olds respond almost twice as often (Pan and Snow, 1999).

Conversations between toddlers usually do not last long, at least not about the same topic. They have difficulty taking turns without getting support, and understanding how the utterances in a conversation relate to each other – many utterances of younger preschool children are unsuccessful attempts at dialogue (Nelson and Gruendel, 1979; Schober-Peterson and Johnson, 1991). Successful conversations are often closely linked to children's actions, such as the following dialogue between two 3-year-olds, Alex and Nicki (Karmiloff and Karmiloff-Smith, 2001, p. 154):

A: *I'm gonna put it there.*
N: *Over there.*
A: *On the green box.*
N: *Yeah, put it on top.*
A: *You wanna do it?*
N: *Okay.*

With age, children contribute more equally to the conversation. They take more initiative in the dialogue and adults do not need to adapt as much to the child's level of comprehension. Dialogues increase in length and there are fewer breaks in communication. The increase in communicative equality seems to be related to the fact that adults leave children with more of the responsibility for keeping the dialogue alive. Whether this is the reason for children's increased contributions or the result of their improved skills is impossible to say – children and adults probably influence each another.

Older children, too, can have difficulty maintaining focus on a single topic over time. In a study of 7-12-year-olds, the children were to pretend to be hosts in a television program. The adults who were interviewed by the children were instructed to answer their questions but not to respond to any more than what the children asked about. The children who did best asked many open questions. Several children were unable to keep the conversation going for the designated 4 minutes, and some of the adults failed to refrain from helping by asking questions of their own, although they had been told not to do so (Schley and Snow, 1992). This shows how slowly these skills evolve and how natural it is for adults to help children in their language development.

Successful conversations require that the communication partners take the other's perspective and adapt the language they produce to the language skills and knowledge of the other person. This adaptive process begins early on. Four-year-olds talk differently to 2-year-olds than to peers and adults (Shatz and Gelman, 1973). In studies of "referential communication," one of the

Children spend much of their time in conversations with parents.

FIGURE 16.4 **Experiment on referential communication.**
The illustration shows a typical experimental situation examining children's ability to describe photographs, geometric shapes and patterns, maps and the like, so someone else who cannot see the referent is able to find or recreate it.

conversation partners has to describe something in such a way that the other person, without having seen it, can find it among several similar objects (Figure 16.4). Adults generally have no difficulty describing geometric shapes so another adult can identify them. The descriptions of preschool children, however, tend to be private and ambiguous, and even adults do not always succeed in finding the correct shape based on their descriptions (Glucksberg et al., 1966). With age, children's descriptions become more precise, and they improve at conveying referential information.

Clarification and repair

Conversations typically involve smaller and larger misunderstandings, which must be detected and resolved to avoid breakdowns in communication, and negotiation is part of the meaning making. Parents ask their children to clarify things even

before starting to talk with them about matters beyond the immediate situation (Pan and Snow, 1999). Starting at a relatively early age, children, too, begin to "repair" or change statements they have discovered to be wrong or that are misunderstood by the person they are talking to. In a study of 2–3 year-olds, Clark (1992) registered between 30 and 50 repairs of this type for each child within a half-hour observation:

Kate (2;8): *What – who's that?*
Zoe (2;11): *Not the – I don't mean the* new *one. The old one.*

Another study found that a third of all the clarifying questions parents asked children aged 2;6 were not "genuine" questions in the sense that the parents did not wait for an answer. Because the children's statements had been unclear, their parents asked them to explain what they meant but failed to wait for an answer, probably because they did not think the child would be able to do so (Shatz and O'Reilly, 1990). The parents tried to guess what the children intended to say, rather than making excessive demands on them. A third of the children's answers did not clarify the misunderstanding and many questions were simply met affirmatively. In some cases, the children asked their parents for clarification and usually received a reply. Nevertheless, this rarely clarified the misunderstanding because the children did not wait for the parents' answer.

Misunderstandings often arise in conversation with preschool children because they do not take sufficient account of the other person's knowledge. Until the age of 5, children rarely notice that the other person seems confused or puzzled at something they have said, and they rarely express that there is something they have not understood. Even 9-year-olds have difficulty discovering ambiguities in what is being said (Lloyd et al., 1995).

Conversations and activities

Changes in children's conversation skills are reflected in the activities they take part in. The first conversations occur in simple activities that place few demands on children's participation. During preschool age, children increasingly participate in smaller and larger groups in connection with games and other activities. Spending time together with peers places new demands on children's ability to maintain conversations without the help usually provided by adults. Children's increased competence leads to greater linguistic freedom and opportunities to use their imagination and initiate play activities, but also more responsibility to adapt their communication to the others and to the situation. Once they start in school, children become part of a broader social reality and have to cope with many new situations and communicative codes. They must learn how to speak in class, in the street together with their peers and with grandma when she comes to visit. During adolescence, with its youth culture and emotions, conversations with peers become a main activity. Thus, the acquisition of conversation skills is closely linked to enculturation in general, as well as to children's and adolescents' developing understanding of themselves and others in a social and cultural context.

Narratives

Story-telling is a common human activity and part of everyday life. Many child–parent conversations are about something that has happened, about what the child or other people did and experienced, and these are important for the child's understanding of the world (Bruner, 1991). A narrative is a story, a representation of a chain of events in time and space in which people (or other characters) engage in action and have intentions, motives, interests and emotions (Labov, 1972). The development of narrative abilities is related to autobiographical memory (see p. 202) and the development of the self (see Chapter 21).

Children begin to share experiences early on, both to tell what is happening and to get help understanding events, starting with declarative pointing (see p. 300) and followed by the early language dialogues. Prior to the narrative below, Philip (aged 10) had let his budgerigar out of its cage. It landed on 18-month-old David's head, and this had frightened him. The boys' mother encouraged David to tell the story to his father, Herb (Clark, 2016, p. 321):

M: *Did you see Philip's bird? Can you tell Herb?*
D: *Head, head, head.*
M: *What landed on your head?*
D: *Bird.*

David began with the story's emotional climax – something happened to his head. His mother helped him bring in another character (the bird) and thus created a slightly larger context. Beginning with the emotional highpoint is typical for children's early narratives, also fragments and lack of coherence. The "fairy tale structure" of narratives, beginning with "once upon a time" and ending with "they lived happily ever after," only develops much later.

At around 3 years of age, children begin to tell more coherent stories, but younger children's stories tend to be descriptive and characters are mainly represented by their physical and external attributes, and many of their narratives lack a temporal structure (Küntay, 2004). Questions from the adult may support coherence in the child's narrative (Silva et al., 2014). Mothers of 3-year-olds asked for more information and repeated the child's utterance more often than mothers of 5-year-olds when co-constructing narratives, as the older children needed less help (Zevenbergen et al., 2016). Five-year-olds include more information about the characters' mental state – their thoughts, feelings and motives – but references to thoughts and perceptions are rare even among 5-6-year-olds (Nelson, 2009; Nicolopoulou and Richner, 2007).

Through school age, children's narratives are gradually longer and more elaborated (see examples in Box 16.6). The children are also becoming more independent in their narrative construction. A mother and a child of school age may have quite different narratives of the same event, but the child may still need help to include emotional and evaluative aspects (Fivush et al., 2008; Veneziano, 2016). Toward adolescence, narratives become more cohesive, detailed and evaluative (Habermas and de Silveira, 2008; Ukrainetz et al., 2005). Narrative skills are important in adolescence because schools expect students to be able to read and retell what they have read. In addition, adolescents spend increasing amounts of time in self-disclosure (see p. 444) and telling stories about themselves and others

BOX 16.6 FICTITIOUS STORIES BY SCHOOL-AGED CHILDREN (Ukrainetz et al., 2005)

A total of 293 children aged 5–12 years were asked to tell a story from the same five pictures from *Test of Narrative Language* (Gillam and Pearson, 2004):

1. A boy is sitting in bed looking at a clock with a distressed expression.
2. The boy is spilling milk as he looks at a wall clock.
3. The boy is snapping a shoelace while putting on shoes.
4. The boy is running after the departing school bus.
5. The boy is walking up the school steps and a woman in a suit is standing outside looking at her watch sternly.

The stories below are typical of each age group.

5–6 YEARS
Once there was a little boy. He was sleeping in his bed. And he went to go eat his breakfast and accidentally took the string out of his shoe and accidentally broke. And then he tried to go to school with the bus. But the bus left already. And he had to walk to school. And then the teacher said he was late.

7–9 YEARS
One morning Bob woke up. And it was twenty after seven. And he was running late for school. And he started pouring a bowl of cereal. And he wasn't paying attention. And he spilled some milk. So he started to clean it up. And then he said I just can't have breakfast this morning. And he went and got dressed. He accidentally tore his shoelace. So he got some tape and taped it. When he got his backpack and ran to the school bus stop he missed the school bus. So he had to run all the way to school. Her teacher got mad at him because he was late. She was wondering if he would come. The end.

10–12 YEARS
One morning a kid woke up. And his name was Todd. He got up and looked at his clock and it turned out he was almost late for school And so he got out of bed. And got dressed hurriedly. And he went into the kitchen. This is where he poured his favorite cereal was out. So he had to do his least favorite which is crunchymunchys. And while he was looking at the clock worrying about time he poured milk over all his cereal. After he got dressed, he started to tie his shoe. And the shoelace snapped. After a long of trying to repair the shoelace he decided to give up. He put on his backpack ran outside and discovered his school bus had raced ahead of him. After a long and treacherous time of walking to school the teacher said he was late. And he had to spend the recess inside.

in an effort to achieve acknowledgement and emotional support (Nippold et al., 2014).

Narrative skills are not always included but may be a useful element in the assessment of language abilities (Norbury and Bishop, 2003). Children from language minorities may have lower narrative skills than their peers and intervention in preschool may give them a better start in school (Petersen and Spencer, 2016). Children and adolescents with disabilities involving communication and language also tend to struggle with narrative construction, including those with intellectual disability (van Bysterveldt et al., 2012), speech and language disorders (Paul et al., 1996; Soto and Hartmann, 2006) and autism spectrum disorders (Baixauli et al., 2016). A low narrative competence may lead to poorer understanding of personal and other social events, and enculturation in general. It may also make it more difficult for children and adolescents with disabilities to tell about personal events and use narration to cope with difficult situations. Studies show that intervention with story retelling in preschool and school may improve narrative abilities (Petersen, 2011; Petersen et al., 2014).

CHILD-DIRECTED LANGUAGE

Adults are children's main source of knowledge about language, and parents vary with regard to how much they speak and in their adaptation when they speak to infants and toddlers. Early child-directed speech is characterized by many short utterances, simple sentence structures and few grammatical errors. Vowels are extended in length. The pronunciation is clear, with distinctly marked stresses on important words, exaggerated intonation and a somewhat lighter vocal register than in speech directed at adults (Fernald and Mazzie, 1991). The intonation seems to draw infants' attention to the speech (Spinelli et al., 2017). Deaf mothers slow down signing in interactions with their infants and toddlers and use rhythmic, slightly exaggerated movements and more repetitions than when they communicate with adults (Masataka, 1992).

Repetition is common when adults talk to young children, but they rarely repeat the same thing in the same way. Parents change their utterances a little or repeat parts of them, producing variation sets with slightly different information,

such as this mother who speaks to her 14-month-old child (Brodsky et al., 2007, p. 834):

M: *You got to push them to school.*
Push them.
Push them to school.
Take them to school.
You got to take them to school.

Parental self-repetition without variation does not provide new information unless the utterance was not heard (or seen) by the child the first time, but partial repetitions may function to highlight prominent sentence elements. A study of 12 mothers' speech to their 2-year-olds found that much of their speech included a small number of "frames" with the same first or last word like *In X, What do X, Are you X, It's X, Let's X, Look X, I think X* or *If X*, as well as many fragments and reduced sentences, consistent with use of variation sets (Cameron-Faulkner et al., 2003).

Repetition of what children say is often combined with recast and *expansion*. For example, if the child says *Daddy cup*, the adult may reformulate and expand it to *Yes, that's Daddy's cup standing on the table*. In this way, the adult shows the child how the utterance has been interpreted, while at the same time giving it a more complete grammatical form. Expansion links new words to the ones the child has already learned; recasting may function as negative evidence and correction (Chouinard and Clark, 2003; Nelson et al., 1973). Both have been shown to be effective strategies in intervention for children with language impairment (Cleave et al., 2015; Nelson, 2001). In sum, this underlines the fact that children do not simply mimic the sentences they have heard before but construct language based on information from different sources (von Tetzchner et al., 2008).

How much parents talk with their children varies considerably. In one study, the number of utterances to 1- to 3-year-olds varied between 34 and 793 utterances per hour. Assuming that children at this age are awake 14 hours a day, some children will hear 476 utterances per day, others 11,102. In the course of 1 year, this adds up to anywhere between 175,000 and 4 million utterances (Hart and Risley, 1992). In a study of families with low socioeconomic background, caregiver speech directed at their 19-month-old child varied from 670 to 12,000 words per day, and the total speech accessible to the child from 2,000 to 29,000 words. The amount of child-directed speech seemed to matter: there was a positive correlation between child-directed speech at 19 months and vocabulary size based on a parent-completed schedule at 24 months (Weisleder and Fernald, 2013). Children of talkative mothers tend to talk a lot themselves and follow up their mother's topic more often than children with less talkative mothers (Hoff, 2006). However, individual differences do not only reflect parents' talkativeness, but also the children's language skills and their reactions to being talked to.

The adaptations of child-directed speech are particularly prominent in the first phase of speech development and they are gradually reduced as the child's language skills improve. By the time children reach the age of 5 years, adults no longer adapt the stress and intonation of their speech when speaking to children. The results cited above indicate that the amount of parents' speech to children matters, and exaggerated stress and intonation seem to help guide infants' attention to the speech. Parents' use of vocabulary affects the words children learn (Rowe, 2012; see p. 313). However, it is still debated how crucial the special characteristics of child-directed speech are for children's language development. Studies have found that the features typical of Western child-directed speech are not as prominent among adult speakers in other language communities, suggesting that this type of speech may be useful but not essential to children's language development (Schaffer, 1989). Children's own spontaneous language use in conversations may be more important. Hoff-Ginsberg (1990) found that the development of children's syntax was best supported by parents who engaged them in linguistic interaction. The structure of the parents' language was less important. This suggests that parents are not so much direct models, but rather supportive interlocutors in social and meaningful contexts.

GENDER DIFFERENCES

Many studies show that girls on average develop comprehension and use of language earlier than boys (e.g., Kimura, 1999; Zambrana et al., 2012),

and language disorders are more prevalent among boys than girls (see p. 60). Differences are observable from the start. There is no difference in the onset of gesture use but girls start to use word-gesture combinations and spoken sentences about 3 months earlier than boys (Özçalışkan and Goldin-Meadow, 2010). Differences in language skills in favor of girls tend to become more evident in school age. Some features that differ between adult males and females first become pronounced after the age of 10, but certain aspects of language use can be observed as early as preschool age (Ladegaard and Bleses, 2003). Six-year-old girls, for example, make more informative statements and talk more about emotions than boys, while boys make more statements involving control (Tenenbaum et al., 2011).

Researchers have unsuccessfully attempted to find a neurological basis for gender differences in language development (see p. 115). Sex hormones seem to influence language development but the mechanism behind this is unknown (Schaadt et al., 2015). The slightly earlier development of girls' language skills may also be related to the fact that they participate more in language-related activities, while boys more often take part in physical play (see Chapter 24). Studies have also shown that, starting at an early age, parents speak somewhat differently to boys than to girls, for example they interrupt girls more often than boys when they talk. Fathers are more directive when they speak to their sons and use more loving expressions such as *my little pet* when talking to their daughters (Andersen, 1990; Gleason and Greif, 1983). Additionally, there are differences in how mothers tell stories and talk about feelings with boys and with girls. It is likely that these influences contribute to shaping some gender-specific language use (Leaper and Smith, 2004).

MULTILINGUALISM

More than half of all children grow up as multilingual (Grosjean, 2010). Multilingualism is defined as the mastery of two or more languages at the level of a native speaker. In its most common form, it involves two languages. In *bilingual first language acquisition* the child is exposed to two languages from birth; in *early second language acquisition*, exposition to the second language begins between the age of 1;6 and 4 years (De Houwer, 2009). When bilingualism is practiced *within* the family, one or both of the two languages are usually part of the external language environment. When bilingualism is practiced *between* the family and the society, the family speaks a different language than most of the community around them. In such cases of *minority language* use, the family often has contact with others who speak the same language, although some children grow up with a home language that is spoken by only a few people in their environment. Moving from one country to another can involve language loss because the use of the first language becomes limited (Bialystok, 2001; De Houwer, 2009). Internationally adopted toddlers may experience a total shift of language, as expressed by one parent: "She didn't have a word of English; we didn't have a word of Vietnamese" (McAndrew and Malley-Keighran, 2017, p. 89). It can be difficult to distinguish language disorders from the language problems of minority language children who have little experience with many topics in the majority language and have received inadequate education (Paradis, 2010; Scheidnes and Tuller, 2016).

Children growing up with two languages must learn two phonological systems, vocabularies and grammars, and when to use each of the two. Children who learn a spoken language and a sign language must learn a system of sounds and a system of movements (Petitto et al., 2001). This is generally no more difficult than learning the sounds or movements of a single language. Children who learn both languages from the start will master both phonological systems equally well if their exposure is the same. Children with both a home language and an outside language are usually exposed to the home language first. They may struggle a bit initially but by the age of 5 children have usually mastered both phonological systems (Werker and Byers-Heinlein, 2008).

Bilingual children acquire their first words at about the same age as monolingual children, but they need to build a far greater inventory of word forms if they are to master each language as well as monolinguals. Their vocabulary develops a bit more slowly in each of the two languages compared with monolingual children, partly because they do not learn the corresponding words simultaneously but in separate language situations.

They also have less time and experience with each language compared with those who learn a single language only. Looking at the two languages in context, however, the picture changes. Many words are initially learned in one language only, but even if words familiar in both languages are only counted once, the total vocabulary of bilingual children often exceeds that of their monolingual peers (Bialystok and Luk, 2012; Hoff et al., 2012).

Bilingual children also need to learn which words correspond to each other in the two languages. Saunders (1988) suggests that up to the age of 2, bilingual children have one common set of words among the two languages, but studies have shown that as early as their second year, many bilingual children use words with the same meaning in both languages, for example *bola* (Portuguese) and *ball* (English), or *Brot* (German) and *pain* (French). Sometimes they say both words, such as *heiss hot*. Until the age of 2, the percentage of words common to both languages is relatively small – typically 20 to 30 percent – but from this age on, it increases significantly (De Houwer, 2009). Grosjean (1982) tells of a 2-year-old girl who combined *chaud* and *hot* into *shot*, although this type of language mixing, also called code-mixing, is rare. Problems with code-mixing usually have to do with words that have the same form but different meanings, such as *gift* in English and *Gift* (poison) in German.

Sometimes bilingual children construct sentences with words from both languages, such as *Und ich bin boy*, but there are major individual differences. Some children never mix languages, others do it half of the time. When children mix languages, their parents usually mix the two languages as well and sometimes even encourage it, leaving the division between the two languages somewhat indistinct (De Houwer, 2009; Lanza, 1997). Bilingual toddlers generally use the correct language when talking to another person 80–90 percent of the time (De Houwer, 2009).

Languages have different syntax and the order of acquisition of grammatical structures essentially corresponds to the monolingual development in each language. The phase without word inflections (see p. 321) seems to be shorter for bilingual than for monolingual children, perhaps because they become aware of the variation in word forms at an earlier point (Genese and Nicoladis, 2007). Since languages differ in their development, bilingual children can to some degree express different grammatical relationships in the two languages. For example, Slobin (1973) reports about two girls who used locative expressions far earlier in Hungarian than in Serbo-Croatian, which has an extremely complex system of locative prepositions. Bilingual children sometimes transfer the word order of the dominant language to the other language for a period.

It has been argued that bilingualism causes problems if the native language has not been acquired before the next language is learned (Hansegård, 1968), but studies show that bilingualism has a positive rather than a negative impact on cognitive development (Bialystok et al., 2012). Bilingual children must learn the different ways their languages categorize the world and realize early on that there is more than one perspective to the same thing. This may be the reason that bilingual children tend to develop better than average executive functions and a flexibility in solving problems and thinking creatively. They consistently do better on tasks that require selective attention and inhibition of responses (Bialystok, 2001).

Bilingualism can be harmonic and successful – there are many examples of children who benefit from growing up with two languages in an active bilingual environment. However, bilingualism does not come entirely by itself; the child must get adequate exposure to both languages. When bilingualism occurs within the family, conversation with both parents becomes more critical for children's language development than in the case of monolingual families. De Houwer (2009) writes about an English-speaking father who spoke little with his daughter because he travelled much. The mother spoke Flemish with the daughter. The father argued on the basis of the theory of an innate universal grammar (see p. 321) that the extent of language stimulation did not matter and that the daughter would develop his language anyway. The result was that at 3 years she neither understood nor used English.

In many countries professionals advise parents to use only a single language with their child, often a language other than that spoken by the parents among themselves. Sometimes, one or both parents are not particularly good at expressing themselves in this language. Using the majority language may lead to a poorer and less varied language environment than if the child grew up with parents speaking their native language, cause the child to feel rejected by being excluded from the parents' language, give rise to more emotional distance and impede the child's relationship with the parents. It is far better to ensure a solid language environment in both languages within and outside the family (De Houwer, 2009).

Bilingualism is as common among children with disabilities as among nondisabled children but research is limited (Kay-Raining Bird et al., 2016). The professional advice of using one language with the child is often given to parents of children with disabilities, as expressed by this Chinese mother of a 3-year-old with autism spectrum disorder (Yu, 2016a, p. 428):

And that speech therapist would say, uh, the way we talk, in two languages, affects his language development. She kept insisting to us that it wasn't the problem of having or not having one–one–one therapy but that we need to speak English at home.

The advice is based on the belief that it is easier for children with language impairment to learn only one language, that the child may be confused and that the home language will interfere with learning the majority language – beliefs that are not supported by research (Peña, 2016; Yu, 2013, 2016b). Bilingual development does not safeguard against disorders but neither does it involve any increased vulnerability (De Houwer, 2013; Kohnert, 2010). Children with Down syndrome, for example, have no more problems with bilingualism than other children (Kay Raining-Bird et al., 2005; Ostad, 2008). Autism spectrum disorder implies difficulties with communication and language but children with this disorder are not negatively affected by a bilingual situation (Lund et al., 2017). However, the exposure to the two languages matters. One study found that children with simultaneous bilingualism do as well in both languages as monolingual children with language impairment in their language, while children with sequential bilingualism do less well in the second language. This is usually the majority language of the society but depends on exposure to each of the languages, and they may need more exposure to the weaker language (Kay-Raining Bird et al., 2016). Language intervention has positive effects but interventions in one language show little generalization to the other, so bilingual children with language impairment often need intervention in both languages (Ebert et al., 2014). In addition, including the home language may increase the parental language input and the family's engagement in the child's bilingual development (Verdon et al., 2016). Today, professionals still tend to regard it as difficult to support bilingual development in children with communication and language impairment but in many countries there seems to be a trend toward more bilingual special education (Marinova-Todd et al., 2016).

LANGUAGE IN OTHER MODALITIES

Language and speech are not the same. Language is independent of a particular sensory modality and can be acquired in various forms. Some children need a visual form of communication due to hearing impairment (Mellon et al., 2015), while others have motor impairments or other physical disabilities and need augmentative and alternative communication (von Tetzchner and Martinsen, 2000).

Sign language

Many deaf children need sign language (for a discussion of different language forms, see p. 138). The developmental process is similar in sign and speech, and like spoken language, sign language development depends on the language environment. Deaf parents who sign adapt their child-directed signing similar to hearing parents' child-directed speech (see p. 327). However, 90 percent of deaf children's parents are hearing and to support their child's signing they first need to learn the national sign language (Napier et al., 2007). They therefore have less developed sign language skills and also adapt their child-directed signing to a lesser degree than deaf parents (Masataka, 1992; Spencer and Harris, 2006). One study found that deaf children of deaf parents showed a typical gradual course of language development, while the increased exposure to sign language when they entered a school for deaf children led to accelerated sign language development in deaf children with hearing parents. The older they were when they entered the school, the lower they later scored on a test of sign language grammar (Novogrodsky et al., 2017).

Provided they have a good signing environment, deaf children who develop sign language begin to use the first signs and multi-sign utterances at about the same age as hearing children speak their first words and phrases (Petitto and Marentette, 1991). They acquire a sign repertoire that matches the vocabulary of hearing children, but with a somewhat larger proportion of verbs, maybe because the manual form of sign languages makes action and motion more salient (Hoiting, 2006; Rinaldi et al., 2014). Without a sign language environment, sign development will be limited (Coppola, 2002; Kegl and Iwata, 1989). Studies show that deaf parents use a richer sign vocabulary and that deaf children with deaf parents have a more developed vocabulary and use more different handshapes than deaf children with hearing parents (Lu et al., 2016). The grammars of signed and spoken language differ considerably within the same society. This means that the development paths differ somewhat, but as long as deaf children grow up in a sign language environment, the complexity of their signed utterances will increase in line with the spoken utterances of their peers. Thus, the development of speech and signing is comparable in these areas as well.

Manual signs and graphic symbols for children with severe speech and language impairment

Also some groups of children with normal hearing may need another communication form than speech (Smith and Murray, 2016; von Tetzchner, 2018; von Tetzchner and Martinsen, 2000). Severe motor impairments may prevent children from speaking or make their speech unintelligible. They must rely on graphic symbols, written words and letters that can support and supplement or replace speech. The cognitive abilities of children in this group vary considerably; some motor disabled children with little or no speech have cognitive abilities in the normal range and can follow the regular school curriculum, others have intellectual disability (Stadskleiv et al., 2017). They may also need other forms of intervention but the function of augmentative and alternative communication (AAC) is to give children with disabilities opportunities for language development, although in an atypical manner (von Tetzchner and Grove, 2003).

Early sign language promotes communication and language development in children with Down syndrome.

Children with autism spectrum disorder, intellectual disability or severe language impairment may also have difficulty acquiring speech normally, even if they grow up in an adequate language environment and receive speech therapy. Many of them benefit from learning manual signs or graphic symbols (von Tetzchner and Martinsen, 2000). Although they do not develop signed or aided language skills comparable to typically developing children, they can improve their communication skills significantly, and often their spoken language as well, provided they have an adequately adapted language environment (von Tetzchner and Stadskleiv, 2016). In many countries, most children with Down syndrome, for example, receive early intervention with manual signs (Clibbens, 2001; Launonen, 1996; Wright et al., 2013).

Augmentative and alternative communication and speech development

There is a long-standing controversy whether the acquisition of manual signs or graphic symbols can inhibit speech development but all the evidence shows that language use promotes language development, independent of the modality being used. In fact, some parents teach their normally developing, hearing toddlers "baby signs" to boost their cognitive and linguistic development (Acredolo and Goodwyn, 2009; Pizer et al., 2007). Studies of deaf children show that sign language promotes both the development of speech and literacy (Miller, 2010; Strong and Prinz, 1997). Similarly, studies of children with severe language and communication impairments show that intervention with manual signs and graphic symbols promotes rather than inhibits the development of speech (Clibbens, 2001; Drager et al., 2010; Millar et al., 2006; Schlosser and Wendt, 2008).

LANGUAGE DISORDERS

Most children develop language without any particular problems, but some struggle on their way into language (see p. 60). There are children who have such severe problems that they affect the children's social functioning and learning as well as their emotional functioning and self-image. Disorders involving impairment of comprehension in particular affect the acquisition of knowledge and social skills (Law et al., 2007).

Articulation disorders alone can also affect children's learning and development, partly because the children may be perceived as younger than they are or to have lower cognitive functioning than they actually do. Children with language disorders experience problems playing with others since many forms of play require a good understanding of the rules of social interaction, and thereby miss important social experiences (Clegg et al., 2015; Glogowska et al., 2006). Language disorders may also influence peer relations later in childhood and adolescence (Durkin and Conti-Ramsden, 2007, 2010).

Early intervention is important to prevent aberrant development and secondary effects (Fricke et al., 2013; Kaiser and Roberts, 2011). Learning a language is not primarily about the ability to point at an object or a picture when someone says a word, or to be able to pronounce words. Language is social, and it is the contexts in which words occur that lend them meaning (Nelson, 2007a). Language stimulation of children who are delayed in language development must therefore be varied and take place in a conversational setting that children are able to make sense of. Also, signing deaf children with language disorders have been found to benefit from support in their narrative development (Herman et al., 2014). All aspects of the language environment are important, not least at school where children learn "school language," that is, words and phrases related to school subjects. Children with language disorders need support to develop adequate academic and social skills. A significant percentage of children with language disorders develop dyslexia and may need special literacy education (see p. 61). Audiobooks, electronic books with speech output and other materials can reduce the loss of knowledge that typically results from lack of reading, and the negative consequences of poor reading skills in adulthood (Chanioti, 2017; Moe and Wright, 2013; Schiavo and Buson, 2014).

Over time, most children with early language disorders develop intelligible speech and use words and sentences in a way not readily noticed by others. Some of them, however, continue to struggle. The majority of children with distinct language disorders at the age of 7 continue to show language problems at the age of 11 (Conti-Ramsden et al., 2001). Additionally, the demands on language increase over time, although less attention is given to language development during

school age (Hollands et al., 2005). Lesser cognitive and language impairments are "invisible" and can be difficult to detect without thorough assessment (Im-Bolter and Cohen, 2007). Language comprehension forms the basis for learning, and undiscovered language disorders can have a major impact on the ability to learn at school. A school environment adapted to the child's abilities can be crucial for developing language and taking full advantage of school.

In adolescence, peer conversations become more central and children with early language disorders may need language support when they reach this age (Clark et al., 2007). Research thus shows that it is essential to follow up all children with moderate or severe language disorders during preschool, when they start school, and throughout school age, even when their speech seems relatively unimpaired once they start in school. Not all children will show persistent problems, but the probability is high enough for all of them to be followed up.

Language disorders and emotional and behavioral disorders

Children with language and communication disorders experience many difficult situations. When adults meet a toddler, they typically say *hi*, ask the child for his name or say something else that requires a response from the child. When the child has delayed language, this implies focusing on the child's difficulties and may contribute to making the child more anxious in interaction with other people. Delayed language development often receives a great deal of attention in the early years, and many parents of children who struggle with language spend a lot of time trying to get their child to repeat words and sentences after them, and to name people and things. This type of "training" often has little effect and may be experienced as pressure by children. Although parents generally are positive communication partners for their children, it is better to let a professional assume the responsibility for activities that may take the form of training. Parents and others in the child's immediate environment may be guided to encourage what the child is able to do instead of focusing on the delayed development of speech. Some children develop selective mutism, meaning that they only speak at home and with their immediate family (see p. 66), and many of them had delayed language development and speech that was difficult for others to understand when they were younger. Although they now have no problems making themselves understood, they do not talk outside the home or with children and adults outside the family (Cline and Baldwin, 2004; Scott and Beidel, 2011). Studies show that selective mutism is more frequent among children in immigrant families, reflecting that the change of language and environment implied in immigration may represent social stress for some children (Muris and Ollendick, 2015).

In addition to the many frustrating situations experienced by children with language disorders, their language problems make it difficult for them to communicate and process problematic experiences. Some react with aggression and by acting out, others become anxious and withdrawn; and some show both internalizing and externalizing behavior (Bornstein et al., 2013). Studies have found that children with language disorders have a higher incidence of mental health problems than those with normal language development, and that children with mental disorders have a higher incidence of language impairments (Im-Bolter and Cohen, 2007; van Daal et al., 2007). Many adolescents with behavioral disorders have language problems as well, especially in the social use of language (Helland et al., 2014; Lundervold et al., 2008). Research as well as clinical experience demonstrates the central role of language for mental health and the importance of including language assessment and intervention in the measures for children and adolescents with emotional and behavioral problems.

SUMMARY

1 Communication and language distinguish human beings from other species and represent two of the main topics in developmental psychology.

2 In the second half of the first year of life, children gradually pay more attention to where others are looking. *Joint attention* means that two or more people are aware of the same thing and are aware of sharing this attention. Joint attention is independent of modality and provides a necessary foundation for the development of communicative skills and language. Children with *autism spectrum disorder* have difficulties with non-verbal communication and establishing and engaging in joint attention.

3 According to Trevarthen, *primary* and *secondary intersubjectivity* reflect an innate basis for communication. In Bloom's *intentionality model*, humans have an intrinsic motive to create and maintain *intersubjectivity*. Tomasello maintains that communication is rooted in a species-specific ability to understand and convey *intentions* and to cooperate.

4 Early *dialogues* largely take place during play or in the context of *daily routines* and involve *turn-taking* between children and adults.

5 Toward the end of the first year of life, children begin to follow *pointing* and other *deictic gestures*. Some theorists consider pointing to be primarily social, rooted in an innate motive to share knowledge and experiences with others. Others view pointing as a way of obtaining information and an extension of children's early exploration with their fingertips. Imitation does not seem to play a major role in the development of pointing. *Symbolic gestures* appear at the same time as children begin to say their first words and probably have their basis in children's imitation of their parents. Gestures are never completely replaced by words and remain part of the communicative repertoire throughout life.

6 *Nativists* claim that children have an innate *language acquisition device* (LAD) in the form of a *universal grammar*. Language stimulation in itself is too "impoverished" to give rise to language, and children must therefore have an innate mechanism that perceives and processes linguistic stimulation based on a set of grammatical rules. *Behaviorism* explains language acquisition just like any other behavior as the result of conditioning and imitation. *Social*

constructivism views language as a *cultural tool* that children learn to apply within a social framework. By adapting their interaction with children, adults represent a *language acquisition support system*, or *scaffolding*. *Emergentism* explains language development as the result of interaction between cognitive abilities and language experience. The language environment has "rich" enough information to allow children to learn a language. The *usage-based theory* maintains that children construct language by using it for communication; an innate predisposition is associated with communication rather than syntax and grammar. Based on current evidence, it is not possible to determine which of the theories provides the most accurate description of the language development process.

7   Children usually begin to *babble* when they approach the age of 6–7 months, and by 10 months their babbling clearly begins to absorb the sound of the surrounding language. Children learn to differentiate, recognize and produce precisely those *speech sounds that distinguish meaning* in the language(s) they grow up with.

8   Children *comprehend* some words before they begin to speak. They usually *produce* their first words around the age of 1 year, with major variation. Toward the end of the second year, their vocabulary rapidly increases. Following the *vocabulary spurt*, children learn between 5.5 and 9 new words per day.

9   The first time children hear a new word, they must *fast map* it, form an assumption about its meaning in order to recognize and use the word later. Early in development, children use words both in a broader sense (overextension) and in a narrower sense (underextension) than adults.

10 Infants spend a lot of time exploring the environment and often ask adults what things are called. Some children's early vocabulary contains many object words, while others have a more expressive early vocabulary. Object words usually make up less than half of children's vocabulary in the second year of life. Other important word classes are verbs and adjectives. Function words are related to sentence formation and many of them are acquired relatively late. Later language development is characterized by the increasing use of *metaphors* and other *figurative language*.

11 The transition from single- to multi-word utterances is the most important qualitative change in language development. Children understand *multi-word utterances* before they themselves begin to produce them. Initially, children use *successive single-word utterances* that are thematically related but not linked together by an intonation contour. As inter-word pauses get progressively shorter, more words fall within the same intonation contour. *Verbs* represent an early conceptual framework for constructing sentences since they implicitly involve someone performing an action and someone or something acting as recipient. *Formulas* turn into more abstract sentence structures. *Complex sentences* are first constructed by combining sentence types that previously were expressed separately. Once children are well on their way to using sentences, they begin to *inflect* words and use function words such as *above* and *below*.

12 Conversation skills include taking initiative, responding, taking turns, clarifying misunderstandings and ending the conversation. Adults guide children's early conversations and support the child's participation. As they grow older, children's contributions become more equal and they become better at resolving misunderstandings, but they continue to have difficulty maintaining long-term focus on a single topic.

13 At an early age, children begin to construct *narratives* and share events they have experienced. The stories of younger children generally describe physical attributes, while descriptions of the characters' thoughts, feelings and motives are rare even among 5- to 6-year-olds. With age, narratives become more coherent, detailed and evaluative.

Continued

14 When adults talk to young infants and young children, they use short utterances and simple sentence structures with clear pronunciation and a somewhat lighter vocal register than in speech directed at adults. However, the characteristics of *child-directed speech* have not been found to be essential for language development. *Variation sets* in adults' language directed at young children demonstrate that children draw on information from different sources when learning to express themselves through language.

15 Girls generally have somewhat better language skills than boys. This is particularly evident during school age, but some differences can be observed as early as preschool age. Parents speak differently to boys and to girls starting at an early age.

16 Multilingual development is common. Children with *bilingual first language acquisition* or *early second language acquisition* must learn the phonetic systems of both languages, learn which words correspond to each other in the two languages, and when to use them. Early in life, this is no more difficult than learning a single language, but children's competence in each language depends on how much it is used. Many bilingual children develop a flexibility in solving problems and thinking creatively.

17 Language can be acquired in different modalities. The development of *sign language* follows the same principles as the development of speech, although its grammar and sentence structure are quite different.

18 Some children with motor impairments, autism spectrum disorder, intellectual disability or severe language disorders have difficulty acquiring spoken language normally, even if they grow up in an adequate language environment and receive speech therapy. Intervention with manual signs and graphic symbols may give them new possibilities for communication and support their development of speech.

19 Language disorders will influence children's learning and development, whether they develop spoken language or sign language. Problems with comprehension are more critical than problems involving expressive language only. Children with language impairments are vulnerable to developing dyslexia. Early intervention is important and with age, most children with language disorders develop relatively inconspicuous language skills. However, some adolescents need additional language support and reduced language understanding may be a major hindrance to their academic success at school.

20 Children with language and communication disorders experience many difficult situations and are vulnerable for developing mental health problems. Children with mental disorders have a higher incidence of language disorders than other children.

CORE ISSUES

- The emergence of communication.
- The biological and experiential bases of language.
- The functions of child-directed speech.
- The influence of non-vocal language on speech development.

SUGGESTIONS FOR FURTHER READING

Bialystok, E., Craik, F. I., Green, D. W., & Gollan, T. H. (2009). Bilingual minds. *Psychological Science in the Public Interest, 10,* 89–129.

Carpendale, J. I., & Carpendale, A. B. (2010). The development of pointing: From personal directedness to interpersonal direction. *Human Development, 53,* 110–126.

Im-Bolter N., & Cohen, N. J. (2007). Language impairment and psychiatric comorbidities. *Pediatric Clinics of North America, 54,* 525–542.

Kuhl, P. K. (2004). Early language acquisition: Cracking the speech code. *Nature Reviews Neuroscience, 5,* 831–843.

MacWhinney, B. (2004). A multiple process solution to the logical problem of language acquisition. *Journal of Child Language, 31,* 883–914.

Naber, F. B. A., Bakermans-Kranenburg, M. J., van IJzendoorn, M. H., Dietz, C., van Daalen, E., Swinkels, S. H. N., Buitelaar, J. K., & van Engeland, H. (2008). Joint attention development in toddlers with autism. *European Child and Adolescent Psychiatry, 17,* 143–152.

Tardif, T., Fletcher, P., Liang, W., Zhang, Z., Kaciroti, N., & Marchman, V. A. (2008). Baby's first 10 words. *Developmental Psychology, 44,* 929–938.

Tomasello, M. (2005). Beyond formalities: The case of language acquisition. *The Linguistic Review, 22,* 183–197.

Zevenbergen, A. A., Holmes, A., Haman, E., Whiteford, N., & Thielges, S. (2016). Variability in mothers' support for preschoolers' contributions to co-constructed narratives as a function of child age. *First Language, 36,* 601–616.

Contents

CHAPTER 17

EMOTIONS AND EMOTION REGULATION

E motions are part of the basic equipment that allows human beings to understand and act in a social world. Children become aware of other people's emotions early in life, showing signs of happiness when they can play and be silly, or getting angry or upset when they cannot have a toy they want or when they see someone get hurt. They can be proud or ashamed of something they have done. Children who are upset look for someone to comfort them; happy children look for playmates or others who can share their happiness. Children who feel ashamed often react by withdrawing, while proud children seek interaction and recognition. Emotional development deals with the types of emotions children understand and express at different ages, and their ability to gradually adapt their emotional expressions and actions to different activities and social contexts.

EMOTIONS

There is no generally accepted definition of "emotion," but it is commonly agreed that emotions include feeling states as a reaction to an event or the result of evaluating a past or present situation or event, including social cues from others (Camras and Shuster, 2013). Emotions are comprised of seven key elements: *expression* includes facial and other gestures, posture, movements, vocalization and linguistic content. *Understanding* is the recognition of emotional expressions in other people. *Experience* is the conscious recognition of one's own emotions,

while *bodily responses* include changes in heart rate, skin temperature, and the like. Fear, for example, results in increased heart rate, shortness of breath and sweating, while shame can lead to a lower heart rate and blushing. *Direction* reflects the fact that emotions always are directed *at* something, such as being in love or angry with someone, being afraid of something or someone, and so on. *Action* means that emotions activate and govern human actions toward or away from something. Happiness serves to maintain an individual's activity, while anger can lead to attempts at overcoming obstacles. *Regulation* involves adaptation to a given situation by modifying one's emotional experience or expression and related actions.

Primary emotions are associated with evaluating an entire situation or specific aspects of it, and include joy, sadness, fear and anger. *Secondary* or *self-referential* emotions are rooted in self-perception and an individual's evaluation according to a personal standard, and include pride, shame, embarrassment, guilt and envy. *Relational emotions*, such as love, hate and jealousy, are directed at others. They will be discussed in Chapter 19.

Reason and emotion are often seen as opposites, but there is no absolute dividing line between emotional and cognitive development. Any emotional response implies an appraisal of the situation – whether it is safe or dangerous, gives reason for concern or joy, and so on (Moors et al., 2013). In order for children to make such evaluations, they must have knowledge of their physical and social environment.

EMOTION REGULATION

Emotion regulation refers to the monitoring and control of one's own emotional experiences and expressions, and the ability to adapt them to one's personal goals and socio-cultural conditions (Campos et al., 1989). Although traditionally it has been common to distinguish between *generating* and *regulating* emotions as two processes with a different neurological basis (Gross and Barrett, 2011), both perceived emotion and emotional expression will depend on the context, one's own preparedness for what will or will not happen, and how well one knows and masters the situation. An emotional expression in itself will thus always be the result of regulation (Campos et al., 2004; Kappas, 2011; Thompson, 2011).

Hence, self-regulation can occur before, during or after an emotion has come to expression and can include the emotion itself, its particular expression and its intensity. Behavior is regulated by adapting emotional expressions and actions to the situation. A child may show less anger, suppress a smile or tears, or refrain from taking an attractive toy. Children can avoid or seek out emotional situations, or someone can prepare them for what is about to happen, such as a blood test, in order to avoid an excessively strong emotional reaction. New and unexpected events will generally elicit stronger emotions than events that are expected, but in some cases, expectations about an emotionally positive or negative event can amplify the child's reactions. Children's expectations about their own birthday, for example, often lead to increasing emotional arousal as the day approaches. As children grow older, their development goes from seeking protection and help from adults to regulating their own emotional state and seeking help from peers (see Figure 17.1), but most people faced with a difficult situation will seek help from others throughout life.

Many studies focus on children's ability to control anxiety, anger and similar emotions, but regulation is more than control. Emotions and regulation strategies are neither good nor bad in themselves but depend on the context. Even strong negative emotions can be adaptive if the child is facing a threatening or dangerous situation. Both over control and under control lead to a more limited emotional repertoire and poorer emotion regulation in children (see p. 389). The goal of regulation is adaptation, but the process can lead to maladaptation when children make the wrong connections between emotions, cognition and actions. In such cases, the developmental outcome can be emotional or behavioral disorders.

CULTURAL DIFFERENCES

The issue of universal emotions and cultural differences is central to an understanding of emotional development. Some emotions, such as fear of dangerous animals, are probably universal in the sense that they share the same type of expression and are triggered by similar situations in all cultures. Other, more complex emotions are likely to be culturally determined. There are significant cultural differences in regard to the types of expressions that are used, the extent to which emotions are valued, and the ways in which children are expected to show emotions and regulate them at different ages (Halberstadt and Lozada, 2011; Keller and Otto, 2009), for example between Cameroon and Germany (Figure 17.2).

For example, the function of anger is to overcome obstacles in order to achieve goals and how and when anger is accepted varies between cultures. Inappropriate anger may repel others and it is therefore an important developmental task

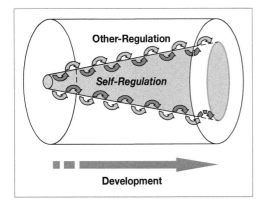

FIGURE 17.1 From other-regulation to self-regulation. Early in development, children need a great deal of external help to regulate their emotions. With age, they steadily improve at self-regulation, but even adults may need external help when their stress levels are high (based on Sameroff and Fiese, 2000, p. 6).

Children express a variety of emotions, some shy, others direct.

to learn to express anger in culturally acceptable ways (Lemerise and Harper, 2010), as illustrated in Box 17.1.

The cultural differences are noticeable early on. In an experimental study, 11-month-old Japanese children waited on average for 48 seconds before approaching an attractive toy after their mothers had said something with an angry voice. American children waited for 18 seconds. When the mother's voice expressed joy or fear, there were no differences between the children (Miyaki et al., 1986). The results reflect

that Japanese mothers protect their children against expressions of anger, especially in public places. The Japanese children were not accustomed to these types of expressions and reacted more strongly to them than US children, who were more accustomed to anger. Another experiment showed stronger negative emotions among German than Japanese 5-year-olds when an adult hindered them from reaching a goal – took away a puzzle before the children were done with it (Holodynski and Friedlmeier, 2006). Differences go beyond Eastern and Western

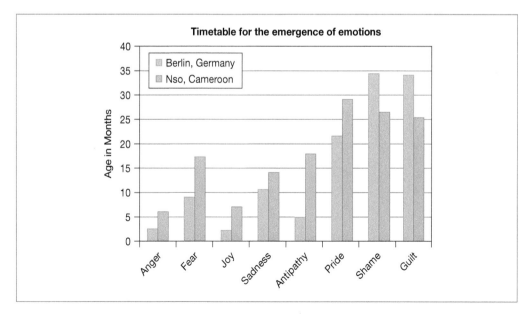

FIGURE 17.2 Mothers in Germany and Cameroon expect their children to show particular emotions at different ages (after Keller and Otto, 2009, p. 1002).

BOX 17.1 CHILD ANGER IN DIFFERENT CULTURES

The Yanomami tribe in northern Brazil raises children to develop anger and aggression. Among the Inuit in Arctic regions of America, children show little anger after the age of 6. In Kenya, Kipsigi children are raised not to show pain or grief. Children of the Tamang people in Eastern Nepal explained that it is useless to get angry at someone who has done something wrong to them, and that they should instead feel shame. Children of the Brahman tribe in Western Nepal believed anger is acceptable, but should not be shown. Likewise, children in Gujarat in India said they felt anger, grief and pain, but did not express these feelings because others might find it unacceptable. Children in the Northeastern part of the United States said they could both feel and show anger as long as they did so in a socially acceptable way (Cole et al., 2002; Oatley et al., 2006; Raval et al., 2007; Wilson et al., 2012).

cultures, however: Japanese 1-year-olds are more expressive than their Chinese peers (Camras et al., 2003).

The fact that studies have found early differences in emotion regulation among Japanese and American children does not mean that Japanese children merely suppress their *expressions* of anger because showing anger is culturally unacceptable, but that they actually *feel* less anger as a result of cultural influences. Thus, emotional development is part of the enculturation process (Lutz, 1988).

MAIN THEORIES OF EMOTIONAL DEVELOPMENT

Most theories of emotional development are based on Darwin's (1872) hypothesis that the emotional expressions of human beings are the result of evolutionary adaptation. According to *differential emotions theory* children begin with two innate forms of *general arousal*: one that may be called "discomfort" or "restlessness," and another that may be called "comfort" or "contentment." These arousals are divided into progressively more demarcated and structurally consistent emotions. Crying and smiling can be seen as part of a warning system that, from the moment of birth, signals important changes in the child or the environment, and may involve

discomfort, contentment or danger for the child and caregiver (Mayer and Salovey, 1997). Early emotional expressions are primarily the result of *physiological* reactions. Over time, they are increasingly driven by *psychological* factors, meaning that emotions are governed by the child's evaluation of people and events in the environment. Children's evaluations change in line with their general cognitive and social development and are determined by their experiences and the cultural meaning they have learned to attribute to different events (Camras, 2011; Sroufe, 1996; Thompson, 2011).

Theories of *discrete emotions* are based on the assumption that human beings have a set of basic innate emotions that are activated early on and appear quickly and automatically (see Table 17.1). According to Izard (2007), children are unable to regulate their emotional expressions in the first 6 months of life, as they are triggered almost reflexively. However, children and adults rarely have a need for spontaneous and automatic reactions. Gradually, children learn to distinguish feelings and facial expressions and become better able to modify their own emotions and expressions, while the importance of the basic emotions decreases as a result of maturation, emotional enculturation, cognitive development and social learning. This process gains momentum as children begin to talk and develop more advanced cognitive skills (Izard et al., 2002).

TABLE 17.1 Basic emotions according to Izard (based on Tomkins and McCarter (1964); Izard (2007))

Emotion	Description
Interest	Eyebrows down, eyes track, look, listen
Enjoyment, joy	Smile, lips widened up and out, smiling eyes (circular wrinkles)
Grief	Arched eyebrows, mouth down, tears, rhythmic sobbing
Anger	Frown, clenched jaw, eyes narrowed, red face
Disgust	Sneer, upper lip up
Fear	Eyes frozen open, pale, cold, sweaty, facial trembling, with hair erect

According to Izard's theory, children are born with a system of emotions that lays the foundation for experiencing and expressing a number of basic emotions. This system gradually undergoes change and transformation as children consciously and non-consciously learn to adapt their emotional states and expressions to the situation. In contrast to theories of differential emotions, discrete emotions are indivisible but can be *combined* into more complex emotions (Camras, 2011; Camras and Shutter, 2010).

From a *behaviorist* point of view, crying and smiling are innate physiological reactions to certain events, such as loss of a supporting surface, hunger, loud sounds or pain. In *classical conditioning*, neutral stimuli are associated with stimuli that trigger emotional responses, causing the neutral stimuli to elicit more differentiated emotional responses (see p. 285). Consequently, emotional development is the result of a differential response (Schlinger, 1995). In one of developmental psychology's most widely discussed experiments, 9-month-old Albert was exposed to an extremely loud sound while playing with a white rat. The sound was intended as an unconditioned stimulus that would elicit fear, leading Albert to associate the rat with the sound and in turn become afraid of the rat (Watson and Rayner, 1920). The results, however, are unclear, and it is uncertain whether Albert actually developed a fear of rats and similar animals (Griggs, 2015; Harris, 1979).

Functionalist theories focus on the relationship between emotions and the "object" at which they are directed. Often, this can be another person, and development reflects the changes in children's goals and ability to regulate their emotions and the social environment. The purpose of emotions is to maintain or change critical aspects of the child's inner state or the environment, and preparing for action is part of the emotion itself (Barrett and Campos, 1987; Campos et al., 2010, 2011).

EARLY EMOTIONAL DEVELOPMENT

Human beings show emotions in different ways, such as by vocalizing or sweating, but above all by movements of the mouth and eyebrows (Figure 17.3). As they develop, children's comprehension and production of emotions change, as well as the situations in which emotions are used, and the way in which they are perceived by others.

Emotional expressions

Positive emotions

Smiling is the first expression of contentment and joy, and a *reflexive smile* is present from birth. The *social smile*, characterized by open eyes and a focused gaze, usually occurs for the first time when children are 6 to 10 weeks old. Reflexive smiles and social smiles have different social consequences: parents tend to interpret the reflexive smile as an expression of the child's physiological state, while the social smile is seen as an expression of the feelings experienced by the child. Many parents report that the social smile, together with eye contact, represented the first clue that their child looked at them with interest, so that they themselves began to look at their child as a person (Freedman, 1974; Wolff, 1963).

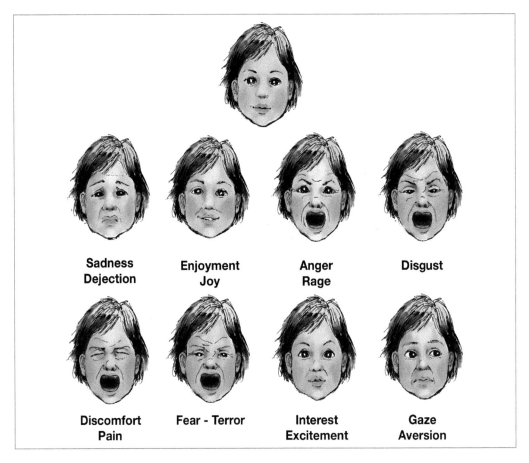

FIGURE 17.3 Some emotional expressions in children.

Early smiles are most easily elicited when the infant is awake and inactive. At the end of the neonatal period, infants also begin to smile in response to external stimulation. They smile when they *recognize* something, such as a colorful toy or a familiar voice. In the first 6 weeks, infants smile more at voices than at faces, and more at hearing the voice of their mother than that of a stranger. At 3 months, the maternal voice is no longer enough. The sound of her voice leads infants to search for her face, and their smile first appears once they have found it (Sroufe, 1996; Wolff, 1963, 1966).

Both people and interesting objects can elicit early infant smiles. Three-month-olds smile most during interaction with others, and there is little difference between familiar and unfamiliar faces. At 5–6 months, regardless of the situation, a stranger will no longer elicit a smile, and if the stranger's face shows no expression, children begin to look worried. Eight-month-olds smile when they see their mother looking at them from a distance, but not when she is reading and not looking at them. In other words, the sight of the mother's face is not enough for children at this age to smile – they must perceive that they have her attention as well (Jones and Hong, 2005).

Infants also smile when they *master* something. Two- to 8-month-olds smiled more often in response to a music box playing a tune when they moved their foot (a ribbon attached to their foot activated the music box) than same-age children who heard the music box just as often, but independent of their own actions (Lewis et al., 1990).

Although the development of smiling does not depend on visual stimulation, a lack of visual stimulation leads to delayed development. Blind

Smiles express joy.

children smile before the age of 3 months, but their smile has a reflexive quality and differs from the smiles of sighted infants of the same age. Their smiles are more difficult to elicit and seem vague and unclear. A prolonged and distinct smile that corresponds to the social smile of sighted children first appears at the age of 6 months (Fraiberg, 1971; Freedman, 1964). Also deafblind children show a variation in emotional expression, but to a lesser degree than sighted children (Eibl-Eibesfeldt, 1973). The fact that children who are unable to see the emotional expressions of others still develop the same types of expressions indicates the presence of a relatively specific genetic basis for expression.

Laughter appears in the first months of life and already then closely resembles that of adults (Kawakami et al., 2006; Sroufe and Waters, 1976). Children often laugh in connection with an abrupt change in activity, such as when someone lifts them up into the air or engages them in other romp and play. In the first year of life, a change takes place in what makes children laugh. Initially, tactile stimulation is most effective, but gradually, social and humorous visual stimulation is most likely to elicit laughter (Sroufe, 1996).

Negative emotions

Crying is the first expression interpreted as distress and discomfort. In newborns, crying is asso-

ciated with high levels of physiological activation and can be triggered by internal and external stimulation. Sound, visual stimulation and room temperature, among other things, can affect how much or how little a child cries. To begin with, crying is acoustically quite uniform, and parents often do not know what it means. During the first weeks of life, crying becomes more varied in its sound patterns and subject to more varied interpretations. There is a certain relationship between the sound of the crying and how it is interpreted, but parents tend to focus on its possible cause, with major differences in whether they believe children cry because they long for company or because they are being difficult or unreasonable (Newson and Newson, 1965). Changes in crying patterns are not only the result of maturation but also of changes in the activities children participate in. The enculturation of crying starts early.

The earliest signs of *fear* in infants are interpreted based on facial expressions and crying. Although newborns blink reflexively when an object approaches, this is hardly an expression of fear. It is not until the age of 8–9 months that children begin to show defensive reactions, an increase in heart rate and other signs of fear in situations that could reasonably be thought to cause the child to be afraid. This development is generally attributed to maturation, since children at this age have no experience with being struck by objects. At about 5 months of age, many infants begin to show fear of strangers. They are now better able to distinguish between familiar and unfamiliar, and it is the unfamiliar itself infants react to, since they usually have no previous experience that could give rise to fear of strangers. They also begin to show fear of loud noises, heights, masks and unfamiliar toys (Scarr and Salapatek, 1970).

It is during early childhood that children show most fear of things. Their fear response is strongest at the end of the second year, after which it decreases, but fear of loud noises and unfamiliar toys, for example, begins to decline in the beginning or middle of the second year. At the same time, there is considerable variation between individuals: some children easily respond with fear, others seem fearless. Individual variation also vary across situations. "Strong" fear-eliciting situations trigger fear in nearly all children, while fear responses in "weak" situations differ depending on the children's experiences. For example, children show little reaction to strangers when engaged in free play, while many will respond with fear to a remote-controlled robot or spider. Children who respond to non-threatening situations with fear are often socially reticent (Buss and McDoniel, 2016; Mischel et al., 2002).

Ethologists (see p. 29) point out that fear is determined by nature as well as culture (Hinde, 1992). This is illustrated in a study where 7–18-month-olds were shown two films at the same time, one with a snake and one with another exotic animal. They looked longer at a film of a snake when they heard a fearful voice than when the voice had a happy character. Without voice-over, they looked equally long at the snake film as other animal films (DeLoache and LoBue, 2009). This demonstrated a special attention to snakes with fearful voices, but not that fear of snakes was innate. In a similar study, infants did not demonstrate accelerated heart rate or a large startle magnitude when they saw the snake film, which are usual physiological reactions indicating fear. However, the special attention to snakes may make children prepared for learning fast to be afraid of snakes (Thrasher and LoBue, 2016). In ethological theory, fear of snakes has evolutionary survival value and is therefore easily established, but also depends on specific experiences (Hinde, 1992).

Early in children's lives, parents also interpret crying as an expression of *anger*, for example when the child cries after losing a pacifier, although clear expressions of anger do not usually show up until the age of 4–6 months. Infants typically show anger when they are impeded in their

movements or when parents and other adults do not fulfill their expectations, such as taking an object they are sucking on from their mouth (Stenberg et al., 1983). Pain can lead to expressions of anger as well (Izard et al., 1987). In the course of toddlerhood, parents show increasingly less tolerance for expressions of anger and try to get children to regulate their emotions according to the cultural standards by "labeling" their expressions, diverting their attention, and similar strategies (Lemerise and Dodge, 2008).

There is less research on *sadness* and *grief* than on discomfort, anger and fear. A possible reason for this may be that sadness is not always linked to a specific aspect of a situation but appears to be more of a basic mood. Children are perceived as sad when they show little facial expression, activity and positive response. This can for example be observed in 3-month-olds who are separated from their caregiver and in infants who live in orphanages with little social stimulation. From an ethological perspective, sadness is associated with loss or expected loss of a loved one (Bowlby, 1980). Sadness reduces children's activity level and preserves their energy in situations in which the caregiver is not available to protect them (LaFreniere, 2000). Children can also show sadness when the people in their environment fail to be emotionally responsive to them. Children of depressed mothers, for example, appear sadder or more despondent than other children.

Distinguishing between early emotional expressions

Infants' earliest facial expressions can be difficult to differentiate. Although they often resemble the emotional expressions of adults, they do not always occur in relevant situations and observers may be uncertain as to their interpretation (Camras and Shutter, 2010). One study observed 10- to 12-month-olds in situations designed to elicit joy (playing with an interesting toy), fear (being placed near a visual cliff) and surprise (seeing an object "disappear"). The happy situation almost exclusively elicited expressions of joy. The fear situation elicited a greater amount of fearful expressions than the other situations, in addition to many other emotional expressions. Although the infants showed more surprise than any other emotion in the surprising situation, surprise was just as frequent in the other

Crying is a clear emotional expression but it is not always easy to find the cause.

situations (Hiatt et al., 1979). Other studies have found that infants show approximately the same facial expression in situations designed to elicit fear or anger (Camras and Witherington, 2005).

There is little doubt that children have a number of innate emotional expressions, as demonstrated by observations of blind children (see p. 345). However, the expressions of newborns do not reflect any expectations. It takes several months for emotions to gain more direction and content and for infants to begin to expect certain reactions from the environment (Emde, 1992; Sroufe, 1996). This means that infants' repertoire of facial expressions gradually finds application and meaning, counter to Izard's assumption that children are born with a limited number of discrete emotional expressions. Instead, the results indicate that children start with relatively undifferentiated states of arousal and that the various emotional expressions initially reflect differences in intensity only (Camras, 2011; Oster et al., 1992). Perhaps they represent a form of "emotional babbling" on the way to a broader emotional repertoire.

Children must be able to adapt to the possibilities as well as the dangers of their environment. They need both the motivation to explore and a set of reactions to possible dangers ranging from caution to escape. Fear of steep cliffs or unknown predators (enemies in the environment) cannot be learned by trial and error. Children would have fallen down the cliff or been devoured before they had the chance to learn how to avoid these dangers. At the same time, it would be unfeasible to maintain a repertoire of hundreds of specific reactions that nonetheless would be insufficient to cover all the environmental dangers a child may face. This means that an *open dynamic system*, along with a handful of action tendencies capable of providing new responses quickly, affords the best adaptation to the environment. A key element of such a system is the ability to learn from the emotional expressions of others. This requires children to quickly develop an understanding of a number of relatively unambiguous emotional expressions.

Understanding emotional expressions in others

The perception of emotions involves the ability to *detect*, *differentiate* and *recognize* expressions, that is, to ascribe value or meaning to them in a given context, and decide a course of action (Walker-Andrews, 1997; Walle and Campos, 2012). Initially, the perception of emotional expressions is *global*, since children have not yet learned to distinguish between different contextual elements. Over time, they perceive emotions as more *referential* (directed at a particular aspect of the situation) and linked to specific types of situations.

Voices

At birth, hearing is more developed than vision, and vocal emotional expressions attract more attention than facial expressions during early development. Hearing does not need to be focused in the same way as vision, and acoustic stimulation is suitable for waking up children as well as to capture their attention. Three-month-olds dishabituate to a happy voice after habituation to a sad voice, but they first dishabituate to a happy face after having habituated to a sad face at the age of 5 months (Caron et al., 1988). This indicates that the voice represents an earlier cue to emotional information than the face.

Around the age of 3 months, infants look for their mother's face when they hear her voice, but do not associate facial expressions with the voice until later. Seven-month-old children, unlike children 4 months younger, spent more time looking at a video with a correspondence between vocal emotional content and facial expression than at a video in which voice and face expressed different emotions (Walker-Andrews, 1986). Infants thus are more attentive to emotional expressions that are presented synchronously in different modalities (see also p. 144).

Facial expressions

The recognition of facial expressions undergoes a gradual development in the first 2 years of life. Field and colleagues (1982) found that 2-day-old children responded differently to faces showing joy, surprise and grief, while Farroni and colleagues (2007) found that 1-day-old children discriminated between a happy and a fearful facial expression, but not between a fearful and a neutral face. This suggests a certain ability to discriminate facial expressions, but also shows that they must be quite dissimilar for newborn infants to notice the difference. Three-month-olds are able to differentiate faces with different intensities of the same emotion, such as a smiling face (Bornstein and Arterberry, 2003; Kuchuk et al., 1986).

Around the age of 5 months, children begin to distinguish between sad, fearful and angry facial expressions (Schwartz et al., 1985). Seven-month-olds generally look longer at a fearful face than a happy one, but reactions are *asymmetrical*: after habituation to a happy face, 7-month-olds dishabituated to a face showing fear, but did not dishabituate to a face showing joy or astonishment after habituation to a fearful face (Nelson and de Haan, 1997). These results suggest that fearful facial expressions have greater attention value than faces showing joy. One possible explanation may be that children have an innate tendency to perceive a fearful face as a danger signal. A more likely explanation is that infants generally have far more experience with happy than with fearful faces, and that they spend more time looking at what is least familiar. Infants at this age rarely see their mothers showing negative facial expressions (Malatesta and Haviland, 1982).

Children's perception of emotional expressions remains limited throughout the first year, and expressions need to be distinct. Ten-month-olds dishabituated to more mixed positive expressions following habituation to prototypically happy expressions, but not vice versa (Ludemann, 1991). This probably reflects the categories the children formed during habituation to facial expressions. When they were shown only typical expressions of joy, they formed a narrow category and dishabituated to mixed facial expressions because they perceived them as novel. After habituation to more mixed expressions, however, they formed a broader category that also could include typical happy expressions. They failed to dishabituate because they did not perceive the typical happy expressions as a change in stimulation (see p. 46). The results of these studies show that early emotional perception is not exclusively governed by a biologically predetermined course of development, but a process based on experience.

Imitation of emotional expressions

It is generally agreed that children are able to perceive and produce emotional facial expressions early on; there is considerable disagreement about *when* children begin to imitate the expressions they observe in others (see also p. 350). According to Field and colleagues (1982) 2-day-old infants showed evidence of imitating some aspects of happy, sad and surprised facial expressions. The infants reacted with eye and mouth widening more often when the face showed surprise than when it showed one of the other two emotions, lip tightening when they saw a sad face, and lip widening when they saw a smile. Since 2 days is unlikely to be enough to learn to recognize facial expressions, Field interprets the results to suggest a connection between newborn infants' systems for perception and action, for example in the form of a mirror neuron system (see p. 112).

However, other researchers have pointed out that Field's study does not necessarily demonstrate imitation but only the fact that the adult expressions elicited an emotional response in the infants (Anisfeld, 2005; Kaitz et al., 1988; Ray and Heyes, 2011). The children's reactions may rather reflect the same type of emotional "contagion" that leads newborns to cry when they hear other infants cry (Geangu et al., 2010). In line with this, Provine (1997) describes this type of response as a preparation for later imitation of emotional expressions. Contrary to this view, Meltzoff (1993) maintains that infants do not only imitate the expressions, imitation leads the infants to experience the emotion that corresponds to the expression they are imitating. Meltzoff thus views imitation as the underlying mechanism for emotional contagion, rather than emotional contagion as the basis for imitation, as Provine argues.

Meltzoff and Moore (1999) suggest that the imitation of emotional expressions and other facial movements leads children to discover they are human beings: infants' sense of human identity is strengthened when they experience belonging to the ones "who do like that with their faces." Furthermore, imitation leads to recognition and affection between parent and child and, from an evolutionary point of view, increases the likelihood of children being cared for and surviving. Parents often imitate the facial expressions of their child, usually with some form of variation. In the first 12 months, parents actually imitate their child more often than the child imitates them. Positive emotional expressions in particular are subject to imitation, while the child's negative emotions are often overlooked or met with a different emotion, such as concern and interest in response to the child's anger (Ray and Heyes, 2011; Lemerise and Dodge, 2008).

Emotion regulation

In early infancy, children lack the cognitive and neurological prerequisites to regulate their innate emotional expressions (Izard, 1991). They need help calming down but also to learn how to calm down without the help of others, a process that begins at birth when parents respond to the infant's signals and offer comfort (Kopp, 1989). In early infancy, parents establish routines to avoid sudden shifts in the child's state and help regulate the child's level of arousal by interpreting the child's signals and adjusting stimulation to a suitable level. Stern (1998) uses the term *affect attunement* to describe adults' adjustment of emotional actions and expressions to those of the child, like in this example (p. 207):.

A nine-month-old boy bangs his hand on a soft toy, at first in some anger but gradually with pleasure, exuberance, and humor. He sets up a steady rhythm. Mother falls into his rhythm and says, "kaaaaa-bam, kaaaaa-bam," the "bam" falling on the stroke and the "kaaaaa" riding with the preparatory upswing and the suspenseful holding of his arm aloft before it falls.

The mother "reformulates" the child's emotional actions. According to Stern, affect attunement helps children understand the emotions that underlie actions (see also p. 439).

With age, children learn to delay as well as to moderate their expressions. Delaying an emotional response is the first step on the way to emotion regulation, a window of time that allows perceptual and cognitive processes to affect the perceived emotion and expression, and reduce excessive stimulation. Six-month-olds, for example, show less distress when, after a little while, they stop looking at a toy fire truck with flashing lights and blaring sirens that they see for the first time (Crockenberg and Leerkes, 2006). An infant who smiles and interacts with the mother may turn away from the mother for a short moment to moderate his emotional arousal and subsequently turn back to continue the interaction with the mother. Sucking on the thumb is an early form of emotional self-regulation that helps children calm down (Saarni et al., 2006). Adults contribute to expanding children's repertoire by allowing them to perceive the state of their own body and form simple patterns of behavior. Without the help of adults to regulate their emotions, children experience discomfort and emotional disorganization (Field, 1994).

Parents are often worried they might "spoil" their children by picking them up when they cry and cause them to cry more often, that picking up will function as a reinforcer and increase crying, as might be expected based on behaviorist theories (see p. 23). However, a classic study found that infants whose mothers responded quickly to their child's crying during the first half year cried less during the second half (Bell and Ainsworth, 1972). This means that a quick response to children's expression of discomfort did not cause them to be "spoiled" and more demanding. Instead, the results indicate that the maternal responsiveness helped the children learn to cope with the causes of their crying. They appeared less overwhelmed by emotions, managed to regulate their own emotions, and cried less. Moreover, the decrease in crying allowed the children more time to become familiar with other activities, sounds and movements. When the mothers waited longer, the intensity of the crying tended to increase and it was more difficult to calm the infants down (Thompson, 1991).

Social referencing

Children react to the emotional expressions of others early on, and toward the end of their first year of life children begin to use other expressions of people as a cue to how they themselves should feel, think and act in unfamiliar and insecure situations. *Emotional social referencing* means that children use the emotional content of other people's expressions as cues for their own feelings in a given situation. *Instrumental referencing* involves using others as a cue to how they themselves should act in a situation. Social referencing provides children with information they cannot extract from the situation itself based on their own experience alone (Feinman et al., 1992). Thus, in these situations children do not try to identify other people's emotions to find out how others feel, but to find out more about their own current situation.

In a classic study of social referencing in 12-month-olds, the infants used the mother's emotional expression to guide them in an uncertain situation (Box 17.2). A similar study found that children crawled across faster when the mother smiled *and* spoke positively than when she spoke with her back turned so the child could not see

BOX 17.2 VISUAL CLIFF AND SOCIAL REFERENCING (Sorce et al., 1985)

The study utilized a customized version of a visual cliff covered by a glass plate (see p. 128). The cliff was shallow but appeared so deep that several of the 12-month-old children were unsure whether it was dangerous as they were led toward the edge. Many of them looked at their mother, who had been instructed to show expressions of joy, fear, anger, sadness or interest. There was clear relation between the mothers' emotional expressions and the children's actions. When the mothers showed fear, none of the 17 children crawled across the drop-off. When they looked angry, 2 of 18 children moved across, while 6 of 18 children crossed the cliff when their mothers looked sad. When the mothers showed interest, 11 of 15 children traversed the cliff, while 14 of 19 children crawled across when their mothers looked happy. The children thus used the mothers' emotional expression as a cue to their safety in an uncertain situation.

Photographs courtesy of Joe Campos.

her face. The children waited the longest time when their mother smiled but did not say anything (Mumme et al., 1996).

Emotional expressions are an important part of children's social world, and many situations involve children's use of emotional information. In one study, 14-month-olds were given either a sad or a fearful message by their mother about a doll who had lost its leg. The children who received a sad message tried to comfort the doll, while the children who received a message accompanied by a fearful expression avoided playing with the doll (Campos et al., 1985). This type of emotional information can affect young children far longer than the situation itself. Eleven- and 14-month-old infants watched an unfamiliar toy out of reach being lowered from the ceiling while the experimenter repeated the nonsense phrase "tat fobble" several times with a voice and a facial expression that expressed either joy or disgust, and then raised the toy to the ceiling again (Hertenstein and Campos, 2004). When the children were allowed to explore the toy an hour later, the 14-month-olds who had heard the voice expressing disgust waited longer before touching the toy than those who had heard the cheerful voice. The 11-month-olds who had been exposed to the disgust condition waited a little longer as well, but the difference from those who had heard the cheerful voice was minor. In other studies, the object exploration of 15- and 18-month-olds was influenced by the observation of a conversation with angry or neutral information not directed at them (Repacholi and Meltzoff, 2007; Repacholi et al., 2014).

The studies show that adults' reactions and attitudes are important for how young children meet new and unfamiliar people and things. Twelve- to 18-month-olds are more kindly disposed to strangers when their parents smile and talk about them in a positive emotional voice. Concerned parents usually have a serious demeanor when their toddler is examined by a doctor. This can lead the child to be reluctant and cry, as the parents' facial expressions are perceived to mean something is wrong with the doctor. Physical exams at the doctor's office may go more smoothly if parents smile and laugh even though they are concerned for their child.

Research on emotional expression has commonly used the child's mother as an emotional reference, but children just as readily follow the father's cues as those of the mother. Siblings, too, can function as a reference when young children feel uncertain (Blackford and Walden, 1998; Hirshberg and Svejda, 1990a, b). In a laboratory environment, 12-month-old infants may spend more time looking at a friendly experimenter than at their own mother (Stenberg, 2009). Thus, children seek emotional information from people they trust, either they are very familiar to the child, or they seem to have control and are part of the situation in which the child finds herself (Walden and Kim, 2005).

The information children gain through social referencing does not alone determine how they relate to new and unfamiliar situations. Some situations are so obviously positive or negative from the child's point of view that no help is needed to define them. Other situations are so unclear that adults represent children's only source of appraisal, but most situations lie somewhere in the middle. Children seek information or use the information adults voluntarily offer to varying degrees. Some may feel uncertain about what to do in a given situation, and some will always act contrary to the information they have been given. In the study involving a visual cliff, five of 19 children did not crawl to their mother when she smiled, and two moved toward her when she looked angry. Some of these differences are due to children's subjective perception of the situation. In addition to individual temperament, children react differently to novelty and unknown things (see p. 370). Earlier experiences can lead to a different perception of the situation as well. Some toddlers, for example, are afraid of Santa Claus in stores at Christmas time, while others readily sit on his lap (Blackford and Walden, 1998).

Although information from adults is important, it is only one of several cues used by children to assess a situation. Sometimes, the temptation to touch and explore something is simply too strong for children, even if their mother has conveyed that it is "dangerous." When this happens, children will occasionally turn to their mother and smile. This is often perceived as defiant or teasing behavior, but the child may just as well intend to reassure the mother and let her know that it was not dangerous after all. Children do not always understand why they are not supposed to touch something, such as an object that easily breaks.

Many 1-year-olds act first and look at their caregiver afterwards. With increasing age, children improve at evaluating new situations and using the emotional information provided by adults. Young toddlers often look at their caregiver before they approach an unfamiliar object. Once they are slightly older, children increasingly ask direct questions to obtain emotional information. Three-year-olds often ask questions

about dangerous things. As children grow older and more independent in their evaluations, "negotiations" about the emotional content of different situations become more common (Walden and Ogan, 1988).

One of the characteristics of emotional referencing is its focus on external circumstances, such as a particular person, object or event. A mere mood change in the child does not qualify as social referencing. The child's feelings must be directed at something the adult has reacted to as well. When an adult shows a particular emotion, the child always seeks to identify the aspect of the situation associated with the emotion. A child who takes the initiative must be able to direct the adult's attention at the element of concern to find out how the adult reacts to this particular element, for example a nearby dog. The principle is the same as for establishing joint attention, which appears around the same age (see p. 299). Occasionally, children can misinterpret the source of the expression of an adult, but in order to be useful at all, social referencing must essentially be secure – information that appears uncertain would undermine its very function. Since children also have to trust the other person, they usually use parents, siblings and other familiar or clearly competent persons for social referencing.

EMOTIONAL DEVELOPMENT IN CHILDHOOD AND ADOLESCENCE

With age children recognize a greater range of emotions and become more familiar with the relationship between emotions and external events, desires and beliefs. At about 3–4 years of age, children are able to name the type of emotions that commonly accompany different situations, and around the age of 5, they begin to gain a broader understanding of the expressions and causes of emotions (Gross and Bailif, 1991; Pons et al., 2004).

Self-referential emotions

Children's emerging recognition of themselves, as a *self-as-known*, or *me*, at the end of the second year (see p. 435) represent the beginning of self-referential (or self-conscious) emotions

(Figure 17.4). These emotions are founded on self-evaluation, personal standards and assumptions about how one is evaluated by others, and are primarily related to social relations (Lagattuta and Thompson, 2007; Zinck, 2008). Emotions based on a personal moral standard are often called *moral emotions* (Dahl et al., 2011; Eisenberg, 2000). Guilt and pride are examples of self-directed emotions that may have their basis in a personal standard, while contempt and disgust are examples of moral emotions that can be directed at others (Tangney et al., 2007; Tracy and Robins, 2004).

Additionally, self-referential emotions have a regulating function. Shame and guilt reduce the likelihood of repeating the action that triggered the emotion, whether it is something unreasonable a child has said or the inability to master a skill that is expected at a certain age. Younger children can feel proud to be able to eat by them-

selves and feel ashamed when they make a mess. At the same time, expressions of guilt and shame show that children have insight into their own actions, and thus reduce the likelihood of negative reactions from others. Pride over good grades will usually increase the time and effort a child spends on homework in the future (Beer and Keltner, 2004).

Pride

Pride is a combination of feeling joy and mastery. In early childhood, pride is a general feeling of doing "well," often as a result of adults' praise or recognition, such as a positive comment about a child's drawing. With age, children begin to develop a personal standard (Sroufe, 1996). Winning a race, for example, increasingly leads to expressions of joy in 2–5-year-olds (Stipek et al., 1992). Pride is associated with achievement.

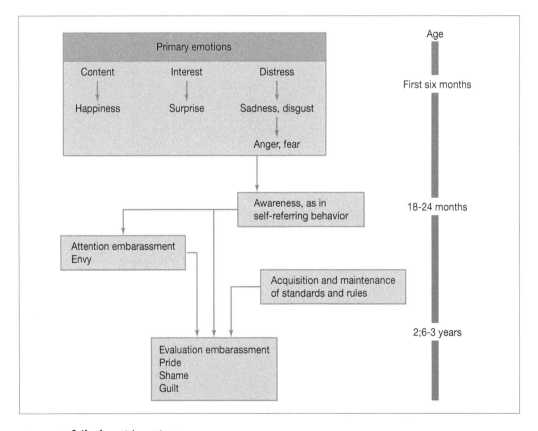

FIGURE 17.4 **Self-referential emotions.**
Early development of self-referential emotions (elaborated from Lewis, 1993, p. 232, 2007, p. 135).

Pride of mastery.

Shame of failure.

Three-year-olds only show pride when they are able to master a task they find difficult, mastery of simple tasks does not lead to expressions of pride (Tracy and Robins, 2007). Children will not feel proud when they are praised for something they have been able to do for a while, but may instead believe that the person praising them has little confidence in their abilities (Dweck, 1999).

The understanding of pride develops somewhat later than the expression of pride. Around the age of 4 years, children begin to recognize pride in the facial expression and posture of others (without supporting situational cues), but until the age of 7, expressions of pride are often perceived as joy. All the way up to the age of 11, children have trouble differentiating between the happiness of getting something they like without having done anything in particular, such as grandpa buying an ice cream, and the pride of getting something after making an effort, such as an award for throwing a ball a long distance after practicing for a long time (Kornilaki and Chlouverakis, 2004; Tracy et al., 2005). The ability to differentiate self-referential emotions thus requires both cognitive skills and social insight.

Shame and guilt

Shame is related to the violation of personal standards. Toddlers only show shame when their wrongdoing is discovered by others. Around 3 years of age, children begin to feel ashamed when they are unable to accomplish a given task. Girls show more shame than boys, but with significant individual differences also early in development. Children who often show shame during preschool age have a tendency to continue to do so at school age as well (Mills, 2003; Mills et al., 2010).

Shame reflects children's perception of how they are evaluated by others. Children who have experienced social trauma or being rejected typically describe feelings of shame. Girls who have been subjected to neglect show less pride when they master something and generally show more shame than girls who have not been victims of neglect. Boys who have been subjected to neglect show less pride as well as shame. Children who have been sexually abused often blame themselves and feel ashamed about the abuse (Mills, 2005).

Guilt is defined as an intense feeling of having transgressed one's own standards. It differs from shame in that it focuses on a failed task rather than a failed self (Lewis, 2007). In one study, the leg of a doll had been attached so it would fall off while 2-year-olds played with it and the experimenter was in another room. Some of the children – the avoiders – reacted in a way similar to shame – they avoided the experimenter when she returned and waited to tell her what had happened. Other children – the amenders – showed more guilt-related behavior; they repaired the doll and promptly told the experimenter about the incident (Barrett et al., 1993). However, most likely, the children's expression of guilt merely reflected their expectations that the adult would scold them or react negatively in other ways. Children usually do not show guilt based on a personal standard until the age of 3–5 years, when they also begin to show signs of a moral standard. Girls' expressions of guilt are more pronounced than those of boys, but only after the age of 3 years (Kochanska et al., 2002). Shame and guilt are complex emotions, and children are well into school age before they are able to distinguish between them based on the underlying events (Ferguson et al., 1991).

Shame and guilt are important for children's social adjustment but can also contribute to maladjustment and a poor self-image. Children who have suffered neglect and abuse often react with shame (see previous page), but also children who have been subjected to excessive control by their parents can develop strong feelings of shame and guilt. Some children take responsibility for situations in which they have no part. They may believe, for example, that it is their fault that their depressed mother or father is distressed (Zahn-Waxler et al., 1984). There is a relationship between excessive guilt and shame and the development of depression and other mental health disorders (Dost and Yagmurlu, 2008; Mills, 2005), while lack of shame and guilt is related to development of psychopathic traits (Frick et al., 2014) (see p. 468).

Embarrassment

Embarrassment is social. *Exposure embarrassment* is an unpleasant emotion associated with feeling observed and exposed, while *evaluative embarrassment* stems from an assumption or fear of being evaluated by others against one's own will (see Figure 17.4). Feelings of insecurity and an inability to take the perspective of others can cause children to think that others pay particular attention to them and focus on their negative sides, and thus lead to embarrassment and social anxiety (Miller, 2007). Children with social-cognitive disorders, such as high-functioning children with autism spectrum disorder, are often anxious and easily embarrassed when they think someone is watching them (Kuusikko et al., 2008).

Cultural differences

The basis for self-referential emotions varies with each culture. Shame, for example, is related to violating the norms of modesty in Japan and China, while in the United States it is usually associated with a shortcoming in personal qualities. Similarly, pride is related to individual traits in the United States, while it is associated with contributing to the benefit of others in China. Chinese parents talk about shame when their children do not behave as expected by society (Fung et al., 2003; Mesquita and Karasawa, 2004).

Further emotional development

The ability to recognize more differentiated and subtle emotional expressions continues to evolve throughout childhood and adolescence (Montirosso et al., 2009). Children gradually gain a better understanding of the types of emotions they might expect and express in different situations. They realize that there are differences in what people feel and how they express themselves, and that they can hide their feelings from others. They can talk about emotions they have experienced in the past and discuss what leads up to emotions and the consequences they can have (Bretherton et al., 1986). In adolescence, self-referential emotions are increasingly related to comparisons with peers.

Toward school age, children become better at putting a name to their own emotional states, as well as those of others. They can explain that they look forward to something or that someone is angry with them because they have done something wrong. Ten-year-olds know, on average, eight words for happy feelings, six words for sad feelings and six words for scary feelings. Fourteen-year-olds know about the same number of words for happy and scary feelings, but they know more words for sad feelings, at least when it comes to girls (Doost et al., 1999). Both children and adolescents are better at labeling the emotions in stories than in facial expressions alone (Widen et al., 2015).

Children also begin to understand mixed emotions, for example that people can feel both pride and sadness at the same time (Denham, 2007). In one study, 5- to 10-years-olds were told a story about a girl who had been rejected by her best friend and then asked what the girl felt when she met her friend again. The youngest children simply based their responses on the current situation and the idea that children are happy to meet their best friends, and answered that the girl would feel happy. The older children also took into account what had happened earlier and said the girl would be upset when she met her friend (Gnepp and Gould, 1985). In late childhood, children begin to understand that the emotional content of a situation can be seen from several angles and that people can have conflicting feelings (Pons et al., 2004).

Emotion regulation

Throughout childhood, children continue to regulate their emotions in cooperation with adults and older children. Parents communicate how and when it is appropriate to express emotions, such as not to laugh at someone who has been hurt, how to react to others' emotional expressions, and how children can regulate their emotional expressions in culturally appropriate ways (Eisenberg et al., 1998; Halberstadt and Lozada, 2011; Morris et al., 2007). Once children are about 6 years old, parents in many cultures begin to expect them to express their emotions according to the culture's norms and rules. Japanese mothers expect more emotional control of their children than American mothers, such as refraining from crying and coping with their anger on their own (Hess et al., 1980).

Preschool children regulate their emotions mostly through action or by seeking help from others. They might crawl underneath the bed to avoid something they do not like, hug a teddy bear when they are upset or ask an adult for comfort. Children evolve from "being their emotion" to representing their emotional state through symbols and language and by processing it through play, imagination and conversations with adults (Greenspan and Greenspan, 1985). Once they enter school age, children make increasing use of *cognitive strategies*, such as saying to themselves "I can do it," redefining the situation or trying to think of something else. Five-year-olds need help with this, while 10-year-olds make spontaneous use of these types of strategies (Brenner and Salovey, 1997).

Children also become better both at hiding their emotions and knowing what situations require it. In preschool age, children are to some extent aware of when to modify, amplify or suppress their emotional expressions. Three- to 4-year-olds who have hurt themselves cry more often when they know that a familiar adult is watching them (Blurton-Jones, 1967). They clearly express disappointment when they open

an uninteresting present by themselves, but moderate their expression when the person who gave the present watches them open the package. Six-year-old girls hide their disappointment more than boys of the same age when receiving a gift that is too childish for their age (Cole, 1986; Saarni, 1984). Children express anger more often when provoked by their peers than when provoked by adults (Gross and Harris, 1988; Saarni, 1988).

The ability to regulate emotions and deal with distress and stress independently and together with one's peers is important for the development of independence in childhood and adolescence. When children of early school age are asked who gives them emotional support, most of them mention their parents. Older children more often respond that they would seek help from friends (Asher and Parker, 1989). Adolescents often ask their peers for advice on how to deal with unfamiliar social and emotional situations (Steinberg and Silk, 2002). Sharing feelings and giving emotional support are key elements in adolescents' descriptions of friendship (see p. 422), and adolescents particularly turn to their friends when they need support in dealing with emotionally difficult situations, also via online contact (Dolev-Cohen and Barak, 2013; Rossman, 1992).

Emotionality in adolescence

Adolescence is often described as a turbulent and emotional period. In one study, 12- to 15-year-olds reported more events involving negative emotions related to family, school and friends than 9- to 11-year-olds (Larson and Ham, 1993). Higher levels of emotionality among adolescents are related to puberty and the body's physical changes, but also to a role that varies between being child and adult. The transfer of responsibility and control from the parents to the adolescent implies greater demands on self-regulation, and social embarrassment and anxiety is common (Cui et al., 2014). Adolescents are sensitive to being evaluated by others, and feelings of both shame and pride increase in frequency and intensity. Many adolescents experience stress in connection with change of school and the growing academic and social demands. Taken together, these factors can lead to greater emotional lability, anxiety and depression among adolescents (Laugesen et al., 2003; Zeman et al., 2006).

THE INFLUENCE OF THE ENVIRONMENT ON CHILDREN'S EMOTIONS

Children's earliest emotional experiences usually occur within the family, and the family's emotional climate has an impact on how children express and regulate emotions. Toddlers tend to spend much time together with their mothers, and when the latter show many positive emotions, the children show more positive emotions than negative ones as well. Toddlers with mothers who are often angry show negative emotions more frequently than positive ones, while toddlers with emotionally intense mothers tend to be more emotional than toddlers whose mothers are less intense (Denham, 1989; Denham and Grout, 1993).

Sensitivity

Parental sensitivity and reactions help shape children's feelings about themselves and others, and are important for whether a child learns that it is acceptable to show emotions and seek help and support from others. A study of maternal reactions to anger in 2-year-old children found that children of mothers who responded quickly to anger were angry less often and reacted more positively to other people when their mother was absent than children whose mothers reacted more slowly to their child's anger. When the mothers responded quickly to their child's expressions of fear, the children showed less fear in other situations and more joy and interest for their surroundings. The children who were encouraged to show emotions when they felt anxious were also more popular in kindergarten and rarely showed anger in socially unacceptable ways. The children whose parents tried to get them to show little emotion, for example by asking them not to make such a fuss about what bothered them, were perceived to be socially less competent by their kindergarten teachers (Denham, 1993).

When parents show little reaction to their child's expressions of distress, children can learn to inhibit these expressions. They may be less likely to seek contact, or may adopt other strategies to reduce their own distress (Bridges and Grolnick, 1995). Likewise, children who are punished for crying and showing negative emotions learn to inhibit these expressions (Morris et al., 2007), with possible consequences for their ability to self-regulate. One study found that boys of mothers with a restrictive attitude to negative emotional expressions showed physiological arousal when they saw negative emotions in others, while at the same time denying that they felt distress (Eisenberg, 1991). For children to learn to manage negative emotions, they need experience with emotionally demanding situations. If children are not given the opportunity to show these types of emotions, they will not be able to learn to regulate them and will feel insecure in situations in which they are likely to occur. It is notable that children who are told by their parents to restrain their display of emotions in order not to hurt someone do not react in this way. It is parents' repeated request for emotional restraint when they themselves are upset or anxious that can lead children to become more aroused in situations involving negative emotions.

The previously mentioned studies suggest that sensitive parents who react quickly are advantageous to children's emotional development, but the relationship between parental reaction and children's emotional regulation is not so simple. Roberts and Strayer (1987) found that children with moderately responsive parents showed the highest level of social competence. Their explanation for this is that adults who are highly responsive to children's negative emotions can hinder children from engaging in difficult social interactions with others and prevent them from getting sufficient opportunities to learn to cope with negative emotions. Other studies have found that children whose parents try to regulate their child's negative emotions with "time out," telling them to go into another room when they are crying, show little anger together with other children. The same applies to children whose parents react with sympathy and comfort (Eisenberg and Fabes, 1994). Consequently, it seems that children who receive help in regulating their own negative emotions show fewer such emotions in interaction with other children. The way in which help is offered is not a deciding factor. At the same time, it is important to remember that parental reactions are affected by children's temperament (see Chapter 18). The ability to regulate emotions is the result of interaction between the child's characteristics and the way in which the environment supports the child's self-regulation.

Talking about emotions

Talking with others about emotions and emotional situations is important for the development of emotion regulation. Children first talk about emotions within the family. In early childhood, mothers largely talk about emotions when children have pain or feel happy, but also when they are angry, upset or agitated about something. These conversations give children insight into emotional states, what they are called how they are expressed, how they affect others and how they can regulate them. Most 2-year-olds use language to express concern, comfort and sympathy when others seem upset. One study found that half of the emotional explanations relating to everyday situations among 3-year-olds involved internal or mental causes, such as: *She is upset because she misses her mom*, or *She was angry because she thought it was her turn*. Most explanations had to do with children not getting their way or their wishes fulfilled (Fabes et al., 1991). Another study found that 3-year-olds who often talked with their parents about the cause of emotions showed better emotional skills 3 years later than children who had not had these types of conversations as often (Dunn et al., 1991).

Girls seem to talk more about emotions than boys. In an American kindergarten, 77 percent of the children's emotional statements came from girls, and in school age, the girls used more emotional words than boys (Doost et al., 1999). One reason for this may be that parents and older siblings of kindergarten-age children ask more questions and comment more on the emotional life of girls than of boys of the same age, although boys and girls initiate these types of conversations equally often (Dunn et al., 1987). There are also differences in the types of emotion talk boys and girls are engaged in. Mothers of 3-year-olds discuss sad emotions in greater detail with their daughters, and anger in more detail with their sons. In addition, they focus more on restoring relationships when their daughters are angry with a girlfriend, while they have more acceptance for retaliation when their sons are angry with a friend (Fivush, 1991). Gender differences continue into later childhood and adolescence. More often than boys, girls say they want to talk to siblings or others when they are sad. They also focus more on the emotion itself than boys do and use more cognitive strategies to try to

suppress feelings. Boys are more likely to use strenuous physical activity to regulate their emotions, for example in situations in which they feel bad, nervous or worried (Brenner and Salovey, 1997).

REACTING TO EMOTIONS IN OTHERS

Children's social world contains a myriad of emotional situations and expressions. Their reactions to the emotional expressions of others reflect their interpretation of these expressions and situations, as well as their own emotional regulation abilities.

Empathy and sympathy

Empathy and sympathy are not emotions in their own right, but *emotional reactions* to the condition or situation of another person. *Empathy* means to feel *with* someone else and to experience an emotion similar to that of the other person. This can be pain or sadness, but also joy or anger, depending on the other person's situation. *Sympathy* or *cognitive empathy* means to feel *for* someone else and implies an understanding that the other person has the feelings he or she has. Both reactions require an awareness of the fact that another person feels something specific; it is not enough for the child to be affected by someone else's mood (de Waal, 2008; Eisenberg et al., 1992).

Hoffman (1987) describes four stages in the development of empathy (Table 17.2). In the first stage, infants can show expressions similar to those they perceive in others, but probably reflecting the child's perception of the situation more than the other person's emotional state (see also social referencing, p. 350). In the second stage, children are aware that someone else is unhappy, rather than they themselves. They try to give comfort, for example by fetching an adult or offering a favorite toy to a crying child. In the third stage, beginning at the age of 2–3 years, children's attempts at comforting are more adapted to the person being comforted. They might fetch the crying child's mother, rather than just any adult (Eisenberg, 1992; Zahn-Waxler et al., 1992). The fourth stage starts during school age. Now, empathy does not only include an understanding of someone else's immediate feelings but

TABLE 17.2 Four stages in the development of empathy (Hoffman, 1987)

1. Global empathy	In the first year of life, children are able to express an emotion they have witnessed, for example by crying when another child is crying, but their emotions are involuntary and undifferentiated.
2. "Egocentric" empathy	Beginning in the second year, children actively offer to help others. They make appropriate efforts to empathize, but in a way they themselves would find comforting, and thus egocentric.
3. Empathy for another's feelings	In the third year of life, when they also begin to engage in role-play, children become aware that other people's feelings can differ from their own. Their response thus becomes more adapted to the needs of others.
4. Empathy for another's general plight	Late childhood or early adolescence brings a growing awareness of the fact that other people have feelings beyond the immediate situation that extend to other general life conditions. Older children and adolescents can feel empathy for entire groups, such as poor or oppressed people, and thereby go beyond the immediate situational experience.

also of the person's experiences and situation. Ten- to 12-year olds, for example, are better than younger schoolchildren at regulating the impact of someone else's grief in order to be able to offer comfort (Saarni, 1992).

The social environment is important for children's development of empathic and sympathetic reactions. Parents who react with empathy and sympathy when children are upset or anxious also seem to foster children who respond with empathy and sympathy when others are sad or upset (Spinrad and Stifter, 2006). Personal negative experiences do not lead to insight and empathy but rather to the contrary. In a study of 1- to 3-year-olds who had been victims of neglect, the children showed little concern for other children who were crying. Some of them threatened or physically attacked the crying child, others became agitated and anxious. Both reactions can be the result of the children's rejection and the lack of help they received in coping with their own and others' emotions. Children of the same age who had not been subjected to neglect also reacted differently, but were generally more caring. They looked at the crying child, touched and caressed her, or tried to comfort her in other ways (Main and George, 1985).

A low degree of empathic arousal can lead to poor motivation to help and comfort others, but a strong empathic response does not necessarily lead to more concern for others. Children who experience strong empathy with another child can become extremely aroused, feel distress and focus more on their own discomfort than on the other child's problems. When they see a child get hurt and start to cry, they can withdraw to avoid having to hear the sound of crying instead of offering help. Children with more moderate emotional reactions to such situations, or with good emotion regulation, are not as overpowered by their own emotional reactions and are able to help and support the crying child (Eisenberg et al., 1997). Therefore, empathy is not always an advantage. A high degree of empathy can increase children's worry and guilt and thus represent vulnerability for developing internalizing disorders (Tone and Tully, 2014). For example, children who become too involved in their depressed mothers tend to blame themselves for the mother's problems and develop excessive guilt (Zahn-Waxler and Kochanska, 1990).

Reactions to negative emotions in others

Children seem to be especially aware of anger and other negative emotions in other people (LoBue, 2009; Vaish et al., 2008). They often become distressed and have problems regulating themselves when they experience such emotions in others. Parental conflicts with lots of quarreling and aggression in children's first months of life increase the likelihood that they will react with withdrawal, negativity and distress to novelty at the age of 6 months (Crockenberg et al., 2007).

In one experiment, 2-year-old children, accompanied by their mother and a friend of the same age, witnessed two women pretending to argue for 5 minutes, followed by a 2-minute conversation during which they resolved their differences. Half of the 2-year-olds became quite distressed during the quarrel, moved toward their mother and expressed verbal and non-verbal concern. One-third of the children did not move during the exchange. Furthermore, children who had witnessed the pretend-quarrel were later more aggressive toward their friend or took away the friend's toy slightly more often than they had done previously. One month later, some of the children witnessed a similar type of quarrel. On this occasion, an even larger number of children became anxious, and their subsequent aggressive behavior was more frequent and intense (Cummings et al., 1985). Hence, the effect increased with number of experiences.

A similar study found that 4- to 5-year-olds became more distressed than the 2-year-olds had been, but had a larger repertoire of regulatory strategies and showed more varied responses. Some of them tried to get away, while others smiled. Some watched the arguing adults and looked back and forth between their mother and their friend, maybe to see how they reacted. The most ambivalent children – those who were both distressed and smiled – also showed the most aggressive behavior afterwards (Cummings, 1987).

Harris (1994) points out that there is no clear explanation for why witnessing a quarrel would lead to greater aggression in young children. Their reaction was not simply imitative: the adults only had a verbal argument, while the children displayed non-verbal aggressive behavior. One explanation may be that seeing adults quarrel counteracted the inhibitions children were brought up to have in connection with both verbal quarrels and physical acts of aggression (Bandura, 1986). Another possibility is that the quarrel elicited greater emotional arousal and in turn led the children to interpret their peers' behavior as provocative rather than positive. The latter explanation is supported by the observation that the most aggressive boys were more aroused after witnessing a pretend-quarrel than the boys who showed less aggression. It is also important to stress that not all children in Cummings' study responded the same way. While

some showed aggressive behavior, others seemed concerned and tried to offer comfort. Several children attempted to get away, perhaps because they were overwhelmed by their own feelings of empathy. In a study of 6- to 9-year-old children, boys had a tendency to react to anger and aggression by showing anger and aggression themselves, while girls expressed distress and anxiousness instead (Cummings et al., 1989). In another study involving a pretend-quarrel, 9- to 11-year-olds showed the strongest aversion to anger in adults, while 17- to 19-year-olds showed the least (Cummings et al., 1991). This suggests that children are more vulnerable to such experiences than adolescents, who have developed a higher level of self-regulation.

The results of these studies emphasize the importance of children's emotional environment. Studies have furthermore shown that children who grow up in families with many conflicts involving anger and aggression have less emotional competence, perform more aggressive actions and more often develop internalizing and externalizing disorders than other children. It is possible that parents who frequently have conflicts expose their children to more stress than parents who quarrel less, and offer their children less help with emotional regulation (Katz et al., 2007; Morris et al., 2007; Raver, 2004). Additionally, parents serve as role models for solving interpersonal problems, and children and adolescents with frequent exposure to parental conflicts have a tendency to try to resolve conflicts with physical aggression and similar strategies (Cummings and Davies, 1994, 2002; Duman and Margolin, 2007; Maxwell and Maxwell, 2003). Some children and adolescents live in conflict areas with high levels of negative emotions. They react with distress and anxiety but may also experience desensitization with reduced reactions to anger and conflict (Cummings et al., 2009, 2017; Tarabah et al., 2016).

Parents with depressive traits

Depressive symptoms are relatively common in mothers of infants and toddlers, and somewhat less common in fathers (Dix and Meunier, 2009; Wilson and Durbin, 2010). Depressive mothers are typically passive and despondent, and their children show less positive emotions and look less often at their mother's face than other children

(Silk et al., 2006). Many of the mothers' emotional expressions are related to their general condition and do not give the child information about the emotional content of the situation, for example the presence of something funny or dangerous. This reduces the children's basis for emotional learning through social referencing (see p. 350) and leaves them with a more limited repertoire of strategies for emotional regulation (Field, 1984; Field et al., 1988, 2009).

Peers

Children share many experiences, norms, challenges and perspectives with their peers. Peer interaction is therefore important for children to learn when and how to express emotions (Burleson and Kunkel, 2002; Denham, 2007). Children typically meet joy with joy, while they meet other children's expressions of sadness with attempts to include them in play or other activities (Strayer, 1980). The reactions change with age. Toddlers react more often to other children's expressions of anger than to expressions of sadness (Denham, 1986). Preschoolers rarely react to someone who seems hurt or angry, and show the strongest reactions to expressions of joy. Since they tend to stay away from children who often seem angry, the latter have poorer chances of social learning and participation (Barth and Archibald, 2003). Children who frequently show anger and little ability to self-regulate are at risk of being teased and bullied by their peers (Hanish et al., 2004).

EMOTIONAL DISORDERS

Symptoms of anxiety, depression and regulation disorders are relatively common in childhood and adolescence, and some children meet the criteria for a diagnosis (see Chapter 4). This also applies to children who show atypical development in other areas, such as children with autism spectrum disorders (Gillberg et al., 2016; Joshi et al., 2010). Anxiety and depression illustrate the complexity in the development of mental disorders in children and adolescents. Children with anxiety often show symptoms of depression, but the two disorders develop along somewhat different paths. An unstable home environment and negative life events seem to have a greater impact on the development of depression than of anxiety (Karevold et al., 2009; McLaughlin and King, 2015).

Depression and anxiety disorders tend to have a major impact on peer relations and school performance, but many children and adolescents are not referred for treatment. Programs at school may increase the likelihood of detecting and preventing disorders (Werner-Seidler et al., 2017).

Anxiety disorders

Among all mental disorders, those involving anxiety appear earliest in life, perhaps because they are so closely associated with children's fundamental need for security (see p. 399). Attention to potential danger is important for children's well-being and survival, and fear fulfills an important function in children's ability to adapt and cope with the environment. The border between natural apprehension and fear on the one hand, and anxiety disorders requiring treatment on the other, is not always clear, and milder forms can be particularly difficult to identify. Unlike fear, anxiety is characterized by excessive and pervasive emotions that occur in situations that are not immediately dangerous or threatening, but perceived as such by the child (Pine and Klein, 2015).

When and how anxiety disorders present themselves coincides to some degree with other developmental traits (Vasey et al., 2014). Phobias emerge at the same time as children begin to show a normal fear response. Separation anxiety is most common in the years following the child's first reactions to being separated from attachment figures (see Chapter 19). In adolescence, social anxiety is the most common disorder, but adolescents generally show more symptoms of worry and anxiety than children and adults (Pine and Klein, 2015). Thus, the basis for anxiety disorders can differ throughout life. Most children with early anxiety disorders do not develop anxiety disorders in adulthood, but many adults with anxiety disorders have experienced problems with anxiety in childhood (Gregory et al., 2007). Most adolescents with symptoms of anxiety do not develop anxiety disorders as adults (Pine and Fox, 2015).

Developmental psychopathology (see p. 14) emphasizes the importance of temperament and attention regulation in the development of anxiety

(Ollendick and Hirshfeld-Becker, 2002; Pérez-Edgar et al., 2014). Genetic vulnerability seems to play a role (Feigon et al., 2001). While heritability is higher in childhood than in adulthood, it also stabilizes over time. This suggests an age-related increase in the impact of cultural and social factors on children's ability to cope with anxiety and stressful situations (Nivard et al., 2015; Zheng et al., 2016). It is possible that the genetic basis is the same as for inhibited temperament (see Chapter 18). Toddlers with this type of temperament are vulnerable to developing anxiety, but only a small percentage of all children with inhibited temperament develop anxiety disorders (Buss and McDoniel, 2016; Pérez-Edgar et al., 2014). One explanation for the relation between inhibited temperament and anxiety disorders may be that children with this temperament type tend to be careful, do not get to know their emotional environment and therefore are unable to distinguish between what is and what is not safe. Their constant alertness to potential threats shows up in the form of anxiety symptoms (Kalin, 1993).

Children with symptoms of anxiety are more attentive to novel events and facial expressions reflecting a possible threat than other children (Dudeney et al., 2015; Mathews and MacLeod, 2005). Although attention to potentially threatening events is important, it becomes non-functional when it persists over time, and can promote and maintain anxiety. A number of factors can contribute to developing this type of sustained attention. One possibility is that toddlers with an inhibited temperament are particularly sensitive to novelty and threatening expressions and events, and therefore overestimate the importance of such events. Another explanation is that the children fail to unlearn the early innate attention with quick reactions to new and uncertain events (Pérez-Edgar et al., 2011, 2014). They develop an attention bias to threats that involve many, or nearly all, novel and slightly more complex situations, including neutral communication from other children and adults (Briggs-Gowan et al., 2015). Britton and colleagues (2011) suggest that these blurred lines between threat and safety may contribute to the development of chronic anxiety disorders in adulthood.

There is no evidence that the family's overall level of functioning and parenting styles contribute to the development of anxiety, but there is a link between anxiety disorders and over-protective, "hostile" upbringing with little autonomy encouragement (Jongerden and Bögels, 2015; Lebowitz et al., 2014). In addition, studies have shown transactional effects: children of anxious parents can become especially attentive to potential dangers, and anxiety in children can lead to overprotective parents (Rapee et al., 2009; Vascy et al., 2014). Mothers of anxious children can become over involved and controlling and thereby contribute to increasing their child's anxiety (Eley et al., 2010, Hudson et al., 2009, 2011).

Anxiety thus seems to be related to social stress and insecurity (Rapee et al., 2009). Research has found that negative life events only have a limited impact, but that an unsafe or threatening childhood environment can increase children's vigilance to non-specific threats. Children's sensitivity to potential threats can furthermore amplify the effect of exposure to domestic violence. Studies have described symptoms of anxiety and depression in underage refugees and others who have experienced war (for example in Vietnam, Bosnia, Kuwait and Lebanon). These symptoms can be exacerbated by factors that maintain children's psychological distress after they have come to more peaceful areas, such as uncertain asylum status, long waiting times, frequent relocations, social isolation and poor housing conditions (Ehntholt and Yule, 2006). Correspondingly, early intervention and social support for children exposed to war trauma can help reduce anxiety many years later (Llabre et al., 2015). Studies of children who experienced Hurricane Katrina in Louisiana in 2005 found that the deployment of social support, especially from parents, had a protective effect (Lai et al., 2015).

Anxiety disorders can lead to negative cascading effects. For example, separation anxiety may manifest itself in sleep disorders during early school age, somatic complaints in late childhood and school refusal in adolescence (Vasey et al., 2014). Avoidance is a common strategy to reduce anxiety, and many children with anxiety try to avoid their peers. A possible consequence of this is that children miss out on play and interaction with their peers, while stress and worries lay hold of their cognitive resources and draw attention away from social interaction and schoolwork. Children with anxiety disorders have fewer friends than other children, are perceived as less competent and are at greater risk of being bullied (Buss and McDoniel, 2016; Rubin et al., 2009).

The extent of the disorder varies: in some adolescents social anxiety is limited to specific situations, others struggle in many situations. Anxiety may interfere with both learning and social life at school, as well as romantic relationships (Kagan and Snidman, 2004). Social anxiety can lead to poor school performance and difficulties coping with the work environment (Ollendick and Hirshfeld-Becker, 2002). Some children with anxiety disorder also fulfill the criteria for behavioral disorders; this group generally does not cope as well as children who have anxiety disorder without behavioral disorders (Halldorsdottir and Ollendick, 2014).

It can be easier to affect the course of the disorder earlier rather than later in development (Pérez-Edgar et al., 2014), and the many potentially negative consequences make a strong argument for preventive measures and early intervention (Paulus et al., 2015). Prevention is especially targeted at children who appear anxious and socially inhibited, and aims to teach them to master new situations and deal with their own anxiety, and thereby support their self-esteem, social participation and well-being (Macklem, 2014). A number of studies have shown that it is possible to influence the developmental course of anxious children as early as preschool age (Chronis-Tuscano et al., 2015; Rapee et al., 2010). For example, the intervention program *Strengthening Early Emotional Development* (SEED) consists of gatherings and group training in socio-emotional skills for preschool children with mild and moderate anxiety symptoms, as well as concurrent discussion groups for parents (Fox et al., 2012).

Late childhood and adolescence is a vulnerable period for developing anxiety, and most preventive programs target this age group. Studies, however, indicate that prevention at age 9–10 is more effective than at 14–16 years of age (Lau and Rapee, 2011). *Coping Cat* includes individual intervention and prevention in groups. Based on cognitive behavioral therapy, it aims to help children and adolescents recognize and cope with difficult situations and anxiety (Gosch et al., 2012; Kendall, 1994). *Friends* (Barrett and Turner, 2001; Barrett et al., 2014) is based on *Coping Cat* and consists of several age-specific

programs with positive group activities for preventing anxiety: *Fun Friends* (4–7 years), *Friends for Life* (8–11 years) and *My Friends Youth* (12–16 years) (Higgins and O'Sullivan, 2015). *Emotion*, designed for children aged 8–13 years, aims to raise awareness about the relationship between experienced emotions and emotions and situations, and to promote a positive sense of self and active social participation (Martinsen et al., 2016). In line with a transactional point of view, several studies involving parents and children have shown reduced levels of anxiety in children and of distress and anxiety in parents (Anticich et al., 2013; Fox et al., 2012).

Treatment includes relaxation exercises, emotional training, strategies for coping with situations involving anxiety, controlled mental or physical exposure to anxiety-inducing things or situations (desensitization), and educating children and parents about anxiety and its treatment (Neil and Christensen, 2009; Weems and Varela, 2011). Medication of children with anxiety disorders is common in the United States but less accepted in other countries (Pine and Klein, 2015). *Cognitive behavioral therapy* aims to change negative thinking patterns and teach children with social anxiety disorder to cope with difficult situations. Treatment includes gradual exposure to situations that trigger anxiety, such as separation from parents or phobia of things or places, use of relaxation techniques and cognitive strategies. Parents often have a central role in following up these initiatives on a daily basis (Rapee et al., 2010). *Attention modification* is a relatively new cognitive method. Treatment applies computer programs that lead the child's attention from threatening to neutral stimuli on the screen (such as faces with an angry expression to faces with a neutral expression) or from neutral to positive expressions (Bar-Haim, 2010; MacLeod and Clarke, 2015). Only a limited number of studies have been conducted with children, but the preliminary results indicate that the method may help reduce symptoms of anxiety, including in children who have had little benefit from traditional cognitive behavior therapy (Bar-Haim et al., 2011; Bechor et al., 2014; Lowther and Newman, 2014). However, not all children with anxiety disorders show increased attention to negative emotional expressions; it is therefore necessary to implement multiple strategies and adapt treatment to the individual child. Assessment of the child's abilities and other possible disorders will be important when choosing a treatment strategy. Moreover, it is important to look for positive resources as well as signs of other disorders in children who show symptoms of anxiety.

Depression

Depression is a developmental disorder with many possible causes and layers of symptoms, and appears related to factors such as temperament, cognitive style and stress (Hankin, 2012). While children with anxiety are wary of potential threats, children with depression ruminate on hopelessness and loss (Hankin, 2012; Hankin et al., 2010). There is some genetic vulnerability, but negative life events in childhood can have a major impact as well. Although adulthood depression is frequent in children subjected to physical, sexual or psychological abuse in childhood, not all individuals in this group develop depression. Children with the short allele of the 5-HTTLPR gene are susceptible to the influence of both good and bad environments (see p. 84). Children with this allele who have been abused are more vulnerable for developing depression than abused children with other alleles of this gene (Saveanu and Nemeroff, 2012). Children of depressed parents have higher rates of depression. This may be due to hereditary factors as well as the transmission of pessimistic attitudes and a negative cognitive style from parent to child (Restifo and Bögels, 2009).

Depression manifests itself somewhat differently depending on age, although always implies a change of mood and behavior. Sleep problems are common during the preschool period; with increasing age, lack of energy and poor concentration become more prominent, along with an unwarranted sense of guilt and worthlessness (Reinfjell et al., 2016). Friends are central to young people's lives, and the breakup of a close friendship can be a difficult experience and lead to depression, guilt and anger (Rubin et al., 2013). Furthermore, depression is often accompanied by other impairments, including regulation disorders (see following page). Children and adolescents who have problems with online gaming have a higher incidence of depression, difficulties at school and behavioral disorders

(Brunborg et al., 2014; Johansson et al., 2009). Adolescents with ADHD have more depressive symptoms than adolescents without ADHD (Seymour et al., 2012). Many children and adolescents with a mild intellectual disability have low self-esteem and symptoms of depression, feeling that others perceive them as "stupid" and look down on them (Dagnan and Sandhu, 1999; Masi, 1998).

Children and adolescents spend a lot of time at school. Here, their problems often become more apparent and their depression is typically aggravated by social isolation and fewer friends. When adolescents are unable to solve the problems they face, they experience even more stress, low self-esteem and depression (Roberts, 2015). If left untreated, adolescent depression represents vulnerability for mental health problems in adulthood.

Different types of treatments are available for depression, including cognitive behavioral therapy and "interpersonal therapy," which builds on the notion that depressive symptoms affect social relations (Gladstone and Beardslee, 2009). Treatments aim to reduce negative thoughts and promote stress management, self-regulation and positive thinking (Corrieri et al., 2013; Horowitz and Garber, 2006; Roberts, 2015). Relaxation and participation in enjoyable activities are key elements, while attempting to change children's thinking and self-perception and improve their social and communicative skills (Corcoran and Hanvey-Phillips, 2013). Conversations focusing on strengthening children's confidence and self-image can also help reduce depression (Roberts, 2015; Sowislo and Orth, 2013). At school, teachers can contribute by establishing good relationships with depressed children and helping them interact positively with other students (Patel et al., 2014). Studies have found that children and adolescents with symptoms of depression who attended the *Penn Resiliency Program* and the *Coping with Stress Course* showed fewer such symptoms after attending the program (Hetrick et al., 2015). Meta-studies which combine results from many studies, however, have shown small or moderate effects of treatment on children (Bastounis et al., 2016; Forti-Buratti et al., 2016), possibly because a number of treatments place excessive demands on the cognitive, social and emotional skills of the individual child or adolescent (Garber et al., 2016).

364 EMOTIONS AND EMOTION REGULATION

The same treatment principles have also been applied to preventive measures for adolescents in general, as well as those who are vulnerable to developing depression. Some studies have found a lower incidence of depression in children and adolescents who followed this type of program, while other studies did not show a similarly positive effect. Many programs lack sufficient evidence, especially long-term effects (Corcoran and Hanvey-Phillips, 2013; Gillham et al., 2007; Horowitz and Garber, 2006; Merry et al., 2012).

Regulation disorders

Emotion dysregulation – both under- and over-regulation – can be found in descriptions of many psychiatric diagnoses (Kring and Werner, 2004; Mullin and Hinshaw, 2007), and developmental psychopathology places particular emphasis on emotion regulation (see p. 15). Many studies have found relations between younger children's ability to regulate emotions and later disorders. Children who are emotionally unstable, restless, readily distracted and negative in preschool age tend to be inattentive, distractible, hyperactive and antisocial in later school age. Children with attention disorders are restless and have problems regulating their emotions (Shaw et al., 2014). Actively aggressive and antisocial behavior in children and adolescents (see Chapter 20) is related to low activation and lack of emotionality (Mullin and Hinshaw, 2007). There are different strategies for regulating emotions, and adolescents with a limited repertoire have a greater incidence of internalizing problems than adolescents with a broader repertoire (Lougheed and Hollenstein, 2012). In children with autism spectrum disorders, cognitive rigidity and poor emotion understanding and sensitivity to changes in the environment contribute to problems with emotion regulation (Mazefsky and White, 2014). Thus, the relationship between emotion regulation, social competence and disorders in children is a complex one.

The main focus of developmental studies has been on children's underregulation of anger and other negative emotions, probably because these can have a highly negative effect on the relationship between children and parents and children's social life in general (Valiente et al., 2004). Emotional dysregulation, however, can involve excessively strong or weak emotional expressions, uninhibited or inhibited behavior, *internalizing* disorders characterized by shyness and withdrawal, and *externalizing* disorders marked by aggressive, disruptive and antisocial behavior (Mullin and Hinshaw, 2007; Nigg, 2000). Depression in girls is usually related to *over controlled* behavior and anxiety, while depression in boys seems to be related to *under controlled* behavior and aggression (Caspi et al., 1995). The relationship between over- and under regulation remains somewhat unclear. Depression in girls may be the result of overregulated positive emotions together with underregulated fear and other negative emotions (Mullin and Hinshaw, 2007). Children who both overregulate positive emotions and underregulate negative emotions are particularly vulnerable to disorders.

Since emotion regulation has a social basis, regulation disorders can have a serious impact on children's social development. Some years into school age, children begin to compare their skills, attitudes, possessions and families with those of their peers. According to Harter (1987), the most serious consequence of low self-esteem based on these types of comparisons is that children can develop mood disturbances, or, in more severe cases, depression. This in turn leads to cascading effects of decreased interest and motivation to participate in peer activities, lower activity levels, and little support and attention from the environment. Similarly, friends who use adaptive strategies can contribute to better self-regulation in adolescents who struggle with emotionally challenging situations (Reindl et al., 2016). Resilience to negative emotions is another factor that helps children cope with comparisons that put them at a disadvantage.

The development and consequences of emotional overregulation are not as well studied as those of underregulation. Overregulation can lead to poor emotional expressivity and inadequate emotional adaptation, whereby the child suppresses emotions instead of seeking help to deal with them. Consequently, the child may have fewer emotional experiences and receive little help and support from others in emotionally difficult situations. This can make for poorer learning and affect the child's attachment behavior, which is a means of seeking security in uncertain and complex situations (Nigg, 2006).

SUMMARY

1 *Emotional development* involves changes in an individual's understanding and use of emotional expressions and emotional regulation. Emotions comprise seven key elements: *expression, understanding, experience, bodily responses, direction, action* and *regulation*. There is no clear distinction between generating and regulating emotions. Development progresses from reactive to largely voluntary regulation, and from seeking adult protection and help to self-regulation and seeking help from one's peers.

2 Some emotions seem to be *universal*; they share similar expressions and are elicited by the same types of situations in all cultures. Others show significant cultural differences in expression, perceived value, and the different ages at which children are expected to show and regulate particular emotions.

3 Nearly all theories of emotional development are based on Darwin. According to *differential emotions theory*, children start with two innate forms of general positive or negative arousal, which are divided into progressively more demarcated and structurally consistent emotions. Theories of *discrete emotions* maintain that infants have an innate capacity to experience and express a number of basic emotions that are gradually combined into more complex emotions. From a *behavioral* point of view, development is determined by classical conditioning and differential responses. *Functionalist theories* focus on the relationship between emotions and the "object" at which they are directed, often another human being. Development reflects the changes in children's goals and their ability to regulate themselves and their social environment.

4 The *reflexive smile* is present at birth, while the *social smile* usually appears at the age of 6–10 weeks. Laughter comes at 3–4 months of age. Blind children begin to smile later than sighted children. This shows that experience is of importance, but also that the development of smiling does not depend on seeing others smile. Newborns *cry* when they experience high levels of physiological activation. Crying patterns are altered due to both maturation and changes in children's activities.

5 In the middle of the first year of life, children begin to show *fear*, and the elicitation of fear depends on the child's development of other skills, such as independent locomotion. In preschool age, children are often scared of fantasy characters, while fear in school age is mostly related to physical injury and danger. In adolescence, social fear becomes dominant. Clear expressions of *anger* commonly emerge at 4–6 months, such as when children are impeded in their movements or when parents do not fulfill their expectations. In the course of early childhood, anger is increasingly less accepted by parents. Children are perceived to be *sad* when they show little facial expression, activity and positive response. Infants show many expressions resembling the emotional expressions of adults, but not always in relevant situations; interpreting the infant's inner state based on these expressions is unreliable.

6 Children show an early ability to distinguish the emotional expressions of voices a little before faces. Initially expressions have to be distinct, but with age, children gradually improve at recognizing more subtle emotional expression. They also develop a better understanding of the relationship between emotions and events, desires and beliefs, the differences between other people's expressions and feelings, and the fact that emotions can be mixed or contradictory.

7 Researchers disagree on when children begin to *imitate* emotional expressions. Some maintain neonate imitation is made possible by a connection between the sensory and action systems, for instance in the form of a mirror neuron system. Others suggest the emotional expressions of adults can trigger emotional reactions in newborns, which prepare them for later imitation of emotional expressions.

Continued

8   Infants have a limited repertoire of self-regulating strategies and depend on help from caregivers. Stern uses the term *affect attunement* to describe adults' adaptation of emotional actions and expressions to those of the child, which helps children understand the emotions that underlie actions. *Social referencing* means that children use other people as a cue to what they themselves should feel, think and do in uncertain situations. With age, children learn to delay, modify or hide their emotional expressions in accordance with the social situation.

9   Self-referential emotions are founded on a personal standard. *Shame* is related to violating this standard, while *pride* is related to exceeding it. Children can be *embarrassed* at being observed and evaluated by others. *Moral emotions* are based on a personal moral standard. *Guilt* and *pride* are aimed at oneself, while (justified) anger, contempt and disgust are directed at others. Self-referential emotions help to identify and correct social errors, and vary across cultures.

10 Children's emotional experiences within the family affect the child's emotions. Parental sensitivity helps shape children's feelings about themselves and others. When children are prevented from showing negative emotions, they are unable to learn to regulate them and feel unsafe in situations that can give rise to these types of emotions. Children who receive help in regulating their negative emotions show fewer such emotions in interaction with other children. The way in which help is offered is not a deciding factor. Children who are able to deal with their emotions are also better at helping others than children with poorer emotional regulation. By the age of 3, conversations with parents often concern the causes of emotions. This gives children the opportunity to learn about emotional states, share their own feelings with others and understand and express emotions in new ways, in turn affecting their reaction to emotional situations.

11 *Empathy* and *sympathy* are emotional reactions to the situation of others. Hoffman describes four stages in the development of empathy. The emotional style of parents and other adults is important to children's development of empathy and sympathy. Negative experiences do not lead to insight and empathy in children. Children with self-regulation problems are often unable to help others who experience difficulties.

12 When parents or other adults show anger and aggression, children usually become anxious and find it difficult to regulate their emotions. Children are more vulnerable than adolescents, who have better self-regulation. Children growing up in families with high levels of anger and aggression are vulnerable to developing internalizing and externalizing problems. Children whose parents are depressed may develop a smaller repertoire for emotion regulation.

13 Since peers share many of the same experiences, norms, challenges and perspectives, *peer interaction* is essential for learning when and how emotions are expressed. Children's ability to self-regulate and deal with anxiety and stress is important for how they are met by their peers and for developing independence and social participation in childhood and adolescence.

14 *Anxiety disorders* appear early in life, and their development seems related to the child's temperament, attention to threats and need for security. When and how they emerge depends on many factors. Although anxiety is not related to the family's overall level of functioning, there is a relation between anxiety disorders and overprotective, "hostile" upbringing with little autonomy encouragement. Anxiety disorders can have negative *cascading effects* on learning and social development. There are many programs to prevent and treat anxiety disorders in children and adolescents, but studies show varying efficiency of such programs.

15 Children and adolescents with *depression* tend to focus on hopelessness and loss, and temperament, cognitive style and environmental factors can contribute to the development

of depression. Adolescence is a particularly vulnerable period. Studies of programs for the prevention and treatment of depression have shown varying results.

16 There is a relationship between behavioral disorders and underregulation of anger, but problems with emotional regulation can involve both excessively strong or weak expressions, uninhibited and inhibited behavior, *internalizing* disorders with shyness and withdrawal, and *externalizing* disorders with aggressive, disruptive and antisocial behavior. Depression in girls is usually related to *over controlled* behavior and anxiety, while depression in boys seems to be associated with *under controlled* behavior and aggression. Regulation disorders can have a major impact on children's social development and academic achievement.

CORE ISSUES

* The presence of inborn discrete emotions.
* Early imitation of emotions.
* Culture and emotions.

SUGGESTIONS FOR FURTHER READING

Cummings, E. M., Ballard, M., & El Sheikh, M. (1991). Responses of children and adolescents to interadult anger as a function of gender, age, and mode of expression. *Merrill-Palmer Quarterly*, *37*, 543–560.

Darwin, C. (1872). *The expression of the emotions in man and animals*. London: Oxford University Press (Reprint, 1998).

Denham, S. A. (2007). Dealing with feelings: How children negotiate the worlds of emotions and social relationships. *Cognitions, Brain, Behaviour*, *11*, 1–48.

Dunn, J., Bretherton, I., & Munn, P. (1987). Conversations about feeling states between mothers and their young children. *Developmental Psychology*, *23*, 132–139.

Hertenstein, M. J., & Campos, J. J. (2004). The retention effects of an adult's emotional displays on infant behavior. *Child Development*, *75*, 595–613.

Hiatt, S. W., Campos, J. J., & Emde, R. N. (1979). Facial patterning and infant emotional expression: Happiness, surprise, and fear. *Child Development*, *50*, 1020–1035.

Llabre, M. M., Hadi, F., La Greca, A. M., & Lai, B. S. (2015). Psychological distress in young adults exposed to war-related trauma in childhood. *Journal of Clinical Child and Adolescent Psychology*, *44*, 169–180.

Spinrad, T. L., & Stifter, C. A. (2006). Toddlers' empathy-related responding to distress: Predictions from negative emotionality and maternal behavior in infancy. *Infancy*, *10*, 97–121.

Tomkins, S. S., & McCarter, R. (1964). What and where are the primary affects? Some evidence for a theory. *Perceptual and Motor Skills*, *18*, 119–158.

Contents

Temperament is often viewed as the starting point for children's personality. From the moment children are born, they meet the world in different ways. Some children are more active, emotional or irritable than others, or more reactive when hindered from doing something. Some children like to explore, while others respond with caution to changes and meeting new people, places and events. Nearly all 1-year-olds briefly check their activity when an unfamiliar adult wearing a mask enters the room, but while some continue with what they were doing almost immediately, others remain still for a long time. Some children are particularly responsive to rewards, others are vulnerable to punishment. All of these differences reflect children's *temperament*, an individual reaction tendency, a behavioral and emotional disposition. *Personality* can be defined as a tendency to feel, think and act in ways that develop into individual patterns of an increasingly complex repertoire of thoughts, actions and emotions. It is commonly assumed that temperament has a strong biological basis, while personality also reflects the individual's experiences. Children with similar temperaments can develop highly different personalities depending on how they cope with the world and other people's reactions to them.

TEMPERAMENT

Temperament can be categorized in a number of ways (see Bornstein et al., 2015; Zentner and Shiner, 2012). In a classic longitudinal study, Thomas and Chess (1977) found three main types of temperament. One group of children was generally cheerful, had regular sleeping and eating patterns, adapted easily to new situations, were positive to strangers, showed moderate emotional reactions and were easily calmed down when they became aroused. This group with an "easy" temperament accounted for about 40 percent of the children. Another group had a tendency to withdraw in unfamiliar situations and generally appeared negative, with strong emotional reactions and irregular sleeping and eating patterns. These children with a "difficult" temperament accounted for about 10 percent. A third group of 15 percent was "slow to warm up." Although they adapted to new situations, they needed time to do so, and were uneven in their daily routines. They were restless and easily started to cry, but their reactions were moderate. Initially, they often seemed similar to the difficult group, but after warming up, they mostly resembled the easy group. The remainder of the children, about one-third, could not be classified in any one of the three main groups.

More recent descriptions of temperament use slightly different categories, but most are related to activity, reactivity, emotionality and sociability (Shiner, 2015). "Activity level" describes the frequency and intensity of children's motor activities, and resistance to having to remain passive. "Positive emotionality" refers to the amount and intensity of positive emotions. "Negative emotionality" includes both fear and shyness, as well as irritability, discomfort, anger and resistance to control. "Sociability" describes the degree of children's extraversion and their interest and enjoyment in being with other people.

Some children are cautious, others activly seek new experiences.

"Self-regulation" refers to the effortful control of attention and distractions, as well as persistence. Some descriptions also include "likeability" or "kindness" and "adaptability" as basic temperamental traits (Rothbart and Bates, 2006; Zentner and Bates, 2008).

Since children experience many new things, "reaction to novelty" is a temperament trait of special importance. "High-reactive" or "inhibited" children tend to be cautious and shy, and withdraw when meeting new people or things. They can find it emotionally challenging, for example, to meet lots of new children and adults when starting in kindergarten, and may need help adapting. "Low-reactive" or "uninhibited" children are more likely to approach others and be social in these types of situations. Most children in this group enjoy meeting other children and adults in kindergarten. Shyness is more problematic for boys than for girls, and the relationship between mothers and shy daughters is usually better than that between mothers and shy sons (Coplan and Arbeau, 2008; Kagan and Snidman, 2004).

Measuring temperament

There are different approaches to measuring temperament, each with strengths and weaknesses, and considerable discussion about which measures describe temperament best. Questionnaires and parent interviews are the most common methods, especially in investigations involving a large number of children (Caspi et al., 2005). However, many studies have found low correlations between different evaluations, such as between mothers and preschool teachers when the mothers evaluate their own child's temperament. The correlation is considerably higher when the child is not the mother's own (Seifer, 2002; Seifer et al., 1994). This indicates that a mother's evaluation does not merely reflect the child's characteristics, but also the mother–child relationship and maternal characteristics, such as the mother's stress level (Räikkönen et al., 2006). The subjective basis of such evaluations is also reflected in moderate correlations (0.29–0.49) between mothers' and fathers' assessments of their child's temperament (Neppl et al., 2010). Also cultural beliefs influence parents' evaluations of their child's temperament (deVries and Sameroff, 1984).

Kagan and Fox (2006) maintain that parent evaluations should be used with caution, since they are highly colored by parental traits and aspirations for the child, and should always be accompanied by observations of physiological measures such as heart rate and respiration. Rothbart and Bates (2006) object to Kagan's views that observations in practice rarely take place in different situations and do not last long enough for the observer to gain insight into how the child generally meets the world, while assessments by parents and preschool teachers reflect their contact with the child over time. They argue that observations cannot replace the information gathered by questionnaires and interviews, which additionally provides a solid basis for observation. Nonetheless, they agree with Kagan that one should not rely on a single method, but assess children's temperament using different approaches, such as both questionnaires and observations of children in various situations.

Heritability

It is a general view that the development of temperament is determined by both genetic and environmental factors (Goldsmith et al., 1999; Saudino, 2009; Saudino and Micalizzi, 2015). Twin studies have generally shown more similar temperaments in identical twins than in fraternal twins, but genetic influence seems to vary across traits. Heritability estimates vary from 0.2 to 0.6 (see p. 83). Torgersen (1989), for example, found a relatively high degree of heritability for the temperament trait "activity level," while "emotionality" showed the lowest heritability.

In recent years, the relationship between temperament and specific genes has been the subject of study in both humans and apes. Current knowledge remains limited, but important genes appear to be those with a general effect on brain metabolism, such as 5-HTTLPR, MAOA and DRD4 (see p. 84). This agrees well with Kagan's description of temperament traits as "root notes" in the nervous system. However, human biology is not about genes alone – prenatal nutrition and health of the mother and child also affect the child's irritability. Even twins can have slightly different fetal environments (Riese, 1990; Saudino, 2009).

Stability of temperament

Developmental research on temperament has focused on infancy, but temperament exists at all age levels. Adult temperament is often described as "introverted" or "extraverted," "inhibited" or "impulsive" (Eysenck, 1967). An important question is the degree to which an individual maintains the same temperament. Mathiesen and Tambs (1999) found moderate correlations, ranging from 0.37 to 0.60 based on maternal ratings of four temperament traits at 1½ and 4 years: "activity," "reaction to novelty," "sociability" and "emotionality." This shows that changes in temperament occur even during the first years. Another study assessed children several times from the age of 2 to 12 years, and found that the largest changes in temperament occurred between the ages of 3 and 5. After this, the chil-

dren showed less intense reactions and better regulation, adaptability and mood, but their activity level as well as degree of sensitivity and reactivity continued to change throughout school age (Guerin and Gottfried, 1994). Parental evaluations of child temperament over extended periods of time show relatively low correlations of around 0.2–0.4 from early to later age levels (Putnam et al., 2002).

Kagan and Snidman's (2004) results illustrate the complexity of temperament development. In a study of 68 children with signs of a "high-reactive" or "inhibited" temperament at an early age, ten were described as shy with strangers at the age of 11. Only one of the 92 children with an early "low-reactive" or "uninhibited" temperament fit this description. Thirty percent of the children in the early uninhibited group were described as "exuberant," while only 5 percent of those with an early inhibited temperament had this characteristic at the age of 11. At the same time, 30 percent of the early inhibited group, and 15 percent of the early uninhibited group, were described as energetic and talkative. Nine of the early uninhibited children, and one inhibited child, were described as rebellious at 11 years of age.

The issue of stability is further complicated by the fact that the behaviors used to measure temperament change with age. "Activity" and "emotionality" are expressed in quite different ways at the ages of 1, 7 and 15 years. Six-month-olds show negative emotionality by crying, while 6-year-olds show worry and concern, and can appear depressed and sad. Children can thus change considerably while maintaining the same temperament (Neppl et al., 2010). Additionally, continuity of temperament is dependent on the environment. Children with early inhibition, for example, more often remain inhibited when their mothers are invasive and critical, while they become less reticent with mothers who actively try to counteract the child's shyness (Rubin et al., 2002).

Temperament and parental behavior

Children's activity level, irritability and reactions to unfamiliar people and situations have an impact on how parents perceive children and relate to them. For example, active children tend to look for a toy themselves while passive children wait until someone brings a toy to them, and they will probably be treated differently. This in turn affects the child's activities and reactions, which then influence the parents, and so on, in a transactional chain (Cheah and Park, 2006; Räikkönen et al., 2006).

Parental response to the child's temperament changes as the child grows older. Studies have found that children whose mothers reported that their child had a difficult temperament at 6 months received more emotional contact and stimulation with objects than children with an easier temperament. The contact may have consisted of attempts to comfort, and stimulation with objects in an effort to divert the attention of the crying child. At 2 years the children with a difficult temperament and resistance to external control were exposed to more negative control by their mothers (Lee and Bates, 1985; Pettit and Bates, 1984). Shy and reserved children are often overprotected and over controlled by their parents (Rubin et al., 1999). In addition, parents bring their own temperament, their ways of meeting others and their cultural values into the interaction with their child, and show a relatively stable parenting style throughout early childhood and preschool age (Dallaire and Weinraub, 2005; Smith, C. L., 2010).

Children with a difficult temperament can be a challenge for parents; it is particularly stressful when typical parenting strategies fail. The experience of not being able to manage their child has a very negative impact on parents with low self-esteem in the first place. Mothers who were insecure and anxious to begin with became more insecure when they failed to calm their child, while secure mothers were not affected by such experiences. Similarly, an irritable temperament in the child can lead vulnerable mothers to become depressed and feel incompetent (Ganiban et al., 2011). Several studies have found a relationship between irritability and negative emotions in children, and poor caregiving and lack of response from parents. Correspondingly, there is a relationship between children's positive emotions and their ability to self-regulate, and parents' responsivity, social interaction and use of rewards (Hinde, 1989; Kiel and Buss, 2010). However, these correlations say nothing about the way in which the patterns arise – both are parts of a transactional chain and affect one another. The temperament and emotional style of the parent as well as of the child contribute to the course of development (Gallagher, 2002; Sameroff, 2009).

Different temperaments are neither good nor bad in themselves, but the temperaments of parent and child can be more or less suited to one another, "goodness of fit" (Chess and Thomas, 1999; McClowry et al., 2008). The development of temperament is not merely a matter of the child's initial temperament alone, but also of how parents respond to it, and how the child in turn responds to the parents' temperament (Bates et al., 2012). This is well illustrated in Box 18.1. The only generally positive parental traits that can be singled out are sensitivity and ability to adapt to the child's temperament and help the child to cope with difficult situations and with self-regulation. This is true regardless of whether the child tends to be active or passive, emotionally positive or negative, or shows strong or weak reactions. The temperament of a child has less explanatory value for the course of development than the context in which the temperaments of the child and the parents interact (Lerner and Lerner, 1983).

Early temperament and later disorders

Much of the research on temperament has a clinical focus and is concerned with the relationship between early temperament traits and later behavioral and emotional disorders, school problems, and alcohol and drug abuse, and the possibilities of prevention and early intervention. Developmental psychopathology builds on the assumption that children's temperament can make it more difficult for them to adapt to the challenges of the environment and thereby contribute to the emergence of such disorders (Nigg, 2006). Studies have found small overall correlations between early temperament and later disorders, but children with very high or low scores on a particular temperament trait are more likely to develop disorders later. More often than other children, those with early inhibition show internalizing disorders later in life, while uninhibited children show more externalizing disorders. Children with early negative emotionality show both types of disorders (Rothbart and Bates, 2006).

It is never temperament alone that leads to later disorders, but an interaction between the child's temperament and the way in which children and parents adjust to one another. For example, studies have found that the combination of an inhibited temperament and a permissive parenting style (see p. 385) increases that risk for internalizing disorders (Williams et al., 2009). Parents who perceive their children as vulnerable sometimes try to protect them from difficult situations. This sort of overprotective behavior may exacerbate the effect of an inhibited temperament, because the children do not learn to deal with difficult situations, but rather to avoid them and withdraw (Coplan et al., 2008; Rubin et al., 2002; see also p. 361). Another study found that infants with difficult or more regular temperaments developed fewer behavioral problems when their mothers were sensitive, while the mother's sensitivity had little consequence for infants with an easier temperament. Maternal sensitivity thus had a different effect on children with different temperaments, and possibly with different alleles of certain genes as well (Bradley and Corwyn, 2008). In line with this, children with a difficult temperament (low inhibition, difficult to comfort, high level of frustration) showed the highest number of behavioral disorders when their mothers lacked in sensitiveness and exercised a great deal of negative control (Kiff et al., 2011; van Aken et al., 2007). Children with an "exuberant" temperament and extremely positive reactions to unfamiliar people and things can develop a high degree of sociability, but can also show a lot of anger, since they often experience being prevented from reaching their goals (Degnan et al., 2011).

The studies illustrate that the consequences of children's early temperament are not given. The majority in all temperamental groups do not develop disorders. Temperament only represents a starting point and whether children with a particular temperament develop disorders will depend on the characteristics of their environment and the interactions they engage in.

Resilience and protection

Research has mainly dealt with temperament as a vulnerability to developing disorders, but temperament traits can also be a source of resilience (Shiner, 2015). Children who are energetic and at the same time easily comforted cope better with a difficult family environment than children with other types of temperaments (Werner and Smith, 1982). An easy temperament can help children cope with stress and uncertainty in their surroundings, for example, if the child's parents divorce (Davis and Suveg, 2014).

BOX 18.1 A TEMPERAMENTAL JOURNEY (Thomas and Chess, 1986, pp. 48–49)

Carl was one of our most extreme cases of difficult temperament from the first few months of life through 5-years-of-age. However, he did not develop behavior disorder, primarily due to optimal handling by his parents and stability of his environment. His father, who himself had an easy temperament, took delight in his son's "lusty" characteristics, recognized on his own Carl's tendency to have intense negative reactions to the new, and had patience to wait for eventual adaptability to occur. It was clear without any orientation by us, that these characteristics were in no way his or his wife's influence. His wife tended to be anxious and self-accusatory over Carl's tempestuous course. However, her husband was supportive and reassuring and this enabled her to take an appropriate objective and patient approach to her son's development. By the middle childhood and adolescent years few new situations arose which evoked the difficult temperament responses. The family, school and social environment was stable and Carl flourished and appeared to be temperamentally easy rather than difficult. An occasional new demand, however, such as the start of piano lessons, again evoked his previous typical response of initial intense negative response, followed by slow adaptability and eventual positive zestful involvement. When Carl went off to college, however, he was faced simultaneously with a host of new situations and demands – an unfamiliar locale, a different living arrangement, new academic subjects and expectations, and a totally new peer group. Within a few weeks his temperamentally difficult traits reappeared in full force. He felt negative about the school [and] his courses, the other students, couldn't motivate himself to study and was constantly irritable. Carl knew something was wrong, discussed the situations with his family and us and developed an appropriate strategy to cope with his problem. He limited new demands by dropping several extracurricular activities, limited his social contacts and policed his studying. Gradually he adapted, his distress disappeared and he was able to expand his activities and social contacts. When seen by us for the early adult follow-up at age 23 his temperamental rating was not in the difficult group.

As pointed out earlier, some children with an inhibited temperament do not become shy and withdrawn because their environment supports the development of other behaviors. Children with a cautious temperament can react by withdrawing when they start in kindergarten, but sensitive and warm mothers seem to offer protection against a development path toward internalizing disorders (Early et al., 2002). Similarly, sensitive parenting can protect children with difficult temperaments from developing behavioral disorders (Bradley and Corwyn, 2008; see Box 18.1). Environments with high levels of stress can increase the risk of disorders in children with a very inhibited or uninhibited temperament, while environments in which adults adapt and help children regulate their emotions may not only prevent the development of disorders, but also take advantage of a child's temperament in a way that promotes a particularly positive development (Sameroff, 2009).

PERSONALITY

Nearly all theories of personality describe human qualities in terms of characteristic traits. Composite traits are sometimes combined into *personality types* such as "resilient," "over controlled" or "under controlled" (Robins et al., 1996). There is a close connection between the traits described by the various theories and their assumptions about how personality develops.

Personality traits

Personality traits can be described in innumerable ways. Children, adolescents and adults are described as "kind," "malicious," "quick," "fun," "honest," "nice," "insecure," and so forth, and there are many ongoing efforts to reduce the number of descriptive traits to a relatively small collection of key dimensional characteristics. It is the position within each of these dimensions that together make up the description of an individual's personality.

Today, personality is commonly described in terms of the "Big Five," based on Goldberg's (1990) analysis of the terminology used to characterize human beings: "extraversion," "agreeableness," "conscientiousness," "neuroticism" (emotional lability) and "openness" (to experience). However, some researchers hold that five

dimensions are insufficient to map the variation in human personality (Block, 1995), while others find that the three major traits "extraversion," "conscientiousness" and "neuroticism" (emotional lability) best describe the personality differences in the population (Eysenck, 1992; Rothbart and Bates, 2006). Costa and McCrae (1992) have assigned sub-characteristics to each of the Big Five for a total of 30 facets (Table 18.1).

Parents begin quite early to assess their child's personality along the same main dimensions as for adults. In one study across seven countries, parents of children aged 3–12 years were asked to describe what characterized their child. Three-quarters of the descriptions fell within the Big Five, with a larger percentage for the older than the younger children, but they also included some age-specific terms. The younger children were often referred to as "independent" and "mature for their age" (Kohnstamm et al., 1995, 1998). In order to provide an adequate description of younger children's personality, Caspi (1998) suggests complementing the Big Five with "activity" and "irritability." With age, the parents' child-specific characteristics are gradually reduced in favor of traits used to describe adults.

General and situation-specific traits

As a rule, personality traits aim to describe an individual's general ways of reacting, independent of the situation. In practice, however, there is often little agreement when several persons assess the personality of the same child. Parents and teachers, for example, can have very different views on a child's personality, degree of aggression, industriousness and sociability (Lewis, 2001a). This undermines the assumption of personality traits as general and situation-independent reaction tendencies.

Bandura (1999) and Mischel (1984) dismiss the notion that children develop general personality traits; a child's tendencies to react and act reflect adaptations to actual situations, and therefore must be seen in light of the child's challenges and relationships. In their view, descriptions of personality traits should include traits that usually characterize the child's reactions and behaviors in specific situations, such as "aggressive during play," "introverted with strangers," "extraverted at home," and so on. These types of traits are

TABLE 18.1 The Big Five and their 30 facets: the "Big Five" personality traits, the six facets describing each trait, and an adjective closely associated with each facet (Costa and McCrae, 1992, p. 49)

The Big Five	The thirty facets	Adjective
Extraversion versus introversion	Gregariousness	Sociable
	Assertiveness	Forceful
	Activity	Energetic
	Excitement seeking	Adventurous
	Positive emotions	Enthusiastic
	Warmth	Outgoing
Agreeableness versus antagonism	Trust	Forgiving
	Straightforwardness	Not demanding
	Altruism	Warm
	Compliance	Not stubborn
	Modesty	Not a show-off
	Tender-mindedness (nurturance)	Sympathetic
Conscientiousness versus lack of direction	Competence	Efficient
	Order	Organized
	Dutifulness	Not careless
	Achievement striving	Thorough
	Self-discipline	Not lazy
	Deliberation	Not impulsive
Neuroticism versus emotional stability	Anxiety	Tense
	Angry hostility	Irritable
	Depression	Not contented
	Self-consciousness	Shy
	Impulsiveness	Moody
	Vulnerability	Not self-confident
Openness versus closedness to experience	Ideas	Curious
	Fantasy	Imaginative
	Aesthetics	Artistic
	Actions	Wide interests
	Feelings	Excitable
	Values	Unconventional

illustrated by a study of children at a summer camp. Although the children showed various types of responses that to some extent were consistent across situations, their reactions varied considerably from one situation to another. Those who showed the most aggression, happiness, sadness, and so on, were not always the same children (Shoda et al., 1994). Figure 18.1 shows observations of verbal aggression in two children who participated in the study. Both made approximately the same number of verbally aggressive statements, but the situations where they occurred differed. According to Shoda, children's reaction tendencies, or personalities, should include such situational variation and are best described by a *situation profile* or *behavioral signature*. Behavioral signatures thus redefine traits by taking into account the child's perception of the situation (Mischel and Shoda, 2008, 2010).

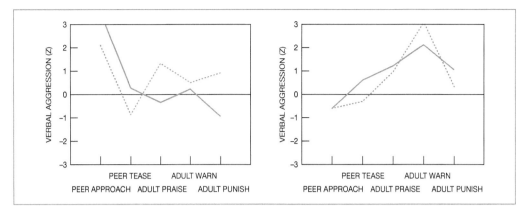

FIGURE 18.1 **Different patterns of verbal aggression in two children.**
A group of 7- to 13-year-old boys and girls were observed for 6 weeks at a summer camp. The figure shows the extent of verbal aggression by two children in relation to the group average in different situations and on two occasions. Most of child A's aggressive statements occurred in connection with being approached by other peers, those of child B when reprimanded by adults (based on Shoda et al., 1994, p. 678).

THEORIES OF PERSONALITY DEVELOPMENT

All theorists assume that an individual's reaction tendencies are affected by past experiences, and search for mechanisms to explain the development of the adult personality. Freud formulated the first comprehensive theory of personality development. His psychoanalytic theory established the basis for psychodynamic theories and has had enormous influence on the understanding of personality development in general (Schultz and Schultz, 2016). Today, Freud's theory is largely of historical interest, as most modern psychodynamic theorists have disclaimed or reformulated many of Freud's most important ideas. If the theory is presented in some detail nonetheless, it is due to its great significance and illustration of *psychodynamic thinking*. Theories about the development of children's relationships and self-development also incorporate assumptions about personality traits. They will be discussed in the following chapters.

Freud's theory

In Freud's theory (see also Chapter 2), personality is a mental structure that derives from the interaction between innate drives common to all human beings and the child's unique experiences (Westen et al., 2008). *Libido* and *Thanatos* represent the basic forces behind all human actions, and the discharge of these drives must be adapted to the physical, social and cultural environment during development. As part of this adaptive process, children form a tripartite mental structure consisting of *id*, *ego* and *superego* (see p. 21). According to Freud, it is the interactions between these three parts, the way in which the drives are dealt with, and internal conflicts during the three psychosexual phases that impact the traits that eventually characterize an adult's personality (Freud, 1905).

In the *oral* phase (0–1 years), children explore the environment with their mouth, and drives are reduced by the consumption of food. When mental energy becomes fixated during the oral period, the individual may become talkative or feel "hunger" for others' attention as an adult. Smoking and excessive eating and drinking are also considered expressions of personality traits originating in this phase, according to Freud (Table 18.2).

Conflicts in the *anal* phase (2–3 years) are particularly linked to control over feces (expelling and withholding) and increasing demands for cleanliness. Overly strict toilet training, for example, can lead to excessive cleanliness in adulthood. The emphasis on cleanliness in this phase leads to the first conflict between the child's desires and the expectations of culture. This is an important aspect of Freud's theory, since it

Sigmund Freud.

notion that boys are sexually attracted to their mother and experience their father as competing for the mother's attention, while girls are attracted to their father. According to the theory, a developmentally favorable solution to this inner conflict is for boys to identify with their father and girls with their mother, an identification that leads to the internalization of the parents' social and cultural attitudes and values, and the formation of the superego. The absence of such identification can result in inadequate moral development.

Following the phallic phase, children enter a *latency phase* that lasts until the age of 13 years, with less sexual drive and without focus on new body zones. With the onset of puberty, sexual instincts awaken once again, as well as attraction to the parent of the opposite sex. According to Freud, this forms the basis for generational conflicts in adolescence.

According to Freud, the psychosexual phases give rise to individual differences in personality, as well as to mental health problems. Unresolved inner conflicts from these phases are maintained and become central and permanent elements of the individual's personality. Each phase can be seen as a form of critical period that depends on specific stimulation (see p. 377). The various phases are characterized by personality traits that may emerge to a greater or lesser degree, a development that largely terminates with the Oedipus and Electra conflicts. This means that in Freud's theory, the adult personality is more or less shaped by the age of 5.

Another central element in Freud's personality theory is the idea that the conflicts between the impulses of the id and the limitations of the superego lead to anxiety and use of *defense*

implies that children are not socially oriented to begin with. Enculturation is not a positive experience for children, but spawns discomfort since it limits the free reign of children's drives.

Conflicts in the *phallic* phase (4–5 years) revolve around children's discovery of their own and others' genitalia. The *Oedipus conflict* and the *Electra conflict* are central to the formation of personality. These conflicts are based on the

TABLE 18.2 The psychosexual phases and their potential impact on personality development if the conflicts in a phase remain unresolved (Pervin and John, 1997, p. 123)

Stage	Personality traits
Oral	Demanding, impatient, envious, covetous, jealous, rageful, depressed (feels empty), mistrustful, pessimistic.
Anal	Rigid, striving for power and control, concerned with should and oughts, pleasure and possessions, anxiety over waste and loss of control, concern with whether to submit or rebel.
Phallic	Male: exhibitionistic, competitive, striving for success, emphasis on being masculine – macho – potent. Female: naive, seductive, exhibitionistic, flirtatious.

mechanisms to reduce the anxiety (see p. 22). These defense mechanisms enable children to adapt to the demands of their surroundings, but their use can also form the basis for developing particular personality traits. Fanaticism, for example, can be the result of strong, unacceptable impulses, such as abstinence due to a craving for alcohol. Defense mechanisms can furthermore lead to pathological conditions. This happens when impulses become so strong and the use of defense mechanisms so extensive, that the individual is unable to cope with everyday challenges (Freud, 1895).

The status of the theory

Freud's theory has been criticized by theorists both within and outside the psychodynamic group. An internal criticism of the theory is its predominant focus on the development of boys, while it is vague and unclear on a number of points regarding the development of girls (Simanowitz and Pearce, 2003). While none of today's psychodynamic theorists completely endorse Freud's theory of personality development in its original form, psychodynamic developmental psychology has no alternative major theory to offer (Westen et al., 2008). Although Freud's explanations use different terminology and models than what is common today, they contain many of the elements of modern developmental theories, such as the emphasis on parent–child relations, self-regulation (ego function) and emotional regulation (defense mechanisms) in the development of personality (Luborsky and Barrett, 2006). Key elements of Freud's theory are being further elaborated by modern psychodynamic psychology. This applies above all to Freud's assumptions about unconscious processes and "psychodynamics" (see also p. 22). Early experiences remain important for the development of personality, but are less crucial than in Freud's theory. Defense mechanisms continue to have a central position as well, and it is assumed that the individual in the course of childhood and adolescence develops a stable *defensive style* to cope with anxiety and external threats. Positive early experiences lead to the development of flexible and adaptive defense mechanisms such as *sublimation* and *intellectualization*, while negative experiences lead to less mature and effective mechanisms such as *repression* and *projection* (Bornstein, 2006; Gilmore,

2008; Rice and Hoffman, 2014). Maternal and paternal relationships, as well as different interpretations of the Oedipus/Electra complexes as organizing elements in personality development, maintain a prominent place in psychodynamic theories (Balsam, 2015; Hindle and Smith, 1999; Westen et al., 2008).

A common criticism raised by other theories is the dearth of studies involving children. Instead, psychoanalytic developmental theory builds on clinical interpretations of adult patients – the psychosexual phases, for example, are based on assumptions about the causes of personality traits and mental disorders in adulthood. No studies exist to support the hypotheses about psychosexual phases or the Oedipus and Electra conflicts. Many critics point out that the theory's assertions, based on clinical interpretations of children and adults' actions, have such a vague basis that they cannot be refuted in practice. Much research continues to focus on the development of personality disorders in studies of adult patients (Shiner, 2009).

Erikson's theory

Erik Homburger Erikson (1963, 1968) belongs to the psychodynamic tradition, but offers a rather different view of development than Freud's description of children driven by instincts. His theory represents ego psychology which emphasizes the regulatory and adaptive functions of the ego, the development of social relations, identity, autonomy, self-regulation, and coping in a social world (see Chapter 2).

Erikson, too, describes biologically determined phases in development in which personality is shaped by experience, but does not share Freud's view that personality traits are formed by conflicts linked to drive impulses. According to Erikson, human beings go through eight psychosocial phases, each associated with social relations and *social crises*. Like in Freud's theory, personality is determined by the way in which each phase is traversed (Table 18.3). In the first phase, children learn to trust that their parents or other caregivers will provide them with food, care and love. The way in which this trust develops impacts the development of autonomy in the second phase. Overprotection during this phase will lead children to doubt their own abilities and opportunities. Experiences in the third phase are important for the development of initiative and

Erik H. Erikson.

adolescence to be of particular importance for the development of personality because adolescents actively define their self and establish their identity (see Chapter 21).

The status of the theory

Erikson's elaboration of Freud's theory continues to exert a major influence on descriptions of personality development, particularly for adolescence and adulthood. Some of the criticism of Freud's theory is also relevant for this theory. Like Freud, Erikson wrote most about the personality development of males. Additionally, his phases are somewhat old-fashioned and do not reflect more recent developments in education and the workplace. Although many of the concepts of ego psychology correspond to modern assumptions about self-regulation, little research exists to document any possible links between events in the various phases and personality traits in adulthood.

McCrae and Costa's five-factor model

McCrae and Costa (1995, 2008) describe the development of personality traits based on temperament and general principles of development. The theory is based on Goldberg's Big Five personality traits (see p. 375), which McCrae and Costa believe to reflect basic personal characteristics formed by evolution. In their theory there is a continuous development from children's earliest temperament traits to the personality characteristics typical of adults. Development is universal and identical in all cultures. Maturation

guilt. The basis of personality is thus formed by social and emotional conflicts.

Erikson's psychosocial phases incorporate a broader age span than Freud's psychosexual phases. The first five phases cover the period up to adolescence, while the last three include the remainder of the life cycle. Unlike Freud, Erikson does not believe personality to be fully formed by the end of the preschool period, and considers

TABLE 18.3 The psychosocial phases (based on Erikson, 1963)

Phase		Psychosocial crisis	Basic strengths
1	0–12 months	Trust versus mistrust	Energy and hope
2	13–24 months	Autonomy versus doubt and shame	Self-control and willpower
3	2–4 years	Initiative versus guilt	Direction and purpose
4	5 years to puberty	Industriousness versus inferiority	Method and competence
5	Adolescence	Identity versus role confusion	Devotion and fidelity
6	Early adulthood	Intimacy versus isolation	Friendship and love
7	Middle adulthood	Generativity versus stagnation	Productivity and care
8	Old age	Ego integrity versus despair	Moderation and wisdom

and other biological processes form the basis for personality traits, especially in the first third of life, but development continues throughout the life span. Individual differences are mainly genetic in origin, but can also be affected by other biological factors, such as disease or brain injury. According to McCrae and Costa, individual experience plays only a minor role: "The course of personality development is determined by biological maturation, not by life experiences" (2008, p. 167).

McCrae and Costa's five model differs fundamentally from other theories, in that personality traits are not the result of the adaptations, but instead form the basis for the child's adaptation. Personality traits represent dispositions that contribute *causally* to a child's feelings, thoughts and actions in different situations. In McCrae and Costa's *model of the person*, personality traits interact with life events and other external factors to determine how the individual adapts in terms of roles, relationships, aspirations and attitudes that in turn affect the individual's self-concept (Figure 18.2). Unlike personality traits, these adaptations change with culture, family conditions and life-course development.

The status of the theory

It is generally agreed that the Big Five describe important aspects of the personality, and McCrae and Costa's theory has considerable influence, although the centrality of these aspects is disputed (see p. 374). McCrae and Costa focus on the relationship between temperament traits and personality traits throughout the life span, and their theory has been criticized for failing to explain the mechanisms behind development, how personality traits are formed and how individual differences arise (Caspi, 1998; Caspi et al., 2005). The assumption that personality is rooted in biology alone, and that the Big Five represent a universal description of personality across cultural boundaries, has also been subject to criticism (Piekkola, 2011).

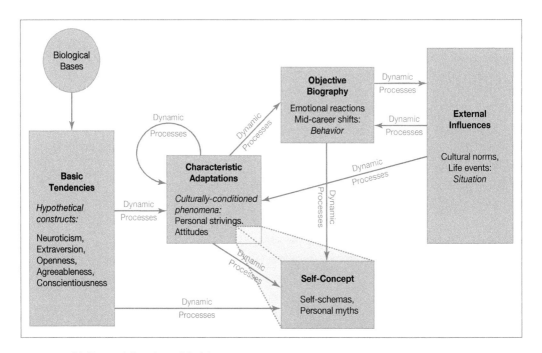

FIGURE 18.2 **McCrae and Costa's model of the person.**

The Big Five represent individual characteristics with origins in genetic and non-genetic biological factors, including maternal health, use of alcohol and narcotic substances, and illness during pregnancy. Personality traits affect the individual's self-concept and personal history, as well as adaptations, aspirations and attitudes (based on McCrae and Costa, 1995, p. 237. With permission from (c) John Wiley & Sons Ltd.).

Behaviorism

In behaviorism, personality is the organization and quality of characteristic action tendencies that an individual has acquired through learning (Novak and Peláez, 2004). There is no inherent mental structure nor a specific set of phases that underlie the development of response tendencies. Personality does not consist of the child's characteristics, since children's inclinations are governed by external factors. According to Skinner (1971) "a person does not act upon the world, the world acts upon him." Skinner sees anomalous personality traits as "wrong" or maladaptive responses and reactions that result from the child not having learned an adequate response, or respond to the wrong stimuli. Depression, for example, is thought to be caused by reduced activity due to lack of positive reinforcements to maintain the individual's activity level.

The status of the theory

A main criticism of the theory is that the assumptions about external control and human actions based on conditioning and imitation represent a simplification that takes insufficient account of the diversity of children's minds and the complex transaction chain that underlies children's emotional and social development and adaptation (Bandura, 2006; Pervin et al., 2005). All the same, much child-rearing advice to parents is based on the idea that children's personalities are learned, formed by reward and punishment, including television programs such as "Supernanny" (Rydland, 2007).

Cognitive behavior theory

Personality development from the perspective of cognitive behavior theory (or social learning theory) differs from traditional behaviorism on a number of important points (see p. 24). In cognitive behavior theory, children's reactions and behaviors are related to their self-image and expectations, especially their perceptions of themselves as *agents*, individuals acting in a social world (Bandura, 1986, 2006). Their behavior is not shaped by the environment, as Skinner argues, but by the children's own active exploration – how they perceive the surroundings and their goals, intentions and conscious self-regulation.

Bandura is skeptical of the idea of general personality traits, since they represent an abstraction of children's and adolescent's action strategies and intentions away from the situations in which they are functional (see p. 374). A child may, for example, be shy in the classroom, but extraverted on the soccer field. It is the specific environment that determines the degree to which an action strategy is functional, making it necessary to identify the situations in which children are extraverted and introverted. Thus, Bandura disagrees with both psychodynamic theories, which view children's personality traits as the result of internal dynamics independent of the child's situation, as well as with McCrae and Costa's (2008) evolution-based trait theory.

As the name indicates, cognitive processes are central in this theory. Personality emerges as a result of how children interpret the reactions of the environment to their own and other people's actions. According to Bandura, a description of personality that fails to take children's reflections and intentions into account portrays them as automatons without subjectivity, conscious regulation and personal identity. There are two main ways in which children acquire action tendencies: either by experiencing the consequences of their own actions, or by observing others, including direct social models and models in mass media such as film and television (see p. 24). Seeing others succeed in achieving a goal or being rewarded can motivate children to try to reach a similar goal; seeing others fail or being punished can have the opposite effect. This was demonstrated in a classic experiment where preschool children first witnessed a man behaving aggressively toward a doll, and receiving different reactions to his behavior. When the children played with the same doll afterwards, their actions reflected both the man's behavior and the other people's reactions (Box 18.2). Moreover, in cognitive behavior theory the child's ability to imagine what *might* happen is important for developing sound action strategies. Children form *expectations* about themselves and their surroundings and establish a standard for their own behavior by internalizing the reactions and valuations of others. The family's reactions are extremely important for younger children, while the attitudes and reactions of peers and adults outside the family become more important with age. This becomes evident in the

BOX 18.2 LEARNING FROM OBSERVING CONSEQUENCES OF AGGRESSION (BANDURA, 1965).

Preschool children aged 3;6 to 5;11 years were shown a video where man acted aggressively towards a doll called Bobo. Sometimes the man was rewarded after beating Bobo, other times he was punished or received no response. When the children were allowed to play with Bobo afterwards, they all performed similarly aggressive actions. The children who had seen the man being punished, however, showed fewer aggressive actions, especially the girls. When the children were encouraged to be aggressive towards Bobo, the children in each of the three groups showed approximately the same amount of aggressive behavior. The children's actions thus reflected both the consequences of the man's actions for himself, and other people's attitudes about the action. This shows that adults can affect children's behavior by what they encourage them to do and not to do, and by letting them know what they think of different events and actions children encounter, for example on television.

change of reference groups during childhood and adolescence, that is groups that children and adolescents use as a yardstick for desirable and appropriate behavior. Children with autism spectrum disorders are both impaired in their ability to form expectations and very insecure when they lack concrete expectations. For example, if they are going to the cinema, they need to know all details about the film itself, the cinema and the schedule, and a change in one of these elements may lead to strong emotional reactions. This is an impairment that can make their everyday life extremely stressful (Martinsen et al., 2015).

A key element of the theory is that children's action tendencies are not determined by standards as such, but rather by how children perceive their own ability to meet these standards, their *self-efficacy* (Bandura, 1997). This affects the goals children set for themselves and how they act in different situations. For example, children will only read up on homework if they believe it will have an influence on their achievement. Some children believe their own efforts have little influence and therefore find it useless to invest any resources. This is where Bandura's theory differs most radically from traditional behaviorism. Children's behaviors are not simply a matter of actual competence and external consequences, but also of internal interpretation and processing. Neither does children's self-regulation merely rely on negative feedback and experienced failure, but equally on positive feedback and sense of mastery. According to Bandura, it is precisely this sense of mastering a skill or knowledge that gives children the motivation to set themselves new goals.

The status of the theory

Bandura's cognitive theory is very influential. Although it is usually placed within the behavioral tradition, the focus on inner mental processes makes it similar to psychodynamic theories. Cognition is a core aspect of the theory but it has been criticized for not integrating knowledge about general cognitive development and children's way of managing social information at different ages. It is criticized for not taking sufficient account of changes due to physical maturation, for example in regard to sexuality, and for lacking an adequate explanation of motivational processes, such as conflicts involving incompatible or contradictory motives for action. Bandura's theory is the basis of *cognitive behavior therapy* and *cognitive developmental therapy* which are used much in school psychology and treatment of children and adolescents. These therapies aim at influencing the child's or adolescents' thought schemas, self-awareness, self-esteem and self-efficacy, and thereby changing the cognitive basis of maladaptive action tendencies (Benjamin et al., 2011; Creed et al., 2016).

THE EMERGENCE OF PERSONALITY

Temperament is generally regarded to be one of the cornerstones of adult personality – even if most researchers do not agree with Costa and McCrae's theory (Chen and Schmidt, 2015). The temperament traits *sociability*, *effortful control* and *negative emotionality* are mirrored in the personality traits *extraversion*, *conscientiousness* and *neuroticism* (emotional lability). However, although they overlap, personality traits describe individual differences that are not captured by temperament (Herzhoff et al., 2017).

Studies of early temperament and later personality traits suggest a certain continuity. The Dunedin study has followed up more than 1,000 children born in 1972 and 1973. Caspi (2000) found limited connection between temperament measures at the age of 3 and personality traits at 18 and 21 years in general. However, 10 percent of the children had the temperament type *under controlled* at 3 years, and they appeared more reckless and aggressive at 21 years than the other children and had a tendency to feel mistreated and deceived by others. Another 8 percent of the children had the temperament type *inhibited* at the age of 3. They tended to become cautious, showed little aggression, avoided physically dangerous activities and disliked guiding or influencing others. At 21 years, other people characterized them as lacking in warmth and confidence. Other studies, too, have found that children who seem extremely inhibited in infancy tend to become introverted as adults (Asendorpf, 2010; Kagan and Snidman, 2004). Shyness is such a prominent part of a child's behavior that others tend to define the child in terms of this characteristic, and this may contribute to maintaining the shyness.

Kagan (1998a) points out that the assumption of early personality formation contradicts the view that personality is the result of adaptation. Although children's early reaction and action tendencies reflect their temperament, children are also part of a dynamic social context that contributes to regulating their reactions and behaviors (Chen and Schmidt, 2015). The extent to which temperament traits prove stable over time will therefore depend on how well they fit with other people and the cultural practices of the environment (Wachs, 1994). Early differences in temperament confirm that children make their own unique contribution to the transactional process. The temperament alone cannot explain the development of personality but theories about the role of temperament still offer alternative or supplementary viewpoints to other theories.

Personality in childhood

The transition to preschool age (3–4 years) is considered a developmental milestone in the sense that a number of person characteristics begin to

be observable at this age, but even when based on Big Five, descriptions of children's personality traits differ from descriptions of those of adults (see p. 374). As children grow older, they show a broader and more complex set of individual differences. At the same time as new differences between children come to the surface, children's personalities become increasingly stable (Shiner, 2006, 2015).

Children who score *high* on *neuroticism* in Big Five are described as anxious, vulnerable and tense. They have difficulties coping with stress, easily feel guilty, have a low frustration threshold, and feel insecure in social relations. Emotionally they are characterized by fear, anxiety and sadness. Anxiety and fear can be impediments to social relationships and to adapting in school and at work. Children who score *low* on this trait are typically stable and relaxed, adapt to new situations, and quickly recover from negative events.

Parents rarely describe their children as *conscientious* before the age of 3, but often after the age of 6. Children who score *high* on this trait are attentive, responsible and have high standards. They plan, think before they act, and persevere. Children with *low* scores are typically described as irresponsible, unreliable, careless and distractible, and easily give up. Conscientiousness is generally associated with adaptability and a prosocial, positive development at school and in children's personal lives.

Children who score *high* on *agreeableness* are described as considerate, empathic, generous, protective and kind. They are compliant and easy to interact with. Agreeableness, too, is associated with positive development, good peer relations, positive progress in school and at work, and a low probability of externalizing problems and criminal behavior. Children who score *low* on this trait are described as aggressive, rude, stubborn, bossy and manipulative. They are often rejected by their peers and are more likely to do poorly at school and in the workplace, and experience conflictual partner relationships.

Children who score high on *openness to experience* are described as eager and quick to learn, clever, knowledgeable, curious and original. This trait first shows up in parents' descriptions when children are about 6–7 years old, and is typically associated with good achievements at school.

However, the picture is not as clear-cut as this brief summary may suggest. The various traits interact and the presence of a positive trait does not always imply a positive development. A trait such as *compliance*, for example, is generally considered positive but can also involve a risk for abuse. Neither will a negative trait be destiny, the developmental outcome depends on the social context of the child.

Stability and change

Children's personality traits vary in stability. Some children show high stability, while the personality development of others is marked by change (Asendorpf, 1992). When children are compared at intervals of 1–2 years, stability is generally high, with correlations around 0.5–0.8. With a wider age span, stability decreases. One study found correlations of about 0.2 between the Big Five measured at 2 and 15 years of age (Lamb et al., 2002). The stability of personality traits lies within a range of 0.4–0.5 for a 3-year period in childhood, and increases throughout the life span to over 0.7 within a 10-year period after the age of 50 (Ibáñez et al., 2016; Roberts and DelVecchio, 2000). Low to moderate correlations indicate considerable variation in the development of children with similar early traits. Moreover, participant attrition is a problem in most longitudinal studies. Families may move or tire of participating in observations and completing research forms (e.g. Magnus et al., 2016; Schreuder and Alsaker, 2014). Children who remain in these types of studies have therefore mostly grown up under stable conditions, which also may contribute to the stability in their personal characteristics.

Stability does not mean that the child does not change, as the behavior that forms the basis for assessing personality traits changes with age. Children can change behavior, while at the same time maintaining their relative position in relation to their peers. In the longitudinal study from 2 to 15 years, the children on average became slightly less extraverted and somewhat more agreeable and conscientious (Lamb et al., 2002). Children with frequent outbursts of anger at the age of 2 have usually learned to control their behavior by the age of 10. Although outbursts have become rare, they may still be perceived as quick-tempered compared with their peers. Thus, assessments of personality traits must account for what is typical at a given age (Caspi and Roberts, 2001).

Personality development in adolescence

Adolescence is a transitional and formative period, during which instability in general is more prominent than stability. Stability in individual traits as well as in personality profile seems higher than in childhood, especially in late adolescence, and lower than in adulthood, but degree of stability varies between studies (Hill and Edmonds, 2017; Klimstra et al., 2009). Adolescents tend to become more agreeable with age, but many of those who scored low on agreeableness when they are younger, continue to do so, although they, too, become more agreeable over time. This indicates that the rank order to some extent is preserved over time. Stability may partly be due to the fact that adolescents seek out activities to fit their personality and thereby reinforce their existing traits. However, it depends on life events: a stable life situation contributes to stability, while parental divorce and other negative life events affect later personality, adaptability, reactions and behaviors (Caspi et al., 2005; Lewis, 2001b; Roberts et al., 2006).

The variation in development of personality in adolescence illustrates the continuous interaction between stability and change that characterizes development in most areas. An individual does not maintain exactly the same personality, but constantly changes from the characteristics developed before. Additionally, there seem to be individual differences in the tendency to change. Some children and adolescents change more than others, underlining the fact that the mature personality is not determined in childhood (Roberts et al., 2006).

FACTORS THAT AFFECT PERSONALITY DEVELOPMENT

Genetic factors, aspects of the general environment and specific life events contribute to individual differences in personality.

Heritability

Genes have been found to influence personality development. A large metastudy found that roughly half of the variance in personality could be attributed to genes and half to the environment, indicating that genes and environment play equal roles in development of personality

(Briley and Tucker-Drob, 2014). However, heritability estimates (see p. 83) for personality traits also vary with the age of the twins (Shiner, 2015). Both identical and fraternal twins growing up separately tend to become more dissimilar with age (McCartney et al., 1990). Viken and colleagues (1994) found that heritability estimates for *extraversion* and *neuroticism* declined from childhood to early adulthood and subsequently stabilized, while heritability of *inhibition* remained more stable. The notion that the influence of genes diminishes with age runs contrary to Scarr and McCartney's (1983) claim that individuals create their own environment (see also p. 87). Based on their theory, similarities between identical twins should increase compared with fraternal twins since the biological basis is "freer" and less bound by their parents' lifestyle.

Genes are not independent: stressful life events can affect the relative impact of genes. One study found less overlap in personality traits among 29-year-old twins who had experienced stressful life events between the ages of 6 and 15 years than among twins without similar experiences during the same period, especially for the traits agreeableness, conscientiousness and openness to experience (Torgersen and Janson, 2002). Moreover, it is likely that parents and others treat identical twins as more alike than fraternal twins since they resemble each other more in appearance (Joseph, 2013). Twins with parents who know or assume they are identical are often considered more similar than they actually are (assimilation effect). Even when they resemble each other strongly, fraternal twins are often attributed complementary characteristics such as "quick" and "sedate," or "happy" and "grumpy" (contrast effect). They are compared to one another rather than to a general norm (Neale and Stevenson, 1989; Plomin et al., 1997).

Recent years have seen the discovery of genes that seem to affect the way in which children respond to positive and negative experiences (see p. 84). Alleles of the genes MAO-A and 5-HTTP, for example, appear to be related to children's temperament and reactions to novelty, and in turn impact their susceptibility to particular parenting styles. The effects of some genetic differences only seem to emerge during development when children have experienced neglect, abuse and similarly serious incidents. Genes do not cause such events, but may affect how the individual copes with them when they do occur (Meaney, 2010; Moffitt et al., 2006; Rutter, 2004). Consequently, it is not particular personality traits that distinguish individuals with different genetic makeups, but rather differences in flexibility and sensitivity to the characteristics of their social surroundings that may influence personality development.

Childhood environment

The social environment is the other major source of individual differences in personality. In most societies, the family represents the main social environment in childhood and adolescence. Parents are an important resource for children's psychological growth, for instance by engaging in conversations about the child herself and others (Dunn et al., 1987; Pomerantz and Thompson, 2008). Parents' personality and their sense of competence and self-efficacy affect their parenting style. Parents who score high on extraversion and agreeableness and perceive themselves as competent parents do not overreact as often and have a warmer parenting style than parents who score lower on these two traits and perceive themselves as less competent (de Haan et al., 2009). Also depression and other mental health problems may have an impact on perceived self-competence and parenting style in both mothers and fathers (Berg-Nielsen et al., 2002; Peláez et al., 2008; Wilson and Durbin, 2010).

Several theoretical perspectives imply that children should become similar to their parents. From a cognitive-behavioral view, parents affect their children by being role models (see p. 24). According to Freud's theory, personality is partly shaped by children's identification with their parents (see p. 377). Research, however, has not found strong similarities between the personality traits of parents and their children. For *extraversion*, the correlation is 0.15, for *neuroticism* it is 0.16 between children and their biological parents, and 0.10 and 0.05 between adopted children and their adoptive parents. The personalities of siblings growing up in the same family can be quite different. Although parenting style shows considerable stability (Dallaire and Weinraub, 2005), this does not mean that parents treat their children equally all the time. The entire family goes through transactional change over time, and parents adjust to their children's age and development.

The differences between siblings and the relative dissimilarity between children and parents have led to discussions about the amount of influence parents actually have on their child's personality. Scarr (1992) concludes that it is pointless for parents to try to influence their children's personalities, but many studies show that parental attitudes and parenting practices have significance for children's personality. In a classic study, Baldwin (1949) found that children of parents with a *democratic* parenting style tended to be active, social and could speak for themselves. Children with *controlling* parents were more obedient, fearful and withdrawn. Other studies have found that children and adolescents with controlling parents tend to be dependent and lacking in sociability, while those with *positive authoritative* parents (decisive, rational and loving) were more independent and socially competent (Baumrind, 1967, 2013). Many adult patients with personality disorders tell that their parents did not understand them in childhood, that they were over controlled and that they did not get the love they needed (Cramer et al., 2007).

This small selection of studies demonstrates that the family impacts children's development in different ways. Children observe their parents' actions and reactions, and parents control, stimulate and challenge their children, encouraging, refusing and helping them to become autonomous and solve the challenges they face on their own. Their influence does not always lead to a personality that resembles their own – the family environment can contribute to both similarity and dissimilarity (Pomerantz and Thompson, 2008). Children growing up in the same family do not necessarily have identical environments. Even when they have a consistent parenting style, parents treat their children differently, and their adaptation to the children's temperament and other individual traits can result in very different environments for siblings. Contrast effects, too, have an impact on siblings: if parents found their first child to be difficult, they often perceive their next child to be easy, and vice versa (Rodgers et al., 1994). Moreover, studies also show that children with different gene variants (alleles) can be differentially susceptible to parent sensitivity and parenting (Pluess and Belsky, 2010). Knowledge of kinship and the parents' living situation is not enough to map the environmental factors that may contribute to children's similarities and differences: the interaction between parenting style and children's characteristics results in a relative influence rather than an absolute one (Collins et al., 2000; Torgersen and Janson, 2002). This means that all children are affected by their home environment, but on different premises and in different ways.

Parents do not only represent their own experiences or personalities. Social norms and cultural values contribute to forming the actions of children and adults, how their emotions are expressed, the relationships between them, and so on. Cultures vary in how much they emphasize control, obedience, cooperation and autonomy (Chen and French, 2008; Rodríguez et al., 2009; Selin, 2014). In collectivist cultures like China, parents stress the importance of the child's contribution to society's goals, while parents in individualistic cultures like the United States emphasize competition and the child's own well-being (Kwan and Herrmann, 2015). Additionally, parenting style is influenced by the immediate surroundings. Parents living in violent or stressful neighborhoods tend to be more controlling and restrictive than parents who live in quieter areas (Furstenberg and Hughes, 1997; Gewirtz and Zamir, 2014).

Once children enter school age, peers become more important and friends gain increasing influence (see Chapter 20). They represent a benchmark when children gain more knowledge about themselves and others. In late adolescence and adulthood, personality development is more influenced by forces outside the family, and positive authoritative parenting has greatest effect when the parents of the children's friends have the same upbringing style (Fletcher et al., 1995).

The significance of early experiences

Both classical and modern theorists consider early childhood to be a particularly important period that sets the developmental course. Studies have especially focused on the consequences of serious neglect, maltreatment and abuse, and how change and improvement in the rearing environment affect children's social adjustment and personality development (Clarke and Clarke, 2000; Fox and Rutter, 2010). Negative experiences early in life seem to contribute to a *vigilance* that increases vulnerability to stressful events, or to the development of behavioral tendencies that increase the likelihood of stress or personal problems later in life, and may leave relatively permanent traces on the individual's personality (see McCrory and Viding, 2015). Early identification of limited family resources and timely intervention are therefore important priorities in a society (Guralnick, 2011; Herskind et al., 2015).

Early neglect

Studies of infant monkeys have lent important insight into the possible consequences of early neglect (see also p. 398). A classic study demonstrates the importance of early active interaction. Harlow (1963) isolated infant monkeys so they could see other monkeys, but not have physical contact with them in the first few months of life. Observations showed that they developed neither playing skills nor ordinary social skills. When they later were brought together with non-isolated monkeys, they had significant problems interacting with them. As adolescents and adults, they were often aggressive and had difficulty engaging in normal sexual activities. Many of the female monkeys developed into incompetent mothers, and some abused their young. Problems were greatest with their firstborns, while later-born infants often were given better care. Individual differences were significant, however, and a third of the mothers in this group showed normal care for their infant (Suomi, 1991).

In this study, the monkeys were directly placed together with the rest of the group after isolation. In another study, similarly isolated infant monkeys were slowly exposed to social stimulation, initially in the company of a non-isolated 3-month-old monkey for 1 hour a day. Gradually, they improved at playing and socializing with others, but the other monkeys continued to be the only ones to take initiative. After a few weeks they, too, started to initiate play and interaction. As adolescents and adults they generally behaved normally, but new and stressful situations initially caused them to respond with rocking movements and other forms of stereotyped behaviors they had shown during their early isolation. They also reacted with strong emotions and by acting out when placed in isolation once again (Novak and Harlow, 1975; Suomi, 1991). The reaction patterns caused by their early isolation thus never

completely disappeared, even though they only emerged under similar conditions.

Corresponding reactions have been observed in studies of children exposed to severe neglect in orphanages or in the home. Especially in countries at war, but also in other contexts, many children grow up in orphanages without adequate physical and emotional care. Several studies have found a significantly higher prevalence of internalizing disorders in children and adolescents who had been victims of neglect than children who had not experienced neglect (Gallo et al., 2017; Sadowski et al., 1999; Zeanah et al., 2009). Studies have found a higher prevalence of suicide attempts, more antisocial personality disorders and alcohol abuse in individuals who had been neglected or abused in childhood (Sachs-Ericsson et al., 2017; Widom, 2000). In a follow-up study of children who had been taken from their parents due to neglect or abuse and placed in orphanages, one-third showed poor adaptation as adults. A comparison group with normal upbringing showed a similar development for 10 percent of the males and none of the females. The difficulties experienced by the follow-up group were not only the result of early neglect, but also of having been separated from their families and growing up in institutions, with a continuous chain of risk factors (Rutter, 1991a).

Still, early neglect is not destiny. Many children are resilient to growing up under such negative conditions (Cicchetti, 2013; Luthar et al., 2014). A number of studies show that the negative consequences of poor childhood conditions are reduced when children are adopted into better home environments. Their age at adoption and the length of time children have spent in orphanages have major significance (Julian, 2013). Children from Romanian orphanages of low quality who were adopted between the ages of 6 and 24 months had somewhat poorer adaptation at the age of 6 years than children adopted before the age of 6 months. This was due not only to the shorter amount of time the children had spent under normal childhood conditions, the advantages of early adoption were also evident when comparing groups that had been adopted equally long. The developmental trajectory seems more difficult to change when a child has spent a longer time adapting to the neglect – longer time indicates to the child that the aversive features of the environment are stable and hence will continue (Chisholm, 1998; Rutter et al., 2010).

Other studies have found poorer social-cognitive and play skills in 4-year-old Romanian than British adoptees, with greater differences for Romanian children adopted between the ages of 6 and 24 months than those who had been younger at the time of adoption. Ten percent of the children had severe social-cognitive problems reminiscent of autism spectrum disorder, including communication and social impairment, trouble understanding other people's thoughts and feelings, narrow interests and stereotyped repetitive movements. However, they took far more initiative in social interaction than children with autism spectrum disorder usually do, and the problems were significantly reduced when the children were 11–12 years old (Kreppner et al., 1999; Rutter et al., 2007).

Early intervention is important, but a number of studies show a positive development also in children who were adopted into stable environments at a relatively late age and offered appropriate treatment after many years in different foster homes (Dumaret et al., 1997). Moskowitz (1985) observed a small group of children who had been interned in German concentration camps during World War II. The children had managed to adapt and had not developed irreparable psychological damage. While adoption studies show that it takes time for children to get over negative experiences, they also give reason to believe that the differences to their peers gradually dissipate once they get older and have lived under positive and stable conditions for longer periods.

Maltreatment and sexual abuse

Maltreatment and sexual abuse shatter the very foundation of children's life – that somebody cares for them. They affect children's perception of themselves and others (see also Chapter 21) and can have profound consequences for the development of their personality and mental health. A longitudinal study of physically abused 2-year-olds found that they showed more anger and were less obedient together with their mothers than other children. A little more than a year later they showed poor self-regulation and a negative self-image. In kindergarten they were negative, angry, disobedient and antagonistic toward their peers. They had learned that the world is a hostile place in which they had to

defend themselves. Children who had been sexually abused before the age of 5 are exceptionally anxious and dependent on adults, while at the same time exhibiting wide mood swings from extreme aggressiveness to strong dependence and passivity (Erickson et al., 1989). Around 6 years of age, children who had been maltreated scored lower on the traits agreeableness, conscientiousness and openness to experience, and higher on neuroticism involving high negative emotionality and low emotion regulation. This personality pattern was maintained at 9 years (Rogosch and Cicchetti, 2004).

Children who have been maltreated or abused often show poor development but their developmental trajectories vary. A strong sense of shame (see p. 353), depression, and a tendency to perceive other people as a threat (see p. 361) are common reactions. Some react with hostility and aggression toward their peers, while others tend to withdraw from them. Some children alternate between aggression and withdrawal, incorporating the actions of both perpetrator and victim in interacting with other children. In school age, some children develop delusions of grandeur, seemingly as a protection against the negative image they perceive others to have of them. In adolescence and early adulthood, some of them develop dissociative personality disorder with disruptions in identity and sense of being a person (Cicchetti, 2016; Cicchetti and Toth, 2015).

Many parents who maltreat or abuse their children have themselves grown up under difficult circumstances and were subjected to abuse in childhood. Since they received little help in regulating their own temperament, they may not have learned to deal with the kind of irritation that a crying or nagging child can provoke. The use of violent strategies to resolve conflicts in childhood may further have led to a lower threshold for these types of abusive actions (see p. 359). Adults who have abused children outside their own family have often experienced prolonged separation from their parents or grown up in institutions, but less than half have been sexually abused themselves (Waterhouse et al., 1994). These studies demonstrate the importance of the conditions under which children grow up, but also that the underlying causes of child abuse and maltreatment are complex, and that they cannot easily be explained (Clarke and Clarke, 2000).

Divorce and death

Among all the single events involving major changes in children's lives, divorce is the most common, and for many children entails less contact with one of their parents, usually the father (Kalmijn, 2015). Numerous studies have shown that divorce can reduce children's confidence, cause them to blame themselves and cope poorly at school, as well as become more dependent on their teachers and the parent they live with. Adolescents can become anxious, depressed and disruptive, with girls reacting stronger than boys (Størksen et al., 2005). Parental divorce may even influence well-being in adult life (Huurre et al., 2006). Studies that include information on the child *before* it was known whether the parents would divorce have found that domestic conditions were different for children whose parents divorced than for those who did not divorce, factors that were important for children's reactions following the divorce (Strohschein, 2005). Some studies show long-term effects, but the direct impact of divorce is usually short-lived. Most children show a typical development, and any long-term effects on their personality development are related to the new type of relationship they establish with their parents (Hetherington, 2003; Wallerstein and Lewis, 2004).

Losing a parent is always a dramatic experience for children and adolescents, and brings with it the risk of internalizing disorders and problems at school (Dyregrov et al., 2015; Stikkelbroek et al., 2016). The strongest grief reactions generally do not last very long. After 1 year, they are usually significantly reduced, but depression in the surviving parent, including inadequate care and reduced parent–child interaction, can intensify and prolong these reactions (Pianta and Nimetz, 1992). Loss of a parent in childhood increases the likelihood of anxiety and depression as an adult, but also depends on the child's vulnerability and other life events (Brent et al., 2012; Howell et al., 2015). Vulnerability is highest when parents die of external causes early in children's lives, such as accidents, murder and suicide (Berg et al., 2016). Although children in most countries do not lose one or both of their parents in childhood or adolescence, it is a common experience for children in countries at war, and many young refugees have lost one or both parents (Shaw, 2003; Werner, 2012). Also in countries with poor health care and high rates of HIV and AIDS, many children lose their parents (Case et al., 2004).

The developmental consequences of early experiences

The studies presented here show that early negative experiences involve a risk of aberrant and delayed development, but also that even severe forms of neglect and abuse can be overcome. Children are often resilient to individual experiences, which rarely have a profound and lasting impact. It is the experience of repeated negative events and continuous neglect or abuse by the surroundings that can affect children's personality development in the long term (Wachs and Gruen, 1982; Sameroff, 2009).

PERSONALITY DEVELOPMENT AND LATER DISORDERS

A personality disorder is a pattern of inner experiences and behavior that deviates from cultural norms. In DSM-5, this diagnosis is not usually given before the age of 18 on the grounds that an individual's personality is not sufficiently stable before that age (American Psychiatric Association, 2013), and personality disorders are not included in Chapter 4. However, some claim that personality disorders are observable in childhood and adolescence, and it is a common assumption that they are rooted in childhood. Both child characteristics and environmental conditions appear to be related to later personality disorders (Shiner, 2009; Tackett, et al., 2009; van den Akker et al., 2016). Klein and associates (2014) hypothesize that maladaptive child development across the self and interpersonal domains play an important role in the genesis of later personality pathology. Harsh parenting as well as physical, emotional and sexual abuse in childhood and adolescence seem to represent increased risk of developing borderline personality disorder. Still, symptoms of personality disorder may be difficult to distinguish from the normal emergence of personality traits in adolescence and such symptoms are more unstable than in adulthood (Klein et al., 2014).

Studies show that children's early personality affects how they later adapt to and shape their own social surroundings. A comprehensive British study generally found a low incidence of emotional disorders in adults, but the incidence was several times higher in those who had shown significant behavioral problems and emotional disorders in childhood (Rutter, 1991b). Children who are social, secure and independent have a lower probability of developing internalizing disorders. In the Dunedin study (see p. 382), children who were under controlled at the age of 3 years have more externalizing disorders in school age and adolescence than other children. At 21 years, they had committed more crimes than their peers, had relatively many conflicts in their relationships, and were often considered unreliable and untrustworthy by others. Over controlled or inhibited children showed a tendency to develop internalizing disorders in the course of adolescence. At age 21, they had smaller social networks and less social support than children who had not been inhibited at the age of 3 (Caspi, 2000). Another study found that under controlled children had a higher incidence of drug problems in adolescence than better regulated children (Shedler and Block, 1990). Some personality disorders in adolescence and adulthood are considered to be maladaptive variants of the Big Five (Shiner, 2009). Psychopathy (see p. 468) is considered a personality disorder and adolescents may show symptoms of psychopathy similar to adults (Lynam and Widiger, 2007).

Although early disorders entail greater vulnerability for later disorders, it is not always the same children who suffer from disorders at all age levels. In a follow-up study of children who had been referred to a psychiatric clinic for anxiety and emotional disorders, only three of 28 who had been referred before the age of 9 years received psychiatric treatment as young adults. A quarter of the children referred between the ages of 10 and 14 years, and half of those referred between 15 and 19 years, received psychiatric treatment when they were 20–24 years old (von Knorring et al., 1987). This indicates that most children with relatively early disorders eventually outgrow them, and that disorders later in childhood and adolescence are more indicative of disorders in adulthood.

PERSONALITY DEVELOPMENT IS A TRANSACTIONAL PROCESS

Children's tendency to feel, think, react and act in particular ways is formed by the possibilities and limitations of their surroundings, as well as by their previous development, while at the same time they contribute to shaping their own environment. Children's personality reflects their development history, their goals and values, and the characteristics of the people in their surroundings. The same event can have different meanings for children with differing backgrounds, interests and goals. Children's individual tendencies to act and react represent a *preparedness* that reflects their individual temperament and understanding of the world. Contrary to Scarr's (1992) claim, children can only create their own environment to a limited extent. They *affect* their parents, but do not create them. The parents' own temperament and established behaviors determine how they initially meet the child's actions and reactions. An insecure father living under difficult conditions can become more secure by experiencing himself as a successful parent of a temperamentally easy child, or become more insecure if the child has a difficult temperament. In that case, the father's insecurity is not caused by the child alone, however. Children born into unstable or war-torn areas are powerless to create peace for their parents. Most children have an important, albeit limited impact on their caregivers and surroundings in general. A basic personality trait may be the ability to act in different ways and to choose action strategies based on the demands of the situation. The most important differences between children do not have to do with how they react in familiar situations, but how they deal with *new* situations (Kagan and Snidman, 2004; Masten, 2014). Sroufe and colleagues (1993) describe *developmental lines* not characterized by fixed behavior patterns, but rather by how consistently children meet and adapt to new contexts. It is this consistency the authors believe best represents what is known as personality.

SUMMARY

1   Children differ with respect to emotionality, irritability, activity level and how they handle emotional situations, novelty and changes. Traditional temperament types include *easy*, *difficult* and *slow to warm up*. More recent categories include *sociability*, *positive* and *negative emotionality*, *extraversion*, *effortful control of attention and distractions*, *endurance*, *likeability* and *adaptability*. *Reaction to novelty* is an especially important trait that indicates whether children are cautious and timid, or approach when they meet strangers and new situations. Temperament can be assessed through *physiological measures*, *questionnaires*, *parent interviews* and *observations*.

2   Temperament heritability ranges from 0.2 to 0.6, changes with age, and shows greater stability over shorter than longer periods. There is generally a moderate continuity of temperament, but more for children with a pronounced trait.

3   Children's temperaments affect the way in which they are treated by their parents, whose reactions change with the child's age and can both strengthen or weaken the effect of the child's temperament. The "goodness of fit" of parents' and children's temperaments differ. A generally positive parental trait is *sensitivity* and the ability to adapt to the child's temperament.

4   Children's temperament can entail both vulnerability to *internalizing* and *externalizing* disorders, and *resilience* to such disorders. Positive environmental characteristics and children's interactions with other people can protect children with a difficult temperament from developing problems. Temperament can contribute to both vulnerability and protection against disorders.

5   *Personality* is the tendency to feel, think and act in certain ways. The "Big Five" personality traits include *extraversion*, *agreeableness*, *conscientiousness*, *neuroticism* (emotional lability) and *openness to experience*, each consisting of six sub-facets. Younger children are typically described as *active*, *irritable*, *independent* and *mature for their age*. According to Bandura and Mischel, children's tendencies to act and react in certain ways are adaptations to actual situations that variously characterize a child in different situations, like a *behavioral signature*.

6   The main elements of Freud's *psychodynamic* theory of personality development are *id*, *ego* and *superego*, *the psychosexual phases* and *the defense mechanisms*. Many modern theorists build on Freud's basic ideas but have changed major parts of his theory. Erikson represents *ego psychology*. Each of eight lifespan phases is associated with a *social crisis* that form the basis for an individual's personality. The theory has been criticized for being too male-oriented and poorly suited to modern society, but is still widely used.

7   McCrae and Costa's theory is based on evolutionary principles and the hypothesis that the Big Five and their 30 facets are universal and develop through maturation. Personality is not the result of individual adaptation, but instead forms the basis for adaptation. The theory has been criticized for failing to explain the mechanisms underlying personality development.

8   *Behaviorism* describes personality in terms of *response tendencies* acquired through conditioning and imitation like all other behavior. The theory has been criticized for taking insufficient account of the diversity of children's minds and the complexity of development. In *cognitive behavior theory*, children's reactions and behaviors are the result of environmental adaptation related to children's self-esteem and expectations, and especially their perception of themselves as *agents* in a social world. They learn from the consequences of their own actions and by observing the consequences of others' actions. Cognitive behavior therapy based on Bandura's theory is very influential in clinical child and adolescent psychology, but he has been criticized for not integrating knowledge of general cognitive development.

Continued

9   Early temperament and later personality are partially related. Descriptions of children's personality traits differ from descriptions of adults. New personal characteristics appear in preschool age, and toward adolescence personality is increasingly described with the same personality traits as adults.

10 Personality traits are stable over shorter time spans and low to moderate over longer time spans. Some children have a *stable* personality development, while others are more characterized by *change*. Although early *disorders* involve a greater risk of later disorders, it is generally not the same children who show disorders at all age levels.

11 Heritability varies for each trait, with estimates rarely exceeding 0.4–0.5, indicating that the genes and environment play equal roles. The influence of genes seems to decrease with age. Some genes have an impact on how vulnerable children are to neglect, parenting style and other environmental factors.

12 The personality traits of parents and their children generally show low correlations. Family affects the development of children's personalities, but not always in such a way that they come to resemble their parents or siblings. Parenting style and behavior reflect parents' experiences, personality and any possible disorders, as well as influences from their children. Children of parents with a *democratic parenting style* tend to be active, social and able to speak up for themselves. Children with *controlling* parents are obedient, fearful and withdrawn. *Friends and activities outside the home* gain increasing influence on the development of personality. Social and cultural factors affect parenting style and thereby contribute to shaping children's personalities.

13 Early childhood is often viewed as a developmentally *sensitive period* that leads to *vigilance* with increased *vulnerability* or *resilience* to stress and problems later in life. Children who have been subjected to severe neglect usually show poor adaptation, but the risk of developing mental health problems can be reduced by improved domestic conditions or by adoption into solid rearing environments. Maltreatment and sexual abuse increase children's vulnerability and can have a profound and lasting impact on their development. It affects children's perception of their surroundings, and some children react by withdrawing from their peers, others by showing aggression and hostility. Divorce involves sudden and major changes in children's lives, but the effects are relatively short-lived.

14 Some children are *resilient* and manage to cope with relatively serious early neglect without apparent damage. It is the continuous exposure to an environment of neglect or abuse, rather than isolated incidents, that can impact the development of children's personality in the long term.

15 The diagnosis "personality disorder" is not usually given before the age of 18 but many claim that such disorders may be observable in adolescence, and it is a common assumption that they are rooted in the individual's experiences in childhood and maladaptive variants of personality traits.

16 Personality development is an adaptive transactional process. The environment can either hinder or promote children's ability to self-regulate and adapt, and is in turn affected by the child's self-regulating mechanisms. One of the most basic personality traits is the ability to choose appropriate action strategies in new situations. *Developmental lines* represent the consistency in children's ability to meet and adapt to new contexts.

CORE ISSUES

- The relationship between temperament and disorders.
- The measurement of temperament.
- The bases of personality traits.
- The importance of early experiences.
- The presence of personality disorders in childhood and adolescence.

SUGGESTIONS FOR FURTHER READING

Bandura, A. (2006). Toward a psychology of human agency. *Perspectives on Psychological Science, 1,* 164–180.

Davis, M., & Suveg, C. (2014). Focusing on the positive: A review of the role of child positive affect in developmental psychopathology. *Clinical Child and Family Psychology Review, 17,* 97–124.

Erikson, E. H. (1963). *Childhood and society.* New York, NY: W. Norton and Company.

Guralnick, M. J. (2011). Why early intervention works: A systems perspective. *Infants and Young Children, 24,* 6–28.

Kagan, J., & Snidman, N. C. (2004). *The long shadow of temperament.* Cambridge, MA: Belknap Press.

Kongerslev, M. T., et al. (2015). Personality disorder in childhood and adolescence comes of age: A review of the current evidence and prospects for future research. *Scandinavian Journal of Child and Adolescent Psychiatry and Psychology, 3,* 31–48.

Rothbart, M. K. (2007). Temperament, development, and personality. *Current Directions in Psychological Science, 16,* 207–212.

Widom, C. S., et al. (2008). Childhood victimization and lifetime revictimization. *Child Abuse and Neglect, 32,* 785–796.

Contents

CHAPTER 19

ATTACHMENT

From birth throughout the life span, human beings are oriented toward social stimulation and participation, making social relations a core area of developmental psychology. This chapter is about children's early social relations and the influence they may have on the child's social functioning and development. According to attachment theories, early close relationships provide children with knowledge about social relations that form the basis for how they meet other people and contribute to forming their later reactions and behaviors.

Attachment behavior is defined as "any behavior that results in a person attaining or maintaining proximity to some other clearly identified individual who is conceived as better able to cope with the world" (Bowlby, 1982, p. 669). Thus, the function of attachment behaviors is to ensure a feeling of safety by reducing the physical distance to specific individuals, *attachment figures*. If a child's attachment system is to perform its function, attachment figures must respond to the child's attachment behavior. Adults react to signaling behavior by reducing the distance to the child when necessary, calling the child or moving closer when the distance exceeds a certain limit, for example when the child has wandered off (Bowlby, 1969).

THEORETICAL PERSPECTIVES ON ATTACHMENT

Views differ with regard to the basis of attachment and the possible outcomes of different types of attachment. John Bowlby presented the first comprehensive theory of attachment and laid the foundation for all later theories (Hinde, 2005). Bowlby's ethological theory will therefore be presented first and in particular detail, although some other views predated his.

Seeking security by the mother.

Ethological theory

Attachment has to do with relationships, whose biological basis, according to Bowlby (1969), is survival. From an evolutionary perspective, the survival value of attachment behavior lies in the fact that human infants would be unable to survive without a caregiver. The same applies to infant monkeys, although their development is somewhat faster (Suomi, 2008). The imprinting behavior of ducks and other birds seems to fulfill a similar function as attachment behavior in humans (see Figure 19.1), with the difference that imprinting in birds must occur within a short critical period to be functional since birds mature quickly. Also birds show distress by separation from their mother after being imprinted. In humans, the attachment process moves far more slowly, and attachment relations can only change over longer periods (Ainsworth and Bowlby, 1991; Bowlby, 1982).

John Bowlby.

According to Bowlby (1969, 1973, 1980), attachment is an innate *behavioral system* whose task is to ensure protection through proximity to an attachment figure. The need for security is an independent drive in line with nutritional needs and sexual behavior. Attachment behavior is regulated by a *control system* comparable to the autonomous parts of the nervous system that regulate blood pressure and body temperature. The function of this control system is to keep the attachment figure within certain boundaries of distance and availability, depending on the child's state and the situation. To achieve this, children use increasingly sophisticated ways of communicating, making the development of communication and language an important element in attachment. Attachment is an active process rather than passive dependence (Ainsworth and Bowlby, 1991).

The theory is based on the premise that attachment behavior must be reciprocated by someone who provides the necessary care. Bowlby proposes that adults have a *caregiving behavioral system* that is activated by the child's attachment behavior. Parents (and other adults) are thus biologically predisposed to react in certain ways to children's attachment behavior. Given a normal development, parents will experience a strong urge to hold their child, give comfort when the child cries, keep the child warm, and protect and feed the child. Since the caregiving system, too, has evolved through evolution, parental behavior will to some extent follow a predetermined pattern, but the parents' social and cultural experiences determine how this behavior manifests itself.

At the core of the theory lies the notion that children form "working models" for their later relationships with other people (Bowlby, 1969). A working model is a "map" based on past experiences that includes information about the interactions with another person in a relationship, and particularly the person's availability and responsiveness to the child. These working models form the basis for children's perceptions and expectations of others and themselves and determine how children meet their social environment and new relational partners. Feelings toward others are an integral part of the working models, and children's feelings, as well as the quality of the relationship, are the result of attachment experiences. By and large, they lead to security and love, but can also give rise to anger and rejection.

FIGURE 19.1 Imprinting in birds.

The imprinting of ducklings relies on the fact that they follow the first moving object or living being they see within a period of 48 hours, and will seek out the imprinting object in situations that elicit attachment behavior. Konrad Lorenz (1935) was able to imprint ducklings to any moving object within the critical period, regardless of whether it was a human being or a rolling ball, providing the eggs were hatched in an incubator. When the mother duck sits on her eggs, she will usually exchange sounds with the unhatched ducklings toward the end of the incubation period. This exchange allows the ducklings and the mother to recognize each other, helping to ensure that imprinting between mother and offspring takes place, and reducing the likelihood that the ducklings will be "malimprinted" (Hess, 1972).

Experiences from early relationships are thus preserved in the form of working models. Since children have a particular need for protection during the first 3–4 years of life, these years can be seen as a primary period in the development of relationships. The formation of working models affects children's security and explorative behavior in the years to come. Although later experiences can lead to changes in working models, change is usually limited and occurs slowly over time, according to Bowlby. Despite any such changes, early working models set a strong precedent for how children relate to other people later in life.

Primary needs

The earliest explanations of attachment behavior suggested that children become attached to the people who fill their primary needs. Psychoanalytic theory viewed attachment behavior as an expression of dependency resulting from the fulfillment of primary needs and oral stimulation (Levert-Levitt and Sagi-Schwartz, 2015).

Behaviorism placed attachment on equal terms with all other behavior, learned through conditioning and reinforced by satisfying primary needs (Dollard and Miller, 1950).

Monkey studies have been used to gain insight into the importance of feeding and nursing in establishing attachment relationships. In a classic study, eight infant monkeys were separated from their mothers 12 hours after birth and grew up in a cage with two "mother figures" – one made of wire, the other of soft cloth (Harlow, 1959; Box 19.1). The infant monkeys spent far less time with the wire mother than with the cloth mother, regardless of where they got the milk, and in situations that normally would elicit attachment behavior, all the monkeys kept near the soft cloth surrogate. This suggests that the cloth "mothers" provided better external comfort and help for the monkeys' ability to regulate their emotional insecurity than the steel wire figures that dispensed milk. The results indicate that attachment behavior is not related to fulfilling basic needs, and thus disclaim the views of early behavioral and psychoanalytic theories.

BOX 19.1 THE ROLE OF PRIMARY NEEDS IN THE DEVELOPMENT OF ATTACHMENT (Harlow, 1959)

Infant monkeys were separated from their mothers 12 hours after birth and placed alone in a cage with two "surrogate mothers" – one made of wire, the other made of soft cloth. Four of the infant monkeys could suck milk from the teat of the wire figure, while the other four could suck milk from the cloth figure. In the first six months of their lives, the monkeys spent 14–18 hours a day with the cloth figures, and far less time with the wire figures. Even when the wire surrogate dispensed milk, the monkeys spent less than 2 hours a day with it. When an unfamiliar mechanical "spider" with blinking lights was placed in the cage, an event that normally would elicit attachment behavior, all the monkeys kept near the soft cloth surrogate (Photographs courtesy of Harlow Primate Laboratory.)

Separation theory

Margaret Mahler represents object-relation theory in the psychodynamic tradition. In psychodynamic theory, a mental "object" is an internal representation of a person or a thing targeted by a drive, or the means by which the drive can achieve its goal (see p. 21). One of the key features of Mahler's theory is newborns' inability to distinguish between internal and external regulation, such as experienced restlessness due to hunger and nourishment provided by the caregiver (Mahler et al., 1975). Mahler believes infants establish their first mental representations of the environment together with their mother and only slowly learn to distinguish between her and themselves through what she calls a "psychological birth." Although infants incorporate a representation of themselves as well as of the maternal object, they are unable to fully distinguish between them until the age of 12–18 months. Therefore, no clear relationship exists between the two objects early in children's lives. The self as an object is gradually distilled through a process of *separation–individuation* that leads children to form a distinct and independent representation of themselves. In Mahler's theory, relationships are not formed as the result of common experiences between caregiver and child, such as Bowlby's theory proposes. Instead, the relationship emerges as a link between self-object and maternal object once children are able to distinguish between mental representations of themselves and their mother. Since the separation and individuation process, according to Mahler, is affected by maternal sensitivity, it is the mother who shapes the child's attachment.

Mahler's description of development and her assumption that children are unable to mentally distinguish between themselves and their mother has met with considerable criticism, also within the psychodynamic tradition. According to Daniel Stern (1998), there is no empirical basis for such an assumption. He maintains that newborns begin by forming a perception of themselves that furnishes the basis for the maternal relationship as well as relationships with other caregivers (see p. 437). Additionally, the results of attachment research are clearly at odds with Mahler's assumption that a child's first relationship exclusively revolves around the biological mother (see p. 400).

Peter Fonagy represents a radical deviation from the common conception of attachment. He builds on Mahler's theory but considers that the function of early relationships and attachment is to pave the way for *mentalizing* and *mind understanding* (see p. 241; Fonagy et al., 2002, 2007). In Fonagy's theory of self-reflection and mentalizing, the experiences in the attachment relation lead to an understanding of self and others. This has limited relevance for attachment as a relational and emotional system, as it is understood by Bowlby and most others. Moreover, studies have found little direct connection between attachment and mind understanding (Ontai and Thompson, 2008).

THE DEVELOPMENT OF ATTACHMENT

Around the age of 2 months, children begin to show selective recognition of familiar persons, but distinct attachment behavior involving *positive selection* of other people does not occur until about 7 months. Children at this age also begin to show *negative selection* in the form of reticence to strangers (see p. 346). However, there are significant individual differences, and the age at which children begin to show clear selectivity can vary from 3½ to 15 months.

There are two main classes of attachment behavior: *signaling behavior* includes facial expressions, smiling, crying, and gestures or postures that cause others to approach; *approach behavior* includes crawling, walking and other forms of locomotion that bring the child closer to the attachment figure. Once children are capable of independent locomotion, their approach behavior increases. Tension is reduced when proximity is achieved, while failing to achieve proximity results in separation anxiety (Table 19.1).

Attachment behavior is activated when a child is at some distance from the attachment figure *and* experiences emotional arousal such as pain, fear, stress, insecurity or anxiety (Bowlby, 1969, 1982). In most such situations there is no actual danger but the child is feeling insecure. In younger children, the absence of an attachment

TABLE19.1 Characteristics of attachment behavior (based on Bowlby, 1982)

- Attachment behavior is selective and directed toward specific figures who elicit attachment behavior in a way and to an extent not found in interaction with other people.
- Attachment behavior involves seeking and trying to maintain physical proximity with the attachment figure.
- Attachment behavior is most readily elicited when children are ill or otherwise in a vulnerable state.
- Attachment behavior creates a sense of comfort and safety as a result of having attained proximity to the attachment figure.
- Attachment behavior leads to separation anxiety when the bond to the attachment figure is severed and proximity cannot be achieved.

figure in insecure situations leads to anxiousness and attachment behavior. Unfamiliar people, places and routines are always alarming to children, especially when they meet them on their own. Illness, fatigue and the like will additionally lower children's threshold for seeking an attachment figure, as they make children more vulnerable and increase their need for protection. It is the combination of the child's condition and the distance from the attachment figure that activate attachment behavior. Children's reaction to the absence of an attachment figure can be mitigated, however, by the presence of a familiar person such as a sibling or a friend, and even an object like a favorite teddy bear can have a mitigating effect.

What causes attachment behavior to *cease* is determined by its emotional intensity. If it is low, the sight or voice of the child's mother or other attachment figure will be sufficient. At higher intensities, it will only cease when the child can touch or cling to the attachment figure. When children are very upset and frightened, prolonged comfort may be necessary. An important consequence of attachment behavior is that the attachment figure helps the child understand and master situations involving insecurity and fear. Children with secure attachment (see the following) associate negative emotions with help and support from an attachment figure, and therefore do not become emotionally overwhelmed by such emotions. They seek help and receive emotional support in directing their attention and resources at evaluating the situation and discovering appropriate coping strategies, while adults represent a *safe base* for exploring objects and places that potentially elicit fear. The attachment process thus forms part of the foundation for the development of emotion regulation in general (Zimmer-Gembeck et al., 2017).

Since infants usually spend most of their time together with the mother, attachment behavior is often directed at her, especially when intensity is high. However, as early as 18 months of age, the majority of children show attachment to several persons (Schaffer and Emerson, 1964), and the loss of a nanny "can be almost as tragic as the loss of a mother" (Bowlby, 1958, p. 7).

Studies of children who were adopted after growing up in poor orphanages with limited access to adults suggest that the first 2 years constitute a sensitive period for establishing primary attachment relations (see p. 387). Attachment

behavior is most apparent in the second and third years of life. Around 4 years of age, the basic attachment period is over, and children's physical and social world greatly expands. From this age on, children no longer react to physical separation from an attachment figure in the same way as during early childhood, since they *know* that the person will be available. Four-year-olds show less anxiety at being separated from their mother than 3-year-olds when the mother's temporary absence has been agreed on in advance. They also begin to feel more secure with people other than attachment figures, providing the person is familiar, such as a teacher or a schoolmate. This also assumes that the child is not ill or distressed about something, and knows that the person will be available in the foreseeable future. In preschool-age children, attachment behavior, including crying and expressions of despair, is particularly common in situations with little overview, for example when a child is separated from the parents in a busy shopping mall. Although children's attachment behavior becomes less pronounced as they approach school age, they continue to seek out their parents or other close individuals when they feel afraid or insecure, and attachment behavior is as important in early school age as in infancy (Marvin et al., 2016). This can also include peers, but friendship and attachment are two different things. Interview studies have found that children like to spend time with their friends, but seek out their parents for security (Seibert and Kerns, 2009).

In the course of childhood, both security and insecurity manifest themselves in new ways. Things that caused children to react with fear or anxiety in preschool age are no longer perceived as threatening. Availability of attachment figures entails that they are receptive and open to communicate about emotional issues. In school age, psychological proximity becomes more important than physical proximity; knowledge about future availability, that an attachment figure will return, takes precedence. Children are now able to be apart from their mother and other attachment figures for longer periods, and do not need to make direct contact to restore a sense of security – a phone call can be enough (Kerns and Brumariu, 2016; Mayseless, 2005).

In adolescence, attachment becomes less distinct and the behavior more varied. The need for security via others not only diminishes, but runs counter to adolescents' need for independence and the growing autonomy typical of this age (Ammaniti et al., 2000). Adolescents more often use their friends when they feel a need for security, and although they begin to develop emotional ties in romantic relationships, these are activated and terminated under different conditions and therefore do not replace the attachment relationship with parents. Romantic relationships are more reciprocal than attachment relationships, in which an older generation protects a younger one.

Still, even in adulthood, attachment to parents and other important persons does not disappear. According to Bowlby, attachment fulfills the same function throughout life: to seek and maintain proximity. Adult relations, too, can be described as either secure or insecure. Signs of insecure attachment in adulthood include lack of openness or undiscriminating intimacy, excessive jealousy, feelings of loneliness in relationships, a reluctance to commit oneself, and excessive demands for attention by the other part (Hazan and Shaver, 1994; Morrison et al., 1997). The unavailability of an attachment figure in difficult situations – either physical or mental – can lead to problems with emotion regulation and occasionally result in a deactivation of the attachment system (Marvin and Britner, 2008; Mikulincer and Shaver, 2008).

Exploration

The attachment system provides children with knowledge about the availability of people who can ensure their safety and whereabouts, but they also need to learn what is safe and what is dangerous in their surroundings, knowledge they acquire through exploration (Bowlby, 1982). Exploratory behavior consists of three basic elements: an orienting response, movement in the direction of the object, and physical investigation of the object by manipulating it or experimenting with it in other ways. Exploration is activated by unfamiliar and/or complex objects and locations. Once an object has been investigated and becomes familiar to the child, exploration ceases.

Attachment and exploration are activated under almost identical conditions, but whereas attachment behavior leads to proximity, exploratory behavior creates more distance to the attachment figure. Attachment behavior is elicited by fear and insecurity, while exploration takes place when something catches children's interest and they feel relatively secure. When the attachment figure moves further away from the child, attachment behavior is activated, while exploratory behavior is more easily activated when the attachment figure approaches, for example in situations involving fascinating objects such as toys or animals. By means of attachment, familiar adults become a secure base for controlled exploration of objects and locations that otherwise can elicit insecurity or fear, a base the child alternately leaves and returns to (Ainsworth, 1963). Young children typically show rapid shifts between attachment and exploratory behavior, skepticism and interest, most often with an initially skeptical attitude.

Thus, attachment and exploration are to some extent complementary ways of meeting new situations, meaning that exploratory behavior is inhibited in situations in which children show attachment behavior. When the two systems come into conflict with each other, children may obtain emotional information by watching others (social referencing, see p. 350) which then determines what system is activated. If the child sees the attachment figure smile, tension is reduced and the exploratory system is activated. If the attachment figure looks worried or frightened, tension increases and the attachment system is activated.

INDIVIDUAL DIFFERENCES IN ATTACHMENT

According to Bowlby (1969, 1982), individual differences in attachment behavior are the result of children's experiences in connection with separation from or loss of an attachment figure. The attachment figure provides the child with information about the environment, alerts the child to danger and safety, and helps the child understand what takes place in the surrounding world, knowledge children eventually seek out themselves through social referencing. When children first seek physical closeness, they do not know what this closeness entails, but the physical proximity fundamental to attachment behavior simultaneously forms the basis for the emotional relationship between child and attachment figure. By being sensitive to children's gradual coping with such situations, caregivers ensure children's cooperation and give them the security to explore the world (Ainsworth, 1983).

Children can show many different reactions in situations that activate attachment behavior, and no other type of behavior is accompanied by stronger emotions. Children's experiences when they seek physical proximity to an attachment figure determine the kinds of feelings they develop for this person. Joy and devotion are the most common. When 4-month-old infants see their mother or another caregiver after a brief separation, their most likely reaction is a smile of recognition, which often leads the caregiver to respond by smiling, chitchatting, and similar. Also later in children's lives, a reunion that leads to the termination of attachment behavior will usually involve expressions of joy.

Most children are met with warmth and care, but some children experience being rejected or even beaten when they approach an attachment figure. Under such conditions, children can associate the relationship with emotions like anger, hatred and insecurity. These emotional reactions are not the result of defunct love, but rather of children's past experiences with situations that activate attachment behavior, telling them that the relationship includes these types of emotions. It is children's way of adapting their emotions to the environment. Although positive feelings are most common, the emotional outcome depends on the availability of attachment figures and the way in which the relationships between children and their attachment figures develop.

How children themselves react to reunion also depends on their state of health and mind. After a brief separation without unfamiliar things or illness in the child's life, the most likely reaction is a smile. If the separation has lasted for a longer period without regular routines, the child will often cry and cling to the attachment figure, or become quiet and less responsive. After prolonged separation, attachment behavior can assume more unusual forms by either increasing in intensity, or being absent altogether. Anger can be a reaction to the unavailability of an attachment figure. In connection with temporary separations, which represent the majority of instances, anger has two functions: first, to empower the child to overcome the obstacles on the way to reunion, and second, to try to ensure that the attachment figure does not disappear again. This type of anger does not destroy the emotional bond between child and attachment figure, but strengthens it. The attachment figure, too, can show anger, for example when a child suddenly runs across the street or otherwise exposes herself to danger.

Thus, both anger and physical approach are behavioral strategies rooted in the attachment system. Children may react to insecurity by wanting to establish maximal access to the attachment figure, and by showing anger to feelings or potential threats of abandonment. It is an emotional balancing act. Children can be furious at the attachment figure, only to seek confirmation and consolation from the same person the next moment. Paradoxically, children who have been abused by their parents show strong signs of attachment. Children who have been adopted away from a neglectful or abusive attachment figure can show anger and rejection for some time before becoming attached to caring adoptive or foster parents (Raby et al., 2017). Since fear and anger are activated under the same conditions, they often occur simultaneously, and an increase in the intensity of one emotion can at times strengthen the other.

Occasionally, anger can become so intense as to damage the emotional bond between child and caregiver. This happens when children are exposed to many separations and threats of abandonment, threats they perceive as real and plausible. Under such circumstances, children can experience tremendous conflicts. They meet the threat of separation with anger, but dare not show their anger for fear of being abandoned, or express it toward other people or in other contexts. They can show a strong sense of ownership, deep insecurity and intense anger toward their attachment figures, sometimes resulting in a vicious circle: their fear of losing the attachment figure creates anger and in turn increases their fear of separation, and so on. They show anxiety, ownership and concern for the other person's welfare, afraid that something might happen to the attachment figure. There is a thin line between love and hate in an attachment relationship.

Measures of attachment

Several ways for measuring attachment have been developed (Solomon and George, 2016). However, the *Strange Situation* is regarded as the "gold standard" for measuring attachment in 1- to 3-year-olds by observing how they react to separation from and subsequent reunion with their mother or another attachment figure in an unfamiliar surrounding (Ainsworth and Wittig,

1969). It consists of seven 3-minute episodes in which the child is either together with the mother and/or a stranger, or left alone (see Table 19.2). Particular emphasis is on the different ways 1-year-olds react to episodes 4 and 7 in which the mother comes back after having left the room and the child has been alone with a stranger.

An observer records the child's level of activity, play, crying and other signs of uneasiness, distance to the mother (or other familiar person), attempts to get her attention, distance to the stranger, and willingness to interact with her or him. Apart from the 30-second introduction (episode 0), each episode lasts for 3 minutes for a total of 21 minutes.

Children's reactions in the Strange Situation are commonly classified into three main groups: A – *insecure-avoidant*, B – *secure* and C – *insecure-resistant* (Ainsworth et al., 1978). Later research has led to an additional category, D – *insecure-disorganized* (Main and Weston, 1981). The behaviors that characterize each of these four types are described in Table 19.3. Secure attach-

ment (B) can be observed when the child shows signs of missing the attachment figure at the time of separation, greets her and shows joy over the reunion, and once again returns to play with toys. Categories A and C do not represent disorders, but alternative strategies for dealing with separation. There is disagreement about whether the behavior in category D actually reflects an attachment relationship or the fact that the child has not formed such a relationship. It is lack of, rather than a quality of, the attachment. Since children in this category often develop mental disorders, their behavior is of major clinical importance (Bernier and Meins, 2008; Rutter et al., 2009). In addition, the classification is not absolute: some children show behaviors that do not clearly fall into any of the four categories.

The purpose behind these categories is not to specify children's general characteristics, such as descriptions of personality traits, but to characterize the quality of the specific relationship between the child and the adult in the Strange Situation. Usually, it is the child's mother

TABLE 19.2 The Strange Situation (Ainsworth et al., 1978, p. 34)

Episode	Persons	Event
0	Mother, child	The observer leads the mother (or another person familiar to the child) and child into the experiment room.
1	Mother, child	The mother places the child on the floor among a collection of toys and leaves to sit down in a chair at the other end of the room. The child observes without the mother's participation. If necessary, the mother encourages the child to play during the last minute.
2	Mother, child, stranger	The stranger enters, remains quiet for 1 minute, and speaks to the mother for 1 minute. Then he or she tries to get the child to play with a toy.
3	Child, stranger	The mother leaves the room inconspicuously. The stranger's behavior depends on the child. If the child neither cries nor shows other signs of uneasiness, the stranger quietly sits down next to the child. If the child cries or seems upset, the stranger tries to comfort the child.
4	Mother, child	The mother returns, greets or comforts the child, and tries to get the child to play while the stranger leaves.
5	Child	The mother leaves and the child is left completely alone.
6	Child, stranger	The stranger enters, his or her behavior depending on the child as in episode 3.
7	Mother, child	The mother returns and the stranger leaves.

An observer records the child's level of activity, play, crying and other signs of uneasiness, distance to the mother (or other familiar person), attempts to get her attention, distance to the stranger, and willingness to interact with her or him. Apart from the 30-second introduction (episode 0), each episode lasts for three minutes for a total of 21 minutes.

TABLE 19.3 Types of attachment

A. *Insecure-avoidant*	Children pay little attention to their mother while she is in the room and often show no signs of distress when she leaves. They turn or look away when their mother returns, rather than seeking closeness and comfort. Some children reject their mother, while others show mixed attempts at interaction and avoiding interaction. They are as easily comforted by the stranger as by the mother.
B. *Secure*	Some children do not care that their mother is leaving, while others become quite upset. When the mother returns after the separation, the child approaches her, is easily quieted if upset and quickly begins to play again. Some children notice their mother returning and immediately continue to play, while others go up to her.
C. *Insecure-resistant*	Children in this category are often upset simply because they are in a foreign environment, even when they are together with their mother. They get quite agitated when she leaves, seeking both proximity and resisting contact when she returns. They can cry in order to be picked up and comforted, and fight to be let go of when they are picked up.
D. *Insecure-disorganized*	These children typically show contradictory behavior, for example by approaching their mother without looking at her. Some children can appear disorganized, unemotional and depressed.

or father, but can also include other people with whom the child has a relationship. Additionally, it is important to emphasize that the differences between children lie in the *quality* of the attachment relationship; its strength or intensity is irrelevant as long as the relationship is intact (Rutter et al., 2009; Sroufe et al., 2005).

Main and Weston (1981) compared children's attachment behavior when they were together with each of the parents. Some children showed secure attachment to the mother and insecure attachment to the father. For others, the reverse was true. Although children often relate in similar ways to both parents in situations that activate attachment, a significant percentage of children show different types of attachment behavior with each parent (Fox et al., 1991). Children's attachment behavior does not always form a consistent pattern, but depends on the individual relationship. The close relationships children engage in, however different they may be, together form the basis for how the children meet other people.

The Strange Situation can provide valuable insights into children's early relationships and has been used extensively in research. Kagan (1998a), on the other hand, maintains that it is unreasonable to assume that a 21-minute observation would be able to capture important qualities of children's relationships that have taken shape over thousands of hours of time spent in company with others. Besides, most studies use only a few of the standard 21 minutes. Cultural differences

in the statistical distribution of attachment behaviors give reason to question what children's reactions in the Strange Situation actually reveal (see p. 407). The Strange Situation should furthermore be used with caution in clinical practice, since its use is limited to the age of 2–3 years, and research has found relatively little correspondence between early insecure attachment and later disorders (Rutter et al., 2009).

Another way of measuring attachment is the *Attachment Q-set* (Waters, 1995). It is an observation form that consists of 90 behavioral types that provide information about the child's behavior in natural situations involving attachment reactions, and is considerably more time-consuming than the Strange Situation. In addition, there are a growing number of questionnaires and interviews to measure various aspects of attachment relationships from infancy to adulthood (Crowell et al., 2008; Fairchild, 2006; Kerns and Brumariu, 2016).

Attachment and adult sensitivity

For a relationship to be secure, the attachment figure must be available, reliable and predictable, characteristics Ainsworth in line with Bowlby's theory refers to as "sensitivity." In a study of 21 children, she found a high correlation (0.78) between the children's attachment behavior and the mothers' sensitivity, meaning how frequently, quickly and adequately they reacted to their child. Mothers of children who showed secure attachment in this situation reacted quickly when the child cried, consistent with what they believed to be the cause of the crying. Mothers of children who showed insecure attachment responded more rarely and inconsistently to the child's crying. Children with insecure-resistant attachment had mothers who seemed little concerned, while mothers of children with insecure-avoidant attachment tended to feed and look after their children based on rules and routines rather than in response to signs indicating that the child had specific needs (Ainsworth et al., 1972).

Other studies have found significantly lower correspondences between maternal sensitivity and children's attachment (correlations of about 0.24). Although this suggests a certain connection between maternal sensitivity and children's attachment behavior, it is fairly modest. Other characteristics of maternal behavior show nearly the same correlation with children's attachment types, such as stimulation strategies, reciprocity and emotional support (Goldsmith and Alansky, 1987; Nievar and Becker, 2008; de Wolff and van IJzendoorn, 1997). One reason may be that maternal sensitivity is not related to attachment alone, but influences many aspects of development. Moreover, within a transactional model the child may influence the mother's sensitivity (see p. 8).

Some parents show very little sensitivity and may instead invoke fear in their child. In particular, children with insecure-disorganized attachment (category D) may have been subjected to abuse, maltreatment or frightening experiences. This form of attachment behavior may be the result of inconsistent parental behavior, with conflicting signals and a mixture of approval and rejection the children are unable to decode and therefore cannot develop strategies to deal with (Crockenberg and Leerkes, 2000).

Mobile phones and parent availability

The mobile phone has become a tool of remote parenting from preschool age to adolescence, and parents often buy the first mobile phone for their child to ensure safety and regulate the child's independence outside the home (Ling and Haddon, 2008; Rudi et al., 2015). Research on mobile phone use and child development is still sparse (Yan, 2018) but the parental availability provided by mobile phones is likely to influence children's attachment behavior and exploration. It may provide a feeling of security by keeping caregivers informed and available, and in addition allow older children to take advantage of several attachment figures, including a divorced parent they are not living with (Ribak, 2009; Ling and Haddon, 2008). Parents tell that they strive to be available to their children when they are at work and many parents are almost constantly available, in order to make their children more secure in situations away from them (Strandell, 2014). Such availability may even imply parenting across borders when mothers have to go to another country to find work (Chib et al., 2014). Some parents use surveillance apps to keep track of their child's whereabouts. This may increase the child's exploration of unfamiliar spaces but many older children and adolescents react negatively to being surveilled (Barron, 2014; Ribak, 2009). However, the mobile phone also represents a disturbing element that may interfere with child–parent interactions, make a parent less emotionally available, and create an "absent presence" (Gergen, 2002; Kildare and Middlemiss, 2017; McDaniel and Radesky, 2018).

Temperament

Some theorists suggest that attachment behaviors have their origins in children's temperament, rather than in the way children have been treated by their caregivers (Kagan, 1982). However, it has proved difficult to formulate alternative descriptions of the four attachment types in Table 19.3 with categories based on temperament traits (see p. 369), and only a limited correspondence has been found between children's temperament and the four attachment categories (Thompson, 1998; Vaughn et al., 2008). The fact that there is a moderate correspondence in attachment behavior toward mother and father also supports the assumption that attachment behavior reflects the child's relationship with the person rather than a general disposition, as in the case of temperament.

Despite these theoretical contradictions, temperament and attachment are often seen in context. In the *unified theory of attachment*, temperament is a contributing factor in determining how infants interpret other people and themselves, and how they respond to separation. Children's temperament thus affects their behavior as well as the reactions of attachment figures (Groh et al., 2017; Stevenson-Hinde, 2005). For example, the temperamental trait *negative emotionality* has been viewed as an important precursor to insecure attachment (van dem Boom, 1989). Mangelsdorf and colleagues (1990) found little direct connection between children's temperament at 9 months and Strange-Situation attachment behavior toward the mother at 13 months, or between maternal personality and children's attachment behavior. However, they found a connection with attachment behavior when the child's temperament was seen in context with the mother's personality: children with an irritable temperament who had mothers with a reserved personality showed a tendency toward insecure attachment behavior at 13 months of age. Another study found that children with irritable temperament tended to show insecure attachment, but only when the mother received little social support from her surroundings (Crockenberg, 1981). Together, these results support the assumption that children's temperaments affect the development of their attachment relationships. Although there is no direct relation between temperament and attachment category, interaction effects between temperament and characteristics of the attachment figure have an impact on the child's attachment behavior. This emphasizes the transactional nature of the attachment process.

Attachment in atypical development

Disabilities can affect the development of attachment behavior and attachment relationships, but the attachment process is robust, and children with disabilities essentially show the same development as children without them. Blind children can show similar attachment behavior as sighted children, although delayed and with later reactions to strangers (Dale and Edwards, 2015). Deaf children with deaf parents show the same patterns as hearing children with hearing parents, while a slightly larger proportion of deaf children with hearing parents show insecure attachment (A and C), probably reflecting the hearing parents' limited competence in signing and insecurity in caring for a deaf child (Dale and Edwards, 2015). Mothers of children with cerebral palsy often report strong separation reactions in their children, and of having to be together with them all the time (Quinn and Gordon, 2011). This is probably related to these children's motor impairments, which inhibit their development of self-propelled and independent approach behavior.

Memory and other aspects of cognitive development are of importance to the attachment

process. For example, *person permanence*, the understanding that persons exist also when they are not perceived by the child (analogue to object permanence, (see p. 169)), is a cognitive basis of the working model (Bowlby, 1969; Sherman et al., 2015). Children with intellectual disability develop attachment relationships with their parents and other adults such as kindergarten personnel just like other children, but development is delayed and behavior patterns can differ somewhat (De Schipper et al., 2006). In a Strange Situation study of 26-month-olds with Down syndrome, many of the children showed behaviors that could not be categorized, but this proportion was lower at 42 months (Atkinson et al., 1999). Children with autism spectrum disorder are impaired in their social interaction, and approximately half show secure early attachment behavior in Strange-Situation studies. In one study, 8- to 12-year-old high functioning children with autism spectrum disorders and typically developing children and their mothers completed the Kerns Security Scales (Kerns et al., 2001), designed to measure attachment security. There were no significant differences between the two groups, neither in the parents' or the children's own assessments of the scale's statements related to attachment security (Chandler and Dissanayake, 2014). However, among children with autism spectrum disorder, those who also have intellectual disability are more likely to show insecure attachment behavior (Rutgers et al., 2004). In addition, more unclear attachment behavior and a demanding caregiving situation may increase the likelihood that parents with children with autism spectrum disorder do not respond to their child's approach behavior in situations the child experiences as insecure (Rutgers et al., 2007).

Some adolescents and adults with severe intellectual disability continue to show approach behavior in new and insecure situations without access to an attachment figure. Often, their behavior is not understood by others as an attempt to seek security and is therefore rejected, increasing the risk of self-injury and other forms of challenging behavior (Janssen et al., 2002; Perry and Flood, 2016; von Tetzchner, 2004).

CONTINUITY OF ATTACHMENT

Attachment can change over time, but once children's working models are established, a high degree of stability is expected. However, observations of attachment behavior toward the same person at different ages show varying results. Studies of children at age 12 and 18 months showed stability ranging from 42 to 96 percent. Despite the fact that two-thirds of all children belong to category B, secure attachment, 40 percent typically change category in the course of these 6 months (Thompson, 2006). This may be related to the increasing mobility that characterizes this age and leads to changes in the repertoire of children's attachment behavior (see Campos et al., 2000). Additionally, specific events can cause relatively major changes in attachment behavior. For example, a sibling represents a potential threat to the mother's availability and after the birth of a younger sister or brother, many firstborns show less secure attachment to their mother in the Strange Situation. The greatest difference can be seen in children whose mothers are depressed or have trouble with their relationship around the time of birth. When mothers feel happy and show affection toward their firstborn, attachment behaviors tend to remain secure (Teti et al., 1996).

At the same time, stability does not seem to increase with age: attachment interviews at quite small intervals in adolescence show only correlations of around 0.5–0.6 or lower. Over longer periods, stability is modest, for example from toddlerhood to middle childhood and adolescence. One study found correlations of around 0.15 between early attachment behavior in the Strange Situation and attachment measured by interview in adulthood (Raby et al., 2013). This may partly be caused by changes in attachment over time, but also by the widely differing methods of measuring attachment at different ages (Allen and Tan, 2016; Kerns and Brumariu, 2016; Solomon and George, 2016).

Attachment theory is based on the assumption of a certain continuity across generations: the attachment figures' own attachment history affects their sensitivity and reactions when children feel afraid or insecure (Bretherton, 1990). Parental reactions to attachment behavior are based on the parents' own working models as well as the experiences with their child, which leads to individual differences in availability (George and Solomon, 2008). However, just as in the case of early and later measures of attachment, only modest correlations have been found between mothers' attachment in their own childhood and the attachment type of their children. The one exception is mothers with early insecure-disorganized attachment (category D) – more than half had children who fell into category D (Raby et al., 2015), suggesting that it was the mothers' own highly deviant development that most clearly affected the children in this group. The attachment relationships of children with more conventional attachment histories can be affected by many factors. However, attachment behavior is thought to be mainly a result of experience, and genes do not seem to have a significant impact on the development of attachment relationships (Raby et al., 2013).

CULTURAL DIFFERENCES

Ainsworth (1967) did her first studies of attachment in Uganda, and studies indicate that children's behavior in the Strange Situation can be classified according to the same categories in all cultures. However, cultural differences in caregiving patterns are mirrored in the distribution of attachment types. Infants among the Aka people in the Central African Republic, for example, have more than 20 different caregivers every day. One-year-olds of the Nso tribe in the Northwest Region of Cameroon do not react to being picked up by a stranger, and will readily follow the stranger's initiative (Otto et al., 2014). Israeli kibbutzim practice communal child rearing, and children sleep away from their parents (Sagi-Schwartz and Aviezer, 2005). Italian 1-year-olds are more accustomed to being separated from their mother daily for shorter periods, for example in day care centers, or with grandparents or baby sitters, and normally do not pay particular attention to their mother when she returns. They are therefore likely to relate in ways that are classified as insecure-avoidant attachment (category A), although half of them show secure attachment (Simonelli et al., 2014). Conversely, Japanese infants are rarely separated from their mother, and many of them react strongly to separation in the Strange Situation. They are difficult to comfort at reunion, and more of them therefore end up in category C (Takahashi, 1990).

These findings do not contradict the assumption that attachment behavior is universal, but do raise questions about the suitability of the Strange Situation as a universal method of measuring reactions to security and stress. Attachment behavior is found among children of all cultures, but the conditions that elicit such behavior vary. This is also demonstrated by cultural variations

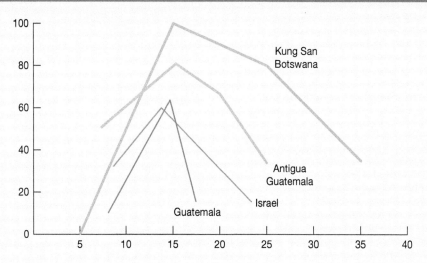

In a Strange Situation study, childen aged 4–40 months from different cultures were observed when their mother left the room. The children were from the Kung San tribe in Botswana, a village in Guatemala, the City of Antigua in Guatemala, and a kibbutz in Israel. The figure shows that the percentage of 1-year-olds who cried when their mother left the room ranged from 60 percent of the children in an Israeli kibbutz to nearly 100 percent of the Kung San children in Botswana. These differences lasted until the age of about 3 and reflect the children's experience with their mother's absence. Among the Kung San, young children spend nearly all their time together with the mother, while kibbutz children from early on are cared for by adults other than the parents during daytime.

in the proportion of children who cry when their mother leaves them in an unfamiliar situation (see Box 19.2), variations that do not reflect cultural differences in children's affection. How much children cry is not related to the quality of caregiving, but to how accustomed children are to separation from their mother.

ATTACHMENT AND LATER FUNCTIONING

According to Bowlby's theory, children's inner working models form the basis for their expectations of social relations and contribute to social adaptation and competence (Sroufe et al., 1999). Some studies have found a moderate connection between children's attachment to parents and their peer relations, others have found little statistical relationship between assessments of early attachment to each parent and social com-

petence and friendships in school age (Elicker et al., 1992; Sroufe et al., 2005; Thompson, 2016). Nonetheless, secure attachment to both parents over time seems to increase the likelihood of positive social development and relationships in later childhood and adolescence, while children with insecure attachment to both parents often show poorer peer relations and are more likely to develop behavioral disorders (Boldt et al., 2014; Kerns and Brumariu, 2014).

It is commonly assumed that secure attachment leads to protection, while insecure attachment may contribute to internalizing disorders, and disorganized attachment to externalizing disorders, but results have been inconsistent (Brumariu and Kerns, 2010; Lowell et al., 2014). Egeland and colleagues (1993) found low correspondences between 18-month-olds' attachment behavior in the Strange Situation and teachers' assessments of children's externalizing or inhibited behavior during the first few years of school.

However, when the same children were assessed at a summer camp, a situation in which children usually form many new relationships, staff evaluations showed that children with secure maternal attachment had somewhat better social skills and self-esteem, were less dependent and had more friends than children with insecure attachment at 18 months of age. No relation was found between attachment behavior at 12 months and later functioning (Sroufe et al., 2005).

Other studies have found a clear relation between early disorganized attachment behavior and later behavioral disorders and oppositional behavior (Theule et al., 2016), as well as between measures of attachment and social competence, and behavioral disorders in school age (Boldt et al., 2016). When children have insecure attachment to the mother, their attachment to the father is of particular importance (Boldt et al., 2014; Kochanska and Kim, 2013).

Although studies generally show that children with early insecure attachment develop anxiety and depression somewhat more often than children with secure attachment, the differences are small. This highlights the fact that attachment is only one of the factors that can contribute to the development of such disorders (Kerns and Brumariu, 2014; Madigan et al., 2013; Sroufe et al., 2005). Attachment behavior is one of several *markers* that to a greater or lesser extent predicts later functioning depending on the changes that occur in the child's life. Since most environments have a high degree of continuity, developmental markers in childhood predict the environment as well as later relationships (Clarke and Clarke, 2000). At the same time, it is possible to influence children's caregiving environment, attachment behavior and parental coping by counseling with a focus on parental sensitivity and responsiveness, both in cases of typical and atypical development (Barlow et al., 2016; Kerr and Cossar, 2014; Letourneau et al., 2015).

On the whole, studies suggest that secure attachment provides the best basis for development, at least in Western middle-class children (Belsky, 2005). Nonetheless, a given type of attachment behavior will not necessarily be equally successful under all social conditions. All forms of attachment entail social learning and adaptation. Children's working models represent a preparedness to meet the social world they have come to know through their attachment relationships. A child with relatively insensitive

and unpredictable caregivers may show a tendency to become aggressive and competitive, traits that may well prepare the child to cope with a stressed and unpredictable environment. Parenting may be influenced by stress in times of war and the development of insecure attachment patterns may be functional (Belsky, 2008). In this perspective, aggressive and competitive relational behavior does not represent a deviation from optimal development, but rather an adequate adaptation to the world as it appears to the child (Belsky, 2005; Hinde, 1992). Besides, in line with the low correlations, an aggressive and competitive behavior pattern is not merely the result of the mother's relational style or that of other attachment figures. From a transactional point of view, the characteristics of the child as well as other people in the environment contribute to the development of these types of behavior patterns.

ATTACHMENT-RELATED DISORDERS

Attachment gives a sense of security when an available and responsive attachment figure is present, and insecurity when the attachment figure is absent. Some children experience prolonged absence from caregivers, such as unaccompanied refugee children and adolescents (Bowlby, 1951; Derluyn and Broekaert, 2007; Smith, T., 2010). Robertson and Bowlby (1952) describe a sequence of reactions to the absence of an attachment figure, from protest via despair to detachment in case of prolonged or permanent separation – the loss of an attachment figure. The protest phase might begin immediately or after some time, lasting from a few hours to weeks and months. In this phase, children often search for the attachment figure and cry. During the despair phase, they continue to focus on the absent attachment figure but are not as preoccupied with finding her. Crying becomes monotonous or ceases altogether. Children become passive, lose their appetite and make no demands on their surroundings. Gradually, they start to show more interest in the people around them and begin to eat once again. This is a process of detachment whereby attachment behavior is no longer activated in relation to the attachment figures the child has been separated from. For children fleeing from war or catastrophe, this can include all former attachment figures. When an attachment figure comes to visit an orphanage or other place where the child is living, the child will not exhibit the attachment behavior typical for such reunions, but remains passive and shows no initiative or interest. The system can be reactivated, however, if child and attachment figure are fully reunited. When children repeatedly lose an attachment figure, they will gradually invest less and less in potentially new attachment figures (Foster et al., 2003; Kobak and Madsen, 2008; Newman and Steel, 2008).

Some children grow up under social conditions that do not offer the necessary qualities to form normal attachment relationships. Two disorders are clearly linked to the caregiving environment: "reactive attachment disorder" and "disinhibited social engagement disorder." Both diagnoses require that the child has been subjected to serious neglect or abuse (see p. 67), and although some children exhibit characteristics of both inhibited and indiscriminate attachment behavior, the two disorders seem to have a different basis (Zeanah et al., 2004).

Children with *reactive attachment disorder* show inadequate or deviant attachment behavior in situations that usually elicit attachment behavior. In a study of children with this diagnosis, approximately half the children showed early insecure disorganized attachment behavior (D), nearly a quarter were so withdrawn as to allow no classification, while the remainder showed secure attachment behavior. Almost none of the children showed other forms of insecure attachment behavior, which could have indicated that they had found strategies to cope with stress and separation. The lower the quality of the caregiving environment, the more distinct the symptoms of reactive attachment disorder. There was clear evidence, in other words, that these disorders had been caused by rearing environments in which children had not developed attachment relationships due to a lack of sufficiently available and consistent attachment figures. However, these disorders disappeared quickly once the children came to a better caregiving environment, such as adoptive care or foster home (Zeanah and Gleason, 2015). Similarly, symptoms of reactive attachment disorder quickly disappeared in a group of children from Romanian orphanages after they had been placed in good foster homes, while children who remained in the orphanage showed the same symptoms 6 years later. One of the decisive factors, however, was whether the

children came to a good caregiving environment before or after the age of 2 years, suggesting that the earliest years may represent a sensitive period for primary attachment (Smyke et al., 2010).

Children with *disinhibited social engagement disorder* show little restraint toward strangers and are "indiscriminately friendly" in situations that elicit attachment behavior. Many children growing up in orphanages develop this disorder, which previously was thought to be caused by inadequate access to permanent attachment figures (Lawler et al., 2014; Zeanah and Gleason, 2015). Studies, however, have only been able to find a moderate link between early attachment type and disinhibited social engagement, suggesting that indiscriminate attachment behavior in new and stressful situations is rather part of a general pattern of poorly adapted social behavior. While children with reactive attachment disorder show a lack of attachment behavior, children with disinhibited social engagement show too much. Since they approach strangers without seeking security or comfort, their behavior is not attachment-related, but a general social impairment involving physical approach behavior with strangers, both in situations that elicit attachment behavior and situations that do not. It is not a matter of establishing indiscriminate attachment relationships, but of indiscriminate social behavior in interaction with strangers, of showing attachment behavior in social situations in which such behavior is inappropriate (Dozier and Rutter, 2008; Zeanah and Gleason, 2015). Adolescents who have been subjected to severe early neglect and placed in different foster homes may also show signs of disinhibited social engagement (Kay and Green, 2013).

The developmental trajectories described in these studies clearly indicate that different disorders are involved. While the symptoms of reactive attachment disorder quickly disappeared once the children had been adopted and established new attachment relationships, the symptoms of children with disinhibited social engagement only showed a slow reduction. Many of the children continued to show signs of disinhibited social engagement in later childhood, also with their peers (Zeanah and Smyke, 2015).

Not all children who grow up under extremely poor caregiving conditions develop reactive attachment or uninhibited social engagement disorder (Zeanah et al., 2004). A poor environment is not enough. Development can be related to differences in genetic vulnerability, resilience and temperament, and even negative environments can include protective elements in the form of persons who are partially available and reduce the environment's negative impact (Soares et al., 2013).

Some children with atypical development show a behavioral pattern similar to attachment-related disorders. Both reactive attachment disorder and autism spectrum disorder (see p. 62) involve social impairment, and it can be difficult to distinguish between them. However, children with reactive attachment disorder show greater social reciprocity, and, unlike children with autism spectrum disorder, are positively affected by moving to a better caregiving environment (Davidson et al., 2015). Similarly, children with Williams syndrome are exuberant, friendly and socially uninhibited (see p. 76), and these are traits that may be confounded with the disinhibited social engagement disorder (Soares et al., 2013).

ATTACHMENT THEORY AND SOCIAL WORK IN PRACTICE

Bowlby's theory was initially based on observations of children in orphanages with little social contact and staff with little stability, or children who otherwise had lost a stable attachment person (Bowlby, 1951). It is therefore only natural that attachment theory has had a major impact on child welfare practice and similar social services. Large orphanages have been closed down in many countries and replaced with foster homes and smaller institutions, with greater emphasis on promoting stable relationships between children and adults. Attachment theory has influenced the way foster care and adoption are organized (Byrne et al., 2005; Dozier and Rutter, 2008; Rutter, 2008), and is used to lend professional support to why it is important for children to maintain ties to both parents after a divorce, spend enough time together with each of them and stay overnight at each parent's home (Kelly and Lamb, 2000).

Attachment theory has also been used to argue that an early start in kindergarten can be harmful to children (Belsky, 2001; Vandell, 2004). Studies, however, do not support such a claim (Borge et al., 2004; Côté et al., 2007). It is the quality of caregiving at home and in kindergarten that determines whether they contribute to the child's positive development (Rutter, 2008).

SUMMARY

1 *Attachment* is about developing relationships and feelings for other people. The function of attachment behaviors is to ensure a feeling of safety by reducing the physical distance to specific individuals, *attachment figures*.

2 In Bowlby's *ethological* theory, attachment is an innate *behavioral system* whose aim is to provide security. Inner *working models* carry information from interaction with important persons, their availability and responsiveness, and form the basis for how children meet their social environment. Adults have a *caregiving behavioral system*. Traditional *psychoanalysis* and *behaviorism* view attachment behavior as a means of satisfying primary needs. According to Mahler's *psychodynamic theory*, attachment relationships are formed as a relation between *self-object* and *maternal object* once children begin to distinguish between mental representations of themselves and their mother.

3 At 2 months of age, children begin to show *selective attention* for familiar people, and positive and negative selection by 7 months. Attachment behavior includes *signaling behavior* and *approach behavior*, activated when children are at a physical distance from the attachment figure and experience pain, anxiety, insecurity and stress. Proximity to an attachment figure provides security and ceases the attachment behavior.

4 Attachment behavior is most pronounced in the second and third year of life, and by around 3–4 years of age, the basic attachment period is over. Children are now able to be apart from

Continued

their attachment figures for longer periods, and do not need to take direct contact to restore a sense of security. With age, attachment reactions become rarer and less intense, and knowledge of future availability becomes more important than physical proximity. Adolescence is characterized by increasing autonomy, but the attachment system remains functional throughout life.

5 *Explorative behavior* is activated when children are interested in something new and do not experience too much insecurity. The attachment figure represents a *secure base* for exploration of new objects and places.

6 Children's experiences in connection with separation or loss lead to *individual differences* in attachment behavior. The *Strange Situation* is based on the fact that separation from an attachment figure in unfamiliar surroundings elicits attachment behavior. Behavior is categorized as *insecure-avoidant* (A), *secure* (B), *insecure-resistant* (C) and *insecure-disorganized* (D). Most children show secure attachment. A secure relationship depends on the availability, reliability and predictability of the attachment figure. Prolonged separation and absence or loss of an attachment figure can lead to protest with crying and despair. As children form attachments with different people, their behavior toward them can vary.

7 According to Bowlby and Ainsworth, the attachment figure's *availability* and *sensitivity* is an essential prerequisite for secure attachment, but studies have found a low correspondence between maternal sensitivity and children's attachment. The mobile phone influences the availability of parents and other attachment figures. Parents seek to be easily available, but mobile telephones can also create "absent presence". A difficult life situation may increase parental stress and contribute to insecure attachment in the child.

8 Some theorists believe differences in attachment are caused by *temperament* rather than how the child is treated by the caregiver. In a *unified theory*, temperament forms part of the basis for infants' interpretations of other people and themselves and their reaction to separation.

9 Attachment is a robust system, and children with intellectual disability, autism spectrum disorders and other disabilities largely show the same distribution of attachment types as children with typical development, even if their behavior may be delayed and somewhat different, and some continue to exhibit physical approach behavior at a much later age than others.

10 A high degree of stability in attachment behavior is expected but observations of attachment behavior toward the same person at different ages show varying results. Correlations are usually modest or low. This may partly be due to different measures. Stability in parental sensitivity in childhood is modest.

11 Attachment is found in all cultures but cultural caregiving patterns result in differences in the proportion of children who show a given attachment type.

12 Secure attachment to both parents increases the likelihood of positive social development and relationships. Disorders are somewhat more common in children with early insecure attachment than children with secure attachment, but the differences are minor. Insecure disorganized attachment carries the greatest risk of developing emotional and behavioral disorders.

13 Robertson and Bowlby describe reactions related to prolonged or permanent separation from an attachment figure. Children with *reactive attachment disorder* have grown up with relatively unavailable and inconsistent attachment figures and show inadequate or deviant attachment behavior. Children with *disinhibited social engagement disorder* show little restraint toward strangers and behave indiscriminately in situations that elicit attachment behavior. This social disorder commonly occurs in children who have lived in orphanages. Children

who are adopted relatively late usually establish attachment relationships with their adoptive parents. Some children are resilient in negative environments.

14 All forms of attachment involve social learning and adaptation. The actions and behaviors of attachment figures are incorporated into working models that provide children with clues to the type of environment they can expect. Insecure attachment behavior is not necessarily a deviation from "healthy" development, but rather an adequate adaptation to the world as experienced by the child.

15 Attachment theory has had a major impact on child welfare practice and similar social services. Large orphanages have been closed down in many countries and replaced with foster homes and smaller institutions, with greater emphasis on promoting stable relationships between children and adults.

CORE ISSUES

- The biological bases of attachment behavior.
- The role of temperament in attachment relations.
- The relationship between adult sensitivity and attachment.

SUGGESTIONS FOR FURTHER READING

Ainsworth, M. D. S., & Bowlby, J. (1991). An ethological approach to personality development. *American Psychologist, 46*, 433–441.

Jin, M. K., et al. (2012). Maternal sensitivity and infant attachment security in Korea: Cross-cultural validation of the Strange Situation. *Attachment and Human Development, 14*, 33–44.

Main, M., & Weston, D. R. (1981). The quality of the toddler's relationship to mother and father: Relation to conflict behavior and readiness to establish new relationships. *Child Development, 52*, 932–940.

Mangelsdorf, S., et al. (1990). Infant proneness-to-distress temperament, maternal personality, and mother–infant attachment: Associations and goodness of fit. *Child Development, 61*, 820–831.

Raby, K. L. (2017). Attachment states of mind among internationally adoptive and foster parents. *Development and Psychopathology, 29*, 365–378.

Rutter, M., et al. (2009). Emanuel Miller Lecture: Attachment insecurity, disinhibited attachment, and attachment disorders: Where do research findings leave the concepts? *Journal of Child Psychology and Psychiatry, 50*, 529–543.

Seibert, A. C., & Kerns, K. A. (2009). Attachment figures in middle childhood. *International Journal of Behavioral Development, 33*, 347–355.

Suomi, S. J. (2005). Mother-infant attachment, peer relationships, and the development of social networks in rhesus monkeys. *Human Development, 48*, 67–79.

Contents

CHAPTER 20

SIBLING AND PEER RELATIONS

eer relations refer to a broad set of direct and indirect experiences with non-familial age mates (Rubin et al., 2015). They constitute a social setting that exerts immediate and proximal influence on the child (Chen et al., 2006). Interactions with siblings and peers are qualitatively different from those with adults, and have a prominent place in children's social lives from an early age. Siblings are part of the child's immediate environment while peers gains a gradually greater role as the child's social world expands.

Peer relations are usually horizontal, while relationships between children and adults are vertical (Hartup, 1992). In vertical relations, one part has more knowledge and social power than the other, and the relationship is asymmetrical and complementary. Adults have control and children are given protection and security. Children seek knowledge and help, and adults provide it. In peer relationships, social power is more equally distributed, although children may have different roles when interacting. One of them throws the ball, the other catches. One dresses the doll, the other pushes the cart. Horizontal relationships offer experiences and learning that vertical relationships cannot provide, including both competition and cooperation. Peer relations can moderate the effects of other positive and negative influences (Bukowski and Adams, 2005).

Friendship is a horizontal reciprocal relationship characterized by a strong emotional bond, and is based on equality and symmetry. *Popularity* is about being accepted and liked within a particular group or more generally, while friend-ship (and being enemies) is a special relationship between two children.

Key developmental issues in this chapter are the nature of sibling relationships, when and how children establish friendships, what factors contribute to some children being more popular and accepted than others, and the importance of sibling and peer relations for children's social and cultural adaptation.

SIBLING RELATIONSHIPS

Children spend much time together with their siblings, often more than with their parents (Howe and Recchia, 2014). Sibling relationships represent both social resources and challenges, and the family's emotional climate affects the relationship between siblings (McHale et al., 2012). During times of parental conflict or divorce, siblings can support each other, but animosity between siblings can also increase in connection with a divorce (Gass et al., 2007; McGuire and Shanahan, 2010). Observations of children's behavior toward their siblings in the Strange Situation as well as in the everyday environment suggest that they often feel attached to their older siblings (Gass et al., 2007; Stewart, 1983). Siblings who have been abused often have a close bond, and siblings who come into foster care together usually show a better development than siblings placed separately (Fraley and Tancredy, 2012; Washington, 2007).

Positive sibling interactions involving play and mutual help occur early on, as do competition and conflict. As early as 16–18 months of

Peer relations are important in childhood.

age, children can purposely destroy an object their sibling is particularly fond of. In the course of their second year, most children have begun to tease their siblings, and before the age of three, they have called their mother's attention to something wrong an older sibling has done (Dunn, 1988, 1993).

Parents and older siblings represent different domains of authority. During play, toddlers usually follow their older siblings' guidance and instruction and are usually more obedient toward their siblings than their parents. In other activities they are less willing to do what their older siblings tell them. Nonetheless, Dunn (1988) found a high correlation (0.90) between younger and older siblings' cooperative actions outside the play situation, indicating that children can have a major influence on how their younger siblings meet their surroundings. Siblings imitate each other, especially younger siblings but older siblings also imitate the younger (Howe et al., 2017). Older siblings engage in "teaching" their younger sibling (Howe et al., 2016).

Children aged 5–10 years are more collaborative as well as conflictual when talking to siblings than when talking to friends (Cutting and Dunn, 2006). Siblings share positive experiences, play together and jointly create fantasies and stories (Kramer, 2014). At the same time, sibling conflicts are more frequent and intense than quarrels in other relationships. The siblings' temperaments affect their relationships, and children with an active temperament experience more sibling conflicts than those who are less active (Brody, 1998). Children with aggressive and uncongenial older siblings are at greater risk of problems in their later relationships than children with siblings who have been warm and loving toward them (Dunn, 1996; Pike et al., 2005).

In school age, sibling conflicts typically have to do with what is fair and reasonable in relation to the siblings' age, sharing of personal belongings, physical aggression and general irritation over something a sibling says or does. Although sibling conflicts decrease in number, physical fights are common around the age of 10–11 and more frequent than when siblings are together with other children. Eventually, fighting is replaced by teasing and other indirect forms of aggression. However, even in later school age, many sibling conflicts are resolved when parents intervene or are dragged into the dispute. In interview studies, children themselves tell that negotiation and compromise rarely resolve the conflicts with their siblings. In step with their development of social cognitive skills, siblings nonetheless solve conflicts increasingly on their own, usually by withdrawing from the situation (McGuire et al., 2000). Moreover, despite spending much time together, children are more like their friends than their siblings when it comes to emotional style and conflict resolution (Lecce et al., 2009). This is not particularly surprising, however, considering that children typically both choose friends who resemble them in important ways and influence each other (see p. 422).

As siblings approach adolescence, their relationship becomes more equal, but they also spend increasingly less time together. This is probably the result of more time spent with friends outside the family, especially among boys (Buhrmester and Furman, 1990; Noller, 2005). An important aspect of the sibling relationship is also the fact that siblings speak differently with each other than with their parents. Girls are generally warmer toward their younger siblings and confide more often in them than boys do (Brown and Dunn, 1992; Dunn, 1996). Sisters tend to talk more about close relationships than brothers, and the closeness between same-sex siblings shows little change throughout childhood and adolescence. In adolescence, the relationship between different-sex siblings increases considerably in closeness, as girls and boys generally spend more time together (Kim et al., 2006).

Sibling relationships thus include cooperation and care as well as disagreement and conflict. It is this combination of warmth and conflict that uniquely contributes to the social learning and development among siblings (Kramer, 2014; McGuire et al., 1996). And it is a special

Siblings usually have a close relationship.

relationship with lasting impact. For example, while the competitive mentality that may have dominated the siblings in childhood decreases, it does not completely disappear. Brothers tend to maintain competition the most, different-sex siblings the least. Siblings who have established their own families tend to experience a strong emotional bond and often confide in each other. It is rare for siblings to lose contact entirely, and about 50 percent of adult siblings talk with each other once a month or more (Cicirelli, 1996). For many people, sibling relationships are the most enduring of all: from childhood to old age.

Siblings with atypical development

Sibling relationships are usually based on some sense of being equals, even though age differences can lead to a number of differences in status and physical strength. When one sibling has a disability, this may change the relationship in some ways (Meltzer and Kramer, 2016). Children with severe disabilities often become "younger siblings," regardless of their actual age rank among the others. In many areas, the relationship is the same as for siblings without disabilities but characterized by more warmth and care than other sibling relationships. When high-functioning adolescents with autism spectrum disorder were asked about their siblings, the feelings and attitudes they expressed were similar to other sibling relationships (Petalas et al., 2015).

A longitudinal study of children with disabled siblings found that they developed an early awareness of the uncommon characteristics of the disabled sibling, and the younger children usually began to comment on their sibling not long after beginning to speak. Around the age of 2, they started to use their parents as a model for how to relate to the disabled sibling, and around the age of 4 began to ask their parents about the future – whether the sibling's disability will change, and whether they will be going to the same school as their sibling. However, younger children do not fully understand disability and find it difficult to tell their peers about it. Once they enter school age, they become more aware of their sibling's need for care, worry about how things will go, and often say they want to take better care of their sibling in the future. By early adolescence, they usually have gained a good understanding of the cause of the disability and are able to explain the extra chromosome in children with Down

The sibling relationship is special when one sibling has a disability.

syndrome, for example (Dew et al., 2008; Hames, 2008). However, even younger adolescents may still have misconceptions about the condition of their sibling with a rare disease, such as stating that a chromosome is a kind of nerve and that the signals are weak (Vatne et al., 2015).

Siblings with and without disabilities generally spend less time together, and therefore experience both less conflict and shared prosocial behavior (Cuskelly and Gunn, 2003; Dallas et al., 1993a, b; Seligman and Darling, 2007). Still, for severely disabled children, who may have difficulties engaging in ordinary peer relations, siblings may have a very special role (Petalas et al., 2015).

PEER RELATIONS

Observations show that children have an early interest in other children. Three-month-olds look longer at other infants than at adults (Fogel, 1979). Vandell and associates (1980) observed simple interactions between 6-month-olds every 4 minutes, and every 3 minutes between 9-month-olds. They mostly consisted of one-way actions in which one child did something without a reciprocal action by the other. Genuine interactions involving looking, vocalizing and smiling did not occur until the end of the first year (Figure 20.1).

In their second year, children show an even greater interest in their peers. A study of 12- to 18-month-olds sitting together with their mother showed that they looked more than twice as long at a child of the same age than at another female adult (Lewis et al., 1975). When 11- and 23-month-old children in another study were paired and engaged in interaction with an adult, they too looked more at the other child than at the adult. When the adult deliberately excluded one of the children from interaction, the excluded child tried to establish contact with the other child far more often than with the adult (Tremblay-Leveau and Nadel, 1996). While most early interaction is dyadic, meaning that one child interacts with another child or adult, 2-year-olds are able to engage in triadic interaction. Occasionally, this involves interaction between all three children, but more often two children interact while the third child watches (Ishikawa and Hay, 2006; Selby and Bradley, 2003).

In the course of early childhood, children spend increasingly more time together. In modern Western societies, children spend much time in organized and unorganized activities with other children, while children in many other cultures are more integrated into adult activities from early on (Lam and McHale, 2015; Rogoff, 2014). As early as 2–3 years of age, children in Western societies spend more of their time outside kinder-

FIGURE 20.1 Four 1-year-olds engaged in interaction without adult guidance (photograph courtesy of Ben S. Bradley).

garten in the company of other children than adults, and as school age approaches, less and less of their leisure time is spent with adults (Ellis et al., 1981).

The relationships between children change with age (Box 20.1). Children of preschool age essentially represent a collection of separate individuals. Over time, they increasingly form into groups with norms and internal organization, and have to harmonize the competing demands of the groups they belong to. Some of these norms are related to relationships with the opposite sex, norms that are strictly adhered to in order to maintain gender boundaries (Sroufe et al., 1999).

Since many peer relations originate in school, children who attend the same class may become life-long friends. School is an important factor in whom children spend their time with, such as children from different social backgrounds as well as children with typical and atypical progress at school (Crosnoe and Benner, 2015).

Emotional involvement and vulnerability increase during adolescence, and peer relationships become an important part of young people's identities (see Chapter 21). Friendships and group relations between the sexes increase in number, as do intimate relationships with friends and sexual partners. All these relationships have to be reconciled with the norms and requirements of each group, and can make it difficult to maintain established relationships in case of misunderstandings and conflicts (Sroufe et al., 1999).

THE DEVELOPMENT OF FRIENDSHIP

Friendships have an important role in children's development: Friends develop social skills and understanding together, talk about themselves and others, and gain insight into moral values, conflict resolution and social and cultural rules (Bagwell and Schmidt, 2011; Dunn, 2004).

As early as children's second year, parents tell about special relationships with other children and how their children miss the playmates when they are away from kindergarten or play at home. Children start to talk about whom they like or dislike in kindergarten and other places early on (Dunn, 2004). Interaction between children increases around the age of 2, but since they still lack adequate independent social skills, the development of their play interactions and emotional relationships would run into problems without adults to facilitate play and offer emotional support (Howes, 1996). It is uncertain whether these early relationships have the necessary qualities to be called friendships, but cooperation is typical for this age nonetheless. Two-year-olds more often offer toys to others than taking a toy someone else is playing with.

By around 4 years of age, children have firmly established preferences and friendship relations.

BOX 20.1 TOPICS IN PEER RELATIONS OF CHILDREN AND ADOLESCENTS (after Sroufe et al., 1999)

PRESCHOOL AGE: POSITIVE ATTENTION TO PEERS

- Choosing specific partners
- Maintaining turns in integrations
  - Negotiating conflicts in interactions
  - Maintaining organization when excited
  - Finding joy in the interaction process
- Participation in groups

SCHOOL AGE: INVESTING IN A WORLD OF PEERS

- Establishing loyal friendships
- Maintaining relations
  - Negotiating conflicts in interactions
  - Tolerating many emotional experiences
  - Promote self in relations
- Functioning in stable, organized groups
  - Follow group norms
  - Maintaining gender borders
- Coordinating friendship and group functioning

ADOLESCENCE: INTEGRATING SELF AND PEER RELATIONS

- Establish intimate relations
  - Self-disclosure in same gender peer relations
  - Cross-gender relations
  - Sexual relationships
- Commitment in relations
  - Negotiating conflicts relevant for self
  - Emotional vulnerability
  - Self-disclosure and identity
- Functioning in a network of relations
  - Mastering systems with multiple rules
  - Establishing flexible borders
- Coordinating multiple relations of same and different gender
  - Intimate relations and functioning in the group

One study found that about 50 percent of a group of 4-year-olds in kindergarten had a special relationship with another child they spent over 30 percent of their time with (Hinde et al., 1985). About 75 percent of all preschool children say they have friends, while 80–90 percent of adolescents say they do (Hay et al., 2009). About 15 percent of all children and adolescents do not have a reciprocal friendship for 6 months or longer (Rubin et al., 2013).

Preschoolers have on average 1–2 friends, while school-age children typically mention 3–5 friends, depending on whether the friendship is reciprocal or not. This figure remains stable throughout adolescence. In childhood girls have a slightly smaller network of friends than boys, but in adolescence, the trend reverses. Both children and adolescents spend much time together with their friends. In adolescence, this amounts to nearly one-third of all their time (Hartup and Stevens, 1997).

Children are more cooperative and positive toward their friends than toward other peers. Friends have more fun together, often engage in more advanced forms of play, and solve school assignments better together than nonfriends. They spend more time talking about the assignment and less time beating about the bush. This probably has to do with their shared interests and the fact that friends are familiar with each other's behavior, strengths and weaknesses. In addition, spending time with friends offers important opportunities to learn how to resolve conflicts. Conflicts arise as often between friends as between nonfriends, and most conflicts in childhood actually occur within the family or between friends. What distinguishes conflicts between friends is the way in which they are resolved. Friends negotiate conflicts, while children who are not friends insist more on their own point of view. Friends more often work out compromises and solutions that do not ruin the friendship, instead of trying to out-trump or defeat each other. Both children and adolescents argue, but adolescents are more concerned with the relationship itself than younger children, who focus more on competition (Bukowski et al., 2009; Hartup and Stevens, 1997; Laursen and Pursell, 2009).

Most childhood friendships are between children of the same sex. As early as the age of 3, children show a distinct preference for playmates of the same sex among mixed groups of children.

In a study of fifth–sixth graders, 94 percent of reciprocal friendships were between children of the same sex (George and Hartmann, 1996). Part of the reason is that many childhood friendships are established through participation in social activities that tend to differ between boys and girls (see Chapter 24). Boys more often participate in group activities with a certain age spread and spend much of their time on competitive team sports with focus on cooperation and leadership. Girls more often collect in smaller groups and are more preoccupied with intimacy and who is in and outside the clique. Girls also prefer to play with other girls because they dislike the rough play of boys (Maccoby, 1990).

In adolescence, friendships are characterized by intimacy and personal issues. In conversations with friends, adolescents "disclose" themselves in an entirely different way than in conversations with their parents, especially girls (see p. 444). At the same time, friendships are the most fragile relationships: many adolescents worry about their friendships and about not being accepted (Coleman, 1980; Dolgin and Kim, 1994). Friendships with the opposite sex and romantic relationships become more common during adolescence, and those with early physical maturity and a high status among the group often lead the way. Others gradually follow suit, and eventually, mixed-gender groups become common. Many adolescents are unsure of themselves and the social relations they engage in. Learning to interact with the opposite sex is an important step in the social development of this phase, and friends play an important part in the process (Dunn, 2004).

Social media are important for young people to stay in touch with their friends, and digital communication with real friends is far more common than with other so-called "friends" on the Internet; it is among "real-life" friends social media can contribute to the quality of friendship (Furman and Rose, 2015).

Developing perceptions of friendship

When preschoolers are asked about their friends, they answer based on whom they do things together with, that they are friends because they play together. Adults, too, tend to perceive and describe younger children's relationships in this way. Joint activities are an important criterion for friendship among older children and adolescents as well, especially among boys. With age, however, perceptions of friendship increasingly involve feelings of perceived closeness and shared emotions. Friends are understanding, loyal and can be trusted. Older children associate friendship to a greater extent with similar attitudes and values. They are friends because they enjoy the same activities and the same music. In adolescence, descriptions of friendships additionally begin to include shared secrets and feelings, and opportunities for emotional support. It is with friends one can talk about one's innermost thoughts. Adolescents who are anxious and withdrawn look at their friends as a source of help and comfort (Bukowski et al., 2009; Mathur and Berndt, 2006; Schneider and Tessier, 2007). At the same time, adolescents are more selective than younger children in whom they consider to be their friends (Poulin and Chan, 2010).

Changes in children's perception of friendship partly reflect their developing mind understanding and the growing realization that not everyone thinks the same way they do (Fink et al., 2015). This creates a need to learn more about others as well as to tell others about oneself. Friendship opens up important opportunities to talk about private issues, including personal likes and dislikes. Children and adolescents tend to gossip more about others with their friends than those who are not friends generally do (Gottman and Mettetal, 1986).

Children's understanding of friendship also varies along cultural lines. Supporting a friend's self-image, for example, is considered a more important friendship quality among children and adolescents in Western, individualistic cultures than in more collectively oriented cultures such as China or Indonesia. Although Chinese and Indonesian children place somewhat greater emphasis on the utility of friendship, they attach equal importance to intimacy and emotional closeness as Canadian children (Chen et al., 2006).

Some children show an atypical understanding of friendship. For example children with autism spectrum disorder may refer to barely familiar children and hired adult assistants as their friends (Petrina et al., 2014). Children with severe motor impairment who lack speech and use communication aids may perceive other children as friends but are not always considered a friend by them (Østvik et al., 2017). There are friendships between children with and without a disability, but the prevalence of true reciprocal friendship involving children with severe disabilities is much lower than friendships among typically developing children. They may depend on adult intervention and typically developing "friends" may sometimes act as helpers rather than as friends (Guralnick et al., 2007; Rossetti and Keenan, 2018; Sterrett et al., 2017).

Stability of friendships

Children's earliest friendships are quite stable, typically lasting for more than a year, and by the age of 4, friendships have often lasted for 2 years. Their stability is probably related to the limited choices offered by the kindergarten, the neighborhood and the playmates introduced by parents. Relationships become more variable with a typical duration of 6–12 months during the preschool period (Dunn, 1993; Howes, 1996, 2009).

Children's radius of action expands and previous groups split up once children start in school, and school-age children regularly change best friends (see Box 20.2). One study found that nearly one-third of children in fourth and eighth grade had replaced all their best friends in the course of 6 months (Berndt et al., 1986). Shifting friendships are typical for early adolescence, but in the years to come, friendships become more stable again (Poulin and Chan, 2010).

Although children change friends, the status of having or not having friends has a high degree of stability. Children with friends at one age level usually also have friends at a later age (Elicker et al., 1992). Friendships lasting for shorter periods can reflect the quality of the friendship. For example, children with ADHD have shorter and less stable friendships (Chupetlovska-Anastasova, 2014). Also children with antisocial behavior often have unsatisfactory and shorter-lasting friendships (Dishion et al., 1995).

Similarities between friends

Friends tend to resemble each other in terms of social background and behavior, and two mechanisms seem to contribute this (Howes, 2009; McDonald et al., 2013). *Social selection* means that children choose their friends based on similarities in age, gender, socioeconomic and ethnic backgrounds, as well as temperament, interests

BOX 20.2 BEST FRIENDS (adapted from Gulbrandsen, 1998, pp. 15–17)

Robert (R) is participating in a longitudinal study where he is interviewed regularly by the researcher (G)

SECOND GRADE, SEPTEMBER

G: *Do you have a best friend?*
R: *Yes, Tom is my best friend*

SECOND GRADE, FEBRUARY

G: *Did you walk to school today?*
R: *Yes, and I bicycled some of the way. My friend and I bicycled together.*
G: *Was it Tom?*
R: *No, it was Magnus. Tom and Martin were driving.*
G: *So only you and Magnus bicycled?*
R: *Hm.*
G: *Did you not want to drive?*
R: *No. because Tom is so stupid. He teased Magnus and said he was slow and such. Magnus is my best friend, and then I don't go with Tom.*

SECOND GRADE, MAY

G: *When you went home from school yesterday, did you go together with somebody?*
R: *Tom.*
G: *Last time I talked with you, Tom and you were a little unfriendly.*
R: *Yes, but we are not anymore.*
G: *You are not unfriendly any more.*
R: *Now we are best friends.*

THIRD GRADE, DECEMBER

G: *Do you see Tom much now?*
R: *No, not much. He plays horse so much and I am tired of that. And at home, then they only play with the computer.*

and values. In an experiment with 7–8-year-olds who had never met and were gathered in groups on several occasions, the very first meeting revealed who liked and disliked each other, and children who liked each other played more alike than children who did not like each other (Rubin et al., 1994). *Social deselection* means that children choose not to become friends with others who differ from themselves in these areas, or end the friendship once they realize that they and their friend develop in different ways (Brown et al., 2008). Social deselection can also include children with intellectual disability, autism spectrum disorder or other disabilities (Schneider, 2016).

There seem to be greater similarities in antisocial behavior, such as fighting and bullying, than in prosocial behavior, such as cooperation and helpfulness (Haselager et al., 1998). One study found that boys (but not girls) who chose a friend with a relatively high level of antisocial behavior, themselves had a tendency for such behavior. Neither boys nor girls with low levels of antisocial behavior chose friends with this type of behavior. Children with high levels of prosocial behavior chose friends with the same behavior (Eivers et al., 2012). When children with antisocial behavior select friends with the same type of behavior, it may mean that they accept this behavior, but this may be because they have been deselected by more prosocial children and thus have few to choose from. Their friendships may not originate in mutual attraction, but in the children's inability to find other friends (Killen et al., 2009; Haselager et al., 1998).

Similarities are also promoted by the fact that friends consolidate their attitudes and behavior patterns when they are together. In this context, *social influence* is a transactional process in which children actively cooperate to construct, support and reject beliefs and attitudes, through conversations about people, events, movies, books, and so on. The older or more popular part in a friendship usually has somewhat greater influence than the younger or less accepted part (Furman and Rose, 2015), but it is rare that one of them is either "good" or "bad" as such, and the other simply has gotten a good or a bad friend. Friendship relations usually involve active *mutual* influence after an initial period of selecting and deselecting potential friends. Some children have friendships with conflicting influences, something that is not uncommon among children with minority backgrounds with friends belonging to both the majority and the minority culture (Berndt and Murphy, 2002; Brown et al., 2008). The degree of similarity between friends also tends to affect whether a friendship is maintained (Hafen et al., 2011; Poulin and Chan, 2010).

Boys who are friends tend to be more similar in terms of physical activity than nonfriends. Girls who are friends are more alike in physical attractiveness and the size of their social network than girls who are not friends. Female friends also share more similarities in prosocial and antisocial behavior than male friends. The opposite is true of shyness, which is a less problematic trait for girls than for boys (Cairns et al., 1995; Haselager et al., 1998).

ENEMIES

Being enemies involves a *relationship of mutual antipathy*. Just as in the case of friendships, there are corresponding degrees of hostile relationships: best friends and worst enemies. Children can be enemies for shorter periods in connection with conflicts among playmates, or have more prolonged hostile relationships that are equally stable as friendships (Casper and Card, 2010). About 35 percent of all children and adolescents report having one or more enemies, with a slight increase during early school age and a decrease in adolescence. More boys than girls report having enemies. Enemies often share a unique negative background (Card, 2010; Rodkin et al.,

2003), while friendship can be maintained by having a common enemy (Rambaran et al., 2015).

Having enemies is not related to general social competence and adaptability, but when a child has many enemies, it usually indicates a problem with social interaction. Adolescents with many enemies are less accepted and bullied more often, and some enemy relationships are founded on bullying and mutual antipathy (Hafen et al., 2013; see also p. 477). Some adolescents with many enemies, particularly boys, show a lot of aggressive behavior. Others tend to be more socially withdrawn than those with few or no enemies, but, unlike unpopular children, do not report feeling lonely (see p. 428). Consequently, having enemies can in a certain sense fulfill a socially "protective" role. Girls who are generally disliked often feel sad. Girls who have enemies, but are not disliked, rarely feel sad. This underlines the role of mutual antipathy as an active relationship and integral part of the social network, even if its dynamic is negative. Additionally, it requires a certain social competence to establish a negative relationship in which both parts must contribute to maintain their antagonism. While adolescents with many enemies show somewhat more antisocial and aggressive behavior than those without enemies, adolescents with prosocial behavior have enemies as well, and the differences are minor (Abecassis et al., 2002; Pope, 2003).

POPULAR AND REJECTED CHILDREN

Some children are popular. Everyone wants to spend time with them, and they get to participate in anything they like. Others are largely excluded from joint play unless organized and supervised by adults (Cillessen and Rose, 2005). Popularity and rejection can be measured by observing which children in a group spend little or much time together with other children. Another method is to ask children whether they want to spend time with a particular child, or to name the three children they would like to be together with the most, and the three they would rather not be together with. One should be careful, however, in asking children to classify their peers in negative ways (Martinsen et al., 2010; Schneider, 2016).

Children's sociometric status is commonly divided into five major groups: popular, rejected, neglected, controversial and neutral (Rubin et al., 2006). Importantly, peer popularity or rejection is not a characteristic that resides in the child. It represents the feelings of others toward the child and only makes sense in the context of a peer group (Bagwell and Schmidt, 2011).

Popular children are actively accepted. Often they are physically strong, with an attractive appearance, but their willingness to share, their ability to cooperate and other social skills are equally important for their popularity among peers (Parker and Asher, 1993; Asher and McDonald, 2009).

Rejected, or *unpopular*, children are actively excluded by other children. Although aggression may be regarded as the primary reason for rejection (Rubin et al., 2015), only 40–50 percent of rejected children actually show particular signs of aggression, while others appear more submissive. Socially withdrawn children make up 10–20 percent of the rejected group, and 25 percent of withdrawn children are rejected (Rubin et al., 2013). This group also includes children who are immature and childish compared with their peers (Berndt, 2002). Nonetheless, aggressive behavior does not necessarily lead to rejection – it depends on how the behavior is expressed. In many situations, popular children are as assertive and aggressive as rejected aggressive children. One study found that only half the children who were considered extremely aggressive had rejected status. Aggressive actions in response to threats from others were seen as positive (Cillessen et al., 1992). Tough children who are able to "speak out" and at times even use their fists, but who rarely show the socially disruptive and aggressive behavior typical of unpopular rejected children, can be quite popular among their peers (Rodkin et al., 2006). Children who behave aggressively while at the same time being able to establish a social network rarely end up in the unpopular group; they have positive qualities that outweigh their aggressive behavior (Cairns et al., 1988; Pedersen et al., 2007).

Neglected children are neither accepted nor rejected, but interact less with their peers than children in the neutral group. They are quite similar to other children, usually show little aggressive behavior and try to avoid aggression somewhat more than other children, but none-theless do not appear anxious or withdrawn. Children with the latter characteristics typically end up in the withdrawn rejected group.

Controversial children are both accepted and rejected, and have traits in common with popular as well as rejected children. At times they can appear active, aggressive, destructive and angry, or socially withdrawn, at other times they can show cooperation, leadership, helpfulness and social sensitivity. Their behavior varies depending on the situation and whom they are together with. Other children tend to perceive their behavior as contradictory since their positive traits do not represent enough of a counterweight to place them in the popular or neutral category, while their negative traits are not dominant enough to make them unpopular.

Neutral children fall in between the other groups. They are neither particularly popular, rejected or controversial, but are not neglected either.

When children are asked whom they like and dislike, their answers are always affected by recent events and changes in mood. Not all children remain in the sociometric category they first start out in, but rejection from peers is more stable than acceptance during childhood (Hardy et al., 2002; Pedersen et al., 2007).

Social strategies and popularity

Initiating contact with other children is a natural start of peer relationships. Some of the differences between popular, rejected and neglected children clearly show up in the social strategies they use, for example when joining a game already in progress. Popular children usually first observe the situation for a moment before gradually joining into the play themselves. Pushy unpopular children tend to throw themselves into play, often in a way that interrupts the activity. They do not understand the rules and therefore are unable to fit in naturally. Their attempts to join into play are an expression of wanting social contact, but their clumsy way of interfering makes them disliked by their peers. Since they are excluded from participating in the activity, they never get a chance to learn the rules. Aggressive unpopular children are usually not aware of their own lack of social skills, and are therefore bewildered and frustrated when other children reject them (Dodge et al., 1983; Martinsen and Nærland, 2009).

Unpopular submissive children are often directly rejected when they seek contact with their peers, and typically ask adults fo help in resolving conflicts with other children. They perceive social conflicts and can identify possible solutions, but are often unable to carry them out. They have insight into their own social problems and express feelings of perceived loneliness to a greater degree than aggressive rejected children (Hymel et al., 1993). Neglected children stand on the sidelines and look on without making an active effort to join in. They are not included in play by other children, but merely observe and do not disturb the other's play. Therefore, they gain a better understanding of the rules of play than children in the aggressive rejected group. Unlike unpopular submissive children, neglected children do not give the impression of experiencing loneliness (Howes, 2009).

In the course of childhood, many factors can affect whether children are accepted by their peers. Toddlers depend on adults to establish interaction and play, and several studies have found a relation between the way parents monitor and intervene in their child's activities and the child's relationships with other children. Children with mothers who indirectly manage the child's activities are better liked than children whose mothers are more direct. For boys, maternal over and under involvement both seem to entail a lower social status among peers. Girls with a high social status among their peers typically have under involved mothers, and their own efforts to make contact with other children considerably exceed those of the mother. Mothers of popular children interfere less with play than mothers of unpopular, rejected children, and tend to address the entire group when explaining something or intervening in children's play activities (Ladd and Hart, 1992). All these differences are not merely the result of maternal characteristics; maternal strategies are equally influenced by the characteristics of the child and the child's friends (Furman and Rose, 2015).

Temperament and the ability to self-regulate influence how children try to establish relationships with other children (Eisenberg et al., 2009). Children with an early inhibited temperament are often socially reticent in company with their peers when they grow older (Rubin et al., 2002). Children with a difficult temperament tend to be more impulsive and aggressive than other chil-

dren, increasing the likelihood of rejection by their peers. A study found that 5- to 10-year-olds who scored high on sociability were more popular and had more positive relationships than children who scored lower on this temperament trait. The children who scored high on the emotionality trait had poorer relationships with their peers than children who were less emotional (Stocker and Dunn, 1990). Similarly, sociable children with poor emotion regulation tend to exhibit aggressive and destructive behaviors that make them unpopular. They would rather join in than be destructive, but are unable to cope with the situation. Sociable children with good emotion regulation tend to be socially competent. Socially wary children with good self-regulation easily blend into play with others, while socially wary children with poor self-regulation appear anxious and cautious (Rubin et al., 1995).

At every age level, children carry with them the expectations and strategies they have developed through earlier peer interactions. Not only do popular and unpopular children act in different ways, they also have a different understanding of other people's perspectives and intentions, and may have quite different expectations of companionship. Aggressive unpopular children often mention rivalry as a motive to spend time with other children, while popular children express interest and pleasure in companionship as such. Some unpopular children put the blame on others when they get into a quarrel. They have a more hostile attitude to solving conflicts and fewer suggestions for prosocial solutions. Other unpopular children believe their social success is the result of external circumstances while blaming social failure on their own personal characteristics (Crick and Dodge, 1994; Dunn, 1999). These types of differences in children's perception of the social environment and themselves can be seen in light of their own experiences with being rejected, but they can also become self-fulfilling prophecies which impact on their later development (Bierman, 2004; Rubin et al., 2006). Thus, the social *life space* (Lewin, 1935) of popular and unpopular children can be quite different.

Cultural differences

The studies referred to here were conducted in Europe and North America. Since cultural norms and characteristics regarded as positive and socially competent vary from one culture to another, the characteristics of popular and unpopular children also show some variation between different countries. Aggression in any form, for example, is frowned upon in China and many other Asian countries, while sensitive, careful and controlled behavior is considered an expression of social maturity and competence. Accordingly, this type of behavior is relatively more prominent in popular children in Asian than in Western countries. In most cultures, popular children and adolescents show cooperation, prosocial behavior, friendliness and sociability, while social withdrawal leads to rejection in many cultures (Rubin et al., 2010, 2013).

Friends, popularity and adaptation

Throughout childhood and adolescence, peer relations play an important role in learning how to adapt. Peer relations help younger children learn to collaborate, resolve conflicts and other social skills. Among older children and adolescents, they contribute to the development of identity and a broader understanding of other people, but can lead to both positive and negative outcomes: when friends show positive social behavior, cooperation and good solutions, they protect against a negative social development. Friends who are cooperative to begin with become more cooperative over time. Similarly, friends with poor social adaptation and conflict resolution skills will increase the likelihood of a negative social development (Berndt, 2002; Hartup and Stevens, 1997). Well-functioning friendships in which one or both parts show deviant behavior increase the risk of negative development (Dishion and Piehler, 2009).

Some children do not have friends their own age and miss out on the social and relational skills brought about by emotionally close, reciprocal friendships. For some, this is due to specific social impairments such as autism spectrum disorder (Attwood, 1998; Petrina et al., 2014), but there are also children without such impairments who do not gain the necessary experience with common social interaction. This increases their likelihood of poor social adaptation and emotional disorders.

Studies show that children who have friends generally are less dominating, controlled and tense, and more independent, emotionally supportive and sensitive to other people's feelings than children without reciprocal friendships. They have better social skills, are more sociable and unselfish, and show better adaptation and performance at school. In school age, play between friends is more reciprocal, cooperative and positive-affective than play between children with few or no friends. Children without friends show poorer interaction with their peers and a reduced ability to take the perspective of others. They are perceived negatively by others as well as themselves. Children without friends are more vulnerable to internalizing than externalizing disorders (Furman and Rose, 2015; Rubin et al., 2013).

Poor social skills can be the result of lack of social experiences, but lack of social experiences can also be the result of poor social skills. Children who have suffered neglect or abuse are socially less competent, less prosocial and more aggressive toward their peers than children who have not been subjected to such harm. They can be withdrawn, although this is more common in children who have suffered neglect than those who have been subjected to physical abuse. Even if their peers take positive initiatives, they may respond with aggression (see p. 482). They can either show a complete lack of trust in other people or appear excessively confident. Both forms of behavior make interaction with other children difficult. These children are often disliked by their peers and have difficulty establishing friendship relations. In one study, children who had never met before were divided into eight play groups, each with one child who had suffered neglect and three children who had received normal care. After 4 weeks, nine of the 24 children who had not been subjected to neglect formed reciprocal friendships. Only one of the eight children who had suffered neglect established this type of friendship in the course of the same period (Price, 1996). This shows that neglect from significant adults may impact children's development of social skills and confidence to establish social relationships with their peers. However, some children who have suffered gross neglect and physical abuse develop resilience and form positive relationships and friendships that to a certain extent mitigate the consequences of their abuse (Dubowitz et al., 2016; Houshyar et al., 2013).

428 SIBLING AND PEER RELATIONS

Friendship and popularity status may have both similar and different consequences. In one study, children in fifth and sixth grade reported having approximately the same number of friends, but the unpopular children had only half as many *reciprocal* friendships as the neutral children, and only one-third as many as the popular children. Additionally, the popular group had the greatest number of popular children as reciprocal friends. Most reciprocal friendships among unpopular children were with neutral children, in addition to a relatively larger proportion of unpopular friends, compared with popular children (George and Hartmann, 1996). The unpopular group in this study also had more reciprocal friendships exclusively outside school, most likely because rejection at school led the unpopular children to seek social recognition and friendship elsewhere. Consequently, peer relations in the long-term stable environment of school were of relatively less importance for these children than for others. This might have contributed to contact with extreme or anti-social groups in adolescence.

Friendships are important for children's self-image, and children without friends generally have a less positive perception of themselves than children with friends. Submissive rejected children in particular have a poor self-image (Rubin et al., 2006). Harter (1987) describes a vicious circle in the development of friendship relations and self-image: children with a low sense of self-worth feel they receive little support from their classmates and friends, adding further to their low self-evaluation, and so on. Relatively speaking, children without best friends are more lonely than children with best friends, no matter how popular they are (Parker and Asher, 1993). Unpopular children are at risk of social isolation, particularly when they have no friends. Most unpopular children say they have friends, in which case their low popularity generally has less severe consequences for their ability to adapt. Friendship thus provides protection against perceived loneliness in both popular and unpopular children. It is the combination of not having friends *and* being unpopular that negatively affects the development process.

It is rare for children to either have or not have friends throughout their entire childhood. Children constantly establish new relationships and sometimes change best friends many times

before reaching adolescence. It is not each individual friendship that is essential, but their positive or negative sum total. Nonetheless, from a transactional perspective on development, it is the quality of former friendships that forms the foundation for new ones and for the expectations children have of friendships and their own contribution to the relationship.

ADOLESCENT GROUPS

A group is a social network within which individuals interact and relationships are embedded (Rubin et al., 2015). As part of the emancipation process, adolescents seek out smaller and larger groups outside the home. Some are "skaters," some are "nerds," others are involved in politics or sports or have an ethnic affiliation outside mainstream society. Some groups have values that differ radically from those of society, but most groups reflect society at large, with typical attitudes and values that generally characterize young people in society. They may function as *reference groups* for the individual, meaning that the groups' rules, values and norms largely determine adolescents' attitudes and behaviors, whether they are prosocial or antisocial. These groups have little stability, however, and change when adolescents switch school or take up other interests, in addition to developments within the group itself and society in general. The individual relationships and attitudes within groups of close friends in particular change in line with development (Faircloth and Hamm, 2011).

Adolescents are particularly vulnerable to rejection from their peers. Many are worried about not being accepted by their peers, and a high degree of conformity with friends and reference groups is typical of adolescence. *Conformity* means to adopt the attitudes and behaviors of others due to actual or perceived pressure from them. In many contexts, it is the attitudes of friends that become decisive, rather than the norms and values of the family or society in general (Berndt, 1979). Adolescents do many things because "everyone else does it." In relation to society, the attitudes and norms of a group can be conformist (comply with society), non-conformist (act independently of society) or anti-conformist (act contrary to society's norms). They might start to smoke, drink or shoplift because their friends tell them they are gutless or childish if they do not participate. Also the negative consequences of placing adolescents with deviant behaviors together with other deviant peers demonstrate adolescents' influence on each other (Prinstein and Dodge, 2008; see also p. 481). However, following the norms of a group is not the same as submitting to the group altogether. Adolescents may seem conformist because they seek out groups whose values they accept and that accept them in return, influencing the groups they are part of as well as being influenced by them.

PEER RELATIONS AND LATER DISORDERS

Peers are a core element of children's social environment and this is reflected in the associations between early social acceptance and later disorders. Children who start school together with friends, for example, are more positive to school and adapt better in first grade than children who do not have friends when they start school – the school environment becomes less alien to children who have friends with them (Dunn, 2004; Ladd, 1990). In later childhood and adolescence, the affiliation with different groups can contribute to a strengthened self-image and protect against the development of mental disorders (Newman et al., 2007).

Children who have been rejected by their peers before starting in school show poorer adaptation at school (Wentzel, 2009). Those in the aggressive rejected group are at risk of behavioral problems, poor impulse control and aggression regulation, hostility and antisocial behavior, even in adolescence. One study found that a higher proportion of 11-year-olds classified as rejected had dropped out of school 7 years later. Compared with popular or neglected children, three times as many had been in contact with the police (Kupersmidt and Coie, 1990). Submissive rejected children are more vulnerable

to developing anxiety, depression and low self-esteem (Rubin et al., 2013; Hymel et al., 1990). Chronic rejection represents a negative developmental spiral and children who experience chronic rather than intermittent rejection have the greatest risk of later disorders (Bierman, 2004; DeRosier et al., 1994).

If friendship is to have a positive social impact, it must have positive qualities. Some friendships are distinguished by little equality and high levels of conflict. When interaction is not based on the relational equality a friendship requires, children's expectations of friendship and their peer interaction strategies can become dominated by negative qualities (Berndt, 1996; Dishion et al., 1995; Newcomb and Bagwell, 1996). Although some friendships are characterized by positive inner qualities such as equality, emotional support and a high degree of loyalty and intimacy, they can still contribute to the development of aggressive and antisocial behavior when friends support and encourage each other in such behavior (Hartup, 1999; Kupersmidt et al., 1995). This type of friendship thus represents a form of negative social capital.

The studies referred to in this chapter provide a complex picture of children's relationships with other children. Many factors are at play when children engage in friendships and other peer relationships: children's own characteristics such as temperament, emotion regulation and social cognitive skills, as well as their accumulated experiences from interaction with other children and adults. It is the totality of all these factors that leads each child to form unique expectations of social relationships and strategies, and that colors their further development. Nonetheless, vulnerability to internalizing and externalizing disorders is not destined – most children do not develop such disorders, and there are various initiatives to reduce rejection, promote social skills and positive relationships between children, and guard against disorders (Bierman, 2004; Schneider, 2016).

SUMMARY

1   Peer relations refer to a broad set of direct and indirect experiences with non-familial age mates, constitute a social setting that exerts immediate and proximal influence on the child. In *vertical* relationships one part has more knowledge and social power than the other. In a *horizontal* relationship, social power is more equally distributed.

2   Siblings are part of the child's immediate environment. They share many experiences and have positive interactions as well as conflicts, which may have to be resolved by their parents. Although they can support each other in difficult situations, these can also put a strain on the relationship. It is a combination of warmth and conflict that uniquely contributes to the social learning and development among siblings.

3   When one of the siblings is disabled, the relationship is often characterized by more warmth and care than other sibling relationships. Since they generally spend less time together, they also experience less conflict and shared prosocial behavior.

4   Children show an early interest in other children and spend increasing amounts of time together throughout childhood, while leisure time with adults decreases. Preschoolers essentially represent a collection of separate individuals, groups begin to form during school age, and children have to reconcile their friendships with the competing demands of the groups they belong to. Adolescence sees a growing number of relationships across the sexes.

5   *Friendship* is a horizontal relationship with a strong emotional bond. By the age of 4 years, children usually have well-established friendship relations, and the number of friends increases slightly with age. For preschoolers, friends are the children they do things together with. For older children and adolescents, friendship is more about perceived closeness and emotional fellowship. While schoolchildren describe their friends as understanding, loyal and trustworthy, older children place more weight on similar values and attitudes. In adolescence, descriptions of friendship include shared secrets and feelings, and opportunities for emotional support. Friends have as many conflicts as non-friends, but they are better at resolving them. In adolescence, intimacy and personal issues becomes increasingly important for friendships.

6   Toddlerhood friendships typically last for 1–2 years. In preschool age, friendships are somewhat more variable, and in school age, many children regularly change best friends. In the course of adolescence, friendships become more stable and selective. In preschool age and childhood, girls have a slightly smaller network of friends than boys, but in adolescence the trend reverses.

7   *Social selection* means children choose friends who are similar to themselves, *social deselection* that they choose not to become friends with children who are different from themselves. Friends affect each other's attitudes and behaviors through *social influence*. Male friends tend to be similar in terms of physical activity, female friends in attractiveness and the size of their social network. Female friends share more similarities in prosocial and antisocial behavior than male friends. The opposite is true of shyness, which is less problematic for girls than for boys.

8   One-third of all children and adolescents say they have *enemies*. Mutual antipathy is an active relationship and integral part of a child's social network, even if its dynamic is negative. Adolescents with many enemies are less accepted and subjected to more bullying. Some enemy relationships are founded on bullying.

9   *Popular children* are often physically strong, with an attractive appearance, but their willingness to share, their ability to cooperate and other social skills are equally important for their popularity. About 50 percent of the *unpopular* group show socially disruptive,

aggressive behavior, while socially withdrawn and submissive children make up 10–20 percent. Some rejected children are immature and childish compared with their peers. *Neglected* children are neither accepted nor rejected. *Controversial* children share common traits with both popular and unpopular children, and are both accepted and rejected. *Neutral* children are neither particularly popular, rejected or controversial, but are not neglected either.

10 Popular and unpopular children have a different understanding of other children's perspectives and intentions, and may have completely different motives and expectations. Aggressive unpopular children often mention rivalry, while popular children express interest and pleasure in companionship as such. Some unpopular children put the blame on others when conflicts and problems arise. Other unpopular children believe their social success is the result of external circumstances, while blaming social failure on their own personal characteristics. *Cultures* differ with regard to the types of characteristics they consider positive, and thus also the characteristics of popular and unpopular children.

11 Most children take part in the process of relational learning and enculturation a reciprocal friendship usually involves. Younger children learn to cooperate, resolve conflicts and other social skills. Among older children and adolescents, peer relations contribute to the development of identity and a broader understanding of other people. Unpopular children are at risk of social isolation and missing out on social skills, especially when they do not have friends.

12 Adolescents influence the groups they are part of and are in turn influenced by them. The groups' rules, values and norms are important for their attitudes and behaviors, and can both promote and inhibit the development of prosocial and antisocial behavior patterns. A high degree of conformity with friends and groups is typical of adolescence, but in relation to society, the attitudes and norms of a group can either be conformist, non-conformist or anti-conformist.

13 Studies have found relations between early social acceptance and later disorders. Friendship and group affiliation can contribute to a strengthened self-image and protect against disorders. Children in the aggressive rejected group are vulnerable to developing behavioral disorders and antisocial behavior, submissive rejected children to developing anxiety, depression and low self-esteem. Children who experience chronic rather than intermittent rejection have the greatest risk of later disorders. Nonetheless, most unpopular children without good peer relations do not develop disorders, and there exist interventions that can reduce rejection, promote social skills and positive relationships, and guard against disorders.

CORE ISSUES

- Emotional closeness and conflict among siblings.
- The behavioral bases of peer acceptance and rejection.
- Selection and deselection processes in friendship formation.
- Risk and protection related to friends and peers.

SUGGESTIONS FOR FURTHER READING

Abecassis, M. (2003). I hate you just the way you are: Exploring the formation, maintenance and need for enemies. *New Directions for Child and Adolescent Development, 102,* 5–22.

Cuskelly, M., & Gunn, P. (2003). Sibling relationships of children with Down syndrome: Perspectives of mothers, fathers, and siblings. *American Journal on Mental Retardation, 108,* 234–244.

Dishion, T. J., et al. (1995). Antisocial boys and their friends in early adolescence: Relationship characteristics, quality, and interactional process. *Child Development, 66,* 139–151.

Dunn, J. (2004). *Children's friendships: The beginnings of intimacy.* Oxford: Blackwell.

Haselager, G. J. T., et al. (1998). Similarities between friends and nonfriends in middle childhood. *Child Development, 69,* 1198–1208.

Howe, N., et al. (2017). "I'm an ogre so I'm very hungry!" "I'm assistant ogre": The social function of sibling imitation in early childhood. *Infant and Child Development, 27,* e2040.

Rubin, K. H., et al. (1994). "Birds of a feather . . .": Behavioral concordances and preferential personal attraction in children. *Child Development, 65,* 1778–1785.

Contents

CHAPTER 21

SELF AND IDENTITY

The key issues in this chapter revolve around the forming of the individual self and the emergence of self-understanding and typical and atypical self-esteem and identity. An important aspect of this development is that the self and the identity both change and remain the same (Hammack and Toolis, 2015; Koh and Wang, 2012). The self is an inner experience and awareness of being a unique individual. Identity is a continuation of reflections of the self and an experience of sameness, difference and affiliation with other people, of being part of a larger social context (Hammack and Toolis, 2015). Self and identity have to do with changing variations and answers to the question "Who am I, and what is my place in the world?" (Brummelman and Thomaes, 2017).

THE BEGINNINGS OF SELF-PERCEPTION

The self comprises two main aspects: the *self as knower*, or *I*, is the experience of being a unique individual. It is a sense of being and acting in the world that comes from within. The *self as known*, or *me*, is the self-perception of an individual, an awareness of being in possession of certain characteristics and qualities and an evaluation of one's own abilities relative to those of others (James, 1890). One method of studying early self-perception is to observe when children recognize themselves in a mirror or a picture. Lewis and Brooks-Gunn (1979) found that children on average have passed the age of 20 months before they touch their nose when they look in a mirror

after their mother unknown to them has put a red mark on their nose (Box 21.1). Other studies have similar results (Courage et al., 2004), but have also found cultural differences. German and Greek toddlers, for example, showed earlier self-recognition than toddlers from a village in Cameroon, a result that did not seem to be related to differences in the children's access to mirrors but rather to different parenting styles. German and Greek children had more face-to-face interaction with adults than the children from Cameroon (Keller et al., 2004, 2005).

The ability to recognize oneself in a mirror is a skill human beings share with few other species. Some elephants seem to understand that they are looking at a mirror image of themselves (Plotnik et al., 2006, 2010), and magpies pass the "mark test" as well (Prior et al., 2008). Self-recognition is rare even among primates: not all chimpanzees show this type of recognition, and only about one-third of all gorillas that have been studied recognize themselves in a mirror (Suddendorf and Collier-Baker, 2009). Most animals with a mirror placed in their cage for some time will explore the mirror rather than what the mirror reflects. This demonstrates that it is cognitively more demanding to recognize oneself than to recognize others, something most animals are capable of.

Studies using variations of the mark test have found that children recognize themselves later on video and in photographs than in a mirror. In one study, the experimenter placed a sticker on the head of 2- to 4-year-olds without their knowledge, and then took a photograph or video-recording and immediately showed it to the child.

BOX 21.1 EARLY SELF-RECOGNITION IN THE MIRROR (Lewis and Brooks-Gunn, 1979)

The study involved 96 children, aged 9, 12, 15, 18, 21 and 24 months, with eight boys and eight girls in each group.

The children and their mothers were first observed in a room with a mirror for 1.5 minutes. The children looked at the mirror but almost none of them touched their nose during the observation. Following this, the mother was given a cloth with rouge and without the child noticing, the mother put a red mark on the child's nose. The mother was instructed not to talk about the nose or direct the child's attention to the nose. She turned the child toward the mirror and he or she was observed for the same length of time, 1.5 minutes.

None of the children in the two younger groups touched their nose when they looked into the mirror after the rouge was applied. Nineteen percent of the 15-month-olds and 25 percent of the 18-month-olds touched their nose when they looked into the mirror. It was only after the age of 21 months that a majority of the children touched their nose: 63 percent of the 21-month-olds and 66 percent of the 24-month-olds.

None of the 2-year-olds and only one-quarter of the 3-year-olds reacted to the sticker on their head when they saw the photograph or video of themselves they had seen being taken moments earlier, while a majority of the 4-year-olds reacted immediately (Povinelli et al., 1996). Experience is of importance for the development of this form of self-recognition, however: toddlers recognize themselves earlier when they have experience using camcorders and digital cameras (see p. 135). The development of self-perception is also reflected in the emergence of self-referential emotions like pride and shame at the same age (p. 352), as well as claims of objects as their own by saying "*It's mine!*" (Levine, 1983; Lewis, 2011).

Another milestone in self development is when children recognize their name. Toddlers begin to refer to themselves by name or *I*, and rarely make a mistake between *you* and *I*. Understanding who is referred to by *you* and *I* requires situational awareness since the personal reference depends on who is talking. Without visual clues, this is more difficult to do, and although blind children generally develop language at the same time as other children, their use of these particular words is often delayed (Fraiberg, 1977). This does not mean, however, that their self-understanding is any less developed.

"Do it myself"

THEORIES OF SELF DEVELOPMENT

Self-awareness and knowledge of oneself as a reflective agent in the world are central to human development, and there are many different views on this process. Here is mainly room for the influential theories of Margaret Mahler, Daniel Stern and Michael Lewis.

Separation-individuation theory

The distinguishing feature of Mahler's psychoanalytic theory is the inability of the newborn child to differentiate between herself and the mother (Mahler et al., 1975). According to this theory, the human child starts in a symbiotic phase where she experiences oneness with the mother and does not distinguish between self-object and mother-object; the early self thus includes both herself and the mother (see p. 398). After about 5 months, the child begins to differentiate an individual concept of self from the early symbiotic concept through what Mahler calls separation-individuation processes. The infant incorporates a representation of herself and the mother, and by the age of 12–18 months she is able to fully distinguish between them, although the processes continue over the first 3 years of life. During the *separation process*, the child's sense of being a self separated from others gradually increases. She develops feelings of both separateness and connection with the outside world, particularly the connection between her own body and that of the mother. The process of *individuation* allows the child to get a sense of herself as an individual with characteristics independent of the mother. The child's increasing mobility plays an important role in this development. Individuation is dependent on the mother's availability and her ability to match the child's feelings, but the primary goal of this process is independence, rather than the development of a mother–child relationship such as in Bowlby's attachment theory (see Chapter 19).

Mahler's theory has been historically important and its basic views are shared by many within psychodynamic psychology (Blom and Bergman, 2013). For example, Donald Winnicott (1960) describes a development where the child first goes through an *undifferentiated phase* in which she cannot be described independently of the mother. The child's development of self-perception is determined by maternal reactions, and the child's experience of self is an extension of how he experiences the mother's subjectivity. It is the mother's *mirroring* of the child's movements during play and other activities that allow the child to perceive himself as powerful and unique. If the mother is sufficiently empathetic, the child will develop a "true self" that reflects his unique potentials. If the mother lacks the necessary empathy, the child will adapt to the mother by developing a "false self" that protects the real self from negative maternal influences. A child's self-perception is therefore directly linked to the

mother and makes significant demands on how the mother relates to the child.

Several authors – also within psychoanalytic and psychodynamic psychology – have pointed out that the assumption that children start with an undifferentiated experience of themselves and their mother is not supported by the early competencies revealed in modern infant research (Blum, 2004; Silverman, 2004; Stern, 1998). Studies have found that newborns show a preference for their mother's voice and learn to distinguish the outline of their mother's head from those of other women early on (see Chapter 8). The fact that infants react to separation from their mother in unfamiliar surroundings is a further indication that they distinguish between themselves and their mother, and between the mother and other people (see Chapter 19). Studies of social referencing show that children seek adult help in evaluating the environment as early as the first year of life (see p. 350). Although very young children have a limited understanding of the fact that other people can have states of mind, intentions, experiences and skills that differ from their own, they have no problem distinguishing between themselves and others.

The criticism of the early symbiotic phase has led to several revisions of the separation-individuation theory, either by omitting this aspect of the theory and instead maintaining the existence of a core self at birth (Blum, 2004; Silverman, 2004), or by redefining the nature of such a self experience (Blom and Bergman, 2013; Pine, 2004). However, the theories still maintain that separation-individuation is a self process from dependence to independence. Separation-individuation is an intra-person process of becoming a separate person, an independent self (Blom and Bergman, 2013).

Six senses of self

Stern (1998) describes the development of a multi-layered self (Figure 21.1) whereby each layer develops in parallel and remains an independent but integrated part of the mature individual's self. An inadequately developed or severely impaired sense of self will lead to aberrant social functioning or mental health disorders. According to Stern, the self develops through transfer of the caregiver's emotions to the child by means of empathy. He rejects the idea that children go through a phase in which they do not distinguish between their mother and themselves, and argues instead that children are born with a sense of independence and agency. Although Stern belongs to the psychodynamic tradition, his description of the development of self-experience differs considerably from those of Mahler and Winnicott.

The emergent self

Children's earliest sense of self is the experience of connecting isolated objects and events and discovering their permanent characteristics. They consist of internal signals, including momentary states, arousal, activation, muscle tension, moti-

vation and satisfaction. All these bodily signals come from the self. According to Stern, newborns experience the *process* itself through an increasing degree of organization. It is a form of "primary consciousness" that is not reflective, cannot be formulated verbally, and only lasts for a brief moment, a "now" of what occupies the mind. It is "an awareness of the process of living an experience. The contents of the experience could be anything" (Stern, 1998, p. xviii).

The core self

The core self is not a cognitive construct, a "concept of" or a "knowledge of," but an "experi-

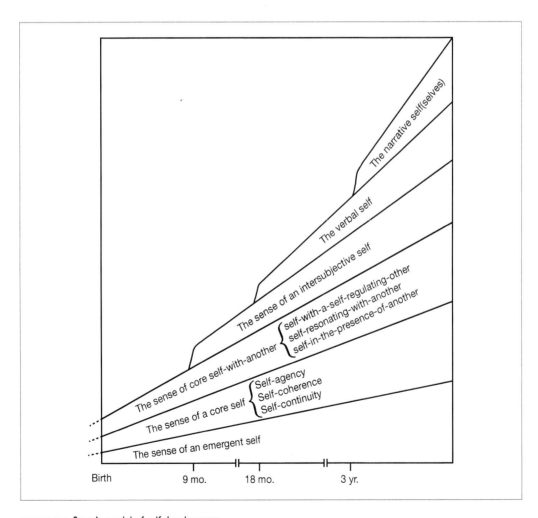

FIGURE 21.1 **Stern's model of self development.**
Three senses of self are present at birth, while the three others emerge at a later age (based on Stern, 1998, p. 47).

ential integration" (Stern, 1998, p. 71). It consists of two parts:

Core self I: Self versus other concerns children's experiences of themselves and is divided into three subcategories. *Self-agency* is the sense of being the force behind one's own actions, as distinct from others. *Self-coherence* is the sense of being a non-fragmented, physical whole with external boundaries and a locus of action. *Self-continuity* is the sense of enduring and, in spite of changes, remaining the same over time.

Core self II: Self with other concerns children's experiences with others and is divided into three subcategories. *Self with a self-regulating other* refers to the child's sense of security, attachment, arousal, activation, pleasure, unpleasure, physiological gratification, self-esteem, and so on. *Self resonating with another* includes the experiences of being in connection with another by way of other-centric participation. *Self in the presence of the other* is the sense of perceiving, thinking, or acting, alone but in the physical proximity of a caregiver, whereby the physical presence (without any interactive, psychological presence) serves as a framing environment in which the infant can continue to be psychologically alone, on his own. This subcategory is a special variation of the self-regulating other.

According to Stern, children form *representations of interactions that have been generalized* (RIGs), which are activated when children have an experience that reminds them of something they have done before. They are a form of early *script*, mental representations of events children have participated in that are modified and eventually become an organized network of self-experience (see p. 202). One example would be the mental representation of a generalized version of peek-a-boo. The game is never exactly the same. This first time, Daddy may be hiding his face behind his hands, something the child remembers as a specific event. The next time, he hides his face behind a teddy bear or a book. With each variation, recollections of the game increasingly change into a generalized event that represents a prototype for the child's experiences with the game.

Mental representations of generalized interactions that include other people allow children to form a basic sense of belonging and to acquire new perspectives: their subjective social world is transformed through human interaction. When children activate a mental representation of events that include being together with someone else, they meet what Stern calls an *evoked companion*. The evoked companion is a sense of being with, or in the presence of, a self-regulating other, a sense the child may be, or not be, aware of. The companion is not a separate working model or the concept of a person but part of a generalized event. Since the companion can be evoked (mentally activated) in the presence as well as absence of the caregiver, the evoked companion represents a form of *internalization* that provides children with a sense of security and continuity in the absence of the caregiver.

The intersubjective self

According to Stern, early on, infants start to sense "that there are other minds out there as well as their own." Although infants' experience of (primary) intersubjectivity nearly goes back to the beginning of life (see p. 301), it is the (secondary) intersubjectivity that emerges around the age of 9 months that Stern describes as the sense of an intersubjective self. Children draw conclusions about mental states that are invisible, ascribe intentions and feelings to other people and "read" their minds. This paves the way for the establishment of joint attention, intersubjectivity, intimacy and closeness. Initially, it involves an *implicit* understanding apart from conscious reflection. Nonetheless, this new relational awareness, based on mind understanding, represents a major qualitative leap compared with the more physical relational experience of the core self, according to Stern.

Shared awareness of emotional states is one of the key aspects of the intersubjective self. Stern particularly emphasizes the importance of *affect attunement* for establishing intersubjectivity. The mother (or another person) mirrors or matches the affective content of the child's action, the feeling underlying the action (see p. 349). Affect attunement results in a sharing of feelings, an intersubjectivity that provides children with knowledge of their own emotional state and contributes to the development of a sense of self.

The verbal self

With the acquisition of language, children's sense of self becomes more explicit and conscious.

Children can tell themselves what they are experiencing, such as, *I am thirsty*. The verbal self begins to form around the age of 15 months, and identifies and categorizes properties, opens up for new relationships, and enables children to share private experiences and coordinate knowledge of themselves and others in new ways and thereby transcend the immediate experience.

The narrative self

The narrative self emerges at the age of about 3. It creates a historical context and represents an individual's autobiography, the official history of one's life. Initially, the development of the narrative self is co-constructed with others, usually parents and older siblings who organize individual event components, order them sequentially and establish the narrative's emotional highpoints. According to Stern, these narratives are shared by the family and thus emphasize the role of the self in a broader social context.

The status of the theory

Stern's theory illustrates the complexity of the self concept and has been of major influence, but has also been criticized for conclusions that are difficult to verify empirically. Although insisting that he takes the child's perspective and interprets what children experience, self-experience is private and relatively inaccessible knowledge. Most of the criticism, however, is directed at his claim that young infants are able to recognize the *process* underlying the development of their sense of self, meaning that very young infants not only experience sensations, feelings and actions but are also capable of experiencing the organizing process underneath, and thus a self as known. Stern believes infants have a level of insight into their own mind and those of others, along with complex beliefs about social issues, for which children at this age lack the developmental prerequisites, according to many theorists (Cushman, 1991; Lewis, 1997).

Four levels of a representational self

Lewis (1991, 2011) describes the development of a representational self in four phases, or levels, that emerge in the first 3 years of life. Level 1 is *knowing*, or *I know*. It is an implicit awareness that exists from birth. Children are able to men-

tally store events and remember, but are not aware of doing so. It is a self that knows, an *I*. Level 2 is *I know I know*. It involves the capacity to reflect on one's own self and knowledge and represents the beginning of self-referential behavior. This level of mental representation is usually described as self-awareness and typically shows up between the ages of 15 and 24 months. Children are not only able to remember events, but are also aware of remembering them. It is a self as known, a *me*. Level 3 is *I know you know*, a form of knowing that begins to develop at the age of 2 and involves children's understanding that they are not the only ones who know that others know something and have a mind. This level forms the basis for sharing opinions. Level 4 is *I know you know I know*, a form of self-awareness that approaches the adult level. Children understand that others can experience events from different perspectives. Additionally, they are aware of the fact that they can be the subject that experiences as well as the "object" being experienced.

Other views on early self-perception

Kagan (1991, 1998b) rejects the notion that children have an early experience of themselves. He maintains that it makes little sense to ascribe self-perception to children before they are able to take an external perspective on themselves, recognize themselves physically and have an awareness of experiencing or doing something, that is, *a self as known*. He points out that it is not enough for children to act and regulate their interactions with the environment since mice do the same thing without anyone claiming they have self-perception. Children must also show that they have the experience of doing so. This, according to Kagan, does not happen until well into their second year, but even this early form of self-awareness is rudimentary in nature.

Thus, the main points of dispute are how to define self-perception and the extent to which very young children can be said to have such a perception of themselves. To a certain extent, the issue revolves around the classic distinction between the self as knower and the self as known. The first represents a sense of being a separate sentient individual who acts and feels; the second involves the capacity for self-reflection, an awareness of one's own abilities. If self-perception is defined as the experience of a meaningful outside world and purposeful action, the only requirement is a "minimal self" (Rochat, 2013), or what Lewis (1991) calls "the machinery of the self," an *I*. There can be little doubt that young infants have such a perception. If one assumes that self-perception implies an understanding of oneself as an individual with certain characteristics subject to opinion and reflection, at least in a simple sense, then an "evaluative" or "personified" self, a *me*, develops in early childhood (Neisser, 1997; Rochat, 2013).

FURTHER DEVELOPMENT OF SELF-PERCEPTION

With age children become more self-aware and begin to distinguish between a private and a public self: their way of being (private self) and how they appear to others (public self). Older children increasingly consider the private self as the one that is "real" (Harter, 2006). Adolescents tend to be conscious about themselves and how they appear to others. Rankin and associates (2004) found that younger adolescents were more self-conscious about public appearance than older adolescents who were more self-reflective and privately self-aware than the younger group, and that girls tended to be more self-aware than boys. Adolescents also describe *several selves*, saying they experience themselves to be different in different contexts with parents, friends, romantic partners, classmates, and so on. An adolescent may, for example, be talkative among close friends and quiet together with the family (Harter, 2006; Ruble, 1987).

Children's development of self-perception cannot be seen separately from their perception of others. They are unable to notice their own characteristics before these have been contrasted with their presence or absence in others. Toddlers with older siblings show more self-awareness than toddlers without an older sibling (Taumoepeau and Reese, 2014). Children have *first-person knowledge* about themselves (from within), but use *third-person knowledge* to understand themselves (from outside). What comes first, is like the question about the chicken and the egg: one is a prerequisite for the other (Bruner and Kalmar, 1998). While the sense of self is private, children use the same categories to describe themselves and others, with parallel shifts in their descriptions (van Aken et al., 1996).

Self-descriptions

Children and adolescents' descriptions of themselves change with age and provide insight into their self-perception. Damon and Hart (1988) divide the contents of these descriptions into four domains or aspects: physical, active, social and psychological (Table 21.1). The *physical* aspect includes properties such as height, weight and gender. *Activity* consists of what the child says and does. *Psychological* refers to inner qualities such as smartness or kindness. *Social* includes children's descriptions of relationships and other social factors, especially those involving family and friends.

According to Damon and Hart, examples of all four aspects can be found in children's descriptions at all ages, but their distribution changes with age. Physical self-descriptions dominate among toddlers, for example that they are a boy or a girl, that they have blue eyes, and so on. These types of descriptions decrease in middle childhood but increase once again in adolescence. In preschool age, children typically describe what they do, for example that they like to play football, help their mother and go bicycling. Around the age of 7, the number of psychological characteristics increases and reaches a peak in the descriptions of adolescents, which are often characterized by soul-searching and reflection on their own inner qualities, the private self. In answer to the question, *who am I?*, children may also comment that their mother works in an office or that they are popular with other children. In adolescence, descriptions include fewer such social relations.

With age, children's descriptions become more differentiated and consistent, and their self-concepts more complex and relative. While younger children use simple categories to describe the properties of the body, older children tend to compare their physical traits more with those of others. Younger adolescents comment on the importance of physical traits for their relationships with others, while older adolescents are concerned with the influence of their physical traits on personal choices. A similar development can be found in children's descriptions of activities. Toddlers talk about what they usually do – play football or fight with their brother. Adolescents talk about actions that reflect personal choices and moral standards, for example that they do not cheat because they think it is wrong, and that

TABLE 21.1 A model of the development of self-understanding (the model includes four forms of the self as object or known (physical, active, social, psychological) and three aspects of the self as subject or knower (continuity, distinctness and agency) at four different age levels: a) early childhood, b) middle and late childhood, c) early adolescence and d) late adolescence (Damon and Hart, 1988, p. 56)

Developmental level	General organizing principle	The self as object				The self as subject		
		Physical self	Active self	Social self	Psychological self	Continuity	Distinctness	Agency
Late adolescence	Systematic beliefs and plans	Physical attributes reflecting volitional choices, or personal and moral standards	Active attributes that reflect choices, personal or moral standards	Moral or personal choices concerning social relations or social-personality characteristics	Belief systems, personal philosophy, self's own thought processes	Relations between past, present and future selves	Unique subjective experience and interpretations of events	Personal and moral evaluations influence self
Early adolescence	Inter-personal implications	Physical attributes that influence social appeal and social interactions	Active attributes that influence social appeal and social interactions	Social-personality characteristics	Social sensitivity, communicative competence and other psychologically related social skills	Ongoing recognition of self by others	Unique combination of psychological and physical attributes	Communication and reciprocal interaction influence self
Middle and late childhood	Comparative assessments	Capability-related physical attributes	Abilities related to others, self or normative standards	Abilities or acts considered in light of others' reactions	Knowledge, cognitive abilities and ability-related emotions	Permanent cognitive and active capabilities and immutable self-characteristics	Comparison between self and other along isolated dimensions	Efforts, wishes and talents influence self
Early childhood	Categorical identifications	Bodily properties or material possessions	Typical behavior	Facts of membership in particular social relations or groups	Momentary moods, feelings, preferences, and aversions	Categorical identifications	Categorical identifications	External, uncontrollable factors determine self

they are good losers. When it comes to psychological characteristics, younger children describe immediate feelings and what they like and dislike. Older children also mention cognitive skills. Younger adolescents talk about their social and communicative skills, while older adolescents describe their values and fundamental philosophical attitudes. Children with disabilities may mention characteristics related to their disability (Cheong et al., 2016).

Autobiographical narrative

Memories are core elements of the self. When children have a memorable experience, such as a trip to an amusement park or to grandma and grandpa, they can reflect over it for a long time after. When children reflect on past events, they become aware of their former self as both different and similar to their current (reflecting) self. It is an external understanding of themselves that requires language skills, and both the development of memory and the cultural categories embedded in language contribute to the temporal stability of the self (Moore and Lemmon, 2001; Nelson, 2007b).

Children's early life histories are mainly formed in conversation with adults who fill out children's descriptions and give context and meaning to their fragmented narratives (see Chapter 11). Children do not distinguish between their own early memories and what others have told them – everything is "self-experience" (Nelson, 2007b). However, toddlers' private "crib talk" without anybody present often have a narrative form. In this monologue, Emily at 32 months is placing herself in several everyday events (Nelson, 2015b, p. 173):

Tomorrow when we wake up from bed, first me and Daddy and Mommy, you, eat breakfast like we usually do, and then we're going to p-l-a = y, and then soon as Daddy comes, Carl's going to come over, and then we're going to play a little while. And then Carl and Emily are both going down the car with somebody, and we're going to ride to nursery school, and then we when we get there, we're all going to get out of the car, go into nursery school, and Daddy's going to give us kisses, then go, and then say and then we will say goodbye, then he's going to work and we're going to play at nursery school. Won't that be funny? Because sometimes I go to nursery school

cause it's a nursery school day. Sometimes I stay with Tanta all week. And sometimes we play mom and dad. But usually, sometimes, I um, oh go to nursery school. But today I'm going to nursery school in the morning.

Nelson suggests that "for Emily her speech for self seemed to serve as a space for exploring her place in an expanding universe of knowing in conjunction with active experience and social speech in conversation with parents" (2015b, p. 178). Such elaborations of events are part of an emergent autobiographical narrative and self development.

Around 3 years of age, children begin to form a clearer understanding of their own life history, and the development continues through childhood. The autobiographical narrative is not an individual collection of memories but the result of co-construction with others (Thompson, 2006). Through conversations with adults children become aware that people experience and remember different events and that different minds can remember the same event in different ways. Peers, too, contribute to children's self-history through self-disclosure (see p. 444) and participation in events parents are not part of, leading children to focus on new aspects of themselves. In adolescence, new life events and participation in a broader range of activities influence the autobiographical narrative and self concept (Negele and Habermas, 2010). Some life histories make up an integrated whole, while others are more independent parts of the life cycle, but they are always unified by the sense of having occurred to the same individual – oneself (Ferrari, 1998).

Cultural perspectives

It is a general assumption that interactions with others contribute to the development of children's self-perception. It is a social construct: children learn to understand themselves through interacting with others (Fivush and Buckner, 1997; Markus and Kitayama, 2010). Cooley (1902) compares other people with a social mirror in which children discover themselves.

Considering the social foundation of the self, it follows that children's self-concepts reflect the culture they grow up in. Adults guide children onto culture-specific "selfways" that reflect the society's self-ideas and self-values. Children's self-perception is thus the result of both cultural selfways and individual experience. It lies at the core of the unique individual, albeit constructed through the cultural filter represented by the surrounding social world (Markus et al., 1997).

The *cultured self* is primarily individualistic and autonomous, or *independent*, in some cultures, and more social and relational, or *interdependent*, in others (Markus and Kitayama, 2010; Wang, 2014). In the United States, the most prominent notion about the self is independence; in Japan, it is relations. The Japanese word for "self" is *jibun* and refers to "one's part of the shared living space." In one study, half of Japanese adolescents' self-descriptions were about relationships with others, compared with only one-quarter of American adolescents' descriptions. The difference is explained by the fact that American adults encourage children to compare themselves with others, and that children develop an early habit of identifying their own positive qualities and the belief that they are better than their peers. In Japan, adults spend far more time talking about children's relations with other people and how children's actions depend on their relationship with others (Dennis et al., 2002; Markus et al., 1997). Another view is that there are two main selves, an individual-oriented self and a social-oriented self, and that it is the strength of these that varies across cultures (Sun, 2017). This means that the two selves change with cultural changes. In China, for example, cultural influences from Western countries seem to increase the role of the individual self (Lu, 2008).

Self-disclosure

Self-disclosure – giving personal information about oneself to others – is an important element in the development of self-perception in older children and adolescents. This can include factual information or opinions, such as how they feel about an event or person (Rotenberg, 1995), and may take place face-to-face or via social media (Valkenburg et al., 2011). Children and adolescents typically communicate this type of information to parents and siblings, and a central characteristic of close friendships among older children and adolescents is the ability to talk about one's innermost thoughts without being ridiculed (see Chapter 20). However, children and adolescents do not usually disclose everything. Experiences that they disclose are part of the narrated and shared self, but experiences that they remember but do not want to tell others about also have an impact on their construction of the self (Pasupathi et al., 2009).

For younger children, parents' acceptance is most important; recognition by peers becomes more important toward the end of adolescence. In the course of development, disclosure to friends increases, while disclosure to parents remains stable or decreases slightly. This means that self-disclosure on the whole increases throughout childhood and adolescence, only to slow down again around the age of 18–20 years (Buhrmester and Prager, 1995). The pattern is similar across cultures, even though the content of disclosure varies (Hunter et al., 2011).

Parents are not always the most fitting partners for these conversations involving self-disclosure. They typically lack the necessary insight into youth culture, and self-disclosure often involves issues young people do not want to share with their parents. Besides, holding back information about oneself is a way of marking one's independence and autonomy (Howe et al., 1995; Hunter et al., 2011). Some adolescents continue to confide mainly in their parents, especially when their mothers are warm and do not control their personal lives too much. Adolescents who fear punishment if they tell a secret to their parents, or who are involved in delinquent activities, have low levels of self-disclosure to their parents (Keijsers et al., 2010; Smetana et al., 2009). Both boys and girls disclose a great deal to their mother, and boys relatively more often to their father than girls. Disclosure to the father declines among adolescent girls but not among boys. Fathers often are more restrictive toward their daughters than their sons, and girls may confide less in their father to avoid being restricted in their freedom of action (Buhrmester and Prager, 1995).

Until the age of about 9, the amount of self-disclosure to peers is the same for boys and girls. After this age, female friends exchange more self-disclosing information than male friends. The increase in self-disclosure usually begins around 10–11 years for girls and 13–14 years for boys, and the transition from mainly confiding in parents to mainly confiding in friends also occurs earlier among girls than boys. These differences are probably related to puberty and physiological maturation in males and females, but the characteristics of social interaction among male and female groups also seem to contribute to differences between genders. The emphasis on status and dominance among boys can inhibit self-disclosure, while emphasis on relationships can create a need for intimacy and promote self-disclosure among girls. These differences, however, only apply to *groups*: many male friendships are characterized by closeness, intimacy and a high degree of disclosure, while many female friendships are not. In middle adolescence, a rapid change takes place in self-disclosure between males and females. Before this age, few relationships between genders are close enough to open up for self-disclosure. In romantic relationships, self-disclosure is expected (Berndt and Hanna, 1995; Buhrmester and Prager, 1995).

Self-disclosure allows children and adolescents to achieve *self-clarification* by formulating their thoughts and ideas. They are either *validated* in their beliefs and attitudes through agreement with and recognition from parents or friends, or they realize that their thoughts and viewpoints are unacceptable (Derlega and Grzelak, 1979). As the amount of self-disclosure increases, conversations between peers progressively include more negative gossip about others. Both help to establish group standards based on shared beliefs and attitudes. Thus, conversations between adolescents about themselves and others are closely linked, just like their perception of themselves and others. Reciprocal disclosure helps adolescents construct each other's life stories (Berndt and Hanna, 1995). For today's adolescents, the use of social media may have a significant role in this process, through online communication about personal topics that are typically not easily disclosed, such as one's feelings, worries and vulnerabilities. The self-disclosure hypothesis states that online self-disclosure may have beneficial effects on social connectedness and well-being (Huang, 2016; Valkenburg and Peter, 2009).

Self-evaluation

As children grow older, their self-concept also includes evaluations of the characteristics they ascribe to themselves and others. Self-esteem is children's subjective evaluation of their own worth as a person (Donnellan et al., 2011). Children develop an internal standard against which they evaluate their characteristics, a standard that also includes an ideal self, how they would like to be. Some develop a positive eval-

uation of themselves, others a more negative perception of their own worth. Self-perception is dynamic and may change over time, but also shows some degree of continuity (Chung et al., 2017).

Views differ on how and when children develop the ability for self-evaluation. From the perspective of attachment theory, children's self-concept develops in parallel with the establishment of *working models* for the child–parent relationship. Relationships are based on reciprocity: when parents are caring, the child is worthy of being cared for (Bowlby, 1969). Working models thus incorporate the beginnings of self-evaluation (see p. 396). According to Neisser (1997), children's *evaluating self* begins to develop around the age of 2–3 years and entails a conscious self-understanding and reflection on their own characteristics. One sign of an evaluative self-perception is children's ability to not only express their feelings, but to talk *about* them. Kagan (1998b), however, maintains that children under the age of 5 years are not capable of self-evaluation since they lack the necessary cognitive development to reflect on whether their characteristics meet their own standards and those of society.

In preschool age, children's self-evaluations generally show little reflection. They confuse effort with achievement, and often have a far too high opinion of their own abilities when they start school. Even when children are told how they are doing compared with others, they do not seem to use this information in evaluating their own performance (Ruble, 1987). Children are well into school age before they start comparing themselves with others in a way that affects their self-evaluations, and their main motive for comparing themselves with peers seems to be to determine their own competence. Adolescence is characterized by self-consciousness, and adolescents make increasing use of comparisons to ascertain reactions to themselves and others, and as a basis for changing their own behavior.

Harter (1987) investigated how children rate their own competence in various areas: academic skills, sports, popularity, acceptance, physical appearance and behavioral conduct, and found that children's self-evaluations gradually became more differentiated. The children below 8 years of age tended to have the same perception of themselves in all areas; they described themselves as capable, bad, kind or mean. Older children evaluated themselves differently in each area. They said they could be good at one thing and bad at another, or kind in some situations and mean in others. Physical appearance has a major impact on self-evaluation in both children and adolescents. Girls focus more on appearance than boys, and many girls perceive themselves as being unattractive. One consequence of this seems to be that girls as a group have lower self-esteem than boys (Baumeister, 1993). It is often maintained that low self-esteem may lead to poor academic achievement and there are many school programs directed at increasing children's self-esteem (Baumeister, 2005). However, the modest correlations found between self-esteem and academic achievement in typically developing children indicate that low school grades lead to low self-esteem rather than the other way around (Baumeister et al., 2003; Trautwein et al., 2006).

The reactions of people in the surroundings is an important basis for self-evaluation. These reactions reflect both the children's behaviors and their compatibility with the characteristics of important people around them. For example, active children, whose parents react negatively because they have trouble dealing with the child's activity level, can develop an image of themselves as being disruptive. Other children may be just as active, but their parents react in a way that leads to a positive self-perception, for example as someone with "lots going on" (Eder and Mangelsdorf, 1997). Many adults believe that praise is the best medicine for raising a child's self-esteem, and parents may lavish their children with praise. Brummelman and associates (2017) found that parents of children with low self-esteem gave more "inflated" praise – "Your drawing is amazing" – than parents of children with average or high self-esteem, probably with the intention of raising their child's self-esteem. However, inflated praise seemed to work in the opposite direction and to lower, rather than raise the child's self-esteem, while inflated praise to children with high self-esteem seemed to increase narcissistic features (see p. 448). Instead of praise, it may be better to influence a child's self-esteem indirectly, by showing affection and positive interest in their activities (Brummelman et al., 2016; Brummelman and Thomaes, 2017). Studies have found that children with warm, sensitive and responsive parents have better self-esteem and evaluate themselves more positively than children with cold and unresponsive parents (Clark and Symons, 2000). Parents with realistic expectations to the child's abilities and needs tend to promote positive self-evaluation. Children with parents whose expectations do not match the child's interests and abilities might believe their parents are dissatisfied with their achievement and develop low self-esteem. A low self-esteem is also a key characteristic of children who have been subjected to mistreatment and abuse. These children may feel that they are little worth and unworthy of love, and can experience themselves as being a bad person, "rotten to the core" (Harter, 2006).

Self-efficacy

Self-efficacy is an important aspect of self-evaluation: the experience of personal agency and control over one's own life (Bandura, 1997, 2008). Children with low self-efficacy feel that they lack such control and that their lives are controlled by external forces. For example, they may believe that they will continue to do poorly in school even if they work harder. Comparisons with others are important for children's development of self-efficacy, for example whether the children they use for comparison succeed in tasks they themselves master or do not master. School is another factor with a major impact on children's self-efficacy (Bouffard and Vezeau, 1998). Adolescents with low self-efficacy may experience learned helplessness, they have learned that what they do will not matter, and do not attempt to succeed because they believe they will be unsuccessful no matter what (Seligman, 1975). It may become a self-fulfilling belief and lead to under achievement and a failure to learn and experience mastery.

SELF-PERCEPTION IN ATYPICAL DEVELOPMENT

It is generally acknowledged that children's self-perception is influenced by how other people react to them. These reactions are influenced by the children's characteristic, including the presence of disabling conditions. In typical development, physical attractiveness is associated with self-esteem (see above) but there is not a direct relation between degree of disability and self-esteem. In children with physical disabilities like cerebral palsy and spina bifida, minor disabilities were found to have a moderate impact and severe disabilities only a mild impact on their general self-esteem (Miyahara and Piek, 2006). One reason may be differential reactions to disabilities: severe disabilities are visible and any achievement by children with such disabilities may be met with positive reactions, while minor disabilities may not be noticed and the children's difficulties seen as a result of a lack of effort, and the children are therefore met with less favorable reactions. Another explanation may be that the results reflect the comparison group the children used when they evaluated themselves. According to social comparison theory, children's self-esteem depends on who they compare themselves with (O'Byrne and Muldoon, 2017). The children with minor disabilities may score lower on self-esteem because they compare themselves to peers with typical development, while children with more severe disabilities feel they do better and have higher self-esteem because they compare themselves with children with similar disabilities.

It has been hypothesized that the social difficulties of children with autism spectrum disorder will have an impact on their self-perception. However, studies have found that the self-images of adolescents with autism spectrum disorder are similar to those of adolescents with typical development, but in line with their problems with mind understanding (see Chapter 13) they had problems telling how others might perceive them (Farley et al., 2010). There is a somewhat higher prevalence of low self-esteem among children with autism spectrum disorder than among children with typical development (16 vs 6 percent). This may reflect the social difficulties of children with autism spectrum experience and their problems understanding what they perceive as the "mindreading abilities" of other people. However, the results also show that most of these children had comparable levels of self-esteem to the children with typical development (McChesney and Toseeb, 2016).

One study found that the self-perception of adolescents with intellectual disability was similar to typically developing children matched for mental age (Nader-Grosbois, 2014). However, in another study, children with intellectual disabilities in the seventh grade had lower self-efficacy than non-disabled children, even when they obtained comparable grades. This probably reflected their struggle with school work, continuous frustration and the large efforts they

invested to achieve comparable to peers. Some of the children in this group said that they felt that they worked all the time and had little life outside school (Lackaye et al., 2006).

SELF-PERCEPTION AND EMOTIONAL AND BEHAVIORAL DISORDERS

It is a common finding that low self-esteem is associated with emotional and behavioral disorders, and that high self-esteem may protect against psychopathology (Zeigler-Hill, 2011). One study found lower self-esteem in 8–14-year-old children with psychiatric disorders than in peers without such disorders (Stadelmann et al., 2017). Other studies have found high correlations between self-report measures of self-esteem and depressive symptoms among children and adolescents with typical development (Moksnes et al., 2016; Pauletti et al., 2012), as well as among children with intellectual disabilities and learning disorders (Alesi et al., 2014). However, correlational studies do not say anything about causal direction. Low mood may influence self-esteem, and low self-esteem can lead to lower mood levels (Harter, 1987). Moreover, it is not easy to distinguish the effect of self-esteem from other factors. Studies suggest that positive or negative self-esteem is a marker and not a causal factor in social and personal development (Baumeister et al., 2003; Boden et al., 2008). Marsh and O'Mara (2008) argue for reciprocal influences, that self-perception influences the way children and adolescents act, and that the reactions from other people to their actions in turn influence their self-perception.

Eating disorders

Self-perception is a main element in eating disorders. These disorders usually start in adolescence, but body dissatisfaction and worries about weight are common already in early school age and may become an adolescent's constant focus of attention (Evans et al., 2017; Saunders and Frazier, 2017). The age at onset seems to be decreasing which may reflect an increasing body focus in today's children (Favaro et al., 2009). Misperception of the physical self, of the weight and size of own body compared to peers, intense fear of gaining weight, and low self-esteem or self-worth are core features of eating disorders, and may also include over-eating and self-induced vomiting. It may start with dieting, sometimes after comments from peers or others about weight, but most adolescents who diet do not develop eating disorders (Carr, 2016; Evans et al., 2013). Eating disorders are often associated with girls but also occur in boys, especially binge eating, although with a lower prevalence. A higher age at onset among boys may be related to the later puberty in boys compared with girls (Mitchison and Mond, 2015).

Amianto and associates (2016) consider anorexia nervosa a deficit in the integrative function of the self, that is, its ability to integrate cognitive, affective and conative – intrinsically motivating – functions. Reported risk factors in preadolescence are perceived pressure to be thin and thin-ideal internalization. Body dissatisfaction has also been seen as a risk factor but may develop in parallel with symptoms of eating disorders and may thus be a sign of the disorder rather than a precursor (Amaral and Ferreira, 2017; Evans et al., 2017; Rohde et al., 2015). Disordered self-perception is a core feature but eating disorders are complex and have been linked to a range of biological and social factors, including puberty and dieting, as well as attachment, sexual abuse and trauma (Bryant-Waugh and Watkins, 2015; Klump, 2014). Eating disorders occur in most countries but the prevalence differs considerably and may be influenced by the focus on beauty and the ideal self in mass media and society (Becker et al., 2011; Smink et al., 2012).

Self-esteem and narcissism

Some years ago, it was a common belief that aggressive behavior and bullying were signs of low self-esteem and insecurity (Baumeister et al., 1996). However, assertiveness and aggression are not typical behaviors of children and adolescents with low self-esteem, who rather tend to be careful and avoid conflict (Baumeister et al., 2003; Zeigler-Hill, 2011). Aggressive and bullying children tend rather to have high but unstable self-esteem and to put the blame on others when their interactions run into problems (Baumeister et al., 1996; Crick and Dodge, 1996). Moreover, bullying and aggression have been connected to narcissism. Narcissistic personality disorder is only diagnosed in adults but narcissistic traits, such as grandiosity in fantasy or behavior, self-enhancement, an unrealistic sense of importance and entitlement, sensitivity to criticism, need for admiration and lack of empathy can be apparent in middle childhood and may be particularly common in adolescence (American Psychiatric Association, 2013; Thomaes et al., 2008). In a longitudinal study, Carlson and Gjerde (2009) found that narcissism scores increased from middle to late adolescence, followed by a decrease into emerging adulthood.

> High self-esteem means thinking well of oneself, whereas narcissism involves passionately wanting to think well of oneself.
> (Bushman and Baumeister, 1998, p. 228)

A high positive self-evaluation is a core feature of narcissism but not all individuals with a high self-evaluation are narcissistic (Baumeister et al., 2003). An important difference is that self-esteem is an evaluation of the actual self, whereas narcissism is characterized by a constant need for social approval and admiration in order to nourish the grandiose self (Pauletti et al., 2012). In young people, genuine high self-esteem is related to positive social relationships and mental health, while narcissistic grand self-evaluation is related to aggression and antisocial behaviors (Bushman and Baumeister, 1998; Tracy et al., 2009). Aggression thus appears to be a feature of narcissism rather than of high self-esteem, elicited by a perceived threat to the individual's ego. Consistent with this view, studies have found small negative correlations between narcissistic traits and self-esteem in 11-year-olds (Pauletti et al., 2012). Different developmental origins are also indicated by the finding that high self-esteem and narcissistic features in 7–12-year-olds were associated with parental over evaluation of their child, overestimation of her intelligence, and overpraising of her performance, while high self-esteem without narcissistic features was related to parental warmth, parents treating their child with affection and appreciation, sharing of positive effect, and fostering in their child the feeling that he or she matters (Brummelman et al., 2015, 2016). Research thus supports a developmental distinction between typical and atypical forms of self-esteem.

IDENTITY FORMATION

Identity formation starts in adolescence and entails both the continuing development of the self and the integration in a "society of minds" (Nelson, 2007a). Personal identity comprises the self-defining characteristic of the individual person, who he thinks he is. Social or collective identity refers to identification with groups and social categories to which the individual belongs, who he or she thinks they belong with, the meanings that they give to these social groups and categories, and the feelings, beliefs and attitudes that result from identifying with them. Being a member of several groups and categories may imply having multiple identities, sometimes contradictory (Vignoles et al., 2011), such as when an adolescent with severe hearing impairment identifies with both the culture of his hearing family and the deaf community (Bat-Chava, 2000).

In adolescence, individuals become more aware of who they are, while at the same time developing new roles, independent positions and a clearer sense of belonging to certain groups in society. Adolescents search for coherence and question the nature and meaning of life in a way not found in children. They explore values and attitudes and search for possible roles, affiliations and their future place as an adult and independent individual in society, in relation to gender, sexual orientation, social class, education, occupation, religion and neighborhood affiliation (McLean and Syed, 2015). In modern multicultural societies, language and ethnicity are important aspects of an individual's identity. Discussions about identity formation are about the *content*, the issues, concerns and topics that adolescents (and adults) are attentive to when they think about who they are and will become, and the *process*, the activities they engage in when they think about this content (McLean et al., 2016). For today's adolescents, the social media represent opportunities for trying out roles and attitudes (Shapiro and Margolin, 2014; Wängqvist and Frisén, 2016).

The central theorist in identity development is Erik Homburger Erikson (1968). In his theory, adolescence is the fifth of eight phases of social crises, each of which leaves a permanent mark on the individual's personal and social development (see p. 380). In phase five, the individual defines himself actively, becomes aware of the future, unites the inner and outer world, and if successful, achieves an identity. The crisis arises because identification with parents that was so important in childhood is not enough for adolescents to develop their own roles and relationships and find their independent place in a wider social context. Therefore, young people have to seek out other sources of knowledge, inspiration and models to live up to in creating their own adult lives.

According to Erikson, adolescents are in a state of psychosocial moratorium during the transition to adult life. Figuratively speaking, the moratorium represents a chasm between the safety of childhood and the autonomy of adulthood, a period in which the individual tries out different roles and can go through frequent changes in attitude and behavior. The outcome of a positive transition through this phase is fidelity and commitment to others. Identity achievement is the experience of being at home in one's own body and knowing what to move toward, as well as an inner certainty of being accepted by the people who are important in one's life. It is not a static experience, but rather a sense of being on the inside of a dynamic process that provides the right direction for a future life. A suboptimal transition through the social crisis in this phase will lead to role confusion and uncertainty about one's own identity. This can take two forms: young people can either become withdrawn and isolate themselves from family and peers, or plunge into a world of peers and lose their identity among the crowd.

Erikson builds on Freud and his theory is met with some of the same criticism as Freud's theory (Arnett, 2015). Since his basis lies in clinical experience, the theory is not easily tested by empirical means. In addition, Erikson's theory is deeply rooted in the social and historical context of his time. According to Erikson, career choice is central to the social crisis of adolescence, but today, this aspect of identity formation is part of emerging adulthood, and far more young people go through a long period of student identity before assuming a more permanent professional identity well into adulthood (see Chapter 27). Another example is Erikson's portrayal of men as oriented toward career and ideology and women toward creating an adult existence centered on taking care of husband and children. Such gender differences are disappearing in modern cultures (see Chapter 24). These examples demonstrate the importance of viewing identity formation in light of the social changes that take place in society (Hammack, 2015; Kroger, 2004). In addition, longitudinal observations suggest that adolescence does not involve a massive identity crisis, and even if identity gradually becomes more stable, the process continues throughout adulthood (Meeus, 2011).

Most other theories of identity development build on, or argue against, Erikson's psychodynamic theory. In recent years, *neo-Eriksonians* have revised and clarified numerous aspects of Erikson's theory (Hammack, 2015; Schwartz, 2001). Adams and Marshall (1996) point to the integrative element in Erikson's theory: the integration of the personal identity that distinguishes the individual from other individuals, such as personal tastes and preferences, and the collective identity that involves affiliation with groups and society by means of language, ethnicity, social class, education, political alignment, and so on. They emphasize the balance between *differentiation processes* that contribute to the establishment of an independent individual, and *integration processes* that involve the individual's affiliation with social and cultural groups – an excessive level of differentiation can lead to rejection *of* others, while a low level of integration can lead to rejection *by* others.

Erikson's theory is also a basis for *theories of narrative identity*, together with theories of autobiographical memory and narrative development (Fivush et al., 2011; Nelson and Fivush, 2004). Autobiographical memory (see p. 202) integrates individual experiences of self and cultural frames, and narratives are important for the individual's sense of personal continuity. Narrative identity formation builds on autobiographical reasoning around relationships, roles and positions with a basis in the individual's life history. It is a process that serves to create meaning and coherence in the individual's life (Habermas and Köber, 2015; McAdams, 2013; McAdams and Cox, 2010). One example would be all the factors that may lead an adolescent to become a carpenter, such as his or her particular skills, prior experience with woodwork, the wish to take up a profession that does not require an academic education, the career choices of friends, and a shortage of carpenters in the local community. This type of integrated identity process requires cognitive and social skills that are not developed until adolescence (Habermas and Reese, 2015). The development of an autobiographical narrative and a sense of continuity, context and social identity are important prerequisites for mental well-being (Habermas and Köber, 2015).

Ethnic identity

An *ethnic group* refers to individuals who identify themselves with a particular culture *and* have an affiliation that provides the basis for interaction. This may be the majority or a minority group such as the indigenous Sami people in Scandinavia or Mexicans living in the United States. The language is often an important identity element of an ethnic group, and many adolescents with severe hearing impairment see themselves as members of a Deaf ethnic group that shares the use of a sign language (Bat-Chava, 2000). When written with a capital D, *Deaf* refers deaf to membership in a social and cultural group, rather than being a bearer of a medical category. An *ethnic category* is defined by an outside source, be it a bureaucrat or a scientist (Gjerde, 2014). Adolescents who are placed in a given ethnic category can be attributed specific ethnic characteristics (which often reflect stereotypical views), without these characteristics being important for their identity.

Young people in modern multicultural societies have to deal with a greater number of value systems than in previous societies. This offers new opportunities, but also leads to a more complex – and perhaps lengthier – process of identity formation. Adolescents from ethnic minorities go through the same process of identity formation as the majority population, but in addition to the usual characteristics and roles, parts of their identity may be linked to an ethnic group and race (Umaña-Taylor et al., 2014). Phinney (1990, 1993) describes three stages in the development of identity as a member of an ethnic minority (Table 21.2).

Ethnic minority adolescents are often in a complex identity situation because they may have to deal with the expectations of society at large, their peers within the majority population, and their own ethnic group (Hedegaard, 2005). Children notice differences in skin color and cultural background and adolescents become more aware of their cultural background, although

TABLE 21.2 The development of identity as an ethnic minority (based on Phinney (1993))

Stage	Age	Characteristics
1 Unexamined ethnic identity	Childhood	No exploration of ethnic issues. Passive acceptance of the majority culture's values.
2 Ethnic identity search/ Moratorium	Early adolescence	Seeking to determine the meaning of ethnicity to oneself. Questioning former attitudes. May include increased political awareness and anger.
3 Ethnic identity achievement	Late adolescence	A clear and secure sense of one's own ethnicity. Uncertainty is resolved and commitments are made. Ethnicity becomes internalized.

the impact of ethnic background on their identity formation varies considerably (Way and Rogers, 2015; Worrell, 2015). The family is important for the development of identity and acquisition of group values and customs in adolescence. Some immigrant parents who have grown up in poverty may warn their children "Don't be like me" and encourage their child to seek education (Maciel and Knudson-Martin, 2014). On the other hand, the obligation to follow tradition and parental expectations are often stronger among minority than majority populations and this may reduce minority adolescents' available options. Generational conflicts can arise when young people from minority groups wish to create an adult existence that differs radically from what their parents have intended for them (Seiffge-Krenke and Haid, 2012), such as when a Norwegian adolescent with Pakistani parents wants to study art rather than work in the family grocery store. Conflicts between generations can also be more extensive and profound. A break with ethnic heritage can have lasting consequences for adolescents' relationship with parents and their ethnic group. At the same time, adolescents can have a strong desire to pattern their adult existence along the same lines as that of their peers in the majority population. For many young people from ethnic minorities, such dilemmas come in the way of

identity formation and can lead to crises in the more literal sense of the word, not least for asylum seekers who come to a new country as children and have strong feelings for both their old and new country (Umaña-Taylor et al., 2014).

Another problem is that young people from ethnic minorities do not always have positive role models to identify with and may therefore struggle to transcend the majority population's expectations of them as members of a minority, even when this has the support of their parents and others. One example is the relationship between the values of the White majority and the Black minority in the United States, which represents an obstacle for many Afro-American adolescents. While some of them identify with the White majority and take on their values, their skin color and cultural background prevents many White people from fully accepting them. Others distance themselves completely from White majority values and ways of life, and thereby limit their own options. Still others try to balance the two value systems in their search for a future role. The same applies to adolescents from Asian and other ethnic backgrounds (Way and Rogers, 2015; Worrell, 2015). Studies show that positive feelings about one's ethnic identity and race contribute to social adjustment and mental health (Rivas-Drake et al., 2014).

SUMMARY

1 The *self as knower*, or *I*, is the experience of being a unique individual acting in the world. The *self as known*, or *me*, is the individual's perception of self, an awareness of being in possession of certain characteristics and qualities.

2 In the middle of their second year of life, children begin to realize that a mirror shows a reflection of themselves, and some time later also recognize themselves in a photograph or a video. Toddlers start referring to themselves by name or *I* and rarely make a mistake between *you* and *I*.

3 According to Mahler, the newborn child is unable to differentiate between herself and the mother. Through a *separation process*, children gradually develop a sense of being a self separate from others. During the *individuation process*, they develop a sense of themselves as autonomous individuals with characteristics independent of the mother. Winnicott suggests children first go through an *undifferentiated phase* and gradually develop a sense of self through the mother's *mirroring* and other maternal reactions. Later theorists are critical to the assumption that infants starts with a differentiated experience of themselves and their mother, and have revised this part of the theory.

4 Stern describes a multi-layered self that experiences being both independent and part of a social world. Some layers are present at birth, others emerge later in development: *emergent self*, *core self I* and *II*, *intersubjective self*, *verbal self* and *narrative self*. Stern emphasizes interaction, social relations and *affect attunement* in the development of the self. His theory has been of major influence, but has been criticized for the assumption that very young infants can recognize the *process* underlying their development of self-perception and conclusions that are difficult to verify.

5 Lewis describes four levels in the development of a *representational self* that emerges in the first 3 years of life: level 1 is *I know*, level 2 is *I know I know*, level 3 is *I know you know* and level 4 is *I know you know I know*. Children become aware that they may be both the subject that experiences and the "object" being experienced.

6 Questions about the self revolve around the distinction between the self as knower and the self as known. Kagan believes children must have a primitive sense of self-as-known before they can acquire a sense of self-perception.

7 Children's self-descriptions include four aspects: *physical*, *activity*, *psychological* and *social*. The distribution of these changes with age, and children's descriptions become more differentiated and integrated. Adolescents experience themselves to be different in different contexts and describe *several selves*. Self-descriptions also reflect the culture.

8 Memories are a core element of the self and the *autobiographical narrative* is an essential part of self-perception, and the result of co-construction with others, initially in conversation with adults, later also with peers.

9 The culture constitutes a foundation for self development. Some cultures are individualistic and autonomous, others are more social and relationally oriented. *Selfways* reflect the culture's ideas and values about the nature of the self, and children's self-perception is the result of cultural selfways and individual experience.

10 *Self-disclosure* is the sharing of personal information with others, face-to-face or on social media. Self-disclosure to friends increases with age, while self-disclosure to parents remains stable or decreases slightly. Children and adolescents achieve *self-clarification*; they are either

validated in their beliefs and attitudes through agreement with and recognition from parents or friends, or they realize that their thoughts and viewpoints are unacceptable. Gender differences in self-disclosure seem to be partly due to the different characteristics of male and female group interaction.

11 Younger children rarely compare themselves with others and use the reactions in their surroundings as a basis for *self-evaluation*. In school age they start comparing themselves with peers, seeming to determine their own competence. Adolescents use comparisons to ascertain reactions to themselves and others, and as a basis for changing their own behavior. Parents with realistic goals for their child promote positive self-evaluation, while parents with expectations that do not match the child's prerequisites can contribute to low self-evaluation. Inflated praise from parents may lead to lower self-esteem, or to an increase in narcissistic features.

12 *Self-efficacy* is the experience of personal agency and control over one's own life. Children with low self-efficacy feel their lives are controlled by external forces. Comparisons with others are important for children's development of self-efficacy, for example whether the children they use for comparison succeed in tasks they themselves master or do not master. Adolescents with low self-efficacy may have learned that what they do will not matter – learned helplessness.

13 Self-perception varies somewhat in children with *atypical development* but most show comparable development to typically developing children. Children with minor disabilities may have lower self-esteem than children with more severe disabilities. The self-images of adolescents with autism spectrum disorder are similar to those of adolescents with typical development, but they have problems telling how others might perceive them.

14 Studies have found associations between emotional and behavioral disorders and self-esteem and the influences may be reciprocal. Disordered self-perception is a core feature of eating disorders but these disorders are complex and have been linked to a range of biological and social factors.

15 Research indicates a developmental distinction between typical and atypical self-esteem. Narcissism may be rooted in parental over evaluation, and high self-esteem in parental warmth. Aggression and bullying may imply unstable self-esteem and have been connected to *narcissism*.

16 *Identity formation* involves the exploration and selection of different values and attitudes, and finding one's place in society. In Erikson's theory, a positive transition through the social crisis of the fifth phase leads to a mature identity, while a suboptimal transition leads to role confusion and uncertainty about one's identity. The theory is deeply rooted in the social and historical context of Erikson's time, and neo-Eriksonians have revised the theory in various ways and adapted it to today's social reality, including an increased emphasis on integration of personal and social identity, and the development of narrative identity theory.

17 *Ethnicity* and *race* are essential elements in identity formation. Adolescents gradually develop an awareness of their cultural background, with varying impact on their identity. Phinney describes three phases in the development of *ethnic identity*. Multicultural societies lead to new processes in identity formation. Young people from ethnic minorities have to deal with the expectations of society at large, their peers within the majority population, and their own ethnic group.

CORE ISSUES

- The newborn infant's ability to distinguish psychologically between herself and the mother.
- The process of self-perception development.
- Self-esteem and narcissism.
- Identity formation and culture.

SUGGESTIONS FOR FURTHER READING

Brummelman, E., et al. (2015). Origins of narcissism in children. *Proceedings of the National Academy of Sciences, 112*, 3659–3662.

Erikson, E. H. (1968). *Identity: Youth and crisis.* New York, NY: Norton.

Fivush, R., et al. (2011). The making of autobiographical memory: Intersections of culture, narratives and identity. *International Journal of Psychology, 46*, 321–345.

Habermas, T., & Reese, E. (2015). Getting a life takes time: The development of the life story in adolescence, its precursors and consequences. *Human Development, 58*, 172–201.

Markus, H. R., & Kitayama, S. (2010). Cultures and selves: A cycle of mutual constitution. *Perspectives on Psychological Science, 5*, 420–430.

Pine, F. (2004). Mahler's concepts of "symbiosis" and separation-individuation: Revisited, reevaluated, refined. *Journal of the American Psychoanalytic Association, 52*, 511–533.

Swanson, S. A., et al. (2011). Prevalence and correlates of eating disorders in adolescents. Results from the national comorbidity survey replication adolescent supplement. *Archives of General Psychiatry, 68*, 714–723.

Umaña-Taylor, A. J., et al. (2014). Ethnic and racial identity during adolescence and into young adulthood: An integrated conceptualization. *Child Development, 85*, 21–39.

Contents

CHAPTER 22

MORAL DEVELOPMENT

Morality is the ability to tell right from wrong and forms the basis for judging whether one's own actions and those of others are just, caring and to the benefit of other people, or unjust, harmful and selfish. Morality is socially oriented, and moral norms and values, as well as the development of conscience, are crucial to human interaction and coexistence within societies. Thus, moral development is a process of enculturation and social functioning in a broader social and societal context. This chapter is about the biological and social bases of moral development and theoretical explanations of the emergence of moral reasoning, how children and adolescents reason about the morality of actions based on their consequences and intentions, and resolve moral dilemmas. Moral development is related to prosocial and anti-social behavior, they are the topic of the next chapter.

THEORETICAL PERSPECTIVES

Most major theories have a view on moral development and offer widely differing explanations. Some theories emphasize children's cognitive abilities as a basis for moral reasoning while others see morality as primarily motivational and driven by emotions. Earlier theories of moral development were concerned with the *transmission* of norms and values and the internalization of norms imposed by authorities, while constructivist theories assume that children develop moral understandings in interaction with their surroundings (Dahl, 2014; Turiel, 2014). Three main perspectives are included here: logical constructivism, evolutionary theory and social domain theory.

Logical constructivism

Logical constructivism is primarily concerned with the cognitive processes underlying moral reasoning, and it is children's ability to reason that determines their moral views.

Piaget's theory

According to Piaget (1932), moral development is a process of differentiation whereby children gradually learn to distinguish actions based on reciprocity and fairness from actions based on ready-made rules by an authority. Early moral judgments reflect children's interaction with adults, while social conflicts with *peers* have greater significance for moral development in later childhood. Piaget examined, for example, how children develop an understanding of rules through marbles and other games. Since no adult authority can provide the correct answer, children are forced to compare their own views with those of other children. The resulting cognitive conflict (see p. 186) in each individual child is the driving force behind moral development.

Piaget describes three stages of moral development with approximate age levels. Until the age of 4–5 years, children are in the *pre-moral* stage. They have a poor understanding of the general rules of right and wrong and follow personal rules

Piaget considered children's participation in games an experiential basis for moral development.

without a fixed system, based on their own desires. They like to play marbles but have little understanding of the rules of the game and may well call the marbles "mummy ball" and "baby balls."

The second stage, *moral realism*, begins around the age of 5. Although children are able to follow rules, they can only do so literally, with little willingness to adapt or change. Children now try to win at marbles, but the rules to them are defined by an inviolable authority rather than something everyone has agreed on. An important characteristic of this age is children's emphasis on the consequences of an action rather than its intent. Piaget asked children who was naughtier – Jean, who accidentally broke 12 cups because he did not know that the cups stood behind a door he opened, or Henri, who broke one cup when he was about to steal some jam and therefore intended to do something wrong. Here Piaget talks with 6-year-old Geo (1932, pp. 120–121).

P: *Have you understood these stories?*
G: *Yes.*
P: *What did the first boy do?*
G: *He broke eleven cups.*
P: *And the second one?*
G: *He broke a cup by moving roughly.*
P: *Why did the first one break the cups?*
G: *Because the door knocked him.*
P: *And the other?*
G: *He was clumsy. When he was getting the jam the cup fell down.*
P: *Is one of the boys naughtier than the other?*
G: *The first is because he knocked over twelve cups.*
P: *If you were the daddy, which one would you punish more?*
G: *The one who broke twelve cups.*
P: *Why did he break them?*
G: *The door shut too hard and knocked them. He didn't do it on purpose.*
P: *And why did the other boy break a cup?*

G: *He wanted to get jam. He moved too far. The cup got broken.*
P: *Why did he want to get the jam?*
G: *Because he was all alone. His mother wasn't there.*
P: *Have you got a brother?*
G: *No, a little sister.*
P: *Well, if it was you who had broken the twelve cups when you went into the room and your little sister had broken one cup while she was trying to get the jam, which of you would be punished most severely?*
G: *Me, because I broke more than one cup.*

The children understood the intention behind the actions and gave many replies such as: *It wasn't his fault, he didn't do it on purpose*, but did not take these insights into account. Their reasoning was solely based on adults saying it is wrong to break cups.

The third stage, *moral subjectivism*, begins around the age of 9–10 years. Children now understand that rules are *conventions*, that is, social constructs based on agreement, and that it is possible to change them if one agrees on it. They consider the *intention* behind an action, and, faced with the broken-cup dilemma, they reply that Henri is naughtiest because he intended to do something wrong. This inclusion of intention in moral evaluation is a significant qualitative step in their moral reasoning.

Later studies have found that children show moral understanding considerably earlier than Piaget had found. Preschool children, for example, seem to distinguish between social conventions and moral dictates. Critics point out that Piaget's studies are biased in favor of language skills, and that his stories are too long and complex for younger children. It is the complexity of the tasks, rather than their moral dilemmas, which makes them difficult for the children. Studies have shown that if the extent of damage caused is equal, younger children make greater allowances for the intent behind the action. When children are told that two children have broken the same number of cups, they say that the naughtier child is the one who did it on purpose (Imamoglu, 1975).

Kohlberg's theory

Kohlberg (1969, 1976) extends Piaget's theoretical framework and adds stages for adolescence and adulthood and introduces the *moral judgment interview*, a predetermined set of stories consisting of moral dilemmas. The best known among these is about Heinz (Kohlberg, 1963, pp. 18–19):

In Europe, a woman was near death from a special kind of cancer. There was one drug that the doctors thought might save her. It was a form of radium that a druggist in the same town had recently discovered. The drug was expensive to make, but the druggist was charging ten times what the drug cost him to make. He paid $200 for the radium and charged $2,000 for a small dose of the drug. The sick woman's husband, Heinz, went to everyone he knew to borrow the money, but he could only get together about $1,000 which is half of what it cost. He told the druggist that his wife was dying and asked him to sell it cheaper or let him pay later. But the druggist said: "No, I discovered the drug and I'm going to make money from it." So Heinz got desperate and broke into the man's store to steal the drug for his wife. Should the husband have done that?

The answers to the interview dilemmas are ranked according to the *reasons* given, rather than whether the actions were considered right or wrong. Kohlberg describes three main levels of moral development, each consisting of two stages and characterized by a specific line of reasoning (Box 22.1). At level 1, *pre-conventional morality*, the authority decides. This stage usually lasts until the age of 10, but pre-conventional moral reasoning can also be found among many adolescents. At stage 1, actions are judged according to their consequences and Heinz's dilemma is justified based on the likelihood of ending up in prison. At stage 2, any action is judged by the extent to which it meets one's own needs. From this point of view, the solution to Heinz's dilemma can be to steal the drug.

Level 2 is *conventional morality*. Most children reach stage 3 around the age of 13, and adolescents are able to incorporate the perspectives and intentions behind other people's actions. "Nobody will think badly about you if you steal the medicine, and your family will think you are inhuman if you don't." Stage 4 also includes orientation toward social order and one's duty as a citizen. "It is natural that Heinz wishes to save his wife's life but it is always wrong to steal."

BOX 22.1 KOHLBERG'S STAGES OF MORAL DEVELOPMENT (adapted from Kohlberg, 1971; Kohlberg and Hersh, 1977)

I: PRE-CONVENTIONAL LEVEL

Stage 1: The punishment and obedience orientation
The physical consequences of an action determine how good or bad it is, for example expectations of punishment. The reason for doing right is to avoid punishment from a superior power of authorities who decides the rules. Motive for moral action: Obey the rules to avoid punishment.

Stage 2: The instrumental relativist orientation
Right action consists of what instrumentally satisfies one's own needs and occasionally the need of others. It is necessary to recognize that other people have their interests, and elements of fairness, reciprocity and equal sharing are present. Motive for moral action: Conform to obtain rewards, have favors returned, and so on.

II: CONVENTIONAL LEVEL

Stage 3: The interpersonal concordance or "good boy-nice girl" orientation
Good behavior is what pleases or helps others and is approved by them. Behavior is frequently judged by intention – "he means well" becomes important for the first time. One earns approval by being "nice." Motive for moral action: Conform to avoid disapproval and dislike from others.

Stage 4: The "law and order" orientation
Right behavior consists in doing one's duty, showing respect for authority, maintaining the given social order for its own sake and avoiding breakdown of the system. Motive for moral action: Conform to avoid censure by legitimate authorities and resultant guilt.

III: POST-CONVENTIONAL, AUTONOMOUS OR PRINCIPLED LEVEL

Stage 5: The social-contract legalistic orientation, generally with utilitarian overtones
Right action tends to be defined in terms of general individual rights and standards that have been critically examined and agreed upon by the whole society. Aside from what is constitutionally and democratically agreed upon, the right is a matter of personal values and opinion. Laws may be changed after rational considerations of social utility. Motive for moral action: Conform to maintain the respect of the impartial spectator judging in terms of community welfare.

Stage 6: The universal ethical-principle orientation
Right is defined by the decision of conscience in accord with self-chosen abstract ethical principles that appeal to logical comprehensiveness, universality and consistency, such as the Golden Rule or the categorical imperative. At heart, these are universal principles of justice, of the reciprocity and equality of the human rights, and of respect for the dignity of human beings as individual persons. Motive for moral action: Conform to avoid self-condemnation.

Level 3, *post-conventional morality*, requires the capacity for formal-operational reasoning (see p. 172). At stage 5, the rights of the individual and the values of society become increasingly important. Rules are still not fixed, however, but remain relative. "One cannot let people steal because they are desperate. The goal may be good but does not justify the means." At stage 6, the individual reasons are based on abstract moral principles. What is morally right depends on the individual's conscience, guided by universal moral principles rather than the laws of a particular society. "If you don't steal the medicine and let your wife die you will condemn yourself afterwards. You will not live up to the standard of your own conscience." According to Kohlberg, only 10 percent of adults reach this stage.

In a longitudinal study, Kohlberg followed the development of moral reasoning in a group of boys from the age of 10 to 16 until they were 36 years old (Colby et al., 1983). Their answers to the dilemmas did not only follow their age, reasoning associated with different stages existed side by side in their development. Pre-conventional moral reasoning was found even in adults, albeit rarely, and none of the answers belonged to stage 6. Nonetheless, the group of boys largely followed Kohlberg's stages. None of them skipped over a stage and regression to an earlier stage was rare. Their reasoning also remained consistent within one or two adjacent stages. Later studies support these findings but take issue with the fact that the stages are not entirely distinct and that stage 6 lacks responses (Boom et al., 2007; Lourenço, 2003). All the boys in Colby's study had normal cognitive development as adults and should therefore have been capable of post-conventional moral reasoning. When some of them did not show such reasoning, it indicates that general cognitive skills are *necessary* but not *sufficient* for advanced moral

Lawrence Kohlberg.

reasoning. The question is: What other conditions have to be met for an individual to develop the ability to make difficult moral judgments?

Cultural factors

According to Kohlberg (1981), the stages of moral development are universal, and children and adolescents in different countries largely show the same development. Stages 5 and 6, however, appear less structured and integrated in cross-cultural comparisons than the other stages. Many people from rural cultures, for example, do not present arguments belonging to the two most advanced stages, although this does not necessarily reflect a lower level of moral or cognitive competence (Snarey, 1985). Furthermore, most studies have used Kohlberg's stories and therefore do not reflect the particular moral dilemmas children and adolescents may face in their own social and cultural context. The reasoning demanded by these types of dilemmas is also affected by practical factors, such as the interests of one's own family and a sense of intuition and of having found a good solution (Snarey, 1985). Some studies have therefore tried to pose ethical questions more relevant to children's or adolescents' daily lives, such as: "Think of a time you made a promise to someone. How important is it that people keep their promises?" or "Think of a time you helped your parents. How important is it for children to help their parents?" (Gibbs et al., 2007b). Also religious rules can be perceived as natural and inevitable, and determine the outcome of a moral dilemma. Some forms of moral reasoning among non-Western cultures are difficult to incorporate into Kohlberg's stages. Neither are arguments based on notions such as non-violence and social harmony easily reconciled with the assumption of fairness and justice as overriding moral goals (Walker and Hennig, 1997). However, Gibbs and associates (2007b) conclude: "Our review bolsters the conclusion that Kohlberg was in principle correct regarding the universality of basic moral judgment development, moral values, and related social perspective-taking processes across cultures" (p. 491).

Justice and caring

Another objection to Kohlberg's theory is that it fails to account for differences between male and female reasoning. Carol Gilligan (1982) argues that male morality is oriented toward justice and female morality toward care, and describes three stages in the development of women's morality. The first stage focuses on caring for oneself, the second stage on caring for other people, while the third stage integrates care for oneself and others. The challenge for women is to find a balance between their own needs and those of others in connection with moral dilemmas.

According to Gilligan, these differences in moral reasoning are not the result of biological factors. Women's upbringing teaches them to be more aware of how their actions affect other people's feelings, while men's upbringing focuses more on independence, self-awareness and result-oriented thinking. Therefore, women approach moral dilemmas from the perspective of caring and taking responsibility for others, while men's reasoning is based on a sense of justice. Since fairness and justice are central to Kohlberg's stages and the dilemmas he presents, Gilligan believes women will inevitably achieve lower scores on Kohlberg's moral judgment interviews, thus underestimating their moral sense. However, Walker (1984) compared the results of a large number of studies and found no systematic differences between the scores of boys and girls on Kohlberg's interview, indicating that any differences in moral reasoning do not affect the scores. One of these differences is that girls seem to provide more arguments based on empathy and care than boys do. This is contrary to Kohlberg's (1981) own assumption that morality is about a sense of justice.

In one study, 80 children were asked to judge both hypothetical moral dilemmas and dilemmas they had experienced in their own daily lives. Gender differences were minor, and only a few subjects reasoned consistently based on either justice or care. The majority showed both types of reasoning, including those who achieved the highest scores on Kohlberg's interview (Walker et al., 1987). This is contrary to Gilligan's assumption that boys and girls develop different forms of morality. Both girls and boys reasoned based on care and justice when this was required by a moral dilemma. No doubt, there are differences in how boys and girls are enculturated (see Chapter 24), but these differences do not seem to lead to radically different ways of reasoning about moral issues. Instead, studies suggest that care and justice are important elements in the morality of both boys and girls. Gilligan's views can thus be seen as an extension rather than an alternative to Kohlberg's theory (Jorgensen, 2006).

Evolutionary theory

The key assumption of evolutionary theories is that the basis of morality is formed by evolution and that human beings have an innate tendency to regard certain actions as right, good and deserving of reward, and others as wrong, bad and deserving of punishment (Hamlin, 2013). According to Hauser (2006), children are fundamentally moral at birth, they react in an intuitively moral way to certain events, and altruism, fairness and care have their basis in human nature. The innate mechanism underlying moral development is a *universal moral grammar* that defines the possibilities and limitations of moral development, similar to the way Chomsky's universal grammar is assumed to impose restrictions on language development (see p. 305). This universal moral grammar contains a set of abstract moral rules, and children's social experiences tell them which of these rules apply in their society. In practice, this happens when children expect other people to act morally, and react emotionally when their expectations are broken. In this way, children's moral sense is formed by the rules of culture, thus allowing for differences in morality across cultures. However, the theory raises the question of why some members of the human species act in immoral ways.

Ethical intuitionism is a related theory arguing that morality is an immediate, unconscious, irrational and intuitive appraisal of something experienced as wrong, and not subject to reasoning. Moral judgments are driven by emotions like disgust and contempt. According to the theory, moral reasoning is a post-hoc construction, generated *after* a moral judgment has been reached, even if such reasoning can sometimes lead to a change in attitude so that the individual's action is not always determined by intuitive judgment (Haidt, 2001, 2008, 2013). Innate intuitions are compared to a set of "moral taste buds" that are biologically conditioned to react to certain stimulation while the sensitivity of their receptors and the trigger for individual intuitions is modulated by cultural input (Rottman and Young, 2015).

Critics of this theory point out that moral judgments are not always immediate and irrational, but just as often intentional and well considered. Moreover, malicious actions are not necessarily judged immoral, for example in war, and also children judge physically harmful acts differently depending on whether they consist of an unprovoked attack or a retaliation to such an attack (Nucci and Turiel, 2009). Assumptions about an innate intuitive morality meet the same criticism as many other assumptions about specific innate characteristics, that development is unnecessary. The child only needs a certain amount of experience to implement what already exists. Besides, the theory remains an assumption: there is no evidence that moral judgments are automatic and intuitive or that children's moral development actually has its basis in an innate predisposition that specific. Instead, results suggest that children's (and adults') judgments of right and wrong are complex and that cognitive, emotional and social factors contribute to moral development (Turiel, 2014).

Social domain theory

Social domain theory is partly based on Piaget's and Kohlberg's model but considers the development of moral reasoning to be domain-specific rather than an expression of general cognitive development (Smetana et al., 2014; Turiel, 2014). It sees morality as one of three forms of social knowledge (the other two are societal and psychological knowledge) – actions may have consequences for the welfare, just treatment and rights of other people. The three domains develop in parallel, but younger children have a better understanding of other people's welfare than of justice. Social domain theory also emphasizes the emotional basis in the development of moral concepts. Children use information about positive and negative emotions – both their own and those of others – in judging whether something is right or wrong. Social domain theory differs from evolutionary theory in that emotions do not govern moral judgments, and the assumption of a dichotomy between emotions and reasoning is seen as a fallacy. Additionally, the theory emphasizes experiences with positive emotions (Dunn, 2014; Smetana et al., 2014). Critics point to the lack of a clear distinction between social conventions as part of social order and moral norms

related to the welfare of others (Rottman and Young, 2015), but moral judgments of older children and adolescents can incorporate both conflicting moral norms and conventional norms, such as when children lie in order not to hurt someone.

Morality is about doing good or bad to others and hence is fundamentally social. Many theorists underline the importance of children's social relations in moral development (Carpendale et al., 2013; Dunn, 1988, 2014). Children gradually become more sensitive to moral issues through social interaction within and outside the family. Since family life provides many opportunities for conflicts involving moral issues, Dunn (1988) views children's interaction within the family as a window to their moral understanding, sensitivity and acquisition of moral norms. Values and norms are not simply transferred but acquired through a *process of collaboration*: children observe, interpret and internalize different aspects of parental behavior, sometimes disagreeing with their parents on what is fair and just, and in turn affect parents by externalizing their own beliefs and attitudes – it is a dialectical and transactional process (Kuczynski and Knafo, 2014).

Elliot Turiel.

THE DEVELOPMENT OF MORAL UNDERSTANDING

The extent to which young children judge actions from a moral perspective in their first 2 years of life is subject to considerable disagreement (e.g., Hamlin, 2015; Killen and Dahl, 2018). There is little doubt that children show *morally relevant* reactions and actions early on. Infants react with unease when they hear other infants cry, for example (see p. 349). In their second year of life, children often help others as long as they understand how to do so (Vaish and Tomasello, 2014). A number of studies in which infants were shown two puppets – one puppet helping and the other preventing a third puppet from reaching a goal such as opening a box – found that more children reached for the helping puppet than the hindering puppet, or looked at them for different lengths of time (Hamlin, 2015; Hamlin and Wynn, 2011). Other studies, however, have not found corresponding reactions (Salvadori et al., 2015) and some have questioned the results (Killen and Dahl, 2018). Nativist researchers interpret early social actions as an expression of a nascent concern for others, rooted in innate moral concepts (Wynn and Bloom, 2014; Hamlin, 2015). However, other researchers point out that children at this age see and perform many actions that are unfair or potentially harmful to others, but these are not interpreted as reflecting an innate tendency to carry out immoral actions (Killen and Dahl, 2018).

Toddlers show better understanding of the consequences actions may have, for example, whether they can cause harm, and what is and is not allowed in the family. They also begin to justify their actions (Dunn, 2014; Killen and Smetana, 2014). They also seem to start to become aware of the difference between conventional rules, for example that it is wrong to throw clothes on the floor instead of hanging them up, and moral "truths," such as the importance of sharing with others and not hitting other children. In one study, 3-year-olds intervened when they saw a puppet destroying a clay figure made by another puppet (Box 22.2). Dunn (1988) observed that toddlers often denied having done something wrong, even when it was obvious that they were responsible for the action. This shows that the children had acquired a certain understanding that the action was wrong and had expectations about the likely reaction of others.

Throughout preschool age, and in agreement with domain theory, children begin to distinguish more clearly between events in the moral, social and personal domain (Killen and Smetana, 2014; Turiel, 2015). Studies of preschool-age children from different cultures have found that the children regard moral transgressions that cause harm to another person, such as pushing someone off a swing, as more serious than transgressions that only affect the one breaking the rule, for example when a boy gets hurt falling off a chair he was not allowed to climb on (Dunn, 1995; Yau and Smetana, 2003). The distinction is not absolute, however: some events can represent a combination of moral issues and conventions (Dahl et al., 2011; Killen and Smetana, 2014). At this age, children also begin to take more account of the intent behind actions (Smetana et al., 2014).

While both younger and older school-age children say that moral transgressions are wrong because they hurt others, older children also begin to include arguments related to equality and justice. One study found that 6- to 13-year-old children were quick to react to transgressions of moral norms, responding with comments about the damage or loss itself, how unfair it was, and how the victim felt. In connection with violations of conventional rules, they merely pointed out the transgression and recalled the rule, or ridiculed the transgressor. The children considered it wrong to steal, even in a country where they were told this was not forbidden, but had no qualms changing the rules of a game if everyone agreed on it (Nucci and Nucci, 1982a, b). When it comes to conventional rules, younger children mainly base their arguments on authority figures (the teacher said so) and avoidance of punishment, while older children point out the importance of following such rules for regulating social interaction.

According to domain theory, children learn to differentiate between domains by the types of emotional reactions and comments they are met with in different domains (Killen and Smetana, 2014; Turiel, 2015). Even younger children are aware that they feel pain when someone hits them or that they become upset and cry when someone makes fun of them. When children violate moral rules, adults usually stress the experience and welfare of the person being subjected to the action. For example, mothers respond by intercepting physically and by reasoning with their children about the consequences (Dahl and Campos, 2013). Children's own justifications

BOX 22.2 THREE-YEAR-OLDS REACT TO THE TRANSGRESSIONS OF OTHERS (Vaish et al., 2011)

Thirty-two 3-year-olds were randomly assigned to a harm condition and a control condition. Together with a child, there were two hand puppets (cow and elephant). One puppet brought four clays pieces, leaving the extra one on the side. One puppet created a clay snail, the other a flower, and the child whatever he wanted. Each puppet happily showed off her sculpture twice, and both puppets took an active interest in the child's sculpture. Then one of the puppets left the room. In the harm condition, the actor said in a neutral but firm manner, 'Well, I don't like the cow's/elephant's flower/snail. I'm going to tear/break it now'. In the control condition, she said in the same manner, 'Well, I don't like the ball of clay. I'm going to tear/break it now'. In both conditions, she

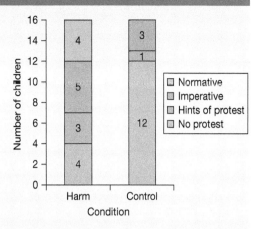

then moved towards the target object and repeated, 'Yes, I'm going to break it now'. Picking up the object, she returned to her position, said, 'Yes, I'm going to break it now', then destroyed the object and threw the pieces into a bin. The actor's intention was repeated and her actions presented in this stepwise manner to provide children with ample occasions to protest.

After the object was destroyed, the recipient reentered, looked into the bin, and neutrally said 'Hmm' to show that she had noticed something there. She looked at the remaining objects on the table, again said 'Hmm' neutrally, and looked back into the bin. In the Harm condition, the recipient then said in a somewhat surprised and sad tone, 'Oh, that was my flower/snail', waited about 6 s, said 'Oh well' mildly despondently, and returned to her seat. In the control condition, the puppet behaved the same way except that she noted in a neutral tone that the object in the bin had been the extra clay.

The children protested in three different ways: a) Normative (No, you're not supposed to do that), b) Imperative (No! Don't destroy it), and c) Hints of protest (Hey! Why are you doing that?). The figure shows that the 12 of 16 children protested when one doll destroyed the sculpture of the other doll. When the doll destroyed the extra clay ball, only four children protested. The results demonstrate that the 3-year-olds can understand and act on moral aspects of situations.

seem to reflect the situations in which moral aspects are commented by adults. When children break conventional rules, adults typically react by asking them to stop what they are doing and telling them how disruptive their actions are to social order. Seven-years-olds react with ridicule and similarly demeaning responses when other children violate such rules (Smetana, 1993). Children aged 4–5 and 10–12 years and their mothers were presented with small stories about prudential transgressions like lighting matches and opening a bottle of poison, moral transgressions like hitting a friend and stealing money, or social convention transgressions like eating lunch with the fingers and staying up past bedtime. Both the younger and the older children

and their mothers said the prudential and moral transgressions were more serious. The older children and the mothers were also more willing to accept corporal punishment (spanking) for acts that would harm others (prudential and moral) than for transgressions of social rules (conventions), while the younger children said all three transgressions should be punished (Catron and Masters, 1993).

With age, discussions with peers outside the family gain increasing importance in the development of morality. In peer discussions, 8-year-old children are engaged and active, while with their mother they are more passive and contribute little to the discussion (Kruger, 1992). This supports the assumption that negotiations are particularly conducive to moral understanding when there is a certain equality between the parts, as Piaget claims.

With age, children are able to consider an increasing number of factors, and in adolescence their moral reasoning becomes more complex. In one study, children between the ages of 7 and 16 years agreed that it was important to help those in need, avoid causing harm to others and respect the right to property, as long as there were no competing considerations. When situations became more complex, such as when helping one person could indirectly harm another, differences in ages became more pronounced. The youngest children responded directly based on moral rules, while the 14-year-olds, and particularly the 16-year-olds, tried to balance different considerations (Nucci and Turiel, 2009).

The development of morality is related to relevant experiences but morality does not reflect actions in the environment in any simple sense. Children and adolescents growing up with war and violence develop an understanding of what is morally right and wrong. However, there can be a large gap between actions they consider to be right, and how they expect themselves and others to act (Posada and Wainryb, 2008; Wainryb and Pasupathi, 2010).

MORALITY AND EMOTIONS

Most theorists believe emotions play a decisive role in moral development, and self-evaluative emotions such as pride, guilt and shame are often referred to as "moral emotions" (Malti and Ongley, 2014). Sensitivity to other people's feelings is therefore central in evaluating emotions, in particular the aspect of care in connection with morality (Dunn, 2014).

Some theorists emphasize the role of negative emotions. Freud (1916, 1930) relates conscience and morality to anxiety and discomfort. Hoffman (2000) describes *empathy-related guilt*, a self-directed negative emotion of distress and remorse rooted in something the child has done that causes another person to be upset. In order to escape this feeling, the child has to avoid performing similarly hurtful actions or try to do something to repair the damage that has been done. Thus, feelings of guilt become a motive for moral action. It is the task of parents and other

adults to direct the child's attention to the harm or suffering inflicted on the other person, and to induce *other-oriented* responses in the child.

Others argue that morality springs from a broader emotional spectrum than guilt and fear (Turiel and Killen, 2010). Dahl and colleagues (2011) stress the importance of *social joy* and parents' positive emotional expressions to young children's helping behavior. Dunn (2014) describes how social interactions with positive emotional content can have an important influence on the development of moral understanding. Children respond empathically to the distress and joy of others, show interest in others' feelings and discover that right and wrong can be linked to different emotions. They can show anger as the result of their moral judgment, for example when seeing others humiliated or treated unjustly, but also joy and pleasure at transgressing something forbidden.

Parents influence children by how they talk with them about moral issues, and the family's emotional climate determines how children react to rules. Dunn and colleagues (1995) found that even 2-year-olds were able to follow simple rules and negotiate about rules in emotionally warm families. The parents who supported a dialogue based on equality seemed to have the most positive influence. Their conversations centered not only on restrictions and punishment, but equally on sharing happiness and giving comfort. When children show shame and guilt, this demonstrates that they take into account other people's judgments (see p. 353). These emotions, too, have an impact on children's moral interactions, but Dunn considers close and positive relationships with parents and siblings an important basis for children's moral development, rather than guilt or the wish for conformity. Studies show that children whose parents engaged in dialogues about moral issues with their children offered emotional support, helped them ask questions and reformulated what they said, had a more positive moral development than children whose parents merely criticized their wrongdoings and told them what was right. Also humor, listening responses and praise promoted moral development, whereas hostility, sarcasm and threats had an inhibiting effect (Walker and Taylor, 1991).

Adolescence is an emotional period (see p. 355) and for adolescents their own and other people's emotions are central to their making sense of events in the social world, and evaluating their own and other people's actions. They can report strong feelings of guilt in connection with having hurt a friend or otherwise acted wrong in a social context (Wainryb and Recchia, 2012).

Understanding the relationship between morality and emotions

Children's own understanding of the relationship between moral transgressions and experienced emotions evolves gradually. Even when they say that an action is wrong, like stealing, they have problems relating the agents' feelings and moral judgment (Krettenauer et al., 2013). Nearly all 4-year-olds say that both the giver and the receiver will be happy when children share something, and that a child will be upset when something is stolen from him (Arsenio and Lover, 1995). At this age, children argue that the person who has stolen something from someone else will feel happy as long as he or she is not found out, termed "happy victimizers." Seventy-four percent of 4-year-olds, 40 percent of 6-year-olds and 10 percent of 8-year-olds thought that someone stealing candy without being discovered would feel happy. In addition, 57 percent of 4-year-olds, 71 percent of 6-year-olds and 41 percent of 8-year-olds said that someone who resisted the temptation to steal the candy would feel upset (Arsenio and Lover, 1995). Thus, younger preschoolers seem to focus on the outcome of the victimizer's action. Although they judged the action wrong, it did not change their belief that the thief would feel happy. Not until school age did children begin to ascribe mixed feelings to the thief based on both personal gain and consequences for the victim. It is possible that young children have difficulty attributing simultaneous conflicting emotions to another person, and that the positive emotion associated with the consequences takes precedence over any possible feelings of guilt, which children usually begin to show around the ages of 3 to 5 (see p. 353). Another related explanation is that younger children focus on the actual experience, while older children increasingly consider how the thief *ought* to feel (Arsenio et al., 2006). Adolescents become increasingly aware of everyday moral conflicts and their complexities, leading to more subtle feelings and reasoning skills (Malti et al., 2012).

CONSCIENCE

Conscience is an inner regulatory system, characterized by negative self-evaluations and feelings of *guilt* in connection with something one has done or failed to do. It is based on an internal standard and an internalization of cultural attitudes that enable children to resist temptations in the absence of adults. The development of conscience begins in early childhood and continues throughout adolescence (Kochanska et al., 2010; Laible et al., 2008).

Although most theorists emphasize the importance of other people's negative reactions for the development of conscience, there are several developmental pathways to conscience. Which path a child follows may depend on the child's temperament, parental reactions to the child's actions and the relationship between child and parents (Kochanska, 1997). Children with a positive relationship to their parents, for example, show *committed compliance*, a willing, eager stance to go along with parental directives, and an implicit internalization of the rules laid out by the parent. Parental warmth and reciprocity are important incentives for moral compliance, but also contribute to feelings of guilt when the child's action is not in agreement with the moral directive (Kochanska and Aksan, 2004, 2006).

The parental strategy best suited depends on the child's characteristics. In anxious children, the development of conscience seems best promoted by parental strategies not based on force but on explanations and warmth. Such strategies are less effective with impulsive children, since they find it more difficult to internalize imposed rules (Kochanska, 1997, 2002). This is not to say that impulsive children necessarily have particular difficulty developing conscience, but rather that they have problems acquiring social skills. Many impulsive children with little self-control develop poor social understanding and inadequate interaction strategies, and thus end up in the unpopular children group. For them, positive directives that lead to compliance may be an effective developmental pathway to conscience (Cornell and Frick, 2007; Kochanska, 1997).

The ability to arrive at a negative emotional evaluation of one's own actions is considered an important characteristic of the mature individual and member of society. It is crucial for both society at large and for the individual's mental health that conscience and guilt develop without major complications. However, conscience shows significant individual variation. Some children and adolescents have too little conscience while others suffer from strong feelings of guilt (Thompson et al., 2006).

CALLOUS-UNEMOTIONAL TRAITS AND PSYCHOPATHY

Atypical developmental pathways provide insight into the importance of emotions for morality and conscience. Some children and adolescents appear callous and unemotional, showing a lack of guilt and remorse, as well as manipulative behavior, impulsiveness and irresponsibility (Marsee and Frick, 2010). Since these traits also lie at the core of psychopathy, the terms *psychopathic traits* and *callous-unemotional traits* are often used interchangeably (Viding and McCrory, 2015).

Studies show a relation between behavioral disorders and emotional understanding. Eight- to 10-year-old children who had been referred to a psychiatric clinic for behavioral disorders (aggression, vandalism, shoplifting and the like) attributed less fear to both a person acting contrary to moral rules and the victim of the action than children of the same age without behavioral disorders. The children with behavioral disorders were also less concerned with the negative consequences for the victim than with the positive consequences for the victimizer. Moreover, their descriptions of negative consequences revolved more around material issues, such as losing a toy, than emotional consequences, such as pain and grief. In addition, they used a single set of conceptual terms for their experienced emotions (happy, sad), while the other children gave more varied emotional descriptions (Arsenio, 1988).

Such results suggest that some children with behavioral disorders lack insight into the emotional consequences of immoral actions for both the victimizers and the victims of these actions. They do not as readily as others recognize sadness and fear, both in facial and vocal expression, while their perception of joy, surprise, disgust and anger does not differ from that of other people. Conscience is the very ability to direct negative emotions toward something one has done to others and requires an understanding of both one's own and the other person's feelings. From a developmental psychopathology perspective (see p. 14), Frick and colleagues (2014) explain atypical conscience development in children with callous-unemotional traits by their reduced ability to experience negative emotional arousal, fearful inhibition and empathy. They can tell right from wrong, but with little emotion attached to their judgment. Attention to positive consequences and lack of attention to negative emotions and punishment lie at the core of these children's inadequate conscience development and their increased risk of developing antisocial behavior (see p. 482).

Studies have found some degree of heritability of callous-unemotional traits, as well as links to early neglect. A genetic basis is most prominent in the children who develop antisocial behavior (Viding et al., 2012). Studies of early neglect include children who have spent their early childhood in orphanages with little stimulation and developed callous-unemotional traits, but often without the presence of behavioral disorders (Bowlby, 1946; Kumsta et al., 2012). In line with this, studies also show that positive and warm parenting strategies reduce the risk of developing callous-unemotional traits and behavioral disorders in children showing signs of such traits (Pasalich et al., 2016; Wall et al., 2016). Children and adolescents with callous-unemotional traits are aware of rewards and other positive aspects, and less so of any potential punishment. Consequently, parenting strategies and interventions based on punishment and negative sanctions are less effective, while initiatives based on reward show more positive changes in these children and adolescents (Viding and McCrory, 2015).

Children with autism spectrum disorder have social impairments and can also appear callous and unemotional, but without any strong connection to conduct disorders and criminal behavior. Unlike children with autism spectrum disorder, children with callous-unemotional traits have no problem understanding other people's thoughts and intentions. They have problems processing emotional information, while children with autism spectrum disorder can become emotionally aroused at seeing others in pain (Leno et al., 2015; Viding and McCrory, 2015).

SUMMARY

1 Morality is the understanding of right and wrong. *Moral reasoning* involves reflection on the correctness of one's own and others' actions.

2 *Logical constructivism* associates morality with cognitive development. Piaget divides moral development into three stages, arguing that social conflicts between peers give rise to cognitive conflicts that drive the development from *premoral reasoning* to *moral realism* and *moral subjectivism*. Critics point out that children show moral understanding earlier than Piaget claims.

3 Kohlberg extends Piaget's stage theory and methodology by introducing the *moral judgment interview*. *Pre-conventional morality* is determined by what others say is good or bad, *conventional morality* is linked to the group's views on morally right actions, while *post-conventional morality* is determined by the values of society. In adulthood, morality is tied to the individual's conscience and universal moral principles. Although children in different countries largely show the same development in moral reasoning, this applies to a lesser extent to post-conventional morality.

4 Gilligan distinguishes between *justice-oriented* male morality and *care-oriented* female morality and describes three stages in the development of women's morality: 1) caring for oneself, 2) caring for other people, 3) integrated care of oneself and others. Both men and women reason based on care and justice, but women are more concerned with relationships and therefore reason more often based on a morality of care.

5 Hauser believes humans have an innate *universal moral grammar* that sets the parameters for moral development. According to the theory of *ethical intuitionism*, moral judgments are immediate, unconscious and intuitive, and moral reasoning only justifies an action *after* a situation has been evaluated.

6 *Social domain theory* views morality as one of three forms of social understanding. The development of norms and values is a collaborative process, and children gradually become more sensitive to moral issues through their experiences with social interaction within and outside the family.

7 Children show different reactions to violations of moral norms and social conventions early on, both in regard to themselves and others, and with increasing age distinguish more clearly between actions belonging to the moral, social and personal domain. With age, they also improve at taking into account several factors at the same time.

8 Most theorists believe emotions to be central to moral development and an understanding of others' feelings. According to Hoffman, *empathy-related guilt* leads children to avoid hurtful actions or try to repair the damage that has been done. Dunn, Campos and Dahl emphasize the importance of *social joy* and parents' positive emotional expressions when young children help others. Children's understanding of the relationship between moral violations and experienced emotions undergoes a gradual development. Children with behavioral disorders have a more immature understanding of transgressions of moral rules and norms.

9 *Conscience* is characterized by negative self-evaluations and feelings of *guilt* directed at one's own actions. Different developmental pathways can lead to a sense of conscience, depending on the child's temperament, the parents' way of meeting the child's actions and the child–parent relationship.

10 Some children with *callous-unemotional* traits may have an atypical conscience development and show signs of *psychopathy*.

CORE ISSUES

- The evolutionary origin of moral reasoning.

- The cognitive and emotional bases of moral development.

- Emergence of early morality.

- The role of positive and negative emotion in development of conscience.

SUGGESTIONS FOR FURTHER READING

Flom, M., & Saudino, K. J. (2017). Callous–unemotional behaviors in early childhood: Genetic and environmental contributions to stability and change. *Development and Psychopathology, 29*, 1227–1234.

Gibbs, J. C., et al. (2007). Moral judgment development across cultures: Revisiting Kohlberg's universality claims. *Developmental Review, 27*, 443–500.

Gilligan, C. (1982). *In a different voice: Psychological theory and women's development.* Cambridge, MA: Harvard University Press.

Hamlin, J. K. (2013). Moral judgment and action in preverbal infants and toddlers: Evidence for an innate moral core. *Current Directions in Psychological Science, 22*, 186–193.

Kochanska, G. (1997). Multiple pathways to conscience for children with different temperaments: From toddlerhood to age 5. *Developmental Psychology, 33*, 228–240.

Kohlberg, L. (1981). *The philosophy of moral development: Moral stages and the idea of justice.* New York, NY: Harper and Row.

Nucci, L., & Turiel, E. (2009). Capturing the complexity of moral development and education. *Mind, Brain, and Education, 3*, 151–159.

Piaget, J. (1965). *The moral judgment of the child.* New York, NY: Free Press.

Contents

CHAPTER 23

PROSOCIAL AND ANTISOCIAL DEVELOPMENT

In all human societies, people share with others and help each other, and such prosocial actions are necessary for societies to function. However, also antisocial actions are part of social life in most societies, both among children and adults. These behaviors are defined according to their functions in social interaction: The intention of prosocial actions is to benefit others, while antisocial actions aim to inflict physical or psychological harm on others. Children are social and gradually learn what is and is not appropriate and approved behavior when interacting with others in their society. Their social orientation can lead to both prosocial and antisocial actions, but these behaviors show opposing developmental trajectories (Padilla-Walker et al., 2017). This chapter describes the emergence of understanding and production of prosocial and antisocial behavior in children, and how parenting styles and other conditions may influence this development.

PROSOCIAL BEHAVIOR

Prosocial action is defined by an intention of doing well for others and having "costs" and no benefits for the actor, such as helping, caring or sharing (Dunfield, 2014; Paulus and Moore, 2012). It is a requirement that the actions are voluntary; actions resulting from external pressure or requirements, such as putting on boots when it rains or when the father says so, are not considered prosocial. Thus, actions motivated by *obedience* are not prosocial as such, but they are

often seen as behavioral precursors to prosocial actions (Eisenberg et al., 2015).

Development in childhood

Typical prosocial actions consist of a) helping someone, such as picking up something a person has dropped or carrying something for another person, b) giving something to someone, such as sharing a toy with another child, or c) comforting someone who is upset, for example a child who has been injured (Dunfield, 2014; Paulus and Moore, 2012). Such actions require a certain degree of empathy and sympathy. Children must be able to understand and react to the "negative" state of another person, such as someone failing to reach a goal or obtain something, or experiencing grief or discomfort, and be motivated to change the negative state. Many factors may influence children's prosocial actions and contribute to individual differences, including mind understanding, motivation and earlier experience with performing and observing prosocial actions, and the three main types of prosocial actions show somewhat different developmental trajectories (Paulus, 2014). The social norms of the society will influence the development of prosocial behavior (House, 2018), and parents guide their children toward actions that are considered prosocial in the culture, and both parental expectations and their strategies to promote prosocial behavior in children change throughout childhood (Dahl, 2015; Pettygrove et al., 2013). Younger children require unambiguous situations to understand the need of another person and show prosocial behavior, while older

Children share with others from an early age.

children understand others' need in more complex situations (Dunfield, 2014).

Helping

Offering help to someone who has lost something or fails to manage a task can be observed from the age of 1 year and shows a rapid development. At around 18 months, children spontaneously help adults without having been asked to do so, as long as the child is able to understand the goal of the action (Warneken and Tomasello, 2007, 2009). Helping becomes common around the age of 2 and does not substantially increase in scope throughout preschool age (Eisenberg et al., 2015).

Children's early help is influenced by their parents' style. In one study 18- to 24-month-old children with mothers who encouraged and supported their children's active participation in cleaning up toys and the like were helping more often than children whose mothers did not support and encourage their participation to the same degree (Hammond and Carpendale, 2015). It is notable, however, that children's early help seems to be intrinsically rather than extrinsically motivated (Martin and Olson, 2015). When 20-month-olds were given a small toy in reward for picking up something an adult had lost, they were *less* helpful afterwards than when the adult praised them or simply took the object and con-

tinued what she was doing (Warneken and Tomasello, 2008). In another study of 4-year-olds, those who were not praised by their mother for helping offered spontaneous help most often (Grusec, 1991). These studies, showing that rewards decreased rather than increased helping, have been used to argue for an inborn tendency to help (Hay, 2009; Warneken and Tomasello, 2008). However, Dahl (2015) argues that the results also can be explained by children's tendency to take part in adult activities and parental reactions to the child in these activities. He found that parental praise and thanks were associated with increase in helping in the second year of life. When children are older, they are more often encouraged to help because adults see more opportunities for them to help, and get less praise because their ability to help is well established and help therefore expected (Dahl, 2015). Praise may not lead to increased helping because children perceive praise as reflecting a low evaluation of their competence (see p. 446).

Children's early tendency to help is general and relatively independent of the characteristics of the person receiving help, but around 2 years of age, helping begins to become more selective: children prefer to help someone they perceive as helpful and kind, or whom they have made music together with, rather than someone who seems little helpful and unkind (Dahl et al., 2013; Dunfield and Kuhlmeier, 2010; Kirschner and Tomasello, 2010). Thus, whatever the motive is for children's early helping, it is still influenced by the behavior of possible recipients of the helping behavior. Moreover, appropriate help depends on the understanding of another person's need for help. Five-year-olds are better at evaluating the situation and provided more help when it was needed, while 3-year-olds gave the same amount of help, whether it was needed or not (Paulus and Moore, 2011).

Sharing

Sharing requires children to discover that another person has less than they do and being motivated to change this. Eighteen-month-olds are able to share, but only if an adult both expresses a wish for something the child has *and* asks directly for it; thus, early sharing is related to compliance. Two-year-olds will share with an adult if the adult expresses a desire for something the child has, but sharing of objects is rare throughout toddler age (Brownell et al., 2009, 2013; Dunfield and Kuhlmeier, 2013).

Principles of reciprocity and fairness have an early influence on sharing. In one study, children aged 2–3 years were placed in pairs on either side of a low fence. Only one side had toys, so the child on that side had to give toys to the other child so that child, too, would have something to play with. After a while, the roles were switched. The child who originally had been toy-deprived now had the toys and generally shared toys with the other child only if that child, too, had shared. When the child who first had the toys did not share, the other child did not share either (Levitt et al., 1985). Similarly, children aged 4–5 years gave less to another child when they themselves had received less than the others in a group of children than when they had received as much as the others (Masters, 1971). In another study, 5-year-olds shared more with an adult when they were in a reciprocal situation where they expected to be a recipient of the adult's sharing later (Xiong et al., 2016). Children are also positively influenced by peer behavior. Seven-year-olds gave more when a same-age peer began to give more (Messer et al., 2017).

The principle of fairness is not fully established until early school age, however, and sharing depends on costs. In one study, children from 4 to 7 years of age accepted that another child got less, but not that they themselves did. The 8-year-olds accepted no disadvantageous inequity (Blake and McAuliffe, 2011). Another study found that sharing steadily increased from 3 to 14 years in all of six different cultures as long as it did not "cost" the child anything, the child got the same amount of food independent of his sharing. However, sharing decreased from 3 to 7–9 years if the child himself got less food when he shared, and then rose again toward the age of 14 years. Early development was similar across cultures, but in middle childhood, cultural differences emerged for actions that had a cost to children, and the 14-year-olds approached the typical adult-level of sharing within their society (House et al., 2013).

One might have assumed that young children with autism spectrum disorder, because of their social difficulties and problems with mind understanding, would show less prosocial behavior than other children. However, a study found that 3–6-year-olds with autism spectrum disorder both gave more of their part to others and

helped spontaneously more often than children with typical development (Paulus and Rosal-Grifoll, 2017).

Comforting

Also giving comfort emerges early. It requires children to understand another person's emotional state. Toddlers have a certain understanding of how they can hurt and comfort others, but less than half of 17-month-olds comfort someone who is hurt or sick. Below is a mother telling about her son comforting a peer (Zahn-Waxler et al., 1979, pp. 321–322):

John [92 weeks] had a friend over, Jerry. Today Jerry was kind of cranky; he just started completely bawling and he wouldn't stop. John kept coming over and handing Jerry toys, trying to cheer him up so to speak. He'd say things like, "Here Jerry," and I said to John, "Jerry's sad; he doesn't feel good; he had a shot today." John would look at me with his eyebrows kind of wrinkled together, like he really understood that Jerry was crying because he was unhappy, not that he was just being a crybaby. He went over and rubbed Jerry's arm and said, "Nice Jerry," and continued to give him toys.

At 29 months, 70–80 percent do so, at least occasionally (Baillargeon et al., 2011). Three-year-olds will comfort a doll whose drawings or playthings have been damaged (Vaish et al., 2011). Such actions are relatively rare in early childhood, however. Both child temperament and the social environment, including the warmth and behavior of parents and preschool teachers, have an impact on how much comfort children give in preschool age (Paulus and Moore, 2012).

Children's comments about prosocial actions change as well. When 4- to 5-year-old children who have spontaneously helped, encouraged or shared with someone are asked why they did it, many children give standard replies such as "it's nice to help," or justify their action based on others' needs or practical aspects. Occasionally, they mention their own benefits. From 5 to 11 years, children increasingly say that prosocial behavior makes them happy. At this age, they also include more prosocial traits in descriptions of other children (Eisenberg, 1982; Eisenberg-Berg and Neal, 1979).

Development in adolescence

Overall, studies show that preschoolers on average perform about twice as many prosocial actions as toddlers, school-age children about twice as many as preschoolers, and adolescents 50 percent more than school-age children. These changes are related to improved cognitive and social-cognitive skills, emotional development and enculturation in general. Adolescents are more aware of social expectations and are better at evaluating social situations. In addition, they show increasing differentiation, with more prosocial behavior toward friends than others. Peers are therefore an important mediator of prosocial behavior in adolescence (Güroğlu et al., 2014).

However, not all prosocial behavior increases in adolescence – the outcome varies depending on the type of behavior and situation. Some studies show that adolescents share more with their peers, but not with adults, and that they do not help others more than children do. Helping victims of aggression is actually on the decline, a fact that may be related to young people not wanting to get involved and risk subjecting themselves to aggression (Eisenberg et al., 2006, 2015). One study found a decline in prosocial behavior, but not in sympathy, from 13 to 17 years, with a subsequent increase until the age of 21. Girls showed somewhat more prosocial behavior than boys, but both showed the same pattern in development (Luengo Kanacri et al., 2013).

ANTISOCIAL BEHAVIOR

Antisocial actions are defined by an intention to inflict physical or psychological harm, or to acquire or damage objects belonging to others. Some antisocial actions involve violations of the law. Aggression is the most studied form of antisocial behavior and will be treated in more detail here as well. Disobedience, vandalism, crime and drug abuse are also commonly referred to as antisocial behaviors (Séguin and Tremblay, 2013).

Instrumental aggression refers to aggressive acts used to achieve something, such as when one child pushes another off a bike to get the bike for himself, or threatens to take another child's money. *Hostile aggression* describes acts whose main objective is to harm someone else, such as when one child bullies another, and consists of two forms: *open aggression* involves acts that cause physical harm to someone, while *relational aggression* aims to harm the relationship between two people, such as backbiting or manipulating a friendship. Another important dividing line runs between reactive and proactive aggression. *Reactive aggression* is a spontaneous reaction to something and is often associated with anger. The experience of a friend who intends to inflict damage, for example, can quickly lead to aggressive retaliation. *Proactive aggression* is instrumental, such as threating to beat up another child to obtain something.

Aggression is part of the normal behavioral repertoire, and most children show occasional aggression without violating norms or moral rules. Some children show atypical development with far more aggression than usual and in situations in which aggression is inappropriate. It is important to distinguish between children's normal aggression and aggressive behavior with an extent and severity that meets the criteria for diagnosing a behavioral disorder (see p. 63).

Prevalence of antisocial behavior

In their second year of life, most children show aggressive actions, which at this age are particularly common in connection with conflicts over toys. In line with the development of language, verbal aggression increases from 2 to 4 years of age and eventually stabilizes. Although early aggression is generally instrumental, it does not always revolve around access to a desired object – the argument itself seems to hold a certain attraction. Toddlers often argue over a toy, even though an identical toy is available (Caplan et al., 1991).

Hitting and many other forms of physical aggression increase throughout early childhood and subsequently become less frequent. Seventy percent of all 2-year-olds hit other children, compared with 20 percent of 4- to 5-year-olds and 12 percent of 8- to 9-year-olds. This decline is the result of improved self-regulation, but also the fact that children with age gain a better understanding of how others experience being hit. Fighting is common among boys throughout childhood, but much of it is make-believe and part of rough-and-tumble play and play fighting. The number of openly aggressive acts continues to decline throughout childhood (Dodge et al., 2006). In school age, hostile aggression becomes more common and relational aggression increases in relation to open aggression. Other forms of antisocial behavior, such as lying, cheating and shoplifting, also become more prevalent (Loeber and Schmaling, 1985).

Adolescent aggression is a major topic of discussion in today's society, but aggressive acts are actually on the decline at this age, while the incidence of other antisocial acts rises, such as skipping school, shoplifting, oppositional behavior and more serious criminal conduct (Figure 23.1). This increase may be related to adolescents' separation from parents and the parents' reduced control over what their children are doing (Morgado and da Luz Vale-Dias, 2013). Some adolescents with a high degree of antisocial behavior are diagnosed with ADHD and behavioral disorders.

Twelve to 14 years is a typical age of onset for many criminal offenses across countries, but the majority are non-serious; more serious offenses like assault or bicycle theft are rare in adolesence (Junger-Tas, 2012). The highest frequencies of criminal offenses occur at the end of adolescence, and the highest frequency of arrests

a little later for both boys and girls but boys are charged by the police or arrested much more often than girls (Elonheimo et al., 2014; Loeber et al., 2012, 2017). Only a small group continues to show high levels of aggressiveness and criminal behavior in adulthood. They include adults who showed antisocial behavior early in life, as well as adults who began to veer onto an antisocial developmental pathway in adolescence (Odgers et al., 2008; Piquero et al., 2012).

Bullying

Bullying stands for a significant share of the aggression among children and adolescent groups. Bullying typically consists of teasing and physical or verbal aggression and differs from other forms of aggression by being repeated over time and directed against one or more individuals or a group. Social media, e-mails and cell phone messages are used in cyberbullying (Navarro et al., 2016; see p. 523). Direct bullying consists of open attacks on the one being bullied, while indirect bullying entails social

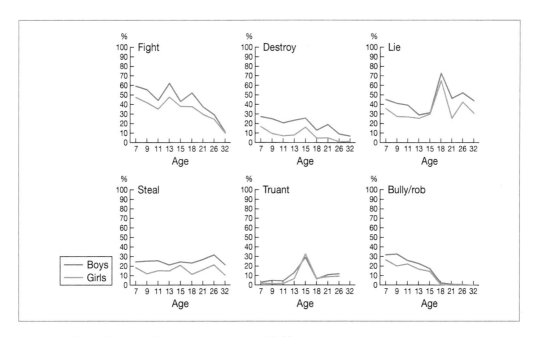

FIGURE 23.1 Antisocial conduct in females and males aged 7–32 years.

The percentage of females and males at different age levels who showed six different types of antisocial conduct problems: fighting, destroying, lying, stealing, truancy and bullying/robbery. The figures are based on reports from parents and teachers in childhood, parents, teachers and adolescents themselves in adolescence, and adults' self-reports in adulthood (based on data from Odgers et al., 2008).

exclusion. It is rare for large groups of children to bully another child – usually, two or three students do the bullying, and a single student can be responsible for 35–40 percent of it. In a school environment, however, a certain contagion effect can occur and encourage many others to participate in the bullying (Olweus, 1993).

Bullying typically begins to show up in middle childhood, and its incidence declines with age. Bullying is a considerable problem in schools (Rosen et al., 2017). At the start of school, bullying can be part of the process of establishing dominance relations between children (see Hinde, 1974). In first grade, popular children often do the bullying and aggressive children in particular become the target for their bullying (Humphreys and Smith, 1987). In one study, about 9 percent of 8- to 16-year-olds were bullied at school, 7 percent bullied others occasionally or regularly, while 1.6 percent bullied others and were bullied themselves. However, the numbers varied with the school climate and the school's preventive measures and interventions (Pellegrini and Long,

2002). The frequency of children who reported being bullied was found to vary considerably across 40 countries, from 5–6 percent in Sweden to around 40 percent in Lithuania, and more boys than girls (Craig et al., 2009). While direct bullying is most common among boys, girls and boys are equally exposed to indirect bullying (Olweus, 1993).

Bullying declines over time, but some aspects of bullying show stability. Children who are bullied in early school age are at risk of being bullied at later age levels, and the same children largely do the bullying at different ages. In some cases, the relationship between bully and victim can last for several years. Among older children who bully, bullying increasingly becomes part of a broader pattern of antisocial behavior. A Swedish study of 14- to 15-year-olds found a link between bullying at school and violence and weapon carrying outside of school. The adolescents who bullied were also themselves subjected to violence outside of school (Andershed et al., 2001). In another study, 60 percent of boys who

Indirect bullying with gossiping may lead to feelings of loneliness and internalizing disorders.

bullied in middle school had been convicted of at least one offense by the time they were 24 years old (Olweus, 1993).

Previously, it was commonly assumed that bullying behavior was rooted in insecurity and lack of social competence, but research does not support such a hypothesis. This group, too, shows variation, but compared with their peers, bullies are generally confident and show unusually low levels of anxiety and insecurity (see also p. 448). Instead, it is the victims of bullying who often are socially insecure and isolated, and without a single good friend (Olweus and Breivik, 2014). Children with intellectual disability, autism spectrum disorder and attention deficit disorder report being victims of bullying more often than other children (Twyman et al., 2010). Bullying involves an asymmetrical power balance, and Olweus (1993) suggests that bully and victim enter into complementary roles in the sense that the bully searches for someone who will not resist aggression. Moreover, children rarely bully when they are emotionally aroused. Thus, bullying is not part of children's and adolescents' ordinary conflicts and differences (Gasser and Keller, 2009). It is not uncommon for bullies to be popular among their peers. As a group, their popularity is slightly below average and decreases with age, but they are generally more popular with their peers than the victims of bullying (Humphreys and Smith, 1987). Moreover, the social capital of popularity may be one reason why anti-bullying programs appear ineffective with popular bullies compared with bullies who are less popular (Garandeau et al., 2014).

To the extent bullying is part of a general antisocial trajectory, other factors influencing development of antisocial behavior will also affect children's bullying. Poor social-cognitive skills can contribute to both bullying behavior and victimization (Shakoor et al., 2012). Generally speaking, the risk of children bullying others is increased by negative attitudes from parents with little warmth and interest, together with parental indifference, lack of boundary setting and use of corporal punishment in childhood. This applies to both boys and girls. Bullying may have severe consequences: being a victim of bullying has been associated with mental health problems, including internalizing disorders, eating disorders and suicidal ideation and behavior (Gunn and Goldstein, 2017; Olweus and Breivik, 2014;

Troop-Gordon, 2017). There are many intervention programs and studies have demonstrated that it is possible to reduce bullying in schools, but the effects may vary with the age, gender and socioeconomic background of the children (Cantone et al., 2015; Farrington and Ttofi, 2009).

Individual differences in antisocial behavior

Throughout childhood, the individual child's level of aggression shows considerable variation. In school age, the extent of aggressive behavior decreases and differences between children gradually become more stable, also over longer periods. For some children, aggressiveness becomes a hallmark of their behavior and relationships, but children with low levels of aggression show the greatest stability. The correlations for assessed aggression at different age levels lie around 0.3–0.5 for 5-year periods in school age and adolescence. These moderate correlations indicate both a certain stability and the fact that many children show changes in aggression over time (Dodge et al., 2006; Piquero et al., 2012).

Children with behavioral disorders are a heterogeneous group. Some may be callous-unemotional (see p. 468), while others show signs of self-regulation problems (Fanti et al., 2016; Frick, 2006). Studies have found much higher rates of callous-unemotional traits in children and adolescents with behavioral disorders (32–46 percent) than among the general population (3–7 percent), and there is clear evidence that such traits involve a vulnerability to severe and persistent behavioral disorders (Herpers et al., 2012; Klingzell et al., 2016). DSM-5 specifies the diagnosis of a small subset of conduct disorders with the label "with limited prosocial emotions" (American Psychiatric Association, 2013). Children with this disorder are particularly characterized by proactive and instrumental aggression, but often show reactive aggression as well (Frick and Morris, 2004). Children with regulation disorders mainly show reactive aggression in response to experienced provocation and tend to perceive other people as threatening (see p. 364). Problems with attention and hyperactivity make an impediment to impulse control and regulation in the children, as well as help from adults in the environment (Moffitt, 1993). Social disorders and unpopularity are common among this group, while children and adolescents with proactive aggression can be popular and be perceived as leaders by their peers (Poulin and Boivin, 2000). However, they tend to have more contact with the police than adolescents with behavioral problems without such traits (Viding and McCrory, 2015). Children with autism spectrum disorder and intellectual disability are vulnerable for developing challenging behavior, especially those who have limited language and communication skills (Emerson and Einfeld, 2011).

Studies indicate a relatively strong genetic influence on the development of antisocial behavior in callous-unemotional children, but not on antisocial behavior without these traits (Hyde et al., 2016). Genes associated with behavioral problems are "susceptibility genes" that can contribute to different developmental trajectories, and do not represent a vulnerability to a particular disorder (see p. 84). For example, studies have shown that neglected children with a low-activity allele of the MAO-A gene were more likely to display antisocial behavior than children with other alleles of this gene. Without neglect, there were no differences in antisocial behavior (Caspi et al., 2002; Foley et al., 2004; see also p. 85). This means that the environment is at least equally important for children's behavior (Caspi et al., 2010). A Swedish follow-up study of 862 adopted boys found that 12 percent of boys with criminal biological parents were arrested in connection with minor offenses as adults (not alcohol-related). The same was the case for 7 percent of the boys without criminal biological parents who had been adopted by parents with a criminal background, while 40 percent of those with both foster parents and biological parents with a criminal background were arrested for such offenses (Cloninger et al., 1982). The combined interaction effect of the genes and the environment was thus significantly higher than the effects of genes and the home environment added together.

Moreover, children's aggressive acts are not merely related to other people's reactions to their behavior. When children frequently see others in conflict involving anger and faces full of fear, they will become distressed and react in accordance with a dangerous world (see Chapter 17). Children and adolescents who regularly experience violent conflict resolutions at home and in their local community can over time become desensitized to violence, increasing the likelihood that they, too, will commit violent acts (Mrug et al., 2016). Not everyone reacts this way, however. Some children growing up in families with high levels of anger and parental conflict show prosocial behavior toward their parents and siblings, but not toward their peers. It is possible they minimize their own negative emotions in order to reduce the conflict level at home, but without developing a corresponding degree of sympathy and prosocial behavior toward others (Eisenberg et al., 2006). One study found that when physically abused children witnessed a female stranger showing anger toward their mother, they reacted by giving more comfort to the mother and reacting more negatively and aggressively toward the stranger than children without such a background (Cummings et al., 1994). Similarly, children can react with anger and aggression when child protective services come to remove them from difficult home circumstances. Mistreated

Some children are witness to conflicts involving anger and violence in the home.

children generally react with stronger emotions than other children, both when supporting their mother and showing aggression toward others (Maughan & Cicchetti, 2002).

There is a link, in other words, between antisocial behavior in children and parenting style (see below). Patterson and colleagues (1989) argue that behavioral problems are related to parents "rewarding" their children's antisocial behavior instead of punishing it. Studies show that a strict and inconsistent parenting style seems to increase the likelihood of antisocial behavior in children with callous traits, while an emotionally warm parenting style seems to reduce it (see p. 468). Children whose parents are cold, punitive and dismissive typically have a high level of aggression (Eisenberg and Fabes, 1994). These observations, however, say nothing about the causal relationship behind parent–child interaction; the children's behavior may have elicited negativity and contributed to stricter and more inconsistent parenting (Kimonis et al., 2013; Waller et al., 2014). Kochanska and colleagues (2017) describe a developmental cascade (see p. 12) from 4-year-olds' carefree transgression of rules via parental attempts at enforcing strict discipline at the age of 8, to antisocial behavior at 10–12 years of age. The prosocial and antisocial behavior of parents themselves can be of importance as well. Increased presence of a prosocial father, for example, may lead to reduced aggression in children, while increased presence of an antisocial father may raise children's level of aggression (Jaffee et al., 2003).

With age, peers gain increasing importance for children's development, including their prosocial and antisocial behavior (Dishion and Tipsord, 2011). Aggressive unpopular children often seek out peers with antisocial attitudes, sometimes because they are rejected by other children (Carlo et al., 2014; Murray and Farrington, 2010). Adolescents with aggressive and antisocial behavior join violent and criminal gangs more often than other adolescents (O'Brien et al., 2013). The influence of peers is also evidenced by a study in which high-risk adolescents' participation in group therapy led to more rather than less antisocial behavior, especially among the children with initial low levels of delinquency (Dishion et al., 1999; Poulin et al., 2001).

Differences in aggressiveness between boys and girls are relatively small, and it is only in preschool age that they become apparent. Boys are involved in more conflicts than girls and show more hostile as well as instrumental aggression (Ostrov and Crick, 2007). There is no gender difference in verbal aggression, but girls show somewhat more relational aggression in the form of gossip, group exclusion and the like (Underwood, 2003). Fighting and other forms of physical aggression are more accepted among boys than girls. Since girls' aggressive actions are often less conspicuous, they are ignored by others, while boys' actions are to a greater extent met with resistance. Ignored behavior often disappears, while resistance leads to more fighting and prolongs the conflicts of boys (Fagot and Hagan, 1985). Gender differences increase in adolescence, mainly because girls' oppositional behavior declines earlier than that of boys (Dodge et al., 2006; Murray-Close et al., 2006).

When it comes to behavioral disorders, gender differences are significant. In the United States and Canada, the incidence of behavioral disorders in school age and adolescence is estimated at 7–9 percent for boys and 2–3 percent for girls. Moreover, compared with girls, boys show far more involvement in all types of serious criminal activity beginning as early as childhood. These differences increase toward adulthood and are greatest for robbery and burglary (Odgers et al., 2008; Rutter et al., 1998).

Culture, too, affects the development of prosocial and antisocial behavior. Some cultures do not attach much importance to helpfulness and other forms of prosocial behavior, and children in these cultures largely take on the same values. One example of this is sharing behavior among the Ik people of Uganda. Sharing virtually disappeared at all age levels when the tribe lost much of its livelihood because their natural hunting and food-gathering grounds were converted into a nature reserve (Turnbull, 1972). Parent perspectives on aggression vary as well. US mothers show a higher tolerance for aggressive behavior in their children than mothers from Japan (Hess et al., 1980).

Antisocial behavior and behavioral disorders can be found in most countries, but their prevalence varies significantly, for example a prevalence for oppositional defiant disorder and conduct disorder of 1.2 percent in Italy, 5.3 percent in Britain and 7.1 percent in Yemen (Scott, 2015). In many countries, prevalence increased from 1970 until the turn of the century. Since then, it has leveled off and declined to some degree in a number of countries, but the reasons for these changes are uncertain (Collishaw, 2015).

Pathways to antisocial behavior

There is a relation between antisocial behavior in childhood and later adaptation, but following different developmental pathways (Jennings and Reingle, 2012). The *early authority conflict* pathway develops from early stubbornness to avoiding authority, such as truancy. The *covert* pathway follows a trajectory of covert antisocial behavior such as lying and shoplifting to more serious forms of delinquency like property damage, car theft, burglary and selling drugs. The *overt* pathway escalates from bullying and harassment of others to physical fighting and violence. According to Loeber and colleagues (1993), children with an overlap between all three pathways are most likely to develop serious forms of antisocial behavior.

Prosocial children have a high probability of peer acceptance and positive adaptation later in life, while children with little prosocial behavior risk being rejected by their peers. Children with high levels of antisocial behavior are often unpopular with their peers and are at greater risk of poor personal relationships and social maladjustment later in life, but only a small minority show persistent aggression and antisocial behavior (Séguin and Tremblay, 2013; Viding and Larsson, 2007). One US study found that children who were rated aggressive by their peers at 8 years of age were often perceived as aggressive at 18 years of age, with a correlation of 0.38 between peer evaluations at 8 and 18 years. At 30 years of age, they continued to be perceived as more aggressive by their peers, had more criminal convictions and a higher rate of spousal abuse, and punished their children more harshly than those who had not shown an aggressive style in childhood (Eron, 1987). Not everyone follows such a development, however. Many adults with antisocial behavior were affected by behavioral disorders in childhood, but well under half of all children with behavioral disorders developed these types of problems as adults (Odgers et al., 2008; Robins, 1978). Neither do adult criminals necessarily have a childhood with behavioral disorders. There is a subgroup of adolescents who transgress the liberal norms of behavior typical for their age and begin to participate in criminal activities. For most members of this group,

however, such behavior is temporary (Moffitt, 1993; Odgers et al., 2008).

Correlations between early development and later antisocial behavior are often statistically significant, but generally low and occasionally moderate. Thus, early development does not determine the future. Many young children with more than usual aggressive behavior show good adaptation later in life, while some children with inconspicuous behavior in childhood show poor adaptation as adults. Maladaptation in adulthood, however, is more prevalent among children with aggression and behavioral problems than among children with early positive adaptation. This is a good argument for early intervention.

A social-cognitive model

Traditionally, theories of antisocial behavior have focused on the underlying motives and external factors maintaining this type of behavior (Freud, 1927; Lorenz, 1963; Skinner, 1971). More recent theories reject the notion of drives or basic motives that make children "helpful" or "aggressive." Based on a model of social information processing, Crick and Dodge (1994) describe six continuously recurring steps in children's social adaptation (Figure 23.2). The model incorporates cognitive and emotional processes and can be applied to all forms of behavior, but Crick and Dodge focus on the development of aggressive behavior in particular. Aggressive children and adolescents have difficulty assuming the perspective of others, take into account fewer social cues and are more attentive to signs of aggression in others than nonaggressive children. Other people's intentions are often interpreted as hostile. A peer who tries to establish positive contact can therefore be perceived as aggressive, accidents can be perceived as intentional, and so on. This reaction pattern has been found among aggressive children in different cultural settings (Dodge et al., 2015).

In one study, popular children and unpopular aggressive children were asked to describe a video with peers at play. More often than the popular group, the unpopular aggressive children interpreted actions as aggressive. Perceiving others as aggressive does not necessarily lead to aggressive behavior, however. Also depressed nonaggressive children interpret people in their environment as hostile more often than other children (Quiggle et al., 1992). Another study found

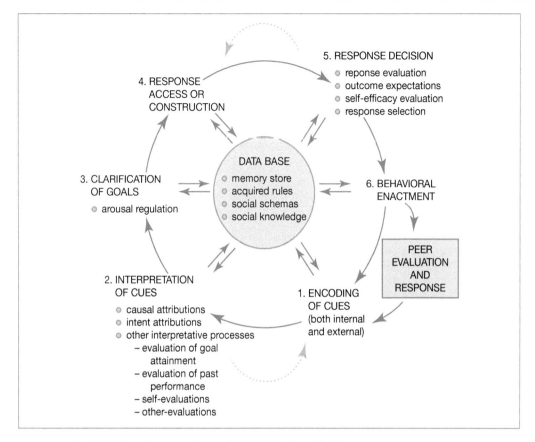

FIGURE 23.2 A social information-processing model of children's social adjustment.
The model consists of six continuously repeated steps. Children begin by interpreting internal and external situational cues, such as other people's facial expressions and their own arousal in the form of increased heart rate. They then use this information to ascribe intentions to others and make causal assumptions. The model also incorporates emotions. The outcome of children's chosen goals and behavioral strategies are stored as knowledge that contributes to later interpretations of the environment and action strategies (based on Crick and Dodge 1994, p. 76. With permission from the American Psychological Association (c)).

that a fake "threat" lead to an emotional preparedness and more perceived hostile intentions in 9- to 10-year-old aggressive unpopular boys than in a same-aged group of nonaggressive and popular boys (Box 23.1).

The model in Figure 23.2 is circular, illustrating that the steps repeat. Over time, the consequences of the child's chosen goals and behavioral strategies are embedded as *social scripts* (generalized expectations of specific social situations), in turn affecting the child's later interpretation of the environment and choice of strategies. For children who tend to interpret others as hostile, the process represents a vicious circle. Expectations of aggression are confirmed because the children themselves create aggression

or interpret the situation to imply that they avoided someone else's aggression through their choice of action strategies. Over time, fewer and fewer situations contradict the children's evaluations and lead them to interpret most actions as a threat. Such scripts largely consist of automated knowledge and can therefore be difficult to change (Fontaine and Dodge, 2009).

The social-cognitive model thus stresses the importance of children's perception of the social world. According to the model, antisocial behavior does not originate in malicious or aggressive drives, but in a tendency to assume that others have negative, competing or hostile intentions. Even positive actions can be interpreted as attempts to cause harm. From a developmental

The study included 65 boys aged 8 to 10 years. Thirty-two of the boys were rejected (unpopular) and aggressive, while 33 were well-adjusted and non-aggressive. Each should watch 12 videos that showed someone doing something wrong on purpose or by accident (e.g., one boy assures his own victory in a painting contest by spilling paint on the other boy's painting). As part of the experimental procedure, after the first four videos, the experimenter would make a break to fetch another boy. The experimenter went to the back room and turned on a tape recorder with a prerecorded conversation that the boy heard through a loudspeaker. In this way, half of the boys would "incidentally" overhear the boy he was going to be together with having a conversation with the experimenter and saying things like "If I go in there, I'm just going to get into a fight with that boy". The experimenters hypothesized that such a "threat" would lead to emotional preparedness even though after the "conversation," the experimenter returned to the front room and explained to the boy that he would soon have to do a task with another boy, but that the other boy was "in a bad mood," so they would have to wait a short while. In the mean time, the subject was to listen to the final eight stories. Thus, the other boy never really appeared.

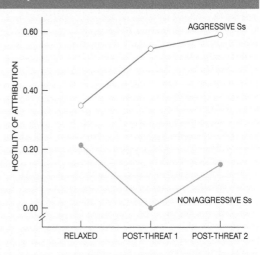

The results supported the hypothesis. The figure showed that without a threat, there was only a small and non-significant difference in how the aggressive and nonaggressive children perceived the situations they watched on video. For the two first videos after hearing the threat (post-threat 1 and 2), the aggressive boys described more hostile intentions, while the nonaggressive children's perceptions of the videos did not change significantly. The emotional level thus had a negative effect on how the situation was perceived: the relaxed situation led to similar evaluations, while the threat situation elicited different responses in the two groups.

psychopathology perspective, attention to threat may have its origin in an early bias toward negative emotions (see p. 360). The model can also incorporate attachment relationships (see Chapter 19). Children gradually construct their own perception of the environment, and their cognitive schemas or working models of human relations based on interaction with parents, siblings, peers and others form part of their social-cognitive development. A lack of social-cognitive skills can lead to profound consequences, for example in children with autism spectrum disorder, who may be anxious because they have major difficulties understanding both emotions and intentions in others (see p. 62). Emotion perception and regulation, too, may have an impact on this development. Some children have been subjected to such severe neglect and abuse that their

experiences have far-reaching consequences for their perception of others' attitudes and intentions (see p. 386). But for most children, social-cognitive schemas are the result of interaction between temperament, parental rearing style and experiences with relationships within and outside the family.

PARENTING INFLUENCES

Parents are the core of children's social environment and parental influence is important for the development of prosocial and antisocial behavior. Both presence and lack of prosocial behavior in situations in which prosocial behavior is expected usually lead to a response from adults (Dahl and Campos, 2013). In one study, mothers reported that they responded to over 90 percent of all incidents in which their 4- to 7-year-old children either showed or failed to show prosocial behavior. When the children were helpful, their mothers generally responded by smiling, thanking them, praising them and expressing appreciation. When their children failed to be helpful, they responded with moral exhortations, admonishments to do the right thing, questions about empathy, expressions of disapproval and direct interventions (Grusec, 1982).

Children's desires and parents' demands will inevitably lead to conflicts. Unambiguous rules and emotionally mediated explanations seem to promote prosocial behavior, whereas prohibitions without further explanations have the opposite effect. Toddlers whose mothers tended to respond to their child's distress with affective explanations more often showed prosocial behavior and comforted others than children whose mothers rarely offered affective explanations. The toddlers with mothers who often imposed unexplained prohibitions showed less altruistic behavior and gave less comfort than children whose mothers rarely imposed such prohibitions (Zahn-Waxler et al., 1979). Praise can promote prosocial behavior, but a study found that 4-year-olds whose prosocial actions usually were taken for granted and not commented upon by the parents were slightly more prosocial than children whose parents gave praise (Grusec, 1991). Praise can thus both undermine and increase children's intrinsic motivation, or have no effect on it (Dweck, 1999).

Baumrind (1997) describes four parenting styles that differ in emotional warmth and control. Parents with an *authoritarian* parenting style are demanding and emotionally unresponsive. Parents with an *authoritative* style set high standards for their children and show a high degree of responsiveness. A *permissive* style means that parents are responsive, but make few demands. Parents with an *uninvolved* style are neither demanding nor responsive. According to Baumrind and associates (2010), it is authoritative parenting with both high demands and high responsiveness that best promotes prosocial behavior.

Parental control is part of raising a child and can be important for preventing or reducing antisocial behavior and norm-violating activities in adolescence (Galambos et al., 2003). Disagreements with parents about parenting issues can

furthermore teach older children and adolescents how to negotiate as well as to comply (Baumrind, 1997; Eisenberg et al., 2006). Thus, it is not control as such that is decisive, but how parents exert it – parents can monitor their children both too little and too much. Authoritative parenting is characterized by emotional warmth, moderate or high levels of control, and negotiation. Authoritarian upbringing consists of a high level of control, little warmth and few negotiations, and, when based on asserting power and demanding (involuntarily) obedience, will impede rather than promote the child's prosocial development. Longitudinal studies have found a relation between strict early upbringing and corporal punishment and later antisocial behavior, and between strict and callous disciplinary upbringing in school age and later acting-out behavior and criminal activities (Bornstein, 2015; Dodge et al., 2006).

Rearing styles reflect the characteristics of both parents and child, and the relationship between children and parents in general. Children who know that their parents are physically and emotionally available perceive disturbing events as less threatening than children with less sensitive and more unavailable parents. When responding slowly and inconsistently, parents increase their children's distress (Grusec, 2011), and, more dramatically, abuse in early childhood often leads to less prosocial and more antisocial behavior in later childhood and adulthood. (Lansford et al., 2002; Luntz and Widom, 1994). Thus, research clearly indicates that assertion of power should not be a key element in children's upbringing; strategies that promote children's empathy, sympathy and understanding of themselves and others show far better outcomes. However, in many countries, corporal punishment remains relatively common (Lansford et al., 2010). One US study found that 28 percent of 1-year-olds had been spanked by their mother, and 7 percent twice or more a week. At 3 years of age, the numbers were 57 percent and 13 percent, respectively. Additionally, the results suggest a transactional effect: maternal physical punishment led to an increased incidence of behavioral disorders, while children's behavioral problems in turn led to an increased incidence of corporal punishment (MacKenzie et al., 2015). Since corporal punishment is common, it alone is unable to explain some children's antisocial development, and depends on the context in which punishment takes place. Occasional use of force need not have a negative effect if it is exercised by parents who are generally supportive; it is the cumulative effect of repeated physical punishment that leads to antisocial behavior in childhood and adolescence (Fréchette, 2016).

The relation between corporal punishment and behavioral disorders is also affected by cultural differences (Lansford, 2010). In countries in which corporal punishment is rare, children subjected to such punishment develop behavioral disorders. In countries in which it is more common, the developmental outcome more often consists of anxiety and aggression (Lansford et al., 2005). Neither is there a clear connection between what would be considered prosocial behavior in Western cultures, and a warm, affectionate parenting style. The Waorani people of Amazonian Ecuador are highly belligerent and constantly at war with neighboring tribes, and their basic philosophy is extremely individual-oriented. If the tribe is attacked, everyone takes responsibility for themselves only, regardless of what happens to family and friends. The Semai people of Malaysia represent the very opposite type of culture, putting extreme emphasis on cooperation, and especially solidarity and support within the family. At the same time, both tribes show themselves to be loving and caring toward their children, with little use of punishment (Robarchek and Robarchek, 1992). These studies show that a loving parenting style promotes collective cultural values, no matter what those values may be. A culture that encourages individuality will promote individual-oriented behavior, while encouragement of cultural unity will lead to traditional prosocial behavior. Similarly, there is an increased likelihood that children from societies with many conflicts will develop poor social skills and manipulative relationships (Trevarthen and Logotheti, 1989). The acquisition of society's values is part of children's adaptation to the society they live in.

SOCIETY AND PREVENTION

Violence and other forms of antisocial behavior are a serious problem in many countries. There are prevention and intervention programs with documented effects in reducing aggression and other forms of antisocial behavior, and increasing non-violent conflict resolution, such as The

Incredible Years (Webster-Stratton, 2006) and *Triple P Programmed* (Sanders, 1999; Sanders et al., 2000). There are also programs directed at children and adolescents with developmental disorders who have challenging behavior (Brosnan and Healy, 2011; McIntyre, 2013; von Tetzchner, 2004). Worries about violence can have a major impact on mental health in children attending schools with a violent school climate. Interventions that focus on educational and social support of students and their sense of belonging to the school may counteract a violent school climate (Eisenbraun, 2007; Gavine et al., 2014).

Theory and research on prosocial and antisocial behavior provide guidelines for how parents and society can promote prosocial behavior and prevent antisocial development. Reducing poverty and preventing child neglect and abuse will contribute to preventing antisocial behavior (Daro and Benedetti, 2014; Gavine et al., 2014). However, it is important not only to focus on reducing risk factors but also on factors that may support positive child development and wellbeing (Daro and Benedetti, 2014; Sameroff, 2009). Problems that may start in early childhood and escalate transactionally into later antisocial behavior are an argument for early intervention: both children's behavior and parental strategies may be more easily changed while children are young (MacKenzie et al., 2015). Additionally, parents have to change strategies as their children grow older; strategies that are effective for toddlers may be ineffective in later childhood and adolescence (Bornstein, 2015).

Although individual intervention is useful, the goal of society is to implement preventive measures aimed at larger groups or entire populations. There are a number of more general or community-wide programs to promote sensitive and positive parenting (Brock and Kochanska, 2016; Enebrink et al., 2015; Skar et al., 2015). Legislation is an important tool for cultural change. In 2015, corporal punishment of children was only prohibited by a minority of the world's countries (46), most of them European (Heilmann et al., 2015). The resources used by society to rehabilitate adolescents and adults are considerable in most countries. In the United States, antisocial behavior costs over a trillion dollars every year, making prevention an important priority in terms of human and economic factors (Dodge, 2009).

SUMMARY

1 Typical prosocial actions are helping, sharing and comforting. Around 1 year of age, children begin to show helping behavior, followed a little later by sharing with and comforting others. Children differ in the development of social skills and disposition for prosocial behavior, and parents in how they guide their children toward such behavior. Extrinsic rewards have little effect, while warm and supportive parenting promotes children's prosocial actions. A sense of justice, regardless of self-interest, is established in school age. In adolescence, various forms of prosocial behavior develop in slightly different ways and depend on the particular situation.

2 The most common form of *antisocial behavior* is *aggression*, and children begin to show aggressive actions in their second year. With age, there is a reduction in openly aggressive acts, while relational aggression increases. Other forms of antisocial behavior, such as lying, cheating and shoplifting, increase during school age. Following adolescence, there is a general decrease in antisocial behavior, but a small group continues to show such behavior.

3 *Bullying* consists of repeated *negative actions* such as teasing and physical or verbal aggression directed at one or more particular individuals over time. Bullying typically begins to show up in middle childhood, and its prevalence declines with age. Boys bully more than girls. Children who are bullied early in school age are at risk of being bullied at later ages. Individuals who bully have a higher probability of developing criminal behavior and alcohol abuse in adulthood, especially adolescents who bully. Bullying relationships can last for many years.

4 Children with behavioral disorders and callous-unemotional traits are characterized by proactive aggression, while children with emotion-regulation problems show more reactive aggression and perceive the environment as threatening. Both genes and the environment are contributing factors. Children whose parents are cold, punitive and dismissive typically show high levels of aggression, which in turn can trigger negative parental reactions. Children are affected by the way in which conflicts are resolved at home and in their local community. With age, peers gain more importance. Antisocial children commonly seek out each other because they are rejected by other children; as adolescents, they are more often involved with violent and criminal gangs than others.

5 Gender differences are generally small. Boys show more hostile and instrumental aggression in both physical and verbal behavior, and are more involved in all types of criminal activity. There is no gender difference in verbal aggression, but girls show somewhat more relational aggression in the form of gossip, group exclusion and the like. Behavioral disorders show significant gender differences in incidence.

6 The relation between antisocial behavior in childhood and later adaptation can follow different developmental pathways. Children with low levels of prosocial behavior risk being rejected by their peers. Children with high levels of antisocial behavior are often unpopular among their peers and have an increased likelihood of poor personal relationships and social maladjustment later in life, but only a small minority show persistent aggression and antisocial behavior. The connections between early development and later antisocial behavior are often statistically significant, but correlations are generally low and occasionally moderate.

7 The model based on social information processing emphasizes children's interpretation of external and internal situational cues and how they use them to ascribe intentions to others and make causal assumptions. Aggressive children are more attentive to signs of aggression in others than nonaggressive children, and their *social scripts* tend to incorporate more hostile elements and can be difficult to change.

8 Parenting styles can both promote and inhibit prosocial and antisocial behavior. Baumrind describes four different *parenting styles*: *authoritarian, authoritative, permissive* and *uninvolved*.

Continued

488 PROSOCIAL AND ANTISOCIAL DEVELOPMENT

Authoritative parenting best promotes prosocial behavior, while an authoritarian style with high demands on obedience and a low degree of emotional responsiveness has the opposite effect. There is a link between strict and callous disciplinary upbringing in school age and later acting-out behavior and criminal activities.

9 The relationship between corporal punishment and behavioral problems is affected by cultural differences and depends on how common such punishment is in a given culture. There is no clear link between the way in which cultural values are conveyed and the specific underlying values. A loving parenting style promotes collective cultural values, no matter what those values may be.

10 Today's knowledge provides guidelines for promoting prosocial and preventing antisocial behavior, and community-wide parenting programs and legislation against corporal punishment can bring about both human and economic gains.

CORE ISSUES

- The biological and social bases of prosocial behavior.
- Factors influencing children who bully.
- The cognitive and emotional bases of antisocial behavior.
- Parenting style and development of prosocial and antisocial behavior.
- Strategies for preventing antisocial behavior in society.

SUGGESTIONS FOR FURTHER READING

Crick, N. R., & Dodge, K. A. (1994). A review and reformulation of social information-processing mechanisms in children's social adjustment. *Psychological Bulletin, 115,* 74–101.

Dahl, A. (2015). The developing social context of infant helping in two US samples. *Child Development, 86,* 1080–1093.

Dishion, T. J., et al. (1999). When interventions harm: Peer groups and problem behavior. *American Psychologist, 54,* 755–764.

Dodge, K. A., et al. (2015). Hostile attributional bias and aggressive behavior in global context. *Proceedings of the National Academy of Sciences of the United States of America, 112,* 9310–9315.

House, B. R. (2017). Diverse ontogenies of reciprocal and prosocial behavior: Cooperative development in Fiji and the United States. *Developmental Science, 20* (6), e12466.

Loeber, R., et al. (2017). *Female delinquency from childhood to young adulthood: Recent results from the Pittsburgh Girls Study.* Cham, Switzerland: Springer.

Olweus, D. (2013). School bullying: Development and some important challenges. *Annual Review of Clinical Psychology, 9,* 751–780.

Contents

CHAPTER 24

GENDER DEVELOPMENT

Gender or sex is a salient biological characteristic, as well as a social and cultural construct, in the sense that societies attribute different abilities and behaviors to being male or female. Gender is a characteristic of both individual and collective identity (I'm a girl/boy; we are girls/boys) and impacts the life patterns of boys and girls, men and women, and society's activities in general. This chapter is about the development of gender knowledge, of the understanding of being a boy or a girl, and biological and environmental factors that may influence the development of gender identity and gender-related behavior.

THE DEVELOPMENT OF GENDER UNDERSTANDING

Most children develop an early awareness of differences between boys and girls, and actively begin to look for traits that distinguish the two groups. At the end of their second year, children show a growing understanding of the words *boy* and *girl*. They acquire concrete knowledge such as the fact that men have beards and women have breasts, as well as cultural knowledge and attitudes related to typical male and female tasks in the society in which they grow up. Although the content of children's gender concepts changes with age, it continuously affects their interpretations and recollections of events involving boys and girls, men and women. Furthermore, children internalize the *gender roles* and *gender stereotypes* of their culture (Martin and Ruble, 2009).

Gender identity, stability and constancy

Kohlberg (1966) describes three stages in children's development of gender awareness. During the first stage, beginning around 2 years of age, children develop gender identity and are able to distinguish boys and girls. Initially, they have slight difficulties answering whether they themselves are a girl or a boy, but manage to choose correctly when they are shown pictures of a boy and a girl and asked which of them is like themselves. Once children begin to identify with their own gender, they also start to perceive gender as a central and positive aspect of themselves (Ruble et al., 2007). However, toddlers are unaware that gender remains stable over time and that boys turn into men and fathers, and girls into women and mothers. During Kohlberg's second stage, beginning at 3–4 years of age, children develop gender stability: the understanding that people maintain the same gender throughout life. The percentage of children who show gender stability increases from age 4 to 5 (Halim et al., 2017). The third stage, gender constancy, begins around 6 years of age. Now children begin to understand that gender is related to biological characteristics, rather than the types of clothes people wear and similar external features. Once children have developed gender constancy, they also become increasingly aware of other aspects of male and female characteristics, and categorize people spontaneously by gender. At this age children often have rigid views on traits that characterize boys and girls (Halim and Ruble, 2010).

It is generally agreed that children's gender awareness develops in the order described by

Kohlberg, but with considerable variation in age for each of the stages and the length of time children remain in a given stage (Ruble et al., 2007). In one study, 40 percent of 3- to 5-year-olds answered that children maintain the same sex even if they put on clothes belonging to the other sex (Bem, 1989), earlier than the average indicated by Kohlberg.

Gender roles

Gender roles consist of all the expectations society has of children and adults by virtue of their gender, that is, how males and females in a given culture are expected to behave in different contexts. These expectations vary within different areas of life, from culture to culture and from era to era (Hewlett, 2000). For example, among the Aka tribe in Central Africa, young children spend much of their time with both parents and gender roles are relatively egalitarian (Box 24.1).

It seems that fathers' greater participation in child care and housekeeping is both a result of and contributes to greater gender equality. This is one reason why some countries have introduced child-birth leave that can only be used by the father (Eydal et al., 2015; Karu and Tremblay, 2017; O'Brien and Wall, 2017). This policy has contributed to a change in the father role as well as an increase in work equality in the home, but in most societies mothers still do most of the child care and housework (Almqvist and Duvander, 2014; O'Brien and Wall, 2017). The general change in gender role taking place is well illustrated by the fact that around 1900, women were not expected to study. One hundred years later, female students outnumbered male students at universities in many countries (Eggins, 2017). For example, in 2014, 56 percent of US students were female (Snyder et al., 2016).

Boys and girls show different preferences for toys early on (see following section). However, preschool children rarely justify their choice of toy based on whether it is fitting for boys or for girls, but on personal preference (Eisenberg-Berg et al., 1982). Thus, young children's behavior is not shaped by gender roles and general expectations of how boys and girls should play. Instead, children's experiences with their own and other children's preferences and behaviors contribute to sex-typing, and eventually lead to a conscious understanding of what being male or female means for oneself and others.

Once children start in school, they already have a good understanding of what is expected of boys and girls, and of characteristics and activities considered male and female. As children gain increasing insight into these expectations (gender roles), they also become less conforming and more flexible in their attitudes toward them (Ruble et al., 2006). It is a developmental trend that the female role is less rigid than the male role, and younger boys are under greater pressure to comply with their gender role than younger girls. It is more acceptable for girls to be boyish than for boys to be girlish (see p. 499).

In adolescence, gender roles once again become less flexible, probably because gender-related expectations are strengthened by the focus on sexual relationships typical for this age (Clemans et al., 2010).

Gender stereotypes

In most societies, social gender categories have evolved, general views about what it means to be a boy, girl, man or woman, and what characterizes typical male and female activities and traits. Within a culture, there is usually widespread agreement on what defines these characteristics and stereotypes are often activated without any awareness on the individual's part (Banse et al., 2010; Brandt, 2011).

Once gender identity has been established, children begin to form gender stereotypes. *Boys hit people*, *Girls talk a lot*, *Girls often need help*, *Boys play with cars* and *Girls give kisses* are examples of statements made by 2½- to 3½-year-olds (Schaffer, 1996, p. 192). In one study, 3- to 5-year-olds were asked what they thought of two infants. Half of the children were told that child A was a boy and child B a girl, while the others were told the opposite. Regardless of whether A or B was a "boy," the "boy" was labeled big, fast, strong, loud, smart and hard, and the "girl" was labeled little, scared, slow, weak, quiet, dumb and soft (Haugh et al., 1980). The children attributed these qualities solely based on their knowledge of who was a boy and a girl. Similar studies have been made with adults (see p. 498), and the gender label appears to have a stronger effect on children and adolescents than on adults (Stern and Karraker, 1989; Vogel et al., 1991). When toddlers are asked what kind of jobs men and women have, they largely respond in line with attitudes typical for their

BOX 24.1 GENDER ROLES AMONG THE AKA TRIBE (Hewlett, 1991, 1992, 2000)

Thanks to Barry S. Hewlett for the photograph.

The Aka tribe lives off hunting and gathering in the tropical forest regions of the southern Central Africa Republic and northern People's Republic of the Congo. The husband–wife relationship is close and cooperative, and the gender roles are relatively egalitarian. Aka husbands and wives engage in a variety of tasks together, including hunting with nets and childcare. Women are held in high esteem and food preparation and childcare are not considered feminine activities. In fact, fathers provide more direct infant care than in other societies. Young children spend much of their time with both parents. The Aka fathers do not play with their children, but they hold them much and talk with them, and they spend much time together. Through this, father and child develop strong attachment and relationships. It is believed that both the shared hunting and housework, and the large amount of time both spend in caregiving, contribute to the egalitarian gender roles in this society. Although hunting methods have changed somewhat and mobility is reduced since the 1980s, the caregiving pattern of mothers and fathers of the Aka tribe has remained stable together with cultural features such as egalitarianism, sharing, and autonomy (Meehan et al., 2017).

society (Gettys and Cann, 1981). From 5 years of age, children increasingly say that men and women have different personality traits. Five-year-olds expect women to be calmer than men, and men to be more aggressive and competitive than women (Best et al., 1977).

Gender stereotypes also affect the way in which children remember events. Children aged 5–6 years were shown pictures depicting a male doctor and a female nurse. A week later, they were asked what the pictures had shown and had no problems describing it. Other children were shown pictures of a female doctor and a male nurse. When asked 1 week later what the pictures had shown, they had a tendency to associate the man with the doctor and the woman with the nurse (Cordua et al., 1979). Children aged 5–9 years were shown a film of a boy playing with a

In many countries, fathers participate more in the care of the children.

doll and another film of a girl playing with a truck. When the children were asked to describe the films, 58 percent of them changed the gender of one of the children and 22 percent of both, with the youngest children relabeling gender more often than the older children.

A common stereotype is that girls are concerned about their appearance. In another study, 4- to 10-year-olds were told: "I think you know a lot of girls (boys). Tell me what you know about girls (boys). Describe them." The most frequent answers dealt with appearance ("girls wear dresses") for girls (31 percent) and personality traits ("boys are mean" or "girls are sensitive") for boys (27 percent). Personality traits came in second place for girls (19 percent) and appearance in third place for boys (13 percent). The same pattern was found from preschool to fifth grade, but descriptions of personality traits and other internal characteristics increased with age (Miller et al., 2009) (see also p. 383).

Gender stereotyping increases until the age of 11–12 years. From 8 years of age, children's perceptions largely coincide with those of adults within the same culture. At the same time, children become more flexible in their own attitudes beginning around 6–8 years of age, with girls somewhat more flexible than boys (Banse et al., 2010; Halim and Ruble, 2010). When school-age children were asked to draw their preferred future occupation, many boys and few girls wanted to be football players and policemen, while the gender pattern was opposite for hairdresser, veterinarian and kindergarten teacher (Tzampazi et al., 2013). To some degree, stereotyping has a normative function with significant social consequences for the relationships between the sexes and choices related to education and work (Brown and Stone, 2016).

SEX-TYPING

Gender roles are about attitudes and expectations, while sex-typing reflects what children actually do. Children gradually learn to act in accordance with what their culture considers appropriate behaviors and attitudes for boys and girls. However, they may have a clear understanding of what is appropriate for boys and for girls, without necessarily conforming to gender roles in every detail themselves. Boys with clear gender stereotypes generally are also more sex-typed in their preferences, but such a connection is not as pronounced among girls (Halim and Ruble, 2010).

Activity preferences

From early on, boys and girls show different play preferences and behaviors, reflecting both their culture's stereotypes and children's own preferences (McHale et al., 2004). Boys engage in more rough-and-tumble play than girls, a fact that may be related to boys' generally higher activity level (Goldstein, 1994). One-year-old boys prefer cars, tools and other forms of active play. Girls prefer dolls, soft toy animals and building blocks. By 20 months of age, these preferences have stabilized. Although girls are somewhat less biased in their choices than boys, they too make clear gender-typical choices at 3 years of age (O'Brien and Huston, 1985; Todd et al., 2017). Gender differences in toy preferences are maintained throughout childhood (Cherney and London, 2006). However, children's actual use of toys depends on availability. During a visit to an orphanage in Uganda where there were almost no toys, I observed what happened when the children were given dolls and doll equipment – toys that are mainly favored by girls. Both boys and girls of all ages played happily with the dolls: caring, dressing, bathing and feeding them.

Gender-specific preferences for color emerge around 2 years and are well established by 3 years (Wong and Hines, 2015). One study found that over half the girls showed "clothing rigidity," with a preference for pink frilly dresses around the age of 3–4 years in particular, but also that about 25 percent never had such a preference. For boys, the opposite was true: approximately one-quarter were preoccupied with clothing, especially with *not* wearing pink, while more than half never went through a period of clothing rigidity (Halim and Ruble, 2010). The preferences of boys and girls thus show clear differences as well as significant overlap.

Boys are often more interested in construction play than girls, but the relatively organized play activities in kindergarten show no differences. In home observations, which may more clearly reveal children's own preferences, 5- to 6-year-old boys spent about 16 percent of the time with construction games and girls less than 7 percent (Christie and Johnson, 1987). Although boys and girls spend about equal time on pretend play, the content varies: while girls prefer activities like shopping and washing the baby, boys pretend to be policemen, firemen, Superman and the like. Generally, girls prefer small groups with one or two best friends, while boys prefer to play in larger groups. These differences in emotional and behavioral style are probably important for sex-typing. Even when boys and girls share the same object preferences, such as a cart and similar items that can be pushed along, they use them in

Girls tend to prefer small group activities and boys play in larger groups.

different ways. Boys tend to bash them around, while girls use toys more gently. Girls who often join in with groups of boys tend to be particularly good at sports. Boys are rougher, engage in more teasing and fighting, have more conflicts and are more competitive and status-oriented than girls. They interrupt each other talking, directing and threatening, and often refuse to follow the directions of others (Liben and Bigler, 2008). Traditionally, boys have spent more time than girls on team activities such as football or other types of ball games, but this is changing. In many countries, handball and soccer have become common sports among girls as well (Figure 24.1).

There are general patterns in sex-typing but also individual differences. By the age of 5, some children have established distinct gender-typical preferences for activities and games. Other children show a slower and more gradual development with stabilization of clear gender-typical preferences around the age of 10 (Trautner, 1992). Studies have found a connection between gender-typical preferences in early childhood and sex-typed behavior in later childhood. Children who show the most sex-typed behavior at the age of 2½ years tended to show the same type of behavior at the age of 5 and 8 years. One reason for this stability may be that the children with the most sex-typed behavior played more with same-sex children, thereby strengthening their sex-typed behavior (Golombok et al., 2008, 2012).

Boys and girls continue to show sex-typed behavior in adolescence, but also more interest in gender-neutral activities. Their activity choices become more varied, and girls continue to be more flexible than boys (Su et al., 2009). It is important to remember, however, that sex-typing refers to *group differences* with a considerable overlap between male and female groups. Within each group there is significant individual variation in degree of sex-typed behavior.

Gender segregated interaction

A preference for same-sex playmates can be observed as early as toddler age, and somewhat earlier among girls than boys. At 3 years of age, girls mainly play with girls and boys with boys.

FIGURE 24.1　In many other countries, soccer has become a common activity among girls.

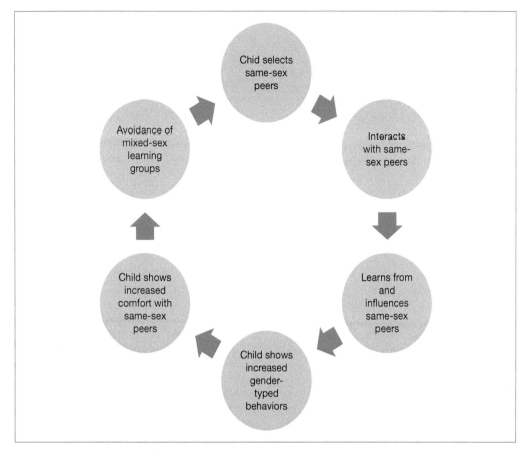

FIGURE 24.2 The gender-segregation cycle (based on Martin et al., 2014, p. 162).

In addition, preschoolers are more positive about their own than the opposite sex and are more open to praise and recognition by same-sex than other-sex peers (Fagot, 1985; Halim et al., 2016). There is little reason to believe that children have an innate tendency to seek out same-sex peers. Neither does research indicate that parents make a particular point of encouraging play with children of the same sex, or are averse to play with children of the opposite sex (Golombok and Fivush, 1994). When children "naturally" seek out same-sex peers, their shared play preferences are probably an important contributing factor, but also the wish to identify with children of the same sex as their own (Martin et al., 2014). Boys play somewhat differently with boys than with girls (and vice versa), and are less aggressive in playing with girls than with boys. Preschoolers, however, prefer children of their own sex in gender-neutral activities as well, such as playing with a swing or laying a puzzle. They also feel more competent and comfortable when playing with children of the same sex as their own. These factors strengthen each other (see Figure 24.2). In my observation of doll play in an orphanage in Uganda mentioned previously, there was a clear gender segregation even though all the children played with dolls.

The tendency to play with children of the same sex becomes more pronounced with age, although joint play and activities are found at all ages (Maccoby, 2002). Participation in physical activity may influence gender segregation. In a study of 3–5-year-olds, the girls with a high activity level spent more time with boys – and thus less time in segregated play – than the less active girls. The boys with a high activity level spent most time in segregated play. This indicates that girls with a high activity level prefer boys with a moderate activity level over girls with a moderate activity level, but not boys who have a high activity level (Bohn-Gettler et al., 2010). In another study, around 6 years of age, US children played 11 times more often with same-sex peers than with peers of the opposite sex (Maccoby and Jacklin, 1987).

School has a major influence on gender-segregated interaction, both in and outside the classroom (see the following) – learning and development seem to be best promoted by mixed-sex classes (Martin et al., 2014). When British children were asked about friends of the opposite sex, 8-year-olds responded that they had several such friends, although these consisted mainly of family and children they had known since preschool age. Eleven-year-olds answered that they would probably have more friends of the opposite sex once they were older (Abrams, 1989). Toward mid-adolescence, gender-segregated groups are gradually replaced by mixed groups as romantic relationships become more common. Also friendships with the opposite sex are increasingly being established (see Chapter 20).

Gender-segregated play can be found in most cultures, albeit to varying degrees (Best, 2010; Boyette, 2016; Munroe and Romney, 2006). This means that most children's upbringing environment provides a basis for sex-typing. Mixed-gender groups are generally the result of limited access to same-sex peers. In such cases, the preferences of boys and girls usually differ, even though the playgroups in practice are mixed. Neither does early play interaction between boys and girls prevent sex-typing and the development of distinct sex-typed behavior patterns in adulthood (Harkness and Super, 1985; Maccoby and Jacklin, 1987). Mixed-gender groups can be encouraged with the support and organization of adults, but children tend to return to gender-segregated interaction patterns as soon as adults stop to encourage mixed groups (Serbin et al., 1994; Thorne, 1986).

Some societies place higher demands on girls' than on boys' participation in housework, leaving girls with less time for games and play. In non-industrialized societies, boys can have up to one-third more leisure time than girls, but around 10 percent is more typical. In industrialized societies, there are no significant gender differences in regard to play time (Larson and Verma, 1999).

Differential treatment

It is a general observation that boys and girls in many ways are met and treated somewhat differently by their environment from an early age. Newborn boys are dressed in blue and girls in pink, and their rooms are decorated in keeping with their gender (LoBue and DeLoache, 2011). Advertisements and shops use pink and blue to mark things for girls and boys (Fine and Rush, 2018). One experimental study found that adults reacted differently to the same 1-year-old, depending on whether they had been told it was a boy or a girl. As a "boy," the child was treated far more roughly than as a "girl" (Bem et al., 1976). In a similar study, adults were shown a video of a 9-month-old who was called either "David" or "Lisa." When the adults were asked to describe the child, David was perceived as angry and Lisa as scared when a jack-in-the-box jumped up, even though the video was identical (Condry and Condry, 1976). These studies demonstrate that external characteristics alone do not lead to different perceptions and treatment of boys and girls. Stereotyped views of children and adults and the different expectations associated with boys and girls are significant as well (see p. 492). Children's behavior, however, is more closely linked to the parents' gendered behaviors than to the parents' gender attitudes and ideologies (Halpern and Perry-Jenkins, 2016). However, same-sex parents do not seem to have much influence on sex-typing. Two- to 4-year-olds who had been adopted by same-sex couples showed typical sex-typed behavior, but with slightly smaller differences between boys and girls than in heterosexual families (Goldberg et al., 2012).

Parents accentuate gender by talking about *boys* and *girls* when referring to other children's actions, instead of using the gender-neutral label *child*, for example, "See that boy running fast" or "The girl is laughing" (Zosuls et al., 2009). They talk more with their daughters than with their sons, make more of an effort to involve them in conversation and talk more with them about emotions, especially positive ones. They also tend to talk about the experience itself with their daughters, while they discuss causes and consequences with their sons, often involving negative emotions such as anger. Girls are encouraged to show their distress, while boys are told to control their anger, influencing boys and girls differently to regulate their own and others' emotional expressions. School-age girls, for example, expect more positive parental responses when they feel sad than boys do (Brody and Hall, 1993; Kuebli and Fivush, 1992).

Studies show that parents respond positively to girls using "girl toys" and boys using "boy toys," but this is more the case for boys than for girls. Parents largely encourage their child's own interests, and children rarely get negative reactions, but as early as 1 year of age, gender-atypical play among boys – but not girls – is actually met with negative reactions. Boys are generally under greater pressure to live up to their gender roles than girls, especially in relation to their fathers. "Tomboy" is not perceived to be as derogatory as "sissy." While it is relatively acceptable for girls to show boyish behavior, boys face considerable social sanctions if they show effeminate behavior (Hines, 2015).

At least as important as the influence of parents and other adults on the development of gendered behavior is the influence of peers (Martin and Fabes, 2001). Children expect gender-typical behavior when playing with same-sex peers and are extremely critical when other children violate their expectations of gender roles. In school age, they tend to tease or otherwise penalize children with friends of the opposite sex. Both children and adolescents respond with severe sanctions to boys who deviate from male gender roles, while they find it more acceptable for girls to participate in boy activities. Atypical gender behavior in preschool age may be associated with open and relational aggression, exclusion and bullying. A similar pattern of negative reactions may be found in school age and adolescence, but friendship and acceptance by same- and other-sex peers can protect against such sanctions (Toomey et al., 2014; Zosuls et al., 2016). Nonetheless, more in-depth studies have shown that the influence of friends is a complex process. One study found that negative peer sanctions led 10-year-old boys with many male friends to become more gender-typical, whereas boys with few male friends had a more atypical development. Girls developed more gender-typical traits, but only those with many male friends. Girls with many female friends and few male friends did not change, possibly because they did not perceive their problems to be related to gender-typical behavior (Ewing Lee and Troop-Gordon, 2011).

School can have a major impact on gender-typical behavior. The way in which teachers relate to students contributes to promoting or reducing students' sex-typed behavior (Bhana, 2016; Stromquist, 2007). Yet some authorities argue that the differences in boys' and girls' brains and their competitive mentalities, cognitive processing, activity levels, and so on, make it impossible to teach them effectively in the same classroom (Gurian, 2011). In 2012, the United States had 699 schools with gender-segregated classes and 106 single-sex schools (67 for girls, 39 for boys) (Klein et al., 2014). Research, however, shows that both girls and boys learn as well or better in mixed- than in single-sex classes. Classes with both boys and girls also seem to have a regulating effect on sex-typed play and other behavior among both sexes; boys, for example, do not engage in physical fights when playing with girls. Segregation of girls and boys, or teachers who in other ways stress gender as a category in the classroom, seem to contribute to underlining and reinforcing gender stereotypes. Mixed-sex classrooms thus lead to more positive gender attitudes than segregation (Hilliard and Liben, 2010; Martin et al., 2014).

The gender roles of society have a general impact, and it is a common finding that boys and girls are treated differently in children's literature and mass media. Since nearly all children watch television, it is likely that television programs affect gender attitudes and that existing gender stereotypes are reflected in how males and females are portrayed. The traditional literature for children and adolescents has represented men and women based on stereotypes. Since the 1980s, authors have placed greater emphasis on equality between the sexes, but women continue to be portrayed as more in need of help than men (Ruble et al., 2006). Moreover, a gender bias may still be found in school books (Moser and Hannover, 2014).

ATYPICAL DEVELOPMENT

Children vary in their development of gendered preferences, behaviors and interests. Despite many emotional experiences, development proceeds without problems in most cases. A minority of around 3 percent have difficulty finding their role as a male or female in society and show a "non-conforming" development of gender identity (Becker et al., 2017). They may experience a discrepancy between their anatomical and their perceived gender, and feel they belong to a different sex than the one they were "assigned." This is a small group, estimated at 2–14 in 100,000, but the numbers are quite uncertain. Boys dominate among those who are referred for sex identity problems, and although slightly more girls than boys report they would rather belong to the other sex, this need not be related to gender identity (Gender Identity Research and Education Society, 2006; Zucker and Seto, 2015).

There seem to be two atypical developmental pathways. The first consists of an "early" group with atypical development from early childhood. The second group begins to show signs closer to puberty when gender identity is affected by the body's first sexual responses and feelings of love. While the majority of children in the early group become homosexual, this is not the case for the latter group, which instead is characterized by cross-dressing and the like. The reasons for atypical development are uncertain, but twin studies suggest both genetic and non-genetic contributions. Individuals with atypical prenatal sex hormones have a far higher incidence than among the general population, but the majority of this group do not show atypical gender development (Hines, 2015; Ristori and Steensma, 2016; Zucker and Seto, 2015).

The experience of atypical gender identity development can be an extremely difficult one for children and adolescents. Younger children can react by crying when their parents tell them that they belong to their anatomical sex. The children might dislike their own genitalia and other bodily sexual characteristics, have a strong desire to belong to the other sex, dress up like the opposite sex and play with other-sex children and their gender-typical toys. They often take on the role of the opposite sex in pretend and fantasy play (Zucker et al., 2014).

When this type of development creates severe distress and problems in daily life, children or adolescents may meet the criteria for a diagnosis of "gender dysphoria" (American Psychiatric Association, 2013) or "gender incongruence of childhood" (Reed et al., 2016; World Health Organization, 2018). The duration of dysphoria varies and for most children it does not last into adolescence (Box 24.2). However, for some, the problem will not desist until they have decided to change gender, and a small percentage choose sex change surgery (Ristori and Steensma, 2016). One interview study found a difference between those who said they *were* the other gender, and those who said they *wished* they were to the other gender. Gender dysphoria was persistent in the first group, while showing more desistence in the second group (Steensma et al., 2011).

Atypical gender behavior and the experience of being different from others typically lead to severe problems with personal relationships in childhood and adolescence. Many among this group develop behavioral disorders and emotional responses involving depression, anxiety

BOX 24.2 DESISTENCE AND PERSISTENCE OF CHILDHOOD GENDER DYSPHORIA (Steensma et al., 2013)

How long gender dysphoria lasts varies considerably. Seventy-nine children with a natal gender of boy and 48 children with a natal gender of girl who had referred to a gender specialist clinic and diagnosed with gender dysphoria before the age of 12 years, were followed up in adolescence and were 15 years and older at the follow-up from 2008 to 2012. Twenty-three of the 79 natal boys and 24 of the 48 natal girls reapplied for treatment and were considered "persisters". Two thirds of the natal boys and half of the natal girls thus did not return to the clinic. It was assumed that they no longer had a desire for gender reassignment and thus that the gender dysphoria had desisted. Those who had more intense gender dysphoria were more likely to persist. When asked "Are you a boy or a girl?" those who expressed cross-gender identification had a greater probability of persisting. Nearly half of the boys who persisted had started the social transition in childhood while only a small minority of the desisters had started early. Among the girls, the difference was small, around half of both the persisters and the desisters had started early. Thus, among the natal males, early transition predicted the developmental course but not among the natal female group.

and social withdrawal. This may be related to a lack of tolerance and acceptance from peers in childhood and adolescence (Bos and Sandfort, 2015; Eden et al., 2012). Self-harm and suicidal ideation are much more common than in the general population and increase through childhood (Aitken et al., 2016).

In line with the broad range of variation among this group, the aim of intervention can differ considerably: reduction of gender-atypical and promotion of gender-typical behavior, conversations with children and parents about social consequences, or determining whether the child actually identifies as transgender. Whatever the goal may be, any intervention entails major professional and ethical issues (Ehrensaft, 2017; Ristori and Steensma, 2016).

THEORETICAL PERSPECTIVES ON GENDER-TYPICAL BEHAVIOR

Theorists largely agree on the development of sex-typed behavior and the role of cultural factors in this development, but differences between the genders have various explanations, particularly with regard to the emphasis on nature versus nurture. Theories must be able to explain the trajectories and variations of both typical and atypical development.

While men and women show clear biological differences related to reproduction, it is not as clear how biological differences affect the development of male and female behavior. According to *evolutionary psychology*, many forms of behavior that typically distinguish the sexes have their origin in hormonal processes related to maturation, such as choice of partner, caring for children and emotional relationships (Buss, 2009; Kennair et al., 2011; Wilson, 1998). A major argument in favor of this theory is that variation in prenatal sex hormones seems to contribute to individual differences in sex-typed behavior (Cohen-Bendahan et al., 2005; Hines et al., 2016). One study found that mothers of young girls with more male-typed behavior had higher testosterone levels than mothers of girls with more female-typical behavior (Hines et al., 2002). Hormones organize the brain and activity interests are linked to prenatal androgen exposure (Berenbaum and Beltz, 2016). Girls

who have been exposed to abnormally large amounts of male hormones during fetal development will exhibit more boy-like characteristics, even if their hormonal balance is restored after birth, their parents encourage them to engage in more girl-typical activities than other parents, and the children clearly develop as females (Hines, 2015). The girls in this group do better than average on tasks requiring spatial perception (an area in which boys generally outperform girls), and tend to be boy-like in their selection of toys, such as choosing cars over dolls (Nordenström et al., 2002; Servin et al., 2003). For the majority of girls, the hormonal disturbance does not lead to changes in gender identity and self-perception as females, but only in the development of gender-typical behavior. Children who are genetically male, but were insufficiently exposed to male hormones during the fetal period, do not have a corresponding tendency to develop female-typed behavior. This may be because the environment places more pressure on boys than on girls to conform to sex-typed behavior. It is easier for girls to follow their actual preferences without incurring social sanctions (Meyer-Bahlburg et al., 2006; Ruble et al., 2006).

Some boys (with sex chromosomes XY) do not have male genitalia due to congenital anomalies, and on rare occasions, the penis has been accidentally cut off during circumcision. In some of these cases, attempts have been made to transform a male into a female by surgically forming a vagina, initiating hormone treatment and raising the child as a girl (Money 1975; Money and Ehrhardt, 1972). Such attempts have shown widely differing results. Although most of the children developed a female identity, nearly all were characterized by male interests. Some experienced themselves as a male in a female body, with a far higher incidence of sex reassignment surgery than among the general population. The results suggest that prenatal hormones impact individual interests, but that hormones alone do not determine gender. Parenting, too, can have a significant effect on gender identity formation (Meyer-Bahlburg, 2005).

Behaviorist theories represent the counterpart to evolutionary psychology, in that the rearing environment is believed to have the greatest impact. Sex-typing is the result of differential treatment, as people in the environment encourage and penalize various types of behavior among boys and girls (Lamb et al., 1980). Furthermore, children observe the behavior of boys, girls, men and women and other people's responses, and thereby get to know their own and the opposite sex. They learn to behave in different ways with different people, and gender is one of the main categories of division. Studies show that children imitate older children and adults of the same sex more than children and adults of the opposite sex (Novak and Peláez, 2004). Just like other acquired behavior, traditional behaviorism views sex-typing as primarily driven by external influences. *Cognitive behavioral theory* unifies learning-based theories with the formation of gender concepts (see below). Bussey and Bandura (1992, 1999) describe a development from external control to internal regulation of gender-typical behavior. By observing many people, children form an abstract and generalized understanding of how boys, girls, men and women behave. It is this understanding, together with the knowledge of their own gender, which forms the basis for children's actions in situations in which gender has a bearing on their choice of action.

Other theories focus on the development of *cognitive gender schemas* or *gender concepts*, the beliefs children form about boys' and girls' behavior. According to Kohlberg (1966), part of children's cognitive development entails that as soon as they have established gender identity and gender constancy (see p. 491), they begin to interpret the outside world based on gender as a main category and to infer what it means to belong to a certain gender. Boys discover that they are boys and instruct themselves to do "boy things." Similarly, girls instruct themselves to do "girl things." What is typical for "boy things" or "girl things" depends on the differences between boys' and girls' activities in the society they grow up in and that "labels" them as belonging to one or the other gender. Kohlberg's theory thus views children's gender-typical behavior as the result of a conscious effort to be like children of the same sex as their own. Therefore, gender constancy is a prerequisite for gender-typical behavior, but studies show that children have gender-typical toy preferences before they know whether they are a boy or a girl. Although 3-year-olds have only developed gender stability, they have a good understanding of typical boy and girl things, and the play preferences of boys and girls (Martin et al., 2002). This suggests that the development of understanding gender as a permanent individual trait occurs in parallel with the acquisition of knowledge about gender roles in society.

Also Bem (1981) suggests that sex-typing has its origins in the development of gender concepts or schemas. Children establish a gender concept through learning to evaluate what is right and wrong from a gender perspective, and thus how they should act based on their own gender. The organization of behavior based on one's own gender identity is not driven by cognitive development but is the result of adults directing children's attention to the gender-typical traits of other children and adults from an early age. Although Bem's *gender schema theory* places greater emphasis on gender as a social construct than Kohlberg's theory, both agree that children seek to be similar to others who share the same biological attributes.

According to *developmental intergroup theory* children identify with other children based on certain characteristics. Gender is an important group characteristic in society, and affiliation with either the "boy" or the "girl" group represents a key element in children's social identity (Bigler and Liben, 2007). Sex-typing is assumed to have its origins in the biological characteristics of males and females as well as in children's perceptions and concepts of what boys and girls do. Their social identity as a boy or a girl makes children see the world through "male lenses" or "female lenses," and represents a strong incentive to act in accordance with what is considered appropriate for one's own sex and avoid acting like the other sex (Liben, 2014; Maccoby, 1998).

This short overview shows that the theoretical perspectives on gender development vary considerably. For example, evolutionary psychology and behaviorism make very dissimilar assumptions about the foundation of gender-typical behavior. Other theories are complementary rather than contradictory, making it possible to unify several theoretical perspectives. Biological factors undoubtedly play an important role in the development of gender-typical behavior, but biological differences alone are unable to explain the variation in interests and behavior among boys and girls. Neither do parents relate so differently to boys and girls that this alone would be able to explain the differences between genders (Hines, 2015; Maccoby, 2000). Besides, these differences only represent an average – men and women show a wide range of characteristics and behaviors, and there are significant cultural differences (Buller, 2005, 2008; Lickliter and Honeycutt, 2003). Overall, research suggests that biology imposes certain constraints that contribute to the different development in males and females. Boys and girls are biologically "primed" to develop gender-typical behavior, but the content of their gender schemas and identities can be affected by upbringing. Although biological factors are of importance to children's early preferences, the social environment can have a decisive impact on whether the differences between boys' and girls' preferences and behaviors are maintained or modified (Archer, 1992). The same developmental processes can result in cultural differences in relation to gender roles and behavior. Cultural differences and the changes that have occurred in many countries with regard to gender roles and

women's participation in the workplace, in team sports and in men and women's choice of profession are examples of how culture contributes to maintain or change areas of activity that may be perceived to be biologically determined and gender-specific in a given culture. However, identifying as a boy or a girl need not be the only reason for gender-specific behavior. Other differences can lead boys and girls to form different concepts and beliefs about the world. Maccoby (2002) points to peer groups as an important influence on sex-typing. It is the multiple interaction between biological differences impacting temperament, cognition and action, the typical activities and experiences of boys and girls, and the responses and influences from their surroundings that form the development of children's perception of the social world.

SUMMARY

1 Gender is a salient biological characteristic as well as a social and cultural construct. Children are at an early age aware of differences between boys and girls, and begin to acquire society's expectations of males and females.

2 Kohlberg describes three stages in the development of *gender awareness*: *gender identity*, *gender stability* and finally *gender constancy*.

3 *Gender roles* consist of the expectations society has of children and adults by virtue of their gender. Boys seem to be under greater pressure than girls to live up to their gender role, and incur more social sanctions for behavior typical of the other sex.

4 *Gender stereotypes* are beliefs about the characteristics of adults and children solely based on their gender. From 3–4 years of age, children gradually adopt culturally transmitted attitudes about the typical vocations and personalities of men and women.

5 *Sex-typing* refers to the acquisition of what culture regards as appropriate play, behavior and attitudes for boys and girls. Children vary in their developmental trajectories of gender-typical activity preferences. Adolescents continue to show sex-typed behavior, but also more interest in gender-neutral activities.

6 Children prefer to play with same-sex peers, but joint play and activities take place at all ages. In mid-adolescence, mixed groups replace gender-segregated groups, and friendships with the other sex become increasingly common.

7 Boys and girls are in different ways met and treated somewhat differently by their environment, in the home, in kindergarten and school, among peers, and in children's literature and mass media.

8 A small percentage of children experience a discrepancy between their anatomical and their perceived gender. Some children and adolescents meet the criteria for a diagnosis of "gender dysphoria" or "gender incongruence." In the majority, the problems are temporary, but for some they do not desist until the person has decided to change gender. Atypical gender

Continued

behavior typically leads to relationship problems and emotional disorders, and any intervention entails major professional and ethical issues.

9 *Evolutionary psychology* stresses the biological basis of gender-typical behavior patterns. One argument in favor of the theory is that variation in the prenatal sex hormones seem to contribute to individual differences in sex-typed behavior, although the influence on gender identity is small. Studies suggest that biology imposes certain constraints, but that gender identity is also affected by upbringing.

10 *Behaviorist theories* largely view gender differences as the result of the environment encouraging and penalizing various types of behavior among boys and girls. According to *cognitive behavioral theory*, children gradually form a generalized understanding of what boys and girls are and how they behave, leading to a development from external control to internal regulation of gender-typical behavior.

11 Kohlberg's theory views children's development of gender concepts as part of their general cognitive development. *Gender identity* forms the basis for developing gender-typical behavior: boys do "boy things" while girls do "girl things." According to Bem, sex-typing is the result of adults helping children to develop gender concepts by directing children's attention to the characteristics of the child's own and others' gender-typical behavior from an early age. *Developmental intergroup theory* views gender as an important group characteristic in society, and therefore as a key element in children's social identity. Children's social identity as a boy or a girl leads them to view the world through "male lenses" or "female lenses," and act in accordance with what is considered appropriate for one's own sex and avoid acting like the other sex.

12 Overall, research suggests that boys and girls are biologically "primed" to develop gender-typical behavior, but that the content of their gender schemas and identities is affected by upbringing. Cultural differences and changes in women's participation in the workplace and sports are examples of how culture affects gender roles. The multiple interaction between biological differences impacting temperament, cognition and action, the typical activities and experiences of boys and girls, and the responses and influences from their surroundings form the development of children's perception of the social world.

CORE ISSUES

- The biological and social bases of gender-typical behavior.
- The evolutionary basis of gender roles.
- The cultural and historical variation in gender roles and behavior.

SUGGESTIONS FOR FURTHER READING

Banse, R., et al. (2010). The development of spontaneous gender stereotyping in childhood: Relations to stereotype knowledge and stereotype flexibility. *Developmental Science*, *13*, 298–306.

Halim, M. L. D. (2016). Princesses and superheroes: Social-cognitive influences on early gender rigidity. *Child Development Perspectives*, *10*, 155–160.

Halpern, H. P., & Perry-Jenkins, M. (2016). Parents' gender ideology and gendered behavior as predictors of children's gender-role attitudes: A longitudinal exploration. *Sex Roles*, *74*, 527–542.

Karu, M., & Tremblay, D. G. (2017). Fathers on parental leave: An analysis of rights and take-up in 29 countries. *Community, Work and Family*, *21*, 344–362.

Maccoby, E. E. (2002). Gender and group process: A developmental perspective. *Current Directions in Psychological Science*, *11*, 54–58.

Munroe, R. L., & Romney, A. K. (2006). Gender and age differences in same-sex aggregation and social behavior: A four-culture study. *Journal of Cross-Cultural Psychology*, *37*, 3–19.

Ristori, J., & Steensma, T. D. (2016). Gender dysphoria in childhood. *International Review of Psychiatry*, *28*, 13–20.

Contents

The activities children participate in is a basis for their enculturation. In the first years of life and throughout childhood, play is an important activity for children in many societies. A clear-cut definition of play is difficult to find. In fact, most authors point to the difficulty defining play and avoid defining it (Glenn et al., 2013; Sheridan et al., 2011). They point out that play is not a group of activities but defined by the underlying motives – play actions are voluntary, do not distinguish between reality and fantasy, are enjoyable and have no goal beyond themselves; they may or may not involve others (Lifter et al., 2011; Pellegrini, 2013). Thus, running up a hill to get to school on time is not play. When children run up and down a hill without any other purpose than perhaps to see who can run the fastest, they are playing. Except on occasions when children don't know what to do with themselves, they need neither encouragement nor reward for playing. Play actions are motivating in and of themselves and are typically accompanied by joy and other positive emotions.

This chapter describes different forms of play and their developmental trajectories, and discusses the functions of play in children with typical and atypical development.

FORMS OF PLAY

Play takes many forms and can be categorized in different ways (Lillard, 2015; Mertala et al., 2016). Some of the more common categories are listed in the following, but the boundaries between them are often blurred.

Sensorimotor play and *exercise play* are forms of *physical play* (Pellegrini and Smith, 1998). Infants and toddlers can keep up rhythmic movements with their arms and legs for long stretches at a time and engage in *locomotor play* involving gross motor activities such as running, jumping, climbing and sliding, or activities such as pulling, grasping and throwing objects, all without a clear outside purpose other than the activity itself. Many animals, too, spend a lot of time on gross motor play (Burghardt, 2005). Objects can be used in fitting ways for play, such as when children have a long "conversation" on a telephone that is not connected, or in unfitting ways, such as when a child persistently hits a toy car on a table top. While very young infants and children engage in pure motor activities, in later activities the physical actions have a broader basis of meaning, often imitations of adult activities. However, the aim of such actions does not lie in their practical consequences, but solely in the pleasure of mastering them. When children do the dishes or sweep the floor in the kitchen or the dollhouse, they do not do so in order to clean, but to master an adult activity. When children perform actions to help adults with their work and perceive their own actions as goal-oriented and helpful they are no longer playing. This type of cooperation also introduces children to culturally valued activities, but here they are "trainees" rather than play partners.

Rough-and-tumble play is physical but also a form of *social play* in which children chase each other – pushing, tickling and the like – or engage in play fighting. The fact that the fighting is not for real is signaled by children's facial expressions and verbal communication, and by the way in which they fight. These episodes usually last for a short time and children do not hit as hard as when they fight for real. Such play can nonetheless lead to arousal, and for children with self-regulation problems, play fighting tends to develop into real fighting (see p. 476). This type of play is also common among many animal species and provides insight into their communication (Palagi et al., 2016; Pellegrini and Smith, 1998).

Constructive play involves creating something, such as building a house with blocks or Lego, forming a clay figure or assembling a Meccano vehicle. Children putting bricks on top of each other and knocking them down again is not considered constructive play. Constructive play can occur alone or together with others, and often has symbolic elements. Children can use their constructions in role and pretend play, often accompanied by a story, such as dolls living in a house built of blocks, or puppets "eating" a clay cake the child has made (Christie and Johnson, 1987). Piaget (1951) and Pellegrini (2013), however, argue against the role of construction as play, contending that construction has an extrinsic goal – the completed structure – and therefore cannot be considered play. There are no clearly defined boundaries, however. Playing out a story in a dollhouse or racing toy cars can be as goal-oriented as building a house with Lego, and neither the act of constructing nor making up a story have a goal other than the joy of carrying out the activity itself.

In *symbolic play* or *pretend play*, children take on the role of a person or an animal and assign a function to objects other than their usual one. It involves both symbolic objects and objects used for their actual function, but without fulfilling that function in reality. When children pretend to be drinking from an empty cup, the cup is used for its intended purpose, but the action is make-believe. One of the characteristics of play is that it can transcend the constraints of reality and incorporate *counterfactual* reasoning (Amsel and Smalley, 2000). The child can be a nurse, a firefighter or a pirate, and a building block can become a house or a car. It is the object's role in the context of play that defines its use and function. When a building block acts as a toy car, it is the properties of cars, rather than blocks, that determine what the block can do and how it can be used in play (even though

"cars" sometimes begin to fly in the air). The same applies to children's make-believe roles. When children become nurses or pirates, it is their make-believe role that determines the possibilities and limitations of their actions. Play reflects children's imagination, but also the basic human tendency to think in metaphors (see Fauconnier and Turner, 2002; Lakoff and Johnson, 1980). Pretend play is often social and particularly common when children play together with their parents or other children.

Symbolic play is often considered the "true" form of play, but many types of play can include symbolic elements and take place both in a social context and alone. For example, children can run on their own for the sake of running, or play cops and robbers and run after each other.

SOLITARY, PARALLEL AND GROUP PLAY

The earliest form of play takes place in interaction with adults, such as playing peek-a-boo or retrieving an object that falls outside the infant's reach. Over time, children become more self-reliant and able to play on their own (Christie and Johnson, 1987; Pellegrini, 2013).

The first form of play involving several children is *parallel play*. Children play *next to* rather than *with* each other. The reason for this may be that coordinating several actions and people at the same time exceeds younger children's cognitive capacity. In the early years, children also spend a good deal of time watching other children's activities without participating themselves (Veiga et al., 2017).

With increasing age, *group play* becomes more common. In *associated group play*, children play with the same toys and interact to a certain extent. They might play side by side with dolls, for example, and occasionally put their own doll in the bed of another child's doll. *Collaborative play* involves complementary roles and tasks. One child bathes the doll while another makes up the doll's bed. One child assembles the train tracks into a circle while the other finds the locomotive and wagons and puts them on the tracks (Parten, 1932).

Among slightly older children, play has traditionally been social and collective, but in the course of the twentieth century, solitary play has become significantly more common in Western industrialized countries among children not attending kindergarten (Sutton-Smith, 1994). This may be due to the smaller size of families, less access to play areas and more time spent playing at home, since parents today often feel it is unsafe for their child to play outside, especially in the cities (Frost, 2012; Wridt, 2004). This development is also reflected in the manufacture of many toys children can play with on their own (including tablets and online games).

Most children spend a lot of time playing, but play patterns vary from one child to another. Solitary play is more common among shy children, not because they are not motivated to play with others, but because they feel anxious about engaging in new activities and being judged and evaluated socially (Coplan et al., 2015). Much time spent on solitary play can also be the result of rejection by other children (Coplan et al., 2014). In preschool age, this can be a warning sign of social isolation or atypical social development, particularly when caused by rejection, but solitary play can also be constructive and creative (Coplan et al., 2015; Luckey and Fabes, 2005). *Nonsocial play* means that children play alone even when possible play partners are present. This can reflect a preference for solitary play that need not be related to developmental problems, while children who actively show *social avoidance* are at risk of being rejected by their peers and developing social anxiety and other internalizing disorders (Coplan et al., 2015).

THE DEVELOPMENT OF PLAY

Different forms of play do not represent separate stages or periods of development. Some appear earlier than others, but continue to be part of children's repertoire as long as they play. Thus, there is no clear timeline between the different play forms.

Exercise play is the most common form of play in the first 3 years of life. Reaching a peak at the age of 4–5 years, it continues throughout childhood, while physically active play becomes common in the first few years of school. Initially, this type of play consists of motor repetitions for the sheer pleasure of executing them and manipulating objects in the environment, but gradually becomes more symbolic and involves more participants (Pellegrini, 2011). Rough-and-tumble

play begins around the age of 3. Play fighting increases throughout childhood, making up 3–5 percent of play in preschool age, peaking at around 8–10 percent in middle childhood and decreasing to 5 percent in early adolescence (Pellegrini and Smith, 1998).

Simple constructive play starts in the beginning of the second year. Around 2 years of age, constructive play increases significantly and represents 40 percent of all play at the age of 3–4, especially in kindergarten which often is well equipped for this type of play. While constructive play stands for about half of all play in kindergarten from the age of 4–6, it makes up only 12–13 percent of the time spent playing at home, and twice as much among boys than girls (Christie and Johnson, 1987). The simple constructions of young children and toddlers are gradually replaced by train sets, complicated Lego structures and model airplanes.

According to Piaget (1951), the earliest symbolic play can be observed in the second year of life, when children begin to perform familiar activities with novel objects. When Piaget's own daughter Jacqueline was 18 months old, she said *cry, cry* to her toy animals and made crying sounds for them. Two months later she was scrubbing the floor with a sea shell, similar to the action she had seen the house cleaner perform with a scrub brush. Pretend play is central to the third of Vygotsky's and Elkonin's six stages of leading activities in the period from 3 to 7 years (see p. 186).

Fenson and Schell (1985) describe three parallel developmental trends in pretend play. The first is related to *decentration*, meaning that play gradually involves other people as well. One example of a developmental sequence is that the child first pretends to be drinking from an empty cup, then feeds a doll from an empty cup, and finally lets the doll drink from the empty cup. Usually, this last type of play action emerges during the second year of life (Largo et al., 1979a, b). The second parallel developmental trend is *decontextualization*. This means that the child gradually moves away from concrete actions, for example by first drinking from an empty cup, then drinking from a shell or similar item, and finally pretending to drink without a cup or other substitute object. Around the age of 3–4 years, children usually use their finger as a toothbrush when asked to pretend to brush their teeth, while children above the age of 6 perform this make-believe action with their hand without replacing the missing toothbrush with a finger or an object. Using invisible objects to make-believe is considered a more advanced form of pretend play, since the absence of a concrete object shows that it exists only in the child's mind (Weisberg, 2015). The third trend is the gradual *integration* of multiple actions in the same play activity. A possible developmental sequence can start with the child pretending to feed a doll, followed by feeding several dolls in turn, and finally feeding, washing and putting the doll to bed. Performing several actions within the same play activity usually also occurs before the age of 2.

The onset of pretend play seems to vary among cultures, depending on the extent to which adults encourage such play, but in all cultures it starts before the age of 3 years. By this age, most children have also developed a good understanding of the difference between reality and fantasy (Ma and Lillard, 2006). Symbolic play has a central place in children's activities between the age of 3 and 5 years (Lillard et al., 2013). In a retrospective survey of university students, 92 percent responded that pretend play had been a daily activity at 4–5 years of age. The percentage decreased in early school age, and after the age of 10–11 years, pretend play gradually became less common, although a small group of students said they continued to play beyond the age of 18 years (Table 25.1).

Many children have an *imaginary companion*, a fantasy person who accompanies them everywhere. This is also considered a form of pretend play (Weisberg, 2015). Some children create extensive worlds that include farms, railways, countries and islands filled with people, animals and things. These companions and worlds can be private and secret, or children can tell their parents and siblings about them (Cohen and MacKeith, 1990). This form of pretend play is most common during preschool age. In one study, 31 of 100 children aged 3;4–4;8 years responded that they had such a companion. Three years later, only three of the children still had one (Taylor et al., 2004). There is a possible relation between imaginary companions and verbal imagination. On average, children with imaginary friends tend to be better at telling stories than children without such friends (Trionfi and Reese, 2009).

Helping children play

Younger children need help to develop play skills. Adults often help children get started with pretend play and thereafter withdraw so children can develop these skills on their own (Shmukler, 1981). How children play also depends on whether they are playing alone or together with someone else. Slade (1987) found that toddlers' play was more advanced and lasted longer when the mother took an active part than when they were playing on their own. Verbal encouragement alone without the mother's participation had little impact on the children's play. Another study found a difference between children's pretend

TABLE 25.1 The development of pretend play (113 students were asked how often they engaged in pretend play throughout childhood and adolescence (based on Smith and Lillard, 2012). Asterisks (*) indicate cells where the observed count was significantly higher than the expected count (p < 0.01).)

Age (years)	Never	Rarely	Monthly	Weekly	Daily
4–5	0	0	0	21	92*
6–7	0	1	2	34	76*
8–9	1	5	16	56*	35*
10–11	7	11	34	46*	15
12–13	11	33	43*	21	5
14–15	29	44*	23	13	4
16–17	35*	52*	13	9	4
18+	48*	43*	8	9	5

play with their mothers and their peers: playing with the mother, children largely followed her suggestions and directions, while peer play was more active, equal and flexible (Howes and Matheson, 1992).

Play is also central to fathers' parenting style. In fact, fathers spend more time playing with the child than in other care-taking activities (Fletcher et al., 2011). There are, however, differences between father–child play and mother–child play. In a study of children aged 2–4½ years, the mothers structured the play, supported learning through teaching, guided the child's behavior and engaged in empathic conversation. The fathers engaged in physical play, behaved more like an age mate, let the child lead the activity, and supported learning by motivating and challenging the child (John et al., 2013). It is suggested that fathers' involvement in rough-and-tumble play may support the child's development of self-regulation (Fletcher et al., 2013).

The influence of parents' participation depends on the play skills of the child and what is being played. O'Connell and Bretherton (1984) observed that explorative and exercise play increased among 20–28-month-olds when their mother was present. Among 28-month-olds, the mother's presence only affected symbolic play. All the mothers supported both forms of play to an equal degree, but maternal interaction only helped children develop their most advanced form of play. The mothers' attempts to help their child with previously mastered play skills were overlooked by the children. This is in line with Vygotsky's theory that learning support must occur in the child's zone of proximal development and within the relevant area (see p. 291). Help from more competent adults and peers is important for children's learning and development, but only as long as the child needs help and is able to understand the task itself and what the help involves. This emphasizes the importance of offering individualized help and support to children with both typical and atypical development.

THE FUNCTIONS OF PLAY

Depending on the theoretical point of view and the type of play involved, psychology offers various explanations and attributes different functions to play in children's development (Burriss and Tsao, 2002). Some give particular weight to the biological basis of play and its importance for children's enculturation. According to evolutionary psychology, exercise play is biologically determined as a way of discovering and practicing new skills in a safe environment before they are applied. It is an adaptive function that has given human beings and other species an evolutionary advantage (Pellegrini et al., 2007; Pellegrini and Smith, 1998). From a different theoretical perspective, Piaget (1951) ascribes a similar function to exercise play.

Other theorists have focused on pretend play. From a psychodynamic perspective, Winnicott (1971) sees play as a "third zone" between inner mental life and external reality. Play promotes the development of emotional relations, allows children to use their creativity fully and contributes to establishing the self (à Beckett et al., 2017). In line with this, psychodynamic psychology uses play as a tool in psychotherapy for children with psychiatric disorders (Axline, 1964; Mumford, 2012; O'Connor and Braverman, 1997).

Building on logical constructivism, Furth and Kane (1992) view pretend play above all as a way of constructing an understanding of society. Children "play society" and co-construct societal knowledge together, such as when two girls play they are going to bed and create going-to-bed rules based on their age in the pretend play role. The lack of access to free play with peers that characterizes many of today's Western urban communities can therefore have an impact on children's enculturation (Jarvis et al., 2014). Others see pretend play in the context of developing mind understanding (Lillard, 2001).

Montessori (1910) believes that constructive play develops sensory and motor skills, but maintains that pretend play is a primitive escape from reality without functional value: children should set real tables and sweep real floors instead of performing such activities in a dollhouse. Piaget (1951) disagrees with Montessori and views imagination and symbolic play as important aspects of cognitive functioning. Pretend play does not primarily fulfill an exercise function: the purpose of washing and putting a doll to bed is not for children to learn to wash themselves and go to bed, but for the sheer joy and sense of mastery.

Vygotsky (1967) mainly discusses pretend play, to which he ascribes major developmental importance, but holds a somewhat different view than Piaget. According to Piaget's theory, pretend play contributes to development through the activities children participate in, but as the *result* of cognitive development, not as a means of promoting such development. Vygotsky's theory views pretend play as a way of overcoming the limitations of the immediate situation and fulfilling unattainable desires, thereby contributing to the development of higher mental functions. Pretend play is acquired through social activities, often in interaction with the parents, but in such a way that children eventually can play on their own, incorporate more people into their pretend play and create more roles by themselves (Bodrova and Leong, 2015; Karpov, 2005; Nicolopoulou, 1993).

Despite the importance often attributed to play in connection with children's learning and development (Ginsberg et al., 2007; Singer et al., 2006), it has been difficult to demonstrate developmental effects of children's participation in play (Lillard et al., 2013). This may be due to the fact that play is not a uniform set of activities, but includes many different elements and forms of interaction. Johnson and colleagues (1982), for example, found a positive relation between children's constructive play and their scores on intelligence tests, but not between role play and intelligence. Connolly and Doyle (1984) found a similar relationship between children's role play and social skills. The results probably reflect the fact that intelligence tests include construction tasks such as puzzles and copying of dice patterns, while social skills require knowledge of social relationships. Thus, it is possible that constructive play promotes skills relevant to many of the typical tasks on intelligence tests, while role play promotes social skills. Another possibility is that an aptitude for construction skills leads to advanced constructive play and an aptitude for social skills to better role play. Whatever the case may be, studies suggest that children's play does not reflect their general cognitive ability, but rather different abilities related to specific activities.

It is commonly asserted that play-based teaching leads to better learning results than other forms of teaching (Weisberg et al., 2015). However, comparisons of play-based and other forms of teaching have not been able to uncover systematic differences, except that play-based teaching seems to promote children's social participation (Smith and Simon, 1984; Trawick-Smith, 1989). Such participation may in itself be positive, but does not necessarily lead to more learning. Moreover, some researchers believe that focusing on educational benefits in play may lead to a loss of the very nature of play, that play has no purpose outside the enjoyment of playing (Singer, 2013). Fun and interesting instruction is not the same as play. If a teacher presents schoolwork as play – that is, without an overriding objective – students may find it disparaging to their effort to learn.

PLAY IN DIFFERENT CONTEXTS

Play does not depend on the presence of playgrounds or the availability of ready-made toys. When children are asked they say they can play anywhere, but the type of play depends on the context: being indoor or outdoor affords different types of play (Glenn et al., 2013). In some countries, manufactured toys are a rarity (Gosso et al., 2007; Göncü et al., 2000).

Culture defines the settings for play, and the environment in which children are raised influences how children play. The same forms of play can be found in many countries, but their specific content varies with the economic and cultural characteristics of each society. For example, in small societies like the Aka and Ngandu people in Central Africa, children tend to spend much more of their play time in pretend work than in other forms of pretend play. The Ngandu people are rather competitive while the Aka people are more group oriented, and a study found that the Ngandu children spent much more time playing games than the Aka children who participated more in various forms of object play (Boyette, 2016).

Also the amount of time children spend playing varies from one country to another. First-graders in Japan and the United States play about 3 hours per day. American fifth-graders play approximately the same amount of time, while Japanese fifth-graders play 1 hour less because they spend more time on schoolwork (Stevenson and Lee, 1990). In a number of non-industrialized societies, children are expected to contribute to adult work from a relatively early age. They spend less time together with other children than children in industrialized societies, and therefore play less and become "apprentices" under adult supervision (Morelli et al., 2003; Rogoff, 2003). This may also be reflected in parental attitudes to play:

US mothers believe play promotes children's cognitive development and Chinese mothers that it benefits social and physical development, while Mexican mothers believe participation in work and work-related activities is more important for the children's development. Japanese mothers see play as a means to promote social interaction and communication, while US mothers see play as a means to get world knowledge. In some cultures it is siblings rather than parents who scaffold children's play (Kazemeini and Pajoheshgar, 2013).

Children's household chores will affect how much they play. In the United States, 5-year-olds spend an average of 15 minutes a day on chores, while 15- to 17-year-olds spend 41 minutes. Western European adolescents spend 10–20 minutes on housework, while the average in Korea is 6 minutes. In Bangladesh, the amount of time girls spend on chores increases from 1.9 hours at 4–5 years to 6.7 hours at 10–12 years. Time for play and other leisure activities is correspondingly reduced (Alsaker and Flammer, 1999; Larson and Verma, 1999). Children's contribution to housework is related to economic factors, but also to cultural attitudes. In Bangladesh, children's work contribution is a necessity, while in the United States , sharing in housework is motivated by the wish to help children become independent and self-reliant individuals. Parents in China and Japan place few demands on children's participation in housework because they are afraid it will affect their children's school performance.

Although children in some cultures have a limited amount of time for play with each other, it has been difficult to ascertain any developmental consequences of participating in housework and other activities rather than play. The extent to which children are given the opportunity to play in the traditional sense has not been shown to affect their development (Sutton-Smith, 1986), and children who spend a lot of time playing do not seem to have an advantage in terms of social or cognitive development. This may be because most children get to play enough, or because their other activities promote development in similar ways as play. It is also possible that most children in Western cultures play so much that it does not make a difference whether they play slightly more or less. Children grow up in different environments and acquire skills and knowledge through play or by performing tasks of various kinds, but this does not seem to lead to general developmental differences between them. Meaningful activities must be part of children's everyday life, but several developmental pathways lead to good cognitive and social functioning (Karpov, 2005; Larson and Verma, 1999; Maccoby, 1990).

PLAY AMONG CHILDREN WITH ATYPICAL DEVELOPMENT

Play reflects children's cognitive, social and language skills and abilities, and an atypical development in these areas will affect both the form and function of children's play. Compared to children without disabilities, children with many types of disabilities more often become spectators and spend more time playing alone and less with peers (Barton, 2015; Hestenes and Carroll, 2000).

Children with intellectual disability typically show a similar delay in play as in other areas and need more help than other children to initiate and carry out play activities (Layton et al., 2014; Venuti et al., 2009).

Children with severe congenital visual impairment are delayed in the development of all forms of play, and generally play less than other children and more often alone (Lewis et al., 2000; Preisler, 1993). Delayed motor development is common in this group, and problems with spatial orientation puts restraints on many forms of exercise play, including social play such as rough-and-tumble. Celeste (2006) describes a 4½-year-old blind girl who showed typical development in most areas, but played little and mostly on her own. In addition to the girl's lack of relevant experiences, this may reflect the fact that it was difficult for the other children to adapt their pretend play so that she, too, could take part in it. Another study with older children (6–9 years) found near normal pretend play in blind children without other social or cognitive disorders (Bishop et al., 2005). The fact that children with visual impairments begin with pretend play, albeit slightly later than others, shows that it is possible to develop such play without the use of visual make-believe cues. Voice and touch, for example, can provide cues that something is make-believe rather than real. With age, blind children usually become more integrated into play as their dependence on specific objects in symbolic play decreases and language gains a more prominent place (see p. 135).

Since much of children's early play involves motor functions, movement disorders affect the development of play (Pfeifer et al., 2011). Even moderate movement disorders can inhibit children's participation in locomotor play and changes of activity in the group. Symbolic play with objects and pretend play can be problematic when children cannot make full use of their hands. Children with more severe motor disorders typically play on their own and together with adults (Skär and Tamm, 2002). This group depends on much help and support from adults and peers in order not to be left out and become spectators rather than active partners in play (Graham et al., 2014). The physical environment can, however, be adapted to facilitate more participation, both indoors and outdoors (Woolley, 2013). When children's motor disorders prevent them from constructing or performing other play actions with their hands, they can use speech, graphic symbols or written text to instruct peers and adults to perform the actions they themselves are physically unable to perform (Batorowicz et al., 2016). In this way, by using *language for action*, they develop personal autonomy in spite of their physical limitations and dependence on others to perform the actions.

Children with autism spectrum disorder generally have difficulty understanding other people, imagining and planning the future and realizing that another person can perceive the world as different from how it actually is (see p. 256). Pretend play appears difficult for this group and a number of studies have shown that children with autism spectrum disorder rarely initiate pretend play,

even if they are able to perform pretend actions when explicitly asked to do so (Jarrold et al., 1996; Kasari et al., 2013; Lam and Yeung, 2012). For example, one boy could sit for long periods and explore an action figure, balancing it, bending its legs and arms, taking it apart, putting it back together again, and the like, seemingly without a play story. He joined peers and adults when they initiated role play, but did not engage in role play on his own (Papacek et al., 2016). In a comparison of 15-minute school recess activities among 51 5- to 12-year-old high-functioning children with autism spectrum disorder and 51 children with typical development, the children with autism spectrum disorder spent three times as much time alone (30 versus 9 percent) and just over half as much time interacting (42 versus 72 percent). The children with autism spectrum disorder initiated fewer interactions than the children with typical development, and in addition were less likely to get a response when they initiated (Locke et al., 2016). At the same time, gender differences in play preferences among boys and girls with autism spectrum disorder are similar to those of other boys and girls (Harrop et al., 2017). Studies have found that support of play activities increases social participation and interaction with peers, and helps children with autism spectrum disorder develop communication and the ability for pretense (Chang et al., 2016; Goods et al., 2013; Papacek et al., 2016).

Strategies to promote play and making physical and social adaptation to enable all the different forms of play are central elements in early intervention for all children with disabilities.

SUMMARY

1 Play is difficult to define. Important characteristics are that play has no extrinsic goal and is motivating in itself. *Exercise play* is the most common form of play in the first 3 years of life. *Rough-and-tumble* play is a form of social play. Exercise play does not aim at the practical consequences of an action, but the joy of mastery. Simple *constructive play* shows up in the beginning of the second year and stands for a major part of toddlers' play, especially in kindergarten. *Symbolic play* or *pretend play* involves imagination and taking on the role of a person or an animal, and using objects for other functions than their usual ones. Pretend play often involves several children, but can also be solitary.

2 The earliest form of play takes place in interaction with adults, while *solitary play* becomes more dominant in the second year. In *parallel play*, children play side by side with each other. In *associated group play*, children play with the same toys and interact to a certain degree, while *collaborative play* involves complementary roles and tasks. *Nonsocial play* can reflect

a preference for solitary play, while children who show active *social avoidance* are at risk of being rejected by their peers and developing internalizing disorders.

3 Different forms of play first appear at different ages and continue as part of children's repertoire as long as they play. Play gradually becomes more symbolic and involves more participants. *Decentration* means that play includes others than the child itself, *decontextualization* that children move away from concrete actions and use substitute or imaginary objects in play, and *integration* that children include several actions in the same play activity. Younger children need help to initiate and sustain play.

4 There are several views on the *function of play*. According to Piaget, play reflects cognitive development, but also contributes to development through the activities children participate in. The increase in interactive play is the result of cognitive development. In Vygotsky's theory, pretend play is acquired through social activities that eventually enable children to play on their own. Although play is fundamentally social and cultural, the individual child gradually develops the ability to create the various roles independently.

5 The same forms of play are found across *cultures*, but their content varies with the economic and cultural characteristics of each society. In some societies, children spend a lot of time playing, while in others they have many tasks in and outside the home. The extent to which the amount of play affects development has been difficult to ascertain.

6 Play reflects children's motor, cognitive, social and language skills and abilities, and any *atypical development* in these areas will affect how they play. Children with disabilities may need help to initiate and carry out play activities. However, play is equally important for children in this group as for other children.

CORE ISSUES

- The evolutionary bases of play.
- The functions of play.
- The role of play in education.

SUGGESTIONS FOR FURTHER READING

Boyette, A. H. (2016). Children's play and culture learning in an egalitarian foraging society. *Child Development*, 87, 759–769.

Christie, J. F., & Johnson, E. P. (1987). Reconceptualizing constructive play: A review of the empirical literature. *Merrill-Palmer Quarterly*, 33, 439–452.

Lewis, P. J. (2017). The erosion of play. *International Journal of Play*, 6, 10–23.

Lifter, K., et al. (2005). Developmental specificity in targeting and teaching play activities to children with pervasive developmental disorders. *Journal of Early Intervention*, 27, 247–267.

Lillard, A. S. (2017). Why do the children (pretend) play? *Trends in Cognitive Sciences*, 11, 826–834.

Papacek, A. M., et al. (2016). Play and social interaction strategies for young children with autism spectrum disorder in inclusive preschool settings. *Young Exceptional Children*, 19, 3–17.

Contents

CHAPTER 26

MEDIA AND UNDERSTANDING OF SOCIETY

This chapter discusses children in a media world and how children come to learn about the functions of society – two quite different aspects of the expansion of the social environment. Through exposure to and exploration of the digital world children get experience with real and fictional realities that are not part of their immediate surroundings. With the use of social media they communicate with friends and a wider circle of people.

The development of societal understanding begins in childhood and gains momentum in adolescence. Children and young people learn about the functions and roles of society, societal groups, local and national political leaders, the importance of money, power and status, and prevailing conflicts of interest. These insights represent important aspects of their societal understanding and becoming citizens.

CHILDREN AND ADOLESCENTS IN A MEDIA SOCIETY

Digital media are an important part of modern life and take up a major amount of children's time from early childhood on (Haughton et al., 2015; Rideout, 2013). Most digital media provide passive or interactive access to information and entertainment. *Social media* involves online communication between two or more people via cell phone, tablet or computer (Calvert, 2015; O'Keeffe, 2016). Key issues are how the new media affect children's knowledge and cognitive development, prosocial and antisocial behavior, and their general well-being. Much knowledge

has been gained about the influence of television and video, but knowledge about other media remains limited, especially their long-term effects (Anderson and Kirkorian, 2015; Calvert, 2015). Since the Internet began to take shape in 1993, development has been rapid, but children who have had today's massive exposure to digital media are barely into adolescence.

> Children are in the midst of a vast, unplanned experiment, surrounded by digital technologies that were not available but five years ago.
> (Hirsh-Pasek et al., 2015, p. 3)

Extent of media use

Most people living in modern societies own a cell phone and almost every home has a television set as well as a computer, tablet or similar device, but in many economically developing countries, electronic media are less common. Television and video (via different sources) continue to be the most prevalent forms of media in environments with children. In the United States, about 40 percent of all children are regularly exposed to television and video from the age of 3 months, and by the age of 2, 90 percent of all US children regularly watch television and video (American Academy of Pediatrics, 2011). One-year-olds watch on average 1 hour a day, increasing to about 1.5 hours by the age of 2, more time than the average child is being read to (Barr et al., 2010; Zimmerman et al., 2007). As a result, many of today's children are experienced media users by the time they start school. In 2015, average daily media use in the United States was nearly 6 hours among 8–12-year-olds. This included about 2½ hours of television, video and DVD, 1½ hours of electronic games, nearly an hour of music, a quarter of an hour of social media and half an hour of reading. Between the ages of 13 and 18 years, the corresponding figures were about 2½ hours of television, video and DVD, 1½ hours of electronic games, 2 hours of music, just over 1 hour of social media and half an hour of reading. The adolescents spent a total of 9 hours in media activity, of which 6½ hours were screen activities (Rideout, 2016). This shows that particularly the use of social media and music were increasing among this age group. Similar time use has been reported in other countries (Kanz, 2016; Padilla-Walker et al., 2016; Yu and Baxter, 2016).

Children and adolescents thus spend a lot of their time on screen-based media. An Australian survey found that this accounted for one-quarter of girls' and one-third of boys' waking time (Olds et al., 2006). By the time they finish high school, and with current media use, today's adolescents in the United States will have spent more time in front of a screen than in school (American Academy of Child and Adolescent Psychiatry, 2015). These average figures conceal large individual differences, however. Some children watch very little television and video and almost never use a tablet or computer, while others spend most of their leisure time on these activities. One study found that some 4-year-olds spent 4 hours a day watching TV at home (Fletcher et al., 2014). The central place of media in modern daily life is evidenced by the fact that around 16 percent of 0- to 1-year-olds in the United States have a television set in their bedroom. This percentage gradually increases to nearly 60 percent among 13- to 18-year-olds. The majority of children and adolescents also own a cell phone and many have gaming consoles, tablets and similar devices (Rideout, 2013, 2016). According to one study, more than 40 percent of 8- to 10-year-olds and 90 percent of 15- to 17-year-olds owned a cell phone. Forty percent of the 8- to 10-year-olds sent daily text messages, and nearly half of the 15- to 17-year-olds sent more than 30 messages a day (Lauricella et al., 2014).

A small group of adolescents spend a great deal of time online. A study of 11- to 16-year-olds from 25 European countries found that 4.4 percent made moderately excessive use of the Internet (over 4 hours a day), while 1.4 percent made very excessive use of it (over 5 hours a day). The average for all the adolescents was 1¾ hours (Blinka et al., 2015). Some adolescents show signs of withdrawal when the Internet is unavailable (see p. 524).

Parental attitudes and children's media environment

In addition to their own active use, many children are passively exposed to media. In some homes, the TV is on all the time, even when no one is watching. One study found that about one-third of parents of children aged 3–27 months left the TV turned on all or most of the time (Wartella et al., 2013). According to another study, the TV was on during half or more of the play time of a large majority of children aged 4–19 months, both when they played alone and with their mother. This reduced some of their attention as well as the quantity and quality of play (Masur et al., 2015). In a study of 0- to 6-year-olds, the children from homes with the TV on in the background much of the time participated less in reading and other activities (Vandewater et al., 2005). Both children and parents talk less when the TV is on, since the sound makes it more difficult to understand what others say (Christakis et al., 2009). Taken as a whole, conditions like these may affect children's language development.

By comparison, American parents daily spend nearly 3 hours watching television, 2 hours using their computer (outside of work) and under 1 hour playing video games (Vittrup et al., 2016). To some degree, parents control how much and what their children get to watch, and naturally there is a relationship between the media use and attitudes of parents and the extent of their children's use. For some people, media takes up a major part of life with an average of over 11 hours of screen exposure per day. Less than 20 percent of US parents of children aged 0–8 years expressed concern for their children's media use (Wartella et al., 2013). In one study, nearly 70 percent of parents of 2- to 7-year-olds agreed with the statement that early use of technology better prepares children for working life, and two-thirds disagreed that children under the age of 2 years should not watch television, as suggested by the American Academy of Pediatrics (Shifrin et al., 2015). Nearly the same number of parents believed that today's children have an early and natural understanding of how to use computers and similar technologies, and generally seemed to overestimate children's competence (Vittrup et al., 2016). But there are cultural differences. Many British parents, for example, are concerned about the use of e-books among their 0- to 8-year-old children (Kucirkova and Littleton, 2016).

To some extent, parents use electronic media – mainly television and video – together with their children, especially at younger ages, and fathers take more part in electronic games than mothers (Connell et al., 2015). Children quickly become independent, however, and the time children and parents spend on media together diminishes significantly between early childhood and the beginning of school (Rideout, 2014; Wartella et al., 2013). The fact that a majority of children have media access in their room also reflects the differences in media use between parents and children. When adults and children watch television together, it is usually to watch the adults' programs. Many preschoolers and younger schoolchildren watch adult-directed programs such as news, entertainment and movies. Younger schoolchildren can become anxious watching news about fires, floods and other disasters, while older children think that reports about murder and other types of crimes are most frightening (Smith and Wilson, 2002; Valerio et al., 1997). Several studies have additionally shown that younger children and adults communicate less while watching television than when reading a book or playing together (Nathanson and Rasmussen, 2011; Pempek et al., 2014).

Many parents establish rules for using games and video, for example that homework and other tasks must be finished first, but what children are allowed to do also depends on the parents' activities. If they themselves are often busy, they allow children more leeway and also use media access as reward or punishment to mediate other behaviors. Many parents, however, try to teach their children to regulate their own time in front of the screen (Jago et al., 2016; Schaan and Melzer, 2015). On the other hand, parents' emotional involvement in children's online use seems to contribute to fewer restrictions (Schaan and Melzer, 2015).

The use of media is an integral part of modern society. The large differences in media use and access among children and families are related to factors such as children's temperament, gender, geographic location (urban or rural), siblings, parenting style, attitudes to and use of media, socioeconomic background and the school's policies on electronic media use. This makes it difficult to separate the effects of media from general changes in technology and society. It becomes a question of whether media contributes to shaping children's worlds, or whether their content merely reflects the world as it is.

Media and learning

Since electronic media occupy such a major part of children's lives, it is important to understand their possible impact on learning and the acquisition of knowledge. A myriad of educational computer programs and apps exists today, but with the exception of television and video, many applications of electronic media are fairly new, and knowledge about their impact on development and learning remains limited. Although the use of electronic media has become part of children's curriculum in many schools, no one knows how the content of these vast electronic offerings affects thinking and learning (Guernsey, 2017; Lauricella et al., 2017).

Research shows a complex picture. It is not simply a question of time use, but of content and how impressionable children are (Guernsey, 2017; Wartella et al., 2016). Any positive or negative impact will depend on a) the content of the media, b) how it is adapted to the child's age, cognition and language, and c) the context in which the media are used, for example, whether the child is alone or together with other children or adults (Barr and Linebarger, 2017). Videos with engaging stories and educational content adapted to the child's age can promote imaginative thinking. Ready-made stories and little quiet and empty time for reflection, on the other hand, can reduce children's creativity and imagination (Calvert, 2015). Although educational videos can benefit children's understanding and knowledge, experiencing two-dimensional images on a screen cannot replace the experience of a three-dimensional physical world. Infants and toddlers in particular have a poorer understanding of something presented on a screen than in the real world – Anderson and Pempek (2005) refer to this as "video deficit." Any possible benefits for very young children are uncertain, especially considering that the time spent in front of the screen inevitably displaces other toys and activities (Haughton et al., 2015). Nonetheless, many parents still consider early media use to be educational and believe that younger children in particular learn a lot by watching television and video (Rideout, 2014). Video series such as *Baby Einstein* claim to promote infants' and toddlers' exploration and learning, but studies show that young children learn little from these videos. When parents were asked to assess how much their child learned from a video, their assessment had more to do with how much the parents themselves liked the video than with how much their child actually learned (DeLoache et al., 2010).

Although slightly older children can benefit from educational media (Gentile, 2011; Gentile et al., 2009), their usage decreases with age (Rideout, 2014) and studies generally find little effect on learning (Anderson and Kirkorian, 2015). A number of US studies found a greater vocabulary increase in preschool children who watched programs that included explanations of vocabulary than in children who did not watch these types of programs (Rice et al., 1990; Wright et al., 2001). Not all television programs designed to promote reading skills had a measurable effect on children's reading skills, however, even if the programs were popular and the children enjoyed watching them. It is possible that the development of good reading skills requires a more active effort, and that the television medium is not suited to this type of learning (Huston and Wright, 1998; Linebarger and Walker, 2005). Furthermore, television programs generally make small demands on vocabulary: 3,000 words stand for 95 percent of the words used in American children's and entertainment programs (Webb and Rodgers, 2009). In addition, television and video can promote passive viewing behavior. The content, often well-designed and ready-made, can reduce children's reflective thinking and problem solving (Anderson and Kirkorian, 2015). Children become consumers and experience the world in a different way than the active and exploratory child Piaget places such emphasis on.

Educational games encouraging active participation can lead to better learning. Some video games, for example, have been found to promote spatial skills (Powers et al., 2013; Redick and Webster, 2014) or enhance performance on tasks requiring visual attention and quick reactions (Spence and Feng, 2010). Educational programs designed to improve children's math skills have also shown positive results (Drivjers et al., 2016). Nonetheless, there remains considerable disagreement about the effect of interactive computer games on everyday cognitive functioning (Bavelier et al., 2010; Owen et al., 2010).

Extent of media exposure and learning

Media use can have both positive and negative effects, but always involves less time for other activities, including sleep. Adolescents in the United States sleep less than just a few years ago: more screen time leads to later bedtimes and less sleep (Hale and Guan, 2015). There is no link between regular television viewing (2 hours per day) and learning, school work and attention problems. A moderate amount of television and video, and with a certain proportion of informational programs, seems to increase children's level of knowledge, while a lot of time spent watching ordinary entertainment content has a negative effect on academic performance (Anderson and Kirkorian, 2015). There is a positive relation between the time spent on educational games and school performance (Hastings et al., 2009), but a negative one between total screen time and school grades (Kirkorian et al., 2008). One study found that 10- to 19-year-old boys who played online games spent 30 percent less time on reading, and the girls 34 percent less time on homework, than those who did not play (Cummings and Vandewater, 2007). Studies show that the acquisition of reading skills can be inhibited by little time spent reading during the first few years of school (Koolstra and Van Der Voort, 1996).

Rideout and associates (2010) found that nearly half of a group of 8- to 18-year-old heavy media users had fair or poor grades, compared to light media users where under a quarter had such grades at school. However, what is cause and effect remains uncertain. It is possible that children watch a lot of television and video because they have little or poor contact with their peers and participate in few other activities. When adolescents spend a lot of time playing video games, it may be that they experience social and personal problems, but feel they master the game (Gentile, 2009; Kowert et al., 2015; Rasmussen et al., 2015). Adolescents in this group have higher rates of depression than those with light or moderate media use, and suicide attempts are more frequent among this group (Johansson and Götestam, 2004; Messias et al.,

2011). One study found that children and adolescents with excessive use of online gaming showed anxiety and depression, and that these symptoms were reduced when they stopped playing online games (Gentile et al., 2011a). Such findings underline the importance of parents and teachers following up children and adolescents with an atypical amount or pattern of media use.

Prosocial and antisocial effects of media

Research has particularly focused on how television and other media content affects the attitudes and behavior of children and adolescents (Anderson et al., 2010; Prot et al., 2014). Television and streaming media offer a wide range of content: family idylls among ethnic groups, everyday environments of adolescents and young adults, or "reality" shows showing young people in a variety of life situations. Observing how relational problems are resolved, for example, can promote development of both prosocial and antisocial attitudes. A study of 13-year-olds in Singapore found that those who preferred TV programs with prosocial content were more positive to helping and sharing and less accepting of aggressive attitudes than children who preferred programs with other content (Gentile et al., 2009). Studies have found that exposure to a number of such programs – rather than total viewing time – had an impact on young people's self-esteem and attitudes toward parenting (Ex et al., 2002; Martins and Jensen, 2014). The way in which problems and moral dilemmas are solved in programs watched by children and adolescents can thus affect their self-perception, values and attitudes.

Television and aggression

Violence is common in media: Studies show that 70 percent of all TV programs for children include physical violence in one form or another, more than programs aimed at adults, with a violent episode about every 4 minutes (Potter, 1999; Wilson et al., 2002). Children and adolescents express a greater preference for violent games than for television and video with violent content (Funk et al., 2004).

There have been two key assumptions about the impact of observing violence and aggressive behavior on television and other media: that it

leads to either an increase or to a decrease in children's aggression. From the perspective of *psychodynamic* theory, observing violence should lead to a reduction in arousal (catharsis) and therefore a reduction in actual violent behavior (Feshbach, 1961). This point of view has little support in research. There are no studies that show a relation between exposure to violent media and a decrease in aggression, while nearly all studies have found positive correlations between exposure and aggression, although the effects are moderate (Greitemeyer and Mügge, 2014; Huesmann et al., 2003).

Studies thus suggest that violent media content can affect children's and adolescents' attitudes to violence and increase their likelihood of getting involved in violent situations themselves (Kanz, 2016). This is in line with most theories of aggression, including Crick and Dodge's social cognitive model (see p. 483). According to *cognitive behavioral theory*, children imitate the people they see on the television, and their aggressive behavior increases when they observe others performing violent actions. In addition, their inhibition to aggression can be weakened by exposure to violence (Bandura, 1994). One US longitudinal study found that boys who watched a lot of videos with violent content at 2–5 years of age showed more antisocial behavior at the age of 7–10 years than boys who did not watch as many violent videos. There was no corresponding connection for girls, and the children's total TV viewing time had no impact on the development of antisocial behavior (Christakis and Zimmerman, 2007). Another explanation is that media content contributes to forming children's and adolescents' expectations of other people's behavior and their perception of how conflicts are resolved. This can result in both prosocial and antisocial behavior, depending on the content and the way it is interpreted. For children who observe a lot of violence in the media, violence will appear to be a normal solution to conflicts. They form scripts (see p. 202) containing aggressive elements, while children who watch prosocial programs more often form scripts with prosocial content (Huesmann, 2007; Huesmann et al., 2003).

Thus, children are affected by their media experiences, but the effects are complex (Anderson et al., 2010; Prot et al., 2014). How children react to screen media depends on characteristics such as age, gender and cognitive skills (Wiedeman et al., 2015), and whether they can identify with the situation. In cases in which it is difficult for children to distinguish between fantasy and reality, media have a greater impact on their perception of the world. Studies show that toddlers more often imitate the actions of real-life people than those they have seen on video (Nielsen et al., 2008). Since cartoons seem less real than movies with people, they more clearly represent fantasy. In one study, many children stated that they enjoyed watching programs designed for adults, but also that they had felt scared and gotten nightmares. This, too, supports the assumption that films in which real people show violent behavior have a greater impact than violence in cartoons (Gunter and McAleer, 1997). Also the presence of adults viewing may influence how children perceive the violence they see. A comment made by an adult can sometimes change a child's view of what is happening, and children can interpret the silence of an adult co-viewer as supporting the behavior observed on the screen (Cantor and Wilson, 2003). Additionally, children are more likely to imitate the violent behavior of a "hero" who is rewarded for his aggressive actions than that of a ruthless killer who is caught and put in jail (Huesmann, 2007). Children do not merely imitate, but make sense of the actions they observe based on their general social understanding.

Computer games

Over 90 percent of computer games considered suitable for 10-year-olds include hitting, shooting and other violent elements (Gentile and Gentile, 2008). Compared with video and television, computer games require more active participation. While children and adolescents who watch television are in a certain sense passive onlookers, computer games often involve performing make-believe destructive actions and being rewarded with a higher point score (Hastings et al., 2009). Much time spent on gaming seems to lead to higher levels of arousal, more aggressive thoughts and behavior, and less empathy and helping behavior. This is mainly related to physical aggression in boys and relational aggression in girls (Anderson et al., 2010; Gentile et al., 2011b; Huesmann, 2010). Playing games alone in particular leads to increased aggression, while gaming together with others can reduce aggression (Velez et al., 2016). Gaming is not a minority phenomenon: many adolescents

spend many hours a week on video games containing a lot of violence (Rideout, 2015) and may therefore bring with it major social consequences (Anderson, 2004). Studies in other countries report similar findings, but the effect on behavior shows some variation depending on cultural attitudes (Krahé, 2016). However, studies have also found that prosocial computer games lead to more prosocial behavior and less aggression (Greitemeyer and Mügge, 2014).

A possible reason for the connection between aggression and violent computer games may be that aggressive children are drawn to such games. A greater likelihood of aggressive behavior may also be due to the fact that games with violent content prime children and adolescents to form scripts containing violent elements (see above), and thus more easily activate aggressive thoughts (Greitemeyer and Mügge, 2014). When violence becomes an appropriate and expected response to certain situations, it will affect the attitudes of children and adolescents. Moreover, exposure to violent games can lead to a *desensitization* to violence and fewer negative emotional reactions to observing violence (Hastings et al., 2009; Krahé et al., 2011; Orue et al., 2011). The effect of violence in videos and games is furthermore compounded: children who are exposed to violent content are affected by the content while at the same time losing out on the positive effects of being exposed to more prosocial content.

Many factors thus contribute to the impact of more or less exposure to electronic media. Studies have generally shown small or moderate correlations between media exposure in childhood and later violent and criminal behavior. This is not to say that their effect is insignificant, but underlines the fact that media is one of several sources that influence children's development of interaction strategies and behaviors (Anderson et al., 2015; Bushman and Anderson, 2015). At the same time, it is important to emphasize that only a small percentage of children and adolescents show high levels of aggression. Neither do most adults become involved in criminal behavior aside from traffic offenses and similar, regardless of whether they do or do not like movies with a lot of violent content.

Social media

Social media such as *Facebook*, *Twitter* and *YouTube* are systems that enable two or more people to communicate and share content. They are used to communicate with individuals and groups, friends, classmates and other people that share a particular interest, such as geology, Harry Potter, bird watching or sports. Some people use social media to spread their views or to sell their music, their fashion designs or other products and services. The most active and frequent users of social media are adolescents and young adults, and their numbers have increased dramatically in recent years. In the Netherlands, about 60 percent of 10 to 11-year-olds and almost 90 percent of 12 to 16-year-olds used the Internet to communicate via chat groups or messaging with an average of 11 hours per week (van den Eijnden et al., 2010, 2011). Similar figures apply to the United States , where 20 percent of adolescents said they checked social media more than five times a day (Lauricella et al., 2014; Rideout, 2012). When children and adolescents spend a lot of time on social media, it leaves less time for face-to-face communication with one or more other persons.

In today's society, cell phones and social media contribute to shaping the social patterns of children and adolescents in significant ways. Gatherings and activities are largely coordinated via e-mail and cell phone calls or text messages; established meeting places play less of a role than before (Kaare et al., 2007; Lenhart et al., 2010). This means that children and adolescents depend on being contacted by others – or initiate contact themselves – in order to take part in social events. Some of them will miss out on many social events, not because they are unpopular or actively being avoided, but because they are overlooked.

Negative social patterns are changing as well, and children and adolescents in many countries are bullied on social media, via e-mail and cell phone messages (Navarro et al., 2016). *Cyberbullying* has the same consequences as other types of bullying: depression, low self-esteem, learned helplessness, social anxiety and alienation (Giumetti and Kowalski, 2016; see p. 477). Moreover, this form of bullying can be more pervasive

The cell phone plays a key role in the social life of children and adolescents.

than direct bullying because it is impossible to protect oneself without severing all electronic connections with the outside world and thereby isolate oneself from the social community at large (Patchin and Hinduja, 2010; Wong-Lo and Bullock, 2011).

Studies show that most children and adolescents follow up existing friends on social media, while some also look for new relationships. Some socially anxious adolescents report that they find it easier to open up for *self-disclosure* (see p. 444) and communicate about intimate topics online than face to face. This applies especially to people they know in real life, while pure online contacts are perceived to be less close (Liu and Brown, 2014; Valkenburg and Peter, 2007). Some children are drawn to social media because they feel socially isolated and have difficulty establishing social relationships in the real world. Some adolescents show atypical development with signs of Internet addiction (see p. 68). Their thoughts are dominated by the Internet, which they use to escape negative thoughts and feelings, experiencing discomfort when they do not have online access and continuing their online activities although they have decided to stop. In many cases, social media is the main factor contributing to dependency (Johansson and Götestam, 2004; van den Eijnden et al., 2011).

The use of social media is considerable and may rise even higher, and the long-term positive and negative consequences of this will only show themselves in the future. From the perspective of developmental psychology, it is important to monitor how they impact the cognitive, emotional and social development of children and adolescents, their communication and interaction patterns and their perceptions of themselves and others.

SOCIETAL KNOWLEDGE

All children grow up in a society. As they grow older, children gain an understanding of how the society functions, of societal structures and social similarities and differences (Buchanan-Barrow, 2005). Societal cognition is an extension and further development of understanding individual thought and action, and entails the construction of a set of concepts and a "theory" of society (Hatano and Takahashi, 2005). Children's experience of themselves and their own position in

society and that of others provide an important basis for the development of societal knowledge (de França, 2016; Killen et al., 2016).

Economics and social structure

As early as toddlerhood, children begin to understand that money is used to buy things, but they have little understanding of where money comes from (Berti, 2005; Webley, 2005). In the following example, Berti talks to 3;6-year-old Esther about work and salary (Berti and Bombi, 1988, p. 61):

B: *How do daddies come to have the money they need?*
E: *They take it.*
B: *How do they take it?*
E: *They take in their pocket.*
B: *The money they have in their pocket, was it also there yesterday?*
E: *Yes.*
B: *And before then?*
E: *It was in their pockets.*
B: *When it's finished what does Daddy do?*
E: *He takes it from his other pocket.*
B: *And when that one's also empty what does he do?*
E: *He takes more.*
B: *Where from?*
E: *From wallets.*

Six-year-olds only have a nascent understanding of economic reality, such as the fact that shop owners have to pay for the goods they sell (Jahoda, 1984, p. 72):

I: *What do you do when you buy something?*
S: *Give the shop lady the money.*
I: *What does she do with it?*
S: *Gives the money back.*
I: *Is it the same money?*
S: *Yes.*
I: *Can you tell more about this?*
S: *The people pays her, she pays the people.*
I: *Where does the milk in the shop come from?*
S: *Cows – the man brings it.*
I: *Does the lady have to pay for the milk?*
S: *The lady pays the man and the man pays the lady because he gives her milk.*

Around the age of 7–8 years, children begin to form a basic understanding of the parts of society they themselves belong to, but have no knowledge of public institutions and governance, and usually are unaware that a shopkeeper makes money by selling things. They believe that any profits are given to poor or disabled people, but their explanations also reflect their personal experiences. Children who have sold things at garage sales or in the street have a more developed understanding of profit than children without this type of experience (Berti, 2005; Webley, 2005).

Around 9 to 10 years of age, children realize that someone must be supplying the supermarket with groceries, and that these are bought from farmers, fishermen and others, but they fail to understand the larger picture and the various functions of the people in the system. Children do not understand the relationship between bank deposits and loans, that a principal has to get money from someone in order to run the school, or that a shopkeeper must generate earnings. This is from an interview with a 10-year-old (Jahoda, 1984, p. 74):

I: *Who pays the shop lady?*
S: *The manager.*
I: *Where does he get the money from?*
S: *Off some of the money out of the till.*
I: *Is the manager doing a job?*
S: *No.*
I: *Where does he get the money for his food?*
S: *He might have another job.*

Not until the age of about 13 do children begin to understand how the person who pays wages earns his or her money.

School is the first social institution children encounter, and by the age of 11 they have gained an understanding of how school works as a system, like Jaqui (Emler, 1992, pp. 71–72):

J: *They [teachers] could make classroom rules but they would not be able to make whole school rules.*
I: *Who can make school rules?*
J: *Headmaster.*
I: *Could he make a rule to say children should come to school.*
J: *No, that would be the government.*

At this age, children accept the teacher's authority in the classroom, but are also aware of its limits. They consider it ridiculous, for example, that the teacher should decide when they have to go to bed. Younger children are more willing to accept this type of authority from teachers (Emler, 1992).

According to Furth (1980), children's general cognitive development furnishes the basis for their understanding of society as a hierarchical structure. Jahoda (1984) emphasizes the fact that children and adolescents construct knowledge based on the information they have about different areas, rather than merely reproducing what they have learned at school or heard from adults. Children's incomplete understanding of societal functions is due to the relative complexity of these issues as well as children's lack of domain-specific knowledge. The answers in the previous dialogues above reflect the children's efforts to use their own experience to create meaning and context in areas they have little knowledge about.

Social inequality

Children notice differences between people early on. In preschool age, many children become aware that some people earn more than others, especially those they perceive to be in a position of power, such as policemen. When asked to describe a person in a picture, they often name the person's profession, such as plumber, doctor or businessman (Emler and Dickinson, 2005). At this age, children also begin to pay attention to clues about wealth and status, such as how people dress and live, and in some areas the color of their skin. Children use these clues to evaluate the abilities and popularity of other people, and whether they themselves would want to be friends with them (Shutts et al., 2013).

Sigelman (2012) found that 6-year-olds had difficulties explaining why some people are rich, even though some of them said they had a good job. Marco, aged 6;8 years, believed that everyone who worked was rich (Berti and Bombi, 1988, p. 70):

B: *How come there are rich people and poor people?*
M: *Because the poor don't have any money.*
B: *And why don't they have any money?*

M: *Because they don't work.*
B: *And the rich, on the other hand?*
M: *They go to work.*

Many of the 10-year-olds in Sigelman's study mentioned a good job in addition to effort and inheritance, while the 14-year-olds additionally included abilities and education. Another study found that children aged 10–12 years had a relatively good understanding of the social class they belonged to, but also associated poor people with fewer positive traits than rich people (Mistry et al., 2015).

At the same time, younger children are concerned with equality and justice, and often argue that differences are unjust (Almås et al., 2010), such as 6-year-old Mary (Leahy, 1983, p. 99):

M: *Some people don't got no refrigerators, nothing to eat . . . if they don't eat they gonna die.*

At 7–8 years of age, children begin using more judgmental terms to describe different professions. Some are great, others are bad jobs or regular jobs. Common explanations for why some people earn more than others is that some jobs are important or strenuous, or require knowledge or education: doctors earn more than bus drivers because "drivers just drive a bus, while doctors cure people."

In late childhood and adolescence, explanations of social inequality involve more psychological factors and differences in traits, thoughts and motives. Social class differences collide with principles of equality or are justified by ideas about equality, as in the case of 12-year-old Dean (Leahy, 1983, p. 99):

D: *I think that they should all be the same, each have the same amount of money because then the rich people won't think they are so big.*

Adolescents use words like responsibility, qualifications and abilities when they argue why some jobs are better paid than others. The rich and the poor are perceived to be different types of people with different thoughts, feelings and characteristics. Until the age of about 14 years, arguments in favor of equality dominate, while such arguments make up less than half of all explanations

after the age of 17 years. Seventeen-year-old Rose is aware of the contradictions on the issue of inequality (Leahy, 1983, p. 99):

R: *If you look at it one way you say, "Why?" It's so unfair. . . . Like why can't it be equally balanced? But I guess people who are rich, they work for what they have.*

Some older adolescents perceive personal economy as a reward merited by individual effort. Seventeen-year-old John argues more clearly in favor of social inequality (Leahy, 1983, p. 99):

J: *They don't want to go for a job. it's their own fault. They deserve to be poor . . . they're just hanging out, doing nothing. A person like that deserves to be poor.*

In later adolescence, factors such as market forces, class and political power become increasingly important (Emler and Dickinson, 2005). People who belong to the same social class are perceived as similar because they share psychological characteristics (Leahy, 1983). Adolescents rank different professional groups approximately the same as adults do, but their own social background impacts their evaluation. Middle-class adolescents are generally more aware of occupational status, while adolescents from working-class backgrounds overestimate the status of skilled workers in society. Middle-class adolescents also estimate the wage differences between people with and without an education to be greater than adolescents with a working-class background do (Emler and Dickinson, 2005).

Becoming citizens

Societal reasoning develops from a primary focus on the individual's own situation to including the needs of others and factors of general importance to a society (Helwig and Turiel, 2002). It is the mental schemas children and adolescents have formed about political processes and the workings of society that are activated when they meet with political dilemmas and begin to fulfill their role as citizens (Torney-Purta, 1992). In adolescence and emergent adulthood, young people come to integrate the understanding of social structure, organization, rules and roles that is necessary to fully become a member of society (de França, 2016).

SUMMARY

1 Children are exposed to electronic media early on, with a continual increase in use throughout childhood and adolescence, but with large individual differences. Parents try to regulate their children's media use and to some extent spend time on media together with their younger children. Media takes away time from other activities.

2 The learning effect of electronic media is small for toddlers, and two-dimensional images cannot replace the experience of a three-dimensional physical world. Slightly older children and adolescents may profit from media with educational content and purpose, but many educational programs only show a minimal learning effect. There is disagreement about potential positive influences of computer games on cognitive functioning. There is a negative relation between a lot of time spent gaming and academic performance.

3 The *psychodynamic* assumption that watching violence leads to a reduction in violent behavior has little support in research. According to *cognitive behavioral theory*, children imitate aggressive behavior when they see others perform violent actions on video and have less inhibition of aggressive behavior. Another explanation is that the content contributes to shaping children's and adolescents' expectations of other people's behavior and their perceptions of how conflicts can be resolved. Children who witness large amounts of violence in the media form *scripts* containing aggressive elements, while children who watch prosocial programs more often form scripts with prosocial content. Exposure to violent games can lead to a *desensitization* to violence.

4 Prosocial games can lead to an increase in prosocial behavior. Many electronic games include make-believe destructive actions that give a higher score and lead to higher levels of arousal, more aggressive thoughts and behavior, and less empathy and helping behavior. There is a moderate relation between children's preference for violent games and later violent and criminal behavior. Excessive amounts of time spent on electronic games can be an expression of social and personal problems.

5 Social media use increases with age, and most adolescents use social media daily. Children and adolescents follow up their existing friends and look for new relationships online. *Cyberbullying* has the same consequences as other types of bullying but can be more pervasive because it is impossible to protect against. Some children are drawn to social media because they are socially isolated and have difficulty establishing social relationships in real life. Some adolescents show atypical use and signs of Internet addiction.

6 *Societal cognition* involves the construction of a set of concepts or a "theory" about society. In preschool age, children have no coherent understanding of society's functions. In early school age, children begin to understand the parts of society they themselves belong to, and on their way to adolescence, children acquire a basic understanding of societal functions and how different systems work.

7 Children notice differences between people early on. In preschool age, they become aware that some people earn more than others. In early school age, children begin to use more judgmental terms to describe different professions, but also give more rational explanations for differences in wages and status. Children typically argue that differences are unjust, while positive justifications become more prominent in adolescence. Social background impacts these evaluations.

CORE ISSUES

- The impact of media use on development and learning.
- The impact of media use on social interaction patterns.
- The impact of media on prosocial and antisocial behavior.
- The bases of political attitudes.

SUGGESTIONS FOR FURTHER READING

Anderson, C. A., et al. (2010). Violent video game effects on aggression, empathy, and prosocial behavior in Eastern and Western countries. *Psychological Bulletin, 136*, 151–173.

Barrett, M., & Buchanan-Barrow, E. (Eds) (2005). *Children's understanding of society.* New York, NY: Psychology Press.

Berti, A. E., & Bombi, A. S. (1988). *The child's construction of economics.* Cambridge: Cambridge University Press.

Blinka, L., et al. (2015). Excessive internet use in European adolescents: What determines differences in severity? *International Journal of Public Health, 60*, 249–256.

Christakis, D. A., et al. (2009). Audible television and decreased adult words, infant vocalizations, and conversational turns: A population-based study. *Archives of Pediatric and Adolescence Medicine, 163*, 554–558.

DeLoache, J. S., et al. (2010). Do babies learn from baby media? *Psychological Science, 21*, 1570–1574.

Huesmann, L. R. (2007). The impact of electronic media violence: Scientific theory and research. *Journal of Adolescent Health, 41*, S6–S13.

Kucirkova, N., & Littleton, K. (2016). *The digital reading habits of children: A National survey of parents' perceptions of and practices in relation to children's reading for pleasure with print and digital books.* Book Trust. Available from: <http://www.booktrust.org.uk/news-andblogs/news/1371>.

Lauricella, A. R., et al. (2015). Young children's screen time: The complex role of parent and child factors. *Journal of Applied Developmental Psychology, 36*, 11–17.

CHAPTER 27

TOWARD ADULTHOOD

hildhood and adolescence are valuable periods in their own right and at the same time form the basis for life as an adult. Adolescence completes the developmental pathways of childhood and marks out the course for a more autonomous and independent existence (Smetana et al., 2006). It is a period characterized by puberty and sexual maturation and brings with it new types of relationships and social activities. Adolescence is replaced by *emerging adulthood*, which extends into the twenties and is described in slightly different ways: as an extension of adolescence (Wyn, 2004), a separate stage of development (Arnett, 2006; Arnett et al., 2014) or a transition period to adulthood (Côté, 2014). Emerging adulthood varies in length and shows major variations along the way, but typical of this period is the transition from one's former family to a new one, from dependence to independence and from mandatory school attendance to personal choices regarding education, occupation and lifestyle, with all the changes in social roles, goals and responsibilities this entails. At the same time, young adults spend more time alone than in the periods before and after, in which they generally live together with family (Larson, 1990). It is an age at which many feel uncertain about their future and the world, but it is also a window of opportunity for individuals to make changes to their existence and the course of their lives, for example when those who have grown up under difficult family circumstances show resilience and exploit their independence to create a good life for themselves as adults (Masten, 2016). Additionally, early adulthood is an important element in the development of societies, and community engagement contributes to a positive development (O'Connor et al., 2011).

Since many of the choices an individual makes in emerging adulthood affect the remainder of adult life, it is an important phase from a life-span perspective (Schulenberg et al., 2004). In the past 100 years, higher education has evolved from an elite privilege for the few to become a natural part of the lives of most adolescents and young adults (Snyder et al., 2016). In industrialized societies, education is an important pursuit for many at this age (Arnett, 2006). The current pattern of education also affects cultural continuity and the relationship between generations in fundamental ways. Previously, occupations were largely "inherited," whether it meant following in the footsteps of a physician or a blacksmith, but many millennials choose an education different from the one their parents chose. This applies equally to working-class children who become academics as to children of university professors who choose a non-academic career or no higher education at all. Early adulthood and the transition to adult life is usually shorter for those who do not continue to study, but move straight on to working life.

The experience of being an adult comes gradually, and many young adults report a sense of standing between adolescence and adulthood (Arnett, 2001). Nelson and Barry (2005) found that 25 percent of 19- to 25-year-olds considered themselves adults, while 69 percent felt they were adults in some, but not in all areas. They have an adult existence in the sense that many of them have left their homes and live on their own, with a spouse or a partner, but are adolescents in the sense that today's financial situation allows parents to influence their child's transition to adulthood, but also to maintain a certain degree of dependence in the relationship (Fingerman and Yahirun, 2015). The key role parents or others of the parental generation have played in enculturating their children is completed, however. They have become independent members of society and are in the process of establishing more stable romantic relationships; for them, the role as parent is not merely a biological option, but a cultural probability. Establishing one's own (first) home is a developmental task that belongs to emerging adulthood, and studies show that it often leads to positive changes in the parent–child relationship. But above all, it is a steady job and the independence that comes with it that distinguish the established adult life (Seiffge-Krenke, 2015).

The metaphor "the child is father of the man" denotes that the adult individual is shaped by his upbringing. Nonetheless, development is not finished at the threshold to adulthood – the transition itself is considered a particularly important part of the life span and can entail both continuity and discontinuity in social development and mental health (Schulenberg et al., 2004). Prosocial and moral reasoning continue to develop (Eisenberg et al., 2005). The formation of identity – which is usually considered part of adolescent development – can in some cases last well into an individual's thirties (Cramer, 2017), and the development of personality undergoes its largest average changes between the ages of 20 and 40 years (Roberts et al., 2006). Neither is it a linear transition – emergent adulthood is characterized by many changes in residence (including moving back home during periods) and partners (Arnett, 2006), as well as in degree of dependence (Cohen et al., 2003). Both the establishment of relationships and experienced loneliness show major individual differences at this age (Bowker et al., 2014).

From a life-span perspective, the functional changes that take place in adulthood can be studied as developmental phenomena in line with the changes taking place in childhood and adolescence (Baltes et al., 2006). This calls for a broader concept of development than, for example, that of Werner (1948), who proposes that traits and abilities become qualitatively and quantitatively more complex, extensive, and the like. In the course of the life span, development also includes periods of declining characteristics and skills, and the need to adapt to weaker functioning. In this perspective, too, developmental changes are time-bound, but with variations in the direction of change.

GLOSSARY

See subject index to find the terms in the text

A-not-B error. Children look for an object where they have previously found it (position A), rather than where they saw the object being hidden (position B).

Abstraction. A cognitive process that gives rise to a generalized category of something concrete, such as people, objects and events that are associated with less detailed features, aspects or similarities.

Accommodation. Alteration or formation of a new cognitive *schema* in order to better adapt the *cognitive structure* to external conditions; see *assimilation*.

Acculturation. The cultural adjustment of individuals or groups in meeting new cultures.

Action potential. The repeated discharges that occur when electrochemical impulses are transmitted through the neuron.

Activity. A stable and complex system of goal-oriented activities or interactions that are related to each other by theme or situation and have taken place over a long period of time.

Activity state. In fetuses, a condition characterized by specific frequency patterns of heartbeat and movement.

Activity theory. The elaboration and revision of Vygotsky's *theory* by neo-Vygotskians.

Activity-specific. Refers to skills and abilities that are unique to a particular activity; see *domain-general* and *domain-specific*.

Adaptation. Changes that increase the ability of a species or an individual to survive and cope with the environment.

Adaptive behavior. Behavior that enables an individual to survive and cope with the physical, social and cultural challenges of the environment.

Adaptive function. Behavioral consequences that contribute to an individual's survival.

Adolescence. The period between *childhood* and adulthood, age 12–18.

Adoption Study. Study comparing adopted children with their biological relatives and/or family members who have adopted them; used to shed light on the importance of genes and the environment.

Affect attunement. See *emotional attunement*.

Affordance. According to Gibson, the relationship between the properties of the physical world and possible actions, such as perceiving an object as "graspable" or a surface as "walkable."

Age score. The average age at which children achieve a certain *raw score* on a *test*; sometimes called mental age in connection with *intelligence tests*.

Aggression. Behavior intended to harm living beings, objects or materials; see *hostile aggression*, *instrumental aggression*, *open aggression* and *relational aggression*.

Agreeableness. One of the *Big Five personality traits*.

Allele. One of several variants of the same gene at the same location on a *chromosome*, and controlling the same genetic characteristics.

Ambidextrous. Equal dexterity with both hands.

Amodal perception. "Without modality," perceptual characteristics that are not specific to a particular sense, but common across two or more senses.

Anal phase. According to *psychoanalytic theory*, the second stage in *psychosexual development*, in which the area around the anus becomes a source of pleasure; age 2–3 years; see *genital phase*, *latency phase*, *oral phase* and *phallic phase*.

Anatomically detailed dolls. Dolls with genitals used in connection with forensic interviews of younger children as well as older children with learning disabilities who may have been victims of sexual abuse.

Angelman syndrome. Genetic syndrome characterized by hyperactivity and severe learning disabilities; caused by a missing part of chromosome pair 15, inherited from the mother; the counterpart to *Prader-Willi syndrome*.

Anorexia nervosa. Eating disorder involving excessive dieting, under-eating and weight loss; see *bulimia*.

Antisocial behavior. Behavior that shows little concern for other people's feelings and needs, and violates the common social and ethical norms of a culture; see *prosocial behavior*.

Archival research. The use of psychological reports and other historical sources in research.

Assessment (in clinical work). The mapping of an individual's strengths and weaknesses, competencies and problem areas.

Assimilation. The adaptation, integration or interpretation of external influences in relation to existing cognitive *schemas*; see *accommodation*.

Associated group play. Form of *group play* in which children engage in the same activities and interact to a certain degree.

Association. A link, such as between a stimulus and a reaction or action, or between ideas or thoughts.

Attachment. A *behavioral system* that includes various forms of *attachment behavior*; the system is activated when a child finds herself at a shorter or a longer distance from the person she is attached to, and experiences emotions such as pain, fear, stress, uncertainty or anxiety; the term is also used to describe emotional attachment to a caregiver; Attachment can be secure, insecure and disorganized; see *exploration*.

Attachment behavior. According to Bowlby, any behavior that enables a person to achieve or maintain closeness with another, clearly identified person who is perceived to be better able to cope with the environment; includes signal behavior and approach behavior.

Attention deficit disorder; ADD. Characterized by impulsivity, low ability to concentrate on a task, and little sustained attention, may experience problems with emotional regulation, motor coordination, working memory, spatial perception and executive function.

Attention deficit hyperactivity disorder; ADHD. Attention deficit disorder with restlessness and a high level of activity.

Atypical development. Course of development that differs significantly from the development of the majority of a *population*; see *individual differences* and *typical development*.

Augmentative and alternative communication. Non-vocal communication methods that can replace and supplement the functions of speech.

Authoritarian parenting. Parenting style that places high demands on the child and in which parents show a large degree of control and *responsivity*; see *authoritative parenting*, *disengaged* and *permissive parenting style*.

Authoritative parenting. Parenting style that places high demands on the child and in which parents show a large degree of warmth and *responsivity*; see *authoritarian parenting*, *disengaged parenting* and *permissive parenting*.

Autism spectrum disorder. Neurodevelopmental disorder that appears in the first years of life; characterized by persistent deficits in social skills, communication and language, and by repetitive behavior and restricted interests.

Autobiographical memory. Memory of chronologically organized sequences of personally experienced events; see *episodic memory*, *long-term memory*, *semantic memory* and *working memory*.

Automatization. Reduced conscious regulation of motor and cognitive processes as a result of repeated execution.

Autonomy. Independence, self-determination. Ability to make independent decisions related to life's everyday tasks; an important element in the formation of *identity* in *adolescence*.

Autosomal chromosome. Chromosome that is not a *sex chromosome*.

Axon. Long, thin neural conductor that transmits impulses to other cells.

Babbling. Speech-like vocalization; usually occurs at 6–7 months of age.

Babinski reflex. *Developmental reflex* elicited when a sharp object is stroked backwards along the sole of the foot, causing a child's big toe to flex upwards and the other toes to fan out; usually disappears at 8–12 months of age.

Basic emotions. A set of *emotions* related to the evaluation of an entire situation or its individual aspects; includes joy, grief, fear and anger; also called primary emotions; see *relational emotions* and *self-referential emotions*.

Basic needs; Primary needs. Needs associated with survival.

Batten disease; Juvenile neuronal ceroid lipofuscinosis (JNCL). Genetic *autosomal* recessive disease; neurodegenerative disorder with blindness at age 5–15 and development of childhood dementia with decline in cognitive and motor functions.

Behavioral disorder. All forms of behavior that are socially unacceptable in one way or another, such as running away from home, screaming, cursing, messy eating manners, bed-wetting, ritual behavior, excessive dependency, poor *emotion regulation*, *aggression*, fighting and *bullying*.

Behavioral genetics. The study of how genes and the environment affect the development of characteristics such as *intelligence*, *temperament* and *personality*.

Behavioral phenotype. Characteristic pattern of motor, cognitive, language and social characteristics that seem to be related to a known

genetic syndrome or the presence of one or more genes.

Behavioral state. The main states of sleep and wakefulness in newborn children.

Behavioral system. Innate system shaped by evolutionary factors; activated under certain conditions and terminated under conditions other than those that activated it; the function of a behavioral system is the likely outcome of the behavior.

Behaviorism; Behavior analysis. Group of psychological theories that emphasize the influence of the environment to explain developmental changes.

Big Five personality traits. Five traits frequently used to describe *personality*: *agreeableness*, *conscientiousness*, *extraversion*, *neuroticism* (emotional lability) and *openness to experience*.

Body image. The subjective image of one's own body.

Bowlby-Robertson syndrome. The typical sequence of reactions among infants who are separated from their caregivers: initial protest followed by despair, and finally, if separation remains prolonged, *detachment*; see *attachment*.

Bulimia. Eating disorder involving binge-eating and "countermeasures" against food intake such as intentional regurgitation or use of a laxative; see *anorexia nervosa*.

Bullying. Negative actions, such as teasing and physical or verbal *aggression*, that are repeated over time and directed toward one or several individuals; direct bullying consists of open attacks on the person being bullied, while indirect bullying entails social exclusion.

Canonical babbling. The most basic or simple form of babbling.

Caregiving system. According to Bowlby, an innate behavioral system that triggers caregiving behavior in adults.

Case description; Case study. Study that involves the detailed description of certain characteristics or developmental processes in a single individual.

Cataract. Eye disease that results in the gradual clouding of the lens.

Causality, understanding of. Understanding of the causal relationship or connection between actions and their consequences; the fundamental connection between things; see *physical causality* and *psychological causality*.

Cell death. Selective loss of cells during the first years of life due to *maturation* and experience.

Cell differentiation; Cell specialization. Process by which a cell achieves a more specialized function.

Cell migration. The movement of cells to another location that occurs during fetal development.

Centering. Focusing attention on specific aspects of a situation or an event; see *decentration*.

Cerebellum. Part of the brain located behind and below the occipital lobe of the cerebrum, lying at an angle between the latter and the continuation of the spinal cord in the skull (medulla oblongata).

Cerebral palsy. Impaired muscle function due to prenatal or early brain damage. Characterized by paralysis, poor motor or postural coordination, and increased or varying muscle tension.

Checklist. Questionnaire or interview with specific observational categories, questions or statements answered by an individual respondent or by others; often used to assess the development of an individual in one or more areas.

Childhood. Age 1–12 years.

Child-directed speech. Adults' and older children's adaptation of pitch, *intonation* and *syntax* when talking to infants and toddlers.

Childhood amnesia. Describes the inability of older children and adults to remember experienced events that took place during the first 2–3 years of life.

Childhood dementia. Cognitive decline with onset in childhood.

Chromosomal abnormality. Change in the number or structure of chromosomes.

Chromosome. Thread-shaped formation in the cellular nucleus that carries genes; always occurs in pairs, with 23 pairs in human beings.

Class inclusion. Refers to a class or category that is part of another class or category; essential feature of a hierarchical structure.

Classical conditioning. See *conditioning*.

Clinical Method. Piaget's term for the combined use of experimental tasks and interviews in the study of child development.

Cognition. Thinking or understanding; includes some type of perception of the world, storage in the form of mental *representation*, different ways of managing or processing new and stored experiences, and action strategies.

Cognitive behavior theory. School within the behavioral tradition built on the basic premise that development is a cumulative learning process, and that learning forms the basis for most individual differences between children; also emphasizes the importance of models and *observational learning*, and cognitive processing and regulation of own behavior; also known as social learning theory.

Cognitive profile. The profile or pattern of performance in various cognitive areas.

Cognitive structure. Complex structure of mental representations and processes that forms the basis for thoughts, actions and the perception of the outside world; evolves and changes throughout development.

Cohort. A group of individuals who share a defining characteristic, such as the same year of birth, and thus experienced certain historical events at the same age.

Collaborative play. Form of *group play* in which children take on complementary roles and tasks.

Collective monologue. Piaget's term for children's *egocentric speech* or *private speech*.

Collectivist society. Emphasize social values and the individual's responsibility and place in society; see *individualistic society*.

Color constancy. Ability to recognize a color under different lighting conditions; see *form constancy* and *size constancy*.

Communication. Intentional conveyance of thoughts, stories, desires, ideas, emotions, etc., to one or more persons.

Communicative intention. Intention to convey a thought or an idea, direct others' attention at ideas or conditions in the outside world, or get others to do something specific; see *communication*.

Comparative psychology. A branch of psychology concerned with the study of animal behavior in developmental psychology often by comparing the developmental pathways of humans and animals.

Concept. Mental *representation* of a category of objects, events, persons, ideas, etc.; see *extension (of a concept)* and *intension (of a concept)*.

Concrete operational stage. According to Piaget, the third of four stages in cognitive development, approximately age 7–11; see *formal operational stage*, *preoperational stage* and *sensorimotor stage*.

Conditioning. The learning of a specific reaction in response to specific stimuli; includes classical and operant conditioning. In *classical conditioning*, a neutral stimulus is associated with an unlearned or *unconditioned stimulus* that elicits an unlearned or *unconditioned response*, eventually transforming the neutral stimulus into a conditioned stimulus that elicits a conditioned response similar to the unconditioned response. In *operant conditioning*, an action is followed by an event that increases or reduces the probability that the action will be repeated under similar circumstances; see *reinforcement*.

Conformity. The adoption of other people's attitudes and behavior due to actual or perceived pressure from them.

Connectionism. Theory within the information-processing tradition; based on a model of mental functioning by which external stimulation leads to various activating and inhibitory processes that may occur sequentially (following one another in time) or in parallel (simultaneously); knowledge is represented as a pattern of activation and inhibition, and new networks give rise to phenomena that differ qualitatively from the processes from which they emerged; see also *emergentism*.

Conscience. Emotional evaluation of one's own actions, often involving feelings of having done something wrong; closely related to shame and guilt.

Conscientiousness. One of the *Big Five personality traits*; see *agreeableness*, *extraversion*, *neuroticism* and *openness to experience*.

Conservation (in cognition). A form of mental constancy; the ability to understand that the material or mass of an object does not change in mass, number, volume or weight unless something is taken away or added, even if external aspects of the object appear changed.

Constancy (in cognition). The ability to understand that the attributes of objects and people remain the same, even if they seem to have changed, for example due to a different viewing angle and lighting conditions; see *color constancy*, *form constancy*, *object permanence* and *size constancy*.

Constraint (in development). The organism's resistance to change and adaptation to new experiences; often used in connection with the nervous system; see *plasticity*.

Constructive play. Form of play that entails that children construct something, such as a Lego house or a clay figure; may be performed alone or together with others; see *exercise play*, *group play*, *pretend play* and *symbolic play*.

Constructivism. Psychological theories based on the notion that an individual constructs his or her understanding of the outside world; see *logical constructivism* and *social constructivism*.

Contingency. Dependency between events; an event follows after the presence of a particular stimulus or action.

Continuity (in development). Development in which later ways of functioning build directly on previous functions and can be predicted based on them; see *discontinuity*.

Contrast principle (in language development). Refers to children's assumption that every new word has a different meaning from the words they have previously learned.

Control group. Group of individuals that is compared with an *experimental group* as similar to the control group as possible in relevant areas, but not exposed to the experimental variable.

Controversial children (sociometry). Children who are both accepted and rejected by their peers, and may appear active, aggressive, destructive and angry, or as socially withdrawn; they can also be helpful, cooperative and assume leadership, and at times display socially sensitive behavior; see *neglected children*, *neutral children*, *popular children* and *unpopular children*.

Conventional morality. According to Kohlberg, the second of three main stages of moral development, in which children emphasize other people's values, attitudes and possible reactions to an action being considered; see *post-conventional morality* and *pre-conventional morality*.

Cooing sounds. The first sounds produced by an infant that do not resemble crying, typically consisting of repeated vowel sounds.

Cooperative learning; Collaborative learning. Two or more children solving problems together.

Core knowledge. In nativist theory, the innate abilities that form the basis for further perceptual, cognitive and linguistic development.

Correlation. Measure of the degree of covariation between two variables, ranging from −1.00 to +1.00; values close to 0.00 show a low degree of correlation; a positive correlation (+) means that a high score on one variable is associated with high score on the other; a negative correlation (−) indicates that a high score on one variable is associated with a low score on the other.

Correspondence (cognitive). In Piaget's New Theory, the perception of structural similarity that provides a basis for comparing people, objects, events, actions, etc.; see *morphism*.

Cortex. The outermost, folded layer of the brain; *phylogenetically* the most recent part of the human brain.

Cortisol. Hormone that usually increases when an individual experiences stress.

Criterion-referenced test. *Test* in which the various tasks are arranged in such a way that the score reflects how far an individual has advanced in mastering skills within a specific area; see *norm-referenced test*.

Critical period. Limited time period in which an individual is especially susceptible to specific forms of positive or negative stimulation and experience; if the stimulation or experience fails to take place during this period, a similar stimulation or experience later in life will neither benefit nor harm the individual to any appreciable extent; see *sensitive period*.

Critical psychology. Theoretical tradition influenced by radical social constructivism and women's studies, as well as postmodern sociology and psychoanalytic interpretation; challenges the idea that regular developmental features have a biological basis.

Cross-cultural developmental study. Study comparing children who grow up in different cultures in order to map the importance of genetic and environmental impacts in the broadest sense.

Cross-sectional study. Research method that traces a developmental change by comparing children at different ages; see *longitudinal study*.

Crystallized intelligence. Ability to solve problems that require cultural and personal knowledge acquired through experience, such as vocabulary or factual information; see *fluid intelligence*.

Cultural tool. According to Vygotsky, a skill that has developed through generations in a culture, and that is passed on to children, such as language, the numerical system or calendar time.

Culture. The particular activities, tools, attitudes, beliefs, values, norms, etc., that characterize a group or a community.

Darwinism. Evolutionary theory based on the premise that all organisms at a given moment in history have evolved from earlier organisms based on the principle of *natural selection*: offspring with attributes well adapted to the current environment are most likely to mature and reproduce, thereby passing on their own attributes to the next generation.

Decentration. Ability to perceive other perspectives than one's own and consider several aspects of a situation at the same time; see *centering*.

Declarative communication. Form of communication with the sole purpose of providing information and directing someone else's attention at something, such as a person, an object or an idea; see *instrumental communication*.

Deductive reasoning. The process of ascertaining whether a statement is true or false based on a given premise; drawing conclusions about a specific case based on general principles; see *hypothetical-deductive reasoning* and *inductive reasoning*.

Defense mechanism. In *psychodynamic theory*, unconscious mental strategies for dealing with inner psychological conflicts and reducing anxiety that follows the drives and impulses of the *id* and threatens control by the *ego*.

Deferred imitation; Delayed imitation. Deliberate repetition of another person's action at some later point in time; see *immediate imitation*.

Deictic gesture. Pointing gesture; gesture that directs others' attention at something in the environment without naming it.

Dendrite. Short, branch-like extension of the cell body that receives impulses from surrounding nerve cells, muscle cells or glands under certain conditions.

Deoxyribonucleic acid (DNA). The basic building block of genes, comprised of long spiral-shaped and sequential threads of *introns* and *exons*. DNA provides the blueprint for *ribonucleic acid* (RNA), which performs a number of cellular functions, controls the production of new proteins and triggers chemical reactions in the body.

Dependent variable. The outcome, conditions resulting from variation in the *independent variable*.

Desegregation (education). The reintegration of a child into an ordinary preschool group or school class after the child has received special education outside the ordinary school system; see *segregation*.

Detachment. Discontinuation of an attachment relationship due to prolonged or permanent separation; see *Bowlby-Robertson syndrome* and *attachment*.

Determinism. The view that the actions of an individual are predetermined.

Development. Changes over time in the structure and functioning of human beings and animals as a result of interaction between biological and environmental factors.

Developmental disorder. Disorder that is congenital or appears in *infancy* or *childhood* without the presence of external injuries or similar.

Developmental pathway. One of several possible courses of development within the same area or domain.

Developmental phase. Time period central to a particular developmental process.

Developmental psychopathology. Multidisciplinary tradition among researchers and practitioners with a basis in developmental psychology; attempts to identify and influence the processes that underlie various psychological disorders, founded on assumptions about vulnerability and resilience in children, and risk and protection in the childhood environment.

Developmental quotient (DQ). *Standard score* in developmental tests; corresponds to the *intelligence quotient (IQ)* in intelligence tests.

Developmental reflex. Early motor reflex that normally disappears within the first year of life.

Dialectical reasoning. The process of basing decisions and conclusions on dialectical reflection or argumentation.

Diary Study (in research on children). Research method based on parents' written record of their child's actions or utterances.

Difficult temperament. According to Thomas and Chess, temperament characterized by a tendency to withdraw in new situations, general negativity, strong emotional reactions and highly irregular sleeping and eating patterns; see *slow-to-warm-up* and *easy temperament*.

Disability. The difference between an individual's abilities and the demands of the environment.

Discontinuity (in development). Development in which new functions are associated with qualitative differences rather than merely a quantitative growth in previously established functions, and where the effect of past development can be altered by subsequent experiences; see *continuity, heterotypic continuity* and *homotypic continuity*.

Disengaged parenting. Parenting style that does not place high demands on the child and in which parents show little *responsivity*; see *authoritarian, authoritative* and *permissive parenting*.

Discriminate. Dustinguish between, react differentially; see *generalize*.

Dishabituation. Increased response to a new stimulus or aspect of a stimulus following a reduction in response intensity due to repeated presentation of a stimulus; see *habituation*.

Distinct emotions. According to Tomkins, the assumption that children are born with a certain set of different emotions.

Dizygotic twins; Fraternal twins. Twins resulting from two separate fertilized eggs and sharing 50 percent of each other's genes; see *monozygotic twins (identical twins)*.

Domain. A delimited sphere of knowledge; an area in which something is active or manifests itself.

Domain-general. Abilities and skills that include most domains of knowledge; see *domain-specific*.

Domain-specific. Abilities and skills within a specific domain of knowledge; see *domain-general*.

Dominant gene. Gene that is expressed even though it is inherited from the mother or the father alone, and resulting in a characteristic that will always be expressed; see *genomic imprinting* and *recessive gene*.

Down syndrome; Trisomy 21. Syndrome that causes varying degrees of *intellectual disability*; caused by an error in cell division that results in a partial or complete extra copy of chromosome 21.

Dynamic assessment. The mapping of children's cognitive abilities by recording how much progress they make in the solution of a certain type of task after having received specific help and training for a given period; see *Learning Potential Assessment Device*.

Dynamic system (in development). A system of nonlinear *self-organizing* and *self-regulating* processes in which qualitatively new functions occur as an *integrated* result of interaction between subsystems that may have different developmental rates.

Dyslexia. Severe reading and writing disorder, despite adequate sensory and intellectual abilities and appropriate training; see *learning disorder*.

Dyspraxia. Partial or complete inability to perform voluntary movements.

Easy temperament. According to Thomas and Chess, temperament characterized by an overall good mood, regular sleeping and eating patterns, easy adaptation to new situations, a positive attitude toward strangers, and moderate emotional reactions; easy to calm down when agitated; see *difficult temperament* and *slow-to-warm-up*.

Echolalia. Meaningless repetition of what other people are saying, or of things heard on the radio or television.

Ecological psychology. According to Bronfenbrenner, a model of child development whereby developmental conditions are determined by the complex interaction between various social systems that impact one another; see *exosystem macrosystem, mesosystem* and *microsystem*.

Ecological validity. The extent to which an observation is representative of the natural environment of the individual being observed; see *concurrent validity, construct validity, external validity, internal validity* and *predictive validity*.

Ego. In *psychoanalytic theory*, one of the three parts of the human psyche; its purpose is to regulate the drives and impulses of the *id* in relation to the realities of the world and the limitations of the *superego*.

Ego ideal. In *psychodynamic theory*, an individual's objectives and frame of reference for acceptable and socially desirable behavior; the person an individual desires to be.

Ego psychology. Branch of *psychodynamic psychology* that emphasizes the autonomous role of the *ego* in the development of personality, independent of drives.

Egocentric speech. According to Piaget, verbal communication that fails to take into account the other person's perspective, see *private speech*.

Egocentrism. Tendency to interpret events from one's own perspective; partial or complete inability to distinguish between one's own and other people's perspective.

Electra conflict. According to psychoanalytic theory, a genetically based psychological conflict rooted in the idea that girls are sexually attracted to their father, and experience the mother as a competitor for the father's affection; equivalent to the *Oedipus conflict* for boys.

Electroencephalography (EEG). Method to record the electrical activity of the brain by means of electrodes attached to the exterior of the skull.

Embryonic period. Weeks 2–8 of prenatal development; see *germinal period* and *fetal period*.

Emergentism. Theoretical approach related to *connectionism*; based on the premise that existing elements and processes interact to give rise to new phenomena that are qualitatively different from the elements and processes they emerged from.

Emotion. A state caused by an event important to the person and characterized by the presence of feelings; involves physiological reactions, conscious inner experience, directed action and outward expression.

Emotion regulation. Implicit and explicit strategies to adapt one's own emotional reactions and those of others in line with social and cultural conventions, especially in regard to the expression, intensity, duration and contexts in which they arise.

Emotional attunement; Affect attunement. A state in which a person is *sensitive* and *responsive* to the emotional state of another. According to Stern, a process by which the caregiver "mirrors" the experiences of the child without using language and allows the child to understand how he or she is perceived.

Emotional competence. The ability to understand one's own and others' feelings, and to make use of and regulate the expression of one's own emotions in problem solving and social interaction.

Emotionality. The mood of an individual; the amount and intensity of positive and negative emotions.

Empathy. Feel with someone; emotional reaction similar to the emotion another person is perceived to experience; see *sympathy*.

Encoding. Conversion of external stimulation to mental *representations*.

Enculturation. Acquisition of a culture's practices, customs, norms, values, and the like; the first foundation in this process is children's innate social orientation.

Epigenesis. Developmental process by which an individual's genetic dispositions are modified by environmental influences and change the structure and behavior of the organism.

Episodic memory. Memory of events in which an individual has participated, such as what he or she did during the summer holidays; see *autobiographical memory*, *long-term memory*, *semantic memory* and *working memory*.

Equifinality. The principle that different conditions and developmental pathways can lead to the same end result.

Equilibration. According to Piaget, a process that leads children to search for solutions to cognitive contradictions and to integrate established cognitive *schemas* and new experiences.

Ethology. The study of human and animal behavior under natural conditions and of the role of behavior in *evolution*. Also a branch of *evolution-based psychology*.

Evolutionary psychology; Evolution-based psychology. School of thought that focuses on the function of a particular behavior pattern during evolution, in the context of explaining human actions.

Executive functions. Cognitive functions that monitor and regulate attention and plan and supervise the execution of voluntary actions, including the inhibition to act on inappropriate impulses.

Exercise play. Non-functional practice in performing different actions; see *constructive play*, *group play*, *rule-based play* and *symbolic play*.

Exon. Active base in a DNA sequence that encodes proteins and other cell products; see *intron*.

Exosystem. Subsystem of Bronfenbrenner's *bio-ecological model* consisting of broader social contexts that do not include the child itself, but that are important to the functioning of family and child, such as the parents' workplace and social networks, distant relatives and parents of friends; see *ecological psychology*, *macrosystem*, *mesosystem* and *microsystem*.

Expansion (in language development). The repetition of what a child is saying by an adult, with longer sentences and greater complexity.

Experiment. Method to test a hypothesis on specific causal relationships or connections. One or several conditions are systematically altered, and the effect is recorded. As many conditions as possible are kept constant in order not to affect the outcome, increasing the probability that the results are solely related to the conditions being studied.

Experimental group. In experiments with two groups, the group that receives the experimental treatment or other influence; see *control group*.

Explicit reasoning. Conscious elaboration of a problem, typically by using language; see *implicit reasoning*.

Exploration. According to Bowlby, a behavioral system whose function is to provide information about the environment and enable the individual to better adapt to it; activated by unfamiliar and/or complex objects; deactivated once the objects have been examined and become familiar to the individual; see *attachment* and *secure base*.

Exploratory behavior. According to Bowlby, exploratory behavior consists of three elements: an *orienting response*, movement in the direction of the object, and physical exploration of the object by moving it and experimenting with it; see *attachment*.

Expressive language. The language that the child produces; see *receptive language*.

Expressive style (in early language development). According to Nelson, speech characterized by social expressions; see *referential style*.

Extension (of a concept). All actual and possible exemplars encompassed by a concept; see *intension (of a concept)*.

Externalizing disorder. Negative emotions directed at others; often expressed in the form of antisocial and aggressive behavior.

Extinction (in conditioning). Reduction or discontinuation of a *conditioned response*.

Extraversion. One of the *Big Five personality traits*; the opposite of *introversion*; see *agreeableness*, *conscientiousness*, *neuroticism* and *openness to experience*.

False belief tasks. Tasks where the child must infer a false belief in another person; used to investigate *theory of mind* in children; see *mind understanding*.

Family study. Study based on the percentage of genes shared among family members; used to study the relationship between heredity and environment.

Feature-based category. *Conceptual category* whose members share a set of common characteristics that distinguishes the category from other conceptual categories; see *prototype category*.

Fetal alcohol syndrome (FAS). Abnormal development caused by the mother's consumption of alcohol or other drugs during pregnancy; common characteristics include a small head, distinctive facial features, malformations of the heart and limbs, *irritability*, attention deficit disorder and *hyperactivity*.

Fetal period. Ninth week of pregnancy until birth; see *embryonic period* and *germinal period*.

Field experiment. Experimental method based on modifying *independent variables* in an individual's natural environment.

Figurative language. Language that makes use of metaphors or similes to express facts or ideas; see *metaphor*.

Fine motor skills. Movements of the hands, fingers and toes; see *gross motor skills*.

First-order belief attribution; First-order theory of mind. The ability to understand what another person is thinking; see *second-order belief attribution*.

Fixed action pattern. Behavior shared in almost identical form among most members of a species (may vary between male and female); triggered by specific types of stimulation, but more complex than *reflexes*.

Fluid intelligence. Basic skills such as memory and spatial perception whose development is relatively independent of specific cultural experiences; see *crystallized intelligence*.

Flynn effect. Increase in skills and knowledge that over time leads to changes in the norms of IQ tests.

Form constancy. The ability to recognize an object from different visual angles; see *color constancy* and *size constancy*.

Formal operational stage. According to Piaget, the fourth and final stage in cognitive development, starting around the age of 11; see *concrete operational stage*, *preoperational stage* and *sensorimotor stage*.

Formal operational thinking. According to Piaget, the highest form of cognitive functioning, where thinking is completely free of specific objects and experiences.

Fragile X syndrome. Hereditary condition that mainly affects boys; caused by damage to the X chromosome. Characterized by the development of an elongated head, a large forehead, a high palate and a prominent chin following *puberty*. Often, but not always, entails *learning disabilities* of widely varying degree, from mild to severe, and occasionally *autism*.

Functional equivalence. Refers to the fact that characteristics, behavior patterns or stimulation fulfill the same function in different individuals (for example in different cultures), or in the same individual at different age levels.

Functional magnetic resonance imaging (fMRI). Method to examine the brain by measuring the oxygen content or changes in oxygen content in different brain areas while the subject performs a specific task, such as looking at something, listening to something or performing mental calculations.

Functional play. See *exercise play*.

Gender constancy. The ability to understand that an individual's gender is linked to certain biological characteristics and remains the same, regardless of clothing and the like.

Gender difference; Sex difference. Characteristic, ability or behavior pattern that differs between the two sexes.

Gender identity. Sense of belonging to a particular gender; according to Kohlberg, the ability to distinguish between male and female.

Gender role; Sex role. Expectations about the actions or behavior of boys, girls, men and women in a particular society under different circumstances.

Gender stereotype. Generalized and often erroneous view of the behavior and characteristics of boys, girls, men and women.

Gender typing; Sex typing. The process of adopting behavior and attitudes that a given culture regards as appropriate for males and females.

General factor; g-factor (in intelligence). *Domain-general* ability; see *specific factor*.

Generalize. To perceive and react in the same way to events that are similar in some respects; see *discriminate*.

Genital phase. According to *psychoanalytic theory*, the mature stage of *psychosexual development*, beginning with *puberty*; see *anal phase*, *latency phase*, *oral phase* and *phallic phase*.

Genome. The sum of all genes of an individual.

Genomic imprinting. Activation of a gene depending on whether the gene is inherited from the father or the mother; see *dominant gene* and *recessive gene*.

Genotype. The genetic makeup of an individual; see *phenotype*.

Germinal period. The first 10 days of prenatal development; see *embryonic period* and *fetal period*.

Gestalt principles (in perception). Principles used for perceptual organization and presumed to be innate.

Gesture. Distinct movement primarily used as a means of communication and interpreted consistently within a social system; see *deictic gesture* and *symbolic gesture*.

Giftedness (intelligence). Scores in the high end of the IQ distribution, above 130.

Goodness of fit. A measure of how well something fits together with something else; often used to describe the degree to which the *temperaments* of parents and children coincide.

Grammar. Rules that describe how sentences are formed in a language; includes *morphology* and *syntax*.

Gross motor skills. Movements of the body, arms and legs; see *fine motor skills*.

Group play. Play in which several children interact; see *associated group play, collaborative play, constructive play, exercise play, rule-based play* and *symbolic play*.

Growth spurt. Rapid growth in body height during early puberty; also used to describe the rapid growth of a characteristic or function within a specific time period.

Habilitation. The effort to improve and support functionality, interaction and quality of life for people with congenital or early-acquired disabilities; see *rehabilitation*.

Habituation. Gradual reduction in the intensity of a reaction or response following repeated stimulation; allows an individual to ignore familiar objects and direct attention at new ones.

Head Start. American preschool program during the 1960s and 1970s with the aim of providing support for children from low-income and socially disadvantaged families.

Heritability estimate. Calculation of heritability based on the difference between the correlations of fraternal and identical twins.

Heterotypic continuity. Refers to the fact that actions differ while function remains the same at different age levels; see *continuity*, *discontinuity* and *homotypic continuity*.

Hierarchical structure (of concepts). Organization of objects or concepts into categories and subcategories that are part of larger categories.

Holophrase. Single-word utterance that in early language development functions as an entire sentence; see *over-extension* and *under-extension*.

Homotypic continuity. Refers to behavior that fulfills the same function at different age levels; see *continuity*, *discontinuity* and *heterotypic continuity*.

Horizontal décalage. According to Piaget, the difference in the development of skills within a certain stage; see *vertical décalage*.

Horizontal relation. Relationship in which both parties share an equal amount of knowledge and social power; see *vertical relation*.

Horizontal structure (in language). Utterances consisting of several words that all lie within the same intonation contour; see *intonation* and *vertical structure*.

Hospitalization syndrome. Bad health and delayed development in children due to being raised in poor institutional environments.

Hostile aggression. Actions whose main objective is to harm someone else, such as when a child bullies another; see *instrumental aggression*, *open aggression* and *relational aggression*.

Huntington disease. A heritable and as yet incurable neurodegenerative disease, characterized by involuntary jerking movements especially in the face, tongue, neck, shoulders, arms and legs; irritability, depression and dementia; usual onset between the ages of 30 and 40. Caused by a *dominant gene* located on chromosome 4.

Hydrocephalus. Abnormal accumulation of fluid in the cavities or exterior part of the brain; can lead to enlargement of the head, brain atrophy, reduced cognitive abilities and epilepsy.

Hyperactivity. Unusually high activity level that is difficult for an individual to control.

Hyperlexia. Mechanical reading ability without understanding.

Hypertonia. Increased tension, such as in the muscles; see *hypotonia*.

Hypoactivity. Unusually low activity level; difficulties taking initiative.

Hypothetical-deductive reasoning. Method of solving problems or seeking knowledge that proceeds from a general assumption about the relationship between different factors and develops hypotheses that can be tested systematically; see *deductive reasoning* and *inductive reasoning*.

Hypotonia. Reduced tension, such as in the muscles; see *hypertonia*.

Id. In *psychoanalytic theory*, one of the three parts of the human psyche, consisting of drives that seek to find an outlet; see *ego* and *superego*.

Identification. Process characterized by a tendency to mimic behavior and assume someone else's points of view.

Identity. An individual's sense of who he or she is, as well as of affiliation with larger and smaller social groups and communities.

Imitation. The deliberate execution of an action to create a correspondence between what oneself does and what someone else does; see *delayed imitation* and *modeling*.

Immediate imitation. Deliberate repetition of another person's action immediately after it has been performed; see *deferred imitation*.

Imperative communication. See *instrumental communication*.

Implicit reasoning. Automatic and nonconscious inferences based on knowledge and experience; see *explicit reasoning*.

Imprinting. A form of rapid learning that takes place during a short and sensitive period immediately after birth; ducklings, for example, will follow the first person, animal or object they see move within a period of 48 hours after hatching.

Incidence. The appearance of new occurrences of a trait, disease or similar in a particular *population* during a particular time span, often expressed as the number of incidences per 1,000 individuals per year; see *prevalence*.

Independent variable. A condition that varies naturally or is deliberately varied to investigate its effect on what is being measured; see *dependent variable*.

Individual differences. Variation in skills and characteristics between the individuals in a *population*; see *atypical development* and *typical development*.

Individualistic society. Society where values emphasize on the uniqueness of each individual; see *collectivist society*.

Induced memory. Memory of an experienced event that is "planted" in a person without the latter actually having experienced the event.

Inductive reasoning. The establishment of a general rule based on specific experience; see *deductive reasoning* and *hypothetical-deductive reasoning*.

Infancy. The first year of life.

Information processing (theory). Psychological theories based on the assumption that all mental phenomena can be described and explained by models in which the flow of information is processed by one or more systems.

Inhibition. Shyness and withdrawal from social challenges.

Instinct. Species-specific behavior with a genetic basis, such as nest-building among birds.

Instrumental aggression. The use of aggressive actions to achieve a goal, such as when one child pushes another off a bike in order to ride the bike themselves; see *hostile aggression*, *open aggression* and *relational aggression*.

Instrumental communication. Communicative action aimed at getting someone else to do something specific; see *declarative communication*.

Integration (in development). Coordination; progress toward greater organization and a more complex structure.

Intellectual disability; Learning disability; Mental retardation. Significant problems learning and adjusting that affect most areas of functioning; graded mild (IQ 70–50), moderate (IQ 49–35), severe (IQ 34–20) and profound (IQ below 20); in clinical contexts, a significant reduction in social adjustment is an additional criterion.

Intelligence quotient (IQ). Numerical representation of an individual's *intelligence* in relation to peers. Formerly, IQ was based on the relationship between mental age and chronological age, calculated by dividing the *age score* on an IQ test by the individual's chronological age; today, IQ tests are based on a *standard score* with a mean of 100 and a *standard deviation* of 15 or 16, depending on the *test* being used.

Intension (of a concept). The content, all of the attributes embraced by a *concept*; see *extension*.

Intentionality. Goal-oriented determination; includes a notion of the goal of an action, and emotions and plans related to achieving the goal.

Inter-observer reliability. The degree of concurrence in the scoring or assessment by two or more persons who observe the same event independent of each other, directly or on video.

Inter-sensory perception. The influence of one *sensory modality* on the processes of another.

Interaction (statistics). The degree of influence of one or several other variables on the relationship between an *independent* and a *dependent variable*; see *moderator*.

Interaction effect. An influence by one or several other factors; see *main effect* and *transaction effect*.

Intermodal perception. Perception of a person, an event or an object whereby information from two or more senses is combined, for example seeing and hearing a cat meow.

Internalization. Process whereby external processes are reconstructed to become internal processes, such as when children independently adopt problem-solving strategies they have previously used in interaction with others, or adopt the attitudes, characteristics and standards of others as their own.

Internalizing disorder. Negative emotions directed at oneself, anxiety, depression; often involving a negative self-image, shyness and seclusion; see *externalizing disorder*.

Interpretative mind. Describes the fact that two people can perceive the same information differently; see *mind understanding*.

Intersubjectivity. The consciously shared subjective experience of an event or phenomenon by two or more individuals simultaneously.

Intonation. The melody or pattern of changes in the pitch of the speaking voice.

Intron. Inactive base of a gene in a DNA sequence; see *exon*.

Introversion. *Personality trait* characterized by shyness, anxiousness and withdrawal from social situations, as opposed to *extraversion*.

Irritability (temperament). Tendency of an individual to become easily agitated and lack patience and tolerance.

Joint attention. Two or more individuals share a common focus of attention, while at the same time being aware that the same focus of attention is shared by the other person(s).

Klinefelter syndrome. Chromosomal disorder caused by an additional X chromosome in males (XXY); symptoms include sterility, small testes, and long arms and legs; see *sex chromosomes*.

Landmark. Distinctive spatial feature used to orient oneself in one's surroundings, such as the color of the walls or the placement of windows, doors and objects.

Language Acquisition Device, LAD. According to Chomsky, an innate grammatical representation, a *module* for language that underlies all languages and enables children to learn to understand the language around them and assemble words into grammatically correct phrases.

Language Acquisition Support System, LASS. According to Bruner, the systematic way in which the environment supports a child's language development; see *scaffold*.

Language function. The purpose of speech; the objective one wants to achieve by conveying something to another person using language.

Latency phase. According to *psychoanalytic theory*, a period of reduced sexual drive without focus on a new area of the body; lasts from the end of the phallic phase until puberty (approx. age 6–13); see *anal phase, genital phase, oral phase* and *phallic phase*.

Laterality. Asymmetry in the functioning of the brain, when some functions are more prominent in one brain hemisphere than in the other.

Learned helplessness. The experience of lacking self-determination and the ability to affect one's environment as a result of having experienced situations in which one felt little control.

Learning. Relatively permanent change in understanding and behavior as the result of experience; see *development* and *maturation*.

Learning disorder. Significant problems developing skills in a specific area of knowledge, such as language impairment, reading/writing disorders (*dyslexia*) and difficulties with math (dyscalculia); often referred to as specific learning disorder as opposed to general learning disability; see *intellectual disability*.

Learning Potential Assessment Device. Test procedure to assess a child's learning abilities; tests are first performed in the traditional way, after which the child receives specific and standardized help with the tasks the child was unable to solve independently; an increase in the test score following instruction is considered a measure of the child's learning potential; see *dynamic assessment*.

Lexical development. The development of vocabulary.

Libido. Sexual or life drive; according to *psychoanalytic theory*, a source of energy aimed at reproduction, but among human beings also converted into other forms of expression. Motivates all action together with *Thanatos*.

Logical constructivism. Psychological tradition that includes Piaget's theory and the theories of others that build on it; its main principle is that children actively construct their own understanding of the outside world, and that *perception* and *cognition* are affected by logical and conceptually driven processes; see *constructivism* and *social constructivism*.

Logical reasoning. Reasoning whose deductions are limited by the rules of logic.

Long-term memory. Part of the memory system that stores memories over time and contains most of an individual's knowledge; see *autobiographical memory*, *episodic memory*, *semantic memory* and *working memory*.

Longitudinal study. Research method that involves the observation of the same individuals at various age levels; see *cross-sectional study*.

Macrosystem. Subsystem of Bronfenbrenner's *bioecological model*; includes social institutions such as government, public services, laws, customs and values of importance to what takes place in the other systems; see *exosystem*, *mesosystem* and *microsystem*.

Magnetic resonance imaging, MRI. Method of studying the brain that yields black-and-white images of the brain's shape and size. MRI is sensitive to the cell differences in various tissue types, such as white and gray brain matter.

Main effect. An influence that is independent of other factors; see *interaction effect* and *transaction effect*.

Maladaptation. *Mental disorder* or antisocial behavior with a basis in an individual's lack of adaptability and difficulties adjusting to the environment.

Maturation. Developmental change caused by genetically determined regulating mechanisms that are relatively independent of the individual's specific experiences; see *development* and *learning*.

Mean length of utterance (MLU). Average number of *morphemes* per utterance; generally calculated on the basis of 100 utterances, and used to measure a child's level of language proficiency.

Mediator. Active factor in the impact of an independent variable on a dependent variable.

Memory span. The amount of information an individual is able to keep in *working memory*, such as the number of digits a child can recall after seeing or hearing them once.

Mental age. See *age score*.

Mental disorder. Behavioral or psychological pattern that occurs in an individual and leads to clinically significant distress or impairment in one or more important areas of functioning.

Mental model. Subjective mind model of how the world functions and how things are connected.

Mentalizing. The interpretation of one's own and others' behavior as an expression of mental states, desires, feelings, perceptions, etc.; according to Fonagy, a process that includes all thoughts about relationships, human interactions and psychological processes in humans.

Mesosystem. Subsystem of Bronfenbrenner's *bioecological model*; consists of connections between two or more microsystems a child actively participates in; see *exosystem*, *macrosystem* and *microsystem*.

Meta-knowledge. Knowledge about knowledge, for example metalinguistic insight into language itself.

Metaphor. A type of *analogy*; meaning expressed illustratively or figuratively.

Microgenetic study. A study in which the development of a skill is mapped from the moment a change takes place until the child masters the skill.

Microsystem. Subsystem of Bronfenbrenner's *bioecological model* that includes the child's closest daily relationships, usually the parents, siblings and other relatives living with the family, preschool, school, youth clubs, neighborhood friends and the like; see *mesosystem*, *exosystem* and *macrosystem*.

Mind understanding. Understanding that other people have internal states, such as knowledge, feelings and plans, that may be different from one's own and may affect their actions; see *social cognition* and *theory of mind*.

Mind-oriented. Relating to other people as cognitive individuals.

Minority language. Language spoken by a minority of a society's population.

Mirror neuron. Nerve cell that is activated both when an individual observes an action and when he or she performs the action.

Modeling. Type of observational learning, whereby an individual learns by observing and imitating other people's behavior and its consequences; see *imitation*.

Moderator. Variable that affects the strength of the relationship between two other variables; see *interaction*.

Module (in cognition). Isolated brain system that deals with a particular type of stimulation and knowledge.

Monozygotic twins; Identical twins. Twins resulting from the splitting of the same fertilized egg, sharing 100 percent of each other's genes; see *dizygotic twins (fraternal twins)*.

Moral dilemma. Situation involving a conflict between two or more solutions that may violate an individual's perception of what is right and wrong.

Moral realism. According to Piaget, the second of three stages in moral development, beginning at 5 years of age; characterized by the child's ability to follow rules, but in an absolute way, i.e. with little ability to adapt or change the rules; see *moral subjectivism* and *premoral stage*.

Moral reasoning. Reasoning about real or hypothetical moral dilemmas.

Moral subjectivism. According to Piaget, the third and final stage in moral development; begins at age 9–10; characterized by the child's understanding that rules are conventional, *social constructions* based on consensus, and that it is possible to change them if consensus can be reached; see *moral realism* and *premoral stage*.

Moro reflex. *Developmental reflex* elicited when an infant extends her arms and the head suddenly loses support, causing the infant's arms to move toward the body's midline; usually disappears at 5–6 months of age.

Morpheme. Smallest *grammatical* unit in a language that changes the meaning of a word; can be a word or part of a word, such as the conjugation of a verb.

Morphism. In Piaget's new theory, *correspondence* beyond identical resemblance.

Morphology. The study of how words are built up; includes the creation of content words like *ball* and *run*, functional words like *and* and *in*, and inflections of word forms like *run*, *ran* and *running*.

Multilingualism. Proficiency in two or more languages at roughly the same level, with bilingualism being the most common form. Multilingualism may be practiced within the family alone, or between the family and society; see *minority language*.

Multiple intelligences. According to Gardner, different forms of intelligence among human beings.

Mutation. Sudden change in a gene.

Myelination. The formation of a thin myelin sheath around the nerve fibers, consisting of proteins and fat and leading to an increase in the transmission of nerve impulses.

Nativism. Theoretical assumption that development proceeds according to a plan that in some way is represented genetically, and that experience has little or no effect on the developmental outcome; see *maturation*.

Natural selection. The principle that genetic changes in a species are due to the fact that offspring with characteristics well-adapted to the current environment are most likely to grow up and propagate, and thus pass on those properties to later generations.

Naturalistic observation. Research method involving the observation of an individual's regular activities in his or her ordinary environment without any attempt at outside influence.

Negative reinforcement (in conditioning). A stimulation or event that, when removed from a situation, increases the probability of an individual performing a specific action; for example, the likelihood of a child doing homework may increase when this results in eliminating the threat of having to stay after school; see *positive reinforcement* and *reinforcement*.

Neglected children (sociometry). Children who are neither accepted nor rejected by their peers; few features distinguish them from other children, but they have less interaction with others, and little attention is paid to them; they typically show little aggressiveness and seem to try to avoid aggression to a somewhat greater degree than other children, but do not appear overly anxious or withdrawn; see *controversial children, neutral children, popular children* and *unpopular children.*

Neonatal period. The first month of life.

Neuroimaging. Using technology to create images of the structures and functions of the brain.

Neuronal group theory. Theory of motor development based on the assumption that evolution has resulted in a structure of primary neuronal groups (nerve cell connections) that control motor functions and changes with experience, i.e. that information from the muscles affects the development of the brain.

Neuroticism. One of the *Big Five personality traits*; see *agreeableness, conscientiousness, extraversion* and *openness to experience.*

Neurotransmitter. Chemical substance released from an *axon* to a *neuron* that affects the activity of another neuron.

Neutral children (sociometry). Children who do not fall into a particular group when their popularity is evaluated by their peers, i.e. who are neither *popular, unpopular* or *controversial,* but who at the same time are not *neglected children.*

New theory. See *The new theory.*

Norm (in a test). A standard or normative score for a certain age level, based on the results from a large number of individuals.

Norm-referenced test. *Test* that is *standardized* based on a representative group and scaled in such a way that the score reflects an individual's performance relative to the performance of the standardized group; see *criterion-referenced test.*

Normal distribution. Statistically defined distribution around a mean; also called Gaussian curve.

Normal expectable environment. Natural variation in environmental conditions associated with the normal development of children born without particular biological abnormalities.

Object (in psychodynamic theory). Mental representation of a person or an object that is the goal of a drive, or through which a drive can achieve its goal; see *object relation.*

Object constancy. Understanding that an object remains the same despite changes in how it appears in different light, perspective or distance.

Object permanence. Understanding that an object continues to exist even though it cannot be perceived by the senses.

Object relation. In psychodynamic theory, the dynamic interaction between an individual's mental *representations* of him or herself, and emotionally significant persons in the environment.

Observational learning. Learning by observing the behavior of others and the consequences of their behavior.

Oedipus conflict. According to *psychoanalytic theory,* a genetically determined psychological conflict rooted in the idea that boys are sexually attracted to their mother and experience the father as a competitor for the mother's affection; equivalent to the *Electra conflict* in girls.

Ontogenesis. The developmental history of an individual.

Open aggression. A form of *hostile aggression;* actions whose purpose is to harm another person physically; see *hostile aggression, instrumental aggression* and *relational aggression.*

Openness to experience. One of the *Big Five personality traits*; see *agreeableness, conscientiousness, extraversion* and *neuroticism.*

Operant conditioning. See *conditioning.*

Operation (cognitive). According to Piaget, the mental *representation* of actions that follow logical rules.

Operationalization (in research). Normative definition or precise description of how to measure what is being studied.

Oppositional defiant disorder. Externalizing disorder characterized by hostility toward adults, reluctance to do what authorities say and to follow normal rules, and maliciousness and vindictiveness when met with resistance.

Oral phase. According to *psychoanalytic theory,* the first stage in *psychosexual development,* in which the area around the mouth becomes a source of pleasure; age 0–1 years; see *anal phase, genital phase, latency phase* and *phallic phase.*

Orienting response. Directing one's attention at a new stimulus.

Orthogenetic principle. The principle that all development involves changes in a positive direction: greater differentiation, integration, organization, etc.

Over-controlled behavior. Inhibited and anxious behavior; see *under-controlled behavior*.

Over-extension. Use of a word beyond its usual meaning; see *under-extension*.

Over-regulation (in language development). Application of a general grammatical rule beyond the particular cases it applies to, for example *goed* instead of *went*.

Over-stimulation. More stimulation than an organism is able to deal with at its current level; see *under-stimulation*.

Painter's cues (depth perception). Information about light, surface, height and similar used as indicators of the position of objects relative to each other, for example the fact that one object can cover another object located further back in the room, and that objects that are further away are positioned "above" objects that are closer; see *stereoscopic vision*.

Palmar grasp reflex. *Developmental reflex* causing the fingers to flex inward when the infant's palm is gently touched; usually disappears at 2–4 months of age.

Parallax movement. Apparent motion of an object located at a short distance, when first looking with one eye only, followed by the other. Also discernable when the head is moved to the side: close objects are shifted to one side of the visual field, and objects further away to the other.

Parallel play. Play in which several children play side by side with similar objects or in a similar way, but without interacting.

Parenting style. General description of how parents raise their children; see *authoritarian, authoritative, disengaged* and *permissive parenting*.

Perception. Knowledge gained through the senses; discernment, selection and processing of sensory input.

Perceptual constancy. Awareness of perceptual characteristics as constant, even though the lighting conditions and the image projected on the retina may vary.

Perceptual preference. Method to examine how a child perceives the surroundings; involves measuring what the child is attentive to for the longest amount of time; see *preference method*.

Perinatal. Period just before and after birth.

Permissive parenting. Parenting style that places few demands on the child, but in which parents are *responsive*; see *authoritarian, authoritative* and *disengaged parenting*.

Personal narrative. See *autobiographical memory*.

Personality. An individual's characteristic tendency to feel, think and act in specific ways.

Personality traits. Summary description of an individual's *personality*.

Phallic phase. According to *psychoanalytic theory*, the third phase in *psychosexual development*, in which the genital area becomes a source of pleasure; age 4–5 years; see *anal phase, genital phase, latency phase* and *oral phase*.

Phenotype. An individual's observable physical and psychological characteristics; see *genotype*.

Phenylketonuria (PKU). Hereditary disorder in the production of the enzyme phenylalanine hydroxylase, leading to elevated levels of phenylalanine in the blood; causes severe mental and physical impairment if left untreated by a dietary regimen.

Phoneme. The smallest unit of sound that distinguishes two words in a language; /m/ and /p/, for example, are different phonemes in English, since *mile* and *pile* are different English words; see *morpheme*.

Phonology. Branch of linguistics dealing with the sounds of spoken language.

Phylogenesis. The evolutionary history of a species or an attribute.

Physical causality, understanding of. Understanding of how physical objects behave and interact with one another; see *causality* and *psychological causality*.

Pincer grip. Grip of the thumb and index finger.

Plantar reflex. *Developmental reflex* that causes the toes to flex inward when the ball of the foot is stimulated; usually disappears at 9–10 months of age.

Plasticity (in development). The ability of an organism to change and adapt in response to experiences; frequently used in connection with the nervous system; see *constraint*.

Pleasure principle. According to *psychoanalytic theory*, one of two principles governing human functioning; seeking the immediate satisfaction of drives, needs and desires regardless of consequences; see *reality principle*.

Polygenic inheritance. Refers to the interaction of several genes in shaping a characteristic that varies among the *population*.

Popular children (sociometry). Children who are actively accepted by other children. Often they are physically strong with an attractive appearance, but their willingness to share, ability to cooperate and other social skills are equally important for their acceptance and popularity among peers; see *controversial children*, *neglected children*, *neutral children* and *unpopular children*.

Population (in statistics). The sum total of individuals, objects, events and the like included in a study. Also used to describe a group of individuals with a common measurable attribute, such as children in a certain school grade or young people in cities.

Positive reinforcement (in conditioning). An event or other factor that, when injected into a situation, increases the likelihood of a particular action; for example, the likelihood of a child doing homework may increase when homework leads to good grades; see *negative reinforcement* and *reinforcement*.

Post-conventional morality. According to Kohlberg, the third and final of three main stages of moral development; characterized by abstract values that are valid under all circumstances and in every society; see *conventional morality* and *pre-conventional morality*.

Postnatal. After birth.

Prader-Willi syndrome. Genetic syndrome characterized by short stature, *hypotonia*, an insatiable appetite and often mild learning disabilities; caused by a missing or unexpressed part of chromosome pair 15, inherited from the father; the counterpart to *Angelman syndrome*; see *genomic imprinting*.

Pragmatic reasoning. Reasoning based on *schemas* abstracted from one's own past experiences in similar situations.

Pragmatics (in language). Functions of language in everyday use; see *semantics*.

Pre-conventional morality. According to Kohlberg, the first of three main stages of moral development; characterized by moral reasoning based on reward, punishment and authority; see *conventional morality* and *post-conventional morality*.

Preference for novelty. Tendency to be more attentive to new rather than familiar stimulation; appears in infants after the age of 3 months.

Preference method. Method of measuring the proportion of time a child is attentive to each of two different stimuli, such as a simple checkerboard and a more complex visual pattern, or the mother's voice and the voice of a stranger; children are said to show a preference for the stimulus they are attentive to for more than half the time.

Pre-linguistic. Refers to children's skills and abilities before they begin to speak, for example pre-linguistic *communication*.

Premoral stage. According to Piaget, the first of three stages in moral development; lasts until 4–5 years of age; during this stage, children show a poor understanding of general rules and follow their own personal rules without a consistent system, based on their own wishes and needs; see *moral realism* and *moral subjectivism*.

Prenatal period. The developmental period before birth.

Preoperational stage. According to Piaget, the second of four stages in cognitive development, approx. age 4–7; see *concrete operational stage*, *formal operational stage* and *sensorimotor stage*.

Preschool age. Age 3–6 years.

Pretend play. Form of *symbolic play* that involves make-believe actions.

Prevalence. Relative presence of for example traits, diseases and syndromes in a particular population at a certain time; see *incidence*.

Primary emotions. See *basic emotions*.

Primary intersubjectivity. According to Trevarthen, younger infants' perception of how they affect others, and the fact that others are aware of them; see *secondary intersubjectivity*.

Private speech. Speech that does not convey enough information to allow the listener to understand what is being communicated.

Procedural memory. Memory of how something is done; includes among other things the ability to form habits, acquire skills and some forms of classical conditioning.

Prosocial behavior. Behavior intended to help others and share objects or other benefits without advantage to the individual itself; see *antisocial behavior*.

Prosody. The patterns of stress and intonation in a spoken language.

Prospective study. Study that follows an individual over time; see *retrospective study*.

Protection (in development). Conditions that reduce the negative effects of *vulnerability* and *risk*.

Prototype. Typical exemplar of a concept.

Prototype category. *Conceptual category* derived from a prototypical exemplar; see *feature-based category*.

Psychoanalytic psychology. Psychological theories based on Freud's theory and psychotherapeutic method (psychoanalysis); founded on the principle that an individual's thoughts and actions are determined by drives and impulses and their internal, often *unconscious*, regulation through interaction between the different parts of the human psyche; both *personality* and mental problems of children and adults are explained on the basis of unconscious processes and conflicts rooted in early childhood; see *ego*, *id*, *psychodynamic theory* and *superego*.

Psychodynamic psychology. Tradition that emphasizes the importance of feelings and needs for an individual's thoughts and actions; describes *personality* and its development based on the assumption that the human psyche involves mental forces that frequently are in conflict with each other, and have an important basis in early childhood; *psychoanalysis* belongs to this tradition.

Psychological causality, understanding of. Understanding of the intent or motivation behind an action; see *causality*.

Psychometrics. Measurement of *individual differences* in psychological characteristics.

Psychopathology. Mental problems and disorders that make everyday functioning difficult.

Psychosexual phase. According to *psychoanalytic theory*, a *critical period* in which a child's mental energy is directed toward a specific area of the body; the development of an individual's personality and sociocultural adaptation depends on certain stimuli and experiences and the resolution of mental conflicts during these periods; see *anal phase*, *genital phase*, *latency phase*, *oral phase* and *phallic phase*.

Psychosocial crisis. According to Erikson, a *critical period* of developmental challenges or tasks related to the formation of specific characteristics; the experience of a psychosocial crisis leaves a permanent mark on an individual's personal and social development, and has consequences for the course of future psychosocial crises.

Psychosocial moratorium. According to Erikson, a period in which adolescents have not yet decided on a future career or role in society, and find themselves between the safety of childhood and the independence of adult life (*autonomy*).

Punishment. In behavioral psychology, any event that reduces the probability of repeating an action under similar circumstances; see *reinforcement*.

Qualitative change. Change in the nature or quality of a phenomenon; see *quantitative change*.

Qualitative method. Research method involving the use of descriptions and categories that need not be quantifiable, and analyses not based on measurements and numerical processing; does not require *replicability*, but the researcher must be able to account for his or her standpoint and the basis for interpreting what has been observed; see *quantitative method*.

Quantitative change. Quantifiable change in the nature or quality of a phenomenon, measurable in degree, amount, number, and the like; see *qualitative change*.

Quantitative method. Research method involving the use of quantifiable descriptions and categories, and analyses based on measurements and statistical processing; requires *replicability*; see *qualitative method*.

Raw score (in testing). The total number of points scored on a test; see *standard score*.

Reaction range. The degree to which a developmental process can be influenced at a particular point during development.

Reaction to novelty. Behavior characterized by shyness and uncertain reactions to new situations, objects and people.

Reality principle. According to *psychoanalytic theory*, one of two principles that govern human functioning; seeking to satisfy drives, needs and desires in relation to what is realistic, i.e. what is possible within a given physical, social and cultural environment; see *pleasure principle*.

Recall. Recollection of an experience without perceptual support; see *recognition*.

Receptive language. The language that the child understands; see *expressive language*.

Recessive gene. Gene that is only expressed when present on both *chromosomes* of a pair, one from each parent; see *dominant gene* and *genomic imprinting*.

Recognition. The process of experiencing something in the moment that has been experienced before, such as when children consciously or nonconsciously show that they have seen a particular image before; see *recall*.

Reductionism. Theoretical model that attempts to explain phenomena at a higher systemic level based on processes and elements at a lower systemic level, such as explaining complex traits and skills based on the notion that they arise from a set of simpler traits and skills.

Reference group. Group that forms the basis for an individual's values, norms, attitudes and behaviors.

Referential communication. Use of language that enables the other person to identify a particular individual, object or event in the current environment.

Referential style (in early language development). According to Nelson, speech characterized by a preponderance of words referring to objects; see *expressive style*.

Reflective abstraction. According to Piaget, knowledge acquired by thinking about one's own thoughts and forming abstractions based on these personal reflections; see *cognitive structure*.

Reflex. Unlearned and involuntary response to an external stimulus.

Refreshment (of memory). Repeated presentation of an object or event previously experienced by an individual.

Regression. The relapse into earlier, more primitive or childish ways of functioning.

Regulating function of language. Use of language to regulate one's own behavior.

Rehabilitation. The effort to build up new or previously existing functions and restore opportunities for interaction and quality of life for people with acquired disabilities; see *habilitation*.

Reinforcement (in conditioning). In *classical conditioning*: presentation of an *unconditioned stimulus* and a *neutral stimulus* that becomes a *conditioned stimulus*, such that the *conditioned response* is triggered more consistently. In *operant conditioning*: events that follow the execution of an action and increase the likelihood of repeating the action under similar circumstances.

Relational aggression. A form of *hostile aggression*; actions whose main intent is to damage the relationship between two people, for example by speaking ill of them; see *hostile aggression*, *instrumental aggression* and *open aggression*.

Relational emotion. Emotion exclusively directed at other people, such as love, hatred or jealousy; see *basic emotions* and *self-referential emotion*.

Reliability. Measure of how dependable a piece of information is, and whether the observational categories and measuring methods lead to the same result after repeated observation; see *validity*.

Replicability (in research). Requirement that another person has to be able to perform a study in precisely the same way it was originally carried out, and arrive at approximately the same result.

Representation (mental). An individual's mental storage of understanding and knowledge about the world.

Representative sample. A group of individuals with the same distribution of relevant characteristics as the *population* represented by the sample, so that the results of the sample can be assumed to be valid for the entire population.

Research design. Plan for how and when to collect scientific data in a study.

Resilience. Attributes that lead to a positive development under difficult childhood conditions, such as children who are biologically or socially at *risk* of aberrant or delayed development; see *vulnerability*.

Responsivity (as a characteristic of play objects). Measure of the extent to which objects "react" when children play with them, for example whether they move, emit a sound or change shape.

Responsivity (as a human trait). The ability to provide a quick and appropriate response to an individual's *signals* and behavior; see *sensitivity*.

Retrospective study. Study in which an individual is asked about earlier events.

Rett syndrome. Genetic syndrome that almost exclusively affects girls; characterized by severe *intellectual disability* and motor and language impairment; development is often normal for the first 6–18 months of life, with a consequent decline in functioning. Believed to be mainly caused by a defective control gene (MeCP$_2$) on the X chromosome that fails to switch off other X chromosome genes at the right time; see *genomic imprinting*.

Reversibility (in cognition). The understanding that a change in one direction can be counteracted by a change in the opposite direction, for example that a ball of clay shaped into a sausage can be reshaped into a ball.

Ribonucleic acid (RNA). Macromolecular compounds carrying genetic information and responsible for cellular protein synthesis.

Rigidity. *Personality trait* characterized by poor social adaptability and lack of flexibility.

Risk. Increased likelihood of a negative developmental outcome; may be linked to biological and environmental factors.

Ritualization. Process whereby involuntary forms of expression, such as facial expressions, evolve into *signals*; or a process whereby a voluntary action becomes a communicative *gesture*, for example when a reaching movement turns into a pointing gesture.

Role. Expectations of certain action patterns and behaviors associated with an individual by virtue of their function or position in society, for example as a girl, teenager or boy scout.

Role-play. Form of *pretend play* in which the participants make-believe they are another person, an animal or a human-like figure.

Rooting reflex. *Developmental reflex* elicited when an infant is lightly touched on the cheek and turns the head toward the side being stimulated; usually disappears at 3 months of age.

Rough-and-tumble play. A type of *exercise play* in which children run after each other, push, tickle, play-fight and similar.

Scaffold. In *social constructivism*, the external regulation, help and support provided by adults or more experienced peers to children, adapted to their level and allowing them to transcend their independent coping skills and develop new skills and knowledge; see *zone of proximal development*.

Schema. Mental *representation* that emerges when actions are generalized by means of repetition and transformed through mental processing, thus shaping the individual's perception of the environment; see *cognitive structure*.

School age. Age 6–12.

Screening test. Brief *test* that aims to identify individuals who should be examined using more thorough and time-consuming methods.

Script (cognition). Generalized mental *representation* of a sequence of events that recur within the context of a specific situation; provides among other things the basis for an individual's expectations of how to behave in different situations, such as at school or at a restaurant.

Second-order belief attribution; Second-order theory of mind. The belief of one person's thoughts about another person's thoughts, what A thinks B is thinking; see *mind understanding*, *theory of mind*.

Secondary intersubjectivity. According to Trevarthen, the *joint attention* of children and adults on something outside themselves, as well as their awareness of each other's attention.

Secure base. Describes the function of caregivers when they give younger children the opportunity for controlled *exploration* of objects and environments that can elicit fear, and to seek refuge when they become apprehensive; see *attachment*.

Segregation (education). Special educational alternative outside the ordinary preschool group or school class a child is part of; see *desegregation*.

Self. Personal awareness, perception or evaluation of oneself.

Self as knower. The *I*, the subject that perceives its own existence and presence in the world; see *self as known*.

Self as known. The *me*, the entire complex of characteristics an individual thinks of when reflecting on their own person; see *self as knower*.

Self-concept. Awareness of having specific and independent traits; see *self as known*.

Self-disclosure. Communicating personal information about oneself to others; typical in *adolescence*.

Self-efficacy. The experience of acting and having control over one's own life; belief in one's own ability to deal with different situations and events.

Self-evaluation; Self-esteem. The assessment of one's own characteristics in relation to an inner standard that includes how and who one wishes to be; can also refer to questionnaires, surveys and the like about a person's characteristics.

Self-image. Positive or negative perception of oneself and one's own characteristics.

Self-organization. The emergence or establishment of new structures not driven by external factors.

Sef-referential emotion; Self-conscious emotions; Secondary emotions. Emotion associated with an individual's self-evaluation in relation to a standard based on personal emotional experiences and information provided by others; includes pride, shame, embarrassment, guilt and envy; see *basic emotions* and *relational emotions*.

Self-regulation. The ability to monitor and adapt one's own thoughts, feelings, reactions and actions in order to cope with the requirements, challenges and opportunities of the environment and be able to achieve one's goals; also referred to as self-control.

Semantic memory. Long-term memory of general facts and knowledge, such as the name of the United States capital; see *autobiographical memory*, *episodic memory*, *long-term memory* and *working memory*.

Semantics. The branch of linguistics concerned with the meaning of words and phrases.

Sensitive period. Limited period of time when an individual is particularly susceptible to specific forms of positive or negative stimulation and experience; if the stimulation or experience does not take place during the given time period, the individual will still be able to take advantage of, or be impaired by, similar types of stimulation or experience later in life, but to a lesser extent; see *critical period*.

Sensitivity (of a caregiver). Ability to understand a child's condition, respond quickly and adequately to the child's *signals* and behavior, and provide challenges the child is able to master; see *responsivity*.

Sensorimotor stage. According to Piaget, the first of four stages in cognitive development, lasting until the age of 2; see *concrete operational stage*, *formal operational stage* and *preoperational stage*.

Sensory integration. Simultaneous use of different types of perceptual information within the same modality or from two or more modalities, such as the visual and acoustic characteristics of a person speaking.

Sensory modality. One of several specific senses, such as vision or hearing.

Separation distress. Emotional reaction elicited when a child is separated from a caregiver; also known as separation anxiety.

Separation syndrome. See *Bowlby-Robertson syndrome*.

Sex. See *gender*.

Sex chromosomes. Chromosomal pair that determines the sex of an individual and differs between males (XY) and females (XX).

Sex-linked inheritance. Inherited characteristic related to the genes on the *sex chromosomes*.

Shaping (of behavior). Step-by-step *reinforcement* of behavior in such a way that it gradually changes and increasingly resembles desired behavior; part of *operant conditioning*.

Sign language. Visual-manual language, primarily using movements of the arms, hands and fingers, supported by body movements, mouth movements and facial gestures.

Signals (in early development). Infant actions and expressions used by adults as an indication of the infant's interests, preferences and general well-being.

Significance (in statistics). Indication of the likelihood that a statistical difference or relationship is based on pure coincidence.

Size constancy. Ability to perceive the size of an object as constant despite changes in the size of the image projected on the retina; see *color constancy*, *constancy* and *form constancy*.

Slow-to-warm-up (temperament). According to Thomas and Chess, slow adaptation to new situations; includes irregularities in daily routines and a tendency to cry and feel restless, but with moderate reactions; may initially resemble *difficult temperament*, but mostly resembles *easy temperament* once the individual has warmed up.

Sociability (temperament). Interest and enjoyment in being in the company of other people.

Social cognition. Cognitive processes that form the basis for understanding one's own and other people's intentions, motives, emotions, thoughts and social relations.

Social construction. Anything rooted in or created by means of social interaction.

Social constructivism. Psychological theories based on the notion that children construct their understanding of the outside world through interaction and cooperation with other people, and that people in different cultures (including the subcultures of a society) can perceive one and the same phenomenon in different ways; see *logical constructivism*.

Social learning theory. See *cognitive behavior theory*.

Social mediation. Social communication of or guidance toward knowledge.

Social referencing. Using other people's emotional reactions to evaluate uncertain situations; see *emotion regulation*.

Social selection. Selectivity in choice of friends and social relations.

Socialization. Term frequently used synonymous with *enculturation*.

Sociobiology. Branch of biology built on the assumption that complex forms of social behavior, such as *aggression* and altruism, have a genetic basis and have been shaped by *evolution* due to their survival value.

Socioeconomic status (SES). Assessment of an individual's economic and social status in society; for children, usually based on information about the parents' education and occupation.

Sociogram. A graphic representation of an individual's social network; see *sociometry*.

Sociometry. Method used to map the popularity and status of individuals in a group, based on the opinions of other group members, such as asking children whom they would most and least like to spend time with; can be graphically represented as a *sociogram*.

Specific factor; s-factor (in intelligence). *Domain-specific* ability; see *general factor*.

Speech act; Language act. Action performed via a linguistic utterance, such as a greeting, question, narration, promise or command.

Stability (in development). Describes the constancy of an individual's position in relation to peers with respect to a particular characteristic; the fact that individual differences in the execution of a skill are constant from one developmental stage to another.

Stage (in development). Delimited period of time in which thoughts, feelings and behavior are organized in a way that is qualitatively different from the preceding or following periods.

Stage theory. Theory based on the assumption that development proceeds in distinct and qualitatively different *stages*.

Standard deviation. Measure of the spread of *quantitative* data; indicates the average degree of deviation in the score or numerical value of a variable from the total average; see *normal distribution*.

Standard score (in testing). Score based on *standard deviation*; indicates the relative ranking of an individual's performance on a test compared with the statistical average and the distribution of scores in the standardization sample; see *raw score*.

Standard theory. See *The standard theory*.

Standardization (of tests). Systematic survey of *test* items among a *representative sample* of the *population* targeted by the test; aims to estimate the distribution of scores among a given population.

Stanford-Binet Intelligence Scales. IQ test for ages 2–23; the 5th revised English-language edition (SB5) was released in 2003.

Stanine scale. STAndard NINE is a method of scaling test scores based on a division of the *normal distribution curve* into nine steps, with a mean of five and a standard deviation of two.

Stereoscopic vision. Ability to perceive space as three-dimensional due to a small difference between the images that are projected on the retina when the eyes are directed at the same point (parallax); see *painter's cues*.

Stereotype. General and often erroneous view of the characteristics of a group of individuals, for example *gender stereotype*.

Strange Situation. Standardized situation to assess the quality of attachment between an adult and a child aged 1–2 years; see *attachment*.

Stranger anxiety. Fear of strangers common in children during the early attachment period; see *attachment*.

Successive one-word utterances. Utterances during early language development that consist of several thematically related words, but articulated in such a way that the words do not lie

within the same intonation contour, but have short pauses between them; see *horizontal structure*, *intonation* and *vertical structure*.

Superego. In *psychoanalytic theory*, one of the three parts of the human psyche, consisting of internalized demands and expectations, primarily from parents, but also from other important persons in the child's environment; its function is to ensure that an individual's actions remain within the norms and values of culture; see *id* and *ego*.

Symbol. Something that represents something other than itself, such as a sign, a word, an image or the like.

Symbolic gesture. Gesture that specifies or names the thing or category it refers to; see *deictic gesture*.

Symbolic play. Play in which children take on the role of a person or an animal, and connect objects with a function unlike the one they usually have, performing a make-believe activity; see *constructive play*, *exercise play*, *group play* and *rule-based play*.

Sympathy. Understanding why another person experiences the emotions that they express.

Synapse. Contact point between the *axon* of a nerve cell and the body of another nerve cell via its *dendrites*; this is where the transmission of impulses occurs.

Synaptic pruning. Selective loss of synapses during the first years of life due to lack of use.

Syndrome. Set of attributes and behavioral characteristics that regularly occur together.

Syntax. The grammatical arrangement of words and phrases in a language.

Tabula rasa. "Blank slate"; common expression based on the assumption that humans are born with an empty mind that acquires content and structure through experience.

Telegraphic speech. Incomplete utterances of only a few words during early language development; consists primarily of content words without functional words such as articles and prepositions.

Temperament. A biologically determined pattern of emotional reactivity and regulation unique to an individual; includes the degree of *emotionality*, *irritability* and *activity level*, and reactions to and ability to cope with emotional situations, new impressions and changes; see *easy temperament*, *difficult temperament* and *slow-to-warm-up*.

Teratogens. Substances that can cause damage to the fetus.

Terrible twos. Common term for the period between 18 and 36 months, when children are often disobedient and defiant toward their parents.

Test. Measurement instrument; a collection of questions or tasks that provide a basis for assessing an individual's performance relative to peers or a specific set of criteria; see *criterion-referenced test* and *norm-referenced test*.

Thanatos. According to *psychoanalytic theory*, the aggressive and destructive drive that together with *libido* motivates all human action.

The new theory. A common term for Piaget's final revision of his theory of cognitive development, which makes allowances for some of the criticism directed at *the standard theory*, in particular issues concerning Piaget's assumptions on *domain-general* development.

The standard theory. A common term for Piaget's theory of cognitive development as it appeared in its basic form in the 1950s and 1960s; see *the new theory*.

Theory of mind. The understanding that human beings are thinking and sentient beings who act according to how they perceive a given situation; see *social cognition* and *mind understanding*.

Toddlerhood. Age 1–3.

Transaction effect. The result of reciprocal influences between an individual and the environment over time, see *main effect* and *interaction effect*.

Transactional model. Developmental model based on mutual interaction between an individual and the environment over time: the environment changes the individual, the individual changes the environment, which in turn changes the individual, and so on.

Transitive relation. Relation that makes it possible to infer the relation between A and C based on the relations A–B and B–C, for example that A must be greater than C when A is greater than B and B is greater than C.

Triarchic model of intelligence. According to Sternberg, a model of intelligence with three integrated sub-theories: 1) *cognition* and the processes that form the basis for intelligent action, 2) experiences of relationships between the inner and the outer world, and 3) use of cognitive mechanisms to adapt to the world one lives in on a practical everyday basis.

Trisomy 21. The most common form of *Down syndrome*, caused by an extra chromosome 21.

Turner syndrome. *Chromosomal abnormality* caused by the presence of only a single X chromosome (X0) in females; characterized by a slightly low weight at birth, heart failure, distinctive facial features, short and chubby fingers, short stature, inability to reproduce and *learning disabilities*.

Twin Study. Study comparing identical and fraternal twins who have grown up together and separately in order to shed light on the importance of genes and the environment in the development of different traits.

Typical development. Course of development that characterizes the majority of a *population*; see *atypical development* and *individual differences*.

Unconditioned response. See *conditioning*.

Unconditioned stimulus. See *conditioning*.

Unconscious. Not within the sphere of conscious attention; in *psychoanalytic theory*, an inaccessible part of consciousness where repressed, often anxiety-eliciting memories and desires are stored.

Under-controlled behavior. Impulsive, disruptive and aggressive behavior; see *over-controlled behavior*.

Under-extension. Use of a word more limited than its usual meaning; see *over-extension*.

Under-stimulation. Deprivation, lack of or a reduction in stimulation considered important for normal development; see *over-stimulation*.

Universal grammar. In Chomsky's theory, an innate grammatical device that contains the grammars of all human languages.

Universality. General validity; phenomena that exist in all cultures, such as language.

Unpopular children (sociometry). Children who are actively rejected by other children; some children in this group appear particularly aggressive and hostile, others are socially withdrawn and often submissive, while others yet are immature and childish compared with their peers; see *controversial children, neglected children, neutral children* and *popular children*.

Validity. The soundness or factual accuracy of knowledge; whether a given method measures what it aims to measure and whether the results provide answers to the research questions posed.

Variation set. A set of statements that express the same information in slightly different ways; common in *child-directed speech*.

Vertical décalage. According to Piaget, the transition from one stage to another; see *horizontal décalage*.

Vertical relation. Relationship in which one part has more knowledge and social power than the other, such as parent–child; see *horizontal relation*.

Vertical structure (in language). Early utterances consisting of several words that do not lie within the same intonation contour, but have short pauses between them; see *horizontal structure, intonation* and *successive one-word utterances*.

Visual perspective. Ability to understand what others are able or unable to see.

Vocable. Vocalization of a speech-like sound without conventional meaning in the child's language environment; typically occurs during early language development.

Vocabulary spurt. A rapid increase in productive vocabulary that typically characterizes children's language from the end of the second year of life; often defined as the first month in which a child's vocabulary increases by 15 words or more, often coinciding with the child's earliest two-word utterances.

Vulnerability. An individual's susceptibility to be adversely affected by particular conditions or circumstances in the environment; see *resilience* and *risk*.

Williams syndrome. Genetic syndrome characterized by heart defects, distinctive facial features, a short stature, developmental delays in the fetal stage and later, problems thriving during *infancy*, mild or moderate *learning disabilities*, good language abilities compared with other skills, and trusting behavior toward other people.

Working memory. Part of the memory system related to what an individual does while trying to remember something for a short period of time or dealing with a problem. Characterized by limited storage and processing capacity, and a rapid reduction in content if not repeated; see *autobiographical memory, episodic memory, long-term memory* and *semantic memory*.

Working model (in social relations). Mental representation of an early relationship that forms the basis for expectations about the nature of social relationships, such as a caregiver's inclination to provide emotional support and be devoted and reliable.

Zone of maintenance. In childhood dementia or other negatively processing pathological conditions, the level of functioning where the individual can perform actions with help after independent performance has been lost.

Zone of modifiability. The reaction range which represents the child's developmental constraints, the upper and lower level of possible deevlopment.

Zone of proximal development. Children's mastery of skills in collaboration with more competent individuals within a specific area of knowledge or expertise, as opposed to self-mastery; see *scaffold*.

Zygote. Cell resulting from the fusion of an egg and a sperm cell.

BIBLIOGRAPHY

à Beckett, C., Lynch, S., & Pike, D. (2017). Playing with theory. In S. Lynch, D. Pike & C. à Beckett (Eds), *Multidisciplinary perspectives on play from birth and beyond* (pp. 1–22). Singapore: Springer.

Abdolmaleky, H. M., Thiagalingam, S., & Wilcox, M. (2005). Genetics and epigenetics in major psychiatric disorders: Dilemmas, achievements, applications, and future scope. *American Journal of Pharmacogenomics, 5*, 149–160.

Abecassis, M. (2003). I hate you just the way you are: Exploring the formation, maintenance and need for enemies. *New Directions for Child and Adolescent Development, 102*, 5–22.

Abecassis, M., Hartup, W. W., Haselager, G. J. T., Scholte, R. H. J., & van Lieshout, C. F. M. (2002). Mutual antipathies and their significance in middle childhood and adolescence. *Child Development, 73*, 1543–1556.

Abrahamsen, E. P., & Smith, R. (2000). Facilitating idiom acquisition in children with communication disorders: Computer vs classroom. *Child Language Teaching and Therapy, 16*, 227–239.

Abrams, D. (1989). Differential association: Social development in gender identity and intergroup relations during adolescence. In S. M. Skevington & D. Baker (Eds), *The social identity of women* (pp. 59–83). London: Sage.

Abravanel, E., & DeYong, N. G. (1997). Exploring the roles of peer and adult video models for infant imitation. *Journal of Genetic Psychology, 158*, 133–150.

Achenbach, T. M., & Rescorla, L. A. (2000). *Manual for the ASEBA preschool forms and profiles: An integrated system of multi-informant assessment.* Burlington, VT: University of Vermont Department of Psychiatry.

Achenbach, T. M., & Rescorla, L. A. (2001). *Manual for the ASEBA school-age forms and profiles.* Burlington, VT: Research Center for Children, Youth, and Families, University of Vermont.

Ackerman, S. (1992). *Discovering the brain.* Washington, DC: National Academy Press.

Acredolo, C. (1997). Understanding Piaget's new theory requires assimilation and accommodation. *Human Development, 40*, 235–237.

Acredolo, L. P., & Goodwyn, S. (2009). *Baby signs: How to talk with your baby before your baby can talk, Third edition.* New York, NY: McGraw Hill.

Adams, G. R., & Marshall, S. K. (1996). A developmental social psychology of identity: Understanding the person-in-context. *Journal of Adolescence, 19*, 429–442.

Adolph, K. E., & Robinson, S. R. (2015). Motor development. In R. M. Lerner, L. Liben & U. Muller (Eds), *Handbook of child psychology and developmental science, Seventh edition, Volume 2: Cognitive processes* (pp. 114–157). New York, NY: Wiley.

Adolph, K. E., & Tamis-LeMonda, C. S. (2014). The costs and benefits of development: The transition from crawling to walking. *Child Development Perspectives, 8*, 187–192.

Adolph, K. E., Tamis-LeMonda, C. S., Ishak, S., Karasik, L. B., & Loboet, S. A. (2008). Locomotor experience and use of social information are posture specific. *Developmental Psychology, 44*, 1705–1714.

Adolphs, R. (2009). The social brain: Neural basis of social knowledge. *Annual Review of Psychology, 60*, 693–716.

Adrian, M., Lyon, A. R., Oti, R., & Tininenko, J. (2010). Developmental foundations and clinical applications of social information processing: A review. *Marriage and Family Review, 46*, 327–345.

Agnew, S. E., & Powell, M. B. (2004). The effect of intellectual disability on children's recall of an event across different question types. *Law and Human Behavior, 28*, 273–294.

Ainsworth, M. D. S. (1963). The development of infant–mother interaction among the Ganda. In B. M. Foss (Ed.), *Determinants of infant behavior, Volume 2* (pp. 67–104). New York, NY: Wiley.

Ainsworth, M. D. S. (1967). *Infancy in Uganda: Infancy and the growth of love.* Baltimore, MD: Johns Hopkins University Press.

Ainsworth, M. D. S. (1983). Patterns of infant–mother attachment as related to maternal care. In D. Magnusson & V. Allen (Eds), *Human development: An interactional perspective* (pp. 35–55). London: Academic Press.

Ainsworth, M. D. S., & Bowlby, J. (1991). An ethological account of personality development. *American Psychologist, 46,* 433–441.

Ainsworth, M. D. S., & Wittig, B. A. (1969). Attachment and exploratory behavior of one-year-olds in a strange situation. In B. M. Foss (Ed.), *Determinants of infant behavior, Volume 4* (pp. 111–136). London: Methuen.

Ainsworth, M. D. S., Bell, S. M., & Stayton, D. J. (1972). Individual differences in strange-situation behavior of one-year-olds. In H. R. Schaffer (Ed.), *The origin of human social relations* (pp. 17–57). London: Academic Press.

Ainsworth, M. D. S., Blehar, M. C., Waters, E., & Wahl, S. (1978). *Patterns of attachment.* Hillsdale, NJ: Erlbaum.

Aitken, M., VanderLaan, D. P., Wasserman, L., Stojanovski, S., & Zucker, K. J. (2016). Self-harm and suicidality in children referred for gender dysphoria. *Journal of the American Academy of Child and Adolescent Psychiatry, 55,* 513–520.

Akhutina, T. V. (2003). L. S. Vygotsky and A. R. Luria: Foundations of neuropsychology. *Journal of Russian and East European Psychology, 41,* 159–190.

Alderson-Day, B., & Fernyhough, C. (2015). Inner speech: Development, cognitive functions, phenomenology, and neurobiology. *Psychological Bulletin, 141,* 931–965.

Alea, N., & Wang, Q. (2015). Going global: The functions of autobiographical memory in cultural context. *Memory, 23,* 1–10.

Alesi, M., Rappo, G., & Pepi, A. (2014). Depression, anxiety at school and self-esteem in children with learning disabilities. *Journal of Psychological Abnormalities in Children, 3,* 125.

Alexander, J. M., & Schwanenflugel, P. J. (1994). Strategy regulation: The role of intelligence, metacognitive attributions, and knowledge base. *Developmental Psychology, 30,* 709–723.

Alexander-Passe, N. (2006). How dyslexic teenagers cope: An investigation of self-esteem, coping and depression. *Dyslexia, 12,* 256–275.

Algozzine, B., Porfeli, E., Wang, C., McColl, A., & Audette, R. (2012). Achievement gaps: Learning disabilities, community capital, and school composition. In W. Sittiprapaporn (Ed.), *Learning disabilities* (pp. 19–30). Rijeka, Croatia: InTech.

Alhusen, J. L. (2008). A literature update on maternal-fetal attachment. *Journal of Obstetric, Gynecological, and Neonatal Nursing, 37,* 315–328.

Allan, K. (1977). Classifiers. *Language, 53,* 285–311.

Allen, J. G. (2003). Mentalizing. *Bulletin of the Menninger Clinic, 67,* 91–112.

Allen, J. P., & Tan, J. S. (2016). The multiple facets of attachment in adolescence. In J. Cassidy & P. R. Shaver (Eds), *Handbook of attachment: Theory, research and clinical applications, Third edition* (pp. 399–415). New York, NY: Guilford Press.

Almås, I., Cappelen, A. W., Sørensen, E. Ø., & Tungodden, B. (2010). Fairness and the development of inequality acceptance. *Science, 328,* 1176–1178.

Almeida, L. S., Prieto, M. D., Ferreira, A. I., Bermejo, M. R., Ferrando, M., & Ferrándiz, C. (2010). Intelligence assessment: Gardner multiple intelligence theory as an altenative. *Learning and Individual Differences, 20,* 225–230.

Almqvist, A.-L., & Duvander, A.-Z. (2014). Changes in gender equality? Swedish fathers' parental leave, division of childcare and housework. *Journal of Family Studies, 20,* 19–27

Alsaker, F. D., & Flammer, A. (1999). *The adolescent experience.* London: Lawrence Erlbaum.

Alt, M., & Plante, E. (2006). Factors that influence lexical and semantic fast mapping of young children with specific language impairment. *Journal of Speech, Language, and Hearing Research, 49,* 941–954.

Altınkamış, N. F., Kern, S., & Sofu, H. (2014). When context matters more than language: Verb or noun in French and Turkish caregiver speech. *First Language, 34,* 537–550.

Amaral, A. C. S., & Ferreira, M. E. C. (2017). Body dissatisfaction and associated factors among Brazilian adolescents: A longitudinal study. *Body Image, 22,* 32–38.

Ambridge, B., & Lieven, E. V. M. (2011). *Child language acquisition: Contrasting theoretical approaches.* Cambridge: Cambridge University Press.

American Academy of Child and Adolescent Psychiatry (2015). Screen time and children. Downloaded from www.aacap.org/AACAP/Families_and_Youth/Facts_for_Families/FFF-Guide/Children-And-Watching-TV-054.aspx.

American Academy of Pediatrics (2011). Media use by children younger than 2 years. *Pediatrics, 128,* 1040–1045.

American Psychiatric Association (2013). *Diagnostic and statistical manual of mental disorders, Fifth edition (DSM-5).* Washington, DC: American Psychiatric Association.

Amianto, F., Northoff, G., Daga, G. A., Fassino, S., & Tasca, G. A. (2016). Is anorexia nervosa a disorder of the self? A psychological approach. *Frontiers in Psychology, 7,* 849.

Amir, R. E., Van den Veyver, I. B., Wan, M., Tran, C. Q., Francke, U., & Zoghbi, H. Y. (1999). Rett syndrome is caused by mutations in X-linked MECP2, encoding methyl-CpG-binding protein 2. *Nature Genetics, 23,* 185–188.

Ammaniti, M., van IJzendoorn, M. H., Speranza, A. M., & Tambelli, R. (2000). Internal working models of attachment during late childhood and early adolescence: An exploration of stability and change. *Attachment and Human Development, 2,* 328–346.

Amsel, E., & Smalley, J. D. (2000). Beyond really and truly: Children's counterfactual thinking about pretend and possible worlds. In P. Mitchell & K. J. Riggs (Eds), *Children's reasoning and the mind* (pp. 121–147). Hove, UK: Psychology Press.

Anazi, S., Maddirevula, S., Faqeih, E., Alsedairy, H., Alzahrani, F., Shamseldin, H. E., Patel, N., Hashem, M., Ibrahim, N., Abdulwahab, F., et al. (2017). Clinical genomics expands the morbid genome of intellectual disability and offers a high diagnostic yield. *Molecular Psychiatry, 22,* 615–624.

Andersen, E. S. (1990). *Speaking with style. The socio-linguistic skills of children*. London: Routledge.

Andersen, G. L., Irgens, L. M., Haagaas, I., Skranes, J. S., Meberg, A. E., & Vik, T. (2008). Cerebral palsy in Norway: Prevalence, subtypes and severity. *European Journal of Paediatric Neurology, 12*, 4–13.

Andersen, P. N., Hovik, K. T., Skogli, E. W., Egeland, J., & Øie, M. (2013). Symptoms of ADHD in children with high-functioning autism are related to impaired verbal working memory and verbal delayed recall. *PloS One, 8* (5), e64842.

Andershed, H., Kerr, M., & Stattin, H. (2001). Bullying in school and violence on the streets: Are the same people involved? *Journal of Scandinavian Studies in Criminology and Crime Prevention, 2*, 31–49.

Anderson, C. A. (2004). An update on the effects of violent video games. *Journal of Adolescence, 27*, 113–122.

Anderson, C. A., Bushman, B. J., Donnerstein, E., Hummer, T. A., & Warburton, W. (2015). SPSSI research summary on media violence. *Analyses of Social Issues and Public Policy, 15*, 4–19.

Anderson, C. A., Shibuya, A., Ihori, N., Swing, E. L., Bushman, B. J., Sakamoto, A., & Saleem, M. (2010). Violent video game effects on aggression, empathy, and prosocial behavior in Eastern and Western countries. *Psychological Bulletin, 136*, 151–173.

Anderson, D. I., Campos, J. J., Rivera, M., Dahl, A., Uchiyama, I., & Barbu-Roth, M. (2014). The consequences of independent locomotion for brain and psychological development. In R. B. Shepherd (Ed.), *Cerebral palsy in infancy* (pp. 199–223). Edinburgh, UK: Elsevier.

Anderson, D. I., Campos, J. J., Witherington, D. C., Dahl, A., Rivera, M., He, M., Uchiyama, I., & Barbu-Roth, M. (2013). The role of locomotion in psychological development. *Frontiers in Psychology, 4*, 440.

Anderson, D. R., & Kirkorian, H. L. (2015). Media and cognitive development. In R. M. Lerner, L. S. Liben & U. Müller (Eds), *Handbook of child psychology and developmental science, Seventh edition, Volume 2: Cognitive processes* (pp. 949–994). Hoboken, NJ: Wiley.

Anderson, D. R., & Pempek, T. A. (2005). Television and very young children. *American Behavioral Scientist, 48*, 505–522.

Anderson, V., Spencer-Smith, M., & Wood, A. (2011). Do children really recover better? Neurobehavioural plasticity after early brain insult. *Brain, 134*, 2197–2221.

Andrés-Roqueta, C., Adrian, J. E., Clemente, R. A., & Katsos, N. (2013). Which are the best predictors of theory of mind delay in children with specific language impairment? *International Journal of Language and Communication Disorders, 48*, 726–737.

Anglin, J. M. (1993). Knowing versus learning words. *Monographs of the Society for Research in Child Development, 58*, 10.

Anholt, G. E., Aderka, I. M., van Balkom, A. J. L. M., Smit, J. H., Schruers, K., van der Wee, N. J. A., Eikelenboom, M., De Luca, V., & van Oppen, P. (2014). Age of onset in obsessive–compulsive disorder: Admixture analysis with a large sample. *Psychological Medicine, 44*, 185–194.

Anisfeld, M. (2005). No compelling evidence to dispute Piaget's timetable of the development of representational imitation in infancy. In S. Hurley & N. Chater (Eds), *Perspectives on imitation: From neuroscience to social science, Volume 2: Imitation, human development, and culture* (pp. 107–131). Cambridge, MA: MIT Press.

Anisfeld, M., Turkewitz, G., Rose, S. A., Rosenberg, F. R., Sheiber, F. J., Couturier-Fagan, D. A., Ger, J. S., & Sommer, I. (2001). No compelling evidence that newborns imitate oral gestures. *Infancy, 2*, 111–122.

Anticich, S. A., Barrett, P. M., Silverman, W., Lacherez, P., & Gillies, R. (2013). The prevention of childhood anxiety and promotion of resilience among preschool-aged children: A universal school based trial. *Advances in School Mental Health Promotion, 6*, 93–121.

Antshel, K. M., & Olszewski, A. K. (2014). Cognitive behavioral therapy for adolescents with ADHD. *Child and Adolescent Psychiatric Clinics, 23*, 825–842.

Apperly, I. A. (2008). Beyond simulation–theory and theory–theory: Why social cognitive neuroscience should use its own concepts to study "Theory of Mind". *Cognition, 107*, 266–283.

Apperly, I. A. (2011). *Mindreaders: The cognitive basis of "theory of mind"*. New York, NY: Psychology Press.

Archer, J. (1992). Childhood gender roles: Social context and organisation. In H. McGurk (Ed.), *Childhood social development: Contemporary perspectives* (pp. 31–61). Hove, UK: Erlbaum.

Arden, R., & Plomin, P. (2006). Sex differences in variance of intelligence across childhood. *Personality and Individual Differences, 41*, 39–48.

Arnett, J. J. (1992). Reckless behavior in adolescence: A developmental perspective. *Developmental Review, 12*, 339–373.

Arnett, J. J. (2000). Emerging adulthood: A theory of development from the late teens through the twenties. *American Psychologist, 55*, 469–480.

Arnett, J. J. (2001). Conceptions of the transition to adulthood: Perspectives from adolescence to midlife. *Journal of Adult Development, 8*, 133–143.

Arnett, J. J. (2006). Emerging adulthood: Understanding the new way of coming of age. *Emerging Adults in America: Coming of Age in the 21st Century, 22*, 3–19.

Arnett, J. J. (2015). *Emerging adulthood: The winding road from the late teens through the twenties, Second edition*. New York, NY: Oxford University Press.

Arnett, J. J., Žukauskienė, R., & Sugimura, K. (2014). The new life stage of emerging adulthood at ages 18–29 years: Implications for mental health. *The Lancet Psychiatry, 1*, 569–576.

Arnheim, R. (1974). *Art and visual perception: A psychology of the creative eye*. Berkeley, CA: University of California Press.

Aronsson, K. (1997). *Barns världar – barns bilder*. Stockholm, Sweden: Natur och Kultur.

Arsenault, D. J., & Foster, S. L. (2012). Attentional processes in children's overt and relational aggression. *Merrill-Palmer Quarterly, 58*, 409–436.

Arsenio, W. F. (1988). Children's conceptions of the situational affective consequences of sociomoral events. *Child Development, 59*, 1611–1622.

Arsenio, W. F., & Lover, A. (1995). Children's conceptions of sociomoral affect: Happy victimizers, mixed emotions, and other expectancies. In M. Killen & D. Hart (Eds), *Morality in everyday life: Developmental perspectives* (pp. 87–128). Cambridge: Cambridge University Press.

Arsenio, W. F., Gold, J., & Adams, E. (2006). Children's conceptions and displays of moral emotions. In M. Killen & J. G. Smetana (Eds), *Handbook of moral development* (pp. 581–609). Mahwah, NJ: Erlbaum.

Åsberg, J., Carlsson, M., Oderstam, A. M., & Miniscalco, C. (2010). Reading comprehension among typically developing Swedish-speaking 10–12-year-olds: Examining subgroups differentiated in terms of language and decoding skills. *Logopedics Phoniatrics Vocology, 35*, 189–193.

Asch, S. & Nerlove, H. (1960). The development of double function terms in children: An exploratory investigation. In B. Kaplan & S. Wapner (Eds), *Perspectives in psychological theory: Essays in honor of Heinz Werner* (pp. 47–60). New York, NY: International Universities Press.

Asendorpf, J. B. (1992). Beyond stability: Predicting inter-individual differences in intra-individual change. *European Journal of Personality, 6*, 103–117.

Asendorpf, J. B. (2010). Long-term development of shyness: Looking forward and looking backward. In K. H. Rubin & R. J. Coplan (Eds), *The development of shyness and social withdrawal* (pp. 157–175). New York, NY: Guilford Press

Asendorpf, J. B., Conner, M., De Fruyt, F., De Houwer, J., Denissen, J. J., Fiedler, K., Fiedler, S., Funder, D. C., Kliegl, R., Nosek, B. A., et al. (2013). Recommendations for increasing replicability in psychology. *European Journal of Personality, 27*, 108–119.

Asher, S. R., & McDonald, K. (2009). The behavioral basis of acceptance, rejection, and perceived popularity. In K. K. Rubin, W. Bukowski & B. Laursen (Eds), *The handbook of peer interactions, relationships, and groups* (pp. 232–248). New York, NY: Guilford Press.

Asher, S. R. & Parker, J. G. (1989). Significance of peer relationship problems in childhood. In B. H. Schneider, G. Attili, J. Nadel & R. P. Weissberg (Eds), *Social competence in developmental perspective* (pp. 5–23). Norwell, MA: Kluwer.

Ashiabi, G. S., & O'Neal, K. K. (2015). Child social development in context: An examination of some propositions in Bronfenbrenner's bioecological theory. *SAGE Open, 5*, 1–14.

Aslin R. N. (2007). What's in a look? *Developmental Science, 10*, 48–53.

Astington, J. W., & Gopnik, A. (1988). Knowing you have changed your mind: Children's understanding of representational change. In J. W. Astington, P. L. Harris & D. R. Olsen (Eds), *Developing theories of mind* (pp. 193–206). Cambridge: Cambridge University Press.

Atkinson, L., Chisholm, V. C., Scott, B., Goldberg, S., Vaughn, B. E., Blackwell, J., Dickens, S., & Tam, F. (1999). Maternal sensitivity, child functional level, and attachment in Down syndrome. *Monographs of the Society for Research in Child Development, 64*, 45–66.

Attwood, T. (1998). *Asperger's syndrome: A guide for parents and professionals*. London: Jessica Kingsley.

Aubusson, P. J., Harrison, A. G., & Ritchie, S. M. (Eds) (2006). *Metaphor and analogy in science education*. Dordrecht, NL: Springer.

Avis, J., & Harris, P. L. (1991). Belief desire reasoning among Baka children: Evidence for a universal conception of mind. *Child Development, 62*, 460–467.

Axline, V. M. (1964). *Dibs: In search of self*. New York, NY: Ballantine.

Ayoub, C., O'Connor, E., Rappolt-Schlictmann, G., Vallotton, C., Raikes, H., & Chazan-Cohen, R. (2009). Cognitive skill performance among young children living in poverty: Risk, change, and the promotive effects of Early Head Start. *Early Childhood Research Quarterly, 24*, 289–305.

Bagwell, C. L., & Schmidt, M. E. (2011). The friendship quality of overtly and relationally victimized children. *Merrill-Palmer Quarterly, 57*, 158–185.

Bahrick, L. E. (2004). The development of perception in a multimodal environment. In G. Bremner & A. Slater (Eds), *Theories of infant development* (pp. 90–120). Malden, MA: Blackwell.

Bahrick, L. E., & Lickliter, R. (2000). Intersensory redundancy guides attentional selectivity and perceptual learning in infancy. *Developmental Psychology, 36*, 190–201.

Bahrick, L. E., & Lickliter, R. (2014). Learning to attend selectively: The dual role of intersensory redundancy. *Current Directions in Psychological Science, 23*, 414–420.

Bahrick, L. E., Walker, A. S., & Neisser, U. (1981). Selective looking by infants. *Cognitive Psychology, 13*, 377–390.

Bailey, D. B., Bruer, J. T., Symons, F. J., & Lichtman, J. W. (2001). *Critical thinking about critical periods*. Baltimore, MD: Paul H. Brookes.

Baillargeon, R. (1987). Young infants' reasoning about the physical and spatial properties of a hidden object. *Cognitive Development, 2*, 179–200.

Baillargeon, R. (1994). How do infants learn about the physical world? *Current Directions in Psychological Science, 3*, 133–140.

Baillargeon, R. (2004). Infants' physical world. *Current Directions in Psychological Science, 13*, 89–94.

Baillargeon, R. (2008). Innate ideas revisited: For a principle of persistence in infants' physical reasoning. *Perspectives on Psychological Science, 3*, 2–13.

Baillargeon, R., Kotovsky, L., & Needham, A. (1995). The acquisition of physical knowledge in infancy. In D. Sperber, D. Premack & A. J. Premack (Eds), *Causal cognition* (pp. 79–116). Oxford: Oxford University Press.

Baillargeon, R., Scott, R. M., & Bian, L. (2016). Psychological reasoning in infancy. *Annual Review of Psychology, 67*, 159–186.

Baillargeon, R., Scott, R. M., & He, Z. (2010). False-belief understanding in infants. *Trends in Cognitive Sciences, 14*, 110–118.

Baillargeon, R., Li, J., Ng, W., & Yuan, S. (2009). An account of infants' physical reasoning. In A. Woodward & A. Needham (Eds), *Learning and the infant mind* (pp. 66–116). New York, NY: Oxford University Press.

Baillargeon, R., He, Z., Setoh, P., Scott, R. M., Sloane, S., & Yang, D. Y. J. (2013). False-belief understanding and why it matters. In M. Banaji & S. Gelman (Eds), *Navigating the social world: What infants, children, and other species can teach us* (pp. 88–95). New York, NY: Oxford University Press.

Baillargeon, R., Morisset, A., Keenanc, K., Normand, C. L., Jeyaganthe, S. Boivinf, M., & Tremblay, R. E. (2011). The development of prosocial behaviors in young children: A prospective population-based cohort study. *The Journal of Genetic Psychology: Research and Theory on Human Development, 172*, 221–251.

Baillieux, H., De Smet, H. J., Paquier, P- F., De Deyn, P. P., & Mariën, P. (2008). Cerebellar neurocognition: Insights into the bottom of the brain. *Clinical Neurology and Neurosurgery, 110*, 763–773.

Baixauli, I., Colomer, C., Roselló, B., & Miranda, A. (2016). Narratives of children with high-functioning autism spectrum disorder: A meta-analysis. *Research in Developmental Disabilities, 59*, 234–254.

Baker, B. L., Marquis, W. A., & Abbott Feinfield, K. (2016). Early intervention and parent education. In A. Carr, S. Linehan, G. O'Reilly, P. N. Walsh & J. McEnvoy (Eds), *The handbook of intellectual disability and clinical psychology practice, Second edition* (pp. 311–338). Abingdon, UK: Routledge.

Baker, D. P., Eslinger, P. J., Benavides, M., Peters, E., Dieckmann, N. F., & Leon, J. (2015). The cognitive impact of the education revolution: A possible cause of the Flynn effect on population IQ. *Intelligence, 49*, 144–158.

Bakermans-Kranenburg, M. J., & van IJzendoorn, M. H. (2006). Gene-environment interaction of the dopamine D4 receptor (DRD4) and observed maternal insensitivity predicting externalizing behavior in preschoolers. *Developmental Psychobiology, 48*, 406–409.

Baldry, A. C. (2003). Bullying in schools and exposure to domestic violence. *Child Abuse and Neglect, 27*, 713–732.

Baldwin, A. L. (1949). The effect of home environment on nursery school behavior. *Child Development, 20*, 49–62.

Balogh, R. D., & Porter, R. H. (1986). Olfactory preferences resulting from mere exposure in human neonates. *Infant Behavior and Development, 9*, 395–401.

Balsam, R. H. (2015). Oedipus Rex: Where are we going, especially with females? *The Psychoanalytic Quarterly, 84*, 555–588.

Baltes, P. B., Lindenberger, U., & Staudinger, U. M. (2006). Lifespan theory in developmental psychology. In W. Damon & R. M. Lerner (Eds), *Handbook of child psychology, Sixth edition, Volume 1: Theoretical models of human development* (pp. 569–664). New York, NY: Wiley.

Bandura, A. (1965). Influence of models' reinforcement contingencies on the acquisition of imitative responses. *Journal of Personality and Social Psychology, 1*, 589–595.

Bandura, A. (1978). The self system in reciprocal determinism. *American Psychologist, 33*, 344–358.

Bandura, A. (1986). *Social foundations of thought and action: A social cognitive theory.* Upper Saddle River, NJ: Prentice Hall.

Bandura, A. (1994). Social cognitive theory of mass communication. In J. Bryant & R. Zillmann (Eds), *Media effects: Advances in theory and research* (pp. 61–90). Hillsdale, NJ: Erlbaum.

Bandura, A. (1997). *Self-efficacy: The exercise of control.* New York, NY: W. H. Freeman.

Bandura, A. (1999). Self efficacy: Toward a unifying theory of behavioral change. In R. F. Baumeister (Ed.), *The self in social psychology* (pp. 285–298). London: Taylor and Francis.

Bandura, A. (2001). Social cognitive theory: An agentic perspective. *Annual Review of Psychology, 52*, 1–26.

Bandura, A. (2006). Toward a psychology of human agency. *Perspectives on Psychological Science, 1*, 164–180.

Bandura, A. (2007). Much ado over a faulty conception of perceived self-efficacy grounded in faulty experimentation. *Journal of Social and Clinical Psychology, 26*, 641–658.

Bandura, A. (2008). Toward an agentic theory of the self. In H. Marsh, R. G. Craven & D. M. McInerney (Eds), *Advances in self research, Volume 3. Self-processes, learning, and enabling human potential* (pp. 15–49). Charlotte, NC: Information Age Publishing.

Banihani, R., Smile, S., Yoon, G., Dupuis, A., Mosleh, M., Snider, A., & McAdam, L. (2015). Cognitive and neurobehavioral profile in boys with Duchenne muscular dystrophy. *Journal of Child Neurology, 30*, 1472–1482.

Bannard, C., & Lieven, E. (2012). Formulaic language in L1 acquisition. *Annual Review of Applied Linguistics, 32*, 3–16.

Banse, R., Gawronski, B., Rebetez, C., Gutt, H., & Morton, J. B. (2010). The development of spontaneous gender stereotyping in childhood: Relations to stereotype knowledge and stereotype flexibility. *Developmental Science, 13*, 298–306.

Bar-Haim, Y. (2010). Research review: Attention bias modification (ABM): A novel treatment for anxiety disorders. *Journal of Child Psychology and Psychiatry, 51*, 859–870.

Bar-Haim, Y., Morag, I., & Glickman, S. (2011). Training anxious children to disengage attention from threat: A randomized controlled trial. *Journal of Child Psychology and Psychiatry, 52*, 861–869.

Bar-Haim, Y., Ziv, T., Lamy, D., & Hodes, R. (2006). Nature and nurture in own-race face processing. *Psychological Science, 17*, 159–163.

Barinaga, M. (1995). Remapping the motor cortex. *Science, 268*, 1696–1698.

Barlow, J., Schrader-McMillan, A., Axford, N., Wrigley, Z., Sonthalia, S., Wilkinson, T., Rawsthorn, M., Toft, A., & oad, J. (2016). Attachment and attachment-related outcomes in preschool children–a review of recent evidence. *Child and Adolescent Mental Health, 21*, 11–20.

Barnes-Holmes, Y., Hayes, S. C., Barnes-Holmes, Y., & Roche, B. (2001). Relational frame theory. Post-Skinnerian account of human language and cognition. *Advances in Child Development and Behavior, 28*, 101–138.

Baron, I. S. (2004). *Neuropsychological evaluation of the child*. New York, NY: Oxford University Press.

Baron-Cohen, S. (1995). *Mindblindness: An essay on autism and theory of mind*. Boston, MA: MIT press.

Baron-Cohen, S., Leslie, A. M., & Frith, U. (1985). Does the autistic child have a "theory of mind"? *Cognition, 21*, 37–46.

Baron-Cohen, S., Leslie, A. M., & Frith, U. (1986). Mechanical, behavioural and intentional understanding of picture stories in autistic children. *British Journal of Developmental Psychology, 4*, 113–125.

Barr, R., & Hayne, H. (2003). It's not what you know, it's who you know: Older siblings facilitate imitation during infancy. *International Journal of Early Years Education, 11*, 7–21.

Barr, R., & Linebarger, D. N. (2017). *Media exposure during infancy and early childhood*. Cham, Switzerland: Springer.

Barr, R., Danziger, C., Hilliard, M. E., Andolina, C., & Ruskis, J. (2010). Amount, content and context of infant media exposure: A parental questionnaire and diary analysis. *International Journal of Early Years Education, 18*, 107–122.

Barrasso-Catanzaro, C., & Eslinger, P. J. (2016). Neurobiological bases of executive function and social-emotional development: Typical and atypical brain changes. *Family Relations, 65*, 108–119.

Barrett, H. C., & Kurzban, R. (2006). Modularity in cognition: Framing the debate. *Psychological Review, 113*, 628.

Barrett, K. C., & Campos, J. J. (1987). Perspectives on emotional development: II. A functionalist approach to emotions. In J. D. Osofsky (Ed.), *Handbook of infant development, Second edition* (pp. 555–578). New York, NY: Wiley.

Barrett, K. C., Zahn-Waxler, C., & Cole, P. M. (1993). Avoiders versus amenders – implication for the investigation of guilt and shame during toddlerhood? *Cognition and Emotion, 7*, 481–505.

Barrett, M., & E. Buchanan-Barrow, E. (Eds) (2005). *Children's understanding of society*. Hove, UK: Psychology Press.

Barrett, M., Harris, M., & Chasin, J. (1991). Early lexical development and maternal speech: A comparison of children's initial and subsequent uses of words. *Journal of Child Language, 18*, 21–40.

Barrett, P. M., & Turner, C. (2001). Prevention of anxiety symptoms in primary school children: Preliminary results from a universal school-based trial. *British Journal of Clinical Psychology, 40*, 399–410.

Barrett, P. M., Cooper, M., & Guajardo, J. G. (2014). Using the FRIENDS programs to promote resilience in cross-cultural populations. In S. Prince-Embury & D. H. Saklofske (Eds), *Resilience interventions for youth in diverse populations* (pp. 85–108). New York, NY: Springer.

Barron, C. M. (2014). "I had no credit to ring you back": Children's strategies of negotiation and resistance to parental surveillance via mobile phones. *Surveillance and Society, 12*, 401–413.

Barrouillet, P. (2015). Theories of cognitive development: From Piaget to today. *Developmental Review, 38*, 1–12.

Barrouillet, P., & Poirier, L. (1997). Comparing and transforming: An application of Piaget's morphisms theory to the development of class inclusion and arithmetic problem solving. *Human Development, 40*, 216–234.

Barth, J. M., & Archibald, A. (2003). The relation between emotion production behavior and preschool social behavior: In the eye of the beholder. *Social Development, 12*, 67–90.

Barton, E. E. (2010). Development of a taxonomy of pretend play for children with disabilities. *Infants and Young Children, 23*, 247–261.

Barton, E. E. (2015). Teaching generalized pretend play and related behaviors to young children with disabilities. *Exceptional Children, 81*, 489–506.

Basser, L. S. (1962). Hemiplegia of early onset and the faculty of speech with special reference to the efffects of hemispherectomy. *Brain, 1985*, 427–460.

Bastounis, A., Callaghan, P., Banerjee, A., & Michail, M. (2016). The effectiveness of the Penn Resiliency Programme (PRP) and its adapted versions in reducing depression and anxiety and improving explanatory style: A systematic review and meta-analysis. *Journal of Adolescence, 52*, 37–48.

Bat-Chava, Y. (2000). Diversity of deaf identities. *American Annals of the Deaf, 145*, 420–428.

Bates, E., Bretherton, I., & Snyder, L. (1988). *From first words to grammar. Individual differences and dissociable mechanisms*. Cambridge: Cambridge University Press.

Bates, E., Dale, P. S., & Thal, D. (1995). Individual differences and their implications for theories of language development. In P. Fletcher & B. MacWhinney (Eds), *Handbook of child language* (pp. 96–151). Oxford: Basil Blackwell.

Bates, E., Elman, J., Johnson, M. H., Karmiloff-Smith, A., Parisi, D., & Plunkett, K. (1998). Innateness and emergentism. In W. Bechtel & G. Graham (Eds), *A companion to cognitive science* (pp. 590–601). Oxford: Basil Blackwell.

Bates, J. E., Schermerhorn, A. C., & Petersen, I. T. (2012). Temperament and parenting in developmental perspective. In M. Zentner & R. L. Shiner (Eds), *Handbook of temperament* (pp. 425–441). New York, NY: Guilford Press.

Batorowicz, B., Stadskleiv, K., von Tetzchner, S., & Missiuna, C. (2016). Children who use communication aids instructing peer and adult partners during play-based activity. *Augmentative and Alternative Communication, 32*, 105–119.

Battistich, V., & Watson, M. (2003). Fostering social development in preschool and the early elementary grades through cooperative classroom activities. In R. M. Gillies & A. F. Ashman (Eds), *Cooperative learning: The social and intellectual outcomes of learning in groups* (pp. 19–35). London: Routledge.

Battro, A. M. (2000). *Half a brain is enough: The story of Nico.* New York, NY: Cambridge University Press.

Bauer, P. J. (1997). Development of memory in early childhood. In N. Cowan (Ed.), *The development of memory in childhood* (pp. 83–111). Hove, UK: Psychology Press.

Bauer, P. J. (2006) Event memory. In D. Kuhn & R. Siegler (Eds), *Handbook of child psychology: Cognition, perception, and language, Sixth edition* (pp. 373–425). London: Wiley.

Bauer, P. J. (2013). Memory. In P. D. Zelazo (Ed.), *Oxford handbook of developmental psychology, Volume 1: Mind and body* (pp. 505–541). New York, NY: Oxford University Press.

Bauer, P. J. (2014). The development of forgetting: Childhood amnesia. In P. Bauer & R. Fivush (Eds), *The Wiley handbook on the development of children's memory, Volume I–II* (pp. 513–544). London: Wiley.

Bauer, P. J. (2015). Development of episodic and autobiographical memory: The importance of remembering forgetting. *Developmental Review, 38*, 146–166.

Bauer, P. J., & Fivush, R. (1992). Constructing event representations: Building on a foundation of variation and enabling relations. *Cognitive Development, 7*, 381–401.

Bauer, P. J., & Larkina, M. (2014). The onset of childhood amnesia in childhood: A prospective investigation of the course and determinants of forgetting of early-life events. *Memory, 22*, 907–924.

Bauer, P. J., & Werkera, S. S. (1995). One- to two-year-olds' recall of events: The more expressed, the more impressed. *Journal of Experimental Child Psychology, 59*, 475–496.

Bauer, P. J., & Werkera, S. S. (1997). Saying is revealing: Verbal expression of event memory in the transition from infancy to early childhood. In P. W. van den Broek, P. J. Bauer & T. Bourg (Eds), *Developmental spans in event comprehension and representation: Bridging fictional and actual events* (pp. 139–168). Hillsdale, NJ: Erlbaum.

Bauer, P. J., Hertsgaard, L. A., & Wewerka, S. S. (1995). Effects of experience and reminding on long term recall in infancy: Remembering not to forget. *Journal of Experimental Child Psychology, 59*, 260–298.

Bauer, P. J., Doydum, A. O., Pathman, T., Larkina, M., Güler, O. E., & Burch, M. (2012). It's all about location, location, location: Children's memory for the "where" of personally experienced events. *Journal of Experimental Child Psychology, 113*, 510–522.

Bauman, M. L., Kemper, T. L., & Arin, D. M. (1995). Microscopic observations of the brain in Rett syndrome. *Neuropediatrics, 26*, 105–108.

Baumeister, R. F. (1993). Self-presentation: Motivational, cognitive, and interpersonal patterns. In G. L. Van Heck, P. Bonaiuto, I. J. Deary & W. Nowack (Eds), *Personality psychology in Europe, Volume 4* (pp. 257–279). Tilburg, NL: Tilburg University Press.

Baumeister, R. F. (2005). Rethinking self-esteem: Why non-profits should stop promoting self-esteem and start endorsing self-control. *Stanford Social Innovation Review, 3*, 34–41.

Baumeister, R. F, Smart, L., & Boden, J. M. (1996). Relation of threatened egotism to violence and aggression: The dark side of high selfesteem. *Psychological Review, 103*, 5–33.

Baumeister, R. F., Campbell, J. D., Krueger, J. I., & Vohs, K. D. (2003). Does high self-esteem cause better performance, interpersonal success, happiness, or healthier lifestyles? *Psychological Science in the Public Interest, 4*, 1–44.

Baumrind, D. (1967). Child care and practices anteceding three patterns of preschool behavior. *Genetic Psychology Monographs, 75*, 43–88.

Baumrind, D. (1993). The average expectable environment is not so good. *Child Development, 64*, 1299–1317.

Baumrind, D. (1997). The disciplinary encounter: Contemporary issues. *Aggression and Violent Behavior, 2*, 321–335.

Baumrind, D. (2013). Authoritative parenting revisited: History and current status. In R. E. Larzelere, A. S. Morris & A. W. Harrist (Eds), *Authoritative parenting: Synthesizing nurturance and discipline for optimal child development* (pp. 11–34). Washington, DC: American Psychological Association.

Baumrind, D., Larzelere, R. E., & Owens, E. B. (2010). Effects of preschool parents' power assertive patterns and practices on adolescent development. *Parenting, 10*, 157–201.

Bavelier, D., Green, C. S., & Dye, M. W. G. (2010). Children, wired: For better and for worse. *Neuron, 67*, 692–701.

Bayley, N. (2006). *Bayley Scales of Infant and Toddler Development, Third edition.* San Antonio, Texas: Harcourt Assessment.

Bechor, M., Pettit, J. W., Silverman, W. K., Bar-Haim, Y., Abend, R., Pine, D. S., Vasey, M. W., & Jaccard, J. (2014). Attention Bias Modification Treatment for children with anxiety disorders who do not respond to cognitive behavioral therapy: A case series. *Journal of Anxiety Disorders, 28*, 154–159.

Becker, A. E., Fay, K. E., Agnew-Blais, J., Khan, A. N., Striegel-Moore, R. H., & Gilman, S. E. (2011). Social network media exposure and adolescent eating pathology in Fiji. *The British Journal of Psychiatry, 198*, 43–50.

Becker, F., & Erlenkamp, S. (2007). Et språkløst liv med cochleaimplantat? *Tidsskrift for Norsk Lægeforening, 127*, 2836–2838.

Becker, I., Ravens-Sieberer, U., Ottová-Jordan, V., & Schulte-Markwort, M. (2017). Prevalence of adolescent gender experiences and gender expression in Germany. *Journal of Adolescent Health, 61*, 83–90.

Becker, J. (2006). Relation of neurological findings on decoupling of brain activity from limb movement to Piagetian ideas on the origin of thought. *Cognitive Development, 21*, 194–198.

Beckett, C., Maughan, B., Rutter, M., Castle, J., Colvert, E., Groothues, C., Hawkins, A., Kreppner, J., O'Connor,

T. G., Stevens, S., & Sonuga-Barke, E. J. (2007). Scholastic attainment following severe early institutional deprivation: A study of children adopted from Romania. *Journal of Abnormal Child Psychology, 35*, 1063–1073.

Bedard, K., & Dhuey, E. (2006). The persistence of early childhood maturity: International evidence of long-run age effects. *The Quarterly Journal of Economics, 121*, 1437–1472.

Bedell, G., Coster, W., Law, M., Liljenquist, K., Kao, Y. C., Teplicky, R., Anaby, D., & Khetani, M. A. (2013). Community participation, supports, and barriers of school-age children with and without disabilities. *Archives of Physical Medicine and Rehabilitation, 94*, 315–323.

Beer, J. S., & Keltner, D. (2004). What is unique about self-conscious emotions? *Psychological Inquiry, 15*, 126–128.

Begeer, S., Dik, M., Marieke, J., Asbrock, D., Brambring, M., & Kef, S. (2014). A new look at theory of mind in children with ocular and ocular-plus congenital blindness. *Journal of Visual Impairment and Blindness, 108*, 17–27.

Behnke, M., Smith, V. C., & Committee on Substance Abuse (2013). Prenatal substance abuse: Short- and long-term effects on the exposed fetus. *Pediatrics, 131*, e1009–e1024.

Beilin, H. (1992). Piaget's new theory. In H. Beilin & P. B. Pufall (Eds), *Piaget's theory: Prospects and possibilities* (pp. 1–17). Hillsdale, NJ: Erlbaum.

Bell, R. Q. (1968). A reinterpretation of the direction of effects in studies of socialization. *Psychological Review, 75*, 81–95.

Bell, S. M., & Ainsworth, M. D. S. (1972). Infant crying and maternal responsiveness. *Child Development, 43*, 1171–1190.

Belli, R. F. (Ed.) (2012). *True and false recovered memories: Toward a reconciliation of the debate.* New York, NY: Springer.

Belmonte, M. K. (2009). What's the story behind "theory of mind" and autism? *Journal of Consciousness Studies, 16*, 118–139.

Belsky, J. (2001). Developmental risks (still) associated with early child care. *Journal of Child Psychology and Psychiatry, 42*, 845–859.

Belsky, J. (2005). Attachment theory and research in ecological perspective. In K. E. Grossman, K. Grossman & E. Waters (Eds), *Attachment from infancy to adulthood: The major longitudinal studies* (pp. 71–97). New York, NY: Guilford Press.

Belsky, J. (2008). War, trauma and children's development: Observations from a modern evolutionary perspective. *International Journal of Behavioral Development, 32*, 260–271.

Belsky, J., & de Haan, M. (2011). Parenting and children's brain development: The end of the beginning. *Journal of Child Psychology and Psychiatry, 52*, 409–428.

Belsky, J., Jonassaint, C., Pluess, M., Stanton, M., Brummett, B., & Williams, R. (2009). Vulnerability genes or plasticity genes? *Molecular Psychiatry, 14*, 746–754.

Bem, S. L. (1981). Gender schema theory: A cognitive account of sex typing. *Psychological Review, 88*, 354–364.

Bem, S. L. (1989). Genital knowledge and gender constancy in preschool children. *Child Development, 60*, 649–662.

Bem, S. L., Martyna, W., & Watson, C. (1976). Sex typing and androgeny: Further explorations of the expressive domain. *Journal of Personality and Social Psychology, 34*, 1016–1023.

Benjamin, C. L., Puleo, C. M., Settipani, C. A., Brodman, D. M., Edmunds, J. M., Cummings, C. M., & Kendall, P. C. (2011). History of cognitive-behavioral therapy in youth. *Child and Adolescent Psychiatric Clinics of North America, 20*, 179–189.

Benson, M. J., & Buehler, C. (2012). Family process and peer deviance influences on adolescent aggression: Longitudinal effects across early and middle adolescence. *Child Development, 83*, 1213–1228.

Berenbaum, S. A., & Beltz, A. M. (2016). How early hormones shape gender development. *Current Opinion in Behavioral Sciences, 7*, 53–60.

Berg, C. A., & Sternberg, R. J. (1985). Response to novelty: Continuity versus discontinuity in the developmental course of intelligence. *Advances in Child Development and Behavior, 19*, 2–47.

Berg, L., Rostila, M., & Hjern, A. (2016). Parental death during childhood and depression in young adults – a national cohort study. *Journal of Child Psychology and Psychiatry, 57*, 1092–1098.

Bergman, L. R., Corovic, J., Ferrer-Wreder, L., & Modig, K. (2014). High IQ in early adolescence and career success in adulthood: Findings from a Swedish longitudinal study. *Research in Human Development, 11*, 165–185.

Bergman, R. L., Piacentini, J., & McCracken, J. T. (2002). Prevalence and description of selective mutism in a school-based sample. *Journal of the American Academy of Child and Adolescent Psychiatry, 41*, 938–946.

Berg-Nielsen, T. S., Vikan, A., & Dahl, A. (2002). Parenting related to child and parental psychopathology: A descriptive review of the literature. *Clinical Child Psychology and Psychiatry, 7*, 529–552.

Berman, R. A. (2007). Developing linguistic knowledge and language use across adolescence. In E. Hoff & M. Shatz (Eds), *Blackwell handbook of language development* (pp. 347–367). Oxford: Blackwell.

Berndt, T. J. (1979). Developmental changes in conformity to peers and parents. *Developmental Psychology, 15*, 608–616.

Berndt, T. J. (1996). Exploring the effects of friendship quality on social development. In W. M. Bukowski, A. F. Newcomb & W. W. Hartup (Eds), *The company they keep: Friendship in childhood and adolescence* (pp. 346–365). Cambridge: Cambridge University Press.

Berndt, T. J. (2002). Friendship, quality and social development. *Current Directions in Psychological Science, 11*, 7–10.

Berndt, T. J. (2007). Children's friendships: Shifts over a half-century in perspectives on their development and their effects. In G. W. Ladd (Ed.), *Appraising the human developmental sciences: Essays in honor of Merrill-Palmer Quarterly* (pp. 138–155). Detroit, MI: Wayne State University Press.

Berndt, T. J., & Hanna, N. A. (1995). Intimacy and self disclosure in friendships. In K. J. Rotenberg (Ed.), *Disclosure processes in children and adolescents* (pp. 57–77). Cambridge: Cambridge University Press.

Berndt, T. J., & Murphy, L. M. (2002). Influences of friends and friendships: Myths, truths, and research recommendations. *Advances in Child Development and Behavior*, 30, 275–310.

Berndt, T. J., Hawkins, J. A., & Hoyle, S. G. (1986). Changes in friendship during a school year: Effects on children's and adolescents' impressions of friendship and sharing with friends. *Child Development*, 57, 1284–1297.

Bernier, A., & Meins, E. (2008). A threshold approach to understanding the origins of attachment disorganization. *Developmental Psychology*, 44, 969–982.

Berninger, V. W. (2015). *Interdisciplinary frameworks for schools: Best professional practices for serving the needs of all students.* Washington, DC: American Psychological Association.

Bernstein, N. (1967). *The coordination and regulation of movements.* Oxford: Pergamon Press.

Bertenthal, B. I., & Clifton, R. K. (1998). Perception and action. In W. Damon, D. Kuhn & R. S. Siegler (Eds), *Handbook of child psychology, Fifth edition, Volume 2: Cognition, perception, and language* (pp. 51–102). New York, NY: Wiley.

Berti, A. E. (2005). Children's understanding of politics. In M. Barrett & E. Buchanan-Barrow (Eds), *Children's understanding of society* (pp. 69–103). New York, NY: Psychology Press.

Berti, A. E., & Bombi, A. S. (1988). *The child's construction of economics.* Cambridge: Cambridge University Press.

Best, C. T. (1993). Emergence of language specific constraints in perception of non-native speech: A window on early phonological development. In B. de Boysson-Bardies, S. D. Schonen, P. E. Jusczyk, P. McNeilage & J. Morton (1993). *Developmental neurocognition: Speech and face processing in the first year of life* (pp. 289–304). Norwell, MA: Kluwer.

Best, C. T. (1995). Learning to perceive the sound patterns of English. *Advances in Infancy Research*, 9, 217–304.

Best, D. L. (2010). Gender. In M. H. Bornstein (Ed.), *Handbook of cultural developmental science* (pp. 209–222). New York, NY: Psychology Press.

Best, D. L., Williams, J. E., Cloud, J. M., Davis, S. W., Robertson, L. S., Edwards, J. R., et al. (1977). Development of sex-trait stereotypes among young children in the United States, England, and Ireland. *Child Development*, 48, 1375–1384.

Best, J. R., Miller, P. H., & Jones, L. L. (2009). Executive functions after age 5: Changes and correlates. *Developmental Review*, 29, 180–200.

Beuker, K. T., Schjølberg, S., Lie, K. K., Swinkels, S., Rommelse, N. N., & Buitelaar, J. K. (2014). ESAT and M-CHAT as screening instruments for autism spectrum disorders at 18 months in the general population: Issues of overlap and association with clinical referrals. *European Child and Adolescent Psychiatry*, 23, 1081–1091.

Bhana, D. (2016). *Gender and childhood sexuality in primary school.* Singapore: Springer.

Bialystok, E. (2001). *Bilingualism in development: Language, literacy, and cognition.* New York, NY: Cambridge University Press.

Bialystok, E., & Luk, G. (2012). Receptive vocabulary differences in monolingual and bilingual adults. *Bilingualism: Language and Cognition*, 15, 397–401.

Bialystok, E., Craik, F. I., & Luk, G. (2012). Bilingualism: Consequences for mind and brain. *Trends in Cognitive Sciences*, 16, 240–250.

Bialystok, E., Craik, F. I., Green, D. W., & Gollan, T. H. (2009). Bilingual minds. *Psychological Science in the Public Interest*, 10, 89–129.

Bidell, T. R., & Fischer, K. W. (1992). Beyond the stage debate: Action, structure, and variability in Piagetian theory and research. In R. J. Sternberg & C. A. Berg (Eds), *Intellectual development* (pp. 100–140). Cambridge: Cambridge University Press.

Biederman, J. (2005). Attention-deficit/hyperactivity disorder: A selective overview. *Biological Psychiatry*, 57, 1215–1220.

Bierman, K. L. (2004). *Peer rejection: Developmental processes and intervention strategies.* New York, NY: Guilford Press.

Bigelow, A. (2003). The development of joint attention in blind children. *Development and Psychopathology*, 15, 259–275

Biggerstaff, D. (2012). Qualitative research methods in psychology. In G. Rossi (Ed.), *Psychology – selected papers* (pp. 175–206). Croatia: InTech Open Science

Bigler, R. S., & Liben, L. S. (2007). Developmental intergroup theory: Explaining and reducing children's social stereotyping and prejudice. *Current Directions in Psychological Science*, 16, 162–166.

Bijou, S. W. (1968). Ages, stages, and the naturalization of human development. *American Psychologist*, 23, 419–427.

Bijou, S. W., & Baer, D. M. (1961). *Child development, Volume 1: A systematic and empirical theory.* New York, NY: Appleton-Century-Crofts.

Binet, A. (1975). *Modern ideas about children.* Menlo Park, CA: Suzanne Heisler.

Binet, A., & Simon, T. (1905). Méthodes nouvelles pour diagnostic du niveau intéllectuel des abnormaux. *L'Année Psychologique*, 11, 191–244.

Biringen, Z., Emde, R. N., Campos, J. J., & Appelbaum, A. (2008). Development of autonomy: Role of walking onset and its timing. *Perceptual and Motor Skills*, 106, 395–414.

Bishop, D. V. M. (2003). Genetic and environmental risks for specific language impairment in children. *International Congress Series*, 1254, 225–245.

Bishop, D. V. M. (2005). *Test for Reception of Grammar, TROG.* London: Psychological Corporation.

Bishop, D. V. M. (2006). What causes specific language impairment in children? *Current Directions in Psychological Science*, 15, 217–221.

Bishop, D. V. M. (2007). Using mismatch negativity to study central auditory processing in developmental language and literacy impairments: Where are we, and where should we be going? *Psychological Bulletin, 133*, 651–672.

Bishop, D. V. M. (2013). Cerebral asymmetry and language development: Cause, correlate, or consequence? *Science, 340* (6138), 1230531.

Bishop, D. V. M. (2015, May). The interface between genetics and psychology: Lessons from developmental dyslexia. *Proceedings of the Royal Society B, 282* (1806), 20143139.

Bishop, D. V. M., Nation, K., & Patterson, K. (2014). When words fail us: Insights into language processing from developmental and acquired disorders. *Philosophical Transactions of the Royal Society of London. Series B, Biological Sciences, 369*, 20120403.

Bishop, D. V. M., & Snowling, M. J. (2004). Developmental dyslexia and specific language impairment: Same or different? *Psychological Bulletin, 130*, 858–886.

Bishop, E. G., Cherny, S. S., Corley, R., Plomin, R., DeFries, J. C., & Hewitt, J. K. (2003). Development genetic analysis of general cognitive ability from 1 to 12 years in a sample of adoptees, biological siblings, and twins. *Intelligence, 31*, 31–49.

Bishop, M., Hobson, R. P., & Lee, A. (2005). Symbolic play in congenitally blind children. *Development and Psychopathology, 17*, 447–465.

Bitner-Glindzicz, M., & Saihan, Z. (2013). Usher syndrome. In T. D. Kenny & P. L. Beales (Eds), *Ciliopathies: A reference for clinicians* (pp. 238–261). Oxford: Oxford University Press.

Bjerkan, B., Martinsen, H., Schjølberg, S., & von Tetzchner, S. (1983, July). Communicative development and adult reactions. Presented at 2nd International Conference on Social Pychology and Language, Bristol.

Björck-Åkesson, E., Wilder, J., Granlund, M., Pless, M., Simeonsson, R., Adolfsson, M., Almqvist, L., Augustine, L., Klang, N., & Lillvist, A. (2010). The International Classification of Functioning, Disability and Health and the version for children and youth as a tool in child habilitation/early childhood intervention – Feasibility and usefulness as a common language and frame for practice. *Disability and Rehabilitation, 32*, 125–138.

Bjørgaas, H. M., Hysing, M., & Elgen, I. (2012). Psychiatric disorders among children with cerebral palsy at school starting age. *Research in Developmental Disabilities, 33*, 1287–1293.

Bjorklund, D. F. (1995). *Children's thinking: Developmental functions and individual differences, Second edition*. Pacific Grove, CA: Brooks.

Bjorklund, D. F., & Harnishfeger, K. K. (1987). Developmental differences in mental effort requirments for the use of an organizational strategy in free recall. *Journal of Experimental Child Psychology, 44*, 109–125.

Bjorklund, D. F., & Pellegrini, A. D. (2002). *The origins of human nature: Evolutionary developmental psychology*. Washington, DC: American Psychological Association.

Bjorklund, D. F., Dukes, C., & Brown, R. D. (2009). The development of memory strategies. In M. L. Courage & N. Cowan (Eds). *The development of memory in infancy and childhood* (pp. 146–175). Hove, UK: Psychology Press.

Blacher, J., Feinfield, K. A., & Kraemer, B. R. (2007). Supporting families who have children with disabilities. In A. Carr, G. O'Reilly, P. N. Walsh & J. McEvoy (Eds), *The handbook of intellectual disability and clinical psychology practice* (pp. 303–335). New York, NY: Routledge.

Blackford, J. U., & Walden, T. A. (1998). Individual differences in social referencing. *Infant Behavior and Development, 21*, 89–102.

Blair, C. (2016). Executive function and early childhood education. *Current Opinion in Behavioral Sciences, 10*, 102–107.

Blair, E. (2010). Epidemiology of the cerebral palsies. *Orthopedic Clinics of North America, 41*, 441–455.

Blake, P. R., & McAuliffe, K. (2011). "I had so much it didn't seem fair": Eight-year-olds reject two forms of inequity. *Cognition, 120* (2), 215–224.

Blakemore, C., & Cooper, G. F. (1970). Development of the brain depends on the visual environment. *Nature, 228*, 477–478.

Bleie, T. (2003). Evolution, brains and the predicament of sex in human cognition. *Sexualities, Evolution and Gender, 5*, 149–189.

Blinka, L., Škařupová, K., Ševčíková, A., Wölfling, K., Müller, K. W., & Dreier, M. (2015). Excessive internet use in European adolescents: What determines differences in severity? *International Journal of Public Health, 60*, 249–256.

Block, J. (1995). A contrarian view of the five-factor approach to personality description. *Psychological Bulletin, 117*, 187–215.

Block, J., & Block, J. H. (2006). Venturing a 30-year longitudinal study. *American Psychologist, 61*, 315–327.

Blom, I., & Bergman, A. (2013). Observing development: A comparative view of attachment theory and separation–individuation theory. In J. E. Bettmann & D. D. Friedman (Eds), *Attachment-based clinical work with children and adolescents* (pp. 9–43). New York, NY: Springer.

Bloom, L. (1973). *One word at a time*. The Hague, NL: Mouton.

Bloom, L. (1993). *The transition from infancy to language: Acquiring the power of expression*. Cambridge: Cambridge University Press.

Bloom, L. (1998). Language acquisition in its developmental context. In W. Damon, D. Kuhn & R. S. Siegler (Eds), *Handbook of child psychology, Fifth edition, Volume 2: Cognition, perception and language* (pp. 309–370). New York, NY: John Wiley.

Bloom, P. (2004). Myths of word learning. In D. G. Hall & S. R. Waxman (Eds), *Weaving a lexicon* (pp. 205–220). Cambridge, MA: MIT Press.

Blowers, G., Cheung, B. T., & Ru, H. (2009). Emulation vs. indigenization in the reception of Western psychology in Republican China: An analysis of the content of Chinese psychology journals (1922–1937). *Journal of the History of the Behavioral Sciences, 45,* 21–33.

Blum, H. P. (2004). Separation-individuation theory and attachment theory. *Journal of the American Psychoanalytic Association, 52,* 535–553.

Blumberg, F. (2008). *Freaks of nature: What anomalies tell us about development and evolution.* Oxford: Oxford University Press.

Blurton-Jones, N. (1967). An ethological study of some aspects of social behaviour of childen in a nursery school. In D. Morris (Ed.), *Primate ethology* (pp. 347–368). Chicago, IL: Aldine.

Boden, J. M., Fergusson, D. M., & Horwood, L. J. (2008). Does adolescent self-esteem predict later life outcomes? A test of the causal role of self-esteem. *Development and Psychopathology, 20,* 319–339.

Bodrova, E., & Leong, D. J. (2015). Vygotskian and post-Vygotskian views on children's play. *American Journal of Play, 7,* 371–388

Bohn-Gettler, C. M., Pellegrini, A. D., Dupuis, D., Hickey, M., Hou, Y., Roseth, C., & Solberg, D. (2010). A longitudinal study of preschool children's (homo sapiens) sex segregation. *Journal of Comparative Psychology, 124,* 219–228.

Boland, A. M., Haden, C. A., & Ornstein, P. A. (2003). Boosting children's memory by training mothers in the use of an elaborative conversational style as an event unfolds. *Journal of Cognition and Development, 4,* 39–65.

Boldt, L. J., Kochanska, G., Grekin, R., & Brock, R. L. (2016). Attachment in middle childhood: Predictors, correlates, and implications for adaptation. *Attachment and Human Development, 18,* 115–140.

Boldt, L. J., Kochanska, G., Yoon, J. E., & Koenig Nordling, J. (2014). Children's attachment to both parents from toddler age to middle childhood: Links to adaptive and maladaptive outcomes. *Attachment and Human Development, 6,* 211–229.

Bond, E. (2010). Managing mobile relationships: Children's perceptions of the impact of the mobile phone on relationships in their everyday lives. *Childhood, 17,* 514–529.

Bondy, A., & Frost, L. (2002). *A picture's worth: PECS and other visual communication strategies in autism.* Bethesda, MD: Woodbine House.

Bonifacci, P., Storti, M., Tobia, V., & Suardi, A. (2016). Specific learning disorders: A look inside children's and parents' psychological well-being and relationships. *Journal of Learning Disabilities, 49,* 532–545.

Bono, K. E., & Bizri, R. (2014) The role of language and private speech in preschoolers' self-regulation. *Early Child Development and Care, 184,* 658–670.

Boom, J., Wouters, H., & Keller, M. (2007). A cross-cultural validation of stage development: A Rasch re-analysis of longitudinal socio-moral reasoning data. *Cognitive Development, 22,* 213–229.

Boorsboom, D., Mellenbergh, G. J., & van Heerden, J (2004). The concept of validity. *Psychological Review, 111,* 1061–1071.

Booth, A. E. (2008). The cause of infant categorization? *Cognition, 106,* 984–993.

Borge, A. I. H. (2010). *Resiliens – Risiko og sunn utvikling, Revidert utgave.* Oslo, NO: Gyldendal Akademisk.

Borge, A. I. H., Rutter, M., Côtè, S., & Tremblay, R. E (2004). Early childcare effects on physical aggression: Differentiating social selection and social causation. *Journal of Child Psychology and Psychiatry, 45,* 367–376.

Borgen, J. (1965). *Barndommens rike.* Oslo: Gyldendal.

Borgstein, J., & Grootendorst, C. (2002). Half a brain. *The Lancet, 359* (9305), 473.

Bornstein, M. H. (1992). Perception across the life span. In M. H. Bornstein & M. E. Lamb (Eds), *Developmental psychology: An advanced textbook, Third edition* (pp. 155–209). Hillsdale, NJ: Lawrence Erlbaum.

Bornstein, M. H. (Ed.) (2010). *Handbook of cultural developmental science.* Hove, UK: Psychology Press.

Bornstein, M. H. (2015). Children and their parents. In M. H. Bornstein & T. Leventhal (Eds), *Handbook of child psychology and developmental science, Seventh edition, Voleme 4: Ecological settings and processes* (pp. 55–132). Hoboken, NJ: Wiley.

Bornstein, M. H., & Arterberry, M. E. (2003). Recognition, discrimination and categorization of smiling by 5-month-old infants. *Developmental Science, 6,* 585–599.

Bornstein, M. H., Hahn, C. S., & Suwalsky, J. T. (2013). Developmental pathways among adaptive functioning and externalizing and internalizing behavioral problems: Cascades from childhood into adolescence. *Applied Developmental Science, 7,* 76–87.

Bornstein, M. H., Putnick, D. L., Gartstein, M. A., Hahn, C. S., Auestad, N., & O'Connor, D. L. (2015). Infant temperament: Stability by age, gender, birth order, term status, and socioeconomic status. *Child Development, 86,* 844–863.

Bornstein, M. H., Cote, L. R., Maital, S., Painter, K., Park, S. Y., Pascual, L., Pêcheux, M. G., Ruel, J., Venuti, P., & Vyt, A. (2004). Cross-linguistic analysis of vocabulary in young children: Spanish, Dutch, French, Hebrew, Italian, Korean, and American English. *Child Development, 75,* 1115–1139.

Bornstein, R. F. (2006). A Freudian construct lost and reclaimed: The psychodynamics of personality pathology. *Psychoanalytic Psychology, 23,* 339–353.

Bos, H., & Sandfort, T. (2015). Gender nonconformity, sexual orientation, and Dutch adolescents' relationship with peers.*Archives of Sexual Behavior, 44,* 1269–1279.

Bouchard, T. J., Lykken, D. T., McGue, M., Segal, N. L., & Tellegen, A. (1990). Sources of human psychological differences: The Minnesota study of twins reared apart. *Science, 250,* 223–228.

Boucher, J. (2012). Research review: Structural language in autistic spectrum disorder – characteristics and causes. *Journal of Child Psychology and Psychiatry, 53,* 219–233.

Bouffard, T., & Vezeau, C. (1998). The developing self-system and self-regulation of primary school children. In M. D. Ferrari & R. J. Sternberg (Eds), *Self awareness:*

Its nature and development (pp. 246–272). New York, NY: Guilford Press.

Bourgeois, J. P. (1997). Synaptogenesis, heterochrony and epigenesis in the mammalian neocortex. *Acta Pædiatrica, Supplement, 422,* 27–33.

Bowerman, M., & Choi, S. (2001). Shaping meanings for language: Universal and language-specific in the acquisition and shaping of semantic categories. In M. Bowerman & S. Levinson (Eds), *Language acquisition and conceptual development* (pp. 475–511). Cambridge: Cambridge University Press.

Bowker, J. C., Nelson, L. J., Markovic, A., & Luster, S. (2014). Social withdrawal during adolescence and emerging adulthood. In R. J. Coplan & J. C. Bowker (Eds), *The handbook of solitude: Psychological perspectives on social isolation, social withdrawal, and being alone* (pp. 167–183). Chichester, UK: Wiley.

Bowlby, J. (1946). *Forty-four juvenile thieves; their characters and home-life.* Oxford: Bailliere, Tindall and Cox.

Bowlby, J. (1951). *Maternal care and mental health.* Geneva: World Health Organization.

Bowlby, J. (1958). The nature of the child's tie to his mother. *The International Journal of Psycho-Analysis, 39,* 350.

Bowlby, J. (1969). *Attachment and loss, Volume 1. Attachment.* Harmonsworth, UK: Penguin.

Bowlby, J. (1973). *Attachment and loss, Volume 2. Separation: Anxiety and anger.* Harmondsworth, UK: Penguin.

Bowlby, J. (1980). *Attachment and Loss: Volume 3. Loss: Sadness and depression.* New York, NY: Basic Books.

Bowlby, J. (1982). Attachment and loss: Retrospect and prospect. *American Journal of Orthopsychiatry, 52,* 664–678.

Boyette, A. H. (2016). Children's play and culture learning in an egalitarian foraging society. *Child Development, 87,* 759–769.

Bradley, R. H., & Corwyn, R. F. (2008). Infant temperament, parenting, and externalizing behavior in first grade: A test of the differential susceptibility hypothesis. *Journal of Child Psychology and Psychiatry, 49,* 124–131.

Braine, M. D. S. (1994). Is nativism sufficient? *Journal of Child Language, 21,* 9–31.

Brambring, L., & Asbrock, D. (2010). Validity of false belief tasks in blind children. *Journal of Autism and Developmental Disorders, 40,* 1471–1484.

Brambring, M. (2007). Divergent development of manual skills in children who are blind or sighted. *Journal of Visual Impairment & Blindness, 101* (4), 212–225.

Brandt, M. J. (2011). Sexism and gender inequality across 57 societies. *Psychological Science, 22,* 1413–1418.

Brant, A. M., Munakata, Y., Boomsma, D. I., DeFries, J. C., Haworth, C. M., Keller, M. C., Martin, N. G., McGue, M., Petrill, S. A., Plomin, R., et al (2013). The nature and nurture of high IQ: An extended sensitive period for intellectual development. *Psychological Science, 24,* 1487–1495

Brem, S., Grünblatt, E., Drechsler, R., Riederer, P., & Walitza, S. (2014). The neurobiological link between OCD and ADHD. *ADHD Attention Deficit and Hyperactivity Disorders, 6,* 175–202.

Bremner, G. (1997). From perception to cognition. In G. Bremner, A. Slater & G. Butterworth (Eds). *Infant development: Recent advances* (pp. 55–74). Hove, UK: Lawrence Erlbaum.

Brenner, E. M., & Salovey, P. (1997). Emotion regulation during childhood: Developmental, interpersonal and individual considerations. In P. Salovey & D. J. Sluyter (Eds), *Emotional development and emotional intelligence* (pp. 168–192). New York, NY: Basic Books.

Brent, D. A., Melhem, N. M., Masten, A. S., Porta, G., & Payne, M. W. (2012). Longitudinal effects of parental bereavement on adolescent developmental competence. *Journal of Clinical Child and Adolescent Psychology, 41,* 778–791.

Bretherton, I. (1990). Communication patterns, internal working models, and the intergenerational transmission of attachment relationships. *Infant Mental Health Journal, 11,* 237–252.

Bretherton, I., Fritz, J., Zahn-Waxler, C., & Ridgeway, D. (1986). Learning to talk about emotions: A functionalist perspective. *Child Development, 57,* 529–548.

Bridges, L. J., & Grolnick, W. S. (1995). The development of emotional self regulation in infancy and early childhood. In N. Eisenberg (Ed.), *Social development* (pp. 185–211). Thousand Oaks, CA: Sage.

Briggs-Gowan, M. J., Pollak, S. D., Grasso, D., Voss, J., Mian, N. D., Zobel, E., McCarthy, K. J., Wakschlag, L. S., & Pine, D. S. (2015). Attention bias and anxiety in young children exposed to family violence. *Journal of Child Psychology and Psychiatry, 56,* 1194–1201.

Briley, D. A., & Tucker-Drob, E. M. (2013). Explaining the increasing heritability of cognitive ability across development: A meta-analysis of longitudinal twin and adoption studies. *Psychological Science, 24,* 1704–1713.

Briley, D. A., & Tucker-Drob, E. M. (2014). Genetic and environmental continuity in personality development: A meta-analysis. *Psychological Bulletin, 140,* 1303–1331.

Brinch, C. N., & Galloway, T. A. (2012). Schooling in adolescence raises IQ scores. *Proceedings of the National Academy of Sciences, 109,* 425–430.

Britten, K. H. (2008). Mechanisms of self-motion perception. *Annual Review of Neuroscience, 31,* 389–410.

Britton, J. C., Lissek, S., Grillon, C., Norcross, M. A., & Pine, D. S. (2011). Development of anxiety: The role of threat appraisal and fear learning. *Depression and Anxiety, 28,* 5–17.

Brock, R. L., & Kochanska, G. (2016). Toward a developmentally informed approach to parenting interventions: Seeking hidden effects. *Development and Psychopathology, 28,* 583–593.

Brodal, P. (2004). *The central nervous system: Structure and function.* Oxford: Oxford University Press.

Brodsky, P., Waterfall, H. R., & Edelman, S. (2007). Characterising motherese: On the computational; structure of child-directed language. In D. S. McNamara & J. G. Trafton (Eds), *Proceedings of the 29th Annual Cognitive Science Society* (pp. 833–838). Austin, TX: Cognitive Science Society.

Brody, G. H. (1998). Sibling relationship quality: Its causes and consequences. *Annual Review of Psychology, 49,* 1–24.

Brody, L., & Hall, J. (1993). Gender and emotion. In M. Lewis & J. Haviland (Eds), *Handbook of emotions* (pp. 447–460). New York, NY: Guilford Press.

Bronfenbrenner, U. (1979). *The ecology of human development.* Cambridge, MA: Harvard University Press.

Bronfenbrenner, U. (2005). *Making human beings human.* Thousand Oaks, CA: Sage.

Bronfenbrenner, U., & Morris, P. A. (2006). The bioecological model of human developmental. In W. Damon & R. M. Lerner (Eds), *Handbook of child psychology, Sixth edition, Volume 1: Theoretical models of human development* (pp. 793–828). New York, NY: John Wiley.

Brosnan, J., & Healy, O. (2011). A review of behavioral interventions for the treatment of aggression in individuals with developmental disabilities. *Research in Developmental Disabilities, 32,* 437–446.

Brossard-Racine, M., Hall, N., Majnemer, A., Shevell, M. I., Law, M., Poulin, C., & Rosenbaum, P. (2012). Behavioural problems in school age children with cerebral palsy. *European Journal of Paediatric Neurology, 16,* 35-41.

Brown, A. L. (1989). Analogical learning and transfer: What develops? In S. Vosniadou & A. Ortony (Eds), *Similarity and analogical reasoning* (pp. 369–412). Cambridge: Cambridge University Press.

Brown, B. B., Bakken, J. P., Ameringer, S. W., & Mahon, S. D. (2008). A comprehensive conceptualization of the peer influence process in adolescence. In M. J. Prinstein & K. Dodge (Eds), *Understanding peer influence in children and adolescents* (pp. 17–44). New York, NY: Guilford Press.

Brown, C. S., & Stone, E. A. (2016). Gender stereotypes and discrimination: How sexism impacts development. *Advances in Child Development and Behavior, 50,* 105–133.

Brown, J. R., & Dunn, J. (1991). You can cry, Mum: The social and developmental implications of talk about internal states. *British Journal of Developmental Psychology, 9,* 237–256.

Brown, J. R., & Dunn, J. (1992). Talk with your mother or your sibling? Developmental changes in early family conversations about feelings. *Child Development, 63,* 336–349.

Brown, R. (1958). *Words and things.* New York, NY: Free Press.

Brown, R. (1973). *A first language.* Cambridge, MA: Harvard University Press.

Brown, T. T., & Jernigan, T. L. (2012). Brain development during the preschool years. *Neuropsychology Review, 22,* 313–333.

Brownell, C. A., Svetlova, M., & Nichols, S. (2009). To share or not to share: When do toddlers respond to another's needs? *Infancy, 14,* 117–130.

Brownell, C. A., Iesue, S. S., Nichols, S. R., & Svetlova, M. (2013). Mine or yours? Development of sharing in toddlers in relation to ownership understanding. *Child Development, 84,* 906–920.

Bruck, M., Ceci, S. J., & Principe, G. F. (2006). The child and the law. In W. Damon, R. M. Lerner, K. A. Renninger & I. E. Sigel (Eds), *Handbook of child psychology, Sixth edition, Volume 4: Child psychology in practice* (pp. 776–816). New York, NY: Wiley.

Bruck, M., Ceci, S. J., Francoeur, E., & Barr, R. (1995a). "I hardly cried when I got my shot": Influencing children's reports about a visit to their pediatrician. *Child Development, 66,* 193–208.

Bruck, M., Ceci, S. J., Francoeur, E., & Renick, A. (1995b). Anatomically detailed dolls do not facilitate preschoolers' reports of a pediatric examination involving genital touching. *Journal of Experimental Psychology: Applied, 1,* 95–109.

Brumariu, L. E., & Kerns, K. A. (2010). Parent–child attachment and internalizing symptoms in childhood and adolescence: A review of empirical findings and future directions. *Development and Psychopathology, 22,* 177–203.

Brummelman, E., & Thomaes, S. (2017). How children construct views of themselves: A social-developmental perspective. *Child Development, 88,* 1763–1773.

Brummelman, E., Thomaes, S., & Sedikides, C. (2016). Separating narcissism from self-esteem. *Current Directions in Psychological Science, 25,* 8–13.

Brummelman, E., Nelemans, S. A., Thomaes, S., & Orobio de Castro, B. (2017). When parents' praise inflates, children's self-esteem deflates. *Child Development, 88,* 1799–1809.

Brummelman, E., Thomaes, S., Nelemans, S. A., De Castro, B. O., Overbeek, G., & Bushman, B. J. (2015). Origins of narcissism in children. *Proceedings of the National Academy of Sciences, 112* (12), 3659–3662.

Brummelman, E., Thomaes, S., Overbeek, G., Orobio de Castro, B., van den Hout, M. A., & Bushman, B. J. (2014). "That's not just beautiful – that's incredibly beautiful!" the adverse impact of inflated praise on children with low self-esteem. *Psychological Science, 25,* 728–735.

Brunborg, G. S., Mentzoni R. A., & Frøyland L. R. (2014). Is video gaming, or video game addiction, associated with depression, academic achievement, heavy episodic drinking, or conduct problems? *Journal of Behavioral Addictions, 3,* 27–32.

Bruner, J. S. (1975). The ontogenesis of speech acts. *Journal of Child Language, 2,* 1–19.

Bruner, J. S. (1983). *Child's talk.* Oxford: Oxford University Press.

Bruner, J. S. (1991). The narrative construction of reality. *Critical Inquiry, 18,* 1–21.

Bruner, J. S., & Kalmar, D. A. (1998). Narrative and meta-narrative in the construction of self. In M. D. Ferrari & R. J. Sternberg (Eds), *Self awareness: Its nature and development* (pp. 308–331). New York, NY: Guilford Press.

Bryant-Waugh, R., & Watkins, B. (2015). Feeding and eating disorders. In A. Thapar, D. S. Pine, F. S. Leckman,

S. Scott, M. J. Snowling & E. Taylor (Eds), *Rutter's child and adolescent psychiatry, Sixth edition* (pp. 1016–1034). Oxford: Wiley.

Buchanan-Barrow, E. (2005). Children's understanding of the school. In M. Barrett & E. Buchanan-Barrow (Eds), *Children's understanding of society* (pp. 17–42). Hove, UK: Psychology Press.

Buck, R. (1984). *The communication of emotion.* New York, NY: Guilford Press.

Bugden, S., & Ansari, D. (2015). How can cognitive developmental neuroscience constrain our understanding of developmental dyscalculia? In S. Chinn (Ed.), *International handbook of dyscalculia and mathematical learning difficulties* (pp. 18–43). London: Routledge.

Bühler, C. (1928). *Kindheit und Jugend: Genese des Bewusstseins.* Leipzig: Hirzel.

Buhrmester, D., & Furman, W. (1990). Perceptions of sibling relationships during middle childhood and adolescence. *Child Development, 61,* 1387–1398.

Buhrmester, D., & Prager, K. (1995). Patterns and functions of self disclosure during childhood and adolescence. In K. J. Rotenberg (Ed.), *Disclosure processes in children and adolescents* (pp. 10–56). Cambridge: Cambridge University Press.

Buică-Belciu, C., & Popovici, D.-V. (2014). Being twice exceptional: Gifted students with learning disabilities. *Procedia-Social and Behavioral Sciences, 127,* 519–523.

Bukowski, W. M., & Adams, R. (2005). Peer relationships and psychopathology: Markers, moderators, mediators, mechanisms, and meanings. *Journal of Clinical Child and Adolescent Psychology, 34,* 3–10.

Bukowski, W. M., Motzoi, C., & Meyer, F. (2009). Friendship as process, function, and outcome. In K. H. Rubin, W. M. Bukowski & B. Laursen (Eds), *Handbook of peer interactions, relationships, and groups* (pp. 217–231). New York, NY: Guilford Press.

Buller, D. J. (2005). Evolutionary psychology: The emperor's new paradigm. *Trends in Cognitive Science, 9,* 277–283.

Buller, D. J. (2008). Four fallacies of pop evolutionary psychology. *Scientific American, 300,* 74–81.

Bulloch, M. J., & Opfer, J. E. (2009). What makes relational reasoning smart? Revisiting the relational shift in cognitive development. *Developmental Science, 12,* 114–122.

Bulteau, C., Jambaqué, I., Chiron, C., Rodrigo, S., Dorfmüller, G., Dulac, O., Hertz-Pannier, L., & Noulhiane, M. (2017). Language plasticity after hemispherotomy of the dominant hemisphere in 3 patients: Implication of non-linguistic networks. *Epilepsy and Behavior, 69,* 86–94.

Burack, J. A., Russo, N., Kovshoff, H., Palma Fernandes, T., Ringo, J., Landry, O., & Iarocci, G. (2016). How I attend – not how well do I attend: Rethinking developmental frameworks of attention and cognition in autism spectrum disorder and typical development. *Journal of Cognition and Development, 17,* 553–567.

Burghardt, G. M. (2005). *The genesis of animal play: Testing the limits.* Cambridge, MA: MIT Press.

Burleson, B. R., & Kunkel, A. (2002). Parental and peer contributions to the emotional support skills of the child: From whom do children learn to express support? *Journal of Family Communication, 2,* 81–97.

Burman, E. (2001). Beyond the baby and the bathwater: Postdualistic developmental psychologies for diverse childhoods. *European Early Childhood Education Research Journal, 9,* 5–22.

Burman, E. (2008). *Developments: Child, image, nation.* Abingdon, UK: Routledge.

Burman, E. (2013a). Conceptual resources for questioning "child as educator". *Studies in Philosophy and Education, 32,* 229–243.

Burman, E. (2013b). Desiring development? Psychoanalytic contributions to antidevelopmental psychology. *International Journal of Qualitative Studies in Education, 26,* 56–74.

Burman, E. (2017). *Deconstructing developmental psychology, Third edition.* Abingdon, UK: Routledge.

Burman, J. T. (2013). Updating the Baldwin effect: The biological levels behind Piaget's new theory. *New Ideas in Psychology, 31,* 363–373.

Burmeister, M., McInnis, M. G., & Zöllner, S. (2008). Psychiatric genetics: Progress amid controversy. *Nature Reviews Genetics, 9,* 527–540.

Burriss, K. G., & Tsao. L.-L. (2002). Review of research: How much do we know about the importance of play in child development? *Childhood Education, 78,* 230–233.

Burton, T. D. (1994). *Introduction to dynamic systems analysis.* New York, NY: McGraw-Hill.

Bush, N. R., & Boyce, W. T. (2014). The contributions of early experience to biological development and sensitivity to context. In M. Lewis and K. Rudolph (Eds), *Handbook of developmental psychopathology* (pp. 287–309). New York, NY: Springer.

Bushman, B. J., & Anderson, C. A. (2015). Understanding causality in the effects of media violence. *American Behavioral Scientist, 59,* 1807–1821.

Bushman, B. J., & Baumeister, R. F. (1998). Threatened egotism, narcissism, self-esteem, and direct and displaced aggression: Does self-love or self-hate lead to violence? *Journal of Personality and Social Psychology, 75,* 219–229.

Bushnell, E. W., McKenzie, B. E., Lawrence, D. A., & Connell, S. (1995). The spatial coding strategies of 1-year-old infants in a locomotor search task. *Child Development, 66,* 937–958.

Bushnell, I. W., Sai, F., & Mullin, J. T. (1989). Neonatal recognition of the mother's face. *British Journal of Developmental Psychology, 7,* 3–15.

Buss, D. M. (2009). How can evolutionary psychology successfully explain personality and individual differences? *Perspectives on Psychological Science, 4,* 359–366.

Buss, D. M., & Duntley, J. D. (2011). The evolution of intimate partner violence. *Aggression and Violent Behavior, 16,* 411–419.

Buss, D. M., & Penke, L. (2015). Evolutionary personality psychology. In M. Mikulincer, P. R. Shaver, M. L.

Cooper, & R. J. Larsen (Eds), *APA handbook of personality and social psychology, Volume 4: Personality processes and individual differences* (pp. 3–29). Washington, DC: American Psychological Association.

Buss, K. A., & McDoniel, M. E. (2016). Improving the prediction of risk for anxiety development in temperamentally fearful children. *Current directions in psychological science, 25*, 14–20.

Bussey, K., & Bandura, A. (1992). Self-regulatory mechanisms governing gender development. *Child Development, 63*, 1236–1250.

Bussey, K., & Bandura, A. (1999). Social cognitive theory of gender development and differentiation. *Psychological Reveiw, 106*, 676–713.

Buttelmann, D., Carpenter, M., & Tomasello, M. (2009). Eighteen-month-old infants show false belief understanding in an active helping paradigm. *Cognition, 112*, 337–342.

Buttelmann, D., Over, H., Carpenter, M., & Tomasello, M. (2014). Eighteen-month-olds understand false beliefs in an unexpected-contents task. *Journal of Experimental Child Psychology, 119*, 120–126.

Butterfill, S. A. (2007). What are modules and what is their role in development? *Mind and Language, 22* (4), 450–473.

Butterworth, B. (2008). Developmental dyscalculia. In J. Reed & J. Warner-Rogers (Eds), *Child Neuropsychology* (pp. 357–274). Oxford: Blackwell.

Butterworth, G. (2003). Pointing is the royal road to language for babies. In S. Kita (Ed.), *Pointing: Where language, culture, and cognition meet* (pp. 9–33). Mahwah, NJ: Lawrence Erlbaum.

Butterworth, G., & Harris, M. (1994). *Principles of developmental psychology*. Hove, UK: Erlbaum.

Bybee, J., & Zigler, E. (1998). Outerdirectedness employed in individuals with and without mental retardation: A review. In R. M. Hodap, J. A. Burack, & E. Zigler (Eds), *Handbook of mental retardation and development* (pp. 434–461). Cambridge: Cambridge University Press.

Byrne, J. G., O'Connor, T. G., Marvin, R. S., & Whelan, W. F. (2005). Practitioner review: The contribution of attachment theory to child custody assessments. *Journal of Child Psychology and Psychiatry, 46*, 115–127.

Caballero, A., Granberg, R., & Tseng, K. Y. (2016). Mechanisms contributing to prefrontal cortex maturation during adolescence. *Neuroscience and Biobehavioral Reviews, 70*, 4–12.

Cairns, R. B. (1991). Multiple metaphors for a singular idea. *Developmental Psychology, 27*, 23–26.

Cairns, R. B., Leung, M. C., Buchanan, L., & Cairns, B. D. (1995). Friendships and social networks in childhood and adolescence: Fluidity, reliability, and interrelations. *Child Development, 66*, 1330–1345.

Cairns, R. B., Cairns, B. D., Neckerman, H. J., Gest, S. D., & Garièpy, J.-L. (1988). Social networks and aggressive behavior: Peer support or peer rejection? *Developmental Psychology, 24*, 815–823.

Callaghan, J., Andenæs, A., & Macleod, C. (2015). Deconstructing developmental psychology 20 years on: Reflections, implications and empirical work. *Feminism and Psychology, 25*, 255–265.

Callaghan, T., Rochat, P., Liilard, A., Claux, M., Odden, H., Itakura, S., Tapanya, S., & Singh, S. (2005). Synchrony in the onset of mental state reasoning: Evidence from five cultures. *Psychological Science, 16*, 378–384.

Calvert, S. L. (2015). Children and digital media. In M. H. Bornstein, T. Leventhal & R. M. Lerner (Eds), *Handbook of child psychology and developmental science, Seventh edition, Volume 1: Ecological settings and processes in developmental systems* (pp. 375–415). Hoboken, NJ: Wiley.

Calvin, C. M., Fernandes, C., Smith, P., Visscher, P. M., & Deary, I. J. (2010). Sex, intelligence and educational achievement in a national cohort of over 175,000 11-year-old schoolchildren in England. *Intelligence, 38*, 424–432.

Camaioni, L., Perucchini, P., Muratori, F., Parrini, B., & Cesari, A. (2003). The communicative use of pointing in autism: Developmental profile and factors related to change. *European Psychiatry, 18*, 6–12.

Cameron-Faulkner, T., Lieven, E., & Tomasello, M. (2003). A construction based analysis of child directed speech. *Cognitive Science, 27*, 843–873.

Campbell, F. A., & Ramey, C. T. (1994). Effects of early intervention on intellectual and academic achievement: A follow up study of children from low income families. *Child Development, 65*, 684–698.

Campbell, F. A., Ramey, C. T., Pungello, E., Sparling, J., & Miller-Johnson, S. (2002). Early childhood education: Young adult outcomes from the Abecedarian Project. *Applied Developmental Science, 6*, 42–57.

Campbell, M. E., & Cunnington, R. (2017). More than an imitation game: Top-down modulation of the human mirror system. *Neuroscience and Biobehavioral Reviews, 75*, 195–202.

Campbell, R. N. (1986). Language acquisition and cognition. In P. Fletcher & M. Garman (Eds), *Language acquisition, Second edition* (pp. 30–48). Cambridge: Cambridge University Press.

Campbell, S. B., Halperin, J. M., & Sonuga-Barke, E. S. J. (2014). A developmental perspective on attention deficit/hyperactivity disorder (ADHD). In M. Lewis & K. Rudolp (Eds), *Handbook of developmental psychopathology* (pp. 427–448). New York, NY: Springer.

Campos, J. G., & de Guevara, L. G. (2007). Landau-Kleffner syndrome. *Journal of Pediatric Neurology, 5*, 93–99.

Campos, J. J., Anderson, D. I., Barbu-Roth, M. A., Hubbard, E. M., Hertenstein, M. J., & Witherington, D. (2000). Travel broadens the mind. *Infancy, 1*, 149–219.

Campos, J. J., Butterfield, P., & Klinnert, M. D. (1985, April). Cardiac and behavioral differentiation of negative emotional signals: An individual differences perspective. Presented at the biennial Meeting of the Society for Research in Child Development, Toronto, Canada.

Campos, J. J., Campos, R. G., & Barrett, K. C. (1989). Emergent themes in the study of emotional development and emotion regulation. *Developmental Psychology, 25,* 394–402.

Campos, J. J., Dahl, A., & He, M. (2010). Beyond breaches and battles: Clarifying important misconceptions about emotion. *Emotion Review, 2,* 100–104.

Campos, J. J., Frankel, C., & Camras, L. (2004). On the nature of emotion regulation. *Child Development, 75,* 377–394.

Campos, J. J., Walle, E. A., Dahl, A., & Main, A. (2011). Reconceptualizing emotion regulation. *Emotion Review, 3,* 26–35.

Campos, J. J., Witherington, D., Anderson, D. I., Frankel, C. I., Uchiyama, I., & Barbu-Roth, M. (2008). Rediscovering development in infancy. *Child Development, 79,* 1625–1632.

Camras, L. A. (1992). Expressive development and basic emotions. *Cognition and Emotion, 6,* 269–283.

Camras, L. A. (2011). Differentiation, dynamical integration and functional emotional development. *Emotion Review, 3,* 138–146.

Camras, L. A., Oster, H., Campos, J. J., & Bakemand, R. (2003). Emotional facial expressions in European-American, Japanese, and Chinese infants. *Annals of the New York Academy of Sciences, 1000,* 135–151.

Camras, L. A., & Shuster, M. M. (2013). Current emotion research in developmental psychology. *Emotion Review, 5,* 321–329.

Camras, L. A., & Shutter, J. (2010). Emotional facial expressions in infancy. *Emotion Review, 2,* 120–129.

Camras, L. A., & Witherington, D. C. (2005). Dynamical systems approaches to emotional development. *Developmental Review, 25,* 328–350.

Cantone, E., Piras, A. P., Vellante, M., Preti, A., Daníelsdóttir, S., D'Aloja, E., Lesinskicnc, S., Angermeyer, M. C., Carta, M. G., & Bhugra, D. (2015). Interventions on bullying and cyberbullying in schools: A systematic review. *Clinical Practice and Epidemiology in Mental Health, 11* (Suppl 1: M4), 58–76.

Cantor, J., & Wilson, B. J. (2003). Media and violence: Intervention strategies for reducing aggression. *Media Psychology, 5,* 363–403.

Caplan, M., Vespo, J., Pedersen, J., & Hay, D. F. (1991). Conflict and its resolution in small groups of one and two year olds. *Child Development, 62,* 1513–1524.

Capron, C., & Duyme, M. (1989). Assessment of effects of socio-economic status on IQ in a full cross-fostering study. *Nature, 340,* 552–554.

Caraballo, R. H., Cejas, N., Chamorro, N., Kaltenmeier, M. C., Fortini, S., & Soprano, A. M. (2014). Landau–Kleffner syndrome: A study of 29 patients. *Seizure, 23,* 98–104.

Caramazza, A., Anzellotti, S., Strnad, L., & Lingnau, A. (2014). Embodied cognition and mirror neurons: A critical assessment. *Annual Review of Neuroscience, 37,* 1–15.

Carbon, C. C. (2014). Understanding human perception by human-made illusions. *Frontiers in Human Neuroscience, 8,* 566.

Card, N. (2010). Antipathetic relationships in child and adolescent development: A meta-analytic review and recommendations for an emerging area of study. *Developmental Psychology, 46,* 516–529.

Cardoos, S. L., & Hinshaw, S. P. (2011). Friendship as protection from peer victimization for girls with and without ADHD. *Journal of Abnormal Child Psychology, 39,* 1035–1045.

Carey, S. (1978). The child as word learner. In M. Halle, J. Bresnan & G. A. Miller (Eds), *Linguistic theory and psychological reality* (pp. 264–293). Cambridge, MA: MIT Press.

Carey, S. (1985). *Conceptual change in childhood.* London: MIT Press.

Carey, S. (1992). Becoming a face expert. *Philosophical Transactions of the Royal Society of London. B: Biological Science, 335,* 95–103.

Carey, S. (1996). Perceptual classification and expertise. In R. Gelman & T.K.-F. Au (Eds), *Perceptual and cognitive development* (pp. 49–69). London: Academic Press.

Carey, S. (2011). Précis of the origin of concepts. *Behavioral and Brain Sciences, 34,* 113–124.

Carey, S., Zaitchik, D., & Bascandziev, I. (2015). Theories of development: In dialog with Jean Piaget. *Developmental Review, 38,* 36–54.

Carlier, M., & Roubertoux, P. L. (2014). Genetic and environmental influences on intellectual disability in childhood. In D. Finkel & C. A. Reynold (Eds), *Behavior genetics of cognition across the lifespan* (pp. 69–101). New York, NY: Springer.

Carlo, G., Mestre, M. V., McGinley, M. M., Tur-Porcar, A., Samper, P., & Opal, D. (2014). The protective role of prosocial behaviors on antisocial behaviors: The mediating effects of deviant peer affiliation. *Journal of Adolescence, 37,* 359–366.

Carlson, K. S., & Gjerde, P. F. (2009). Preschool personality antecedents of narcissism in adolescence and young adulthood: A 20-year longitudinal study. *Journal of Research in Personality, 43,* 570–578.

Carlson, S. M., Zelazo, P. D., & Faja, S. (2013). Executive function. In P. Zelazo (Ed.), *The Oxford handbook of developmental psychology, Volume 1* (pp. 706–743). Oxford: Oxford University Press.

Carney, R. N., & Levin, J. R. (2002). Pictorial illustrations still improve students' learning from text. *Educational Psychology Review, 14,* 5–26.

Caron, A. J. (2009). Comprehension of the representational mind in infancy. *Developmental Review, 29,* 69–95.

Caron, A. J., Caron, R. F., & McLean, D. T. (1988). Infant discrimination of naturalistic emotional expressions: The role of face and voice. *Child Development, 59,* 604–616.

Carpendale, J. I. M., & Carpendale, A. B. (2010). The development of pointing: From personal directedness to interpersonal direction. *Human Development, 53,* 110–126.

Carpendale, J. I. M., & Chandler, M. J. (1996). On the distinction between false belief understanding and subscribing to an interpretative theory of mind. *Child Development, 67,* 1686–1706.

Carpendale, J. I. M., Hammond, S. I., & Atwood, S. (2013). A relational developmental systems approach to moral development. *Advances in Child Development and Behavior, 45*, 125–153.

Carpendale, J. I. M., & Lewis, C. (2004). Constructing an understanding of mind: The development of children's social understanding within social interaction. *Behavioral and Brain Sciences, 27*, 79–151.

Carpendale, J. I. M., & Lewis, C. (2015). The development of social understanding. In R. M. Lerner, L. S. Liben & U. Mueller (Eds), *Handbook of child psychology and developmental science, Seventh edition, Volume 2: Cognitive processes* (pp. 381–424). Hoboken, NJ: Wiley.

Carpendale, J. I. M., Lewis, C., Susswein, N., & Lunn, J. (2009). Talking and thinking: The role of speech in social understanding. In A. Winsler, C. Fernyhough & I. Montero (Eds), *Private speech, executive functioning, and the development of verbal self-regulation* (pp. 83–94). Cambridge: Cambridge University Press.

Carpenter, M., & Call, J. (2002). The chemistry of social learning. *Developmental Science, 5*, 23–25.

Carpenter, M., & Liebal, K. (2011). Joint attention, communication, and knowing together in infancy. In A. Seemann (Ed.), *Joint attention: New developments in psychology, philosophy of mind, and social neuroscience* (pp. 159–181). Cambridge, MA: The MIT Press.

Carpenter, M., Nagell, K., & Tomasello, M. (1998). Social cognition, joint attention and communicative competence from 9 to 15 months of age. *Monographs of the Society for Research in Child Development, 63* (4), 1–174.

Carr, A. (2016). *The handbook of child and adolescent clinical psychology: A contextual approach.* Hove, UK: Routledge.

Carr, A., & O'Reilly, G. (2016a). Diagnosis, classification and epidemiology. In A. Carr, G. O'Reilly, P. N. Walsh & J. McEvoy (Eds), *The handbook of intellectual disability and clinical psychology practice* (pp. 3–44). Hove, UK: Routledge.

Carr, A., & O'Reilly, G. (2016b). Lifespan development and the family lifecycle. In A. Carr, G. O'Reilly, P. N. Walsh & J. McEvoy (Eds), *The handbook of intellectual disability and clinical psychology practice* (pp. 45–74). Hove, UK: Routledge.

Carr, A., Linehan, C., O'Reilly, G., Walsh, P. N., & McEvoy, J. (Eds) (2016). *The handbook of intellectual disability and clinical psychology practice.* Hove, UK: Routledge.

Carruth, B. R., Ziegler, P. J., Gordon, A., & Barr, S.I. (2004). Prevalence of picky eaters among infants and toddlers and their caregivers' decisions about offering a new food. *Journal of the American Dietetic Association, 104* (Supplement 1), S57–S64.

Carruthers, P. (2006). *The architecture of the mind: Massive modularity and the flexibility of thought.* Oxford: Oxford University Press.

Carruthers, P. (2008). Précis of the architecture of the mind: Massive modularity and the flexibility of thought. *Mind and Language, 23*, 257–262.

Case, A., Paxson, C., & Ableidinger, J. (2004). Orphans in Africa: Parental death, poverty, and school enrollment. *Demography, 41*, 483–508.

Case, R. (1985). *Intellectual development: Birth to adulthood.* London: Academic Press.

Case, R. (1998). The development of conceptual structures. In W. Damon & N. Eisenberg (Eds), *Handbook of child psychology, Fifth edition, Volume 3. Cognition, perception, and language* (pp. 311–388). New York, NY: Wiley.

Casey, B. J., Tottenham, N., Liston, C., & Durston, S. (2005). Imaging the developing brain: What have we learned about cognitive development? *Trends in Cognitive Science, 9*, 104–110.

Casper, D. M., & Card, N. A. (2010). "We were best friends, but. . .": Two studies of antipathetic relationships emerging from broken friendships. *Journal of Adolescent Research, 25*, 499–526

Caspi, A. (1998). Personality development across the life course. In W. Damon & N. Eisenberg (Eds), *Handbook of child psychology, Fifth edition, Volume 2. Social, emotional, and personality development* (pp. 745–800). New York, NY: Wiley.

Caspi, A. (2000). The child is the father of the man: Personality continuities from childhood to adulthood. *Journal of Personality and Social Psychology, 78*, 158–172.

Caspi, A., & Roberts, B. W. (2001). Personality development across the life course: The argument for change and continuity. *Psychological Inquiry, 12*, 49–66.

Caspi, A., Roberts, B. W., & Shiner, R. L. (2005). Personality development: Stability and change. *Annual Review of Psychology, 56*, 453–484.

Caspi, A., Hariri, A. R., Holmes, A., Uher, R., & Moffitt, T. E. (2010). Genetic sensitivity to the environment: The case of the serotonin transporter gene and its implications for studying complex diseases and traits. *Focus, 8*, 398–416.

Caspi, A., Henry, B., McGee, R. O., Moffitt, T. E., & Silva, P. A. (1995). Temperamental origins of child and adolescent behavior problems: From age three to age fifteen. *Child Development, 66*, 55–68.

Caspi, A., Houts, R. M., Belsky, D. W., Harrington, H., Hogan, S., Ramrakha, S., Poulton, R., & Moffitt, T. E. (2016). Childhood forecasting of a small segment of the population with large economic burden. *Nature Human Behaviour, 1*, 0005.

Caspi, A., McClay, J., Moffitt, T. E., Mill, J., Martin, J., Craig, I. W., Taylor, A., & Poulton, R. (2002). Role of genotype in the cycle of violence in maltreated children. *Science, 297*, 851–854.

Catron, T. F., & Masters, J. C. (1993). Mothers' and children's conceptualizations of corporal punishment. *Child Development, 64*, 1815–1828.

Cattaneo, L., & Rizzolatti, G. (2009). The mirror neuron system. *Archives of Neurology, 66*, 557–560.

Cattell, R. B. (1963). Theory of fluid and crystallized intelligence: A critical experiment. *Journal of Educational Psychology, 54*, 1–22.

Ceci, S. J. (1991). How much does schooling influence general intelligence and its cognitive components? A reassessment of the evidence. *Developmental Psychology, 27*, 703–722.

Ceci, S. J., & Kanaya, T. (2010). "Apples and oranges are both round": Furthering the discussion on the Flynn effect. *Journal of Psychoeducational Assessment, 28*, 441–447.

Ceci, S. J., Kulkofsky, S., Klemfuss, Z., Sweeney, C. D., & Bruck, M. (2007). Unwarranted assumptions about children's testimonial accuracy. *Annual Review of Clinical Psychology, 3*, 311–328.

Celeste, M. (2006). Play behaviors and social interactions of a child who is blind: In theory and practice. *Journal of Visual Impairment and Blindness, 100*, 75–90.

Cernoch, J. M., & Porter, R. H. (1985). Recognition of maternal axillary odors by infants. *Child Development, 56*, 1593–1598.

Chabris, C. F., Hebert, B. M., Benjamin, D. J., Beauchamp, J., Cesarini, D., Van der Loos, M., Johannesson, M., Magnusson, P. K., Lichtenstein, P., Atwood, C. S., et al. (2012). Most reported genetic associations with general intelligence are probably false positives. *Psychological Science, 23*, 1314–1323.

Chahboun, S., Vulchanov, V., Saldaña, D., Eshuis, H., & Vulchanova, M. (2016). Can you play with fire and not hurt yourself? A comparative study in figurative language comprehension between individuals with and without autism spectrum disorder. *PloS one, 11* (12), e0168571.

Chaiklin, S. (2003). The zone of proximal development in Vygotsky's analysis of learning and instruction. In A. Kozulin, B. Gindis, V. Ageyev & S. Miller (Eds), *Vygotsky's educational theory in cultural context* (pp. 39–64). Cambridge: Cambridge University Press.

Chandler, F., & Dissanayake, C. (2014). An investigation of the security of caregiver attachment during middle childhood in children with high-functioning autistic disorder. *Autism, 18*, 485–492.

Chang, F., Dell, G. S., & Bock, K. (2006). Becoming syntactic. *Psychological Review, 113*, 234–272.

Chang, H.-W., & Trehub, S. E. (1977). Auditory processing of relational information by young infants. *Journal of Experimental Child Psychology, 24*, 324–331.

Chang, Y. C., Shire, S. Y., Shih, W., Gelfand, C., & Kasari, C. (2016). Preschool deployment of evidence-based social communication intervention: JASPER in the classroom. *Journal of Autism and Developmental Disorders, 46*, 2211–2223.

Chanioti, E. (2017). Dyslexia in primary school: A new platform for identifying reading errors and improving reading skills. In P. Anastasiades & N. Zaranis (Eds), *Research on e-learning and ICT in education* (pp. 257–271). Cham, Switzerland; Springer.

Charman, T. (2000). Theory of mind and the early diagnosis of autism. In S. Baron-Cohen, H., Tager-Flusberg & D. J. Cohen (Eds), *Understanding other minds, Second edition* (pp. 422–441). Oxford: Oxford University Press.

Chatterjee, M., Zion, D. J., Deroche, M. L., Burianek, B. A., Limb, C. J., Goren, A. P., Kulkarni, A. M., & Christensen, J. A. (2015). Voice emotion recognition by cochlear-implanted children and their normally-hearing peers. *Hearing Research, 322*, 151–162.

Cheah, C. S. L., & Park, S.-Y. (2006). South Korean mothers' beliefs regarding aggression and social withdrawal in preschoolers. *Early Childhood Research, 21*, 61–75.

Chen, J.-Q., & Gardner, H. (1997). Alternate assessment from a multiple intelligences theoretical perspective. In D. P. Flanagan, J. L. Genshaft & P. L. Harrison (Eds), *Contemporary intellectual assessment* (pp. 105–212). London: Guilford Press.

Chen, X., & French, D. (2008). Children's social competence in cultural context. *Annual Review of Psychology, 59*, 591–616.

Chen, X., French, D., & Schneider. B. H. (2006). Culture and peer relationships. In X. Chen, D. C. French & B. H. Schneider (Eds), *Peer relationships in a cultural context* (pp. 3–20). Cambridge: Cambridge University Press.

Chen, X., & Schmidt, L. A. (2015). Temperament and personality. In R. M. Lerner, M. E. Lamb & C. G. Coll (Eds), *Handbook of child psychology and developmental science, Seventh edition, Volume 3: Social and emotional development* (pp. 152–200). Hoboken, NJ: Wiley.

Chen, Z., & Klahr, D. (2008). Remote transfer of scientific reasoning and problem-solving strategies in children. In R. V. Kail (Ed.), *Advances in child development and behavior, Volume 36* (pp. 419–470). Amsterdam: Elsevier.

Cheng, P. W., & Holyoak, K. J. (1985). Pragmatic reasoning schema. *Cognitive Psychology, 17*, 391–416.

Cheng, Y.-L., & Mix, K. S. (2014). Spatial training improves children's mathematics ability. *Journal of Cognition and Development, 15*, 2–11.

Chcong, S. K., Lang, C. P., Hemphill, S. A., & Johnston, L. M. (2016). What constitutes self-concept for children with CP? A Delphi consensus survey. *Journal of Developmental and Physical Disabilities, 28*, 333–346.

Cherney, I. D., & London, K. (2006). Gender-linked differences in the toys, television shows, computer games, and outdoor activities of 5- to 13-year-old children. *Sex Roles, 54*, 717–726

Chess, S., & Thomas, A. (1999). *Goodness of fit: Clinical applications from infancy through adult life.* London: Bunner/Mazel.

Chi, M. T. H. (1978). Knowledge structures and memory development. In R. S. Siegler (Ed.), *Children's thinking: What develops?* (pp. 73–96). Hillsdale, NJ: Lawrence Erlbaum.

Chi, M. T. H., & Koeske, R. D. (1983). Network representation of a child's dinosaur knowledge. *Developmental Psychology, 19*, 29–39.

Chiao, J. Y., Hariri, A. R., Harada, T., Mano, Y., Sadato, N., Parrish, T. B., & Iidaka, T. (2010). Theory and methods in cultural neuroscience. *Social Cognitive and Affective Neuroscience, 5*, 356–361.

Chib, A., Malik, S., Aricat, R. G., & Kadir, S. Z. (2014). Migrant mothering and mobile phones: Negotiations of transnational identity. *Mobile Media and Communication, 2*, 73–93.

Chinn, S. (2015). The Routledge international handbook of dyscalculia and mathematical learning difficulties: An overview. In S. Chinn (Ed.), *The Routledge international handbook of dyscalculia and mathematical learning difficulties* (pp. 1–17). New York, NY: Routledge.

Chisholm, K. (1998). A three-year follow-up of attachment and indiscriminate friendliness in children adopted from Romanian orphanages. *Child Development, 69,* 1092–1106.

Chomsky, N. (1959). Review of Skinner's Verbal Behavior. *Language, 35,* 26–58.

Chomsky, N. (1968). *Language and mind.* New York: Harcourt Brace Jovanovich.

Chomsky, N. (1986). *Knowledge of language: Its nature, origin, and use.* London: Praeger.

Chomsky, N. (1988). *Language and problems of knowledge.* Cambridge, MA: MIT Press.

Chomsky, N. (2000). *New horizons in the study of language and mind.* Cambridge: Cambridge University Press.

Choufani, S., & Weksberg, R. (2016). Genomic imprinting. In D. P. Bazett-Jones & G. Dellaire (Eds), *The functional nucleus* (pp. 449–465). Switzerland: Springer.

Chouinard, M. M., & Clark, E. V. (2003). Adult reformulations of child errors as negative evidence. *Journal of Child Language, 30,* 637–669.

Christakis, D. A., Gilkerson, J., Richards, J. A., Zimmerman, F. J., Garrison, M. M., Xu, D., Gray, S., & Yapanel, U. (2009). Audible television and decreased adult words, infant vocalizations, and conversational turns: A population-based study. *Archives of Pediatrics and Adolescent Medicine, 163,* 554–558.

Christakis, D. A., & Zimmerman, F. J. (2007). Violent television viewing during preschool is associated with antisocial behavior during school age. *Pediatrics, 120,* 993–999.

Christiansen, M. H., & Chater, N. (2008). Language as shaped by the brain. *Behavioral and Brain Sciences, 31,* 489–558.

Christianson, S. Å., Azad, A., Leander, L., & Selenius, H. (2013). Children as witnesses to homicidal violence: What they remember and report. *Psychiatry, Psychology and Law, 20,* 366–383.

Christie, J. F., & Johnson, E. P. (1987). Reconceptualizing constructive play: A review of the empirical literature. *Merrill-Palmer Quarterly, 33,* 439–452.

Chronis-Tuscano, A., Rubin, K. H., O'Brien, K. A., Coplan, R. J., Thomas, S. R., Dougherty, L. R., Cheah, C. S., Watts, K., Heverly-Fitt, S., Huggins, S. L., et al. (2015). Preliminary evaluation of a multimodal early intervention program for behaviorally inhibited preschoolers. *Journal of Consulting and Clinical Psychology, 83,* 534–540.

Chugani, H. T., Phelps, M. E., & Mazziotti, J. C. (1987). Positron emission tomography study of human brain functional development. *Annals of Neurology, 22,* 487–497.

Chung, J. M., Hutteman, R., van Aken, M. A., & Denissen, J. J. (2017). High, low, and in between: Self-esteem development from middle childhood to young adulthood. *Journal of Research in Personality, 70,* 122–133.

Chupetlovska-Anastasova, A. (2014). Longitudinal exploration of friendship patterns of children and early adolescents with and without Attention-Deficit/Hyperactivity Disorder. Doctoral dissertation, University of Ottawa.

Cicchetti, D. (2002). The impact of social experience on neurobiological systems: Illustration from a constructivist view of child maltreatment. *Cognitive Development, 17,* 1407–1428.

Cicchetti, D. (2013). Annual research review: Resilient functioning in maltreated children—past, present, and future perspectives. *Journal of Child Psychology and Psychiatry, 54* (4), 402–422.

Cicchetti, D. (2016). Socioemotional, personality, and biological development: Illustrations from a multilevel developmental psychopathology perspective on child maltreatment. *Annual Review of Psychology, 67,* 187–211.

Cicchetti, D., & Cohen, D. (Eds). (2006). *Developmental psychopathology.* New York, NY: Wiley.

Cicchetti, D., & Toth, S. L. (2009). The past achievements and future promises of developmental psychopathology: The coming of age of a discipline. *Journal of Child Psychology and Psychiatry, 50,* 16–25.

Cicchetti, D., & Toth, S. L. (2015). Child maltreatment. In R. M. Lerner, M. E. Lamb & C. G. Coll (Eds), *Handbook of child psychology and developmental science, Seventh edition, Volume 3: Social and emotional development* (pp. 513–563). Hoboken, NJ: Wiley.

Cicirelli, V. G. (1996). Sibling relationships in middle and old age. In G.-H. Brody (Ed.), *Sibling relationships: Their causes and consequences* (pp. 47–73). Stamford, CT: Ablex.

Cillessen, A. H. N., & Rose, A. J. (2005). Understanding popularity in the peer system. *Current Directions in Psychological Science, 14,* 102–105.

Cillessen, A. H. N., van IJzendoorn, H. W., van Lieshout, C. F. M., & Hartup, W. W. (1992). Heterogeneity among peer-rejected boys: Subtypes and stabilities. *Child Development, 63,* 893–905.

Clark, A. (2008). Pressing the flesh: A tension in the study of the embodied, embedded mind? *Philosophy and Phenomenological Research, 76,* 37–59.

Clark, A., O'Hare, A., Watson, J., Cohen, W., Cowie, H., Elton, R., Nasir, J., & Seckl, J. (2007). Severe receptive language disorder in childhood – familial aspects and long-term outcomes: Results from a Scottish study. *Archives of Disease in Childhood, 92,* 614–619.

Clark, E. V. (1973). What's in a word? On the child's acquisition of semantics in his first language. In T. E. Moore (Ed.), *Cognitive development and the acquisition of language* (pp. 65–110). New York, NY: Academic Press.

Clark, E. V. (1980). Lexical innovations: How children learn to create new words. *Papers and Reports on Child Language Development, 18,* 1–24.

Clark, E. V. (1981). Lexical innovations: How children learn to create new words. In W. Deutsch (Ed.), *The child's construction of language* (pp. 299–328). London: Academic Press.

Clark, E. V. (1992). Conventionality and contrast: Pragmatic principles with lexical consequences. In A. Lehrer & E. F. Kittay (Eds), *Frames, fields and contrasts* (pp. 171–188). Hove, UK: Lawrence Erlbaum.

Clark, E. V. (2016). *First language acquisition, Second edition*. Cambridge: Cambridge University Press.

Clark, I. (2012). Formative assessment: Assessment is for self-regulated learning. *Educational Psychology Review*, 24, 205–249.

Clark, S. E., & Symons, D. K. (2000). A longitudinal study of Q-sort attachment security and self-processes at age 5. *Infant and Child Development*, 9, 91–104.

Clarke, A., & Clarke, A. (2000). *Early experience and the life path*. London: Jessica Kingsley.

Clarke, B., Doabler, C. T., Smolkowski, K., Baker, S. K., Fien, H., & Strand Cary, M. (2016). Examining the efficacy of a Tier 2 kindergarten mathematics intervention. *Journal of Learning Disabilities*, 49, 152–165.

Cleave, P. L., Becker, S. D., Curran, M. K., Van Horne, A. J. O., & Fey, M. E. (2015). The efficacy of recasts in language intervention: A systematic review and meta-analysis. *American Journal of Speech-Language Pathology*, 24, 237–255.

Clegg, J., Law, J., Rush, R., Peters, T. J., & Roulstone, S. (2015). The contribution of early language development to children's emotional and behavioural functioning at 6 years: An analysis of data from the Children in Focus sample from the ALSPAC birth cohort. *Journal of Child Psychology and Psychiatry*, 56, 67–75.

Clemans, K. H., DeRose, L. M., Graber, J. A., & Brooks-Gunn, J. (2010). Gender in adolescence: Applying a personin-context approach to gender identity and roles. In J. C. Chrisler & D. R. McCreary (Eds), *Handbook of gender research in psychology* (pp. 527–558). New York, NY: Springer.

Clibbens, J. (2001). Signing and lexical development in children with Down syndrome. *Down Syndrome Research and Practice*, 7, 101–105.

Clifton, R. K. (1992). The development of spatial hearing in human infants. In L. A. Werner & E. W. Rubel (Eds), *Developmental psychoacoustics* (pp. 135–157). Washington, DC: American Psychological Association.

Cline, T., & Baldwin, S. (2004). *Selective mutism in children, Second edition*. London: Whurr/Wiley.

Clinton, D. (2010). Towards an ecology of eating disorders: Creating sustainability through the integration of scientific research and clinical practice. *European Eating Disorders Review*, 18, 1–9.

Cloninger, C. R., Sigvardsson, S., Bohman, M., & Knorring, A. L. von (1982). Predisposition to petty criminality in Swedish adoptees: II. Cross fostering analysis of gene environment interaction. *Archives of General Psychiatry*, 39, 1242–1247.

Cnattingius, S. (2004). The epidemiology of smoking during pregnancy: Smoking prevalence, maternal characteristics, and pregnancy outcomes. *Nicotine and Tobacco Research*, 6 (Suppl-2), S125–S140.

Cohen, D., & MacKeith, S. (1990). *The development of imagination*. London: Routledge.

Cohen, L. B., & Cashon, C. H. (2006). Infant cognition. In W. Damon & R. M. Lerner (Eds), *Handbook of child psychology, Sixth edition, Volume 1: Theoretical models of human development* (pp. 793–828). New York, NY: Wiley.

Cohen, L. B., Chaput, H. H., & Cashon, C. H. (2002). A constructivist model of infant cognition. *Cognitive Development*, 17, 1323–1343.

Cohen, P., Kasen, S., Chen, H., Hartmark, C., & Gordon, K. (2003). Variations in patterns of developmental transmissions in the emerging adulthood period. *Developmental Psychology*, 39, 657–669.

Cohen-Bendahan, C. C. C., van de Beek, C., & Berenbaum, S. A. (2005). Prenatal sex hormone effects on child and adult sex-typed behavior: Methods and findings. *Neuroscience and Biobehavioral Reviews*, 29, 353–384.

Colby, A., Kohlberg, L., Gibbs, J., & Lierberman, M. (1983). A longitudinal study of moral development. *Monographs for the Society for Research in Child Development*, 48 (1–2).

Cole, M. (2005). Cross-cultural and historical perspectives on developmental consequences of education. *Human Development*, 48, 195–216.

Cole, M. (2006). Internationalization in psychology: We need it now more than ever. *American Psychologist*, 61, 904–917.

Cole, P. M. (1986). Children's spontaneous control of facial expression. *Child Development*, 57, 1309–1321.

Cole, P. M., Bruschi, C. J., & Tamang, B. L. (2002). Cultural differences in children's emotional reactions to difficult situations. *Child Development*, 73, 983–996.

Coleman, J. C. (1980). Friendship and the peer group in adolescence. In J. Adelson (Ed.), *Handbook of adolescent psychology* (pp. 408–431). New York, NY: Wiley.

Coleman, P. K., & Karraker, K. H. (1998). Self-efficacy and parenting quality: Findings and future applications. *Developmental Review*, 18, 47–85.

Collier, K., Bickel, B., van Schaik, C. P., Manser, M. B., & Townsend, S. W. (2014). Language evolution: Syntax before phonology? *Proceedings of the Royal Society B: Biological Sciences*, 281, 20140263.

Collins, W. A., Maccoby, E. E., Steinberg, L., Hetherington, E. M., & Bornstein, M. H. (2000). Contemporary research on parenting. *American Psychologist*, 55, 218–232.

Collis, G. M., & Schaffer, H. R. (1975). Synchronization of visual attention in mother–infant pairs. *Journal of Child Psychology and Psychiatry*, 16, 315–320.

Collishaw, S. (2015). Annual research review: Secular trends in child and adolescent mental health. *Journal of Child Psychology and Psychiatry*, 56, 370–393.

Colombo, J. (2001). Infants' detection of contingency: A cognitive-neuroscience perspective. *Bulletin of the Menninger Clinic*, 65, 321–334.

Condry, J., & Condry, S. (1976). Sex differences: A study of the eye of the beholder. *Child Development*, 47, 812–819.

Condry, K. F., Smith, W. C., & Spelke, E. S. (2001). Development of perceptual organization. In F. Lacerda, C. von

Hofsten & M. Heimann (Eds), *Emerging cognitive abilities in early infancy* (pp. 1–28). Mahwah, NJ: Erlbaum.

Conn, C. (2014). Investigating the social engagement of children with autism in mainstream schools for the purpose of identifying learning targets. *Journal of Research in Special Educational Needs*, 14, 153–159.

Connell, S. L. Lauricella, A. R., & Wartella, E. (2015). Parental co-use of media technology with their young children in the USA. *Journal of Children and Media*, 9, 5–21.

Connolly, J. A., & Doyle, A. B. (1984). Relation of social fantasy play to social competence in preschoolers. *Developmental Psychology*, 20, 797–806.

Connolly, K. J., & Dalgleish, M. (1993). Individual patterns of tool use by infants. In A. F. Kalverboer, B. Hopkins & R. Geuze (Eds), *Motor development in early and later childhood: Longitudinal approaches* (pp. 174–204). Cambridge: Cambridge University Press.

Constable, H., Campbell, B., & Brown, R. (1988). Sectional drawings from science textbooks: An experimental investigation into pupil's understanding. *British Journal of Educational Psychology*, 58, 89–102.

Conti-Ramsden, G., Botting, N., Simkin, Z., & Knox, E. (2001). Follow-up of children attending infant language units: Outcomes at 11 years of age. *International Journal of Language and Communication Disorders*, 36, 207–219.

Conti-Ramsden, G., Simkin, Z., & Botting, N. (2006). The prevalence of autistic spectrum disorders in adolescents with a history of specific language impairment (SLI). *Journal of Child Psychology and Psychiatry*, 47, 621–628

Conway, A. R., & Kovacs, K. (2015). New and emerging models of human intelligence. *Wiley Interdisciplinary Reviews: Cognitive Science*, 6, 419–426.

Cook, M. (2008). Students' comprehension of science concepts depicted in textbook illustrations. *Electronic Journal of Science Education*, 12, 1–14.

Cook, R., Bird, G., Catmur, C., Press, C., & Heyes, C. (2014). Mirror neurons: From origin to function. *Behavioral and Brain Sciences*, 37, 177–192.

Cook, T. D., & Campbell, D. T. (1979). *Quasi-experimentation: Design and analysis for field settings*. Boston, MA: Houghton Mifflin.

Cooley, C. H. (1902). *Human nature and the social order*. New York, NY: Charles Schribner's Sons.

Coplan, R. J., & Arbeau, K. A. (2008). The stresses of a brave new world: Shyness and adjustment in kindergarten. *Journal of Research in Childhood Education*, 22, 377–389.

Coplan, R. J., Arbeau, K. A., & Armer, M. (2008). Don't fret, be supportive! Maternal characteristics linking child shyness to psychosocial and school adjustment in kindergarten. *Journal of Abnormal Child Psychology*, 36, 359–371.

Coplan, R. J., Ooi, L. L., & Nocita, G. (2015). When one is company and two is a crowd: Why some children prefer solitude. *Child Development Perspectives*, 9, 133–137.

Coplan, R. J., Ooi, L. L., Rose-Krasnor, L., & Nocita, G. (2014). "I want to play alone": Assessment and correlates of self-reported preference for solitary play in young children. *Infant and Child Development*, 23, 229–238.

Coppola, M. (2002). The emergence of the grammatical category of Subject in home sign: Evidence from family-based gesture systems in Nicaragua. Doctoral Dissertation, University of Rochester, USA.

Corcoran, J., & Hanvey-Phillips, J. (2013). Effective interventions for adolescents with depression. In C. Franklin, M. B. Harris & P. Allen-Meares (Eds), *The school services sourcebook: A guide for school-based professionals* (pp. 149–157). Oxford: Oxford University Press.

Cordier, R., Munro, N., Speyer, R., Wilkes-Gillan, S., & Pearce, W. (2014). Reliability and validity of the Pragmatics Observational Measure (POM): A new observational measure of pragmatic language for children. *Research in Developmental Disabilities*, 35, 1588–1598.

Cordón, I. M., Pipe, M. E., Sayfan, L., Melinder, A., & Goodman, G. S. (2004). Memory for traumatic experiences in early childhood. *Developmental Review*, 24, 101–132.

Cordua, G. D., McGraw, K. O., & Drabman, R. S. (1979). Doctor or nurse: Children's perception of sextyped occupations. *Child Development*, 50, 590–593.

Cormier, E. (2008). Attention deficit/hyperactivity disorder: A review and update. *Journal of Pediatric Nursing*, 23, 345–357.

Cornell, A. H., & Frick, P. J. (2007). The moderating effects of parenting styles in the association between behavioral inhibition and parent-reported guilt and empathy in preschool children. *Journal of Clinical Child and Adolescent Psychology*, 36, 305–318.

Corrieri. S., Heider, D., Conrad, I., Blume, A., König, H. H., & Riedel-Heller, S. G. (2013). School-based prevention programs for depression and anxiety in adolescence: A systematic review. *Health Promotion International*, 29, 427–441.

Corrigan, R., & Denton, P. (1996). Causal understanding as a developmental primitive. *Developmental Review*, 16, 162–202.

Cortese, S., Ferrin, M., Brandeis, D., Buitelaar, J., Daley, D., Dittmann, R. W., Holtmann, M., Santosh, P., Stevenson, J., Stringaris, A., et al. (2015). Cognitive training for attention-deficit/hyperactivity disorder: Meta-analysis of clinical and neuropsychological outcomes from randomized controlled trials. *Journal of the American Academy of Child and Adolescent Psychiatry*, 54, 164–174.

Cortina, M., & Liotti, G. (2010). Attachment is about safety and protection, intersubjectivity is about sharing and social understanding. *Psychoanalytic Psychology*, 27, 410–441.

Cosmides, L., & Tooby, J. (1994). Origins of domain specificity: The evolution of functional organization. In L. Hirschfeld & S. Gelman (Eds), *Mapping the mind: Domain-specificity in cognition and culture* (pp. 85–116). New York, NY: Cambridge University Press.

Costa, P. T., & McCrae, R. R. (1992). *Revised NEO Personality Inventory (NEO-PI-R) and NEO Five Factor*

Inventory (NEO-FFI). Professional manual. Odessa, FL: Psychological Assessment Resources.

Côté, J. E. (2014). The dangerous myth of emerging adulthood: An evidence-based critique of a flawed developmental theory. *Applied Developmental Science, 18,* 177–188.

Côté, S. M., Boivin, M., Nagin, D. S., Japel, C., Xu, Q., Zoccolillo, M., Junger, M., & Tremblay, R. A. (2007). The role of maternal education and nonmaternal care services in the prevention of children's physical aggression problems. *Archives of General Psychiatry, 64,* 1305–1312.

Coull, G. J., Leekam, S. R., & Bennett, M. (2006). Simplifying second-order belief attribution: What facilitates children's performance on measures of conceptual understanding? *Social Development, 15,* 260–275.

Couperus, J. W., & Nelson, C. A. (2006). Early brain development and plasticity. In K. McCartney & D. Phillips (Eds). *Blackwell handbook of early childhood development* (pp. 85–105). Malden, MA: Blackwell.

Courage, M. L., Edison, S. C., & Howe, M. L. (2004). Variability in the early development of visual self-recognition. *Infant Behavior and Development, 27,* 509–532.

Cowan, N. (2014). Short-term and working memory in childhood. In P. J. Bauer & R. Fivush (Eds), *The Wiley handbook on the development of children's memory, Volume 2* (pp. 202–229). Chichester, UK: Wiley.

Cox, D. R., Skinner, J. D., Carruth, B. R., Moran, J., & Houck, K. S. (1997). A food variety index for toddlers (VIT): Development and application. *Journal of the American Dietetic Association, 97,* 1382–1386.

Cox, M. J., Mills-Koonce, R., Propper, C., & Gariépy, J. L. (2010). Systems theory and cascades in developmental psychopathology. *Development and Psychopathology, 22,* 497–506.

Cozby, P. C. (1993). *Methods in behavioral research, Fifth edition.* London: Mayfield.

Craig, W., Harel-Fisch, Y., Fogel-Grinvald, H., Dostaler, S., Hetland, J., Simons-Morton, B., Molcho, M., de Mato, M. G., Overpeck, M., Due, P., et al. (2009). A cross-national profile of bullying and victimization among adolescents in 40 countries. *International Journal of Public Health, 54,* 216–224.

Craik, F. I. M., & Schloerscheidt, A. M. (2011). Age-related differences in recognition memory: Effects of materials and context change. *Psychology and Aging, 26,* 671–677.

Cramer, P. (2017). Identity change between late adolescence and adulthood. *Personality and Individual Differences, 104,* 538–543.

Cramer, V., Torgersen, S., & Kringlen, E. (2007). Socio-demographic conditions, subjective somatic health, Axis I disorders and personality disorders in the common population: The relationship to quality of life. *Journal of Personality Disorders, 21,* 552–567.

Creed, A. T., Waltman, H. S., Frankel, A. S., & Williston, A. M. (2016). School-based cognitive behavioral therapy: Current status and alternative approaches. *Current Psychiatry Reviews, 12,* 53–64.

Creswell, J. W., & Miller, D. L. (2000). Determining validity in qualitative inquiry. *Theory into Practice, 39,* 124–130.

Crick, N. R., & Dodge, K. A. (1994). A review and reforl-mulation of social information-processing mechanisms in children's social adjustment. *Psychological Bulletin, 115,* 74–101.

Crick, N. R., & Dodge, K. A. (1996). Social information processing mechanisms on reactive and proactive aggression. *Child Development, 67,* 993–1002.

Crippa, A., Marzocchi, G. M., Piroddi, C., Besana, D., Giribone, S., Vio, C., Maschietto, D., Fornaro, E., Repossi, S., & Sora, M. L. (2015). An integrated model of executive functioning is helpful for understanding ADHD and associated disorders. *Journal of Attention Disorders, 19,* 455–467.

Crockenberg, S. B. (1981). Infant irritability, mother responsiveness, and social support influences on the security of infant mother attachment. *Child Development, 52,* 857–865.

Crockenberg, S. C., & Leerkes, E. (2000). Infant social and emotional development in family context. In C. H. Zeanah (Ed.), *Handbook of infant mental health, Second edition* (pp. 60–90). London: Guilford Press.

Crockenberg, S. C., & Leerkes, E. (2006). Infant and mother behavior moderate reactivity to novelty to predict anxious behavior at 2.5 years. *Development and Psychopathology, 18,* 1–18.

Crockenberg, S. C., Leerkes, E. M., & Lekka, S. K. (2007). Pathways from marital aggression to infant emotion regulation: The development of withdrawal in infancy. *Infant Behavior and Development, 30,* 97–113.

Cronch, L. E., Viljoen J. L., & Hansen, D. J. (2006). Forensic interviewing in child sexual abuse cases: Current techniques and future directions. *Aggression and Violent Behavior, 11,* 195–207.

Crosnoe, R., & Benner, A. D. (2015). Children at school. In M. Bornstein, T. Leventhal & R. M. Lerner (Eds), *Handbook of child psychology and developmental science, Seventh edition. Volume 4. Ecological settings and processes* (pp. 268–304). London: Wiley.

Crow, J. F. (2000). The origins, patterns and implications of human spontaneous mutation. *Nature Review Genetics, 1,* 40–47.

Crowell, J. A., Fraley, R. C., & Shaver, P. R. (2008). Measurement of individual differences in adolescent and adult attachment. In J. Cassidy & P. R. Shaver (Eds), *Handbook of attachment: Theory, research, and clinical applications, Second edition* (pp. 599–634). New York, NY: Guilford Press.

Crusio, W. E. (2015). Key issues in contemporary behavioral genetics. *Current Opinion in Behavioral Sciences, 2,* 89–95.

Csibra, G. (2010). Recognizing communicative intentions in infancy. *Mind and Language, 25,* 141–168.

Cuevas, K., Rajan, V., Morasch, K. C., & Bell, M. A. (2015). Episodic memory and future thinking during early childhood: Linking the past and future. *Developmental Psychobiology, 57,* 552–565.

Cui, L., Morris, A. S., Criss, M. M., Houltberg, B. J., & Silk, J. S. (2014). Parental psychological control and adolescent adjustment: The role of adolescent emotion regulation. *Parenting, 14,* 47–67.

Cummings, E. M. (1987). Coping with background anger in early childhood. *Child Development*, *58*, 976–984.

Cummings, E. M., & Davies, P. T. (1994). *Children and marital conflict: The impact of family dispute and resolution*. New York, NY: Guilford Press.

Cummings, E. M., & Davies, P. T. (2002). Effects of marital conflict on children: Recent advances and emerging themes in process-oriented research. *Journal of Child Psychology and Psychiatry*, *43*, 31–63.

Cummings, E. M., Ballard, M., & El Sheikh, M. (1991). Responses of children and adolescents to interadult anger as a function of gender, age, and mode of expression. *Merrill-Palmer Quarterly*, *37*, 543–560.

Cummings, E. M., Hennessy, K. D., Rabideau, G. J., & Cicchetti, D. (1994). Responses of physically abused boys to interadult anger involving their mothers. *Development and Psychopathology*, *6*, 31-41.

Cummings, E. M., El-Sheikh, M., Kouros, C. D., & Buckhalt, J. A. (2009). Children and violence: The role of children's regulation in the marital aggression–child adjustment link. *Clinical Child and Family Psychology Review*, *12*, 3–15.

Cummings, E. M., Iannotti, R. J., & Zahn-Waxler, C. (1985). Influence of conflict between adults on the emotions and aggression of young children. *Developmental Psychology*, *21*, 495–507.

Cummings, E. M., Merrilees, C. E., Taylor, L. K., & Mondi, C. F. (2017). *Political violence, armed conflict, and youth adjustment*. Cham, Switzerland: Springer.

Cummings, E. M., Vogel, D., Cummings, J. S., & El-Sheikh, M. (1989). Children's responses to different forms of expression of anger between adults. *Child development*, 1392–1404.

Cummings, H. M., & Vandewater, E. A. (2007). Relation of adolescent video game play to time spent in other activities. *Archives of Pediatrics & Adolescent Medicine*, *161*, 684–689.

Cummings, L. (2008). *Clinical linguistics*. Edinburgh: Edinburgh University Press.

Cummings, L. (2014). *Pragmatic disorders*. Dordrecht: Springer.

Cushman, P. (1991). Ideology obscured. Political uses of the self in Daniel Stern's infant. *American Psychologist*, *46*, 206–219.

Cuskelly, M. & Gunn, P. (2003). Sibling relationships of children with Down syndrome: Perspectives of mothers, fathers, and siblings. *American Journal on Mental Retardation*, *108*, 234–244.

Cutting, A. L., & Dunn, J. (2002). The cost of understanding other people: Social cognition predicts young children's sensitivity to criticism. *Journal of Child Psychology and Psychiatry and Allied Disciplines*, *43*, 849–860.

Cutting, A. L., & Dunn, J. (2006). Conversations with siblings and with friends: Links between relationship quality and social understanding. *British Journal of Developmental Psychology*, *24*, 73–87.

D'Souza, D., & Karmiloff-Smith, A. (2011). When modularization fails to occur: A developmental perspective. *Cognitive Neuropsychology*, *28*, 276–287.

Dagnan, D., & Sandhu, S. (1999). Social comparison, self-esteem and depression in people with intellectual disability. *Journal of Intellectual Disability Research*, *43*, 372–379.

Dahl, A. (2014). Definitions and developmental processes in research on infant morality. *Human Development*, *57* (4), 241–249.

Dahl, A. (2015). The developing social context of infant helping in two US samples. *Child Development*, *86*, 1080–1093.

Dahl, A., & Campos, J. J. (2013). Domain differences in early social interactions. *Child Development*, *84*, 817–825.

Dahl, A., Campos, J. J., & Witherington, D. (2011). Emotional action and communication in early moral development. *Emotion Review*, *3*, 147–157.

Dahl, A., Schuck, R. K., & Campos, J. J. (2013). Do young toddlers act on their social preferences? *Developmental Psychology*, *49*, 1964–1970.

Dahlgren, S. O., Dahlgren Sandberg, A., & Larsson, M. (2010). Theory of mind in children with severe speech and physical impairments. *Research in Developmental Disabilities*, *31*, 617–624.

Dahlgren Sandberg, A. (2006). Reading and spelling abilities in children with severe speech impairments and cerebral palsy at 6, 9, and 12 years of age in relation to cognitive development: A longitudinal study. *Developmental Medicine and Child Neurology*, *48*, 629–634.

Dakin, S., & Frith, U. (2005). Vagaries of visual perception in autism. *Neuron*, *48*, 497–507.

Dale, N., & Edwards, L. (2015). Children with specific sensory impairments. In A. Thapar, D. S. Pine, J. F. Leckman, S. Scott, M. J. Snowling & E. Taylor (Eds), *Rutter's child and adolescent psychiatry, Sixth edition* (pp. 612–622). Chichester, UK: Wiley.

Dale, P. S., & Goodman, J. C. (2005). Commonality and individual differences in vocabulary growth. In M. Tomasello & D. I. Slobin (Eds), *Beyond nature-nurture: Essays in honor of Elizabeth Bates* (pp. 41–78). Mahwah, NJ: Erlbaum.

Daley, T. C., Whaley, S. E., Sigman, M. D., Espinosa, M.P., & Neumann, C. (2003). IQ on the rise: The Flynn effect in rural Kenyan children. *Psychological Science*, *14*, 215–219.

Dallaire, D. H., & Weinraub, M. (2005). The stability of parenting behaviors over the first 6 years of life. *Early Childhood Research Quarterly*, *20*, 201–219.

Dallas, E., Stevenson, J., & McGurk, H. (1993a). Cerebral palsied children's interactions with siblings: I. Influence of severity of disability, age and birth order. *Journal of Child Psychology and Psychiatry*, *34*, 621–647.

Dallas, E., Stevenson, J., & McGurk, H. (1993b). Cerebral palsied children's interactions with siblings: II. Interactional structure. *Journal of Child Psychology and Psychiatry*, *34*, 649–671.

Dammeyer, J. (2010). Prevalence and aetiology of congenitally deafblind people in Denmark. *International Journal of Audiology*, *49*, 76–82.

Dammeyer, J. (2014). Deafblindness: A review of the literature. *Scandinavian Journal of Public Health, 42*, 554–562.

Damon, W. (1984). Peer education: The untapped potential. *Journal of Applied Developmental Psychology, 5*, 331–343.

Damon, W., & Hart, D. (1988). *Self understanding in childhood and adolescence*. Cambridge: Cambridge University Press.

Damon, W., & Phelps, E. (1989). Strategic uses of peer learning in children's education. In T. J. Berndt & G.-W. Ladd (Eds), *Peer relationships in child development* (pp. 135–157). New York, NY: Wiley.

Danby, S., Ewing, L., & Thorpe, K. (2011). The novice researcher: Interviewing young children. *Qualitative Inquiry, 17*, 74–84.

Danforth, J. S., Connor, D. F., & Doerfler, L. A. (2016). The development of comorbid conduct problems in children with ADHD: An example of an integrative developmental psychopathology perspective. *Journal of Attention Disorders, 20*, 214–229.

Dapul, H., & Laraque, D. (2014). Lead poisoning in children. *Advances in Pediatrics, 61*, 313–333.

Daro, D., & Benedetti, G. (2014). Sustaining progress in preventing child maltreatment: A transformative challenge. In J. E. Korbin & R. D. Krugman (Eds), *Handbook of child maltreatment* (pp. 281–300). Dordrecht, NL: Springer.

Darwin, C. (1859). *On the origin of species by means of natural selection or the preservation of favored races in the struggle for life*. London: Murray.

Darwin, C. (1872). *The expression of the emotions in man and animals*. London: Oxford University Press (Reprint, 1998).

Darwin, C. (1877). A biographical sketch of an infant. *Mind, 2*, 285–294.

Daselaar, S. M., Rice, H. J., Greenberg, D. L., Cabeza, R., LaBar, K. S., & Rubin, D. C. (2006). The spatiotemporal dynamics of autobiographical memory: Neural correlates of recall, emotional intensity, and reliving. *Cerebral Cortex, 18*, 217–229.

Davidson, C., O'Hare, A., Mactaggart, F., Green, J., Young, D., Gillberg, C., & Minnis, H. (2015). Social relationship difficulties in autism and reactive attachment disorder: Improving diagnostic validity through structured assessment. *Research in Developmental Disabilities, 40*, 63–72

Davidson, R. J. (2003). Darwin and the neural bases of emotion and affective style. *Annals of the New York Academy of Sciences, 1000*, 316–336.

Davies, J., & Wright, J. (2008). Children's voices: A review of the literature pertinent to looked-after children's views of mental health services. *Child and Adolescent Mental Health, 13*, 26–31.

Davies, J. R., Dent, C. L., McNamara, G. I., & Isles, A. R. (2015). Behavioural effects of imprinted genes. *Current Opinion in Behavioral Sciences, 2*, 28–33.

Davis, M., & Suveg, C. (2014). Focusing on the positive: A review of the role of child positive affect in developmental psychopathology. *Clinical Child and Family Psychology Review, 17*, 97–124.

Dawson, G. (1994). Development of emotional expression and emotion regulation in infancy: Contributions of the frontal lobe. In G. Dawson & K. W. Fischer (Eds), *Human behavior and the developing brain* (pp. 346–379). New York, NY: Guilford Press.

Dawson, G., Hessl, D., & Frey, K. (1994). Social influences on early developing biological and behavioral systems related to risk for affective disorder. *Development and Psychopathology, 6*, 759–779.

de Colibus, L., Li, M., Binda, C., Edmondson, D. E., & Mattevi, A. (2005). *Proceedings of the National Academy of Science in United States of America, 102*, 2684–12689.

de França, D. X. (2016). From a sense of self to understanding relations between social groups. In J. Vala, S. Waldzus & M. M. Calheiros (Eds), *The social developmental construction of violence and intergroup conflict* (pp. 35–53). Cham, Switzerland: Springer.

de Frias, C. M., Lovden, M., Lindenberger, U., & Nilsson, L. G. (2007). Revisiting the dedifferentiation hypothesis with longitudinal multicohort data. *Intelligence, 35*, 381–392.

de Haan, A. D., Prinzie, P., & Dekovic, M. (2009). Mothers' and fathers' personality and parenting: The mediating role of sense of competence. *Developmental Psychology, 45*, 1695–1707.

de Haan, M., & Johnson, M. (2003). Mechanisms and theories of brain development. In M. de Haan & M. Johnson (Eds), *The cognitive neuroscience of development* (pp. 1–18). Hove, UK: Psychology Press.

De Houwer, A. (2009). *Bilingual first language acquisition*. Bristol, UK: Multilingual Matters.

De Houwer, A. (2013). Harmonious bilingual development: Young families' well-being in language contact situations. *International Journal of Bilingualism, 19*, 169–184.

De Los Reyes, A., & Kazdin, A. E. (2005). Informant discrepancies in the assessment of childhood psychopathology: A critical review, theoretical framework, and recommendations for further study. *Psychological Bulletin, 131*, 483–509.

de Rosnay, M., Pons, F., Harris, P. L., & Morrell, J. (2004). A lag between understanding false belief and emotion attribution in young children: Relationships with linguistic ability and mothers' mental-state language. *British Journal of Developmental Psychology, 22*, 197–218.

De Ruiter, M. A., Van Mourik, R., Schouten-van Meeteren, A. Y., Grootenhuis, M. A., & Oosterlaan, J. (2013). Neurocognitive consequences of a paediatric brain tumour and its treatment: A meta-analysis. *Developmental Medicine and Child Neurology, 55*, 408–417.

De Santis, M., Cavaliere, A. F., Straface, G., & Caruso, A. (2006). Rubella infection in pregnancy. *Reproductive Toxicology, 21*, 390–398.

de Saussure, F. (1974). *Course in general linguistics*. Glasgow: Collins.

De Schipper, J. C., Stolk, J., & Schuengel, C. (2006). Professional caretakers as attachment figures in day care centers for children with intellectual disability and behavior problems. *Research in Developmental Disabilities 27*, 203–216.

de Vries, J. I. P., Visser, G. H. A., & Prechtl, H. F. R. (1982). The emergence of fetal behavior: I. Qualitative aspects. *Early Human Development, 7*, 301–322.

de Vries, J. I. P., Visser, G. H. A., & Prechtl, H. F. R. (1985). The emergence of fetal behaviour: II. Quantitative aspects. *Early Human Development, 12*, 99–120.

de Vries, J. I. P., Visser, G. H. A., & Prechtl, H. F. R. (1988). The emergence of fetal behaviour: III. Individual differences and consistencies. *Early Human Development, 16*, 85–103.

de Waal, F. B. (2008). Putting the altruism back into altruism: The evolution of empathy. *Annual Review of Psychology, 59*, 279–300.

de Wolff, M. S., & van Ijzendoorn, M. H. (1997). Sensitivity and attachment: A meta-analysis on parental antecedents of infant attachment. *Child Development, 68*, 571–591.

Deary, I. J., Pattie, A., & Starr, J. M. (2013). The stability of intelligence from age 11 to age 90 years: The Lothian birth cohort of 1921. *Psychological Science, 24*, 2361–2368.

Degnan, K. A., Hane, A. A., Henderson, H. A., Moas, O. L., Reeb-Sutherland, B. C., & Fox, N. A. (2011). Longitudinal stability of temperamental exuberance and social-emotional outcomes in early childhood. *Developmental Psychology, 47*, 765–780.

Dekker, T. M., & Karmiloff-Smith, A. (2011). The dynamics of ontogeny: A neuroconstructivist perspective on genes, brains, cognition and behavior. *Progress in Brain Research, 189*, 23–33.

Delgado, B., Gómez, J. C., & Sarriá, E. (2009). Private pointing and private speech: Developing parallelisms. In A. Winsler, C. Fernyhough & I. Montero (Eds), *Private speech, executive functioning, and the development of verbal self-regulation* (pp. 163–162). New York, NY: Cambridge University Press.

Delgado, B., Gómez, J. C., & Sarriá, E. (2011). Pointing gestures as a cognitive tool in young children: Experimental evidence. *Journal of Experimental Child Psychology, 110*, 299–312.

DeLoache, J. S. (1987). Rapid change in the symbolic functioning of very young children. *Science, 238*, 1556–1557.

DeLoache, J. S., & Burns, N. M. (1994). Early understanding of the representational function of pictures. *Cognition, 52*, 83–110.

DeLoache, J. S., & LoBue, V. (2009). The narrow fellow in the grass: Human infants associate snakes and fear. *Developmental Science, 12*, 201–207.

DeLoache, J. S., & Marzolf, D. P. (1995). The use of dolls to interview young children: Issues of symbolic representation. *Journal of Experimental Child Psychology, 60*, 155–173.

DeLoache, J. S., Miller, K. F., & Pierroutsakos, S. L. (1998). Reasoning and problem solving. In W. Damon, D. Kuhn & R. S. Siegler (Eds), *Handbook of child psychology, Fifth edition, Volume 2: Cognition, perception, and language* (pp. 801–850). New York, NY: Wiley.

DeLoache, J. S., Strauss, M., & Maynard. J. (1979). Picture perception in infancy. *Infant Behavior and Development, 2*, 77–89.

DeLoache, J. S., Chiong, C., Sherman, K., Islam, N., Vanderborght, M., Troseth G. L., Strouse, G. A., & O'Doherty, K. (2010). Do babies learn from baby media? *Psychological Science, 21*, 1570–1574.

DeMarie, D., & López, L. M. (2014). Memory in schools. In P. J. Bauer & R. Fivush (Eds), *The Wiley handbook on the development of children's memory, Volume 2* (pp. 836–864). Chichester, UK: Wiley.

Demetriou, A., Spanoudis, G., & Mouyi, A. (2011). Educating the developing mind: Towards an overarching paradigm. *Educational Psychology Review, 23*, 601–663.

Demetriou, A., Christou, C., Spanoudis, G., & Platsidou, M. (2002). The development of mental processing: Efficiency, working memory, and thinking. *Monographs of the Society of Research in Child Development, 67*, 268.

Dempster, F. N. (1981). Memory span: Sources of individual and developmental differences. *Psychological Bulletin, 89*, 63–100.

Denham, S. A. (1986). Social cognition, prosocial behavior, and emotion in preschoolers: Contextual validation. *Child Development, 57*, 194–201.

Denham, S. A. (1989). Maternal affect and toddlers' social emotional competence. *American Journal of Orthopsychiatry, 59*, 368–376.

Denham, S. A. (1993). Maternal emotional responsiveness and toddlers' social emotional competence. *Journal of Child Psychology and Psychiatry, 34*, 715–728.

Denham, S. A. (2007). Dealing with feelings: How children negotiate the worlds of emotions and social relationships. *Cognitions, Brain, Behaviour, 11*, 1–48.

Denham, S. A., & Grout, L. (1993). Socialization of emotion: Pathway to preschoolers' emotional and social competence. *Journal of Nonverbal Behavior, 17*, 205–227.

Dennis, E. L., & Thompson, P. M. (2013). Typical and atypical brain development: A review of neuroimaging studies. *Dialogues in Clinical Neuroscience, 15*, 359–384.

Dennis, M., Landry, S. H., Barnes, M., & Fletcher, J. M. (2006). A model of neurocognitive function in spina bifida over the life span. *Journal of the International Neuropsychological Society, 12*, 285–296.

Dennis, T. A., Cole, P. M., Zahn-Waxler, C., & Mizuta, I. (2002). Self in context: Autonomy and relatedness in Japanese and U.S. mother–preschooler dyads. *Child Development, 73*, 1803–1817.

Deocampo, J. A., & Hudson, J. A. (2005). When seeing is not believing: Two-year-olds' use of video representations to find a hidden toy. *Journal of Cognition and Development, 6*, 229–260.

Derlega, V. J., & Grzelak, J. (1979). Appropriateness of self-disclosure. In G. J. Chelune (Ed.), *Self-disclosure: Origins, patterns, and implications of openness in interpersonal relationships* (pp. 151–176). San Francisco: Jossey-Bass.

Derluyn, I., & Broekaert, E. (2007). Different perspectives on emotional and behavioural problems in unaccompanied refugee children and adolescents. *Ethnicity and Health, 12*, 141–162.

DeRosier, M., Kupersmidt, J. B., & Patterson, C. J. (1994). Children's academic and behavioral adjustment as a function of the chronicity and proximity of peer rejection. *Child Development*, 65, 1799–1813.

Derwing, B. L., & Baker, W. J. (1986). Assessing morphological development. In P. Fletcher & M. Garman (Eds), *Language acquisition, Second edition* (pp. 326–338). Cambridge: Cambridge University Press.

Desforges, C. (1998). Learning and teaching: Current views and perspectives. In D. Shorrocks-Taylor (Ed.), *Directions in educational psychology* (pp. 5 -18). London: Whurr.

Desrochers, S., Morisette, P., & Richard, M. (1995). Two perspectives on pointing in infancy. In C. Moore & P. J. Dunham (Eds), *Joint attention: Its origins and role in development* (pp. 85–101). Hillsdale, NJ: Erlbaum.

deVries, M. W., & Sameroff, A. J. (1984). Culture and temperament: Influences on infant temperament in three East African societies. *American Journal of Orthopsychiatry*, 54, 83–96.

deVries, R. (2000). Vygotsky, Piaget, and education: A reciprocal assimilation of theories and educational practices. *New Ideas in Psychology*, 18, 187–213.

Dew, A., Balandin, S., & Llewellyn, G. (2008). The psychosocial impact on siblings of people with lifelong physical disability: A review of the literature. *Journal of Developmental and Physical Disabilities*, 20, 485–507.

Di Martino, A., Fair, D. A., Kelly, C., Satterthwaite, T. D., Castellanos, F. X., Thomason, M. E., Craddock, R. C., Luna, B., Leventhal, B. L., Zuo, X. N., et al. (2014). Unraveling the miswired connectome: A developmental perspective. *Neuron*, 83, 1335–1353.

Diamond, A. (2013). Executive functions. *Annual Review of Psychology*, 64, 135–168.

Diamond, A., & Lee, K. (2011). Interventions shown to aid executive function development in children 4 to 12 years old. *Science*, 333 (6045), 959–964.

Diamond, A., & Ling, D. S. (2016). Conclusions about interventions, programs, and approaches for improving executive functions that appear justified and those that, despite much hype, do not. *Developmental Cognitive Neuroscience*, 18, 34–48.

Dickens, W. T., & Flynn, J. R. (2006a). Black Americans reduce the racial IQ gap: Evidence from standardization samples. *Psychological Science*, 17, 913–920.

Dickens, W. T., & Flynn, J. R. (2006b). Common ground and differences. *Psychological Science*, 17, 923–924.

Dietz, A., Löppönen, T., Valtonen, H., Hyvärinen, A., & Löppönen, H. (2009). Prevalence and etiology of congenital or early acquired hearing impairment in Eastern Finland. *International Journal of Pediatric Otorhinolaryngology*, 73, 1353–1357.

Dilks, D. D., Hoffman, J. E., & Landau, B. (2008). Vision for perception and vision for action: Normal and unusual development. *Developmental Science*, 11, 474–486.

Ding, X. P., Wellman, H. M., Wang, Y., Fu, G., & Lee, K. (2015). Theory-of-mind training causes honest young children to lie. *Psychological Science*, 26, 1812–1821.

DiPietro, J. A. (2010). Psychological and psychophysiological considerations regarding the maternal–fetal relationship. *Infant and Child Development*, 19, 27–38.

Dishion, T. J., & Piehler, T. F. (2009). Deviant by design: Peer contagion in development, interventions and schools. In K. H. Rubin, W. Bukowski & B. Laursen (Eds), *Handbook of peer interactions, relationships, and groups* (pp. 589–602). New York, NY: Guilford Press.

Dishion, T. J., & Tipsord, J. M. (2011). Peer contagion in child and adolescent social and emotional development. *Annual Review of Psychology*, 62, 189–214.

Dishion, T. J., Andrews, D. W., & Crosby, L. (1995). Antisocial boys and their friends in early adolescence: Relationship characteristics, quality, and interactional process. *Child Development*, 66, 139–151.

Dishion, T. J., McCord, J., & Poulin, F. (1999). When interventions harm: Peer groups and problem behavior. *American Psychologist*, 54, 755–764.

Dix, T., & Meunier, L. N. (2009). Depressive symptoms and parenting competence: An analysis of 13 regulatory processes. *Developmental Review*, 29, 45–68.

Dodd, B. (1975). Children's understanding of their own phonological forms. *Quarterly Journal of Experimental Psychology*, 27, 165–172.

Dodge, K. A. (2009). Community intervention and public policy in the prevention of antisocial behavior. *Journal of Child Psychology and Psychiatry*, 50, 194–200.

Dodge, K. A., & Somberg, D. (1987). Hostile attributional biases among aggressive boys are exacerbated under conditions of threats to the self. *Child Development*, 58, 213–224.

Dodge, K. A., Coie, J. D., & Lynam, D. (2006). Aggression and antisocial behavior in youth. In W. Damon, R. M. Lerner & N. Eisenberg (Eds), *Handbook of child psychology, Sixth edition, Volume 3: Social, emotional, and personality development* (pp. 437–472). New York, NY: Wiley.

Dodge, K. A., Schlundt, D. G., Schocken, I., & Delugach, J. D. (1983). Social competence and children's social status: The role of peer group entry strategies. *Merrill-Palmer Quarterly*, 29, 309–336.

Dodge, K. A., Malone, P. S., Lansford, J. E., Sorbring, E., Skinner, A. T., Tapanya, S., Tirado, L. M., Zelli, A., Alampay, L. P., Al-Hassan, S. M., et al. (2015). Hostile attributional bias and aggressive behavior in global context. *Proceedings of the National Academy of Sciences of the United States of America*, 112, 9310–9315.

Doggett, A. M. (2004). ADHD and drug therapy: Is it still a valid treatment? *Journal of Child Health Care*, 8, 69–81.

Doherty, M. J. (2009). *Theory of mind: How children understand others' thoughts and feelings*. Hove, UK: Psychology Press.

Doherty, M. J., Anderson, J. R., & Howieson, L. (2009). The rapid development of explicit gaze judgment ability at 3 years. *Journal of Experimental Child Psychology*, 104, 296–312.

Doherty, M. J., Tsuji, H., & Phillips, W. A. (2008). The context-sensitivity of visual size perception varies across cultures. *Perception*, 37, 1426–1433.

Doise, W. (1978). *Groups and individuals: Explanantions in social psychology*. Cambridge: Cambridge University Press.

Dolev-Cohen, M., & Barak, A. (2013). Adolescents' use of Instant Messaging as a means of emotional relief. *Computers in Human Behavior, 29*, 58–63.

Dolgin, K. G., & Kim, S. (1994). Adolescents' disclosure to best and good friends: The effects of gender and topic intimacy. *Social Development, 3*, 146–157.

Dollaghan, C. (1985). Child meets word: "Fast mapping" in preschool children. *Journal of Speech and Hearing Research, 28*, 449–454.

Dollard, J., & Miller, N. (1950). *Personality and psychotherapy: An analysis in terms of learning, thinking, and culture.* New York, NY: McGraw-Hill

Donaldson, M. (1978). *Children's minds.* London: Fontana.

Donlan, C. (2015). Linguistic factors in the development of basic calculation. In S. Chinn (Ed.), *The Routledge international handbook of dyscalculia and mathematical learning difficulties* (pp. 346–356). Abingdon, UK: Routledge.

Donnellan, M. B., & Lucas, R. E. (2008). Age differences in the Big Five across the life span: Evidence from two national samples. *Psychology and Aging, 23*, 558–566.

Donnellan, M. B., Trzesniewski, K. H., & Robins, R. W. (2011). Self-esteem: Enduring issues and controversies. In T. Chamorro-Premuzic, S. von Stumm & A. Furnham (Eds), *The Wiley-Blackwell handbook of individual differences* (pp. 718–746). New York, NY: Wiley-Blackwell.

Doost, H. T. N., Moradi, A. R., Taghavi, M. R., Yule, W., & Dalgleish, T. (1999). The development of a corpus of emotional words produced by children and adolescents. *Personality and Individual Differences, 27*, 433–451.

Dore, J. (1977). "Oh them sheriff": A pragmatic analysis of children's responses to questions. In S. Ervin Tripp & C. Mitchell-Kernan (Eds), *Child Discourse* (pp. 139–163). New York, NY: Academic Press.

Dore, J. (1986). The development of conversational competence. In R. L. Schiefelbusch (Ed.), *Language competence: Assessment and intervention* (pp. 3–60). London: Taylor and Francis.

Dost, A., & Yagmurlu, B. (2008). Are constructiveness and destructiveness essential features of guilt and shame feelings respectively? *Journal for the Theory of Social Behaviour, 38*, 109–129.

Dowker, A. (2017). Interventions for primary school children with difficulties in mathematics. *Advances in Child Development and Behavior, 53*, 255–287.

Dozier, M., & Rutter, M. (2008). Challenges to the development of attachment relationships faced by young children in foster and adoptive care. In J. Cassidy & P. R. Shaver (Eds), *Handbook of attachment: Theory, research, and clinical applications, Second edition* (pp. 698–717). New York, NY: Guilford Press.

Drager, K., Light, J., & McNaughton, D. (2010). Effects of AAC interventions on communication and language for young children with complex communication needs. *Journal of Pediatric Rehabilitation Medicine, 3* (4), 303–310.

Dramé, C., & Ferguson, C. J. (2017). Measurements of intelligence in sub-Saharan Africa: Perspectives gathered from research in Mali. *Current Psychology*, 1–6.

Drevon, D. D., Knight, R. M., & Bradley-Johnson, S. (2017). Nonverbal and language-reduced measures of cognitive ability: A review and evaluation. *Contemporary School Psychology, 21*, 255–266.

Drijvers, P., Ball, L., Barzel, B., Heid, M. K., Cao, Y., & Maschietto, M. (Eds) (2016). *Uses of technology in lower secondary mathematics education.* Cham, Switzerland: Springer.

Drillien, C. M., & Wilkinson, E. M. (1964). Emotional stress and mongoloid births. *Developmental Medicine and Child Neurology, 6*, 140–143.

Dromi, E. (1993). The mysteries of early lexical development: Underlying cognitive and linguistic pocesses in meaning acquisition. In E. Dromi (Ed.), *Language and cognition: A developmental perspective* (pp. 32–60). Norwood, NJ: Ablex.

Dubowitz, H., Thompson, R., Proctor, L., Metzger, R., Black, M. M., English, D., Poole, G., & Magder, L. (2016). Adversity, maltreatment, and resilience in young children. *Academic Pediatrics, 16*, 233–239.

Dudeney, J., Sharpe, L., & Hunt, C. (2015). Attentional bias towards threatening stimuli in children with anxiety: A meta-analysis. *Clinical Psychology Review, 40*, 66–75.

Duman, S., & Margolin, G. (2007). Parents' aggressive influences and children's aggressive problem solutions with peers. *Journal of Clinical Child and Adolescent Psychology, 36*, 42–55.

Dumaret, A. C., Coppel-Batsch, M., & Courand, S. (1997). Adult outcome of children reared for long term periods in foster families. *Child Abuse and Neglect, 21*, 911–927.

Duncan, R., & Tarulli, D. (2009). On the persistence of private speech: Empirical and theoretical considerations. In A. Winsler, C. Fernyhough & I. Montero (Eds), *Private speech, executive functioning, and the development of verbal self-regulation* (pp. 176–187). New York, NY: Cambridge University Press.

Dunfield, K. A. (2014). A construct divided: Prosocial behavior as helping, sharing, and comforting subtypes. *Frontiers in Psychology, 5*, 958.

Dunfield, K. A., & Kuhlmeier, V. A. (2010). Intention-mediated selective helping in infancy. *Psychological Science, 21*, 523–527.

Dunfield, K. A., & Kuhlmeier, V. A. (2013). Classifying prosocial behavior: Children's responses to instrumental need, emotional distress, and material desire. *Child Development, 84*, 1766–1776.

Dunn, J. (1988). *The beginnings of social understanding.* Cambridge, MA: Harvard University Press.

Dunn, J. (1993). *Young children's close relationships: Beyond attachment.* Thousand Oaks, CA: Sage.

Dunn, J. (1995). Children as psychologists: The later correlates of individual differences in understanding of emotions and other minds. *Cognition and Emotion, 9*, 187–201.

Dunn, J. (1996). Brothers and sisters in middle childhood and early adolescence: Continuity and change in individual differences. In G. H. Brody (Ed.), *Sibling relationships: Their causes and consequences* (pp. 31–46). Stamford, CO: Ablex.

Dunn, J. (1999). Siblings, friends, and the development of social understanding. In W. A. Collins & B. Laursen (Eds), *Relationships as developmental contexts* (pp. 263–279). Mahwah, NJ: Erlbaum.

Dunn, J. (2004). *Children's friendships: The beginnings of intimacy*. Oxford: Blackwell.

Dunn, J. (2014). Moral development in early childhood and social interaction in the family. In M. Killen & J. G. Smetana (Eds), *Handbook of moral development, Second edition* (pp. 135–160). Hove, UK: Psychology Press.

Dunn, J., Bretherton, I., & Munn, P. (1987). Conversations about feeling states between mothers and their young children. *Developmental Psychology, 23*, 132–139.

Dunn, J., Brown, J. R., & Beardsall, J. (1991). Family talk about feeling states and children's later understanding of others' emotions. *Developmental Psychology, 27*, 448–455.

Dunn, J., Brown, J. R., & Maguire, M. (1995). The development of children's moral sensibility: Individual differences and emotion understanding. *Developmental Psychology, 31*, 649–659.

Dunn, J., & Cutting, A. L. (1999). Understanding others, and individual differences in friendship interactions in young children. *Social Development, 8*, 201–219.

Dunn, L., & Dunn, D. (2007). *Peabody Picture Vocabulary Test, Fourth edition* (PPVT-IV). Bloomington, MN: Pearson.

Durand, K., Baudon, G., Freydefont, L., & Schaal, B. (2008). Odorization of a novel object can influence infant's exploratory behavior in unexpected ways. *Infant Behavior and Development, 31*, 629–636.

Durand, V. M., & Merges, E. (2001). Functional communication training: A contemporary behavior analytic intervention for problem behaviors. *Focus on Autism and Other Developmental Disabilities, 16*, 110–119.

Durkin, K., & Conti-Ramsden, G. (2007). Language, social behavior, and the quality of friendships in adolescents with and without a history of specific language impairment. *Child Development, 78*, 1441–1457.

Durkin, K., & Conti-Ramsden, G. (2010). Young people with specific language impairment: A review of social and emotional functioning in adolescence. *Child Language Teaching and Therapy, 26*, 105–121.

Durrant, R., & Ward, T. (2012). The role of evolutionary explanations in criminology. *Journal of Theoretical and Philosophical Criminology, 4*, 1–37.

Dweck, C. S. (1999). Caution – praise can be dangerous. *American Educator, 23*, 4–9.

Dye, M. W., & Hauser, P. C. (2014). Sustained attention, selective attention and cognitive control in deaf and hearing children. *Hearing Research, 309*, 94–102.

Dyregrov, A., Dyregrov, K., Endsjø, M., & Idsoe, T. (2015). Teachers' perception of bereaved children's academic performance. *Advances in School Mental Health Promotion, 8*, 187–198.

Early, D. M., Rimm-Kaufman, S. E., Cox, M. J., Saluja, G., Pianta, R. C., Bradley, R. H., & Payne, C. C. (2002). Maternal sensitivity and child wariness to the transition to kindergarten. *Parenting: Science and Practice, 2*, 355–377.

Ebert, K. D., Kohnert, K., Pham, G., Disher, J. R., & Payesteh, B. (2014). Three treatments for bilingual children with primary language impairment: Examining cross-linguistic and cross-domain effects. *Journal of Speech, Language, and Hearing Research, 57*, 172–186.

Eckstein, M. K., Guerra-Carrillo, B., Singley, A. T. M., & Bunge, S. A. (2017). Beyond eye gaze: What else can eye-tracking reveal about cognition and cognitive development? *Developmental Cognitive Neuroscience, 25*, 69–91.

Edelman, G. M. (1989). *Neural Darwinism. The theory of neuronal group selection*. Oxford: Oxford University Press.

Eden, K., Wylie, K., & Watson, E. (2012). Gender dysphoria: Recognition and assessment. *Advances in Psychiatric Treatment, 18*, 2–11.

Eder, D., & Fingerson, L. (2001). Interviewing children and adolescents. In A. Holstein & J. F. Gubrium (Eds), *Inside interviewing: New lenses, new concerns* (pp. 33–53). Thousand Oaks, CA: Sage.

Eder, R. A., & Mangelsdorf, S. C. (1997). The emotional basis of early personality development: Implications for the emergent self concept. In R. Hogan, J. A. Johnson & S. Brigga (Eds), *Handbook of personality psychology* (pp. 209–240). London: Academic Press.

Egeland, B. R., Carlson, E., & Sroufe, L. A. (1993). Resilience as process. *Development and Psychopathology, 5*, 517–528.

Eggins, H. (Ed.) (2017). *The changing role of women in higher education*. Dordrecht, the Netherlands: Springer.

Ehntholt, K. A., & Yule, W. (2006). Practitioner Review: Assessment and treatment of refugee children and adolescents who have experienced war-related trauma. *Journal of Child Psychology and Psychiatry, 47*, 1197–1210.

Ehrensaft, D. (2017). Gender nonconforming youth: Current perspectives. *Adolescent Health, Medicine and Therapeutics, 8*, 57–67.

Ehrhart, F., Coort, S. L., Cirillo, E., Smeets, E., Evelo, C. T., & Curfs, L. M. (2016). Rett syndrome–biological pathways leading from MECP2 to disorder phenotypes. *Orphanet Journal of Rare Diseases, 11*, 158.

Eibl-Eibesfeldt, I. (1973). The expressive behavior of the deaf-and-blind-born. In M. von Cranach & I. Vine (Eds), *Social communication and movement* (pp. 163–194). London: Academic Press.

Eimas, P. D. (1985). The perception of speech in early infancy. *Scientific American, 252*, 46–52, 120.

Eimas, P. D., & Quinn, P. C. (1994). Studies on the formation of perceptually based basic-level categories in young infants. *Child Development, 65*, 903–917.

Eisen, M. L., Goodman, G. S., Qin, J. J., & Davis, S. L. (2002). Memory and suggestibility in maltreated children: Age, stress arousal, dissociation, and psychopathology. *Journal of Experimental Child Psychology, 83*, 167–212.

Eisenberg, N. (1982). The development and reasoning regarding prosocial behavior. In N. Eisenberg (Ed.), *The *development of prosocial behavior* (pp. 219–249). London: Academic Press.

Eisenberg, N. (1983). The relation between empathy and altruism: Conceptual and methodological issues. *Academic Psychology Bulletin, 5*, 195–207.

Eisenberg, N. (1991). Meta-analytic contributions to the literature on prosocial behavior. *Personality and Social Psychology Bulletin, 17*, 273–282.

Eisenberg, N. (1992). *The caring child*. London: Harvard University Press.

Eisenberg, N. (2000). Emotion, regulation, and moral development. *Annual Review in Psychology, 51*, 665–697.

Eisenberg, N., Cumberland, A., Guthrie, I. K., Murphy, B. C., & Shepard, S. A. (2005). Age changes in prosocial responding and moral reasoning in adolescence and early adulthood. *Journal of Research on Adolescence, 15*, 235–260.

Eisenberg, N., Cumberland, A., & Spinrad, T. L. (1998). Parental socialization of emotion. *Psychological Inquiry, 9*, 241–273.

Eisenberg, N., & Fabes, R. A. (1994). Mothers' reactionsto children's negative emotions: Relations to children's temperament and anger behavior. *Merrill-Palmer Quarterly, 40*, 138–156.

Eisenberg, N., Fabes, R. A., Carlo, G., & Karbon, M. (1992). Emotional responsiveness to other: Behavioral correlates and socialization antecedents. *New Directions for Child Development, 5*, 57–73.

Eisenberg, N., Fabes, R. A., & Spinrad, T. L. (2006). Prosocial development. In W. Damon, R. M. Lerner & N. Eisenberg (Eds), *Handbook of child psychology, Sixth edition, Volume 3. Social, emotional, and personality development* (pp. 646–718). New York: John Wiley.

Eisenberg, N., Murphy, B. C., & Shepard, S. (1997). The development of empathic accuracy. In W. J. Ickes (Ed.), *Empathic accuracy* (pp. 73–116). New York, NY: Guilford Press.

Eisenberg, N., Spinrad, T. L., & Knafo-Noam, A. (2015). Prosocial development. In R. M. Lerner, M. E. Lamb & C. G. Coll (Eds), *Handbook of child psychology and developmental science, Seventh edition, Volume 3: Social and emotional development* (pp. 610–656). Hoboken, NJ: Wiley.

Eisenberg, N., Vaughan, J., & Hofer, C. (2009). Temperament, self-regulation, and peer social competence. In K. H. Rubin, W. M. Bukowski & B. Laursen (Eds), *Handbook of peer interactions, relationships, and groups* (pp. 473–489). New York, NY: Guilford Press.

Eisenberg-Berg, N., Murray, E., & Hite, T. (1982). Children's reasoning regarding sex typed toy choices. *Child Development, 53*, 81–86.

Eisenberg-Berg, N., & Neal, C. (1979). Children's moral reasoning about their own spontaneous prosocial behaviour. *Development Psychology, 15*, 228–229.

Eisenbraun, K. D. (2007). Violence in schools: Prevalence, prediction, and prevention. *Aggression and Violent Behavior, 12*, 459–469.

Eivers, A. R., Brendgen, M. R., Vitaro, F., & Borge, A. I. H. (2012). Links between children's prosocial and antiso-

cial behaviour and their nominated friends in early childhood. *Early Childhood Research Quarterly, 27*, 137–146.

Eley, T. C., Napolitano, M., Lau, J. Y., & Gregory, A. M. (2010). Does childhood anxiety evoke maternal control? A genetically informed study. *Journal of Child Psychology and Psychiatry, 51*, 772–779.

Elicker, J., Englund, M., & Sroufe, L. A. (1992). Predicting peer competence and peer relationships in childhood from early parent child relationships. In R. D. Parke & G. W. Ladd (Eds), *Family peer relationships: Modes of linkage* (pp. 77–106). Hillsdale, NJ. Erlbaum.

Elkind, D. (1967). Egocentrism in adolescence. *Child Development, 38*, 1025–1034.

Elkind, D. (1976). *Child development and education*. Oxford: Oxford University Press.

Elkind, D., Koegler, R. R., & Go, E. (1964). Studies in perceptual development: II Part-whole perception. *Child Development, 35*, 81–90.

Ellefson, M. R., Ng, F. F. Y., Wang, Q., & Hughes, C. (2017). Efficiency of executive function: A two-generation cross-cultural comparison of samples from Hong Kong and the United Kingdom. *Psychological Science, 28*, 555–566.

Elliott, J. G., & Grigorenko, E. L. (2014). *The dyslexia debate*. Cambridge: Cambridge University Press.

Ellis, S., Rogoff, B., & Cromer, C. C. (1981). Age segregation in children's social interactions. *Developmental Psychology, 17*, 399–407.

Ellison, P. T. (2010). Fetal programming and fetal psychology. *Infant and Child Development, 19*, 6–20.

Elman, J. L. (2005). Connections models of development: Where next? *Trends in Cognitive Science, 9*, 111–117.

Elman, J. L., Bates, E. A., Johnson, M. H., Karmiloff-Smith, A., Parisi, D., & Plunkett, K. (1996). *Rethinking innateness. A connectionist perspective on development*. London: MIT Press.

Elonheimo, H., Gyllenberg, D., Huttunen, J., Ristkari, T., Sillanmäki, L., & Sourander, A. (2014). Criminal offending among males and females between ages 15 and 30 in a population-based nationwide 1981 birth cohort: Results from the FinnCrime Study. *Journal of Adolescence, 37*, 1269–1279.

Elsner, B. (2005). Novelty and complexity: Two problems in animal (and human) imitation. In S. L. Hurley & N. Chater (Eds), *Perspectives on imitation: From neuroscience to social science, Volume 1* (pp. 287–290). Cambridge, MA: MIT Press.

Elsner, B. (2007). Infants' imitation of goal-directed actions: The role of movements and action effects. *Acta Psychologica, 124*, 44–59.

Emde, R. N. (1992). Social referencing research: Uncertainty, self, and the search for meaning. In S. Feinman (Ed.), *Social referencing and the social construction of reality in infancy* (pp. 79–94). London: Plenum.

Emde, R. N. (1998). Early emotional development: New modes of thinking for research and intervention. *Pediatrics, 102* (Supplement E1), 1236–1243.

Emerson, E., & Einfeld, S. (2011). *Challenging behaviour, Third edition*. Cambridge: Cambridge University Press.

Emerson, J. (2015). The enigma of dyscalculia. In S. Chinn (Ed.), *International handbook of dyscalculia and mathematical learning difficulties* (pp. 217–227). Abingdon, UK: Routledge.

Emery, A. E., Muntoni, F., & Quinlivan, R. C. (2015). *Duchenne muscular dystrophy, Fouth edition.* Oxford: Oxford University Press.

Emler, N. (1992). Childhood origins of beliefs about institutional authority. *New Directions for Child Development, 56,* 65–78.

Emler, N., & Dickinson, J. (2005). Children's understanding of social class and occupational groupings. In M. Barrett & E. Buchanan-Barrow (Eds), *Children's understanding of society* (pp. 169–198). Hove, UK: Psychology Press.

Enard, W., Przeworski, M., Fisher, S. E., Lai, C. S., Wiebe, V., Kitano, T., Monaco, A. P., & Paabo, S. (2002). Molecular evolution of FOXP2, a gene involved in speech and language. *Nature, 418,* 869–872.

Enebrink, P., Danneman, M., Mattsson, V. B., Ulfsdotter, M., Jalling, C., & Lindberg, L. (2015). ABC for parents: Pilot study of a universal 4-session program shows increased parenting skills, self-efficacy and child well-being. *Journal of Child and Family Studies, 24,* 1917–1931.

Ensor, R., Devine, R. T., Marks, A., & Hughes, C. (2014). Mothers' cognitive references to 2-year-olds predict Theory of Mind at ages 6 and 10. *Child Development, 85,* 1222–1235.

Erickson, L. C., & Thiessen, E. D. (2015). Statistical learning of language: Theory, validity, and predictions of a statistical learning account of language acquisition. *Developmental Review, 37,* 66–108.

Erickson, M. F., Egeland, B. R., & Pianta, R. (1989). The effects of maltreatment on the development of young children. In D. Cicchetti & V. Carlson (Eds), *Child maltreatment: Theory and research on the causes and consequences of child abuse and neglect* (pp. 647–684). Cambridge: Cambridge University Press.

Erikson, E. H. (1963). *Childhood and society.* London: Norton.

Erikson, E. H. (1968). *Identity: Youth and crisis and the life cycle.* London: Norton

Erola, J., Jalonen, S., & Lehti, H. (2016). Parental education, class and income over early life course and children's achievement. *Research in Social Stratification and Mobility, 44,* 33–43.

Eron, L. D. (1987). The development of aggressive behavior from the perspective of a developing behaviorism. *American Psychologist, 42,* 435–442.

Evans, E. H., Tovée, M. J., Boothroyd, L. G., & Drewett, R. F. (2013). Body dissatisfaction and disordered eating attitudes in 7-to 11-year-old girls: Testing a sociocultural model. *Body Image, 10,* 8–15.

Evans, E. H., Adamson, A. J., Basterfield, L., Le Couteur, A., Reilly, J. K., Reilly, J. J., & Parkinson, K. N. (2017). Risk factors for eating disorder symptoms at 12 years of age: A 6-year longitudinal cohort study. *Appetite, 108,* 12–20.

Evans, V. (2014). *The language myth: Why language is not an instinct.* Cambridge: Cambridge University Press.

Evrard, P., Marret, S., & Gressens, P. (1997). Environmental and genetic determinant of neural migration and post-migratory survival. *Acta Pædiatrica, Supplement, 422,* 20–26.

Ewing, D., Zeigler-Hill, V., & Vonk, J. (2016). Spitefulness and deficits in the social–perceptual and social–cognitive components of Theory of Mind. *Personality and Individual Differences, 91,* 7–13.

Ewing Lee, E. A., & Troop-Gordon, W. (2011). Peer socialization of masculinity and femininity: Differential effects of overt and relational forms of peer victimization. *British Journal of Developmental Psychology, 29,* 197–213.

Ex, C. T. G. M., Janssens, J. M. A. M., & Korzilius, H. P. L. M. (2002). Young females' images of motherhood in relation to television viewing. *Journal of Communication, 52,* 955–971.

Eydal, G. B., Gíslason, I. V., Rostgaard, T., Brandth, B., Duvander, A. Z., & Lammi-Taskula, J. (2015). Trends in parental leave in the Nordic countries: Has the forward march of gender equality halted? *Community, Work and Family, 18,* 167–181.

Eysenck, H. J. (1967). *The biological basis of personality.* Springfield, IL: Charles C. Thomas.

Eysenck, H. J. (1992). Four ways five factors are not basic. *Personality and Individual Differences, 13,* 667–673.

Ezkurdia, I., Juan, D., Rodriguez, J. M., Frankish, A., Diekhans, M., Harrow, J., Vazquez, J., Valencia, A., & Tress, M. L. (2014). Multiple evidence strands suggest that there may be as few as 19 000 human protein-coding genes. *Human Molecular Genetics, 23,* 5866–5878.

Fabbri-Destro, M., & Rizzolatti, G. (2008). Mirror neurons and mirror systems in monkeys and humans. *Physiology, 23,* 171–179.

Fabes, R., Eisenberg, N., Nyman, M., & Michealieu, Q. (1991). Young children's appraisal of others' spontaneous emotional relations. *Developmental Psychology, 27,* 858–866.

Fabes, R. A., Martin, C. L., & Hanish, L. D. (2009). Children's behaviors and interactions with peers. In K. H. Rubin, W. M. Bukowski & B. Laursen (Eds), *Handbook of peer interactions, relationships, and groups* (pp. 45–62). New York, NY: Guilford Press.

Fagan, J. F. (1979). The origin of facial pattern perception. In M. H. Bornstein & W. Kessen (Eds), *Psychological development from infancy: Image to intention* (pp. 83–113). Hillsdale, NJ: Lawrence Erlbaum.

Fagan, J. F., & Detterman, D. K. (1992). The Fagan Test of Infant Intelligence: A technical summary. *Journal of Applied Developmental Psychology, 13,* 173–193.

Fagan, J. F., & Holland, C. R. (2007). Racial equality in intelligence: Predictions from a theory of intelligence as processing. *Intelligence, 35* (4), 319–334.

Fagan, J. F., Holland, C. R., & Wheeler, K. (2007). The prediction from infancy of adult IQ and achievement. *Intelligence, 35,* 22–231.

Fagan, M. K. (2015). Why repetition? Repetitive babbling, auditory feedback, and cochlear implantation. *Journal of Experimental Child Psychology, 137,* 125–136.

Fagot, B. I. (1985). Beyond the reinforcement principle: Another step toward understanding sex role development. *Developmental Psychology, 21,* 1097–1104.

Fagot, B. I., & Hagan, R. (1985). Aggression in toddlers: Responses to the assertive acts of boys and girls. *Sex Roles, 12,* 341–351.

Fairbairn, W. R. D. (1952). *Psychoanalytic studies of the personality.* London: Routledge and Kegan Paul.

Fairchild, S. R. (2006). Understanding attachment: Reliability and validity of selected attachment measures for preschoolers and children. *Child and Adolescent Social Work Journal, 23,* 235–261.

Faircloth, B. S., & Hamm, J. V. (2011). The dynamic reality of adolescent peer networks and sense of belonging. *Merrill-Palmer Quarterly, 57,* 48–72.

Fan, J. (2013) Attentional network deficits in autism spectrum disorders. In J. D. Buxbaum & P. R. Hof (Eds), *The neuroscience of autism spectrum disorders* (pp. 281–288). Oxford: Elsevier.

Fanti, K. A., Panayiotou, G., Lazarou, C., Michael, R., & Georgiou, G. (2016). The better of two evils? Evidence that children exhibiting continuous conduct problems high or low on callous–unemotional traits score on opposite directions on physiological and behavioral measures of fear. *Development and Psychopathology, 28,* 185–198.

Fantz, R. L. (1956). A method for studying early visual development. *Perceptual and Motor Skills, 6,* 13–15.

Fantz, R. L. (1958). Pattern vision in young infants. *Psychological Record, 8,* 43–47.

Fantz, R. L. (1961). The origin of form perception. *Scientific American, 204,* 66–72.

Fantz, R. L., & Fagan, J. F. (1975). Visual attention to size and number of pattern details by term and preterm infants during the first six months. *Child Development, 46,* 3–18.

Fantz, R. L., & Miranda, S. B. (1975). Newborn infant attention to form of contour. *Child Development, 46,* 224–228.

Faraone, S. V., Smoller, J. W., Pato, C. N., Sullivan, P., & Tsuang, M. T. (2008). The new neuropsychiatric genetics. *American Journal of Medical Genetics Part B: Neuropsychiatric Genetics, 147,* 1–2.

Farley, A., López, B., & Saunders, G. (2010). Self-conceptualisation in autism: Knowing oneself versus knowing self-through-other. *Autism, 14,* 519–530.

Farrington, D. P., & Ttofi, M. M. (2009). School-based programs to reduce bullying and victimization. *Campbell Systematic Reviews, 2009,* 6.

Farroni, T., Menon, E., Rigato, S., & Johnson, M. H. (2007). The perception of facial expressions in newborns. *European Journal of Developmental Psychology, 4,* 2–13.

Fauconnier, G., & Turner, M. (2002). *The way we think: Conceptual blending and the mind's hidden complexities.* New York, NY: Basic Books.

Favaro, A., Caregaro, L., Tenconi, E., Bosello, R., & Santonastaso, P. (2009). Time trends in age at onset of anorexia nervosa and bulimia nervosa. *Journal of Clinical Psychiatry, 16),* 1715–1721.

Fazzi, E., Lanners, J., Ferrari-Ginevra, O., Achille, C., Luparia, A., Signorini, S., & Lanzi, G. (2002). Gross motor development and reach on sound as critical tools for the development of the blind child. *Brain Development, 24,* 269–275.

Fazzi, E., Signorini, S. G., Bomba, M., Luparia, A., Lanners, J., & Balottin, U. (2011). Reach on sound: A key to object permanence in visually impaired children. *Early Human Development, 87,* 289–296.

Fazzi, E., Signorini, S. G., La Piana, R., Bertone, C., Misefari, W., Galli, J., Balottinm U., & Bianchi, P. E. (2012). Neuro-ophthalmological disorders in cerebral palsy: Ophthalmological, oculomotor, and visual aspects. *Developmental Medicine and Child Neurology, 54,* 730–736.

Feigon, S. A., Wladman, I. D., Levy, F., & Hay, A. D. (2001). Genetic and environmental influences on separation anxiety disorder symptoms and their moderation by age and sex. *Behavior Genetics, 31,* 403–411.

Feinfield, K. A., Lee, P. P., Flavell, E. R., Green, F. L., & Flavell, J. H. (1999). Young children's understanding of intention. *Cognitive Development, 14,* 463–486.

Feinman, S., Roberts, D., Hsieh, K.-F., Sawyer, D., & Swanson, D. (1992). A critical review of social referencing in infancy. In S. Feinman (Ed.), *Social referencing and the social construction of reality in infancy* (pp. 15–54). London: Plenum.

Fekkes, M., Pijpers, F. I., & Verloove-Vanhorick, S. P. (2005). Bullying: Who does what, when and where? Involvement of children, teachers and parents in bullying behavior. *Health Education Research, 20,* 81–91.

Feldman, D., Banerjee, A., & Sur, M. (2016). Developmental dynamics of Rett syndrome. *Neural Plasticity, 2016,* 6154080.

Feldman, D. H. (2004). Piaget's stages: The unfinished symphony of cognitive development. *New Ideas in Psychology, 22,* 175–231.

Fenson, L., & Schell, R. E. (1985). The origins of exploratory play. *Early Child Development and Care, 19,* 3–24.

Ferdenzi, C., Coureaud, G., Camos, V., & Schaal, B. (2008). Human awareness and uses of odor cues in everyday life: Results from a questionnaire study in children. *International Journal of Behavioral Development, 32,* 417–426.

Ferguson, C. A. (1978). Learning to pronounce: The earliest stages of phonological development in the child. In F. D. Minifie & L. L. Lloyd (Eds), *Communicative and cognitive abilities – Early behavioral assessment* (pp. 273–297). Baltimore, MD: University Park Press.

Ferguson, K. T., Kulkofsky, S., Cashon, C. H., & Casasola, M. (2009). The development of specialized processing of own-race faces in infancy. *Infancy, 14,* 263–284.

Ferguson, T., Stegge, H., & Damhuis, I. (1991). Children's understanding of guilt and shame. *Child Development, 62,* 827–839.

Fernald, A., & Mazzie, C. (1991). Prosody and focus in speech to infants and adults. *Developmental Psychology, 27,* 209–221.

Ferrara, K., & Landau, B. (2015). Geometric and featural systems, separable and combined: Evidence from reorientation in people with Williams syndrome. *Cognition*, *144*, 123–133.

Ferrari, M. (1998). Being and becoming self-aware. In M. D. Ferrari & R. J. Sternberg (Eds), *Self awareness: Its nature and development* (pp. 387–422). New York, NY: Guilford Press.

Feshbach, S. (1961). The stimulating versus cathartic effects of vicarious aggressive activity. *Journal of Abnormal and Social Psychology*, *63*, 381–385.

Fessakis, G., Gouli, E., & Mavroudi, E. (2013). Problem solving by 5–6 years old kindergarten children in a computer programming environment: A case study. *Computers and Education*, *63*, 87–97.

Feuerstein, R., Feuerstein, R., & Gross, S. (1997). The Learning Potential Assessment Device. In D. P. Flanagan, J. L. Genshaft & P. L. Harrison (Eds), *Contemporary intellectual assessment* (pp. 297–313). London: Guilford Press.

Fias, W., Menon, V., & Szucs, D. (2013). Multiple components of developmental dyscalculia. *Trends in Neuroscience and Education*, *2*, 43–47.

Field, T. (1984). Early interactions between infants and their postpartum depressed mothers. *Infant Behavior and Development*, *7*, 517–522.

Field, T. (1994). The effects of mother's physical and emotional unavailability on emotion regulaton. *Monographs of the Society for Research in Child Development*, *59* (2–3), 208–227.

Field, T. (2011). Prenatal depression effects on early development: A review. *Infant Behavior and Development*, *34*, 1–14.

Field, T., Diego. M., & Hernandez-Reif, M. (2009). Depressed mothers' infants are less responsive to faces and voices. *Infant Behavior and Development*, *32*, 239–244.

Field, T., Healy, B., Goldstein, S., Perry, S., Bendell, D., Schanberg, S., Zimmerman, E. A., & Kuhn, C. (1988). Infants of depressed mothers show "depressed" behavior even with nondepressed adults. *Child Development*, *59*, 1569–1579.

Field, T., Woodson, R., Greenberg, R., & Cohen, D. (1982). Discrimination and imitation of facial expressions by neonates. *Science*, *218*, 179–181.

Fifer, W. P., Monk, C. E., & Grose-Fifer, J. (2004). Prenatal development and risk. In G. Bremner & A. Fogel (Eds), *Blackwell handbook of infant development* (pp. 505–542). Malden, MA: Blackwell.

Fifer, W. P., & Moon, C. M. (1995). The effects of experience with fetal sound. In J.-P. Lecanuet, W. P. Fifer, N. A. Krasnegor & W. P. Smotherman (Eds), *Fetal development* (pp. 351–366). Hove, UK: Lawrence Erlbaum.

Fine, C. (2014). His brain, her brain? *Science*, *346* (6212), 915–916.

Fine, C., & Rush, E. (2018). "Why does all the girls have to buy pink stuff?" The ethics and science of the gendered toy marketing debate. *Journal of Business Ethics*, *159*, 769–784.

Fingerman, K. L., & Yahirun, J. J. (2015). Emerging adulthood in the context of family. In J. J. Arnett (Ed.), *The Oxford handbook of emerging adulthood* (pp. 163–176). New York, NY: Oxford University Press.

Fink, E., Begeer, S., Peterson, C. C., Slaughter, V., & Rosnay, M. (2015). Friendlessness and theory of mind: A prospective longitudinal study. *British Journal of Developmental Psychology*, *33*, 1–17.

Finne, P. H., Seip, M., & Salomonsen, L. (2001). *Propedeutisk pediatri*. Oslo: Universitetsforlaget.

Fintoft, K., Bollingmo, M., Feilberg, J., Gjettum B., & Mjaavatn, P. E. (1983). *Fire år: En undersøkelse av normalspråket hos norske 4-åringer*. Trondheim: Universitetet i Trondheim.

Fischer, K. W. (1980). A theory of cognitive development: The control and construction of hierarchies of skills. *Psychological Review*, *87*, 477–531.

Fischer, K. W., & Connell, M. W. (2003). Two motivational systems that shape development: Epistemic and self-organizing. *British Journal of Educational Psychology: Monograph Series II*, *2*, 103–123.

Fischer, K. W., Shaver, P. R., & Carnochan, P. (1990). How emotions develop and how they organise development. *Cognition and Emotion*, *4*, 81–127.

Fitzgerald, J., & Pavuluri, M. (2015). Bipolar disorder. In T. P. Gullotta, R. W. Plant & M. A. Evans (Eds), *Handbook of adolescent behavioral problems* (pp. 193–208). New York, NY: Springer.

Fivush, R. (1991). Gender and emotion in mother–child conversations about the past. *Journal of Narrative and Life History*, *1*, 325–341.

Fivush, R. (1997). Event memory in early childhood. In N. Cowan (Ed.), *The development of memory in childhood* (pp. 139–161). Hove, UK: Psychology Press.

Fivush, R. (2009). Coconstructing memories and meaning over time. In J. A. Quas & R. Fivush (Eds), *Emotion and memory in development* (pp. 343–354). Oxford: Oxford University Press.

Fivush, R. (2011). The development of autobiographical memory. *Annual Review of Psychology*, *62*, 559–582.

Fivush, R., & Buckner, J. (1997). The self as socially constructed: A commentary. In U. Neisser & D. A. Jopling (Eds), *The conceptual self in context: Culture, experience, self-understanding* (pp. 176–181). Cambridge: Cambridge University Press.

Fivush, R., Habermas, T., Waters, T. E., & Zaman, W. (2011). The making of autobiographical memory: Intersections of culture, narratives and identity. *International Journal of Psychology*, *46*, 321–345.

Fivush, R., Haden, C. A., & Reese, E. (2006). Elaborating on elaborations: The role of maternal reminiscing style on children's cognitive and socioemotional development. *Child Development*, *77*, 1568–1588.

Fivush, R., & Hamond, N. R. (1989). Time and again: Effects of repetition and retention interval on 2-year-olds' event recall. *Journal of Experimental Child Psychology*, *47*, 259–273.

Fivush, R., & Hamond, N. R. (1990). Autobiographical memory across the preschool years: Toward reconceptualizing childhood amnesia. In R. Fivush & J. A. Hudson (Eds), *Emory symposia in cognition, Volume 3. Knowing and remembering in young children* (pp. 223–248). New York, NY: Cambridge University Press.

Fivush, R., Kuebli, J., & Clubb, P. A. (1992). The structure of events and event representations: A developmental analysis. *Child Development, 63,* 188–201.

Fivush, R., & Nelson, K. (2004). Culture and language in the emergence of autobiographical memory. *Psychological Science, 15,* 573–577.

Fivush, R., Sales, J. M., & Bohanek, J. G. (2008). Meaning making in mothers' and children's narratives of emotional events. *Memory, 16,* 579–594

Fivush, R., Sales, J. M., Goldberg, A., Bahrick, L., & Parker, J. (2004). Weathering the storm: Children's long-term recall of Hurricane Andrew. *Memory, 12,* 104–118.

Flanigan, K. M. (2012). The muscular dystrophies. *Seminars in Neurology, 32,* 255–263.

Flavell, J. H. (1971). Stage related properties of cognitive development. *Cognitive Psychology, 2,* 421–453.

Flavell, J. H. (1992). Perspectives on perspective taking. In H. Beilin & P. B. Pufall (Eds), *Piaget's theory: Prospects and possibilities* (pp. 107–139). Hillsdale, NJ: Erlbaum.

Flavell, J. H. (2004). Development of knowledge about vision. In D. T. Levin (Ed.), *Thinking and seeing: Visual metacognition in adults and children* (pp. 13–36). Cambridge, MA: MIT Press.

Flavell, J. H., Beach, D. R., & Chinsky, J. M. (1966). Spontaneous verbal rehearsal in a memory task as a function of age. *Child Development, 37,* 283–299.

Flavell, J. H., Botkin, P. T., Fry, C. L., Wright, J. V., & Jarvis, P. E. (1968). *The development of role-taking and communication skills in children.* New York, NY: John Wiley.

Fletcher, A., Darling, N., Steinberg. L., & Dornbusch, S. (1995). The company they keep: Relation of adolescents' adjustment and behavior to their friends' perception of authoritative parenting in the social network. *Developmental Psychology, 31,* 300–310.

Fletcher, E. N., Whitaker, R. C., Marino, A. J., & Anderson, S. E. (2014). Screen time at home and school among low-income children attending Head Start. *Child Indicators Research, 7,* 421–436.

Fletcher, J. M., Stuebing, K. K., & Hughes, L. C. (2010). IQ scores should be corrected for the Flynn effect in high-stakes decisions. *Journal of Psychoeducational Assessment, 28,* 469–473.

Fletcher, R., May, C., St George, J., Morgan, P. J., & Lubans, D. R. (2011). Fathers' perceptions of rough-and-tumble play: Implications for early childhood services. *Australasian Journal of Early Childhood, 36,* 131–138.

Fletcher, R., St George, J., & Freeman, E. (2013). Rough and tumble play quality: Theoretical foundations for a new measure of father–child interaction. *Early Child Development and Care, 183,* 746–759.

Fletcher-Watson, S., Collis, J. M., Findlay, J. M., & Leekam, S. R. (2009). The development of change blindness: Children's attentional priorities whilst viewing naturalistic scenes. *Developmental Science, 12,* 438–445.

Fletcher-Watson, S., McConnell, F., Manola, E., & McConachie, H. (2014). Interventions based on the Theory of Mind cognitive model for autism spectrum disorder (ASD). *The Cochrane Library.*

Flom, M., & Saudino, K. J. (2017). Callous–unemotional behaviors in early childhood: Genetic and environmental contributions to stability and change. *Development and Psychopathology, 29,* 1227–1234.

Floyd, R. G. (2010). Assessment of cognitive abilities and cognitive processes: Issues, applications and fit with a problem-solving model. In G. G. Pedacock, R. A. Ervin, E. J. Daly & K. W. Merrell (Eds), *Practical handbook of school psychology: Effective practices for the 21st century* (pp. 48–66). New York, NY: Guilford Press.

Flynn, E., Pine, K. J., & Lewis, C. (2007). Using the microgenetic method to investigate cognitive development: An introduction. *Infant and Child Development, 15,* 1–6.

Flynn, J. R. (1998). IQ gains over time: Toward finding the causes. In U. Neisser (Ed.), *The rising curve* (pp. 25–66). Washington, DC: American Psychological Association.

Flynn, J. R. (2007). *What is intelligence? Beyond the Flynn effect.* Cambridge: Cambridge University Press.

Flynn, J. R. (2016). *Does your family make you smarter? Nature, nurture and human autonomy.* Cambridge: Cambridge University Press.

Flynn, J. R., & Shayer, M. (2018). IQ decline and Piaget: Does the rot start at the top? *Intelligence, 66,* 112–121.

Fodor, J. (1983). *Modularity of mind: An essay on faculty psychology.* Cambridge, MA: MIT Press.

Fodor, J. (1985). Précis of "Modularity of mind". *Behavioral and Brain Sciences, 8,* 1–42.

Fogassi, L., & Ferrari, P. F. (2011). Mirror systems. *WIREs Cognitive Science, 2,* 22–38.

Fogel, A. (1979). Peer vs. mother directed behavior in 1-to 3-month-old infants. *Infant Behavior and Development, 2,* 215–226.

Foley, D. L., Eaves, L. J., Wormley, B., Silberg, J. L., Maes, H. H., Kuhn. J., & Riley, B. (2004). Childhood adversity, monoamine oxidase a genotype, and risk for conduct disorder. *Archives of General Psychiatry, 61,* 738–744.

Fonagy, P., Gergely, G., & Jurist, E. L. (Eds) (2004). *Affect regulation, mentalization and the development of the self.* London: Karnac books.

Fonagy, P., Gergely, G., Jurist, E., & Target. (2002). *Affect regulation, mentalization and the development of the self.* New York, NY: Other Press.

Fonagy, P., Gergely, G., & Target, M. (2007). The parent–infant dyad and the construction of the subjective self. *Journal of Child Psychology and Psychiatry, 48* (3–4), 288–328.

Fontaine, R. G. (2010). New developments in developmental research on social information processing and antisocial behavior. *Journal of Abnormal Child Psychology, 38,* 569–573.

Fontaine, R. G., & Dodge, K. A. (2009). Social information processing and aggressive behavior: A transactional perspective. In A. J. Sameroff (Ed.), *The transactional model of development: How children and contexts shape each other* (pp. 117–135). Washington, DC: American Psychological Association.

Forte, L. A., Timmer, S., & Urquiza, A. (2014). A brief history of evidence-based practice. In S. Timmer & A. Urquiza (Eds), *Evidence-based approaches for the treatment of maltreated children* (pp. 13–18). New York, NY: Springer.

Forti-Buratti, M. A., Saikia, R., Wilkinson, E. L., & Ramchandani, P. G. (2016). Psychological treatments for depression in pre-adolescent children (12 years and younger): Systematic review and meta-analysis of randomised controlled trials. *European Child and Adolescent Psychiatry, 25,* 1045–1054.

Foster, D., Davies, S., & Steele, H. (2003). The evacuation of British children during World War II: A preliminary investigation into the long-term psychological effects. *Aging and Mental Health, 7,* 398–408.

Fox, J. K., Warner, C. M., Lerner, A. B., Ludwig, K., Ryan, J. L., Colognori, D., Lucas, C. P., & Brotman, L. M. (2012). Preventive intervention for anxious preschoolers and their parents: Strengthening early emotional development. *Child Psychiatry and Human Development, 43,* 544–559.

Fox, L., Carta, J. J., Strain, P. S., Dunlap, G., & Hemmeter, M. L. (2010). Response to intervention and the Pyramid Model. *Infants and Young Children, 23,* 3–13.

Fox, N. A., Kimmerly, N. L., & Schafer, W. D. (1991). Attachment to mother/attachment to father: A meta-analysis. *Child Development, 62,* 210–225.

Fox, N. A., & Rutter, M. (2010). Introduction to the special section on the effects of early experience on development. *Child Development, 81,* 23–27.

Fraiberg, S. (1971). Smiling and stranger reaction in blind infants. In J. Hellmuth (Ed.), *The exceptional infant, Volume 2* (pp. 110–127). New York, NY: Brunner/Mazel.

Fraiberg, S. (1977). *Insights from the blind.* New York, NY: Basic Books.

Fraley, R. C., & Tancredy, C. M. (2012). Twin and sibling attachment in a nationally representative sample. *Personality and Social Psychology Bulletin, 38,* 308–316.

Frances, A. J., & Nardo, J. M. (2013). ICD-11 should not repeat the mistakes made by DSM-5. *British Journal of Psychiatry, 203,* 1–2.

Franco, F., & Butterworth, G. (1996). Pointing and social awareness: Declaring and requesting in the second year. *Journal of Child Language, 23,* 307–336.

Franklin, T. (2017). Best practices in multicultural assessment of cognition. In R. S. McCallum (Ed.), *Handbook of nonverbal assessment, Second edition* (pp. 39–46). Cham, Switzerland: Springer.

Fréchette, S. (2016). Corporal punishment: National trends, longer-term consequences, and parental perceptions of physical discipline. Doctoral dissertation, University of Ottawa.

Freedman, D. A., & Cannady, C. (1971). Delayed emergence of prone locomotion. *Journal of Nervous and Mental Disease, 153,* 108–117.

Freedman, D. G. (1964). Smiling in blind infants and the issue of innate vs. acquired. *Journal of Child Psychology and Psychiatry, 5,* 171–184.

Freedman, D. G. (1974). *Human infancy: An evolutionary perspective.* Hillsdale, NJ: Erlbaum.

Freeman, N. H., & Lacohée, H. (1995). Making explicit 3-year-olds' implicit competence with their own false beliefs. *Cognition, 56,* 31–60.

Freud, A. (1966). *Normality and pathology in childhood.* London: Hogarth Press.

Freud, A. (1992). *The ego and the mechanisms of defence, Revised edition.* London: Karnac Books.

Freud, S. (1894). The neuro-psychoses of defence. In *The standard edition of the complete works of Sigmund Freud* (pp. 43–61). London: Hogarth Press.

Freud, S. (1895) Project for a scientific psychology. In *The standard edition of the complete works of Sigmund Freud, Volume 1.* London: Hogarth Press.

Freud, S. (1905). *Three essays on the theory of sexuality.* London: Allen and Unwin.

Freud, S. (1911). Two principles in mental functioning. In *The standard edition of the complete works of Sigmund Freud, Volume 12* (pp. 213–226), London: Hogarth Press.

Freud, S. (1915). The unconscious. In *The standard edition of the complete works of Sigmund Freud, Volume 14* (pp. 159–205). London: Hogarth Press.

Freud, S. (1916). *A general introduction to psychoanalysis.* New York, NY: Liveright.

Freud, S. (1927). *The ego and the id.* London: Hogarth Press.

Freud, S. (1930). *Civilization and its discontents.* Oxford: Hogarth Press.

Frick, P. J. (2006). Developmental pathways to conduct disorder. *Child and Adolescent Psychiatric Clinics of North America, 1,* 311–331.

Frick, P. J., & Morris, A. S. (2004). Temperament and developmental pathways to conduct problems. *Journal of Clinical Child and Adolescent Psychology, 33,* 54–68.

Frick, P. J., & Nigg, J. T. (2012). Current issues in the diagnosis of attention deficit hyperactivity disorder, oppositional defiant disorder, and conduct disorder. *Annual Review of Clinical Psychology, 8,* 77–107.

Frick, P. J., Ray, J. V., Thornton, L. C., & Kahn, R. E. (2014). Annual research review: A developmental psychopathology approach to understanding callous-unemotional traits in children and adolescents with serious conduct problems. *Journal of Child Psychology and Psychiatry, 55,* 532–548.

Fricke, S., Bowyer-Crane, C., Haley, A. J., Hulme, C., & Snowling, M. J. (2013). Efficacy of language intervention in the early years. *Journal of Child Psychology and Psychiatry, 54,* 280–290.

Friedman, W. J. (2005). Developmental and cognitive perspectives on humans' sense of the times of past and future events. *Learning and Motivation, 36,* 145–158.

Friedman, W. J. (2014). The development of memory for the times of past events. In P. J. Bauer & R. Fivush (Eds),

The Wiley-Blackwell handbook on the development of children's memory (pp. 394–407). Chichester, UK: Wiley-Blackwell.

Friedman, W. J., Gardner, A. G., & Zubin, N. R. E. (1995). Children's comparisons of the recency of two events from the past year. *Child Development, 66*, 970–983.

Friedman, W. J., Cederborg, A.-C., Hultman, E., Änghagen, O., & Magnusson, K. F. (2010). Children's memory for the duration of a paediatric consultation. *Applied Cognitive Psychology, 24*, 545–556.

Friedman, W. J., Reese, E., & Dai, X. (2011). Children's memory for the times of events from the past years. *Applied Cognitive Psychology, 25*, 156–165.

Frost, J. L. (2012). The changing culture of play. *International Journal of Play, 1*, 117–130.

Fukushima, S. (2011). The deafblind and disability studies. In A. Matsui, O. Nagase, A. Sheldon, D. Goodley & Y. Sawada (Eds), *Creating a society for all: Disability and economy* (pp. 50–58). Leeds, UK: The Disability Press.

Funamoto, A., & Rinaldi, C. M. (2015). Measuring parent–child mutuality: A review of current observational coding systems. *Infant Mental Health Journal, 36*, 3–11.

Fung, H., Lieber, E., & Leung, P. W. L. (2003). Parental beliefs about moral socialization in Taiwan, Hong Kong and United States. In K. S. Yang, K. K. Wang, P. B. Pedersen & I. Daibo (Eds), *Progress psychology: Conceptual and empirical contributions* (pp. 83–109). Westport, CO: Praeger.

Funk, J. B., Baldacci, H. B., Pasold, T., & Baumgardner, J. (2004). Violence exposure in real-life, video games, television, movies, and the internet: Is there desensitization? *Journal of Adolescence, 27*, 23–39.

Furman, W., & Rose, A. J. (2015). Friendships, romantic relationships, and peer relationships. In R. M. Lerner, M. E. Lamb & C. G. Coll (Eds), *Handbook of child psychology and developmental science, Seventh edition, Volume 3: Social and emotional development* (pp. 1–43). Hoboken, NJ: Wiley.

Furstenberg, F. F., & Hughes, M. E. (1997). The influence of neighborhoods on children's development: A theoretical perspective and a research agenda. In J. Brooks-Gunn, G. J. Duncan & J. L. Aber (Eds), *Neighborhood poverty, Volume 2* (pp. 23–47). New York, NY: Sage.

Furth, H. G. (1980). *The world of grown-ups. Children's conceptions of society*. Amsterdam, NL: Elsevier.

Furth, H. G., & Kane, S. R. (1992). Children constructing society: A new perspective on children at play. In H. McGurk (Ed.), *Childhood social development: Contemporary perspectives* (pp. 149–173). Hillsdale, NJ: Erlbaum.

Furth, H. G., & Wachs, H. (1975). *Thinking goes to school: Piaget's theory in practice*. Oxford: Oxford University Press.

Gagné, F. (2004) Transforming gifts into talents: The DMGT as a developmental theory. *High Ability Studies, 15*, 119–147.

Gagnon, R. (1992). Fetal behaviour in relation to stimulation. In J. G. Nijhuis (Ed.), *Fetal behavior* (pp. 209–226). Oxford: Oxford Medical Publications.

Galambos, N. L., Barker, E. T., & Almeida, D. M. (2003). Parents do matter: Trajectories of change in externalizing and internalizing problems in early adolescence. *Child Development, 74*, 578–594.

Gallagher, K. C. (2002). Does child temperament moderate the influence of parenting on adjustment? *Developmental Review, 22*, 623–643.

Gallahue, D. L., & Ozmun, J. C. (1997). *Understanding motor development: Infants, children, adolescents and adults, Fourth edition*. Boston, MA: McGraw-Hill.

Gallahue, D. L., & Ozmun, J. C. (2006). *Understanding motor development: Infants, children, adolescents, adults, Sixth edition*. Boston, MA: McGraw-Hill.

Gallese, V., Fadiga, L., Fogassi, L., & Rizzolatti, G. (1996). Action recognition in the premotor cortex. *Brain. 119*, 593–609.

Gallo, E. A. G., De Mola, C. L., Wehrmeister, F., Gonçalves, H., Kieling, C., & Murray, J. (2017). Childhood maltreatment preceding depressive disorder at age 18 years: A prospective Brazilian birth cohort study. *Journal of Affective Disorders, 217*, 218–224.

Ganiban, J. M., Ulbricht, J., Saudino, K. J., Reiss, D., & Neiderhiser, H. M. (2011). Understanding child-based effects on parenting: Temperament as a moderator of genetic and environmental contributions to parenting. *Developmental Psychology, 47*, 676–692.

Gapp, K., Woldemichael, B. T., Bohacek, J., & Mansuy, I. M. (2014). Epigenetic regulation in neurodevelopment and neurodegenerative diseases. *Neuroscience, 264*, 99–111.

Garandeau, C. F., Lee, I. A., & Salmivalli, C. (2014). Differential effects of the KiVa anti-bullying program on popular and unpopular bullies. *Journal of Applied Developmental Psychology, 35*, 44–50.

Garber, J., & Rao, U. (2014). Depression in children and adolescents. In M. Lewis & K. D. Rudolph (Eds), *Handbook of developmental psychopathology, Third edition* (pp. 489–520). New York, NY: Springer.

Garber, J., Frankel, S. A., & Herrington, C. G. (2016). Developmental demands of cognitive behavioral therapy for depression in children and adolescents: Cognitive, social, and emotional processes. *Annual Review of Clinical Psychology, 12*, 181–216.

Gardner, H. (1983). *Frames of mind: The theory of multiple intelligence*. New York, NY: Basic Books.

Gardner, H. (1993). *Multiple intelligences: The theory in practice*. New York, NY: Basic Books.

Gardner, H. (2006). *Multiple intelligences: New horizons*. New York, NY: Basic Books.

Garmezy, N. (1991). Resiliency and vulnerability to adverse developmental outcomes associated with poverty. *American Behavioral Scientist, 34*, 416–430.

Garvey, C. (1977). The contingent query: A dependent act in conversation. In M. Lewis & L. A. Rosenblum (Eds), *Interaction, conversation and the development of language* (pp. 63–93). New York, NY: Wiley.

Gass, K., Jenkins, J., & Dunn, J. (2007). Are sibling relationships protective? A longitudinal study. *Journal of Child Psychology and Psychiatry, 48*, 167–175.

Gasser, L., & Keller, M. (2009). Are the competent the morally good? Perspective taking and moral motivation of children involved in bullying. *Social Development, 18*, 798–816.

Gathercole, S. E., Pickering, S. J., Ambridge, B., & Wearing, H. (2004). The structure of working memory from 4 to 15 years of age. *Developmental Psychology, 40*, 177–190.

Gathercole, V. C. (1987). The contrastive hypothesis for the acquisition of word meaning: A reconsideration of the theory. *Journal of Child Language, 14*, 493–531.

Gauvain, M., & Perez, S. (2015). Cognitive development and culture. In R. M. Lerner, L. S. Liben & U. Müller (Eds), *Handbook of child psychology and developmental science, Seventh edition, Volume 2: Cognitive processes* (pp. 854–896) Hoboken, NJ: Wiley.

Gavine, A., MacGillivray, S., & Williams, D. J. (2014). Universal community-based social development interventions for preventing community violence by young people 12 to 18 years of age. *The Cochrane Library, No. 8.*

Geangu, E., Benga, O., Stahl, D., & Striano, T. (2010). Contagious crying beyond the first days of life. *Infant Behavior and Development, 33*, 279–288.

Geary, D. C. (2015). The classification and cognitive characteristics of mathematical disabilities in children. In R. C. Kadosh & A. Dowker (Eds), *Oxford handbook of numerical cognition* (pp. 767–786). Oxford: Oxford University Press.

Geary, D. C., & Bjorklund, D. F. (2000). Evolutionary developmental psychology. *Child Development, 71*, 57–65.

Geary, D. C., Hoard, M. K., Nugent, L., & Bailey, H. D. (2013). Adolescents' functional numeracy is predicted by their school entry number system knowledge. *Plos One, 8* (1), e54651.

Geddie, B. E., Bina, M. J., Miller, M. M., Bathshaw, M. L., Roizen, N. J., & Lotrecchiano, G. R. (2013). Vision and visual impairment. In G. Lotrecchiano, N. Roizen & M. Batshaw (Eds), *Children with disabilities, Seventh edition* (pp. 169–188). Baltimore, MD: Brookes.

Gee, D. G., Gabard-Durnam, L. J., Flannery, J., Goff, B., Humphreys, K. L., Telzer, E. H., Hare, T. A., Bookheimer, S. Y., & Tottenham, N. (2013). Early developmental emergence of human amygdala–prefrontal connectivity after maternal deprivation. *Proceedings of the National Academy of Sciences, 110*, 15638–15643.

Geers, A. E., Moog, J. S., Biedenstein, J., Brenner, C., & Hayes, H. (2009). Spoken language scores of children using cochlear implants compared to hearing age-mates at school entry. *The Journal of Deaf Studies and Deaf Education, 14*, 371–385.

Geldart, S., Mondloch, C., Maurer, D, de Schonen, S., & Brent, H. (2002). The effect of early visual deprivation on the development of face processing. *Developmental Science, 5*, 490–501.

Gelman, R., & Williams, E. M. (1998). Enabling constraints for cognitive development and learning: Domain specificity and epigenesis. In W. Damon, D. Kuhn & R. S. Siegler (Eds), *Handbook of child psychology, Volume 2: Cognition, perception and language* (pp. 575–630). New York, NY: Wiley.

Gender Identity Research and Education Society (GIRES) (2006). Atypical gender development – A review. *International Journal of Transgenderism, 9*, 29–44,

Genese, F., & Nicoladis, E. (2007). Bilingual first language development. In E. Hoff & M. Shatz (Eds), *Handbook of child language development* (pp. 324–342). Oxford: Blackwell.

Gentile, D. A. (2009). Pathological video-game use among youth ages 8 to 18: A national study. *Psychological Science, 20*, 594–602.

Gentile, D. A. (2011). The multiple dimensions of video game effects. *Child Development Perspectives, 5*, 75–81.

Gentile, D. A., & Gentile, J. R. (2008). Violent video games as exemplary teachers: A conceptual analysis. *Journal of Youth and Adolescence, 37*, 127–141.

Gentile, D. A., Mathieson, L. C., & Crick, N. R. (2011b). Media violence associations with the form and function of aggression among elementary school children. *Social Development, 20*, 213–232.

Gentile, D. A., Anderson, C. A., Yukawa, S., Ihori, N., Saleem, M., Ming, L. K., Shibuya, A., Liau, A. K., Bushman, B. J., Rowell Huesmann, L., & Sakamoto, A. (2009). The effects of prosocial video games on prosocial behaviors: International evidence from correlational, longitudinal, and experimental studies. *Personality and Social Psychology Bulletin, 35*, 752–763.

Gentile, D. A., Choo, H., Liau, A., Sim, T., & Li, D. (2011a). Pathological video game use among youths: A two-year longitudinal study. *Pediatrics, 127*, e319–e329.

Gentner, D., & Bowerman, M. (2009). Why some spatial semantic categories are harder to learn than others: The typological prevalence hypothesis. In J. Guo, E. Lieven, N. Budwig, S. Ervin-Tripp, K. Nakamura & S. Özcaliskan, (Eds), *Crosslinguistic approaches to the psychology of language: Research in the tradition of Dan Isaac Slobin* (pp. 465–480). New York, NY: Psychology Press.

George, C., & Solomon, J. (2008). The caregiving system: A behavioral systems approach to parenting. In J. Cassidy & P. R. Shaver (Eds), *Handbook of attachment: Theory, research, and clinical applications, Second edition* (pp. 833–856). New York, NY: Guilford Press.

George, T. P., & Hartmann, D. P. (1996). Friendship networks of unpopular, average, and popular children. *Child Development, 67*, 2301–2316.

Gerber, P. J. (2012). The impact of learning disabilities on adulthood: A review of the evidenced-based literature for research and practice in adult education. *Journal of Learning Disabilities, 45*, 31–46.

Gergen, K. J. (2002). The challenge of absent presence. In J. E. Katz & M. Aakhus (Eds), *Perpetual contact: Mobile communication, private talk, public performance* (pp. 227–241). Cambridge: Cambridge University Press.

Gershoff, E. T., Lansford, J. E., Sexton, H. R., Davis-Kean, P., & Sameroff, A. J. (2012). Longitudinal links between spanking and children's externalizing behaviors in a national sample of White, Black, Hispanic, and Asian American families. *Child Development, 83*, 838–843.

Gerstein, M. B., Bruce, C., Rozowsky, J. S., Zheng, D., Du, J., Korbel. J. O., Emanuelsson, O., Zhang, Z. D.,

Weissman, S., & Snyder, M. (2007). What is a gene, post-ENCODE? History and updated definition. *Genome Research, 17*, 669–681.

Gersten, R., Chard, D. J., Jayanthi, M., Baker, S. K., Morphy, P., & Flojo, J. (2009). Mathematics instruction for students with learning disabilities: A meta-analysis of instructional components. *Review of Educational Research, 79*, 1202–1242.

Gersten, R., Rolfhus, E., Clarke, B., Decker, L. E., Wilkins, C., & Dimino, J. (2015). Intervention for first graders with limited number knowledge: Large-scale replication of a randomized controlled trial. *American Educational Research Journal, 52*, 516–546.

Geschwind, D. H. (2011). Genetics of autism spectrum disorders. *Trends in Cognitive Sciences, 15*, 409–416.

Geschwind, D. H., & Flint, J. (2015). Genetics and genomics of psychiatric disease. *Science, 349* (6255), 1489–1494.

Geschwind, N., & Galaburda, A. M. (1985). Cerebral lateralization: Biological mechanisms, associations, and pathology: I. A hypothesis and a program for research. *Archives of Neurology, 42*, 428–459.

Gesell, A., & Thompson, H. (1929). Learning and growth in identical infant twins. *Genetic Psychology Monographs, 6*, 1–124.

Gettys, L. D., & Cann, A. (1981). Children's perceptions of occupational sex stereotypes. *Sex Roles, 7*, 301–308.

Gewirtz, A. H., & Zamir, O. (2014). The impact of parental deployment to war on children: The crucial role of parenting. *Advances in Child Development and Behavior, 46*, 89–112.

Gibbs, J., Appleton, J., & Appleton, R. (2007a). Dyspraxia or developmental coordination disorder? Unravelling the enigma. *Archives of Disease in Childhood, 92*, 534–539

Gibbs, J. C., Basinger, K. S., Grime, R. L., & Snary, J. R. (2007b). Moral judgment development across cultures: Revisiting Kohlberg's universality claims. *Developmental Review, 27*, 443–500.

Gibson, E. J. (1982). The concept of affordances in development: The renaissence of functionalism. In W. A. Collins, *Minnesota symposia on child psychology, Volume 15* (pp. 55–81). Hillsdale, NJ: Erlbaum.

Gibson, E. J., Riccio, G., Schmuckler, M. A., Stoffregen, T. A., Rosenberg, D., & Taormina, J. (1987). Detection of the traversability of surfaces by crawling and walking infants. *Journal of Experimental Psychology: Human Perception and Performance, 13*, 533–544.

Gibson, E. J., & Schmuckler, M. A. (1989). Going somewhere: An ecological and experimental approach to development of mobility. *Ecological Psychology, 1*, 3–25.

Gibson, E. J., & Walk, R. D. (1960). The "visual cliff". *Scientific American, 202*, 64–71.

Gibson, J. J. (1979). *The ecological approach to visual perception.* Boston: Houghton Mifflin.

Gifford, S., & Rockliffe, F. (2012). Mathematics difficulties: Does one approach fit all? *Research in Mathematics Education, 14*, 1–15.

Gigerenzer, G., & Gaissmaier, W. (2011). Heuristic decision making. *Annual Review of Psychology, 62*, 451–482.

Gillam, R. B., & Pearson, N. (2004). *Test of narrative language.* Austin, TX: Pro-Ed.

Gillberg, I. C., Helles, A., Billstedt, E., & Gillberg, C. (2016). Boys with Asperger syndrome grow up: Psychiatric and neurodevelopmental disorders 20 years after initial diagnosis. *Journal of Autism and Developmental Disorders, 46*, 74–82.

Gillham, J. E., Reivich, K. J., Freres, D. R., Chaplin, T. M., Shatté, A. J., Samuels, B., Elkon, A. G. L., Litzinger, S., Lascher, M., Gallop, R., & Seligman, M. E. P. (2007). School-based prevention of depressive symptoms: A randomized controlled study of the effectiveness and specificity of the Penn Resiliency Program. *Journal of Consulting and Clinical Psychology, 75*, 9–19.

Gillies, R. M. (2003). The behaviors, interactions, and perceptions of junior high school students during small-group learning. *Journal of Educational Psychology, 95*, 137.

Gillies, R. M. (2014). Cooperative learning: Developments in research. *International Journal of Educational Psychology, 3*, 125–140.

Gilligan, C. (1982). *In a different voice: Psychological theory and women's development.* Cambridge, MA: Harvard University Press.

Gillum, J. (2012). Dyscalculia: Issues for practice in educational psychology. *Educational Psychology in Practice, 28*, 287–297.

Gilman, B. J., Lovecky, D. V., Kearney, K., Peters, D. B., Wasserman, J. D., Silverman, L. K., Postma, M. G., Robinson, N. M., Amend, E. R., Ryder-Schoeck, M., et al. (2013). Critical issues in the identification of gifted students with co-existing disabilities: The twice-exceptional. *Sage Open, 3*, 2158244013505855.

Gilmore, K. (2008). Psychoanalytic developmental theory: A contemporary reconsideration. *Journal of the American Psychoanalytic Association, 56*, 885–907.

Ginsberg, K. R., & American Academy of Pediatrics. (2007). Committee on Communications, Committee on Psychological Aspects of Child and Family Health. The importance of play in promoting healthy child development and maintaining strong parent–child bonds. *Pediatrics, 119*, 182–911.

Girotto, V., Light, P., & Colbourn, C. (1988). Pragmatic schemas and conditional reasoning in children. *The Quarterly Journal of Experimental Psychology, 40*, 469–482.

Giumetti, G. W., & Kowalski, R. M. (2016). Cyberbullying matters: Examining the incremental impact of cyberbullying on outcomes over and above traditional bullying in North America. In R. Navarro, S. Yubero & E. Larranaga (Eds), *Cyberbullying across the globe: Gender, family and mental health* (pp. 117–130). Cham, Switzerland: Springer.

Gjerde, P. F. (2014). An evaluation of ethnicity research in developmental psychology: Critiques and recommendations. *Human Development, 57*, 176–205.

Gladstone, T. R., & Beardslee, W. R. (2009). The prevention of depression in children and adolescents: A review. *The Canadian Journal of Psychiatry, 54* (4), 212–221,

Glaser, D. (2000). Child abuse and neglect and the brain: A review. *Journal of Child Psychology and Psychiatry*, *41*, 97–116.

Gleason, J. B., & Greif, E. (1983). Men's speech to young children. In B. Thorne, C. Kraemerae & N. Henley (Eds), *Language, gender and society* (pp. 140–150). Rowley, MA: Newbury House.

Gleason, J. B., Phillips, B. C., Ely, R., & Zaretsky, E. (2009). Alligators all around: The acquisition of animal terms in English and Russian. In J. Guo, E. Lieven, N. Budwig, S. Ervin-Tripp, K. Nakamura & S. Özcaliskan (Eds), *Crosslinguistic approaches to the psychology of language: Research in the tradition of Dan Isaac Slobin* (pp. 17–26). New York, NY: Psychology Press.

Glenberg, A. M. (2010). Embodiment as a unifying perspective for psychology. *Wiley Interdisciplinary Reviews: Cognitive Science*, *1*, 586–596.

Glenn, N. M., Knight, C. J., Holt, N. L., & Spence, J. C. (2013). Meanings of play among children. *Childhood*, *20*, 185–199.

Glogowska, M., Roulstone, S., Peters, T. J., & Enderby, P. (2006). Early speech- and language-impaired children: Linguistic, literacy and social outcomes. *Developmental Medicine and Child Neurology*, *48*, 489–494.

Gluckman, P. D., & Hanson, M. A. (2010). The plastic human. *Infant and Child Development*, *19*, 21–26.

Glucksberg, S., Krauss, R. M., & Weisberg, R. (1966). Referential communication in nursery school children: Method and some preliminary findings. *Journal of Experimental Child Psychology*, *3*, 333–342.

Gnepp, J., & Gould, M. E. (1985). The development of personalized inferences: Understanding other people's emotional reactions in light of their prior experiences. *Child Development*, *56*, 1455–1464.

Gögele, M., Pattaro, C., Fuchsberger, C., Minelli, C., Pramstaller, P. P., & Wjst, M. (2011). Heritability analysis of life span in a semi-isolated population followed across four centuries reveals the presence of pleiotropy between life span and reproduction. *Journal of Gerontology, Series A: Biological Sciences*, *66A*, 26–37.

Goldberg, A. E., Kashy, D. A., & Smith, J. Z. (2012). Gender-typed play behavior in early childhood: Adopted children with lesbian, gay, and heterosexual parents. *Sex roles*, *67*, 503–515.

Goldberg, S. (1990). Attachment in infants at risk: Theory, research, and practice. *Infants and Young Children*, *2*, 11–20.

Golden, S. D., McLeroy, K. R., Green, L. W., Earp, J. A., & Lieberman, L. D. (2015). Upending the social ecological model to guide health promotion efforts toward policy and environmental change. *Health Education and Behavior*, *42* (1 Suppl), 8S–14S.

Goldfield, E. C., & Wolff, P. H. (2004). A dynamical systems perspective on infant action and its development. In G. Bremner & A. Slater (Eds), *Theories of infant development* (pp. 3–29). Oxford: Blackwell.

Goldin-Meadow, S. (2015). Gesture and cognitive development. In R. M. Lerner, L. Liben & U. Muller (Eds), *Handbook of child psychology and developmental science, Seventh edition, Volume 2: Cognitive processes* (pp. 339–380). New York, NY: Wiley.

Goldman, A., & Mason, K. (2007). Simulation. In P. Thagard (Ed.), *Philosophy of psychology and cognitive science* (pp. 267–293). Amsterdam, NL: North Holland/ Elsevier.

Goldsmith, H. H., & Alansky, J. A. (1987). Maternal and infant temperamental predictors of attachment: A meta-analytic review. *Journal of Consulting and Clinical Psychology*, *55*, 805–816.

Goldsmith, H. H., Lemery, K. S., Buss, K. A., & Campos, J. J. (1999). Genetic analyses of focal aspects of infant temperament. *Developmental Psychology*, *35*, 972.

Goldstein, J. H. (1994). Sex differences in toy play and use of video games. In J. H. Goldstein (Ed.), *Toys, play and child development* (pp. 110–129). Cambridge: Cambridge University Press.

Goldstein, M. H., & West, M. J. (1999). Consistent responses of human mothers to prelinguistic infants: The effect of prelinguistic repertoire size. *Journal of Comparative Psychology*, *113*, 52–58.

Goldstein, S. (2015). The evolution of intelligence. In S. Goldstein, D. Princiotta & J. A. Naglieri (Eds), *Handbook of intelligence* (pp. 3–7). New York, NY: Springer.

Goldstein, S., &. Naglieri, J. A. (Eds) (2014). *Handbook of executive functioning*. New York, NY: Springer.

Golinkoff, R. M., Ma, W., Song, L., & Hirsh-Pasek, K. (2013). Twenty-five years using the intermodal preferential looking paradigm to study language acquisition: What have we learned? *Perspectives on Psychological Science*, *8*, 316–339.

Golinkoff, R. M., Hirsh-Pasek, K., Mervis, C. B., Frawley, W. B., & Parillo, M. (1995). Lexical principles can be extended to the acquisition of verbs. In M. Tomasello & W. E. Merriman (Eds), *Beyond names for things: Young children's acquisition of verbs* (pp. 185–221). Hillsdale, NJ: Erlbaum.

Golombok, S., & Fivush, R. (1994). *Gender development*. Cambridge: Cambridge University Press.

Golombok, S., Rust, J., Zervoulis, K., Golding, J., & Hines, M. (2012). Continuity in sex-typed behavior from preschool to adolescence: A longitudinal population study of boys and girls aged 3–13 years. *Archives of Sexual Behavior*, *41*, 591–597.

Golombok, S., Rust, J., Zervoulis, K., Croudace, T., Golding, J., & Hines, M. (2008). Developmental trajectories of sex-typed behavior in boys and girls: A longitudinal general population study of children aged 2.5–8 years. *Child Development*, *79*, 1583–1593.

Gómez, J. C. (2004). *Apes, monkeys, children and the growth of mind*. Cambridge, MA: Harvard University Press.

Gómez, J. C. (2005). Species comparative studies and cognitive development. *Trends in Cognitive Science*, *9*, 118–125.

Göncü, A., Mistry, J., & Mosier, C. (2000). Cultural variations in the play of toddlers. *International Journal of Behavioral Development*, *24*, 321–329.

Goodman, G. S., & Reed, R. S. (1986). Age differences in eyewitness testimony. *Law and Human Behavior, 10,* 317–322.

Goodman, G. S., Bottoms, B., Schwartz-Kenney, B., & Rudy, L. (1991). Children's memory for a stressful event: Improving children's reports. *Journal of Narrative and Life History, 1,* 69–99.

Goodman, G. S., Rudy, L., Bottoms, B., & Aman, C. (1990). Children's concerns and memory: Issues of ecological validity in the study of children's eyewitness testimony. In R. Fivush & J. Hudson (Eds), *Knowing and remembering in young children* (pp. 249–284). Cambridge: Cambridge University Press.

Goods, K. S., Ishijima, E., Chang, Y. C., & Kasari, C. (2013). Preschool based JASPER intervention in minimally verbal children with autism: Pilot RCT. *Journal of Autism and Developmental Disorders, 43* (5), 1050–1056.

Goos, L. M., & Silverman, I. (2001). The influence of genomic imprinting on brain development and behavior. *Evolution and Human Behavior, 22,* 385–407.

Gopnik, A., & Astington, J. W. (1988). Children's understanding of representational change and its relation to the understanding of false belief and the appearance–reality distinction. *Child Development, 59,* 26–37.

Gopnik, A., & Bonawitz, E. (2015). Bayesian models of child development. *Wiley Interdisciplinary Reviews: Cognitive Science, 6,* 75–86.

Gopnik, A., & Choi, S. (1995). Names, relational words, and cognitive development in English and Korean speakers: Nouns are not always learned before verbs. In M. Tomasello & W. E. Merriman (Eds), *Beyond names for things: Young children's acquisition of verbs* (pp. 63–80). Hillsdale, NJ: Erlbaum.

Gopnik, A., & Meltzoff, A. N. (1997). *Words, thoughts and theories.* London: MIT Press.

Gordon, N. B. (1983). Maternal perception of child temperament and observed mother–child interaction. *Child Psychiatry and Human Development, 13,* 153–167.

Gordon, R. M. (1986). Folk psychology as simulation. *Mind and Language, 1,* 158–171.

Goren, C. C., Sarty, M., & Wu, P. (1975). Visual following and pattern discrimination of face-like stimuli by newborn infants. *Pediatrics, 56,* 544–545.

Gosch, E. A., Flannery-Schroeder, E., & Brecher, R. J. (2012). Anxiety disorders: School-based cognitive behavioral interventions. In R. B. Mennuti, R. W. Christner & A. Freeman (Eds), *Cognitive-behavioral interventions in educational settings: A handbook for practice* (pp. 117–160). New York, NY: Routledge.

Gosling, S. D., & Mason, W. (2015). Internet research in psychology. *Annual Review of Psychology, 66,* 877–902.

Gosso, Y., Morais, M., & Otta, E. (2007). Pretend play of Brazilian children: A window into different cultural worlds. *Journal of Cross-Cultural Psychology, 38,* 539–558.

Goswami, U. (1992). *Analogical reasoning in children.* Hillsdale, NJ: Lawrence Erlbaum.

Gottesman, I. I. (1963). Genetic aspects of intelligent behavior. In N. R. Ellis (Ed.), *Handbook of mental deficiency:* *Psychological theory and research* (pp. 253–296). New York, NY: McGraw-Hill.

Gottesman, I. I., & Hanson, D. R. (2005). Human development: Biological and genetic processes. *Annual Review of Psychology, 56,* 263–286.

Gottlieb, G. (1992). *Individual development and evolution.* Oxford: Oxford University Press.

Gottlieb, G. (1995). Some conceptual deficiencies in "developmental" behavior genetics. *Human Development, 38,* 131–141.

Gottlieb, G. (2002). Developmental-behavioral initiation of evolutionary change. *Pychological Review, 109,* 211–218.

Gottlieb, G. (2007). Probabilistic epigenesis. *Developmental Science, 10,* 1–11.

Gottlieb, G., Wahlsten, D., & Lickliter, R. (2006). The significance of biology for human development: A developmental psychobiological systems view. In R. W. Damon & R. M. Lerner (Eds), *Handbook of child development, Sixth edition, Volume 1: Theoretical models of human development* (pp. 210–257). New York, NY: Wiley.

Gottman, J., & Mettetal, G. (1986). Speculations about social and affective development: Friendship and acquaintanceship through adolescence. In J. M. Gottman & J. G. Parker (Eds), *Conversations of friends: Speculations on affective development* (pp. 192–240). Cambridge: Cambridge University Press.

Gouze, K. R. (1987). Attention and social problem solving as correlates of aggression in preschool males. *Journal of Abnormal Child Psychology, 15,* 181–197.

Graefen, J., Kohn, J., Wyschkon, A., & Esser, G. (2015). Internalizing problems in children and adolescents with math disability. *Zeitschrift für Psychologie, 22,* 93–101.

Graham, N., Truman, J., & Holgate, H. (2014). An exploratory study: Expanding the concept of play for children with severe cerebral palsy. *British Journal of Occupational Therapy, 77,* 358–365.

Granrud, C. E., & Schmechel, T. T. N. (2006). Development of size constancy in children: A test of the proximal mode sensitivity hypothesis. *Perception and Psychophysics, 68,* 1372–1381.

Grant, C. M., Grayson, A., & Boucher, J. (2001). Using tests of false belief with children with autism: How valid and reliable are they? *Autism, 5,* 135–145.

Grant, C. M., Riggs, K. J., & Boucher, J. (2004). Counterfactual and mental state reasoning in children with autism. *Journal of Autism and Developmental Disorders, 34,* 177–188.

Grayson, D. S., & Fair, D. A. (2017). Development of large-scale functional networks from birth to adulthood: A guide to the neuroimaging literature. *NeuroImage, 160,* 15–31.

Gredebäck, G., Johnson, S., & von Hofsten, C. (2010). Eye tracking in infancy research. *Developmental Neuropsychology, 35,* 1–19.

Green, A. E., Kenworthy, L., Mosner, M. G., Gallagher, N. M., Fearon, E. W., Balhana, C. D., & Yerys, B. E. (2014). Abstract analogical reasoning in high-functioning children with autism spectrum disorders. *Autism Research, 7,* 677–686.

Green, K. B., & Gallagher, P. A. (2014). Mathematics for young children: A review of the literature with implications for children with disabilities. *Başkent University Journal of Education, 1,* 81–92.

Green, S., Pring, L., & Swettenham, J. (2004). An investigation of first-order false belief understanding of children with congenital profound visual impairment. *British Journal of Developmental Psychology, 22,* 1–17.

Green, S. K., & Gredler, M. E. (2002). A review and analysis of constructivism for school-based practice. *School Psychology Review, 31,* 53–70.

Greenfield, P. M. (1998). The cultural evolution of IQ. In U. Neisser (Ed.), *The rising curve* (pp. 81–123). Washington, DC: American Psychological Association.

Greenspan, S. I., & Greenspan, N. T. (1985). *First feelings: Milestones in the emotional development of your infant and child from birth to age 4.* New York, NY: Viking Press.

Greenspan, S. I., & Woods, G. W. (2014). Intellectual disability as a disorder of reasoning and judgement: The gradual move away from intelligence quotient-ceilings. *Current Opinion in Psychiatry, 27,* 110–116.

Greenwood, P. M., & Parasuraman, R. (2010). Neuronal and cognitive plasticity: A neurocognitive framework for ameliorating cognitive aging. *Frontiers in Aging Neuroscience, 2,* 1–14.

Greer, R. D., & Keohane, D. D. (2005). The evolution of verbal behavior in children. *Behavioral Development Bulletin, 12,* 31–47.

Gregory, A. M., Caspi, A., Moffitt, T. E., Koenen, K., Eley, T. C., & Poulton, R. (2007). Juvenile mental health histories of adults with anxiety disorders. *American Journal of Psychiatry, 164,* 301–308.

Greitemeyer, T., & Mügge, D. O. (2014). Video games do affect social outcomes: A meta-analytic review of the effects of violent and prosocial video game play. *Personality and Social Psychology Bulletin, 40,* 578–589.

Griffiths, P. (1986). Early vocabulary. In P. Fletcher & M. Garman (Eds), *Language acquisition, Second edition* (pp. 279–306). Cambridge: Cambridge University Press.

Griggs, R. A. (2015). Psychology's lost boy: Will the real Little Albert please stand up? *Teaching of Psychology, 42,* 14–18.

Grigorenko, E. L. (2007). Rethinking disorders of spoken and written language: Generating workable hypotheses. *Journal of Developmental and Behavioral Pediatrics, 28,* 478–486.

Grigorenko, E. L. (2009). Dynamic assessment and response to intervention: Two sides of one coin. *Journal of Learning Disabilities, 42,* 111–132.

Grigorenko, E. L., Klin, A., & Volkmar, F. (2003). Annotation: Hyperlexia: Disability or superability? *Journal of Child Psychology and Psychiatry, 44,* 1079–1091.

Groh, A. M., Narayan, A. J., Bakermans-Kranenburg, M. J., Roisman, G. I., Vaughn, B. E., Fearon, R. M., &

van IJzendoorn, M. H. (2017). Attachment and temperament in the early life course: A meta-analytic review. *Child Development, 88,* 770–795.

Grosjean, F. (1982). *Life with two languages: An introduction to bilingualism.* Cambridge, MA: Harvard University Press.

Grosjean, F. (2010). *Bilingual.* Cambridge, MA: Harvard University Press.

Gross, A. L., & Bailif, B. (1991). Children's understanding of emotion from facial expressions and situations: A review. *Developmental Review, 11,* 368–398.

Gross, D., & Harris, P. L. (1988). False belifs about emotion: Children's understanding of misleading emotional displays. *International Journal of Behavioral Development, 11,* 475–488.

Gross, H., Shaw, D. S., Burwell, R. A., & Nagin, D. S. (2009). Transactional processes in child disruptive behavior and maternal depression: A longitudinal study from early childhood to adolescence. *Development and Psychopathology, 21,* 139–156.

Gross, J. J., & Barrett, L. F. (2011). Emotion generation and emotion regulation: One or two depends on your point of view. *Emotion Review, 3,* 8–16.

Grossman, S. W., Churchill, J. D., McKinney, B. C., Kodish, I. M., Otte, S. L., & Greenough, W. T. (2003). Experience effects on brain development: Possible contributions to psychopathology. *Journal of Child Psychology and Psychiatry, 44,* 33–63.

Grusec, J. E. (1982). The socialization of altruism. In N. Eisenberg-Berg (Ed.), *The development of prosocial behavior* (pp. 65–90). London: Academic Press.

Grusec, J. E. (1991). Socializing concern for others in the home. *Developmental Psychology, 27,* 338–342.

Grusec, J. E. (2011). Socialization processes in the family: Social and emotional development. *Annual Review of Psychology, 62,* 243–269.

Gudgeon, S., & Kirk, S. (2015). Living with a powered wheelchair: Exploring children's and young people's experiences, *Disability and Rehabilitation: Assistive Technology, 10,* 118–125.

Guerin, D. W., & Gottfried, A. W. (1994). Temperamental consequences of infant difficultness. *Infant Behavior and Development, 17,* 413–421.

Guernsey, L. (2017). Who's by their side? Questions of context deepen the research on children and media: Commentary on Chapter 1. In R. Barr & D. Nichols Linebarger (Eds), *Media exposure during infancy and early childhood* (pp. 25–32). Cham, Switzerland: Springer.

Guerrini, I., Thomson, A. D., & Gurling, H. D. (2007). The importance of alcohol misuse, malnutrition and genetic susceptibility on brain growth and plasticity. *Neuroscience and Biobehavioral Reviews, 31,* 212–220.

Guilford, J. P. (1988). Some changes in the structure of intellect model. *Educational and Psychological Measurement, 48,* 1–4.

Guillaume, P. (1926). *Imitation in children.* Chicago: University of Chicago Press.

Gulbrandsen, L. M. (1998). *I barns dagligliv.* Oslo, NO: Universitetsforlaget.

Gunn, J. F., & Goldstein, S. E. (2017). Bullying and suicidal behavior during adolescence: A developmental perspective. *Adolescent Research Review, 2*, 77–97.

Gunter, B., & McAleer, J. (1997). *Children and television: The one-eyed monster, Second edition*. London: Routledge.

Guralnick, M. J. (2011). Why early intervention works: A systems perspective. *Infants and Young Children, 24*, 6–28.

Guralnick, M. J. (2017). Early intervention for children with intellectual disabilities: An update. *Journal of Applied Research in Intellectual Disabilities, 30*, 211–229.

Guralnick, M. J., Neville, B., Hammond, M. A., & Connor, R. T. (2007). The friendships of young children with developmental delays: A longitudinal analysis. *Journal of Applied Developmental Psychology, 28*, 64–79.

Gurian, M. (2011). *Boys and girls learn differently! A guide for teachers and parents, Second edition*. San Francisco, CA: Jossey-Bass.

Güroğlu, B., van den Bos, W., & Crone, E. A. (2014). Sharing and giving across adolescence: an experimental study examining the development of prosocial behavior. *Frontiers in Psychology, 5*, 291.

Guthke, J. (1993). Development in learning potential assessment. In J. H. M. Hamers, K. Sijtsma & A. J. J. M. Ruijssenaars (Eds), *Learning potential assessment* (pp. 43–67). Amsterdam, NL: Swets and Zeitlinger.

Gutteling, B. M., de Weerth, C., Willemsen-Swinkels, S. H. N., Huizink, A. C., Mulder, E. J. H., Visser, G. H. A., & Buitelaar, J. K. (2005). The effects of prenatal stress on temperament and problem behavior of 27-month-old toddlers. *European Child and Adolescent Psychiatry, 14*, 41–51.

Gutteling, B. M., de Weerth, C., Zandbelt, N., Mulder, E. J., Visser, G. H., & Buitelaar, J. K., (2006). Does maternal prenatal stress adversely affect the child's learning and memory at age six? *Journal of Abnormal Child Psychology, 34*, 789–798.

Guyer, A. E., Silk, J. S., & Nelson, E. E. (2016). The neurobiology of the emotional adolescent: From the inside out. *Neuroscience and Biobehavioral Reviews, 70*, 74–85.

Guyon-Harris, K. L., Humphreys, K. L., Fox, N. A., Nelson, C. A., & Zeanah, C. H. (2018). Course of disinhibited social engagement disorder from early childhood to early adolescence. *Journal of the American Academy of Child and Adolescent Psychiatry, 57*, 329–335.

Haak, K. V., Langers, D. R., Renken, R., van Dijk, P., Borgstein, J., & Cornelissen, F. W. (2014). Abnormal visual field maps in human cortex: A mini-review and a case report. *Cortex, 56*, 14–25.

Habermas, T., & de Silveira, C. (2008). The development of global coherence in life narratives across adolescence: Temporal, causal, and thematic aspects. *Developmental Psychology, 44*, 707–721.

Habermas, T., & Köber, C. (2015). Autobiographical reasoning in life narratives buffers the effect of biographical disruptions on the sense of self-continuity. *Memory, 23*, 664–674.

Habermas, T., & Reese, E. (2015). Getting a life takes time: The development of the life story in adolescence, its precursors and consequences. *Human Development, 58*, 172–201.

Hadders-Algra, M. (2002). Variability in infant motor behavior: A hallmark of the healthy nervous system. *Infant Behavior and Development, 25*, 433–451.

Hafen, C. A., Laursen, B., Burk, W. J., Kerr, M., & Stattin, H. (2011). Homophily in stable and unstable adolescent friendships: Similarity breeds constancy. *Personality and Individual Differences, 51*, 607 612.

Hafen, C. A., Laursen, B., Nurmi, J. E., & Salmela-Aro, K. (2013). Bullies, victims, and antipathy: The feeling is mutual. *Journal of Abnormal Child Psychology, 41*, 801–809.

Haidt, J. (2001). The emotional dog and its rational tail: A social intuitionist approach to moral judgment. *Psychological Review, 108*, 814–834.

Haidt, J. (2007). The new synthesis in moral psychology. *Science, 316*, 998–1002.

Haidt, J. (2008). Morality. *Perspectives on Psychological Science, 3*, 65–72.

Haidt, J. (2013). Moral psychology for the twenty-first century. *Journal of Moral Education, 42*, 281–297

Håkansson, G., & Westander, J. (2013). *Communication in humans and other animals*. Amsterdam: John Benjamins.

Hala, S., & Carpendale, J. I. M. (1997). All in the mind: Children's understanding of mental life. In S. Hala (Ed.), *The development of social cognition* (pp. 189–329). Hove, UK: Psychology Press.

Halberstadt, A. G., & Lozada, F. T. (2011). Emotion development in infancy through the lens of culture. *Emotion Review, 3*, 158–168.

Hale, L., & Guan, S. (2015). Screen time and sleep among school-aged children and adolescents: A systematic literature review. *Sleep Medicine Reviews, 21*, 50–58.

Hales, C. N., & Barker, D. J. (2001). The thrifty phenotype hypothesis. *British Medical Bulletin, 60*, 5–20.

Halford, G. S. (1989). Reflections on 25 years of Piagetian cognitive psychology. *Human Development, 32*, 325–357.

Halford, G. S. (1992). Analogical reasoning and conceptual complexity in cognitive development. *Human Development, 35*, 193–217.

Halford, G. S., & Andrews, G. (2004). The development of deductive reasoning: How important is complexity? *Thinking and Reasoning, 10*, 123–145.

Halford, G. S., & Andrews, G. (2006). Reasoning and problem solving. In D. Kuhn & R. Siegler (Eds), *Handbook of child psychology, Volume 2. Cognitive, language and perceptual development* (pp. 557–608). Hoboken, NJ: Wiley.

Halford, G. S., & Andrews, G. (2011). Information processing models of cognitive development. In U. Goswami (Ed.), *The Wiley-Blackwell handbook of childhood cognitive development* (pp. 697–722). Oxford: Blackwell.

Halim, M. L. D. (2016). Princesses and superheroes: Social-cognitive influences on early gender rigidity. *Child Development Perspectives, 10*, 155–160.

Halim, M. L. D., Bryant, D., & Zucker, K. J. (2016). Early gender development in children and links with mental and physical health. In M. R. Korin (Ed.), *Health promotion for children and adolescents* (pp. 191–213). New York, NY: Springer.

Halim, M. L. D., & Ruble, D. (2010). Gender identity and stereotyping in early and middle childhood. In J. C. Chrisler & D. R. McCreary (Eds), *Handbook of gender research in psychology* (pp. 495–525). New York, NY: Springer.

Halim, M. L. D., Ruble, D. N., Tamis-LeMonda, C. S., Shrout, P. E., & Amodio, D. M. (2017). Gender attitudes in early childhood: Behavioral consequences and cognitive antecedents. *Child Development*, 88, 882–899.

Hall, I., Strydom, A., Richards, M., Hardy, R., Bernal, J., & Wadsworth, M. (2005). Social outcomes in adulthood of children with intellectual impairment: Evidence from a birth cohort. *Journal of Intellectual Disability Research*, 49, 171–182.

Halldorsdottir, T., & Ollendick, T. H. (2014). Comorbid ADHD: Implications for the treatment of anxiety disorders in children and adolescents. *Cognitive and Behavioral Practice*, 21, 310–322.

Halonen, A., Aunola, K., Ahonen, T., & Nurmi, J. E. (2006). The role of learning to read in the development of problem behaviour: A cross-lagged longitudinal study. *British Journal of Educational Psychology*, 76, 517–534.

Halpern, D. F., Benbow, C. P., Geary, D. C., Gur, R., Hyde, J. S., & Gernsbacher, M. A. (2007). The science of sex differences in science and mathematics. *Psychological Science in the Public Interest*, 8, 1–51.

Halpern, H. P., & Perry-Jenkins, M. (2016). Parents' gender ideology and gendered behavior as predictors of children's gender-role attitudes: A longitudinal exploration. *Sex roles*, 74, 527–542.

Hames, A. (2008). Siblings' understanding of learning disability: A longitudinal study. *Journal of Applied Research in Intellectual Disabilities*, 21, 491–501.

Hamilton, A. F. de C. (2009). Research review: Goals, intentions and mental states: Challenges for theories of autism. *Journal of Child Psychology and Psychiatry*, 50, 881–892.

Hamlin, J. K. (2013). Moral judgment and action in preverbal infants and toddlers: Evidence for an innate moral core. *Current Directions in Psychological Science*, 22, 186–193.

Hamlin, J. K. (2015). The case for social evaluation in preverbal infants: Gazing toward one's goal drives infants' preferences for Helpers over Hinderers in the hill paradigm. *Frontiers in Psychology*, 5, 1563.

Hamlin, J. K., & Wynn, K. (2011). Young infants prefer prosocial to antisocial others. *Cognitive Development*, 26, 30–39.

Hammack, P. L. (2008). Narrative and the cultural psychology of identity. *Personality and Social Psychology Review*, 12, 222–247.

Hammack, P. L. (2015). Theoretical foundations of identity. In K. C. McLean & M. Syed (Eds) *The Oxford handbook of identity development* (pp. 11–30). Oxford, UK: Oxford University Press.

Hammack, P. L., & Toolis, E. E. (2015). Putting the social into personal identity: The master narrative as root metaphor for psychological and developmental science. *Human Development*, 58, 350–364.

Hammond, S. I., & Carpendale, J. I. (2015). Helping children help: The relation between maternal scaffolding and children's early help. *Social Development*, 24, 367–383.

Handler, S. M., Fierson, W. M., & The Section on Ophthalmology and Council on Children with Disabilities, American Academy of Ophthalmology, American Association for Pediatric Ophthalmology and Strabismus (2011). Learning disabilities, dyslexia, and vision. *Pediatrics*, 127, e818–e856.

Hanish, L. D., Eisenberg, N., Fabes, R. A., Spinrad, T. L., Ryan, P., & Schmidt, S. (2004). The expression and regulation of negative emotions: Risk factors for young children's peer victimization. *Development and Psychopathology*, 16, 335–353.

Hankin, B. L. (2012). Future directions in vulnerability to depression among youth: Integrating risk factors and processes across multiple levels of analysis. *Journal of Clinical Child and Adolescent Psychology*, 41, 695–718.

Hankin, B. L., & Abramson, L. Y. (2001). Development of sex differences in depression: An elaborated cognitive vulnerability–transactional stress theory. *Psychological Bulletin*, 127, 773–796.

Hankin, B. L., Gibb, B. E., Abela, J. R., & Flory, K. (2010). Selective attention to affective stimuli and clinical depression among youths: Role of anxiety and specificity of emotion. *Journal of Abnormal Psychology*, 119, 491–501.

Hankin, B. L., Young, J. F., Gallop, R., & Garber, J. (2018). Cognitive and interpersonal vulnerabilities to adolescent depression: Classification of risk profiles for a personalized prevention approach. *Journal of Abnormal Child Psychology*, doi.org/10.1007/s10802-018-0401-2.

Hannon, E. E., & Johnson, S. P. (2005). Infants use meter to categorize rhythms and melodies: Implications for musical structure learning. *Cognitive Psychology*, 50, 354–377.

Hannula, M. M., Lepola, J., & Lehtinen, E. (2010). Spontaneous focusing on numerosity as a domain-specific predictor of arithmetical skills. *Journal of Experimental Child Psychology*, 107, 394–406.

Hanscombe, K. B., Trzaskowski, M., Haworth, C. M., Davis, O. S., Dale, P. S., & Plomin, R. (2012). Socioeconomic status (SES) and children's intelligence (IQ): In a UK-representative sample SES moderates the environmental, not genetic, effect on IQ. *PLoS One*, 7 (2), e30320.

Hansegård, N. E. (1968). *Tvåspråklighet eller halvspråklighet?* Stockholm, Sweden: Aldas.

Happé, F. G. E. (1994). *Autism: An introduction to psychological theory*. London: University College London Press.

Happé, F. G. E. (1995). Understanding minds and metaphors: Insights from the study of figurative language in autism. *Metaphor and Symbolic Activity*, 10, 275–295.

Happé, F. G. E. (1996). Studying weak central coherence at low levels: Children with autism do not succumb to visual illusions. A research note. *Journal of Child Psychology and Psychiatry*, 37, 873–877.

Happé, F. G. E., & Conway, J. R. (2016). Recent progress in understanding skills and impairments in social cognition. *Current Opinion in Pediatrics*, 28, 736–742.

Happé, F. G. E., & Ronald, A. (2008). The "fractionable autism triad": A review of evidence from behavioural, genetic, cognitive and neural research. *Neuropsychology Review*, 18, 287–304.

Hardy, C. L., Bukowski, W. M., & Sippola, L. K. (2002). Stability and change in peer relationships during the transition to middle level school. *Journal of Early Adolescence*, 22, 117–142.

Hargreaves, D. J. (1986). *The developmental psychology of music*. Cambridge: Cambridge University Press.

Hari, R., & Kujala, M. (2009). Brain basis of human social interaction: From concepts to brain imaging. *Physiological Reviews*, 89, 453–479.

Harkness, S., & Super, C. M. (1985). The cultural context of gender segregation in children's peer groups. *Child Development*, 56, 219–224.

Harlow, H. F. (1959). Love in infant monkeys. *Scientific American*, 200, 68–74.

Harlow, H. F. (1963). The maternal affectional system. In B. M. Foss (Ed.), *Determinant of infant behaviour* (pp. 3–29). London: Methuen.

Harner, L. (1975). Yesterday and tomorrow: Development of early understanding of the terms. *Developmental Psychology*, 11, 864–865.

Harré, R. (1986). *The social construction of emotions*. Oxford: Blackwell.

Harris, B. (1979). Whatever happened to Little Albert? *American Psychologist*, 34, 151–160.

Harris, G. (1997). Development of taste perception and appetite regulation. In G. Bremner, A. Slater & G. Butterworth (Eds), *Infant development: Recent advances* (pp. 9–30). Hove, UK: Erlbaum.

Harris, J. C., & Greenspan, S. (2016). Definition and nature of intellectual disability. In N. N. Singh (Ed.), *Handbook of evidence-based practices in intellectual and developmental disabilities* (pp. 11–39). Cham, Switzerland: Springer.

Harris, M. (1992). *Language experience and early language development: From input to uptake*. London: Erlbaum.

Harris, P. L. (1992). From simulation to folk psychology: The case for development. *Mind and Language*, 7, 120–144.

Harris, P. L. (1994). Understanding pretense. In C. Lewis & P. Mitchell (Eds), *Children's early understanding of mind* (pp. 235–260). Hillsdale, NJ: Erlbaum.

Harris, P. L., Kavanaugh, R. D., & Dowson, L. (1997). The depiction of imaginary transformations: Early comprehension of a symbolic function. *Cognitive Development*, 12, 1–19.

Harris, P. L., & Núñez, M. (1996). Understanding of permission rules by preschool children. *Child Development*, 67, 1572–1591.

Harris, P. L., & Want, S. (2005). On learning what not to do: The emergence of selective imitation in tool use by young children. In S. Hurley & N. Chater (Eds) *Perspectives on imitation: From neuroscience to social science, Volume 2* (pp. 149–162). Cambridge, MA: MIT Press.

Harrison, L. J., & McLeod, S. (2010). Risk and protective factors associated with speech and language impairment in a nationally representative sample of 4-to-5-year-old children. *Journal of Speech, Language, and Hearing Research*, 53, 508–529.

Harrop, C., Green, J., Hudry, K., & PACT Consortium. (2017). Play complexity and toy engagement in preschoolers with autism spectrum disorder: Do girls and boys differ? *Autism*, 21, 37–50.

Hart, B., & Risley, T. R. (1992). American parenting of language learning children: Persisting differences in family–child interactions observed in natural home environments. *Developmental Psychology*, 28, 1096–1105.

Harter, S. (1987). The determinants and mediation role of global self-worth in children. In N. Eisenberg (Ed.), *Contemporary issues in developmental psychology* (pp. 219–242). New York, NY: Wiley.

Harter, S. (2006). The self. In W. Damon, R. M. Lerner & N. Eisenberg (Eds), *Handbook of child psychology, Volume 3: Social, emotional, and personality development* (pp. 505–570). New York, NY: Wiley.

Hartshorn, K. (2003). Reinstatement maintains a memory in human infants for 1(1/2) years. *Developmental Psychobiology*, 42, 269–282.

Hartup, W. W. (1992). Friendships and their developmental significance. In H. McGurk (Ed.), *Childhood social development: Contemporary perspectives* (pp. 175–205). Hillsdale, NJ: Erlbaum.

Hartup, W. W. (1999). Peer experience and its developmental significance. M. Bennett (Ed.), *Developmental psychology: Achievements and prospects* (pp. 106–125). London: Psychology Press.

Hartup, W. W., & Stevens, N. (1997). Friendship and adaptation in the life course. *Psychological Bulletin*, 121, 355–370.

Haselager, G. J. T., Hartup, W. W., van Lieshout, C. F. M., & Riksen-Walraven, M. A. (1998). Similarities between friends and nonfriends in middle childhood. *Child Development*, 69, 1198–1208.

Hassold, T., & Sherman, S. (2000). Down syndrome: Genetic recombination and the origin of the extra chromosome 21. *Clinical Genetics*, 57, 95–100.

Hastings, E. C., Karas, T. L., Winsler, A., Way, E., Madigan, A., & Tyler, S. (2009). Young children's video/computer game use: Relations with school performance and behavior. *Issues in Mental Health Nursing*, 30, 638–649.

Hatano, N., & Takahashi, J. (2005). The development of societal cognition: A commentary. In M. Barrett & E. Buchanan-Barrow (Eds), *Children's understanding of society* (pp. 287–304). Hove, UK: Psychology Press.

Haugh, S. S., Hoffman, C. D., & Cowan, G. (1980). The eye of the very young beholder: Sex typing of infants by young children. *Child Development*, 51, 598–600.

Haughton, C., Aiken, M., & Cheevers, C. (2015). Cyber Babies: The impact of emerging technology on the developing infant. *Psychology Research, 5*, 504–518.

Hauser, M. D. (2006). *Moral minds: How nature designed our universal sense of right and wrong*. New York, NY: Ecco Press.

Hay, D. F. (2009). The roots and branches of human altruism. *British Journal of Psychology, 100*, 473–479.

Hay, D. F. (2014). Social cognition: Commentary: Do theory of mind deficits lead to psychopathology or is it the other way around? *Journal of Personality Disorders, 28*, 96–100.

Hay, D. F., Caplan, M., & Nasch, A. (2009). The beginnings of peer relations. In K. H. Rubin, W. M. Bulowski & B. Laursen (Eds), *The handbook of peer interactions, relationship and group* (pp. 121–142). New York, NY: Guilford Press.

Hayes, B. K., Heit, E., & Swendsen, H. (2010). Inductive reasoning. *Wiley Interdisciplinary Reviews: Cognitive Science, 1*, 278–292.

Hayne, H. (1990). The effect of multiple reminders on long term retention in human infants. *Developmental Psychobiology, 23*, 453–477.

Hayne, H. (2004). Infant memory development: Implications for childhood amnesia. *Developmental Review, 24*, 33–73.

Hayne, H., & Jack, F. (2011). Childhood amnesia. *Wiley Interdisciplinary Reviews: Cognitive Science, 2*, 136–145.

Hayne, H., MacDonald, S., & Barr, R. (1997). Developmental changes in the specificity of memory over the second year of life. *Infant Behavior and Development, 20*, 237–249.

Hazan, C., & Shaver, P. R. (1994). Attachment as an organizational framework for research on close relationships. *Psychological Inquiry, 5*, 1–22.

Heard, E., & Martienssen, R. A. (2014). Transgenerational epigenetic inheritance: Myths and mechanisms. *Cell, 157*, 95–109.

Hearold, S. (1986). A synthesis of 1043 effects of television on prosocial behavior. In G. Comstock (Ed.), *Public communications and behavior, Volume 1* (pp. 1019–1026). New York, NY: Macmillan.

Hedegaard, M. (2005). Strategies for dealing with conflicts in value positions between home and school: Influences on ethic minority students' development of motives and identity. *Culture and Psychology, 11*, 187–205.

Heilmann, A., Kelly, Y., & Watt, R. G. (2015). Equally Protected? A review of the evidence on the physical punishment of children. Report commissioned by the NSPCC Scotland, Children 1st, Barnardo's Scotland and the Children and Young People's Commissioner Scotland.

Heimann, M., Nelson, K. E., & Schaller, J. (1989). Neonatal imitation of tongue protrusion and mouth opening: Methodological aspects and evidence of early individual differences. *Scandinavian Journal of Psychology, 30*, 90–101.

Held, R., & Hein, A. (1963). Movement produced stimulation in the development of visually guided behavior.

Journal of Comparative and Physiological Psychology, 56, 872–876.

Helland, I. B., Smith, L., Saarem, K., Saugstad, O. D., & Drevon, C. A. (2003). Maternal supplementation with very-long-chain n-3 fatty acids during pregnancy and lactation augments children's IQ at 4 years of age. *Pediatrics, 111*, e39–e44.

Helland, W. A., Lundervold, A. J., Heimann, M., & Posserud, M. B. (2014). Stable associations between behavioral problems and language impairments across childhood – The importance of pragmatic language problems. *Research in Developmental Disabilities, 35*, 943–951.

Helwig, C. C., & Turiel, E. (2002). Civil liberties, autonomy, and democracy: Children's perspectives. *International Journal of Law and Psychiatry, 25*, 253–270.

Hemmer, I., Hemmer, M., Neidhardt, E., Obermaier, G., Uphues, R., & Wrenger, K. (2015). The influence of children's prior knowledge and previous experience on their spatial orientation skills in an urban environment. *Education 3–13, 43*, 184–196.

Henik, A., Rubinsten, O., & Ashkenazi, S. (2011). The "where" and "what" of developmental dyscalculia. *Clinical Neuropsychologist, 25*, 989–1008.

Henry L. A., & Gudjonsson, G. H. (2003). Eyewitness memory, suggestibility and repeated recall sessions in children with mild and moderate intellectual disabilities. *Law and Human Behavior, 27*, 481–505.

Hensch, T. K. (2004). Critical period regulation. *Annual Review of Neuroscience, 27*, 549–579.

Hepper, P. G. (1992). Fetal psychology: An embryonic science. In J. G. Nijhuis (Ed.), *Fetal behavior* (pp. 129–156). Oxford: Oxford Medical Publications.

Hepper, P. G. (2015). Behavior during the prenatal period: Adaptive for development and survival. *Child Development Perspectives, 9*, 38–43.

Hepper, P. G. (2016). Observing the fetus' behavior to assess health: The behavior of the human fetus in response to maternal alcohol consumption. In N. Reissland & B. S. Kisilevsky (Eds), *Fetal development* (pp. 317–330). Cham, Switzerland: Springer.

Herba, C., & Phillips, M. (2004). Development of facial expression recognition from childhood to adolescence: Behavioural and neurological perspectives. *Journal of Child Psychology and Psychiatry, 45*, 1185–1198.

Herbart, J. F. (1841). *Umriss pädagogischer Vorlesungen*. Göttingen, Germany: Göttingen Druck.

Herman, L. M. (2010). What laboratory research has told us about dolphin cognition. *International Journal of Comparative Psychology, 23*, 310–330.

Herman, R., Rowley, K., Mason, K., & Morgan, G. (2014). Deficits in narrative abilities in child British Sign Language users with specific language impairment. *International Journal of Language and Communication Disorders, 49*, 343–353.

Herpers, P. C., Rommelse, N. N., Bons, D. M., Buitelaar, J. K., & Scheepers, F. E. (2012). Callous–unemotional traits as a cross-disorders construct. *Social Psychiatry and Psychiatric Epidemiology, 47*, 2045–2064.

Herrmann, E., Call, J., Hernandez-Lloreda, M., Hare, B., & Tomasello, M. (2007). Humans have evolved specialized skills of social cognition: The cultural intelligence hypothesis. *Science, 317*, 1360–1366.

Herrnstein, R. J., & Murray, C. (1994). *The bell curve: The reshaping of American life by differences in intelligence.* New York, NY: Free Press.

Herskind, A., Greisen, G., & Nielsen, J. B. (2015). Early identification and intervention in cerebral palsy. *Developmental Medicine and Child Neurology, 57*, 29–36.

Hertenstein, M. J., & Campos, J. J. (2004). The retention effects of an adult's emotional displays on infant behavior. *Child Development, 75*, 595–613.

Herzhoff, K., Smack, A. J., Reardon, K. W., Martel, M. M., & Tackett, J. L. (2017). Child personality accounts for oppositional defiant disorder comorbidity patterns. *Journal of Abnormal Child Psychology, 45*, 327–335.

Hess, E. H. (1972). "Imprinting" in a natural laboratory. *Scientific American, 227*, 24–31.

Hess, R. D., Kashiwagi, K., Azuma, K., Price, G. G., & Dickson, W. P. (1980). Maternal expectations for mastery of developmental tasks in Japan and the United States. *International Journal of Psychology, 15*, 259–271.

Hestenes, L. L., & Carroll, D. E. (2000). The play interactions of young children with and without disabilities: Individual and environmental influences. *Early Childhood Research Quarterly, 15*, 229–246.

Hetherington, E. M. (2003). Social support and the adjustment of children in divorced and remarried families. *Childhood, 10*, 217–236.

Hetland, L. (2000). Listening to music enhances spatial–temporal reasoning: Evidence for the 'Mozart Effect'. *Journal of Aesthetic Education, 34*, 105–48.

Hetrick, S. E., Cox, G. R., & Merry, S. N. (2015). Where to go from here? An exploratory meta-analysis of the most promising approaches to depression prevention programs for children and adolescents. *International Journal of Environmental Research and Public Health, 12*, 4758–4795.

Hewlett, B. S. (1991). *Intimate fathers.* Ann Arbor, MI: University of Michigan Press.

Hewlett, B. S. (Ed.) (1992). *Father-child relations: Cultural and biosocial contexts.* New York, NY: Aldine de Gruyter.

Hewlett, B. S. (2000). Culture, history, and sex. *Marriage and Family Review, 29*, 59–73,

Heyman, G. D., Phillips, A. T., & Gelman, S. A. (2003). Children's reasoning about physics within and across ontological kinds. *Cognition, 89*, 43–61.

Hiatt, S. W., Campos, J. J., & Emde, R. N. (1979). Facial patterning and infant emotional expression: Happiness, surprise, and fear. *Child Development, 50*, 1020–1035.

Hibel, J., Farkas, G., & Morgan, P. L. (2010). Who is placed into special education? *Sociology of Education, 83*, 312–332.

Hickok, G. (2013). Do mirror neurons subserve action understanding? *Neuroscience Letters, 540*, 56–58.

Higgins, E., & O'Sullivan, S. (2015). "What works": Systematic review of the "FRIENDS for Life" programme as a universal school-based intervention programme for the prevention of child and youth anxiety. *Educational Psychology in Practice, 31*, 424–438.

Hilgetag, C. C., & Barbas, H. (2009). Sculpting the brain. *Scientific American, 300*, 66–71.

Hill, P. L., & Edmonds, G. W. (2017). Personality in adolescence. In J. Specht (Ed.), *Personality accross the life span* (pp. 25–38). London: Elsevier.

Hilliard, L. J., & Liben, L. S. (2010). Differing levels of gender salience in preschool classrooms: Effects on children's gender attitudes and intergroup bias. *Child Development, 81*, 1787–1798.

Himmeltvei, H., Oppenheim, A., & Vince, P. (1958). *Television and the child.* London: Oxford University Press.

Hinde, R. A. (1974). *Biological bases of human social behavior.* New York, NY: McGraw-Hill.

Hinde, R. A. (1988). Continuities and discontinuities: Conceptual issues and methodological considerations. In M. Rutter (Ed.), *Studies of psychosocial risk: The power of longitudinal data* (pp. 367–383). Cambridge: Cambridge University Press.

Hinde, R. A. (1989). Temperament as an intervening variable. In G. A. Kohnstamm, J. E. Bates & M. K. Rothbarth (Eds), *Temperament in childhood* (pp. 27–33). Chichester, UK: John Wiley.

Hinde, R. A. (1992). Human social development: An ethological/relationship perspective. In H. McGurk (Ed.), *Childhood social development: Contemporary perspectives* (pp. 13–29). Hove, UK: Lawrence Erlbaum.

Hinde, R. A. (2005). Ethology and attachment theory. In K. Grossman, E. Waters & K. Grossman (Eds), *Attachment from infancy to adulthood: The major longitudinal studies* (pp. 1–12). New York; NY: Guilford Press.

Hinde, R. A., Titmus, G., Easton, D., & Tamplin, A. (1985). Incidence of "friendship" and behavior toward strong associates versus nonassociates in preschoolers. *Child Development, 56*, 234–245.

Hindle, D., & Smith, M. V. (Eds) (1999). *Personality development: A psychoanalytic perspective.* London: Routledge.

Hines, M. (2015). Gendered development. In R. M. Lerner, M. E. Lamb & C. G. Coll (Eds), *Handbook of child psychology and developmental science, Seventh edition, Volume 3: Social and emotional development* (pp. 842–887). Hoboken, NJ: Wiley.

Hines, M., Golombok, S., Rust, J., Johnston, K. J., Golding, J., & Parents and Children Study Team. (2002). Testosterone during pregnancy and gender role behavior of preschool children: A longitudinal, population study. *Child Development, 73*, 1678–1687.

Hines, M., Pasterski, V., Spencer, D., Neufeld, S., Patalay, P., Hindmarsh, P. C., Hughes, I. A., & Acerini, C. L. (2016). Prenatal androgen exposure alters girls' responses to information indicating gender-appropriate behaviour. *Philosophical Transactions of the Royal Society B: Biological Sciences, 371* (1688), 20150125.

Hinshaw, S. P. (2018). Attention deficit hyperactivity disorder (ADHD): Controversy, developmental mechanisms, and multiple levels of analysis. *Annual Review of Clinical Psychology*, 14, 291–316.

Hinshaw, S. P., & Scheffler, R. M. (2014). *The ADHD explosion: Myths, medication, money, and today's push for performance*. Oxford: Oxford University Press

Hirsh-Pasek, K., Zosh, J. M., Golinkoff, R. M., Gray, J. H., Robb, M. B., & Kaufman, J. (2015). Putting education in "educational" apps: Lessons from the science of learning. *Psychological Science in the Public Interest*, 16, 3–34.

Hirshberg, L. M., & Svejda, M. (1990a). When infants look to their parents: I. Infants' social referencing of mothers compared to fathers. *Child Development*, 61, 1175–1186.

Hirshberg, L. M., & Svejda, M. (1990b). When infants look to their parents: II. Twelve month olds' response to conflicting parental emotional signals. *Child Development*, 61, 1187–1191.

Hobson, P. R., & Bishop, M. (2003). The pathogenesis of autism: Insights from congenital blindness. *Philosophical Transactions of the Royal Society B: Biological Sciences*, 358 (1430), 335–344.

Hochberg, J., & Brooks, V. (1962). Pictorial recogniton as an unlearned ability: A study of one child's performance. *American Journal of Psychology*, 75, 624–628.

Hodapp, R. M. (1997). Direct and indirect behavioral effects of different genetic disorders of mental retardation. *American Journal on Mental Retardation*, 102, 67–79.

Hodge, S., & Eccles, F. (2013). *Loneliness, social isolation and sight loss*. London: Thomas Pocklington Trust.

Hoff, E. (2006). How social contexts support and shape language development. *Developmental Review*, 26, 55–88.

Hoff, E. (2013). Interpreting the early language trajectories of children from low-SES and language minority homes: Implications for closing achievement gaps. *Developmental psychology*, 49, 4–14.

Hoff, E., Core, C., Place, S., Rumiche, R., Señor, M., & Parra, M. (2012). Dual language exposure and early bilingual development. *Journal of Child Language*, 39, 1–27.

Hoff-Ginsberg, E. (1990). Maternal speech and the child's development of syntax: A further look. *Journal of Child Language*, 17, 85–99.

Hoffman, M. L. (1987). The contribution of empathy to justice and moral judgment. In N. Eisenberg & J. Strayer (Eds), *Empathy and its development* (pp. 47–80). Cambridge: Cambridge University Press.

Hoffman, M. L. (2000). *Empathy and moral development*. New York, NY: Cambridge University Press.

Hogan, A. E., & Quay, H. C. (2014). Bringing a developmental perspective to early childhood and family interventionists: Where to begin. *Advances in Child Development and Behavior*, 46, 245–279.

Hoiting, N. (2006). Growing attention: From getting attention to signing variation sets. Presented at the 8th Oslo Workshop on early Attention, Interaction and Communication, University of Oslo, October 24th, 2006.

Hollands, K., van Kraayenoord, C. E., & McMahon, S. (2005). Support to adolescents experiencing language difficulties: A survey of speech-language pathologists. *International Journal of Speech-Language Pathology*, 7, 113–129.

Holle, B. (1981). *Læse/skrive parat?* Copenhagen, DK: Munksgaard.

Hollich, G. J., Hirsh-Pasek, K., Golinkoff, R. M., Brand, R. J., Brown, E., Chung, H. L., Hennon, E., Rocroi, C., & Bloom, L. (2000). Breaking the language barrier: An emergentist coalition model for the origins of word learning. *Monographs of the Society for Research in Child Development*, 65, 3.

Holm, A. M., & Thau, L. (1984). *Børns billedverden*. Copenhagen, DK: Børn & Unge.

Holmes, C. J., Kim-Spoon, J., & Deater-Deckard, K. (2016). Linking executive function and peer problems from early childhood through middle adolescence. *Journal of Abnormal Child Psychology*, 44, 31–42.

Holmes, J., & Gathercole, S. E. (2014). Taking working memory training from the laboratory into schools. *Educational Psychology*, 34, 440–450.

Holmes, W., & Dowker, A. (2013). Catch up numeracy: A targeted intervention for children who are low-attaining in mathematics. *Research in Mathematics Education*, 15, 249–265.

Holodynski, M., & Friedlmeier, W. (2006). *Development of emotions and emotion regulation*. New York, NY: Springer.

Holyoak, K. J. (2005). Analogy. In K. J. Holyoak & R. G. Robinson (Eds), *The Cambridge handbook of thinking and reasoning* (pp. 315–340). Cambridge: Cambridge University Press.

Hoogenhout, M., & Malcolm-Smith, S. (2014). Theory of mind in autism spectrum disorder: Does DSM classification predict development? *Research in Autism Spectrum Disorders*, 8, 597–607.

Hoogenhout, M., & Malcolm-Smith, S. (2017). Theory of mind predicts severity level in autism. *Autism*, 21, 242–252.

Hoon, A. H., & Tolley, F. (2012). Cerebral palsy. In G. Lotrecchiano, N. Roizen & M. Batshaw (Eds), *Children with disabilities, Seventh edition* (pp. 423–450). Baltimore, MD: Brookes.

Hopkins, B., Beek, P. J., & Kalverboer, A. F. (1993). Theoretical issues in the longitudinal study of motor development. In A. F. Kalverboer, B. Hopkins & R. Geuze (Eds), *Motor development in early and later childhood: Longitudinal approaches* (pp. 343–371). Cambridge: Cambridge University Press.

Hopkins, B., & Butterworth, G. (1997). Dynamical systems approaches to development of action. In G. Bremner, A. Slater & G. Butterworth (Eds), *Infant development: Recent advances* (pp. 75–100). Hove, UK: Lawrence Erlbaum.

Horowitz, J. L., & Garber, J. (2006). The prevention of depressive symptoms in children and adolescents: A meta-analytic review. *Journal of Consulting and Clinical Psychology*, 74, 401–415.

Horowitz, P. D. (1987). *Exploring developmental theories.* London: Erlbaum.

Horwitz, B., & Horovitz, S. G. (2012). Introduction to research topic–brain connectivity analysis: Investigating brain disorders. Part 1: The review articles. *Frontiers in Systems Neuroscience, 6,* 3.

House, B. R. (2017). Diverse ontogenies of reciprocal and prosocial behavior: Cooperative development in Fiji and the United States. *Developmental Science, 20* (6), e12466.

House, B. R. (2018). How do social norms influence prosocial development? *Current Opinion in Psychology, 20,* 87–91.

House, B. R., Silk, J. B., Henrich, J., Barrett, H. C., Scelza, B. A., Boyette, A. H., Hewlett, B. S., McElreath, R., & Laurence, S. (2013). Ontogeny of prosocial behavior across diverse societies. *Proceedings of the National Academy of Sciences, 110,* 14586–14591.

Houshyar, S., Gold, A., & deVries, M. (2013). Resiliency in maltreated children. In S. Goldstein, & R. B. Brooks (Eds), *Handbook of resilience in children* (pp. 161–179). New York, NY: Springer.

Hovik, K. T., Saunes, B. K., Aarlien, A. K., & Egeland, J. (2013). RCT of working memory training in ADHD: Long-term near-transfer effects. *PLoS One, 8,* e80561.

Howe, C. (2009). Collaborative group work in middle childhood. *Human Development, 52,* 215–239.

Howe, C. (2010). *Peer groups and children's development.* Oxford: Wiley-Blackwell

Howe, M. J. A., Davidson, J. W., & Sloboda, J. A. (1998). Innate talents: Reality or myth? *Behavioral and Brain Sciences, 21,* 399–407.

Howe, M. L. (2015). Memory development. In R. M. Lerner, L. S. Liben & U. Müller (Eds), *Handbook of child psychology and developmental science, Seventh edition, Volume 2: Cognitive processes* (pp. 203–249). Hoboken, NJ: Wiley.

Howe, N., Aquan-Assee, J., & Bukowski, W. M. (1995). Self disclosure and the sibling relationship: What did Romulus tell Remus? In K. J. Rotenberg (Ed.), *Disclosure processes in children and adolescents* (pp. 78–99). Cambridge: Cambridge University Press.

Howe, N., Della Porta, S., Recchia, H., & Ross, H. (2016). "Because if you don't put the top on, it will spill": A longitudinal study of sibling teaching in early childhood. *Developmental Psychology, 52,* 1832.

Howe, N., & Recchia, H. (2014). Sibling relations and their impact on children's development. In M. Boivin (Ed.), *Encyclopedia of early childhood development, December 2014 edition* (pp. 17–24).

Howe, N., Rosciszewska, J., & Persram, R. J. (2017). "I'm an ogre so I'm very hungry!" "I'm assistant ogre": The social function of sibling imitation in early childhood. *Infant and Child Development, 27,* e2040.

Howell, K. H., Shapiro, D. N., Layne, C. M., & Kaplow, J. B. (2015) Individual and psychosocial mechanisms of adaptive functioning in parentally bereaved children. *Death Studies, 39,* 296–306.

Howes, C. (1996). The earliest friendships. In W. M. Bukowski, A. F. Newcomb & W. W. Hartup (Eds), *The company they keep: Friendship in childhood and adolescence* (pp. 66–86). Cambridge: Cambridge University Press.

Howes, C. (2009). Friendship in early childhood. In K. H. Rubin, W. M. Bulowski & B. Laursen (Eds), *The handbook of peer interactions, relationship and group* (pp. 180–194). New York, NY: Guilford Press.

Howes, C., & Matheson, C. C. (1992). Sequences in the development of competent play with peers: Social and social pretend play. *Developmental Psychology, 28,* 961–974.

Huang, H. Y. (2016). Examining the beneficial effects of individual's self-disclosure on the social network site. *Computers in Human Behavior, 57,* 122–132.

Huber-Okrainec, J., Blaser, S. E., & Dennis, M. (2005). Idiom comprehension deficits in relation to corpus callosum agenesis and hypoplasia in children with spina bifida meningomyelocele. *Brain and Language, 93,* 349–368.

Hudson, J. A. (1993). Reminiscing with mothers and others: Autobiographical memory in young two-year-olds. *Journal of Narrative and Life History, 3,* 1–32.

Hudson, J. A., & Mayhew, E. M. Y (2009). The development of memory for recurring events. In M. L. Courage & N. Cowan (Eds), *The development of memory in infancy and childhood, Second edition* (pp. 69–91). Hove, UK: Psychology Press.

Hudson, J. A., & Sheffield, E. (1995). Extending young children's event memory: Effects of reminder on 16–24-month-olds long-term recall. Paper presented at American Psychological Society, New York, USA.

Hudson, J. L., Doyle, A. M., & Gar, N. (2009). Child and maternal influence on parenting behavior in clinically anxious children, *Journal of Clinical Child and Adolescent Psychology, 38,* 256–262.

Hudson, J. L., Dodd, H. F., Lyneham, H. J., & Bovopoulous, N. (2011). Temperament and family environment in the development of anxiety disorder: Two-year followup. *Journal of the American Academy of Child and Adolescent Psychiatry, 50,* 1255–1264.

Hudziak, J. J., & Faraone, S. V. (2010). The new genetics in child psychiatry. *Journal of the American Academy of Child and Adolescent Psychiatry, 49,* 729–735.

Huesmann, L. R. (2007). The impact of electronic media violence: Scientific theory and research. *Journal of Adolescent Health, 41,* S6–S13.

Huesmann, L. R. (2010). Nailing the coffin shut on doubts that violent video games stimulate aggression: Comment on Anderson et al. (2010). *Psychological Bulletin, 136,* 179–181.

Huesmann, L. R., Moise T. J., Podolski, C. L., & Eron, L. D. (2003). Longitudinal relations between children's exposure to TV violence and their aggressive and violent behavior in young adulthood: 1977–1992. *Developmental Psychology, 39,* 201–221.

Hughes, C., & Devine, R. T. (2015). Individual differences in theory of mind from preschool to adolescence: Achievements and directions. *Child Development Perspectives, 9,* 149–153.

Hughes, C., & Dunn, J. (1998). Understanding mind and emotion: Longitudinal associations with mental-state talk between young friends. *Developmental Psychology, 34*, 1026–1034.

Hughes, C., & Leekam, S. (2004). What are the links between theory of mind and social relations? Review, reflections and new directions for studies of typical and atypical development. *Social Development, 13*, 590–619.

Hughes, C., Devine, R. T., & Wang, Z. (2017). Does parental mind-mindedness account for cross-cultural differences in preschoolers' Theory of Mind? *Child Development*, doi:10.1111/cdev.12746.

Hughes, J. R. (2009). Update on autism: A review of 1300 reports published in 2008. *Epilepsy and Behavior, 16*, 569–589.

Hughes-Scholes, C. H., & Gavidia-Payne, S. (2016). Development of a routines-based early childhood intervention model. *Educar em Revista, 59*, 141–154.

Humphreys, A. P., & Smith, P. K. (1987). Rough and tumble, friendship, and dominance in schoolchildren: Evidence for continuity and change with age. *Child Development, 58*, 201–212.

Hundeide, K. (1977). *Piaget i kritisk lys* (Critical light on Piaget). Oslo, Norway: Cappelen.

Hunt, R. H., & Thomas, K. M. (2008). Magnetic resonance imaging methods in developmental science: A primer. *Development and Psychopathology, 20*, 1029–1051.

Hunter, S., Hurley, R. A., & Taber, K. H. (2013). A look inside the mirror neuron system. *The Journal of Neuropsychiatry and Clinical Neurosciences, 25*, 170–175.

Hunter, S. B., Barber, B. K., Olsen, J. A., McNeely, C. A., & Bose, K. (2011). Adolescents' self-disclosure to parents across cultures: Who discloses and why. *Journal of Adolescent Research, 26*, 447–478.

Huston, A. C., & Bentley, A. C. (2010). Human development in societal context. *Annual Review of Psychology, 61*, 411–437.

Huston, A. C., & Wright, J. C. (1998). Mass media and children's development. In W. Damon, I. E. Siegel & K. A. Renninger (Eds), *Handbook of child psychology, Fifth edition, Volume 4: Child psychology in practice* (pp. 999–1058). New York, NY: Wiley.

Hutt, S. J., Hutt, C., Lenard, H. G., von Bernuth, H., & Muntjewerff, W. J. (1968). Auditory responsivity in the human neonate. *Nature, 218*, 888–890.

Huttenlocher, P. R. (1990). Morphometric study of human cerebral cortex development. *Neuropsychologia, 28*, 517–527.

Huurre, T., Junkkari, H., & Aro, H. (2006). Long–term psychosocial effects of parental divorce. *European Archives of Psychiatry and Clinical Neuroscience, 256*, 256–263.

Hyde, J. S., Fennema, E., & Lamon, S. J. (1990). Gender differences in mathematics performance: A meta-analysis. *Psychological Bulletin, 107*, 139–155.

Hyde, L. W. (2015). Developmental psychopathology in an era of molecular genetics and neuroimaging: A develop-mental neurogenetics approach. *Development and Psychopathology, 27*, 587–613.

Hyde, L. W., Waller, R., Trentacosta, C. J., Shaw, D. S., Neiderhiser, J. M., Ganiban, J. M., Reiss, D., & Leve, L. D. (2016). Heritable and nonheritable pathways to early callous-unemotional behaviors. *American Journal of Psychiatry, 173*, 903–910.

Hymel, S., Bowker, A., & Woody, E. (1993). Aggressive versus withdrawn unpopular children: Variations in peer and self-perceptions in multiple domains. *Child Development, 64*, 879–896.

Hymel, S., Rubin, K. H., Rowden, L., & Le Mare, L. (1990). Children's peer relation ships: Longitudinal prediction of internalizing and externalizing problems from middle to late childhood. *Child Development, 61*, 2004–2021.

Iacoboni, M. (2005). Neural mechanisms of imitation. *Current Opinion in Neurobiology, 15*, 632–637.

Ibáñez, M. I., Viruela, A. M., Mezquita, L., Moya, J., Villa, H., Camacho, L., & Ortet, G. (2016). An investigation of five types of personality trait continuity: A two-wave longitudinal study of Spanish adolescents from age 12 to age 15. *Frontiers in Psychology, 7*, 512.

Imamoglu, E. O. (1975). Children's awareness and usage of intention cues. *Child Development, 46*, 39–45.

Im-Bolter, N., & Cohen, N. J. (2007). Language impairment and psychiatric comorbidities. *Pediatric Clinics of North America, 54*, 525–542.

Immordino-Yang, M. H. (2007). Compensation after losing half of the brain. In A. Nava (Ed.), *Critical issues in brain science and pedagogy* (pp. 45–54) San Francisco, CA: McGraw Hill.

Ingalhalikar, M., Smith, A., Parker, D., Satterthwaite, T. D., Elliott, M. A., Ruparel, K., Hakonarson, H., Gur, R. E., Gur, R. C., & Verma, R. (2014). Sex differences in the structural connectome of the human brain. *Proceedings of the National Academy of Sciences, 111*, 823–828.

Ingesson, S. G. (2007). Growing up with dyslexia: Interviews with teenagers and young adults. *School Psychology International, 28*, 574–591.

Inhelder, B., & Piaget, J. (1964). *The early growth of logic in the child: Classification and seriation.* London: Routledge and Kegan Paul.

Ionescu, T. (2012). Exploring the nature of cognitive flexibility. *New Ideas in Psychology, 30*, 190–200.

Irner, T. B. (2012). Substance exposure in utero and developmental consequences in adolescence: A systematic review, *Child Neuropsychology, 18*, 521–549,

Isbell, E., Fukuda, K., Neville, H. J., & Vogel, E. K. (2015). Visual working memory continues to develop through adolescence. *Frontiers in Psychology, 6*, 696.

Ishikawa, F., & Hay, D. F. (2006). Triadic interaction among newly acquainted 2-year-old. *Social Development, 15*, 145–168.

Iverson, J. M. (2010). Developing language in a developing body: The relationship between motor development and language development. *Journal of Child Language, 37*, 229–261.

Izard, C. E. (1991). *The psychology of emotions.* New York, NY: Plenum Press.

Izard, C. E. (2007). Basic emotions, natural kinds, emotion schemas, and a new paradigm. *Perspectives on Psychological Science, 2,* 260–280.

Izard, C. E., Fine, S. E., Mostow, A. J., Trentacosta, C. J., & Campbell, J. (2002). Emotion processes in normal and abnormal development and preventive intervention. *Development and Psychopathology, 14,* 761–787.

Izard, C. E., Hembree, E. A., & Huebner, R. R. (1987). Infants' emotion expressions to acute pain: Developmental change and stability of individual differences. *Developmental Psychology, 23,* 105–113.

Jackendoff, R. (2002). *Foundations of language.* Oxford: Oxford University Press.

Jackendoff, R. (2006). *Language, culture, consciousness: Essays on mental structure.* Cambridge, MA: MIT Press.

Jackson, J. F. (1993). Human behavioural genetics, Scarr's theory, and her views on intervention: A critical review and commentary on their implications for African American Children. *Child Development, 64,* 1318–1332.

Jacob, P. (2009). The tuning-fork model of human social cognition: A critique. *Consciousness and Cognition, 18,* 229–243.

Jacob, P. (2013). How from action-mirroring to intention-ascription? *Consciousness and Cognition, 22,* 1132–1141.

Jaffee, S. R., Moffitt, T. E., Caspi, A., & Taylor, A. (2003). Life with (or without) father: The benefits of living with two biological parents depend on the father's antisocial behavior. *Child Development, 74,* 109–126.

Jago, R., Zahra, J., Edwards, M. J., Kesten, J. M., Solomon-Moore, E., Thompson, J. L., & Sebire, S. J. (2016). Managing the screen-viewing behaviours of children aged 5–6 years: A qualitative analysis of parental strategies. *BMJ Open, 6,* e010355.

Jahoda, G. (1984). The development of thinking about socio-economic systems. In H. Tajfel (Ed.), *The social dimension, Volume 1* (pp. 69–88). Cambridge: Cambridge University Press.

James, D. K. (2010). Fetal learning: A critical review. *Infant and Child Development, 19,* 45–54.

James, W. (1890). *The principles of psychology.* New York, NY: Holt.

Janssen, C. G. C., Schuengel, C., & Stolk, J. (2002). Understanding challenging behaviour in people with severe and profound intellectual disability: A stress-attachment model. *Journal of Intellectual Disability Research, 46,* 445–453.

Jarrold, C., Boucher, J., & Smith, P. K. (1996). Generativity deficits in pretend play in autism. *British Journal of Developmental Psychology, 14,* 275–300.

Jarvis, P., Newman, S., & Swiniarski, L. (2014). On "becoming social": The importance of collaborative free play in childhood. *International Journal of Play, 3,* 53–68.

Jeltova, I., Birney, D., Fredine, N., Jarvin, L., Sternberg, R. J., & Grigorenko, E. L. (2007). Dynamic assessment as a process-oriented assessment in educational settings. *Advances in Speech Language Pathology, 9,* 273–285.

Jennings, W. G., & Reingle, J. M. (2012). On the number and shape of developmental/life-course violence, aggression, and delinquency trajectories: A state-of-the-art review. *Journal of Criminal Justice, 40,* 472–489.

Jensen, A. R. (1985). The nature of the Black–White difference on various psychometric tests: Spearman's hypothesis. *Behavioral and Brain Sciences, 8,* 193–219.

Jensen, L. A. (2012). Bridging universal and cultural perspectives: A vision for developmental psychology in a global world. *Child Development Perspectives, 6,* 98–104.

Jenson, W. R., Harward, S., & Bowen, J. M. (2011). Externalizing disorders in children and adolescents: Behavioral excess and behavioral deficits. In M. A. Bray & T. J. Kehle (Eds), *The Oxford handbook of school psychology* (pp. 379–410). New York, NY: Oxford University Press.

Jersild, A. T., & Bienstock, S. F. (1935). *Development of rhythm in young children. Child Development Monographs, number 22.* New York, NY: Teachers College, Columbia University.

Jiang, Y., Guo, X., Zhang, J., Gao, J., Wang, X., Situ, W., Yi, J., Zhang, X., Zhu, X., Yao, S., & Huang, B. (2015). Abnormalities of cortical structures in adolescent-onset conduct disorder. *Psychological Medicine, 45,* 3467–3479.

Jimenez-Gomez, A., & Standridge, S. (2014). A refined approach to evaluating global developmental delay for the international medical community. *Pediatric Neurology, 51,* 198–206.

Jin, M. K., Jacobvitz, D., Hazen, N., & Jung, S. H. (2012). Maternal sensitivity and infant attachment security in Korea: Cross-cultural validation of the Strange Situation. *Attachment and Human Development, 14,* 33–44.

Johansson, A., & Götestam, K. G. (2004). Internet addiction: Characteristics of a questionnaire and prevalence in Norwegian youth (12–18 years). *Scandinavian Journal of Psychology, 45,* 223–229.

Johansson, A., Grant, J. E., Kim, S. W., Odlaug, B. L., & Götestam, K. G. (2009). Risk factors for problematic gambling: A critical literature review. *Journal of Gambling Studies, 25,* 67–92.

John, A., Halliburton, A., & Humphrey, J. (2013). Child–mother and child–father play interaction patterns with preschoolers. *Early Child Development and Care, 183,* 483–497.

Johnson, D. W., & Johnson, R. T. (2009). An educational psychology success story: Social interdependence theory and cooperative learning. *Educational Researcher, 38,* 365–379.

Johnson, J. E., Ershler, J., & Lawton, J. T. (1982). Intellective correlates of preschoolers' spontaneous play. *The Journal of General Psychology, 106,* 115–122.

Johnson, M. H. (1998). The neural basis of cognitive development. In W. Damon, D. Kuhn & R. S. Siegler (Eds), *Handbook of child psychology, Fifth edition, Volume 2: Cognition, perception and language* (pp. 1–49). New York, NY: Wiley.

Johnson, M. H. (2011). Interactive specialization: A domain-general framework for human functional brain development? *Developmental Cognitive Neuroscience, 1,* 7–21.

Johnson, M. H., Dziurawiec, S., Ellis, H. D., & Morton, J. (1991). Newborns' preferential tracking of face-like stimuli and its subsequent decline. *Cognition, 40*, 1–19.

Johnson, M. H., Grossmann, T., & Cohen Kadosh, K. (2009). Mapping functional brain development: Building a social brain through interactive specialization. *Developmental Psychology, 45*, 151–159.

Johnson, M. H., Halit, H., Grice, S. J. & Karmiloff-Smith, A. (2002). Neuroimaging of typical and atypical development: A perspective from multiple levels of analysis. *Development and Psychopathology, 14*, 521–536.

Johnson, S. P. (2004). Development of perceptual completion in infancy. *Psychological Science, 15*, 769–775.

Johnson, S. P. (2005). Building knowledge from perception in infancy. In L. Gershkoff-Stowe & D. Rakison (Eds), *Building object categories in developmental time* (pp. 33–62). Mahwah, NJ: Erlbaum.

Johnson, S. P., & Hannon, E. E. (2015). Perceptual development. In L. S. Liben, U. Müller & R. M. Lerner (Eds), *Handbook of child psychology and developmental science, Seventh edition, Volume 2: Cognitive processes* (pp. 63–112). Hoboken, NJ: Wiley.

Johnson, W., Carothers, A., & Deary, I. J. (2008). Sex differences in variability in general intelligence: A new look at the old question. *Perspectives on Psychological Science, 3*, 518–531.

Johnson, W., Carothers, A., & Deary, I. J. (2009). A role for the X chromosome in sex differences in variability in general intelligence? *Perspectives on Psychological Science, 4*, 598–611.

Johnson-Laird, P. N. (1999). Deductive reasoning. *Annual Review of Psychology, 50*, 109–135.

Jones, C. M., Braithwaite, V. A., & Healy, S. D. (2003). The evolution of sex differences in spatial ability. *Behavioral Neuroscience, 117*, 403–411.

Jones, E. A., Carr, E. G., & Feeley, K. M. (2006). Multiple effects of joint attention intervention for children with autism. *Behavior Modification, 30*, 782–834.

Jones, S. S. (1996). Imitation or exploration? Young infants' matching of adults' oral gestures. *Child Development, 67*, 1952–1969.

Jones, S. S. (2006). Exploration or imitation? The effect of music on 4-week old infants' tongue protrusions. *Infant Behavior and Development, 29*, 126–130.

Jones, S. S. (2007). Imitation in infancy: The development of imitation. *Psychological Science, 18*, 593–599.

Jones, S. S. (2009). The development of imitation in infancy. *Philosophical Transactions of the Royal Society, B Biological Sciences, 364*, 2325–2335.

Jones, S. S., & Hong, H. W. (2005). How some infant smiles get made. *Infant Behavior and Development, 28*, 194–205.

Jongerden, L., & Bögels, S. M. (2015). Parenting, family functioning and anxiety-disordered children: Comparisons to controls, changes after family versus child CBT. *Journal of Child and Family Studies, 24*, 2046–2059.

Jorgensen, G. (2006). Kohlberg and Gilligan: Duet or duel? *Journal of Moral Education, 35*, 179–196.

Joseph, J. (2013). The use of the classical twin method in the social and behavioral sciences: The fallacy continues. *The Journal of Mind and Behavior, 34*, 1–39.

Joseph, R. (2000). Fetal brain behavior and cognitive development. *Developmental Review, 21*, 81–98.

Josephs, I. E., & Valsiner, J. (2007). Developmental science meets culture: Cultural developmental psychology in the making. *European Journal of Developmental Science, 1*, 47–64.

Joshi, R. M., Padakannaya, P., & Nishanimath, S. (2010), Dyslexia and hyperlexia in bilinguals. *Dyslexia, 16*, 99–118.

Julian, M. M. (2013). Age at adoption from institutional care as a window into the lasting effects of early experiences. *Clinical Child and Family Psychology Review, 16*, 101–145.

Junger-Tas, J. (2012). Delinquent behaviour in 30 countries. In J. Junger-Tas, I. H. Marshall, D. Enzmann, M. Killias, M. Steketee & B. Gruszczynska (Eds), *The many faces of youth crime* (pp. 69–93). New York, NY: Springer.

Kaare, B. H., Brandtzæg, P. B., Heim, J., & Endestad T. (2007). In the borderland between family orientation and peer culture: The use of communication technologies among Norwegian tweens. *New Media Society, 9*, 603–624.

Kagan, J. (1982). The construct of difficult temperament: A reply to Thomas, Chess, and Korn. *Merrill-Palmer Quarterly, 28*, 21–24.

Kagan, J. (1991). The theoretical utility of constructs of self. *Developmental Review, 11*, 244–250.

Kagan, J. (1992). Temperamental contributions to emotion and social behavior. In M. S. Clark (Ed.), *Review of personality and social psychology, Volume 14* (pp. 99–118). Thousand Oaks, CA: Sage.

Kagan, J. (1998a). *Three seductive ideas.* Cambridge, MA: Harvard University Press.

Kagan, J. (1998b). Is there a self in infancy? In M. D. Ferrari & R. J. Sternberg (Eds), *Self awareness: Its nature and development* (pp. 137–147). New York, NY: Guilford Press.

Kagan, J. (2007). *What is emotion?* New Haven, CT: Yale University Press.

Kagan, J. (2008a). In defense of qualitative changes in development. *Child Development, 79*, 1606–1624.

Kagan, J. (2008b). Using the proper vocabulary. *Developmental Psychobiology, 50*, 4–8.

Kagan, J. (2009). *The three cultures: Natural sciences, social sciences, and the humanities in the 21st century.* Cambridge: Cambridge University Press.

Kagan, J., & Fox, N. (2006). Biology, culture, and temperamental biases. In W. Damon, R. M. Lerner & N. Eisenberg (Eds), *Handbook of child psychology, Sixth edition, Volume 3: Social, emotional and personality development* (pp. 167–225). New York, NY: Wiley.

Kagan, J., Kearsley, R. B., & Zelazo, P. R. (1978). *Infancy: Its place in human development.* Cambridge, MA: Harvard University Press.

Kagan, J., & Snidman, N. C. (2004). *The long shadow of temperament.* Cambridge, MA: Belknap Press.

Kahneman, D. (2011). *Thinking, fast and slow*. New York, NY: Farrar, Straus and Giroux.

Kail, R. V. (2004). Cognitive development includes global and domain-specific processes. *Merrill-Palmer Quarterly, 50*, 445–455.

Kail, R. V., & Bisanz, J. (1992). The information-processing perspective on cognitive development in childhood and adolescence. In R. J. Sternberg & C. A. Berg (Eds), *Intellectual development* (pp. 229–260). Cambridge: Cambridge University Press.

Kail, R. V., & Miller, C. A. (2006) Developmental change in processing speed: Domain specificity and stability during childhood and adolescence. *Journal of Cognition and Development, 7*, 119–137.

Kaiser, A. P., & Roberts, M. Y. (2011). Advances in early communication and language intervention. *Journal of Early Intervention, 33*, 298–309.

Kaitz, M., Meschulach-Sarfaty, O., Auerbach, J., & Eidelman, A. (1988). A reexamination of newborns' ability to imitate facial expressions. *Developmental Psychology, 24*, 3–7.

Káldy, Z., & Kovács, I. (2003). Visual context integration is not fully developed in 4-year-old children. *Perception, 32*, 657–666.

Kalin, N. H. (1993). The neurobiology of fear. *Scientific American, 268*, 94–101.

Kalmijn, M. (2015). Father-child relations after divorce in four European countries: Patterns and determinants. *Comparative Population Studies, 40*, 251–276.

Kan, K. -J., Wicherts, J. M., Dolan, C. V., & van der Maas, H. L. J. (2013). On the nature and nurture of intelligence and specific cognitive abilities: The more heritable, the more culture dependent. *Psychological Science, 24*, 2420–2428.

Kana, R. K., Uddin, L. Q., Kenet, T., Chugani, D., & Müller, R. A. (2014). Brain connectivity in autism. *Frontiers in Human Neuroscience, 8*, 349.

Kanaya, T., & Ceci, S. J. (2011). The Flynn Effect in the WISC subtests among children tested for special education services. *Journal of Psychoeducational Assessment, 29*, 125–136.

Kanaya, T., & Ceci, S. J. (2012). The impact of the Flynn Effect on LD diagnoses in special education. *Journal of Learning Disabilities, 45*, 319–326.

Kang, C., & Drayna, D. (2011). Genetics of speech and language disorders. *Annual Review of Genomics and Human Genetics, 12*, 145–164.

Kanner, L. (1943). Autistic disturbances of affective contact. *Nervous Child, 12*, 17–50.

Kanz, K. M. (2016). Mediated and moderated effects of violent media consumption on youth violence. *European Journal of Criminology, 13*, 149–168.

Kappas, A. (2011). Emotion and regulation are one! *Emotion Review, 3*, 17–25.

Karayanidis, F., Kelly, M., Chapman, P., Mayes, A., & Johnston, P. (2009). Facial identity and facial expression matching in 5–12-year-old children and adults. *Infant and Child Development, 18*, 404–421.

Karevold, E., Røysamb, E., Ystrom, E., & Mathiesen, K. S. (2009). Predictors and pathways from infancy to symptoms of anxiety and depression in early adolescence. *Developmental Psychology, 45*, 1051–1060.

Karmiloff, K., & Karmiloff-Smith, A. (2001). *Pathways to language: From fetus to adolescent*. Cambridge, MA: Harvard University Press.

Karmiloff-Smith, A. (1998). Development itself is the key to understanding developmental disorders. *Trends in Cognitive Sciences, 2*, 389–398.

Karmiloff-Smith, A. (2005). Bates's emergentist theory and its relevance to understanding genotype/phenotype relations. In M. Tomasello & D. I. Slobin (Eds), *Beyond nature-nurture: Essays in honor of Elizabeth Bates*. (pp. 219–236). Mahwah, NJ: Erlbaum.

Karmiloff-Smith, A. (2007). Atypical epigenesis. *Developmental Science, 10*, 84–88.

Karmiloff-Smith, A. (2009). Nativism versus neuroconstructivism: Rethinking the study of developmental disorders. *Developmental Psychology, 45*, 56–63.

Karmiloff-Smith, A. (2010). A developmental perspective on modularity. In B. Glatzeder, V. Goel & A. Müller (Eds), *Towards a theory of thinking on thinking, Part 3* (pp. 179–187). Berlin: Springer.

Karmiloff-Smith, A. (2011). Static snapshots versus dynamic approaches to genes, brain, cognition and behaviour in neurodevelopmental disabilities. *International Review of Research in Developmental Disabilities, 40*, 1–16.

Karmiloff-Smith, A. (2015). An alternative to domain-general or domain-specific frameworks for theorizing about human evolution and ontogenesis. *AIMS neuroscience, 2*, 91–104.

Karns, C. M., Isbell, E., Giuliano, R. J., & Neville, H. J. (2015). Auditory attention in childhood and adolescence: An event-related potential study of spatial selective attention to one of two simultaneous stories. *Developmental Cognitive Neuroscience, 13*, 53–67.

Karpov, Y. V. (2005). *The neo-Vygotskian approach to child development*. Cambridge: Cambridge University Press.

Karpov, Y. V. (2014). *Vygotsky for educators*. Cambridge: Cambridge University Press.

Karu, M., & Tremblay, D. G. (2017). Fathers on parental leave: An analysis of rights and take-up in 29 countries. *Community, Work and Family, 21*, 344–362.

Kasari, C., Chang, Y. C., & Patterson, S. (2013). Pretending to play or playing to pretend: The case of autism. *American Journal of Play, 6*, 124–135.

Kashdan, T. B., & McKnight, P. E. (2010). The darker side of social anxiety: When aggressive impulsivity prevails over shy inhibition. *Current Directions in Psychological Science, 19*, 47–50.

Katz, L. F., Hessler, D. M., & Annest, A. (2007). Domestic violence, emotional competence, and child adjustment. *Social Development, 16*, 513–538.

Kaufmann, L., Mazzocco, M. M., Dowker, A., von Aster, M., Goebel, S. M., Grabner, R. H., Henik, A., Jordan, N. C., Karmiloff-Smith, A., Kucia, K., et al. (2013)

Dyscalculia from a developmental and differential perspective. *Frontiers in Psychology*, 4, 516.

Kavale, K. A., Holdnack, J. A., & Mostert, M. P. (2005). Responsiveness to intervention and the identification of specific learning disability: A critique and alternative proposal. *Learning Disability Quarterly*, 29, 113–127.

Kavšek, M. (2004). Predicting later IQ from infant visual habituation and dishabituation: A meta-analysis. *Journal of Applied Development Psychology*, 25, 369–393.

Kavşek , M., Granrud, C. E., & Yonas, A. (2009). Infants' responsiveness to pictorial depth cues in preferential-reaching studies: A meta-analysis. *Infant Behavior and Development*, 32, 245–253.

Kawakami, K., Takai-Kawakami, K., Tomonaga, M., Suzuki, J., Kusaka, T., & Okai, T. (2006). Origins of smile and laughter: A preliminary study. *Early Human Development*, 82, 61–66.

Kay, C., & Green, J. (2013). Reactive attachment disorder following early maltreatment: Systematic evidence beyond the institution. *Journal of Abnormal Child Psychology*, 41, 571–581.

Kay-Raining Bird, E., Cleave, P., Trudeau, N., Thordardottir, E., Sutton, A., & Thorpe, A. (2005). The language abilities of bilingual children with Down syndrome. *American Journal of Speech–Language Pathology*, 14, 187–199.

Kay-Raining Bird, E., Genese, F., & Verhoeven, L. (2016). Bilingualism in children with developmental disorders: A narrative review. *Journal of Communication Disorders*, 63, 1–14.

Kaye, K., & Fogel, A. (1980). The temporal structure of face-to-face communication between mothers and infants. *Developmental Psychology*, 16, 454–464.

Kazemcini, T., & Pajoheshgar, M. (2013). Children's play in the context of culture: Parental ethnotheories. *Journal of Science and Today's World*, 2, 265–281.

Keehn, B., Müller, R. A., & Townsend, J. (2013). Atypical attentional networks and the emergence of autism. *Neuroscience and Biobehavioral Reviews*, 37, 164–183.

Kegl, J., & Iwata, G. (1989). Lenguaje de Signos Nicaragüense: A pidgin sheds light on the "creole?" ASL. In R. Carlson, S. DeLancey, S. Gilden, D. Payne & A. Saxena (Eds), *Proceedings of the Fourth Annual Meeting of the Pacific Linguistics Conference* (pp. 266–294). Eugene, OR: University of Oregon.

Keijsers, L., Branje, S. J., VanderValk, I. E., & Meeus, W. (2010). Reciprocal effects between parental solicitation, parental control, adolescent disclosure, and adolescent delinquency. *Journal of Research on Adolescence*, 20, 88–113.

Keil, F. C. (1986). Conceptual domains and the acquisition of metaphor. *Cognitive Development*, 1, 72–96.

Keil, F. C. (1990). Constraints on constraints: Surveying the epigenetic landscape. *Cognitive Science*, 14, 135–168.

Keller, H. (2016). Psychological autonomy and hierarchical relatedness as organizers of developmental pathways. *Philosophical Transactions of the Royal Society B: Biological Sciences*, 371 (1686), 1–9.

Keller, H., Kaertner, J., Yovsi, R., Borke, J., & Kleis, A. (2005). Parenting styles and the development of the categorical self: A longitudinal study on mirror self-recognition in Cameroonian Nso and German families. *International Journal of Behavioral Development*, 29, 496–504.

Keller, H., & Otto, H. (2009). The cultural socialization of emotion regulation during infancy. *Journal of Cross-Cultural Psychology*, 40, 996– 1011.

Keller, H., Yovsi, R., Borke, J., Kärtner, J., Jensen, H., & Papaligoura, Z. (2004). Developmental consequences of early parenting experiences: Self-recognition and self-regulation in three cultural communities. *Child Development*, 75, 1745–1760.

Kellman, P. J. (1996). The origins of object perception. In R. Gelman & T. K. F. Au (Eds), *Perceptual and cognitive development* (pp. 3–48). London: Academic Press.

Kellman, P. J., & Spelke, E. S. (1983). Perception of partly occluded objects in infancy. *Cognitive Psychology*, 15, 483–524.

Kelly, D. J., Liu, S., Lee, K., Quinn, P. C., Pascalis, O., Slater, A. M., & Ge, L. (2009). Development of the other-race effect in infancy: Evidence towards universality? *Journal of Experimental Child Psychology*, 104, 105–114.

Kelly, J. B., & Lamb, M. E. (2000). Using child development research to make appropriate custody and access decisions for young children. *Family Court Review*, 38, 297–311.

Kelly-Vance, L., Ryalls, B. O., & Gill-Glover, K. (2002). The use of play assessment to evaluate the cognitive skills of two- and three-year-old children. *School Psychology International*, 23, 169–185.

Kendall, P. C. (1994). Treating anxiety disorders in children: Results of a randomized clinical trial. *Journal of Consulting and Clinical Psychology*, 62, 100–110.

Kendall, P. C., Peterman, J. S., & Cummings, C. M. (2015). Cognitive-behavioral therapy, behavioral therapy, and related treatments in children. In A. Thapar, D. S. Pine, F. S. Leckman, S. Scott, M. J. Snowling & E. Taylor (Eds), *Rutter's child and adolescent psychiatry, Sixth edition* (pp. 496–509). Oxford: Wiley.

Kendon, A. (2004). *Gesture: Visible action as utterance.* Cambridge: Cambridge University Press.

Kennair, L. E. O., Nordeide, J., Andreassen, S., Strønen, J., & Pallesen, S. (2011). Sex differences in jealousy: A study from Norway. *Nordic Psychology*, 63, 20–34.

Kerbel, D., & Grunwell, P. (1998a). A study of idiom comprehension in children with semantic-pragmatic difficulties. Part I: Task effects on the assessment of idiom comprehension in children. *International Journal of Language and Communication Disorders*, 33, 1–22.

Kerbel, D., & Grunwell, P. (1998b). A study of idiom comprehension in children with semantic-pragmatic difficulties. Part II: Between-groups results and discussion. *International Journal of Language and Communication Disorders*, 33, 23–44.

Kercood, S., Grskovic, J. A., Banda, D., & Begeske, J. (2014). Working memory and autism: A review of literature. *Research in Autism Spectrum Disorders*, 8, 1316–1332.

Kermoian, R., & Campos, J. J. (1988). Locomotor experience: A facilitator of spatial cognitive development. *Child Development, 59*, 908–917.

Kerns, C. M., & Kendall, P. C. (2014). Autism and anxiety: Overlap, similarities, and differences. In T. E. Davis III, S. W. White & T. H. Ollendick (Eds), *Handbook of autism and anxiety* (pp. 75–89). New York, NY: Springer.

Kerns, K. A., Aspelmeier, J. E., Gentzler, A. L., & Grabill, C. M. (2001). Parent–child attachment and monitoring in middle childhood. *Journal of Family Psychology, 15,* 69–81.

Kerns, K. A., & Brumariu, L. E. (2014). Is insecure parent–child attachment a risk factor for the development of anxiety in childhood or adolescence? *Child Development Perspectives, 8*, 12–17.

Kerns, K. A., & Brumariu, L. E. (2016). Attachment in middle childhood. In J. Cassidy & P. R. Shaver (Eds), *Handbook of attachment: Theory, research and clinical applications, Third edition* (pp. 349–365). New York, NY: Guilford Press.

Kerr, L., & Cossar, J. (2014). Attachment interventions with foster and adoptive parents: A systematic review. *Child Abuse Review, 23*, 426–439.

Kesiktas, A. D. (2009). Early childhood special education for children with visual impairments: Problems and solutions. *Educational Sciences: Theory and Practice, 9,* 823–832.

Kestenbaum, R., Termine, N., & Spelke, E. S. (1987). Perception of objects and object boundaries by three-month-old infants. *British Journal of Developmental Psychology, 5*, 361–383.

Ketelaars, M. P., Weerdenburg, M. van, Verhoeven, L., Cuperus, J. M., & Jansonius, K. (2010). Dynamics of the Theory of Mind construct: A developmental perspective. *European Journal of Developmental Psychology, 7,* 85–103.

Key, E. (1900). *Barnets århundrade: Studie.* Stockholm: Bonniers.

Khundrakpam, B. S., Reid, A., Brauer, J., Carbonell, F., Lewis, J., Ameis, S., et al. (2013). Developmental changes in organization of structural brain networks. *Cerebral Cortex, 23*, 2072–2085.

Kidd, C., Palmeri, H., & Aslin, R. N. (2013). Rational snacking: Young children's decision-making on the marshmallow task is moderated by beliefs about environmental reliability. *Cognition, 126*, 109–114.

Kiel, E. J., & Buss, K. A. (2010). Maternal expectations for toddlers' reactions to novelty: Relations of maternal internalizing symptoms and parenting dimensions to expectations and accuracy of expectations. *Parenting, 10,* 202–218.

Kiff, C. J., Lengua, L. J., & Zalewski, M. (2011). Nature and nurturing: Parenting in the context of child temperament. *Clinical Child and Family Psychology Review, 14,* 251.

Kildare, C. A., & Middlemiss, W. (2017). Impact of parents' mobile device use on parent-child interaction: A literature review. *Computers in Human Behavior, 75,* 579–593.

Killen, M., & Dahl, A. (2018). Moral judgment: Reflective, interactive, spontaneous, challenging, and always evolving. In K. Gray & J. Graham (Eds), *Atlas of Moral Psychology.* New York, NY: Guilford Press.

Killen, M., Rutland, A., & Jampol, N. S. (2009) Social exclusion in childhood and adolescence. In K. H. Rubin, W. M. Bulowski & B. Laursen (Eds), *The handbook of peer interactions, relationship and group* (pp. 249–266). New York, NY: Guilford Press.

Killen, M., Rutland, A., & Yip, T. (2016). Equity and justice in developmental science: Discrimination, social exclusion, and intergroup attitudes. *Child Development, 87,* 1317–1336.

Killen, M., & Smetana, J. G. (Eds). (2014). *Handbook of moral development, Second edition.* Hove, UK: Psychology Press.

Kim, S. H., & Lord, C. (2013). The behavioral manifestations of autism spectrum disorders. In J. D. Buxbaum & P. R. Hof (Eds), The *neuroscience of autism spectrum disorders* (pp. 25–37). Amsterdam, NL: Elsevier.

Kim, J.-Y., McHale, S. M., Wayne Osgood, D., & Crouter, A. C. (2006). Longitudinal course and family correlates of sibling relationships from childhood through adolescence. *Child Development, 77*, 1746–1761.

Kim-Cohen, J., Caspi, A., Taylor, A., Williams, B., Newcombe, R., Craig, I., & Moffitt, T. E. (2006). MAOA, maltreatment, and gene-environment interaction predicting children's mental health: New evidence and a meta-analysis. *Molecular Psychiatry, 11,* 903–913.

Kimhi, Y. (2014). Theory of mind abilities and deficits in autism spectrum disorders. *Topics in Language Disorders, 34,* 329–343.

Kimonis, E. R., Cross, B., Howard, A., & Donoghue, K. (2013). Maternal care, maltreatment and callous-unemotional traits among urban male juvenile offenders. *Journal of Youth and Adolescence, 42,* 165–177.

Kimura, D. (1992). Sex differences in the brain. *Scientific American, 267*, 81–87.

Kimura, D. (1999). *Sex and cognition.* Cambridge, MA: MIT Press.

Kimura, D. (2004). Human sex differences in cognition, fact, not predicament. *Sexualities, Evolution and Gender, 6,* 45–53.

King, D. L., Haagsma, M. C., Delfabbro, P. H., Gradisar, M. S., & Griffiths, M. D. (2013). Toward a consensus definition of pathological video-gaming: A systematic review of psychometric assessment tools. *Clinical Psychology Review, 33*, 331–342

King, S., Waschbusch, D. A., Pelham Jr, W. E., Frankland, B. W., Andrade, B. F., Jacques, S., & Corkum, P. V. (2009). Social information processing in elementary-school aged children with ADHD: Medication effects and comparisons with typical children. *Journal of Abnormal Child Psychology, 37*, 579–589.

Kinzler, K. D., & Spelke, E. S. (2007). Core systems in human cognition. *Progress in Brain Research, 164,* 257–264.

Kirk, H., Gray, K., Ellis, K., Taffe, J., & Cornish, K. (2017). Impact of attention training on academic achievement, executive functioning, and behavior: A randomized controlled trial. *American Journal on Intellectual and Developmental Disabilities*, 122, 97–117.

Kirkorian, H. L., Wartella, E. A., & Anderson, D. R. (2008). Media and young children's learning. *The Future of Children*, 18, 39–61.

Kirschner, S., & Tomasello, M. (2010). Joint music making promotes prosocial behavior in 4-year-old children. *Evolution and Human Behavior*, 31, 354–364.

Kisilevsky, B. S. (2016). Fetal auditory processing: Implications for language development? In N. Reissland & B. S. Kisilevsky (Eds), *Fetal development* (pp. 133–152). Cham, Switzerland: Springer.

Kisilevsky, B. S., Chambers, B., Parker, K., & Davies, G. A. L. (2014). Auditory processing in growth restricted fetuses and newborns and later language development. *Clinical Psychological Science*, 2, 495–513.

Kisilevsky, B. S., Hains, S. M. J., Brown, C. A., Lee, C. T., Cowperthwaite, B., Stutzman, S. S., Swansburg, M. L., Lee, K., Xie, X., Huang, H., et al. (2009). Foetal sensitivity to properties of maternal speech and language. *Infant Behavior and Development*, 32, 59–71.

Klassen, R. M., Tze, V. M., & Hannok, W. (2013). Internalizing problems of adults with learning disabilities: A meta-analysis. *Journal of Learning Disabilities*, 46, 317–327.

Kleefstra, T., Schencka, A., Kramera, J. M., & van Bokhove, H. (2014). The genetics of cognitive epigenetics. *Neuropharmacology*, 80, 83–94.

Klein, D. N., Bufferd, S. J., Dyson, M. W., & Danzig, A. P. (2014). Personality pathology. In M. Lewis & K. D. Rudolph (Eds), *Handbook of developmental psychopathology* (pp. 703–719). Boston, MA: Springer.

Klein, M. (1948). A contribution to the theory of anxiety and guilt. In *The writings of Melanie Klein, Volume 1* (pp. 25–42). New York, NY: The Free Press.

Klimstra, T. A., Hale III, W. W., Raaijmakers, Q. A., Branje, S. J., & Meeus, W. H. (2009). Maturation of personality in adolescence. *Journal of Personality and Social Psychology*, 96, 898–912.

Klingberg, T., Forssberg, H., & Westerberg, H. (2002). Training of working memory in children with ADHD. *Journal of Clinical and Experimental Neuropsychology*, 24, 781–791.

Klingzell, I., Fanti, K. A., Colins, O. F., Frogner, L., Andershed, A. K., & Andershed, H. (2016). Early childhood trajectories of conduct problems and callous-unemotional traits: The role of fearlessness and psychopathic personality dimensions. *Child Psychiatry and Human Development*, 47, 236–247.

Klump, K. L. (2014). Developmental trajectories of disordered eating: Genetic and biological risk during puberty. In M. Lewis & K. D. Rudolph (Eds), *Handbook of developmental psychopathology, Third edition* (pp. 621–629). New York, NY: Springer.

Kobak, R., & Madsen, S. (2008). Disruptions in attachment bonds: Implications for theory, research, and clinical intervention. In J. Cassidy & P. R. Shaver (Eds), *Handbook of attachment: Theory, research, and clinical applications, Second edition* (pp. 23–47). New York, NY: Guilford Press.

Kochanska, G. (1997). Multiple pathways to conscience for children with different temperaments: From toddlerhood to age 5. *Developmental Psychology*, 33, 228–240.

Kochanska, G. (2002). Mutually responsive orientation between mothers and their young children: A context for the early development of conscience. *Current Directions in Psychological Science*, 11, 191–195.

Kochanska, G., & Aksan, N. (2004). Development of mutual responsiveness between parents and their young children. *Child Development*, 75, 1657–1676.

Kochanska, G., & Aksan, N. (2006). Children's conscience and self-regulation. *Journal of Personality*, 74, 1587–1618.

Kochanska, G., Brock, R. L., & Boldt, L. J. (2017). A cascade from disregard for rules of conduct at preschool age to parental power assertion at early school age to antisocial behavior in early preadolescence: Interplay with the child's skin conductance level. *Development and Psychopathology*, 29, 875–885.

Kochanska, G., Gross, J. N., Lin, M. H., & Nichols, K. E. (2002). Guilt in young children: Development, determinants, and relations with a broader system of standards. *Child Development*, 73, 461–482.

Kochanska, G., & Kim, S. (2013). Early attachment organization with both parents and future behavior problems: From infancy to middle childhood. *Child Development*, 84, 283–296.

Kochanska, G., Koenig, J. L., Barry, R. A., Kim, S., & Yoon, J. E. (2010). Children's conscience during toddler and preschool years, moral self, and a competent, adaptive developmental trajectory. *Developmental Psychology*, 46, 1320–1332.

Koelch, M., Singer, H., Prestel, A., Burkert, J., Schulze, U., & Fegert, J. M. (2009). "...because I am something special" or "I think I will be something like a guinea pig": Information and assent of legal minors in clinical trials – assessment of understanding, appreciation and reasoning. *Child and Adolescent Psychiatry and Mental Health*, 3, 1–13.

Koh, J. B. K., & Wang, Q. (2012). Self-development. *Wiley Interdisciplinary Reviews: Cognitive Science*, 3, 513–524.

Kohlberg, L. (1963). The development of children's orientations toward a moral order. *Vita Humana*, 6, 11–33.

Kohlberg, L. (1966). Moral education in schools: A developmental review. *School Review*, 74, 1–30.

Kohlberg, L. (1969). Stage and sequence: The cognitive-developmental approach. In D. A. Goslin (Ed.), *Handbook of socialization theory and research* (pp. 347–480). Chicago, IL: Rand McNally.

Kohlberg, L. (1971). Stages of moral development. *Moral Education*, 1, 23–92.

Kohlberg, L. (1976). Moral stages and moralization: The cognitive-developmental approach. In T. Lickona (Ed.), *Moral development and behavior: Theory, research and social issues* (pp. 31–53). New York, NY: Holt, Rinehart and Winston.

Kohlberg, L. (1981). *The philosophy of moral development: Moral stages and the idea of justice*. New York, NY: Harper and Row.

Kohlberg, L., & Hersh, R. H. (1977). Moral development: A review of the theory. *Theory into Practice*, 16, 53–59.

Kohnert, K. (2010). Bilingual children with primary language impairment: Issues, evidence and implications for clinical actions. *Journal of Communication Disorders*, 43, 456–473.

Kohnstamm, G. A., Halverson, C. F., Mervielde, I., & Havill, V. L. (1998). Analyzing parental free descriptions of child personality. In G. A. Kohnstamm, C. F. Halverson, I. Mervielde & V. L. Havill (Eds), *Parental descriptions of child personality: Developmental antecedents of the Big Five?* (pp. 1–19). Mahwah, NJ: Erlbaum.

Kohnstamm, G. A., Mervielde, I., Besevegis, I., & Halverson, C. F. (1995). Tracing the Big Five in parents' free descriptions of their children. *European Journal of Personality*, 9, 283–304.

Kohut, H. (1977). *The restoration of the self*. New York, NY: International Universities Press.

Kolb, B., Mychasiuk, R., Muhammad, A., & Gibb, R. (2013). Brain plasticity in the developing brain. *Progress in Brain Research*, 207, 35–64.

Kolb, D. A. (1984). *Experiential learning: Experience as the source of learning and development*. Englewood Cliffs, NJ: Prentice-Hall.

Kokin, J., Younger, A., Gosselin, P., & Vaillancourt, T. (2016). Biased facial expression interpretation in shy children. *Infant and Child Development*, 25, 3–23.

Kongerslev, M. T., Chanen, A. M., & Simonsen, E. (2015). Personality disorder in childhood and adolescence comes of age: A review of the current evidence and prospects for future research. *Scandinavian Journal of Child and Adolescent Psychiatry and Psychology*, 3, 31–48.

Konner, M. J. (1976). Maternal care, infant behavior and development among the !Kung. In R. B. Lee & I. DeVore (Eds), *Kalahari hunter-gatherers: Studies of the !Kung San and their neighbors* (pp. 218–245). Cambridge, MA: Harvard University Press.

Konrad, K., Firk, C., & Uhlhaas, P. J. (2013). Brain development during adolescence: Neuroscientific insights into this developmental period. *Deutsches Ärzteblatt International*, 110, 425–431.

Koolstra, C. M., & Van Der Voort, T. H. (1996). Longitudinal effects of television on children's leisure-time reading: A test of three explanatory models. *Human Communication Research*, 23, 4–35.

Kopp, C. B. (1989). Regulation of distress and negative emotions: A developmental view. *Developmental Psychology*, 25, 343–354.

Kopsida, E., Mikaelsson, M. A., & Davies, W. (2011). The role of imprinted genes in mediating susceptibility to neuropsychiatric disorders. *Hormones and Behavior*, 59, 375–382.

Kornilaki, E. N., & Chlouverakis, G. (2004). The situational antecedents of pride and happiness: Developmental and domain differences. *British Journal of Developmental Psychology*, 22, 605–619.

Kosc, L. (1974). Developmental dyscalculia. *Journal of Learning Disabilities*, 7, 164–177.

Kovács, I. (2000). Human development of perceptual organization. *Vision Research*, 40, 1301–1310.

Kowert, R., Vogelgesang, J., Festl, R., & Quandt, T. (2015). Psychosocial causes and consequences of online video game play. *Computers in Human Behavior*, 45, 51–58.

Kozulin, A. (2002). Sociocultural theory and the mediated learning experience. *School Psychology International*, 23, 7–35.

Kozulin, A., Gindis, B., Ageyev, V. S., & Miller, S. M. (Eds) (2003). *Vygotsky's educational theory in cultural context*. Cambridge: Cambridge University Press.

Krahé, B. (2016). Violent media effects on aggression: A commentary from a cross-cultural perspective. *Analyses of Social Issues and Public Policy*, 16, 439–442.

Krahé, B., Möller, I., Huesmann, R., Kirwil, L., Felber, J., & Berger, A. (2011). Desensitiation to media violence: Links with habitual media violence exposure, aggressive cognitions, and aggressive behaviors. *Journal of Personality and Social Psychology*, 100, 630–646.

Kramer, L. (2014). Learning emotional understanding and emotion regulation through sibling interaction. *Early Education and Development*, 25, 160–184.

Kreppner, J. M., O'Connor, T. G., Dunn, J., Andersen-Wood, L., & the English and Romanian Adoptees Study Team (1999). The pretend play and social role play of children exposed to early severe deprivation. *British Journal of Developmental Psychology*, 17, 319–332.

Kretch, K. S., Franchak, J. M., & Adolph, K. E. (2014). Crawling and walking infants see the world differently. *Child Development*, 85, 1503–1518.

Krettenauer, T., Campbell, S., & Hertz, S. (2013). Moral emotions and the development of the moral self in childhood. *European Journal of Developmental Psychology*, 10, 159–173.

Kring, A. M., & Werner, K. H. (2004). Emotion regulation in psychopathology. In P. Philippot & R. S. Feldman (Eds), *The regulation of emotion* (pp. 359–385). Mahwah, NJ: Erlbaum.

Kroger, J. (2004). *Identity in adolescence: The balance between self and other, Third edition*. London: Routledge.

Kruger, A. C. (1992). The effect of peer and adult–child transductive discussions on moral reasoning. *Merrill-Palmer Quarterly*, 38, 191–211.

Kruger, A. C. (1993). Peer collaboration: Conflict, cooperation, or both? *Social Development*, 2, 165–182.

Kuchuk, A., Vibert, M., & Bornstein, M. H. (1986). The perception of smiling and its experiential correlates in three month old infants. *Child Development*, 57, 1054–1061.

Kucirkova, N., & Littleton, K. (2016) *The digital reading habits of children: A National survey of parents' perceptions of and practices in relation to children's reading for pleasure with print and digital books*. Book Trust. Available from: www.booktrust.org.uk/news-and-blogs/news/1371.

Kuczaj II, S. A. (1982). Language play and language acquisition. *Advances in Child Development and Behavior*, 17, 197–232.

Kuczynski, L., & Knafo, A. (2014). Innovation and continuity in socialization, internalization and acculturation. In M. Killen & J. G. Smetana (Eds), *Handbook of moral development, Second edition* (pp. 93–112). New York, NY: Taylor and Francis.

Kuebli, J., & Fivush, R. (1992). Gender differences in parent–child conversations about past emotions. *Sex Roles, 27,* 683–698.

Kuebli, J., & Fivush, R. (1994). Children's representations and recall of event alternatives. *Journal of Experimental Child Psychology, 58,* 25–45.

Kuehn, D. P., & Moller, K. T. (2000). The state of the art: Speech and language issues in the cleft palate population. *The Cleft Palate-Craniofacial Journal, 37,* 1–35.

Kuhl, P. K. (1992). Psychoacoustics and speech perception: Internal standards, perceptual anchors, and prototypes. In L. A. Werner & E. W. Rubel (Eds), *Developmental Psychoacoustics* (pp. 293–332). Washington, DC: American Psychological Association.

Kuhl, P. K. (1993). Early linguistic experience and phonetic perception: Implications for theories of developmental speech perception. *Journal of Phonetics, 21,* 125–139.

Kuhl, P. K. (2004). Early language acquisition: Cracking the speech code. *Nature Reviews Neuroscience, 5,* 831–843.

Kuhl, P. K. (2010). Brain mechanisms in early language acquisition. *Neuron, 67,* 713–727.

Kuhn, D. (2013). Reasoning. In P. D. Zelazo (Ed.), *The Oxford handbook of developmental psychology, Volume 1: Body and mind* (pp. 744–764). Oxford: Oxford University Press.

Kuhn D., & Franklin, S. (2008). The second decade: What develops (and how). In. W. Damon & R. M. Lerner (Eds), *Child psychology and adolescent psychology: An advanced course* (pp. 517–550). New York, NY: Wiley.

Kumsta, R., Sonuga-Barke, E., & Rutter, M. (2012). Adolescent callous–unemotional traits and conduct disorder in adoptees exposed to severe early deprivation. *The British Journal of Psychiatry, 200,* 197–201.

Küntay, A. C. (2004). Lists as alternative discourse structures to narratives in preschool children's conversations. *Discourse Processes, 38,* 95–118.

Kuo, Z. Y. (1967). *The dynamics of behavior development: An epigenetic view.* New York, NY: Random House.

Kupersmidt, J. B., Burchinal, M., & Patterson, C. J. (1995). Developmental patterns of childhood peer relations as predictors of externalizing behavior problems. *Development and Psychopathology, 7,* 825–843.

Kupersmidt, J. B., & Coie, J. D. (1990). Preadolescent peer status, aggression, and social adjustment as predictors of self-reported behavior problems in preadolescence. *Child Development, 61,* 1350–1362.

Kuppler, K., Lewis, M., & Evans, A. K. (2013). A review of unilateral hearing loss and academic performance: Is it time to reassess traditional dogmata? *International Journal of Pediatric Otorhinolaryngology, 77,* 617–622.

Kurmanaviciute, R., & Stadskleiv, K. (2017). Assessment of verbal comprehension and non-verbal reasoning when standard response mode is challenging: A comparison of different response modes and an exploration of their clinical usefulness. *Cogent Psychology, 4,* 1275416.

Kurzban, R., Burton-Chellew, M. N., & West, S. A. (2015). The evolution of altruism in humans. *Annual Review of Psychology, 66,* 575–599.

Kuss, D. J., van Rooij, A., Shorter, G. W., Griffiths, M. D., & van de Mheen, D. (2013). Internet addiction in adolescents: Prevalence and risk factors. *Computers in Human Behavior, 29,* 1987–1996.

Kuusikko, S., Pollock-Wurman, R., Jussila, K., Carter, A. S., Mattila, M. L., Ebeling, H., Pauls, D., & Moilanen, I. (2008). Social anxiety in high-functioning children and adolescents with autism and Asperger syndrome. *Journal of Autism and Developmental Disorders, 38,* 1697–1709.

Kwan, V. S. Y., & Herrmann, S. D. (2015). The interplay between culture and personality. In M. Mikulincer & P. R. Shaver (Eds), *APA handbook of personality and social psychology, Volume 4: Personality processes and individual differences* (pp. 553–574). Washington, DC: American Psychological Association.

Kyllonen, P., & Kell, H. (2017). What is fluid intelligence? Can it be improved? In M. Rosen, K. Y. Hansen & U. Wolff (Eds), *Cognitive abilities and educational outcomes* (pp. 15–38). Cham, Switzerland: Springer.

LaBlonde, C. E., & Chandler, M. J. (1995). False belief understanding goes to school: On the social-emotional consequences of coming early or late to a first theory of mind. *Cognition and Emotion, 9,* 167–185.

Labov, W. (1972). The transformation of reality in narrative syntax. In W. Labov (Ed.), *Language in the inner city* (pp. 354–396). Philadelphia, PA: University of Pennsylvania Press.

Labov, W., & Labov, T. (1978). The phonetics of *cat* and *mama. Language, 54,* 816–852.

Lackaye, T., Margalit, M., Ziv, O., & Ziman, T. (2006). Comparisons of self-efficacy, mood, effort, and hope between students with learning disabilities and their non-LD-matched peers. *Learning Disabilities Research and Practice, 21,* 111–121.

Ladd, G. W. (1990). Having friends, keeping friends, making friends and being liked by peers in the classroom: Predictors of children's early school adjustment? *Child Development, 61,* 1081–1090.

Ladd, G. W., & Hart, C. H. (1992). Creating informal play opportunities: Are parents' and preschoolers' initiations related to the children's competence with peers? *Developmental Psychology, 28,* 1179–1187.

Ladefoged, P. (2004). *Vowels and consonants.* Oxford: Blackwell.

Ladegaard, H. J., & Bleses, D. (2003). Gender differences in young children's speech: The acquisition of sociolinguistic competence. *International Journal of Applied Linguistics, 13,* 222–233.

LaFreniere, P. J. (2000). *Emotional development.* London: Wadsworth.

Lagattuta, K. H., Kramer, H. J., Kennedy, K., Hjortsvang, K., Goldfarb, D., & Tashjian, S. (2015). Beyond Sally's missing marble: Further development in children's understanding of mind and emotion in middle childhood. *Advances in Child Development and Behavior, 48,* 185–217.

Lagattuta, K. H., & Thompson, R. A. (2007). The development of self-conscious emotions: Cognitive processes and social influences. In J. L. Tracy, R. W. Robins & J. P. Tangney (Eds), *The self-conscious emotions: Theory and research* (pp. 91–113). New York, NY: Guilford Press.

Lai, B. S., Kelley, M. L., Harrison, K. M., Thompson, J. E., & Self-Brown, S. (2015). Posttraumatic stress, anxiety, and depression symptoms among children after Hurricane Katrina: A latent profile analysis. *Journal of Child and Family Studies, 24,* 1262–1270.

Lai, C. S. L., Fisher, S. E., Hurst, J. A., Vargha-Khadem, F., & Monaco, A. P. (2001). A forkhead-domain gene is mutated in a severe speech and language disorder. *Nature, 413,* 519–523.

Laible, D., Eye, J., & Carlo, G. (2008). Dimensions of conscience in mid-adolescence: Links with social behavior, parenting, and temperament. *Journal of Youth and Adolescence, 37,* 875–887.

Lakoff, G. (1987). *Women, fire and dangerous things.* Chicago, IL: University of Chicago Press.

Lakoff, G., & Johnson, M. H. (1980). *Metaphors we live by.* Chicago, IL: Chicago University Press.

Lam, C. B., & McHale, S. M. (2015). Time use as cause and consequence of youth development. *Child Development Perspectives, 9,* 20–25.

Lam, Y. G., & Yeung, S. S. S. (2012). Cognitive deficits and symbolic play in preschoolers with autism. *Research in Autism Spectrum Disorders, 6,* 560–564.

Lamarck, J. B. P. (1809). *Philosophie zoologique.* Paris: L'Imprimerie de Duminil-Lesueur.

Lamb, M. E., Chuang, S. S., Wessels, H., Broberg, A. G., & Hwang, C. P. (2002). Emergence and construct validation of the Big Five Factors in early childhood: A longitudinal analysis of their ontogeny in Sweden. *Child Development, 73,* 1517–1524.

Lamb, M. E., Easterbrooks, M. A., & Holden, G. W. (1980). Reinforcement and punishment among preschoolers: Characteristics, effects, and correlates. *Child Development,* 1230–1236.

Lamb, M. E., La Rooy, D. J., Malloy, L. C., & Katz, C. (Eds) (2011). *Children's testimony: A handbook of psychological research and forensic practice, Second edition.* Chichester, UK: Wiley.

Lambek, R., Sonuga-Barke, E., Psychogiou, L., Thompson, M., Tannock, R., Daley, D., Damm, D., & Thomson, P. H. (2017). The Parental Emotional Response to Children Index. A questionnaire measure of parents' reactions to ADHD. *Journal of Attention Disorders, 21,* 494–507.

Landau, B., & Ferrara, K. (2013). Space and language in Williams syndrome: Insights from typical development. *Wiley Interdisciplinary Reviews: Cognitive Science, 4,* 693–706.

Landau, B., & Gleitman, L. R. (1985). *Language and experience: Evidence from the blind child.* Cambridge, MA: Harvard University Press.

Landerl, K. (2015). How specific is the specific disorder of arithmetic skills? In S. Chinn (Ed.), *The Routledge international handbook of dyscalculia and mathematical learning difficulties* (pp. 115–124). New York, NY: Routledge.

Landerl, K., & Moll, K. (2010). Comorbidity of learning disorders: Prevalence and familial transmission. *Journal of Child Psychology and Psychiatry, 51,* 287–294.

Lang-Roth, R. (2014). Hearing impairment and language delay in infants: Diagnostics and genetics. *GMS Current Topics in Otorhinolaryngology, Head and Neck Surgery, 13,* 05.

Lansford, J. E. (2010). The special problem of cultural differences in effects of corporal punishment. *Law and Contemporary Problems, 73,* 89–106.

Lansford, J. E., Alampay, L. P., Al-Hassan, S., Bacchini, D., Bombi, A. S., Bornstein, M. H., Chang, L., Deater-Deckard, K., Di Giunta, L., Dodge, K. A., et al. (2010). Corporal punishment of children in nine countries as a function of child gender and parent gender. *International Journal of Pediatrics, 2010,* 672780.

Lansford, J. E., Chang, L., Dodge, K. A., Malone, P. S., Oburu, P., Palmérus, K., Bacchini, D., Pastorelli, C., Bombi, A. S., Zelli, A., et al. (2005). Physical discipline and children's adjustment: Cultural normativeness as a moderator. *Child Development, 76,* 1234–1246.

Lansford, J. E., Dodge, K. A., Pettit, G. S., Bates, J. E. Crozier, J., & Kaplow, J. (2002). A 12-year prospective study of the long-term effects of early child physical maltreatment on psychological, behavioral, and academic problems in adolescence. *Archives of Pediatric and Adolescence Medicine, 156,* 824–830.

Lanza, E. (1997). *Language mixing in infant bilingualism: A sociolinguistic perspective.* Oxford: Clarendon Press.

Laraway, S., Snycerski, S., Michael, J., & Poling, A. (2003). Motivating operations and terms to describe them: Some further refinements. *Journal of Applied Behavior Analysis, 3,* 407–414.

Largo, R. H., & Howard, J. A. (1979a). Developmental progression in play behavior of children between nine and thirty months, I: Spontaneous play and language development. *Developmental Medicine and Child Neurology, 21,* 492–503.

Largo, R. H., & Howard, J. A. (1979b). Developmental progression in play behavior of children between nine and thirty months: II. Spontaneous play and imitations. *Developmental Medicine and Child Neurology, 21,* 299–310.

Largo, R. H., Kundu, S., & Thun-Hohenstein, L. (1993). Early motor development in term and preterm children. In A. F. Kalverboer, B. Hopkins & R. Geuze (Eds), *Motor development in early and later childhood: Longitudinal approaches* (pp. 247–265). Cambridge: Cambridge University Press.

Largo, R. H., Molinari, L., Weber, M., Pinto, L. C., & Duc, G. (1985). Early development of locomotion: Significance of prematurity, cerebral palsy and sex. *Developmental Medicine and Child Neurology, 27,* 183–191.

Largo, R. H., Caflisch, J. A., Hug, F., Muggli, K., Molnar, A. A., & Molinari, L. (2001b). Neuromotor development from 5 to 18 years. Part 2: Associated movements. *Developmental Medicine and Child Neurology, 43,* 444–453.

Largo, R. H., Caflisch, J. A., Hug, F., Muggli, K., Molnar, A. A., Molinari, L., Sheehy, A., Gasser, T. (2001a). Neuromotor development from 5 to 18 years. Part 1:

Timed performance. *Developmental Medicine and Child Neurology, 43*, 436–443.

Larson, R. W. (1990). The solitary side of life: An examination of the time people spend alone from childhood to old age. *Developmental Review, 10*, 155–183.

Larson, R. W., & Ham, M. (1993). Stress and "Storm and Stress" in early adolescence: The relationship of negative events with dysphoric affect. *Developmental Psychology, 29*, 130–140.

Larson, R. W., & Verma, S. (1999). How children and adolescents spend time across the world: Work, play, and developmental opportunities. *Psychological Bulletin, 125*, 701–736.

Latham, J., & Wilson, A. (2010). The great DNA data deficit: Are genes for disease a mirage? *The Bioscience Research Project*, 18–21.

Lau, E. X., & Rapee, R. M. (2011). Prevention of anxiety disorders. *Current Psychiatry Reports, 13*, 258–266.

Laugesen, N., Dugas, M. J., & Bukowski, W. M. (2003). Understanding adolescent worry: The application of a cognitive model. *Journal of Abnormal Child Psychology, 31*, 55–64.

Launonen, K. (1996). Enhancing communication skills of children with Down syndrome: Early use of manual signs. In S. von Tetzchner & M. H. Jensen (Eds), *Augmentative and alternative communication: European perspectives* (pp. 213–231). London: Whurr/Wiley.

Lauricella, A. R., Blackwell, C. K., & Wartella, E. (2017). The "new" technology environment: The role of content and context on learning and development from mobile media. In R. Barr & D. Nichols Linebarger (Eds), *Media exposure during infancy and early childhood* (pp. 1–23). Cham, Switzerland: Springer.

Lauricella, A. R., Cingel, D. P., Blackwell, C., Wartella, E., & Conway, A. (2014). The mobile generation: Youth and adolescent ownership and use of new media. *Communication Research Reports, 31*, 357–364.

Lauricella, A. R., Wartella, E., & Rideout, V. (2015). Young children's screen time: The complex role of parent and child factors. *Journal of Applied Developmental Psychology, 36*, 11–17.

Laursen, B., & Pursell, G. (2009). Conflict in peer relationships. In K. H. Rubin, W. M. Bulowski & B. Laursen (Eds), *The handbook of peer interactions, relationship and group* (pp. 267–286). New York, NY: Guilford Press.

Lave, J., & Wenger, E. (1991). *Situated learning.* Cambridge: Cambridge University Press.

Law, J., Gaag, A., Hardcastle, W. J., Beckett, D. J., MacGregor, A., & Plunkett, C. (2007). *Communication support needs: A review of the literature.* Edinburgh: Scottish Executive.

Law, J., Garrett, Z., & Nye, C. (2003). Speech and language therapy interventions for children with primary speech and language delay or disorder. *The Cochrane Library, 3*.

Lawler, J. M., Hostinar, C. E., Mliner, S. B., & Gunnar, M. R. (2014). Disinhibited social engagement in postinstitutionalized children: Differentiating normal from atypical behavior. *Development and Psychopathology, 26*, 451–464.

Lawton, C. A. (2010). Gender, spatial abilities, and wayfinding. In J. Chrisler & D. McCreary (Eds), *Handbook of gender research in psychology* (pp. 317–341). New York, NY: Springer.

Layton, T., Chuang, M. C., & Hao, G. (2014). Play behaviors in chinese toddlers with Down syndrome. *Journal of Psychological Abnormalities in Children, 3*, 131.

Lazar, I., & Darlington, R. (1982). Lasting effects of early education. *Monographs of the Society for Research in Child Development, 47*, 2–3.

Lazinski, M. J., Shea, A. K., & Steiner, M. (2008). Effects of maternal prenatal stress on offspring development: A commentary. *Archives of Women's Mental Health, 11*, 363–375.

Leader, L. R. (1995). The potential value of habituation in the neonate. In J.-P. Lecanuet, W. P. Fifer, N. A. Krasnegor & W. P. Smotherman (Eds), *Fetal development* (pp. 383–404). Hove, UK: Lawrence Erlbaum.

Leader, L. R. (2016). The potential value of habituation in the fetus. In N. Reissland & B. S. Kisilevsky (Eds), *Fetal development* (pp. 189–209). Cham, Switzerland: Springer.

Leahy, R. L. (1983). The development of the conception of social class. In R. L. Leahy (Ed.), *The child's construction of social inequality* (pp. 79–107). London: Academic Press.

Leaper, C., & Smith, T. E. (2004). A meta-analytic review of gender variations in children's language use: Talkativeness, affiliative speech, and assertive speech. *Developmental Psychology, 40*, 993–1027.

Learmonth, A. E., Newcombe, N. S., Sheridan, N., & Jones, M. (2008). Why size counts: Children's spatial reorientation in large and small enclosures. *Developmental Science, 11*, 414–426.

Lebowitz, E. R., Scharfstein, L. A., & Jones, J. (2014). Comparing family accommodation in pediatric obsessive-compulsive disorder, anxiety disorders, and nonanxious children. *Depression and Anxiety, 31*, 1018–1025.

Lecanuet, J.-P., & Schaal, B. (2002). Sensory performances in the human foetus: A brief summary of research. *Intellectica, 34*, 29–56.

Lecce, S., Caputi, M., Pagnin, A., & Banerjee, R. (2017). Theory of mind and school achievement: The mediating role of social competence. *Cognitive Development, 44*, 85–97.

Lecce, S., & Hughes, C. (2010). The Italian job? Comparing theory of mind performance in British and Italian children. *British Journal of Developmental Psychology, 28*, 747–766.

Lecce, S., Pagnin, A., & Pinto, G. (2009). Agreement in children's evaluations of their relationships with siblings and friends. *European Journal of Developmental Psychology, 6*, 153–169.

Lederberg, A. R., Schick, B., & Spencer, P. E. (2013). Language and literacy development of deaf and hard-of-hearing children: Successes and challenges. *Developmental Psychology, 49*, 15–30.

Lederer, S. H., & Battaglia, D. (2015). Using signs to facilitate vocabulary in children with language delays. *Infants and Young Children, 28*, 18–31.

Lee, C., & Johnston-Wilder, S. (2015). Mathematical resilience. In S. Chinn (Ed.), *The Routledge international handbook of dyscalculia and mathematical learning difficulties* (pp. 337–345). New York, NY: Routledge.

Lee, C. L., & Bates, J. E. (1985). Mother–child interaction at age two years and perceived difficult temperament. *Child Development*, 56, 1314–1325.

Lee, K. (2013). Little liars: Development of verbal deception in children. *Child Development Perspectives*, 7, 91–96.

Leekam, S. (2016). Social cognitive impairment and autism: What are we trying to explain? *Philosophical Transactions of the Royal Society B: Biological Sciences*, 371 (1686), 20150082.

Leevers, H. J., & Harris, P. L. (2000). Counterfactual syllogistic reasoning in normal 4-year-olds, children with learning disabilities, and children with autism. *Journal of Experimental Child Psychology*, 76, 64–87.

Legerstee, M., & Barillas, Y. (2003). Sharing attention and pointing to objects at 12 months: Is the intentional stance implied? *Cognitive Development*, 18, 91–110.

Leibenluft, E., & Dickstein, D. P. (2015). Bipolar disorder in childhood. In A. Thapar, D. S. Pine, F. S. Leckman, S. Scott, M. J. Snowling & E. Taylor (Eds), *Rutter's child and adolescent psychiatry, Sixth edition* (pp. 866–873). Oxford: Wiley.

Leibold, L. J. (2012). Development of auditory scene analysis and auditory attention. In L. A. Werner, A. N. Popper & R. R. Fay (Eds), *Human auditory development* (pp. 137–161). New York, NY: Springer.

Lemerise, E. A., & Dodge, K. A. (2008). The development of anger and hostile interactions. In M. Lewis, J. M. Haviland & L. F. Barrett (Eds), *Handbook of emotions, Third edition* (pp. 740–741). New York, NY: Guilford Press.

Lemerise, E. A., & Harper, B. D. (2010). The development of anger from preschool to middle childhood: Expressing, understanding, and regulating anger. In M. Potegal, G. Stemmler & C. Spielberger (Eds) *International handbook of anger constituent and concomitant biological, psychological, and social processes* (pp. 219–229). New York, NY: Springer.

Lenhart, A., Purcell, K., Smith, A., & Zickuhr, K. (2010). *Social media and mobile Internet use among teens and young adults*. Washington, DC: Pew Internet and American Life Project.

Leno, V. C., Charman, T., Pickles, A., Jones, C. R., Baird, G., Happé, F., & Simonoff, E. (2015). Callous–unemotional traits in adolescents with autism spectrum disorder. *The British Journal of Psychiatry*, 207, 392–399.

Lenroot, R. K., & Giedd, J. N. (2006). Brain development in children and adolescents: Insights from anatomical magnetic resonance imaging. *Neuroscience and Biobehavioral Reviews*, 30, 718–729.

Lenroot, R. K., & Giedd, J. N. (2008). The changing impact of genes and environment on brain development during childhood and adolescence: Initial findings from a neuroimaging study of pediatric twins. *Developmental Psychopathology*, 20, 1161–1175.

Leonard, H., & Wen, X. (2002). The epidemiology of mental retardation: Challenges and opportunities in the new millennium. *Developmental Disabilities Research Reviews*, 8, 117–134.

Leopold, W. F. (1947). *Speech development of a bilingual child: A linguist's record. Volume 2. Sound-learning in the first two years*. Evanston, IL: Nortwestern University Press.

Lerner, J. V., & Lerner, R. M. (1983). Temperament and adaptation across life: Theoretical and empirical issues. In P. B. Baltes & O. G. Brim (Eds), *Life-span development and behavior, Volume 5* (pp. 197–231). London: Academic Press.

Lerner, R. M. (2002). *Concepts and theories of human development, Third edition*. Mahwah, NJ: Erlbaum.

Lerner, R. M. (2015). Eliminating genetic reductionism from developmental science. *Research in Human Development*, 12, 178–188.

Lerner, R. M., & Castellino, D. R. (2002). Contemporary developmental theory and adolescence: Developmental systems and applied developmental science. *Journal of Adolescent Health*, 31, 122–135.

Lerner, R. M., Schwartz, S. J., & Phelps, E. (2009). Problematics of time and timing in the longitudinal study of human development: Theoretical and methodological issues. *Human Development*, 52, 44–68.

Leslie, A. M. (2005). Developmental parallels in understanding minds and bodies. *Trends in Cognitive Sciences*, 9, 459–462.

Leslie, A. M., Friedman, O., & German, T. (2004). Core mechanisms in "theory of mind". *Trends in Cognitive Sciences*, 8, 528–533.

Letourneau, N., Tryphonopoulos, P., Giesbrecht, G., Dennis, C. L., Bhogal, S., & Watson, B. (2015). Narrative and meta-analytic review of interventions aiming to improve maternal–child attachment security. *Infant Mental Health Journal*, 36, 366–387.

Levels, M., Dronkers, J., & Kraaykamp, G. (2008). Immigrant children's educational achievement in western countries: Origin, destination, and community effects on mathematical performance. *American Sociological Review*, 73, 835–853.

Levert-Levitt, E., & Sagi-Schwartz, A. (2015). Integrated attachment theory. In J. D. Wright (Ed.), *International encyclopedia of the social and behavioral sciences, Second edition, Volume 12* (pp. 228–234). Amsterdam, NL: Elsevier.

Levin, I. (1977). The development of time concepts in young children: Reasoning about duration. *Child Development*, 48, 435–444.

Levin, I. (1989). Principles underlying time measurement: The development of children's constraints on counting time. In I. Levin & D. Zakay (Eds), *Time and human cognition: A life-span perspective* (pp. 145–183). Amsterdam, NL: Elsevier.

Levine, L. E. (1983). Mine: Self definitions in two-year-old boys. *Developmental Psychology*, 19, 544–549.

Levitt, M. J., Weber, R. A., Clark, M. C., & McDonnell, P. (1985). Reciprocity of exchange in toddler sharing behavior. *Developmental Psychology*, 21, 122–123.

Levorato, M. C., & Cacciari, C. (2002). The creation of new figurative expressions: Psycholinguistic evidence on children, adolescents and adults. *Journal of Child Language, 29*, 127–150.

Lewin, K. (1931). Environmental forces in child behavior and development. In C. Murchison (Ed.), *A handbook of child development, Second edition* (pp. 590–625). Worcester, MA: Clark University Press.

Lewin, K. (1935). *A dynamic theory of personality*. New York, NY: McGraw-Hill.

Lewis, C., Freeman, N. H., Hagestadt, C., & Douglas, H. (1994). Narrative access and production in preschoolers' false belief reasoning. *Cognitive Development, 9*, 397–424.

Lewis, M. (1991). Ways of knowing: Objective self-awareness or consciousness. *Developmental Review, 11*, 231–243.

Lewis, M. (1993). The emergence of human emotions. In M. Lewis & J. Haviland (Eds), *Handbook of emotions* (pp. 223–235). New York, NY: Guilford Press.

Lewis, M. (1997). The development of a self. Comments on the paper of Neisser. *Annals New York Academy of Sciences, 818*, 279–283.

Lewis, M. (2001a). Issues in the study of personality development. *Psychological Inquiry, 12*, 67–83.

Lewis, M. (2001b). Continuity and change: A reply. *Psychological Inquiry, 12*, 110–112.

Lewis, M. (2005). Self-organizing individual differences in brain development. *Developmental Review, 25*, 252–277.

Lewis, M. (2007). Self-conscious emotional development. In J. L. Tracy, R, W. Robins, & J. P. Tangney (Eds), *The self-conscious emotions: Theory and research* (pp. 134–149). New York, NY: Guilford Press.

Lewis, M. (2011). Problems in the study of infant emotional development. *Emotion Review, 3*, 131–137.

Lewis, M., & Brooks-Gunn, J. (1979). *Social cognition and the acquisition of self*. New York, NY: Plenum Press.

Lewis, M., Alessandri, S. M., & Sullivan, M. V. (1990). Violation of expectancy, loss of control and anger expressions in young infants. *Developmental Psychology, 26*, 745–751.

Lewis, M., & Rudolph, K. (Eds) (2014). *Handbook of developmental psychopathology, Third edition*. New York, NY: Springer.

Lewis, M., Stanger, C., & Sullivan M. W. (1989). Deception in three-year-olds. *Developmental Psychology, 25*, 439–443.

Lewis, M., Young, G., Brooks, J., & Michalson, L. (1975). The beginning of friendship. In M. Lewis & L. Rosenblum (Eds), *Friendship and peer relations* (pp. 27–66). New York, NY: Wiley.

Lewis, M. M. (1936). *Infant speech*. London: Routledge and Kegan Paul.

Lewis, P. J. (2017). The erosion of play. *International Journal of Play, 6*, 10–23.

Lewis, T. L., & Maurer, D. (2005). Multiple sensitive periods in human visual development: Evidence from visually deprived children. *Developmental Psychobiology, 46*, 163–183.

Lewis, T. L., & Maurer, D. (2009). Effects of early pattern deprivation on visual development. *Optometry and Vision Science, 86*, 640–646.

Lewis, V., Norgate, S., Collis, G., & Reynolds, R. (2000). The consequences of visual impairment for children's symbolic and functional play. *British Journal of Developmental Psychology, 18*, 449–464.

Lewkowicz, D. J. (1994). Development of intersensory perception in human infants. In D. J. Lewkowicz & R. Lickliter (Eds), *The development of intersensory perception: Comparative perspectives* (pp. 165–203). Hillsdale, NJ: Erlbaum.

Lewontin, R. (1970). Race and intelligence. *Bulletin of the Atomic Scientists, 26*, 2–8.

Li, P., Huang, B., & Hsiao, Y. (2010). Learning that classifiers count: Mandarin-speaking children's acquisition of sortal and mensural classifiers. *Journal of East Asian Linguistics, 19*, 207–230.

Li, W. S., & Ho, C. S. H. (2011). Lexical tone awareness among Chinese children with developmental dyslexia. *Journal of Child Language, 38*, 793–808.

Liao, X., Vasilakos, A. V., & He, Y. (2017). Small-world human brain networks: Perspectives and challenges. *Neuroscience and Biobehavioral Reviews, 77*, 286–300.

Liben, L. S. (2014). The individual ↔ context nexus in developmental intergroup theory: Within and beyond the ivory tower. *Research in Human Development, 11*, 273–290.

Liben, L. S., & Bigler, R. S. (2008). Developmental gender differentiation: Pathways in conforming and nonconforming outcomes. *Journal of Gay and Lesbian Mental Health, 12*, 95–119.

Lickliter, R., & Honeycutt, H. (2003). Developmental dynamics: Towards a biologically plausible evolutionary psychology. *Psychological Bulletin, 129*, 819–835.

Lickliter, R., & Honeycutt, H. (2015). Biology, development, and human systems. In R. M. Lerner, W. F. Overton & P. C. M. Molenaar (Eds), *Handbook of child psychology and developmental science, Seventh edition. Volume 1: Theory and method* (pp. 162–207). New York, NY: Wiley.

Lidz, C. S. (1997). Dynamic assessment approaches. In D. P. Flanagan, J. L. Genshaft & P. L. Harrison (Eds), *Contemporary intellectual assessment. Theories, tests, and issues* (pp. 281–296). London: Guilford Press.

Lidz, C. S., & Peña, E. D. (2009). Response to intervention and dynamic assessment: Do we just appear to be speaking the same language? *Seminars in Speech and Language, 30*, 121–133.

Lieberman, A. F., Compton, N. C., Van Horn, P., & Ghosh Ippen, C. (2003). *Losing a caregiver to death in the early years: Guidelines for the treatment of traumatic bereavement in infancy and early childhood*. Washington, DC: Zero to Three.

Lieu, J. E., Tye-Murray, N., & Fu, Q. (2012). Longitudinal study of children with unilateral hearing loss. *The Laryngoscope, 122*, 2088–2095.

Lieven, E. (2014). First language development: A usage-based perspective on past and current research. *Journal of Child Language, 41*, 48–63.

Lieven, E. (2016). Usage-based approaches to language development: Where do we go from here? *Language and Cognition, 8*, 346–368.

Lieven, E., Behrens, H., Speares, J., & Tomasello, M. (2003). Early syntactic creativity: A usage-based approach. *Journal of Child Language, 30*, 333–370.

Lieven, E., Salomo, D., & Tomasello, M. (2009). Two-year-old children's production of multiword utterances: A usage-based analysis. *Cognitive Linguistics, 20*, 481–508.

Lifter, K., Ellis, J., Cannon, B., & Anderson, S. R. (2005). Developmental specificity in targeting and teaching play activities to children with pervasive developmental disorders. *Journal of Early Intervention, 27*, 247–267.

Lifter, K., Foster-Sanda, S., Arzamarski, C., Briesch, J., & McClure, E. (2011). Overview of play: Its uses and importance in early intervention/early childhood special education. *Infants and Young Children, 24*, 225–245.

Light, P., & Glachan, M. (1985). Facilitation of individual problem solving through peer interaction. *Educational Psychology, 5*, 217–225.

Light, P. H., Girotto, V., & Legrenzi, P. (1990). Children's reasoning on conditional promises and permissions. *Cognitive Development, 5*, 369–383.

Lillard, A. S. (1993). Pretend play skills and the child's theory of mind. *Child Development, 64*, 348–371.

Lillard, A. S. (2001). Pretend play as Twin Earth. *Developmental Review, 21*, 1–33.

Lillard, A. S. (2015). The development of play. In L. S. Liben & U. Mueller (Eds), *Handbook of child psychology and developmental science, Seventh edition, Volume 2: Cognitive processes* (pp. 425–468). New York, NY: Wiley.

Lillard, A. S. (2017). Why do the children (pretend) play? *Trends in Cognitive Sciences, 11*, 826–834.

Lillard, A. S., Lerner, M. D., Hopkins, E. J., Dore, R. A., Smith, E. D., & Palmquist, C. M. (2013). The impact of pretend play on children's development: A review of the evidence. *Psychological Bulletin, 139*, 1–34.

Linebarger, D. L., & Walker, D. (2005). Infants' and toddlers' television viewing and language outcomes. *American Behavioral Scientist, 48*, 624–645.

Ling, R., & Haddon, L. (2008). Children, youth and the mobile phone. In K. Dortner & L. Livingstone (Eds), *International handbook of children, media and culture* (pp. 137–151). London: Sage.

Lingwood, J., Blades, M., Farran, E. K., Courbois, Y., & Matthews, D. (2015). The development of wayfinding abilities in children: Learning routes with and without landmarks. *Journal of Environmental Psychology, 41*, 74–80.

Linnanmäki, K. (2004). Självuppfattning och utveckling av matematikprestationer. *Nordisk Tidsskrift for Spesialpedagogikk, 81*, 210–220.

Lisina, M. I. (1985). *Child, adults, peers: Patterns of communication*. Moscow: Progress Publishers.

Liszkowski, U., Carpenter, M., Striano, T., & Tomasello, M. (2006). Twelve- and 18-month-olds point to provide information for others. *Journal of Cognition and Development, 7*, 173–187.

Litovsky, R. Y. (1997). Developmental changes in the precedence effect: Estimates of minimal audible angle. *Journal of the Acoustical Society of America, 102*, 1739–1745.

Little, A. H. Lipsitt, L. P., & Rovee-Collier, C. (1984). Classical conditioning and retention of the infant's eyelid response: Effects of age and interstimulus interval. *Journal of Experimental Child Psychology, 37*, 512–524.

Little, C. M. (2011). Genetics and twins. *Newborn and Infant Nursing Reviews, 11*, 185–189.

Liu, D., & Brown, B. B. (2014). Self-disclosure on social networking sites, positive feedback, and social capital among Chinese college students. *Computers in Human Behavior, 38*, 213–219.

Llabre, M. M., Hadi, F., La Greca, A. M., & Lai, B. S. (2015). Psychological distress in young adults exposed to war-related trauma in childhood. *Journal of Clinical Child and Adolescent Psychology, 44*, 169–180.

Lloyd, P., Camaioni, L., & Ercolani, P. (1995). Assessing referential communication skills in the primary school years: A comparative study. *British Journal of Developmental Psychology, 13*, 13–29.

LoBue, V. (2009). More than just another face in the crowd: Detection of threatening facial expressions in children and adults. *Developmental Science, 12*, 305–313.

LoBue, V., & DeLoache, J. S. (2011). Pretty in pink: The early development of gender-stereotyped colour preferences. *British Journal of Developmental Psychology, 29*, 656–667.

Lock, A. (1980). *The guided reinvention of language*. London: Academic Press.

Lock, A., Young, A., Service, V., & Chandler, P. (1990). Some observations on the origin of the pointing gesture. In V. Volterra & C. Erting (Eds), *From gesture to language in hearing and deaf children* (pp. 42–55). Berlin: Springer.

Locke, J., Shih, W., Kretzmann, M., & Kasari, C. (2016). Examining playground engagement between elementary school children with and without autism spectrum disorder. *Autism, 20*, 653–662.

Loeber, R., Jennings, W. G., Ahonen, L., Piquero, A. R., & Farrington, D. P. (2017). *Female delinquency from childhood to young adulthood: Recent results from the Pittsburgh Girls Study*. Cham, Switzerland: Springer.

Loeber, R., Menting, B., Lynam, D. R., Moffitt, T. E., Stouthamer-Loeber, M., Stallings, R., Farrington, D. P., & Pardini, D. (2012). Findings from the Pittsburgh Youth Study: Cognitive impulsivity and intelligence as predictors of the age–crime curve. *Journal of the American Academy of Child and Adolescent Psychiatry, 51*, 1136–1149.

Loeber, R., & Schmaling, K. B. (1985). Empirical evidence for overt and covert patterns of antisocial conduct problems: A meta-analysis. *Journal of Abnormal Child Psychology, 13*, 337–353.

Loeber, R., Wung, P., Keenan, K., Giroux, B., Stouthamer-Loeber, M., van Kammen, W. B., & Maughan, B. (1993). Developmental pathways in disruptive child behavior. *Development and Psychopathology, 5*, 103–133.

Loftus, E. F. (1993). The reality of repressed memories. *American Psychologist, 48,* 518–537.

Loftus, E. F., & Davis, D. (2006). Recovered memories. *Annual Review of Clinical Psychology, 2,* 469–498.

Lord, C., Bishop, S., & Anderson, D. (2015, June). Developmental trajectories as autism phenotypes. *American Journal of Medical Genetics Part C: Seminars in Medical Genetics, 169,* 198–208.

Lorenz, K. (1935). Der Kumpan in der Umwelt des Vogels. *Journal für Ornithologie, 83,* 137–213 & 289–413.

Lorenz, K. (1963). *On aggression.* London: Methuen.

Lougheed, J. P., & Hollenstein, T. (2012). A limited repertoire of emotion regulation strategies is associated with internalizing problems in adolescence. *Social Development, 21,* 704–721.

Lourenço, O. M. (2003). Making sense of Turiel's dispute with Kohlberg: The case of the child's moral competence. *New Ideas in Psychology, 21,* 43–68.

Lourenço, O. M. (2016). Developmental stages, Piagetian stages in particular: A critical review. *New Ideas in Psychology, 40,* 123–137.

Lovaas, O. I. (1993). The development of a treatment-research project for developmentally disabled and autistic children. *Journal of Applied Behavior Analysis, 26,* 617–630.

Lovett, B. J., & Lewandowski, L. J. (2006). Gifted students with learning disabilities: Who are they? *Journal of Learning Disabilities, 39,* 515–527.

Low, J., & Perner, J. (2012). Implicit and explicit theory of mind: State of the art. *British Journal of Developmental Psychology, 30,* 1–13.

Lowell, A., Renk, K., & Adgate, A. H. (2014). The role of attachment in the relationship between child maltreatment and later emotional and behavioral functioning. *Child Abuse and Neglect, 38,* 1436–1449.

Lowther, H., & Newman, E. (2014). Attention bias modification (ABM) as a treatment for child and adolescent anxiety: A systematic review. *Journal of Affective Disorders, 168,* 125–135.

Loye, D. (2002). The moral brain. *Brain and Mind, 3,* 133–150.

Lu, J., Jones, A., & Morgan, G. (2016). The impact of input quality on early sign development in native and non-native language learners. *Journal of Child Language, 43,* 537–552.

Lu, L. (2008). The individual-oriented and social-oriented Chinese bicultural self: Testing the theory. *The Journal of Social Psychology, 148,* 347–374.

Luborsky, L., & Barrett, M. S. (2006). The history and empirical status of key psychoanalytic concepts. *Annual Review of Clinical Psychology, 2,* 1–19.

Lucariello, J. (1998). Together wherever we go: The ethnographic child and the developmentalist. *Child Development, 69,* 355–358.

Lucariello, J., & Nelson, K. (1985). Slot-filler categories as memory organizers for young children. *Developmental Psychology, 21,* 272–282.

Lucariello, J., & Nelson, K. (1987). Remembering and planning talk between mothers and children. *Discourse Processes, 10,* 219–235.

Luciana, M., Conklin, H. M., Hooper, C. J., & Yarger, R. S. (2005). The development of nonverbal working memory and executive control processes in adolescents. *Child Development, 76,* 697–712.

Luckey, A. J., & Fabes, R. A. (2005). Understanding nonsocial play in early childhood. *Early Childhood Education Journal, 33,* 67–72.

Ludemann, P. M. (1991). Generalized discrimination of positive facial expressions by seven- and ten-month-old infants. *Child Development, 62,* 55–67.

Luengo Kanacri, B. P., Pastorelli, C., Eisenberg, N., Zuffianò, A., & Caprara, G. V. (2013). The development of prosociality from adolescence to early adulthood: The role of effortful control. *Journal of Personality, 81,* 302–312.

Lukowski, A. F., Phung, J. N., & Milojevich, H. M. (2015). Language facilitates event memory in early childhood: Child comprehension, adult-provided linguistic support and delayed recall at 16 months. *Memory, 23,* 848–863.

Luna, B., Garver, K. E., Urban, T. A., Lazar, N. A., & Sweeney, J. A. (2004). Maturation of cognitive processes from late childhood to adulthood. *Child Development, 75,* 1357–1372.

Lund, E. M., Kohlmeier, T. L., & Durán, L. K. (2017). Comparative language development in bilingual and monolingual children with autism spectrum disorder: A systematic review. *Journal of Early Intervention, 39,* 106–124.

Lund, T. (2005). The qualitative–quantitative distinction: Some comments. *Scandinavian Journal of Educational Research, 49,* 115–132.

Lundervold, A. J., Heimann, M., & Manger, T. (2008). Behaviour–emotional characteristics of primary-school children rated as having language problems. *British Journal of Educational Psychology, 78,* 567–580.

Luntz, B. K., & Widom, C. S. (1994). Antisocial personality disorder in abused and neglected children grown up. *American Journal of Psychiatry, 151,* 670–674.

Lupyan, G. (2016). The centrality of language in human cognition. *Language Learning, 66,* 516–553.

Luquet, G. H. (1927). *Le dessin enfantin.* Paris: Alcan.

Luria, A. R. (1961). *The role of speech in the regulation of normal and abnormal behavior.* Oxford: Pergamon Press.

Luria, A. R. (1976). *Cognitive development: Its cultural and social foundations.* London: Harvard University Press.

Luthar, S. S. (Ed.) (2003). *Resilience and vulnerability: Adaptation in the context of childhood adversities.* New York, NY: Cambridge University Press.

Luthar, S. S., Lyman, E. L., & Crossman, E. J. (2014). Resilience and positive psychology. In M. Lewis & K. Rudolph (Eds), *Handbook of developmental psychopathology* (pp. 125–140). New York, NY: Springer.

Lutz, C. (1988). Ethnographic perspectives on the emotion lexicon. In V. Hamilton, G. H. Bower, H. Gordon & N. H. Frijda (Eds), *Cognitive perspectives on emotion and motivation* (pp. 399–419). Norwell, MA: Kluwer.

Lyall, A. E., Shi, F., Geng, X., Woolson, S., Li, G., Wang, L., Hamer, R. M., Shen, D., & Gilmore, J. H. (2015). Dynamic development of regional cortical thickness and surface area in early childhood. *Cerebral Cortex*, *25*, 2204–2212.

Lynam, D. R., & Widiger, T. A. (2007). Using a general model of personality to identify the basic elements of psychopathy. *Journal of Personality Disorders*, *21*, 160–178.

Lynch, M. P., & Eilers, R. E. (1992). A study of perceptual development for musical tuning. *Perception and Psychophysics*, *52*, 599–608.

Lyst, M. J., & Bird, A. (2015). Rett syndrome: A complex disorder with simple roots. *Nature Reviews Genetics*, *16*, 261–275.

Ma, L., & Lillard, A. S. (2006). Where is the real cheese? Young children's ability to discriminate between real and pretend acts. *Child Development*, *77*, 1762–1777.

Maccoby, E. E. (1990). Gender and relations: A developmental account. *American Psychologist*, *45*, 513–520.

Maccoby, E. E. (1998). *The two sexes: Growing up apart, coming together*. Cambridge, MA: Harvard University Press.

Maccoby, E. E. (2000). Perspectives on gender development. *International Journal of Behavioral Development*, *24*, 398–406.

Maccoby, E. E. (2002). Gender and group process: A developmental perspective. *Current Directions in Psychological Science*, *11*, 54–58.

Maccoby, E. E., & Jacklin, C. N. (1987). Gender segregation in childhood. *Advances in Child Development and Behavior*, *20*, 239–288.

Maciel, J. A., & Knudson-Martin, C. (2014). Don't end up in the fields: Identity construction among Mexican adolescent immigrants, their parents, and sociocontextual processes. *Journal of Marital and Family Therapy*, *40*, 484–497.

Macintyre, C. (2000). *Dyspraxia in the early years. Identifying and supporting children with movement difficulties*. London: David Fulton Publishers.

Macintyre, C. (2001). *Dyspraxia 5–11: A practical guide*. London: David Fulton Publishers.

MacKenzie, M. J., Nicklas, E., Brooks-Gunn, J., & Waldfogel, J. (2015). Spanking and children's externalizing behavior across the first decade of life: Evidence for transactional processes. *Journal of Youth and Adolescence*, *44*, 658–669.

Macklem, G. L. (2014). *Preventive mental health at school*. New York, NY: Springer.

MacLeod, C., & Clarke, P. J. (2015). The attentional bias modification approach to anxiety intervention. *Clinical Psychological Science*, *3*, 58–78.

Macnamara, J. (1982). *Words for things*. Cambridge, MA: MIT Press.

MacPherson, A. C., & Moore, C. (2007). Attentional control by gaze cues in infancy. In R. Flom, K. Lee & D. Muir (Eds), *Gaze-following: Its development and significance* (pp. 53–75). Mahwah, NJ: Lawrence Erlbaum.

MacWhinney, B. (1982). Basic syntactic processes. In S. Kuczaj (Ed.), *Language development. Volume 1. Syntax and semantics* (pp. 73–136). Hillsdale, NJ: Erlbaum.

MacWhinney, B. (2004). A multiple process solution to the logical problem of language acquisition. *Journal of Child Language*, *31*, 883–914.

MacWhinney, B. (2015). Language development. In R. M. Lerner, L. Liben & U. Muller (Eds), *Handbook of child psychology and developmental science, Seventh edition, Volume 2: Cognitive processes* (pp. 296–338). New York, NY: Wiley.

MacWhinney, B., & O'Grady, W. (Eds) (2015). *Handbook of language emergence*. New York, NY: Wiley.

Macy, M. (2012). The evidence behind developmental screening instruments. *Infants and Young Children*, *25*, 19–61.

Madge, N., & Fassam, M. (1982). *Ask the children. Experiences of physical disability in the school years*. London: Batsford.

Madigan, S., Atkinson, L., Laurin, K., & Benoit, D. (2013). Attachment and internalizing behavior in early childhood: A meta-analysis. *Developmental Psychology*, *49*, 672–689.

Magnus, P., Birke, C., Vejrup, K., Haugan, A., Alsaker, E., Daltveit, A. K., Handal, M., Haugen, M., Høiseth, G., Knudsen, G. P., et al. (2016). Cohort profile update: The Norwegian mother and child cohort study (MoBa). *International Journal of Epidemiology*, *45*, 382–388.

Mahler, M. S., Pine, F., & Bergman, A. (1975). *The psychological birth of the human infant symbiosis and individuation*. New York, NY: Basic Books.

Mahy, C. E., Moses, L. J., & Pfeifer, J. H. (2014). How and where: Theory-of-mind in the brain. *Developmental Cognitive Neuroscience*, *9*, 68–81.

Main, M., & George, C. (1985). Responses of abused and disadvantaged toddlers to distress in agemates: A study in the daycare setting. *Developmental Psychology*, *21*, 407–412.

Main, M., & Weston, D. R. (1981). The quality of the toddler's relationship to mother and father: Relation to conflict behavior and readyness to establish new relationships. *Child Development*, *52*, 932–940.

Majid, A., Boster, J. S., & Bowerman, M. (2008). The cross-linguistic categorization of everyday events: A study of cutting and breaking. *Cognition*, *109*, 235–250.

Malatesta, C. Z., & Haviland, J. M. (1982). Learning display rules: The socialization of emotion expression in infancy. *Child Development*, *53*, 991–1003.

Malti, T., Dys, S., Ongley, S. F., & Colasante, T. (2012). The development of adolescents' emotions in situations involving moral conflict and exclusion. *New Directions for Youth Development*, *136*, 12–41.

Malti, T., & Ongley, S. F. (2014). The development of moral emotions and moral reasoning. In M. Killen & J. Smetana (Eds), *Handbook of moral development, Second edition* (pp. 163–183). New York, NY: Psychology Press.

Mandler, J. M. (2004). *The foundations of mind: Origins of conceptual thought*. Oxford: Oxford University Press.

Mandler, J. M. (2008). On the birth and growth of concepts. *Philosophical Psychology*, *21*, 207–230.

Mandler, J. M. (2010). The spatial foundations of the conceptual system. *Language and Cognition*, *2*, 21–44.

Mandler, J. M. (2012). On the spatial foundations of the conceptual system and its enrichment. *Cognitive Science*, *36*, 421–451.

Mandler, J. M., Bauer, P. J., & McDonough, L. (1991). Separating the sheep from the goats: Differing global categories. *Cognitive Psychology*, *23*, 263–298.

Mandler, J. M., & McDonough, L. (1996). Drinking and driving don't mix: Inductive generalization in infancy. *Cognition*, *59*, 307–335.

Manfra, L., Davis, K. D., Ducenne, L., & Winsler, A. (2014). Preschoolers' motor and verbal self-control strategies during a resistance-to-temptation task. *The Journal of Genetic Psychology*, *175*, 332–345.

Mangelsdorf, S., Gunnar, M., Kestenbaum, M., Lang, S., & Andreas, D. (1990). Infant proneness-to-distress temperament, maternal personality, and mother–infant attachment: Associations and goodness of fit. *Child Development*, *61*, 820–831.

Manuck, S. B., & McCaffery, J. M. (2014). Gene-environment interaction. *Annual Review of Psychology*, *65*, 41–70.

Marchand, H. (2012). Contributions of Piagetian and post-Piagetian theories to education. *Educational Research Review*, *7*, 165–176.

Marcus, G. F. (1995). Children's overregularization of English plurals: A quantitative analysis. *Journal of Child Langue*, *22*, 447–459.

Mareschal, D., Johnson, M. H., Sirois, S., Spratling, M., Thomas, M., & Westermann, G. (2007a). *Neuroconstructivism, Volume I. How the brain constructs cognition*. Oxford: Oxford University Press.

Mareschal, D., Sirois, S., Westermann, G., & Johnson, M. H. (2007b). *Neuroconstructivism, Volume II. Perspectives and prospects*. Oxford: Oxford University Press.

Marfo, K. (2011). Envisioning an African child development field. *Child Development Perspectives*, *5*, 140–147.

Mari, F., Kilstrup-Nielsen, C., Cambi, F., Speciale, C., Mencarelli, M. A., & Renieri, A. (2005). Genetics and mechanisms of disease in Rett syndrome. *Drug Discovery Today: Disease Mechanisms*, *2*, 419–425.

Marini, Z., & Case, R. (1994). The development of abstract reasoning about the physical and social world. *Child Development*, *65*, 147–159.

Marinova-Todd, S. H., Colozzo, P., Mirenda, P., Stahl, H., Kay-Raining Bird, E., Parkington, K., Cain, K., Scherba de Valenzuela, J., Segers, E., MacLeod, A. A., & Genesee, F. (2016). Professional practices and opinions about services available to bilingual children with developmental disabilities: An international study. *Journal of Communication Disorders*, *63*, 47–62.

Markman, E. M. (1992). Constraints on word learning: Speculations about their nature, origins and domain specificity. In M. R. Gunnar & M. P. Maratsos (Eds), *Minnesota symposia on child psychology, Volume 25* (pp. 59–101). Hillsdale, NJ: Lawrence Erlbaum.

Markovits, H., Schleifer, M., & Fortier, L. (1989). Development of elementary deductive reasoning in young children. *Developmental Psychology*, *25*, 787–793.

Markus, H. R., & Kitayama, S. (2010). Cultures and selves: A cycle of mutual constitution. *Perspectives on Psychological Science*, *5*, 420–430.

Markus, H. R., Mullally, P. R., & Kitayama, S. (1997). Selfways: Diversity in modes of cultural participation. In U. Neisser & D. A. Jopling (Eds), *The conceptual self in context: Culture, experience, self understanding* (pp. 13–61). Cambridge: Cambridge University Press.

Marschark, M., Schick, B., & Spencer, P. E. (2006). Understanding sign language development of deaf children. In B. Schick, M. Marschark & P. E. Spencer (Eds), *Advances in the sign language development of deaf children* (pp. 3–19). New York, NY: Oxford University Press.

Marschark, M., Spencer, P. E., Adams, J., & Sapere, P. (2011). Evidence-based practice in educating deaf and hard-of-hearing children: Teaching to their cognitive strengths and needs. *European Journal of Special Needs Education*, *26*, 3–16.

Marsee, M. A., & Frick, P. J. (2010). Callous unemotional traits and aggression in youth. In E. A. William & L. Elizabeth (Eds), *Emotions, aggression and morality in children: Bridging development and psychopathology* (pp. 137–156). Washington: American Psychological Association.

Marsh, H. W., & O'Mara, A. (2008). Reciprocal effects between academic self-concept, self-esteem, achievement, and attainment over seven adolescent years: Unidimensional and multidimensional perspectives of self-concept. *Personality and Social Psychology Bulletin*, *34*, 542–552.

Marshall, P. J. (2016). Embodiment and human development. *Child Development Perspectives*, *10*, 245–250.

Martí, E. (1996). Piaget and school education: A socio-cultural challenge. *Prospects*, *26*, 141–158.

Martí, E., & Rodríguez, C. (Eds) (2012). *After Piaget*. New Brunswick, NJ: Transaction Publishers.

Martin, A., & Olson, K. R. (2015). Beyond good and evil: What motivations underlie children's prosocial behavior? *Perspectives on Psychological Science*, *10*, 159–175.

Martin, C. L., & Fabes, R. A. (2001). The stability and consequences of young children's same-sex peer interactions. *Developmental Psychology*, *37*, 431–446.

Martin, C. L., Fabes, R. A., & Hanish, L. D. (2014). Gendered-peer relationships in educational contexts. *Advances in Child Development and Behavior*, *47*, 151–187.

Martin, C. L., & Ruble, D. N. (2009). Patterns of gender development. *Annual Review of Psychology*, *61*, 353–381.

Martin, C. L., Ruble, D. N., & Szkrybalo, J. (2002). Cognitive theories of early gender development. *Psychological Bulletin*, *128*, 903–933.

Martin, S. (2014). Play in children with motor disabilities. Doctoral Dissertation, University of Kentucky, USA.

Martins, N., & Jensen, R. E. (2014). The relationship between "teen mom" reality programming and teenagers' beliefs about teen parenthood. *Mass Communication and Society*, *17*, 830–852.

Martinsen, H., & Nærland, T. (2009). *Sosial utvikling i førskolealder. Vennskap, konflikter & kommunikasjon i barnehagen.* Oslo, NO: Gyldendal Akademisk.

Martinsen, H., Nærland, T., & Vereijken, B. (2010). Observation-based descriptions of social status in the preschool. *Early Child Development and Care, 180,* 1231–1241.

Martinsen, H., Nærland, T., & von Tetzchner, S. (2015). *Språklig høytfungerende barn og voksne med autismespekterforstyrrelse: Prinsipper for opplæring og tilrettelegging, Annen utgave (High functioning children and adults with autism spectrum disorder: Principles for teaching and adaptation, Second edition).* Oslo: Gyldendal Akademisk.

Martinsen, K. D., Kendall, P. C., Stark, K., & Neumer, S. P. (2016). Prevention of anxiety and depression in children: Acceptability and feasibility of the transdiagnostic EMOTION program. *Cognitive and Behavioral Practice, 23,* 1–13.

Martinussen, R., Hayden, J., Hogg-Johnson, S., & Tannock, R. (2005). A meta-analysis of working memory impairments in children with attention-deficit/hyperactivity disorder. *Journal of the American Academy of Child and Adolescent Psychiatry, 44,* 377–384.

Martlew, M., & Connolly, K. J. (1996). Human figure drawings by schooled and unschooled children in Papua New Guinea. *Child Development, 67,* 2743–2762.

Marvin, R. S., & Britner, P. (2008). Normative development: The ontogeny of attachment. In J. Cassidy & P. R. Shaver (Eds), *Handbook of attachment: Theory, research, and clinical applications, Second edition* (pp. 269–294). New York, NY: Guilford Press.

Marvin, R. S., Britner, P., & Russell, B. S. (2016). Normative development: The ontogeny of attachment in childhood. In J. Cassidy & P. R. Shaver (Eds), *Handbook of attachment: Theory, research, and clinical applications* (pp. 273–290). New York, NY: Guilford Press.

Masangkay, Z. S., McCluskey, K. A., McIntyre, C. W., Sims-Knight, J., Vaughn, B. E., & Flavell, T. H. (1974). The early development of inferences about the visual percepts of others. *Child Development, 45,* 357–366.

Masataka, N. (1992). Motherese in a signed language. *Infant Behavior and Development, 15,* 453–460.

Masataka, N. (2006). Preference for consonance over dissonance by hearing newborns of deaf parents and of hearing parents. *Developmental Science, 9,* 46–50.

Masi, G. (1998). Psychiatric illness in mentally retarded adolescents: Clinical features. *Adolescence, 33,* 425–434.

Massaro, D. W., & Cowan, N. (1993). Information processing models: Microscopes of the mind. *Annual Review of Psychology, 44,* 383–425.

Masten, A. S. (2014). Global perspectives on resilience in children and youth. *Child Development, 85,* 6–20.

Masten, A. S. (2016). Resilience in developing systems: The promise of integrated approaches. *European Journal of Developmental Psychology, 13,* 297–312

Masten, A. S., & Cicchetti, D. (2010). Developmental cascades. *Development and Psychopathology, 22,* 491–495.

Masters, J. C. (1971). Social comparison by young children. *Young Children, 27,* 7–60.

Masur, E. F. (1997). Maternal labelling of novel and familiar objects: Implications for children's development of lexical constraints. *Journal of Child Language, 24,* 427–439.

Masur, E. F., Flynn, V., & Olson, J. (2015). The presence of background television during young children's play in American homes. *Journal of Children and Media, 9,* 349–367.

Mathews, A., & MacLeod, C. (2005). Cognitive vulnerability to emotional disorders. *Annual Review of Clinical Psychology, 1,* 167–195.

Mathiesen, K. S., & Tambs, K. (1999). The EAS Temperament Questionnaire – Factor structure, age trends, reliability, and stability in a Norwegian sample. *Journal of Child Psychology and Psychiatry, 40,* 431–439.

Mathur, R., & Berndt, T. J. (2006). Relations of friends' activities to friendship quality. *Journal of Early Adolescence, 26,* 365–388.

Matson, J. L., & Kozlowski, A. M. (2011). The increasing prevalence of autism spectrum disorders. *Research in Autism Spectrum Disorders, 5,* 418–425.

Matsuda, F. (2001). Development of concepts of interrelationship among duration, distance, and speed. *International Journal of Behavioral Development, 25,* 466–480.

Maughan, A., & Cicchetti, D. (2002). Impact of child maltreatment and interadult violence on children's emotion regulation abilities and socioemotional adjustment. *Child Development, 73* (5), 1525–1542.

Maurer, D., & Werker, J. F. (2014). Perceptual narrowing during infancy: A comparison of language and faces. *Developmental Psychobiology, 56,* 154–178.

Maxwell, C., & Maxwell, S. (2003). Experiencing and witnessing familial aggression and their relationship to physical aggressive behaviors among Filipino adolescents. *Journal of Interpersonal Violence, 18,* 1432–1451.

Mayer, A., & Träuble, B. E. (2013). Synchrony in the onset of mental state understanding across cultures? A study among children in Samoa. *International Journal of Behavioral Development, 37,* 21–28.

Mayer, J. D., & Salovey, P. (1997). What is emotional intelligence? In P. Salovey & D. J. Sluyter (Eds), *Emotional development and emotional intelligence* (pp. 3–31). New York, NY: Basic Books.

Mayes, S. D., Calhoun, S. L., Bixler, E. O., & Zimmerman, D. N. (2009). IQ and neuropsychological predictors of academic achievement. *Learning and Individual Differences, 19,* 238–241.

Mayseless, O. (2005). Ontogeny of attachment in middle childhood: Conceptualization of normative changes. In K. A. Kerns & R. A. Richardson (Eds), *Attachment in middle childhood* (pp. 1–23). New York, NY: Guilford Press.

Mazefsky, C. A., & White, S. W. (2014). Emotion regulation: Concepts and practice in autism spectrum disorder. *Child and Adolescent Psychiatric Clinics of North America, 23,* 15–24.

McAdams, D. P. (2013). The psychological self as actor, agent, and author. *Perspectives on Psychological Science, 8*, 272–295.

McAdams, D. P., & Cox, K. S. (2010). Self and identity across the life span. In R. Lerner, A. Freund & M. Lamb (Eds), *Handbook of life span development, Volume 2* (pp. 158–207). New York, NY: Wiley.

McAlister, A., & Peterson, C. C. (2007). A longitudinal study of child siblings and theory of mind development. *Cognitive Development, 22*, 258–270.

McAllister, R., & Gray, C. (2007). Low vision: Mobility and independence training for the early years child. *Early Child Development and Care, 177*, 839–852.

McAndrew, B., & Malley-Keighran, M. P. O. (2017). "She didn't have a word of English; we didn't have a word of Vietnamese": Exploring parent experiences of communication with toddlers who were adopted internationally. *Journal of Communication Disorders, 68*, 89–102.

McCall, R. B. (1989). Commentary. *Human Development, 32*, 177–186.

McCall, R. B. (1994). What process mediates predictions of childhood IQ from infant habituation and recognition memory? Speculations on the roles of inhibition and rate of information processing. *Intelligence, 18*, 107–125.

McCall, R. B., Applebaum, M. I., & Hogarty, P. S. (1973). Developmental changes in mental performance. *Monographs of the Society for Research in Child Development, 38*, 3.

McCall, R. B., & Carriger, M. S. (1993). A meta-analysis of infant habituation and recognition memory performance as predictors of later IQ. *Child Development, 64*, 57–79.

McCarthy, M. M., Pickett, L. A., VanRyzın, J. W., & Kight, K. E. (2015). Surprising origins of sex differences in the brain. *Hormones and Behavior, 76*, 3–10.

McCartney, K., Harris, M. J., & Bernieri, F. (1990). Growing up and growing apart: A developmental meta-analysis of twin studies. *Psychological Bulletin, 107*, 226–237.

McChesney, G., & Toseeb, U. (2016). Happiness, self–esteem, and prosociality in children with and without autism spectrum disorder: Evidence from a UK population cohort study. *Journal of Autism and Developmental Disorders*.

McClowry, S. G., Rodriguez, E. T., & Koslowitz, R. (2008). Temperament-based intervention: Re-examining goodness of fit. *International Journal of Developmental Science, 2*, 120–135.

McCoach, D. B., Kehle, T., Bray, M. A., & Siegle, D. (2001). Best practices in the identification of gifted students with learning disabilities. *Psychology in the Schools, 38*, 403–411.

McCormack, T. (2015). The development of temporal cognition. In R. M. Lerner, L. S. Liben & U. Mueller (Eds), *Handbook of child psychology and developmental science, Seventh edition, Volume 2: Cognitive Processes* (pp. 624–670). Hoboken, NJ: Wiley-Blackwell.

McCormack, T., & Hanley, M. (2011). Children's reasoning about the temporal order of past and future events. *Cognitive Development, 26*, 299–314.

McCorry, N. K., & Hepper, P. G. (2007). Fetal habituation performance: Gestational age and sex effects. *British Journal of Developmental Psychology, 25*, 277–292.

McCrae, R. R., & Costa, P. T. (1995). Trait explanations in personality psychology. *European Journal of Personality, 9*, 231–252.

McCrae, R. R., & Costa, P. T. (2008). The Five-Factor Theory of personality. In O. P. John, R. W. Robins & L. A. Pervin (Eds), *Handbook of personality: Theory and research, Third edition* (pp. 159–181). New York, NY: Guilford Press.

McCrory, E., Henry, L. A., & Happé, F. (2007). Eye-witness memory and suggestibility in children with Asperger syndrome. *Journal of Child Psychology and Psychiatry, 48*, 482–489.

McCrory, E. J., & Viding, E. (2015). The theory of latent vulnerability: Reconceptualizing the link between childhood maltreatment and psychiatric disorder. *Development and Psychopathology, 27*, 493–505.

McDaniel, B. T., & Radesky, J. S. (2018). Technoference: Parent distraction with technology and associations with child behavior problems. *Child Development, 89*, 100–109.

McDonald, K. L., Dashiell-Aje, E., Menzer, M. M., Rubin, K. H., Oh, W., & Bowker, J. C. (2013). Contributions of racial and sociobehavioral homophily to friendship stability and quality among same-race and cross-race friends. *The Journal of Early Adolescence, 33*, 897–919.

McGarrigle, J., Grieve, R., & Hughes, M. (1978). Interpreting inclusions: A contribution to the study of the child's cognitive and linguistic development. *Journal of the Experimental Child Psychology, 28*, 528–550.

McGillion, M., Herbert, J. S., Pine, J., Vihman, M., DePaolis, R., Keren-Portnoy, T., & Matthews, D. (2017). What paves the way to conventional language? The predictive value of babble, pointing, and socioeconomic status. *Child Development, 88*, 156–166.

McGonigle-Chalmers, M., Slater, H., & Smith, A. (2014). Rethinking private speech in preschoolers: The effects of social presence. *Developmental Psychology, 50*, 829–836.

McGoron, L., Gleason, M. M., Smyke, A. T., Drury, S. S., Nelson, C. A., III, Gregas, M. C., Fox, N. A., & Zeanah, C. H. (2012). Recovering from early deprivation: Attachment mediates effects of caregiving on psychopathology. *Journal of the American Academy of Child and Adolescent Psychiatry, 51*, 683–693.

McGowan, P. O., & Szyf, M. (2010). The epigenetics of social adversity in early life: Implications for mental health outcomes. *Neurobiology of Disease, 39*, 66–72.

McGrath, L. M., Pennington, B. F., Shanahan, M. A., Santerre-Lemmon, L. E., Barnard, H. D., Willcutt, E. G., DeFries, J. C., & Olson, R. K. (2011). A multiple deficit model of reading disability and attention-deficit/hyperactivity disorder: Searching for shared cognitive deficits. *Journal of Child Psychology and Psychiatry, 52*, 47–557.

McGraw, M. B. (1943). *The neuromuscular maturation of the human infant.* New York, NY: Columbia University Press.

McGuire, S., Manke, B., Eftekhari, A., & Dunn, J. (2000). Children's perceptions of sibling conflict during middle childhood: Issues and sibling (dis)similarity. *Social Development, 9,* 173–190.

McGuire, S., McHale, S. M., & Updegraff, K. (1996). Children's perception of the sibling relationship in middle childhood: Connections within and between family relationships. *Personal Relationships, 3,* 229–239.

McGuire, S., & Shanahan, L. (2010). Sibling experiences in diverse family contexts. *Child Development Perspectives, 4,* 72–79.

McHale, S. M., Updegraff, K. A., & Whiteman, S. D. (2012). Sibling relationships and influences in childhood and adolescence. *Journal of Marriage and Family, 74,* 913–930.

McHale, S. M., Shanahan, L., Updegraff, K. A., Crouter, A. C., & Booth, A. (2004). Developmental and individual differences in girls' sex-typed activities in middle childhood and adolescence. *Child Development, 75,* 1575–1593.

McIntosh, G. C., Olshan, A. F., & Baird, P. A. (1995). Paternal age and the risk of birth-defects in offspring. *Epidemiology, 6,* 282–288.

McIntyre, L. L. (2013). Parent training interventions to reduce challenging behavior in children with intellectual and developmental disabilities. *International Review of Research in Developmental Disabilities, 44,* 245–279.

McKelvie, P., & Low, J. (2002). Listening to Mozart does not improve children's spatial ability: Final curtains for the Mozart Effect. *British Journal of Developmental Psychology, 20,* 241–258.

McLaughlin, K. A., & King, K. (2015). Developmental trajectories of anxiety and depression in early adolescence. *Journal of Abnormal Child Psychology, 43,* 311–323.

McLaughlin, K. A., & Lambert, H. K. (2017). Child trauma exposure and psychopathology: Mechanisms of risk and resilience. *Current Opinion in Psychology, 14,* 29–34.

McLean, K. C., & Syed, M. (2015). Personal, master, and alternative narratives: An integrative framework for understanding identity development in context. *Human Development, 58,* 318–349.

McLean, K. C., Syed, M., & Shucard, H. (2016). Bringing identity content to the fore: Links to identity development processes. *Emerging Adulthood, 4,* 356–364.

McLeod, S., & Bleile, K. (2003, November). Neurological and developmental foundations of speech acquisition. Invited seminar presentation at the annual convention of the American Speech-Language-Hearing Association, Chicago, IL.

McMahon, E., Wintermark, P., & Lahav, A. (2012). Auditory brain development in premature infants: The importance of early experience. *Annals of the New York Academy of Sciences, 1252,* 17–24.

McNally, R. J. (2012). Searching for repressed memory. In R. F. Belli (Ed.), *Nebraska Symposium on Motivation: True and false recovered memories. Toward a reconciliation of the debate, Volume 58* (pp. 121– 147). New York, NY: Springer.

McQueen, J. M., Tyler, M. D., & Cutler, A. (2012). Lexical retuning of children's speech perception: Evidence for knowledge about words' component sounds. *Language Learning and Development, 8,* 317–339.

McWilliams, K., Narr, R., Goodman, G. S., Ruiz, S., & Mendoza, M. (2013). Children's memory for their mother's murder: Accuracy, suggestibility, and resistance to suggestion. *Memory, 21,* 591–598.

Meaney, M. J. (2010). Epigenetics and the biological definition of gene × environment interactions. *Child Development, 81,* 41–79.

Meehan, C. L., Hagen, E. H., & Hewlett, B. S. (2017). Persistence in infant care patterns among Aka foragers. In V. Reyes-García & A. A. Pyhälä (Eds), *Hunter-gatherers in a changing world* (pp. 213–232). Cham, Switzerland: Springer.

Meeus, W. (2011). The study of adolescent identity formation 2000–2010: A review of longitudinal research. *Journal of Research on Adolescence, 21,* 75–94.

Mehler, J., Bertoncini, J., Barriere, M., & Jassik-Gerschenfeld, D. (1978). Infant recognition of mother's voice. *Perception, 7,* 491–497.

Meins, E., & Fernyhough, C. (1999). Linguistic acquisitional style and mentalising development: The role of maternal mind-mindedness. *Cognitive Development, 14,* 363–380.

Meins, E., Fernyhough, C., Wainwright, R., Clark-Carter, D., Das Gupta, M., Fradley, E., & Tuckey, M. (2003). Pathways to understanding mind: Construct validity and predictive validity of maternal mind-mindedness. *Child Development, 74,* 1194–1211.

Meissner, W. W. (2008). Mind-brain and consciousness in psychoanalysis. *Bulletin of the Menninger Clinic, 72,* 283–312.

Melby-Lervåg, M., Redick, T. S., & Hulme, C. (2016). Working memory training does not improve performance on measures of intelligence or other measures of "far transfer": Evidence from a meta-analytic review. *Perspectives on Psychological Science, 11,* 512–534.

Melinder, A., Alexander, K., Cho, Y. I., Goodman, G. S., Thoresen, C., Lonnum, K., & Magnussen, S. (2010). Children's eyewitness memory: A comparison of two interviewing strategies as realized by forensic professionals. *Journal of Experimental Child Psychology, 105,* 156–177.

Mellon, N. K., Niparko, J. K., Rathmann, C., Mathur, G., Humphries, T., Napoli, D. J., Handley, T., Scambler, S., & Lantos, J. D. (2015). Should all deaf children learn sign language? *Pediatrics, 136,* 170–176.

Meltzer, A., & Kramer, J. (2016). Siblinghood through disability studies perspectives: Diversifying discourse and knowledge about siblings with and without disabilities. *Disability and Society, 31,* 17–32.

Meltzoff, A. N. (1993). The centrality of motor coordination and proprioception in social and cognitive development: From shared actions to shared minds. In G. J. P. Savelsbergh (Ed.), *The development of coordination in infancy* (pp. 463–496). Amsterdam, NL: Elsevier.

Meltzoff, A. N., & Moore, M. K. (1983). Newborn infants imitate adult facial gestures. *Child Development, 54,* 702–709.

Meltzoff, A. N., & Moore, M. K. (1989). Imitation in newborn infants: Exploring the range of gestures imitated and the underlying mechanisms. *Developmental Psychology, 25,* 954–962.

Meltzoff, A. N., & Moore, M. K. (1994). Imitation, memory, and the representations of persons. *Infant Behavior and Developmental, 17,* 83–99.

Meltzoff, A. N., & Moore, M. K. (1997). Explaining facial imitation: A theoretical model. *Early Development and Parenting, 6,* 179–192.

Meltzoff, A. N., & Moore, M. K. (1999). Persons and representation: Why infant imitation is important for theories of human development. In J. Nadel & G. Butterworth (Eds), *Imitation in infancy* (pp. 9–35). Cambridge: Cambridge University Press.

Memon, A., Cronin, O., Eaves, R., & Bull, R. (1993). The cognitive interview and child witnesses. *Issues in Criminological and Legal Psychology, 20,* 3–9.

Memon, A., Meissner, C. A., & Fraser, J. (2010). The cognitive interview: A meta-analytic review and study space analysis of the past 25 years. *Psychology, Public Policy, and Law, 16,* 340–372.

Mendez, L. M. R. (2017). *Cognitive behavioral therapy in schools: A tiered approach to youth mental health services.* New York, NY: Routledge.

Menon, V. (2013). Developmental pathways to functional brain networks: Emerging principles. *Trends in Cognitive Sciences, 17,* 627–640.

Menon, V. (2016). Working memory in children's math learning and its disruption in dyscalculia. *Current Opinion in Behavioral Sciences, 10,* 125–132.

Mercer, N. (2013). The social brain, language, and goal-directed collective thinking: A social conception of cognition and its implications for understanding how we think, teach, and learn. *Educational Psychologist, 48,* 148–168.

Merriman, W. E. (1986). Some reasons for the occurrence and eventual correction of children's naming errors. *Child Development, 57,* 942–952.

Merry, S. N., Hetrick, S. E., Cox, G. R., Brudevold-Iversen, T., Bir, J. J., & McDowell, H. (2012). Psychological and educational interventions for preventing depression in children and adolescents. *Evidence-Based Child Health, 7,* 1409–1685.

Mertala,. P., Karikoski, H., Tähtinen, L., & Sarenius, V.-M. (2016). The value of toys: 6–8-year-old children's toy preferences and the functional analysis of popular toys. *International Journal of Play, 5,* 11–27.

Mervis, C. B., & Rosch, E. (1981). Categorization of natural objects. *Annual Review of Psychology, 32,* 89–115.

Mesquita, B., & Karasawa, M. (2004). Self-conscious emotions as dynamic cultural processes. *Psychological Inquiry, 15,* 161–166.

Messer, E. J., Burgess, V., Sinclair, M., Grant, S., Spencer, D., & McGuigan, N. (2017). Young children display an increase in prosocial donating in response to an upwards shift in generosity by a same-aged peer. *Scientific Reports, 7,* 2633.

Messias, E., Castro, J., Saini, A., Usman, M., & Peeples, D. (2011). Sadness, suicide, and their association with video game and Internet oeruse among teens: Results from the Youth Risk Behavior Survey 2007 and 2009. *Suicide and Life-Threatening Behavior, 41,* 307–315.

Meyer-Bahlburg, H. F. L. (2005). Gender identity outcome in female-raised 46XY persons with penile agenesis, cloacal exstrophy of the bladder, or penile ablation. *Archives of Sexual Behavior, 34,* 423–438.

Meyer-Bahlburg, H. F. L., Dolezal, C., Baker, S. W., Ehrhardt, A. A., & New, M. I. (2006). Gender development in women with congenital adrenal hyperaplasia as a function of disorder severity. *Archives of Sexual Behavior, 35,* 667–684.

Miao, X., & Wang, W. (2003). A century of Chinese developmental psychology. *International Journal of Psychology, 38,* 258–273.

Mikulincer, M., & Shaver, P. R. (2008). Adult attachment and affect regulation. In J. Cassidy & P. R. Shaver (Eds), *Handbook of attachment: Theory, research, and clinical applications, Second edition* (pp. 503–531). New York, NY: Guilford Press.

Millan, M. J. (2013). An epigenetic framework for neurodevelopmental disorders: From pathogenesis to potential therapy. *Neuropharmacology, 68,* 2–82.

Millar, D. C., Light, J. C., & Schlosser, R. W. (2006). The impact of augmentative and alternative communication intervention on the speech production of individuals with developmental disabilities: A research review. *Journal of Speech, Language, and Hearing Research, 49,* 248–264.

Miller, C. A. (2001). False belief understanding in children with specific language impairment. *Journal of Communication Disorders, 34,* 73–86.

Miller, C. A. (2011). Auditory processing theories of language disorders: Past, present, and future. *Language, Speech, and Hearing Services in Schools, 42,* 309–319.

Miller, C. F., Lurye, L. E., Zosuls, K. M., & Ruble, D. N. (2009). Accessibility of gender stereotype domains: Developmental and gender differences in children. *Sex roles, 60,* 870–881.

Miller, G. A. (2010). Mistreating psychology in the Decade of the Brain. *Perspectives on Psychological Science, 5,* 716–743.

Miller, J. F. (Ed.) (1981). *Assessing children's language production: Experimental procedures.* Baltimore: University Park Press.

Miller, L., Gillam, R. B., & Peña, E. D. (2001). *Dynamic assessment and intervention: Improving children's narrative abilities.* Austin, TX: Pro-Ed.

Miller, L. K. (1989). *Musical savants: Exceptional skills in the mentally retarded.* Hillsdale, NJ: Erlbaum.

Miller, M. R., Müller, U., Giesbrecht, G. F., Carpendale, J. I., & Kerns, K. A. (2013). The contribution of executive function and social understanding to preschoolers' letter and math skills. *Cognitive Development, 28,* 331–349.

Miller, R. S. (2007). Is embarrassment a blessing or a curse? In J. L. Tracy, R. W. Robins & J. P. Tangney (Eds), *The self-conscious emotions: Theory and research* (pp. 245–262). New York, NY: Oxford University Press.

Miller, S. A. (2009). Children's understanding of second-order mental states. *Psychological Bulletin, 135,* 749–773.

Milligan, K., Astington, J. W., & Dack, L. A. (2007). Language and theory of mind: Meta-analysis of the relation between language ability and false-belief understanding. *Child Development, 78,* 622–646.

Mills, K. L. (2015). Social development in adolescence: Brain and behavioural changes. Doctoral dissertation, University College London.

Mills, R. S. L. (2003). Possible antecedents and developmental implications of shame in young girls. *Infant and Child Development, 12,* 29–349.

Mills, R. S. L. (2005). Taking stock of the developmental literature on shame. *Developmental Review, 25,* 26–63.

Mills, R. S. L., Arbeau, K. A., Lall, D. I. K., & De Jaeger, A. E. (2010). Parenting and child characteristics in the prediction of shame in early and middle childhood. *Merrill-Palmer Quarterly, 56,* 500–528.

Millum, J., & Emanuel, E. J. (2007). The ethics of international research with abandoned children. *Science, 318,* 1874–1875.

Mink, D., Henning, A., & Aschersleben, G. (2014). Infant shy temperament predicts preschoolers theory of mind. *Infant Behavior and Development, 37,* 66–75.

Minton, H. L., & Schneider, F. W. (1980). *Differential psychology.* Monterey, CA: Brooks/Cole.

Mirenda, P. (1997). Supporting individuals with challenging behavior through functional communication training and AAC: Research review. *Augmentative and Alternative Communication, 13,* 207–225.

Mischel, W. (1984). Convergences and challenges in the search for consistency. *American Psychologist, 39,* 351–364.

Mischel, W., & Shoda, Y. (2008). Toward a unifying theory of personality: Integrating dispositions and processing dynamics within the cognitive-affective processing system. In L. A. Pervin & O. P. John (Eds), *Handbook of personality: Theory and research, Third edition* (pp. 209–241). New York, NY: Guilford Press.

Mischel, W., & Shoda, Y. (2010). The situated person. In B. Mesquita, L. Feldman Barrett & E. R. Smith (Eds), *The mind in context* (pp. 149–173). New York, NY: Guilford Press.

Mischel, W., Shoda, Y., & Mendoza-Denton, R. (2002). Situation-behavior profiles as a locus of consistency in personality. *Current Directions in Psychological Science, 11,* 50–54.

Mischel, W., Shoda, Y., & Rodriguez, M. I. (1989). Delay of gratification in children. *Science, 244* (4907), 933–938.

Mistry, J. (1997). The development of remembering in cultural context. In N. Cowan (Ed.), *The development of memory in childhood* (pp. 343–368). London: Psychology Press.

Mistry, J., Rogoff, B., & Herman, H. (2001). What is the meaning of meaningful purpose in children's remembering? Istomina Revisited. *Mind, Culture, and Activity, 8,* 28–41.

Mistry, R. S., Brown, C. S., White, E. S., Chow, K. A., & Gillen-O'Neel, C. (2015). Elementary school children's reasoning about social class: A mixed-methods study. *Child Development, 86,* 1653–1671.

Mitchell, L. E., Adzick, N. S., Melchionne, J., Pasquariello, P. S., Sutton, L. N., & Whitehead, A. S. (2004). Spina bifida. *Lancet, 364,* 1885–1895.

Mitchell, P., & Lacohée, H. (1991). Children's early understanding of false belief. *Cognition, 39,* 107–127.

Mitchell, R. E., & Karchmer, M. A. (2004). Chasing the mythical ten percent: Parental hearing status of deaf and hard of hearing students in the United States. *Sign Language Studies, 4,* 138–163.

Mitchell, R. E., & Karchmer, M. A. (2006). Demographics of deaf education: More students in more places. *American Annals of the Deaf, 151,* 95–104.

Mitchell, S. A. (1988). *Relational concepts in psychoanalysis.* Cambridge, MA: Harvard University Press.

Mitchison, D., & Mond, J. (2015). Epidemiology of eating disorders, eating disordered behaviour, and body image disturbance in males: A narrative review. *Journal of Eating Disorders, 3,* 20.

Miyahara, M., & Piek, J. (2006). Self-esteem of children and adolescents with physical disabilities: Quantitative evidence from meta-analysis. *Journal of Developmental and Physical Disabilities, 18,* 219–234.

Miyaki, K., Campos, J., Bradshaw, D., & Kagan, J. (1986). Issues in socioemotional development. In H. Stevenson, H. Azuma & K. Hakuta (Eds), *Child development and education in Japan* (pp. 239–261). New York, NY: Freeman.

Moe, S., & Wright, M. (2013, July). Can accessible digital formats improve reading skills, habits and educational level for dyslectic youngsters? In C. Stephanidis & M. Antona (Eds), Universal access in human-computer interaction. Applications and services for quality of life. UAHCI 2013. *Lecture Notes in Computer Science,* vol 8011 (pp. 203–212). Heidelberg, Germany: Springer.

Moffitt, T. E. (1993). The neuropsychology of conduct disorder. *Development and Psychopathology, 5,* 135–152.

Moffitt, T. E., Caspi, A., Harkness, A. R., & Silva, P. A. (1993). The natural history of change in intellectual performance: Who changes? How much? Is it meaningful? *Journal of Child Psychology and Psychiatry, 34,* 455–506.

Moffitt, T. E., Caspi, A., & Rutter, M. (2006). Measured gene–environment interactions in psychopathology: Concepts, research strategies, and implications for research, intervention, and public understanding of genetics. *Perspectives on Psychological Science, 1,* 5–27.

Moksnes, U. K., Bradley Eilertsen, M. E., & Lazarewicz, M. (2016). The association between stress, self-esteem and depressive symptoms in adolescents. *Scandinavian Journal of Psychology, 57,* 22–29.

Mole, S. E., Williams, R. E., & Goebbel, H. H. (2011). *The neuronal ceroid lipofuscinoses (Batten disease), Second edition*. Oxford: Oxford University Press.

Moll, H., & Tomasello, M. (2004). 12- and 18-month-old infants follow gaze to spaces behind barriers. *Developmental Science, 7*, F1–F9.

Money, J. (1975). Ablatio penis: Normal male infant sex-reassigned as a girl. *Archives of Sexual Behavior, 4*, 65–71.

Money, J., & Ehrhardt, A. A. (1972). *Man and woman, boy and girl: Differentiation and dimorphism of gender identity from conception to maturity*. Oxford: Johns Hopkins University Press.

Monk, C., Spicer, J., & Champagne, F. A. (2012). Linking prenatal maternal adversity to developmental outcomes in infants: The role of epigenetic pathways. *Development and Psychopathology, 24*, 1361–1376.

Monnery-Patris, S., Rouby, C., Nicklaus, S., & Issanchou, S. (2009). Development of olfactory ability in children: Sensitivity and identification. *Developmental Psychobiology, 5*, 268–276.

Montessori, M. (1910). *The advanced method*. Harlow, UK: Longmans.

Montgomery, J. W. (2003). Working memory and comprehension in children with specific language impairment: What we know so far. *Journal of Communication Disorders, 36*, 221–231.

Montgomery, J. W., Polunenko, A., & Marinellie, S. A. (2009). Role of working memory in children's understanding spoken narrative: A preliminary investigation. *Applied Psycholinguistics, 30*, 485–509.

Montirosso, R., Peverelli, M., Frigerio, E., Crespi, M., & Borgatti, R. (2009). The development of dynamic facial expression recognition at different intensities in 4- to 18-year-olds. *Social Development, 19*, 71–92.

Moog, H. (1963). Beginn und erste Entwicklung des Musikerlebens im Kindesalter: Eine empirisch-psychologishe Untersuchung. Dissertation, University of Cologne.

Moore, C., & Lemmon, K. (Eds). (2001). *The self in time*. London: Lawrence Erlbaum.

Moore, K. L., & Persaud, T. V. N. (2008). *The developing human brain, Eighth edition*. Philadelphia, PA: W. B. Saunders.

Moors, A., Ellsworth, P. C., Scherer, K. R., & Frijda, N. H. (2013). Appraisal theories of emotion: State of the art and future development. *Emotion Review, 5*, 119–124.

Morelli, G., Rogoff, B., & Angelillo, C. (2003). Cultural variation in young children's access to work or involvement in specialised child-focused activities. *International Journal of Behavioral Development, 27*, 264–274.

Morgado, A. M., & da Luz Vale-Dias, M. (2013). The antisocial phenomenon in adolescence: What is literature telling us? *Aggression and Violent Behavior, 18*, 436–443.

Morgan, G., Herman, R., & Woll, B. (2007). Language impairments in sign language: Breakthroughs and puzzles. *International Journal of Language and Communication Disorders, 42*, 97–105.

Morra, S., & Borella, E. (2015). Working memory training: From metaphors to models. *Frontiers in Psychology, 6*, 1097.

Morra, S., Gobbo, C., Marini, Z., & Sheese, R. (2008). *Cognitive development: Neo-Piagetian perspectives*. New York, NY: Lawrence Erlbaum.

Morris, A. S., Silk, J. S., Steinberg, L., Myers, S. S., & Robinson, L. R. (2007). The role of the family context in the development of emotion regulation. *Social Development, 16*, 361–388.

Morris, D., Collett, P., Marsh, P., & O'Shaughnessy, M. (1979). *Gestures: Their origin and distribution*. London: Cape.

Morrison, T. L., Goodlin-Jones, B. L., & Urquiza, A. J. (1997). Attachment and the representation of intimate relationships in adulthood. *Journal of Psychology, 131*, 57–71.

Morrongiello, B. A. (1990). The study of individual differences in infants: Auditory processing measures. In J. Colombo & J. W. Fagen (Eds), *Individual differences in infancy: Reliability, stability, prediction* (pp. 271–320). Hillsdale, NJ: Erlbaum.

Morss, J. R. (1996). *Growing critical: Alternatives to developmental psychology*. London: Routledge.

Moser, F., & Hannover, B. (2014). How gender fair are German schoolbooks in the twenty-first century? An analysis of language and illustrations in schoolbooks for mathematics and German. *European Journal of Psychology of Education, 29*, 387–407.

Moser, M. B., & Moser, E. I. (2016). Where am I? Where am I going? Scientists are figuring out how the brain navigates. *Scientific American, 614*, 26–33.

Moskowitz, S. (1985). Longitudinal follow-up of child survivors of the Holocaust. *American Academy of Child Psychiatry, 24*, 401–407.

Moultrie, R. R., Kish-Doto, J., Peay, H., & Lewis, M. A. (2016). A review on spinal muscular atrophy: Awareness, knowledge, and attitudes. *Journal of Genetic Counseling, 25*, 892–900.

Mrug, S., Madan, A., & Windle, M. (2016). Emotional desensitization to violence contributes to adolescents' violent behavior. *Journal of Abnormal Child Psychology, 44*, 75–86.

Mugnaini, D., Lassi, S., La Malfa, G., & Albertini, G. (2009). Internalizing correlates of dyslexia. *World Journal of Pediatrics, 5*, 255–264.

Mulder, E. J. H., de Medina, P. G. R., Huizink, A. C., Van den Bergh, B. R. H., Buitelaar, J. K., & Visser, G. H. A. (2002). Prenatal maternal stress: Effects on pregnancy and the (unborn) child. *Early Human Development, 70*, 3–14.

Mulder, E. J. H., & Visser, G. H. (2016). Fetal behavior: Clinical and experimental research in the human. In N. Reissland & B. S. Kisilevsky (Eds), *Fetal development* (pp. 87–105). Cham, Switzerland: Springer.

Mullen, E. M. (1995). *Mullen Scales of Early Learning*. Circle Pines: American Guidance Service.

Mullen, M. K. (1994). Earliest recollections of childhood: A demographic analysis. *Cognition, 52*, 55–79.

Mullin, B. C., & Hinshaw, S. P. (2007). Emotion regulation and externalizing disorders in children and adolescents. In J. J. Gross (Ed.), *Handbook of emotion regulation* (pp. 523–541). New York, NY: Guilford Press.

Mullin, J. (2014). *Drawing autism.* New York, NY: Akashic Books.

Mumford, S. (2012). Play therapy. In W. M. Klykylo & J. Kay (Eds), *Clinical child psychiatry, Third edition* (pp. 120–129). Oxford: Wiley.

Mumme, D. L., Fernald, A., & Herrera, C. (1996). Infants' responses to facial and vocal emotional signals in a social referencing paradigm. *Child Development, 67,* 3219–3237.

Munakata, Y. (2006). Information processing approaches to development. In W. Damon, R. M. Lerner, D. Kuhn & R. S. Siegler (Eds), *Handbook of child psychology, Sixth edition, Volume 2: Cognition, perception, and language* (pp. 426–463). New York, NY: Wiley.

Mund, M., Louwen, F., Klingelhoefer, D., & Gerber, A. (2013). Smoking and pregnancy – a review on the first major environmental risk factor of the unborn. *International Journal of Environmental Research and Public Health, 10,* 6485–6499.

Mundy, P., Block, J., Delgado, C., Pomares, Y., Van Hecke, A. V., & Parlade, M. V. (2007). Individual differences and the development of joint attention in infancy. *Child Development, 78,* 938–954.

Munro, J. (2003). Dyscalculia: A unifying concept in understanding mathematics learning disabilities. *Australian Journal of Learning Difficulties, 8,* 25–32.

Munroe, R. L., & Romney, A. K. (2006). Gender and age differences in same-sex aggregation and social behavior: A four-culture study. *Journal of Cross-Cultural Psychology, 37,* 3–19.

Muris, P., & Ollendick, T. H. (2015). Children who are anxious in silence: A review on selective mutism, the new anxiety disorder in DSM-5. *Clinical Child and Family Psychology Review, 18,* 151–169.

Murray, A. D., Johnson, J., & Peters, J. (1990). Fine-tuning of utterance length to preverbal infants: Effects on later language development. *Journal of Child Language, 17,* 511–525.

Murray, F. B. (1990). The conversation of truth into necessity. In W. F. Overton (Ed.), *Reasoning, necessity and logic: Developmental perspectives* (pp. 183–203). Hillsdale, NJ: Erlbaum.

Murray, J., & Farrington, D. P. (2010). Risk factors for conduct disorder and delinquency: Key findings from longitudinal studies. *The Canadian Journal of Psychiatry, 55,* 633–642.

Murray-Close, D., Crick, N. R., & Galotti, K. M. (2006). Children's moral reasoning regarding physical and relational aggression. *Social Development, 15,* 345–372.

Murza, K. A., Schwartz, J. B., Hahs-Vaughn, D. L., & Nye, C. (2016). Joint attention interventions for children with autism spectrum disorder: A systematic review and meta-analysis. *International Journal of Language and Communication Disorders, 51,* 236–251.

Näätänen, R. (2003). Mismatch negativity: Clinical research and possible applications. *International Journal of Psychophysiology, 48,* 179–188.

Naber, F. B. A., Bakermans-Kranenburg, M. J., van IJzendoorn, M. H., Dietz, C., van Daalen, E., Swinkels, S. H. N., Buitelaar, J. K., & van Engeland, H. (2008). Joint attention development in toddlers with autism. *European Child and Adolescent Psychiatry, 17,* 143–152.

Nadel-Brulfert, J., & Baudonniere, P. M. (1982). The social function of reciprocal imitation in 2-year-old peers. *International Journal of Behavioral Development, 5,* 95–109.

Nader-Grosbois, N. (2014). Self-perception, self-regulation and metacognition in adolescents with intellectual disability. *Research in Developmental Disabilities, 35,* 1334–1348.

Nafstad, A., & Rødbroe, I. (2016). *Communicative relations.* Aalborg, Denmark: Materialecentret.

Naglieri, J. A. (2015). Hundred years of intelligence testing: Moving from traditional IQ to second-generation intelligence tests. In S. Goldstein, D. Princiotta & J. A. Naglieri (Eds), *Handbook of intelligence: Evolutionary theory, historical perspective and current concepts* (pp. 295–316). New York, NY: Springer.

Nagy, E., Pal, A., & Orvos, H. (2014). Learning to imitate individual finger movements by the human neonate. *Developmental Science, 17,* 841–857.

Nagy, E., Pilling, K., Orvos, H., & Molnar, P. (2013). Imitation of tongue protrusion in human neonates: Specificity of the response in a large sample. *Developmental Psychology, 49,* 1628–1638.

Nagy, W. E., & Anderson, R. C. (1984). How many words are there in printed school English? *Reading Research Quarterly, 19,* 304–330.

Nagy, W. E., & Townsend, D. (2012). Words as tools: Learning academic vocabulary as language acquisition. *Reading Research Quarterly, 47,* 91–108.

Nahum, M., Lee, H., & Merzenich, M. M. (2013). Principles of neuroplasticity-based rehabilitation. *Progress in Brain Research, 207,* 141–171.

Namy, L. L., & Waxman, S. R. (1998). Words and gestures: Infants' interpretations of different forms of symbolic reference. *Child Development, 69,* 295–308.

Nanez, J. E. (1988). Perception of impending collision in 3- to 6-week-old human infants. *Infant Behavior and Development, 11,* 447–463.

Napier, J., Leigh, G., & Nann, S. (2007). Teaching sign language to hearing parents of deaf children: An action research process. *Deafness and Education International, 9,* 83–100.

Nathanson, A. I., & Rasmussen, E. E. (2011). TV viewing compared to book reading and toy playing reduces responsive maternal communication with toddlers and preschoolers. *Human Communication Research, 37,* 465–487.

Nation, K., Cocksey, J., Taylor, J. S., & Bishop, D. V. (2010). A longitudinal investigation of early reading and language skills in children with poor reading comprehension. *Journal of Child Psychology and Psychiatry, 51,* 1031–1039.

Nation, K., & Norbury, C. F. (2005). Why reading comprehension fails: Insights from developmental disorders. *Topics in Language Disorders*, 25, 21–32.

Navarro, R., Yubero, S., & Larrañaga, E. (Eds) (2016). *Cyberbullying across the globe: Gender, family, and mental health*. Cham, Switzerland: Springer.

Neale, M.-C., & Stevenson, J. (1989). Rater bias in the EASI temperament scales: A twin study. *Journal of Personality and Social Psychology*, 56, 446–455 & 845.

Needleman, H. (2004). Lead poisoning. *Annual Review of Medicine*, 55, 209–222.

Negele, A., & Habermas, T. (2010). Self-continuity across developmental change in and of repeated life narratives. In K. C. McLean & M. Pasupathi (Eds), *Narrative development in adolescence: Creating the storied self* (pp. 1–22). New York, NY: Springer.

Negen, J., & Nardini, M. (2015). Four-year-olds use a mixture of spatial reference frames. *PloS One*, 10, e0131984.

Neil, A. L., & Christensen, H. (2009). Efficacy and effectiveness of school-based prevention and early intervention programs for anxiety. *Clinical Psychology Review*, 29, 208–215.

Neil, P. A., Chee-Ruiter, C., Scheier, C., Lewkowicz, D. J., & Shimojo, S. (2006). Development of multisensory spatial integration and perception in humans. *Developmental Science*, 9, 454–464.

Neisser, U. (1997). Concepts and self-concepts. In U. Neisser & D. A. Jopling (Eds), *The conceptual self in context* (pp. 3–12). Cambridge: Cambridge University Press.

Neisser U. (2004). Memory development: New questions and old. *Developmental Review*, 24, 154–158.

Neisser, U., Boodoo, G., Bouchard, T. J., Boykin, A. W., Brody, N., Ceci, S. J., Halpern, D. F., Loehlin, J. C., Perloff, R., Sternberg, R. J., & Urbina, S. (1996). Intelligence: Knowns and unknowns. *American Psychologist*, 51, 77–101.

Nelson, C. A., & Bosquet, M. (2000). Neurobiology of fetal and infant development: Implications for infant mental health. In C. H. Zeanah (Ed.), *Handbook of infant mental health, Second edition* (pp. 37–59). New York, NY: Guilford Press.

Nelson, C. A., & de Haan, M. (1997). A neurobehavioral approach to the recognition of facial expressions in infancy. In J. A. Russell & J. M. Fernandez-Dols (Eds), *The psychology of facial expression* (pp. 176–204). Cambridge: Cambridge University Press.

Nelson, C. A., Moulson, M. C., & Richmond, J. (2006a). How does neuroscience inform the study of cognitive development? *Human Development*, 49, 260–272.

Nelson, C. A., Thomas, K. M., & de Haan, M. (2006b). Neural bases of cognitive development. In W. Damon, R. M. Lerner, D. Kuhn, R. & S. Siegler (Eds), *Handbook of child psychology, Sixth edition, Volume 2: Cognition perception, and language* (pp. 3–57). Hoboken, NJ: Wiley.

Nelson, D. K., O'Neill, K., & Asher, Y. M. (2008). A mutually facilitative relationship between learning names and learning concepts in preschool children: The case of artifacts. *The Journal of Cognition and Development*, 9, 171–193.

Nelson, K. (1973). Structure and strategy in learning to talk. *Monographs of the Society for Research in Child Development*, 38.

Nelson, K. (1981). Individual differences in language development: Implications for development and language. *Developmental Psychology*, 17, 170–187.

Nelson, K. (1988). Constraints on word learning? *Cognitive Development*, 3, 221–246.

Nelson, K. (1996). *Language in cognitive development*. Cambridge: Cambridge University Press.

Nelson, K. (2003). Self and social functions: Individual autobiographical memory and collective narrative. *Memory*, 11, 125–136.

Nelson, K. (2004). Construction of the cultural self in early narratives. In C. Daiute & C. Lightfoot (Eds), *Narrative analysis: Studying the development of individuals in society* (pp. 87–109). Thousand Oaks, CA: Sage.

Nelson, K. (2007a). *Young minds in social worlds: Experience, meaning and memory*. Cambridge, MA: Harvard University Press.

Nelson, K. (2007b). Development of extended memory. *Journal of Physiology*, 101, 223–229.

Nelson, K. (2009). Wittgenstein and contemporary theories of word learning. *New Ideas in Psychology*, 27, 275–287.

Nelson, K. (2010). Developmental narratives of the experiencing child. *Child Development Perspectives*, 4, 42–47.

Nelson, K. (2011). "Concept" is a useful concept in developmental research. *Journal of Theoretical and Philosophical Psychology*, 31, 96–101.

Nelson, K. (2014). Pathways from infancy to the community of shared minds/El camino desde la primera infancia a la comunidad de mentes compartidas. *Infancia y Aprendizaje*, 37, 1–24.

Nelson, K. (2015a). Quantitative and qualitative research in psychological science. *Biological Theory*, 10, 263–272.

Nelson, K. (2015b). Making sense with private speech. *Cognitive Development*, 36, 171–179.

Nelson, K., & Fivush, R. (2004). The emergence of autobiographical memory: A social cultural developmental theory. *Psychological Review*, 11, 486–511.

Nelson, K., & Gruendel, J. M. (1979). At morning it's lunchtime: A scriptal view of children's dialogues. *Discourse Processes*, 3, 73–94.

Nelson, K., & Gruendel, J. M. (1981). Generalized event representations: Basic building blocks of cognitive development. In M. E. Lamb & A. L. Brown (Eds), *Advances in developmental psychology, Volume 1* (pp. 131–158). Hillsdale, NJ: Erlbaum.

Nelson, K., Skwerer, D. P., Goldman, S., Henseler, S., Presler, N., & Walkenfeld, F. F. (2003). Entering a community of minds: An experiential approach to "theory of mind". *Human Development*, 46, 24–46.

Nelson, K. E. (2001). Dynamic tricky mix theory suggests multiple analyzed pathways as an intervention approach for children with autism and other language delays. In S. von Tetzchner & J. Clibbens (Eds), *Understanding the theoretical and methodological bases of augmentative and alternative communication. Proceedings of the Sixth*

Biennial Research Symposium of the International Society of Augmentative and Alternative Communication (ISAAC), Washington, DC, August 2000 (pp. 141–159). Toronto, Canada: ISAAC.

Nelson, K. E., Camarata, S. M., Welsh, J., Butkovsky, L., & Camarata, M. (1996). Effects of imitative and conversational recasting treatment on the acquisition of grammar in children with specific language impairment and younger language-normal children. *Journal of Speech and Hearing Research, 39,* 850–859.

Nelson, K. E., Carskaddon, G., & Bonvillian, J. D. (1973). Syntax acquisition: Impact of experimental variation in adult verbal interaction with the child. *Child Development, 44,* 497–504.

Nelson, L. J., & Barry, C. M. (2005). Distinguishing features of emerging adulthood: The role of self-classification as an adult. *Journal of Adolescent Research, 20,* 242–262.

Neppl, T. K., Donnellan, M. B., Scaramellac, L. V., Widamand, K. F., Spilmana, S. K., Ontai, L. L., & Conger, R. D. (2010). Differential stability of temperament and personality from toddlerhood to middle childhood. *Journal of Research in Personality, 44,* 386–396.

Neubauer, S., & Hublin, J. J. (2012). The evolution of human brain development. *Evolutionary Biology, 39,* 568–586.

Newbury, D. F., Bonora, E., Lamb, J. A., Fisher, S. E., Lai, C. S., Baird, G., Jannoun, L., Slonims, V., Stott, C. M., Merricks, M. J., et al. (2002). FOXP2 is not a major susceptibility gene for autism or specific language impairment. *The American Journal of Human Genetics, 70,* 1318–1327.

Newcomb, A. F., & Bagwell, C. L. (1996). The developmental significance of children's friendship relations. In W. M. Bukowski, A. F. Newcomb & W. W. Hartup (Eds), *The company they keep: Friendship in childhood and adolescence* (pp. 289–321). Cambridge: Cambridge University Press.

Newcombe, N. S. (2002). The nativist-empiricist controversy in the context of recent research on spatial and quantitative development. *Psychological Science, 13,* 395–401.

Newcombe, N. S. (2013). Cognitive development: Changing views of cognitive change. *Wiley Interdisciplinary Reviews: Cognitive Science, 4,* 479–491.

Newcombe, N. S., & Huttenlocher, J. (1992). Children's early ability to solve perspective-taking problems. *Developmental Psychology, 28,* 635–643.

Newcombe, N. S., Huttenlocher, J., Drummey, A. B., & Wiley, J. G. (1998). The development of spatial location coding: Place learning and dead reckoning in the second and third years. *Cognitive Development, 13,* 185–200.

Newcombe, N. S., Uttal, D. H., & Sauter, M. (2013). Spatial development. In P. Zelazo (Ed.), *Oxford handbook of developmental psychology, Volume 1* (pp. 564–590). New York, NY: Oxford University Press.

Newman, B. M., Lohman, B. J., & Newman, P. R. (2007). Peer group membership and a sense of belonging: Their relationship to adolescent behavior problems. *Adolescence, 42,* 241–263.

Newman, G. E., Choi, H., Wynn, K., & Scholl, B. J. (2008). The origins of causal perception: Evidence from post-dictive processing in infancy. *Cognitive Psychology, 57,* 262–291.

Newman, L. K., & Steel, Z. (2008). The child asylum seeker: Psychological and developmental impact of immigration detention. *Child and Adolescent Psychiatric Clinics, 17,* 665–683.

Newson, J., & Newson, E. (1965). *Patterns of infant care in an urban community.* Harmondsworth, UK: Penguin.

Nguyen, S. P., & Murphy, G. L. (2003). An apple is more than just a fruit: Cross-classification in children's concepts. *Child Development, 74,* 1783–1806.

Nichols, P. L. (1984). Familial mental retardation. *Behavior Genetics, 14,* 161–170.

Nicklaus, S. (2009). Development of food variety in children. *Appetite, 52,* 53–55.

Nicklaus, S., Boggio, V., Chabanet, C., & Issanchou, S. (2005). A prospective study of food variety seeking in childhood, adolescence and early adult life. *Appetite, 44,* 289–297.

Nicolopoulou, A. (1993). Play, cognitive development, and the social world: Piaget, Vygotsky, and beyond. *Human Development, 36,* 1–23.

Nicolopoulou, A., & Richner, E. S. (2007). From actors to agents to persons: The development of character representation in young children's narratives. *Child Development, 78,* 412–429.

Nielsen, M., & Haun, D. (2016). Why developmental psychology is incomplete without comparative and cross-cultural perspectives. *Philosophical Transactions of the Royal Society B: Biological Sciences, 371* (1686), 1–7.

Nielsen, M., Simcock, G., & Jenkins, L. (2008). The effect of social engagement on 24-month-olds' imitation from live and televised models. *Developmental Science, 11,* 722–731.

Nievar, M. A., & Becker, B. J. (2008). Sensitivity as a privileged predictor of attachment: A second perspective on de Wolff and van IJzendoorn's meta-analysis. *Social Development, 17,* 102–114.

Nigg, J. T. (2000). On inhibition/disinhibition in developmental psychopathology: Views from cognitive and personality psychology and a working inhibition taxonomy. *Psychological Bulletin, 126,* 220–246.

Nigg, J. T. (2006). Temperament and developmental psychopathology. *Journal of Child Psychology and Psychiatry, 47,* 395–422.

Nilsson, K. K., & de López, K. J. (2016). Theory of mind in children with specific language impairment: A systematic review and meta-analysis. *Child Development, 87,* 143–153.

Nippold, M. A. (1998). *Later language development, Second edition.* Austin, TX: Pro-Ed.

Nippold, M. A., Frantz-Kaspar, M. W., Cramond, P. M., Kirk, C., Hayward-Mayhew, C., & MacKinnon, M. (2014). Conversational and narrative speaking in adolescents: Examining the use of complex syntax. *Journal of Speech, Language, and Hearing Research, 57,* 876–886.

Nisbett, R. E. (2005). Heredity, environment, and race differences in IQ: A commentary on Rushton and Jensen. *Psychology, Public Policy, and Law, 11,* 302–310.

Nisbett, R. E., Aronson, J., Blair, C., Dickens, W., Flynn, J., Halpern, D. F., & Turkheimer, E. (2012). Intelligence: New findings and theoretical developments. *American Psychologist, 67,* 130–159.

Nisbett, R. E., & Norenzayan, A. (2002). Culture and cognition. In H. Pashler & D. L. Medin (Eds), *Stevens' handbook of experimental psychology, Third edition* (pp. 561–597). New York, NY: Wiley.

Nivard, M. G., Dolan, C. V., Kendler, K. S., Kan, K. J., Willemsen, G., van Beijsterveldt, C. E. M., Lindauer, R. J., van Beek, J. H., Geels, L. M., Bartels, M., et al. (2015). Stability in symptoms of anxiety and depression as a function of genotype and environment: A longitudinal twin study from ages 3 to 63 years. *Psychological Medicine, 45,* 1039–1049.

Noel, K. K., & Westby, C. (2014). Applying theory of mind concepts when designing interventions targeting social cognition among youth offenders. *Topics in Language Disorders, 34,* 344–361.

Noller, P. (2005). Sibling relationships in adolescence: Learning and growing together. *Personal Relationships, 12,* 1–22.

Nomura, K., Okada, K., Noujima, Y., Kojima, S., Mori, Y., Amano, M., Ogura, M., Hatagaki, C., Shibata, Y., & Fukumoto, R. (2014). A clinical study of attention-deficit/hyperactivity disorder in preschool children – Prevalence and differential diagnoses. *Brain and Development, 36,* 778–785.

Norbury, C. F., & Bishop, D. V. (2003). Narrative skills of children with communication impairments. *International Journal of Language and Communication Disorders, 38,* 287–313.

Nordenström, A., Servin, A., Bohlin, G., Larsson, A., & Wedell, A. (2002). Sex-typed toy play behavior correlates with the degree of prenatal androgen exposure assessed by CYP21 genotype in girls with congenital adrenal hyperplasia. *The Journal of Clinical Endocrinology and Metabolism, 87,* 5119–5124.

Nosek, B. A., & Bar-Anan, Y. (2012). Scientific utopia: I. Opening scientific communication. *Psychological Inquiry, 23,* 217–243.

Nosek, B. A., Spies, J. R., & Motyl, M. (2012). Scientific utopia: II. Restructuring incentives and practices to promote truth over publishability. *Perspectives on Psychological Science, 7,* 615–631.

Novak, G., & Peláez, M. (2004). *Child and adolescent development: A behavioral systems approach.* London: Sage.

Novak, M., & Harlow, H. F. (1975). Social recovery of monkeys isolated for the first year of life: I. Rehabilitation and therapy. *Developmental Psychology, 11,* 453–465.

Novogrodsky, R., Henner, J., Caldwell-Harris, C., & Hoffmeister, R. (2017). The development of sensitivity to grammatical violations in American Sign Language: Native versus nonnative signers. *Language Learning, 67,* 791–818.

Nsamenang, B. A., & Lo-Oh, J. L. (2010). Afrique Noire. In M. H. Bornstein (Ed.), *Handbook of cultural developmental science* (pp. 383–408). New York, NY: Psychology Press.

Nucci, L. P., & Nucci, M. S. (1982a). Children's social interactions in the context of moral and conventional transgressions. *Child Development, 53,* 403–412.

Nucci, L. P., & Nucci, M. S. (1982b). Children's responses to moral and social conventional transgressions in free-play settings. *Child Development, 53,* 1337–1342.

Nucci, L. P., & Turiel, E. (2009). Capturing the complexity of moral development and education. *Mind, Brain, and Education, 3,* 151–159.

Nunes, T., & Bryant, P. (2015). The development of quantitative reasoning. In R. M. Lerner, L. S. Liben & U. Müller (Eds), *Handbook of child psychology and developmental science, Seventh edition, Volume 2: Cognitive processes* (pp. 715–764). Hoboken, NJ: Wiley.

Nunes, T., Schlieman, A. D., & Carraher, D. W. (1993). *Street mathematics and school mathematics.* Cambridge: Cambridge University Press.

O'Brien, K., Daffern, M., Chu, C. M., & Thomas, S. D. (2013). Youth gang affiliation, violence, and criminal activities: A review of motivational, risk, and protective factors. *Aggression and Violent Behavior, 18,* 417–425.

O'Brien, M., & Huston, A. C. (1985). Development of sex-typed play behavior in toddlers. *Developmental Psychology, 21,* 866–871.

O'Brien, M., & Wall, K. (Eds) (2017). *Comparative perspectives on work-life balance and gender equality: Fathers on Leave Alone.* Cham, Switzerland: Springer.

O'Byrne, C., & Muldoon, O. (2017). Stigma, self-perception and social comparisons in young people with an intellectual disability. *Irish Educational Studies, 36,* 307–322.

O'Connell, B., & Bretherton, I. (1984). Toddlers' play alone and with mother: The role of maternal guidance. In I. Bretherton (Ed.), *Symbolic play: The development of social understanding* (pp. 337–368). London: Academic Press.

O'Connor, K. J., & Braverman, L. M. (Eds) (1997). *Play therapy theory and practice: A comparative presentation.* New York, UK: Wiley.

O'Connor, M., Sanson, A., Hawkins, M. T., Letcher, P., Toumbourou, J. W., Smart, D., Vassallo, S., & Olsson, C. A. (2011). Predictors of positive development in emerging adulthood. *Journal of Youth and Adolescence, 40,* 860–874.

O'Connor, T. G., & Hirsch, N. (1999). Intra-individual differences and relationship-specificity of mentalising in early adolescence. *Social Development, 8,* 256–274.

O'Connor, T. G., Monk, C., & Fitelson, E. M. (2014). Practitioner review: Maternal mood in pregnancy and child development–implications for child psychology and psychiatry. *Journal of Child Psychology and Psychiatry, 55,* 99–111.

O'Donnell, K. J., Glover, V., Barker, E. D., & O'Connor, T. G. (2014). The persisting effect of maternal mood in pregnancy on childhood psychopathology. *Developmental Psychopathology, 26,* 393–403.

O'Keeffe, G. S. (2016). Social media: Challenges and concerns for families. *Pediatric Clinics, 63,* 841–849.

O'Keeffe, G. S., & Clarke-Pearson, K. (2011). The impact of social media on children, adolescents and families. *Pediatrics, 127*, 800–804.

O'Leary, C. M., & Bower, C. (2012). Guidelines for pregnancy: What's an acceptable risk, and how is the evidence (finally) shaping up? *Drug and Alcohol Review, 31*, 170–183.

O'Neill, Y. V. (1980). *Speech and speech disorders in Western thought before 1600*. London: Greenwood Press.

Oakes, L. M. (1994). Development of infants' use of continuity cues in their perception of causality. *Developmental Psychology, 30*, 869–879.

Oakes, L. M., & Luck, S. J. (2014). Short-term memory in infancy. In P. J. Bauer & R. Fivush (Eds), *The Wiley handbook on the development of children's memory* (pp. 157–180). New York, NY: Wiley.

Oakland, T. (2004). Use of educational and psychological tests internationally. *Applied Psychology, 53*, 157–172.

Oatley, K., Keltner, D., & Jenkins, J. M. (2006). *Understanding emotions*. Oxford: Blackwell.

Odding, E., Roebroeck, M. E., & Stam, H. J. (2006). The epidemiology of cerebral palsy: Incidence, impairments and risk factors. *Disability and Rehabilitation, 28*, 183–191.

Odgers, C. L., Moffitt, T. E., Broadbent, J. M., Dickson, N. P., Hancox, R., Harrington, H., Poulton, R., Sears, M. R., Thompson, W. M., & Caspi, A. (2008). Female and male antisocial trajectories: From childhood origins to adult outcomes. *Development and Psychopathology, 20*, 673–716.

Olds, T., Ridley, K., & Dollman, J. (2006). Screenieboppers and extreme screenies: The place of screen time in the time budgets of 10–13 year-old Australian children. *Australian and New Zealand Journal of Public Health, 30*, 137–142.

Ollendick, T. H., & Hirshfeld-Becker, D. R. (2002). The developmental psychopathology of social anxiety disorder. *Biological Psychiatry, 51*, 44–58.

Olsho, L. W., Koch, E. G., & Halpin, C. F. (1987). Level and age effects in infant frequency discrimination. *The Journal of the Acoustical Society of America, 82*, 454–464.

Olson, D. R. (2003). *Psychological theory and educational reform: How school remakes mind and society*. New York, NY: Cambridge University Press.

Olson, I. R., & Newcombe, N. S. (2014). Binding together the elements of episodes: Relational memory and the developmental trajectory of the hippocampus. In P. J. Bauer & R. Fivush (Eds), *Handbook on the development of children's memory* (pp. 285–308). New York, NY: Wiley.

Olweus, D. (1993). *Bullying at school: What we know and what we can do*. Malden, MA: Blackwell.

Olweus, D. (2013). School bullying: Development and some important challenges. *Annual Review of Clinical Psychology, 9*, 751–780.

Olweus, D., & Breivik, K. (2014). The plight of victims of school bullying: The opposite of well-being. In B.-A. Asher, F. Casas, I. Frønes & J. E. Korbin. (Eds), *Handbook of child well-being* (pp. 2593–2616). Heidelberg, Germany: Springer.

Onishi, K. H., & Baillargeon, R. (2005). Do 15-month-old infants understand false beliefs? *Science, 308*, 255–258.

Ontai, L. L., & Thompson, R. A. (2008). Attachment, parent–child discourse and Theory-of-Mind development. *Social Development, 17*, 47–60.

Oostenbroek, J., Slaughter, V., Nielsen, M., & Suddendorf, T. (2013). Why the confusion around neonatal imitation? A review. *Journal of Reproductive and Infant Psychology, 31*, 328–341.

Oostenbroek, J., Suddendorf, T., Nielsen, M., Redshaw, J., Kennedy-Costantini, S., Davis, J., Clark, S., & Slaughter, V. (2016). Comprehensive longitudinal study challenges the existence of neonatal imitation in humans. *Current Biology, 26*, 1334–1338.

Orbach, Y., & Lamb, M. E. (2007). Young children's references to temporal attributes of allegedly experienced events in the course of forensic interviews. *Child Development, 78*, 1100–1120.

Ornstein, P. A., & Light, L. L. (2010). Memory development across the life span. In W. F. Overton & R. M. Lerner (Eds), *The handbook of life-span development, Volume 1: Cognition, biology, and methods* (pp. 259–305). Hoboken, NJ: Wiley.

Ortigo, K. M., Bradley, B., & Westen, D. (2010). An empirically based prototype diagnostic system for DSM–V and ICD–11. In T. Millon, R. Krueger & E. Simonsen (Eds), *Contemporary directions in psychopathology: Scientific foundations of the DSM–V and ICD–11* (pp. 374–390). New York, NY: Guilford Press.

Orue, I., Bushman, B. J., Calvete, E., Thomaes, S., de Castro, B. O., & Hutteman, R. (2011). "Monkey see, Monkey do, Monkey hurt": Longitudinal effects of exposure to violence on children's aggressive behavior. *Social Psychological and Personality Science, 2*, 432–437.

Osborne, J. (2010). Arguing to learn in science: The role of collaborative, critical discourse. *Science, 328* (5977), 463–466.

Ostad, J. (2008). *Zweisprachigkeit bei Kindern mit Down-Syndrom*. Hamburg: Verlag Dr. Kovač.

Oster, H., Hegley, D., & Nagel, L. (1992). Adult judgments and fine grained analysis of infant facial expressions: Testing the validity of a priori coding formulas. *Developmental Psychology, 28*, 1115–1131.

Ostrov, J. M., & Crick, N. R. (2007). Forms and functions of aggression during early childhood: A short-term longitudinal study. *School Psychology Review, 36*, 22–43.

Østvik, J., Ytterhus, B., & Balandin, S. (2017). "So, how does one define a friendship?": Identifying friendship among students using AAC in inclusive education settings. *European Journal of Special Needs Education, 33*, 334–348.

Otto, H., Potinius, I., & Keller, H. (2014). Cultural differences in stranger–child interactions: A comparison between German middle-class and Cameroonian Nso stranger–infant dyads. *Journal of Cross-Cultural Psychology, 45*, 322–334.

Overton, W. F. (2015). Processes, relations, and relational-developmental-systems. In R. M. Lerner, W. F. Overton & P. C. M. Molenaar (Eds), *Handbook of child psychology and developmental science, Seventh edition,*

Volume 1: Theory and method (pp. 9–62). Hoboken, NJ: Wiley.

Overton, W. F., & Lerner, R. M. (2014). Fundamental concepts and methods in developmental science: A relational perspective. *Research in Human Development, 11*, 63–73.

Overton, W. F., Ward, S. L., Noveck, I. A., Black, J., & O'Brien, D. P. (1987). Form and content in the development of deductive reasoning. *Developmental Psychology, 23*, 22–30.

Owen, A. M., Hampshire, A., Grahn, J. A., Stenton, R., Dajani, S., Burns, A. S., Howard, R. J., & Ballard, C. G. (2010). Putting brain training to the test. *Nature, 465* (7299), 775–779.

Özçalişkan. Ş., & Goldin-Meadow, S. (2010). Sex differences in language first appear in gesture. *Developmental Science, 13*, 752–760.

Padilla-Walker, L. M., Coyne, S. M., & Collier, K. M. (2016). Longitudinal relations between parental media monitoring and adolescent aggression, prosocial behavior, and externalizing problems. *Journal of Adolescence, 46*, 86–97.

Padilla-Walker, L. M., Memmott-Elison, M. K., & Coyne, S. M. (2017). Associations between prosocial and problem behavior from early to late adolescence. *Journal of Youth and Adolescence, 47* (5), 961–975.

Palacios, J., & Brodzinsky, D. (2010). Adoption research: Trends, topics, outcomes. *International Journal of Behavioral Development, 34*, 270–284.

Palagi, E., Burghardt, G. M., Smuts, B., Cordoni, G., Dall'Olio, S., Fouts, H. N., Řeháková-Petrů, M., Siviy, S. M., & Pellis, S. M. (2016). Rough-and-tumble play as a window on animal communication. *Biological Reviews, 91*, 311–327.

Pan, B. A., & Snow, C. E. (1999). The development of conversational and discourse skills. In M. Barrett. (Ed.), *Development of Language* (pp. 229–249). Hove, UK: Psychology Press.

Papacek, A. M., Chai, Z., & Green, K. B. (2016). Play and social interaction strategies for young children with autism spectrum disorder in inclusive preschool settings. *Young Exceptional Children, 19*, 3–17.

Paradis, J. (2010). The interface between bilingual development and specific language impairment. *Applied Psycholinguistics, 31*, 227–252.

Parish-Morris, J., Mahajan, N., Hirsh-Pasek, K., Golinkoff, R. M., & Collins, M. F. (2013). Once upon a time: Parent–child dialogue and storybook reading in the electronic era. *Mind, Brain, and Education, 7*, 200–211.

Parker, J. G., & Asher, S. R. (1993). Friendship and friendship quality in middle childhood: Links with peer group acceptance and feelings of loneliness and social dissatisfaction. *Developmental Psychology, 29*, 611–621.

Parker, R. I., & Hagan-Burke, S. (2007). Single case research results as clinical outcomes. *The Journal of School Psychology, 45*, 637–653.

Parten, M. B. (1932). Social participation among preschool children. *Journal of Abnormal and Social Psychology, 27*, 243–269.

Pasalich, D. S., Witkiewitz, K., McMahon, R. J., Pinderhughes, E. E., & Conduct Problems Prevention Research Group (2016). Indirect effects of the fast track intervention on conduct disorder symptoms and callous-unemotional traits: Distinct pathways involving discipline and warmth. *Journal of Abnormal Child Psychology, 44*, 587–597.

Pascual-Leone, J. (1970). A mathematical model for the transition rule in Piaget's developmental stages. *Acta Psychologica, 32*, 301–345.

Pasupathi, M., McLean, K. C., & Weeks, T. (2009). To tell or not to tell: Disclosure and the narrative self. *Journal of Personality, 77*, 89–124.

Patchin, J. W., & Hinduja, S. (2010). Cyberbullying and self-esteem. *Journal of School Health, 80*, 614–621.

Patel, P. G., Stark, K. D., Metz, K. L., & Banneyer, K. N. (2014). School-based interventions for depression. In M. D. Weisst, N. A. Lever, C. P. Bradshaw & J. S. Owens (Eds), *Handbook of school mental health* (pp. 369–383). New York, NY: Springer.

Patterson, G. R., DeBaryshe, B. D., & Ramsey, E. (1989). A developmental perspective on antisocial behavior. *American Psychologist, 44*, 329–335.

Paul, R., Hernandez, R., Taylor, L., & Johnson, K. (1996). Narrative development in late talkers: Early school age. *Journal of Speech, Language, and Hearing Research, 39*, 1295–1303.

Pauletti, R. E., Menon, M., Menon, M., Tobin, D. D., & Perry, D. G. (2012). Narcissism and adjustment in preadolescence. *Child development, 83* (3), 831–837.

Paulus, F. W., Backes, A., Sander, C. S., Weber, M., & von Gontard, A. (2015). Anxiety disorders and behavioral inhibition in preschool children: A population-based study. *Child Psychiatry and Human Development, 46*, 150–157.

Paulus, M. (2014). The emergence of prosocial behavior: Why do infants and toddlers help, comfort, and share? *Child Development Perspectives, 8*, 77–81.

Paulus, M., & Moore, C. (2011). Whom to ask for help? Children's developing understanding of other people's action capabilities. *Experimental Brain Research, 211*, 593–600.

Paulus, M., & Moore, C. (2012). Producing and understanding prosocial actions in early childhood. *Advances in Child Development and Behavior, 42*, 271–305

Paulus, M., & Rosal-Grifoll, B. (2017). Helping and sharing in preschool children with autism. *Experimental Brain Research, 235*, 2081–2088.

Pavarini, G., de Hollanda Souza, D., & Hawk, C. K. (2013). Parental practices and theory of mind development. *Journal of Child and Family Studies, 22*, 844–853.

Pedersen, S., Vitaro, F., Barker, E. D., & Borge, A. I. H. (2007). The timing of middle-childhood peer rejection and friendship: Linking early behaviour to early-adolescent adjustment. *Child Development, 78*, 1037–1051.

Peláez, M., Field, T., Pickens, J. N., & Hart, S. (2008). Disengaged and authoritarian parenting behavior of depressed mothers with their toddlers. *Infant Behavior and Development, 31*, 145–148.

Pellegrini, A. D. (2011). The development and function of locomotor play. In A. Pellegrini (Ed.), *The Oxford handbook of the development of play* (pp. 172–184). New York, NY: Oxford University Press.

Pellegrini, A. D. (2013). Play. In P. D. Zelazo (Ed.), *Oxford handbook of developmental psychology, Volume 2: Self and other* (pp. 276–298). New York, NY: Oxford University Press.

Pellegrini, A. D., Dupuis, D., & Smith, P. K. (2007). Play in evolution and development. *Developmental Review*, 27, 261–276.

Pellegrini, A. D., & Long, J. D. (2002). A longitudinal study of bullying, dominance, and victimization during the transition from primary school through secondary school. *British Journal of Developmental Psychology*, 20, 259–280.

Pellegrini, A. D., & Smith, P. K. (1998). Physical activity play: The nature and function of a neglected aspect of play. *Child Development*, 69, 577–598.

Pelsser, L. M., Frankena, K., Toorman, J., Savelkoul, H. F., Dubois, A. E., Pereira, R. R., Haagen, T. A., Rommelse, N. N., & Buitelaar, J. K. (2011). Effects of a restricted elimination diet on the behaviour of children with attention-deficit hyperactivity disorder (INCA study): A randomised controlled trial. *The Lancet*, 377 (9764), 494–503.

Peltonen, K., Kangaslampi, S., Qouta, S., & Punamäki, R. L. (2017). Trauma and autobiographical memory: Contents and determinants of earliest memories among war-affected Palestinian children. *Memory*, 25, 1347–1357.

Pempek, T. A., Kirkorian, H. L., & Anderson, D. R. (2014). The effects of background television on the quantity and quality of child-directed speech by parents. *Journal of Children and Media*, 8, 211–222.

Peña, E. D. (2016). Supporting the home language of bilingual children with developmental disabilities: From knowing to doing. *Journal of Communication Disorders*, 63, 85–92.

Pennington, B. F. (2015). Atypical cognitive development. In R. M. Lerner, L. S. Liben & U. Mueller (Eds), *Handbook of child psychology and developmental science, Seventh edition, Volume 2: Cognitive processes* (pp. 995–1037). New York, NY: Wiley.

Pennington, B. F., McGrath, L. M., Rosenberg, J., Barnard, H., Smith, S. D., Willcutt, E. G., Friend, A., DeFires, J. C., & Olson, R. K. (2009). Gene-environment interactions in reading disability and attention deficit/ hyperactivity disorder. *Developmental Psychology*, 45, 77–89.

Peretz, I., & Hyde, K. L. (2003). What is specific to music processing? Insights from congenital amusia. *Trends in Cognitive Sciences*, 7, 362–367.

Perez, J. D., Rubinstein, N. D., & Dulac, C. (2016). New perspectives on genomic imprinting, an essential and multifaceted mode of epigenetic control in the developing and adult brain. *Annual Review of Neuroscience*, 39, 347–384.

Pérez-Edgar, K., Reeb-Sutherland, B. C., McDermott, J. M., White, L. K., Henderson, H. A., Degnan, K. A., Hane, A. A., Pine, D. S., & Fox, N. A. (2011). Attention biases to threat link behavioral inhibition to social withdrawal over time in very young children. *Journal of Abnormal Child Psychology*, 39, 885–895.

Pérez-Edgar, K., Taber-Thomas, B., Auday, E., & Morales, S. (2014). Temperament and attention as core mechanisms in the early emergence of anxiety. In K. H. Lagattuta (Ed.), *Children and emotion* (pp. 42–56). Basel, Switzerland: Karger.

Pérez-Pereira, M. (2014). Contrasting views on the pragmatic abilities of blind children. *Enfance*, 2014, 73–88.

Pérez-Pereira, M., & Conti-Ramsden, G. (1999). *Language development and social interaction in blind children.* Hove, UK: Psychology Press.

Perner, J., Ruffman, T., & Leekam, S. R. (1994). Theory of mind is contagious: You catch it from your sibs. *Child Development*, 65, 1228–1238.

Perner, J., & Wimmer, H. (1985). "John thinks that Mary thinks that": Attribution of second-order beliefs by 5–10 year old children. *Journal of Experimental Child Psychology*, 39, 437–471.

Perraudin, S., & Mounoud, P. (2009). Contribution of the priming paradigm to the understanding of the conceptual developmental shift from 5 to 9 years of age. *Developmental Science*, 12, 956–977.

Perry, E., & Flood, A. (2016). Autism spectrum disorder and attachment: A clinician's perspective. In H. K. Fletcher, A. Flood & D. J. Hare (Eds), *Attachment in intellectual and developmental disability: A clinician's guide to practice and research* (pp. 79–103). Oxford: Wiley.

Perry, N. W., & Wrightsman, L. S. (1991). *The child witness: Legal issues and dilemmas.* Newbury Park, CA: Sage.

Persico, A. M., & Napolioni, V. (2013). Autism genetics. *Behavioural Brain Research*, 251, 95–112. Pervin, L. A., & John, O. P. (1997). *Personality.* New York, NY: John Wiley.

Pervin, L. A., Cervone, D., & John, O. P. (2005). *Personality: Theory and research, Ninth edition.* New York, NY: Wiley.

Peskin, J. (1992). Ruse and representations: On children's ability to conceal information. *Developmental Psychology*, 28, 84–89.

Pessoa, L., & Adolphs, R. (2010). Emotion processing and the amygdala: From a "low road" to "many roads" of evaluating biological significance. *Nature Reviews Neuroscience*, 11, 773.

Petalas, M. A., Hastings, R. P., Nash, S., & Duff, S. (2015). Typicality and subtle difference in sibling relationships: Experiences of adolescents with autism. *Journal of Child and Family Studies*, 24, 38–49.

Petalas, M. A., Hastings, R. P., Nash, S., Hall, L. M., Joannidi, H., & Dowey, A. (2012). Psychological adjustment and sibling relationships in siblings of children with autism spectrum disorders: Environmental stressors and the broad autism phenotype. *Research in Autism Spectrum Disorders*, 6, 546–555.

Peters, A. M. (1995). Strategies in the acquisition of syntax. In P. Fletcher & B. MacWhinney (Eds), *The hand-*

book of child language (pp. 462–482). Oxford: Basil Blackwell.

Petersen, D. B. (2011). A systematic review of narrative-based language intervention with children who have language impairment. *Communication Disorders Quarterly*, 32, 207–220.

Petersen, D. B., Brown, C. L., Ukrainetz, T. A., Wise, C., Spencer, T. D., & Zebre, J. (2014). Systematic individualized narrative language intervention on the personal narratives of children with autism. *Language, Speech, and Hearing Services in Schools*, 45, 67–86.

Petersen, D. B., & Spencer, T. D. (2016). Using narrative intervention to accelerate canonical story grammar and complex language growth in culturally diverse preschoolers. *Topics in Language Disorders*, 36, 6–19.

Peterson, C. (2012). Children's autobiographical memories across the years: Forensic implications of childhood amnesia and eyewitness memory for stressful events. *Developmental Review*, 32, 287–306.

Peterson, C., Baker-Ward, L., & Grovenstein, T. N. (2016). Childhood remembered: Reports of both unique and repeated events. *Memory*, 24, 240–256.

Peterson, C., & Rideout, R. (1998). Memory for medical emergencies experienced by one and two year olds. *Developmental Psychology*, 34, 1059–1072.

Peterson, C., & Warren, K. L. (2009). Injuries, emergency rooms and children's memory: Factors contributing to individual differences. In J. A. Quas & R. Fivush (Eds), *Emotion and memory in development* (pp. 60–85). Oxford: Oxford University Press.

Peterson, C., Warren, K. L., & Short, M. M. (2011). Infantile amnesia across the years: A 2-year follow-up of children's earliest memories. *Child Development*, 82, 1092–1105.

Peterson, C., & Whalen, N. (2001). Five years later: Children's memory for medical emergencies. *Applied Cognitive Psychology*, 15, 7–24.

Peterson, C. C. (2002). Children's long-term memory for autobiographical events. *Developmental Review*, 22, 370–402.

Peterson, C. C. (2009). Development of social-cognitive and communication skills in children born deaf. *Scandinavian Journal of Psychology*, 50, 475–483.

Peterson, C. C. (2014). Theory of mind understanding and empathic behavior in children with autism spectrum disorders. *International Journal of Developmental Neuroscience*, 39, 16–21.

Peterson, C. C. (2016). Empathy and theory of mind in deaf and hearing children. *Journal of Deaf Studies and Deaf Education*, 21, 141–147.

Peterson, D. J., Jones, K. T., Stephens, J. A., Gözenman, F., & Berryhill, M. E. (2016). Childhood memory: An update from the cognitive neuroscience perspective. In W. T. O'Donohue & M. Fanetti (Eds), *Forensic interviews regarding child sexual abuse* (pp. 81–105). Cham, Switzerland: Springer.

Peterson, R. L., & Pennington, B. F. (2015). Developmental dyslexia. *Annual Review of Clinical Psychology*, 11, 283–307.

Petitto, L. A. (1992). Modularity and constraints in early lexical acquisition: Evidence from children's early language and gesture. In M. R. Gunnar & M. Maratsos (Eds), *Minnesota symposium on child psychology*, Volume 25 (pp. 25–58). Hillsdale, NJ: Lawrence Erlbaum.

Petitto, L. A., Katerelos, M., Levy, B. G., Gauna, K., Tetreault, K., & Ferraro, V. (2001). Bilingual signed and spoken language acquisition from birth: Implications for the mechanisms underlying early bilingual language acquisition. *Journal of Child Language*, 28, 453–496.

Petitto, L. A., & Marentette, P. F. (1991). Babbling in the manual mode: Evidence for the ontogeny of language. *Science*, 251, 1493–1496.

Petretic, P. A., & Tweney, R. D. (1977). Does comprehension precede the production? The development of children's responses to telegraphic sentences of varying grammatical adequacy. *Journal of Child Language*, 4, 201–209.

Petrina, N., Carter, M., & Stephenson, J. (2014). The nature of friendship in children with autism spectrum disorders: A systematic review. *Research in Autism Spectrum Disorders*, 8, 111–126.

Pettit, G. S., & Bates, J. E. (1984). Continuity of individual differences in the mother infant relationship from six to thirteen months. *Child Development*, 55, 729–739.

Pettygrove, D. M., Hammond, S. I., Karahuta, E. L., Waugh, W. E., & Brownell, C. A. (2013). From cleaning up to helping out: Parental socialization and children's early prosocial behavior. *Infant Behavior and Development*, 36, 843–846.

Pfeifer, L. I., Pacciulio, A. M., Santos, C. A. D., Santos, J. L. D., & Stagnitti, K. E. (2011). Pretend play of children with cerebral palsy. *Physical and Occupational Therapy in Pediatrics*, 31, 390–402.

Pfeiffer, J. P., & Pinquart, M. (2014). Bullying in German boarding schools: A pilot study. *School Psychology International*, 35, 580–591.

Phinney, J. S. (1990). Ethnic identity in adolescents and adults: Review of research. *Child Development*, 65, 499–514.

Phinney, J. S. (1993). A three-stage model of ethnic identity development in adolescence. In M. E. Bernal & G. P. Knights (Eds), *Ethnic identity: Formation and transmission among Hispanics and other minorities* (pp. 61–79). Albany, NY: State University of New York Press.

Piaget, J. (1928). *The child's conception of the world.* London: Routledge and Kegan Paul.

Piaget, J. (1932). *The moral judgment of the child.* London: Kegan Paul.

Piaget, J. (1950). *The psychology of the child.* London: Routledge and Kegan Paul.

Piaget, J. (1951). *Play, dreams and imitation in childhood.* London: Heineman.

Piaget, J. (1952). *The origin of intelligence in the child.* London: Routledge and Kegan Paul.

Piaget, J. (1954). *The construction of reality in the child.* New York, NY: Routledge and Kegan Paul.

Piaget, J. (1959). *The language and thought of the child, Third edition*. London: Routledge.

Piaget, J. (1969a). *The child's conception of time*. London: Routledge and Kegan Paul.

Piaget, J. (1969b). *Psychology and pedagogy*. Paris: Denoel.

Piaget, J. (1970). *The child's conception of movement and speed*. London: Routledge and Kegan Paul.

Piaget, J. (1972). Intellectual evolution from adolescence to adulthood. *Human Development, 15*, 1–12.

Piaget, J. (1983). Piaget's theory. In P. Mussen (Ed.), *Hand book of child psychology, Fourth edition* (pp. 103–128). New York, NY: Wiley.

Piaget, J., Henriques, G., & Ascher, E. (Eds). (1992). *Morphisms and categories: Comparing and transforming*: London: Lawrence Erlbaum.

Piaget, J., & Inhelder, B. (1956). *The child's conception of space*. London: Routledge and Kegan Paul.

Piaget, J., & Inhelder, B. (1975). *The origin of the idea of chance in children*. London: Routledge and Kegan Paul.

Pianta, R. C., & Nimetz, S. L. (1992). Development of young children in stressful contexts: Theory, assessment, and prevention. In M. Gettinger, S. N. Elliott & T. R. Kratochwill (Eds), *Preschool and early childhood treatment directions* (pp. 151–185). Hillsdale, NJ: Erlbaum.

Picci, G., & Scherf, K. S. (2016). From caregivers to peers: Puberty shapes human face perception. *Psychological Science, 27*, 1461–1473.

Picton, T. W., & Taylor, M. J. (2007). Electrophysiological evaluation of human brain development. *Developmental Neuropsychology, 31*, 249–278.

Piek, J. P. (2002). The role of variability in early motor development. *Infant Behavior and Development, 25*, 452–465.

Piekkola, B. (2011). Traits across cultures: A neo-Allportian perspective. *Journal of Theoretical and Philosophical Psychology, 31*, 2–24.

Pietschnig, J., & Voracek, M. (2015). One century of global IQ gains: A formal meta-analysis of the Flynn effect (1909–2013). *Perspectives on Psychological Science, 10*, 282–306.

Pijnacker, J., Vervloed, M. P., & Steenbergen, B. (2012). Pragmatic abilities in children with congenital visual impairment: An exploration of non-literal language and advanced theory of mind understanding. *Journal of Autism and Developmental Disorders, 42*, 2440–2449.

Pike, A., Coldwell, J., & Dunn, J. F. (2005). Sibling relationships in early/middle childhood: Links with individual adjustment. *Journal of Family Psychology, 19*, 523–532.

Pillai, M., & James, D. (1990). Development of human fetal behavior: A review. *Fetal Diagnosis and Therapy, 5*, 15–32.

Pillemer, D. B., Picariello, M. L., & Pruett, J. C. (1994). Very long-term memories of a salient preschool event. *Applied Cognitive Psychology, 8*, 95–106.

Pillemer, D. B., & White, S. H. (1989). Childhood events recalled by children and adults. In H. W. Reese (Ed.), *Advances in child development and behavior, Volume 21* (pp. 297–340). London: Academic Press.

Pine, D. S., & Fox, N. A. (2015). Childhood antecedents and risk for adult mental disorders. *Annual Review of Psychology, 66*, 459–485.

Pine, D. S., & Klein, R. G. (2015). Anxiety disorders. In A. Thapar, D. S. Pine, F. S. Leckman, S. Scott, M. J. Snowling & E. Taylor (Eds), *Rutter's child and adolescent psychiatry, Sixth edition* (pp. 822–840). Oxford: Wiley.

Pine, F. (2004). Mahler's concepts of "symbiosis" and separation-individuation: Revisited, reevaluated, refined. *Journal of the American Psychoanalytic Association, 52*, 511–533.

Pingault, J. B., Côté, S. M., Vitaro, F., Falissard, B., Genolini, C., & Tremblay, R. E. (2014). The developmental course of childhood inattention symptoms uniquely predicts educational attainment: A 16-year longitudinal study. *Psychiatry Research, 219*, 707–709.

Pingault, J. B., Tremblay, R. E., Vitaro, F., Carbonneau, R., Genolini, C., Falissard, B., & Côté, S. M. (2011). Childhood trajectories of inattention and hypera-ctivity and prediction of educational attainment in early adulthood: A 16-year longitudinal population-based study. *American Journal of Psychiatry, 168*, 1164–1170.

Pinhas, L., Morris, A., Crosby, R. D., & Katzman, D. K. (2011). Incidence and age-specific presentation of restrictive eating disorders in children: A Canadian Paediatric Surveillance Program study. *Archives of Pediatrics and Adolescent Medicine, 165*, 895–899.

Pinker, S. (1994). *The language instinct*. London: Allen Lane.

Pinker, S. (1997). *How the mind works*. New York, NY: Norton.

Pinker, S., & Jackendoff, R. (2005). The faculty of language: What's special about it? *Cognition, 95*, 201–236.

Piontelli, A., Ceriani, F., Fabietti, I., Fogliani, R., Restelli, E., & Kustermann, A. (2015). Fetal sensory abilities. In A. Piontelli (Ed.), *Development of normal fetal movements* (pp. 111–126). Milan: Springer.

Pipe, M-E., & Salmon, K. (2009). Dolls, drawings, body diagrams, and other props: Role of props in investigative interviews. In K. Kuehnle & M. Connell (Eds), *The evaluation of child sexual abuse allegations: A comprehesive guide to assessment and testimony* (pp. 365–395). Hoboken, NJ: Wiley.

Piper, M. C., & Darrah, J. (1994). *Motor assessment of the developing infant*. Philadelphia, PA: W. B. Saunders.

Piquero, A. R., Carriaga, M. L., Diamond, B., Kazemian, L., & Farrington, D. P. (2012). Stability in aggression revisited. *Aggression and Violent Behavior, 17*, 365–372.

Pizer, G., Walters, K., & Meier R. P. (2007). Bringing up baby with baby signs: Language ideologies and socialization in hearing families. *Sign Language Studies, 7*, 387–430.

Plantinga, J., & Trehub, S. E. (2014). Revisiting the innate preference for consonance. *Journal of Experimental Psychology: Human Perception and Performance, 40*, 40–49.

Plomin, R., Corley, R., Caspi, A., Fulker, D. W., & DeFries, J. (1998). Adoption results for self-reported personality: Evidence for nonadditive genetic effects? *Journal of Personality and Social Psychology, 75*, 211–218.

Plomin, R., & Deary, I. J. (2015). Genetics and intelligence differences: Five special findings. *Molecular Psychiatry*, *20*, 98–108.

Plomin, R., DeFries, J. C., & Fulker, D. W. (1988). *Nature and nurture during infancy and early childhood*. Cambridge: Cambridge University Press.

Plomin, R., DeFries, J. C., Knopik, V. S., & Neiderhiser, J. M. (2016). Top 10 replicated findings from behavioral genetics. *Perspectives on Psychological Science*, *11*, 3–23.

Plomin, R., DeFries, J. C., McClearn, G. E., & McGuffin, P. (2008). *Behavioral genetics, Fifth edition*. New York, NY: Worth.

Plomin, R., DeFries, J. C., McClearn, G. E., & Rutter, M. (1997). *Behavioral genetics, Third edition*. New York, NY: W. H. Freeman.

Plomin, R., Haworth, C. M., Meaburn, E. L., Price, T. S., Wellcome Trust Case Control Consortium 2, & Davis, O. S. (2013). Common DNA markers can account for more than half of the genetic influence on cognitive abilities. *Psychological Science*, *24*, 562–568.

Plotnik, J., de Waal, F. B. M., & Reiss, D. (2006). Self-recognition in an Asian elephant. *Proceedings of the National Academy of Sciences of the United States of America*, *103*, 17053–17057.

Plotnik, J. M., de Waal, F. B. M., Moore, D., & Reiss, D. (2010). Self-recognition in the Asian elephant and future directions for cognitive research with elephants in zoological settings. *Zoo Biology*, *29*, 179–191.

Pluess, M., & Belsky, J. (2010). Differential susceptibility to parenting and quality child care. *Developmental Psychology*, *46*, 379–390.

Pluess, M., & Belsky, J. (2011). Prenatal programming of postnatal plasticity? *Development and Psychopathology*, *23*, 29–38.

Pluess, M., & Belsky, J. (2013). Vantage sensitivity: Individual differences in response to positive experiences. *Psychological Bulletin*, *139*, 901–916.

Poldrack, R. A. (2010). Interpreting developmental changes in neuroimaging signals. *Human Brain Mapping*, *31*, 872–878.

Pomerantz, E. M., & Thompson, R. A. (2008). Parents' role in children's personality development: The psychological resource principle. In O. P. John, R. W. Robins & L. A. Pervin (Eds), *Handbook of personality: Theory and research, Third edition* (pp. 351–374). New York, NY: Guilford Press.

Pons, F., Harris, P. L., & de Rosnay, M. (2004). Emotion comprehension between 3 and 11 years: Developmental periods and hierarchical organization. *European Journal of Developmental Psychology*, *1*, 127–152.

Poole, D. A., & White, L. T. (1991). Effects of question repetition on the eyewitness testimony of children and adults. *Developmental Psychology*, *27*, 975–986.

Pope, A. W. (2003). Developmental risk associated with mutual dislike in elementary school children. *New Directions for Child and Adolescent Development*, *102*, 89–110.

Popper, K. R. (1959). *The logic of scientific discovery*. London: Hutchinson.

Porath, M. (2014). Meeting the needs of gifted learners. In J. Holliman (Ed.), *The Routledge international companion to educational psychology* (pp. 327–336). London: Routledge.

Posada, R., & Wainryb, C. (2008). Moral development in a violent society: Colombian children's judgments in the context of survival and revenge. *Child Development*, *79*, 882–898.

Posne, M. I., & Rothbart, M. K. (2000). Developing mechanisms of self-regulation. *Development and Psychopathology*, *12*, 427–441.

Potter, W. J. (1999). *On media violence*. London: Sage.

Poulin, F., & Boivin, M. (2000). Reactive and proactive aggression: Evidence of a two-factor model. *Psychological Assessment*, *12*, 115–122.

Poulin, F., & Chan, A. (2010). Friendship stability and change in childhood and adolescence. *Developmental Review*, *30*, 257–272.

Poulin, F., Dishion, T. J., & Burraston, B. (2001). Three-year iatrogenic effects associated with aggregating high-risk adolescents in cognitive-behavioral preventive interventions. *Applied Developmental Science*, *5*, 214–224.

Poulin-Dubois, D., Brooker, I., & Chow, V. (2009). The developmental origins of naive psychology in infancy. *Advances in Child Development and Behavior*, *37*, 55–104.

Poulin-Dubois, D., & Graham, S. A. (1994). Infant categorization and early object–word meaning. In A. Vyt, H. Bloch & M. H. Bornstein (Eds), *Early child development in the French tradition: Contributions from current research* (pp. 207–225). Hillsdale, NJ: Erlbaum.

Povinelli, D. J., Landau, K. R., & Perilloux, H. K. (1996). Self-recognition in young children using delayed versus live feedback: Evidence for a developmental asynchrony. *Child Development*, *67*, 1540–1554.

Povinelli, D. J., Landry, A. M., Theall, L. A., Clark, B. R., & Castille, C. M. (1999). Development of young children's understanding that the recent past is causally bound to the present. *Developmental Psychology*, *35*, 1426–1439.

Powers, K. L., Brooks, P. J., Aldrich, N. J., Palladino, M. A., & Alfieri, L. (2013). Effects of video-game play on information processing: A meta-analytic investigation. *Psychonomic Bulletin and Review*, *20*, 1055–1079.

Prado, E. L., & Dewey, K. G. (2014). Nutrition and brain development in early life. *Nutrition Reviews*, *72*, 267–284.

Pramling, N. (2015). Learning and metaphor: Bridging the gap between the familiar and the unfamiliar. In M. Fleer & N. Pramling (Eds), *A cultural-historical study of children learning science* (pp. 125–132). Dordrecht, The Netherlands: Springer.

Pratt, C., & Bryant, P. (1990). Young children understand that looking leads to knowing (so long as they are looking into a single barrel). *Child Development*, *61*, 973–982.

Prebble, S. C., Addis, D. R., & Tippett, L. J. (2013). Autobiographical memory and sense of self. *Psychological Bulletin*, *139*, 815–840.

Prechtl, H. F. R. (1993). Principles of early motor development in the human. In A. F. Kalverboer, B. Hopkins & R. Geuze (Eds), *Motor development in early and later childhood: Longitudinal approaches* (pp. 35–50). Cambridge: Cambridge University Press.

Preisler, G. M. (1993). A descriptive study of blind children in nurseries with sighted children. *Child Care, Health and Development*, 19, 295–315.

Premack, D., & Woodruff, G. (1978). Does the chimpanzee have a theory of mind? *Behavioural and Brain Sciences*, 4, 515–526.

Presson, A. P., Partyka, G., Jensen, K. M., Devine, O. J., Rasmussen, S. A., McCabe, L. L., & McCabe, E. R. (2013). Current estimate of Down syndrome population prevalence in the United States. *The Journal of Pediatrics*, 163, 1163–1168.

Preyer, W. (1882/1988). *The mind of the child*. New York, NY: Appleton.

Price, J. M. (1996). Friendships of maltreated children and adolescents: Contexts for expressing and modifying relationship history. In W. M. Bukowski, A. F. Newcomb & W. W. Hartup (Eds), *The company they keep: Friendship in childhood and adolescence* (pp. 262–285). Cambridge: Cambridge University Press.

Price-Williams, D., Gordon, W., & Ramirez, M. (1969). Skill and conservation: A study of pottery making children. *Developmental Psychology*, 1, 769.

Prino, C. T., & Peyrot, M. (1994). The effect of child physical abuse and neglect on aggressive, withdrawn, and prosocial behavior. *Child Abuse and Neglect*, 18, 871–884.

Prinstein, M. J., & Dodge, K. A. (2008). *Understanding friendship in children and adolescents* New York, NY: Guilford Press.

Prior, H., Schwarz, A., & Güntürkün, O. (2008). Mirror-induced behavior in the magpie (Pica pica): Evidence of self-recognition. *PLoS Biol*, 6, e202, 1642–1650.

Prot, S., Gentile, D. A., Anderson, C. A., Suzuki, K., Swing, E., Lim, K. M., Horiuchi, Y., Jelic, M., Krahé, B., Liuqing, W., et al. (2014). Long-term relations among prosocial-media use, empathy, and prosocial behavior. *Psychological Science*, 25, 358–368.

Provence, S., & Lipton, R. C. (1962). *Infants in institutions*. New York, NY: International Universities Press.

Provine, R. R. (1997). Yawns, laughs, smiles, tickles, and talking: Naturalistic and laboratory studies of facial action and social communication. In J. A. Russell & J. M. Fernandez-Dols (Eds), *The psychology of facial expression* (pp. 158–175). Cambridge: Cambridge University Press.

Putnam, S. P., Sanson, A. V., & Rothbart, M. K. (2002). Child temperament and parenting. In M. H. Bornstein (Ed.), *Handbook of parenting, Second edition, Volume 1: Children and parenting* (pp. 163–179), Mahwah, NJ: Erlbaum.

Qin, J., Quas, J. A., Redlich, A., & Goodman, G. S. (1997). Children's eyewitness testimony: Memory development in the legal context. In N. Cowan (Ed.), *The development of memory in childhood* (pp. 301–341). London: Psychology Press.

Quas, J. A., & Fivush, R. (Eds) (2009). *Emotion and memory in development*. Oxford: Oxford University Press.

Quas, J. A., Malloy, L. C., Melinder, A., Goodman, G. S., D'Mello, M., & Schaaf, J. (2007). Developmental differences in the effects of repeated interviews and interviewer bias on young children's event memory and false reports. *Developmental Psychology*, 43, 823–837.

Querleu, D., Renard, X., Versyp, F., Paris-Delrue, L., & Crépin, G. (1988). Fetal hearing *European Journal of Obstetrics and Reproductive Biology*, 29, 191–212.

Quiggle, N. L., Garber, J., Panak, W. F., & Dodge, K. A. (1992). Social information processing in aggressive and depressed children. *Child Development*, 63, 1305–1320.

Quinn, P. C. (2002). Beyond prototypes: Asymmetries in infant categorization and what they teach us about the mechanisms guiding early knowledge acquisition. *Advances in Child Development and Behavior*, 29, 161–193.

Quinn, P. C. (2006). On the emergence of perceptual organization and categorization in young infants: Roles for perceptual process and knowledge access. In L. Balter & C. Tamis-Le Monda (Eds), *Child psychology: A handbook of contemporary issues, Second edition* (pp. 109–131). Philadelphia, PA: Psychology Press.

Quinn, P. C. (2008). In defense of core competencies, quantitative change, and continuity. *Child Development*, 79, 1633–1638.

Quinn, P. C., Bhatt, R. S., Brush, D., Grimes, A., & Sharpnack, H. (2002). Development of form similarity as a Gestalt grouping principle in infancy. *Psychological Science*, 13, 320–328.

Quinn, P. C., Eimas, P. D., & Rosenkrantz, S. L. (1993). Evidence for representations of perceptually similar natural categories by 3-month-old and 4-month-old infants. *Perception*, 22, 463–475.

Quinn, P. C., Lee, K., Pascalis, O., & Tanaka, J. W. (2016). Narrowing in categorical responding to other-race face classes by infants. *Developmental Science*, 19, 362–371.

Quinn, T., & Gordon, C. (2011). The effects of cerebral palsy on early attachment: Perceptions of rural South African mothers. *Journal of Human Ecology*, 36, 191–197.

Raaheim, K. (1969). *Opplevelse, erfaring & intelligens*. Oslo: Universitetsforlaget.

Rabipour, S., & Raz, A. (2012). Training the brain: Fact and fad in cognitive and behavioral remediation. *Brain and Cognition*, 79, 159–179.

Raby, K. L., Cicchetti, D., Carlson, E. A., Egeland, B., & Andrew Collins, W. (2013). Genetic contributions to continuity and change in attachment security: A prospective, longitudinal investigation from infancy to young adulthood. *Journal of Child Psychology and Psychiatry*, 54, 1223–1230.

Raby, K. L., Steele, R. D., Carlson, E. A., & Sroufe, L. A. (2015). Continuities and changes in infant attachment patterns across two generations. *Attachment and Human Development*, 17, 414–428.

Raby, K. L., Yarger, H. A., Lind, T., Fraley, R. C., Leerkes, E., & Dozier, M. (2017). Attachment states of mind among internationally adoptive and foster parents. *Development and Psychopathology, 29*, 365–378.

Racz, S. J., Putnick, D. L., Suwalsky, J. T., Hendricks, C., & Bornstein, M. H. (2017). Cognitive abilities, social adaptation, and externalizing behavior problems in childhood and adolescence: Specific cascade effects across development. *Journal of Youth and Adolescence, 46*, 1688–1701.

Radford, A. (1990). *Syntactic theory and the acquisition of English syntax*. Cambridge, MA: Blackwell.

Raghubar, K. P., Barnes, M. A., & Hecht, S. A. (2010). Working memory and mathematics: A review of developmental, individual difference, and cognitive approaches. *Learning and Individual Differences, 20*, 110–122.

Räikkönen, K., Pesonen, A., Heinonen, K., Komsi, N., Järvenpää, A., & Strandberg, T. (2006). Stressed parents: A dyadic perspective on perceived infant temperament. *Infant and Child Development, 15*, 75–87.

Rakic, P., Bourgeois, J. P., Eckenhoff, M. F., Zecevic, N., & Goldman-Rakic, P. S. (1986). Concurrent overproduction of synapses in diverse regions of the primate cerebral cortex. *Science, 232*, 232–235.

Rakison, D. H. (2003). Parts, categorization, and the animate-inanimate distinction in infancy. In D. H. Rakison & L. K. Oakes (Eds), *Early category and concept development: Making sense of the blooming, buzzing confusion* (pp. 159–192). Oxford: Oxford University Press.

Rakison, D. H., & Cohen, L. B. (1999). Infants' use of functional parts in basic-like categorization. *Developmental Science, 2*, 423–432.

Rakoczy, H. (2012). Do infants have a theory of mind? *British Journal of Developmental Psychology, 30*, 59–74.

Rakoczy, H. (2017). In defense of a developmental dogma: Children acquire propositional attitude folk psychology around age 4. *Synthese, 194*, 689–707.

Rakova, M. (2003). *The extent of the literal: Metaphor, polysemy and theories of concepts*. Basingstoke, UK: Palgrave Macmillan.

Rambaran, J. A., Dijkstra, J. K., Munniksma, A., & Cillessen, A. H. (2015). The development of adolescents' friendships and antipathies: A longitudinal multivariate network test of balance theory. *Social Networks, 43*, 162–176.

Ramer, A. (1976). Syntactic styles in emerging language. *Journal of Child Language, 3*, 49–62.

Ramey, C. T., & Ramey. S. L. (1998a). Early intervention and early experience. *American Psychologist, 53*, 109–120.

Ramey, C. T., & Ramey, S. L. (1998b). Prevention of intellectual disabilities: Early interventions to improve cognitive development. *Preventive Medicine, 27*, 224–232.

Randell, A. C., & Peterson, C. C. (2009). Affective qualities of sibling disputes, mothers' conflict attitudes, and children's theory of mind development. *Social Development, 18*, 857–874.

Rankin, J. L., Lane, D. J., Gibbons, F. X., & Gerrard, M. (2004). Adolescent self-consciousness: Longitudinal age changes and gender differences in two cohorts. *Journal of Research on Adolescence, 14*, 1–21.

Rapee, R. M., Kennedy, S. J., Ingram, M., Edwards, S. L., & Sweeney, L. (2010). Altering the trajectory of anxiety in at-risk young children. *The American Journal of Psychiatry, 167*, 1518–1525.

Rapee, R. M., Schniering, C. A., & Hudson, J. L. (2009). Anxiety disorders during childhood and adolescence: Origins and treatment. *Annual Review of Clinical Psychology, 5*, 311–341.

Rapin, I., Dunn, M. A., Allen, D. A., Stevens, M. C., & Fein, D. (2009). Subtypes of language disorders in school-age children with autism. *Developmental Neuropsychology, 34*, 66–84.

Rapport, M. D., Orban, S. A., Kofler, M. J., & Friedman, L. M. (2013). Do programs designed to train working memory, other executive functions, and attention benefit children with ADHD? A meta-analytic review of cognitive, academic, and behavioral outcomes. *Clinical Psychology Review, 33*, 1237–1252.

Raskin, L. A., Maital, S., & Bornstein, M. H. (1983). Perceptual categorization of color: A life span study. *Psychological Research, 45*, 135–145.

Rasmussen, M., Meilstrup, C. R., Bendtsen, P., Pedersen, T. P., Nielsen, L., Madsen, K. R., & Holstein, B. E. (2015). Perceived problems with computer gaming and Internet use are associated with poorer social relations in adolescence. *International Journal of Public Health, 60*, 179–188.

Rauscher, F. H., & Hinton, S. C. (2006). The Mozart effect: Music listening is not music instruction. *Educational Psychologist, 41*, 233–238.

Rauscher, F. H., Shaw, G. L., & Ky, K. N. (1993). Music and spatial task performance. *Nature, 365*, 611.

Raval, V. V., Martini, T. S., & Raval, P. H. (2007). "Would others think it is okay to express my feelings?" Regulation of anger, sadness and physical pain in Gujarati children in India. *Social Development, 16*, 79–105.

Raven, J., Raven, J. C., & Court, J. H. (1998). *Coloured Progressive Matrices*. Oxford: Oxford Psychologist Press.

Raver, C. C. (2004). Placing emotional self-regulation in sociocultural and socioeconomic contexts. *Child Development, 75*, 346–353.

Ray, E., & Heyes, C. (2011). Imitation in infancy: The wealth of the stimulus. *Developmental Science, 14*, 92–105.

Reddy, V. (1991). Playing with others' expectations: Teasing and mucking about in the first year. In A. Whiten (Ed.), *Natural theories of mind: Evolution, development and simulation of everyday mindreading* (pp. 143–158). Oxford: Basil Blackwell.

Redick, T. S., & Webster, S. B. (2014). Videogame interventions and spatial ability interactions. *Frontiers in Human Neuroscience, 8*, 183.

Reed, G. M., Drescher, J., Krueger, R. B., Atalla, E., Cochran, S. D., First, M. B., Arango-de Montis, I., Parish, S. J., Cottler, S., Briken, P., & Saxena, S. (2016). Disorders related to sexuality and gender identity in the ICD-11: Revising the ICD-10 classification based on current scientific evidence, best clinical practices, and human rights considerations. *World Psychiatry, 15*, 205–221.

Reese, H. W. (1999). Strategies for replication research exemplified by replications of the Istomina study. *Developmental Review, 19,* 1–30.

Reesman, J. H., Day, L. A., Szymanski, C. A., Hughes-Wheatland, R., Witkin, G. A., Kalback, S. R., & Brice, P. J. (2014). Review of intellectual assessment measures for children who are deaf or hard of hearing. *Rehabilitation Psychology, 59,* 99–106.

Reeve, R. A., & Gray, S. (2015). Number difficulties in young children. Deficits in core number? In S. J. Chinn (Ed.), *The Routledge international handbook of dyscalculia and mathematical learning difficulties* (pp. 44–59). London: Routledge

Reeve, R. A., & Waldecker, C. (2017). Evidence-based assessment and intervention for dyscalculia and maths disabilities in school psychology. In M. Thielking & M. D. Terjesen (Eds), *Handbook of Australian school psychology* (pp. 197–213). Cham, Switzerland: Springer.

Reilly, D., Neumann, D. L., & Andrews, G. (2017). Gender differences in spatial ability: Implications for STEM education and approaches to reducing the gender gap for parents and educators. In M. S. Khine (Ed.), *Visual-spatial ability: Transforming research into practice* (pp. 195–224). Cham, Switzerland: Springer.

Reindl, M., Gniewosz, B., & Reinders, H. (2016). Socialization of emotion regulation strategies through friends. *Journal of Adolescence, 49,* 146–157.

Reinfjell, T., Kårstad, S. B., Berg-Nielsen, T. S., Luby, J. L., & Wichstrøm, L. (2016). Predictors of change in depressive symptoms from preschool to first grade. *Development and Psychopathology, 28,* 1517–1530.

Reissland, N., & Kisilevsky, B. S. (Eds) (2016). *Fetal development: Research on brain and behavior, environmental influences, and emerging technologies.* Cham, Switzerland: Springer.

Repacholi, B. M., & Gopnik, A. (1997). Early reasoning about desires: Evidence from 14–18-months-olds. *Developmental Psychology, 33,* 12–21.

Repacholi, B. M., & Meltzoff, A. N. (2007). Emotional eavesdropping: Infants selectively respond to indirect emotional signals. *Child Development, 78,* 503–521.

Repacholi, B. M., Meltzoff, A. N., Rowe, H., & Toub, T. S. (2014). Infant, control thyself: Infants' integration of multiple social cues to regulate their imitative behavior. *Cognitive Development, 32,* 46–57.

Rescorla, L. A., Bochicchio, L., Achenbach, T. M., Ivanova, M. Y., Almqvist, F., Begovac, I., Bilenberg, N., Bird, H., Dobrean, A., Erol, N., et al. (2014). Parent–teacher agreement on children's problems in 21 societies. *Journal of Clinical Child and Adolescent Psychology, 43,* 627–642.

Restifo, K., & Bögels, S. (2009). Family processes in the development of youth depression: Translating the evidence to treatment. *Clinical Psychology Review, 29,* 294–316.

Reynolds, G. D., Courage, M. L., & Richards, J. E. (2013). The development of attention. In D. Reisberg (Ed.), *The Oxford handbook of cognitive psychology* (pp. 1000–1013). Oxford: Oxford University Press.

Reznick, J. S. (2009). Working memory in infants and toddlers. In M. L. Courage & N. Cowan (Eds), *The development of memory in infancy and childhood, Second edition* (pp. 343–365). New York, NY: Psychology Press.

Reznick, J. S. (2013). Research design and methods: Toward a cumulative developmental science. In P. D. Zelazo (Ed.), *The Oxford handbook of developmental psychology, Volume 1: Body and mind* (pp. 35–61). Oxford: Oxford University Press.

Reznick, J. S., & Goldfield, B. A. (1992). Rapid change in lexical development in comprehension and production. *Developmental Psychology, 28,* 406–413.

Rhodes, M., & Wellman, H. (2013). Constructing a new theory from old ideas and new evidence. *Cognitive Science, 37,* 592–604.

Ribak, R. (2009). Remote control, umbilical cord and beyond: The mobile phone as a transitional object. *British Journal of Developmental Psychology, 27,* 183–196.

Rice, M. L., Huston, A. C., Truglio, R., & Wright, J. C. (1990). Words from "Sesame Street": Learning vocabulary while viewing. *Developmental Psychology, 26,* 421–428.

Rice, T. R., & Hoffman, L. (2014). Defense mechanisms and implicit emotion regulation: A comparison of a psychodynamic construct with one from contemporary neuroscience. *Journal of the American Psychoanalytic Association, 62,* 693–708.

Richards, J. E. (2001). Cortical indices of saccade planning in infants. *Infancy, 2,* 123–133.

Richardson, K. (1998). *Models of cognitive development.* Hove, UK: Psychology Press.

Richland, L. E., Chan, T. K., Morrison, R. G., & Au, T. K. F. (2010). Young children's analogical reasoning across cultures: Similarities and differences. *Journal of Experimental Child Psychology, 105,* 146–153.

Richland, L. E., Morrison, R. G., & Holyoak, K. J. (2006). Children's development of analogical reasoning: Insights from scene analogy problems. *Journal of Experimental Child Psychology, 94,* 249–271.

Ricketts, J. (2011). Research review: Reading comprehension in developmental disorders of language and communication. *Journal of Child Psychology and Psychiatry, 52,* 1111–1123.

Rideout, V. (2012). *Social media, social life: How teens view their digital lives.* San Francisco, CA: Common Sense Media.

Rideout, V. (2013). *Zero to eight: Children's media use in America.* San Francisco, CA: Common Sense Media.

Rideout, V. (2014). *Learning at home: Families' educational media use in America.* New York, NY: Joan Ganz Cooney Center.

Rideout V. (2015). *The Common Sense Census: Media use by tweens and teens.* San Francisco, CA: Common Sense Media.

Rideout, V. (2016). Measuring time spent with media: The Common Sense census of media use by US 8- to 18-year-olds. *Journal of Children and Media, 10,* 138–144.

Rideout, V., Foehr, U. G., & Roberts, D. F. (2010). *Generation M: Media in the lives of 8- to 18-year-olds.* Menlo Park, CA: Henry J. Kaiser Family Foundation.

Riese, M. L. (1990). Neonatal temperament in monozygotic and dizygotic twin pairs. *Child Development, 61,* 1230–1237.

Riesen, A. H. (1947). The development of visual perception in man and chimpanzee. *Science, 106,* 107–108.

Riley, E. P., Infante, M. A., & Warren, K. R. (2011). Fetal alcohol spectrum disorders: An overview. *Neuropsychology Review, 21,* 73.

Rinaldi, L., & Karmiloff-Smith, A. (2017). Intelligence as a developing function: A neuroconstructivist approach. *Journal of Intelligence, 5,* 18.

Rinaldi, P., Caselli, M. C., Di Renzo, A., Gulli, T., & Volterra, V. (2014). Sign vocabulary in deaf toddlers exposed to sign language since birth. *Journal of Deaf Studies and Deaf Education, 19,* 303–318.

Ristic, J., & Enns, J. T. (2015). The changing face of attentional development. *Current Directions in Psychological Science, 24,* 24–31.

Ristori, J., & Steensma, T. D. (2016). Gender dysphoria in childhood. *International Review of Psychiatry, 28,* 13–20,

Rivas-Drake, D., Syed, M., Umaña-Taylor, A., Markstrom, C., French, S., Schwartz, S. J., & Lee, R. (2014). Feeling good, happy, and proud: A meta-analysis of positive ethnic–racial affect and adjustment. *Child Development, 85,* 77–102.

Rizzolatti, G. (2005). The mirror neuron system and its function in humans. *Anatomy and Embryology, 210,* 419–421.

Rizzolatti, G., & Sinigaglia, C. (2010). The functional role of the parieto-frontal mirror circuit: Interpretations and misinterpretations. *Nature Review Neuroscience, 11,* 264–274.

Robarchek, C. A., & Robarchek, C. J. (1992). Cultures of war and peace: A comparative study of Waorani and Semai. In J. Silverberg & J. P. Gray (Eds), *Aggression and peacefulness in humans and other primates* (pp. 189–213). Oxford: Oxford University Press.

Roberts, B. W., & DelVecchio, J. F. (2000). The rank-order consistency of personality traits from childhood to old age: A quantitative review of longitudinal studies. *Psychological Bulletin, 126,* 3–25.

Roberts, B. W., Walton, K. E., & Viechtbauer, W. (2006). Patterns of mean-level change in personality traits across the life course: A meta-analysis of longitudinal studies. *Psychological Bulletin, 132,* 1–25.

Roberts C. (2015). Depression. In T. Gullotta, R. Plant & M. Evans (Eds), *Handbook of adolescent behavioral problems, Second edition* (pp. 173–191). Boston, MA: Springer.

Roberts, G., Quach, J., Spencer-Smith, M., Anderson, P. J., Gathercole, S., Gold, L., Sia, K.-L., Mensah, F., Rickards, F., Ainley, J., & Wake, M. (2016). Academic outcomes 2 years after working memory training for children with low working memory: A randomized clinical trial. *JAMA Pediatrics, 170,* e154568–e154568.

Roberts, K. P. (2002). Children's ability to distinguish between memories from multiple sources: Implications for the quality and accuracy of eyewitness statements. *Developmental Review, 22,* 403–435

Roberts, K. P., & Powell, M. B. (2001). Describing individual incidents of sexual abuse: A review of research on the effects of multiple sources of information on children's reports. *Child Abuse and Neglect, 25,* 1643–1659.

Roberts, R. M., Ejova, A., Giallo, R., Strohm, K., Lillie, M., & Fuss, B. (2015). A controlled trial of the SibworkS group program for siblings of children with special needs. *Research in Developmental Disabilities, 43,* 21–31.

Roberts, W. L., & Strayer, J. (1987). Parents' responses to the emotional distress of their children: Relations with children's competence. *Developmental Psychology, 23,* 415–422.

Robertson, J., & Bowlby, J. (1952). Responses of young children to separation from their mothers. *Courrier Centre Internationale Enfance, 2,* 131–142.

Robins, L. N. (1978). Sturdy childhood predictors of adult antisocial behavior: Replications from longitudinal studies. *Psychological Medicine, 8,* 611–622.

Robins, R. W., John, O. P., Stouthamer-Loeber, M., Caspi, A., & Moffitt, T. E. (1996). Resilient, overcontrolled, and undercontrolled boys: Three replicable personality types. *Journal of Personality and Social Psychology, 70,* 157–171.

Robinson, C. W., & Sloutsky, V. M. (2004). Auditory dominance and its change in the course of development. *Child Development, 75,* 1387–1401.

Robinson, M., Mattes, E., Oddy, W. H., Pennell, C. E., van Eekelen, A., McLean, N. J., Jacoby, P., Li, J., De Klerk, N. H., Zubrick, S. R., et al. (2011). Prenatal stress and risk of behavioral morbidity from age 2 to 14 years: T he influence of the number, type, and timing of stressful life events. *Development and Psychopathology, 23,* 507–520.

Robson, C. (2002). *Real world research: A resource for social scientists and practitioner-researchers, Second edition.* Oxford: Blackwell.

Robson, C., & McCartan, K. (2016). *Real world research, Fourth edition.* Chichester, UK: Wiley.

Rochat, P. (1993). Hand mouth coordination in the newborn: Morphology, determinants, and early development of a basic act. In G. J. P. Savelsbergh (Ed.), *The development of coordination in infancy* (pp. 265–288). Amsterdam, NL: North Holland/Elsevier.

Rochat, P. (2013). Self-conceptualizing in development. In P. D. Zelazo (Ed.), *Oxford handbook of developmental psychology, Volume 2: Self and other* (pp. 378–397). New York, NY: Oxford University Press.

Rodgers, J. L., Rowe, D. C., & Li, C. (1994). Beyond nature versus nurture: DF analysis of nonshared influences on problem behaviors. *Developmental Psychology, 30,* 374–384.

Rodkin, P. C., Farmer, T. W., Pearl, R., & Acker, R. V. (2006). They're cool: Social status and peer group supports for aggressive boys and girls. *Social Development, 15,* 175–204.

Rodkin, P. C., Pearl, R., Farmer, T. W., & van Acker, R. (2003). Enemies in the gendered societies of middle childhood: Prevalence, stability, association with social status and aggression. *New Directions for Child and Adolescent Development, 102,* 73–88.

Rodríguez., M. M. D., Dononvick, M. R., & Crowley, S. L. (2009). Parenting styles in a cultural context: Observations of "protective parenting" in first-generation latinos. *Family Process, 48*, 195–210.

Roe, J. (2008). Social inclusion: Meeting the socio-emotional needs of children with vision needs. *British Journal of Visual Impairment, 26*, 147–158.

Roessner, V., Ehrlich, S., & Vetter, N. C. (2016). Child and adolescent psychiatry in ICD-11: An opportunity to overcome mistakes made in DSM-5? *European Child and Adolescent Psychiatry, 9*, 935–938.

Rogers, M., Boggia, J., Ogg, J., & Volpe, R. (2015). The ecology of ADHD in the schools. *Current Developmental Disorders Reports, 2*, 23–29.

Rogoff, B. (1998). Cognition as a collaborative process. In W. Damon, D. Kuhn & R. S. Siegler (Eds), *Handbook of child psychology, Fifth edition, Volume 2: Cognition, perception, and language* (pp. 679–744). New York, NY: John Wiley.

Rogoff, B. (2003). *The cultural nature of human development.* London: Oxford University Press.

Rogoff, B. (2014). Learning by observing and pitching in to family and community endeavors: An orientation. *Human Development, 57*, 69–81.

Rogosch, F. A., & Cicchetti, D. (2004). Child maltreatment and emergent personality organization: Perspectives from the five-factor model. *Journal of Abnormal Child Psychology, 32*, 123–145.

Rohde, P., Stice, E., & Marti, C. N. (2015). Development and predictive effects of eating disorder risk factors during adolescence: Implications for prevention efforts. *International Journal of Eating Disorders, 48*, 187–198.

Roid, G. H. (2003). *Stanford-Binet Intelligence Scale manual, Fifth edition.* Itasca, IL: Riverside

Roid, G. H., Miller, L. J., Pomplun, M., & Koch, C. (2013). *Leiter International Performance Scale, Third edition.* Los Angeles, CA: Western Psychological Services.

Roisman, G. I., Newman, D. A., Fraley, R. C., Haltigan, J. D., Groh, A. M., & Haydon, K. C. (2012). Distinguishing differential susceptibility from diathesis–stress: Recommendations for evaluating interaction effects. *Development and Psychopathology, 24*, 389–409.

Roitblat, H. L., Herman, L. M., & Nachtigall, P. E. (Eds) (1993). *Language and communication: Comparative perspectives.* Hillsdale, NJ: Erlbaum.

Rommetveit, R. (1974). *On message structure.* London: Wiley.

Ronca, A. E., & Alberts, J. R. (1995). Maternal contributions to fetal experience and the transition from prenatal to postnatal life. In J.-P. Lecanuet, W. P. Fifer, N. A. Krasnegor & W. P. Smotherman (Eds), *Fetal development* (pp. 331–350). Hove, UK: Lawrence Erlbaum.

Ronca, A. E., & Alberts, J. R. (2016). Fetal and birth experiences: Proximate effects, developmental consequences, epigenetic legacies. In N. Reissland & B. S. Kisilevsky (Eds), *Fetal development* (pp. 15–42). Cham, Switzerland: Springer.

Roopnarine, J. L., & Davidson, K. L. (2015). Parent-child play across cultures: Advancing play research. *American Journal of Play, 7*, 228–252.

Ropar, D., & Mitchell, P. (2001). Susceptibility to illusions and performance on visuospatial tasks in individuals with autism. *Journal of Child Psychology and Psychiatry, 42*, 539–549.

Rosander, K., & von Hofsten, C. (2004). Infants' emerging ability to represent occluded object motion. *Cognition, 91*, 1–22.

Rosch, E. H. (1973). On the internal structure of perceptual and semantic categories. In T. E. Moore (Ed.), *Cognitive development and the acquisition of language* (pp. 111–144). New York, NY: Academic Press.

Rosch, E. H. (1999). Reclaiming concepts. *Journal of Consciousness Studies, 6*, 61–77.

Rosch, E. H., Mervis, C. B., Gray, W., Johnson, D., & Boyes-Braem, P. (1976). Basic objects in natural categories. *Cognitive Psychology, 3*, 382–439.

Rose, S. A., Feldman, J. F., & Jankowski, J. J. (2004). Infant visual recognition memory. *Developmental Review, 24*, 74–100.

Rose, S. A., & Ruff, H. A. (1987). Cross modal abilities in human infants. In J. D. Osofsky (Ed.), *Handbook of infant development, Second edition* (pp. 318–362). New York, NY: John Wiley.

Rose, S. P. R. (1997). Rise of neurogenetic determinism. *Acta Pædiatrica, Supplement 86*, 38–40.

Rosen, L. H., DeOrnellas, K., & Scott, S. R. (Eds) (2017). *Bullying in school: Perspectives from school staff, students, and parents.* New York, NY: Palgrave Macmillan.

Rosenbaum, P., Paneth, N., Leviton, A., Goldstein, M., Bax, M., Damiano, D., Dan, B., & Jacobsson, B. (2007). A report: The definition and classification of cerebral palsy April 2006. *Developmental Medicine and Child Neurology, 49* (Supplement 109), 8–14.

Rosenstein, D., & Oster, H. (1988). Differential facial responses to four basic tastes in newborns. *Child Development, 59*, 1555–1568.

Rosenthal, R. (1994). Interpersonal expectancy effects: A 30-year perspective. *Current Directions in Psychological Science, 3*, 176–179.

Rosenthal, R., & Jacobsen, L. (1968). *Pygmalion in the classroom: Teacher expectation and pupils' intellectual development.* New York, NY: Holt, Rinehart and Winston.

Rossetti, Z., & Keenan, J. (2018). The nature of friendship between students with and without severe disabilities. *Remedial and Special Education, 39*, 195–210.

Rossman, B. R. (1992). School age children's perceptions of coping with distress: Strategies for emotion regulation and the moderation of adjustment. *Journal of Child Psychology and Psychiatry, 33*, 1373–1397.

Rotenberg, K. J. (1995). Moral development and children's differential disclosure to adults versus peers. In K. J. Rotenberg (Ed.), *Disclosure processes in children and adolescents* (pp. 135–147). Cambridge: Cambridge University Press.

Roth, B., Becker, N., Romeyke, S., Schäfer, S., Domnick, F., & Spinath, F. M. (2015). Intelligence and school grades: A meta-analysis. *Intelligence, 53*, 118–137.

Roth, T. L., & Sweatt, J. D. (2011). Annual research review: Epigenetic mechanisms and environmental shaping of the brain during sensitive periods of development. *Journal of Child Psychology and Psychiatry*, 52, 398–408.

Rothbart, M. K. (2007). Temperament, development, and personality. *Current Directions in Psychological Science*, 16, 207–212.

Rothbart, M. K., & Bates, J. E. (2006). Temperament. In W. Damon, R. M. Lerner & N. Eisenberg (Eds), *Handbook of child psychology, Sixth edition, Volume 3: Social, emotional, and personality development* (pp. 99–166). New York, NY: John Wiley.

Rothenberger, A., & Banaschewski, T. (2004). Informing the ADHD debate. *Scientific American Mind*, 14 (5), 50–55.

Rothenberger, A., & Banaschewski, T. (2007). Informing the ADHD debate. *Scientific American*, 17, 36–41.

Rottman, J., & Young, L. (2015). Mechanisms of moral development. In J. Decety & T. Wheatley (Eds), *The moral brain: A multidisciplinary perspective* (pp. 123–142). Cambridge, MA: MIT Press.

Rousseau, J. (1763). *Emile, or, concerning education*. London: Heath and Company.

Rovee-Collier, C., & Barr, R. (2001). Infant learning and memory. In J. G. Bremner & A. Fogel (Eds), *Blackwell handbook of infant development* (pp. 139–168). Oxford: Blackwell.

Rovee-Collier, C., & Cuevas, K. (2008). Infant memory. In J. H. Byrne & H. Roediger (Eds), *Learning and memory: A comprehensive reference, Volume 2: Cognitive psychology* (pp. 687–713). Oxford: Elsevier.

Rovee-Collier, C., & Cuevas, K. (2009a). The development of infant memory. In M. L. Courage & N. Cowan (Eds), *The development of memory in infancy and childhood, Second edition* (pp. 11–41). New York, NY: Psychology Press.

Rovee-Collier, C., & Cuevas, K. (2009b). Multiple memory systems are unnecessary to account for infant memory development: An ecological model. *Developmental Psychology*, 45, 160–174.

Rovee-Collier, C., & Gerhardstein, P. (1997). The development of infant memory. In N. Cowan (Ed.), *The development of memory in childhood* (pp. 5–39). London: Psychology Press.

Rovee-Collier, C., Greco-Vigorito, C., & Hayne, H. (1993). The time window hypothesis: Implications for categorization and memory modification. *Infant Behavior and Development*, 16, 149–176.

Rovee-Collier, C., Hartshorn, K., & DiRubbo, M. (1999) Long-term maintenance of infant memory. *Developmental Psychobiology*, 35, 91–102.

Rowe, M. L. (2012). A longitudinal investigation of the role of quantity and quality of child-directed speech in vocabulary development. *Child Development*, 83, 1762–1774.

Rozin, P. (1989). Disorders of food selection: The compromise of pleasure. In L. H. Schneider, S. J. Cooper & K. A. Halmi (Eds), *The psychobiology of human eating disorders: Preclinical and clinical perspectives* (pp. 376–386). New York, NY: New York Academy of Sciences.

Ruban, L. M., & Reis, S. M. (2005). Identification and assessment of gifted students with learning disabilities. *Theory into Practice*, 44, 115–124.

Rubie-Davies, C. M. (2006). Teacher expectations and student self-perceptions: Exploring relationships. *Psychology in the Schools*, 43, 537–552.

Rubin, D. C. (2000). The distribution of early childhood memories. *Memory*, 8, 265–269.

Rubin, K. H., Bukowski, W., & Bowker, J. C. (2015). Children in peer groups. In R. M. Lerner, M. H. Bornstein & T. Leventhal (Eds), *Handbook of child psychology and developmental science, Volume 4: Ecological settings and processes* (pp. 175–222). New York, NY: Wiley.

Rubin, K. H., Bowker, J. C., McDonald, K. L., & Menzer, M. (2013). Peer relationships in childhood. In P. D. Zelazo (Ed.), *The Oxford handbook of developmental psychology, Volume 2* (pp. 242–275). New York, NY: Oxford University Press.

Rubin, K. H., Bukowski, W., & Parker, J. G. (2006). Peer interactions, relationships and groups. In W. Damon & N. Eisenberg (Eds), *Handbook of child psychology, Sixth edition, Volume 3: Social, emotional, and personality development* (pp. 619–700). New York, NY: Wiley.

Rubin, K. H., Burgess, K. B., & Hastings, P. D. (2002). Stability and social-behavioral consequences of toddlers' inhibited temperament and parenting. *Child Development*, 73, 483–495.

Rubin, K. H., Cheah, C. S. L., & Menzer, M. (2009). Peer relationships. In M. Bornstein (Ed.), *Handbook of cross-cultural developmental science* (pp. 223–238). New York, NY: Psychology Press.

Rubin, K. H., & Coplan, R. J. (Eds) (2010). *The development of shyness and social withdrawal*. New York, NY: Guilford Press.

Rubin, K. H., Lynch, D., Coplan, R. J., Rose-Kasnor, L., & Booth, C. L. (1994). "Birds of a feather...": Behavioral concordances and preferential personal attraction in children. *Child Development*, 65, 1778–1785.

Rubin, K. H., Nelson, L. J., Hastings, P. D., & Asendorpf, J. (1999). The transaction between parents' perceptions of their children's shyness and their parenting styles. *International Journal of Behavioral Development*, 23, 937–958.

Rubin, K. H., Root A. K., & Bowker, J. (2010). Parents, peers, and social withdrawal in childhood: A relationship perspective. *New Directions for Child and Adolescent Development*, 127, 79–94.

Rubin, K. H., Stewart, S. L., & Coplan, R. J. (1995). Social withdrawal in childhood. Conceptual and empirical perspectives. *Advances in Clinical Child Psychology*, 17, 157–196.

Ruble, D. N. (1987). The acquisition of self-knowledge: A self-socialization perspective. In N. Eisenberg (Ed.), *Contemporary issues in developmental psychology* (pp. 243–270). New York, NY: Wiley.

Ruble, D. N., Martin, C. L., & Berenbaum, B. A. (2006). Gender development. In W. Damon, R. M. Lerner & N. Eisenberg (Eds), *Handbook of child psychology, Sixth edition, Volume 3: Social, emotional, and personality development* (pp. 858–932). New York, NY: Wiley.

Ruble, D. N., Taylor, L. J., Cyphers, L., Greulich, F. K., Lurye, L. E., & Shrout, P. E. (2007). The role of gender constancy in early gender development. *Child Development*, *78*, 1121–1136.

Rudi, J., Dworkin, J., Walker, S., & Doty, J. (2015). Parents' use of information and communications technologies for family communication: Differences by age of children. *Information, Communication and Society*, *18*, 78–93.

Rueda, M. R., & Cómbita, L. M. (2013). The nature and nurture of executive attention development. In B. R. Kar (Ed.), *Cognition and brain development: Converging evidence from various methodologies* (pp. 33–59). Washington, DC: American Psychological Association.

Ruff, H. A. (1984). Infants' manipulative exploration of objects: Effects of age and object characteristics. *Developmental Psychology*, *20*, 9–20.

Ruffman, T., Perner, J., Naito, M., Parkin, L., & Clements, W. A. (1998). Older (but not younger) siblings facilitate false belief understanding. *Developmental Psychology*, *34*, 161–174.

Rushton, J. P., & Jensen, A. R. (2005). Thirty years of research on race differences in cognitive ability. *Psychology, Public Policy, and Law*, *11*, 235–294.

Rushton, J. P., & Jensen, A. R. (2010). Race and IQ: A theory-based review of the research in Richard Nisbett's intelligence and how to get it. *The Open Psychology Journal*, *3*, 9–35.

Russell, J. (1999). Cognitive development as an executive process – in part: A homeopathic dose of Piaget. *Developmental Science*, *2*, 247–270.

Rutgers, A. H., Bakermans-Kranenburg, M. J., van IJzendoorn, M. H., & Berckelaer-Onnes, I. A. (2004). Autism and attachment: A meta-analytic review. *Journal of Child Psychology and Psychiatry*, *45*, 1123–1134.

Rutgers, A. H., van IJzendoorn, M. H., Bakermans-Kranenburg, M. J., Swinkels, S. H. N., van Daalen, E., Dietz, C., Naber, F. B. A., Buitelaar, J. K., & van Engeland, H. (2007). Autism, attachment and parenting: A comparison of children with autism spectrum disorder, mental retardation, language disorder, and non-clinical children. *Journal of Abnormal Child Psychology*, *35*, 859–870.

Rutter, M. (1991a). A fresh look at "maternal deprivation". In P. Bateson (Ed.), *The development and integration of behaviour* (pp. 331–374). Cambridge: Cambridge University Press.

Rutter, M. (1991b). Childhood experiences and adult social functioning. In G. R. Bock & J. Whelan (Eds), *The childhood environment and adult disease* (pp. 189–208). Chichester, UK: John Wiley.

Rutter, M. (2004). Pathways of genetic influences on psychopathology. *European Review*, *12*, 19–33.

Rutter, M. (2005). Environmentally mediated risks for psychopathology: Research strategies and findings. *Journal of American Academy of Child and Adolescent Psychiatry*, *44*, 3–18.

Rutter, M. (2006). *Genes and behavior: Nature–nurture interplay explained*. Oxford: Blackwell.

Rutter, M. (2008). Institutional effects on children: Design issues and substantive findings. *Monographs of the Society for Research in Child Development*, *73*, 271–278.

Rutter, M. (2013). Annual research review: Resilience–clinical implications. *Journal of Child Psychology and Psychiatry*, *54*, 474–487.

Rutter, M. (2014). Nature-nurture integration. In M. Lewis & K. Rudolph (Eds), *Handbook of developmental psychopathology, Third edition* (pp. 45–65). New York, NY: Springer.

Rutter, M., Colvert, E., Kreppner, J., Beckett, C., Castle, J., Groothues, C., Hawkins, A., O'Connor, T. G., Stevens, S. E., & Sonuga-Barke, E. J. (2007). Early adolescent outcomes for institutionally-deprived and non-deprived adoptees. I: Disinhibited attachment. *Journal of Child Psychology and Psychiatry*, *48*, 17–30.

Rutter, M., Giller, H., & Hagell, A. (1998) *Antisocial behavior by young people*. Cambridge: Cambridge University Press.

Rutter, M., Graham, P., Chadwick, O., & Yule, W. (1976). Adolescent turmoil: Fact or fiction? *Journal of Child Psychology and Psychiatry*, *17*, 35–56.

Rutter, M., Kim-Cohen, J., & Maughan, B. (2006). Continuities and discontinuities in psychopathology between childhood and adult life. *Journal of Child Psychology and Psychiatry*, *47*, 276–295.

Rutter, M., Kreppner, J., & Sonuga-Barke, E. (2009). Emanuel Miller Lecture: Attachment insecurity, disinhibited attachment, and attachment disorders: Where do research findings leave the concepts? *Journal of Child Psychology and Psychiatry*, *50*, 529–543.

Rutter, M., & Pine, D. S. (2015). Diagnosis, diagnostic formulation and classification. In A. Thapar, D. S. Fine, J. F. Leckman, S. Scott, M. J. Snowling & E. Taylor (Eds), *Rutter's child and adolescent psychiatry* (pp. 17–30). Chicester, UK: Wiley.

Rutter, M., Sonuga-Barke, E. J., Beckett, C., Castle, J., Kreppner, J., Kumsta, R., Schlotz, W., Stevens, S., Bell, C. A., & Gunnar, M. R. (2010). Deprivation-specific psychological patterns: Effects of institutional deprivation. *Monographs of the Society for Research in Child Development*, *75*, 1.

Rutter, M., & Sroufe, L. A. (2000). Developmental psychopathology: Concepts and challenges. *Developmental Psychopathology*, *12*, 265–296.

Rydland, A. B. (2007). Barneoppdragelse i fjernsynet – en analyse av oppdragelsesstrategier og syn på barns utvikling formidlet i "Nannyhjelpen". Professional Thesis, University of Oslo, Norway.

Saarni, C. (1984). An observational study of children's attempts to monitor their expressive behaviour. *Child Development*, *55*, 1504–1513.

Saarni, C. (1988). Children's understanding of the interpersonal consequences of dissemblance of nonverbal emotional-expressive behavior. *Journal of Nonverbal Behavior*, *12*, 275–294.

Saarni, C. (1992). Children's emotional expressive behaviors as regulators of others' happy and sad emotional states. *New Directions for Child Development*, *55*, 91–106.

Saarni, C., Campos, J. J., Camras, L., & Witherington, D. (2006). Emotional development: Action, communication, and understanding. In W. Damon, R. M. Lerner &

N. Eisenberg (Eds), *Handbook of child psychology, Sixth edition, Volume 3: Social, emotional, and personality development* (pp. 226–299). New York, NY: Wiley.

Sachs, J., & Truswell, L. (1978). Comprehension of two word instructions by children in the one word stage. *Journal of Child Language, 5*, 17–24.

Sachs-Ericsson, N. J., Stanley, I. H., Sheffler, J. L., Selby, E., & Joiner, T. E. (2017). Non-violent and violent forms of childhood abuse in the prediction of suicide attempts: Direct or indirect effects through psychiatric disorders? *Journal of Affective Disorders, 215*, 15–22.

Sadowski, H. S., Ugarte, B., Kolvin, I., Kaplan, C., & Barnes, J. (1999). Early life family disadvantages and major depression in adulthood. *British Journal of Psychiatry, 174*, 112–120.

Sagi-Schwartz, A., & Aviezer, O. (2005). Correlates of attachment to multiple caregiver in kibbutz children from birth to emerging adulthood: The Haifa longitudinal study. In K. E. Grossmann, K. Grossmann & E. Watters (Eds), *Attachment from infancy to adulthood: The major longitudinal studies* (pp. 165–197). New York, NY: Guilford Press.

Sai, F. Z. (2005). The role of the mother's voice in developing mother's face preference: Evidence for intermodal perception at birth. *Infant and Child Development, 14*, 29–50.

Saine, N. L., Lerkkanen, M. K., Ahonen, T., Tolvanen, A., & Lyytinen, H. (2011). Computer-assisted remedial reading intervention for school beginners at risk for reading disability. *Child Development, 82*, 1013–1028.

Salekin, R. T. (2016). Psychopathy in childhood: Toward better informing the DSM–5 and ICD-11 conduct disorder specifiers. *Personality Disorders: Theory, Research, and Treatment, 7*, 180–181.

Salminen, A. L., & Karhula, M. E. (2014). Young persons with visual impairment: Challenges of participation. *Scandinavian Journal of Occupational Therapy, 21*, 267–276.

Salminen, J., Koponen, T., Räsänen, P., & Aro, M. (2015). Preventive support for kindergarteners most at-risk for mathematics difficulties: Computer-assisted intervention. *Mathematical Thinking and Learning, 17*, 273–295.

Salmon, M. H., & Zeitz, C. M. (1995). Analysing conversational reasoning. *Informal Logic, 17*, 1–23.

Salvadori, E., Blazsekova, T., Volein, A., Karap, Z., Tatone, D., Mascaro, O., & Csibra, G. (2015). Probing the strength of infants' preference for helpers over hinders: Two replication attempts of Hamlin and Wynn (2011). *PloS One, 10*, e0140570.

Sameroff, A. J. (Ed.) (2009). *The transactional model of development: How children and contexts shape each other.* Washington, DC: American Psychological Association.

Sameroff, A. J. (2010). A unified theory of development: A dialectic integration of nature and nurture. *Child Development, 81*, 6–22.

Sameroff, A. J. (2014). A dialectic integration of development for the study of psychopathology. In M. Lewis &

K. Rudolph (Eds), *Handbook of developmental psychopathology* (pp. 25–44). Boston, MA: Springer.

Sameroff, A. J., & Fiese, B. H. (2000). Models of development and developmental risk. In C. H. Zeanah (Ed.), *Handbook of infant mental health, Second edition* (pp. 3–19). London: Guildford Press.

Sameroff, A. J., Seifer, R., Baldwin, A., & Baldwin, C. (1993). Stability of intelligence from preschool to adolescence: The influence of social and family risk factors. *Child Development, 64*, 80–97.

Sanders, M. R. (1996). New directions in behavioral family intervention with children. In T. H. Ollendick & R. J. Prinz (Eds), *Advances in clinical child psychology* (pp. 283–330). Boston, MA: Springer.

Sanders, M. R. (1999). Triple P-Positive Parenting Program: Towards an empirically validated multilevel parenting and family support strategy for the prevention of behavior and emotional problems in children. *Clinical Child and Family Psychology Review, 2*, 71–90.

Sanders, M. R., Markie-Dadds, C., Tully, L. A., & Bor, W. (2000). The Triple P-Positive Parenting Program: A comparison of enhanced, standard, and self-directed behavioral family intervention for parents of children with early onset conduct problems. *Journal of Consulting and Clinical Psychology, 68*, 624–640.

Saraswathi, T. S., & Dutta, R. (2010). India. In M. H. Bornstein (Ed.), *Handbook of cultural developmental science* (pp. 465–483). London: Psychology Press.

Sarria, E., Gomez, J. C., & Tamarit, J. (1996). Joint attention and alternative language intervention in autism: Implications of theory for practice. In S. von Tetzchner & M. H. Jensen (Eds), *Augmentative and alternative communication: European perspectives* (pp. 49–64). London: Whurr/Wiley.

Sasser, T. R., Kalvin, C. B., & Bierman, K. L. (2016). Developmental trajectories of clinically significant attention-deficit/hyperactivity disorder (ADHD) symptoms from grade 3 through 12 in a high-risk sample: Predictors and outcomes. *Journal of Abnormal Psychology, 125*, 207–219.

Sattler, J. M. (2002). *Assessment of children: Behavioral and clinical applications, Fourth edition.* San Diego, CA: J. M. Sattler Publications.

Saudino, K. J. (2009). The development of temperament from a behavioral genetics perspective. *Advances in Child Development and Behavior, 37*, 201–231.

Saudino, K. J., & Micalizzi, L. (2015). Emerging trends in behavioral genetic studies of child temperament. *Child Development Perspectives, 9* (3), 144–148.

Saunders, G. (1988). *Bilingual children: From birth to teens.* Clevedon, OH: Multilingual Matters.

Saunders, J. F., & Frazier, L. D. (2017). Body dissatisfaction in early adolescence: The coactive roles of cognitive and sociocultural factors. *Journal of Youth and Adolescence, 46*, 1246–1261.

Saveanu, R. V., & Nemeroff, C. B. (2012). Etiology of depression: Genetic and environmental factors. *Psychiatric Clinics, 35*, 51–71.

Saxe, R., & Carey, S. (2006). The perception of causality in infancy. *Acta Psychologica, 123*, 144–165.

Saywitz, K. J., & Nathanson, R. (1993). Children's testimony and their perceptions of stress in and out of the courtroom. *Child Abuse and Neglect*, 17, 613–622.

Scammacca, N. K., Roberts, G., Vaughn, S., & Stuebing, K. K. (2015). A meta-analysis of interventions for struggling readers in Grades 4–12: 1980–2011. *Journal of Learning Disabilities*, 48, 369–390.

Scarr, S. (1992). Developmental theories for the 1990s: Development and individual differences. *Child Development*, 63, 1–19.

Scarr, S. (1996). How people make their own environments: Implications for parents and policy makers. *Psychology, Public Policy, and Law*, 2, 204–228.

Scarr, S., & McCartney, K. (1983). How people make their own environments: A theory of genotype → environment effects. *Child Development*, 54, 424–435.

Scarr, S., & Salapatek, P. (1970). Patterns of fear development during infancy. *Merrill-Palmer Quarterly*, 16, 53–90.

Schaadt, G., Hesse, V., & Friederici, A. D. (2015). Sex hormones in early infancy seem to predict aspects of later language development. *Brain and Language*, 141, 70–76.

Schaafsma, S. M., Pfaff, D. W., Spunt, R. P., & Adolphs, R. (2015). Deconstructing and reconstructing theory of mind. *Trends in Cognitive Sciences*, 19, 65–72.

Schaal, B., Orgeur, P., & Rognon, C. (1995). Odor sensing in the human fetus: Anatomical, functional, and chemoecological bases. In J.-P. Lecanuet, W. P. Fifer, N. A. Krasnegor & W. P. Smotherman (Eds), *Fetal development* (pp. 205–237). Hove, UK: Erlbaum.

Schaan, V. K., & Melzer, A. (2015). Parental mediation of children's television and video game use in Germany: Active and embedded in family processes. *Journal of Children and Media*, 9, 58–76.

Schaffer, H. R. (1989). Language development in context. In S. von Tetzchner, L. S. Siegel & L. Smith (Eds), *The social and cognitive aspects of normal and atypical language development* (pp. 1–22). New York, NY: Springer.

Schaffer, H. R. (1996). *Social development*. Oxford: Blackwell.

Schaffer, H. R., & Emerson, P. E. (1964). The development of social attachment in infancy. *Monographs of the Society for Research in Child Development*, 29, 1–77.

Schank, R. C., & Abelson, R. P. (1977). *Scripts, plans, goals and understanding*. Hillsdale, NJ: Lawrence Erlbaum.

Scheidnes, M., & Tuller, L. (2016). Assessing successive bilinguals in two languages: A longitudinal look at English-speaking children in France. *Journal of Communication Disorders*, 64, 45–61.

Schiavo, G., & Buson, V. (2014). Interactive e-books to support reading skills in dyslexia. Presented at IBOOC 2014 – 2nd Workshop on Interactive eBook for Children at IDC 2014.

Schiff, R., Bauminger, N., & Toledo, I. (2009). Analogical problem solving in children with verbal and nonverbal learning disabilities. *Journal of Learning Disabilities*, 42, 3–13.

Schiff, R., & Joshi, R. M. (Eds) (2016). *Interventions in learning disabilities: A handbook on systematic training programs for individuals with learning disabilities*. Cham, Switzerland: Springer.

Schlesinger, M., & McMurray, B. (2012). The past, present, and future of computational models of cognitive development. *Cognitive Development*, 27, 326–348.

Schley, S., & Snow, C. E. (1992). The conversational skills of school aged children. *Social Development*, 1, 18–35.

Schlinger, H. D. (1995). *A behavior analytic view of child development*. New York, NY: Plenum Press.

Schlosser, R. W., & Wendt, O. (2008). Effects of augmentative and alternative communication intervention on speech production in children with autism: A systematic review. *American Journal of Speech-Language Pathology*, 17, 212–230.

Schmuckler, M. A. (2013). Perceptual-motor relations in obvious and non-obvious domains: A history and review. In P. D. Zelazo (Ed.), *Oxford handbook of developmental psychology* (pp. 237–270). Oxford: Oxford University Press.

Schneider, B. H. (2016). *Childhood friendships and peer relations: Friends and enemies, Second edition*. Abingdon, UK: Routledge.

Schneider, B. H., & Tessier, N. G. (2007). Close friendship as understood by socially withdrawn, anxious early adolescents. *Child Psychiatry and Human Development*, 38, 339–351.

Schneider, W. (2015). *Memory development from early childhood through emerging adulthood*. Cham, Switzerland: Springer.

Schneider, W., & Bjorklund, D. E. (1992). Expertise, aptitude, and strategic remembering. *Child Development*, 63, 461–473.

Schneider, W., Niklas, F., & Schmiedeler, S. (2014). Intellectual development from early childhood to early adulthood: The impact of early IQ differences on stability and change over time. *Learning and Individual Differences*, 32, 156–162.

Schober-Peterson, D., & Johnson, C. J. (1991). Non-dialogue speech during preschool interactions. *Journal of Child Language*, 18, 153–170.

Schoenberg, M. R., & Scott, J. G. (2011). Cognitive decline in childhood or young adulthood. In M. R. Schoenberg & J. G. Scott (Eds), *The little black book of neuropsychology: A syndrome-based approach* (pp. 839–861). New York, NY: Springer.

Schöner, G., & Dineva, E. (2007). Dynamic instabilities as mechanisms for emergence. *Developmental Science*, 10, 69–74.

Schooler, C. (1998). Environmental complexity and the Flynn effect. In U. Neisser (Ed.), *The rising curve* (pp. 67–79). Washington, DC: American Psychological Association.

Schreuder, P., & Alsaker, E. (2014). The Norwegian Mother and Child Cohort Study (MoBa) – Recruitment and logistics. *Norsk Epidemiologi*, 24, 23–27.

Schrott, L. M. (1997). Effect of training and environment on brain morphology and behavior. *Acta Pædiatrica, Supplement*, 422, 45–47.

Schulenberg, J. E., Sameroff, A. J., & Cicchetti, D. (2004). The transition to adulthood as a critical juncture in the course of psychopathology and mental health. *Development and Psychopathology*, 16, 799–806.

Schulte-Körne, G. (2010). The prevention, diagnosis, and treatment of dyslexia. *Deutsches Ärzteblatt International*, 107, 718–727.

Schultz, D. P., & Schultz, S. E. (2016). *Theories of personality*. Boston, MA: Cengage Learning.

Schultz, T. R. (2003). *Computational developmental psychology*. Cambridge, MA: MIT Press.

Schulz, L. E., & Gopnik, A. (2004). Causal learning across domains. *Developmental Psychology*, 40, 162–176.

Schunk, D. H. (2012). *Learning theories – An educational perspective, Sixth edition*. Boston, MA: Pearson.

Schwartz, G. M., Izard, C. E., & Ansul, S. E. (1985). The 5 month old's ability to discriminate facial expressions of emotion. *Infant Behavior and Development*, 8, 65–77.

Schwartz, S. J. (2001). The evolution of Eriksonian and Neo-Eriksonian identity theory and research: A review and integration. *Identity*, 1, 7–58.

Scollon, R. T. (1976). *Conversations with a one year old*. Honolulu: University of Hawaii Press.

Scollon, R. T. (2001). *Mediated discourse: The nexus of practice*. London: Routledge.

Scott, I. A., & Attia, J. (2017). Cautionary tales in the interpretation of observational studies of effects of clinical interventions. *Internal Medicine Journal*, 47, 144–157.

Scott, L. S., Pascalis, O., & Nelson, C. A. (2007). A domain-general theory of the development of perceptual discrimination. *Current Directions in Psychological Science*, 16, 197–201.

Scott, S. (2015). Oppositional and conduct disorders. In A. Thapar, D. S. Fine, J. F. Leckman, S. Scott, M. J. Snowling & E. Taylor (Eds), *Rutter's child and adolescent psychiatry* (pp. 913–930). Chicester, UK: Wiley.

Scott, S., & Beidel, D. C. (2011). Selective mutism: An update and suggestions for future research. *Current Psychiatry Reports*, 13, 251–257.

Seehagen, S., Schneider, S., Miebach, K., Frigge, K., & Zmyj, N. (2017). "Should I or shouldn't I?" Imitation of undesired versus allowed actions from peer and adult models by 18- and 24-month-old toddlers. *Infant Behavior and Development*, 49, 1–8.

Séguin, J. R., & Tremblay, R. E. (2013). Aggression and antisocial behavior: A developmental perspective. In P. D. Zelazo (Ed.), *The Oxford handbook of developmental psychology, Volume 2: Self and other* (pp. 507–526). Oxford: Oxford University Press.

Seibert, A. C., & Kerns, K. A. (2009). Attachment figures in middle childhood. *International Journal of Behavioral Development*, 33, 347–355.

Seifer R. (2002). What do we learn from parent reports of their children's behavior? Commentary on Vaughn et al.'s critique of early temperament assessments. *Infant Behavior and Development*, 25, 117–120.

Seifer, R., Sameroff, A. J., Barrett, L. C., & Krafchuk, E. (1994). Infant temperament measured by multiple observations and mother report. *Child Development*, 65, 1478–1490.

Seiffge-Krenke, I. (2015). Leaving home: Antecedents, consequences, and cultural patterns. In J. J. Arnett (Ed.), *The Oxford handbook of emerging adulthood* (pp. 177–189). New York, NY: Oxford University Press.

Seiffge-Krenke, I., & Haid, M. L. (2012). Identity development in German emerging adults: Not an easy task. *New Directions for Child and Adolescent Development*, 138, 35–59.

Seim, S. (1997). Tenåringen blir pensjonist. *NOVA Rapport* 23.

Selb, M., Kohler, F., Nicol, M. M. R., Riberto, M., Stucki, G., Kennedy, C., & Üstün, B. (2015). ICD-11: A comprehensive picture of health, an update on the ICD–ICF joint use initiative. *Journal of Rehabilitation Medicine*, 47, 2–8.

Selby, J. M., & Bradley, B. S. (2003). Infants in groups: A paradigm for the study of early social experience. *Human Development*, 46, 197–231.

Seligman, M., & Darling, R. B. (2007). *Ordinary families, special children: A systems approach to childhood disability, Third edition*. London: Guilford Press.

Seligman, M. E. P. (1975). *Helplessness: On depression, development, and death*. San Francisco, CA: Freeman.

Selin, H. (2014). *Parenting across cultures*. Dordrecht, The Netherlands: Springer.

Serbin, L. A., Moller, L. C., Gulko, J., Powlishta, K. K., & Colburne, K. A. (1994). The emergence of gender segregation in toddler playgroups. *New Directions for Child and Adolescent Development*, 65, 7–17.

Service, V., Lock, A., & Chandler, P. (1989). Individual differences in early communicative development: A social constructivist perspective. In S. von Tetzchner, L. S. Siegel & L. Smith (Eds), *The social and cognitive aspects of normal and atypical language development* (pp. 23–49). New York, NY: Springer.

Servin, A., Nordenström, A., Larsson, A., & Bohlin, G. (2003). Prenatal androgens and gender-typed behavior: A study of girls with mild and severe forms of congenital adrenal hyperplasia. *Developmental Psychology*, 39, 440–450.

Seymour, K. E., Chronis-Tuscano, A., Halldorsdottir, T., Stupica, B., Owens, K., & Sacks, T. (2012). Emotion regulation mediates the relationship between ADHD and depressive symptoms in youth. *Journal of Abnormal Child Psychology*, 40, 595–606.

Shakoor, S., Jaffee, S. R., Bowes, L., Ouellet-Morin, I., Andreou, P., Happé, F., Moffitt, T. E., & Arseneault, L. (2012). A prospective longitudinal study of children's theory of mind and adolescent involvement in bullying. *Journal of Child Psychology and Psychiatry*, 53, 254–261.

Shapiro, L. A. S., & Margolin, G. (2014). Growing up wired: Social networking sites and adolescent psychosocial development. *Clinical Child and Family Psychology Review*, 17, 1–18.

Shatz, M., & Gelman, R. (1973). The development of communication skills: Modification in the speech of young children as a function of the listener. *Monographs of the Society for Research in Child Development*, 38.

Shatz, M., & O'Reilly, A. W. (1990). Conversational or communicative skill? A reassessment of two year olds' behaviour in miscommunication episodes. *Journal of Child Language*, 17, 131–146.

Shaul, S., & Schwartz, M. (2014). The role of the executive functions in school readiness among preschool-age children. *Reading and Writing*, 27, 749–768.

Shaw, J. A. (2003). Children exposed to war/terrorism. *Clinical Child and Family Psychology Review*, 6, 237–246.

Shaw, P., Stringaris, A., Nigg, J., & Leibenluft, E. (2014). Emotion dysregulation in attention deficit hyperactivity disorder. *American Journal of Psychiatry*, 171, 276–293.

Shayer, M., & Wylam, H. (1978). The distribution of Piagetian stages of thinking in British middle and secondary school children: II. *British Journal of Educational Psychology*, 48, 62–70.

Shaywitz, S. E., Morris, R., & Shaywitz, B. A. (2008). The education of dyslexic children from childhood to young adulthood. *Annual Review of Psychology*, 59, 451–475.

Shaywitz, S. E., & Shaywitz, B. A. (2013). Making a hidden disability visible: What has been learned from the neurobiological studies of dyslexia. In H. L. Swanson, K. R. Harris & S. Graham (Eds), *Handbook of learning disabilities, Second edition* (pp. 643–657). New York, NY: Guilford Press.

Shaywitz, S. E., Shaywitz, B. A., Pugh, K. R., Fulbright, R. K., Constable, R. T., Mencl, W. E., Shankweiler, D. P., Liberman, A. M., Skudlarski, P., Fletcher, J. M., et al. (1998). Functional disruption in the organization of the brain for reading in dyslexia. *Proceedings of the National Academy of Sciences*, 95, 2636–2641.

Shechner, T., Britton, J. C., Pérez-Edgar, K., Bar-Haim, Y., Ernst, M., Fox, N. A., Leibenluft, E., & Pine, D. S. (2012). Attention biases, anxiety, and development: Toward or away from threats or rewards? *Depression and Anxiety*, 29, 282–294.

Shedler, J., & Block, J. (1990). Adolescent drug use and psychological health: A longitudinal inquiry. *American Psychologist*, 45, 612–630.

Sheingold, K., & Tenney, Y. J. (1982). Memory for a salient childhood event. In U. Neisser (Ed.), *Memory observed: Remembering in natural contexts* (pp. 201–212). San Francisco, CA: Freeman.

Sheridan, M. D., Howard, J., & Alderson, D. (2011). *Play in early childhood: From birth to six*. Abingdon, UK: Routledge.

Sherman, L. J., Rice, K., & Cassidy, J. (2015). Infant capacities related to building internal working models of attachment figures: A theoretical and empirical review. *Developmental Review*, 37, 109–141.

Shifrin, D., Brown, A., Hill, D., Jana, L., & Flinn, S. K. (2015). *Growing up digital: Media research symposium*. Itasca, IL: American Academy of Pediatrics.

Shiner, R. L. (2006). Temperament and personality in childhood. In D. K. Mroczek & T. D. Little (Eds), *Handbook of personality development* (pp. 213–230). Mahwah, NJ: Erlbaum.

Shiner, R. L. (2009). The development of personality disorders: Perspectives from normal personality development in childhood and adolescence. *Development and Psychopathology*, 21, 715–734.

Shiner, R. L. (2015). The development of temperament and personality traits in childhood and adolescence. In M. Mikulincer, P. Shaver, M. L. Cooper & R. Larsen (Eds), *APA handbook of personality and social psychology, Volume 3: Personality processes and individual differences* (pp. 85–105). Washington, DC: American Psychological Association.

Shinn, M. W. (1900). *The biography of a baby*. New York, NY: Miffli.

Shmukler, D. (1981). Mother–child interaction and its relationship to the predisposition to imaginative play. *Genetic Psychology Monographs*, 104, 215–235.

Shoda, Y., Mischel, W., & Wright, J. C. (1994). Intraindividual stability in the organization and patterning of behavior: Incorporating psychological situations into the idiographic analysis of personality. *Journal of Personality and Social Psychology*, 67, 674–687.

Shuter-Dyson, R., & Gabriel, C. (1981). *The psychology of musical ability*. London: Methuen.

Shuttleworth-Edwards, A. B., Kemp, R. D., Rust, A. L., Muirhead, J. G., Hartman, N. P., & Radloff, S. E. (2004). Cross-cultural effects on IQ test performance: A review and preliminary normative indications on WAIS-III test performance. *Journal of Clinical and Experimental Neuropsychology*, 26, 903–920.

Shutts, K., Roben, C. K. P., & Spelke, E. S. (2013). Children's use of social categories in thinking about people and social relationships. *Journal of Cognition and Development*, 14, 35–62.

Sibley, M. H., Kuriyan, A. B., Evans, S. W., Waxmonsky, J. G., & Smith, B. H. (2014). Pharmacological and psychosocial treatments for adolescents with ADHD: An updated systematic review of the literature. *Clinical Psychology Review*, 34, 218–232.

Siegal, M. (1991). *Knowing children: Experiments in conversation and cognition*. Hillsdale, NJ: Lawrence Erlbaum.

Siegal, M., & Beattie, K. (1991). Where to look first for children's knowledge of false beliefs. *Cognition*, 38, 1–12.

Siegler, R. S. (1994). Cognitive variability: A key to understanding cognitive development. *Current Directions in Psychological Science*, 3, 1–5.

Siegler, R. S. (2000). The rebirth of children's learning. *Child Development*, 71, 26–35.

Siegler, R. S. (2006). Microgenetic analyses of learning. In W. Damon, R. M. Lerner, D. Kuhn & R. S. Siegler (Eds), *Handbook of child psychology, Sixth edition, Volume 2: Cognition, perception, and language* (pp. 464–510). Hoboken, NJ: Wiley.

Siegler, R. S., & Jenkins, E. (1989). *How children discover new strategies*. Hillsdale, NJ: Lawrence Erlbaum.

Sigelman, C. K. (2012). Rich man, poor man: Developmental differences in attributions and perceptions. *Journal of Experimental Child Psychology, 113,* 415–429.

Sigman, M., & Whaley, S. E. (1998). The role of nutrition in the development of intelligence. In U. Neisser (Ed.), *The rising curve* (pp. 155–182). Washington, DC: American Psychological Association.

Sigurdardottir, S., Eiriksdottir, A., Gunnarsdottir, E., Meintema, M., Arnadottir, U., & Vik, T. (2008). Cognitive profile in young Icelandic children with cerebral palsy. *Developmental Medicine and Child Neurology, 50,* 357–362.

Silk, J. S., Shaw, D. S., Forbes, E. E., Lane, T. L., & Kovacs, M. (2006). Maternal depression and child internalizing: The moderating role of child emotion regulation. *Journal of Clinical Child and Adolescent Psychology, 35,* 116–126.

Silva, M., Straesser, K., & Cain, K. (2014). Early narrative skills in Chilean preschool: Questions scaffold the production of coherent narratives. *Early Childhood Research Quarterly, 29,* 205–213.

Silverman, D. (2004). Early developmental issues reconsidered: Commentary on Pine's ideas on symbiosis. *Journal of the American Psychoanalytic Association, 53,* 239–251.

Simanowitz, V., & Pearce, P. (2003). *Personality development.* Berkshire, UK: Open University Press.

Simcock, G., & DeLoache, J. S. (2006). Get the picture? The effects of iconicity on toddlers' re-enactment from picture books. *Developmental Psychology, 42,* 1352–1357.

Simcock, G., & Hayne, H. (2002). Breaking the barrier? Children fail to translate their preverbal memories into language. *Psychological Science, 13,* 225–231.

Simkin, Z., & Conti-Ramsden, G. (2006). Evidence of reading difficulty in subgroups of children with specific language impairment. *Child Language Teaching and Therapy, 22,* 315–331.

Simmons, D. R., Robertson, A. E., McKay, L. S., Toal, E., McAleer, P., & Pollick, F. E. (2009). Vision in autism spectrum disorders. *Vision Research, 49,* 2705–2739.

Simms, M. D. (2007). Language disorders in children: Classification and clinical syndromes. *Pediatric Clinics of North America, 54,* 437–467.

Simon, H. A. (1962). An information processing theory of intellectual development. *Monographs of the Society for Research in Child Development,* 150–161.

Simonelli, A., De Palo, F., Moretti, M., Baratter, P. M., & Porreca, A. (2014). The strange situation procedure: The role of the attachment patterns in the Italian culture. *American Journal of Applied Psychology, 3,* 47–56.

Simons, G. M. (1964). Comparisons of incipient music responses among very young twins and singletons. *Journal of Research in Music Education, 12,* 212–226.

Simonsen, H. G. (1983). *En norsk femårings språkbruk.* Oslo, NO: Novus.

Simpson, A. E., & Stevenson-Hinde, J. (1985). Temperamental characteristics of three- to four-year-old boys and girls and child family interactions. *Journal of Child Psychology and Psychiatry, 26,* 43–53.

Singer, D. G., Golinkoff, R. M., & Hirsh-Pasek, K. (Eds) (2006). *Play=Learning: How play motivates and enhances children's cognitive and social-emotional growth.* New York, NY: Oxford University Press.

Singer, E. (2013). Play and playfulness, basic features of early childhood education. *European Early Childhood Education Research Journal, 21,* 172–184.

Singer-Freeman, K. E., & Bauer, P. J. (2008). The ABCs of analogical abilities: Evidence for formal analogical reasoning abilities in 24-month-olds. *British Journal of Developmental Psychology, 26,* 317–335.

Sirois, S., Spratling, M., Thomas, M. S., Westermann, G., Mareschal, D., & Johnson, M. H. (2008). Precis of neuroconstructivism: How the brain constructs cognition. *Behavior and Brain Science, 31,* 321–331, Discussion, 331–356.

Skar, A. M. S., von Tetzchner, S., Clucas, C., & Sherr, L. (2015). The long-term effectiveness of the International Child Development Programme (ICDP) implemented as a community-wide parenting programme. *European Journal of Developmental Psychology, 12,* 54–68.

Skär, L., & Tamm, M. (2002). Disability and social network. A comparison between children and adolescents with and without restricted mobility. *Scandinavian Journal of Disability Research, 4,* 118–137.

Skeels, H., & Dye, H. B. (1939). A study of the effects of differential stimulation on mentally retarded children. *Proceedings of the American Association of Mental Deficiency, 44,* 114–136.

Skinner, B. F. (1938). *The behavior of organisms.* New York, NY: Appleton-Century-Crofts.

Skinner, B. F. (1957). *Verbal behavior.* New York, NY: Appleton-Century-Crofts.

Skinner, B. F. (1969). *Contingencies of reinforcement: A theoretical analysis.* Englewood Cliffs, NJ: Prentice-Hall.

Skinner, B. F. (1971). *Beyond freedom and dignity.* New York, NY: Knopf.

Skinner, B. F. (1977). Why I am not a cognitive psychologist. *Behaviorism, 5,* 1–10.

Skinner, B. F. (1981). Selection by consequences. *Science, 213* (4507), 501–504.

Skinner, B. F. (1984). The phylogeny and ontogeny of behavior. *Behavioral and Brain Sciences, 7,* 669–677.

Skinner, B. F. (1989). *Recent issues in the analysis of behavior.* Columbus, OH: Merrill.

Skoczenski, A. M., & Norcia, A. M. (2002). Late maturation of visual hyperacuity. *Psychological Science, 13,* 537–541.

Skogli, E. W., Teicher, M. H., Andersen, P. N., Hovik, K. T., & Øie, M. (2013). ADHD in girls and boys – gender differences in co-existing symptoms and executive function measures. *BMC Psychiatry, 13,* 298.

Skretting, A., Lund, K. E., & Bye, E. K. (2014). *Rusmidler i Norge* (Drugs in Norway). Oslo: Statens institutt for rusmidler.

Slade, A. (1987). A longitudinal study of maternal involvement and symbolic play during the toddler period. *Child Development, 58,* 367–375.

Slater, A. (1995). Individual differences in infancy and later IQ. *Journal of Child Psychology and Psychiatry, 36,* 69–112.

Slater, A. (2001). Visual perception. In G. Bremner & A. Fogel (Eds), *Blackwell handbook of infant development* (pp. 5–34). Oxford: Blackwell.

Slater, A., & Butterworth, G. (1997). Perception of social stimuli: Face perception and imitation. In G. Bremner, A. Slater & G. Butterworth (Eds), *Infant development: Recent advances* (pp. 223–245). Hove, UK: Erlbaum.

Slater, A., Cooper, R., Rose, D., & Morison, V. (1989). Prediction of cognitive performance from infancy to early childhood. *Human Development, 32,* 137–147.

Slater, A., Mattock, A., & Brown, E. (1990). Size constancy at birth: Newborn infants' responses to retinal and real size. *Journal of Experimental Child Psychology, 49,* 314–322.

Slater, A., Morison, V., Town, C., & Rose, D. (1985). Movement perception and identity constancy in the new born baby. *British Journal of Developmental Psychology, 3,* 211–220.

Slater, A., Rose, D., & Morison, V. (1984). New born infants' perception of similarities and differences between two and three dimensional stimuli. *British Journal of Developmental Psychology, 2,* 287–294.

Slobin, D. I. (1973). Cognitive prerequisites for development of grammar. In C. A. Ferguson & D. I. Slobin (Eds), *Studies of child language development* (pp. 175–208). New York, NY: Holt, Rinehart and Winston.

Sloutsky, V. M. (2003). The role of similarity in the development of categorization. *Trends in Cognitive Sciences, 7,* 246–251.

Sloutsky, V. M. (2015). Conceptual development. In R. M. Lerner, L. S. Liben & U. Müller (Eds), *Handbook of child psychology and developmental science, Seventh edition, Volume 2: Cognitive processes* (pp. 469–518). Hoboken, NJ: Wiley.

Smetana, J. G. (1993). Understanding of social rules. In M. Bennett (Ed.), *The child as a psychologist* (pp. 111–141). London: Harvester Wheatsheaf.

Smetana, J. G., Campione-Barr, N., & Metzger, A. (2006). Adolescent development in interpersonal and societal contexts. *Annual Review of Psychology, 57,* 255–284.

Smetana, J. G., Jambon, M., & Ball, C. (2014). The social domain approach to children's social and moral judgments. In M. Killen & J. G. Smetana (Eds), *Handbook of moral development, Second edition* (pp. 23–45). Hove, UK: Psychology Press.

Smetana J. G., Villalobos M., Tasopoulos-Chan M., Gettman, D. C., & Campione-Barr, N. (2009). Early and middle adolescents' disclosure to parents about activities in different domains. *Journal of Adolescence, 32,* 693–713.

Smink, F. R., Van Hoeken, D., & Hoek, H. W. (2012). Epidemiology of eating disorders: Incidence, prevalence and mortality rates. *Current Psychiatry Reports, 14,* 406–414.

Smith, C. L. (2010). Multiple determinants of parenting: Predicting individual differences in maternal parenting behavior with toddlers. *Parenting, 10,* 1–17.

Smith, D. W., & Amato, S. (2012). Synthesis of available accommodations for students with visual impairments on standardized assessments. *Journal of Visual Impairment and Blindness, 106,* 299–304.

Smith, E. D., & Lillard, A. S. (2012). Play on: Retrospective reports of the persistence of pretend play into middle childhood. *Journal of Cognition and Development, 13,* 524–549.

Smith, L., Fagan, J. F., & Ulvund, S. E. (2002). The relation of recognition memory in infancy and parental socioeconomic status to later intellectual competence. *Intelligence, 30,* 247–259.

Smith, L., & von Tetzchner, S. (1986). Communicative, sensorimotor, and language skills of young children with Down syndrome. *American Journal of Mental Deficiency, 91,* 57–66.

Smith, L. B., & Thelen, E. (2003). Development as a dynamic system. *Trends in Cognitive Sciences, 7,* 343–348.

Smith, M. M. (2005). *Literacy and augmentative and alternative communication.* London: Academic Press.

Smith, M. M., & Murray, J. (Eds) (2016). *The silent partner? Language, interaction and aided communication.* Albury, UK: J&R Press.

Smith, P. K., & Simon, T. (1984). Object play, problem-solving and creativity in children. In P. K. Smith (Ed.), *Play in animals and humans* (pp. 199–216). Oxford: Blackwell.

Smith, S. L., & Wilson, B. J. (2002). Children's comprehension of and fear reactions to television news. *Media Psychology, 4,* 1–26.

Smith, T. (Ed.) (2010). *Statement of good practice, Fourth edition.* Copenhagen, DK: Save the Children.

Smitsman, A. W. (2001). Action in infancy: Perspectives, concepts and challenges, development of reaching and grasping. In J. G. Bremner & A. Fogel (Eds), *Blackwell handbook of infant development* (pp. 71–98). Oxford: Blackwell.

Smyke, A. T., Zeanah, C. H., Fox, N. A., Nelson, C. A., & Guthrie, D. (2010). Placement in foster care enhances quality of attachment among young institutionalized children. *Child Development, 81,* 212–223.

Snapp-Childs, W., & Corbetta, D. (2009). Evidence of early strategies in learning to walk. *Infancy, 14,* 101–116.

Snarey, J. R. (1985). Cross-cultural universality of social moral development: A critical review of Kohlbergian research. *Psychological Bulletin, 97,* 202–232.

Snow, C. E. (1977). Mothers' speech research: From input to interaction. In C. E. Snow & C. A. Ferguson (Eds), *Talking to children* (pp. 31–49). Cambridge: Cambridge University Press.

Snow, C. E. (2010). Academic language and the challenge of reading for learning about science. *Science, 328* (5977), 450–452.

Snow, C. E., Pan, B., Imbens-Bailey, A., & Herman, J. (1996). Learning how to say what one means: A longitudinal study of children's speech act use. *Social Development, 5,* 56–84.

Snowling, M. J. (2013). Early identification and interventions for dyslexia: A contemporary view. *Journal of Research in Special Educational Needs, 13,* 7–14.

Snyder, T. D., de Brey, C., & Dillow, S. A. (2016). *Digest of Education Statistics 2015, 51st Edition*. Washington, DC: National Center for Education Statistics.

Soares, I., Belsky, J., Mesquita, A. R., Osório, A., & Sampaio, A. (2013). Why do only some institutionalized children become indiscriminately friendly? Insights from the study of Williams Syndrome. *Child Development Perspectives, 7*, 187–192.

Søbstad, P. I. (1974). Musikalsk utvikling hos barn i førskolealderen (Musical development in preschool age). Thesis, University of Oslo.

Sodian, B. (1994). Early deception and the conceptual continuity claim. In C. Lewis & P. Mitchell (Eds), *Children's early understanding of mind* (pp. 385–401). Hove, UK: Erlbaum.

Sokol, B. W., & Martin, J. (2006). Good fences make good neighbors: A response to Overton and Ennis. *Human Development, 49*, 173–179.

Solomon, J., & George, C. (2016). The measurement of attachment security and related constructs in infancy and early childhood. In J. Cassidy & P. R. Shaver (Eds), *Handbook of attachment, Third edition* (pp. 366–398). New York, NY: Guilford Press.

Sommer, D. (2012). *A childhood psychology: Young children in changing times*. New York, NY: Palgrave Macmillan.

Sonuga-Barke, E. J. S., & Taylor, E. (2015). ADHD and hypergenetic disorder. In A. Thapar, D. S. Fine, J. F. Leckman, S. Scott, M. J. Snowling & E. Taylor (Eds), *Rutter's child and adolescent psychiatry* (pp. 738–756). Chicester, UK: Wiley.

Sorce, J. F., Emde, R. N., Campos, J. J., & Klinnert, M. D. (1985). Maternal emotional signaling: Its effect on the visual cliff behavior of 1-year-olds. *Developmental Psychology, 21*, 195–200.

Soto, G., & Hartmann, E. (2006). Analysis of narratives produced by four children who use augmentative and alternative communication. *Journal of Communication Disorders, 39*, 456–480.

Southgate, V., Senju, A., & Csibra, G. (2007a). Action anticipation through attribution of false belief by 2-year-olds. *Psychological Science, 18*, 587–592.

Southgate, V., & Vernetti, A. (2014). Belief-based action prediction in preverbal infants. *Cognition, 130*, 1–10.

Southgate, V., Van Maanen, C., & Csibra, G. (2007b). Infant pointing: Communication to cooperate or communication to learn? *Child Development, 78*, 735–740.

Søvik, N. (1993). Development of children's writing performance: Some educational implications. In A. F. Kalverboer, B. Hopkins & R. Geuze (Eds), *Motor development in early and later childhood: Longitudinal approaches* (pp. 229–241). Cambridge: Cambridge University Press.

Sowislo, J. F., & Orth, U. (2013). Does low self-esteem predict depression and anxiety? A meta-analysis of longitudinal studies. *Psychological Bulletin, 139*, 213–240.

Spanoudis, G. (2016). Theory of mind and specific language impairment in school-age children. *Journal of Communication Disorders, 61*, 83–96.

Sparrow, S. S., Ciccetti, D. V., & Balla, D. A. (2005). *Vineland Adaptive Behavior Scales, Second edition*. Circle Pines, MN: American Guidance Service.

Spearman, C. (1927). *The abilities of man*. New York, NY: Macmillan.

Spelke, E. S. (1990). Principles of object perception. *Cognitive Science, 14*, 29–56.

Spelke, E. S., & Kinzler, K. D. (2007). Core knowledge. *Developmental Science, 10*, 89–96.

Spelke, E. S., & Newport, E. L. (1998). Nativism, empiricism, and the development of knowledge. In W. Damon & R. M. Lerner (Eds), *Handbook of child psychology, Volume 1: Theoretical models of human development* (pp. 275–340). New York, NY: Wiley.

Spence, I., & Feng, J. (2010). Video games and spatial cognition. *Review of General Psychology, 14*, 92–104.

Spencer, J. P., & Perone, S. (2008). Defending qualitative change: The view from dynamical systems theory. *Child Development, 79*, 1639–1647.

Spencer, P. E., & Harris, M. (2006). Patterns and effects of language input to deaf infants and toddlers from Deaf and hearing mothers. In B. Schick, M. Marschark & P. E. Spencer (Eds), *Advances in sign language development of deaf children* (pp. 71–101). New York, NY: Oxford University Press.

Spencer, P. E., & Marschark, M. (2010). *Evidence-based practice in educating deaf and hard-of-hearing students*. New York, NY: Oxford University Press.

Sperber, D. (2001). In defense of massive modularity. In E. Dupoux (Ed.), *Language, brain and cognitive development: Essays in honor of Jacques Mehler* (pp. 47–57). Cambridge, MA: MIT Press.

Spinath, F. M., Price, T. S., Dale, P. S., & Plomin, R. (2004). The genetic and environmental origins of language disability and ability. *Child Development, 75*, 445–454.

Spinelli, M., Fasolo, M., & Mesman, J. (2017). Does prosody make the difference? A meta-analysis on relations between prosodic aspects of infant-directed speech and infant outcomes. *Developmental Review, 44*, 1–18.

Spinrad, T. L., & Stifter, C. A. (2006). Toddlers' empathy-related responding to distress: Predictions from negative emotionality and maternal behavior in infancy. *Infancy, 10*, 97–121.

Spitz, R. A. (1946). Hospitalism: A follow-up report on an investigation described in Volume 1, 1945. *Psycho-Analytic Study of the Child, 2*, 313–342.

Sroufe, L. A. (1996). *Emotional development*. Cambridge: Cambridge University Press.

Sroufe, L. A. (1997). Psychopathology as an outcome of development. *Development and Psychopathology, 9*, 251–268.

Sroufe, L. A. (2007). The place of development in developmental psychopathology. In A. S. Masten (Ed.), *Multilevel dynamics in developmental psychopathology: Pathways to the future* (pp. 285–299). New York, NY: Lawrence Erlbaum.

Sroufe, L. A., Carlson, E., & Shulman, S. (1993). Individuals in relationships: Development from infancy through adolescence. In D. C. Funder, R. D. Parke, C. Tomlinson-

Keasey & K. Widaman (Eds), *Studying lives through time* (pp. 315–342). Washington, DC: American Psychological Association.

Sroufe, L. A., Coffino, B., & Carlson, E. A. (2010). Conceptualizing the role of early experience: Lessons from the Minnesota longitudinal study. *Developmental Review, 30*, 36–51.

Sroufe, L. A., Egeland, B., & Carlson, E. (1999). One social world: The integrated development of parent–child and peer relationships. In W. A. Collins & B. Laursen (Eds), *Development during the transition to adolescence* (pp. 241–261). Hove, UK: Lawrence Erlbaum.

Sroufe, L. A., Egeland, B., Carlson, E., & Collins, W. A. (2005). *The development of the person: The Minnesota study of risk and adaptation from birth to adulthood.* New York, NY: Guilford Press.

Stadelmann, S., Grunewald, M., Gibbels, C., Jaeger, S., Matuschek, T., Weis, S., Klein, A. M., Hiemisch, A., von Klitzing, K., & Döhnert, M. (2017). Self-esteem of 8–14-year-old children with psychiatric disorders: Disorder- and gender-specific effects. *Child Psychiatry and Human Development, 48*, 40–52.

Sroufe, L. A., & Waters, E. (1976). The ontogenesis of smiling and laughter: A perspective on the organization of development in infancy. *Psychological Review, 83*, 173–189.

Stadskleiv, K., Jahnsen, R., Andersen, G. L., & von Tetzchner, S. (2017). Neuropsychological profiles of children with cerebral palsy. *Developmental Neurorehabilitation, 28*, 108–120.

Stadskleiv, K., von Tetzchner, S., Batorowicz, B., van Balkom, H., Dahlgren-Sandberg, A., & Renner, G. (2014). Investigating executive functions in children with severe speech and movement disorders using structured tasks. *Frontiers in Psychology, 5*, 992.

Steensma, T. D., Biemond, R., de Boer, F., & Cohen-Kettenis, P. T. (2011). Desisting and persisting gender dysphoria after childhood: A qualitative follow-up study. *Clinical Child Psychology and Psychiatry, 16*, 499–516.

Steensma, T. D., McGuire, J. K., Kreukels, B. P., Beekman, A. J., & Cohen-Kettenis, P. T. (2013). Factors associated with desistence and persistence of childhood gender dysphoria: A quantitative follow-up study. *Journal of the American Academy of Child and Adolescent Psychiatry, 52*, 582–590.

Steinberg, L., & Silk, J. S. (2002). Parenting adolescents. In M. H. Bornstein (Ed.), *Handbook of parenting, Second edition, Volume 1: Children and parenting* (pp. 103–133). Mahwah, NJ: Erlbaum.

Steinberg, L., & Chein, J. M. (2015). Multiple accounts of adolescent impulsivity. *Proceedings of the National Academy of Sciences, 112*, 8807–8808.

Steiner, J. E., Glaser, D., Hawilo, M. E., & Berridge, K. C. (2001). Comparative expression of hedonic impact: Affective reactions to taste by human infants and other primates. *Neuroscience Biobehavioral Reviews, 25*, 53–74.

Steinhausen, H. C., Wachter, M., Laimböck, K., & Metzke, C. W. (2006). A long-term outcome study of selective mutism in childhood. *Journal of Child Psychology and Psychiatry, 47*, 751–756.

Steinhorst, A., & Funke, J. (2014). Mirror neuron activity is no proof for action understanding. *Frontiers in Human Neuroscience, 8*, 333.

Steinman, K. J., Mostofsky, S. H., & Denckla, M. B. (2010). Toward a narrower, more pragmatic view of developmental dyspraxia. *Journal of Child Neurology, 25*, 71–81.

Steinschneider, A., Lipton, E. L., & Richmond, J. B. (1966). Auditory sensitivity in the infant: Effect of intensity on cardiac and motor responsivity. *Child Development, 1966*, 233–252.

Stenberg, C. R., Campos, J. J., & Emde, R. N. (1983). The facial expression of anger in seven-month-old infants. *Child Development, 54*, 178–184.

Stenberg, G. (2009). Selectivity in infant social referencing. *Infancy, 14*, 457–473.

Stenberg, N., Bresnahan, M., Gunnes, N., Hirtz, D., Hornig, M., Lie, K. K., Lipkin, W. I., Lord, C., Magnus, P., Reichborn-Kjennerud, T., et al. (2014). Identifying children with autism spectrum disorder at 18 months in a general population sample. *Paediatric and Perinatal Epidemiology, 28*, 255–262.

Stern, D. N. (1998). *The interpersonal world of the infant: A view from psychoanalysis and developmental psychology.* New York, NY: Karnac Books.

Stern, D. N. (2007). Applying developmental and neuroscience finding on other-centred participation to the process of change in psychotherapy. In S. Bråten (Ed.), *On being moved: From mirror neurons to empathy* (pp. 35–47). Amsterdam, NL: John Benjamins.

Stern, M., & Karraker, K. H. (1989). Sex stereotyping of infants: A review of gender labeling studies. *Sex Roles, 20*, 501–522.

Stern, W. (1912). *The psycholigical methods of testing intelligence.* Baltimore, MD: Warwick and York.

Sternberg, R. J. (1997). The triarchic theory of intelligence. In D. P. Flanagan, J. L. Genshaft & P. L. Harrison (Eds), *Contemporary intellectual assessment* (pp. 92–104). London: Guilford Press.

Sternberg, R. J. (2014). The development of adaptive competence: Why cultural psychology is necessary and not just nice. *Developmental Review, 34*, 208–224.

Sternberg, R. J. (2015). Multiple intelligences in the new age of thinking. In S. Goldstein, D. Princiotta & J. A. Naglieri (Eds), *Handbook of intelligence: Evolutionary theory, historical perspective, and current concepts* (pp. 229–241). New York, NY: Springer.

Sternberg, R. J., Grigorenko, E. L., & Bundy, D. A. (2001). The predictive value of IQ. *Merrill-Palmer Quarterly, 47*, 1–41.

Sternberg, R. J., Grigorenko, E. L., & Kidd, K. K. (2005). Intelligence, race, and genetics. *American Psychologist, 60*, 46–59.

Sterrett, K., Shire, S., & Kasari, C. (2017). Peer relationships among children with ASD: Interventions targeting social acceptance, friendships, and peer networks. *International Review of Research in Developmental Disabilities, 52*, 37–74.

Stetsenko, A., & Arievitch, I. M. (2004). The self in cultural-historical activity theory: Reclaiming the unity of social and individual dimensions of human development. *Theory and Psychology*, *14*, 475–503.

Stevenson, H. W., & Lee, S. Y. (1990). Contents of achievement: A study of American, Chinese and Japanese children. *Monographs of the Society for Research in Child Development*, *55*, 3–4.

Stevenson, J., Kreppner, J., Pimperton, H., Worsfold, S., & Kennedy, C. (2015). Emotional and behavioural difficulties in children and adolescents with hearing impairment: A systematic review and meta-analysis. *European Child and Adolescent Psychiatry*, *24*, 477–496.

Stevenson-Hinde, J. (2005). The interplay between attachment, temperament, and maternal style: A Madinglet perspective. In K. E. Grossmann, K. Grossmann & E. Waters (Eds), *Attachment from infancy to adulthood* (pp. 198–222). New York, NY: Guilford Press.

Stewart, R. B. (1983). Sibling attachment relationships: Child–infant interaction in the strange situation. *Developmental Psychology*, *19*, 192–199.

Stikkelbroek, Y., Bodden, D. H., Reitz, E., Vollebergh, W. A., & van Baar, A. L. (2016). Mental health of adolescents before and after the death of a parent or sibling. *European Child and Adolescent Psychiatry*, *25*, 49–59.

Stiles, J., Brown, T. T., Haist, F., & Jernigan, T. (2015). Brain and cognitiive development. In R. M. Lerner, L. S. Liben & U. Mueller (Eds), *Handbook of child psychology and developmental science, Seventh edition, Volume 2: Cognitive processes* (pp. 9–62). Hoboken, NJ: Wiley.

Stipek, D. J., Recchia, S., & McClintic, S. (1992). Self-evaluation in young children. *Monographs of the Society for Research in Child Development*, *57*, 1–98.

Stock, P., Desoete, A., & Roeyers, H. (2010). Detecting children with arithmetic disabilities from kindergarten: Evidence from a 3-year longitudinal study on the role of preparatory arithmetic abilities. *Journal of Learning Disabilities*, *43*, 250–268.

Stocker, C., & Dunn, J. (1990). Sibling relationships in childhood: Links with friendship and peer relationships. *British Journal of Developmental Psychology*, *8*, 227–244.

Stoiber, K. C., & DeSmet, J. L. (2010). Guidelines for evidence-based practice in selecting interventions. In G. G. Pedacock, R. A. Ervin, E. J. Daly & K. W. Merrell (Eds), *Practical handbook of school psychology: Effective practices for the 21st century* (pp. 213–234). New York, NY: Guilford Press.

Stoiber, K. C., Purdy, S., & Klingbeil, D. A. (2016). Evidence-based practices. In N. N. Singh (Ed.), *Handbook of evidence-based practices in intellectual and developmental disabilities* (pp. 41–68). Cham, Switzerland: Springer.

Stoltz, T., Piske, F. H. R., de Fátima Quintal de Freitas, M., D'Aroz, M. S., & Machado, J. M. (2015). Creativity in gifted education: Contributions from Vygotsky and Piaget. *Creative Education*, *6*, 64–70.

Størksen, I., Røysamb, E., Moum, T., & Tambs, K. (2005). Adolescents with a childhood experience of parental divorce: A longitudinal study of mental health and adjustment. *Journal of Adolescence*, *28*, 725–739.

Stott, D. H. (1973). Follow-up study from birth of the effects of prenatal stresses. *Developmental Medicine and Child Neurology*, *15*, 770–787.

Stotz, K. (2008). The ingredients for a postgenomic synthesis of nature and nurture. *Philosophical Psychology*, *21*, 359–381.

Strandell, H. (2014). Mobile phones in children's after-school centres: Stretching of place and control. *Mobilities*, *9*, 256–274.

Strange, W., & Broen, P. A. (1980). Perception and production of approximant consonants by 3-year-olds: A first study. In G. H. Yeni-Komshian, J. F. Kavanagh & C. A. Ferguson (Eds), *Child phonology. Volume 2: Perception* (pp. 117–154). New York, NY: Academic Press.

Strayer, J. (1980). A naturalistic study of empathic behaviours and their relation to affective states and perspective-taking skills in preschool children. *Child Development*, *51*, 815–822.

Stroebe, W. (2016). Are most published social psychological findings false? *Journal of Experimental Social Psychology*, *66*, 134–144.

Stroebe, W., Postmes, T., & Spears, R. (2012). Scientific misconduct and the myth of self-correction in science. *Perspectives on Psychological Science*, *7*, 670–688.

Strohner, H., & Nelson, K. E. (1974). The young child's development of sentence comprehension: Influence of event probability, nonverbal context, syntactic form, and strategies. *Child Development*, *45*, 567–576.

Strohschein, L. (2005). Parental divorce and child mental health trajectories. *Journal of Marriage and Family*, *67*, 1286–1300.

Strømme, P., & Valvatne, K. (1998). Mental retardation in Norway: Prevalence and subclassification in a cohort of 30 037 children born between 1980 and 1985. *Acta Pædiatrica*, *87*, 291–296.

Stromquist, N. P. (2007). The gender socialization process in schools: A cross-national comparison. Paper commissioned for the EFA Global Monitoring Report 2008, Education for All by 2015: Will we make it?

Strong, M., & Prinz, P. M. (1997). A study of the relationship between American Sign Language and English literacy. *The Journal of Deaf Studies and Deaf Education*, *2*, 37–46.

Su, R., Rounds, J., & Armstrong, P. I. (2009). Men and things, women and people: A meta-analysis of sex differences in interests. *Psychological Bulletin*, *135*, 859–884.

Suddendorf, T., & Collier-Baker, E. (2009). The evolution of primate visual self-recognition: Evidence of absence in lesser apes. *Proceedings of the Royal Society B: Biological Sciences*, *276*, 1671–1677.

Suddendorf, T., Oostenbroek, J., Nielsen, M., & Slaughter, V. (2013). Is newborn imitation developmentally homologous to later social-cognitive skills? *Developmental Psychobiology*, *55*, 52–58.

Suddendorf, T., Simcock, G., & Nielsen, M. (2007). Visual self-recognition in mirrors and live videos: Evidence for a developmental asynchrony. *Cognitive Development*, *22*, 185–196.

Sullivan, K., Zaitchick, D., & Tager-Flusberg, H. (1994). Preschoolers can attribute second-order beliefs. *Developmental Psychology, 30,* 395–402.

Sun, C. R. (2017). An examination of the four-part theory of the Chinese self: The differentiation and relative importance of the different types of social-oriented self. *Frontiers in Psychology, 8,* 1106.

Sundet, J. M., Barlaug, D., & Torjussen, T. M. (2004). The end of the Flynn effect? A study of secular trends in mean intelligence test scores of Norwegian conscripts during half a century. *Intelligence, 32,* 349–362.

Suomi, S. J. (1991). Early stress and adult emotional reactivity in rhesus monkeys. In G. R. Bock & J. Whelan (Eds), *The childhood environment and adult disease* (pp. 171–188). Chichester, UK: John Wiley.

Suomi, S. J. (2005). Mother-infant attachment, peer relationships, and the development of social networks in rhesus monkeys. *Human Development, 48,* 67–79.

Suomi, S. J. (2008). Attachment in rhesus monkeys. In J. Cassidy & P. R. Shaver (Eds), *Handbook of attachment, Second edition* (pp. 173–191). New York, NY: Guilford Press.

Super, C. M. (1981). Environmental effects on motor development: The case of "African infant precocity". *Developmental Medicine and Child Neurology, 18,* 561–567.

Supkoff, L. M., Puig, J., & Sroufe, L. A. (2012). Situating resilience in developmental context. In M. Ungar (Ed.), *The social ecology of resilience* (pp. 127–142). New York, NY: Springer.

Sutton, J. E. (2006). The development of landmark and beacon use in young children: Evidence from a touch-screen search task. *Developmental Science, 9,* 108–123.

Sutton-Smith, B. (1986). *Toys as culture.* New York, NY: Gardner Press.

Sutton-Smith, B. (1994). Does play prepare the future? In J. H. Goldstein (Ed.), *Toys, play and child development* (pp. 131–146). Cambridge: Cambridge University Press.

Swaab, D. F. (2007). Sexual differentiation of the brain and behavior. *Best Practice and Research: Clinical Endocrinology and Metabolism, 21,* 431–444.

Swaney, W. T. (2011). Genomic imprinting and mammalian reproduction. *Hormones and Behavior, 59,* 369–374.

Swanson, S. A., Crow, S. J., Le Grange, D., Swendsen, J., & Merikangas, K. R. (2011). Prevalence and correlates of eating disorders in adolescents: Results from the national comorbidity survey replication adolescent supplement. *Archives of General Psychiatry, 68,* 714–723.

Swingler, M. M., Perry, N. B., & Calkins, S. D. (2015). Neural plasticity and the development of attention: Intrinsic and extrinsic influences. *Development and Psychopathology, 27,* 443–457.

Symons, D. K. (2004). Mental state discourse, theory of mind, and an internalization of self-other understanding. *Developmental Review, 24,* 159–188.

Tackett, J. L., Balsis, S., Oltmanns, T. F., & Krueger, R. F. (2009). A unifying perspective on personality pathology across the life span: Developmental considerations for the fifth edition of the Diagnostic and Statistical Manual of Mental Disorders. *Development and Psychopathology, 21,* 687–713.

Tadić, V., Pring, L., & Dale, N. (2009). Attentional processes in young children with congenital visual impairment. *British Journal of Developmental Psychology, 27,* 311–330.

Tafreshi, D., Thompson, J. J., & Racine, T. P. (2014). An analysis of the conceptual foundations of the infant preferential looking paradigm. *Human Development, 57,* 222–240.

Takahashi, K. (1990). Are the key assumptions of the "Strange Situation" procedure universal? A view from Japanese research. *Human Development, 33,* 23–30.

Takesian, A. E., & Hensch, T. K. (2013). Balancing plasticity/stability across brain development. *Progress in Brain Research, 207,* 3–34.

Talwar, V., Arruda, C., & Yachison, S. (2015). The effects of punishment and appeals for honesty on children's truth-telling behavior. *Journal of Experimental Child Psychology, 130,* 209–217.

Talwar, V., & Lee, K. (2002). Emergence of white-lie telling in children between 3 and 7 years of age. *Merrill-Palmer Quarterly, 48,* 160–181.

Talwar, V., Murphy, S. M., & Lee, K. (2007). White lie-telling in children for politeness purposes. *International Journal of Behavioral Development, 31,* 1–11.

Tamm, L., Nakonezny, P. A., & Hughes, C. W. (2014). An open trial of a metacognitive executive function training for young children with ADHD. *Journal of Attention Disorders, 18,* 551–559.

Tammen, S. A., Friso, S., & Choi, S. W. (2013). Epigenetics: The link between nature and nurture. *Molecular Aspects of Medicine, 34,* 753–764.

Tangney, J. P., Stuewig, J., & Mashek, D. J. (2007). Moral emotions and moral behavior. *Annual Review of Psychology, 58,* 345–372.

Tannock, R. (2007). *The educational implications of attention deficit hyperactivity disorder.* Toronto, Ontario: Literacy and Numeracy Secretariat.

Tannock, R., Frijters, J. C., Martinussen, R., White, E. J., Ickowicz, A., Benson, N. J., & Lovett, M. W. (2018). Combined modality intervention for ADHD with comorbid reading disorders: A proof of concept study. *Journal of Learning Disabilities, 51,* 55–72.

Tappan, M. B. (2006). Mediated moralities: Sociocultural approaches to moral development. In M. Killen & J. G. Smetana (Eds), *Handbook of moral development* (pp. 351–374). Mahwah, NJ: Erlbaum.Tarabah, A., Badr, L. K., Usta, J., & Doyle, J. (2016). Exposure to violence and children's desensitization attitudes in Lebanon. *Journal of Interpersonal Violence, 31,* 3017–3038.

Tardif, T. (1996). Nouns are not always learned before verbs: Evidence from Mandarin speakers' early vocabularies. *Developmental Psychology, 32,* 492–504.

Tardif, T. (2006). But are they really verbs? Chinese words for action. In K. Hirsh-Pasek & R. M. Golinkoff (Eds), *Action meets word: How children learn verbs* (pp. 477–498). New York, NY: Oxford University Press.

Tardif, T., Fletcher, P., Liang, W., Zhang, Z., Kaciroti, N., & Marchman, V. A. (2008). Baby's first 10 words. *Developmental Psychology, 44,* 929–938.

Tardif, T., & Miao, X. (2000). Developmental psychology in China. *International Journal of Behavioral Development, 24,* 68–72.

Taumoepeau, M., & Reese, E. (2014). Understanding the self through siblings: Self-awareness mediates the sibling effect on social understanding. *Social Development, 23,* 1–18.

Taylor, H. G., & Alden, J. (1997). Age-related differences in outcomes following childhood brain insults: An introduction and overview. *Journal of the International Neuropsychological Society, 3,* 555–567.

Taylor, M., Carlson, S. M., Maring, B. L., Gerow, L., & Charley, C. M. (2004). The characteristics and correlates of fantasy in school-age children: Imaginary companions, impersonation, and social understanding. *Developmental Psychology, 40,* 1173–1187.

Taylor, S. E., Way, B. M., Welch, W. T., Hilmert, C. J., Lehman, B. J., & Eisenberger, N. I. (2006). Early family environment, current adversity, the serotonin transporter promoter polymorphism, and depressive symptomatology. *Biological Psychiatry, 60,* 671–676.

Tenenbaum, H. R., Ford, S., & Alkhedairy, B. (2011). Telling stories: Gender differences in peers' emotion talk and communication style. *British Journal of Developmental Psychology, 29,* 707–721.

Terrace, H. S. (1979). *Nim: A chimpanzee who learned sign language.* New York, NY: Washington Square Press.

Tessler, M., & Nelson, K. (1994). Making memories: The influence of joint encoding on later recall by young children. *Consciousness and Cognition: An International Journal, 3,* 307–326.

Teti, D. M., Sakin, J. W., Kucera, E., Corns, K. M., & Eiden, R. D. (1996). And baby makes four: Predictors of attachment security among preschool age firstborns during the transition to siblinghood. *Child Development, 67,* 579–596.

Thapar, A., Pine, D. S., Leckman, J. F., Scott, S., Snowling, M., & Taylor, E. A. (Eds) (2015). *Rutter's child and adolescent psychiatry, Sixth edition.* London: Wiley.

Thapar, A., & Rutter, M. (2015). Neurodevelopmental disorders. In A. Thapar, D. Pine, J. Leckman, S. Scott, M. Snowling & E. Taylor (Eds), *Rutter's child and adolescent psychiatry, Sixth edition* (pp. 31–40). London: Wiley.

Thelen, E. (1995). Motor development: A new synthesis. *American Psychologist, 50,* 79–95.

Thelen, E., & Smith, L. B. (1994). *A dynamic systems approach to the development of cognition and action.* London: MIT Press.

Theule, J., Germain, S. M., Cheung, K., Hurl, K. E., & Markel, C. (2016). Conduct disorder/oppositional defiant disorder and attachment: A meta-analysis. *Journal of Developmental and Life-Course Criminology, 2,* 232–255.

Thomaes, S., Stegge, H., Bushman, B. J., Olthof, T., & Denissen, J. (2008). Development and validation of the Childhood Narcissism Scale. *Journal of Personality Assessment, 90,* 382–391.

Thomas, A., & Chess, S. (1977). *Temperament and development.* New York, NY: Bruner/Mazel.

Thomas, A., & Chess, S. (1986). The New York Longitudinal Study: From infancy to early adult life. In R. Plomin & J. Dunn (Eds), *The study of temperament: Changes, continuities and challenges* (pp. 39–52). London: Erlbaum.

Thomas, M. S., Davis, R., Karmiloff-Smith, A., Knowland, V. C., & Charman, T. (2016). The over-pruning hypothesis of autism. *Developmental Science, 19,* 284–305.

Thomas, M. S. C., & Johnson, M. H. (2008). New advances in understanding sensitive periods in brain development. *Current Directions in Psychological Science, 17,* 1–5.

Thomas, M. S. C., Purser, H. R. M., & Richardson, F. M. (2013). Modularity and developmental disorders. In P. D. Zelazo (Ed.), *Oxford handbook of developmental psychology* (pp. 481–505). Oxford: Oxford University Press.

Thomas, R. M. (2005). *Comparing theories of child development, Sixth edition.* Belmont, CA: Wadsworth.

Thommen, E., Avelar, S., Sapin, V. Z., Perrenoud, S., & Malatesta, D. (2010). Mapping the journey from home to school: A study on children's representation of space. *International Research in Geographical and Environmental Education, 19,* 191–205.

Thompson, R. A. (1991). Emotional regulation and emotional development. *Educational Psychology Review, 3,* 269–307.

Thompson, R. A. (1998). Early sociopersonality development. In W. Damon & N. Eisenberg (Eds), *Handbook of child psychology, Fifth edition, Volume 3. Social, emotional, and personality development* (pp. 25–104). New York, NY: John Wiley.

Thompson, R. A. (2006). The development of the person: Social understanding, relationship, conscience, self. In W. Damon, R. M. Lerner & N. Eisenberg (Eds), *Handbook of child psychology, Sixth edition, Volume 3: Social, emotional, and personality development* (pp. 24–98). New York, NY: Wiley.

Thompson, R. A. (2011). Emotion and emotion regulation: Two sides of the developing coin. *Emotion Review, 3,* 53–61.

Thompson, R. A. (2016). Early attachmnet and later deevlopment: Reframing the questions. In J. Cassidy & P. R. Shaver (Eds), *Handbook of attachment: Theory, research, and clinical applications, Third edition* (pp. 330–348). New York, NY: Guilford Press.

Thompson, R. A., Meyer, S., & McGinley, M. (2006). Understanding values in relationships: The development of conscience. In M. Killen & J. G. Smetana (Eds), *Handbook of moral development* (pp. 267–297). Mahwah, NJ: Erlbaum.

Thoresen, C., Lønnum, K., Melinder, A., & Magnussen, S. (2009). Forensic interviews with children in CSA cases: A large-sample study of Norwegian police interviews. *Applied Cognitive Psychology, 23,* 999–1011.

Thoresen, C., Lønnum, K., Melinder, A., Stridbeck, U., & Magnussen, S. (2006). Theory and practice in interviewing young children: A study of Norwegian police interviews 1985–2002. *Psychology, Crime and Law, 12,* 629–640.

Thorne, B. (1986). Boys and girls together, but mostly apart. In W. W. Hartup & Z. Rubin (Eds), *Relationship and development* (pp. 167–184). Hillsdale, NJ: Lawrence Erlbaum.

Thorne, S. L., & Tasker, T. (2011). Sociocultural and cultural-historical theories of language development. In J. Simpson (Ed.), *Routledge handbook of applied linguistics* (pp. 487–500). New York, NY: Routledge.

Thorseng, L. A. (1997). Danske & engelske børns tilegnelse av termer for rumlige relasjoner: En kognitiv lingvistisk undersøgelse. Doctoral dissertation, Aarhus University.

Thrasher, C., & LoBue, V. (2016). Do infants find snakes aversive? Infants' physiological responses to "fear-relevant" stimuli. *Journal of Experimental Child Psychology*, 142, 382–390.

Tidmarsh, L. (1997). Mood disorder: Prolonged bereavement/grief reaction. In A. Lieberman, S. Wieder & E. Fenichel (Eds), *DC: 0 -3 Case Book* (pp. 69–79). Washington, DC: Zero to Three.

Tiedemann, T. (1787). Beobachtungen über die Entwicklung der Seelesfähigkeiten bei Kindern. *Hessische Beiträge zur Gelehrsamkeit und Kunst*, 2 (6–7).

Tillman, C. M., Bohlin, G., Sørensen, L., & Lundervold, A. J. (2009). Intellectual deficits in children with ADHD beyond central executive and non-executive functions. *Archives of Clinical Neuropsychology*, 24, 769–782.

Tisdale, S., & Pellizzoni, L. (2015). Disease mechanisms and therapeutic approaches in spinal muscular atrophy. *Journal of Neuroscience*, 35, 8691–8700.

Todd, B. K., Barry, J. A., & Thommessen, S. A. (2017). Preferences for "gender-typed" toys in boys and girls aged 9 to 32 months. *Infant and Child Development*, 26, doi:10.1002/icd.1986.

Tolan, P. H., & Deutsch, N. L. (2015). Mixed methods in developmental science. In R. M. Lerner, I. W. Overton & P. C. M. Molenaar (Eds), *Handbook of child psychology and developmental science, Seventh edition, Volume 1: Theoretical models of human development* (pp. 713–757). Hoboken, NJ: Wiley.

Tomalski, P., & Johnson, H. (2010). The effects of early adversity on the adult and developing brain. *Current Opinion in Psychiatry*, 23, 233–238.

Tomasello, M. (1992). *First verbs*. Cambridge: Cambridge University Press.

Tomasello, M. (1995). Language is not an instinct. *Cognitive Development*, 10, 131–156.

Tomasello, M. (1999). *The cultural origins of human cognition*. London: Harvard University Press.

Tomasello, M. (2003). *Constructing a language. A usage-based theory of language acquisition*. London: Harvard University Press.

Tomasello, M. (2005). "Cultural constraints on grammar and cognition in Piraha: Another look at the design features of human language": Comment. *Current Anthropology*, 46, 640–641.

Tomasello, M. (2006). Acquiring linguistic constructions. In W. Damon, R. M. Lerner, D. Kuhn & R. S. Siegler (Eds), *Handbook of child psychology, Sixth edition,*

Volume 2: Cognition, perception and language (pp. 371–384). New York, NY: Wiley.

Tomasello, M. (2008). *The origins of human communication*. Cambridge, MA: MIT Press.

Tomasello, M. (2009). *Why we cooperate*. London: MIT Press.

Tomasello, M. (2016). The ontogeny of cultural learning. *Current Opinion in Psychology*, 8, 1–4.

Tomasello, M., & Akhtar, N. (1995). Two-year-olds use pragmatic cues to differentiate reference to objects and actions. *Cognitive Development*, 10, 201–224.

Tomasello, M., & Camaioni, L. (1997). A comparison of the gestural communication of apes and human infants. *Human Development*, 40, 7–24.

Tomasello, M., Carpenter, M., & Lizskowski, U. (2007). A new look at infant pointing. *Child Development*, 78, 705–722.

Tomasi, D., & Volkow, N. D. (2011). Functional connectivity hubs in the human brain. *Neuroimage*, 57, 908–917.

Tomkins, S. S., & McCarter, R. (1964). What and where are the primary affects? Some evidence for a theory. *Perceptual and Motor Skills*, 18, 119–158.

Tone, E. B., & Tully, E. C. (2014). Empathy as a "risky strength": A multilevel examination of empathy and risk for internalizing disorders. *Development and Psychopathology*, 26 (4pt2), 1547–1565.

Toomey, R. B., Card, N. A., & Casper, D. M. (2014). Peers' perceptions of gender nonconformity: Associations with overt and relational peer victimization and aggression in early adolescence. *The Journal of Early Adolescence*, 34, 463–485.

Torgersen, A. M. (1989). Genetic and environmental influences on temperament development: Longitudinal study of twins from infancy to adolescence. In S. Doxiadis & S. Stewart (Eds), *Early influences shaping the individual* (pp. 269–281). New York, NY: Plenum.

Torgersen, A. M., & Janson, H. (2002). Why do identical twins differ in personality: Shared environment reconsidered. *Twin Research*, 5, 44–52.

Torney-Purta, J. (1992). Cognitive representations of the political system in adolescents: The continuum from prenovice to expert. *New Directions for Child Development*, 56, 11–25.

Tosto, M. G., Petrill, S. A., Halberda, J., Trzaskowski, M., Tikhomirova, T. N., Bogdanova, O. Y., Ly, R., Wilmer, J. B., Naiman, D. Q., Germine, L., et al. (2014). Why do we differ in number sense? Evidence from a genetically sensitive investigation. *Intelligence*, 43, 35–46.

Touwen, B. C. L. (1976). *Neurological development in infancy*. London: Spastics International.

Tracy, J. L., Cheng, J. T., Robins, R. W., & Trzesniewski, K. H. (2009). Authentic and hubristic pride: The affective core of self-esteem and narcissism. *Self and Identity*, 8, 196–213.

Tracy, J. L., & Robins, R. W. (2004). Putting the self into self-conscious emotions: A theoretical model. *Psychological Inquiry*, 15, 103–125.

Tracy, J. L., & Robins, R. W. (2007). Emerging insights into the nature and function of pride. *Current Directions in Psychological Science, 16*, 147–150.

Tracy, J. L., Robins, R. W., & Lagattuta, K. H. (2005). Can children recognize the pride expression? *Emotion, 5*, 251–257.

Trainor, L. J., & He, C. (2013). Auditory and musical development. In P. R. Zelazo (Ed.), *The Oxford handbook of developmental psychology, Volume 1: Body and mind* (pp. 310–337). New York, NY: Oxford University Press.

Trainor, L. J., & Trehub, S. E. (1994). Key membership and implied harmony in Western tonal music: Developmental perspectives. *Perception and Psychophysics, 56*, 125–132.

Trainor, L. J., & Unrau, A. J. (2012). Development of pitch and music perception. In L. Werner, R. R. Fay & A. N. Popper (Eds), *Springer handbook of auditory research: Human auditory development* (pp. 223–254). New York, NY: Springer.

Trautner, H. M. (1992). The development of sex typing in children: A longitudinal analysis. *German Journal of Psychology, 16*, 183–199.

Trautwein, U., Lüdtke, O., Köller, O., & Baumert, J. (2006). Self-esteem, academic self-concept, and achievement: How the learning environment moderates the dynamics of self-concept. *Journal of Personality and Social Psychology, 90*, 334–349.

Trawick-Smith, J. (1989). Play is not learning: A critical review of the literature. *Child and Youth Care Quarterly, 18*, 161–170.

Trehub, S. E., & Schellenberg, E. G. (1995). Music: Its relevance to infants. *Annals of Child Development, 11*, 1–24.

Tremblay-Leveau, H., & Nadel, J. (1996). Exclusion in triads: Can it serve "meta-communicative" knowledge in 11- and 23-month-old children? *British Journal of Developmental Psychology, 14*, 145–158.

Trevarthen, C. (1979). Communication and cooperation in early infancy: A description of primary intersubjectivity. In M. Bullowa (Ed.), *Before speech* (pp. 321–347). Cambridge: Cambridge University Press.

Trevarthen, C. (2015). Infant semiosis: The psycho-biology of action and shared experience from birth. *Cognitive Development, 36*, 130–141.

Trevarthen, C., & Logotheti, K. (1989). Child in society, and society in children: The nature of basic trust. In S. Howell & R. Willis (Eds), *Societies at peace: Anthropological perspectives* (pp. 165–186). London: Routledge.

Trionfi, G., & Reese, E. (2009). A good story: Children with imaginary companions create richer narratives. *Child Development, 80*, 1301–1313.

Troop-Gordon, W. (2017). Peer victimization in adolescence: The nature, progression, and consequences of being bullied within a developmental context. *Journal of Adolescence, 55*, 116–128.

Troseth, G. L. (2003). Getting a clear picture: Young children's understanding of a televised image. *Developmental Science, 6*, 247–253.

Troseth, G. L., & DeLoache, J. S. (1998). The medium can obscure the message: Young children's understanding of video. *Child Development, 69*, 950–965.

Troseth, G. L., Pickard, M. E., & DeLoache, J. S. (2007). Young children's use of scale models: Testing an alternative to representational insight. *Developmental Science, 10*, 763–69.

Troseth, G. L., Pierroutsakos, S. L., & DeLoache, J. S. (2004). From the innocent to the intelligent eye: The early development of pictorial competence. *Advances in Child Development and Behavior, 32*, 1–35.

Tröster, H., & Brambring, M. (1992). Early social-emotional development in blind infants. *Child: Care, Health and Development, 18*, 207–227.

Tucker-Drob, E. M., Briley, D. A., & Harden, K. P. (2013). Genetic and environmental influences on cognition across development and context. *Current Directions in Psychological Science, 22*, 349–355.

Tucker-Drob, E. M., Rhemtulla, M., Harden, K. P., Turkheimer, E., & Fask, D. (2011). Emergence of a gene × socioeconomic status interaction on infant mental ability between 10 months and 2 years. *Psychological Science, 22*, 125–133.

Turati, C., Valenza, E., Leo, I., & Simion, F. (2005). Three-month-olds' visual preference for faces and its underlying visual processing mechanisms. *Journal of Experimental Child Psychology, 90*, 255–273.

Turiel, E. (2014). Morality, epistemology, development, and social opposition. In M. Killen & J. G. Smetana (Eds), *Handbook of moral development, Second edition* (pp. 3–22). New York, NY: Psychology Press.

Turiel, E. (2015). Moral development. Biology, development, and human systems. In R. M. Lerner, W. F. Overton & P. C. M. Molenaar (Eds), *Handbook of child psychology and developmental science, Seventh edition. Volume 1: Theory and method* (pp. 484–522). New York, NY: Wiley.

Turiel, E., & Killen, M. (2010). Taking emotions seriously: The role of emotions in moral development. In W. Arsenio & E. Lemerise (Eds), *Emotions in aggression and moral development* (pp. 33–52). Washington, DC: American Psychological Association.

Turkewitz, G., & Kenny, P. A. (1985). The role of developmental limitations of sensory input on sensory/perceptual organization. *Journal of Developmental and Behavioral Pediatrics, 6*, 302–306.

Turkheimer, E., Haley, A., Waldron, M., D'Onofrio, B., & Gottesman, I. I. (2003). Socioeconomic status modifies heritability of IQ in young children. *Psychological Science, 14*, 623–628.

Turkheimer, E., Pettersson, E., & Horn, E. E. (2014). Phenotypic null hypothesis for the genetics of personality. *Annual Review of Psychology, 65*, 515–540.

Turnbull, C. M. (1972). *The mountain people.* New York, NY: Simon and Schuster.

Turnbull, W., Carpendale, J. I. M., & Racine, T. (2009). Talk and children's understanding of the mind. *Journal of Consciousness Studies, 16*, 140–166.

Turner, L. M., & Stone, W. L. (2007). Variability in outcome for children with an ASD diagnosis at age 2.

Journal of Child Psychology and Psychiatry, 48, 793–802.

Twyman, K. A., Saylor, C. F., Saia, D., Macias, M. M., Taylor, L. A., & Spratt, E. (2010). Bullying and ostracism experiences in children with special health care needs. *Journal of Developmental and Behavioral Pediatrics, 31,* 1–8.

Tzampazi, F., Kyridis, A., & Christodoulou, A. (2013). "What will I be when I grow up?" Children's preferred future occupations and their stereotypical views. *International Journal of Social Science Research, 1,* 19–38.

Tzuriel, D. (2005). Dynamic assessment of learning potential: A new paradigm. *Transylvanian Journal of Psychology, 1,* 7–16.

Udwin, O., & Kuczynski, A. (2007). Behavioural phenotypes in genetic syndromes associated with intellectual disability. In A. Carr, G. O'Reilly, P. N. Walsh & J. McEvoy (Eds). *The handbook of intellectual disability and clinical psychology practice* (pp. 488–528). London: Routledge.

Ukrainetz, T. A., Justice, L. M., Kadaravek, J. N., Eisenberg, S. N., Gillam, R. B., & Horn, M. (2005). The development of expressive elaboration in fictional narratives. *Journal of Speech, Language, and Hearing Research, 48,* 1363–1377.

Ullstadius, E. (1998). Neonatal imitation in a mother–infant setting. *Early Development and Parenting, 7,* 1–8.

Umaña-Taylor, A. J., Quintana, S. M., Lee, R. M., Cross, W. E., Rivas-Drake, D., Schwartz, S. J., Syed, M., Yip, T., Seaton, E., & Ethnic and Racial Identity in the 21st Century Study Group (2014). Ethnic and racial identity during adolescence and into young adulthood: An integrated conceptualization. *Child Development, 85,* 21–39.

Underwood, M. A. (2003). *Social aggression among girls.* New York, NY: Guilford Press.

Undheim, A. M., & Drugli, M. B. (2012). Age for enrolling in full-time childcare: A qualitative study of parent and caregiver perspectives. *Early Child Development and Care, 182,* 1673–1682.

Uzgiris, I. C. (1999). Imitation as activity: Developmental aspects. In J. Nadel & G. Butterworth (Eds), *Imitation in infancy* (pp. 186–206). Cambridge: Cambridge University Press.

Vaillend, C., Poirier, R., & Laroche, S. (2008). Genes, plasticity and mental retardation. *Behavior and Brain Research, 192,* 88–105.

Vaish, A., Grossmann, T., & Woodward, A. (2008). Not all emotions are created equal: The negativity bias in social-emotional development. *Psychological Bulletin, 134,* 383–403.

Vaish, A., Missana, M., & Tomasello, M. (2011). Three-year-old children intervene in third-party moral transgressions. *British Journal of Developmental Psychology, 29,* 124–130.

Vaish, A., & Tomasello, M. (2014). The early ontogeny of human cooperation and morality. In M. Killen & J. G. Smetana (Eds), *Handbook of moral development* (pp. 279–298). New York, NY: Psychology Press.

Valerio, M., Amodio, P., Zio, M. D., Vianello, A., & Zacchello, G. P. (1997). The use of television in 2- to 8-year-old children and the attitude of parents about such use. *Archives of Pediatric and Adolescence Medicine, 151,* 22–26.

Valiente, C., Eisenberg, N., Fabes, R. A., Shepard, S. A., Cumberland, A., & Losoya, S. H. (2004). Prediction of children's empathy-related responding from their effortful control and parents' expressivity. *Developmental Psychology, 40,* 911–926.

Valkenburg, P. M., & Peter, J. (2007). Preadolescents' and adolescents' online communication and their closeness to friends. *Developmental Psychology, 43,* 267–277.

Valkenburg, P. M., & Peter, J. (2009). Social consequences of the Internet for adolescents: A decade of research. *Current Directions in Psychological Science, 18,* 1–5.

Valkenburg, P. M., Sumter, S. R., & Peter, J. (2011). Gender differences in online and offline self-disclosure in pre-adolescence and adolescence. *British Journal of Developmental Psychology, 29,* 253–269.

Valsiner, J. (1987). *Culture and the development of children's action.* New York, NY: Wiley.

Valsiner, J. (2012). *A guided science: History of psychology in the mirror of its making.* New Brunswick, NJ: Transaction Publishers.

van Aken, C., Junger, M., Verhoeven, M., van Aken, M. A. G., & Deković, M. (2007). The interactive effects of temperament and maternal parenting on toddlers' externalizing behaviours. *Infant and Child Development, 16,* 553–572.

van Aken, M. A. G., van Lieshout, C. F. M., & Haselager, G. J. T. (1996). Adolescents' competence and the mutuality of their self-descriptions and descriptions of them provided by others. *Journal of Youth and Adolescence, 25,* 285–306.

van Bysterveldt, A. K., Westerveld, M. F., Gillon, G., & Foster-Cohen, S. (2012). Personal narrative skills of school-aged children with Down syndrome. *International Journal of Language and Communication Disorders, 47,* 95–105.

van Daal, J., Verhoeven, L., & van Balkom, H. (2007). Behaviour problems in children with language impairment. *Journal of Child Psychology and Psychiatry, 48,* 1139–1147.

Vandell, D. L. (2004). Early child care: The known and the unknown. *Merrill-Palmer Quarterly, 50,* 387–414.

Vandell, D. L., Wilson, K. S., & Buchanan, N. R. (1980). Peer interaction in the first year of life: An examination of its structure, content, and sensitivity to toys. *Child Development, 51,* 481–488.

van dem Boom, D. C. (1989). Neonatal irritability and the development of attachment. In G. A. Kohnstamm, J. E. Bates & M. K. Rothbart (Eds), *Temperament in childhood* (pp. 299–318). Chichester, UK: John Wiley.

van den Akker, A. L., Prinzie, P., & Overbeek, G. (2016). Dimensions of personality pathology in adolescence: Longitudinal associations with Big Five personality dimensions across childhood and adolescence. *Journal of Personality Disorders, 30,* 211–231.

van den Bergh, B. R. (2011). Developmental programming of early brain and behaviour development and mental health: A conceptual framework. *Developmental Medicine and Child Neurology*, *53*, 19–23.

van den Bos, W., Rodriguez, C. A., Schweitzer, J. B., & McClure, S. M. (2015). Adolescent impatience decreases with increased frontostriatal connectivity. *Proceedings of the National Academy of Sciences*, *112*, E3765–E3774.

van den Eijnden, R. J. J. M., Spijkerman, R., Vermulst, A. A., van Rooij, T. J., & Engels, R. C. M. E. (2010). Compulsive internet use among adolescents: Bidirectional parent-child relationships. *Abnormal Child Psychology*, *38*, 77–89.

van den Eijnden, R. J. J. M., Vermulst, A. A., van Rooij, A., Scholte, R., & van de Mheen, D. (2011). Online and real life victimisation and adolescents' psychosocial problems: What is the cause and what is the consequence? *Psychology and Health*, *26*, 204–205.

van der Donk, M., Hiemstra-Beernink, A. C., Tjeenk-Kalff, A., Van Der Leij, A., & Lindauer, R. (2015). Cognitive training for children with ADHD: A randomized controlled trial of cogmed working memory training and "paying attention in class". *Frontiers in Psychology*, *6*, 1081.

van der Maas, H. L., Kan, K. J., & Borsboom, D. (2014). Intelligence is what the intelligence test measures. Seriously. *Journal of Intelligence*, *2*, 12–15.

van der Steen, S., Steenbeek, H., Wielinski, J., & van Geert, P. (2012). A comparison between young students with and without special needs on their understanding of scientific concepts. *Education Research International*, *2012* (260403), 1–12.

Vandewater, E., Bickham, D., Lee, J., Cummings, H., Wartella, E., & Rideout, V. (2005). When the television is always on: Heavy television exposure and young children's development. *American Behavioral Scientist*, *48*, 562–577.

van Geert, P., & Steenbeek, H. (2005). The dynamics of scaffolding. *New Ideas in Psychology*, *23*, 115–128.

van IJzendoorn, M. H., Luijk, M. P., & Juffer, F. (2008). IQ of children growing up in children's homes: A meta-analysis on IQ delays in orphanages. *Merrill-Palmer Quarterly*, *54*, 341–366.

van IJzendoorn, M. H., Palacios, J., Sonuga-Barke, E. J., Gunnar, M. R., Vorria, P., McCall, R. B., Le Mare, L., Bakermans-Kranenburg, M. J., Dobrova-Kroll, N. A., & Juffer, F. (2011). Children in institutional care: Delayed development and resilience. *Monographs of the Society for Research in Child Development*, *76*, 8–30

van Nieuwenhuijzen, M., & Vriens, A. (2012). (Social) Cognitive skills and social information processing in children with mild to borderline intellectual disabilities. *Research in Developmental Disabilities*, *33*, 426–434.

VanTassel-Baska, J., & Stambaugh, T. (2008). *What works: 20 years of curriculum development and research*. Williamsburg, VA: Center for Gifted Education.

van Wieringen, A., & Wouters, J. (2015). What can we expect of normally-developing children implanted at a young age with respect to their auditory, linguistic and cognitive skills? *Hearing Research*, *322*, 171–179.

Vargha-Khadem, F., Carr, L. J., Isaacs, E., Brett, E., Adams, C., & Mishkin, M. (1997). Onset of speech after left hemispherectomy in a nine-year-old boy. *Brain*, *120*, 159–182

Váša, F., Seidlitz, J., Romero-Garcia, R., Whitaker, K. J., Rosenthal, G., Vértes, P. E., Shinn, M., Alexander-Bloch, A., Fonagy, P., Dolan, R. J., et al. (2017). Adolescent tuning of association cortex in human structural brain networks. *Cerebral Cortex*, *28*, 281–294.

Vasey, M. W., Bosmans, G., & Ollendick, T. H. (2014). The developmental psychopathology of anxiety. In M. Lewis & K. Rudolph (Eds), *Handbook of developmental psychopathology, Third edition* (pp. 543–560). New York, NY: Springer.

Vasilyeva, M., & Lourenco, S. F. (2010). Spatial development. In R. M. Lerner & W. Overton (Eds), *Handbook of lifespan human development, Volume 1: Methods, biology, neuroscience and cognitive development* (pp. 720–753). Hoboken, NJ: Wiley.

Vasilyeva, M., & Lourenco, S. F. (2012). Development of spatial cognition. *Wiley Interdisciplinary Reviews: Cognitive Science*, *3*, 349–362.

Vassilieva, J. (2010). Russian psychology at the turn of the 21st century and post-Soviet reforms in the humanities disciplines. *History of Psychology*, *13*, 138–159.

Vatne, T. M., Helmen, I. Ø., Bahr, D., Kanavin, Ø., & Nyhus, L. (2015). "She came out of mum's tummy the wrong way" (Mis)conceptions among siblings of children with rare disorders. *Journal of Genetic Counseling*, *24*, 247–258.

Vaughn, B. E., Bost, K. K., & van IJzendoorn, M. H. (2008). Attachment and temperament: Additive and interactive influences on behavior, affect, and cognition during infancy and childhood. In J. Cassidy & P. R. Shaver (Eds), *Handbook of attachment: Theory, research, and clinical applications, Second edition* (pp. 192–216). New York, NY: Guilford Press.

Vaughn, S., Roberts, G., Wexler, J., Vaughn, M. G., Fall, A. M., & Schnakenberg, J. B. (2014). High school students with reading comprehension difficulties: Results of a randomized control trial of a two-year reading intervention. *Journal of Learning Disabilities*, *48*, 546–559.

Veiga, G., Ketelaar, L., De Leng, W., Cachucho, R., Kok, J. N., Knobbe, A., Neto, C., & Rieffe, C. (2017). Alone at the playground. *European Journal of Developmental Psychology*, *14*, 44–61.

Velez, J. A., Greitemeyer, T., Whitaker, J. L., Ewoldsen, D. R., & Bushman, B. J. (2016). Violent video games and reciprocity: The attenuating effects of cooperative game play on subsequent aggression. *Communication Research*, *43*, 447–467.

Vendetti, M. S., Matlen, B. J., Richland, L. E., & Bunge, S. A. (2015). Analogical reasoning in the classroom: Insights from cognitive science. *Mind, Brain, and Education*, *9*, 100–106.

Veneziano, E. (2016). The development of narrative discourse in French by 5 to 10 years old children: Some insights from a conversational interaction method. In J. Perera, M. Aparici, E. Rosado & N. Salas (Eds), *Written and spoken language development across the lifespan:*

Essays in honour of Liliana Tolchinsky (pp. 141–160). New York, NY: Springer.

Venuti, P., De Falco, S., Esposito, G., & Bornstein, M. H. (2009). Mother–child play: Children with Down syndrome and typical development. *American Journal on Intellectual and Developmental Disabilities, 114*, 274–288.

Verdon, S., Wong, S., & McLeod, S. (2016). Shared knowledge and mutual respect: Enhancing culturally competent practice through collaboration with families and communities. *Child Language Teaching and Therapy, 32*, 205–221.

Vervloed, M. P., van Dijk, R. J., Knoors, H., & van Dijk, J. P. (2006). Interaction between the teacher and the congenitally deafblind child. *American Annals of the Deaf, 151*, 336–344.

Vicario, C. M., Yates, M., & Nicholls, M. (2013). Shared deficits in space, time, and quantity processing in childhood genetic disorders. *Frontiers in Psychology, 4*, 43.

Viding, E., Fontaine, N. M., & McCrory, E. J. (2012). Antisocial behaviour in children with and without callous-unemotional traits. *Journal of the Royal Society of Medicine, 105*, 195–200.

Viding, E., & Larsson, H. (2007, November). Aetiology of antisocial behaviour. *International Congress Series, 1304*, 121–132.

Viding, E., & McCrory, E. (2015). Developmental risk for psychopathy. In A. Thapar, D. Pine, J. Leckman, S. Scott, M. Snowling & E. Taylor (Eds), *Rutter's child and adolescent psychiatry, Sixth edition* (pp. 966–980). London: Wiley.

Vig, S. (2007). Young children's object play: A window on development. *Journal of Developmental and Physical Disabilities, 19*, 201–215.

Vignoles, V. L., Schwartz, S. J., & Luyckx, K. (2011). Introduction: Toward an integrative view of identity. In S. J. Schwartz, K. Luyckx & V. L. Vignoles (Eds), *Handbook of identity theory and research* (pp. 1–28). New York, NY: Springer.

Vihman, M. (1993). Variable paths to early word production. *Journal of Phonetics, 21*, 61–82.

Viken, R. J., Rose, R. J., Kaprio, J., & Koskenvuo, M. (1994). A developmental genetic analysis of adult personality: Extraversion and neuroticism from 18 to 59 years of age. *Journal of Personality and Social Psychology, 66*, 722–730.

Vinden, P. (2002). Understanding minds and evidence for belief: A study of Mofu children in Cameroon. *International Journal of Behavioral Development, 26*, 445–452.

Visser, B. A., Ashton, M. C., & Vernon, P. A. (2006). Beyond *g*: Putting multiple intelligence theory to the test. *Intelligence, 34*, 487–502.

Visser, G. H., Bekedam, D. J., Mulder, E. J., & van Ballegooie, E. (1985). Delayed emergence of fetal behaviour in type 1 diabetic women. *Early Human Development, 12*, 167–172.

Vissers, L. E., Gilissen, C., & Veltman, J. A. (2016). Genetic studies in intellectual disability and related disorders. *Nature Reviews Genetics, 17*, 9–18.

Vittrup, B., Snider, S., Rose, K. K., & Rippy, J. (2016). Parental perceptions of the role of media and technology in their young children's lives. *Journal of Early Childhood Research, 14*, 43–54.

Voegtline, K. M., Costigan, K. A., Pater, H. A., & DiPietro, J. A. (2013). Near-term fetal response to maternal spoken voice. *Infant Behavior and Development, 36*, 526–533.

Vogel, D. A., Lake, M. A., Evans, S., & Karraker, K. H. (1991). Children's and adults' sex-stereotyped perceptions of infants. *Sex Roles, 24*, 605–616.

Vogt, P., & Lieven, E. (2010). Verifying theories of language acquisition using computer models of language evolution. *Adaptive Behavior, 18*, 21–35.

Volkmar, F., Siegel, M., Woodbury-Smith, M., King, B., & McCracken, J. (2014). Practice parameter for the assessment and treatment of children and adolescents with autism spectrum disorder. *Journal of the American Academy of Child and Adolescent Psychiatry, 53*, 237–257.

von Bastian, C. C., & Oberauer, K. (2014). Effects and mechanisms of working memory training: A review. *Psychological Research, 78*, 803–820.

von Eye, A., Bergman, L. R., & Hsieh, C.-A. (2015). Person-oriented methodological approaches. In R. M. Lerner, W. F. Overton & P. C. M. Molenaar (Eds), *Handbook of child psychology and developmental science, Seventh edition, Volume 1: Theory and method* (pp. 789–841). New York, NY: Wiley.

von Hofsten, C. (1993). Studying the development of goal-directed behaviour. In A. F. Kalverboer, B. Hopkins & R. Geuze (Eds), *Motor development in early and later childhood: Longitudinal approaches* (pp. 109–124). Cambridge: Cambridge University Press.

von Hofsten, C. (2004). An action perspective on motor development. *Trends in Cognitive Sciences, 8*, 266–272.

von Hofsten, C. (2007). Action in development. *Developmental Science, 10*, 54–60.

von Hofsten, O., von Hofsten, C., Sulutvedt, U., Laeng, B., Brennen, T., & Magnussen, S. (2014). Simulating newborn face perception. *Journal of Vision, 14*, 16.

von Knorring, A. L., Andersson, O., & Magnusson, D. (1987). Psychiatric care and course of psychiatric disorders from childhood to early adulthood in a representative sample. *Journal of Child Psychology and Psychiatry, 28*, 329–341.

von Tetzchner, S. (1998). *Noonan syndrome. Characteristics, development, and intervention.* Oslo, Norway: Centre for Rare Disorders, The National Hospital.

von Tetzchner, S. (2004). Early intervention and prevention of challenging behaviour in children with learning disabilities. *Perspectives in Education, 22*, 85–100.

von Tetzchner, S. (2009). Suporte ao desenvolvimento da comunicação suplementar e alternative. In D. Deliberato, M. de J. Gonçalves & E. C. de Macedo (Eds), *Comunicação alternative: Teoria, prática, tecnologias e pesquisa* (pp. 14–27). São Paulo: Memnon Edições Científicas.

von Tetzchner, S. (2018). Introduction to the special issue on aided language processes, development, and use: An international perspective. *Augmentative and Alternative Communication, 34*, 1–15.

von Tetzchner, S., Brekke, K. M., Sjøthun, B., & Grindheim, E. (2005). Constructing preschool communities of learners that afford alternative language development. *Augmentative and Alternative Communication, 21*, 82–100.

von Tetzchner, S., Fosse, P., & Elmerskog, B. (2013). Juvenile neuronal ceroid lipofuscinosis and education. *Biochimica et Biophysica Acta (BBA)-Molecular Basis of Disease, 1832*, 1894–1905.

von Tetzchner, S., & Grove, N. (Eds) (2003). *Augmentative and alternative communication: Developmental issues.* London: Whurr/Wiley.

von Tetzchner, S., Hoiting, N., Küntay, A. C., & Slobin, D. I. (2008). Variation sets in child-directed language – implication for intervention with alternative means of communication. Presented at 13th Biennial Conference of the International Society for Augmentative and Alterntive Communication, Montreal, Canada, 4–9 August, 2008.

von Tetzchner, S., & Martinsen, H. (2000). *Introduction to augmentative and alternative communication.* London: Whurr/Wiley.

von Tetzchner, S., Rogne, S. O., & Lilleeng, M. K. (1997). Literacy intervention for a deaf child with severe reading disorder. *Journal of Literacy Research, 29*, 25–46.

von Tetzchner, S., & Sedberg, T. (2005). Young blind children in activities with joint attention. Presented at X. International Conference for the Study of Child Language, Berlin, Germany, 25–29 July 2005.

von Tetzchner, S., & Stadskleiv, K. (2016). Constructing a language in alternative forms, In M. M. Smith & J. Murray (Eds), *The silent partner? Language, interaction and aided communication* (pp. 17–34). Guildford, UK: J&R Press

Vulchanova, M., Foyn, C. H., Nilsen, R. A., & Sigmundsson, H. (2014). Links between phonological memory, first language competence and second language competence in 10-year-old children. *Learning and Individual Differences, 35*, 87–95.

Vygotsky, L. S. (1962). *Thought and language.* Cambridge, MA: MIT Press.

Vygotsky, L. S. (1967). Play and its role in the mental development of the child. *Soviet Psychology, 5*, 6–18.

Vygotsky, L. S. (1978). *Mind in society: The development of higher mental processes.* Cambridge, MA: Harvard University Press.

Vygotsky, L. S. (1935a/1982). Undervisning & udvikling i førskolealderen. In *Om barnets psykiske udvikling* (pp. 89–104). København: Nyt Nordisk Forlag Arnold Busck.

Vygotsky, L. S. (1935b/1982). Spørsmålet om undervisning & den intellektuelle udvikling i skolealderen. In *Om barnets psykiske udvikling* (pp. 105–124). København: Nyt Nordisk Forlag Arnold Busck.

Wachs, T. D. (1994). Fit, context, and the transition between temperament and personality. In C. F. Halverson, G. A. Kohnstamm & R. P. Martin (Eds), *The developing structure of temperament and personality from infancy to adulthood* (pp. 209–220). Hillsdale, NJ: Lawrence Erlbaum.

Wachs, T. D. (2003). Expanding our view of context: The bio-ecological environment and development. In R. Kail (Ed.). *Advances in child development and behavior, Vol 31* (pp. 365–411). San Diego, CA: Academic Press.

Wachs, T. D., & Gruen, G. E. (1982). *Early experience and human development.* New York, NY: Plenum Press.

Wagner, K. R. (1985). How much do children say in a day? *Journal of Child Language, 12*, 475–487.

Wai, J., Cacchio, M., Putallaz, M., & Makel, M. C. (2010). Sex differences in the right tail of cognitive abilities: A 30 year examination. *Intelligence, 38*, 412–423.

Wai, J., Putallaz, M., & Makel, M. C. (2012). Studying intellectual outliers: Are there sex differences, and are the smart getting smarter? *Current Directions in Psychological Science, 21*, 382–390.

Wainryb, C., & Pasupathi, M. (2010). Political violence and disruptions in the development of moral agency. *Child Development Perspectives, 4*, 48–54.

Wainryb, C., & Recchia, H. E. (2012). Emotion and the moral lives of adolescents: Vagaries and complexities in the emotional experience of doing harm. *New Directions for Student Leadership, 2012*, 13–26.

Wainryb, C., Shaw, L. A., Langley, M., Cottam, K., & Lewis, R. (2004). Children's thinking about diversity of belief in the early school years: Judgments of relativism, tolerance, and disagreeing persons. *Child Development, 75*, 687–703.

Walden, T., & Kim, G. (2005). Infants' social looking toward mothers and strangers. *International Journal of Behavioral Development, 29*, 356–360.

Walden, T. A., & Ogan, T. A. (1988). The development of social referencing. *Child Development, 59*, 1230–1240.

Walker, L. J. (1984). Sex differences in the development of moral reasoning: A critical review. *Child Development, 55*, 677–691.

Walker, L. J., & Hennig, K. H. (1997). Moral development in the broader context of personality. In S. Hala (Ed.), *The development of social cognition* (pp. 297–327). Hove, UK: Psychology Press.

Walker, L. J., de Vries, B., & Trevathan, S. D. (1987). Moral stages and moral orientations in real-life and hypothetical dilemmas. *Child Development, 58*, 842–858.

Walker, L. J., & Taylor, J. H. (1991). Family interactions and the development of moral reasoning. *Child Development, 62*, 264–283.

Walker-Andrews, A. S. (1986). Intermodal perception of expressive behaviors: Relation of eye and voice? *Developmental Psychology, 22*, 373–377.

Walker-Andrews, A. S. (1997). Infants' perception of expressive behaviors: Differentiation of multimodal information. *Psychological Bulletin, 121*, 437–456.

Walker-Andrews, A. S. (2008). Intermodal emotional processes in infancy. In M. Lewis, J. M. Haviland & L. Feldman-Barrett (Eds), *Handbook of emotions* (pp. 364–375). New York, NY: Guilford Press.

Wall, T. D., Frick, P. J., Fanti, K. A., Kimonis, E. R., & Lordos, A. (2016). Factors differentiating callous-unemotional children with and without conduct problems. *Journal of Child Psychology and Psychiatry, 57,* 976–983.

Wallace, P. (2014). Internet addiction disorder and youth. *EMBO Reports, 15,* 12–16.

Walle, E. A., & Campos, J. J. (2012). Interpersonal responding to discrete emotions: A functionalist approach to the development of affect specificity. *Emotion Review, 4,* 413–422.

Waller, R., Gardner, F., Viding, E., Shaw, D. S., Dishion, T. J., Wilson, M. N., & Hyde, L. W. (2014). Bidirectional associations between parental warmth, callous unemotional behavior, and behavior problems in high-risk preschoolers. *Journal of Abnormal Child Psychology, 42,* 1275–1285.

Wallerstein, J. S., & Lewis, J. M. (2004). The unexpected legacy of divorce: Report of a 25-year study. *Psychoanalytic Psychology, 21,* 353–370.

Wallin, A. R., Quas, J. A., & Yim, H. S. (2009). Thysiological stress responses and children's event memory. In J. A. Quas & R. Fivush (Eds), *Emotion and memory in development* (pp. 313–339). Oxford: Oxford University Press.

Wang, Q. (2001). "Did you have fun?": American and Chinese mother – child conversations about shared emotional experiences. *Cognitive Development, 16,* 693–715.

Wang, Q. (2004). The emergence of cultural self-constructs: Autobiographical memory and self-description in European American and Chinese children. *Developmental Psychology, 40,* 3–15.

Wang, Q. (2014). The cultured self and remembering. In P. Bauer & R. Fivush (Eds), *The Wiley handbook on the development of children's memory* (pp. 605–625). Malden, MA: Wiley.

Wang, S., Kaufman, L., & Baillargeon, R. (2003). Should all stationary objects move when hit? Developments in infants' causal and statistical expectations about collision events. *Infant Behavior and Development, 26,* 529–568.

Wang, Z., Devine, R. T., Wong, K. K., & Hughes, C. (2016). Theory of mind and executive function during middle childhood across cultures. *Journal of Experimental Child Psychology, 149,* 6–22.

Wang, Z., Wong, R. K. S., Wong, P. Y. H., Ho, F. C., & Cheng, D. P. W. (2017). Play and theory of mind in early childhood: A Hong Kong perspective. *Early Child Development and Care, 187,* 1389–1402.

Wängqvist, M., & Frisén, A. (2016). Who am I online? Understanding the meaning of online contexts for identity development. *Adolescent Research Review, 1,* 139–151.

Want, S. C., Pascalis, O., Coleman, M., & Blades, M. (2003). Recognizing people from the inner or outer parts of their faces: Developmental data concerning "unfamiliar" faces. *British Journal of Developmental Psychology, 21,* 125–135.

Warneken, F., & Tomasello, M. (2007). Helping and cooperation at 14 months of age. *Infancy, 11,* 271–294.

Warneken, F., & Tomasello, M. (2008). Extrinsic rewards undermine altruistic tendencies in 20-month-olds. *Developmental Psychology, 44,* 1785–1788.

Warneken, F., & Tomasello, M. (2009). The roots of human altruism. *British Journal of Psychology, 100,* 455–471.

Warren, A. R., Hulse-Trotter, K., & Tubbs, E. C. (1991). Inducing resistance to suggestibility in children. *Law and Human Behavior, 15,* 273–285.

Warren, A. R., & Tate, C. S. (1992). Egocentrism in children's telephone conversations. In R. M. Diaz & L. E. Berk (Eds), *Private speech: From social interaction to self regulation* (pp. 245–264). Hillsdale, NJ: Erlbaum.

Warren, S. F., Brady, N., Sterling, A., Fleming, K., & Marquis, J. (2010). Maternal responsivity predicts language development in young children with Fragile X syndrome. *American Journal on Intellectual and Developmental Disabilities, 115,* 54–57.

Wartella, E., Beaudoin-Ryan, L., Blackwell, C. K., Cingel, D. P., Hurwitz, L. B., & Lauricella, A. R. (2016). What kind of adults will our children become? The impact of growing up in a media-saturated world. *Journal of Children and Media, 10,* 13–20.

Wartella, E., Rideout, V., Lauricella, A. R., & Connell, S. L. (2013). *Parenting in the age of digital technology. A national survey.* Evanston, IL: Center on Media and Human Development. School of Communication. Northwestern University.

Washington, K. (2007). Research review: Sibling placement in foster care: A review of the evidence. *Child and Family Social Work, 12,* 426–433.

Wason, P. C. (1977). The theory of formal operations: A critique. In B. Geber (Ed.), *Piaget and knowing: Studies in genetic epistemology* (pp. 119–135). London: Routledge and Kegan Paul.

Wass, S. V., Scerif, G., & Johnson, M. H. (2012). Training attentional control and working memory – Is younger, better? *Developmental Review, 32,* 360–387.

Watanabe, H., & Taga, G. (2006). General to specific development of movement patterns and memory for contingency between actions and events in young infants. *Infant Behavior and Development, 29,* 402–422.

Waterhouse, L. (2006a). Multiple intelligences, the Mozart effect, and emotional intelligence: A critical review. *Educational Psychologist, 41,* 207–225.

Waterhouse, L. (2006b). Inadequate evidence for multiple intelligences, Mozart effect, and emotional intelligence theories. *Educational Psychologist, 41,* 247–255.

Waterhouse, L., Dobash, R. P., & Carnie, J. (1994). *Child sexual abuse.* Edinburgh: The Scottish Office Central Research Unit.

Waters, A. M., Lipp, O., & Spence, S. H. (2008). Visual search for animal fear-relevant stimuli in children. *Australian Journal of Psychology, 60,* 112–125.

Waters, E. (1995). Appendix A: The Attachment Q-Set (Version 3.0). *Monographs of the Society for Research in Child Development, 60,* 234–246.

Watson, J. B., & Rayner, R. (1920). Conditioned emotional responses. *Journal of Experimental Psychology, 3,* 1–14.

Waxman, S. R., & Braun, I. (2005). Consistent (but not variable) names as invitations to form categories: New evidence from 12-month-old infants. *Cognition*, *95*, B59–B68

Waxman, S. R., & Gelman, S. A. (2009). Early word-learning entails reference, not merely associations. *Trends in Cognitive Sciences*, *13*, 258–263.

Way, B. M., & Lieberman, M. D. (2010). Is there a genetic contribution to cultural differences? Collectivism, individualism and genetic markers of social sensitivity. *Social Cognitive and Affective Neuroscience*, *5*, 203–211.

Way, N., & Rogers, O. (2015). "They say black men won't make it, but I know I'm gonna make it": Ethnic and racial identity development in the context of cultural stereotypes. In K. McLean & M. Syed (Eds), *The Oxford handbook of identity development* (pp. 269–282). Oxford: Oxford University Press.

Webb, S., & Rodgers, M. P. H. (2009). Vocabulary demands of television programs. *Language Learning*, *59*, 335–366.

Webley, P. (2005). Children's understanding of economics. In M. Barrett & E. Buchanan-Barrow (Eds), *Children's understanding of society* (pp. 43–65). New York, NY: Psychology Press.

Webster, A., & Roe, J. (1998). *Children with visual impairments. Social interaction, language and learning*. New York, NY: Routledge.

Webster-Stratton, C. (2006). *The Incredible Years: A trouble-shooting guide for parents of children aged 3–8*. Seattle, WA: Incredible Years Press.

Wechsler, D. (2014). *Wechsler Intelligence Scale for Children, Fifth edition*. San Antonio, TX: NCS Pearson.

Weems, C. F., & Varela, R. E. (2011). Generalized anxiety disorder. In D. McKay & E. Storch (Eds), *Handbook of child and adolescent anxiety disorders* (pp. 261–274). New York, NY: Springer.

Weindrich, D., Steinmetz, C. J., Laucht, M., Esser, G., & Schmidt, M. (2000). Epidemiology and prognosis of specific disorders of language and scholastic skills. *European Child and Adolescent Psychiatry*, *9*, 186–194.

Weisberg, D. S. (2015). Pretend play. *Wiley interdisciplinary reviews: Cognitive Science*, *6*, 249–261.

Weisberg, D. S., Kittredge, A. K., Hirsh-Pasek, K., Golinkoff, R. M., & Klahr, D. (2015). Making play work for education. *Phi Delta Kappan*, *96*, 8–13.

Weisleder, A., & Fernald, A. (2013). Talking to children matters: Early language experience strengthens processing and builds vocabulary. *Psychological Science*, *24*, 2143–2152.

Wellman, H. M. (1990). *The child's theory of mind*. Cambridge, MA: MIT Press.

Wellman, H. M., Cross, D., & Watson, J. (2001). Meta-analysis of theory of mind development: The truth about false belief. *Child Development*, *72*, 655–684.

Wellman, H. M., & Lagattuta, K. H. (2004). Theory of mind for learning and teaching: The nature and role of explanation. *Cognitive Development*, *19*, 479–497

Wells, G. (2008). Dialogue, inquiry and the construction of learning communities. In B. Lingard, J. Nixon &

S. Ranson (Eds), *Transforming learning in schools and communities: The remaking of education for a cosmopolitan society* (pp. 236–256). London: Continuum.

Wells, J. C. K. (2007). The thrifty phenotype as an adaptive maternal effect. *Biological Reviews*, *82*, 143–172.

Welsh, M. C., Friedman, S. L., & Spieker, S. J. (2006). Executive functions in developing children: Current conceptualizations and questions for the future. In K. McCartney & D. Phillips (Eds), *Blackwell handbook of early childhood development* (pp. 167–187). Oxford: Blackwell.

Wentzel, K. R. (2009). Peer relationships and motivation at school. In K. Rubin, W. Bukowski, & B. Laursen (Eds), *Handbook on peer relationships* (pp. 531–547). New York, NY: Guilford Press.

Werker, J. F. (1991). The ontogeny of speech perecption. In G. Mattingly & M. Studdert-Kennedy (Eds), *Modularity and the motor theory of speech perception* (pp. 91–109). Hillsdale, NJ: Erlbaum.

Werker, J. F., & Byers-Heinlein, K. (2008). Bilingualism in infancy: First steps in perception and comprehension. *Trends in Cognitive Sciences*, *12*, 144–151.

Werner, E. A., Myers, M. M., Fifer, W. P., Cheng, B., Fang, Y., Allen, R., & Monk, C. (2007). Prenatal predictors of infant temperament. *Developmental Psychobiology*, *49*, 474–484.

Werner, E. E. (2012). Children and war: Risk, resilience, and recovery. *Development and Psychopathology*, *24*, 553–558.

Werner, E. E., & Smith, R. S. (1982). *Vulnerable but invincible*. New York,NY: McGraw-Hill.

Werner, H. (1948). *Comparative psychology of mental development, Revised edition*. New York, NY: International Universities Press.

Werner, H. (1961). *Comparative psychology of mental development*. New York, NY: Science Editions.

Werner, L. A. (1992). Interpreting developmental psychoacoustics. In L. A. Werner & E. W. Rubel (Eds), *Developmental psychoacoustics* (pp. 47–88). Washington, DC: American Psychological Association.

Werner, L. A. (2007). Issues in human auditory development. *Journal of Communication Disorders*, *40*, 275–283.

Werner, L. A., Fay, R. R., & Popper, A. N. (Eds) (2012). *Human auditory development*. London: Springer.

Werner-Seidler, A., Perry, Y., Calear, A. L., Newby, J. M., & Christensen, H. (2017). School-based depression and anxiety prevention programs for young people: A systematic review and meta-analysis. *Clinical Psychology Review*, *51*, 30–47.

Wertheimer, M. (1961). Psychomotor coordination of auditory and visual space at birth. *Science*, *134*, 1692.

Wertsch, J. V. (1991). *Voices of the mind: A sociocultural approach to mediated action*. London: Harvester Wheatsheaf.

Westen, D. (1998). The scientific legacy of Sigmund Freud: Toward a psychodynamically informed psychological science. *Psychological Bulletin*, *124*, 333–371.

Westen, D., Gabbard, G. O., & Ortigo, K. M. (2008). Psychoanalytic approaches to personality. In O. P. John, R. W. Robins & L. A. Pervin (Eds), *Handbook of personality: Theory and research, Third edition* (pp. 61–113). New York, NY: Guilford Press.

Westermann, G., Ruh, G., & Plunkett, K. (2009). Connectionist approaches to language learning. *Linguistics, 47,* 413–452.

Wexler, K. (1999). Maturation and growth of grammar. In W. C. Ritchie & T. K. Bhatia (Eds), *Handbook of child language acquisitoion* (pp. 55–109). London: Academic Press.

Wheldall, K., & Limbrick, L. (2010). Do more boys than girls have reading problems? *Journal of Learning Disabilities, 43,* 418–429.

Whitaker, S. (2017). Assessing the intellectual ability of asylum seekers. *International Journal of Developmental Disabilities,* DOI:10.1080/20473869.2017.1322343.

White, S., Milne, E., Rosen, S., Hansen, P., Swettenham, J., Frith, U., & Ramus, F. (2006). The role of sensorimotor impairments in dyslexia: A multiple case study of dyslexic children. *Developmental Science, 9,* 237–255.

Whitman, T. L., O'Callaghan, M., & Sommer, K. (1997). Emotion and mental retardation. In W. E. MacLean (Ed.), *Ellis' handbook of mental deficiency, psychological theory and research, Third edition* (pp. 77–98) Mahwah, NJ: Lawrence Erlbaum.

Wickenden, M. (2011). Talking to teenagers: Using anthropological methods to explore identity and the lifeworlds of young people who use AAC. *Communication Disorders Quarterly, 32,* 151–163.

Widen, S. C., Pochedly, J. T., & Russell, J. A. (2015). The development of emotion concepts: A story superiority effect in older children and adolescents. *Journal of Experimental Child Psychology, 131,* 186–192.

Widom, C. S. (2000). Childhood victimization: Early adversity, later psychopathology. *National Institute of Justice Journal, 242,* 3–9.

Widom, C. S., Czaja, S. J., & Dutton, M. A. (2008). Childhood victimization and lifetime revictimization. *Child Abuse and Neglect, 32,* 785–796.

Wiedeman, A. M., Black, J. A., Dolle, A. L., Finney, E. J., & Coker, K. L. (2015). Factors influencing the impact of aggressive and violent media on children and adol-escents. *Aggression and Violent Behavior, 25,* 191–198.

Wieder, S. (1994). *Diagnostic Classification of Mental Health and Developmental Disorders of Infancy and Early Childhood. Diagnostic Classification: 0–3.* Zero to Three. Arlington, VA: /National Center for Clinical Infant Programs.

Wiggins, J. L., Mitchell, C., Hyde, L. W., & Monk, C. S. (2015). Identifying early pathways of risk and resilience: The codevelopment of internalizing and externalizing symptoms and the role of harsh parenting. *Development and Psychopathology, 27* (4pt1), 1295–1312.

Wilkening, F., Levin, I., & Druyan, S. (1987). Children's counting strategies for time quantification and integration. *Developmental Psychology, 23,* 823–831.

Wilkinson, L. S., Davies, W., & Isles, A. R. (2007). Genomic imprinting effects on brain development and function. *Nature Reviews Neuroscience, 8,* 832–843.

Willatts, P. (1989). Development of problem-solving in infancy. In A. Slater & G. Bremner (Eds), *Infant development* (pp. 143–182). Hove, UK: Lawrence Erlbaum.

Williams, J., & Hill, P. D. (2012). *Handbook for the assessment of children's behaviours.* Chicester, UK: Wiley.

Williams, L. R., Degnan, K. A., Pérez-Edgar, K., Henderson, H. A., Rubin, K. H., Pine, D. S., Steinberg, L., & Fox, N. A. (2009). Impact of behavioral inhibition and parenting style on internalizing and externalizing problems from early childhood through adolescence. *Journal of Abnormal Child Psychology, 37,* 1063–1075.

Willingham, D. T. (2004). Reframing the mind. *Education Next, 4,* 19–24.

Wilson, B., & Wilson, M. (1977). An iconoclastic view of the imagery sources in the drawings of young people. *Art Education, 30,* 5–11.

Wilson, B. J., Smith, S. L., Potter, W. J., Kunkel, D., Linz, D., Colvin, C. M., & Donnerstein, E. (2002). Violence in children's television programming: Assessing the risks. *Journal of Communication, 52,* 5–35.

Wilson, E. O. (1975). *Sociobiology.* Cambridge, MA: Harvard University Press.

Wilson, E. O. (1998). *Consilience: The unity of knowledge.* New York, NY: Knopf.

Wilson, R. S. (1983). The Louisville twin study: Developmental synchronies in behavior. *Child Development, 54,* 298–316.

Wilson, S., & Durbin, C. E. (2010). Effects of paternal depression on fathers' parenting behaviors: A meta-analytic review. *Clinical Psychology Review, 30,* 167–180.

Wilson, S. L., Raval, V. V., Salvina, J., Raval, P. H., & Panchal, I. N. (2012). Emotional expression and control in school-age children in India and the United States. *Merrill-Palmer Quarterly, 58,* 50–76.

Wimmer, H., & Hartl, H. (1991). Against the Cartesian view on mind: Young children's difficulty with own false beliefs. *British Journal of Developmental Psychology, 9,* 125–138.

Wimmer, H., & Perner, J. (1983). Beliefs about beliefs: Representation and constraining function of wrong beliefs in young children's understanding of deception. *Cognition, 13,* 103–128.

Winner, E. (1988). *The point of words: Children's understanding of metaphor and irony.* Cambridge, MA: Harvard University Press.

Winner, E. (2006). Development in the arts: Drawing and music. In W. Damon, R. M. Lerner, D. Kuhn & R. S. Siegler (Eds), *Handbook of child psychology, Sixth edition, Volume 2: Cognition, perception and language* (pp. 859–904). New York, NY: Wiley.

Winnicott, D. W. (1960). The theory of parent–infant relationship. *International Journal of Psycho-Analysis, 41,* 585–595.

Winnicott, D. W. (1965). Dependence towards independence. In D. W. Winnicott, *The maturational process and the facilitating environment* (pp. 83–92). London: Hogarth Press.

Winnicott, D. W. (1971). *Playing and reality*. London: Routledge.

Winnicott, D. W. (1992). Birth memories, birth trauma, and anxiety. *International Journal of Prenatal and Perinatal Studies*, 4, 17–33.

Winsler, A. (2009). Still talking to ourselves after all these years: A review of current research on private speech. In A. Winsler, C. Fernyhough & I. Montero (Eds) *Private speech, executive functioning, and the development of verbal self-regulation* (pp. 3–41). New York, NY: Cambridge University Press.

Winsler, A., & Naglieri, J. A. (2003). Overt and covert verbal problem-solving strategies: Developmental trends in use, awareness, and relations with task performance in children age 5 to 17. *Child Development*, 74, 659–678.

Witherington, D. C. (2014). Self-organization and explanatory pluralism: Avoiding the snares of reductionism in developmental science. *Research in Human Development*, 11, 22–36.

Witten, M. R. (1997). Mood disorder: Depression of infancy and early childhood. In A. Lieberman, S. Wieder & E. Fenichel (Eds), *DC: 0–3 Case book* (pp. 81–107). Washington, DC: Zero to Three.

Wolcott, H. F. (1994). *Transforming qualitative data: Description, analysis and interpretation*. Thousand Oaks, CA: Sage.

Wolff, P. H. (1963). Observations on early development of smiling. In B. M. Foss (Ed.), *Determinants of infant behaviour, Volume 2* (pp. 113–138). London: Methuen.

Wolff, P. H. (1966). The causes, controls, and organization of behavior in the neonate. *Psychological Issues*, 5, 1–105.

Woll, B., & Morgan, G. (2012). Language impairments in the development of sign: Do they reside in a specific modality or are they modality independent deficits? *Bilingualism: Language and Cognition*, 15, 75–87.

Wong, S., Chan, K., Wong, V., & Wong, W. (2002). Use of chopsticks in Chinese children. *Child Care, Health and Development*, 28, 157–161.

Wong, W. I., & Hines, M. (2015). Preferences for pink and blue: The development of color preferences as a distinct gender-typed behavior in toddlers. *Archives of Sexual Behavior*, 44, 1243–1254.

Wong-Lo, M., & Bullock, L. M. (2011). Digital aggression: Cyberworld meets school bullies. *Preventing School Failure: Alternative Education for Children and Youth*, 55, 64–70.

Wood, D., Bruner, J. S., & Ross, G. (1976). The role of tutoring in problem solving. *Journal of Child Psychology and Psychiatry*, 17, 89–100.

Woodward, A. L., & Markman, L. (1998). Early word learning. In W. Damon, D. Kuhn & R. S. Siegler (Eds), *Handbook of child psychology, Fifth edition, Volume 2: Cognition, perception and language* (pp. 371–420). New York, NY: Wiley.

Woolley, A. W., Aggarwal, I., & Malone, T. W. (2015). Collective intelligence and group performance. *Current Directions in Psychological Science*, 24, 420–424.

Woolley, G. (2010). A multiple strategy framework supporting vocabulary development for students with reading comprehension deficits. *Australasian Journal of Special Education*, 34, 119–132.

Woolley, H. (2013). Now being social: The barrier of designing outdoor play spaces for disabled children. *Children and Society*, 27, 448–458.

World Health Organization (WHO) (1992). *The ICD-10 classification of mental and behavioural disorders: clinical descriptions and diagnostic guidelines*. Geneve, Switzerland: World Health Organization.

World Health Organization (WHO) (2001). *International classification of functioning, disability and health*. Geneve, Switzerland: World Health Organization.

World Health Organization (WHO) (2007). *International classification of functioning, disability and health: Children and youth version*. Geneve, Switzerland: World Health Organization.

World Health Organization (WHO) (2018). *The international statistical classification of diseases and related health problems, ICD-11*. Geneve, Switzerland: World Health Organization.

Worrell, F. C. (2015). Racial and ethnic identity. In C. M. Rubie-Davies, J. M. Stephens & P. Watson (Eds), *Routledge international handbook of social psychology of the classroom* (pp. 111–120). Abingdon, UK: Routledge.

Wridt, P. J. (2004). An historical analysis of young people's use of public space, parks and playgrounds in New York City. *Children Youth and Environments*, 14, 86–106.

Wright, B. (2008). Development in deaf and blind children. *Psychiatry*, 7, 286–289.

Wright, C. A., Kaiser, A. P., Reikowsky, D. I., & Roberts, M. Y. (2013). Effects of a naturalistic sign intervention on expressive language of toddlers with Down syndrome. *Journal of Speech, Language, and Hearing Research*, 56, 994–1008.

Wright, J. C., Huston, A. C., Murphy, K. C., Peters, M. S. Pinon, M., Scantlin, R., & Kotler, J. (2001). The relations of early television viewing to school readiness and vocabulary of children from low-income families: The early window project. *Child Development*, 72, 1347–1366.

Wunderlich, D. (2004). Why assume UG? *Studies in Language. International Journal sponsored by the Foundation "Foundations of Language"*, 28, 615–641.

Wyn, J. (2004). Becoming adult in the 2000s. *Family Matters*, 68, 6–12.

Wynn, K., & Bloom, P. (2014). The moral baby. In M. Killen & J. G. Smetana (Eds), *Handbook of moral development, Second edition* (pp. 435–453). New York, NY: Psychology Press.

Xia, F. (2014). *Finding Monet*. Shanghai: Changning Special Education Center.

Xiong, M., Shi, J., Wu, Z., & Zhang, Z. (2016). Five-year-old preschoolers' sharing is influenced by anticipated reciprocation. *Frontiers in Psychology*, 7, 460.

Xu, F. (2002). The role of language in acquiring object kind concepts in infancy. *Cognition*, 85, 223–250.

Xu, F., & Carey, S. (1996). Infants' metaphysics: The case of numerical identity. *Cognitive Psychology*, 30, 111–153.

Yan, Z. (2018). Child and adolescent use of mobile phones: An unparalleled complex developmental phenomenon. *Child Development*, 89, 5–16.

Yang, D., Sidman, J., & Bushnell, E. W. (2010). Beyond the information given: Infants' transfer of actions learned through imitation. *Journal of Experimental Child Psychology*, 106, 62–81.

Yau, J., & Smetana, J. G. (2003). Conceptions of moral, social-conventional, and personal events among Chinese preschoolers in Hong Kong. *Child Development*, 74, 647–658.

Yecco, G. J. (1993). Neurobehavioral development and developmental support of premature infants. *The Journal of Perinatal and Neonatal Nursing*, 7, 56–65.

Yermolayeva, Y., & Rakison, D. H. (2014). Connectionist modeling of developmental changes in infancy: Approaches, challenges, and contributions. *Psychological Bulletin*, 140, 224–255.

Yiend, J., Parnes, C., Shepherd, K., Roche, M. K., & Cooper, M. J. (2014). Negative self-beliefs in eating disorders: A cognitive-bias-modification study. *Clinical Psychological Science*, 2, 756–766.

Yin, R. K. (2009). *Case study research: Design and methods, Fourth edition*. Thousand Oaks, CA: Sage.

Yonas, A., Elieff, C. A., & Arterberry, M. E. (2002). Emergence of sensitivity to pictorial depth cues: Charting development in individual infants. *Infant Behavior and Development*, 25, 495–514.

Yoshida, H., & Smith, L. B. (2008). What's in view for toddlers? Using a head camera to study visual experience. *Infancy*, 13, 229–248.

Yoshikawa, H., Weisner, T. S., Kalil, A., & Way, N. (2008). Mixing qualitative and quantitative research in developmental science: Uses and methodological choices. *Developmental Psychology*, 44, 344–354.

Yoshinaga-Itano, C. (2013). Principles and guidelines for early intervention after confirmation that a child is deaf or hard of hearing. *Journal of Deaf Studies and Deaf Education*, 19, 143–175.

Yu, B. (2013). Issues in bilingualism and heritage language maintenance: Perspectives of minority-language mothers of children with autism spectrum disorders. *American Journal of Speech-Language Pathology*, 22, 10–24.

Yu, B. (2016a). Bilingualism as conceptualized and bilingualism as lived: A critical examination of the monolingual socialization of a child with autism in a bilingual family. *Journal of Autism and Developmental Disorders*, 46, 424–435.

Yu, B. (2016b). Code-switching as a communicative resource within routine, bilingual family interactions for a child on the autism spectrum. *Perspectives of the ASHA Special Interest Groups*, 1, 17–28.

Yu, M., & Baxter, J. (2016). Australian children's screen time and participation in extracurricular activities. In *The Longitudinal Study of Australian Children Annual Statistical Report 2015* (pp. 99–125). Melbourne: AIFS.

Yumoto, C., Jacobson, S. W., & Jacobson, J. L. (2008). Fetal substance exposure and cumulative environmental risk in an African American cohort. *Child Development*, 79, 1761–1776.

Zahir, F. R., & Brown, C. J. (2011). Epigenetic impacts on neurodevelopment: Pathophysiological mechanisms and genetic modes of action. *Pediatric Research*, 69 (5 Pt 2), 92R–100R.

Zahn-Waxler, C., & Kochanska, G. (1990). The origins of guilt. In R. A. Thompson (Ed.), *The Nebraska symposium on motivation 1988: Socioemotional development, Volume 36* (pp. 182–258). Lincoln, NE: University of Nebraska Press.

Zahn-Waxler, C., Radke-Yarrow, M., & King, R. A. (1979). Child rearing and children's prosocial initiations toward victims of distress. *Child Development*, 50, 319–330.

Zahn-Waxler, C., Cummings, E. M., Ianotti, R. J., & Radke-Yarrow, M. (1984). Young offspring of depressed parents: A population at risk for affective problems. *New Directions for Child Development*, 26, 81–105.

Zahn-Waxler, C., Radke-Yarrow, M., Wagner, E., & Chapman, M. (1992). Development of concern for others. *Developmental Psychology*, 28, 126–136.

Zambo, D. (2004). Using qualitative methods to understand the educational experiences of students with dyslexia. *The Qualitative Report*, 9, 80–93.

Zambrana, I. M., Ystrom, E., & Pons, F. (2012). Impact of gender, maternal education, and birth order on the development of language comprehension: A longitudinal study from 18 to 36 months of age. *Journal of Developmental & Behavioral Pediatrics*, 33, 146–155.

Zeanah, C. H., & Gleason, M. M. (2015). Annual research review: Attachment disorders in early childhood–clinical presentation, causes, correlates, and treatment. *Journal of Child Psychology and Psychiatry*, 56, 207–222.

Zeanah, C. H., & Smyke, A. T. (2015). Disorders of attachment and social engagement related to deprivation. In A. Thapar, D. S. Pine, J. F. Leckman, S. Scott, M. J. Snowling & E. Taylor (Eds), *Rutter's child and adolescent psychiatry, Sixth edition* (pp. 793–805). London: Wiley-Blackwell.

Zeanah, C. H., Scheeringa, M., Boris, N. W., Heller, S. S., Smyke, A. T., & Trapani, J. (2004). Reactive attachment disorder in maltreated toddlers. *Child Abuse and Neglect*, 28, 877–888.

Zeanah, C. H., Egger, H. L., Smyke, A. T., Nelson, C. A., Fox, N. A., Marshall, P. J., & Guthrie, D. (2009). Institutional rearing and psychiatric disorders in Romanian preschool children. *American Journal of Psychiatry*, 166, 777–785.

Zebehazy, K. T., Zigmond, N., & Zimmerman, G. J. (2012). Ability or access-ability: Differential item functioning of items on alternate performance-based assessment tests for students with visual impairments. *Journal of Visual Impairment and Blindness*, 106, 325–338.

Zeigler-Hill, V. (2011). The connections between self-esteem and psychopathology. *Journal of Contemporary Psychotherapy*, 41, 157–164.

Zelazo, P. D. (2013). Developmental psychology: A new synthesis. In P. D. Zelazo (Ed.), *The Oxford handbook of developmental psychology, Volume 2* (pp. 2–12). New York, NY: Oxford University Press.

Zelazo, P. D. (2015). Executive function: Reflection, iterative reprocessing, complexity, and the developing brain. *Developmental Review, 38*, 55–68.

Zeman, J., Cassano, M., Perry-Parrish, C., & Stegall, S. (2006). Emotion regulation in children and adolescents. *Journal of Developmental and Behavioral Pediatrics, 27*, 155–168.

Zentner, M., & Bates, J. E. (2008). Child temperament: An integrative review of concepts, research programs, and measures. *International Journal of Developmental Science, 2*, 7–37.

Zentner, M., & Shiner, R. (2012). Fifty years of progress in temperament reseach: A synthesis of major themes, findings, and challenges and a look forward. In M. Zentner & R. L. Shiner (Eds), *Handbook of temperament* (pp. 673–700). New York, NY: Guilford Press.

Zevenbergen, A. A., Holmes, A., Haman, E., Whiteford, N., & Thielges, S. (2016). Variability in mothers' support for preschoolers' contributions to co-constructed narratives as a function of child age. *First Language, 36*, 601–616.

Zhang, T. Y., & Meaney, M. J. (2010). Epigenetics and the environmental regulation of the genome and its function. *Annual Review of Psychology, 61*, 439–466.

Zheng, Y., Rijsdijk, F., Pingault, J. B., McMahon, R. J., & Unger, J. B. (2016). Developmental changes in genetic and environmental influences on Chinese child and adolescent anxiety and depression. *Psychological Medicine, 46*, 1829–1838.

Zhong, S., He, Y., Shu, H., & Gong, G. (2017). Developmental changes in topological asymmetry between hemispheric brain white matter networks from adolescence to young adulthood. *Cerebral Cortex, 27*, 2560–2570.

Zigler, E., & Valentine, J. (Eds) (1979). *Project Head Start: A legacy of the war on poverty.* New York, NY: Free Press.

Zihl, J., & Dutton, G. N. (2015). *Cerebral visual impairment in children.* Wien, Austria: Springer.

Zill, N. (1996). Family change and student achievement: What we have learned, what it means for schools. In A. Booth & J. F. Dunn (Eds), *Family-school links* (pp. 139–174). Mahwah, NJ: Erlbaum.

Zimmer-Gembeck, M. J., Webb, H. J., Pepping, C. A., Swan, K., Merlo, O., Skinner, E. A., Avdagic, E., & Dunbar, M. (2017). Is parent–child attachment a correlate of children's emotion regulation and coping? *International Journal of Behavioral Development, 41*, 74–93.

Zimmerman, F., Christakis, D., & Meltzoff, A. (2007) Associations between media viewing and language development in children under age 2 years. *Journal of Pediatrics, 4*, 364–368.

Zinck, A. (2008). Self-referential emotions. *Consciousness and Cognition, 17*, 496–505.

Ziv, Y. (2013). Social information processing patterns, social skills, and school readiness in preschool children. *Journal of Experimental Child Psychology, 114*, 306–320.

Zosuls, K. M., Andrews, N. C., Martin, C. L., England, D. E., & Field, R. D. (2016). Developmental changes in the link between gender typicality and peer victimization and exclusion. *Sex Roles, 75*, 243–256.

Zosuls, K. M., Ruble, D. N., Tamis-LeMonda, C. S., Shrout, P. E., Bornstein, M. H., & Greulich, F. K. (2009). The acquisition of gender labels in infancy: Implications for gender-typed play. *Developmental Psychology, 45*, 688–701.

Zucker, K. J., & Seto, M. C. (2015). Gender dysphoria and paraphilic sexual disorders. In A. Thapar, D. S. Pine, F. S. Leckman, S. Scott, M. J. Snowling & E. Taylor (Eds), *Rutter's child and adolescent psychiatry, Sixth edition* (pp. 981–998). Oxford: Wiley.

Zucker, K. J., Wood, H., & VanderLaan, D. P. (2014). Models of psychopathology in children and adolescents with gender dysphoria. In B. P. C. Kreukels, T. D. Steensma & A. L. C. de Vries (Eds), *Gender dysphoria and disorders of sex development: Progress in care and knowledge* (pp. 171–192). New York, NY: Springer.

Zwaigenbaum, L., Thurm, A., Stone, W., Baranek, G., Bryson, S., Iverson, J., Kau, A., Klin, A., Lord, C., Landa, R., et al. (2007). Studying the emergence of autism spectrum disorders in high-risk infants: Methodological and practical issues. *Journal of Autism and Developmental Disorders, 37*, 466–480.

INDEX